RITUAL IN EARLY BRONZE AGE GRAVE GOODS

AN EXAMINATION OF RITUAL AND DRESS EQUIPMENT FROM CHALCOLITHIC AND EARLY BRONZE AGE GRAVES IN ENGLAND

Ann Woodward and John Hunter

with

David Bukach, Stuart Needham and Alison Sheridan

and with contributions by

Peter Bray, Mary Davis, Sheila Hamilton-Dyer, Duncan Hook, Rob Ixer, Mick Jones, Mark Maltby, Sonia O'Connor, Philip Potts, Fiona Roe, Lore Troalen, John Watson and Peter Webb

Oxbow Books

Oxford & Philadelphia

Published in the United Kingdom in 2015 by
OXBOW BOOKS
10 Hythe Bridge Street, Oxford OX1 2EW

and in the United States by
OXBOW BOOKS
908 Darby Road, Havertown, PA 19083

Hardcover Edition: ISBN 978-1-7829-694-3
Digital Edition: ISBN 978-1-78297-695-0

A CIP record for this book is available from the British Library

Printed in the United Kingdom by Short Run Press, Exeter

For a complete list of Oxbow titles, please contact:

UNITED KINGDOM
Oxbow Books
Telephone (01865) 241249, Fax (01865) 794449
Email: oxbow@oxbowbooks.com
www.oxbowbooks.com

UNITED STATES OF AMERICA
Oxbow Books
Telephone (800) 791-9354, Fax (610) 853-9146
Email: queries@casemateacademic.com
www.casemateacademic.com/oxbow

Oxbow Books is part of the Casemate Group

Front cover: gold-covered shale pendant or button from Upton Lovell G2e, Wiltshire (ID 1450)
Back cover: amber necklace from Little Cressingham, Norfolk (ID 999)

Contents

APPENDICES (on CD)

Appendix I. A Revised Classification and Chronology for Daggers and Knives by Stuart Needham

Appendix II. The Role and Use of Daggers in British Early Bronze Age Society: Insights from their Chemical Composition by Peter Bray

Appendix III. Animal Bone and Antler by Mark Maltby

Appendix IV. Identification of Bronze Age Pommels and other Osseous Objects by Sonia O'Connor

Appendix V. The Study and Analysis of Jet and Jet-like Materials: methods and results by Mary Davis, Duncan Hook, Mick Jones, Alison Sheridan and Lore Troalen

Appendix VI. Stone: PXRF Analysis, Magnetic Susceptibility and Petrography by Rob Ixer, Philip Potts, Peter Webb and John Watson

Appendix VII. Necklaces: additional data by Alison Sheridan and Ann Woodward

Acknowledgements

The work for this volume was undertaken during a six-year research programme, the first three years of which (2007–9) were spent at the University of Birmingham undertaking fieldwork and recording. This work was funded by the Leverhulme Trust and we are indebted to the Trust's generosity in supporting the venture. It involved the two of us (Professor John Hunter and Dr Ann Woodward) aided by a post-doctoral assistant Dr David Bukach. The team was also supported in the field by other researchers: Dr Alison Sheridan and Mary Davis (jet and jet-like materials); Dr Stuart Needham (gold and selected other objects); Mark Maltby, Dr Sonia O'Connor and Sheila Hamilton-Dyer (animal bone); Dr Rob Ixer and Fiona Roe (lithics), and colleagues from the Open University, Dr Philip Potts, Dr Peter Webb and John Watson (PXRF). During the programme compositional analysis was also carried out by Lore Troalen (National Museums Scotland), Duncan Hook (British Museum) and the late Dr J. M. Jones (University of Newcastle). We are indebted to them all for their support, enthusiasm and expertise.

The material was examined at thirteen museums and involved considerable work on behalf of their respective curators in locating and making available appropriate material, and in arranging space for examination, often for several days at a time. Without this level of co-operation and support none of this research would have been possible and the authors are especially grateful to the following for their efforts: Alison Roberts and Suzanne Anderson (Ashmolean Museum, Oxford); Gail Boyle (Bristol City Museum and Art Gallery); Dr Ben Roberts (British Museum, London); Anne Taylor (Museum of Archaeology and Anthropology, University of Cambridge); Dr David Dawson and Lisa Webb, now Lisa Brown (Wiltshire Heritage Museum, Devizes); Peter Woodwood (Dorset County Museum, Dorchester); Claire Jones (English Heritage Store, Fort Cumberland, Portsmouth); Heather Fitch, now Heather York (Hove Museum, Brighton); Paula Gentil and Martin Foreman (Hull and East Riding Museum); Emma O'Connor (Barbican House Museum, Lewes); Alan West (Norwich Castle Museum); Peter Saunders and Jane Ellis-Schön (Salisbury and South Wiltshire Museum), and Gill Woolrich (Weston Park Museum, Sheffield).

Collation of the data and most of the writing up process was undertaken by the two of us from 2009 in our so-called 'retirement' and, somewhat apologetically, we would like to thank our partners and families who may have expected more of our time and attention during the last three years. David Bukach has returned to his native Canada and has followed a new career as a professional photographer. We wish him well.

A number of other researchers have added significantly to the text and we are grateful to be able to integrate their specialist knowledge with our own ideas. They brought with them not only their own expertise, but also that of a network of other colleagues. The full list of contributors appears on the title page. Contributions by Dr Alison Sheridan (jet and jet-like materials), Dr Stuart Needham (gold and various other objects), Dr Sonia O'Connor (animal bone), and Dr Peter Bray (analysis of copper alloys) all appear under their own names in the main text and in the appendices. Moreover, we are particularly pleased to be able to incorporate their novel research ideas for the first time, notably in Alison Sheridan's discussion of jet and jet-like necklaces (Chapter 7.3) and Stuart Needham's discussion on gold objects (Chapter 6.3). The volume has gained new richness and importance as a result.

Illustrations play a major part in the presentation of the data. The original photographs are the result of David Bukach's splendid photography; several of the collations are also his work. Nadine Ross also produced page collations in some of the earlier chapters. The majority of the line drawings have been provided by Henry Buglass (formerly of the University of Birmingham), with others by Marion O'Neil (freelance illustrator) and Peter Woodward. We are indebted to their skills and understanding of what we have been trying to achieve.

Copyright for the text, line drawings, diagrams and tables rest with Oxbow Books and the individual authors. For reproduction of any colour plate permission also needs to be sought from the museums which hold the relevant objects. In the case of a plate which illustrates objects from more than one museum it would be necessary to contact each of the museums concerned (for details see the table below). Attributions of objects within any one colour plate can be determined by consulting the Lists of Objects Studied and Illustrated, which appear at the end of each object type section in the text.

There are countless other individuals who have contributed in their own way. Among these we would like to single out Professor Mike Parker Pearson and Dr Mandy Jay who kindly allowed us to use unpublished radiocarbon dates from the Beaker People Project, and Terry Manby for his help in defining regional find locations. Dr Alistair Barclay and Dr Chris Evans provided details of unpublished finds and the X-rays were scanned by Dr Sonia O'Connor. Mary Cahill kindly commented on the discussion of gold objects.

We would also like to thank our professorial colleagues, Richard Bradley, Anthony Harding, John Barrett, Tim Darvill and Stephen Shennan, along with Dr Ian Longworth who, in many different ways, have supported the venture from its inception. In addition, Richard Bradley kindly read and commented upon a final draft of the volume. Gratitude is also due to the staff of Oxbow books, notably Dr Julie Gardiner. Finally, this volume would never have seen the light of day without publication support from the Marc Fitch Fund under the guidance of Dr Christopher Catling. We are indebted to all and trust they will be pleased with the outcome.

Ann Woodward and John Hunter, summer 2013

Abbreviation in tables	Museum	Copyright
Ash	Ashmolean, Oxford	University of Oxford The Ashmolean Museum
Brist	Bristol	Bristol Museums and Art Gallery
BM	British Museum	The British Museum
Camb	Cambridge	University of Cambridge Museum of Archaeology and Anthropology
Dev	Wiltshire Heritage Museum, Devizes	Wiltshire Archaeological and Natural History Society
Dor	Dorset County Museum, Dorchester	Dorset Natural History and Archaeological Society at the Dorset County Museum
Hove	Hove	The Royal Pavilion, Libraries and Museums (Brighton and Hove)
Hull	Hull	Hull and East Riding Museum
Lewes	Barbican House Museum, Lewes	Sussex Archaeological Society
Nor	Norwich Castle Museum	Norfolk Museums and Archaeology Service
Sal	Salisbury	Salisbury and South Wiltshire Museum
Sheff	Weston Park Museum, Sheffield	Sheffield Galleries and Museums Trust

List of Figures and Tables

List of Figures

List of Tables

1. INTRODUCTION

The exotic and impressive grave goods from burials of the 'Wessex Culture' in Early Bronze Age Britain are well known and have inspired influential social and economic hypotheses, invoking the former existence of chiefs, warriors and merchants (Piggott 1938; Gerloff 1975) and high-ranking pastoralists (Fleming 1971). However, more recent studies have begun to express doubts over these ideas, and alternative theories have been proposed. For example, society may have been an amalgam of family-based groups roughly equal in status but where differences in individual social standing were played out through the wearing of visible emblems or exotic equipment and the conspicuous disposal of valuable goods (e.g. Parker Pearson 1999). Moreover, the burial of rich objects within barrows could well have prevented the accumulation of wealth and power through inheritance in aristocratic families, and the deposition of so much richness in the graves may have been designed specifically as a striking display of social standing within the community. In particular it may be that such display was related to *religious and ritual activity* rather than to economic status, and that groups of artefacts found in certain graves may have belonged to religious specialists. The costumes and paraphernalia that characterise the Wessex Bronze Age may have been used at periodic or seasonal religious festivals or other communal meetings of a ritual nature, or in more private contexts possibly involving the practices of medicine or divination by individuals who may have practised shamanism (Woodward 2000, 109–122; Sheridan and Shortland 2003).

Interestingly, these new avenues of enquiry are reviving in part an idea originally put forward by Piggott in relation to the finds from the Upton Lovell G2a barrow (Piggott 1962). He concluded that the arrangement of the sets of perforated bone points and tusks found on the body may have ornamented a special garment worn by a religious specialist or shaman, and cited parallels from graves in Russia to complement his argument. Despite the obvious importance of the material remains in underpinning these theories, it is remarkable that the grave assemblages which provide the raw data have never been comprehensively listed

nor consistently investigated or catalogued. This volume is, in part, directed at rectifying this particular shortcoming.

Most of the finds relevant to our study were recovered from antiquarian excavations undertaken in the late 18th and 19th centuries. The earliest extensive campaigns were concentrated on Salisbury Plain, and especially in the environs of Stonehenge. The exceptional partnership between a wealthy and enlightened banker – Sir Richard Colt Hoare of Stourhead House – and the more humble William Cunnington, a draper and wool merchant from Warminster, led to the carefully observed excavation of the centres of many round barrows. The disposition of grave goods was described in brief and most of the objects were beautifully illustrated, by Philip Crocker, in the two volumes of *Ancient Wiltshire* (Hoare 1812 and 1821). Sadly they were less interested in the remains of the people interred, and it is assumed that they redeposited the bones in the trenches before they were backfilled. The Stourhead Collection of grave goods was purchased by the museum at Devizes, and an illustrated catalogue has been published (Annable and Simpson 1964). The results of antiquarian activities in Dorset, undertaken by a series of different individuals were summarised by Warne (1866) in his *The Celtic Tumuli of Dorset*, although the records are far less detailed and accurate than those provided by Hoare. Much of the detail from these campaigns of excavation in Wessex, and of more modern excavations, was usefully listed and correlated by Grinsell (1957, 1959 and 1982).

Less well known are the two major campaigns of barrow excavation carried out on the chalk wolds of East Yorkshire. Here not only have the objects survived but also details of the age and sex of the people buried were often recorded. Canon William Greenwell was a cleric with a vast literary output. After serving in various curacies he was appointed a minor canon of Durham Cathedral, later becoming librarian for the large collection of charters and rolls belonging to the cathedral. The results of the excavations undertaken by Greenwell (e.g. Greenwell 1868; 1881; Greenwell and Rolleston 1877) are curated in the British Museum and have been fully published to modern standards (Kinnes and Longworth 1985). The finds recovered in the same region by John Mortimer, a corn chandler in the East Yorkshire town of Driffield, were fully illustrated by his daughter Agnes in his volume *Forty Years' Researches in the British and Saxon Burial Mounds of East Yorkshire* (1905), along with many details, and even accurate plans, of the disposition of burials under each barrow. Both Greenwell and Mortimer saved many of the human remains from the burials that they excavated and attempted age and sex estimations within their reports. Finally, in the Peak District of Derbyshire and Staffordshire, Thomas Bateman, known as the 'Barrow Knight' (Marsden 2007) excavated many barrows. He published summaries of his findings (Bateman 1848; 1861) and the objects are housed in the Sheffield City Museum. Many of the grave goods were illustrated within a catalogue of the Bateman Collection (Howarth 1899) and, more recently, by Vine (1982). Useful listings and correlations of the burials and barrows have been compiled by Barnatt (1996). Like Mortimer, Bateman was very interested in the human remains, and he kept large numbers of them in his collections, especially the skulls, which are particularly informative to scholars today.

Following the initial recognition of the shared characteristics of the 'Wessex' graves and their initial listing by Piggott (1938), certain categories of the more exotic artefacts have been studied in detail, and exhaustive catalogues prepared. Such studies include *corpora* of goldwork, copper and copper alloy daggers and items of amber, and an ongoing analysis of faience beads. The *corpus* of goldwork provided by Taylor (1980) included summary listing of all items from the British Isles and a selective photographic record, along with discussion of the results of compositional analysis. In relation to the gold objects from Wessex graves she discussed the occurrence of similar techniques of manufacture that may indicate the former existence of a single craftsman, and that many of the objects may have been produced within a very short time period. Her more recent publications have developed this theme, using suites of new compositional analyses. This work is assessed within this volume, along with detailed descriptions and new interpretations of the major gold items from Wessex graves.

The major *corpus* of daggers published by Gerloff (1975) provided an exhaustive catalogue illustrated with line drawings. This included extensive discussion relating to the interpretation of the Wessex graves, much of which is still useful although some has been overtaken by more recent research and programmes of dating; a revised typo-chronology for the daggers is included within this volume. A major *corpus* of objects made from amber (Beck and Shennan 1991) included an extensive programme of compositional analysis which confirmed that all the amber derived from Baltic sources, and a fully illustrated catalogue. Following on from the pioneering work on the sourcing of faience carried out by Beck and Stone in the 1930's, new techniques for the study and scientific analysis of this exotic glass-like material have been developed, and a full catalogue and discussion of all the British material is in preparation (Sheridan and Shortland 2004).

Preliminary results indicate that most of the faience beads were not imported from central Europe but were made at varying locations within Britain. Furthermore, it can be postulated that there was a very strong link between faience manufacture and the tin trade, with the British and Irish beads displaying a relatively high tin content in comparison with European examples

A major contribution to the publication of exotic artefacts of Beaker and Early Bronze Age date was the illustrated catalogue of the exhibition entitled *Symbols of Power*, which was held in Edinburgh in 1985 (Clarke *et al.* 1985). Along with coloured photographs of many key grave assemblages, it included detailed consideration of manufacturing techniques and craftsmanship. More recent research has also tended to concentrate on the more exotic items, for example on daggers and goldwork (Needham 2000); or on amber, faience and gold (Sheridan and Shortland 2003). Of particular note is the study of cups made from precious materials (Needham *et al.* 2006). This provided a fully illustrated catalogue of these important artefacts, and the ensuing discussion isolated a zone of activity along the south coast which was related to cross-channel relations rather than to the concentration of other rich materials which is centred in the inland Wessex region. By contrast, the more mundane items, notably many types of bead and objects of stone and bone, have received comparatively little attention.

Stone objects of Early Bronze Age date are relatively rare, but some are finely finished, and their morphology and compositional analysis form a significant part of our project. Artefacts made from animal bone, teeth and antler are far more common in rich Early Bronze Age grave groups. However such material has seldom been described or studied in detail, and this category of material figures prominently here. The bone from which such artefacts were manufactured often can be identified to both species and body part. As well as being of general interest, such information is particularly relevant to potential interpretations of objects in relation to the symbolic significance of different species of animal, both wild and domestic, and the possible cosmological referencing of right and left body parts.

Recent innovative studies of the sourcing, potential function and wear history for items of jet, shale, cannel coal and lignite have encompassed material from Wales and Scotland respectively (Sheridan and Davis 1998; 2002). Preliminary analyses of jet and jet-like artefacts from selected Early Bronze Age graves in England have also been carried out (Bussell *et al.* 1981). The research undertaken by Sheridan and Davis provided a major stimulus for further work on sourcing of jet and jet-like materials, and for studying traces of manufacture and wear, and such studies have formed a major part of the primary research undertaken for this volume. Further work by Sheridan has also considered the traces of manufacture and wear visible on items made from amber, for example in the study and replication of amber artefacts from the Knowes of Trotty burial in Orkney (Sheridan *et al.* 2003).

Although many types of beads have never been listed and studied in detail, some important recent research has been highly relevant. In a series of reports Sheridan has defined the concept of 'composite necklaces', and has explained their importance in terms of the variety of materials selected, the methods of manufacture employed and the inclusion of reused items defined by differential patterns of use wear, for example from Exloo (Haveman and Sheridan 2006), Thomas Hardye School (Sheridan 2007b) and Cossington (Sheridan 2008). A second aspect of such studies has been the realisation of the supreme symbolic significance of many of the materials employed. This applies particularly to gold, jet and amber, which possess some very unusual and exciting physical properties. Amber can be polished so that it shines like gold, and both may symbolise the life-giving rays of the sun. But amber is more mysterious than gold because its colours show more variety, and its texture and reflective nature can vary across a single object. Furthermore amber has a traditional medicinal function. Also it possesses electrostatic properties when rubbed with substances such as fur, and it can be burned as aromatic incense. Jet, another substance of dramatic appearance when polished, also possesses electrostatic properties and is sometimes known as 'black amber'. These characteristics were highlighted within the *Symbols of Power* volume (Clarke *et al.* 1985, 204), and the discussion of the magical properties of materials used in Early Bronze Age jewellery and other costume elements was developed in Sheridan and Shortland's (2003) article on *Supernatural Power Dressing*. It is research such as this that has inspired much of the content of this volume.

Moreover, in recent years archaeologists have come to realise that it is very important to study the degree of fragmentation within suites of objects under study. It has been recognised that certain objects were deliberately placed in graves or other deposits in an incomplete state (e.g. Woodward 2002). Sometimes this was because the items were already very old, and may have acquired status as an heirloom or relic; sometimes because a part or parts of the object had been deliberately removed and then retained either for personal veneration or for use within systems of social exchange (e.g. Chapman 2000 on ceramics, especially figurines, from the Balkans; Woodward 2002 on amber beads in Britain and Europe). Such observations are of importance in assessing the function, and of course the original date of manufacture, of individual artefacts in group deposits. However, usually the necessary observations cannot be made from published descriptions or illustrations of individual objects. By contrast it is essential in most cases to visually examine the objects themselves, in the museum collections where they are housed, in order to assess the degree of completeness, the nature of any fractured surfaces (were the breaks ancient, or possibly formed at the time of excavation?) and any overall pattern of freshness or wear. A key example of how such approaches could be applied to all the artefacts present within a single grave assemblage, from the Beaker grave at Raunds, Northamptonshire, was published by Healy and Harding (2004).

An ambitious research project designed to address gaps in the current state of research, and to further consideration of the topics of material sourcing, manufacturing processes and fragmentation/use wear histories was formulated in 2004 at the University of Birmingham. The main aim was to review burial assemblages from relevant Beaker and Early Bronze Age contexts in England.

The classes of material to be studied included beads, pendants, amulets, buttons, pins, points, belt fittings, costume fittings, wrist guards, tools, whetstones and spatulae, along with selected categories of weapons and regalia. The raw materials involved were highly varied: gold, copper alloy, jet or jet-like products, amber, faience, stone, bone, antler, teeth, fossils and minerals. There was a single key objective within the project: to produce a detailed analysis of the nature, function and significance of these grave goods and to test the hypothesis that many of the artefacts were originally designed for use as components of ritual costume or as equipment for use in religious acts and ceremonies. Within this lay a series of sub-topics including, *inter alia*, the exploitation of materials, the phenomenon of 'heirloom' deposition, and regionalisation. To achieve this required a staged process of investigation which is amplified in Chapter 2, necessitating, where possible:

- classification of artefacts by size, shape and idio-syncratic features
- characterisation (and possible sourcing) of the materials of objects made from stone, jet or jet-like materials, fossils and minerals
- identification of the origin, in terms of species and body part, of objects made from bone, teeth and antler
- recognition of manufacturing processes and methods
- analysis and assessment of wear patterning and damage

Primary research was initially funded as a small pilot project by the Leverhulme Trust in order to test feasibility. The potential of the project soon became apparent and, as a result, the Leverhulme Trust generously agreed to fund a major three-year programme of research in 2006. The funding permitted the applicant (Professor John Hunter) to employ a lead researcher (Dr Ann Woodward) and an additional post-doctoral researcher (Dr David Bukach) to carry out the work. The main findings of the overall project, including the pilot study, are set out in this volume, but some of the findings have already been described in earlier publications. These include a general preliminary analysis of the subject (Woodward *et al.* 2005), a more specialised investigation of a selection of stone bracers or wrist guards (Woodward *et al.* 2006), and three reviews of assemblages from specific graves, relating to Bush Barrow (Wilsford G5, Wiltshire; Needham *et al.* 2010), the Clandon Barrow (Winterborne St Martin G31, Dorset; Needham and Woodward 2008) and Wilsford G58, Wiltshire (Woodward and Needham 2012). Although the research was directed at a range of different objects and materials one artefact type, stone bracers, was singled out for more detailed examination and analysis. This resulted in a monograph in its own right (Woodward and Hunter 2011) although summary findings are also included in this volume. The core group of researchers was fortunate in being able to draw into the project other scholars who were already working on some of the artefact types under review. These scholars, together with their areas of expertise and their contributions to the volume, are detailed in Chapter 2.

The volume is divided into 13 chapters and a series of appendices. Chapter 2 deals with the various methodologies which were used to generate the data; it explains why particular methods were used, the levels of confidence which could be achieved, and the rationale for material selection, including the criteria which resulted in identifying the various geographical areas for study. A total of 887 artefacts and 81 necklaces were examined in 13 different museums or institutions (see Chapter 2, Table 2.2 for location of objects). If individual necklace beads are included the total rises to 5665. There are six main descriptive chapters (Chapter 3 to Chapter 8) which deal specifically with artefacts. These are divided under broad headings and some clarification may be useful in explaining the rationale by which individual objects are grouped. Any rigid forensic approach would divide the artefacts into either object type (e.g. beads, buttons, daggers *etc*) or material type (e.g. copper alloy, bone, jet or jet-like materials *etc*) for investigation and discussion purposes. However, many objects are composed of more than one material (e.g. pendants which combine gold and amber), others can be made of different materials (e.g. necklaces composed of beads of jet or jet-like materials, amber or shell), and some are significant in having close associations with other objects made of different materials (e.g. copper alloy daggers and bone pommels). In general, a classification by object type has been followed. However, some artefacts conform to no particular object type and cannot be easily assigned to a particular category; there are also problems in assigning those artefacts which started life with one function and ended, after re-working, with another. As a result it became impossible to conform strictly to either object or material as a primary criterion. It was eventually decided to group the artefacts in terms of perceived associations within the burial context itself: artefacts likely to have been deposited with the body (*Items of Equipment)*, and artefacts adorning the body itself (*Personal Adornment*). In view of the quantity of material under study, both categories required breaking down into smaller sections. These headings and divisions are shown below in Table 1.1.

This grouping transpired to be an effective working system, although there was some inevitable duplication and occasional ambiguity. The division of artefacts in this way may not be entirely satisfactory from the point of view of scientific rigor, but it allows the researcher to identify either object or material with little difficulty using a unique identification number within the volume (see Chapter 2), and to access the discussions which are housed at the end of each section, or sub-section. Each section contains a table at the end whereby object type and find location can be cross-referenced.

Chapter 3 (*daggers, pommels and belt fittings*) is divided into four sections: daggers and knives; pommels; belt hooks, and belt rings and pulley objects. It essentially considers those artefacts which were considered to be associated around the belt area, the main materials being copper alloy (for which there is additional analytical data) and bone or other similar materials (antler, whalebone *etc*). Daggers have been intensively researched by Gerloff (1975) and in part by Jockenhövel (1980). These remain the main sources for study, and are advanced here by a detailed analysis of 143 examples and the introduction of a new typological sequence devised by Stuart Needham. Chapter 3 also includes a revised analysis of pommels (19 examples), again by Stuart Needham, which updates the previous (1974) classification produced by Hardaker. It also includes important new identification of the (animal) bone material used to fashion the pommels. Belt hooks, however, have been more recently investigated by Alison Sheridan (2007a), although not all fall within the geographical parameters of this study. Research into the final object type in this section, belt rings and pulley objects, had traditionally relied on the work of Clarke (1970, 262–3) and is explored further here using 19 examples.

Chapter 4 comprises those objects seen as being less specific in location around the body than those in Chapter 3; all the objects investigated in this chapter have traditionally been viewed as representing working tools, or accoutrements placed with the body at burial, but not as part of the dress or regalia of the body itself. They consist of stone, bone and copper alloy objects. In the stone sections, sponge finger stones were originally listed by Smith and Simpson (1966, Appendix VI) and ten examples have been studied in detail here; the current listing of grooved stones previously relied on pre-war studies (Newall 1932) with eight examples being examined in the project, and the study of perforated stones still relies on the work of Proudfoot (1963, Appendix III) (17 examples here). The group of objects described as 'stones without perforations' has not been subject to any previous listing or typological appraisal as far as is known (six examples). Many of these stone objects were the subject of chemical analysis (X-ray fluorescence) for provenance purposes and the results are incorporated in the relevant sections.

The bone sections are divided into: antler/bone spatulae; bone points; bone tweezers; bone tubes; bone plates, and bone toggles. The spatulae were first analysed in any detail by Smith and Simpson (1966), but subsequent excavations have produced numerous further examples allowing 25 to be studied here. Bone points have been considered by Longworth in relation to their associations with Collared Urns (Longworth 1984, 63–5), but not as a single artefact group, and it was possible to examine a total of 184 examples in the project. The results indicated however that many of the bone points may have formed elements of costume or adornment rather than tools or general equipment. Bone tweezers have been listed by Proudfoot (1963, Appendix IV and 412–4); no listing has previously been made for bone tubes, plates or toggles although some of these items have

Table 1.1. List of chapter sections and number of items examined.

Chapter	Object type	Number studied
Ch. 3	**Items of Equipment I: daggers, pommels and belt fittings**	
Ch. 3.1	Daggers/knives	143
Ch. 3.2	Pommels	19
Ch. 3.3	Belt hooks	10
Ch. 3.4	Belt and pulley rings	19
Ch. 4	**Items of Equipment II: stone, bone, copper alloy and miscellaneous objects**	
Ch. 4.1	Sponge finger stones	10
Ch. 4.2	Grooved stones	8
Ch. 4.3	Perforated stones	17
Ch. 4.4	Whetstones without perforations	6
Ch. 4.5	Bone and antler spatula	25
Ch. 4.6	Copper alloy awls	59
Ch. 4.7	Bone points	184
Ch. 4.8	Bone tweezers	10
Ch. 4.9	Bone tubes	7
Ch. 4.10	Bone plates	4
Ch. 4.11	Bone toggles	6
Ch. 4.12	Miscellaneous objects of bone and antler	24
Ch. 4.13	Miscellaneous copper alloys	6
Ch. 4.14	Miscellaneous jet and jet-like materials	11
Ch. 5	**Personal Adornment I: jet and jet-like materials, amber, bone and copper alloy**	
Ch. 5.1	Tusks and teeth	47
Ch. 5.2	V-perforated buttons	65
Ch. 5.3	Button sets	44
Ch. 5.4	Earrings	7
Ch. 5.5	Dress pins	28
Ch. 5.6	Studs	10
Ch. 5.7	Beads (singletons)	17
Ch. 5.8	Spacer plates (singletons)	9
Ch. 5.9	Pendants and individual necklace fasteners	44
Ch. 5.10	Bronze neck and head ornaments	2
Ch. 6	**Personal Adornment II: gold and the regalia from Bush Barrow**	
Ch. 6.1	Gold objects	31
Ch. 6.2	Regalia from Wilsford G5 (Bush Barrow)	15
Total non-necklace items		**887**
Ch. 7	**Necklaces I: disc beads and spacer plate necklaces**	
Ch. 7.1	Disc bead necklaces	12
Ch. 7.2	Spacer plate necklaces of jet or jet-like materials	13
Ch. 7.4	Amber necklaces	4
Ch. 8	**Necklaces II: simple and composite necklaces**	
Ch. 8.1	Simple necklaces	18
Ch. 8.2	Composite necklaces with two materials	16
Ch. 8.3	Composite necklaces with three materials	11
Ch. 8.4	Composite necklaces with four materials	4
Ch. 8.5	Composite necklaces with five materials	3
Total		**968**

been considered by Thomas (1954). There is an additional section in Chapter 4 that draws in miscellaneous objects of bone and antler which do not fall satisfactorily into any of these categories. The metal sections include copper and copper alloy awls; these have been little studied and no overall corpus has ever been compiled although a useful classification has been provided by Thomas (2005, 220–222). Fifty-nine individual awls were examined in the project. Other copper alloy objects studied include small axes, most recently studied by Needham *et al.* (2010, 19) and which are also the subject of physical analysis here, and the unusual pronged object from Wilsford G58, Wiltshire.

There is a final section containing miscellaneous objects of jet and jet-like materials.

The remaining four descriptive chapters are specifically concerned with personal adornment. Chapter 5 deals with those objects traditionally viewed as belonging to the dressing of the body itself and which can be more safely ascribed a function from the outset; these are grouped into ten sections. The first of these deals with tusks and teeth for which there has been no existing overall consideration apart from comments on a small number of sites (Moore and Rowlands 1972, 48). There are 47 such objects considered here, including a shark tooth. By contrast V-perforated buttons from Britain and Ireland have been fully listed and discussed by Shepherd (1973; 2009). Most examples from England are examined here (54 made from jet or jet-like materials and 11 of bone or amber). There has, however, been little previous work on button sets (predominantly jet or jet-like materials) of which four have been included, providing a total of 44 individual buttons. Nor has much attention been paid to copper alloy earrings (seven examples) or studs (ten examples of jet or jet-like materials and fired clay) both of which are allocated separate sections. Pendants have not previously been considered as a functional group either. Those examined here (44 examples) are derived from raw materials ranging from gold, bronze and jet to amber and bone, often involving a combination of these materials. Dress pins manufactured from bronze or animal bone have been listed by Gerloff (1975, Appendix C) and associated by her with the Wessex Culture. Many of these have been studied in detail, and in addition further bone examples have been identified; a total of 28 pins are studied in this volume. A number of graves contained individual beads (17 examples) or individual spacer plates (nine examples) as opposed to necklaces or parts of necklaces. These were considered to be significant depositions, denoted as 'singletons', and are discussed in two separate sections. The final section in Chapter 5 contains two copper alloy/bronze items, one a head ornament, and the other an armlet.

Chapter 6 deals predominantly with gold objects, or objects decorated with gold; there is inevitably slight duplication with other chapter sections. Gold objects have been well discussed previously (e.g. Needham 2000c). The first section (Chapter 6.1) examines 31 examples including those from the Little Cressingham, Upton Lovell G2e Golden Barrow and Clandon grave groups, notably with regard to gold sheet covered artefacts – discs, button covers, plaques and pendants. Chapter 6.2 is devoted to the Bush Barrow (Wilsford G5) burial which has also been the subject of more recent discussion (Needham *et al.* 2010) and also includes non-gold items in association. Of the 15 items discussed, key objects are the gold belt hook cover (including an explanation of its likely construction method), the studded dagger hilt, and the bone shaft mounts for which new interpretations are suggested. Stuart Needham's discussion here in Chapter 6.3, based on the material from both sections, marks a significant milestone in the study of goldwork in the Early Bronze Age.

The final two object chapters both deal with necklaces. No large-scale study of necklaces has ever been conducted, although study of individual sets, or of bead typologies have been addressed (e.g. Beck and Stone 1935; Shepherd 2009). Recently, however, major strides in the study of necklaces have been made by Alison Sheridan, particularly with regard to their nature, significance and dating (Sheridan and Davis 2002; Sheridan 2007b; 2008), and she contributes significantly to the examination and interpretation of the material here. The project presented the opportunity to examine specific types of necklace in great detail and effectively involved the examination of almost 4800 individual beads, together with terminal and spacer plates, representing a total of 81 different necklaces. Of particular interest in the examination is the interpretation of stringing, the re-use or mobility of individual necklace elements through time, and the interpretation of use wear on bead and spacer perforations. Chapter 7 divides these necklaces into three types: disc bead necklaces of jet and jet-like materials (12 examples); necklaces of jet and jet-like materials containing spacer plates (13 examples), and necklaces of amber (4 examples). Chapter 8 considers necklaces with fewer numbers of beads. These include small sets of beads made from a single material, but with components of variable shape, and composite necklaces, which are composed of elements of more than one material. The chapter is divided into five subsections according to the number of different materials employed. As well as jet, jet-like materials and amber beads, other materials represented include stone, bone, faience and fossils. A further 52 necklaces are covered in this chapter. In order to maintain a consistent style within Chapter 8 some of the necklace descriptions have been slightly shortened. Each of the two necklace chapters includes separate detailed discussion sections.

Chapter 9 *Chronology* presents a discussion of the dating of the periods which are covered within the study as a whole. The material described in the volume covers a time period of about 1000 years, lasting from the inception of copper artefacts *c.* 2500 cal BC until the end of the Early Bronze Age *c.* 1500 cal BC. This millennium encompasses three major archaeological periods. The Copper Age, which in recent times has come to be termed the Chalcolithic, using continental usage (Allen *et al.* 2012) can be dated to *c.* 2450/2400 to 2200/2150 cal BC. Bronze daggers come into use at around 2200 cal BC and Needham's 'fission horizon', relating to the wider distribution and variety of Beaker pottery, occurs at a similar time (Needham 2005). Thus the Bronze Age, defined by the development of new metal types begins *c.* 2200 cal BC. The mature Early Bronze Age, characterised by more complex bronze daggers and the Wessex series graves, starts at the turn of the millennium *c.* 2000 cal BC. This roughly correlates with the inception of new dagger types from *c.* 1950 cal BC. The period covered in this volume therefore includes three major periods: the Chalcolithic *c.* 2500–2200 cal BC, the initial Early Bronze Age *c.* 2200–2000 cal BC and the mature Early Bronze Age *c.* 2000–1500 cal BC. However where ceramic associations exist within the initial Early

Bronze Age they are predominately of Beaker style. As one of the main aims of the project was to compare the results obtained from rich grave assemblages associated with Beakers with those from Early Bronze Age contexts, for the purpose of this volume, the 1000 years covered has been divided simply into two periods, each lasting roughly 500 years. The first, which encompasses the Chalcolithic and initial Early Bronze Age, covers the main currency of Beaker graves and the second relates to the assemblages of the mature Early Bronze Age, including those from the Wessex series graves.

For most object categories the chronological summary provided in the main descriptive chapters is brief and succinct. However, within the necklace chapter discussions (Chapter 7.3, Chapter 7.5 and Chapter 8.6) a more detailed consideration of dating has been included. This detail usefully explains the complexity of the development of the different forms of necklace through time, and establishes the substantial longevity of the necklace traditions. Where radiocarbon determinations relating to objects studied are referred to within the main descriptive texts only the calibrated date range is provided. Full citation of dates, including laboratory reference numbers, may be found in Chapter 9.

Discussion in a wider context occurs in subsequent chapters. *Object Life Stories* (Chapter 10) discusses the occurrence of specially valued objects and the incidence of the recycling of heirloom items. This synthesis brings together and analyses the evidence for ancient fragmentation and wear. It highlights contrasts within the two chronological periods defined for the project and between the different patterns perceived within different geographical regions. *Object Function* (Chapter 11) summarises the evidence gathered relating to object design and use and, once again, analyses the data in relation to the two major periods defined and by geographical region. Distribution maps for selected artefact types are provided in the next chapter *Regional Variation* (Chapter 12). The distributions of further categories are summarised in histograms and the patterns of artefact distribution through space and time are discussed. The extent to which finds of certain categories are concentrated in the Wessex region, or elsewhere, forms a major theme. Finally, some key *Conclusions* are presented in Chapter 13.

In addition there are a series of appendices (housed on CD) which contain more detailed material and methodological information likely to be of use to the specialist researcher rather than the general reader. These contain further detail on the typo-chronology of copper/copper alloy daggers (Appendix I), the results of analytical work on a broader range of copper/copper alloy material (Appendix II), and archival data relating to animal bone identifications and discussion concerning the analysis of cetacean bone objects

(Appendix III and Appendix IV respectively). Technical data relating to the analytical methods used for jet and jet-like objects and stone objects, together with the full results and discussion of provenance follow (Appendix V and Appendix VI respectively). A final appendix contains more detailed information and discussion on the necklaces, notably those of jet and jet-like materials (Appendix VII).

The degree of detail presented within the descriptive chapters (Chapters 3 to 8) is intentionally uneven. This variation relates to the perceived overall significance of groups of objects and of individual items. In particular, two categories of material have been given specially detailed treatment. These are the objects made from gold (Chapter 6) and the major necklaces made from jet or jet-like materials and amber (Chapter 7). The reason for this decision is that these highly important artefacts have seldom been described since the original reports of their discovery by antiquarian excavators, and because they have never previously been the subject of intensive microscopic study.

The items studied within the volume were selected in relation to the research questions that were being addressed by the project. Thus, the book was never intended to form a complete catalogue of all the relevant artefacts from England, nor of all the data collected during our period of research. As far as the latter is concerned, many of the observed details relating to each object, and other elements such as object weights, museum registration numbers and full referencing to existing literature, occur only within the databases and on the primary record forms. However, although not intended as a catalogue raisonné for items from Beaker and Early Bronze Age graves, the volume does provide an extensive, and intensively illustrated, overview of a large proportion of the grave goods from English burial sites, albeit excluding items of pottery and of flint.

The digital databases are deposited with the Archaeological Data Service, University of York while the full paper record is housed at the Society of Antiquaries of London, Burlington House, Piccadilly, London. In addition copies of the relevant primary record forms and photographs have been supplied to each museum visited during the project.

The main aim of the project – to investigate Chalcolithic and Early Bronze Age grave goods in relation to their possible use as special dress accessories or as equipment employed within ritual activities and ceremonies – has been fulfilled in a most positive and dramatic manner. Many items of adornment can be shown to have formed elements of elaborate costumes, probably worn by individuals, both male and female, who held important ritual roles within society. Furthermore, our analysis shows that various categories of object long interpreted as mundane types of tool were in fact items of bodily adornment or implements used in ritual contexts, or in the special embellishment of the human body.

2. METHODOLOGY

THE RESOURCE AND INVESTIGATIVE PROGRAMME

One of the original aims of the Leverhulme project was to define 'rich' graves belonging to the Wessex Culture. To test how such definitions might be achieved it was decided to prepare a site database which lists and records all graves of Beaker and Early Bronze Age date from England which are 'well furnished', this being a less loaded term than 'rich'. The main questions to be addressed were: do the so-called Wessex graves really stand out? And if so, by which criteria? And how do the patterns in the Early Bronze Age relate to the nature and distribution of well-furnished graves of the preceding Beaker tradition?

The definition of well-furnished graves was initially formulated to include grave assemblages which possessed two or more objects made from gold, copper or copper alloy, amber, faience, jet or jet-like materials, bone/antler or stone. Thus, grave groups which contained only pottery vessels, only items of flint, or both pottery and flint were excluded. As the compilation of lists of objects for study commenced, it soon became apparent that it would be more useful to include all grave assemblages that included one item made from the materials listed above. Thus we could include graves with a single dagger only, those with one jet V-perforated button only and those with one perforated bone point *etc*. Where pottery and flints occur in well-furnished graves, they are recorded in the database, but 'pot only' or 'flint only' graves are not recorded. Within the grave groups selected for study, the pottery vessels were not studied in detail. Most ceramic types are covered in the existing literature and published typologies were utilised (e.g. Clarke 1970 and Needham 2005 for Beakers; Longworth 1984 for Collared Urns). Neither were the listed flint objects studied in detail, firstly as there are just too many of them, and secondly because they need a higher level of magnification than was employed in this project to study any use wear. Specific types such as barbed-and-tanged arrowheads have been categorised by Green (1980) and flint daggers are the subject of current study and research by several specialists.

In the time available it was not possible to study the objects of gold, copper or copper alloy, amber, faience, jet and jet-like materials, bone/antler or stone from all the grave assemblages defined as well furnished. Consequently it was decided to concentrate on the items recovered during the main campaigns of antiquarian activity in England, and to take in the objects from more modern excavations that were housed in the relevant museums. The main study sessions were therefore concentrated in six museums. These included the finds from the activities of Mortimer (Hull and East Riding Museum) and Greenwell (The British Museum) on the Yorkshire Wolds, Bateman (Weston Park Museum, Sheffield) in the Peak District, Cunnington and Colt Hoare in Wessex (Wiltshire Heritage Museum, Devizes) and of Warne and his associates in Dorset (Dorset County Museum, Dorchester). We also included extensive study visits at the Salisbury and South Wiltshire Museum, which holds a fine and substantial collection of more recently excavated Beaker and Early Bronze Age grave goods, and shorter visits to other collections that hold key items. The latter included the Museum of Archaeology and Ethnology, Cambridge (key grave groups from East Anglia), Norwich City Museum (for the Little Cressingham group), Bristol City Museum (for major finds from barrows on Mendip), the English Heritage store at Fort Cumberland (for finds from Raunds barrow 1) and single items of stone or bone at Lewes Castle Museum and the Ashmolean Museum, Oxford. These last two items were studied whilst collecting data for our previous detailed research on Beaker-age bracers (Woodward and Hunter 2011). The stone items at the Ashmolean had been specially put aside for us prior to the closure of the museum for major refurbishment, but it was not possible to study other items relevant to our project, deriving from the Upper Thames Valley, due to the museum closure coinciding with the currency of our research project. The abbreviations used within this volume for the museums visited are shown in Table 2.1, and the quantities of objects studied in the various museums are summarised in Table 2.2. Overall, a total of 5665 items was studied in detail; these derived from 780 individual grave groups (211 from the Beaker-age and 569 from the Early Bronze Age; for regional breakdown see Table 2.3). Of the

Table 2.1. *Museums visited, and abbreviations employed in this volume.*

Museum	Abbreviation
The Ashmolean Museum, Oxford	Ash
Bristol City Museum	Brist
The British Museum	BM
Museum of Archaeology and Anthropology, University of Cambridge	Camb
Wiltshire Heritage Museum, Devizes	Dev
Dorset County Museum, Dorchester	Dor
English Heritage store, Fort Cumberland, Portsmouth	EH
Hove Museum	Hove
Hull and East Riding Museum, Hull	Hull
Lewes Castle Museum	Lewes
Norwich City Museum	Nor
Salisbury and South Wiltshire Museum, Salisbury	Sal
Weston Park Museum, Sheffield	Sheff

Table 2.2. *Number of objects studied (necklace elements are not included in the main raw material columns).*

Museum	Gold	Copper/ bronze	Amber	Jet or jet-like material	Bone	Stone	Clay	Necklace	Necklace elements
Ash	-	-	-	-	-	2	-	-	-
Brist	-	5	-	-	1	3	-	1	3
Camb	-	3	-	5	14	-	-	2	30
BM	4	47	3	76	95	4	-	24	1063
Dev	32	64	17	19	110	23	1	28	780
Dor	3	33	5	4	10	5	-	1	15
EH	-	-	1	5	-	2	-	-	-
Hove	-	-	-	-	-	1	-	-	-
Hull	-	24	1	41	38	-	-	7	1947
Lewes	-	-	-	-	1	-	-	-	-
Nor	5	2	-	-	-	-	-	1	48
Sal	-	23	2	3	48	6	-	9	101
Sheff	-	35	-	10	51	-	1	8	791
Totals	**44**	**235**	**29**	**163**	**368**	**46**	**2**	**81**	**4778**

Table 2.3. *Total numbers of grave groups containing objects studied within the project.*

Region	Beaker- age	Early Bronze Age	Total
East Yorkshire	47	131	178
Peak District	36	76	112
Wessex	50	274	324
Rest of country	78	88	166
Total	**211**	**569**	**780**

5665 items, 4778 were individual beads or pendants within necklaces (see also Chapter 1, Table 1.1 for a breakdown of numbers of object types).

Many of the assemblages and objects discussed in this volume were on museum display, while many were in storage. All required complex accession procedures. Examinations were conducted on a museum-to-museum basis with the full body of material kindly made available from display and store by the relevant curators in order that the researchers could view the material *in toto*, sometimes over a period of several days, and often during multiple visits.

SITE DATABASE

The site database was compiled using existing *corpora*, the antiquarian accounts, Heritage Environment Records (HERs) and county journals for recent finds from *c.*1970 onwards. The site database recorded basic contextual data, covering details of the context of discovery for each well-furnished grave assemblage, the published reference to any grave plan, a copy of the grave plan where available, the details of any associated burial, a listing of the associated grave goods within the assemblage and information relating to the placement of objects in relation to the body. The data was recorded manually using the project Assemblage Form (Figure 2.1). As mentioned in Chapter 1, the volume chapters dealing with gold objects and necklaces (Chapters 6 to 8) contain more detailed descriptions than the chapters dealing with individual items (Chapters 3 to 5). The more

Table 2.4. Concordance with Piggott Wessex Interment numbers (Piggott 1938, 102–6). Graves where items lost not included; graves where no objects studied in Leverhulme project not included; H denotes Hoare; G denotes Grinsell.

Wessex Interment	Piggott site name	Grinsell parish and/or barrow number	Chapter section (this volume)
5	Bloxworth Down	G4a	4.8; 8.2
6	Clandon Barrow	Winterborne St Martin G31	3.1; 6.1
8	Dewlish	G7	3.1; 4.3; 4.8; 5.5
9	Fordington	Dorchester G15	3.1; 4.7
10	Fordington, Laurence Barrow	Dorchester G4	3.1
11	Lords Down, Dewlish	G8	3.1
12	Martinstown	Winterborne St Martin G46	3.1
14	Oakley Down (H8)	Wimborne St Giles G8	3.1; 4.6; 7.3
15	Oakley Down (H13)	Wimborne St Giles G13	5.2
17	Oakley Down (H20)	Wimborne St Giles G20	3.1; 4.7
20	Ridgeway, Barrow 7	Weymouth G8	3.1; 3.2, 4.13
21	Winterbourne Came	G38	3.1
26	Camerton	Timsbury G1	3.1; 4.3; 5.5
30	Ablington, Figheldean	Figheldean G12	3.1
31	Aldbourne (Greenwell CCLXXVI)	G1	4.7; 8.1
32	Aldbourne (Greenwell CCLXXVII)	G2	3.1
33	Aldbourne (Greenwell CCLXXX)	G6	4.6; 5.2; 8.5
34	Aldbourne (Greenwell CCLXXXV)	G12	8.2
36	Amesbury (G85)	G85	3.1; 4.2; 4.4; 4.7
37	Amesbury (H26)	G39	8.2
38	Amesbury (H33)	G48	8.3
49	Bishops Cannings (G46)	G46 (Tan Hill)	8.2
51	Brigmerston, Silk Hill	Milston G3 or G7	4.3; 5.5
53	Bush Barrow, Normanton	Wilsford G5	3.1; 6.2
54	Collingbourne Ducis	G4	3.1; 5.5
56	Durrington (H101)	G47	8.2
58	Easton Down	Winterslow G21	8.4
59	Edington (Row Barrow)	G2	3.1
61	Idmiston	G9d	3.1
67	Lake (H Normanton 21)	Wilsford G47, G49 or G50	6.1; 7.3
68	Manton (G Preshute Ia)	Preshute G1a	3.1; 3.2; 7.1; 8.5
69	Newton, South (G1)	G1	8.2
70	Normanton (H139)	Wilsford G23	3.1; 4.3; 4.9; 5.5
71	Normanton (H155)	Wilsford G8	6.1; 8.5
72	Normanton (H156)	Wilsford G7	8.4
73	Normanton (H160)	Wilsford G3	8.3
74	Normanton (H164)	Amesbury G15	3.1
75	Normanton (H177)	Wilsford G27	3.1
76	Normanton (H182)	Wilsford G56	3.1; 4.8; 5.5
77	Norton Bavant (H1)	G1	3.1; 5.5; 8.1
78	Overton Hill	West Overton G1	5.5
81	Upton Lovell (Gold Barrow)	G2e	3.1; 4.6; 6.1; 7.3
82	Upton Lovell (H4)	G2a (shaman)	4.6; 4.7; 5.1; 8.2
83 ??	Upton Lovell (H5)	G2	3.1
84	Upton Lovell (H6)	G1	8.3
88	Wilsford (H Lake 15)	G46	8.2
89	Wilsford (H18)	G58	4.2; 4.9; 4.10; 4.13; 5.1
91	Wilsford (H8)	G43	3.1; 4.3
92	Winterbourne Stoke (H15)	G4	3.1; 3.2; 4.8
93	Winterbourne Stoke (H16)	G5	3.1; 4.6; 4.12
94	Winterbourne Stoke (H18)	G14	8.1
95	Winterbourne Stoke (H25)	G8	4.4; 4.6; 5.1; 8.3
98	Winterbourne Stoke (H West 10)	G67	5.2; 8.3
99	Winterbourne Stoke (H West 12)	G68	8.2

detailed chapters contain the published references and full discussion of burial contexts. For all other objects, such detailed data is included within the project archive and is summarised at the beginning of the section dealing with each object type.

It was intended at the outset that detailed site data would be compiled for all well furnished grave assemblages in England, and this was achieved for all such grave assemblages of Beaker age. However, for the Early Bronze Age period, it became apparent that the time required to undertake such a task was too great to be encompassed within the project programme, and a selective approach needed to be devised. It was therefore decided to concentrate on the collection of detailed Early Bronze Age site data for three regions of the country that had produced the largest numbers of well furnished graves, and which were widely distributed within England.

The three regions chosen were Wessex, the Peak District and the East Yorkshire Wolds, and all site data for relevant burials in these regions were entered in an *Access* database. Using this database, and the full database prepared for the Beaker-age burials, interrogations were undertaken to inform the various analyses discussed in Chapter 10 (*Object Life Stories*) and Chapter 11 (*Object Function*). The Wessex region was defined as including sites within the counties of Dorset and Wiltshire only. Theoretically it would have been useful to include relevant grave groups from Hampshire and from the Upper Thames Valley. However, for logistic reasons, the few grave assemblages from Hampshire, housed in various small museums, were not studied in detail, and the Thames Valley grave groups housed in the Ashmolean Museum were not available for study. Our detailed studies have included the items from many of the burials listed as Wessex Interments by Piggott (1938). The identifications of these burials in terms of Grinsell barrow numbering, and a listing of where the items concerned are considered in this volume, are shown in Table 2.4.

The Peak District region was defined as the counties of Derbyshire and Staffordshire, with most of the relevant finds being housed at the Weston Park Museum, Sheffield. For Yorkshire, we wished to include only the graves that were located on the chalklands of the Yorkshire Wolds. These occur within the parishes which before 1974 occupied the East Riding of Yorkshire. The relevant parishes are listed in Table 2.5. This shows the county designations of the selected parishes, which often had changed twice in recent times. In this project, the parishes on the Wolds have been described as occupying E. Yorks., as opposed to the few relevant sites from other parts of the three-part region which are designated as being located in N. Yorks. or W. Yorks. For the rest of the country the compilation of data relating to burial types, human remains and associations of objects was gathered more rapidly, but using all the same sources, and entered within a simple *Excel* database. The data were used, in combination with the more detailed data from the three selected regions, for the analysis presented in Chapter 12 (*Regional Variation*).

OBJECT IDENTIFICATION

The methodology for recording all objects is addressed below. In summary all were recorded on specially devised proformas in an *Object Database*. This was undertaken by measurement using plastic callipers and by microscopic examination for evidence of manufacture, fracture and use wear. The majority of objects studied were made from animal bone, copper and copper alloy, or jet and jet-like materials (see Table 2.2). Another common material was amber, while items made from gold, stone and fired clay existed in smaller numbers. All analysis involved the three primary team members. A number of other scholars were already heavily involved in researching certain of the object types or materials and generously agreed to contribute to the project by applying their own expertise and knowledge. Notable here were the contributions of Dr Alison Sheridan (jet and jet-like materials) and Dr Stuart Needham (gold and bronze/copper alloy objects).

Alison Sheridan was a key member of the team involved in the identification and recording of artefacts of jet and jet-like materials at the British Museum and at the museums in Sheffield, Hull, Devizes, Salisbury and Cambridge, following a protocol developed by her and Mary Davis for a broader study of prehistoric jet and jet-like jewellery (Sheridan and Davis 2002). The methods of observation and analysis are described in detail in Appendix V. Dr Sheridan also continued analysis of several large necklaces at Weston Park Museum, Sheffield, subsequent to the main phase of project recording. At the British Museum Mary Davis joined the recording team, and she also undertook a programme of XRF analysis of selected objects there, in conjunction with Duncan Hook of the British Museum laboratory.

A number of jet/shale items were also analysed in the NMS laboratories in Edinburgh and by the late Dr J. M. Jones, formerly of the University of Newcastle (for details of all these scientific analyses see below, and Appendix V). All the basic records of the jet and jet-like objects and necklaces were the result of cooperative teamwork, but the synthetic text descriptions of the necklaces presented in Chapter 7, and a few of those in Chapter 8, were prepared by Alison Sheridan. The methods used to record objects made from jet and jet-like materials were also applied to the study of items made from amber, with this work being undertaken by members of the primary team (AW and DB).

Stuart Needham's involvement also provided an invaluable asset in the examination and interpretation of both gold and copper/copper alloy objects. He worked with the team at Devizes, Norwich and Hull, especially in relation to the exotic assemblages from Bush Barrow, The Golden Barrow (Upton Lovell G2e) and Little Cressingham. He has provided detailed descriptions of the gold objects, of all the items recovered from Bush Barrow and a general discussion relating to the gold objects (Chapter 6). In addition, he worked with the team on several groups of copper alloy objects and has contributed a new classification for copper and copper alloy daggers (see Chapter 3.1 and Appendix I), and a revised classification

Table 2.5. Yorkshire parishes: concordance between old and new county designations, and attributions used in this volume (prepared in conjunction with Terry Manby).

Parish	Current county	'New county' (1974) (Kinnes and Longworth)	'Old county' (Kinnes and Longworth 1984)
'East Yorkshire' (E. Yorks.) in this volume			
Acklam	North Yorkshire	North Yorkshire	Yorkshire: East Riding
Aldro, Birdsall	North Yorkshire	North Yorkshire	Yorkshire: East Riding
Birdsall	North Yorkshire	North Yorkshire	Yorkshire: East Riding
Bishop Wilton	East Riding of Yorkshire	Humberside	Yorkshire: East Riding
Brough	East Riding of Yorkshire	North Humberside	Yorkshire: East Riding
Butterwick	North Yorkshire	North Yorkshire	
Cowlam	East Riding of Yorkshire	North Humberside	Yorkshire: East Riding
Driffield	East Riding of Yorkshire	North Humberside	Yorkshire: East Riding
Easington	East Riding of Yorkshire	Humberside	Yorkshire: East Riding
Etton	East Riding of Yorkshire	North Humberside	Yorkshire: East Riding
Fimber	East Riding of Yorkshire	Humberside	Yorkshire: East Riding
Folkton	North Yorkshire	North Yorkshire	Yorkshire: East Riding
Ganton	North Yorkshire	North Yorkshire	Yorkshire: East Riding
Garton-on-the-Wolds	East Riding of Yorkshire	Humberside	Yorkshire: East Riding
Goodmanham	East Riding of Yorkshire	North Humberside	Yorkshire: East Riding
Helperthorpe	North Yorkshire	North Yorkshire	Yorkshire: East Riding
Heslerton	North Yorkshire	North Yorkshire	Yorkshire: East Riding
Huggate	East Riding of Yorkshire	North Humberside	Yorkshire: East Riding
Hunmanby	North Yorkshire	North Yorkshire	Yorkshire: East Riding
Kirby Underdale	East Riding of Yorkshire	North Humberside	Yorkshire: East Riding
Kirkburn	East Riding of Yorkshire	Humberside	Yorkshire: East Riding
Langton	North Yorkshire	North Yorkshire	Yorkshire: East Riding
Melton (Quarry)	East Riding of Yorkshire	Humberside	Yorkshire: East Riding
Middleton-on-the-Wolds	East Riding of Yorkshire	Humberside	Yorkshire: East Riding
Rudston	East Riding of Yorkshire	North Humberside	Yorkshire: East Riding
Sledmere	East Riding of Yorkshire	Humberside	Yorkshire: East Riding
Thixendale	North Yorkshire	North Yorkshire	Yorkshire: East Riding
Thwing	East Riding of Yorkshire	North Humberside	Yorkshire: East Riding
Towthorpe, Fimber	East Riding of Yorkshire	Humberside	Yorkshire: East Riding
Warter	East Riding of Yorkshire	North Humberside	Yorkshire: East Riding
Weaverthorpe	North Yorkshire	North Yorkshire	Yorkshire: East Riding
Wetwang	East Riding of Yorkshire	Humberside	Yorkshire: East Riding
Wharram Percy	North Yorkshire	North Yorkshire	Yorkshire: East Riding

Parish	Current county	'New county' (1974) (Kinnes and Longworth)	'Old county' (Kinnes and Longworth 1984)

'North Yorkshire' (N. Yorks.) in this volume

Parish	Current county	'New county' (1974) (Kinnes and Longworth)	'Old county' (Kinnes and Longworth 1984)
Ayton	North Yorkshire	North Yorkshire	Yorkshire: North Riding
Beadlam	North Yorkshire	North Yorkshire	Yorkshire: North Riding
Egton	North Yorkshire	North Yorkshire	Yorkshire: North Riding
Holwick in Teesdale	North Yorkshire	North Yorkshire	Yorkshire: North Riding
Fylingdales	North Yorkshire	North Yorkshire	Yorkshire: North Riding
Hutton Buscel	North Yorkshire	North Yorkshire	Yorkshire: East Riding
Pickering	North Yorkshire	North Yorkshire	Yorkshire: North Riding
Pockley	North Yorkshire	North Yorkshire	Yorkshire: North Riding
Rosedale	North Yorkshire	North Yorkshire	Yorkshire: North Riding
Scamridge, Ebberston	North Yorkshire	North Yorkshire	Yorkshire: North Riding
Slingsby	North Yorkshire	North Yorkshire	Yorkshire: North Riding
Stranghow Moor, Lockwood	Redcar and Cleveland	Cleveland	Yorkshire: North Riding
Westerdale	North Yorkshire	North Yorkshire	Yorkshire: North Riding

'West Yorkshire' (W. Yorks.) in this volume

Parish	Current county	'New county' (1974) (Kinnes and Longworth)	'Old county' (Kinnes and Longworth 1984)
Ferry Fryston	West Yorkshire	West Yorkshire	Yorkshire: West Riding
Todmorden	West Yorkshire	West Yorkshire	Yorkshire: West Riding

for pommels of all materials (see Chapter 3.2). A digest of existing metal analyses relating to the objects of copper and copper alloy studied within the project has been provided by Dr Peter Bray (see below, Chapter 3.1 and Appendix II).

The main specialist team member involved in the study of items made from animal bone and antler was Mark Maltby. The material was identified and recorded by Mark Maltby and the project team at the British Museum stores and at the museums in Sheffield, Hull, Devizes, Salisbury and Cambridge; his findings are incorporated into the relevant chapters and presented in full in Appendix III. Details of the methodology employed are also provided in Appendix III. Sheila Hamilton-Dyer provided second opinions on the identifications of some of the objects at the British Museum and at Salisbury, and microscopic examination of selected objects was subsequently carried out by Dr Sonia O'Connor (Chapter 3.2 and Appendix IV).

Examination of the stone objects was undertaken by the main project team members in association with geochemists Peter Webb and John Watson and petrographer Dr Rob Ixer. Fiona Roe was also a member of this sevenfold team, and contributed her extensive knowledge of lithic artefacts of different kinds. All were involved in visits to the British Museum, the Ashmolean Museum, and to the museums in Bristol, Hove, Devizes and Salisbury. Stone objects were subjected to petrographic examination, X-ray fluorescence analysis and measurement of magnetic susceptibility (see below and Appendix VI). The use of portable analytical equipment throughout enabled analysis to be carried out in the museums themselves and thus enabled the whole examination programme to be undertaken as a single team exercise. Additionally, all objects were photographed to

provide both general and detailed images. Key conclusions are incorporated within the relevant sections of Chapter 4, while the full results are presented in Appendix VI.

A project of this nature offered significant logistical challenges in addition to those of having the material collected for study and study space made available. Partly for this reason it was agreed that each item should be examined as comprehensively as possible on the one occasion only: this pre-empted the need for a further examination and, moreover, meant that the items were only unwrapped and handled on the single occasion. In a few cases it was however necessary to revisit particular items, either to check certain details, or to discuss material identifications with further specialists. A strict set of *Handling Guidelines* was formulated, and these were followed by all team members in each museum.

As part of the pre-visit programme each individual item was given a project identification (ID) number for the purpose of the research; this could be cross-referenced with the respective museum accession number concerned and with any other existing classification system that had already been applied (e.g. Gerloff 1975; Shepherd 2009). Each ID number was unique and is used to identify that item throughout the volume. The objects were numbered and examined; sequential sets of numbers were used for each material type, but with gaps in the overall sequence between the sets of individual material numbers to allow for any later additions. A small number of problems were encountered when implementing this, for example with respect to necklaces containing large numbers of individual beads. For working purposes, rather than attach ID numbers to each individual bead, the whole necklace was allocated a single number, but suffixed by 'N' (N = necklace), for example ID 247(N); this enabled the more ubiquitous beads (typically fusiform and disc beads) to be described generically. However, all beads were recorded individually using a numerical sub-classification. In the few cases where it was necessary to comment on a particular bead within the volume the sub-classification could be used, for example ID 247.12 indicating Necklace ID 247, bead 12, identified on a suitably numbered illustration. Another problem arose with a small number of objects constructed of more than one material. These tended to be classified according to the dominant material, for example a shale cone covered in gold foil would be numbered under gold; but there were other instances, for example where a bronze dagger and its detached bone pommel would require two separate numbered classifications, but with cross-referencing.

EXAMINATION PROCESS

Each object available for study was examined in detail and recorded on a generic proforma; this is illustrated in Figure 2.2. There were some exceptions to this: notably multiple beads in necklaces (Figure 2.3), V-perforated buttons and sets of bone pins or points (Figure 2.4). There was also a bespoke recording form for stone bracers which were the subject of separate study and publication (Woodward and Hunter 2011). The findings from the bracer study are cross-referenced here, but not reported in full. Objects of animal bone were also recorded on a separate form as the nature of the object interrogation differed somewhat from non-organic materials. Once the proformas had been completed, the information was subsequently transferred into a relational database (*Access*). Direct transfer from examination to database was rejected as the researchers found that not only did interim transfer of data to paper form allow for easier review and checking, but also that it facilitated annotations of drawings and sketches; in several instances it was found that it was more efficient to sort and analyse paper records than to employ a computer directly.

BASIC RECORD

Part of the examination was to create a *basic record*; this consisted of the various defined contextual, material and typological fields listed in the published catalogue, plus additional fields which would allow any future researcher to obtain more refined details of each object, together with its condition and, where available, its life history. There were some additions or variants to this, notably with regards to objects of bone which required basic data on the nature of the material (whether bone, antler or tooth), species identification (e.g. sheep/goat), size category (e.g. large mammal, sheep-sized mammal) and the bone element in question (e.g. metacarpal or mandible). The examination of beads and necklaces of jet and jet-like materials also required a more elaborate examination in order to satisfy basic record requirements, notably on complex dimensional and shape characteristics, the nature of different raw materials, and the nature and type of use wear. The use wear information was used to provide clues as to the probable original arrangement of the components, as well as to the way in which the jewellery and dress accessories had been worn. The overall purpose was to create a record which was as consistent and as comprehensive as possible in coverage, which would present data in the most objective manner possible, and which would also allow the researchers to include 'free text' on observations, interpretations and hypotheses which seemed appropriate at the time.

Part of the basic record involved the weight of many of the items. This was more to create a marker than provide a typological criterion, but it would enable future researchers to identify any minor loss not evident visually, or to provide an additional future check on object veracity. Weighing was normally carried out to one decimal place.

The project dealt with a wide spectrum of different materials and object types with a range of shapes and sizes. Each material or object type possessed its own idiosyncratic attributes, problems and recording nuances. The largest objects included daggers and bone objects, and the smallest awls, buttons and beads; some involved particular measurement difficulties in terms of reference points, notably belt rings and earrings; others exhibited severe surface degradation and/or oxidation such as amber, while others (notably stone) were highly durable. Decorative qualities were particularly evident on gold objects and on some of the necklace plates, while use wear was often highly pronounced on beads of jet and jet-like materials. All these various attributes and differences required consideration in the recording process. There were also a number of limitations: a few items (notably necklaces) were mounted for display and were not able to be detached to allow a consistent level of examination, and some objects had suffered from early conservation and display techniques. This was mostly by the use of thick consolidants, heavy glue mends and display fixing marks all of which inhibited examination of the original surfaces.

Some of the objects had already been studied or described individually, in varying degrees of detail, in previous publications. Data from these were recorded on the proformas but were reviewed rather than accepted. Any differences that occurred were noted; many of these differences had implications for post-depositional damage or wear. Where possible, each record form contained a line drawing of the individual object, either from a previous publication or one sketched during the examination. This was roughly to scale and showed both surfaces as well as the profile for working purposes. It allowed the researchers to annotate particular attributes or decorative features and to record observable wear, fractures, and any other observations that were thought to be important during the examination.

PHOTOGRAPHY

Digital photographs were taken of each object, and a total of 5860 archive images were recorded during the project. These consisted of basic views (front, back and any necessary side view) together with close-up images of any specific feature identified during examination at higher magnification, often with aid of macro extension tubes. Typically these might include striation patterns, details of use wear or fracture and specific evidence of manufacture, flaw or aspect of profile. Photography was undertaken using a Nikon D50 DSLR camera and macro lens, and an illuminating copy stand. Lighting was normally placed at oblique angles for specific close-up work in order to best illustrate manufacturing striations and aspect of use wear. Images were captured in RAW image format and imported into image editing software where basic retouching was completed. Colour correction was minimized using daylight light sources, and when necessary was applied on-site using the object for reference.

One of the advantages of the photography, apart from supporting the basic record, lay in its potential to allow a visual comparison between similar objects and object types held in different museums. Images of individual objects could be cut from their backgrounds, rescaled and pasted adjacent to images of similar objects. The majority of the illustrations in this volume demonstrate the value of this, enabling similar objects from different museums to be viewed to a common scale on the same page. It also enabled different sides of an individual object to be set next to each other in a manner traditionally carried out by line drawing. This was an extremely time-consuming exercise, but one which presents a unique record of the material studied. Objects are shown with a scale bar of either 20mm or 40mm, with some exceptions, and pasted against either a white or black background depending on material. Objects are shown to scale per page but, in view of the size diversity of some of the object types, it was not always possible to keep the scale consistent from one page to the next. The process utilised various commercial softwares, and was also concerned with accuracy of colour. This was particularly awkward with regard to illustrating details of objects, for example decorative elements, which required different angles and levels of light to be achieved effectively.

MEASUREMENT

Dimensional measurements were undertaken using plastic callipers to a theoretical accuracy of 0.1mm, although in terms of the three basic measurements (length, breadth and thickness) unevenness of reference points for some object types would suggest that replicable accuracy was likely to be to the nearest 0.5mm only. With regard to measurement of smaller features (e.g. perforations), a greater degree of accuracy could be argued providing that reference points were clearly visible. In all cases measurements were taken at *maximum* points, although some examples necessitated measuring minimum points in addition. All observations other than basic measurements were undertaken using a binocular microscope (up to ×50) with a cold light source which could be adjusted to provide oblique lighting. This

enabled manufacturing striations, wear marks, possible re-use, surface textures and fractures to be interpreted and recorded clearly, and with a higher degree of confidence. Each item was initially examined visually, its main dimensions recorded and any obvious significant features discussed before being examined microscopically. Some object types or materials, notably spacer plates, required a slightly different approach and necessitated the generation of further quantities of data (both numerical and descriptive) which are held in the various appendices housed in a CD at the end of the volume.

MANUFACTURE

Manufacturing marks were best detected under the microscope with the light source angled to pick out even the faintest of markings or striations reflecting production methods. These might indicate saw marks, the use of abrasive materials or how, in the case of beads made from jet or jet-like materials, a roughout might have been ground into the desired shape. Such features were recorded in terms of their location, size and orientation, together with observations on finishing and polishing. Some objects had also been drilled or perforated; this gave the opportunity to determine how, and from which side, the drilling had been carried out, any changes of direction, and the width of the drill bit. A small number of X-ray photographs were taken of certain necklaces to assist such studies (Chapter 7.2). From the rilling (the concentric lines seen within the perforations caused by drilling) it was possible to see how the drilling might have been undertaken, and to interpret the type of drill used. With bone objects it was possible to identify butchery marks from disarticulation or from splitting, or evidence for skinning.

USE WEAR

Use wear factors were often more difficult to identify, especially on hard or durable materials such as stone, in contrast to more 'mobile' objects such as pendants or strings of beads, and was also best detected under a microscope. It became possible, for example, to detect wear on particular areas of decoration (notably on 'soft' materials such as gold) indicative of a particular angle of action or rubbing, the honing and/or wear of a dagger on a particular part of the blade, or the wear and angle of wear around the perforation on a bone pin. Animal bone might also exhibit burning, or gnaw marks. With beads it was essential to identify evidence for thread-wear, thread-pull, bead-on-bead (and bead-on-plate) wear and 'fabric rub' (the position of the object in relation to fabric). All these have a bearing on how a particular necklace might have been composed and worn. Overall, these various factors are indicative of use and nature of use. It was equally important to identify *absence* of use wear as this also offered important implications regarding the life history of the individual object and its significance in the burial. When the full record of each object was complete, a general estimate of its degree of wear was attempted. The categories employed ranged from 'fresh' to 'very worn'.

One issue that could not fully be addressed was the length of time that might have been involved for different degrees of wear to have developed on objects made from different raw materials. For instance, would heavy wear on a bone tool have occurred more rapidly than the wear observed on an item made of jet? Such questions would need to be addressed through programmes of experimental study, using replica artefacts made from different raw materials. Unfortunately time did not allow for such experimental work to be included within the project, but such experimentation could usefully form part of future research programmes relating to use wear.

DAMAGE

Many of the objects showed fragmentation either through fracture, chipping or flaking; each element of fragmentation was identified, numbered, recorded and located on the drawing or sketch. In most instances it was also possible to determine whether the damaged elements occurred during manufacture (e.g. during drilling a perforation), during use, or post-depositionally. Microscopic analysis usually enabled any wear to be noted on a damaged section, indicating that fracture occurred prior to burial. Reference to previous illustrations of individual objects, especially in early publications, also provided a useful indicator of any subsequent damage. A general estimate of percentage presence was also made for each item.

SCIENTIFIC ANALYSIS

METALS

No new compositional analyses for metal objects were undertaken within the project. Many of the gold objects had been analysed by Hartmann (1982) while new analyses, using laser-ablation induction-coupled plasma mass spectrometry (Taylor 1999; 2004; 2005) have yet to be published in full. Aspects of compositional analysis relevant to the objects studied within the project are described and discussed by Stuart Needham in Chapter 6.

Major programmes of scientific analysis relating to artefacts made from copper and copper alloy (bronze) were undertaken, mainly in the second half of the 20th century. However these mainly concentrated on the sampling of daggers, and very few beads, awls or ornaments have ever been analysed. Existing results have recently been reconsidered by Peter Bray (2009). By combining this consolidated data with the results from other aspects of Bronze Age archaeology, such as excavated sites and the nature of technology, it has been possible to consider the social and economic aspects of Bronze Age metallurgy in more detail. A summary of Bray's research into the role and use of daggers in British Early Bronze Age society is provided in Appendix II. Using Bray's data, a summary of the occurrence of the main metal types through time

is supplied in Chapter 3.1 (Tables 3.1.3 and 3.1.4). Of particular interest to the present project are the possible correlations between metal types in use through time and use wear; a discussion of these aspects is also included in Chapter 3.1.

JET AND JET-LIKE MATERIALS

Objects made from black raw materials such as jet, shale, lignite and cannel coal can be differentiated to some extent by eye. However in many cases firm identifications can only be made through the use of scientific techniques. Numerous numbers of objects made from jet and shale housed in the Wiltshire Heritage Museum at Devizes, the Dorset County Museum at Dorchester, the Salisbury and South Wiltshire Museum and the Ashmolean Museum at Oxford had previously been analysed by Bussell in the early 1980s (Pollard *et al.* 1981; Bussell *et al.* 1982) using X-ray fluorescence spectrometry. This followed from Bussell's earlier work using Neutron Activation Analysis (NAA) directed at Early Bronze Age samples from Sheffield Museums and the Hull and East Riding Museum (Bussell 1976). The results were compared with those obtained from a series of geological control samples of Whitby jet, cannel coals and Kimmeridge shale.

Bussell's research, however, did not include jet and jet-like objects housed in the British Museum. Consequently a major part of the project here involved the compositional analysis of a selection of these items. This analysis was undertaken by project member Mary Davis in association with Duncan Hook of the British Museum. In addition, selected necklaces, buttons and other objects made from jet and jet-like materials housed in the Hull and East Riding Museum and Sheffield Museums were lent to National Museums Scotland for scientific study. They were compositionally analysed by Lore Troalen, also using X-ray fluorescence spectrometry, and with samples of raw Whitby jet and of cannel coal as *comparanda*. On a further front, when studying various objects made from jet or jet-like materials in museum stores, tiny fragments of material detached from the object were located in the storage bags or boxes. With permission, some of these were submitted to the late Dr J. M. Jones, formerly of the University of Newcastle, who analysed them using reflected light microscopy.

The results obtained from these various analytical programmes are incorporated, as appropriate, in the descriptions of the necklaces in Chapter 7 and Chapter 8. The full data, together with details of the respective analytical methods are housed in Appendix V.

Throughout this volume the following abbreviations are used: B – Gill Bussell, AS – Alison Sheridan, MD – Mary Davis, DH – Duncan Hook.

STONE

In order to investigate the possible provenance of objects made from stone, a suite of analytical techniques were employed. The aim was to provide detailed petrographic and chemical descriptions of the stone sources used, for comparison with the signatures of known rock types within Britain and beyond. Stone objects were studied at a number of the museums visited (above). Larger stone objects were chemically analysed using portable X-ray fluorescence spectrometry (XRF), undertaken by Peter Webb and John Watson of the Open University. The most reliable quantitative results from this method rely on smooth flat homogeneous sample surfaces and thus the technique was particularly suited to whetstones and objects of similar shape, such as sponge finger stones. A total of 43 artefacts were analysed (9 sponge finger stones, 7 grooved stones, 17 perforated stones, 6 unperforated stones, and 4 miscellaneous items); the technical data are presented in Appendix VI and the results incorporated into the discussion of the relevant objects in Chapter 4. Magnetic susceptibility readings were also taken, using an Exploranium G.S KT-5 instrument.

All stone objects, including beads which were not examined using XRF, were studied petrographically by Dr Rob Ixer using a standard ×10 hand lens and/or a low power binocular microscope. Particular attention was paid to breaks/fractures in the artefact as these provided 'fresh', unpolished surfaces and the true colour of the rock. All lithological features, including mean grain size, presence of clasts, megacrysts, fossils, veining, bedding, laminae and foliation planes were noted and measured. The colour of the polished and any broken, natural surface was recorded and standardised using the geological Society of America's 'rock-color' chart. Clast grain size within sediments was standardised using the standard grain size scale. A lithological identification for each object was made based upon these macroscopic characteristics. The detailed petrographic descriptions are also presented in Appendix VI.

BURIAL AND AGE CRITERIA

Part of the interpretation of the material rests on the age determination of human remains associated with the grave goods; some explanation may be needed as to how this was defined, and the validity of the information used. The majority of sites were excavated in the 19th century by antiquarian scholars, and in nearly all cases human remains were not retained for deposition in museum collections. Furthermore, some later scholars synthesising these results throughout the first half of the 20th century have made identifications of sex based largely on object associations rather than on actual skeletal observations (e.g. Grinsell and Gerloff tended to ascribe a male attribution to graves associated with daggers). It was therefore necessary to develop a system to rate the accuracy of different age and

sex characteristics for all sites referred to in the volume. Four categories were devised, listed in descending levels of reliability.

The most reliable data comes from excavation reports which include a human bone report, frequently from a named specialist (Category 1, including 28% of sites of all periods and regions with either age or sex data). Although this consists largely of modern excavation reports from the 1950s onwards, several earlier sources fulfil this requirement. A very small number of sites excavated using modern archaeological methods had age and sex data but no specific bone report, and these were considered the next most reliable (Category 2, 2%). The largest number of sites are those with data taken from antiquarian sources and which are widely recognised as having fairly reliable age and sex classifications (Category 3, 60%). Primarily, this includes the published work of Greenwell (summarised in Kinnes and Longworth 1985), some of the graves described by Colt Hoare (1812) and rather more of those described by Mortimer (1905) and Bateman (1848; 1861). The final group contains those where data concerning age or gender could not be reliably considered (Category 4, 10%). In all cases of antiquarian identifications, data from original accounts were obtained where possible, and this resulted in significantly reducing the total number of sites with unreliable information. All analysis relating to the bodies interred has been restricted to the first three categories of data, namely reliable antiquarian sources and data from modern excavations (i.e. *c.* 90%).

The evidence for age at death has been summarised according to a system of four age grades, as follows:

- Child < 12 years
- Youth 12–18 years
- Adult 19–40 years
- Mature > 40 years

Given the variability of the published information (above), these divisions are necessarily arbitary. They do not coincide with the four age divisions devised for bracer graves of Beaker age (Woodward and Hunter 2011, Table 8.5) because in the case of bracer graves, more have been excavated in recent times and more detail of age at death was available. Thus for bracers all four age grades relate to youths or adults. In the present study, there are only two grades relating to adults, and the generic group of children is used for all the bodies described as children in the antiquarian literature, as well as those identified as having been aged less than 12 years at death by modern analysis. Of course, when these criteria were strictly applied, the resulting datasets are not large: the useable age data set comprises only 152 graves, and that for sex data is only slightly more at 165 (out of a total 780 burials studied).

University of Birmingham Institute of Archaeology and Antiquity					
Leverhulme Research Project: EBA Grave Goods **Early Bronze Age Material from Round Barrows**					**ASSEMBLAGE FORM**

Assemblage Code:	County:	Parish:		Barrow No.:	Grid Ref:

Site Name:	

References:

ID	Object Description	Type	Association	Figure	Corpus	Notes

Plan of Burial:
Source:
Scale

Human Remains:

Sex:	Age:	Cremation v. Inhumation:	Crouched/Extended:

Notes:

Completed by:	Inputted by:
Date:	Date:

Figure 2.1 Site assemblage recording form.

University of Birmingham Institute of Archaeology and Antiquity				
Leverhulme research project: EBA grave goods				
ID number	County	Parish	Barrow number	Site name
Material	Artefact type (generic)	Artefact type (specific)		
Piggott interment no.	Corpus type number	Corpus type code/descriptor		
References 1				
2				
Museum		Museum accession number		
Weight (g)	Illustration			
Length or diameter (mm)	Scale Source			
Width (mm)				
Max thickness (mm)				
Other dimensions				
PERFORATION (if any) Diam at front Diam narrowest Diam at rear				
Colour				
Surface texture/ fabric				
Corrosion				
Photo by	Photo number	XRF number/details		Animal bone code
Completed by	Date	Entered by	Date	Checked

Figure 2.2. Front (this page) and rear (next page) of object recording sheet.

Form SHAPE (outline): rectangular/ovoid/circular/elongated/other: SHAPE (section): rectangular/circular/flat/plano-convex/lentoid/domed/other: FACETS/FLANGES: present/absent DESCRIBE   Ht (mm):
Fragmentation: % present
Fragmentation: description (number the breaks if more than one) Front: Rear: Ends:
Fragmentation: nature of breaks Break 1: ancient at manufacture/ancient in use/ancient in burial/modern Break 2: ancient at manufacture/ancient in use/ancient in burial/modern Break 3: ancient at manufacture/ancient in use/ancient in burial/modern Extra description:

Traces of manufacture
SURFACES
Front: rough/polished/high polish
Rear: rough/polished/high polish
STRIATIONS
Front: longitudinal/lateral/diagonal/multi-directional/other:
        faint/marked
        ends/sides/all over/other
        regular/irregular
Rear: longitudinal/lateral/diagonal/multi-directional/other:
        faint/marked
        ends/sides/all over/other
        regular/irregular
Other: DESCRIBE

Traces of manufacture PERFORATION   present/absent Drilled from: front/back/front and back Form: straight/hourglass/funnel Inside perforation: front: smooth/circumferential rilling/other   Rear: smooth/circumferential rilling/other

Condition	Very worn/slightly worn/worn/fresh

Wear traces Front: Rear: Ends: In/around perforations:
Other notes/final comments

Completed by	Date
Entered by	Date

Figure 2.2. Continued

University of Birmingham Leverhulme project: EBA grave goods BEAD RECORDING FORM			
Project ID number/material (if not 'jet')			
Parish			
County			
Barrow number/site name			
Reference			
Museum			
Accession no.			
Illustration (source)			
TYPE (barrel, fusiform, globular etc)			
DIMENSIONS Weight (g)			
Length (mm)			
Max D or W x Th			
Perf diameter			
Profile (e.g. slender,med,plump)			
Section shape			
Shape of ends			
Perf asymmetrical?			
COLOUR/TEXTURE Colour			
Texture e.g.woodgrain			
Coated?			
Sheen (matt,low,med,high)			
Criss-cross (hairline,mod,deep)?			
Concentric (hairline,mod,deep)?			
Longitudinal cracking?			
Lamination?			
FRAGMENTATION % complete			
Nature of damage			
Location of damage			
Age of damage (manuf,ancient,modern)			
MANUFACTURE facet traces?			
Striations (near end, at middle)			
Direction (uni, multi)			
Crisp,mod crisp,faint,v.faint			
Perf bored from both ends?			
Rilling in perf?			
WEAR: thread wear			
Smoothing round outer edge perfs?			
Smoothing of edge of perfs: sketch above			
Thread-pull groove?			
WEAR: bead-on-bead: sketch			
Overall WEAR: fresh/slight/mod/heavy			
MATERIAL ID			

Figure 2.3. Recording sheet for multiple beads in necklaces.

Leverhulme research project: EBA grave goods: BONE PINS AND POINTS				
ID	*Site*		*Parish*	*County*
Museum		Accession no.		% present
Reference(s)				Fig
Length (mm)	Width (mm)	Max. thickness	Colour	Burnt/unburnt
Wt (g)	Perf.diameter (max)	Perf.diameter (min)	Perf. section	Surface texture
Cross-section: circular/square/ovoid/rectangular			Decoration	
Description e.g. head shape				
Breaks (1)	Where?	ancient/modern	What?	
Breaks (2)	Where?	ancient/modern	What?	
Traces of manufacture	Where?	What?		
Traces of wear	Where?	What?		
Notes:			Recorder:	Date:
ID	*Site*		*Parish*	*County*
Museum		Accession no.		% present
Reference(s)				Fig
Length (mm)	Width (mm)	Max. thickness	Colour	Burnt/unburnt
Wt (g)	Perf.diameter (max)	Perf.diameter (min)	Perf. section	Surface texture
Cross-section: circular/square/ovoid/rectangular			Decoration	
Description e.g. head shape				
Breaks (1)	Where?	ancient/modern	What?	
Breaks (2)	Where?	ancient/modern	What?	
Traces of manufacture	Where?	What?		
Traces of wear	Where?	What?		
Notes:			Recorder:	Date:
ID	*Site*		*Parish*	*County*
Museum		Accession no.		% present
Reference(s)				Fig
Length (mm)	Width (mm)	Max. thickness	Colour	Burnt/unburnt
Wt (g)	Perf.diameter (max)	Perf.diameter (min)	Perf. section	Surface texture
Cross-section: circular/square/ovoid/rectangular			Decoration	
Description e.g. head shape				
Breaks (1)	Where?	ancient/modern	What?	
Breaks (2)	Where?	ancient/modern	What?	
Traces of manufacture	Where?	What?		
Traces of wear	Where?	What?		
Notes:			Recorder:	Date:

Figure 2.4. Summary recording sheet for bone pins or points.

3. ITEMS OF EQUIPMENT I: DAGGERS, POMMELS AND BELT FITTINGS

3.1 DAGGERS AND KNIVES

TYPO-CHRONOLOGY (by Stuart Needham)
Prior to the more extensive employment of radiocarbon dating, much discussion of Final Neolithic and Early Bronze Age chronology has hinged upon detailed typological analysis of the morphology and contexts of metal daggers. The standard corpus and typological scheme for daggers and knives is that devised by Gerloff (1975), while a further scheme concentrating on razor-like implements has been provided by Jockenhövel (1980). These remain key sources for any detailed consideration of daggers, knives and razors, but new grave finds since the 1970s, some of them well dated, combined with renewed research has encouraged refinement of classifications and the revision of some chronological relationships (e.g. Needham 2000a; 2000b; 2004; 2007; 2012; Needham and Woodward 2008). The result is a seven-fold categorisation at the broadest level, defining *Series* of blades of distinct character. These Series are sub-divided in different ways according to what attributes best define perceived morphological trends (Table 3.1.1 and Table 3.1.2; Figure 3.1.1 and Figure 3.1.2). Details of this new classification are summarised in Appendix I, with a synopsis of the dating evidence included below.

Series 1: Tanged daggers/knives (copper) (Tanged hilting with flat blade).
The associations and likelihood of a predominantly temporal succession for these groups has been discussed recently elsewhere (Needham 2012); in summary the dating proposed is:

Early group
    Early Chalcolithic, *c.* 2450/2400–2300 cal BC
Later group
    Later Chalcolithic, *c.* 2300–2200/2150 cal BC
Transitional types
    Chalcolithic/Early Bronze Age, *c.* 2200–2100 cal BC

Series 2: Butt-riveted flat daggers (bronze) (Butt-riveted hilting with flat blade).

Gerloff originally envisaged that flat riveted daggers were roughly contemporary with the Wessex daggers of her Armorico-British types (Gerloff 1975, 47–9, 51–2, 56–7, 61–3, 65 and 67–8), but subsequent research recognised that they must be largely earlier (see Appendix I on CD). Radiocarbon dates for a number of dagger-associated graves have since confirmed their earlier emergence, around the 22nd century BC. The overall currency of Series 2 daggers is thus now relatively well established to between 2200/2150 and 1950/1900 cal BC. The following rolling sequence of overlapping currencies may be ventured:

2200–2050 BC
    2F1 Gravelly Guy, 2C Milston
2150–1950 BC
    2D Newton Grange, 2E Masterton, 2F2 Grindon
2100–1900 BC
    2A Butterwick, 2B Garrowby, 2F3 Merthyr Mawr

Series 3: Thin lenticular-section daggers (Butt-riveted hilting with only slightly lenticular blade sections).
The main group, 3A Winterbourne Stoke, has traditionally been seen as a type-fossil of Wessex 1 graves (ApSimon 1954), currently seen as falling within Period 3 (*c.*1950–1750/1700 cal BC). On current evidence, it would seem that the Armorico-British style of dagger in its 'flat'-bladed form may have begun to be introduced to and adopted by British communities rather earlier, during later Period 2, when Series 2 daggers were still the norm. By Period 3 it may have effectively supplanted the pre-existing dagger suite, at the same time stimulating *ad hoc* local imitations (Sub-series 3B).

Series 4: Ribbed flat-bladed daggers (Butt-riveted hilting; flat or near-flat blade carrying midrib or spaced bead-ribs). No radiocarbon dates are yet associated with Armorico-British daggers with midrib (4A Towthorpe) and associated grave groups do not suggest an origin prior to Period 3 (*c.*1950–1750/1700 cal BC). On the other hand, the pointillé decorated blade from Normanton Down (Wilsford G23), is exceptional on weapons prior to Period 4 and probably implies closeness in date to the 3/4 transition. Daggers of

Table 3.1.1. Key to definitions for the revised classification of Copper and Early Bronze Age daggers (Needham).

Series	Definition on:	Sub-series	Definition on:	Type	Definition on:
1 *Tanged, flat blade (dagger sized)*	tang for hilting; blade section flat	A	no rivets	1–6 *(no type names)*	detailed tang and shoulder shape ('types' cross-cut with sub-series)
		B	riveted tang		
		C	riveted shoulders (and tang)	5 *Ferry Fryston*	short trapezoid tang; strong shoulders
2 *Butt-riveted, flat blade*	shallow hilt-plate with rivets; flat blade section	A *Butterwick*	combinations of blade proportions, blade shape, butt shape, hilt line, rivet disposition and rivet thickness		
		B *Garrowby*			
		C *Milston*			
		D *Newton Grange*			
		E *Masterton*			
		F		1 *Gravelly Guy*	combinations of blade proportions, blade shape, butt shape, hilt line, rivet disposition and rivet thickness
				2 *Grindon*	
				3 *Merthyr Mawr*	
		G *Miscellaneous four-rivet*	four rivets; not similar to A–F		
3 *Butt-riveted, lenticular-section blade*	slightly lenticular blade section	A *Winterbourne Stoke*	6 thin rivets in line; groove-sets relatively close to edges		
		B *Raunds*	2–4 rivets; blade furrows (or grooves)		
4 *Butt-riveted, ribbed flat blade*	rib or ribs on flat/near-flat blade section	A *Towthorpe*	single narrow midrib; 6 thin rivets in line; groove-sets relatively close to edges		
		B *Mauldslie*	single narrow midrib; 2 or 3 thicker rivets		
		C *Auchterhouse*	triple-reeded midrib		
		D *Blackwaterfoot*	spaced bead-ribs		
5 *Butt-riveted, thick blade*	thickening towards blade centre – various sectional forms	A *Totland*	broad midrib (usually keeled); no grooves		
		B	thickened mid-blade (lozenge/ lenticular)	1 *Plymstock*	blade furrows, no grooves
				2 *Bridgemere*	full-lozenge blade section; no grooves or furrows
		C	thickened mid-blade (or broad midrib) hemmed by groove bands; 6 rivets in line	1 *Norton Bavant*	otherwise similar to 3A and 4A daggers
				2 *Bourbriac*	rapid taper of blade below hilt-plate
		D *Camerton-Snowshill*	thickened mid-blade (or broad midrib) hemmed by groove bands; 3 rivets in triangle		
		E	thickened mid-blade incorporating rib- and step-mouldings in various ways	1 *Hammersmith*	rib- and/or step-mouldings
				2 *Gavel Moss*	triple-moulded mid-blade
				3 *Ashford*	spaced bead-ribs

the other three sub-series, which can be seen to be derived from indigenous Series 2 daggers, probably emerged earlier. Despite their origins in late Period 2, it is likely that 4B, 4C and 4D daggers continued long enough to overlap the emergence of Sub-series 4A.

Series 5: Thick-bladed daggers (Butt-riveted hilting; significantly thickened blades of lenticular, lozengic, concave-lozengic or complex moulded section).

There is abundant dating evidence from grave and hoard associations to suggest that the great majority of Series 5

Table 3.1.2. Key to definitions for the revised classification of Copper and Early Bronze Age knives/razors (implements under about 100 to 110mm, depending on Series (Needham).

Series	Definition on:	Sub-series	Definition on:	Type	Definition on:
1 *Tanged, flat blade (knife sized)*	tang for hilting; blade section flat	A	no rivets	1–6	detailed tang and shoulder shape ('types' cross-cut with sub-series)
		B	riveted tang		
		C	riveted shoulders (and tang)		
6 *Tanged, small blade implements*	tang for hilting (excludes Series 1 forms)	A *Broad-tanged small blades*	relatively broad tang; almost always with single rivet	1	smooth-curved tang/blade junction
				2	marked shoulders at tang/blade junction
		B *Narrow-tanged small blades*	relatively narrow tang, without rivet	1	leaf-shaped blade
				2	blade shapes ranging from triangular to ivy-leaf
7 *Butt-riveted, small blade implements*	broad, shallow hilt-plate with rivets	A *Flat blade*	Flat or thin blades lacking distinctive morphology (other than edge bevels)		
		B *Midribbed blade*	midrib (varied widths) flanked by flat or furrowed blade wings		
		C *Thickened blade*	Lozenge or lenticular blade section		

daggers belong to Period 4 (*c.* 1750/1700–1500 BC). Type 5C1 Norton Bavant is transitional from Period 3, leading to the dominant Period 4 type, 5D Camerton-Snowshill. 5C2 Bourbriac daggers are essentially contemporary with 5D but were probably imports from Brittany. Of the other sub-series, 5A Totland tends to be earlier in Period 4, while 5B Bridgemere and the three 5E types tend to be later in the period. Some of these last (5B, 5E) foreshadow the styles of early Middle Bronze Age daggers/dirks.

Series 6: Tanged small blades (knives/razors) (with or without single rivet).

These small knives and razors belong to the Early Bronze Age proper (Periods 2 to 4), their Chalcolithic equivalents having been included within Series 1. Although many occur in graves with other goods, the latter are only occasionally closely datable types. Series 6 blades are almost universally from cremation burials, often with urns – Collared, Cordoned or Biconical. The frequency of these ceramic types, especially the last two, could well suggest that the great majority of these small bronze blades were deposited in graves during Periods 3 and 4 and some radiocarbon-dated contexts support this bracket. There are, however, occasional finds of both 6A1 and 6B for which associations indicate Period 2 origins; this is to be expected given their presumed derivation from late Chalcolithic forms.

Series 7: Butt-riveted small blades (knives/razors)

As for the Series 6 implements, there is a considerable number of grave associations for Series 7 a minority of which offer some closer dating within the Early Bronze Age. There are plenty datable to the mature Early Bronze Age (Periods 3 to 4), but also some evidence that butt-riveted small implements emerged in tandem with their larger counterparts in Period 2. It is reasonable to suppose that the flat and near-flat blade sections (7A) would have had chronological primacy over others. Even so, midribbed forms (7B) could easily have emerged alongside midribbed daggers, late in Period 2. Some examples of both 7A and 7B are certainly as late as Period 4, so the general forms at least had a long currency. Datable blades with lozenge or lenticular section (7C) currently all fall within Periods 3 and 4.

MATERIAL (with Peter Bray)

Recent appraisal of the chemical composition of all the British Early Bronze Age copper and bronze objects that have been analysed has led to the definition and discussion of many interesting trends (Bray 2009). Peter Bray made available all chemical composition data relating to the objects studied within the Leverhulme project (collated from published sources and with the kind assistance of Stuart Needham and Peter Northover). The occurrence of the main metal types, and their source areas, is summarised in Table 3.1.3. The table shows the distribution of the metal types according to the new Needham dagger series (Series 1 to 7). An approximate correlation with the Metal Assemblages, MA 1 to MA 6, as defined in Needham (1996) is given in the second row. A full discussion of these results, and their wider context within Britain, is provided by Bray in Appendix II (Bronze Analysis). In brief, at the outset of metal use the Ross Island A Metal and Bell Beaker Metal were most prominent. It is interesting to note that Bell Beaker Metal, probably sourced from Continental Europe, dominates the total copper dagger assemblage (summarised in Table 3.1.4). The daggers presumably came to Britain as the personal equipment of individuals, and eventually these novel items were deposited in graves. By contrast, most

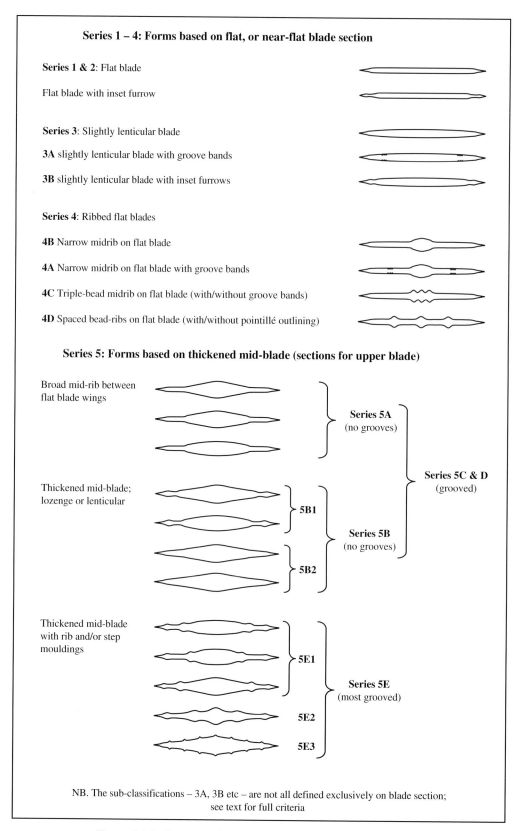

Figure 3.1.1. Copper and bronze dagger sections (Series 1 to 5).

artefacts of Irish A Metal are axes, although some daggers were also produced. As time went on, the incidence of Clean Metal, largely from newly opened mines in Wales, and recycled metal (objects whose chemistry show significant changes from the source geology) gradually increased (see Table 3.1.4 and Appendix II, Figure 2 and Figure 3).

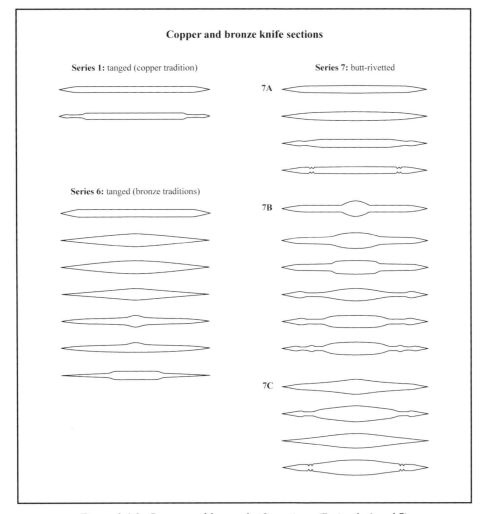

Figure 3.1.2. Copper and bronze knife sections (Series 1, 6 and 7).

DETAILED DESCRIPTIONS

(A full list of items studied and illustrated is shown in Table 3.1.8)

Series 1 n=10 (Figure 3.1.3)

Manufacture

Most examples are too corroded for any signs of manufacture to have survived. However four have faint longitudinal polishing striations on the blade surfaces, and there is one example of diagonal striations.

Completeness and damage

Most are almost complete, with four at 100%, and only one (ID 1327 Standlow, Figure 3.1.3) survives at less than 95%. Modern breaks usually are located at the tip of the blade, while one is on the shoulder.

Wear

The few ancient breaks are variously located at the tip (two), blade edge (one) and top of the tang (ID 1182 Shrewton, Figure 3.1.3). Where the degree of wear could be estimated one is fresh, two are slightly worn, four worn and one very worn. Wear traces comprise wear to the blade edges, scratches and traces of use. In three cases the tang or hilt plate had been bent in antiquity, and in four cases the longitudinal profile displays deliberate bowing or twisting (e.g. ID 1319, Figure 3.1.12).

Hilt and sheath

One dagger had traces of a wooden sheath surviving on discovery (ID 1312 Kelleythorpe, Figure 3.1.3), while three have traces of wooden or horn hilt material on the hilt plate (e.g. ID 1312, Figure 3.1.12) and two more have possible traces of such organic material. Measurement of the rivets from the three examples with central rivet placement (ID 1182, 1312, 1319) provides indication of the thickness of the original hilts. The thickness of the central spine of the hilt would have varied between 9 and 12.1mm.

Conclusions

The tanged copper daggers studied all survive well but tend to have been used extensively. A fair number seem to have

Table 3.1.3. The occurrence of metal types against Needham dagger series (number of daggers studied in detail within the Leverhulme project which have been chemically analysed in the past (Bray).

Needham dagger Series		1	2	3	4	5	6	7
Metal type	**Source area**	MA 1–2	MA 3	MA 4 and 5		MA 6		
A metal	Ross Island, Ireland	4	2	2		2		
F metal	Irish, possibly Ross Ireland	1						
Bell Beaker	Multiple sources. Major early one on the European mainland. Also probably North Wales post *c.* 2100 B.C.	3		1	3			2
A plus Bell Beaker	Recycled mixture					1	1	1
Arsenic only	Cornwall/Devon			1	2	1		1
Antimony/silver	Midi/Languedoc, France	1	1					
Clean Metal	A range of Irish, Welsh, English sources. Probably based on relatively pure chalcopyrite			1	2	1		3
Recycled	Re-melting of single source material					9		3
Total		**9**	**6**	**7**	**5**	**13**	**1**	**10**

Table 3.1.4. Complete dataset of chemically analysed British Early Bronze Age daggers (Bray).

Metal type	**Source area**	**MA 1–2**	**MA 3**	**MA 4**	**MA 5**	**MA 6**
A metal	Ross Island, Ireland	5	9	1	2	3
F metal	Irish, possibly Ross Ireland	1	1	0	0	2
Bell Beaker	Multiple sources. Major early one on the European mainland. Also probably North Wales post *c.* 2100 B.C.	11	5	1	5	6
A plus Bell Beaker	Recycled mixture	0	2	1	0	5
Arsenic only	Cornwall/Devon, Iberian Peninsular	0	1	1	5	0
Antimony/silver	Midi/Languedoc, France	2	1	0	0	0
Clean Metal	A range of Irish, Welsh, English sources. Probably based on relatively pure chalcopyrite	0	0	2	3	8
Recycled	Re-melting of single source material	1	1	2	5	12
Total		**20**	**20**	**8**	**20**	**36**

been buried with the hilt in place, and one also retained its tanged bone pommel of Class 1a (ID 1182 Shrewton, Figure 3.1.3; see also pommel ID 1018, Figure 3.2.1). However, the occurrence of bent tangs and one damaged hilt plate, all of which had been suffered in antiquity, may indicate that some hilts were deliberately removed before the dagger was deposited. Furthermore the ancient bending or twisting of four of the blades may have resulted from deliberate acts, possibly again prior to deposition.

Series 2 n=29 (Figure 3.1.4 and Figure 3.1.5)

Manufacture

Traces of manufacture survive in 83% of cases. Most often these comprised polishing striations on the blade surfaces. They are usually longitudinal (15 examples) but single examples of marked longitudinal or diagonal and faint diagonal or multidirectional striations also occur. Polishing on the bevel is evidenced in two cases: one with diagonal marks and one with lateral (e.g. ID 1209, Figure 3.1.12). Traces of polishing also extend onto the hilt plates in ten cases: usually faint or marked longitudinal striations, but multidirectional and diagonal striations are also represented.

Completeness and damage

In 21 cases the daggers survive at the 95% level or above. Others cluster around the 80 to 85% level, with only one each at 70% and 75%. Modern breaks, totalling 25, occur equally in three locations: at the tip, on the blade edges and at the hilt plate.

Wear

Ancient breaks occur mainly on the hilt plates (six on the margins, six where rivet holes are broken out), with five only at the blade tip and two on blade edges. Wear comprises blade wear, sharpening and ancient scratching and damage. Where the degree of wear could be categorised, most are slightly worn (19 examples: 63%), with four worn, one very worn and only two fresh. Apparently deliberate ancient breaks across the blade occur in four cases (ID 1206; ID 1220, Figure 3.1.4; ID 1328, and ID 1378 Milston where the two pieces have been rejoined in conservation, Figure 3.1.4) and deliberate twisting in three more cases (ID 1207, Figure 3.1.12; 1209 and 1296).

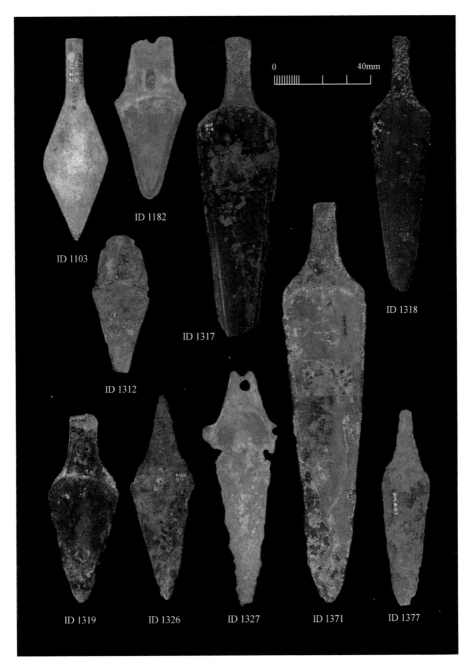

Figure 3.1.3. Examples of Series 1 tanged (copper) daggers/knives: ID 1103 Saffron Walden; ID 1182 Shrewton 5K, type 1B2/4; ID 1312 Kellythorpe, type 1C4; ID 1317 Hundon, type 1A1; ID 1318 Sutton Courtenay, type 1A1; ID 1319 Sittingbourne, type 1B2; ID 1326 Barnack, type 1A3; ID 1327 Standlow, type 1C5; ID 1371 Roundway G8, type 1A1; ID 1377 Mere G6a, type 1A3.

Hilt and sheath

Six of the daggers have associated pommels surviving, and in a seventh case a wooden pommel can be inferred (ID 1206 Net Low); all these also have traces of organic hilt material on the hilt plate, and three of them also have traces of an organic sheath on the blade (e.g. ID 1215, Figure 3.1.12). Five further examples have traces of both hilt and sheath. And in addition there are five more with hilt traces only, and two with sheath traces only. Measurements of the lengths of the rivet sets (usually three per dagger) allow

some estimation of the thickness of the original hilts to be made. The lengths of the outer rivets vary between 10.2 and 19mm while the central ones measure between 10.4 and 20.3mm. The difference between the average length of the two outer rivets and the length of the central rivet varies from 0.9 to 2.1mm. Thus it can be deduced that the hilts were thinner at the sides with a gentle but distinct rise along the central spine. The surviving pommels (see Chapter 3.2 below) are relatively large, varying from 43.9 to 52.7mm in maximum width.

Conclusions

The Series 2 daggers studied survive fairly well and traces of polishing striations at manufacture are common. These polishing striations are not worn away by use and a generally low level of overall wear has been detected. The daggers were often buried with hilt and pommel intact, but ancient breaks, bending and twisting in relation to the blades themselves may be evidence of deliberate acts, perhaps undertaken at the time of deposition. Ancient damage to the hilt plates and rivet holes is generally minor and in all of the 14 cases except one the rivets are still *in situ*. This suggests that in these cases the hilts were still attached at the time of deposition, and the damage to the hilt plates did not result from removal of the hilts.

Series 3 n=9 (Figure 3.1.6)

Manufacture

The survival of polishing marks on the blade surfaces is common, with presence of faint longitudinal striations occurring on the front in seven cases, and rear in five. Also there is one case of faint lateral striations. There is only one case of longitudinal striations also visible on the hilt plate.

Completeness and damage

Only four of the daggers survive at the 95% level or above, with the others present at levels between 80% and 90%. However modern breaks are very few, comprising just two at the blade tip, one on a blade edge and one on the right side of the hilt plate.

Wear

Most of the damage results from ancient breaks which occur most commonly on the hilt plate (present on nine of the daggers, three times on both sides of the hilt plate). Ancient breaks also occur on the blade edges (three times) and at the tip (six times). Traces of marked use wear are rare but include evidence of blade sharpening and dulling of the grooves (in one case). Overall most of the daggers are fresh or only slightly worn (seven cases), with one classified as worn, and two as very worn. Also the one Series 3B dagger (ID 1451 Kilmington) had been cut down in size and reworked (Figure 3.1.6).

Hilt and sheath

Apart from the wooden hilt with gold pin decoration on the dagger from Bush Barrow (ID 1395 Wilsford G5; see gold objects Chapter 6.2) no pommels have been found with Series 3 daggers. Organic traces of both hilt and sheath are visible on four out of the ten examples, sheath only on three and hilt only on one of the daggers. Only two examples have no organic traces. Survival of the rivets however is poor. A full suite of six rivets survives only on two of the examples studied (ID 1185 and ID 1395, both Figure 3.1.6). From the surviving rivet lengths measured it can be deduced that the maximum thicknesses of the hilts was *c.*19mm for the six-riveted types and 14.5mm for a four-riveted example (ID 1129). The difference between the lengths of the various inner and outer rivets indicates a thickening at the centre of the hilt of 1.5mm (four-riveted example) or 3 to 5.2mm (for the six-riveted examples).

Conclusions

The degree of survival for the Series 3 daggers is only moderate. Traces of manufacture are fairly common on the blade. Overall wear traces are only slight, but there is evidence of many ancient breaks, especially in the area of the hilt plate, and loss of rivets. This may indicate that some hilts were removed intentionally prior to deposition of the daggers in graves. However, of the nine daggers with hilt plate damage, five have traces of organic hilt material surviving. Thus, if the hilts had been removed, some of the hilt material must have remained in place. This could have occurred if the hilt elements had been fixed to the hilt plate with adhesive as well as by the rivets themselves. In addition, three out of the ten daggers (ID 1236; ID 1395, Figure 3.1.6 and Figure 3.1.12; ID 1455) had been bent or broken, probably intentionally, prior to deposition.

Series 4 n=12 (Figure 3.1.7 and Figure 3.1.8)

Manufacture

Polishing traces, which are mainly in the form of faint longitudinal striations, occur fairly commonly on the blade faces, three times on the front and five times on the rear. In addition there is one case of concentric striations on one of the midribs. Longitudinal or diagonal striations also are visible on the hilt plate in three cases. Of particular interest is the presence of part of a metal 'belt hook' adhering to the front face of the dagger from Wilsford G23 (ID 1391, Figure 3.1.7 and Figure 3.3.4).

Completeness and damage

Only three daggers survive at the 95% level or over. Others are only present between the 70% and 90% levels. Modern damage is much more common than was the case for the Series 3 daggers. This includes six breaks around the hilt plate, three at blade edges and three at the tip.

Wear

In comparison, the level of ancient breakage at the hilt plate is relatively low (three cases on Series 4A items only). Single cases of ancient damage also occur twice on the blade edge, and once at the tip. Use wear evidenced by dulling of the grooves occurs three times, and obvious sharpening twice only. Overall half of the examples (five) are fresh or only slightly worn, with four worn and none at all heavily worn (in two cases the wear category is indeterminate). Deliberate damage includes one bowed

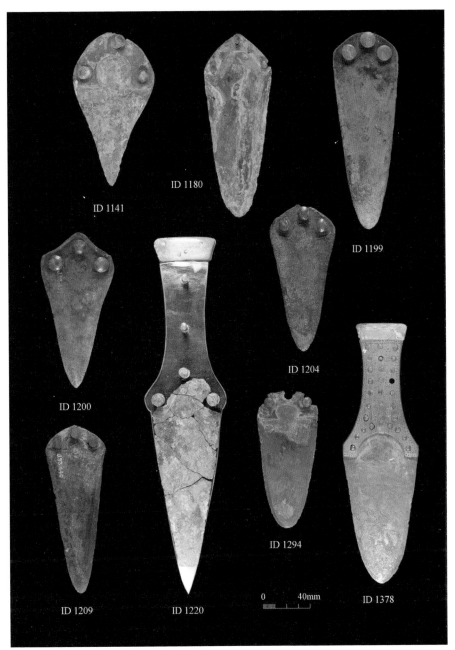

Figure 3.1.4. Examples of Series 2 butt-riveted (bronze) flat daggers/knives: ID 1141 Garrowby Wold 32, type 2B; ID 1180 Amesbury G85, type 2D; ID 1199 Bole Hill, Wormhill, type 2E; ID 1200 Carder Low, type 2B; ID 1204 Parsley Hay, type 2A; ID 1209 Deepdale, Barnet's Low, type 2F2; ID 1220 Scamridge, type 2E; ID 1294 Butterwick, type 2A; ID 1378 Milston G51, type 2C.

blade (ID 1476, Figure 3.1.7) and one hilt plate corner which had been bent, presumably during the removal of the hilt (ID 1301, Figure 3.1.7).

Hilt and sheath

No associated pommels survive. Organic traces of both hilt and sheath occur on half of the examples studied, and sheath traces on a further two. The rivets are present at a slightly higher level than in the case of the Series 3 daggers. Maximum thickness of the organic hilt can be estimated

to be 20.5mm for six-riveted forms and 18.5mm for the three-riveted version. The central thickening indicated by the variation in rivet lengths is 1.5 to 4.6mm (six-riveted dagger) and 1.8 to 2.6mm for the three-riveted examples.

Conclusions

Series 4 daggers survive at a relatively poor level, mainly due to the incidence of many modern breaks. Traces of polishing marks are fairly common. Ancient breaks are few, and overall most of the examples studied are only slightly

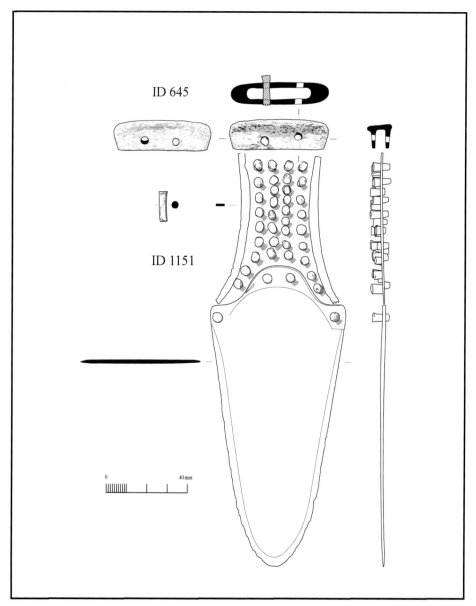

Figure 3.1.5. Example of Series 2 butt-rivetted (bronze) flat dagger/knife ID 1151 Garton Slack 107, type 2C. Drawings by Henry Buglass.

worn. There is better survival of the rivets, and less damage to the hilt plates. This may indicate that these daggers were deposited with their hilts in place. However in one case ancient bending of the corner of a hilt plate suggests that sometimes a hilt had been removed. In a further case there is also evidence that the blade was deliberately bowed prior to deposition.

Series 5 n=30 (Figure 3.1.9)

Manufacture

Traces of manufacture in the form of polishing marks survive on many of the daggers. On the blades they are always faint and longitudinal, occurring 19 times on front faces and 17 on the rear. There are also faint longitudinal or multidirectional traces on five hilt plates.

Completeness and damage

Survival is at the 95% or above level for 18 daggers, with the rest surviving at between 70% and 90%. However, much of the damage is due to modern breakage. Modern breaks occur on 19 of the daggers, and occur as breaks across the blade (five cases), around the hilt plate (nine cases), on blade edges (eight cases) or at the tip (six times).

Wear

There are also some ancient breaks. These occur on 23 daggers, and include mainly damage to the hilt plate (20 instances), plus six cases of damage to the tip. The breaks on the hilt plates are often extensive; on seven daggers there are breaks on both sides of the plate and in a further eight the damage extend from both sides onto the top margin

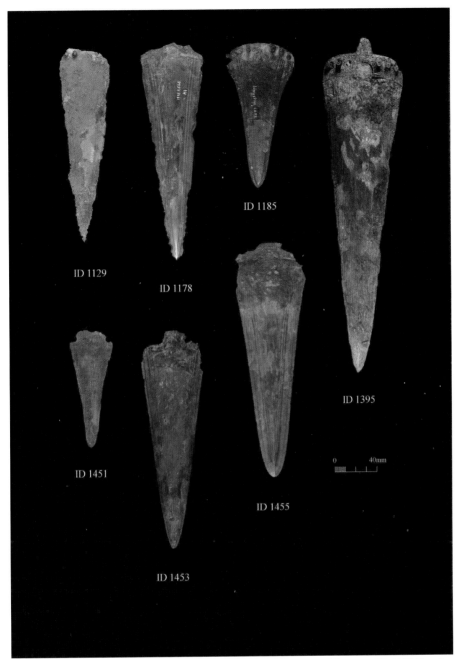

Figure 3.1.6. Examples of Series 3 thin lenticular-section Armorico-British and related daggers: ID 1129 Towthorpe 139; ID 1178 Ablington, Figheldean G25c; ID 1185 Idmiston ?G9d; ID 1395 Wilsford G5; ID 1451 Kilmington G1; ID 1453 Winterbourne G5; ID 1455 Winterbourne Stoke G5 (all type 3A, except ID 1451, type 3B).

also. Traces of use wear include evidence of sharpening and wear to the grooves or decorative pointillé designs. Overall 19 daggers can be categorised as fresh or only slightly worn, with nine worn and only one very worn. Evidence of deliberate damage prior to deposition can be detected in five cases: bending of the tip (ID 1252 and ID 1389, Figure 3.1.9), breaks right across (ID 1322, Figure 3.1.9), slight twisting of the blade (ID 1419, Figure 3.1.9) and bending of one side of the hilt causing fracture (ID 1479, Figure 3.1.7).

Hilt and sheath

No pommels have been found in association with Series 5 daggers. Traces of organic materials are relatively few with six instances of daggers with traces of both hilt and sheath, six with hilt traces only, and three with patches of sheath material only. It can be noted also that three of the daggers with hilt plus sheath remains belong to sub-Series 5A and 5B. Rivets show a fair survival. Measured rivet lengths indicate that hilt thicknesses were 18.7mm (for six-rivet dagger ID 1181), and between 15 and 22mm (average of seven 19.5mm) for three-riveted examples. The estimated

Figure 3.1.7. Examples of Series 4 ribbed flat-bladed daggers: ID 1131 Towthorpe 233, type 4A; ID1213 Musden Low 4, type 4B; ID 1234 Weymouth G8, type 4B; ID 1301 Cheswick, type 4B; ID 1303 Brough UN69, type 4A; ID 1391 Wilsford G23, type 4A; ID 1396 Wilsford G5, type 4A; ID 1476 Wilsford G43, type 4A.

thickening to the centre of the hilt would have been 6.6mm for the six-riveted example and 5.1mm (average of five) for the three-riveted ones.

Conclusions

The survival rate is good, with 60% of daggers complete or almost complete. Also much of the damage is modern, so at deposition the daggers in fact survived to an even higher level than that suggested by the percentage estimates. Traces of manufacture are common, but not as prevalent as on the daggers of Series 2 or 3. Ancient breaks show definite concentration in the area of the hilt plate, and the breaks often occur on both sides, or all around the margin of the plate. A full complement of rivets survives only nine times. Thus it seems that the hilts may have been ripped off in many cases, prior to deposition of the dagger. In spite of this extensive damage, the overall categorisation of wear from other criteria shows that two-thirds of the daggers were only slightly worn, and only one of them very worn. Five items were bent or broken before they were deposited in the grave.

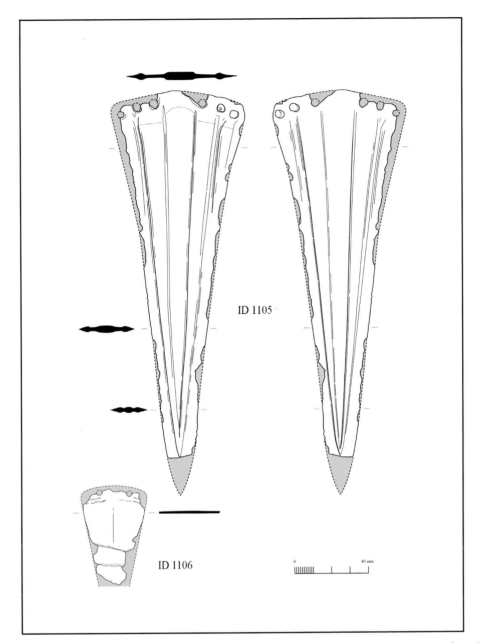

Figure 3.1.8. Series 4 midribbed dagger ID 1105 Little Cressingham, type 4A, and Series 7 butt-riveted small blade ID 1106 Little Cressingham, type 7A. Drawings by Henry Buglass.

Series 6 n=6 (Figure 3.1.10)

Manufacture

Traces of manufacture are visible on four out of the six items studied in detail. These comprise faint longitudinal striations on the blade faces, and multidirectional shaping at the tang or shoulders.

Completeness and damage

Only two items survive at the 95% level or above, but some of the damage on two pieces is due to modern breaks: once at the tang, once on the blade edge, and once across the blade.

Wear

Ancient breaks occur on four pieces. These are usually located in the area of the tang but there are also instances at blade edges and at the tip. Overall wear is difficult to assess but includes one slightly worn example and two which are probably very worn. Deliberate ancient damage comprises bending and bowing of the blade in two cases.

Hilt and sheath

The only organic materials that survive are traces of wood on one of the tangs (ID 1142, Figure 3.1.10). The two examples with single rivet holes do not possess surviving rivets.

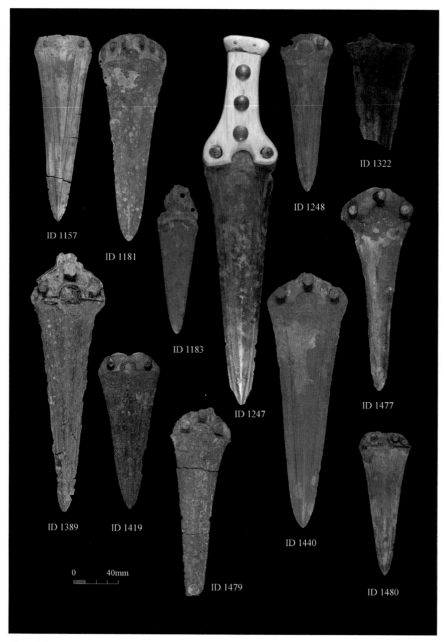

Figure 3.1.9. Examples of Series 5 thick-bladed daggers: ID 1157 Camerton, type 5D; ID 1181 Amesbury G85, type 5C1; ID 1183 Winterbourne Stoke G47, type 5D; ID 1247 Winterbourne St Martin G50, type 5D; ID 1248 Dewlish G8, type 5D; ID 1322 Rillaton, type 5D; ID 1389 Wilsford G56, type 5D; ID 1419 Collingbourne Ducis G4, type 5D; ID 1440 Winterbourne Stoke G4, type 5D; ID 1477 Wilsford G27, type 5D; ID 1479 Edington G2, type 5D; ID 1480 Wimborne St Giles G20, type 5D (with four rivets).

Conclusions

Survival of the Series 6 blades is relatively poor, probably due to the thinness of the blades and fragility of the tangs. Where visible, manufacturing traces survive well, including on the tang and shaping of the shoulders. Ancient breaks occur particularly at the tang end and no rivets survive on the sub-series A1 examples. Handles may therefore have been removed in antiquity. General wear is variable, but two pieces exhibit signs of deliberate damage prior to deposition.

Series 7 n=43 (Figure 3.1.11; see also Figure 3.1.8)

Manufacture

Traces of polishing are very common, particularly on the blade faces. They are usually faint and longitudinal, occurring 22 times on front faces and 22 times on the rear. Diagonal and lateral striations are also represented. On hilt plates longitudinal striations are also the most common, but diagonal, lateral and multidirectional marks are also in evidence.

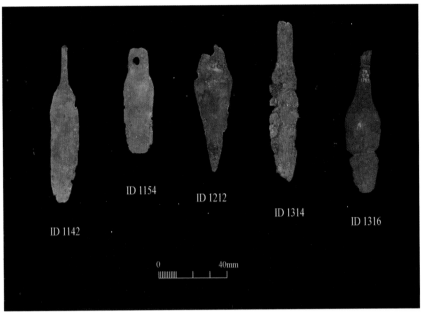

Figure 3.1.10. Examples of Series 6 tanged small blades (knives/razors): ID 1142 Calais Wold 170, type 6B1; ID 1154 Blanch 2, type 6A1; ID 1212 Moot Low, type 6A1; ID 1314 Lambourn 298,1, type 6B1; ID 1316 Ulverston UN8, type 6B2.

Completeness and damage

Just over half of the examples survive at the 95% level or above, but survival is generally rather poor, with nine pieces surviving at 75% or less. Modern breaks occur on nearly half of the items, and these occur mainly on the hilt plate (13 times), with some also at blade edges or the tip.

Wear

Ancient breaks are also common, with 23 daggers displaying damage to the hilt plate. And 15 of these cases involve damage on both sides of the plate or all around its margin. Other ancient damage occurs at the tip (10 instances) or more rarely at the blade edges or right across the blade. General wear traces include ancient scratching and uneven sharpening of one blade edge. Most blades are categorised as slightly worn (16 examples), with none worn and only one very worn. However deliberate damage prior to deposition is evident in ten cases. On five examples this damage is at the hilt plate and probably relates to ancient removal of the hilt, but four are bent (ID 1188; ID 1259, Figure 3.1.11; ID 1267 and ID 1439, Figure 3.1.11) and one appears to have been deliberately broken across the blade (ID 1490, Figure 3.1.11).

Hilt and sheath

Organic traces of hilt or sheath are not common in Type 7 blades, totalling only 15 examples out of the 42 items studied. Also rivet survival is extremely poor. There are only seven full sets on the two-rivet blades and only one set relating to a three-rivet blade. However four blades were found associated with pommels, and two of these were of exotic materials: amber (ID 1430) and gold (ID

1238). From the rivets that do survive it can be estimated that maximum central hilt thicknesses varied from 6.2mm to 11.2 mm, with one much thicker at 17.4mm (ID 1188), and the rise from side to centre of the hilt ranged from 0.3mm to 2.3mm.

Conclusions

Survival of the Series 7 knife daggers is poor, but there is a high incidence of modern breaks, especially at the hilt plate. However, ancient breaks are also very common, sometimes at the tip or across the blade, but in 62% of cases at the hilt plate. Of the ancient hilt breaks, many are extensive, and also rivet survival is very poor. This, linked to the general lack of any traces of organic hilt or sheath materials, may suggest that hilts were generally removed. However some organic traces do survive, and four blades survived with their pommels, two of which are exotic. In general, the wear on the blades was classified as slight, but five examples had been bent or broken across prior to deposition.

GENERAL CONCLUSIONS

Key statistics relating to the overall study of knife and dagger blades are summarised in the following two tables (Tables 3.1.5 and 3.1.6). From these tables, and from the preceding sections, some general conclusions can be reached.

Wear

As far as general level of survival is concerned, daggers of Series 1 (tanged copper blades) and Series 5 (Camerton-

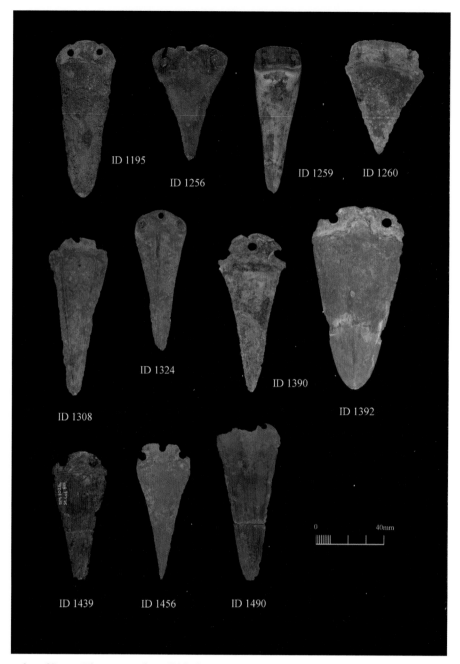

Figure 3.1.11. Examples of Series 7 butt-riveted small blades (knives/razors): ID 1195 Amesbury G58, type 7C; ID 1256 Bradford Peverell G22, type 7A; ID 1259 Dorchester, Fordington Farm, type 7A; ID 1260 Thomas Hardye School, type 1B4/7A; ID 1308 Aldbourne 277, type 7C; ID 1324 Lambourn, type 7B; ID 1390 Wilsford G56, type 7B; ID 1392 Wilsford G23, type 7B; ID 1439 Winterbourne Stoke G4, type 7C; ID 1456 Wilsford G60, type 7A; ID 1490 Knook G1a, type 7B.

Snowshill) survive best. These groups are followed by Series 2 (flat riveted blades), and then Series 3 (mainly Armorico-British A). By comparison the Armorico-British B blades of Series 4, and the Series 6 knives display relatively poor survival, and the Series 7 knife daggers have survived least well. These levels of survival are not closely linked to the occurrence of modern breaks, which tend to occur on about half of the daggers in any one Series. Traces of manufacture in the form of polishing striations are particularly common on Series 2 and Series 5 blades, and extremely evident on the Armorico-British A blades of

Series 3. They occur at a lower level on blades of Series 4 and 7 and are much less common on blades of Series 1 and 6 (although for these groups the samples studied in detail were small). For most Series, overall wear was categorised as slightly worn. This statistic was roughly similar for blades belonging to Series 4, 5 and 7. However, Series 1 daggers appeared to be overall more worn, while those of Series 3 displayed a higher level of slight wear, and for the flat riveted daggers of Series 2, 81% of those where wear could be determined are only slightly worn. Ancient breaks occur on every blade of Series 3 examined, and

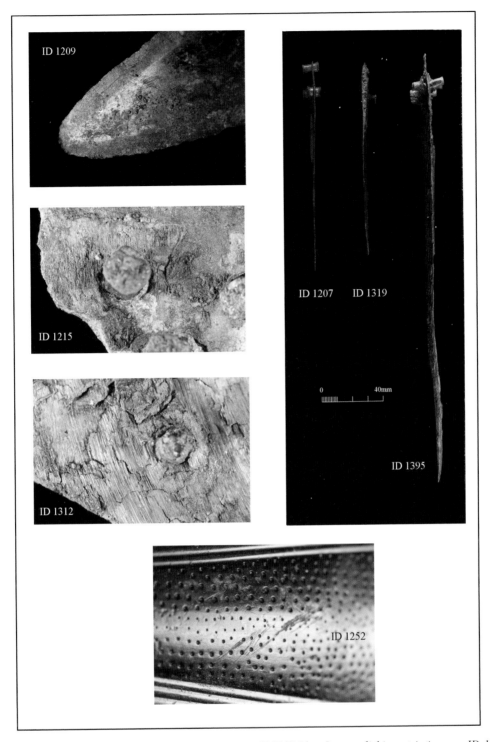

Figure 3.1.12. Detailed images showing deliberate twisting on ID1207 New Inns, polishing striations on ID 1209 Deepdale, Barnet's Low, organic remains of hilt plate and blade on ID 1215 Thorncliff Low, pointillé decoration on ID 1252 Bincombe 1, organic remains on ID 1312 Kelleythorpe, bowing and twisting of blade on ID 1319 Sittingbourne,and deliberate twisting on ID 1395 Wilsford G5.

are also common on Series 5 daggers. However in both cases they occur mostly on the hilt plate, and may relate to removal of the hilts (see below). Otherwise the incidence of ancient breaks is fairly even, although the Series 1 tanged copper daggers seem to be relatively less damaged.

Deliberate damage, usually in the form of bending of the blade, prior to deposition occurs amongst all seven Series. However it is most common in blades of Series 1 and 3. This may indicate that this fashion was one that declined slightly through time.

Table 3.1.5. Knives and daggers: condition, manufacture and wear (manufacturing traces and modern breaks: number of daggers, not total instances).

Series	Quantity	95–100%	Manuf. traces	Modern Breaks	Fresh/ slightly worn	Worn	Very worn	Indet. Wear
1	10	9	4	4	3	4	1	2
2	29	21	23	15	21	4	1	3
3	9	4	9	3	6	1	2	-
4	12	3	7	10	6	4	-	2
5	30	18	21	19	19	9	1	1
6	6	2	4	2	1	-	2	3
7	43	22	27	20	16	10	1	16

Table 3.1.6. Knives and daggers: ancient breaks and damage, organic traces and estimated hilt dimensions (ancient breaks are total number of breaks).

Series	Ancient breaks		Organic traces			Pommel	Estimated hilt dimensions (mm)		Delib. damage
	Hilt	Other	Hilt and sheath	Hilt only	Sheath Only		Max Thickness	Rise to centre	
1	1	2	1	2	-	1	9–12.1	n/a	5
2	12	8	7	8	3	7	10.4–20.3	0.9–2.1	7
3	9	5	4	1	3	1	14.5–19	1.5–5.2	3
4	3	6	5	-	2	-	18.5–20.5	1.5–4.6	1
5	20	8	6	6	3	-	15–24	Av 5.1 (and 6.6)	5
6	3	3	-	1	-	-	n/a	n/a	2
7	24	15	5	7	3	4	6.2–11.2 (and 17.4)	0.3–2.3	10

Wear against chemical composition (with Peter Bray)

Patterns within the wear data appear to match well with inferences drawn from the chemical compositions of the daggers. Two main trends stand out as priorities for further research; see Appendix II for a full discussion of the wear and chemistry datasets in the context of the British Early Bronze Age. The copper daggers (Needham Series 1) show, on average, far higher levels of wear than any other typological group (Figure 3.1.13). This fits well with a scenario wherein the daggers were treasured personal possessions, possibly acting as heirlooms for several generations after originally being made in Continental Europe. This contrasts significantly with the pattern for daggers manufactured at the end of the study period. Those in Needham Series 5 tend to show relatively low levels of wear, if any at all, coupled with extremely high tin levels. As described in detail in Appendix II there is a loose correlation between larger dagger surface areas and higher tin levels. This clearly indicates the importance to the social role of daggers played by both display and the consumption of rare materials. The lack of wear may underline the importance of manufacturing daggers just for exhibition, or even in rare cases solely for the purpose of deposition within a burial.

The changing chemical composition of daggers during the Early Bronze Age makes interpretation of the wear dataset very difficult. Copper objects are relatively soft when compared to the tough, late-Early Bronze Age

daggers that on average contain around 12% tin. If copper and high-tin daggers had experienced the same amount of work-use the copper dagger would show far more wear traces and to a greater degree (see Appendix II). Thus further experimental work is required to decouple the effects of change in the length and degree of dagger use from the influence of changing compositions.

Hilts and sheaths

Traces of organic hilts and/or sheaths occur most commonly on daggers of Series 3 and 4 (Armorico-British A and B), and slightly less so on flat riveted daggers of Series 2. The occurrence of organic traces on the Series 5 (Camerton-Snowshill) daggers is noticeably lower, and incidence on Series 1 tanged copper daggers and Series 7 knife daggers very low indeed. The survival of hilt and sheath traces may indicate that daggers were buried with their organic accoutrements in place. However where there is evidence that the hilt plate was severely damaged in antiquity, and rivets missing, it is possible that only some of the hilt material may have remained in place. Taking all the recorded evidence together, it can be suggested that some hilts may have been deliberately removed within each of the seven chronological series. However for Series 2 it would seem that the hilts were usually still attached at the time of burial. The same probably applies to the Series 4 blades, but in the case of the Series 3 (Armorico-British A) and Series 5 (Camerton-Snowshill) daggers, many hilts appear

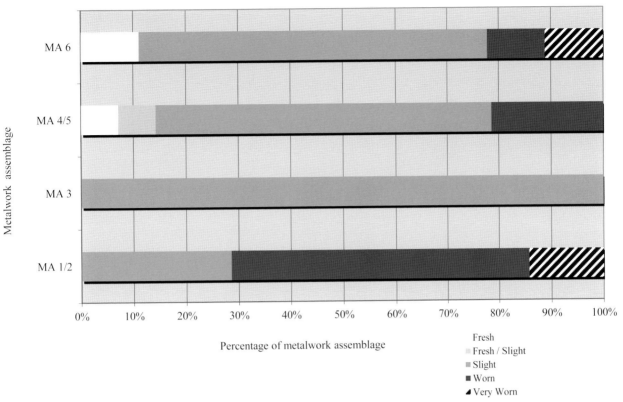

Figure 3.1.13. Wear levels for Early Bronze Age daggers with a known chemical composition.

Table 3.1.7. Knives and daggers: general conclusions (n = 139).

Series	Survival	Manufacture	Wear	Deliberate damage	Hilt removal
1	Very good	Rare	Heavy	Much	Some
2	Fair	Common	Slight	Medium	Very few
3	Moderate	Very common	Slight	Medium	Most
4	Fairly poor	Common	Slight to worn	Little	Very few
5	Good	Very common	Slight to worn	Little	Most
6	Fairly poor	Rare	n/a	Medium	Some
7	Poor	Common	Slight to worn	Medium	Most

to have been deliberately removed. Burial of the Series 2 daggers intact is also indicated by the high occurrence of pommels found associated with them. Interestingly the other group which has a significant number of pommels associated is Series 7, the knife daggers. Although smaller in size, these blades may not have been any less valuable as possessions or as grave goods. Estimation of hilt dimensions from the lengths of surviving rivets indicates that the thickest and most curvy hilts may have been those associated with the Series 5 (Camerton-Snowshill) daggers, but those for Armorico-British daggers of Series 3 and 4 were not far behind (see Table 3.1.6). Series 2 hilts may have been slightly thinner, and those for the Series 1 blades were notably thinner. As one might expect, the hilts belonging to the smaller knife daggers of Series 7 tend to be considerably thinner.

These general conclusions can also be considered by Series as in the above table (Table 3.1.7).

Series 1 tanged copper daggers were heavily used items, but had not been subjected to much ancient damage. The riveted daggers of Series 2 were usually deposited complete with their organic hilts, and some with their pommels surviving, but polishing striations are often visible and overall wear traces slight. Taking into account the incidence of ancient breaks, the Series 3 Armorico-British A daggers, and those of Series 4 (Armorico-British B), were more worn, and some of the hilts appear to have been removed and retained prior to deposition. Although classified as slightly worn to worn in general, the Series 5 Camerton-Snowshill daggers have very few ancient breaks apart from those around the hilt plate and overall survival is good. They are thus overall a less worn class of blade. However

Table 3.1.8. List of daggers and knives studied and illustrated.

Object	Site (Parish), County	Series	Museum	Illustration
Series 1: tanged daggers/knives (copper)				
ID 1317	Hundon, Suffolk	1A1	BM	Figure 3.1.3
ID 1318	Sutton Courtenay, Oxon.	1A1	BM	Figure 3.1.3
ID 1371	Roundway G8, Wilts.	1A1	Dev	Figure 3.1.3
ID 1326	Barnack, Cambs.	1A3	BM	Figure 3.1.3
ID 1377	Mere G6a, Wilts.	1A3	Dev	Figure 3.1.3
ID 1319	Sittingbourne, Kent	1B2	BM	Figure 3.1.3; Figure 3.1.12
ID 1182	Shrewton G5k, Wilts.	1B(2/4)	Sal	Figure 3.1.3
ID 1312	Kelleythorpe (Driffield), E. Yorks.	1C4	BM	Figure 3.1.3 Figure 3.1.12
ID 1327	Standlow (Kniveton), Derbys.	1C5	Shef	Figure 3.1.3
ID 1103	Saffron Walden, Essex	Ethno?	Camb	Figure 3.1.3
Series 2: butt-riveted flat daggers (bronze)				
ID 1102	Litlington, Cambs.	2A	Camb	Not illustrated
ID 1135	Acklam Wold 205 (Acklam), E. Yorks.	2A	Hull	Not illustrated
ID 1202	Brier Low (Hartington Upper), Derbys.	2A	Shef	Not illustrated
ID 1203	Dow Low (Hartington Upper), Derbys.	2A	Shef	Not illustrated
ID 1204	Parsley Hay (Hartington Middle), Derbys.	2A	Shef	Figure 3.1.4
ID 1210	Kenslow (Middleton and Smerrill), Derbys.	2A	Shef	Not illustrated
ID 1233	Charminster, Dorset	2A	Dor	Not illustrated
ID 1294	Butterwick 39, burial 1, E. Yorks.	2A	BM	Figure 3.1.4
ID 1141	Garrowby Wold 32 (Bishop Wilton), E. Yorks.	2B	Hull	Figure 3.1.4
ID 1200	Carder Low (Hartington Middle), Derbys.	2B	Shef	Figure 3.1.4
ID 1151	Garton Slack 107 (Garton-on-the-Wolds), E. Yorks.	2C	Hull	Figure 3.1.5
ID 1206	Net Low (Eaton and Alsop), Derbys.	2C	Shef	Figure 3.2.2
ID 1328	East Kennet G1c, Wilts.	2C	BM	Not illustrated
ID 1378	Milston G51, Wilts.	2C	Dev	Figure 3.1.4
ID 1180	Amesbury G85, Wilts.	2D	Sal	Figure 3.1.4
ID 1207	New Inns (Newton Grange), Derbys.	2D	Shef	Figure 3.1.12
ID 1199	Bole Hill (Wormhill), Derbys.	2E	Shef	Figure 3.1.4
ID 1220	Scamridge (Pickering), N. Yorks.	2E	Shef	Figure 3.1.4
ID 1295	Helperthorpe 49, burial 6, E. Yorks.	2E	BM	Not illustrated
ID 1302	North Charlton UN33, burial 2, Northumb.	2E?	BM	Not illustrated
ID 1296	Rudston 68, burial 6, E. Yorks.	2F1	BM	Not illustrated
ID 1380	Wilsford G54, Wilts.	2F1	Dev	Not illustrated
ID 1201	End Low (Hartington Town), Derbys.	2F2	Shef	Not illustrated
ID 1209	Deepdale, Barnet's Low (Grindon), Staffs.	2F2	Shef	Figure 3.1.4; Figure 3.1.12
ID 1215	Thorncliff Low (Calton Moor), Staffs.	2F2?	Shef	Figure 3.1.12
ID 1205	Shuttlestone (Hartington Nether), Derbys.	2F3	Shef	Not illustrated
ID 1214	Stanshope (Alstonefield), Staffs.	2G	Shef	Not illustrated
ID 1372	Wimborne St Giles G9, Dorset	2G	Dev	Not illustrated
ID 1133	Aldro 116 (Birdsall), E. Yorks.	2	Hull	Not illustrated
Series 3: thin lenticular-section Armorico-British and related daggers				
ID 1129	Towthorpe 139, E. Yorks.	3A	Hull	Figure 3.1.6
ID 1178	Ablington (Figheldean G25c), Wilts.	3A	Sal	Figure 3.1.6
ID 1185	Idmiston ?G9d, Wilts.	3A	Sal	Figure 3.1.6
ID 1236	Ridgeway 7 (Weymouth G8), Dorset	3A	Dor	Not illustrated
ID 1237	Ridgeway 7 (Weymouth G8), Dorset	3A	Dor	Not illustrated
ID 1395	Bush Barrow (Wilsford G5), Wilts.	3A	Dev	Figure 3.1.6; Figure 3.1.10
ID 1453	Winterbourne Stoke G5, Wilts.	3A	Dev	Figure 3.1.6
ID 1455	Winterbourne Stoke G5, Wilts.	3A	Dev	Figure 3.1.6
ID 1451	Kilmington G1	3B	Dev	Figure 3.1.6
Series 4: ribbed flat-bladed daggers				
ID 1105	Little Cressingham, Norfolk	4A	Norwich	Figure 3.1.8
ID 1131	Towthorpe 233, E. Yorks.	4A	Hull	Figure 3.1.7
ID 1297	Hutton Buscel 152, burial 1, E. Yorks.	4A	BM	Not illustrated
ID 1303	Brough UN69, E. Yorks.	4A	BM	Figure 3.1.7
ID 1391	Wilsford G23, Wilts.	4A	Dev	Figure 3.1.7

ID 1396	Bush Barrow (Wilsford G5), Wilts.	4A	Dev	Figure 3.1.7
ID 1476	Wilsford G43, Wilts.	4A	Dev	Figure 3.1.7
ID 1239	Clandon (Winterborne St Martin G31), Dorset	4A(?)	Dor	Not illustrated (see Needham and Woodward 2008, fig. 4)
ID 1213	Musden Low 4 (Waterhouses), Derbys.	4B	Shef	Figure 3.1.7
ID 1234	Ridgeway 7 (Weymouth G8), Dorset	4B	Dor	Figure 3.1.7
ID 1298	Hinton 287, burial 1 (N. Bishopstone), Wilts.	4B	BM	Not illustrated
ID 1301	Cheswick UN16, Northumb.	4B	BM	Figure 3.1.7

Series 5: thick-bladed daggers (Camerton-Snowshill)

ID 1179	Norton Bavant Borrow Pit, Wilts.	5C1	Sal	Not illustrated
ID 1181	Amesbury G85, Wilts.	5C1	Sal	Figure 3.1.9
ID 1240	Two Barrows (Winterborne Came G15), Dorset	5C2	Dor	Not illustrated
ID 1241	Cranborne, Dorset	5C2	Dor	Not illustrated
ID 1242	Dorchester G4, Dorset	5C2?	Dor	Not illustrated
ID 1100	Chippenham 1, Cambs.	5D	Camb	Not illustrated
ID 1157	Camerton (Timsbury G1), Somerset	5D	Brist	Figure 3.1.9
ID 1183	Winterbourne Stoke G47, Wilts.	5D	Sal	Figure 3.1.9
ID 1184	Amesbury, Wilts.	5D	Sal	Not illustrated
ID 1243	Cranborne G4, Dorset	5D	Dor	Not illustrated
ID 1244	Winterborne St Martin G46, Dorset	5D	Dor	Not illustrated
ID 1245	Dewlish G7, Dorset	5D	Dor	Not illustrated
ID 1246	Winterborne Came G15, Dorset	5D	Dor	Not illustrated
ID 1247	Winterborne St Martin G50a, Dorset	5D	Dor	Figure 3.1.9
ID 1248	Dewlish G8, Dorset	5D	Dor	Figure 3.1.9
ID 1249	Edmonsham G2, Dorset	5D	Dor	Not illustrated
ID 1252	Bincombe 1, Dorset (metal detector find)	5D	Dor	Figure 3.1.12
ID 1254	Cowleaze (Winterborne Steepleton), Dorset	5D	Dor	Not illustrated
ID 1299	Snowshill 297, burial 1, Gloucs.	5D	BM	Not illustrated
ID 1320	Loose Howe (Rosedale), N. Yorks.	5D	BM	Not illustrated
ID 1322	Rillaton, Cornwall	5D	BM	Figure 3.1.9
ID 1389	Wilsford G56, Wilts.	5D	Dev	Figure 3.1.9
ID 1419	Collingbourne Ducis G4, Wilts.	5D	Dev	Figure 3.1.9
ID 1440	Winterbourne Stoke G4, Wilts.	5D	Dev	Figure 3.1.9
ID 1477	Wilsford G27, Wilts.	5D	Dev	Figure 3.1.9
ID 1478	Upton Lovell G2, Wilts.	5D	Dev	Not illustrated
ID 1479	Edington G2, Wilts.	5D	Dev	Figure 3.1.9
ID 1480	Wimborne St Giles G20, Dorset	5D four rivets	Dev	Figure 3.1.9
ID 1481	Amesbury G15, Wilts.	5D	Dev	Not illustrated
ID 1171	Marshfield 7, Gloucs.	5D?	Brist	Not illustrated

Series 6: tanged small blades (knives/razors)

ID 1154	Blanch 2 (Huggate), E. Yorks.	6A1	Hull	Figure 3.1.10
ID 1212	Moot Low (Grangemill), Derbys.	6A1	Shef	Figure 3.1.10
ID 1142	Calais Wold 170 (Bishop Wilton), E. Yorks.	6B1	Hull	Figure 3.1.10
ID 1314	Lambourn 289, burial 1, Berks.	6B1	BM	Figure 3.1.10
ID 1316	Ulverston UN8, Cumbria	6B2	BM	Figure 3.1.10
ID 1217	Stanton Moor 3A, Derbys.	6?	Shef	Not illustrated

Series 7: butt-riveted small blades (knives/razors)

ID 1260	Thomas Hardye School (Dorchester), Dorset	1B4*/ 7A	Dor	Figure 3.1.11
ID 1106	Little Cressingham, Norfolk	7A	Norwich	Figure 3.1.8
ID 1143	Life Hill 294 (Sledmere), E. Yorks.	7A	Hull	Not illustrated
ID 1188	Amesbury G85, Wilts.	7A	Sal	Not illustrated
ID 1189	Fonthill Bishop G3, Wilts.	7A	Sal	Not illustrated
ID 1211	Mare Hill (Throwley), Derbys.	7A	Shef	Not illustrated
ID 1238	Ridgeway 7 (Weymouth G8), Dorset	7A	Dor	Not illustrated
ID 1255	Bradford Peverell G30, Dorset	7A	Dor	Not illustrated
ID 1256	Bradford Peverell G22, Dorset	7A	Dor	Figure 3.1.11
ID 1258	Dorchester G4, Dorset	7A	Dor	Not illustrated
ID 1259	Fordington Farm (Dorchester), Dorset	7A	Dor	Figure 3.1.11
ID 1430	Manton Barrow (Preshute G1a), Wilts.	7A	Dev	Not illustrated
ID 1456	Wilsford G60, Wilts.	7A	Dev	Figure 3.1.11

ID 1457	Roundway G5b, Wilts.	7A	Dev	Not illustrated
ID 1497	Wimborne St Giles G8, Dorset	7A	Dev	Not illustrated
ID 1512	Winterbourne Stoke G66, Wilts.	7A	Dev	Not illustrated
ID 1198	Minninglow (Ballidon), Derbys.	7A?	Shef	Not illustrated
ID 1267	Winterborne Came G15, Dorset	7A?	Dor	Not illustrated
ID 1483	Amesbury G56, Wilts.	7A/C	Dev	Not illustrated
ID 1162	Green Barrow (Priddy G3), Somerset	7B	Brist	Not illustrated
ID 1187	Norton Bavant Borrow Pit, Wilts.	7B	Sal	Not illustrated
ID 1216	Stanton Moor 1926 (Birchover), Derbys.	7B	Shef	Not illustrated
ID 1257	Church Knowle G9, Dorset	7B	Dor	Not illustrated
ID 1261	Thomas Hardye School (Dorchester), Dorset	7B	Dor	Not illustrated
ID 1266	Cowleaze (Winterborne Steepleton), Dorset	7B	Dor	Not illustrated
ID 1309	Aldbourne 282, burial 1, Wilts.	7B	BM	Not illustrated
ID 1323	Lambourn, Berks.	7B	BM	Not illustrated
ID 1324	Lambourn, Berks.	7B	BM	Figure 3.1.11
ID 1325	Ablington (Figheldean), Wilts.	7B	BM	Not illustrated
ID 1390	Wilsford G56, Wilts.	7B	Dev	Figure 3.1.11
ID 1392	Wilsford G23, Wilts.	7B	Dev	Figure 3.1.11
ID 1446	Upton Lovell G2e, Wilts.	7B	Dev	Not illustrated
ID 1482	Amesbury G46, Wilts.	7B	Dev	Not illustrated
ID 1490	Knook G1a, Wilts.	7B	Dev	Figure 3.1.11
ID 1470	Amesbury Park, Wilts.	7B?	Dev	Not illustrated
ID 1186	Ablington (Figheldean G25c), Wilts.	7C	Sal	Not illustrated
ID 1195	Amesbury G58, Wilts.	7C	Sal	Figure 3.1.11
ID 1208	Bee Low (Youlgreave), Derbys.	7C	Shef	Not illustrated
ID 1308	Aldbourne 277, burial 2, Wilts.	7C	BM	Figure 3.1.11
ID 1310	Aldbourne 286, burial 1, Wilts.	7C	BM	Not illustrated
ID 1439	Winterbourne Stoke G4, Wilts.	7C	Dev	Figure 3.1.11
ID 1486	Amesbury G4, Wilts.	7C	Dev	Not illustrated
ID 1489	Wilsford G65, Wilts.	7	Dev	Not illustrated

Type unknown: unclassifiable blade fragment				
ID 1136	Hanging Grimston 10 (Thixendale), E. Yorks.	Frag.	Hull	Not illustrated
ID 1137	Hanging Grimston 26 (Thixendale), E. Yorks.	Frag.	Hull	Not illustrated
ID 1140	Garrowby Wold 63 (Bishop Wilton), E. Yorks.	Frag.	Hull	Not illustrated
ID 1190	Norton Bavant G1, Wilts.	Frag.	Sal	Not illustrated

the hilts appear to have been removed much more often prior to burial, and no pommels survive in association with them. Finally the Series 7 knife daggers survive relatively badly. Wear is medium, and yet again it would appear that many hilts may have been removed prior to burial.

3.2 POMMELS

The following classification of Early Bronze Age dagger and knife pommel-pieces has been contributed by Stuart Needham. Nineteen individual items were studied in detail (Table 3.2.1) and these are marked in italics in the classification below.

TYPO-CHRONOLOGY (by Stuart Needham)
Hardaker published a corpus of known pommels in 1974 and formulated a six-group classification (Groups I to VI). With some corrections and inevitable additions, it is possible to put forward a somewhat revised classification. Some of the pommel-pieces associated with cremated remains actually went into the pyre and are thus heat-contorted and fractured to some degree; this may distort original morphology. The following new classification is suggested:

Class 1a: Tanged pommels (Figure 3.2.1).
Shrewton 5k (ID 1018); Standlow (ID 834); Pyecombe (ID 1074); Gravelly Guy; Leicester.
Tanged pommels are either squat elliptical or long oval in plan, the latter anticipating the norm for Class 2. The long oval ones can also be lipped in side profile. Leicester is of composite construction – a bronze plate sandwiched between two bone pieces extends as the tang. Setting aside the slightly early radiocarbon determination from Shrewton, these appear to belong to a limited horizon in the later Chalcolithic (late Period 1) and very earliest part of Period 2. Burial rite is known in all but one case and is consistently inhumation. Pommel widths are in the range 32 to 46mm.

Class 1b: Shanked pommels (Figure 3.2.2).
Net Low (ID 1206); Ferry Fryston.
In two cases two long-shanked studs were evidently embedded vertically within an inferred wooden pommel-piece; the shanks would have been sunk into the top of the handle. This is in effect a variation on the tang principle of attachment, although it did not require transverse securing pegs. This short-lived experiment with means of attachment took place at the very beginning of Period 2.

Class 2: Long oval socketed pommel-pieces with trapezoidal face profile (Figure 3.2.3; for Milston G51 see ID 1378 Figure 3.1.4).
Scamridge (ID 708); Lockton Warren; *Garton Slack 107 (ID 645); Helperthorpe (ID 833); Milston G51 (ID 1072);* Ashgrove; *Amesbury G85 (ID 1019);* through-slotted variant: *Garrowby Wold 32 (ID 771).*
These all furnished Series 2 daggers and accompanied inhumation burials of Period 2. Widths fall between 44 and 52mm. Scamridge and Lockton Warren are both composite sandwiches of bone held together by thin rivets (Manby 2009, 24–5 fig. 2). The Garrowby example differs in having a sub-rectangular profile as well as being through-slotted; it is conceivable that its thin slot actually accommodated a separate perishable tang component, thereby linking it to Class 1a.

Class 2/3: Long oval socketed pommel-piece with strongly expanded profile.
Gristhorpe
This pommel may be alone in combining the more oval plan of Class 2 with the strongly expanded profile of class

Table 3.2.1. List of pommels studied and illustrated.

Object	Site (Parish), County	Museum	Illustration
ID 645	Garton Slack 107 (Garton-on-the-Wolds), E. Yorks.	Hull	Figure 3.1.5; Figure 3.2.2; Figure 3.2.3; Figure 3.2.7
ID 659	Galley Low (Brassington), Derbys.	Shef	Figure 3.2.4; Figure 3.2.7; Figure 3.2.9
ID 663	Stanton Moor 1926, Derbys.	Shef	Figure 3.2.5
ID 703	Narrowdale Hill (Alstonefield), Derbys.	Shef	Figure 3.2.5
ID 708	Scamridge, N Yorks.	Shef	Figure 3.2.3
ID 771	Garrowby Wold 32 (Bishop Wilton), E. Yorks.	Hull	Not illustrated
ID 833	Helperthorpe 49, burial 6, E. Yorks.	BM	Not illustrated
ID 834	Standlow (Kniveton), Derbys.	BM	Figure 3.2.1; Figure 3.2.9
ID 906	Winterbourne Stoke G66, Wilts.	Dev	Figure 3.2.4
ID 907	Winterbourne Stoke G4, Wilts.	Dev	Not illustrated
ID 1018	Shrewton 5k, Wilts.	Sal	Figure 3.2.1
ID 1019	Amesbury G85, Wilts.	Sal	Figure 3.2.3
ID 1047	Ridgeway 7, Weymouth G8, Dorset	Dor	Figure 3.2.5; Figure 3.2.9
ID 1072	Milston G51, Wilts.	Dev	Not illustrated
ID 1074	Pyecombe, E. Sussex	Lewes	Figure 3.2.1
ID 1206	Net Low (Eaton and Alsop), Derbys.	Shef	Figure 3.2.2
ID 1238	Ridgeway 7, Weymouth G8, Dorset	Dor	Figure 3.2.6
ID 1395	Bush Barrow, Wilsford G5, Wilts.	Dev	Figure 3.2.7
ID 1429	Manton Barrow, Preshute G1a, Wilts.	Dev	Not illustrated

3. There are other indications, from the typology of the blade and the radiocarbon date, that it may be intermediate chronologically. As for Class 2, the associated burial is an inhumation.

Class 3: Elliptical or pointed oval socketed pommel-pieces with strongly expanded profiles (Figure 3.2.4).
Bedd Branwen (x2); *Winterbourne Stoke G66 (ID 906)*; *Galley Low (ID 659)*; Radwell; Beech Hill House; Merddyn; Bwlch y Rhiw; Wilmslow; Rounds; *Manton (amber) (ID 1429)*; Ringlemere; Winterbourne Stoke G9; River Thames; Shaw Cairn; ?Gayhurst Quarry (fragment). Through-slotted variant: Marian Bach, Balleymoney (Ireland); composite variant (two-material quadrant construction): *Winterbourne Stoke G4 (ID 907)*. Note: the 'long oval pommels with pronounced lips' described in the Raunds report (Needham 2011b) are a subset of this class, excluding a few of the narrowest examples – this width division is not now thought to be significant.

Manton, Ringlemere and Winterbourne Stoke G9 are of amber, the Thames example of bronze and cast in one with the handle, the rest of bone-like materials (see below); Balleymoney may be horn. The three of amber are amongst the smallest, presumably because of the difficulty of obtaining large pieces of the raw material. Overall, most widths range fairly evenly from 21 to 38mm, but Balleymoney and the Thames examples are much wider (57, 70mm respectively). The latter two are from wet places, the rest being from cremation burials.

This type almost certainly spans both Periods 3 and 4. Nine examples were associated with urns, usually Collared Urns, and various other accompaniments are dominated by ornaments. The associations at Raunds, Manton, Winterbourne Stoke G66, probably Ringlemere and possibly Winterbourne Stoke G9 are of Period 3, while the radiocarbon date for Beech Hill House points to very early in the overall currency. Nevertheless, some contexts are likely to be Period 4 and this is reinforced by the associated Camerton-Snowshill dagger for the unusual variant at Winterbourne Stoke G4 and the metal-hilted dagger from the River Thames. Associated blades can also be smaller implements (Winterbourne Stoke G66, Manton).

Class 4: Squat oval through-slotted pommel-pieces with expanded or lipped profiles (Figure 3.2.5).
Weymouth G8 (ID 1047); Eynsham; *Stanton Moor (ID 663)*; Kernonen (Brittany); variant with socket: *Narrowdale Hill (ID 703)*.
Widths are mainly between 32 and 40mm, but Narrowdale is only 19.5mm wide. Some examples are associated with small implements (Eynsham, Stanton Moor). The associated examples amongst Class 4 suggest a currency starting in Period 2 (Eynsham: its more subtle expansion recalling Class 2 pommels), with Weymouth G8 and Kernonen more likely of Period 3.

Class 5: Squat elliptical double-socketed pommel-pieces with strongly expanded profiles and flattened lip (Figure 3.2.6).

Weymouth G8 (gold) (ID 1238); Hammeldon Down; Grange (Ireland); Liscahane (Ireland).
These are highly crafted in exotic materials. The two British examples are embellished with gold – a total sheet cover in the case of Ridgeway, and gold wire studs in cruciform pattern on Hammeldon Down. The latter pommel and Liscahane are of amber, while Grange is of ivory. The presumed wooden core of Ridgeway is absent, but the other three all have double-sockets; at Hammeldon the partition between the sockets extends as a small tang. Widths fall between about 40 and 60mm. The Liscahane example is unusually shallow, but this may be a function of the amber lump available for its manufacture.

Despite the apparent specialisation and high material value of this form, it is not limited to a narrow horizon. Grange and Ridgeway were associated with Period 3 daggers, Hammeldon with one of Period 4, although the pommel had been repaired and may have been old on deposition. Liscahane is less precisely dated within this overall bracket.

Gold bands as under-pommel mounts.
Collessie; Skateraw; Blackwaterfoot; Forteviot; Topped Mountain (Ireland).

Five graves containing daggers also have corrugated gold bands which, on the evidence of the new Forteviot find, encircled the hilt immediately below the pommel. Forteviot, Collessie, Skateraw and probably Blackwaterfoot are datable to Period 2, whereas Topped Mountain is Period 3.

Ungrouped (Figure 3.2.7)
Bush Barrow (ID 1395); see also Chapter 6.

MORPHOLOGY
The variations in overall shape and form for the 19 pommels studied have been summarised in the new typology outlined in the previous section. In terms of size the different classes appear to group fairly tightly, as shown in the graph (Figure 3.2.8). The Class 2 pommels, which are associated with Series 2 flat riveted daggers are slightly larger, but mainly more narrow than the tanged pommels of Class 1, which are slightly earlier. Otherwise the pommels seem to become smaller through time, although the Class 3 pommels of Period 2 to 3 tend to be wider than those of the Period 3/4 Class 4 examples. The Class 5 gold pommel cover from Ridgeway 7 (ID 1238) and the composite pommel of Class 3 from Winterbourne Stoke G4 are both particularly large. The number of rivets used to attach the pommel to the hilt varies from two to five, and there is no clear correlation between number of rivets and class of pommel. However the Class 2 pommels always have holes for two or four rivets. The rivets or rivet holes, where no rivets survive, are all narrow, varying in diameter from 1.2 to 3.5mm. Again there is no correlation between rivet size and pommel class.

MATERIAL
Some pommels were made from wood or amber, and some embellished with gold pins or sheet, as specified in the class summaries above. However most of them were

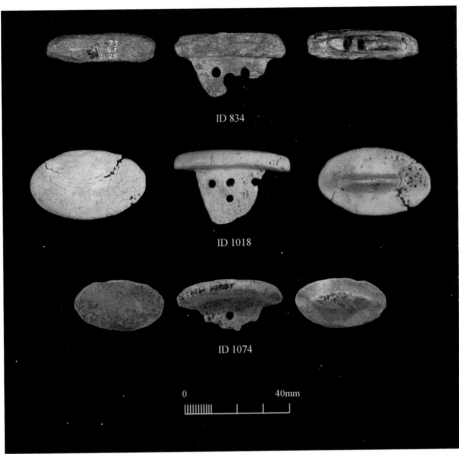

Figure 3.2.1. Class 1a, tanged pommels: ID 834 Standlow; ID 1018 Shrewton; ID 1074 Pyecombe.

Table 3.2.2. Identification of materials used to manufacture pommels (arranged in class order). MM = Mark Maltby; SH-D = Sheila Hamilton-Dyer; SO'C = Sonia O'Connor.

Object	Site, County	Class	Material	Species	Identified by
ID 834	Standlow, Derbys.	1a	Mammal bone	Possibly cetacean	MM and SH-D, plus BMNH; SO,C photo only
ID 1018	Shrewton G5k, Wilts.	1a	Mammal bone	Cetacean	MM, SH-D and SO'C
ID 1074	Pyecombe, E. Sussex	1a	Mammal bone	Cetacean	SO,C
ID 645	Garton Slack 107, E. Yorks.	2	Mammal bone	Cetacean	MM and SO'C
ID 771	Garrowby Wold, E. Yorks.	2	Mammal bone	Probably cetacean	MM and SO'C
ID 708	Scamridge, N. Yorks.	2	Large mammal	Cattle or horse	MM and SO'C
ID 833	Helperthorpe, E. Yorks.	2	Mammal bone	Possibly cetacean	MM, SH-D and SO'C
ID 1019	Amesbury G85, Wilts.	2	Mammal bone	Cetacean	MM and SH-D
ID 1072	Milston G51, Wilts.	2	Mammal bone	Probably cetacean	MM, SH-D and SO'C
ID 659	Galley Lowe, Derbys.	3	Large mammal longbone	Cattle or horse	MM and SO'C
ID 906	Winterbourne Stoke G66, Wilts.	3	Large mammal bone	Cetacean	MM, SH-D and SO'C
ID 907	Winterbourne Stoke G4, Wilts.	3	Antler or bone	Possibly antler or possibly cetacean bone	MM, SH-D and SO'C
ID 663	Stanton Moor 1926, Derbys.	4	Antler or pedicle	Prob. red deer; poss. roe deer	MM and SO'C
ID 703	Narrowdale, Alstonefield, Derbys.	4	Large mammal longbone	Cattle or horse	MM and SO'C
ID 1047	Weymouth G8 (Ridgeway 7), Dorset	4	Large mammal bone	Cetacean	MM and SO'C

manufactured from bone-like materials. The materials used for making the pommels are of particular interest. On first study, by Mark Maltby, it was noted that the materials were

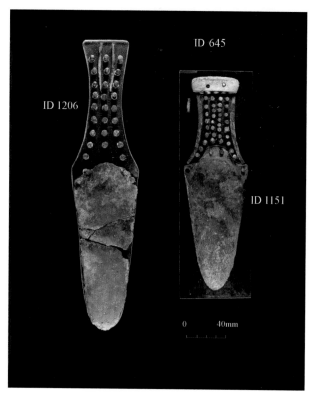

Figure 3.2.2. Class 1b, shanked pommels: ID 1206 Net Low; also Class 2 ID 645 Garton Slack mounted (on dagger ID 1151, see also Figure 3.2.3 and drawing in Figure 3.1.5).

especially dense and displayed some unusual characteristics. It was thought that some might have been made from ivory, horn or other unusual materials and it was therefore decided to study these items further. Thus Sheila Hamilton-Dyer viewed the relevant items at the British Museum and at Salisbury, while Dr Sonia O'Connor was able to accompany Mark Maltby on second visits to the museums at Hull and Sheffield. Dr O'Connor also studied selected pommels at Devizes, Dorchester, Salisbury and Lewes, and studied further unusual examples using the project photographs. The final results of all their examinations and discussions are summarised in the following table (Table 3.2.2), while an illustrated report by Dr O'Connor appears in Appendix IV. The pommel from Standlow had already been identified as having probably been made from sperm whale ivory (Kinnes 1985, A14), although Dr O'Connor's new study indicated that the material was whale (cetacean) bone.

The materials employed were various, including large mammalian longbone, antler, and cetacean mammal (whalebone). The marine material all will have derived ultimately from the sea. Whether whales were hunted at this time, or whether all the material was obtained from dead creatures or beached carcases is not known. Any resource the sea threw up would be avidly collected, but hunting of small cetaceans cannot be ruled out (see discussion below).

MANUFACTURE

The pommels are complex items which have been manufactured to a high level of craftsmanship. Where the degree of original polish can be determined, all except two are polished, and of these two are categorised as highly polished (ID 708, ID 833, both of Class 2). Traces of manufacture

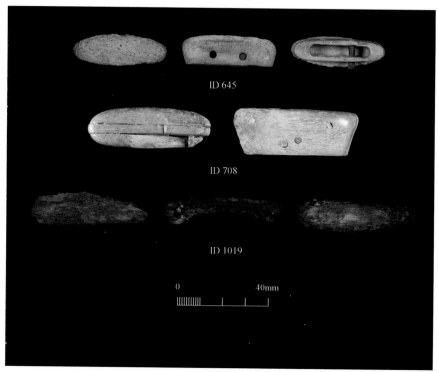

Figure 3.2.3. Class 2, long oval socketed pommel-pieces with trapezoidal face profile: ID 645 Garton Slack 107 (see also drawing on Figure 3.1.5 with dagger ID 1151); ID 708 Scamridge; ID 1019 Amesbury G85.

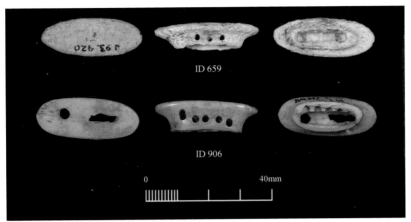

Figure 3.2.4. Class 3, elliptical or pointed oval socketed pommel pieces with strongly expanded profiles: ID 659 Galley Low; ID 906 Winterbourne Stoke G66.

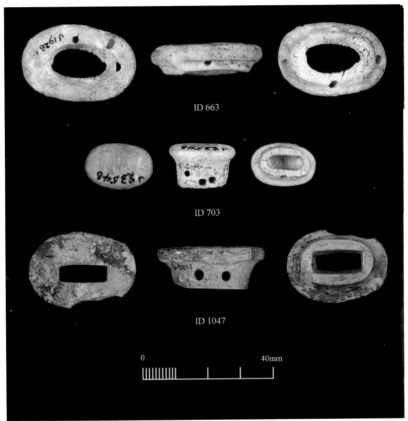

Figure 3.2.5. Class 4, oval through-slotted pommel-pieces with expanded or lipped profiles: ID 663 Stanton Moor; ID 703 Narrowdale Hill; ID 1047 Ridgeway 7.

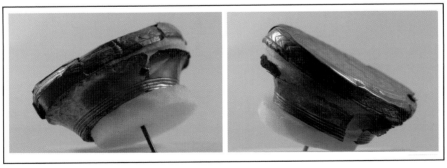

Figure 3.2.6 Class 5, squat elliptical double-socketed pommel-pieces with strongly expanded profiles and flattened lip: ID 1238 Ridgeway 7.

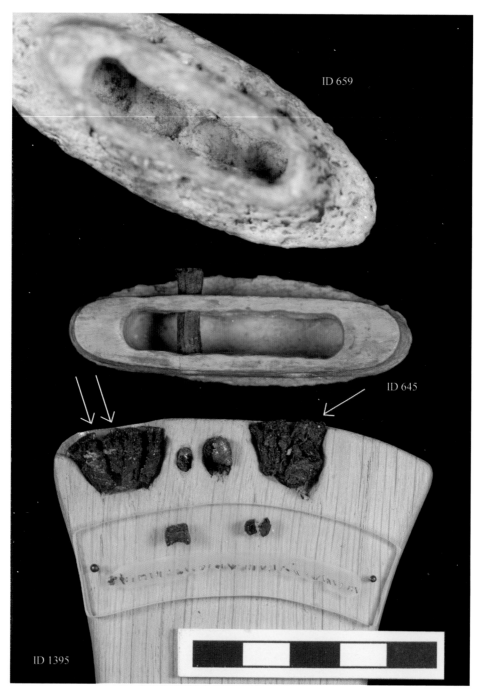

Figure 3.2.7. Top and centre, examples of drilling of basal slots: ID 659 Galley Low; ID 645 Garton Slack 107 (see also drawing on Figure 3.1.3). Bottom, Ungrouped class: ID 1395 Bush Barrow. Note the use of gold pins (selection arrowed).

have therefore mainly been polished out, but are visible on three pommels. These include faint longitudinal striations on the sides of the pommel from Ridgeway 7 (ID 1047), and marked longitudinal or lateral marks on the lower face of the top flange on ID 834 and ID 1047. There are also tool marks situated on the tang of the Pyecombe Class 1a pommel (ID 1074). Under the microscope it is possible to discern how the basal slots were made. Each slot consists of a series of contiguous or overlapping drill holes, three to five in number, made with drills with a diameter equal to the width of the slot (Figure 3.2.7). The through rivet holes had always been drilled in a single operation but

the alignment was not always quite perpendicular to the pommel. Also in a few examples there are traces of starter holes from aborted perforations (Figure 3.2.9).

COMPLETENESS AND DAMAGE

The pommels do not survive particularly well. Only seven of the pieces studied in detail survive at the 95% level or above. And the incidence of modern damage is slight, comprising chips or flakes at the top or slot edges, or minor cracking. This occurs on nine pommels in total. Two of the pommels studied had been burnt, although one was associated with an unburnt dagger. These are grey/blue and

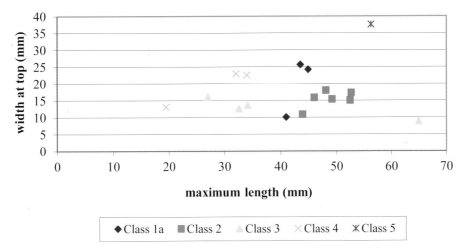

Figure 3.2.8. Pommels: the relationship between length and top width, by class.

white/grey in colour. Others vary in colour from cream to buff, brown and dark brown/black, reflecting the different raw materials employed.

WEAR

All the pommels studied except for one example show signs of ancient damage. This damage includes breaks to the edges of the pommel top in ten cases and to the sides of the pommel twice (Figure 3.2.9). In five cases there is damage to the edge of the slot on the lower surface, and all three tangs of the Class 1a pommels were also damaged in antiquity (see Figure 3.2.1). General wear comprises traces of rubbing and differential smoothing in various locations on the pommel, but often on the top margins (ID 659 and ID 906, Figure 3.2.4; ID 708, Figure 3.2.3). Even the gold pommel cover shows extreme wear, with many small tears around the edges of the top plate (Figure 3.2.6). Overall seven pommels were classed as worn, and nine as very worn. Only one pommel was only slightly worn, and this object category is one of those that displays the greatest degree of wear detected in the project. In addition to these traces of extreme wear on the pommels, there is also evidence of reworking and re-use on six examples. This evidence will be summarised individually.

- *Shrewton G5k (ID 1018).* The break on the tang was re-smoothed in antiquity, as if to prepare the pommel for insertion in a second dagger (Figure 3.2.1).
- *Pyecombe (ID 1074).* Damage to the tang on this pommel may also have related to modification for use on a subsequent dagger (Figure 3.2.1).
- *Helperthorpe (ID 833).* A major break on the lower margin had been repolished. This may have related to preparation of the pommel for use on a second dagger.
- *Milston G51 (ID 1072).* A break along one top edge had been re-polished.
- *Winterbourne Stoke G66 (ID 906).* After breakage at the base, the edge of the slot had been intentionally bevelled. This may have been undertaken so that the pommel could be fitted to a different hilt.

- *Preshute G1a (ID 1429).* The amber pommel from the Manton Barrow also displays strong ancient damage to the basal slot. Once again this may have related to re-fitting of the pommel to a second dagger/knife (not illustrated).

CONCLUSIONS

Pommels made from various materials: bone, horn, antler, marine ivory and whalebone, amber, wood and gold were made throughout the periods under study, and varied in size, overall shape and construction through time. They are all very carefully made, and originally finished to a high degree of polish. Their manufacture would have involved highly skilled craftsmanship and, in particular, expert control of drilling, both for forming the rivet holes and the various slots involved. The selection of unusual materials for many of the earlier pommels may have been deliberate, and symbolic in nature (see more detailed discussion by O'Connor below). In particular the employment of materials derived from the northern seas, and their icy depths, may have represented concepts of mystery and distance (in both space and depth), along with the powers of water and the ocean.

The pommels do not survive particularly well, but modern damage is extremely slight. Most breaks and damage are ancient, and overall traces of wear are very common. Almost all those studied are worn or very worn, with a high complement of examples in the very worn category. In addition to this, in six cases there was evidence that ancient breaks or other damage had been smoothed out, polished over or otherwise reworked. And in most of these cases the modification of tang or lower slot may have related to the need to fit the pommel to a subsequent dagger. Overall the evidence gathered indicates that the pommels were highly valuable items made from exotic and expertly worked materials. They show signs of extreme wear and often were re-used. In other words, the pommels themselves may have been more valuable than the metal knife and dagger blades to which they were attached.

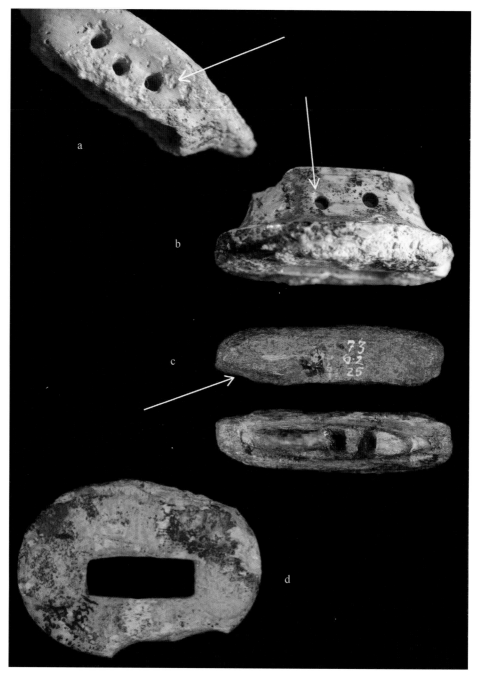

Figure 3.2.9. Traces of starter holes (arrowed) on (a) ID 659 Galley Low and (b) ID1047 Ridgeway 7; breakage on edge of pommel top on (c) ID 834 Standlow and (d) ID 1047 Ridgeway 7.

The very high value of the pommels is further indicated by the fashion for depositing the pommels in graves as individual pieces; in other words without any associated metal blade. This applies particularly to the later pommels of Hardaker's Group II (eight belonging to Needham Class 3 and one to Class 4). Two more recent finds also were found without blades, but in association with various ornaments. These are the Class 3 pommels from Radwell 1 (Hall and Woodward 1977, fig. 4, D) and, in amber, from Ringlemere (Needham *et al.* 2006, fig. 24, a). Both of these pommels also show signs of ancient damage. In this connection it is also of interest to note the finding

of the pommel and dagger blade from Raunds 1. In size the two items are mismatched, and only the pommel was burnt. It would appear that this pommel might not have belonged to the dagger which was found in the grave (Harding and Healy 2007, 245). Amongst the pommels not studied in detail, final mention should be made of the remarkable amber pommel from Hammeldon, which sadly was destroyed in the Second World War. This large piece, decorated with a geometric design formed from rows of inlaid gold pins, had been damaged in antiquity. The broken piece had been replaced and held invisibly by a series of horizontal pegs and gold pins. Later the separate piece had broken away once more, thus revealing the detail of how the repair had been effected (Hardaker 1974, 27–8).

From all available analyses of the skeletal or cremated remains it can be shown that pommels most commonly occurred with male burials. These include two pommels of Class 1a, five of Class 2, four of Class 3 and one of Class 4. However two Class 3 pommels and one of Class 4 have been found with women. There is some suggestion that the pommels associated with female graves tend to be smaller, and associated with knife daggers rather than with dagger blades.

Discussion on cetacean bone (by Sonia O'Connor)
The range of materials used for the pommels is of particular interest. Of the 15 pommels studied, one was antler, one was possibly antler, 13 were bone and none was shown to be horn or ivory of any species. All the bone had the characteristics of large mammal bone but six were clearly cetacean bone. Another two pommels were most probably bone from small cetaceans, and a further three, including one that appeared to share some of the characteristics of antler, were possibly cetacean bone, but as these were identified from photographs alone it is not possible to be more certain. Even ignoring the 'probable' and 'possible' identifications, the use of cetacean bone accounts for over 30% of the pommels in the study.

This is a surprisingly high percentage as cetacean bone is rarely represented in finds assemblages. Exceptions to this are coastal communities as evidenced by the Bronze and Iron Age sites of Atlantic Scotland, where scavenging of strandings as much as active hunting probably contributed to the harvesting of this resource (Mulville 2002). However, although a single whale may present a prolific source of large bones, very little of the skeleton has any thickness of compact tissue suitable for pommel production. Apart from a few elements such as whale ribs and the ramus of the toothed whales' mandible, most of the bone is relatively coarse cancellous tissue encased in only a thin layer of compact bone. A considerable amount of the cetacean bone material recovered from these coastal sites is butchery waste, large more-or-less complete bones employed as architectural elements or charred debris, indicating the use of the oil-rich bone as fuel.

It could be suggested that the size of the pommels might have contributed to this unusual bias towards cetacean bone. Certainly several of the pommels are cut from rather large single pieces of bone that would be difficult, but not necessarily impossible, to source from readily available, large terrestrial mammal fauna, such as horse or cow. It is also possible that elk survived into the Bronze Age, at least in Scotland (Kitchener 2010), and this certainly could have provided both bone and antler of sufficient size for these pommels. However a more probable source of substantial antler compact tissue would have been red deer, which at this time was present in large numbers across the country and had larger and more robust antlers than those of present day populations. However, that antler is not being utilised underlines even more strongly that size alone was not the determining factor for the preferential selection of cetacean bone for dagger pommel production.

Through the recent research undertaken to improve the confidence of the identification of worked and decayed animal hard tissues (O'Connor forthcoming), it is becoming increasingly apparent that cetacean material is being preferentially selected for handle components of cutting edge weapons, from the Bronze Age through the Iron Age to the Viking period. This could indicate a belief that a weapon (or perhaps its owner?) could be invested with the power of the 'beast' whose bones or teeth where fashioned to form its hilt.

3.3 BELT HOOKS

TYPO-CHRONOLOGY

A total of 20 so-called belt hooks known from the British Isles, made mainly from bone, have been listed and discussed by Sheridan (2007a). The non-bone examples are the gold two-piece hook from Bush Barrow (which is considered in detail below in Chapter 6) and a cannel coal trapezoid plate with a V-perforation in the rear surface from Law Hill, Dundee (Clarke *et al.* 1985, fig. 5.47). This may in fact be imitating the similarly shaped piece from Bush Barrow. Of the 20 belt hooks listed by Sheridan eight bone examples from England (Figure 3.3.1), together with the Bush Barrow gold example (Figure 3.3.2), have been studied in detail, together with a newly-discovered example in bronze. In terms of shape, Sheridan has been able to define two main categories, with narrow and broad plates respectively (see below). Associations, which are summarised in detail by Sheridan (2007a, table A3.1) include four Collared Urns, two Food Vessel graves, an accessory vessel, two stone battle-axes, four Armorico-British daggers (Series 3 or 4), a jet bead, a whetstone, four bone pins or toggles and a bone pendant. Such associations place the graves containing belt hooks firmly within the mature Early Bronze Age period, between the 20th and 17th centuries cal BC, and this dating is confirmed by radiocarbon dates from Bargrennan, Fan Foel and Norton Bavant (for details see Sheridan *ibid*). Thus the belt hooks are generally later than the series of belt and pulley rings, which are mainly associated with Beakers (see Chapter 3.4). Most of the belt hooks come from cremation burials, and indeed most examples are burnt, having passed through the fire with the body. There are, however, two

examples found with inhumation burials, and five other belt hooks were not burnt. The age and sex of the bodies concerned has not often been determined. However, of those burials where sex has been analysed, three are male and three more possibly or probably so. The age range represented is wide, varying from juveniles to mature and elderly adults. Those studied here are all listed in Table 3.3.1.

MORPHOLOGY

The hooks are generally D-shaped in side profile and rectangular or square in plan. The curved hook lies in front of a flat back plate. However the gold and cannel coal examples are trapezoid in plan. Two categories have been defined by Sheridan (*ibid*). Key dimensions for the items studied in detail are given in Table 3.3.1. They can be categorised thus:

- Type 1: narrow, rectangular, and relatively small, with the hook being as wide, or nearly as wide, as the plate. Plate lengths vary from *c.* 25 to 30mm.
- Type 2: broad, rectangular, squarish or trapezoidal, and large, with the hook/s being significantly narrower than the plate. One example from Ireland has two hooks projecting from the plate.
- Intermediate: hooks comparable in length to Type 1 examples, but with a squarish plate, wider than the hook.

It can be seen that the hooks are quite variable in size, even within Type 1, whose form and shape is fairly standardised. The gold plate and hook from Bush Barrow (ID 1401 Wilsford G5) is particularly large and ornate,

Table 3.3.1. Belt hooks: typology and dimensions (Int. denotes Intermediate type; Indet. denotes indeterminate measurement); L length; W width; Th: thickness).

Object	Site (Parish), County	Type	Material	Max L (mm)	Hook W (mm)	Hook Th (mm)	Plate W (mm)	Plate Th (mm)	Museum	Illustration
ID 622	Painsthorpe 201 (Kirby Underdale), E. Yorks.	1	Bone	23	20	9.2	n/a	n/a	Hull	Figure 3.3.1
ID 744	Slingsby 145, burial 1, N. Yorks.	1	Bone	27	15–6.5	3.7	-	3	BM	Figure 3.3.1
ID 745	Wytham UN2, burial 1, Oxon.	Int.	Bone	25	25–12.5	2.5	25	3–3.5	BM	Figure 3.3.1
ID 881	Probably Wilts.	2	Bone	Indet.	16.5	Indet.	61	4.2	Dev	Figure 3.3.1
ID 882	Wilsford G15, Wilts.	1	Bone	28.5	17.4–9.9	6.8	-	2.7	Dev	Figure 3.3.1
ID 883	Wilsford G18, Wilts.	1	Bone	29.2	16.1–9.7	8.2	-	6	Dev	Figure 3.3.1; Figure 3.3.3
ID 884	W. Overton G4, Wilts.	1	Bone	30.2	14–9.5	5.8	-	4	Dev	Figure 3.3.1; Figure 3.3.3
ID1014	Norton Bavant, Borrow Pit, Wilts.	Indet.	Bone	30.5	20–10	3	30.6	4.5	Sal	Figure 3.3.1
ID 1391	Wilsford G23, Wilts.	Indet.	Bronze	Indet.	*c.* 30	Indet.	-	Indet.	Dev	Not illustrated.
ID 1401	Wilsford G5, Wilts.	2	Gold	75.9	24.1–13.9	6.5	71	5.5	Dev	Figure 3.3.2

and would have been attached with small tacks or threads through small holes present at each corner (see Chapter 6). The only other hook to possess a perforation is that from Painsthorpe (ID 622). This is also unusual in that there is no clear back plate, and both arms of the hook are similar in shape. The perforation runs at right angles to the hook and is of hourglass form with a diameter ranging between 2.0 and 4.8mm.

Decoration occurs on eight of the hooks studied in detail. This is always linear and usually comprises grooves running along the length of the hook. In four cases there is a single groove running down each side of the front of the hook, and in two cases there are double grooves at the margins. The Painsthorpe hook (ID 622) has three decorative grooves. The grooves sometimes define prominent ridges and both ridges and grooves follow the curved outline of the hook. The grooves vary in width from less than 1mm to 3.5mm, but most are less than 1mm across. Most complex is the decoration on the Bush Barrow hook; this also consists of grooves, but in this case arranged in four zones, each of three grooves, running parallel to each side of the trapezoidal plate.

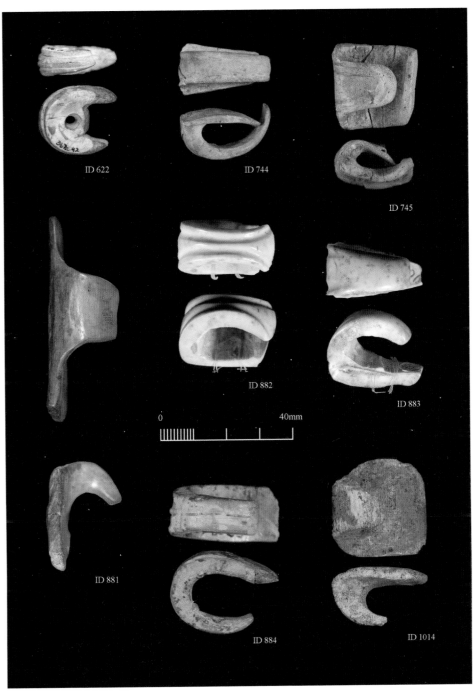

Figure 3.3.1. ID 622 Painsthorpe 201; ID 744 Slingsby 145; ID 745 Wytham UN2; ID 881 probably Wiltshire; ID 882 Wilsford G15; ID 883 Wilsford G18; ID 884 West Overton G4; ID 1014 Norton Bavant.

Although most of the 20 belt hooks listed by Sheridan (see above) were burnt at the time of cremation, this only applies to three of the examples studied in detail (ID 622, ID 744 and ID 745). These pieces are cracked and grey in colour. The non-burnt items vary in colour from white and cream to buff and dark brown.

MATERIAL

Apart from the hooks made from gold or bronze, all are fashioned from bone. In five cases the raw material was identified as the limb shaft of a large mammal (ID 622, ID 744–45, ID 881 and ID 1014). This includes the larger pieces of Intermediate type. The smaller hooks, all of Type 1, are made from the more triangular-sectioned part of a femur (IDs 882, 883 and 884). They are too small to have come from the bone of a large mammal, such as cattle or red deer, and too large for sheep/goat. The exact form of the bone used suggests that it was in fact *human* femurs that were employed. The example from Arreton Down, which is

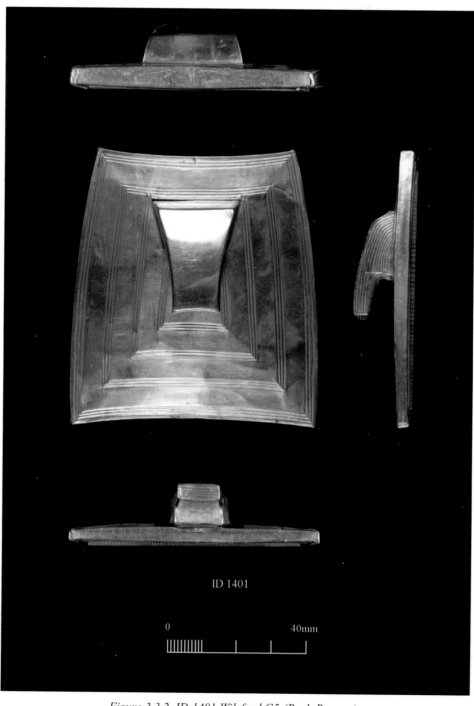

ID 1401

0   40mm

Figure 3.3.2. ID 1401 Wilsford G5 (Bush Barrow).

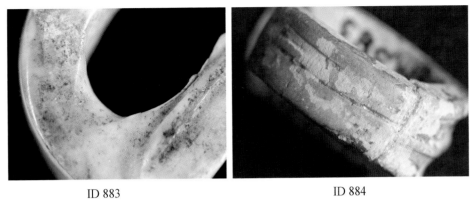

ID 883   ID 884

Figure 3.3.3. Details of wear on the angle of the hook on ID 883 Wilsford G18, and on the decoration of ID 884 West Overton G4.

slightly smaller, was identified as having been made from a sheep-sized long bone (Alexander and Ozanne 1960, 276).

MANUFACTURE

Apart from two cases where the surface is corroded it can be seen that the surfaces are shiny and polished. In three cases the degree of polish was categorised as high, and the decoration is all executed neatly and expertly. Traces of faint initial polishing striations are visible on all eight of the bone examples. These occur twice on the front or top of the hook (longitudinal and lateral), three times on the sides (diagonal, longitudinal and lateral) and five times on the back plate (marked/faint diagonal and multidirectional). There are also chisel marks on the plate of ID 883 and tool marks within one decorative groove on ID 744.

COMPLETENESS AND DAMAGE

Most of the belt hooks are complete or very nearly so (seven examples at 95% survival or above). Two have modern chips and two others have been broken across since excavation, and glued together.

WEAR

Much ancient damage on the burnt examples results from the hooks having passed through the cremation pyre, and there are ancient small chips on two unburnt items. Two pieces however display more serious damage, and appear to have been deposited in the grave in a broken state. The one from Norton Bavant (ID 1014) has a broken hook and damage to the edges of the back plate, and that probably from Wiltshire (ID 881) has much of the plate missing, as well as a broken hook. Evidence of wear is highly variable, and one piece (ID 882) has sharp edges and pristine decoration, indicating that it is a fresh and unused item. Three hooks have obvious wear traces within the angle of the hook (ID 881, ID 883 and ID 884), in two cases extreme (ID 883, Figure 3.3.3; ID 884). And the edges and interior surfaces of the gold hook from Bush Barrow (ID 1401) also show definite signs of use. The outer edge of the perforation on ID 622 also shows strong wear traces. In

ID 1391

Figure 3.3.4. The dagger from ID 1391 Wilsford G23 showing the metal hook attached to the corrosion products of the sheath.

three cases the decoration also shows signs of considerable wear (ID 883; ID 884, Figure 3.3.3; ID 1014). Overall one hook is fresh, four slightly worn, one worn and three very worn. The hook from Bargrennan has green metal staining within the angle of the hook, and Sheridan (2007a) suggested that this may have been caused by the decay of a metal belt ring. Similar staining occurs in the hook angle on examples ID 881 and ID 883, but the metal staining on ID 1014 (Norton Bavant) occurs on the rear and inner edges of the back plate only.

CONCLUSIONS

The high degree of finish and quality of the decoration on this series of hooks indicates that they were items of high value. This conclusion is also amplified by the use of special exotic materials such as gold and cannel coal, and by the careful selection of bone of a particular shape, including human femurs. The latter may have been long bones from known and named individuals, such as relatives of the owner, or 'ancestral' bones recovered from older interments.

It has always been assumed that the hooks functioned as belt fasteners, and Sheridan (2007a, fig. A3.3) has shown how they may have been sewn horizontally into one end of a belt, and hooked over a metal ring which was attached to the other. Metal stains on two of the hooks studied in this project would also fit in with such a reconstruction. However, the finding of the remains of the metal hook attached to the corrosion products of the sheath of the larger dagger from Wilsford G23 (ID 1391, Figure 3.3.4) may suggest a different interpretation. It may be that the hooks were attached vertically into the front of a sheath of scabbard, with the hook providing anchorage for a narrow thong or cord which provided attachment to the belt above.

In the Bush Barrow burial, the gold hook was found in the area of the waist of the body, but was also touching the pair of sheathed daggers (Needham *et al.* 2010, fig. 3). Other information concerning body placement is unhelpful. For instance, at Norton Bavant the belt hook was found with a group of other objects in a cache deposited behind the head of the body (Butterworth 1992, fig. 3).

Many of the hooks from southern England are remarkably similar in form and style. They are narrow, beautifully finished and decorated with neat grooves and ridges following the sinuous outline of the hook. In addition to the examples of this kind studied here (ID 744, ID 882–84), the other two southern items known are also of similar style. These are the hooks from Twyford Down, Hampshire (Walker and Farwell 2000, fig. 31,15) and from Arreton Down, Isle of Wight (Alexander and Ozanne 1960, fig.5a). These similarities may indicate that such highly finished items were manufactured by a single craftsman or school of makers. Sheridan (2007a) further suggests that the hooks may have been made and used during a relatively short period of time, and that the scatter of examples to the north of the Wessex heartland may represent the emulation of a fashion which originated in the south.

3.4 BELT AND PULLEY RINGS

TYPO-CHRONOLOGY

A typology for belt and pulley rings, which are a phenom-enon of the Beaker tradition, was first worked out by Clarke (1970, 262–3) and summarised in a series of useful illustrations (*ibid*, figs. 143–4). The scheme, which has stood the test of time, can best be introduced in his own words as follows: "The earliest belt rings from Britain are simple shanked or unshanked bone rings with Middle Rhineland parallels. From this series in bone and probably in wood, an indigenous British series of prestige versions in jet developed, at first simple rings and then with lateral V-borings for attachment, and finally with a grooved edge form…..Copies of this series can probably be seen in…… the Scottish bone pulley-rings with identical decoration and attachments" (*ibid*, 262). (It should be noted that the links with jet belt sliders, found in association with Peterborough Ware, can no longer be sustained chronologically). Clarke divided the rings into a series of Classes as follows:

- Class I: simple shanked or unshanked bone belt rings, mostly matching continental types (Figure 3.4.1).
- Class II: simple intermediate forms of pulley belt ring, mainly in jet; no continental parallels; no lateral perforations. (Only one example of this type is known, from Cassington, Oxon: Clarke 1970, fig. 240).
- Class IIIa: fully evolved pulley belt ring, usually jet, one or two lateral V-perforations; sometimes with incised radial decoration (Figure 3.4.2).
- Class IIIb: bone versions of Class IIIa pulley ring, similar perforations and decoration, but more elaborate grooved rim sections. (Although not of bone, the ring with elaborate grooved rim from Tring (ID 483) has been placed in this category) (Figure 3.4.3).
- Class IV: pulley belt ring, usually jet, with deep groove around outer edge: often no lateral perforations (Figure 3.4.3).

Examples of rings belonging to each class are listed in Table 3.4.1. The 19 rings which were the subject of detailed study in the project, several of which have been excavated since Clarke's study, are shown differentiated from other examples, the latter being shown in italic. This table also displays the known grave associations. Table 3.4.2 lists the items studied in ID sequence together with cross-reference to illustrations. The associations with Beakers of known type were used by Clarke to devise a chronological sequence for the main classes of ring (*ibid*, 263). Classes I and II are the earliest, associated with European or Middle Rhenish Beaker types. These are followed by Classes III and IV which are associated with Beakers of the later Southern and Northern series. The latest known example may be the Class IV example from Wimborne St Giles G9 (ID 479; Figure 3.4.3), associated with a flat riveted dagger of Series 2. Early tanged copper daggers (Series 1) are found with Class I rings twice, and stone bracers are another common association. With Class I rings there are bracers of unusual red and black materials, and one

each of amphibolite and Group VI rock. The four bracers associated with rings belonging to the later Classes are all of Group VI rock, and such bracers tend to occur later in the Beaker period as a whole (see Woodward and Hunter 2011). The later Classes tend to be associated with other exotic grave goods, such as flint daggers, jet V-perforated buttons and sponge finger stones, all of which are typical accompaniments for later style Beakers (see Needham 2005, fig. 12). It would appear that pulley belt rings did not continue to be used in the mature Wessex Early Bronze Age, and this may well indicate a significant change in body adornment. However there is one Class I ring from an Early Bronze Age grave, Upton Lovell G2a (the 'shaman' burial), but this is worn and may have been an heirloom item (ID 493, Figure 3.4.1). There are a few simple rings of thicker cross section which may date from the Early Bronze Age, two of which were studied (ID 358 and ID 377), but these may not have been used as belt fasteners. They may be related to the simple, but slightly larger, shale ring found on the arm bones of a female inhumation inserted into the long barrow at Raunds, a burial that was also associated with a late style Beaker and a bronze earring (Harding and Healy 2007, fig.4.8).

MORPHOLOGY

The rings are fairly consistent in terms of size, with maximum external diameter ranging from 20.8 to 47.2mm (see Figure 3.4.4). The width of the hoop varies from 4.5 to 15.2mm, with most occurring between 6 and 10mm. From Figure 3.4.4 it can be seen that rings belonging to Classes I and IIIa are all very similar in size, with one exception (ID 287 Little Downham, Figure 3.4.2). However the Class I rings, mostly made from bone, tend to be thinner. The mainly jet rings belonging to Class IIIa show a particularly tight size grouping (with the exception of ID 287), and a constricted distribution of thickness, between 6.0 and 8.7mm. The three amber rings (ID 1359 Kniveton, ID 1565 Raunds and Ferry Fryston) also fall within this cluster. The rings belonging to Classes IIIb and IV are significantly larger and thicker.

Some of the Class I bone rings are more complex in shape with one large ring at one end and a smaller ring at the other end, the so-called 'magnifying glass' shape (ID 657, ID 720, ID 1073, and ID 750 and Stanton Harcourt, see Figure 3.4.1). Cross sections of the hoop are variable. In the Class I examples they are simple, relatively flat and D-shaped or rectangular in section. The inner face of the hoop is straight except in the case of the shale ring with the Amesbury Archer (ID 471, Figure 3.4.1) which is slightly convex due to working from both faces. The hoop sections of the Class III and IV rings, which are mainly made from jet or shale, are much more square and chunky. The outer face may be straight (four examples) or slightly convex (five examples). Inner faces are even more variable, with two concave, three straight and four convex in profile. In two Class IIIa cases the decorated front and rear faces of the hoop are slightly dished (ID 313 and ID

318, Figure 3.4.2). Two of the Class IV shale pieces are distinctly wedge-shaped in overall profile, with one side of the hoop much thinner than the other (ID 474 and ID 480, Figure 3.4.3).

The jet, shale and amber rings of Classes III and IV are characterised by the presence of V-perforations on one side, to facilitate fastening of the ring to fabric or leather. Examples of Class III always have two adjacent V-perforations, while the occurrence of such sets of perforations on the Class IV items is more variable: one on ID 474, two on ID 480 and three in the case of ID 479 (Figure 3.4.3). Due to extreme wear of the perforations,

and loss of many of the bridges, mostly in antiquity, as well as the patterns of re-working the fastenings, it proved difficult to measure the sizes of the original perforations. They tend to be oval in shape, with the long axis along the circumference of the ring. Lengths of individual perforations vary from 4.1 to 7.9mm, and the diameters of the secondary perforations present on several items are much more variable, ranging from 1.7 to 8.0mm.

Six rings, one of Class I (ID 493, Figure 3.4.1) and five of Class IIIa, are decorated. In all cases the decoration occurs on both front and rear faces and on the outer surface of the ring. The designs, which are remarkably uniform, comprise

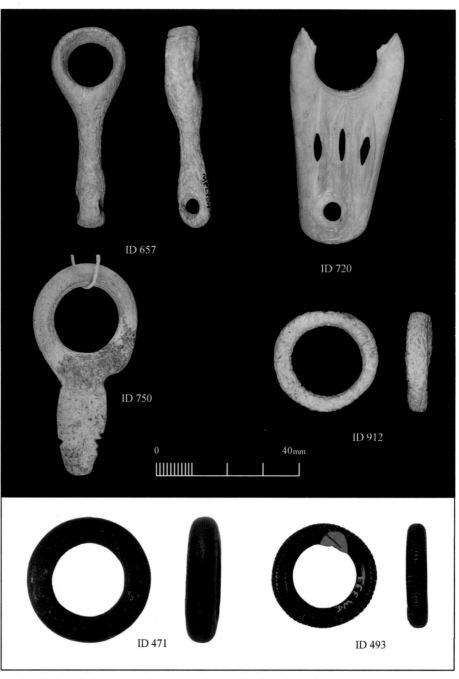

ID 657

ID 720

ID 750

ID 912

0   40mm

ID 471   ID 493

Figure 3.4.1. Examples of Class I objects: ID 657 Melton Quarry; ID 720 Sittingbourne; ID 750 Folkton 245; ID 912 Wilsford G1a; ID 471 Amesbury Archer; ID 493 Upton Lovell G2a.

grooves from 0.1 to 0.5mm in width, made with a sharp gouge or awl. The patterns on the faces are formed from radially placed short grooves. On one ring (ID 313, Figure 3.4.2) the radial lines are arranged at a slight angle. Mostly the grooves are close-set, but in two cases (ID 287, Figure 3.4.2 and ID 315) the lines are more widely spaced. And on the ring from Rudston 61 (ID 315) the lines are very unevenly distributed, with some overlaps forming rough crosses: these appear to be errors rather than intentional. In two cases (ID 477 and ID 318) the decorated faces are slightly dished. The radial decoration is contained within two concentric bounding grooves in three cases (Figure 3.4.2: ID 287, ID 313 and ID 318). Decoration on the edges of the rings is similar, comprising vertical (four cases) or diagonal (two cases) grooves. The three rings which had concentric bounding grooves on the faces also display bounding grooves on the edges of the side decoration. This most complex design, with bounding grooves on faces and edge, is also found on the decorated ring from Ysgwennant (Sheridan and Davis 1998, fig. 12.4.a). There is a distinct variation in the level of craftsmanship, with the two rings with more widely spaced grooves having slightly uneven (ID 287 Little Downham, Figure 3.4.2) or extremely uneven (ID 315 Rudston 61) designs. The decoration on the

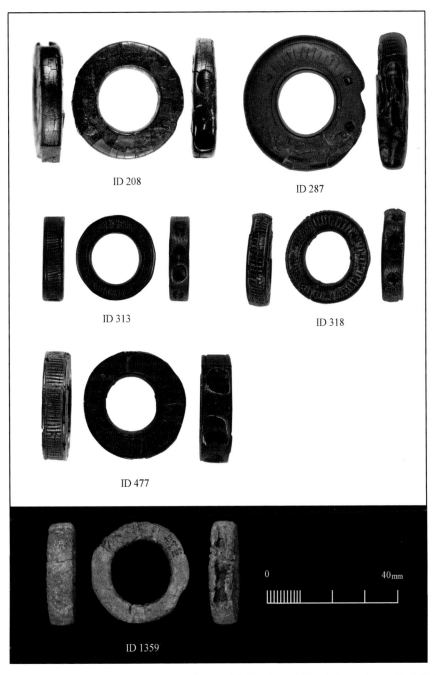

ID 208

ID 287

ID 313

ID 318

ID 477

ID 1359

Figure 3.4.2. Examples of Class IIIa objects: ID 208 Acklam Wold 124; ID 287 Little Downham; ID 313 Thwing 60; ID 318 Rudston 68; ID 477 Winterbourne Monkton; ID 1359 Kniveton.

other three pieces, together with that from Ysgwennant, is executed to a high level of accuracy, and two of them have the slightly dished faces which enhance the overall effect.

MATERIAL

The six bone rings are all made from sections of limb bone shaft, from a large mammal. This was probably cattle, but

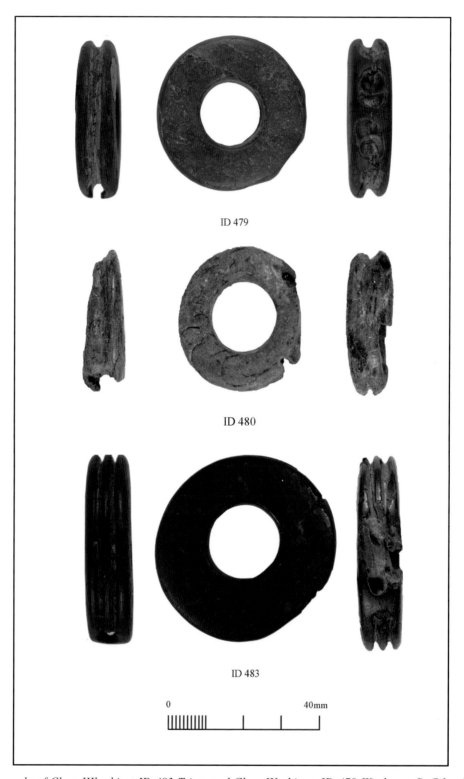

Figure 3.4.3. Example of Class IIIb object ID 483 Tring, and Class IV objects ID 479 Wimborne St Giles G9, and ID 480 Durrington Walls.

Table 3.4.1. Belt rings: classification and associations. Clarke numbers refer to Clarke 1970. b&t denotes one or more barbed and tanged arrowheads. Scottish examples not included.

Site	Beaker	Jet	Amber	Metal	Stone	Flint	Ref.
Class I							
Wilsford G1(a)	W/MR						ID 912
Farleigh Wick	*N/MR*			*gold caps*		*b&t*	*Clarke no.1111*
Amesbury Archer	E			daggers	bracers	b&t	ID 471
Wilsford Shaft							ID 469
Sittingbourne				dagger	bracer		ID 720
Melton Quarry	W/MR?				bracer		ID 657
Wilsford G1 (b)	W/MR						ID 1073
Folkton 245	AOC	disc beads					ID 750
Upton Lovell G2a		bead		awl	battle-axes; grooved stone		ID 493
Stanton Harcourt	*N/MR*					*b&t*	*Clarke no.772*
Class II							
Cassington	*N/MR*						*Clarke no.717*
Class IIIa							
Acklam Wold 124	S1	button	button		fire kit	dagger	ID 208
Winterbourne Monkton	S2(W)	buttons			cushion stone		ID 477
Little Downham	S3(W)	button				dagger	ID 287
Ysgwennant	*S2(W)*	*buttons*			*sponge fingers; fire kit*		*Clarke nos. 1854–5*
Thwing 60		dec button					ID 313
Rudston 61		*button*					*ID 315*
Rudston 68		buttons; 1 dec		dagger	sponge finger		ID 318
Kniveton	u/s						ID 1359
Raunds	Late	buttons			bracer; sponge finger	dagger	ID 1565
Ferry Fryston	Late				bracer		*Brown et al. 2007*
Class IIIb							
Tring					bracers	b&t	ID 483
Class IV							
Winterbourne Stoke G54	S2(W)	button			sponge fingers		ID 474
Wimborne St Giles G9		button		dagger; awl		b&t	ID 479
Durrington Walls		button			sponge finger; chalk discs	dagger	ID 480

could have been red deer. One amber ring (ID 1565) was made from shiny transparent orange amber, while the other (ID 1359) is of more opaque material, but also bright orange in colour. Of the nine jet examples identified ID 433, ID 477 and ID 493 were analysed by Bussell (nos. B48, B52 and B22 respectively) and visually confirmed by AS; ID 208, ID 287, ID 313, ID 318 and ID 483 were visually identified by AS. The two rings from Ysgwennant, also of jet, were analysed by MD. The two simple flattened rings

(ID 471 and ID 469) are made from Kimmeridge shale, the former analysed by MD and the latter visually identified by AS. Three further items were identified as Kimmeridge shale by AS (ID 474, ID 479 and ID 480) and the first two of these had also been identified as non-jet by Bussell's analysis (her nos. B57 and B24 respectively). Item ID 315 could not be located at The British Museum, but Kinnes and Longworth (1985, 60) have described the material as 'shale or lignite'. The two rings of later type (ID 358 and

Table 3.4.2. List of belt and pulley rings studied and illustrated.

Object	Site (Parish), County	Museum	Illustration
ID 208	Acklam Wold 124 (Acklam), E. Yorks.	Hull	Figure 3.4.2
ID 287	Little Downham, Cambs.	Camb	Figure 3.4.2; Figure 3.4.6
ID 313	Thwing 60, burial 3, E. Yorks.	BM	Figure 3.4.2
ID 318	Rudston 68, burial 6, E. Yorks.	BM	Figure 3.4.2; Figure 3.4.6
ID 469	Wilsford Shaft G33a, Wilts.	Sal	Not illustrated
ID 471	Amesbury Archer, Wilts.	Sal	Figure 3.4.1
ID 474	Winterbourne Stoke G54, Wilts.	Dev	Not illustrated
ID 477	Winterbourne Monkton, Wilts.	Dev	Figure 3.4.2; Figure 3.4.5; Figure 3.4.6
ID 479	Wimborne St Giles G9, Dorset	Dev	Figure 3.4.3; Figure 3.4.6
ID 480	Durrington Walls, Wilts.	Dev	Figure 3.4.3
ID 483	Tring, The Grove, Herts.	Dev	Figure 3.4.3
ID 493	Upton Lovell G2a, Wilts.	Dev	Figure 3.4.1; Figure 3.4.5; Figure 3.4.6
ID 657	Melton Quarry, E. Yorks.	Hull	Figure 3.4.1
ID 720	Sittingbourne, Kent	BM	Figure 3.4.1; Figure 3.4.6
ID 750	Folkton 245, grave fill, E. Yorks.	BM	Figure 3.4.1; Figure 3.4.5
ID 912	Wilsford G1(a), Wilts.	Dev	Figure 3.4.1
ID 1073	Wilsford G1(b), Wilts.	Sal	Not illustrated
ID 1359	Kniveton, Derbys.	BM	Figure 3.4.2
ID 1565	Raunds, Northants.	EH	Not illustrated

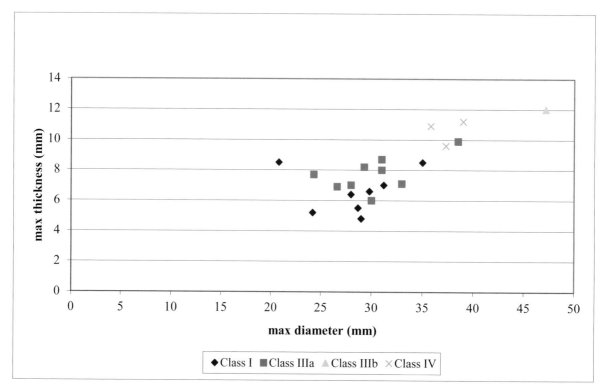

Figure 3.4.4. Belt and pulley rings: key dimensions by Class.

ID 377) are both made from jet, identified visually by AS/MD. Interestingly two black examples of Clarke Class I belt rings are of Kimmeridge shale and one of jet, Class IIIa are all of jet except one, and the Class IV items studied in detail are all of Kimmeridge shale.

MANUFACTURE

Most of the bone belt rings had been polished to a very fine finish, and had been neatly and carefully formed. In only one case (ID 750 Folkton, Figure 3.4.5c) do any polishing striations survive and these are longitudinal and diagonal traces located towards the end of the shaft. Traces of shaping within the rings are also rare, although there are some circumferential striae inside the main ring of ID 1073 (Wilford G1), rilling within the smaller ring and a mark from the bow drill employed next to this smaller ring. The stem of the ring from Folkton 245 (ID 750) has some irregular opposed nicks on either side and these may have been designed to hold fastening threads or binding in place (Figure 3.4.5d). The pieces made from shale are unpolished or finished to low or medium sheen only. Sometimes only the outer surfaces are polished, with the interior of the hoop left matt (ID 479 and ID 480, Figure 3.4.3). The jet rings also tend not to have been highly polished. Most are more shiny on the faces and outer edge surface, but only one example (ID 208 Acklam Wold 124, Figure 3.4.2) was finished to a high sheen. The original finish of the amber rings is indeterminate due to the oxidised surfaces. All but one of the jet rings have traces of polishing striations visible on the front and rear faces. These are circumferential or diagonal and survive between the radial grooves on the decorated items. There are also faint multidirectional striations on the rear of the ring from Tring (ID 483). Within and around the decorative grooves traces of fine tool marks are sometimes evident (ID 477, Figure 3.4.5a). Striations also occur on one of the shale rings (ID 474), faint lateral on the front and multidirectional on the rear. Eight of the rings made from jet or shale have traces of original manufacture inside the hoop. These are usually faint or marked circumferential striations (e.g. ID 493, Figure 3.4.5b) but also include tiny gouge marks in three cases (ID 313, ID 471 and ID 493). The outer face of the ring retains faint polishing striations in five cases, and on one of the rings which possess outer grooves, there are tool marks within the base of the groove (ID 479). In four cases, all of jet, there is a distinct zone of faint or marked striations, in various directions, in the area where the V-perforations are placed. Rilling is visible within the perforations of all six of the jet rings and in two out of three of the ones made from shale. In only one case (ID 477, second V-perforation of the sequence) was a change of drill direction evident. The outer groove on the shale ring from Winterbourne Stoke G54 (ID 474) has a crisp and deep knife cut surviving in its base. The rings of amber are in poor condition but it can be detected that the Raunds ring (ID 1565) had been very carefully shaped, and that on the Kniveton example (ID 1359) one of the original V-perforations had inadvertently been over-bored and had just pierced the inner face of the hoop.

COMPLETENESS AND DAMAGE

Most of the rings survive at the 90% level or above, and the remainder between 75% and 85%. Much of the damage results from the loss of bridges associated with the V-perforations, suffered in antiquity. Major damage since excavation included the loss of some of the main ring on the Sittingbourne bone example (ID 720), major loss of surface material from the two amber rings, and the breakage of one bridge on the ring from Acklam Wold 124 (ID 208). Other modern damage includes minor chips and flakes or spalls in seven cases, and major fractures which have been glued in four cases.

WEAR

Most of the ancient damage on the belt rings, and very clear evidence of long usage, comprises the breaking through of various sets of V-perforations. Out of the eleven rings of jet, shale or amber that have V-perforations, in only four cases are the bridges of the V-perforations intact (ID 477, ID 313, ID 318 and ID 479). Other major ancient breaks include the loss of most of the main ring on the bone example from Folkton 245 (ID 750, Figure 3.4.1) and a break along a cleavage plane on one side of the simple shale ring from the Wilsford Shaft (ID 469). Minor ancient flakes and spalls are also visible on four of the jet or shale examples. Wear histories for many of the rings are complex, and they will therefore be summarised individually.

- *ID 720 Sittingbourne* (bone). All surfaces show overall smoothing (Figure 3.4.6), and there is marked thread-wear on the outer edge of the small ring and all round the surviving (inner) portion of the large ring. Very worn.
- *ID 657 Melton Quarry* (bone). Evidence of wear or fabric rub is visible on the inner edge, both sides, of the larger ring. Very worn.
- *ID 1073 Wilsford G1* (bone). Wear occurs on the outer edge of the large ring, and the outer margin of the small ring. Slightly worn.
- *ID 471 Amesbury Archer* (shale). Detailed traces obscured by consolidant, but there was certainly no heavy wear. Slightly worn.
- *ID 469 Wilsford Shaft* (shale). Slight sheen from wear is visible on the front and rear surfaces. Following the break, the fractured surface was re-smoothed and decorated with a series of four radial grooves. Worn.
- *ID 493 Upton Lovell G2a* (jet). There is slight wear all round the outer edge; inside the hoop wear polish at the central ridge is intense (Figure 3.4.6), especially over one quarter to one third of the diameter. Worn.
- *ID 208 Acklam Wold 245* (jet). There is heavy thread-wear in both sets of V-perforations, and following breakage of the bridge the surviving outer holes continued in use as one wide V-perforation. But there is no obvious sign of differential wear on the hoop. Very worn.
- *ID 477 Winterbourne Monkton* (jet). There is wear-polish on the marginal ridges but the decoration is not much worn (Figure 3.4.5a). All four drill holes in the two V-perforations show thread-polishing and softened edges, and there is fabric rub, in the form of high sheen, on the outer surface in the vicinity of the perforations (Figure 3.4.6). Both bridges are intact. Slightly worn.
- *ID 287 Little Downham* (jet). Taking the two V-perforations as being the top of the piece, the decoration is worn away at the top, and completely worn away on the left hand side (Figure 3.4.6). There is evidence of heavy thread- wear prior to both bridges being broken away. The ring may then have been tied simply at one side, giving rise to the heavy wear on the other (left

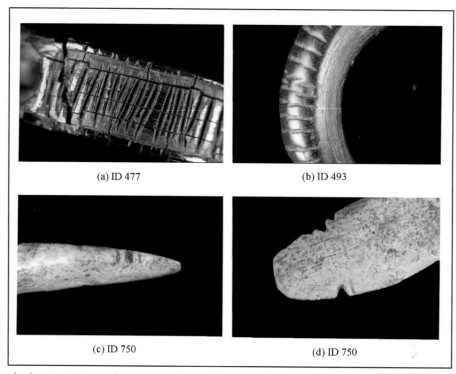

Figure 3.4.5. Details showing (a) manufacturing marks and absence of wear on decoration on ID 477 Winterbourne Monkton, (b) circumferential striations on ID 493 Upton Lovell G2a, (c) manufacturing striations on ID 750 Folkton 245, and (d) nicks on ID 750 Folkton 245.

hand) side, before a later stage of use when two new straight perforations were drilled through the face of the ring near to the previous V-perforations. These straight holes also exhibit thread-wear. Very worn.

- *ID 313 Thwing 60* (jet). The decoration has been worn away in places and all edge angles are smoothed. Thread-wear demonstrates former pulling towards the surviving bridge of each of the two V-perforations and there is evidence of fabric rub in between the two V-perforations. Worn.
- *ID 315 Rudston 61* (shale or lignite). Not located so not studied in detail. One of the two V-perforations had broken through, and was later replaced by a straight hole bored directly through the hoop.
- *ID 318 Rudston 68* (jet). All the edge angles are smoothed. Two sets of V-perforations survive intact and there is evidence of general thread-wear in all four holes (Figure 3.4.6). Worn.
- *D 1359 Kniveton* (amber). The bridges of both V-perforations had broken through. There is no sign of reboring but the ring could have continued in use. Wear category indeterminate.
- *ID 483 Tring* (jet). The bridge of one of the two V-perforations is broken and there is evidence of thread-wear in all four holes. Fabric rub is evident next to the sites of the V-perforations, while inside the hoop there are signs of extra sheen in the zone opposite the perforations. Wear over the edge of the broken-out perforations shows that the ring continued in use after this fracture. Very worn.

- *ID 474 Winterbourne Stoke G54* (shale). All edges of the main aperture are smoothed. The bridge of the heavily worn single V-perforation had broken through during use. Subsequently the circumferential groove was redefined, and attempts were made to provide a new straight-through perforation to replace the V-perforation. There are two aborted holes and a single central hole piercing the hoop. This final perforation also displays thread-wear. Very worn.
- *ID 479 Wimborne St Giles* (shale). Three sets of V-perforations, two of which are partly broken away, show evidence of thread-pulls towards the bridge in each case (Figure 3.4.6). There are also traces of wear within the circumferential groove, and there is fabric rub on the outer surface in the zone of the V-perforations. Worn.
- *ID 480 Durrington Walls* (shale) (Figure 3.4.3). All four drill holes of the two broken out V-perforations show thread-wear, but there is no trace of wear within the circumferential groove. The area where the V-perforations had broken was smoothed through further wear and then a single through-perforation was inserted. In time this also broke through, but use of the ring continued as the broken edge of this single perforation also shows smoothing and wear. Very worn.

Overall the rings can be categorised as worn in thirteen cases and slightly worn in only five cases. None are in fresh condition, and amongst the worn items, seven of them were classified as very worn.

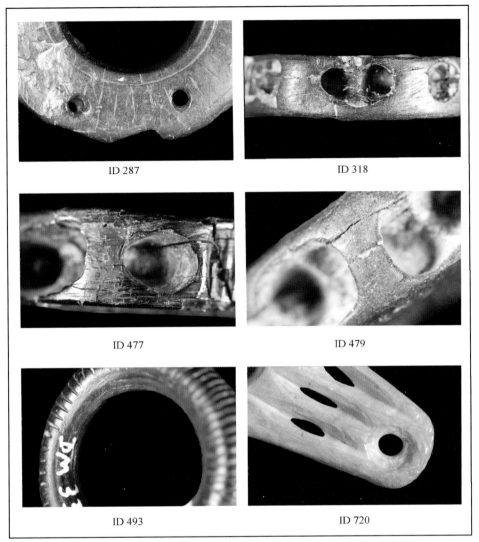

ID 287

ID 318

ID 477

ID 479

ID 493

ID 720

Figure 3.4.6. Details showing wear around the perforations on ID 287 Little Downham, general thread-wear on ID 318 Rudston 68, thread-polishing and fabric rub on ID 477 Winterbourne Monkton, thread-pulls towards the perforation bridge on ID 479 Wimborne St Giles, internal hoop wear-polish on ID 493 Upton Lovell G2a, and overall smoothing on ID 720 Sittingbourne.

CONCLUSIONS

The rings, whether made from bone, jet, shale or amber, are all of fine workmanship and are elegant in both design and execution. They appear to have been valuable items which, on the evidence of use wear and re-working for reuse, possessed very long biographies. In some cases the ring had gone through three or four different use versions, with replacement holes inserted and further wear ensuing over subsequently broken perforations. The earliest black rings seem to be those in Wessex, imitating the simple rings of bone, and these are made from shale, probably obtained from Dorset (one decorated Wessex example is of jet, but is an heirloom in an Early Bronze Age grave). A complex series of very finely made jet rings with two V-perforations on one side (Class IIIa), and often decorated, then followed. The uniform nature of their general morphology, and particularly the incised decoration, might indicate that these pieces were made by a single craft operation, probably close to the jet source in east Yorkshire. The addition of

V-perforations may well have been connected to the same technology that was used to make the large V-perforated jet buttons, which also occur very commonly in east Yorkshire. If such a production centre existed, then examples of this group certainly were taken as far south as the midlands and to Wessex (ID 477 Winterbourne Monkton), and also reached north Wales (Ysgwennant). The very large Class IIIb ring from Tring, Hertfordshire (ID 483) is also made from Whitby jet, and it may be these 'imports' from the north that inspired the slightly later range of simpler, and undecorated, rings with a more variable incidence of V-perforations, and made always from Kimmeridge shale.

Although it has long been assumed that the rings were used to fasten belts of perishable substances such as leather or textile, such a function does need to be demonstrated. In the case of the Class I rings, use wear may have occurred generally all around the ring, although on one example (ID 493) uneven 'belt wear' is evident. In the case of those with fixed fastening points, one might expect to detect more localised signs of wear of this type. Most wear in all cases is evident around the V-perforations or other perforations supplied for attachment to the putative belt. This is often extreme. However, one might also expect to find traces of wear and fabric rub from the end of the belt that was strung through the ring, either in the zone directly opposite the fastening perforations, or, if the belt was tied in the manner suggested by Clarke (1970, fig. 144) at the top and bottom of the ring. In spite of our intensive microscopic study, very few traces of such wear have been detected. In only one case is wear opposite the perforations present (Tring ID 483). The Little Downham ring (ID 287) shows extreme wear on one side, but it is the top or bottom only. In four cases (see above) there is evidence of wear to the hoop all around its circumference which may imply general wear from a belt end which was placed in varying detailed positions during the life of the ring. A further slight problem with the belt ring interpretation is that, however the belt was slotted through the ring, much of the valuable, and sometimes intensively decorated, hoop would have been obscured by the belt. Perhaps an alternative interpretation involving use as a hanging ornament or badge, perhaps suspended *from* a belt or other decorative body strapping, should also be considered. Similar problems apply to the Class I bone rings of magnifying glass form. Whilst the pattern of use wear on the pieces from Sittingbourne (ID 720) and Wilsford G1 (ID 1073) might be consistent with usage as a belt ring, that detected on the inner segments of both hoops on the Melton Quarry example (ID 656) could not. An alternative interpretation for these rings, as a bow stringer, has previously been suggested (Barclay *et al.* 1995, 99), and in this connection, it is interesting to note the occurrence of these early belt rings with archery-related equipment such as stone bracers and fancy arrowheads (see Table 3.4.1).

Overall the list of associated grave goods (Table 3.4.1) is impressive, with many items made from exotic raw materials, and many finely crafted artefacts, involved. This serves to enhance the perceived value and importance of the rings throughout the Beaker period. Links with the series of V-perforated buttons, made usually from jet but also found in shale, are extremely strong. As well as the possible connections between these two types implied by their means of manufacture (see above) they also occur together regularly in grave groups. This phenomenon has been discussed in detail by Shepherd (1973; 2009). The elaborate rings associated with a single jet button, a pair of these, or indeed a set of small buttons, may indicate the existence of a pouch which was fastened and decorated by the button or buttons, and hung from a belt. These finds are also sometimes found in close association with 'fire kits': a lump of iron ore and a flint striker, which may have been contained within the pouch along with other valuable possessions.

There are very few instances of a detailed record of where the ring was found on the body in the grave. Some were found in caches of material, probably originally contained in a perishable bag, placed next to the body (Raunds, Amesbury Archer and Tring) and so provide no useful information concerning where on the body the ring might have originally been placed. The ring from Winterbourne Stoke G54 (ID 474), recorded as being found at the feet of the body, may have been part of a similar cache. Other recorded body positions include near the lower end of the femur (ID 208), beneath the right tibia (ID 315), at the chest (ID 318) and on the middle of the right arm (ID 313). The only ring which is recorded as coming from the waist area of a body is the bone example from Stanton Harcourt (Barclay *et al.* 1995, fig.53), and this is of the type which may have been bow stringers. Whatever their detailed use the various forms of exotic ring were in use throughout the currency of British Beakers. They were valuable and much used items, which probably functioned as inherited ancestral property through more than one generation. However, the fashion for using such rings had disappeared by the time that rich dagger graves were being interred in the mature Early Bronze Age.

4. ITEMS OF EQUIPMENT II: STONE, BONE, COPPER ALLOY AND MISCELLANEOUS OBJECTS

4.1 SPONGE FINGER STONES

TYPO-CHRONOLOGY

Of the ten stratified examples of sponge finger stones listed by Smith and Simpson (1966, Appendix VI), seven have been studied in detail. In addition record of three pieces excavated more recently has also been possible. The latter comprise one from Gravelly Guy (ID 76) and two from Rounds (ID 117 and 125). The list of stones studied and illustrated here is shown in Table 4.1.1. The stones form a very specific morphological type (Figure 4.1.1) and also occur in a restricted range of grave associations, as noted by Smith and Simpson (1966, Table 1). They are found with Beaker-age crouched inhumation burials, five times with later style necked Beakers, four times with sets of jet/shale pulley rings and V-perforated buttons, and once with a single very large shale button. In addition the Gravelly Guy grave also contained a flat riveted dagger and a stone bracer, possibly of heirloom status, while the Rounds assemblage included another relict bracer, this time re-used as a tool, and a set of six V-perforated buttons. All these artefact types occur together in a period just after the fission horizon, probably between c. 2200 and 2000 cal BC (see diagrams in Needham 2005, figs.12 and 13). The radiocarbon dates for the two more recently excavated grave groups are listed in Chapter 9. Another recent find, but not studied, is the group of five sponge finger stones from the entrance shaft of the Charterhouse Warren Farm Swallet. In Horizon 4 these items were loosely associated with foetal or neonate and infant bones, an antler spatula, a flint dagger and a 'button' scraper of Beaker type (Levitan et al. 1988, figs. 8 and 23 to 26).

MORPHOLOGY

The stones studied are all long and narrow, ranging in length from 70 to 119mm and from 15.2 to 22mm in width. Maximum thickness is also fairly consistent, varying between 5.3 and 8.8mm. All are very neatly made, with one end usually slightly narrower than the other. The cross-section is most often plano-convex (seven instances) and otherwise rectangular, but very slightly curved. Thus all pieces tend to have a gently curved upper surface. In five cases there are also marked vertical facets running along the long sides, for example ID 35 Durrington Walls (Figure 4.1.2). The ends are always carefully tapered, rounded and neatly finished.

MATERIAL

All the examples studied were grey to dark grey in colour, with two of them almost black. Seven are made from hard meta-mudstone or meta-siltstone and are in many respects similar to the composition of several of the whetstones

Table 4.1.1. List of sponge finger stones studied and illustrated.

Object	Site (Parish), County	Museum	Illustration
ID 20	Rudston 68, burial 6, E. Yorks.	BM	Figure 4.1.1
ID 33	Winterbourne Stoke G54a, Wilts.	Dev	Figure 4.1.1; Figure 4.1.2
ID 34	Winterbourne Stoke G54b, Wilts.	Dev	Figure 4.1.1; Figure 4.1.2
ID 35	Durrington Walls, Wilts.	Dev	Figure 4.1.1; Figure 4.1.2
ID 36	West Overton G6b, a, Wilts.	Dev	Figure 4.1.1; Figure 4.1.2
ID 37	West Overton G6b, b, Wilts.	Dev	Figure 4.1.1; Figure 4.1.2
ID 68	Lynchard (Langton Matravers), Dorset	Dor	Figure 4.1.1
ID 76	Gravelly Guy (Stanton Harcourt), Oxon.	?	Figure 4.1.1
ID 117	Rounds, Northants.	EH	Figure 4.1.1; Figure 4.1.2
ID 125	Rounds, Northants.	EH	Not illustrated

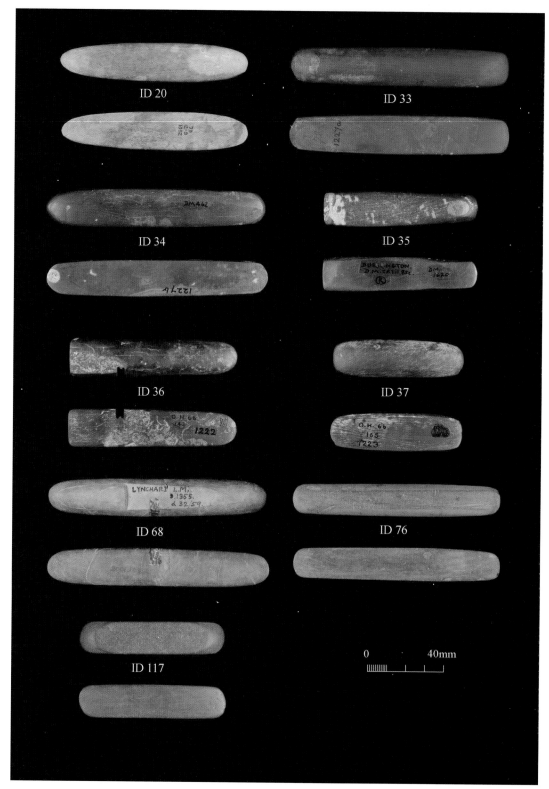

Figure 4.1.1. Sponge finger stones. ID 20 Rudston 68. ID 33 Winterbourne Stoke G54a; ID 34 Winterbourne Stoke G54b; ID 35 Durrington Walls; ID 36 West Overton G6b, a; ID 37 West Overton G6b, b; ID 68 Lynchard; ID 76 Gravelly Guy; ID 117 Raunds.

(Chapter 4.3); the nine stones comprise a tight lithological group and may be sourced from the Devonian killas of the south-west peninsula (see Appendix VI). ID 33, ID 34, ID 76 and ID 117 are very similar to each other, while ID 36 and ID 37 are slightly more silty and ferruginous. Most of these examples come from sites in Wessex, but one is from the midlands (Raunds, ID 117). This may be made from rock derived from the south-west but a source in the local Jurassic cannot entirely be ruled out. A further two sponge finger stones are also mudstones or siltstones,

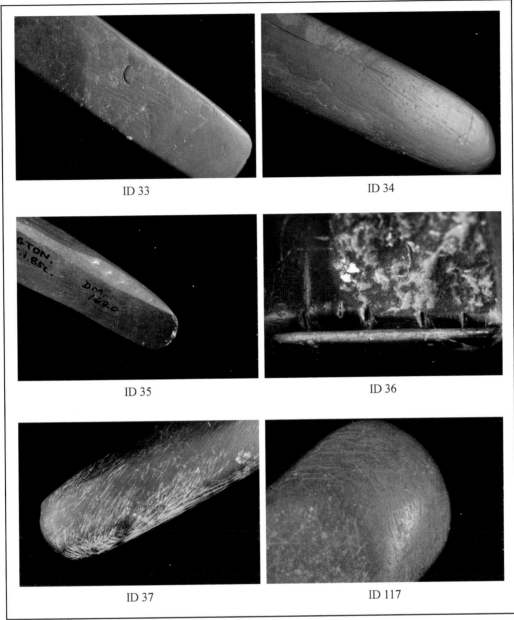

Figure 4.1.2. Details of sponge finger stones. ID 33 Winterbourne Stoke G54a; ID 34 Winterbourne Stoke G54b; ID 35 Durrington Walls; ID 36 West Overton G6b, a; ID 37 West Overton G6b, b; ID 117 Raunds.

but made from beach cobbles. Interestingly, these two items, Rudston 68 (ID 20) and Lynchard (ID 68) are also those found nearest to the coast, in Yorkshire and Dorset respectively. Finally the white copy from Raunds (ID 125) is made from chalk. The nearest outcrop is *c.* 48km to the east, but chalk does occur close to the site within the boulder clay (Harding and Healy 2007, 251). In contrast, the pair of sponge finger stones found in a grave at Ysgwennant in north Wales were made from local Silurian rock, but again a siltstone (Savory 1980, fig. 50, 347:14 and 15 and page 135). All the rocks used were very hard and fine-grained.

MANUFACTURE

Most surfaces on each piece retain traces of striations from the original shaping. These are usually longitudinal, on both front and rear, although those on the front are more often marked and those on the rear are usually faint. Some diagonal striations are also visible. In seven cases there are marked traces of dense striations following the curve of one or more of the ends, surviving from the neat and careful tapering in these areas, for example ID 117 (Figure 4.1.2). Where side facets are present these also carry longitudinal striations, usually faint. In one case, Durrington Walls (ID 35), one end may have been broken in use and then re-shaped to a rougher bevel. Eight pieces are highly polished, four on both sides and four on the rear surface only.

COMPLETENESS AND DAMAGE

Nearly all of the stones are complete or virtually complete, apart from ID 68 which has an ancient fracture on its upper surface. There are very few traces of modern damage.

WEAR

Most of the stones display wear traces in the form of longitudinal and diagonal scratches, mainly on the front surface, but sometimes also on the rear (Figure 4.1.2, ID 33 and ID 34). In addition there are usually dense and marked scratches and grooves near the narrower end of the piece (Figure 4.1.2, ID 37). This occurs in six cases, and in another instance strong wear is visible at both ends (ID 117). In one case (ID 36) there are very marked deep and regular spaced grooves on a faceted end as well as on the front surface (Figure 4.1.2, ID 36), and on ID 76 wear on the rear face of the end was extreme and dished. Only one stone showed no appreciable wear traces at either end (ID 68) and this piece also had fractured along a bedding plane on the front face. In five other cases there is slight ancient damage in the form of minor chips. All the pieces were classified as worn or very worn, apart from the chalk item (ID 125) which appears to be a copy of a standard sponge finger stone and is fresh, but broken into two pieces in antiquity.

CONCLUSIONS

All the sponge finger stones made from hard rock have been used extensively, and they seem to have functioned as tools. Usually one end was used in a repetitive smoothing or polishing action, and it may be that some of the polish on the surfaces also resulted from such use. It can be suggested that such tools had been used in leather working (Smith and Simpson 1966, 134), and our detailed studies would confirm such a hypothesis. Certainly the stones had been held in one hand and worn down relatively slightly against a fairly soft material, and had not been used for whetting metal. The shape of the working end is reminiscent of some tools still used by cobblers in the finishing of leather boots and shoes, although a more general purpose in the treating of leather for garments, bags or pouches and/or containers may be indicated for these prehistoric examples. In two cases the stones occurred as pairs in the grave. The materials of the two items in each pair were not identical, although the two from Winterbourne Stoke G54 (ID 33 and 34) were very similar petrographically, and also similar in size and shape. The significance of the occurrence of such pairs is not clear.

The even grey to black colouring is distinctive and these items, with their partly polished finish, may have been valued as rare exotic items acquired from a distance as well as highly efficient craft tools. An exotic status is also suggested by their associations with jet/shale button and ring sets, which occur rarely in the south. Maybe there was a direct or symbolic connection between the stone tools and special dress items such as a cloak or pouch which had been made from leather, and fastened with the jet accessories. The chalk piece is totally fresh and may have been made as a replica item for deposition in the grave. If so, it was deliberately broken, possibly in a ritual act, before it was placed with the burial.

4.2 GROOVED STONES

TYPO-CHRONOLOGY

A total of 15 grooved stones were listed by Newall in 1932, and to these may be added the pair from Breach Farm, Glamorgan (Grimes 1938, fig. 4). Of these eight have been studied in detail (Table 4.2.1; Figure 4.2.1). In comparison with similar items found in Mesolithic contexts in northern Europe they have generally been interpreted as arrowshaft smoothers (Clark 1963, 74). However, in only two cases (Roundway G5b ID 47–49 and Breach Farm) have they been found in association with flint arrowheads. The stones all derive from graves, either inhumations or cremations, of Early Bronze Age date, although no relevant radiocarbon dates are available. The associations include a Series 5 dagger, two knife daggers, a miniature bronze axe or chisel and the unusual bronze pronged object from Wilsford G58. Other associations include various unusual items of equipment made from bone or antler, and one of the stones was found in the 'shaman burial', Upton Lovell G2a.

MORPHOLOGY

The eight grooved stones studied are all roughly rectangular in shape, varying in length from 54.5 to 81.0mm (with one rather longer at 143mm) and 27 to 55mm wide. They are often about twice as long as wide, and their thickness varies from 20.6 to 26.0mm, with two much thicker and irregular examples which are 34mm thick (ID 49 and 61). They are characterised by a flat upper surface and a rounded lower surface and sides. In three cases the ends are neatly flattened, but most have rounded ends also. Thus the cross sections are usually plano-convex, although in two cases the section is sub-rectangular or sub-square. Along the centre of the upper surface there is usually a single, centrally placed, sub-V-sectioned groove. These grooves vary in width from 10.5 to 19.0mm, and are from 1.5 to 5.5mm deep. Most of the grooves are about 12.0mm wide and 2.5mm deep. Therefore they tend to be more than twice as wide as deep and are by no means semi-circular in profile. In one case (ID 61) three separate grooves are present.

MATERIAL

The grooved stones vary in colour from cream and buff to grey and rust brown and they are all made from medium grained, highly siliceous, vuggy rocks (see Appendix VI). Three are of sarsen, two of ferruginous sandstone, two are siliceous sinter and one feldspathic sandstone. All these materials would have been available in central southern England, with the ferruginous sandstones deriving from Upper Greensand deposits. Three medium-grained quartz-rich unperforated stones, ID 64 Amesbury G85, ID 51 Winterbourne Stoke G8 and ID 49 Roundway G5b (see Chapter 4.3) share these and many other compositional and petrographic features with the grooved stones here. The three items from Roundway G5b are all made from different rock types. The hardness of these rocks would

not be suitable for whetting metal blades, but could have been used to shape long shafts made from wood or bone.

MANUFACTURE

The main surfaces do not retain any traces of shaping, although in one case (ID 54) the corners at one end had been worked, apparently to provide finger holds (Figure 4.2.2), and in two cases the ends show signs of pecking. In most cases the surfaces were left rough, but one rear side was partly polished and one end surface had been deliberately smoothed. The interior of the central grooves usually displays diagonal, or sometimes transverse, wide striations on the sides of the groove. In two cases these are marked (e.g. ID 50, Figure 4.2.1). These could derive from either original shaping or from a partly rotational grinding action during use.

COMPLETENESS AND DAMAGE

Only two of the grooved stones are broken. One (ID 50) has a major chip which occurred at the time of manufacture, and another (ID 62) has one end broken away during ancient use.

WEAR

Use wear within the grooves is visible in all but one case. As well as the wide striations mentioned above there are faint longitudinal scratches or scoring in the base of the groove. And in two cases there were longitudinal areas of smoothing on the rear surface which appear to have been caused by finger pressure, causing very slight longitudinal indentations (ID 46 and ID 50). One piece stands out from the others in that it possesses three separate grooves, none of which are straight (ID 61). The straightest groove may have been original, while a second shows signs of use and a third is fresh (Figure 4.2.2). Overall most pieces were classed as worn (one very worn) while only two were fresh (ID 49) or slightly worn (ID 62).

CONCLUSIONS

This series of stones appear to have been designed for a particular purpose. They would have been held in one hand, and used to smooth the surfaces of some longitudinal item, probably made from wood or bone. The objects have previously been interpreted as arrowshaft-straighteners (see above). However, if the arrowshafts in use were in the order of 7 to 10mm in diameter, as surviving examples might imply (Clark 1963, 74), then the grooves on these stones would be over-large for the purpose. They could have been used in pairs, clamped round a shaft of larger diameter, to trim thicker shafts for other artefacts such as shaft-hole implements (battle-axes or mace-heads); the grinding could have been a combination of longitudinal and rotational actions. Some of the grooves are not completely straight, and it may be that some of the stones were employed in the

Figure 4.2.1. Grooved stones. ID 46 Collingbourne Kingston G4; ID 47 Roundway G5b; ID 48 Roundway G5b; ID 49 Roundway G5b; ID 50 Wilsford G58; ID 54 Upton Lovell G2a; ID 61 Goddard 85 F9; ID 62 Goddard 85 F10.

Table 4.2.1. List of grooved stones studied and illustrated.

Object	Site (Parish), County	Museum	Illustration
ID 46	Collingbourne Kingston G4, Wilts.	Dev	Figure 4.2.1
ID 47	Roundway G5b, Wilts.	Dev	Figure 4.2.1
ID 48	Roundway G5b, Wilts.	Dev	Figure 4.2.1
ID 49	Roundway G5b, Wilts.	Dev	Figure 4.2.1
ID 50	Wilsford G58, Wilts.	Dev	Figure 4.2.1
ID 54	Upton Lovell G2a, Wilts.	Dev	Figure 4.2.1; Figure 4.2.2
ID 61	Amesbury G85, Wilts.	Sal	Figure 4.2.1; Figure 4.2.2
ID 62	Amesbury G85, Wilts.	Sal	Figure 4.2.1

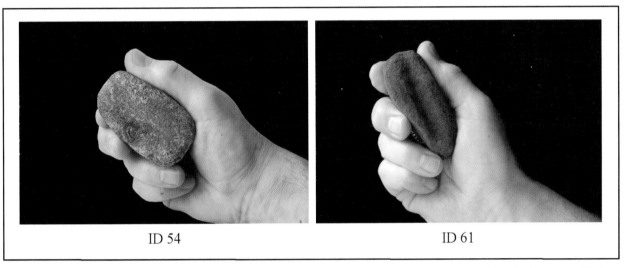

ID 54   ID 61

Figure 4.2.2. Details showing grooves and possible finger grips: ID 54 (Upton Lovell G2a) and ID 61 (Amesbury G85).

general production of various tools and equipment made from bone or wood. Such tools may have been for leather working (Moore and Rowlands 1972, 45). And some of them may also have been used as multi-purpose tools and rubbers. This applies particularly in the case of ID 61, where the three slightly curving grooves could provide finger keying for use as a rubber.

Although they tend not to be associated with flint arrowheads, they are found in a series of richly furnished graves which contain metal items alongside other unusual pieces of equipment made from bone or antler. These sets of equipment may have belonged to specialist craftsmen, and one of their activities may have been the expert working of leather. The stones do not appear to be particularly attractive visually, so their value may have related more to their function rather than their appearance.

4.3 PERFORATED STONES

TYPO-CHRONOLOGY

A series of perforated stones found in Early Bronze Age graves have variously been described as perforated whetstones or pendants. A list of 16 items from England were listed by Proudfoot (1963, Appendix III) and their distribution mainly between Cornwall and Oxfordshire, with a concentration in Wessex, was also plotted (*ibid,* fig. 10, 2). Of these items, 11 were available for detailed study, along with six further examples, two of them from more recent excavations (Table 4.3.1). The perforated stones can be divided into two main groups on the basis of their flat and square cross sections respectively (see below, also Figures 4.3.1 and 4.3.2). Where the contexts are known, all derive from cremation burials in barrows, with the exception of the coffined inhumation from Hove; and where the human remains have been identified they are from adult men. Perforated stones nearly all form part of rich grave groups belonging to both stages of the Wessex Early Bronze Age. They are often accompanied by daggers, as well as occasional occurrences of beads, battle-axes, ceramic accessory cups, a bone belt hook and bone flute. Two types of associated grave good are of particular note: fancy pins of bone or bronze, and bone 'tweezers', and in several cases these occur as sets. Whilst the flat examples occur with daggers belonging to both series of the Wessex graves, the square-sectioned items are only associated with later daggers (Series 5, Camerton-Snowshill), and in one case a Collared Urn. There is a radiocarbon date for the Camerton-Snowshill grave group from Edmonsham (see Chapter 9).

MORPHOLOGY

The key dimensions for perforated stones, the length and maximum thickness, are summarised in Figure 4.3.3. The flat-sectioned stones tend to be thinner, with four being particularly thin (ID 5, 19, 38 and 42), and the square-sectioned ones tend to be longer. Two examples of flat examples with uneven outlines have also been defined.

In overall shape, the flat stones are neatly formed to rectangular or oval outlines, and all possess facets either on all edges, or on all edges apart from the perforated top end. In two cases the longitudinal profile is distinctly lentoid and on ID 39 there is a semicircular projection devised to enclose the perforation. The square-sectioned stones are less well shaped and finished, although in two cases from Dorset (ID 70 and ID 71) the perforated end has been deliberately bevelled and rounded, and in five cases one or both ends have been flattened. In both types, the surfaces have been polished.

MATERIAL

The perforated stones are all made from fine-grained sediments or meta-sediments, ranging in grain size from mudstone and silty mudstone up to fine-grained sandstone (see Appendix VI). Several of the perforated stones are particularly rich in Fe_2O_3, especially ID 41 Warminster, ID 60 Norton Bavant and ID 72 Cowleaze. Although fine-grained sediments these all have low K_2O contents making it unlikely that they are derivatives of ordinary mudstones – possibly they are ferruginous concretions. Their high raw magnetic susceptibility matches their elevated iron contents. They are similar in many respects to the more ferruginous of the sponge finger stones, ID 37 and ID 68. Indeed, sponge finger stone ID 37 West Overton and the perforated stone ID 39 Wilsford G23, with high Fe_2O_3 and Y, low K_2O, Rb and Ba, are almost identical, making a similar source a strong possibility.

The grain sizes are those found normally amongst hones and whetstones used for sharpening metal blades. Although the lithologies are very coherent, the sources of such rocks

Table 4.3.1. List of perforated stones studied and illustrated.

Object	Site (Parish), County	Museum	Illustration
ID 5	Stanton Harcourt, Oxon.	AM	Figure 4.3.1
ID 19	Aldbourne, Wilts.	BM	Figure 4.3.1; Figure 4.3.4
ID 38	Milston G3 or 7, Wilts.	Dev	Figure 4.3.1
ID 39	Wilsford G23, Wilts.	Dev	Figure 4.3.1; Figure 4.3.4
ID 40	Shrewton G1,2 or 3, Wilts.	Dev	Figure 4.3.2
ID 41	Warminster, Wilts.	Dev	Figure 4.3.2
ID 42	Wilsford G43, Wilts.	Dev	Figure 4.3.1
ID 43	Wilsford G60, Wilts.	Dev	Figure 4.3.1; Figure 4.3.4
ID 44	Clyffe Pypard, Wilts.	Dev	Figure 4.3.2
ID 45	Knighton Down (Broadchalke), Wilts.	Dev	Figure 4.3.2; Figure 4.3.4
ID 60	Norton Bavant, Borrow Pit, Wilts.	Sal	Figure 4.3.1
ID 70	Dewlish G7, Dorset	Dor	Figure 4.3.2
ID 71	Edmondsham G2, Dorset	Dor	Figure 4.3.2
ID 72	Cowleaze, Cremation 5, Dorset	Dor	Figure 4.3.1; Figure 4.3.4
ID 109	Camerton (Timsbury G1), Somerset	Brist	Figure 4.3.2; Figure 4.3.4
ID 110	Priddy, Somerset	Brist	Figure 4.3.2; Figure 4.3.4
ID 131	Hove, W. Sussex	Hove	Figure 4.3.1; Figure 4.3.4

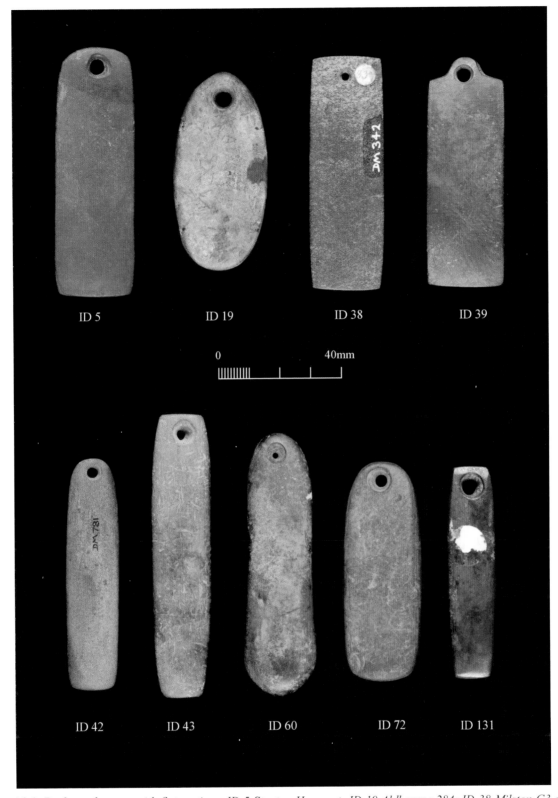

Figure 4.3.1. Perforated stones with flat sections. ID 5 Stanton Harcourt; ID 19 Aldbourne 284; ID 38 Milston G3 or 7; ID 39 Wilsford G23; ID 42 Wilsford G43; ID 43 Wilsford G60; ID 131 Hove, and with uneven flat sections ID 60 Norton Bavant; ID 72 Cowleaze.

are widespread and their geographical origins may be variable. Colour does not seem to have been standardised and ranges from brown-grey and green-grey to all shades of grey and almost black. However all except four items are made from rocks which are non-regional in character. The local rocks employed are Mesozoic (ID 42, ID 45), Devonian (ID 110) or sarsen (ID 70). Amongst the non-regional examples, three cannot be sourced in detail, five

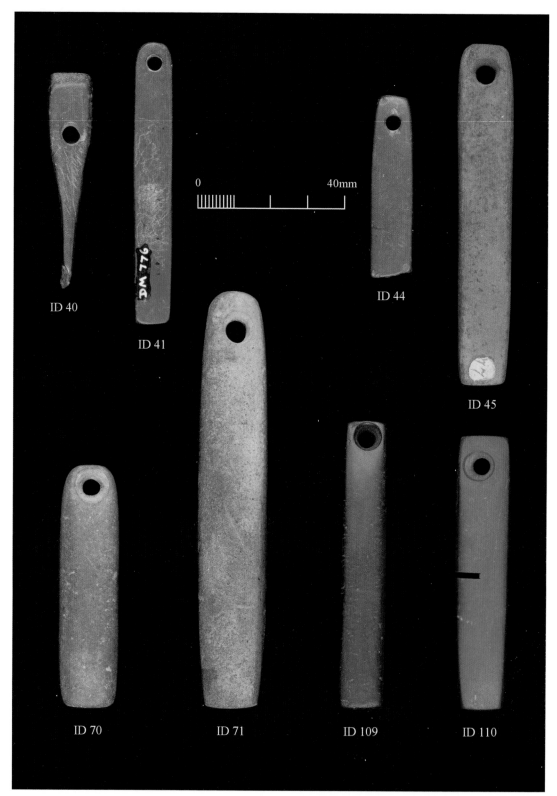

Figure 4.3.2. Perforated stones with square sections. ID 40 Shrewton G1, 2 or 3; ID 41 Warminster G5; ID 44 Clyffe Pypard; ID 45 Knighton Down; ID 70 Dewlish G7; ID 71 Edmondsham G2; ID 109 Camerton; ID 110 Priddy.

are probably from the south-west peninsula (ID 40, 41, 43, 44, 109) and one may be of rock derived from the Severn estuary area (ID 71). Stones with flat cross section are all of non-local rocks except in one case, and two of them closely match sponge finger stones in composition (ID 5 matches

ID 35; ID 39 matches ID 37). This suggests that the relevant stone sources in Devon or Cornwall were still known, and exploited, in the developed Early Bronze Age period. The two uneven flat-sectioned stones are both iron-rich and derive from similar non-local sources. The examples with

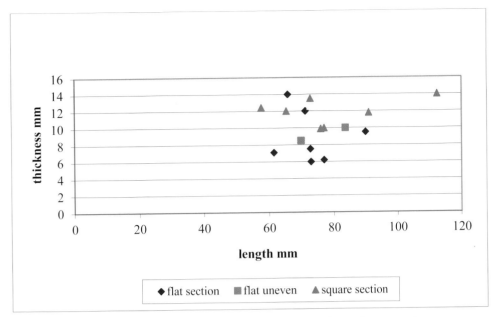

Figure 4.3.3. Perforated stones: size in relation to type of cross section.

square cross-section are more variable. Four are of rocks deriving from the south-west, one from the Severn area, and three are made from local or regional materials. Five items had previously studied by Robinson (2007). He also had identified two materials as having come from Cornwall (ID 41 and ID 44), and he suggested that the rock of ID 45 had come from the Mendips (see Appendix VI).

MANUFACTURE

In spite of heavy use wear the traces of polishing striations are still visible on the front surfaces of 12 examples, on nine rear faces, on all the side facets of the flat examples and on the side surfaces of six square-sectioned stones. These striations are usually longitudinal or diagonal, and faint in nature. Traces of the forming of the projection for the perforation on ID 39 are particularly clear (Figure 4.3.4) and the perforated end of ID 131 is neatly faceted and bevelled (Figure 4.3.4). In all but two cases, rilling is visible in the perforations, for example ID 19 and ID 72 (Figure 4.3.4). The holes are mostly hourglass in profile, although on three of the square-sectioned pieces, they are almost straight. On most of the flat stones the perforations are positioned centrally, but those piercing the square-sectioned stones are all asymmetrically placed.

COMPLETENESS AND DAMAGE

Most of the stones are complete or virtually so, and there are very few instances of modern chips or other damage. Two square-sectioned ones however were broken, and then reworked, in antiquity (see below).

WEAR

The stones all show signs of wear which often are marked and extensive. These usually consist of sets of multidimensional nicks and scratches (e.g. IDs 43 and 109, Figure 4.3.4). On the flat stones they occupy the front and rear surfaces, while on the square-sectioned ones most scratches occur on the side faces and they are more often longitudinal or transverse. There are also minor chips resulting from use on eight of the stones, for example on the end of ID 110 (Figure 4.3.4). Nearly all of them are classed as worn, with three very worn, and only three appear to be only slightly worn. Wear at the perforation occurs as smoothing all round the hole in three cases and at the upper margin only in a further four instances (e.g. ID 19, Figure 4.3.4). Two square-sectioned stones had been broken during their use life, and then re-worked for further usage (ID 40 and 44), and one of them was then utilised almost beyond use. Two whetstones carry streaks of metal. The gold-coloured streaks on the Camerton piece (ID 109) probably post-date the excavation, but the green copper alloy traces on the Knighton Down piece (ID 45) appear to be more embedded (Figure 4.3.4).

CONCLUSIONS

When perforated stones were originally discussed by Proudfoot she surmised, on the basis of published illustrations, that all except Hove were fresh and relatively unused. She suggested that the items were in fact not used as whetstones but had been 'treasured and seldom used' (Proudfoot 1963, 411). Our studies have shown that in all cases there are in fact clear indications of use, and it is probable that these items had been used, to varying

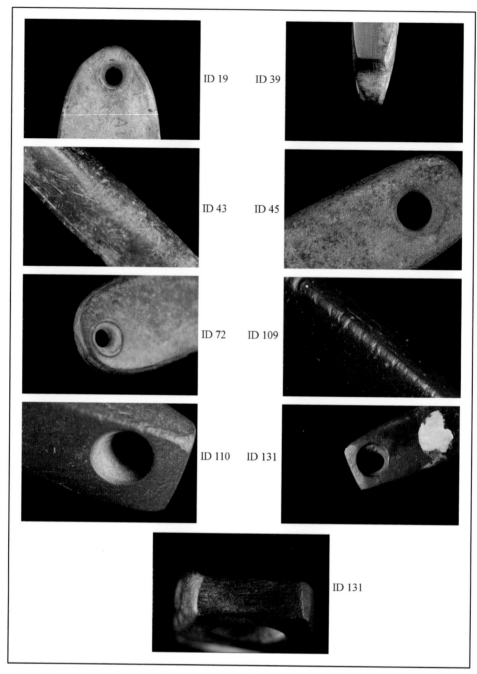

Figure 4.3.4. Details showing smoothing on the upper margin of the perforation and rilling on ID 19, Aldbourne 284; traces of the forming of the projection on ID 39, Wilsford G23; nicks and scratches on ID 43, Wilsford G60; green copper alloy traces on ID 45, Knighton Down; rilling on ID 72, Cowleaze; nicks and scratches on ID 109, Camerton; minor chips on ID 110, Priddy; a neatly faceted and bevelled end on ID 131, Hove (two images).

degrees, in the whetting of metal blades. And indeed in nine cases they had been found in grave groups that contained bronze daggers. It may be that the square-sectioned pieces had suffered greater use, and certainly the flat stones were more finely shaped and finished, with symmetrically placed perforations and delicate faceting of the edges. It would seem therefore that these items at least may have been treasured and valuable items. The perforations in many cases showed signs of thread or string wear, but whether this results from them having been worn around the neck as a pendant, or suspended from a belt alongside the dagger sheath, cannot readily be determined. All are attractive polished items, and the fact that five of them are made from the same kind of south-western rocks as had been used for some of the Beaker-age sponge finger stones may indicate very long term usage, and knowledge of, some rock outcrops that were imbued with special powers.

4.4 WORKED STONES WITHOUT PERFORATIONS

TYPO-CHRONOLOGY

Non-perforated worked stones from graves have seldom been described and no synthesis is available. The six items studied in detail (Table 4.4.1; Figure 4.4.1) derive from both inhumation and cremation burials in barrows, and they were sometimes included in groups containing other items such as daggers, bronze awls, beads, an accessory cup and equipment made from bone. These associations date from early and late stages of the Wessex Early Bronze Age.

Figure 4.4.1. Worked stones without perforations: ID 21 Folkton 241; ID 51 Winterbourne Stoke G8; ID 52 Winterbourne Stoke G8; ID 53 Wilsford G60; ID 59 Shrewton G23; ID 64 Amesbury G85 F17.

Table 4.4.1. List of unperforated stones studied and illustrated.

Object	Site (Parish), County	Museum	Illustration
ID 21	Folkton 241, E. Yorks.	BM	Figure 4.4.1
ID 51	Winterbourne Stoke G8, Wilts.	Dev	Figure 4.4.1; Figure 4.4.2
ID 52	Winterbourne Stoke G8, Wilts.	Dev	Figure 4.4.1
ID 53	Wilsford G60, Wilts.	Dev	Figure 4.4.1
ID 59	Shrewton G23, Wilts.	Sal	Figure 4.4.1
ID 64	Amesbury G85, Wilts.	Sal	Figure 4.4.1; Figure 4.4.2

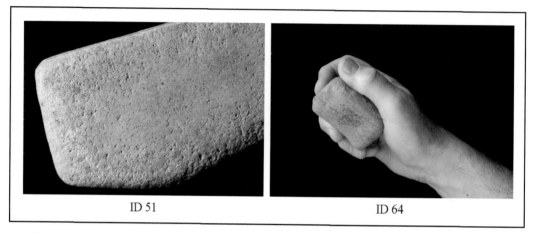

ID 51   ID 64

Figure 4.4.2. Examples of wear on ID 51 (Winterbourne Stoke G8) and ID 64 (Amesbury G85).

MORPHOLOGY

The six stones vary in size and shape but most are long and roughly rectangular in outline. ID 53 is deliberately tapered in shape and ID 52, with its very regular outline might have been classed as a sponge finger stone if it had not been for the distinctly tapering longitudinal cross section.

MATERIAL

The stones vary in colour from cream to brown and grey. All are made from rocks with the appropriate grain size for metalworking whetstones. Three are of sandstone, one of silty mudstone and one is mudstone/meta-mudstone. The latter two may be of material derived from the south-west peninsula, while a final item may be of Pennant Grit from the Severn area (see Appendix VI). The three sandstone items may be made from rocks available locally or regionally, and are similar to the materials used for the grooved stones, discussed above, while the finer rocks recall the materials used for the perforated whetstones.

MANUFACTURE

Three items have visible striations surviving from the initial shaping and finishing processes. These are usually longitudinal and faint.

COMPLETENESS AND DAMAGE

All are almost complete, apart from ID 53 which had been broken, but not reworked, in antiquity.

WEAR

All of the stones display use wear, in the form of scratches, on one or more of the major surfaces. One (ID 51) has a distinct rectangular area of smoothing on the front surface (Figure 4.4.2), while ID 59 has a different form of wear comprising patches of scuffing and sheen. The worn surface of ID 64 is slightly dished, and an area of deep scratches in its centre shows dark staining (Figure 4.4.2).

CONCLUSIONS

The patterns of wear on these items, and the rocks used, suggest that most of the pieces were hones used in the whetting of metal blades. One piece however (ID 59) appears to be a polisher, possibly used in the finishing of pottery vessels or leather.

4.5 BONE AND ANTLER SPATULAE

TYPO-CHRONOLOGY

A series of distinctive spatulate objects made from bone or antler were first discussed in detail by Smith and Simpson (1966) in relation to the fine example excavated from a primary burial in barrow West Overton G6b. They listed 11 items from eight Beaker graves (*ibid* Appendix V, table 1 and fig. 5), and provided further discussion of 13 further examples from six sites (*ibid*, 138). Since then, many more spatulae have been excavated. These include 15 items from ten sites, and in view of the increased number (a total of 42 are now known), an updated listing of the objects is provided in Table 4.5.1. This table also lists the 25 that have been studied in detail here and those illustrated (Figures 4.5.1 and 4.5.2).

From Table 4.5.1 it can be seen that most of the spatulae come from graves in Wessex and the upper Thames valley, or from the Peak District. There are also a few examples from the east Midlands, and two from Yorkshire. However the latter two are slightly different in that they have single perforations. Details of the associated burials and selected associations are shown in Table 4.5.2. As discussed by Smith and Simpson (1966), most of the spatulae come from Beaker inhumation graves. These are all burials of adult men, often mature or middle-aged. However three bodies have been aged between 20 and 30 years, and one was identified as a young adult. Fourteen graves contained Beakers and eight contained barbed and tanged flint arrowheads. These are the most common associations. Other grave goods present, which are listed in the database, show that many of the graves were rich or relatively rich.

Table 4.5.1. Spatulae of bone and antler.

Object	Site (Parish), County	Museum	Qty	Illustration or Reference
ID 621	Painsthorpe 4 (Kirby Underdale), E. Yorks.	Hull	1	Figure 4.5.1
ID 653	Huggate/Water Wold 249, grave C (Huggate), E. Yorks.	Hull	1	Not illustrated
ID 667	Ribden Low (Cotton), Staffs.	Shef	2	Figure 4.5.1
ID 668				Figure 4.5.1
ID 670	Green Lowe (Eaton and Alsop), Derbys.	Shef	3	Figure 4.5.1
ID 671				Figure 4.5.1
ID 672				Not illustrated
ID 683	Top Low (Blore with Swinscoe), Derbys.	Shef	2	Not illustrated
ID 684				Not illustrated
ID 685	Smerrill Moor (Middleton and Smerrill), Derbys.	Shef	1	Not illustrated
ID 686	Mouse Low (Grindon), Staffs.	Shef	2	Figure 4.5.1
ID 687				Figure 4.5.1
ID 701	Haddon Fields (Nether Haddon), Derbys.	Shef	1	Figure 4.5.1
ID 1071	G6a (Mere), Wilts.	Dev	1	Figure 4.5.1
ID 909–10	G5b (Roundway), Wilts.	Dev	4	Not illustrated
ID 915				Figure 4.5.1
ID 987				Figure 4.5.1
ID 1003–4	G85 (Amesbury), Wilts.	Dev	3	Figure 4.5.2; Figure 4.5.4
ID 1005				Figure 4.5.1
ID 1070	G6b (West Overton), Wilts.	Dev	1	Figure 4.5.1
ID 1062–4	Amesbury Archer (Amesbury), Wilts.	Sal	3	Not illustrated
	XV, 1/1 (Stanton Harcourt), Oxon.		1	Barclay *et al.* 1995, fig. 51,2
	Gravelly Guy (Stanton Harcourt), Oxon.		1	Barclay *et al.* 1995, fig. 48, D
	G51, burial A (Amesbury), Wilts.		1	Ashbee 1978, fig. 12, 6
	Easton Lane burial 2752 (Winchester), Hants.		4	Fasham *et al.* 1989, figs. 96, 1–2; 97, 3–4
	Primary grave (Chilbolton), Hants.		1	Russel 1990, fig. 6, 2
	Horizon 4, infant bones (Charterhouse Swallet), Somerset		1	Levitan *et al.* 1988, fig. 24, m
	Barrow Hills grave 203 (Radley), Oxon.		1	Barclay and Halpin 1999, fig. 4.79, WB13
	Barrow Hills grave 4660 (Radley), Oxon.		1	Barclay and Halpin 1999, fig. 4.23, WB3
	(Ravenstone), Bucks.		1	Allen 1981, fig. 9, a
	(Aldwinckle), Northants.		2	Green 1980, 333
	Raunds barrow 1 (Irthlingborough), Northants.		3	Harding and Healy 2007, fig. 4.6

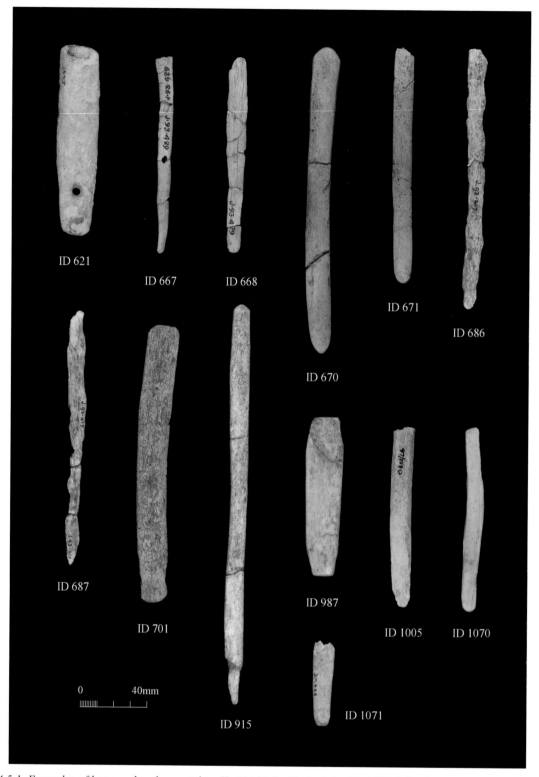

Figure 4.5.1. Examples of bone and antler spatulae: ID 621 Kirby Underdale; ID 667 Ribden Lowe; ID 668 Ribden Lowe; ID 670 Green Lowe; ID 671 Green Lowe; ID 686 Mouse Low; ID 687 Mouse Low; ID 701 Haddon Fields; ID 915 Roundway G5b; ID 987 Roundway G5b; ID 1004 Amesbury G85; ID 1005 Amesbury G85; ID 1070 West Overton G6b; ID 1071 Mere G6a.

The associated Beakers include both early and late forms, and radiocarbon dates relating to eight graves (Amesbury G51, Chilbolton, Amesbury Archer, Gravelly Guy, Raunds 1, Barrow Hills 203, Barrow Hills 4660 and Green Lowe) range in date from the mid-third millennium cal BC to the middle of the second millennium (see Chapter 9). Within the later part of this date range, some of the burials with spatulae were cremations (see Table 4.5.2), and some of these were associated with assemblages of finds more typical of the earlier phase of the Early Bronze Age (graves

Table 4.5.2. Spatulae: burials and selected associations (SN: Stuart Needham; DCL: David Clarke).

Site	Beaker (SN)	Beaker (DLC)	B and T arrowheads	Burial	Sex	Age (years)
Green Lowe	LN	S1	3	Inhumation	Male	Mature
Smerrill Moor	LN	S2(W)	-	Inhumation	Male	Young adult
Mouse Low	LN	S2(E)	4	Inhumation	Male	Mature
Haddon Fields	LN	S1	1	Inhumation	Male	>40
Mere G6a	LC	W/MR	-	Inhumation	Male plus juvenile	
W. Overton G6b	LN	S2(W)	-	Inhumation	Male	>40
Amesbury Archer	LC x 2, SP(low bellied), 2 x ?	E x4	15 min	Inhumation	Male	35–45
Amesbury G51	LN	S2(E)	-	Inhumation	Male	25–30
Stanton Harcourt XV, 1/1	LC	W/MR	-	Inhumation	Male	Adult
Gravelly Guy	LN	Necked	-	Inhumation	Male	45+
Chilbolton	LC	E	-	Inhumation	Male	20–30
Barrow Hills 203	LN	S4	6	Inhumation	Male	20–30
Barrow Hills 4660	LC	E	2	Inhumation	Male	40–45
Raunds 1	LN	Necked	-	Inhumation	Male	Adult
Aldwinkle	-	-	1	Inhumation	-	Adult
Easton Lane	-	-	6	Inhumation	Male	35–45
Painsthorpe 4	-	-	-	Inhumation	Male	Adult
Huggate/Waterwold 249	-	-	-	Cremation	Female	Young
Ribden Low	-	-	-	Cremation	-	-
Top Low	-	-	-	Cremation	-	-
Roundway G5b	-	-	-	Cremation	-	-
Amesbury G85	-	-	-	Cremation	-	-
Ravenstone	-	-	-	Cenotaph?	-	-

of Wessex series 1). These include knife-daggers and grooved whetstones at Roundway G5b and Amesbury G85, and bone points at Top Low and Amesbury G85. This group of cremations also includes the only burial with spatulae that has been identified as female.

Several authorities have discussed the possible function of these objects. Smith and Simpson (1966) thought that the wear on the West Overton G6b spatula, and its association with two sponge finger stones indicated a possible use as leatherworking tools. Clarke however thought this might be unlikely due to the consistent associations with male burials; whereas the most commonly found tool thought to have been used for working leather, the copper or bronze awl, is mainly found with women (Clarke 1970, 203; but see next section for an alternative interpretation for awl function). He noted the associations with arrowheads and bracers and suggested that the spatulae may have been connected with archery. Sets of spatulate bone objects used by Eskimo peoples for twisting bowstrings, tensioning sinew bow backing and preparing feather flights were cited as possible parallels. Use in the manufacture of netting (Thurnam 1871, 436–7) was also thought to be unlikely as none of the objects have a forked end (Clarke 1970, 203). Bateman (1861, 103) had suggested a possible use as pottery burnishers, while another possible function is as parts of composite bows or quivers (Ashbee 1960, 105; Harding and Healy 2007, 254). The only previous use wear analysis to have been undertaken is that by Olsen in relation to the set of spatulae from Easton Lane (in Fasham *et al.* 1989, 104). Parallel transverse striations on the narrower end, pitting on the tip and some longitudinal striae up the shaft resulting from slippage suggested a use as pressure flakers in the manufacture of fine flintwork, and specifically barbed and tanged arrowheads. A little polish on one spatulate tip was not deemed to be enough to indicate use on leather or plants, and was more likely to be localised handling polish.

MORPHOLOGY

The spatulae are all long and narrow items with cross sections which are fairly flat, plano-convex or ovoid, and occasionally concavo-convex. The section shapes are a direct reflection of the raw materials employed (see below). The thicker ones, usually made from antler, tend to have ovoid cross sections and may also possess distinctive flattened side facets (e.g. ID 1003 and ID 1004, Figure 4.5.2). Three examples also display a marked longitudinal curvature, which again reflects the shape of the bone or antler used. The variation in size is shown in Figure 4.5.3. Many of the spatulae have at least one end missing due to breakage. The plot only includes those items where both ends survive, and includes data taken from scale illustrations of examples not studied in detail in order to produce a viable dataset. It can be seen that the spatulae have a very restricted range as far as width is concerned (8.4 to 25.0mm, but mainly between 10 and 20mm), but that overall lengths are much more variable (between 90

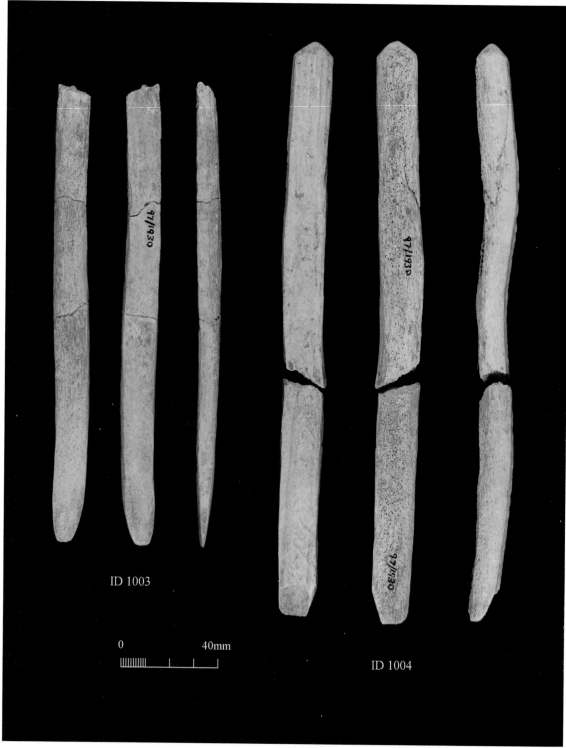

Figure 4.5.2. ID 1003 and ID 1004 from Amesbury G85.

and 340mm), although with a marked cluster in the 100 to 180mm range. It can also be seen that the variation is not related to differences in the raw material used. In all surviving cases studied in detail, both ends of the spatula have been very carefully and intentionally shaped. The distal or main 'business' end may be squared off (seven cases), rounded (six cases) or tapered (six cases), and in two further cases is worked to a blunt point. Fewer proximal ends survive, and these also may be squared (six examples) or rounded (twice). Also one proximal end is necked and squared off (ID 987) and two are faceted to give a neat pyramidal end to the piece (ID 915 and ID 1004, Figure 4.5.4). Two examples have slight waisting towards the distal end, and one has what seems to be a deliberately fashioned thumb or finger groove about one third of the way up from the distal end (ID 915).

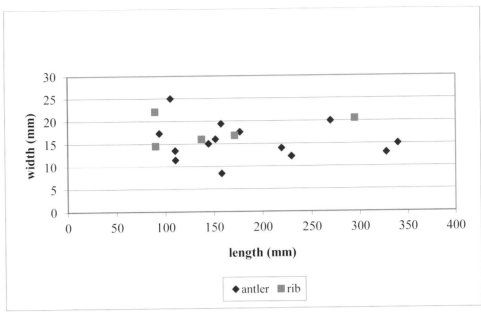

Figure 4.5.3. Bone and antler spatulae: dimensions according to raw material.

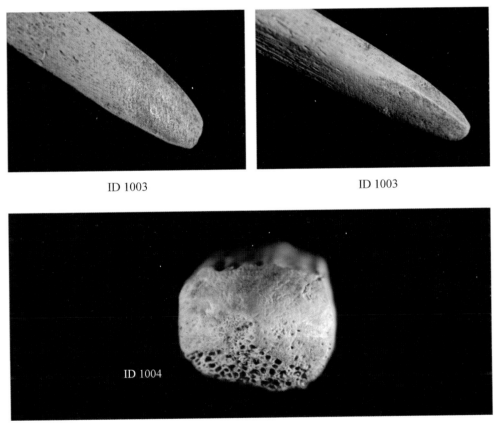

ID 1003   ID 1003

ID 1004

Figure 4.5.4. ID 1003 Amesbury G85 showing diagonal striae on faceted end; ID 1004 Amesbury G85 showing pyramidal head.

MATERIAL

Taking the whole dataset of 42 spatulae, where material has been identified, 25 are made from antler and 14 from animal rib bones. Within those studied in detail the antler was always taken from the stem of a red deer antler, and the ribs were always from large mammals of cattle size. In colour they vary from cream through grey to brown, and only two pieces are burnt (ID 667–68). Both raw materials used are highly resilient and would have withstood careful but firm pressure, and a degree of bending.

MANUFACTURE

The antler strips had been obtained by the groove and splinter technique, and the rib bones had been split longitudinally. As noted above the ends had received particularly careful treatment in the form of specific shaping, including two pieces with pyramidal terminals at the proximal end. Eight spatulae had been left rough, but 11 have traces or original polish. Most of the rough pieces are, as one might suspect, of antler, with its very rough natural outer surface. Most of the polished items (six cases) are on ribs, which are a smoother raw material in the first place, but five antler spatulae also show signs of polish. Quite a few of the spatulae have eroded surfaces, so traces of manufacture cannot always be determined. In three cases any manufacturing marks appear to have been polished out, but a variety of such marks do survive. These include all-over faint or marked longitudinal striations (three cases), similar marks on one side only, marked lateral striations or chop marks on side facets and longitudinal or diagonal striations near the distal tip (three examples).

COMPLETENESS AND DAMAGE

Of the 25 spatulae studied in detail, only 11 survive at the 95% level or above. Most of the breaks however are modern, perhaps suffered at the time of excavation. Several pieces have been broken right across at several points and then glued back together, including some of the complete examples. There are also a few nicks and some with major damage at the sides, but very few modern chips or other damage near to surviving ends.

WEAR

Ancient breaks are very few. Only three items have major breaks that would have led to loss of one of the ends in antiquity (ID 683 Top Low, ID 1071 Mere G6a and ID 1004 Amesbury G85). Otherwise only four cases of chip damage were recorded. General scuffing and scratching is present all over on eight spatulae, near the centre only (diagonal or multidirectional scratching) on two, and on one side in a further two. The most obvious wear occurs at the distal end (e.g. ID 1003, Figure 4.5.4). This included general wear polish (ID 671 and ID 685) and striations or shallow grooves. These are usually diagonal (ID 672, ID 684, ID 915, ID 923, ID 1003, ID 1004, ID 1062 and ID 1070) but sometimes longitudinal (ID 670) or lateral (ID 1064). In two cases there is evidence that both ends of the spatula had been used (ID 1070 and ID 1064). Signs of how the spatula had been held also survived in a few cases. This includes patches of wear on the upper halves of ID 1003 and ID 1004 and the possible rear thumb or finger groove on ID 915. Overall most of the spatulae were categorised as worn (15 examples), with three very worn and only four classed as slightly worn.

CONCLUSIONS

The spatulae are of standardised width, but vary more in length. There are two types of raw material employed, antler and animal rib, but both materials possess the same characteristics, in particular their resilience. These materials may have been selected for such physical and practical reasons, but the choice of material from large animals, both wild and domestic, may have also involved symbolic overtones. There is some evidence of surface polish, but a variety of marks resulting from original manufacture are also visible. Many of the items have become broken in modern times, or at the time of excavation, but most appear to have been deposited whole. Ancient damage is rare but traces of use are widespread, and quite varied. The distal end, which is usually rounded or tapered in shape, shows most traces of use wear. This comprises mainly close-set and fairly regular striae or shallow grooves, but only in one case did the grooves resemble the transverse/lateral marks described for the Easton Lane spatulae (see above). However, the overall use wear evidence does seem to be in support of the pressure flaking function. Of the 18 sites where the spatulae were found in graves with other items, eight included barbed-and-tanged flint arrowheads (see Table 4.5.2). Fancy arrowheads are not a common grave good in Beaker graves, so this level of association may well be significant. Interpretations as netting tools, components for bows (which would not have shown use wear) or pot modelling tools can safely be ruled out, and the marks are probably too distinct to have been the result of burnishing leather.

4.6 COPPER ALLOY AWLS

TYPO-CHRONOLOGY

Awls have been little studied and no overall corpus has ever been compiled. However a useful classification of the main types has been provided by Thomas (2005, 220–222), superseding his previous typology presented in his report on the awl from Carrickinab, Co Down (in Collins and Evans 1968). Thomas has divided the awls into three main Groups, the first being double-pointed, the second single-pointed and the third being of exceptional length. The Groups are subdivided as follows:

Group 1. Double-pointed, central swelling (transition), one or both ends used (Figure 4.6.1).
1A: square section throughout
1B: square at transition, two pointed ends of circular section
1C: circular section throughout
1D: square at transition, one end of circular section, other end of square section

Group 2. Single-pointed with tang, pointed end always of circular section (Figures 4.6.2 and 4.6.3).
2A: chisel-ended tang; formed by hammering/squashing
2B: chisel-ended tang; formed by filing and grinding
2C: square-section tang with squared end; gradual transition to pointed end
2D: marked expansion at transition, tang usually chisel-ended

Group 3. Exceptional length (Figure 4.6.4).
3A: expansion at transition, double-pointed, square section throughout
3B: square section at transition, chisel tang, pointed end of circular section
3C: square section at transition, double points, both of circular section
3D: single-pointed, chisel tang, pointed end of circular section

This typology has been followed in the present study, although sub-groups 2A and 2B have been grouped together. 58 items were studied in detail and a further three listed but not examined (Table 4.6.1). Thomas noted that the Group 1 awls tended to be found in Beaker graves, while those of Group 2 were often found in association with Collared Urns or Food Vessels of developed Bronze Age date. The Group 3 awls are more variable in date, deriving from contexts of the Early Bronze Age or later Bronze Age. Our study encompasses a total of 58 awls, comprising most of the stratified examples from our main study areas: Wessex, the Peak District and the Yorkshire Wolds. The incidence of key associations for these 58 awls is shown in Table 4.6.2.

From the table it can be discerned that the patterns of association are not quite as clear-cut as indicated by Thomas, although the general trend that he observed is confirmed. Group 1 awls do mainly occur in graves of the Beaker period, but they also are associated with Early Bronze Age ceramics and, once, in a Wessex series grave (Winterbourne Stoke G8). Clarke noted that Beaker awls were mainly found with Beakers of his later styles (N2, N3, S1, S2 and S4: Clarke 1970, 448, chart). Interestingly, in the Early Bronze Age, the 2A/B and 2C awls tend to occur with Collared Urns while those of sub-group 2D (with expanded transition) tend to occur with Food Vessels. Both however are found in Wessex series graves and with jet or jet-like necklaces or studs. The large Group 3 items mainly derive from Wessex series graves. Awls belonging to the different groups are all represented within the three main study regions and no clear geographical patterning is therefore apparent.

MORPHOLOGY

The dataset of 58 awls studied in detail includes 14 of Group 1, 27 of Group 2, 6 of Group 3 and 11 of indeterminate type. The key characteristics of the groups and sub-groups have been outlined above, and were followed during the classification of the items recorded. Variation in size according to Group is demonstrated in Figure 4.6.5, where length is plotted against maximum width, a measure which usually relates to the point of transition.

The figure shows that the Group 1 awls have a fairly tight length range (23.5 to 53.3mm) and that they are all of roughly similar width (1.8 to 3.2mm). However two items not plotted (as full length did not survive) are 3.5mm wide. These awls are chunky in nature, often with strongly faceted sides. One is of polygonal cross section (ID 1153) and in five cases there are one or more lozenge-shaped facets at the point of transition (e.g. ID 1283, Figure 4.6.6). Group 2A/B awls show a very tight length variation (24.2 to 42.2mm) but a rather wider range for maximum width in comparison with the Group 1 awls. The awls of Group 2D, those tanged examples with a marked expansion at the point of transition, tend to be longer (up to 54.3mm) and some are rather wider than most of the Group 2A/B examples. Group 3 awls are, by definition, considerably longer, and the maximum widths tend to be proportionately larger also.

An investigation of the relative position of the point of transition demonstrates the relative lengths of the tangs, and, in the case of Group 1 awls, the relative length of the two pointed ends. Table 4.6.3 shows the percentage of the length that occurs above the transition.

It can be seen that the two points of double-pointed Group 1 awls tend to be equal or nearly equal in length. The tangs of the Type 2A/B awls are mainly shorter than those on awls of Types 2C and 2D, and the Type 3 awls have a tendency to possess very short tangs.

MATERIAL

Some of the Beaker awls have been analysed and are known to have been made from unalloyed copper. Awls of the Early Bronze Age have never been analysed systematically.

Table 4.6.1 List of copper alloy awls studied and illustrated.

Object	Site (Parish), County	Museum	Type	Illustration
ID 1132	Aldro 116A (Birdsall), E. Yorks.	Hull	Indet.	Not illustrated
ID 1134	Aldro 113 (Birdsall), E. Yorks.	Hull	2D	Figure 4.6.3
ID 1138	Garrowby 101, A (Kirby Underdale), E. Yorks.	Hull	1B	Figure 4.6.1
ID 1139	Garrowby 64 (Bishop Wilton), E. Yorks.	Hull	2D	Not illustrated
ID 1144	Life Hill (Wetwang), E. Yorks.	Hull	2D	Figure 4.6.3
ID 1145	Garton Slack 152, 1 (Garton-on-the-Wolds), E. Yorks.	Hull	Indet.	Not illustrated
ID 1148	Garton Slack 156 (Garton-on-the-Wolds), E. Yorks.	Hull	2C	Not illustrated
ID 1149	Garton Slack 75, 1 (Garton-on-the-Wolds), E. Yorks.	Hull	2D	Figure 4.6.3
ID 1153	Huggate and Warter Wold 254, 1, E. Yorks.	Hull	1A	Figure 4.6.1
ID 1170	Marshfield G5, Gloucs.	Brist	2A/B	Not illustrated
ID 1174	?Amesbury, Wilts.	Sal	2C	Figure 4.6.3
ID 1175	Shrewton G23, Wilts.	Sal	Indet.	Figure 4.6.4
ID 1176	Winterbourne Stoke G47, Wilts.	Sal	2A/B	Figure 4.6.2
ID 1177	Winterbourne Stoke G50, Wilts.	Sal	2D	Not illustrated
ID 1196	Amesbury G72, Wilts.	Sal	2A/B	Not illustrated
ID 1197	Winterbourne Stoke G47, Wilts.	Sal	2A/B	Not illustrated
ID 1222	Waggon Low (Hartington Middle), Derbys.	Shef	1B	Figure 4.6.1
ID 1223A	Bee Low A (Youlgreave), Derbys.	Shef	Indet.	Not illustrated
ID 1223B	Bee Low B (Youlgreave), Derbys.	Shef	2A/B	Not illustrated
ID 1223C	Bee Low C (Youlgreave), Derbys.	Shef	Indet.	Not illustrated
ID 1223D	Bee Low D (Youlgreave), Derbys.	Shef	1C	Not illustrated
ID 1224	Staker Hill (Hartington Upper), Derbys.	Shef	2D	Figure 4.6.3
ID 1225	Ilam Tops Low (Ilam), Derbys.	Shef	2D	Not illustrated
ID 1226	Warslow and Elkstone, Staffs.	Shef	2A/B	Figure 4.6.2
ID 1227	Stanton Moor 3B.1, Derbys.	Shef	Indet.	Not illustrated
ID 1230	Larks Low (Middleton), Derbys.	Shef	1B	Figure 4.6.1
ID 1231	Rolley Low (Great Longstone), Derbys.	Shef	3D	Figure 4.6.4
ID 1232	Throwley, Staffs.	Shef	3D	Figure 4.6.6
ID 1262	Winterbourne Steepleton (cremation 2), Dorset	Dor	2D	Not illustrated
ID 1263	Frampton G4, Dorset	Dor	2D	Figure 4.6.3
ID 1264	Hilton G2, Dorset	Dor	2C	Figure 4.6.3
ID 1265	Gussage St Michael II (Thickthorn Down), Dorset	Dor	1A	Figure 4.6.1
ID 1280	Langton 2, burial 2, E. Yorks.	BM	2B	Figure 4.6.2
ID 1281	Langton 2, burial 2, E. Yorks.	BM	2A/B	Figure 4.6.2
ID 1282	Langton 2, burial 2, E. Yorks.	BM	Indet.	Not illustrated
ID 1283	Butterwick 39, burial 1, E. Yorks.	BM	1B	Figure 4.6.6
ID 1284	Rudston 62, burial 1, E. Yorks.	BM	2D	Figure 4.6.3; Figure 4.6.6
ID 1285	Rudston 62, burial 4, E. Yorks.	BM	1B	Not illustrated
ID 1286	Rudston 62, burial 4, E. Yorks.	BM	1B	Figure 4.6.1
ID 1287	Folkton 71, burial 6, E. Yorks.	BM	1B	Figure 4.6.1
ID 1288	Goodmanham 115, burial 1, E. Yorks.	BM	2D	Not illustrated
ID 1289	Goodmanham 115, E. Yorks.	BM	2D	Not illustrated
ID 1290	Ferry Fryston 161, burial 9, W. Yorks.	BM	Indet.	Not illustrated
ID 1291A	Aldbourne 280, burial 1, Wilts.	BM	Indet.	Not illustrated
ID 1291B	Aldbourne 280, burial 1, Wilts.	BM	Indet.	Not illustrated
ID 1292	Fowberry UN21, burial 1 (Chatton), Northumb.	BM	1B	Not illustrated
ID 1373	Wimborne St Giles G9, Dorset	Dev	1C	Figure 4.6.1
ID 1426	Preshute G1a (Manton), Wilts.	Dev	3D	Not illustrated
ID 1427	Preshute G1a (Manton), Wilts.	Dev	3D	Not illustrated
ID 1428	Preshute G1a (Manton), Wilts.	Dev	2D	Not seen
ID 1442	Upton Lovell G2e (Golden), Wilts.	Dev	3A	Figure 4.6.4
ID 1452	Upton Lovell G2a (shaman), Wilts.	Dev	2A/B	Figure 4.6.2; Figure 4.6.6
ID 1454	Winterbourne Stoke G5, Wilts.	Dev	Indet.	Not illustrated
ID 1464	Winterbourne Stoke G8, Wilts.	Dev	1B	Figure 4.6.6
ID 1471	Amesbury Park H3, Wilts.	Dev	2A/B	Not illustrated
ID 1487	Wilsford-cum-Lake G42, Wilts.	Dev	3D	Not illustrated
ID 1503	Sutton Veny G11c, Wilts.	Dev	2A	Figure 4.6.2
ID 1508	Winterbourne Stoke G28, Wilts.	Dev	2D	Figure 4.6.3
ID 1515	Amesbury G51, Wilts.	Dev	1B	Figure 4.6.1

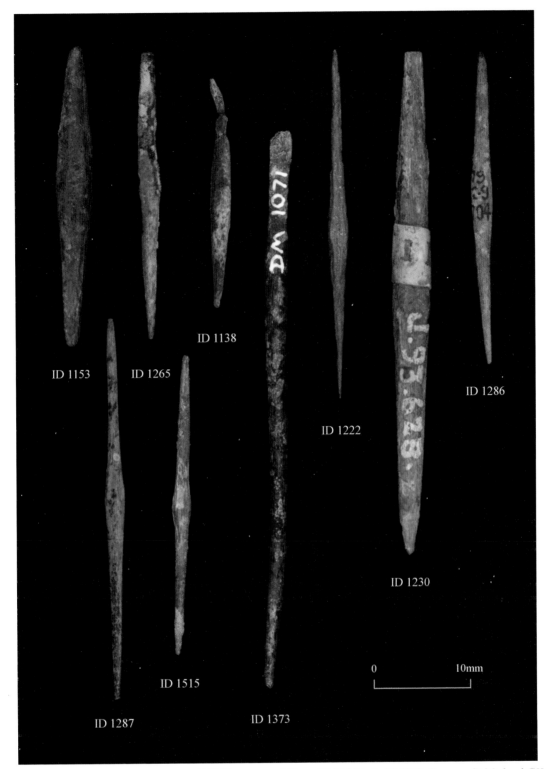

Figure 4.6.1 Copper alloy awls. Group 1A: ID 1153 Huggate and Water Wold 254, 1; ID 1265 Gussage St Michael GII; Group 1B: ID 1138 Garrowby 101, A; ID 1222 Waggon Low; ID 1230 Larks Low; ID 1286 Rudston 62, 4; ID 1287 Folkton 71,6; ID 1515 Amesbury Archer G51; Group 1C: ID 1373 Wimborne St Giles G9.

MANUFACTURE

Owing to the degree of corrosion on the awls studied it was not always possible to detect any signs of manufacture. However, such traces were recorded for 33 items. Polishing striations were visible at both the tang and pointed ends. Of 18 instances recorded at the tang end, most are faint lateral (nine cases) (e.g. ID 1452, Figure 4.6.6) or diagonal (six cases) striations, with only three cases of longitudinal ones. Among the 18 observations made at the pointed end, most are faint and longitudinal (11 cases), but lateral, diagonal and multidirectional striations are also represented. There are also two cases on the facets of Group 1 awls, and two

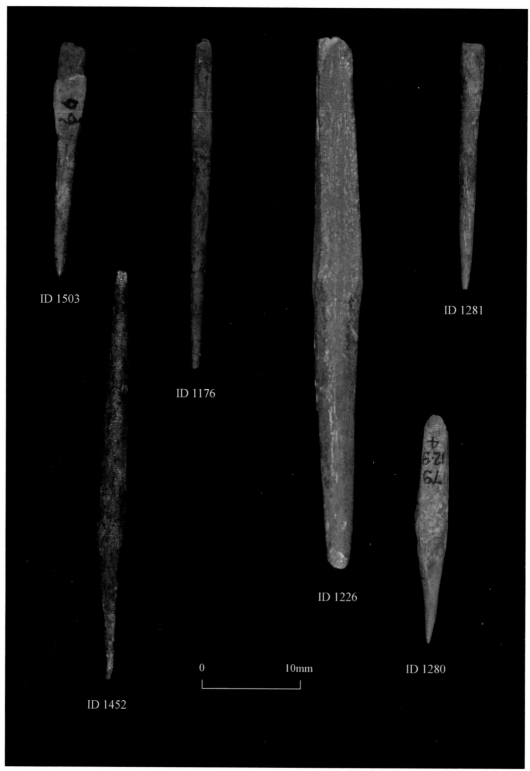

Figure 4.6.2. Copper alloy awls Groups 2A and 2B: ID 1503 Sutton Veny G11c; ID 1176 Winterbourne Stoke G47; ID 1226 Warslow and Elkstone; ID 1281 Langton 2, 2; ID 1452 Upton Lovell G2a; ID 1280 Langton 2, 2.

cases where one end has been re-worked, presumably for re-use (one of Group 1 and one of indeterminate group). Striations immediately below the point of transition on ID 1232 may have related to the hafting process (Figure 4.6.6).

COMPLETENESS AND DAMAGE

In 43 cases it was possible to determine the percentage of the object present. Of these 22 are complete or virtually so (98 to 100%) and 33 are present at the 90% level or above. There is no significant variation in degree of completeness

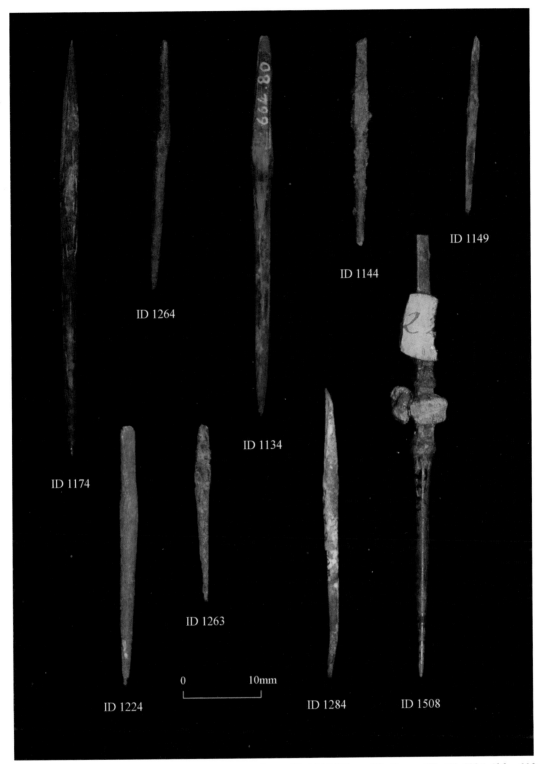

Figure 4.6.3. Copper alloy awls. Group 2C: ID 1174 ?Amesbury; ID 1264 Hilton G2. Group 2D: ID 1134 Aldro 113; ID 1144 Life Hill, Wetwang; ID 1149 Garton Slack 75, 1; ID 1224 Staker Hill, Hartington Upper; ID 1263 Frampton G4; ID 1284 Rudston 62, 1; ID 1508 Winterbourne Stoke G28.

amongst the Groups. Modern breaks were observed on 22 awls. These include 14 breaks at the tip of the point, five cases of damage to the tang, and three cases of glued multiple breaks (the latter all on the large Group 3 awls).

WEAR

A total of 48 ancient breaks are present on 37 awls. They occur amongst examples belonging to all the Groups, and a fair number of the items have more than one ancient break: usually one at each end. This is not surprising considering the extreme fineness and fragility of many of the awls, and

Figure 4.6.4. Copper alloy awls. Group 3A: ID 1442 Upton Lovell G2e; Group 3D: ID 1231 Rolley Low; indeterminate group: ID 1175 Shrewton G23.

the damage may have occurred within the grave rather than prior to deposition. There are 21 ancient breaks at the tang or proximal end, and 27 at the tip of the pointed end. Positive traces of use include six instances of striations or slight wear near the tip of the point (e.g. ID 1232, Figure 4.6.6) five instances of more general wear traces, and two cases of scratches near the proximal end. In addition one tang was slightly bent in antiquity (ID 1284, Figure 4.6.6), and two items appeared to have been re-worked (see above). In ten cases it was noted particularly that the point survived in a pristine and sharp condition (e.g. ID 1464, Figure 4.6.6). There is no observable variation in

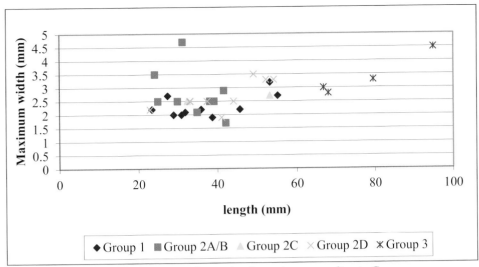

Figure 4.6.5. Copper alloy awls: dimensions according to Group.

Table 4.6.2. Copper alloy awls: grave contexts.

Group	Beaker	Beaker Age	Jet/ Jet-like	Collared Urn	Food Vessel	'Wessex' group	Single find
1	6	2	-	1	2	1	1
2A/B	-	-	2	2	-	5	3
2C	-	-	-	2	-	-	1
2D	1	-	2	-	4	2	5
3	1	-	-	-	-	4	-
Indeterminate	2	-	-	1	-	4	4
TOTAL	**10**	**2**	**4**	**6**	**6**	**16**	**14**

wear patterns amongst the different Groups. An overall wear category could be ascribed for a total of 30 of the awls studied. Amongst these the majority (26) are slightly worn or fresh, with six described as fresh. Only four items are classified as worn, and none at all as very worn.

CONCLUSIONS

Awls have a long currency, and the specific types can be ascribed, on the basis of associated grave goods, to the Beaker and developed Early Bronze Age periods respectively. They are mainly associated with the burials of adult women. Of a total of 11 British Beaker awls recorded by Clarke, eight were found in female graves and five with men. Of the Early Bronze Age examples studied in the present project, sex of the body is recorded in 14 cases. Of these the majority (10) were women, with a further two possible women and two possible males. In 16 cases the age is recorded. There were 11 adults, one middle-aged individual and one elderly (Manton). There were also two 'young' persons and one aged between 10 and 14 years. So throughout the two periods it can be concluded that awls tended to be deposited in the burials of adult women.

A high percentage of the awls were complete or almost complete when deposited, although some may have suffered minor damage within the grave context. This aspect is further confirmed by the presence of *in situ* organic

Table 4.6.3. Copper alloy awls: percentage length above point of transition, by Group.

Group	10%	20%	30%	40%	50%
1	-	1	-	3	6
2A/B	-	2	3	2	1
2C and 2D	-	-	1	1	2
3	1	2	-	1	-

handles in the grave. These include the outline traces of four bulbous wooden handles, recorded by Mortimer on awls from East Yorkshire (including ID 1132 and ID 1144), the deer antler handle on the awl from Winterbourne Stoke G5 (ID 889 on ID 1454), and organic traces on two further examples (ID 1175 and ID 1508). Wear traces are few, indicating minimal use, and some of the points are in fresh and pristine condition. Only two or three items may have been re-worked for reuse.

The question of possible function was discussed in detail by Thomas (2005, 222). The female associations suggest a use in some domestic craft and it has often been proposed that awls were used to pierce leather prior to sewing, or in decoration by pricking or scoring. However, as Thomas pointed out, the points are rather too fine for such purposes, and, as we have seen, our use wear studies show little signs of wear towards the points, and many of the points are in fact pristine. If used for piercing, then the material

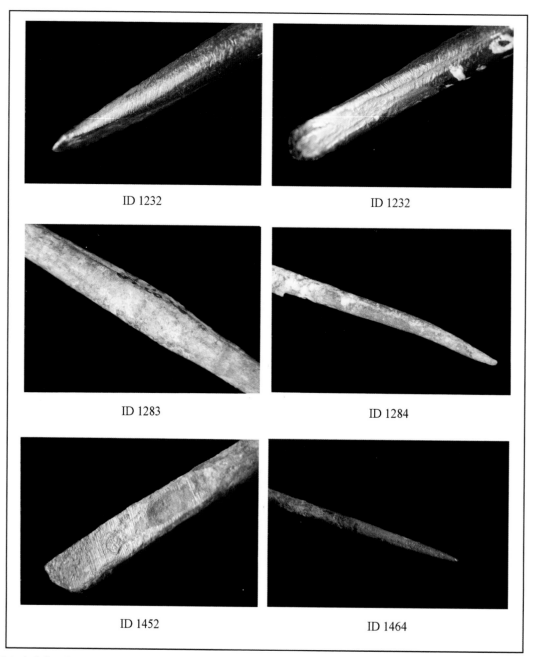

Figure 4.6.6. Awl details. ID 1232 Throwley showing diagonal scratching from use wear (top left); ID 1232 Throwley showing chisel end and likely roughening for hafting (top right); ID 1283 Butterwick 39, 1 with diamond-shaped facets; ID 1284 Rudston 62,1 showing bent tang; ID 1452 Upton Lovell G2a showing lateral faint striations on tang; ID 1464 Winterbourne Stoke G8 illustrating absence of use.

pierced must have been very soft, and thus the suggestion of use in tattooing or scarification (Woodward 2000, 115; Thomas 2005, 222), in which the points would have been employed to pierce human flesh, is an attractive one. Such bodily decoration is known from this period: on the Chalcolithic 'Ice Man' (Spindler 1994). Finally, it is of great interest to note that the awls were sometimes deposited in groups of two or three, with each group comprising awls of slightly different size and/or form. The four sets studied are as follows:

Langton ID 1280–82: Group 2B, Group 2A/B, indeterminate type

Rudston 62, 1 ID 1285–86: Group 1B, Group 1B
Aldbourne 280,1 ID 1291 A and B: two of indeterminate type
Manton ID 1426–28: Group 3D, Group 3D, Group 2D

This may relate to the need for differing points required to execute different kinds of designs in tattooing or scarification. Alternatively the awls may have had a use connected to medical procedures. Again, use within operations would have involved only the piercing or manipulation of human flesh, with little resulting use wear.

4.7 BONE POINTS

TYPO-CHRONOLOGY

Points made from animal bone or antler have received very little attention in Bronze Age research so far. The only attempt at typology has been provided by Longworth within his consideration of the classes of artefacts found in association with Collared Urns (Longworth 1984, 63–5). He defined a few skewer pins, similar to those found in the Neolithic period (his Type 1), carefully formed ring-headed pins (Type 3), pins made from splinters of bone in which the articular end is retained, either imperforate or perforated (Type 4), and similar pins but with the articular end removed (Type 5). Other minor types are only represented in Scotland or Ireland, and many were classified as miscellaneous (Type 8) or of unknown form (Type 9). Longworth pointed out that the ring-headed pins of Type 3 were bone copies of the Central European ring-headed bronze pin, as previously discussed by Gerloff (1975, 110 and Appendix 3), and the pins of this type which have been studied in the current project are considered separately in the section on Dress Pins (Chapter 5.5). In 46% of the English cases listed by Longworth, line drawings of the pins were provided, but they have provoked little interest within modern research. For this reason it was decided to study a large number of such points during the current project (n = 184). These are tabulated at the end of this section in Table 4.7.6.

Associations are diverse. A few points (four of those studied in detail) occur in Beaker-age graves, but these do tend to be larger and more varied in shape than the general series of bone points. The majority derive from Early Bronze Age grave groups, mostly with cremation burials, but a fair number have also been found with inhumations. Female associations are more common than male ones, and, amongst the burials that could be aged, there appears to be a distinct occurrence of points with young adults, adolescents and children. In many graves a single bone point is the only object present; otherwise the most common accompaniment is a Collared Urn. Other goods that occur several times are Food Vessels, flint tools, jet or amber beads, and bronze awls. The incidence of daggers (mainly of Series 5 and 6/7) is also notable. Other associations include a very wide range of items, ranging from battle-axes, bone tubes, bronze axes, complex bone items (e.g. belt hook, decorated bead, tweezers or dress pin), stone pendants and grooved stones. Several of these types may be regarded as exotic, and other such items found in graves with bone points include a jet spacer plate (ID 803 Crosby Garrett, Cumbria) and the Folkton decorated chalk drums (with ID 776).

MORPHOLOGY

As mentioned above, bone pins with a distinct ring head or other complex treatment of the head have been separated out and considered alongside other dress pins made from copper and copper alloy. The decorative heads on these items are relatively large and there is a distinct angle between the base of the ring and the shaft of the pin. The remainder of the pins can be divided into two major groups: those which retain the articular end of the bone, and possess a concavo-convex profile which reflects the morphology of the bone splinter employed; and those in which all the surfaces are worked, and the articular end of the bone has been removed. The latter are usually of circular or ovoid cross-section. Both groups contain examples which may be perforated or not perforated, and thus the following classification may be suggested:

Class 1. Articular end retained, concavo-convex section, imperforate (Figure 4.7.1).
Class 2. Articular end retained, concavo-convex section, perforated through head (Figure 4.7.2).
Class 1 or 2. Articular end retained, concavo-convex section, head missing.
Class 3. Worked all round, circular or ovoid section, imperforate rounded head (Figure 4.7.3).
Class 4. Worked all round, circular or ovoid section, head perforated. The head may be expanded but there is no angle between head and shaft (Figure 4.7.4).
Class 3 or 4. Worked all round, circular or ovoid section, head missing.

In four cases the points occur in distinct sets within single grave groups. These sets, and the occurrence of points studied by class are summarised in Table 4.7.1 (see also Figure 4.7.12).

This indicates that points of Class 2 are most common, but this total is skewed by the occurrence of the large set of such points from the Upton Lovell G2a 'shaman' grave. Otherwise the Class 1 points are very well represented. There is no correlation between class and region, with all classes of point occurring throughout the country.

Many bone points were broken, either in antiquity or recent times (see below), so the measurement of total original length could only be recorded in selected cases. When this data was listed it was found that there were clear groupings of length statistics in the 'short' (40 to 80mm and especially below 75mm) and the 'medium' (81 to 100mm and especially between 91 and 100mm) sectors. In Figure 4.7.5 the occurrence of these size groupings, and of points measuring more than 100mm in length, is plotted according to class. For Classes 1 and 2, most points are 'short' or 'medium' in length. Those of Class 1 are slightly more often 'medium' and Class 2 (the perforated ones) are slightly more often 'short'. In contrast, the Class 3 and 4 pins show a more bimodal distribution, with more 'short' and 'long' examples, and fewer in the 'medium' category. However, overall the size data does not seem to indicate any clear differences in function amongst the different classes. Amongst the four sets of pins, those from Snailwell A (11 pins; Figures 4.7.6 and 4.7.12, left) and the Wilsford Shaft (8 pins; Figure 4.7.7) are mainly 'small', while those from Aldro (5 pins; Figures 4.7.8 and 4.7.12, right) and Upton Lovell G2a (44 pins; Figures 4.7.9 and 4.7.13) are mainly 'medium' in length.

For the Upton Lovell set of points, a particular study of

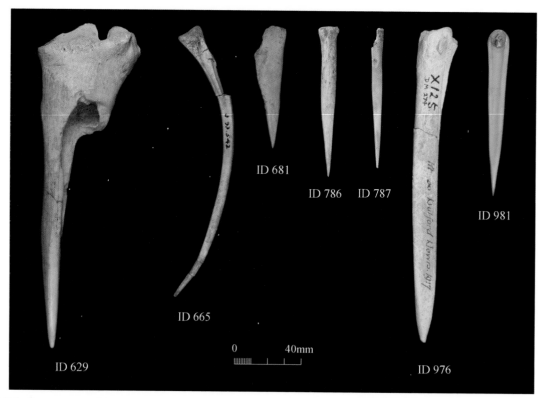

Figure 4.7.1. Bone points, Class 1 examples. From left to right: ID 629 Calais Wold 100; ID 665 Throwley 1; ID 681 Staker Hill, Hartington Upper; ID 786 Lambourn 289; ID 787 Aldbourne 282, 1; ID 976 Bulford Down; ID 981 Norton Bavant G2.

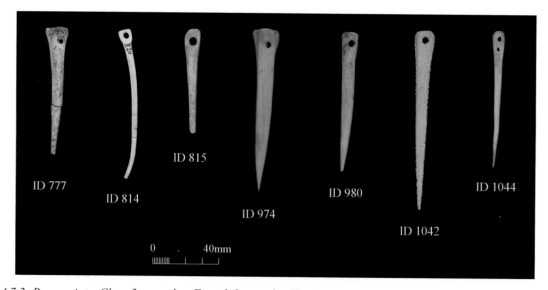

Figure 4.7.2. Bone points, Class 2 examples. From left to right: ID 777 Folkton 241, 2; ID 814 Aldbourne 278, 1; ID 815 Aldbourne 276, 3; ID 974 Wimborne St Giles G20; ID 980 Collingbourne Kingston G4; ID 1042 Amesbury G85; ID 1044 Handley G29.

Table 4.7.1. Occurrence of bone points by class.

Set	Class 1	Class 2	Class 1or2	Class 3	Class 4	Class 3or4
Aldro 113, E. Yorks.	5	-	-	-	-	-
Snailwell A, Cambs.	-	9	-	2	-	-
Wilsford Shaft, (Wilsford G33a),Wilts.	-	8	-	-	-	-
Upton Lovell G2a, Wilts.	-	44	-	-	-	-
Remainder	28	19	18	15	15	19
Total	**33**	**80**	**18**	**17**	**15**	**19**

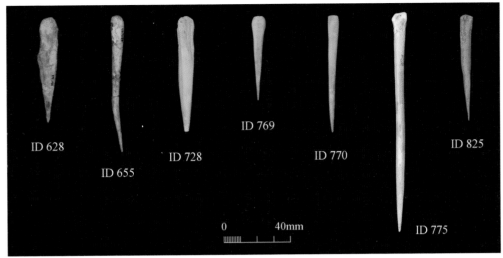

Figure 4.7.3, Bone points, Class 3 examples. From left to right: ID 628 Garrowby Wold 120; ID 655 Blanch 241; ID 728 Roughridge Down, Bishops Cannings; ID 769 Wilsford-cum-Lake; ID 770 Wilsford-cum-Lake; ID 775 Ganton 28,8; ID 825 Barnack.

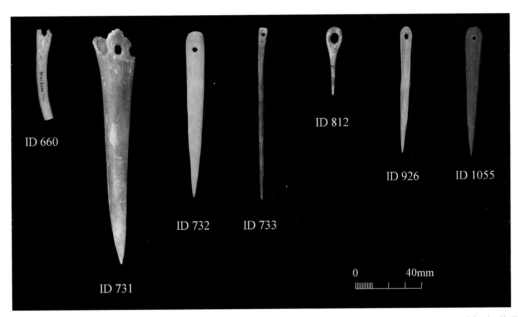

Figure 4.7.4, Bone points, Class 4 examples. From left to right: ID 660 Stanton Moor 17a; ID 731 Mildenhall Fen; ID 732 Wilsford-cum-Lake; ID 733 Wilsford-cum-Lake; ID 812 Slingsby 145,1; ID 926 Amesbury Park; ID 1055 Dorchester G15.

the perforations was undertaken. The shape of the section of the perforation was usually hourglass (45%) or funnel (28%), with only seven perforations (17%) which had been cut straight through. Thus there was a fair degree of variation. The range of size of the perforations was rather more standardised. Most (29) were 4 to 6mm in diameter, 11 were larger, between 6 and 9mm, and only two were between 3 and 4mm in diameter. Occasionally the drill was repositioned, leaving an aborted hole nearby (e.g. Figure 4.7.10, ID 840)

MATERIAL

Most of the points were made from animal bone, with only five items having been formed from antler (for full listings

see Appendix III). The type of bone that was most often chosen as the raw material was the lower leg bone of sheep/goat, most probably sheep. The occurrence of the bones employed, according to species and type is summarised in Table 4.7.2. It can be seen that, apart from sheep limb bones, the main materials chosen were limb bones from large mammals (cattle or red deer), red and roe deer, and occasionally horse or pig. It might have been thought that there would be some correlation between bone species and class of bone point. This is because larger bones may have been more suitable for the production of points that had been finished all round their circular or ovoid cross-section. However the incidence of large mammal (cattle and red deer) bone material within the points studied is roughly equal for all four of the typological classes defined.

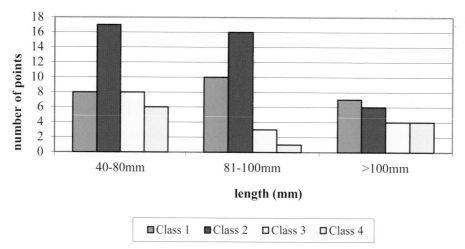

Figure 4.7.5. Bone points: the occurrence of length groups by class.

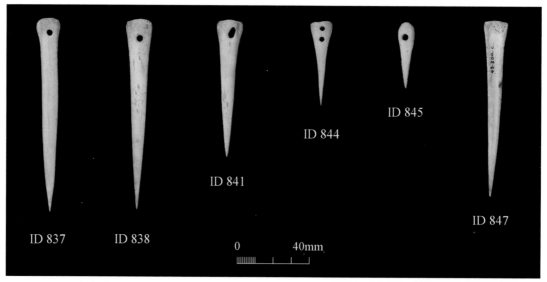

Figure 4.7.6. Selection from Snailwell A set of bone points. From left to right (Class 1) ID 837; ID 838; ID 841; ID 844; ID 845;(Class 2) ID 847.

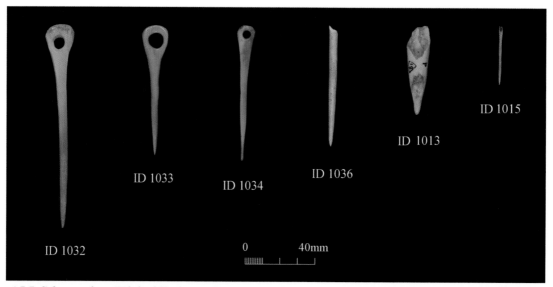

Figure 4.7.7. Selection from Wilsford Shaft set of bone points. From left to right: (Class 2) ID 1032; ID 1033; ID 1034; (Class 3or4) ID 1036; (other) ID 1013; (needle) ID 1015.

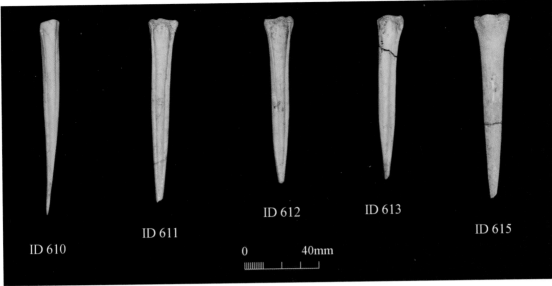

Figure 4.7.8. Aldro 113 set of bone points (Class 1). From left to right: ID 610; ID 611; ID 612; ID 613; ID 615.

Table 4.7.2. Bone points: raw material employed by species and bone type.

Species	Bone type	No of bone points	% by species
Cattle	Metatarsal	2	1%
Cattle	Distal rib shaft	1	
Red deer	Proximal metatarsal	2	1%
Red deer	Radius	1	
Roe deer	Proximal metatarsal	5	2%
Horse	Peripheral metapodial	2	1%
Pig (probable)	Limb shaft	1	0%
Large mammal (cattle or red deer)	Proximal metapodial	5	11%
Large mammal (cattle or red deer)	Limb shaft	20	
Sheep/goat	Proximal metatarsal	124	80%
Sheep/goat	Proximal metacarpal	16	
Sheep/goat	Metapodial	7	
Sheep/goat	Tibia shaft	8	
Sheep/goat	Limb shaft	31	
Mammal	Limb shaft	9	4%
Total identifiable		**234**	**100%**

Table 4.7.3. Bone points: bone sector and body side for sheep/goat limb bones.

Bone	Sector	Upton Lovell G2a	Remainder	Total
Proximal metatarsal	Lateral	14	19	33
(rear leg)	Medial	6	6	12
	Medial/lateral	12	12	24
	Unknown	0	2	2
	Right body side	7	12	19
	Left body side	23	11	34
Proximal metacarpal	Lateral	4	1	5
(front leg)	Medial	0	2	2
	Unknown	0	2	2
	Right body side	4	3	7
	Left body side	0	0	0
	Left body side	0	2	2

Among the metapodials identified it was often possible to determine the sector of the bone that had been selected, following splitting of the shaft. Also in many cases the bone could be identified as having come from the right or left leg of the animal concerned. This data for the sheep/goat metapodials is listed in Table 4.7.3. Much of the best data came from analysis of the large set of points found in the Upton Lovell G2a 'shaman' grave, so these are listed separately, for detailed comparison.

Several interesting patterns emerge from these figures.

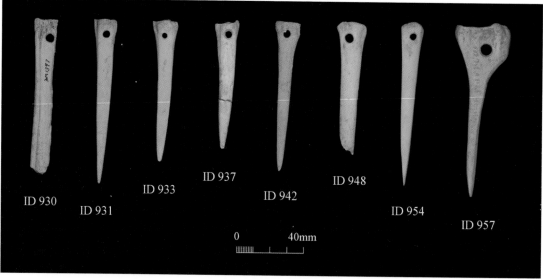

Figure 4.7.9. Selection from Upton Lovell G2a set of bone points (Class 2). From left to right: ID 930; ID 931; ID 933; ID 937; ID 942; ID 948; ID 954; ID 957.

Table 4.7.4. Bone points: the occurrence of breaks.

Class	shaft	Modern head/perf	tip	shaft	Ancient head/perf	tip
Sets	*14*	*12*	*18*	*4*	*14*	*29*
1	9	3	4	1	6	5
2	9	3	5	1	5	7
1or2	4	3	8	12	2	4
3	2	2	1	2	2	4
4	6	3	5	0	4	5
3or4	11	1	4	9	5	9
non-set total	*41*	*15*	*27*	*25*	*24*	*34*
Overall total	**55**	**27**	**45**	**29**	**38**	**63**

Firstly it can be seen that the metapodial from the rear leg was much more often utilised than that from the front leg of the sheep. Secondly the lateral side (outside) of the bone was more commonly used than the medial (inside) section of the split bone, although the medial/lateral section was also sometimes preferred. In the main set of data metatarsals from either side of the body were almost equally represented, but within the particular set from Upton Lovell G2a a preference for those from the left side of the body is evident. In contrast the results for the front leg, although they are few, seem to indicate that in this case bones from the right hand side of the body were selected. The possible reasons for such selections are not clear. However what is abundantly clear is that the material selected for the manufacture of bone points was highly standardised, and this standardisation occurred throughout the country.

MANUFACTURE

The points were made by cutting the selected bone, or bone splinter, and then shaping the point, shaft and head. Very occasionally, a few butchery marks survive (e.g. Figure 4.7.10, ID 629). Most of them were then polished. Of the

161 examples where the original nature of the surface could be determined, 79% were polished. For Classes 1, 2 and 1or2, and also for Classes 3, 4 and 3or4, in each case 84% were polished, while amongst the sets a slightly lower percentage of the points were polished (72%). The polish was achieved through a process which produced longitudinal striations, usually faint, which survived on many items (e.g. Figure 4.7.10, ID 839, ID 843). Such traces of manufacture were recorded on 71% of the non-set Class 1, 2 and 1or2 points, and on 63% of the non-set Class 3, 4 and 3or4 points. This may indicate that the latter group, which had received more initial working and shaping, may also have been polished to a higher degree i.e. the striations had been more often polished out. Interestingly, the points in the four sets were less well finished, with much higher incidences of surviving striations (88% to 100%).

In only two cases were any traces of decoration observed (Figure 4.7.10). These include two grooves on the front top surface of a Class 3 point (ID 728) and faceting on the head (ID 979). Also the all-over green metal staining on a point from Dorchester G15 (ID 1055) may have been deliberate colouring, as was found on several bone dress pins, including other items from this same grave (Figure 4.7.10; see also Chapter 5.5).

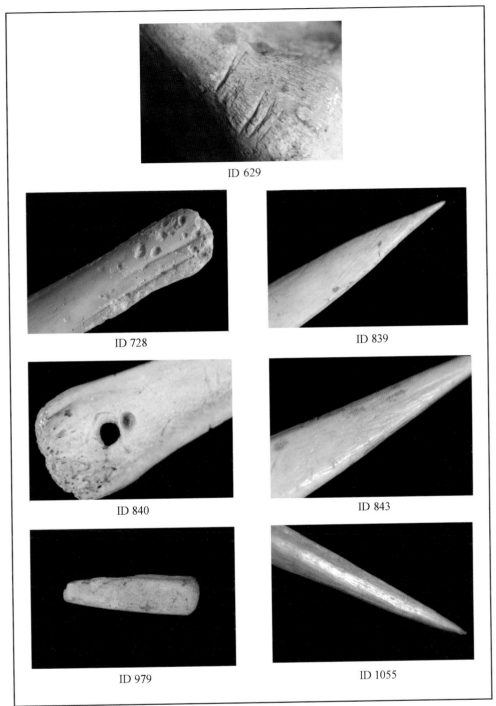

Figure 4.7.10. Details showing: butchery marks on ID 629 Calais Wold 100; decorative grooves on ID 728 Roughridge Down, Bishops Cannings; striations on ID 839 Snailwell A; an aborted perforation on ID 840 Snailwell A; striations and polishing on ID 843 Snailwell A; a faceted head on ID 979 Collingbourne Kingston G4; green staining on ID 1055 Dorchester G15.

COMPLETENESS AND DAMAGE

The points display a very high level of breakage; this is probably a reflection of their fragile morphology, with long and thin shafts and vulnerable margins to any perforations which are present. Further fragmentation has occurred as a result of burning, usually due to the item having gone through the cremation process. For this reason the presence of burning was systematically recorded. None of the points within the four sets were burnt, but amongst the

remainder significant proportions of burning were noted: 38% for points of Class 1, 2 and 1or2, and 24% for Class 3, 4 and 3or4. The occurrence of breaks, according to their location on the point, Class and age, modern or ancient, is summarised in Table 4.7.4.

Modern breaks occur most commonly on the shaft; they usually comprise fractures across the section which have subsequently been glued. This is particularly common amongst the non-set points. Within the sets, modern damage

Table 4.7.5. Bone points: incidence of wear categories by class.

Class	Fresh	Slight wear	Worn	Very worn	Indeterminate
Aldro	-	2	2	-	1
Snailwell A	4	6	-	-	1
Wilsford Shaft	1	3	3	-	1
Upton Lovell G2a	2	42	-	-	-
1	5	13	5	-	5
2	3	8	5	-	3
1or2	1	6	5	-	6
3	3	5	3	2	2
4	1	3	9	-	2
3or4	3	5	3	1	7
Total	**23**	**93**	**35**	**3**	
% of identifiable wear category	15%	60%	23%	2%	

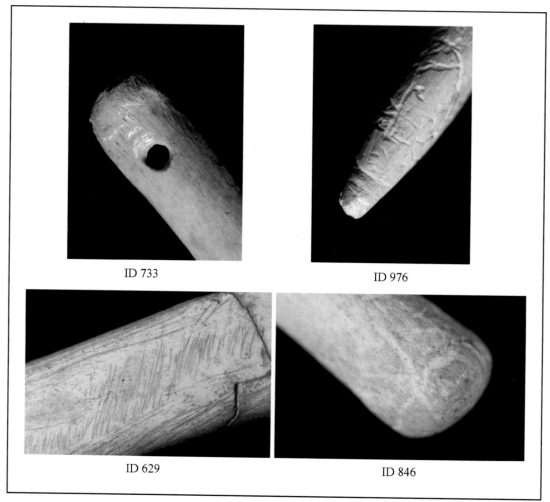

ID 733

ID 976

ID 629

ID 846

Figure 4.7.11. Details showing general scratchings on ID 629 Calais Wold 100; wear around perforation on ID 733 Wilsford-cum-Lake; copper staining on ID 846 Snailwell A, and probable tool use on the tip of ID 976 Bulford Down.

to the tips is slightly more common, and this is particularly the case for the Upton Lovell set, which appears to have suffered damage due to repeated handling, probably at the time of the excavation and subsequently in a series of display situations.

WEAR

The location of ancient breaks shows a different pattern to that for the modern breaks (see Table 4.7.4). More breaks occur at the tip, and this may indicate damage or extreme wear during use. However breaks at the head or shaft are also fairly well represented and again may reflect the overall fragility of these slender items. Ancient tip damage is particularly common within the set of points from Upton Lovell G2a, and this may be related to their particular function (see below). Most wear traces were located at the perforations (e.g. ID 733, Figure 4.7.11), and are indicative of cord- or thread-wear. This probably indicates that the points were suspended, maybe on a necklace or girdle, or fastened to a garment or headdress. Generalised scratching may also have occurred during any of these uses (e.g. Figure 4.7.11, ID 629). In general the points showed low incidences of wear, and in particular wear at the tip was extremely uncommon. It was only observed in 17 cases. In two cases only there was evidence that the tip had been used in a circular motion to facilitate a boring action (Figure 4.7.11, ID 976). These items were of unusual morphology, with wider shafts and tapering points, and may have functioned as tools. The overall incidence of wear categories is summarised in Table 4.7.5.

The figures in Table 4.7.5 demonstrate the overall low incidence of wear among the bone points. Most are only slightly worn, and a significant proportion is fresh, while amongst the worn items, the incidence of heavy wear is very low indeed (at 2%). This lack of wear is even more noticeable amongst the four sets of points.

A total of eleven points showed traces of green metal staining. In one case the all-over colouration may have been deliberate (see above), and in two further cases the grave group also contained bronze items, against which the bone point may have been resting in the grave. However, seven of the examples belong to the set of Class 2 points from Snailwell. They retained flecks of green material in various locations, but no metal objects were recovered within this grave group (Figure 4.7.11, ID 846). So it may be that some copper alloy, perhaps in the form of wire, had been employed in relation to the points. Such wire may have served to join the points together in some way, perhaps as part of a headdress or hair ornament.

CONCLUSIONS

The large number of bone points studied fall into four clear typological groups, although all four classes occur throughout the country. Size is relatively standardised, but does vary from class to class. The choice of bones as raw material for the points is very specific and concentrates on lower limb bones (metapodials) from small-sized animals such as roe deer, sheep or goat. The use of sheep metatarsals (back leg) is particularly common. The employment of such bones may have been determined in part by their suitability for manufacture into points of the desired size. However the choice of sheep over roe deer and goat appears to have been deliberate and may have had symbolic intent. Similarly the selection of bones from the rear legs may have been intentional. Within the large group of points from Upton Lovell G2a, the 'shaman' grave, there was also a strong tendency for the bones from the left-hand back leg to have been utilised. The possible symbolic reasons for such a choice however remain obscure. Most of the

points were polished to a fine degree, while only very few were decorated.

The points display a high level of breakage, dating from both modern and ancient times. No doubt this is due to their slender morphology and fragility, and further damage has sometimes occurred as a result of the cremation process. Ancient breaks occur at both tip and head and relate to use in antiquity. Most wear traces were located at the perforations, and are indicative of cord- or thread-wear. This probably indicates that the points were suspended, maybe on a necklace or girdle, or fastened to a garment or headdress. In only very few cases were any wear traces at or near the tip indicative of use as a tool. Overall the traces of wear are fairly slight, with 75% of points where a level of wear could be determined falling in the fresh or slightly worn categories. It can therefore be concluded that most of the points were used for some other purpose, presumably as items of adornment. These could have included hair pins, head ornaments or headdresses, or embellishments for clothing and costume. Record of body placement in some of the graves provides some clues. In Beaker graves bone points tend to be placed at or near the side or pelvis, while in Early Bronze Age inhumations numerous points were located near the head and shoulders. This appears to indicate a clear shift from placement near the waist or hip to an association with the head (see Chapter 11 for object function). The Beaker-age examples may have been tools, perhaps suspended at the waist or contained in a pouch. A good example is provided by the burial from Acklam Wold 124 (ID 618) which contained a Beaker, and in a group near the pelvis a jet button and jet pulley ring along with the bone point and some flint tools. In contrast the Early Bronze Age items probably functioned as hair pins or ornaments. Within graves where the human remains could be sexed, Beaker-age points were always associated with males, and this applies across the whole country (see Chapter 11). In the Early Bronze Age graves containing points more often were burials of females (57%) and this trend was especially marked in East Yorkshire, where 79% were females.

The use of bone points in adornment of the body or costume is particularly well demonstrated by consideration of the points that were found in groups within the grave. This includes the four main sets which have already been mentioned in this section, together with the traces of further possible sets as follows:

Class 1; Throwley (ID 664–45), Stanshope (ID 704–5), Nether Swell 218, 2 (ID 778–79)
Class 2: Wimborne St Giles G19 (ID 928–29), Amesbury G85 (ID 1041–43)
Class 3: Top Low, Blore with Swinscoe (ID 683–84)
Class 1or2: Bamburgh 198, 1 (ID 799, ID 800, ID 808 and ID 809)

All four of the main sets contain an array of points which are slightly graduated in length, as if they had been designed as decorative sets. This is clearly visible within the sets

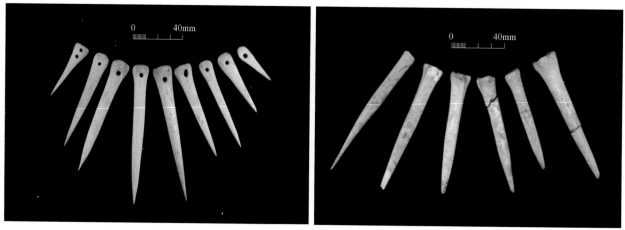

Figure 4.7.12. Sets of bone points from Snailwell A (left) and from Aldro 113 (right).

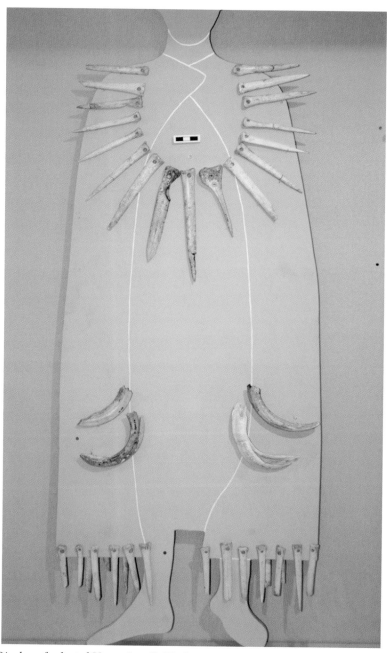

Figure 4.7.13. Display of selected Upton Lovell G2a bone points at the Wiltshire Heritage Museum, Devizes.

Table 4.7.6. List of bone points studied and illustrated.

Object	Site (Parish), County	Museum	Illustration
ID 604	Wharram Percy 71 (Wharram Percy), E. Yorks.	Hull	Not illustrated
ID 605	Wharram Percy 65 (Birdsall), E. Yorks.	Hull	Not illustrated
ID 608	Aldro 52 (Birdsall), E. Yorks.	Hull	Not illustrated
ID 610	Aldro 113 (Birdsall), E. Yorks.	Hull	Figure 4.7.8; Figure 4.7.12
ID 611	Aldro 113 (Birdsall), E. Yorks.	Hull	Figure 4.7.8; Figure 4.7.12
ID 612	Aldro 113 (Birdsall), E. Yorks.	Hull	Figure 4.7.8; Figure 4.7.12
ID 613	Aldro 113 (Birdsall), E. Yorks.	Hull	Figure 4.7.8; Figure 4.7.12
ID 615	Aldro 113 (Birdsall), E. Yorks.	Hull	Figure 4.7.8; Figure 4.7.12
ID 616	Aldro 113 (Birdsall), E. Yorks.	Hull	Figure 4.7.8; Figure 4.7.12
ID 618	Acklam Wold 124 (Acklam), E. Yorks.	Hull	Not illustrated
ID 623	Painsthorpe 121 (Wharram Percy), E. Yorks.	Hull	Not illustrated
ID 626	Painsthorpe 98 (Kirby Underdale), E. Yorks.	Hull	Not illustrated
ID 628	Garrowby Wold 120 (Bishop Wilton), E. Yorks.	Hull	Figure 4.7.3
ID 629	Calais Wold 100 (Bishop Wilton), E. Yorks.	Hull	Figure 4.7.1; Figure 4.7.10; Figure 4.7.11
ID 631	Fimber 133 (Fimber), E. Yorks.	Hull	Not illustrated
ID 649	Garton Slack 112 (Kirkburn), E. Yorks.	Hull	Not illustrated
ID 652	Huggate and Warter Wold 249 (Huggate), E. Yorks.	Hull	Not illustrated
ID 654	Blanch 189 (Huggate), E. Yorks.	Hull	Not illustrated
ID 655	Blanch 241 (Warter), E. Yorks.	Hull	Figure 4.7.3
ID 658	Galley Lowe (Brassington), Derbys.	Shef	Not illustrated
ID 660	Stanton Moor 17a, Derbys.	Shef	Figure 4.7.4
ID 661	Stanton Moor 1926, Derbys.	Shef	Not illustrated
ID 662	Stanton Moor 1926, Derbys.	Shef	Not illustrated
ID 664	Throwley 1, Staffs.	Shef	Not illustrated
ID 665	Throwley 1, Staffs.	Shef	Figure 4.7.1
ID 669	Green Low, Alsop Moor (Eaton and Alsop), Derbys.	Shef	Not illustrated
ID 673	Arbor Low (Middleton and Smerrill), Derbys.	Shef	Not illustrated
ID 674	Little Lea 1, Staffs.	Shef	Not illustrated
ID 677	Little Lea 3, Staffs.	Shef	Not illustrated
ID 678	Throwley (Mare Hill), Staffs.	Shef	Not illustrated
ID 681	Staker Hill (Hartington Upper), Derbys.	Shef	Figure 4.7.1
ID 682	Staker Hill (Hartington Upper), Derbys.	Shef	Not illustrated
ID 683	Top Low (Blore with Swinscoe), Staffs.	Shef	Not illustrated
ID 684	Top Low (Blore with Swinscoe), Staffs.	Shef	Not illustrated
ID 704	Stanshope (Alstonefield), Staffs.	Shef	Not illustrated
ID 705	Stanshope (Alstonefield), Staffs.	Shef	Not illustrated
ID 706	Hay Top (Little Longstone), Derbys.	Shef	Not illustrated
ID 710	Throwley 1, Staffs.	Shef	Not illustrated
ID 712	Throwley 1, Staffs.	Shef	Not illustrated
ID 715	Stanton Moor, Derbys.	Shef	Not illustrated
ID 726	Normanby, N. Yorks.	BM	Figure 4.7.10
ID 727	Brading Down, Isle of Wight.	BM	Not illustrated
ID 728	Roughridge Down (Bishops Cannings), Wilts.	BM	Figure 4.7.3; Figure 4.7.10
ID 729	Obadiah's Barrow, Gugh, Scilly	BM	Not illustrated
ID 730	Obadiah's Barrow, Gugh, Scilly	BM	Not illustrated
ID 731	Mildenhall Fen, Suffolk	BM	Figure 4.7.4
ID 732	Wilsford-cum-Lake (Duke Coll.), Wilts.	BM	Figure 4.7.4
ID 733	Wilsford-cum-Lake (Duke Coll.), Wilts.	BM	Figure 4.7.4; Figure 4.7.11
ID 768	Wilsford-cum-Lake (Duke Coll.), Wilts.	BM	Not illustrated
ID 769	Wilsford-cum-Lake (Duke Coll.), Wilts.	BM	Figure 4.7.3
ID 770	Wilsford-cum-Lake (Duke Coll.), Wilts.	BM	Figure 4.7.3
ID 771	Goodmanham 111, burial 4, E. Yorks.	BM	Not illustrated
ID 772	Goodmanham 109, burial 1, E. Yorks.	BM	Not illustrated
ID 773	Etton 82, burial 2, E. Yorks.	BM	Not illustrated
ID 775	Ganton 28, burial 8, E. Yorks.	BM	Figure 4.7.3
ID 776	Folkton 245, burial 1, E. Yorks.	BM	Not illustrated
ID 777	Folkton 241, burial 2, E. Yorks.	BM	Figure 4.7.2
ID 778	Nether Swell 218, burial 2, Gloucs.	BM	Not illustrated
ID 779	Nether Swell 218, burial 2, Gloucs.	BM	Not illustrated
ID 780	Crosby Garrett 174, cairn, Cumbria	BM	Not illustrated
ID 782	Rudston 64, mound, E. Yorks.	BM	Not illustrated
ID 783	Rudston 63, burial 3, E. Yorks.	BM	Not illustrated
ID 784	Rudston 61, burial 6, E. Yorks.	BM	Not illustrated
ID 785	Weaverthorpe 44, burial 1, E. Yorks.	BM	Not illustrated
ID 786	Lambourn 289, mound, Berks.	BM	Figure 4.7.1
ID 787	Aldbourne 282, burial 1 (G8), Wilts.	BM	Figure 4.7.1

Object	Site (Parish), County	Museum	Illustration
ID 788	Ganton 24, burial 2, E. Yorks.	BM	Not illustrated
ID 790	Ganton 16, burial 1, E. Yorks.	BM	Not illustrated
ID 791	Hackpen (Avebury), Wilts.	BM	Not illustrated
ID 792	Tan Hill (All Cannings), Wilts.	BM	Not illustrated
ID 793	Stonehenge (Amesbury), Wilts.	BM	Not illustrated
ID 794	Roughridge Down (Bishops Cannings), Wilts.	BM	Not illustrated
ID 796	Alwinton 205, burial 3, Northumb.	BM	Not illustrated
ID 797	Goodmanham 89, burial 12, E. Yorks.	BM	Not illustrated
ID 799	Bamburgh 198, burial 1, Northumb.	BM	Not illustrated
ID 800	Bamburgh 198, burial 1, Northumb.	BM	Not illustrated
ID 801	Ford 187, burial 2, Northumb.	BM	Not illustrated
ID 802	Ford 187, burial 3, Northumb.	BM	Not illustrated
ID 803	Crosby Garrett 176, burial 2, Cumbria	BM	Not illustrated
ID 806	Aldbourne 283, burial 1 (G11), Wilts.	BM	Not illustrated
ID 807	Alwinton 205, burial 1, Northumb.	BM	Not illustrated
ID 808	Bamburgh 198, burial 1, Northumb.	BM	Not illustrated
ID 809	Bamburgh 198, burial 1, Northumb.	BM	Not illustrated
ID 810	Easton Hill (Bishops Cannings), Wilts.	BM	Not illustrated
ID 811	Gunnerton UN25, burial 1, Northumb.	BM	Not illustrated
ID 812	Slingsby 145, burial 1, N. Yorks.	BM	Figure 4.7.4
ID 813	Aldbourne 284, burial 1 (G13), Wilts.	BM	Not illustrated
ID 814	Aldbourne 278, burial 1 (G3), Wilts.	BM	Figure 4.7.2
ID 815	Aldbourne 276, burial 3 (G1), Wilts.	BM	Figure 4.7.2
ID 816	Alwinton 205, burial 1, Northumb.	BM	Not illustrated
ID 818	Hunmanby 250, burial 1, E. Yorks.	BM	Not illustrated
ID 825	Barnack, Cambs.	BM	Figure 4.7.3
ID 826	Cowlam (Cottam), E. Yorks.	BM	Not illustrated
ID 828	Hemp Knoll (Bishops Cannings), Wilts.	BM	Not illustrated
ID 829	Hemp Knoll (Bishops Cannings), Wilts.	BM	Not illustrated
ID 830	Hemp Knoll (Bishops Cannings), Wilts.	BM	Not illustrated
ID 832	Nether Swell 220, burial 1, Gloucs.	BM	Not illustrated
ID 837-847	Snailwell A, Cambs.	Camb	Figure 4.7.12 (selection)
ID 837	Snailwell A, Cambs.	Camb	Figure 4.7.6
ID 838	Snailwell A, Cambs.	Camb	Figure 4.7.6
ID 839	Snailwell A, Cambs.	Camb	Figure 4.7.10
ID 840	Snailwell A, Cambs.	Camb	Figure 4.7.10
ID 841	Snailwell A, Cambs.	Camb	Figure 4.7.6
ID 842	Snailwell A, Cambs.	Camb	Not illustrated
ID 843	Snailwell A, Cambs.	Camb	Figure 4.7.10
ID 844	Snailwell A, Cambs.	Camb	Figure 4.7.6
ID 845	Snailwell A, Cambs.	Camb	Figure 4.7.6
ID 846	Snailwell A, Cambs.	Camb	Figure 4.7.11
ID 847	Snailwell A, Cambs.	Camb	Figure 4.7.6
ID 926	Amesbury Park, Wilts.	Dev	Figure 4.7.4
ID 927	Wilsford G64, Wilts.	Dev	Not illustrated
ID 928	Wimborne St Giles G19, Dorset	Dev	Not illustrated
ID 929	Wimborne St Giles G19, Dorset	Dev	Not illustrated
ID 930-970	Upton Lovell G2a (shaman), Wilts.	Dev	Figure 4.7.13 (display)
ID 930-l, 933, 937, 942, 948, 954, 957		Dev	Figure 4.7.9
ID 974	Wimborne St Giles G20, Dorset	Dev	Figure 4.7.2
ID 976	Bulford Down, Wilts.	Dev	Figure 4.7.1; Figure 4.7.11
ID 977	Collingbourne Kingston G4, Wilts.	Dev	Not illustrated
ID 978	Collingbourne Kingston G4, Wilts.	Dev	Not illustrated
ID 979	Collingbourne Kingston G4, Wilts.	Dev	Figure 4.7.10
ID 980	Collingbourne Kingston G4, Wilts.	Dev	Figure 4.7.2
ID 981	Norton Bavant G2, Wilts.	Dev	Figure 4.7.1
ID 982-985	Upton Lovell G2a (shaman), Wilts.	Dev	Figure 4.7.13 (display)
ID 982-985		Dev	Not illustrated
ID 1013	Wilsford G33a (Shaft), Wilts.	Sal	Figure 4.7.7
ID 1015	Wilsford G33a (Shaft), Wilts.	Sal	Figure 4.7.7
ID 1026	Norton Bavant Borrow Pit, Wilts.	Sal	Not illustrated
ID 1028	Wilsford G74, Wilts.	Sal	Not illustrated
ID 1029	Amesbury G85, Wilts.	Sal	Not illustrated
ID 1030	Amesbury G72, Wilts.	Sal	Not illustrated
ID 1031	Wilsford (Normanton Down), Wilts.	Sal	Not illustrated
ID 1032	Wilsford G33a (Shaft), Wilts.	Sal	Figure 4.7.7

Object	Site (Parish), County	Museum	Illustration
ID 1033	Wilsford G33a (Shaft), Wilts.	Sal	Figure 4.7.7
ID 1034	Wilsford G33a (Shaft), Wilts.	Sal	Figure 4.7.7
ID 1035	Wilsford G33a (Shaft), Wilts.	Sal	Not illustrated
ID 1036	Wilsford G33a (Shaft), Wilts.	Sal	Figure 4.7.7
ID 1037	Wilsford G33a (Shaft), Wilts.	Sal	Not illustrated
ID 1038	Wilsford G33a (Shaft), Wilts.	Sal	Not illustrated
ID 1040	Winterslow G21, Wilts.	Sal	Not illustrated
ID 1041	Amesbury G85, Wilts.	Sal	Not illustrated
ID 1042	Amesbury G85, Wilts.	Sal	Figure 4.7.2
ID 1043	Amesbury G85, Wilts.	Sal	Not illustrated
ID 1044	Handley G29, Dorset	Sal	Figure 4.7.2
ID 1048	Weymouth G8 (Ridgeway 7), Dorset	Dor	Not illustrated
ID 1055	Dorchester G15, Dorset	Dor	Figure 4.7.4; Figure 4.7.10

from Aldro and from Snailwell A (Figure 4.7.12). The Class 1 points from Aldro, found behind the head of a female inhumation, are not perforated, but these or indeed the Class 2 set from Snailwell could well have been mounted, points upward, within a perishable head band in order to form an impressive headdress. In the case of the Snailwell set the presence of metal stain traces suggest that this might have been achieved by the use of metal connecting wires. Alternatively sets of perforated points could have been suspended as pendants or as part of necklaces. The evidence of the location of string or cord wear recorded within the perforations on many of the Class 2 and Class 4 points suggests however that in many cases the points were not strung simply so that they hung from a position at the top of the object. The occurrence of cord-wear at positions either side of the top (top right or top left) is fairly common, and it also occurs at the sides of some perforations, or even towards the base. This may indicate that the points were attached or loosely sewn into exact locations on items of dress or costume. These may have included headdresses, as discussed above, or garments of varying type. In three cases (ID 608 Aldro 52, ID 644–45 Throwley and the set from Snailwell A) bone pins were associated with bone tubes. These have been interpreted tentatively as musical instruments (see Chapter 4.9) but an alternative interpretation may be that they functioned in conjunction with the bone pin in some form of elaborate hair ornament. If so, this would recall the pairing of fancy bone dress pins and bone 'tweezers', from a small number of graves in southern England, which have been interpreted in a similar way as having been connected with exotic hairdressing.

Evidence for a special garment was obtained from the 'shaman' grave at Upton Lovell G2a, where the points occurred in two locations on the body: more than three dozen at the feet and a further two dozen 'near the breast' (Figure 4.7.13). Piggott (1962) suggested that these bone items had functioned as the elements of ornamental fringes, sewn on to special garments. He compared them to similar finds from Mesolithic and Bronze Age graves in northern Eurasia, and to historic records of the costumes worn by shamans in Siberia (*ibid*, 95–6). The wear patterns discerned around the perforations of many of these points might indicate that some of the points were sewn or otherwise fixed at varying angles upon the leather, buckskin or textile, perhaps to form curved or other ornate patterns. Of further interest is the fact that three of the sets studied, Aldro 113, Snailwell A and Upton Lovell G2a, contained points made from large mammal (cattle or red deer) metapodials, alongside the main groups of sheep metatarsals. It may be that these materials were chosen so that one or more larger points could be inserted as focal elements in the design of a head ornament or embellishment to a costume; or it may be that the inclusion of these less preferred bones were incorporated for symbolic reasons.

4.8 BONE TWEEZERS

TYPO-CHRONOLOGY

A series of 12 bone objects thought to be tweezers were listed by Proudfoot (1963, Appendix IV and 412–4). Ten of these were examined (Table 4.8.1) and are illustrated in Figure 4.8.1.They are mainly found in Wessex (*ibid*, fig. 10), with the addition of one more recently excavated example from Barrow Hills, Oxfordshire (Barclay and Halpin 1999, figs. 4.82 and 4.83) and a probable fragment from Carsington, Derbyshire (Harding *et al.* 2005, fig.5). Proudfoot drew attention to the variations in head form and placement of perforations, and discussed the grave associations. Where the nature of the burial is known, all were cremations and, where identified, these were of adult men. Six were associated with daggers (usually of Series 5), four with perforated whetstones and one with beads of jet, amber and probably faience (Kingston Deverill G9, lost). Another commonly occurring association however is a bone pin (six instances). In many cases these pins are finely polished and various special forms are represented: crutch-headed (with ID 1050), spirally decorated (with ID 1052) and ring-headed at Wilsford G56 (ID 918) and Barrow Hills (see above; also Chapter 5.5). The tweezers appear to be a British type, although some have similarities with bronze tweezers in Europe (Proudfoot 1963, 412). It had been thought that the Wessex items were made from bird bones, but Proudfoot felt that they were more likely made from long bones of pig or sheep. The first definitive identifications of the bones employed will be found below. A further single find of possible tweezers that are triangular in shape is known from Derbyshire (ID 695).

MORPHOLOGY

The tweezers all have a round or oval head, reflecting the shape of the bone used, and two wide and rigid arms extending below. They vary in length from 31.1 to 70.5mm, but most examples are around 5.0 to 5.5mm long (see Figure 4.8.2). The one from Edmonsham (ID 1052) is significantly smaller, and that from Wilsford G56 (ID 918) the longest. Several of the items have an oval cross-section and this, plus the fairly standard diameters of the heads (8.1 to 11mm, and see Figure 4.8.2) are related to the shape and size of the animal bones employed for their manufacture.

In five cases the head is simply formed and slightly squared in profile. However one of these (ID 1025, Figure 4.8.3d) has a slight neck, and with longer necks there are four examples which also have a lipped top formed by a pronounced flange (ID 766, ID 916, Upton Lovell G2d and ID 1052). On two of these (ID 916, Figure 4.8.3c and Upton Lovell G2d) there are further embellishments in the form of flanges extending part way down the two arms. All the pieces are finely finished and well polished. All are perforated through the top, with the holes varying between 2.0 and 7.5mm in diameter. Four have further perforations through the neck, twice from arm to arm (ID 1024 and Upton Lovell G2d) and twice above the junction of the two arms (ID 919 and ID 1025). These holes vary in diameter from 2.0 to 4.8mm. In only one case do the two arms touch each other at their tips; otherwise the gap between the arms varies (see ID 766, Figure 4.8.3a) and is sometimes as wide as 7mm.

MATERIAL

All the tweezers are made from limb bones of a medium-sized mammal, of sheep/goat size, except for one piece (ID 1050) which is formed from the limb bone of a large mammal. Amongst the sheep/goat bones used, seven were the distal shaft of the tibia and one only the proximal shaft of a metatarsal (ID 1024). The Barrow Hills tweezers are made from a metapodial, again from sheep or goat (Barclay and Halpin 1999, 148).

MANUFACTURE

All the pieces are finely finished and well polished. Four items are recorded as having high polish and this also applies to the tweezers from Barrow Hills (Barclay and Halpin 1999, 148). Although well polished, seven out of the nine items studied in detail retain traces of the polishing striations. These are usually longitudinal and faint, but a few examples of lateral or multidirectional striations on the top or neck (Figure 4.8.3c) also occur. In one case (ID 766) gouge marks are still visible below the head. In general the workmanship displays a high level of skill.

COMPLETENESS AND DAMAGE

Although three of the sets of tweezers are complete, or

Table 4.8.1. List of bone tweezers studied and illustrated.

Object	Site (Parish), County	Museum	Illustration
ID 695	Hanson Grange, Derbys.	Shef	Figure 4.8.1
ID 766	Aldbourne 284, 1, Wilts.	BM	Figure 4.8.1; Figure 4.8.3
ID 767	Bloxworth G4a, Dorset	BM	Figure 4.8.1
ID 916	Amesbury G11, Wilts.	Dev	Figure 4.8.1; Figure 4.8.3
ID 918	Wilsford G56, Wilts.	Dev	Figure 4.8.1
ID 919	Winterbourne Stoke G4, Wilts.	Dev	Figure 4.8.1
ID 1024	Handley G24, Dorset	Sal	Figure 4.8.1
ID 1025	Laverstock and Ford, Wilts.	Sal	Figure 4.8.1; Figure 4.8.3
ID 1050	Dewlish G7, Dorset	Dor	Figure 4.8.1
ID 1052	Edmondsham G2, Dorset	Dor	Figure 4.8.1; Figure 4.8.3

virtually so, four have lost one or both of the arms, and survive at 30% to 70% levels. This damage appears to have occurred since excavation and is a factor of the extreme fragility of these finely crafted pieces.

WEAR

All the tweezers seem to have been used, although seven are only slightly worn. One is classified as worn, and two as with heavy wear. Most of the wear traces are general ancient scuffs and scratches which lie over the polishing striations. These may occur all over the surfaces, or in four cases on the mid to lower exterior surfaces of the arms.

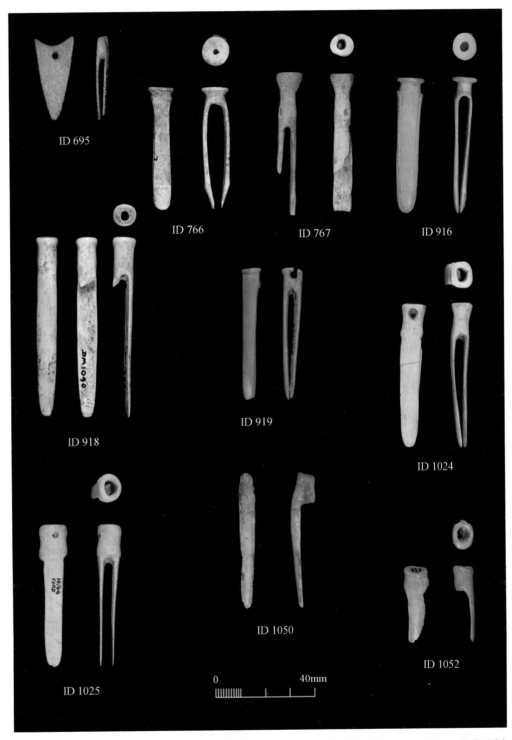

Figure 4.8.1. Examples of bone tweezers studied. ID 695 Hanson Grange; ID 766 Aldbourne 284, 1; ID 767 Bloxworth G4a; ID 916 Amesbury G11; ID 918 Wilsford G56; ID 919 Winterbourne Stoke G4; ID 1024 Handley G24; ID 1025 Laverstock and Ford; ID 1050 Dewlish G7; ID 1052 Edmonsham G2 (part of).

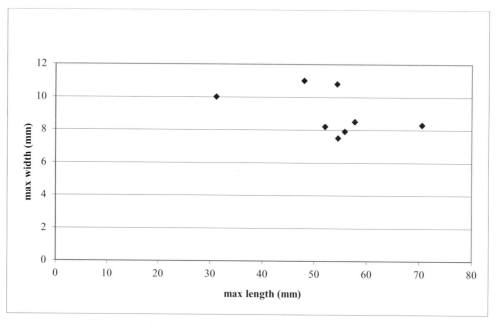

Figure 4.8.2. Bone tweezers: dimensions.

Where the tips survive there are no obvious traces of wear at the tips of the arms (ID 916, Figure 4.8.3b). Detailed study of all perforations showed that mostly these show no signs of thread- or string-wear. However in one case (ID 1052) the perforation in the top surface has a strong thread- or string-pull (Figure 4.8.3e).

CONCLUSIONS

With the exception of the triangular pair from the Peak district, the sets of tweezers form a very unified group with a tight geographic distribution. Also most are made from a similar sheep or goat bone. However details of the forming of the head, location of perforations and addition of flanges or lips are quite variable. The use of the sheep/goat tibiae and metapodials may have been determined by practical factors: these may have been the best bones from which such a complex item could be fashioned. This, taken together with the variations in detailed form might argue against the tweezers having been made by a single craftsman or workshop.

Thomas (1966) pointed out that these items were probably not tweezers, as the arms are too inflexible for depilatory use. Also there is no sign of particular wear at the tips of the arms that might have been expected if they had been used regularly to remove hair from the chin, eyebrows or elsewhere on the human body. Although all had been used, the various perforations only show evidence of strong thread- or string-wear in one case. However, in the larger holes, a free-moving string is unlikely to have formed such wear traces. The perforations may have been employed to facilitate suspension from a belt or the neck, or may have held strings, or perhaps thongs, of a more practical nature, used in securing another item, or for encircling a bun of human hair.

Thomas (*ibid*) suggested that they may have been special clips, used perhaps to display ritual feathers, cloth, or even a scalp. Alternatively, as indicated above, they may have been used to secure a special hairstyle. The tweezers are often found in association with an elaborate bone pin and the two artefact types seem to have functioned as a very particular 'set'. Also the elements of such sets were often found placed next to each other in the grave (e.g. Barclay and Halpin 1999, fig. 4.83).

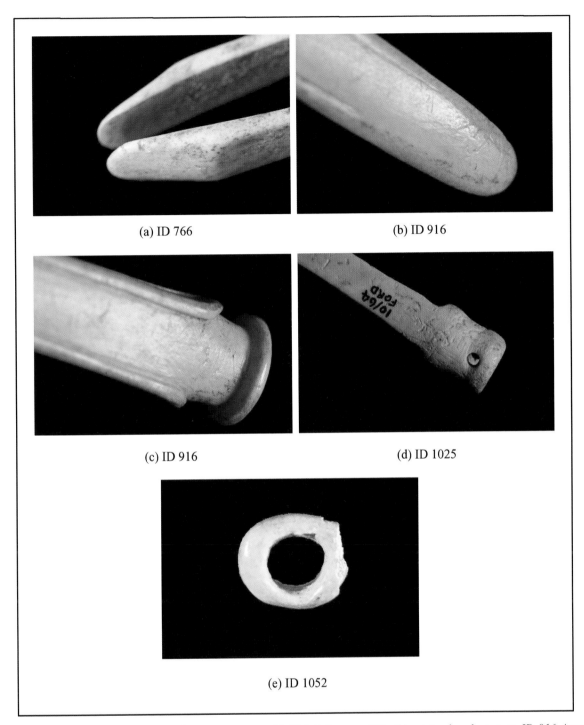

Figure 4.8.3. Details showing (a) gap between arms on ID 766 Aldbourne 284; (b) minimal end wear on ID 916 Amesbury G11; (c) striations on ID 916 Amesbury G11; (d) neck morphology on ID 1025 Laverstock and Ford; (e) stringwear on ID 1052 Edmonsham G2.

4.9 BONE TUBES

TYPO-CHRONOLOGY

A series of objects made from naturally hollow bones have not previously been considered as a group. Some or all of them may have functioned as wind instruments (flutes) or whistles. Seven items have been studied in detail, four of them with one or more perforations (Table 4.9.1; Figure 4.9.1). Six items were found in association with Early Bronze Age cremations. At Aldro (ID 609) the tube was burnt and the associated objects were a set of bone points and flint tools. In three other cases, urns were also present: a Collared Urn at Snailwell A (ID 848–49), along with a further set of antler and bone objects, and a Cordoned Urn at Eagleston Flat (ID 702). In the latter case the 'whistle' had been placed vertically within the top of the cremated bones of a child aged 5 to 8 years. Two of the cremations possessed rich accompaniments: a battle-axe, bronze awl, two bone points and a lost urn of unidentifiable type at Throwley (ID 666), and a group containing two daggers, a bronze crutch-headed pin and perforated whetstone at Wilsford G23 (ID 887). The inhumation of a man at Wilsford G58 (ID 922) included a battle-axe, bronze flanged axe, a unique pronged object, a bone plate, an antler handle, a tusk and a grooved stone. The cremation with ID 702 contained datable charcoal (see Chapter 9).

MORPHOLOGY

With the exception of ID 922, the tubes are all roughly similar in diameter, but highly variable in length (see Table 4.9.1), with evidence of cut marks (Figure 4.9.2d). The interiors are hollow, which is a natural characteristic of the bones used, and the walls relatively thin (Figure 4.9.1). In only one case (ID 922) has the interior of the bone been significantly scraped out. Two of them have been partly distorted by burning, either on the pyre, or through contact with the bones when they were still hot. Four of the tubes have perforations. In three cases there is just one hole, which pierces the front of the tube only, one placed centrally and in two cases at one end. One perforation is straight through (ID 702) and the other two funnel-shaped (e.g. Figure 4.9.2c). In all three cases the narrowest diameter of the hole, which would have been the functional dimension controlling air entry for a whistle, was similar at 3.2 to 3.9mm. A longer tube (ID 887) is made from a different kind of bone (see below) and appears to have had two original holes, of rather larger diameter. Although ID 609 has no perforations, there is an ancient notch on the medial surface of the bone, which forms the rear of the object (Figure 4.9.2a). This may have been a finger-hold, or have served to hold an organic element of the object, such as a reed. The longest tube, from Wilsford G58 (ID 922) has been damaged in recent years, but originally Goddard recorded that there was a side hole at the now damaged end (Thomas 1954, 323). Thomas tentatively suggested that this piece might have been a horn.

MATERIAL

All items except ID 887 and ID 922 are made from the tibia of a sheep or goat, using the portion towards the distal end of the bone in each case. Slight differences in size are due to the age of the animal exploited: for instance ID 849 is made from the bone of a smaller, probably younger, animal than ID 848. The longer piece, ID 887, is made from the shaft of a radius from a crane, again towards the distal end. The use of bones from this bird in prehistory is rare. The much more substantial piece from Wilsford G58 (ID 922) is made from a human femur. Colour varies from cream to grey and brown and reflects the natural colour of the bone employed.

MANUFACTURE

All the tubes have been very carefully finished, with high polish on all surfaces, and carefully formed ends which are often facetted. The polish also is sometimes more intense towards the ends. In five cases traces of faint or marked longitudinal polishing striations survive on the outer

Table 4.9.1. Bone tubes: dimensions and condition.

Object	Site (Parish), County	Museum	L. (mm)	Diam. top end (mm)	Perf. Diam. (mm)	Colour	Condition	Illustrations
ID 609	Aldro 52 (Birdsall), E. Yorks.	Hull	122	11.5 by 8.8	none	grey to black	Burnt	Figure 4.9.1; Figure 4.9.2
ID 666	Throwley, Staffs.	Shef	22.7	10 by 11	6 to 3.5	brown	Unburnt	Figure 4.9.1
ID 702	Eagleston Flat (Curbar), Derbys.	Shef	49.6	12.4 by 9.5	3.2	white/ cream	Partly burnt	Figure 4.9.1; Figure 4.9.2
ID 848	Snailwell A, Cambs.	Camb	106.7	14.2 by 14.5	7 to 3.9	cream	Unburnt	Figure 4.9.1; Figure 4.9.2
ID 849	Snailwell A, Cambs.	Camb	77	11.9 by 10.6	none	cream	Unburnt	Figure 4.9.1
ID 887	Wilsford G23, Wilts.	Dev	188	10 by 11.8	7	grey	Unburnt	Figure 4.9.1; Figure 4.9.2; Figure 4.9.3
ID 922	Wilsford G58, Wilts.	Dev	214	30.4 by 23.5	? side hole	grey	Unburnt	Figure 4.9.1

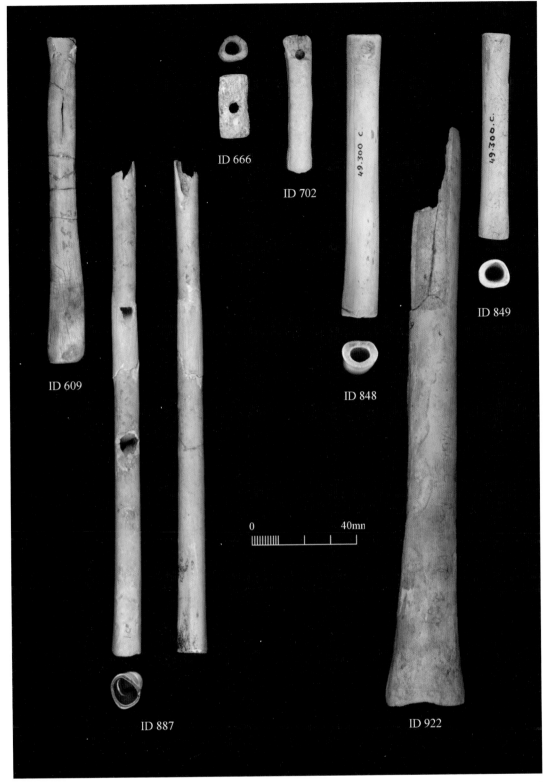

Figure 4.9.1. Bone tubes. ID 609 Aldro 52; ID 666 Throwley; ID 702 Eagleston Flat; ID 848 Snailwell A; ID 849 Snailwell A; ID 887 Wilsford G23; ID 922 Wilsford G58.

surfaces (e.g. Figure 4.9.2e), and in one case (ID 702) there are signs of marked longitudinal smoothing inside the tube. The facets on the two tubes from Snailwell A (ID 848 and 849) also display striations which are circumferential and faint on both pieces, and also diagonal on ID 849. In the case of ID 702 the perforation sits within a neatly formed horizontal groove (Figure 4.9.2b).

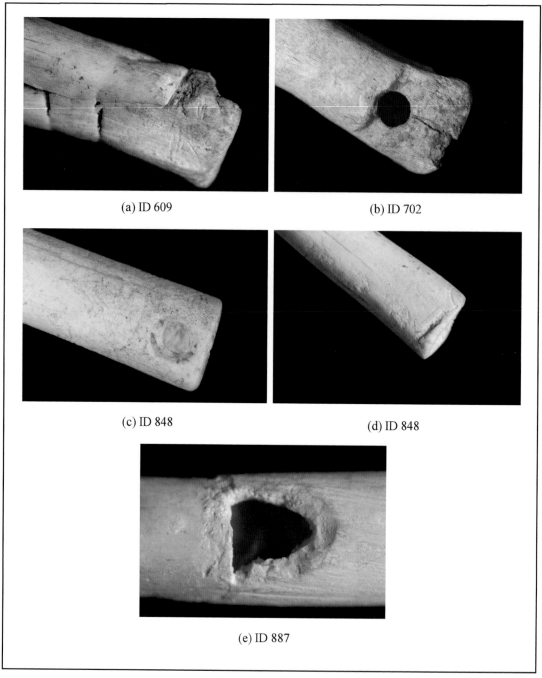

Figure 4.9.2. Details showing (a) notch on ID 609 Aldro 52;(b) perforation and groove on ID 702 Eagleston Flat; (c) funnel-shaped perforation and drilling on ID 848 Snailwell A; (d) cut mark on ID 848 Snailwell A; (e) striations and perforation on ID 887 Wilsford G23.

COMPLETENESS AND DAMAGE

All but one of the pieces survive at the 90% level or above. More broken is ID 609 (at 80%) where modern fractures and loss of material have been caused by the fragile nature of the burnt bone. Other pieces with modern breaks are ID 922 (see above) and ID 887. In the case of ID 887 the breaks are glued and it is known that the object was more complete when excavated by Colt Hoare and Cunnington.

WEAR

All items except ID 887 show evidence of ancient damage which is indicative of use. This damage includes some major breaks, but mainly comprises chips and nicks, often around the upper margin. Traces of use in the form of ancient scratches and scuffs are visible in four cases. On two tubes, ID 666 and ID 887, such wear was greater on the front side, and in the case of ID 849 use sheen was most prominent towards the wider end. On ID 887 the major break lies at the point where the thumb and first

ID 702

Figure 4.9.3. ID 887 Wilsford G23 as a possible flute.

finger of the left hand would have rested, so therefore this may have been a worn and weak point. Overall three tubes were classed as slightly worn, three as worn and one (ID 666) as very worn.

CONCLUSIONS

All examples except the 'flute' from Wilsford G23 (ID 887) and the 'horn' from Wilsford G58 (ID 922) are made from the same animal bone and have one perforation or none. These may have functioned as simple whistles, with those lacking holes cross-blown. The finely made longer tube ID 609 also has a notch which may have served to hold an additional acoustic device such as a reed. The use of sheep/goat tibiae may have been determined by the need for a bone of particular form and dimensions, but also it

may have been chosen for symbolic reasons. Certainly the tube made from the wing bone of a crane is very unusual, and the choice of a bone from this bird may have had important ritual connotations. This piece, ID 887, had at least two perforations, and may originally have also had a thumb hole on the rear. It has been interpreted as a simple flute (Megaw 1968) (Figure 4.9.3). The fine finish on all items suggests that they were valuable and highly prized items, and such a conclusion is further indicated by their occurrence in three rich Early Bronze Age grave groups. Although the interpretation of these objects as possible wind instruments is preferred, it is also possible that some of the tubes, which sometimes occur in association with groups of bone points, may alternatively have functioned as elements within sets of hair ornaments (see Chapter 4.8 above).

4.10 BONE PLATES

TYPO-CHRONOLOGY

A series of five flat bone objects derive only from barrow contexts in Wiltshire. Four of these have been studied in detail (Table 4.10.1; Figure 4.10.1). Three of the plates possess perforations and these have previously been drawn together for discussion by Thomas (1954). The one from Norton Bavant G2 (ID 908) had previously been described as a wristguard (bracer), but Thomas was of the opinion that these perforated examples were versions of spacer plates for use in complex necklaces (*ibid*, 313, 319 and 324). Bone plates were associated with inhumations three times and cremation burials twice. All the grave groups belong to the Early Bronze Age and four of them are rich in goods, including the so-called shaman burial from Upton Lovell G2a (ID 904, not studied in detail). Two of the groups include a bronze axe (ID 902 Collingbourne Kingston G4; Wilsford G58; the former a miniature) and another a dagger (Wilsford G60). Other associations include grooved, perforated and plain whetstones, pins of bone and antler, a battle-axe, a bone mace-head and other items made from bone. No examples of beads are included. The sex of the body deposited has only been identified in one case: the 'very tall, stout man' from bell barrow Wilsford G58.

MORPHOLOGY

All the plates are rectangular in shape, and of fairly even thickness. They vary in length from 60.3 to 82.5mm. Most are between 14.9 and 21mm wide, but the example from Upton Lovell G2a (ID 904) would have been at least 48mm wide. They vary in thickness from 3 to 10.5mm. The plain plate from Wilsford G60 (ID 903) has evenly formed facets down the sides and the ends are carefully bevelled. Two pieces are curved longitudinally, reflecting the nature of the raw material employed (see below; also ID 902 and ID 903, Figure 4.10.2a and b). The placing of perforations is variable. On ID 908 they form a pair at one end, and there may have been a further pair at the other, missing, end. Two straight-through holes have been bored from side to side through the ends of ID 905, while ID 902 has two angled holes at one end and one at the other. On one piece, the broken item from Norton Bavant G2 (ID 908), there are transverse marks which reflect original binding, and microscopic study revealed the traces of copper alloy which had probably taken the form of wires; these wires would have been less than 1mm in width (Figure 4.10.2c).

MATERIAL

All the plates are made from rib shafts, derived from a large mammal, probably cow. Cancellous tissue is visible at the sawn ends, and within breaks.

MANUFACTURE

As stated above, all the plates have been neatly shaped and finished, with low to high polish. Two pieces have surviving faint longitudinal polishing striations on one or both faces, and three have diagonal or lateral striations on or near the ends. The perforations have been carefully drilled, but are in various different positions. The most complex are the three angled perforations near the ends of ID 902 (Figure 4.10.2d). In the published drawing (Annable and Simpson 1964 no. 383) these are shown as being curved, but in fact they are straight borings.

COMPLETENESS AND DAMAGE

The plates do not survive very well (60 to 95%, with only one at 95%); being thin they are rather fragile items. Much of the damage however is modern, including breaks at sides, ends and corners as well as some severe scratching on ID 903.

WEAR

Ancient breaks are not very common, but include the damage to the end of one side of ID 903 and the catastrophic break right across ID 908 from Norton Bavant G2. General wear is apparent only in two cases (ID 902 and ID 905), but the edges of the perforations seem to be crisp and unworn, where this can be determined (see Figure 4.10.2e, ID 908). It would appear that one of the plates was quite worn, but the perforations are very fresh (Figure 4.10.2d, ID 902) This may mean that the perforations were added as a later modification of this particular piece. Overall one plate is fresh, two slightly worn and one worn.

CONCLUSIONS

A small series of bone plates, all from Wiltshire burials, are variable in size and form. However all are made from ribs, probably of cattle. They are neatly made objects with a polished finish and three of them bear perforations in varying configurations. These items occur in rich grave groups of Early Bronze Age date. Due to their fragility they have not survived well, but most damage is modern. Wear is not heavy, and the perforations in particular

Table 4.10.1. List of bone plates studied and illustrated.

Object	Site (Parish), County	Museum	Illustration
ID 902	Collingbourne Kingston G4, Wilts.	Dev	Figure 4.10.1; Figure 4.10.2
ID 903	Wilsford G60, Wilts.	Dev	Figure 4.10.1; Figure 4.10.2
ID 905	Wilsford G58, Wilts.	Dev	Figure 4.10.1
ID 908	Norton Bavant G2, Wilts	Dev	Figure 4.10.1; Figure 4.10.2

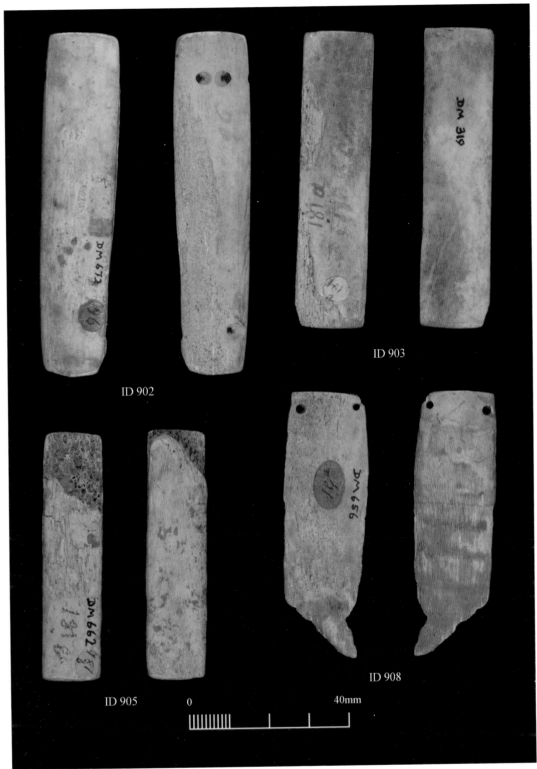

Figure 4.10.1. Bone plates. ID 902 Collingbourne Kingston G4; ID 903 Wilsford G60; ID 905 Wilsford G58; ID 908 Norton Bavant G2.

show no obvious signs of use for strings or cordage. The lack of thread wear in the perforations argues against an interpretation as spacer plates for necklaces, the suggestion that was made by Thomas (1954). Also they are not at all similar to the spacer plates in bone known from East Anglia (e.g. ID 1058–60 Feltwell Fen, all with notable thread

wear in various of the elbow perforations). It is difficult to see how the plates could have functioned in a necklace, and none of them are associated with beads of any kind. The lack of wear at the perforations would also rule out their use as belt fasteners or strap runners. The plates are very thin and one of them was embellished with further

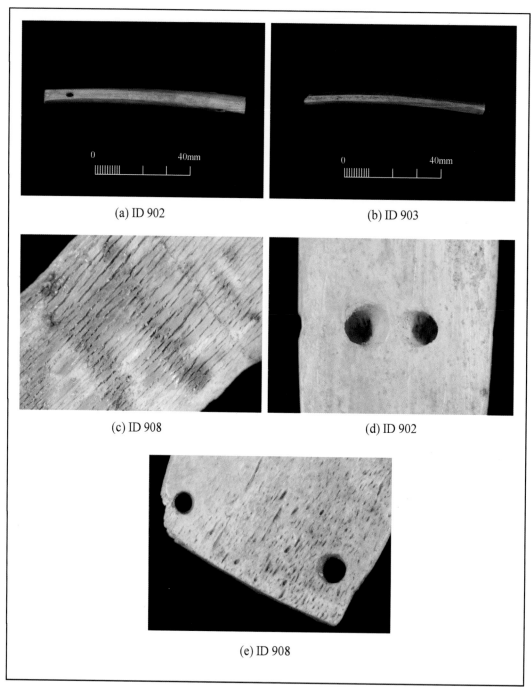

(a) ID 902

(b) ID 903

(c) ID 908

(d) ID 902

(e) ID 908

Figure 4.10.2. Details showing: curve of natural material (a) ID 902 Collingbourne Kingston G4 and (b) ID 903 Wilsford G6; (c) staining from possible copper alloy wire ID 908 Norton Bavant; (d) complex, fresh perforations on ID 902 Collingbourne Kingston G4; (e) crisp unworn perforations on ID 908 Norton Bavant.

fastenings in the form of contrasting copper wire. Although Thomas thought that an interpretation as wristguards was unlikely, it could be that these plates were intended to be fixed to leather or textile as ornaments for the lower arm. It is now accepted that the bracers made from stone

may often has functioned as *arm ornaments* rather than as functional wristguards (Woodward and Hunter 2011). Although unlikely to be wristguards as such, these plates could have been employed as ornaments for the lower arm, or indeed elsewhere on the body.

4.11 BONE TOGGLES

TYPO-CHRONOLOGY

Toggles are a rare form of grave good. They are always made from bone but occur in various forms (Figure 4.11.1). Five bone toggles have been found in rich Beaker graves which also contain stone bracers (although one of these is in Scotland). The simplest form of toggle are the tubes of small diameter with a single transverse perforation, occurring at Sewell (ID 722) and Thomas Hardye School (Gardiner *et al.* 2007, fig. 9,b) Six examples have been studied in detail here (Table 4.11.1). The long narrow toggle with protruding side perforation from Barnack grave 28 (ID 724) has no clear parallels. The broken perforated ring found at Hemp Knoll (ID 721) is also very unusual. On first glance it might be compared to the rare bone Class IIIb pulley rings found in Scotland (see Chapter 3.4). However the Beaker-age Class IIIb rings from Broomend and Mainsriddle (Clarke 1970, 360, figs 660 and 662), although of similar diameter to the Hemp Knoll example, are much more shallow. The ring from Culduthel Mains, also in Scotland (Clarke *et al.* 1985, fig. 4.16) is more similar in height to the Hemp Knoll piece, but neither of them could easily have functioned as belt rings, and both appear to be something rather different. The simpler elongated toggle with side perforation from burial 2 at Kelleythorpe (ID 723; *not* from the bracer grave which is burial 1) was associated with a Food Vessel. It can best be paralleled by a similar toggle, found with a second unusual bone perforated object and a Food Vessel, associated with a child inhumation in barrow 162 at Garton Slack (Mortimer 1905, fig. 531–2; not found at Hull Museum). The toggle with expanded ends (ID 914) probably came from a burial in a barrow at Bishops Cannings. It was found with a fragment of an amphibolite bracer reworked as a pendant. This type of toggle appears to imitate faience beads in form, and dates from the later part of the Early Bronze Age (Piggott 1958). Finally the long decorated toggle from Western Howe (ID 749) was found with an Early Bronze Age cremation, along with a battle-axe, accessory cup and fragments of four bone points.

MORPHOLOGY

As already seen the group of toggles vary greatly in both form and size. The simplest item is the cylindrical piece from Sewell (ID 722), 28mm long with a single perforation of diameter 7.5mm in one side only. The longer toggles from Kelleythorpe 2 and Barnack (ID 723, length 53mm and ID 724, length 65.3mm) both have through-perforations in a protruding expansion roughly half way along the length. These perforations measure 4.2 by 3.8 by 6mm across respectively. The terminals of the Barnack example are also expanded. The broken ring from Hemp Knoll (ID 721) is of a different style, 28mm in diameter and 22.4mm deep. It has a double perforation with angled holes reminiscent of a V-perforation, measuring on average 7.3 by 6mm (Figure 4.11.2c). It is decorated with two deep circumferential grooves at top and bottom. The long narrow toggle from Western Howe (ID 749: of length 40.1 mm) is decorated with a single continuous spiral shallow groove, 1.5mm wide and less than 1mm in depth. In colour the pieces vary from buff to grey and light brown, with the example from Barnack stained green, probably from a copper alloy item in the grave.

MATERIAL

Most of the items studied in detail are made from the shafts of limb bones. The two smaller pieces, ID 722 and ID 914, are made from sheep-sized limb bones. Those which are rather longer, and with side loops, are made from the tibia of a cow (ID 723) and a long bone shaft from an unspecified large mammal i.e. cow or red deer (ID 724). The decorated piece (ID 749) is made from the distal shaft of a sheep-sized tibia. The broken ring from Hemp Knoll (ID 721) however is made from the stem of a red deer antler.

MANUFACTURE

In four cases the level of original surface finish could be determined. All were polished, with the degree of finish varying from low to high polish. All the toggles were neatly and carefully made. Due to the polish, traces of manufacture were not often visible. The only striations noted were on the non-perforated side of the Barnack toggle (ID 724) and, very faint, on the surfaces of the Western Howe piece (ID 749), while traces of shaping in the form of nicks and inclined chop marks are visible in the grooves on items ID 721 (Figure 4.11.2a) and ID 914.

COMPLETENESS AND DAMAGE

All the toggles survived entire in the grave, apart from one modern chip on one end of ID 723. In the case of the toggle

Table 4.11.1. List of bone toggles studied and illustrated.

Object	Site (Parish), County	Museum	Illustrations
ID 721	Hemp Knoll (Bishops Cannings), Wilts.	BM	Figure 4.11.1; Figure 4.11.2
ID 722	Sewell, Beds.	BM	Figure 4.11.1
ID 723	Kelleythorpe UN101, burial 1 (Great Driffield), E. Yorks.	BM	Figure 4.11.1
ID 724	Barnack 28, Cambs.	BM	Figure 4.11.1; Figure 4.11.2
ID 749	Western Howe (Westerdale: NYM10), N. Yorks.	BM	Figure 4.11.1
ID 914	Bishops Cannings, Wilts.	Dev	Figure 4.11.1; Figure 4.11.2

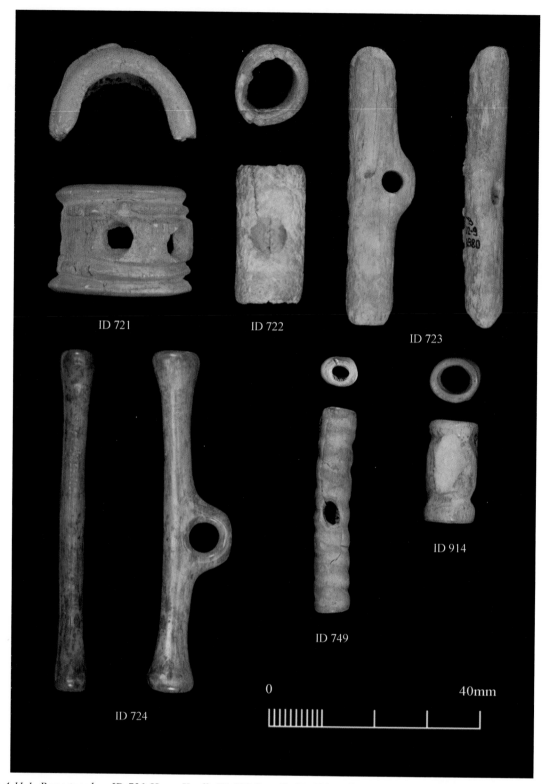

Figure 4.11.1. Bone toggles. ID 721 Hemp Knoll; ID 722 Sewell; ID 723 Kelleythorpe; ID 724 Barnack 28; ID 749 Western Howe; ID 914 Bishops Cannings.

from Hemp Knoll (ID 721) only half of the original ring survives, but in its secondary use life, it survived at 100%.

WEAR

The only ancient break on any of the toggles is that right

across the Hemp Knoll piece. The broken edges had been smoothed over in order that the piece could be re-used, presumably in a slightly different way. Any wear on ID 722 could not be determined due to erosion of the surface. The Kelleythorpe toggle, ID 723, displays extreme wear and tear on all surfaces, and there are several rows of diagonal

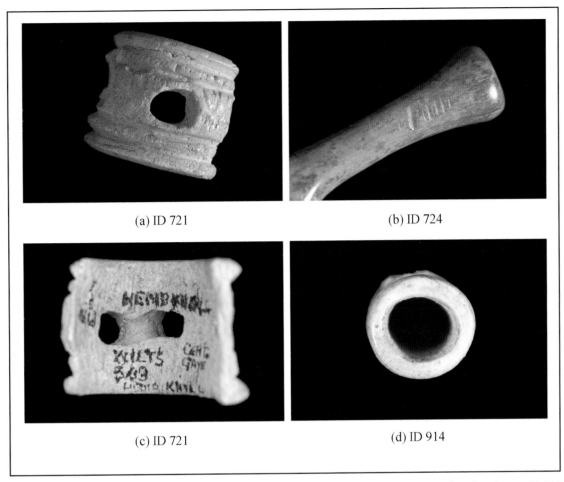

(a) ID 721

(b) ID 724

(c) ID 721

(d) ID 914

Figure 4.11.2. Details showing (a) chop marks within grooves and string wear on outer margin of perforation on ID 721 Hemp Knoll; (b) nicks on ID 724 Barnack; (c) rear of angled holes on ID 721 Hemp Knoll; (d) string/cord wear on end of ID 914 Bishops Cannings.

nicks on the Barnack toggle (ID 724, Figure 4.11.2b). How these nicks had occurred is not entirely clear, but they do seem to have been due to use. Otherwise this piece seemed to be very fresh. String- or cord-wear is visible in three cases: on the outer margins of the perforation pair on ID 721 (Figure 4.11.2a), on the outer margin of the side perforation on the Kellythorpe toggle (ID 723) and in one end of the toggle with expanded ends from Bishops Cannings (ID 914, Figure 4.11.2d). Overall one toggle was classified as fresh (Barnack), two as slightly worn and two as very worn (ID 723 and ID 749).

CONCLUSIONS

The varied set of perforated toggles is made from animal limb bones or antler. They are highly variable in terms of size, overall morphology and the location of side perforations, but they seem to form a functional group of items which are found in Beaker graves of mature males that also contain stone bracers, and also in Food Vessel graves in Yorkshire. Of a total eight examples known from bracer graves, the position in relation to the body was recorded in five cases (Woodward and Hunter 2011, Ch 8). Three times the toggle was placed on the left side of the body:

once at the thigh (ID 721 Hemp Knoll), once at the left elbow (ID 724 Barnack) and once at the left arm (Thomas Hardye School). Another was positioned on the chest (ID 722 Sewell). It therefore seems unlikely that these toggles functioned as belt fasteners. Instead they were all situated in a zone that would have been close to the bracer, which in all these cases was situated on the left lower arm. It seems possible therefore that the toggles may have possessed a specific function that was related to the use of the stone bracers. The two toggles from Food Vessel graves also seem to have been special pieces of equipment. That from Kelleythorpe was found with a ball of metal and a strip of metal and wood. The metal was described as iron by the excavator (Londesborough 1851), but may well have been of some alloy or mineral. All the items were found in the hand of one of the two skeletons in the grave. The similar toggle and a second perforated bag-shaped toggle from Garton Slack 162 (not available for study) were found beside the skull in the burial of a child. Composite pieces of equipment seem to be implied. The toggle with expanded ends from Bishops Cannings (ID 914) and the decorated piece from Western Howe (ID 749) are of different style and were found with cremation burials: they probably date rather later than the other toggles considered in this section.

4.12 MISCELLANEOUS OBJECTS OF BONE AND ANTLER

4.12.1 ANTLER HANDLES

TYPO-CHRONOLOGY

Antler handles have never been listed or discussed previously. The items from graves considered here are probably the only handles of Early Bronze Age date which have survived in the archaeological record, and thus they are of great importance (Figure 4.12.1). The five examples (Table 4.12.1) all derive from primary graves: two inhumations, one cremation and two of unknown type. The associations are wide-ranging, within a series of rich, but lesser known, Wessex Series graves. They include four grooved whetstones, four daggers, three bone plates, two bone/antler spatulae, one awl, one bronze pronged object, one bronze miniature chisel, one miniature bronze axe, one battle-axe, one barbed-and-tanged arrowhead, one tusk and one antler point.

MORPHOLOGY

One long and narrow handle (ID 889), of length 42mm, was found *in situ* on the bronze awl from Winterbourne Stoke G5. The others are wider and less uniform in shape; lengths vary from 73.4 to 120.1mm, widths from 24.4 to 41.2mm and their thicknesses from 17.2 to 24.8mm. They usually have one main perforation, to hold a blade, at one end only. However one (ID 888) has another attempted perforation at the proximal end, and another two (ID 891 and ID 1002) have perforations, of varying dimensions, at both ends.

MATERIAL

All the handles are made from deer antler, the larger ones all of red deer. The material derives from the stem and tine or stem and top of the antler, and colours vary from cream to brown.

MANUFACTURE

The original rough surface of the antler is usually evident, but three items are polished in part. These display longitudinal polishing striations or faceting.

COMPLETENESS AND DAMAGE

All survive at the 95% level or above except for ID 988 (65%). There is a little damage, but most of the breaks are ancient.

WEAR

Ancient damage comprises splits at the main perforated end, or at both ends. Most also have scuffing and scratches, or smoothing of the handle surface resulting from use. Altogether, three are classified as worn, and two as very

Table 4.12.1. List of antler and miscellaneous bone objects studied and illustrated.

Object	Site (Parish), County	Museum	Illustration
4.12.1 Antler Handles			
ID 888	Collingbourne Kingston G4, Wilts.	Dev	Figure 4.12.1
ID 889	Winterbourne Stoke G5, Wilts.	Dev	Figure 4.12.1
ID 891	Wilsford G58, Wilts.	Dev	Figure 4.12.1
ID 988	Roundway G5b, Wilts.	Dev	Figure 4.12.1
ID 1002	Amesbury G85, Wilts.	Sal	Figure 4.12.1
4.12.2 Bone and Antler Tools			
ID 619	Acklam Wold 211 (Acklam), E. Yorks.	Hull	Figure 4.12.2
ID 620	Hanging Grimston 26 (Thixendale), E. Yorks.	Hull	Figure 4.12.2; Figure 4.12.3
ID 639	Garton Slack 162 (Garton-on-the-Wolds), E. Yorks.	Hull	Figure 4.12.2; Figure 4.12.3
ID 747	Crosby Garrett 176, 2, Cumbria	BM	Figure 4.12.2
ID 836	Snailwell A, Cambs.	Camb	Figure 4.12.2; Figure 4.12.3
ID 893	Wilsford G60, Wilts.	Dev	Figure 4.12.2; Figure 4.12.3
ID 1001	Amesbury G85, Wilts.	Sal	Figure 4.12.2
4.12.3 Antlers			
ID 633	Life Hill 270, E.Yorks.	Hull	Figure 4.12.4; Figure 4.12.5
ID 700	Galley Low (Brassington), Derbys.	Shef	Figure 4.12.4
ID 1006	Amesbury G85, Wilts.	Sal	Figure 4.12.4
ID 1008-10	Rockbourne, Hants.	Sal	Figure 4.12.4; Figure 4.12.5
ID 1011-12	Figheldean G25c, Wilts.	Sal	Figure 4.12.4; Figure 4.12.5
4.12.4 Other Items			
ID 835	Bloxworth, Dorset	BM	Not illustrated
ID 892	Winterbourne Stoke G28, Wilts.	Dev	Figure 4.12.6
ID 900	Wimborne St Giles, Dorset	Dev	Figure 4.12.6
ID 1016	Wilsford Shaft G33a, Wilts.	Sal	Not illustrated

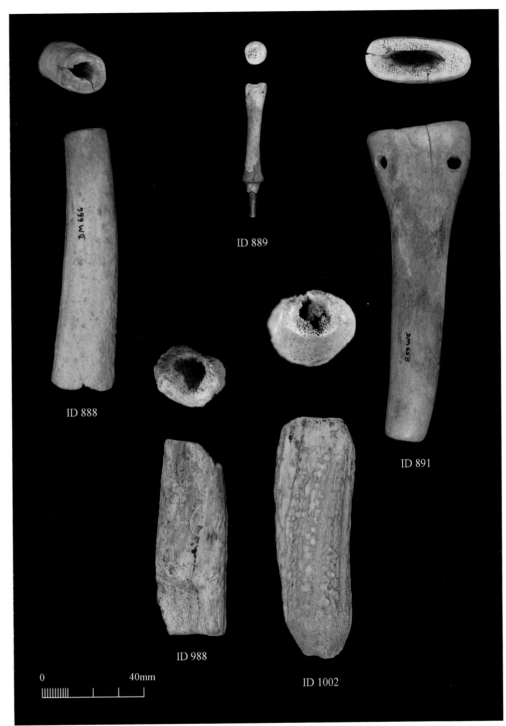

Figure 4.12.1. Antler handles. ID 888 Collingbourne Kingston G4; ID 889 Winterbourne Stoke G5; ID 891 Wilsford G58; ID 988 Roundway G5b; ID 1002 Amesbury G85.

worn. Also two items show signs of re-use: after the splitting of ID 888 during use, a new perforation was attempted at the other end, and in the case of ID 891 there are perforations at both ends. The perforation at the wider end may have held the associated bronze axe-head (ID 1438), or a flint knife, dagger or sickle, while the top socket may have supported a pommel. The pair of pristine perforations may have been original or secondary additions (Figure 4.12.1).

CONCLUSIONS

This small group of handles for bronze tools is of particular interest. All were much-used and some much-modified during their use life, and thus they appear to have been important and valuable items. Some were selected as grave goods even though they were separated from the tool with which they were last associated. It may be therefore that, like some of the dagger pommels, made from bone, antler and ivory, the handles were significant heirlooms or valuables in their own right. Although some are apparently unprepossessing in their form, it is possible that the raw material used, red deer antler, was specifically chosen and symbolically charged.

4.12.2 BONE AND ANTLER TOOLS

TYPO-CHRONOLOGY

Bone or antler tools have not been gathered together or discussed previously. The seven items (Figure 4.12.2; Table 4.12.1) all come from Early Bronze Age graves, some of them inhumations and some cremations. In two cases the sex of the burial could be determined, both being female (ID 639 and ID 747). Morphology varies, so the pieces will be described individually.

ID 619 and ID 620. Two flat tools made on cattle ribs. Both are broken at the proximal end, but the widths are 39 and 23.8mm, thicknesses 10 and 6.5mm respectively. Although superficially similar to the spatulae from Beaker graves these later pieces are wider, thicker and more uneven in shape. ID 619 was found in a Food Vessel burial. Both are polished, and both display breaks of modern and ancient date. Longitudinal marked striations on one side of ID 620 may be from polishing (Figure 4.12.3), but those on the front of ID 619 result from the initial defleshing of the bone. Wear traces include diagonal and multidirectional scratching, and both are classified as very worn. Unlike the Beaker-associated spatulae wear was not concentrated at the oval ends and their specific use remains unknown.

ID 639. Pointed tool or weapon 265mm long, termed a 'dagger' by Mortimer, made from a human tibia. The piece shows signs of gnawing (Figure 4.12.3) but was found below the cremation burial in the grave of an elderly female. It is whole, but broken across in two places in modern times. There are faint longitudinal polishing striations present towards the pointed end, and the tip is rounded and worn through use, but the degree of wear is classified as indeterminate.

ID 747. Fragment of a bone tool with a tapered end, possibly a chisel, of width 11.5mm and thickness 7mm. It is made from a metatarsal, probably deer, and was found in the grave of a woman and two infants, along with a decorated bone barrel bead, bone point and a single jet spacer plate. The side facets are polished and breakage appears to have been suffered during use. Wear is especially evident on one facet, and the piece is classified as worn.

ID 836. A double-perforated antler object formed from the stem and tine of a roe deer antler. The maximum width is 25mm and the diameter of the basal perforation 17mm. It was found with a cremation under a Collared Urn, in association with a set of perforated bone points and two bone tubes. The surface is rough and it is 95% present. Most damage is modern, but there is an ancient chip on the basal margin. The upper and lower facets of the wider element have faint concentric striations related to manufacture, and there are six grooves below the tine (Figure 4.12.3), and one near the top, all of which relate to the initial butchery and

tidying up of the object. All the surfaces display smoothing due to use but unfortunately the tip of the tine, which may have been the main business end, is missing. The two end perforations join to form a large hourglass profiled hole, but no signs of use or wear are visible on the edges of the perforations. Overall the item is classified as very worn, but its actual use remains unknown.

ID 893. Mace-head or hammer made from a stem of red deer antler. This is the only such item to have been found in the Early Bronze Age graves studied. It was found in association with a cremation, dagger, whetstones and a bone plate. The piece measures 62.7 by 25.0 by 21.5mm, and is perforated with a hole of hourglass shape with external diameter 17mm and minimum diameter 11mm. The surface is rough and one corner of the narrower tapered end is broken off. This damage is ancient and may have occurred at the time of manufacture. The piece may be unfinished and there is a shallow trial hole on one side of the tapered end. Also there is an aborted perforation in the tapered terminal (Figure 4.12.3), and hack marks towards that same end. It may be a trial piece, or perhaps an attempt had been made to convert it to a handle. The overall wear category is indeterminate. The piece was obviously important, possibly under conversion to a handle, and made from the same raw material as the handles discussed above.

ID 1001. Broken fragment of an elongated artefact made from antler, probably red deer. The piece is too uneven and thick to have been part of a spatula, and the broken end appears to have been reworked as a facet. The head end is roughly pyramidal in form. The width is 14.4mm and the thickness 6.5mm, increasing to 10.0mm at the head. It was found in a rich Early Bronze Age grave, along with antler ID 1006, below. The surfaces are smoothed through wear, but there are no signs of particular wear at the refashioned tip. It is classfied as worn.

4.12.3 ANTLERS

TYPO-CHRONOLOGY

Worked antlers from graves have not previously been listed or discussed. Eight are discussed here (Figure 4.12.4; Table 4.12.1). They mostly derive from Early Bronze Age graves. One (ID 633) comes from a probably female Food Vessel grave, while others (ID 1006 and ID 1011–12) derive from rich Early Bronze Age graves associated with daggers, tusks and grooved whetstones.

ID 633. Unshed complete roe deer antler 22.5mm long, with cuts and skinning marks from the original butchery of the skull (Figure 4.12.5a). Two tines have been sliced off neatly and the end of the surviving tine carefully smoothed. A zone of diagonal scratches near the point results from use and the surviving tine shows general smoothing of the rough surface through use. It is classified as worn. Lack of wear at the tip itself suggests that the antler was not used as a tool. Any wear at the lower end is not visible due to modern breakage at the pedicle.

ID 700. The shaft of a tine from a red deer antler, of

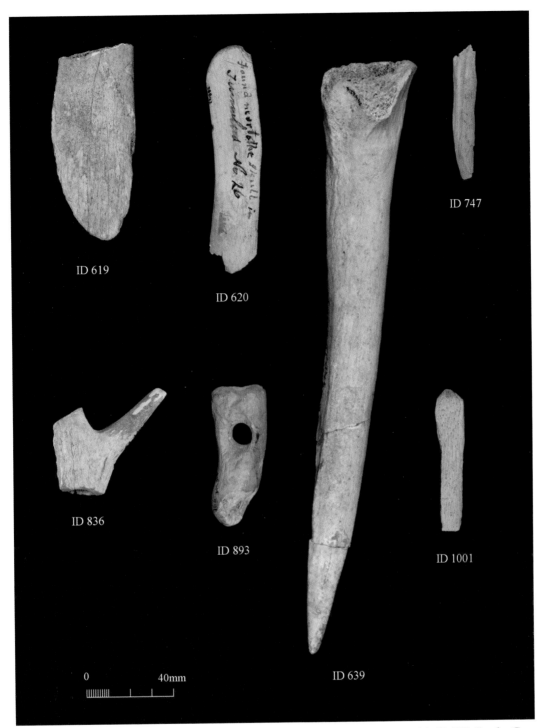

Figure 4.12.2. Bone and antler tools. ID 619 Acklam Wold 211; ID 620 Hanging Grimston 26; ID 747 Crosby Garrett 176, 2; ID 639 Garton Slack 162; ID 893 Wilsford G60; ID 836 Snailwell A; ID 1001 Amesbury G85.

maximum diameter 15mm, had been sawn through and deliberately pointed towards the thicker end. The surfaces are polished, but the tip was damaged in antiquity such that any wear at that point cannot be determined.

ID 1006. Tops from a red deer antler, maximum length 185mm, maximum thickness of shaft 28mm. Two grooves on the longer tine and one on the shaft are deliberate and may date from the time of manufacture. One tip has been broken in recent times and glued in place. Overall the surface is very smoothed from much handling, and it is classified as very worn. There are no signs that the points had been used as tools.

ID 1008–1010. Three pieces from a complete red deer antler – stem, trez tine and tops – were found separately at the head of a crouched inhumation which may have been of Beaker date. The antler is white and fresh, and the three pieces join exactly. Thus the antler, which is otherwise not humanly worked, was deliberately cut into three pieces

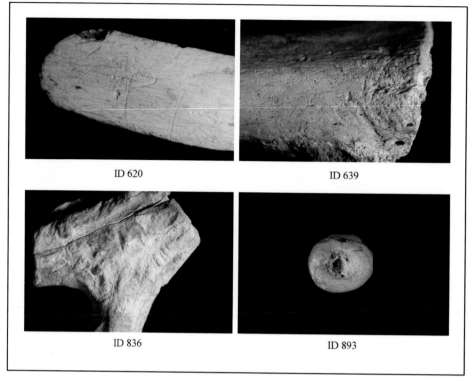

Figure 4.12.3. Bone and antler tools. Details showing polishing on ID 620 Hanging Grimston 26; gnaw marks on ID 639 Garton Slack 162; manufacture marks on ID 836 Snailwell A; an aborted attempt to form a handle on ID 893 Wilsford G60.

prior to its deposition in the grave (Figure 4.12.5b). All four points are polished all round. Wear traces in the form of random but marked, multidirectional scratches is present near all terminal tips, but not at the tips themselves. It is classed as worn (Figure 4.12.5c).

ID 1011–12. Two shed sets of roe deer tops. They are from opposite sides of the head but probably not from the same animal, due to the difference in size. The lengths are 232 and 168mm, maximum widths 24 and 18mm respectively. The surfaces are mainly rough and ID 1011 has some modern damage at the base, and ancient damage to both tips. There are clear signs of polishing, in the form of longitudinal and diagonal striations, on both tines of ID 1011, and on ID 1012 both tines have been slightly trimmed to enhance the shape. The lower end of ID 1012 has been modified by chop marks and smoothing to form a roughly faceted terminal (Figure 4.12.5d), and there has also been minor enhancement of the shape of the butt end of ID 1011. There are no clear signs of use wear apart from sporadic scratches on ID 1011, and wear traces are absent at the tips of the tines. This indicates that the antlers are unlikely to have been used as tools. ID 1011 is classed as worn and ID 1012 as slightly worn.

CONCLUSIONS

Piggott (1962) originally suggested that antlers such as these, with no signs of use as tools, may have formed part of cult head-dresses. Moore and Rowlands (1972, 48) thought that the fact that the ends of some of the tines on ID 1011–12 show wear and polishing indicated possible

use as tools in some craft process. However, our detailed microscopic study suggests that there is no relevant use wear to support this idea, and the polishing was achieved in order to enhance the appearance of the antlers. The shaping of the base areas would not be necessary for a tool, as it is unlikely that such large items would ever have been hafted, and this shaping may rather have been designed to facilitate the mounting of the antlers in some kind of head gear made primarily from perishable materials, such as cloth or leather.

4.12.4 OTHER ITEMS *(Table 4.12.1)*

ID 835. Bloxworth. The upper portion of a broken point or pendant of surviving length 16.5mm, width 6.3mm and thickness 5.6mm. The oval hourglass perforation measures 2.8 by 3.2mm. This piece does not fall into the size or shape range of perforated bone points, so may be an unusual pendant of elongated shape. It is made from the limb bone of a large mammal, not ivory as has previously been thought. It was found beneath a Collared Urn with a cremation, along with seven jet beads, four of faience and a set of bone tweezers. The piece is burnt, so probably went through the pyre and was broken as a result of that process. Its wear category is indeterminate.

ID 892. A circular domed object with a central perforation, made from the acetabulum of a human femur (Figure 4.12.6a). It was found with a primary cremation, an awl and a Food Vessel Urn. The diameter is 37.5mm and the diameter of the perforation, which is slightly eccentrically placed, is 9.5mm. One side of the piece, which survives

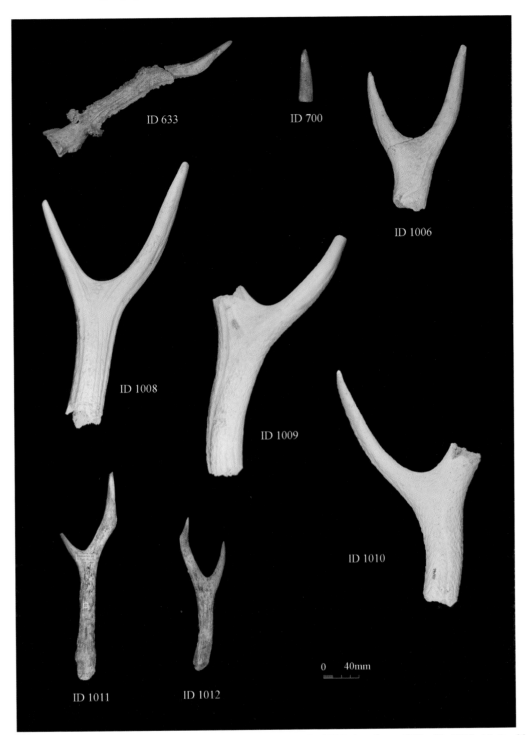

Figure 4.12.4. Antlers. ID 633 Life Hill 270; ID 700 Galley Low; ID 1006 Amesbury G85; ID 1008–10 Rockbourne; ID 1011–12 Figheldean G25c.

at the 70% level, was broken away in antiquity. There is possible string wear on one zone of the upper edge of the perforation. This object is unlikely to be a spindle whorl as the base is neither flat nor solid. It may have functioned as a large decorative stud, attached to a garment, or as a pendant within a necklace. It is classified as worn.

ID 900. This unique piece is formed from shed roe deer tops times three (Figure 4.12.6b). The distinct bend in the shaft is probably the result of abnormal growth on the animal. It was found as the sole grave good with a primary inhumation. The maximum length is 130mm. All surfaces are smooth and polished. One tine was broken away in antiquity, but a modern fracture across the centre is glued. There are longitudinal and diagonal polishing striations in patches all around the main shaft, and faint lateral striae towards the right angle bend. Towards the proximal end the shaft has been worked to produce a necked effect, and the resulting gouge marks survive. A straight perforation part way along the shaft measures 8 by 7mm. There is a bow drill mark surviving on one side. There is no wear of

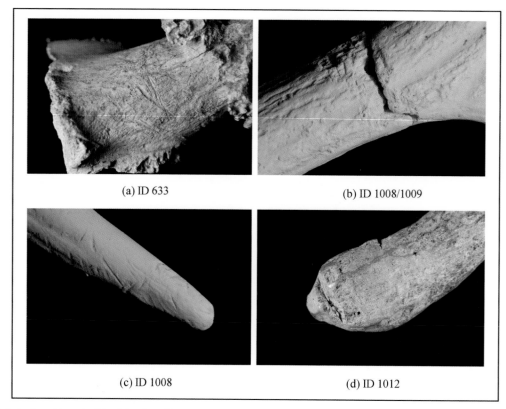

Figure 4.12.5. Antlers. Details. ID 633 Life Hill showing cut marks; ID 1008–9 Rockbourne showing deliberate chopped fracture; ID 1008 Rockbourne showing wear near tip; ID 1012 Figheldean G25c showing possible faceted terminal.

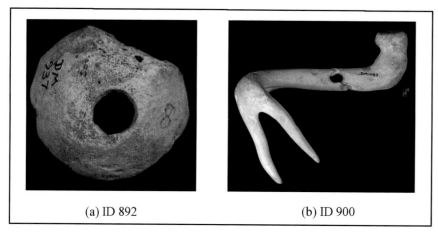

Figure 4.12.6. ID 892 Winterbourne Stoke G28 from part of human femur; ID 900 Wimborne St Giles G18 deer tops showing perforation.

any kind on the tines and none at the perforation either. However the proximal end has straight scratches on the flat end, and in general this end is rounded, blunted and very worn. The object does not appear to have functioned as a pendant, due to the absence of wear at the perforation. It is possible that it was designed and used as a soft hammer or possibly a drumstick, and it is classified as very worn.

ID 1016. A length of worked bone found in the fill of the Wilsford Shaft. It was near to a perforated bone point, but above the level of deposition of sherds of Globular Urn

(Middle Bronze Age). It appeared to the excavator to have been marked with a series of deliberate notches. The piece is made from the limb bone of a large mammal and bears longitudinal and lateral striations from initial polishing. The notches seem to be part of the initial shaping of the artefact and do not relate to use (e.g. as tally marks). The piece does not appear to have been used as an artefact, but does display signs of animal gnawing. The wear category is therefore indeterminate.

4.13 MISCELLANEOUS OBJECTS OF COPPER ALLOY (with Stuart Needham)

Table 4.13.1. List of miscellaneous copper alloys studied and illustrated.

Object	Site (Parish), County	Museum	Illustrations
4.13.1 Copper Alloy Axes			
ID 1293	Butterwick 39, burial 1, E.Yorks.	BM	Figure 4.13.1
ID 1403	Wilsford G5 (Bush Barrow), Wilts.	Dev	Figure 4.13.1; Figure 4.13.2
ID 1438	Wilsford G58, Wilts.	Dev	Figure 4.13.1
ID 1268	Weymouth G8 (Ridgeway 7), Dorset	Dor	Figure 4.13.1; Figure 4.13.2
4.13.2 Sheet Fragments			
ID 1441	Winterbourne Stoke G4, Wilts.	Dev	Not illustrated
4.13.3 Pronged Object			
ID 1437	Wilsford G58, Wilts.	Dev	Figure 4.13.3

4.13.1 COPPER ALLOY AXES

TYPO-CHRONOLOGY

Flat, low-flanged and flanged axes mostly occur in hoards, and very rarely derive from burial contexts. Thirteen well recorded examples are known across Britain (Needham *et al.* 2010, 19), the axes in question ranging from full size examples to very diminutive representations. Of these funerary finds, four have been studied in detail (Figure 4.13.1; Table 4.13.1). Three were associated with rich burials of the Wessex series: Bush Barrow (ID 1403 Wilsford G5), Ridgeway 7 (ID 1268, Weymouth G8) and Wilsford G58 (ID 1438, associated with the pronged object described below). These axes are all low-flanged, two being of indigenous Type Willerby, the third (Wilsford G58) being of Armorican style or inspiration (Woodward and Needham 2012). Other axes from graves belong to Needham's slightly earlier Mile Cross Assemblage, including the flat axe associated with a Series 2 (F3) dagger in the Shuttlestone barrow, Parwich, Derbyshire, which has recently been radiocarbon dated (Needham *et al.* 2010). The fourth axe studied in detail is of the still earlier Migdale type (ID 1293 Butterwick), found with a Series 2 (A) dagger and a set of jet/jet-like and stone V-perforated buttons.

MORPHOLOGY

In detail the axes studied present a variety of forms and sizes. The relatively broad body of the Butterwick example is typical of those early in the sequence, whereas the Bush Barrow example shows in extreme the trend towards a narrowing of the body. Nevertheless, cutting edges remain broad throughout so that the lower expansion becomes more pronounced. Of the indigenous types (i.e. excluding Wilsford G58), only Butterwick lacks a central stop bevel. Lengths vary from 82.9 to 158mm, maximum widths from 16.1 to 66.5mm and thicknesses from 6.6 to 10.5mm. ID 1438 appears to be a particularly small example, in line with some others from grave contexts (Needham 1988, 233).

MATERIAL

Three of the axes have been analysed. That from Butterwick (ID 1293) is of Irish A metal, the Bush Barrow one (ID 1403) is of recycled metal and that from Wilsford G58 (ID 1438) is of clean metal (information from Peter Bray).

MANUFACTURE

Two of the axes retain traces of final polishing, in the form of longitudinal striations on the upper zones of both faces. The Butterwick axe, ID 1293, was polished to a high degree.

COMPLETENESS AND DAMAGE

All except Weymouth G8 (ID 1268) survive at the 95% level or above. The axe from Weymouth G8 is broken across the butt, and on one side of the blade edge. This damage was in part modern in date; however, more than 90% of the axe still survives. Small modern chips on a blade corner or the blade edge are also present on the other three axes studied in detail. Two items, ID 1403 Wilsford G5 (Figure 4.13.2) and ID 1268 Weymouth G8 retain traces of finely woven textiles such as linen.

WEAR

Use wear in the form of ancient scratches or scuffing is visible on two items, and the unevenness of the blade edge on ID 1438 may also be evidence of ancient use. Overall two axes were classified as slightly worn, one as worn and one as indeterminate.

CONCLUSIONS

The inclusion of an axe in an Early Bronze Age grave is a very rare occurrence. They tend to be associated with other items of high value, within rich grave groups. The traces of fine cloth on some of the blades may indicate that the axes had been carefully wrapped, rather than the

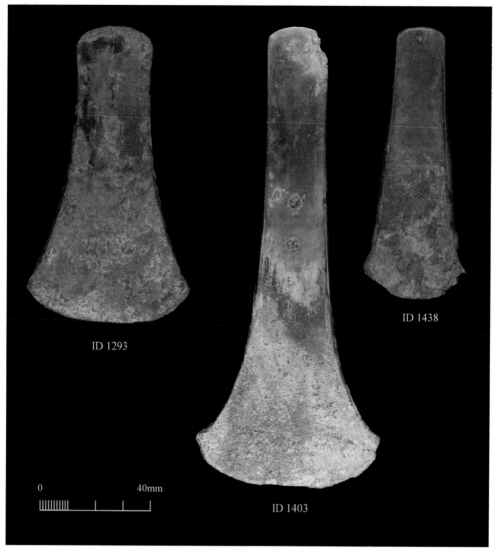

Figure 4.13.1. Axes. ID 1293 Butterwick; ID 1403 Wilsford G5; ID 1438 Wilsford G58; ID 1268 Weymouth G8.

Figure 4.13.2. Details showing traces of textiles from ID 1403 Wilsford G5.

Table 4.13.2. Pronged object ID 1437 Wilsford G58: dimensions of interlocking rings.

Ring	Diameter (mm)	Width of hoop (mm)	Thickness of hoop (mm)
Originally within aperture	*c.*19 (broken)	1.5	2.8
Central	22.1 by 21.8	2.8	3.7
Lower	20.2 by 19.9	3.5	3.3

impressions having derived from proximity to clothing in the grave. Differential corrosion patterns on ID 1438 suggest that the axe was hafted when deposited, and the same can be suggested for the axe at Bush Barrow. The few gold pins observed to be adhering to the axe from Bush Barrow probably came originally from the inlaid dagger handle, but it is not certain whether they became attached in antiquity or after recovery.

4.13.2 COPPER ALLOY SHEET FRAGMENTS FROM WINTERBOURNE STOKE G4

ID 1441 (not illustrated). Two joining fragments of flat sheet, measuring 64 by 17.8mm in total, are only 0.2 to 0.3mm thick i.e. much thinner than any of the knife daggers studied. The original width of the piece is 17.8mm but the original length of the strip is unknown. No traces of any rivet holes are present. All the broken edges appear to have been fractured in antiquity, although possibly in the grave context. There are faint longitudinal polishing striations on the front of one of the fragments. The original size of the strip cannot be estimated, and there are no visible traces of use wear. The degree of wear cannot be determined.

The sheet fragments were found in association with a primary cremation which had, very unusually, been placed within a small wooden coffin measuring 3.5 feet by 2 feet (Colt Hoare 1812, 122). The other grave goods included two daggers, one with a composite pommel, bone tweezers, a bone pin (lost) and a number of bronze rivets which are also lost. Colt Hoare thought that the rivets and the bronze strip were fastenings and fittings for the coffin.

4.13.3 PRONGED OBJECT FROM WILSFORD G58

CONTEXT

ID 1437 "….amongst these numerous relicks, the most curious article is one of twisted brass, whose ancient use, I leave to my learned brother antiquaries to ascertain." (Hoare 1812, 209)

The object was found within a cache of remarkable items at the foot of a "very tall, stout man": greenstone battle-axe, low-flanged axe (see above), grooved whetstone, antler handle, perforated bone plate, tusk and a bone tube. This is one of the more unusual large grave groups within the Wessex barrow cemeteries (also see Woodward and Needham 2012).

MORPHOLOGY

This fork-like object with two twisted prongs is 150mm long, 112mm wide and 6.3mm thick at its maximum (Figure 4.13.3). The weight is 93.8g, plus 6.55g for the rings. When found, the slightly flanged tang (23mm wide, 1.8mm thick) was complete with an arched butt and four holes in a diamond formation, one containing a long rivet (now lost; Hoare 1812, pl. XXIX). The surviving holes in the tang are 3.3 to 3.4mm in diameter. The tang is linked to the prong bases through an expanded zone (measuring 38.7 by 25mm) enclosing a rectangular aperture (27.5 by 12.5mm), the margins of which are decorated on both faces with a row of stroke-filled triangles. The leading edge of the aperture bears a tight lattice design framed by transverse groove bands. Originally, three interlocking metal rings dangled from the rectangular aperture, but the closest one has since broken, thus detaching the others, which are still inter-connected. They have sub-D sections and varying dimensions (see Table 4.13.2). The prongs spring from the sides of the central rectangular zone and then turn through near right-angles. They curve inwards a little towards their tips and are also gently curled in profile. They are tapering, squared bars, one (no. 1) 11.5mm wide at the base decreasing to 3.7mm at a break, the other (no. 2) 10.7mm decreasing to 4mm, again at a break. The twisting of both prongs is clockwise, two and three-quarter twists surviving on no. 1, two and a half surviving on no. 2.

MATERIAL

The material has a brown to gold, smooth shiny surface, blemished by scattered corrosion pits; a corrosion layer has evidently been removed (below). The main object and inner ring have been analysed (Britton 1961, 48 nos. 52–3).

MANUFACTURE

All surfaces are polished. Both front and rear of the tang have marked lateral striations, probably from ancient grinding (Figure 4.13.3a); they extend a little onto the adjacent part of the rectangular frame, but they also cut into the side flanges and would appear to be a secondary feature. Most of the prong twisting is regular, but the spacing is less consistent in the lower part of prong 2. Recurrent deformation fissures aligned along the prong facets may have been picked out by later corrosion etching (Figure 4.13.3c). There are also faint diagonal striations on both prongs, not parallel to the twists and perhaps due to polishing prior to twisting (Figure 4.13.3c).

COMPLETENESS AND DAMAGE

Crocker's illustration in Hoare (1812) shows the object to have a certain amount of corrosion encrustation and this has clearly been cleaned off at some point since. While the end of the tang has been broken off since excavation, it is possible that the prong tips were already missing in the grave and the now-glued break (prong 2) shown detached by Crocker also already broken. The end of prong 1 appears to have suffered some modern damage and prong 2 is shorter (relative to no. 1) than depicted by Crocker, although his drawing is not accurate. Despite loss of the tips, most of the object must be extant (c. 90 to 95%). The ring linking to the aperture has broken since discovery (perhaps during analysis in the late 1950s); three extant fragments seem to be totally de-mineralised with much of the surface plaster coated. The other two interlocking rings, now detached from the main object, are in better condition, but still pitted.

WEAR

The presumed secondary grinding marks on the tang are more worn on the front than on the rear and this may suggest continued use after the original handle had been removed and the tang modified. The only significant wear is around the inner edges of the rectangular aperture, being most intense at one corner (closer to prong 2) and less so at the other, positions where the first ring would come to rest if the object was tilted to one side or other (Figure 4.13.3b). By contrast, there is very little wear of the external angles flanking the lattice decoration (Figure 4.13.3d), although the greatest relative wear is at the same, left-hand corner. There is also internal wear on the bar between the two front corners and the pattern makes it clear that the object was not primarily shaken with prongs pointing upwards, for this would have produced more wear around the lattice-decorated face. Instead, the rings were in motion when the shaft was more horizontal or slightly dipping, the prong ends being curled upwards; moreover, the head was tilted more often clockwise (prong 2 lowered), than anticlockwise. The condition of the rings precludes confident assessment of wear, but it is possible that internal attrition has accentuated the angles flanking the inner faces. Slight rounding of the prong angles may be due to wear. The object was classified as very worn.

CONCLUSIONS

This is a unique object for the period and some scholars have felt unable to speculate on its function (Hoare 1812, 209; Evans 1881, 51, 405). Nevertheless, various possible functions have been entertained, including standard mount (Smith 1921; Ashbee and ApSimon 1954), exotic vessel handle (Grinsell 1957, 212), horse goad (Piggott 1973, 361) and flesh-hook (dismissed in Needham and Bowman 2005, 117). Any concerns that the object may somehow have been intrusive in its Early Bronze Age context may be assuaged by its composition (Britton 1961, 48 nos. 52–3): that for the main object is consistent with, in particular, Period 3 metalwork, while the ring analysed has a more unusual composition. Moreover, the low-flanging of the tang is a classic feature of axe-heads of the period, as seen in the associated example.

The flanged-and-riveted tang suggests that the instrument was mounted at the end of a handle or shaft; the length of the lost rivet would have indicated the thickness of the shaft end. While it would have made an impressive standard mount (even if the Anatolian parallels sought by Ashbee and ApSimon are extremely tenuous), the wear pattern along the bar of the aperture does not support such a function. Likewise, that pattern is not consistent with a predominantly down-pointing orientation, so it is unlikely the object was simply suspended by its tang or handle as an ornament.

Piggott's goad hypothesis is more appealing; the rings would have rattled whenever it was brought down on the animal's rump and soon the beast (perhaps draught ox rather than horse) would have associated noise with action. However, it appears that the prong tips were not normally curling downwards in use as would be expected when a goad was actively prodding the beast. This could simply mean that most often the prongs were turned more upwards, the rattle of the rings producing the desired reaction in the beast. However, this flashy metal instrument might well be a ceremonial or ritual version of ones more generally made in perishable materials and, if so, it may no longer have served the original function of the prototype. Its flashiness could have been further enhanced by, for example, ribbons attached to the rings.

It may not be unconnected to either a utilitarian or other function that the prongs can be viewed as schematic representations of bos horns. This could tie in with the miniature horned pendant from Wilsford G8, ID 1417, Figure 5.9.2 (which is equally schematic) as well as more generally with the importance of cattle in Early Bronze Age society as evidenced by such sites as Hemp Knoll, Raunds and Gayhurst. The curvature of the prongs, if original, recalls that of cattle, but the exaggerated twisting suggests the excesses of metalworker prowess. This is one of the earliest examples of bar twisting, a technique seen otherwise on a few Early Bronze Age pins, including some bone imitations (e.g. Gerloff 1975, 249–51), and occasional other Continental ornaments, such as the clasp-like ornament of twisted gold rod from Tanwedou, Côtes d'Armor (Briard 1984, 212–5). The interlocking rings represent another exceptional technical achievement at this date, requiring either cire perdue casting, or, conceivably, sequential casting-on in a tricky procedure using bivalve moulds. Again, it can be paralleled on a bronze pin, that from Collingbourne Ducis G4 (ID 1418, Figure 5.5.3; Ashbee and ApSimon 1954; Annable and Simpson 1964, 47, no. 193). The filled triangle and lattice incised motifs are, by contrast, familiar on Early Bronze Age artefacts of many types and media.

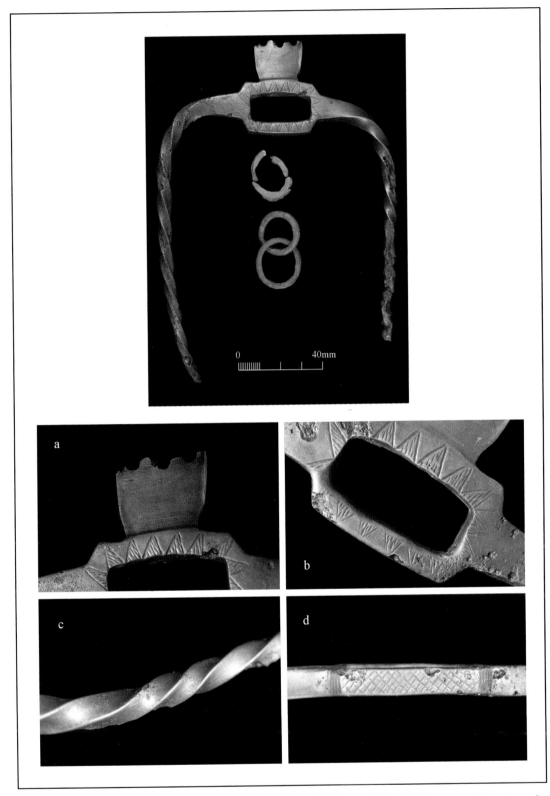

Figure 4.13.3. Pronged object ID 1437 from Wilsford G58 and details showing (a) and (b) wear on the rectangular opening. (a) also shows lateral polishing striations on the tang; (c) striations and fatigue on the twisted prongs and (d) relative lack of wear on the cross-hatched exterior of the lower bar of the rectangular opening.

Object	Site (Parish), County	Museum	Illustration
4.14.1 Debris from working jet and jet-like materials			
ID 311 (3 frags)	Cowlam 58, E. Yorks.	BM	Not illustrated
ID 336	Folkton 239, E. Yorks.	BM	Figure 4.14.1
ID 456	Stanhope, Co. Durham	BM	Figure 4.14.1
ID 459	Pockley, N. Yorks.	BM	Figure 4.14.1
4.14.2 Rings			
ID 280	Eagleston Flat (Curbar), Derbys.	Shef	Figure 4.14.2
ID 437	Fylingdales, N. Yorks.	BM	Figure 4.14.2
ID 438	Fylingdales, N. Yorks.	BM	Figure 4.14.2
ID 450	Nawton, NYM88 (Beadlam), N. Yorks.	BM	Figure 4.14.2
4.14.3 Individual items			
ID 223	Garton Slack 153 (Garton-on-the-Wolds), E. Yorks.	Hull	Figure 4.14.3
ID 253	Garton Slack 153 (Garton-on-the-Wolds), E. Yorks.	Hull	Figure 4.14.3
ID 378	Alwinton, Northumb.	BM	Figure 4.14.3

4.14 MISCELLANEOUS OBJECTS MADE FROM JET AND JET-LIKE MATERIALS

This section describes six items, from four sites, related to working of jet, four rings which do not obviously belong within the series of final Neolithic/Early Bronze Age belt rings, along with two unusual objects and a fossil that was associated with one of the latter (Table 4.14.1).

4.14.1 WORKING DEBRIS FROM JET AND JET-LIKE MATERIALS

TYPO-CHRONOLOGY

Two objects which are unstratified or from an unknown context are described as they are of particular interest, while four unworked fragments are from Yorkshire barrow burials (Figure 4.14.1). One set was associated with a Food Vessel inhumation (ID 336) while ID 311 was found with a male inhumation burial which also included a stone battle-axe.

MORPHOLOGY

ID 336 (Folkton) comprises three irregularly shaped flat pieces of tabular jet, fresh from the outcrop and not beach pebbles. The large tabular piece (ID 311) appears to have snapped during manufacture (Figure 4.14.1 detail) and may have been intended originally as a roughout for a spacer plate. An unstratified perforated object from the barrow at Pockley (ID 459) may have been a roughout for a pendant, although it is of a very unusual hooked shape. The surviving maximum length is 32.5mm, the thickness 14.4mm and minimum diameter of the perforation 7.6mm. Finally, a highly unusual, grooved cigar-shaped object of a compact, stony black material from Stanhope (ID 456) attracted the attention of the project since, on first impressions, it appeared to resemble an abandoned roughout for making large disc beads. The presence of a funnel-shaped transverse borehole, measuring 4.75 by

4.5mm at the front, and 3.95 by 3.9mm at the rear, was interpreted as indicating its conversion into a pendant. Shallow holes at either end were initially thought to be abortive longitudinal boreholes, and the grooving around part of the length of the object had been seen as roughing out in preparation for splitting or sawing off individual disc beads, each up to *c.* 2mm wide (see Figure 4.14.1 detail). However, further research on this object by Kate Verkooijen has provided a compelling corrective to this view. The hollows at either end have been identified as lathe divot scars, and the grooving reinterpreted as being decorative in nature. Other aspects of this object lend support to Verkooijen's idea that it might always have been intended to be a pendant (Verkooijen and Sheridan forthcoming); and if, as seems likely, the identification of lathe divot depressions is correct, then a date in the Roman period, rather than the Early Bronze Age, seems much more likely for this unusual artefact. Parallels can indeed be found among the Roman jet handles in the Yorkshire Museum, including a tapering rod with a lathe scar at one end and a few incised lines near the other, which may have been the handle of a medical instrument (Allason-Jones 1996, 48, no. 306; see also No. 301 and, without the scorings, no. 300). In the light of these *comparanda*, it may indeed be that the transverse perforation on the Stanhope example had been an afterthought. Roman activity in the Stanhope area is attested by the discovery of an altar.

MATERIAL

All items are of Whitby jet, identified visually by AS/MD.

MANUFACTURE

The tabular fragments show some initial scratches (ID 311) or multidirectional faint striations on the side facets (ID 336). The pendant rough out (ID 459) has multi-directional polishing striations on the front and longitudinal ones on the rear, and rilling is present within the perforation (see Figure 4.14.1 detail). On ID 456 there are multidirectional striations on one side only.

COMPLETENESS AND DAMAGE

There are no traces of modern damage on these objects.

WEAR

Edge breaks on the tabular fragments show slight wear, and appear to have been handled after breakage. The pendant rough-out was not used prior to breakage but was subject to subsequent ancient smoothing (classified as slight wear). The object from Stanhope (ID 456) however was much more worn with multidirectional scratches all over the surfaces.

CONCLUSIONS

This group of items are all pieces of raw material or partly finished objects. However, all exhibit ancient wear to varying degrees, so probably were handled and used as amulets after breakage or conversion. Thus the perceived value of the fine raw material, which is Whitby jet in every case, seems to have outweighed the uneven and unusual shapes of these pieces.

4.14.2 RINGS

A group of four rings are of unusual size and hoop section (Figure 4.14.2).

TYPO-CHRONOLOGY

Two rings (ID 437 and 438) were found in a Yorkshire barrow. A third ring (ID 450) was also found in a barrow. The barrow contained the burial of a probable female individual of *c.*14 years and the ring was found with three jet studs and five fusiform jet beads. The fourth ring (ID 280) was found unstratifed on the site of the Early Bronze Age cremation cemetery at Eagleston Flat, Derbyshire. It does appear that these rings may be of Early Bronze Age date, but none are associated with Beakers and they seem to belong to a tradition which is different from, and slightly later than, the series of Beaker-associated circular belt rings (see belt ring section, Chapter 3.4).

MORPHOLOGY

The four rings vary in maximum diameter between 28.5 and 39.2mm, and thickness between 4.5 and 8.4mm. They are all slightly oval in outline and the hoop sections vary from roughly circular (ID 280) to D-shaped with flat interior face (ID 437), tapered interior and curved outer face (ID 438) and flat with tapered interior and outer edges (ID 450). The latter two rings therefore have hourglass perforations.

MATERIAL

Two of the rings are made from jet: ID 437 and ID 450 (the latter analysed by MD/DH), while the other ring from Fylingdales, ID 438, is of cannel coal or shale (MD/DH) and the Derbyshire item, ID 280, is also made from shale or cannel coal, possibly at the known Bronze Age shale/cannel coal working site at Swine Sty (Beswick 1994, 333).

MANUFACTURE

Two of the rings retain traces of manufacture. On ID 438 there are concentric striations on the inner slopes of the hoop (Figure 4.14.2 detail) and ID 450 has longitudinal faint striations on the flat rear face. All the rings are unsymmetrical in form, and finished to a fairly low level of workmanship.

COMPLETENESS AND DAMAGE

All the rings survive at the 90% level or above, with ID 280 being complete. Modern damage includes chips, loss from criss-cross cracking of the jet (ID 437) and one marginal break.

WEAR

Ancient breaks comprise small chips and flaws suffered in antiquity. The ring from Derbyshire (ID 280) shows no signs of wear and is classified as fresh. The Yorkshire items however are all classed as worn, with patches of scratches on the surfaces, and particularly on the inner faces or cusps of the hoops.

CONCLUSIONS

These four rings, of inferior workmanship and of later date when compared with the series of Beaker-age belt rings, may have functioned as ornaments or fasteners. There is no wear evidence to indicate use as belt rings, although such use may not have caused strong wear unless the ring was in a fixed position on the belt. They are also larger, and much thicker, that the series of flat rings, often made from Kimmeridge shale, which are found within composite necklaces in the Wessex region.

4.14.3 INDIVIDUAL ITEMS

ID 223 (spindle object) and ID 253 (ammonite). These two items (Figure 4.14.3) were found in association with a child inhumation and a pair of copper alloy ear rings (ID 1146–7), plus some ochre at Garton Slack 153. The main object is in the shape of a long cylindrical spindle, of length 33.2mm and diameter 13.7mm. There are six ribs and one end is neatly squared off. The other end, however, is deliberately shaped to an uneven profile. The whole item appears to have been made to imitate a piece of ammonite, similar to the one with which it was associated, with the uneven terminal intended to copy a naturally broken end

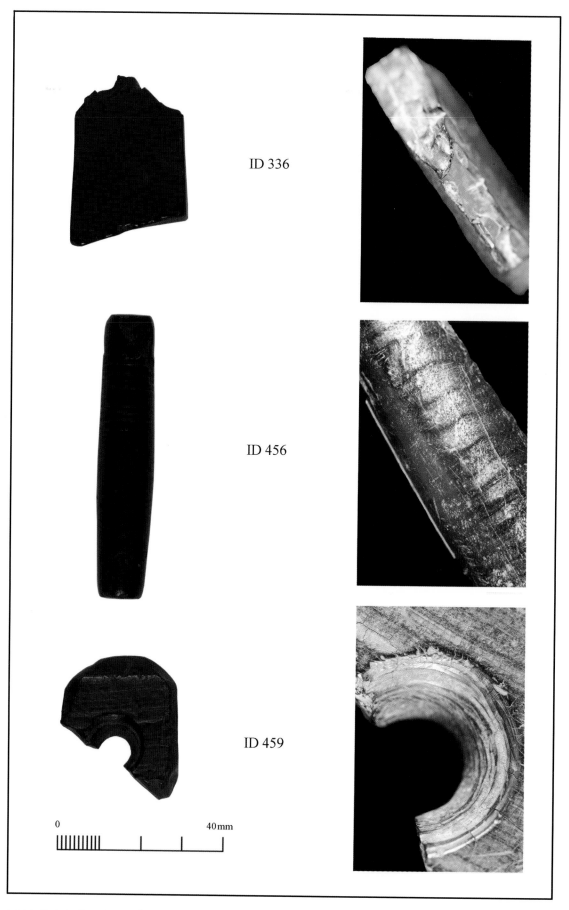

Figure 4.14.1. Debris from jet working. ID 336 Folkton 239 showing detail of snapped end; ID 456 Stanhope showing detail of striations and ribbing; ID 459 Pockley showing detail of rilling.

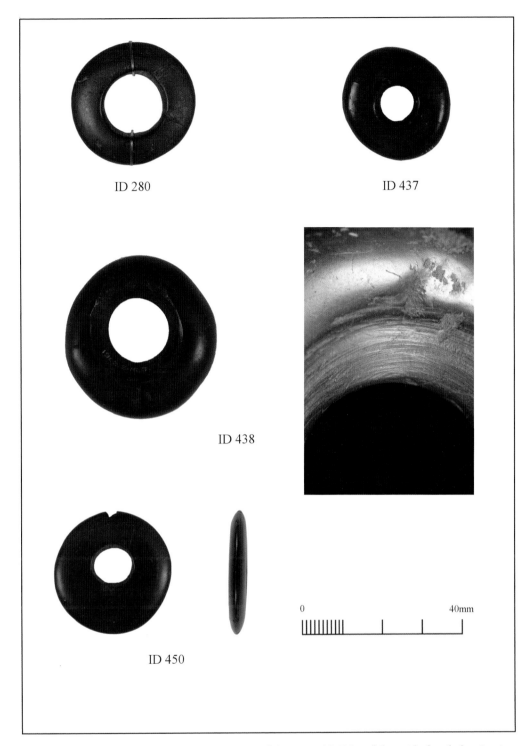

Figure 4.14.2. Rings. ID 280 Eagleston Flat; ID 437 Fylingdales; ID 438 Fylingdales with detail showing inner concentric striations; ID 450 Nawton.

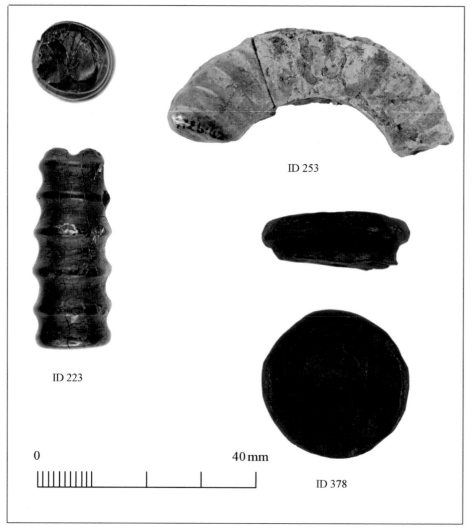

Figure 4.14.3. Individual items ID 223 Garton Slack 153; ID 253 Garton Slack 153; ID 378 Alwinton.

of an ammonite segment. The material was confirmed as jet by XRF analysis (NMS), polished to a low sheen. The object is almost complete, with just a few minor spalls which are of both modern and ancient date. Detailed traces of manufacture include longitudinal faint polishing striations within the hollows between the decorative ribs. The surfaces of the ribs are worn very smooth and the object is categorised as very worn. Although the jet object is much rounder in section than a segment of ammonite fossil, it is clearly intended as a skeuomorph, and probably functioned as an amulet. No doubt the colour contrast between the shiny black jet and the pale creamy hue of the fossil may also have been symbolically significant.

ID 378 (broken disc). A circular disc of maximum diameter 26.5mm and surviving thickness 8.8mm is from an unknown context at Alwinton (Figure 4.14.3). It carries a top facet of depth 4.8mm. Analysis by XRF (NMS) was unable to determine whether the material was jet or cannel coal. Signs of manufacture include lateral and diagonal marked polishing striations on the top surface and cut marks on the facet and in the 'neck' area. There are a few modern flaws, but the main fracture occurred in antiquity. Traces of use wear are present on the facet edges and the object is classified as worn. It is possible that the object is approximately half of a necked stud (see Chapter 5.6), but it is rather rough in terms of finish. Possibly it broke during manufacture and then was subjected to heavy wear in subsequent use as an amulet.

5. ITEMS OF PERSONAL ADORNMENT I: JET AND JET-LIKE MATERIALS, AMBER, BONE AND COPPER ALLOY

5.1 TUSKS AND TEETH

TUSKS

TYPO-CHRONOLOGY

No detailed consideration of modified and unmodified tusks and teeth from Beaker and Early Bronze Age graves has been published. The only comments in print are those by Moore and Rowlands (1972, 48) concerning the three tusks from the Ablington Barrow, Figheldean, Wiltshire. They were described as boars' tusks and it was noted that 'all three have been shaved off at the tip so as to come to a sharper point, presumably for use as a tool'. However, during the Leverhulme pilot project of 2004, Mark Maltby observed that the apparent shaving of the tips was in fact largely due to natural wear of the tusks during the lifetime of the animals from which they were derived (Woodward *et al.* 2006, 45). A more recent find is of particular interest. The single apparently unmodified pig tusk from the large Beaker grave group at Raunds Barrow 1 was dated by the radiocarbon method and was found to have been 420 to 990 years old when it was buried. It was therefore a curated or found relic and may even have been originally of Early Neolithic date, when a series of tusk artefacts are known from Neolithic barrows (Harding and Healy 2007, fig. 4.6 and table 4.9). The series of Neolithic tusks has been discussed by Kinnes, who allocated them to his chronological stages D and E (Kinnes 1979, figs. 3.2–3, 18.5 and 18.9). The group of 12 Middle Neolithic tusks from Duggleby Howe, Yorkshire was also described in more detail (Kinnes *et al.* 1983, 87–90; Gibson 2012) and throughout these artefacts were interpreted as modified blades, in other words as tools. In the light of these previous studies it was decided to include detailed study of ten tusks of Neolithic date, from both round and long barrows, alongside our study of 27 deriving from Beaker and Early Bronze Age graves. Amongst these six were found with Beakers, five with Food Vessels and six with beads, or other ornaments and artefacts of mature Early Bronze Age date. The Amesbury Archer grave has been

subjected to radiocarbon dating, as has the Raunds grave discussed above, but none of the Early Bronze Age graves with tusks are closely dated (for dates see Chapter 9).

MORPHOLOGY

The group comprises 37 pig or boar tusks (ten of them Neolithic in date), which are listed in Table 5.1.1. The tusks are usually more or less entire, with the proximal end, where undamaged, showing the ragged outline of the natural tooth margin that existed within the jaw. They are sometimes unmodified, but others have been split in half longitudinally to provide a flatter, curved artefact with a slightly concave cross-section. Other modifications include some cases of sharpening towards the distal end and the provision of one or more perforations, usually at the proximal end. In two cases the distal end of the tusk had been cut off and used to make a perforated pendant.

MATERIAL

The tusks are all pig canines from mature male animals, usually taken from the mandible, but in two (Early Bronze Age) cases from the upper jaw. The size variation is great (83 to 130mm in length, measured across the chord), with seven large examples definitely deriving from wild boars, and some of the smaller items from domestic animals. Large and small tusks occur in both period groups. Where side of body could be determined, eight were from the left side of the mouth and 15 from the right. Both sides are represented in both the Neolithic and Early Bronze Age samples. However, in the Neolithic group right and left are equally represented, including two possible pairs from single animals. In the later group right hand tusks are twice as common as left hand ones. In two grave groups all the tusks were right hand examples (Amesbury Archer and Figheldean, Figure 5.1.1), and three out of the five left hand tusks were found in a single burial (Upton Lovell G2a 'shaman', Figure 5.1.1). In colour the tusk artefacts vary from creamy-white to grey and buff.

Table 5.1.1. List of tusks and teeth studied and illustrated (FV: Food Vessel).

Object	Site (County), County	Date	Museum	Illustration
	Tusks			
ID 607	Aldro 88, E. Yorks.	Neolithic	Hull	Not illustrated
ID 627	Garrowby Wold 101 (Kirby Underdale), E. Yorks.	EBA (FV)	Hull	Not illustrated
ID 632	Fimber 133 (Fimber), E. Yorks.	EBA (FV)	Hull	Not illustrated
ID 634	Life Hill 294 (Sledmere), E, Yorks.	EBA (FV)	Hull	Figure 5.1.1
ID 641	Garton Slack 40 (Garton-on-the-Wolds), E. Yorks.	EBA	Hull	Not illustrated
ID 696	Baley Hill (Newton Grange), Derbys.	EBA (FV)	Shef	Figure 5.1.1
ID 698	Netherlow (Chelmorton), Derbys.	?EBA	Shef	Figure 5.1.1
ID 751	Folkton 70, burial 13, E. Yorks.	EBA	BM	Not illustrated
ID 752	Cowlam 57, burial 1, E. Yorks.	Neolithic?	BM	Not illustrated
ID 753	Ayton E UN113, burial 4, N. Yorks.	Neolithic	BM	Not illustrated
ID 754	Ayton E UN113, burial 4, N. Yorks.	Neolithic	BM	Not illustrated
ID 755	Uley, Gloucs.	Neolithic	BM	Not illustrated
ID 756	Uley, Gloucs.	Neolithic	BM	Not illustrated
ID 757	Rodmarton, Gloucs.	Neolithic	BM	Not illustrated
ID 758	Aldbourne 280, mound, Wilts.	Indet	BM	Not illustrated
ID 759	Langton 2, burial 2, E. Yorks.	EBA	BM	Figure 5.1.1; Figure 5.1.2
ID 760	Uley, Gloucs.	Neolithic	BM	Figure 5.1.2
ID 761	Goodmanham 117, burial 1, E. Yorks.	?EBA	BM	Figure 5.1.1
ID 762	Folkton 70, burial 13, E. Yorks.	EBA	BM	Figure 5.1.1
ID 763	Aldbourne 280, mound, Wilts.	Indet	BM	Not illustrated
ID 764	Crosby Garrett 174, burial 1, Cumbria	Neolithic	BM	Not illustrated
ID 765	Crosby Garrett 174, burial 1, Cumbria	Neolithic	BM	Not illustrated
ID 850	Upton Lovell G2a, shaman, Wilts.	EBA	Dev	Figure 5.1.1
ID 851	Upton Lovell G2a, shaman, Wilts.	EBA	Dev	Figure 5.1.1
ID 852	Upton Lovell G2a, shaman, Wilts.	EBA	Dev	Figure 5.1.1
ID 924	Wilsford G58, Wilts.	EBA	Dev	Figure 5.1.1
ID 993	Wilsford G1, Wilts.	Beaker	Dev	Figure 5.1.1; Figure 5.1.2
ID 994	Upton Lovell, Wilts.	?	Dev	Not illustrated
ID 995	Unknown, Wilts.	?	Dev	Not illustrated
ID 1021	Figheldean G25c, Wilts.	?EBA	Sal	Figure 5.1.1
ID 1022	Figheldean G25c, Wilts.	?EBA	Sal	Figure 5.1.1
ID 1023	Figheldean G25c, Wilts.	?EBA	Sal	Figure 5.1.1
ID 1065	Amesbury Archer, Wilts.	Beaker	Sal	Not illustrated
ID 1066	Amesbury Archer, Wilts.	Beaker	Sal	Not illustrated
ID 1067	Amesbury Archer, Wilts.	Beaker	Sal	Not illustrated
ID 1068	Amesbury Archer, Wilts.	Beaker	Sal	Not illustrated
ID 1069	Amesbury Archer Companion, Wilts.	Beaker	Sal	Not illustrated
	Beaver teeth			
ID 625	Painsthorpe 98 (Kirby Underdale), E. Yorks.	EBA (FV)	Hull	Not illustrated
ID 880	Winterbourne Stoke G8, Wilts.	EBA	Dev	Figure 8.3.4
	Canine teeth			
ID 688	Kenslow (Middleton and Smerrill), Derbys.	?Beaker	Shef	Figure 5.1.4
ID 689	Kenslow (Middleton and Smerrill), Derbys.	?Beaker	Shef	Figure 5.1.4
ID 690	Kenslow (Middleton and Smerrill), Derbys.	?Beaker	Shef	Figure 5.1.4
ID 691	Kenslow (Middleton and Smerrill), Derbys.	?Beaker	Shef	Figure 5.1.4
ID 692	Kenslow (Middleton and Smerrill), Derbys.	?Beaker	Shef	Figure 5.1.4
ID 693	Kenslow (Middleton and Smerrill), Derbys.	?Beaker	Shef	Figure 5.1.4
ID 694	Kenslow (Middleton and Smerrill), Derbys.	?Beaker	Shef	Figure 5.1.4
	Shark teeth			
ID 1020	Sutton Veny, Wilts.	Not found	Sal	Not illustrated

MANUFACTURE

Many of the tusks display slight damage around the uneven proximal margin which would have taken place when the tusk was removed from the jaw bone. Seven out of the ten Neolithic tusks had been split longitudinally, but only three in the larger Early Bronze Age sample. And in two Neolithic cases only the tusk had been cut across near the root end.

The surfaces of most of the tusks do not show any traces of modification (or wear, see below), but in one Neolithic case, and seven Early Bronze Age cases, there are faint longitudinal, or occasionally diagonal, polishing striations, usually located on the inner surface of the tusk, and often towards the distal end. Particular attention was paid to the identification of any human enhancement of the pointed ends of the tusks. Mark Maltby concluded that deliberate enhancement (i.e. sharpening of the ends) is evident in two out of the ten Neolithic cases and in only six out of the 27 Early Bronze Age examples, two of them slight.

Seven of the tusks studied, from four sites, are perforated. One of them is one of the Neolithic examples from Uley, Gloucestershire, where a single large perforation near the laterally cut proximal end is provided with a distinct groove, made at the time of manufacture, presumably to hold the thread at a particular angle (ID 760, Figure 5.1.2). Amongst the Early Bronze Age items, that from Folkton 70, Yorkshire has at least four funnel-shaped perforations towards the broken proximal end (ID 762, Figure 5.1.1) and the three tusks from Upton Lovell G2a have parts of one perforation surviving at the proximal end of each (ID 850–52, Figure 5.1.1). The other two perforated items are pendants made from the distal ends of tusks (ID 761, Figure 5.1.1 and ID 993, Figure 5.1.2), although in the Goodmanham, Yorkshire case the perforation may have broken through at the time of manufacture. Finally the tusk from Langton, Yorkshire has a series of four incised grooves near the proximal end; these may have been designed to hold threads or strings in place (ID 759, Figure 5.1.2).

COMPLETENESS AND DAMAGE

Tusks are relatively fragile items and many of those studied had suffered breakage since the time of excavation; glue is much in evidence. Indeed of the total of 74 breaks suffered in ancient or modern times, 57 (77%) are modern. The breaks are usually at the ends, or right across the item, and subsequently rejoined with adhesive. Others include damage at the tip, or around perforations. However, overall 13 items were 90% or more present.

WEAR

Breaks during use are relatively uncommon, only four on the Neolithic tusks and ten on the Early Bronze Age ones. They include minor damage to the tip and sometimes at the proximal end. The only trace of wear observed on the Neolithic tusks is a group of four nicks on one of the broken examples from Uley, Gloucestershire. The perforation on ID 760 (Figure 5.1.2) shows no thread-wear. The Early Bronze Age items show varying types of wear, including scratches on the sides or outer edges (three instances) and all over ancient scuffing (two examples). On the tusk from Folkton (ID 762, Figure 5.1.1) there are some scratches at the perforations but the edges of the holes are not significantly worn. On two of the Amesbury Archer tusks (ID 1067 and ID 1068) the tip is gently worn, perhaps due to fabric rub. In only three cases is there any sign of wear which might have been due to use of the tusk as a tool. These are marks on the humanly enhanced facet on two of the tusks from Figheldean (ID 1022 and ID 1023, Figure 5.1.1), and general wearing down of the tip on one tusk from Upton Lovell G2a (ID 851, Figure 5.1.1).

CONCLUSIONS

Pig tusks, which often have been modified, are known from graves dating from the Early Neolithic through to the Early Bronze Age. The Neolithic examples are associated with multiple burials, usually in a disarticulated state. The Beaker/Early Bronze Age graves with tusks include 16 inhumations and just one cremation. Few of the bodies have been sexed but both men (two examples) and women (three examples) are represented. The size of tusks utilised in the two periods of use is summarized in Figure 5.1.3. This shows that a wide range of tusks were used in both periods. The ones from Neolithic contexts show a wider range of sizes, but small and large tusks occur throughout; this indicates that tusks from both domestic and wild animals were being used in both periods.

Our detailed analysis shows that only eight out of the 37 items studied had been sharpened by human enhancement of the distal pointed end. However there are very few traces of use wear, and in only three cases is wear that *might* have been caused by using the tusk as a tool visible. Some tusks found in continental graves were associated with metalworking tools such as cushion stones and have been interpreted as tools for planishing or burnishing metals. The modified tusks from the Amesbury Archer's grave may fall into this category (Fitzpatrick 2011, 61, 163 and 222). However, we suggest that the previous overarching interpretations of tusks as blades or tools are incorrect, and that most of the tusks were in fact designed to perform as ornaments. Further evidence can be cited in favour of this hypothesis. Firstly, two of the Early Bronze Age tusks are designed as pendants, and two Neolithic ones had been cut across deliberately at the proximal end and one of them perforated. A further Neolithic example (not studied) has also been cut across and perforated centrally (Tideswell, Derbyshire; Radley and Plant 1971, fig. 4). Altogether four of the tusks studied, in addition to the two pendants, have surviving perforations. The fact that the edges of these perforations are not worn suggests that they did not hang by a string from a belt, as might have been the case if they had functioned as tools. The only groove at a perforation (ID 760 Uley, Figure 5.1.2) is at an angle, and this may indicate that the tusk was sewn onto a garment such that the tusk lay in a particular chosen position. We know that the perforated tusks with the burial at Upton Lovell G2a (ID 850–52 and 994, Figure 5.1.1) were found on the legs, and that, in association with a large number of perforated bone points (see Chapter 4.7), these probably served to decorate an elaborate costume (Piggott 1962, 93). In general the little wear that was observed under the microscope comprises general scuffing and smoothing which is probably due to fabric rub, so this also adds to the ornamental interpretation.

It can be concluded that the tusks functioned mainly as ornaments, both in the Early Neolithic and Beaker/Early Bronze Age period. One final piece of evidence that can be brought to play is the association of tusks with other types of ornaments within several of the grave assemblages. They occur with a dress pin at Crosby Garrett (Neolithic

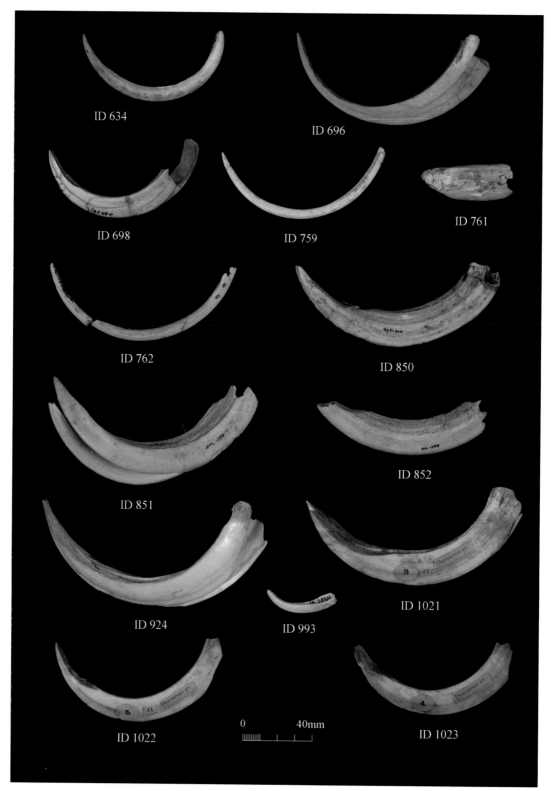

Figure 5.1.1. Examples of tusks: ID 634 Life Hill 294; ID 696 Baley Hill; ID 698 Netherlow; ID 759 Langton 2, 2; ID 761 Goodmanham 117, 1; ID 762 Folkton 70, 13; ID 850–52 Upton Lovell G2a; ID 924 Wilsford G58; ID 993 Wilsford G1; ID 1021–23 Figheldean G25c.

ID 764–65), with a clay button at Garton Slack 40 (ID 641) and with various beads at Langton (ID 759, Figure 5.1.1), Winterbourne Stoke G8 (ID 880) and Netherlow (ID 698, Figure 5.1.1). Like the dated examples from Raunds Barrow

1 many of the tusks may have been old when deposited: they may have functioned as important ancestral relics and/or hunting trophies. Also they may have symbolised the whole animal. Pig meat was consumed in large

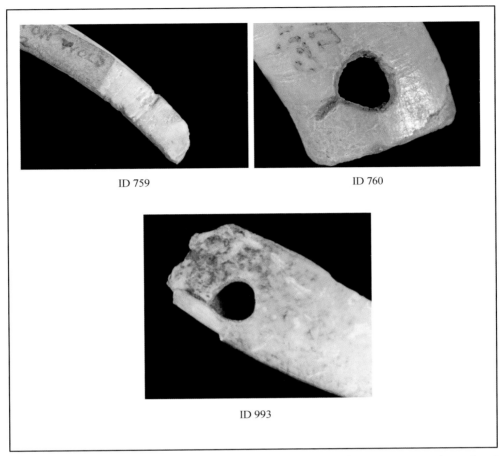

Figure 5.1.2. Details of tusks showing incised grooves on ID 759 Langton 2, 2, the groove next to the perforation on ID 760 Uley, and the pendant perforation on ID 993 Wilsford G1.

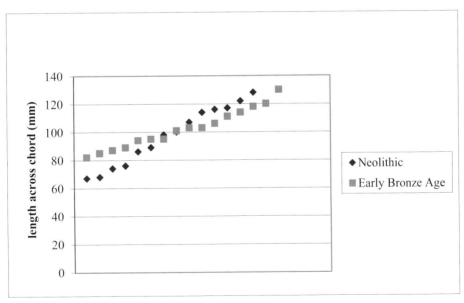

Figure 5.1.3. Pig tusks: variation in size.

quantities on the ritual feasting sites (henge monuments) of the Late Neolithic period, in association with Grooved Ware (Albarella and Payne 2005; Albarella *et al.* 2007), and pig bones were seldom used for the manufacture of bone artefacts in either the Neolithic or Early Bronze Age periods. Such evidence may imply that pigs, both domestic and wild, were of special ritual and symbolic importance in early prehistory.

BEAVER TEETH

TYPO-CHRONOLOGY

The incidence of beavers in Britain and the utilisation of body parts has been the subject of recent detailed research by Bryony Coles (2006). From ethnographic records, mainly from North America, it appears that beaver teeth were used variously as tools, dice and for decoration (Coles 2006, 53 and fig. 4.8). Incisors were particularly valued and were employed mainly in woodworking, and also for cutting human hair (*ibid*, 55). Coles describes several instances of beaver incisors found in Early Bronze Age graves, including one from the composite set of objects from Langton (see composite necklaces section, Chapter 8.4.4), although the beaver tooth is lost and not recorded by Kinnes and Longworth (1985), and one from Amesbury G61a, which was found with an accessory cup, cremation of unknown sex, and a group of beads made from various materials (Ashbee 1985). This lower incisor had been cut down and may have been old when deposited, but it showed no signs of use as a tool (*ibid*, 75).

MORPHOLOGY, MANUFACTURE AND WEAR

Two instances of beaver teeth were studied in detail, one from Painsthorpe, Yorkshire (ID 625) and one from Winterbourne Stoke G8, Wiltshire (ID 880). Both are incisors, one of them definitely from the lower jaw. They have a distinctive deep red-brown colour. There are no signs of any enhancement or modification, and neither of them shows any signs of use as a tool. The Yorkshire example was found together with a Food Vessel in association with an unsexed inhumation, while the one from Wiltshire (ID 880) was found with an accessory cup, an awl, whetstones, beads, fossil shells and a piece of stalactite i.e. a composite necklace (see Chapter 8.3.6).

CONCLUSIONS

There is no evidence that beaver teeth were used as wood-working tools. They seem to be in pristine condition, although sometimes have been cut down at the proximal, root end. Their distinctive colour may have been of great significance, and they tend to be found with groups of other highly coloured beads or small items of natural origin. Thus their function may have been more symbolic in nature, and they may have been employed as amulets. In this respect it is interesting to note that in the Anglo-Saxon period beaver incisors have been found, mainly with the remains of babies, children and young women, in graves within 13 cemeteries in eastern England (Coles 2006, 130–2). The teeth selected were usually lower incisors and they were used as pendants, with a cap or collar of bronze or gold attached to aid suspension (*ibid*, figs. 9.3 and 9.4).

CANINE TEETH

GENERAL OBSERVATIONS

Two grave groups studied contain modified teeth from dog or wolf. One set of teeth is beads, two made from dog canines and 16 from wolf (ID 853–70, South Newton G1). They were found with a further bead made from amber and will be described in the section on composite necklaces in Chapter 8.2.8. The second set comprises a group of seven items from Kenslow (ID 688–94, Figure 5.1.4). Each piece comprises half of a canine tooth from large dog or wolf which has been split axially to provide a crescent-shaped object with plano-convex profile. In each case the tip and root have been removed and the ends are neatly squared off. They are very uniform in size, varying in length from 50.7 to 52.2mm. Widths of most lie between 12.5 and 12.9mm, but one is slightly wider at 13.6mm. All are fixed by threads to a permanent display mounting, but the thicknesses can be estimated to be *c.* 6mm. Each crescent has two small perforations, very neatly executed from the rear and measuring between 1.5 to 2.6mm across. The upper enamel surfaces are mainly in good condition, with a little erosion. Five display breaks, two at the ends and otherwise minor flakes and cracks. All these are modern breaks. There are no traces of manufacture beyond the basic careful shaping of each piece. In terms of wear, most of the perforations have fairly sharp edges but overall the pieces do seem to have been used and they can be categorised as slightly worn. It is difficult to see how the crescents could have been strung in a necklace, and there is no differential wear at the perforations which might have supported such an interpretation. It seems likely that they were sewn permanently onto a garment as ornaments, in a similar way to some of the sets of jet/jet-like buttons (see button sets, Chapter 5.3). The set is remarkably uniform, undoubtedly made by a single person, and none of the items seem to have been heavily worn or re-used. They were found with a secondary inhumation of unknown type, and no further grave goods were recorded.

SHARK'S TOOTH

GENERAL OBSERVATIONS

A single find of a shark's tooth (not a fossil) comes from an extended male inhumation grave in a barrow at Sutton Veny (ID 1020). This was found on the chest of the body and, although damaged, most probably served as a pendant. It cannot now be located but was studied by Alwyne Wheeler at the Natural History Museum (Johnston 1980, 43). The tooth is from the right side of the lower jaw of the mako shark, *Isurus oxyrhinchus*, and probably derived from a carcass on a beach rather than from a caught fish, and would have come from a shark weighing as much as

100 kg. This large and fierce species of shark now occurs in British seas only in the summer and autumn months, but only in deep water more that 15 km from the shore. In tropical seas it can be dangerous to man.

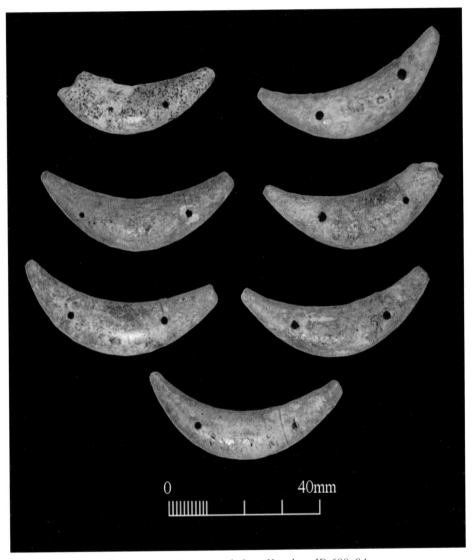

Figure 5.1.4. Canine teeth from Kenslow, ID 688–94.

5.2 V-PERFORATED BUTTONS

This section deals with buttons found in graves as individual items or as pairs. It does not include the large numbers of buttons that occur as elements within jet necklaces in middle and northern England. These necklace buttons are considered within the texts relating to each relevant necklace in Chapter 7. Nor does it include the buttons which occur as larger 'sets' within individual graves, which are described in a separate section, Chapter 5.3, following.

JET AND JET-LIKE MATERIALS

TYPO-CHRONOLOGY

The jet buttons of Great Britain and Ireland have been fully listed and discussed by Shepherd (1973; 2009), and all those from Ireland were also illustrated by Harbison (1975, pls. 21–24). The total of nearly 400 buttons (including necklace buttons) were divided into types by Shepherd. The types were based mainly on the nature of profile, with size as a secondary characteristic. The definition of the types is summarised in Table 5.2.1, and the number of buttons of each type studied in this project is also indicated. Shepherd Types 3b (gold-covered cones), 8 (long necklace fasteners), 9 (pendants) and 10 (through-bored buttons) are not included in this section. Examples of six of the key groups studied are illustrated in Figure 5.2.1. Photographs of examples of specific groups are shown in Figure 5.2.2 (Type 1), Figure 5.2.3 (Types 2, 4 and 5) and Figure 5.2.4 (Types 6a and 6b). A full list of those studied and illustrated is given in Table 5.2.2.

Of the 55 buttons studied in detail, 23 were associated with other grave goods. Most of the grave groups relate to the larger buttons of Types 1, 6a and 6b and contain items such as Beakers, daggers of flint or copper alloy, jet or jet-like material pulley rings and copper alloy earrings. The Beakers belong to the later Southern or Northern series defined by Clarke (1970) and the assemblages fall within

the post-fission horizon period outlined by Needham (2005, fig. 12). Two sites have produced buttons in association with Food Vessels, while in four cases, mainly in Wessex, smaller button types are associated with grave goods of mature Early Bronze Age date.

Radiocarbon dates relating to graves which contained large V-perforated buttons are listed in Chapter 9. These fall within the final few centuries of the third millennium cal BC. This correlates with the stage after the fission horizon, but before the beginning of the Wessex 1 phase of the Early Bronze Age (*cf* Needham 2005, fig. 13).

MORPHOLOGY

The basic variations in button morphology are summarised in Table 5.2.1. Key variables include overall size, the relative height of the dome and the profile of the sides of the dome (whether convex, straight/flat or concave) as well as the profile of the base (flat or convex). In addition, some of the buttons possess a distinct facet at the base of the dome and adjacent to the base. Such facets may be vertical or slightly inclined outwards. Facets are present on 28 of the 55 buttons studied in detail. They occur on approximately half of the buttons of Type 1 and of Type 2, while nearly all of the Type 6a and 6b buttons have facets. The size range of the measurable buttons studied is shown in Figure 5.2.5 where maximum diameter is plotted against dome height. No clear groupings are apparent, but Type 1 buttons, by definition, tend to be larger than those of Type 2. However the special buttons of Types 6a and 6b show a wide range of sizes, from 20.4 to 64.8mm in diameter.

During study it was noticed that often the pair of holes forming the V-perforation was not placed centrally, but was located nearer the top of the button than the bottom. This eccentric placing of the perforations occurs in 21 cases (40% of the total). Some special features were also observed. These appear to have been related to the difficulty of boring a V-perforation in buttons of relatively low height.

Table 5.2.1. V-perforated button typology according to Shepherd.

Type	Profile (sides)	Profile (base)	Height	Size	Material	Total examples	Project examples
1	Conical (straight or convex)	Flat	5–16mm	>25mm diameter	Jet or jet-like material, Stone ×1	59	17
2	Conical (straight or convex)	Flat	4–12mm	<25mm diameter	Jet, bone	201 (many in necklaces)	11
3a	Slightly hipped	Flat	High	Variable	Jet, amber	21	2
4	Smoothly rounded	Flat, oval	Medium	Small	Amber, jet	23	1
5	Conical (straight or convex)	Convex	Medium	Large	Jet, amber	13	2
6a	Reflexly conical (concave)	Flat	Low	Large	Jet or jet-like material	26	11
6b	Reflexly conical (concave)	Convex	Low	Large	Jet or jet-like material	15	3
7	Prismatic	Flat	Low	Small	Amber	13	-

Table 5.2.2. List of jet or jet-like material objects studied and illustrated.

Object	Site (Parish), County	Museum	Illustration
Type 1			
ID 203	Acklam Wold 123 (Thixendale), E. Yorks.	Hull	Not illustrated
ID 215	Painsthorpe 200 (Kirby Underdale), E. Yorks.	Hull	Not illustrated
ID 216	Painsthorpe 200 (Kirby Underdale), E. Yorks.	Hull	Not illustrated
ID 220	Garton Slack 37 (Garton-on-the-Wolds), E. Yorks.	Hull	Not illustrated
ID 221	Garton Slack 161 (Garton-on-the-Wolds), E. Yorks.	Hull	Figure 5.2.1
ID 230	Easington, E. Yorks.	Hull	Figure 5.2.2; Figure 5.2.6
ID 231	Prescott's Pit (Brough), E. Yorks.	Hull	Figure 5.2.2
ID 258	Beechenhill/Castern, Staffs.	Shef	Figure 5.2.2
ID 286	Little Downham, Cambs.	Camb	Figure 5.2.2
ID 314	Rudston 61, burial 2, E. Yorks.	BM	Figure 5.2.7
ID 316	Rudston 68, burial 7, E. Yorks.	BM	Figure 5.2.6; Figure 5.2.7
ID 370	Wooler UN47, burial 1, Northumb.	BM	Figure 5.2.6; Figure 5.2.7
ID 396	Gospel Hillock (Taddington), Derbys.	BM	Not illustrated
ID 415	Huggate Wold (Huggate), E. Yorks.	BM	Figure 5.2.2; Figure 5.2.7
ID 473	Winterbourne Stoke G54, Wilts.	Dev	Figure 5.2.2
ID 475	Winterbourne Monkton, sarsen, Wilts.	Dev	Figure 5.2.2
ID 478	Wimborne St Giles G9, Wilts.	Dev	Figure 5.2.2
Type 2			
ID 255	Blanch 238 (Warter), E. Yorks.	Hull	Figure 5.2.1
ID 274	nr Dow Low (Hartington Upper), Derbys.	Shef	Not illustrated
ID 302	Ganton 27, burial 4, E. Yorks.	BM	Figure 5.2.3; Figure 5.2.7
ID 310	Cowlam 58, grave fill, E. Yorks.	BM	Figure 5.2.7
ID 333	Ford 186, burial 3, Northumb.	BM	Not illustrated
ID 363	Aldbourne 280, burial 1, Wilts.	BM	Figure 5.2.3
ID 373	Helperthorpe UN95, Feature A, E. Yorks.	BM	Not illustrated
ID 419	Wilsford, Lake G50a, Wilts.	BM	Figure 5.2.3
ID 476	Winterbourne Monkton, sarsen, Wilts.	Dev	Not illustrated
ID 512	Amesbury G39, Wilts.	Dev	Figure 5.2.3; Figure 5.2.7
ID 529	Winterbourne Stoke G67, Wilts.	Dev	Figure 5.2.3
Type 3a			
ID 206	Acklam Wold 124 (Acklam), E. Yorks.	Hull	Figure 5.2.1
ID 255	Middleton-on-the-Wolds, E. Yorks.	Hull	Not illustrated
Type 4			
ID 481	Durrington Walls, Wilts.	Dev	Figure 5.2.3
Type 5			
ID 205	Acklam Wold 123 (Thixendale), E. Yorks.	Hull	Figure 5.2.1
ID 368	Great Tosson UN22, burial 2, Northumb.	BM	Figure 5.2.3
Type 6a			
ID 210	Hanging Grimston 55 (Thixendale), E. Yorks.	Hull	Figure 5.2.4
ID 212	Painsthorpe 99 (Kirby Underdale), E. Yorks.	Hull	Figure 5.2.4
ID 213	Painsthorpe 99 (Kirby Underdale), E. Yorks.	Hull	Not illustrated
ID 226	Kemp Howe 209a, E. Yorks.	Hull	Figure 5.2.1
ID 271	Net Low (Eaton and Alsop), Derbys.	Shef	Figure 5.2.4
ID 272	Net Low (Eaton and Alsop), Derbys.	Shef	Figure 5.2.4; Figure 5.2.6
ID 317	Rudston 68, burial 7, E. Yorks.	BM	Figure 5.2.4; Figure 5.2.7
ID 319	Rudston 68, burial 6, E. Yorks.	BM	Figure 5.2.4
ID 320	Rudston 68, burial 6, E. Yorks	BM	Figure 5.2.4
ID 367	Great Tosson UN22, burial 1, Northumb.	BM	Not illustrated
ID 416	Lambourn 7 Barrows, Berks.	BM	Not illustrated
Type 6b			
ID 209	Hanging Grimston 57 (Thixendale), E. Yorks.	Hull	Figure 5.2.4
ID 222	Garton Slack 152 (Garton-on-the-Wolds), E. Yorks.	Hull	Figure 5.2.1
ID 312	Thwing 60, burial 3, E. Yorks.	BM	Figure 5.2.4
Others			
ID 202	Acklam Wold 123 (Thixendale), E. Yorks.	Hull	Not illustrated
ID 285	Shippea Hill (Littleport), Cambs.	Camb	Not illustrated
ID 395	Gospel Hillock (Taddington), Derbys.	BM	Not illustrated
ID 534	Unlocated, Wilts.	Dev	Not illustrated
ID 535	Unlocated, Wilts.	Dev	Not illustrated
ID 541	Cowleaze (Winterbourne Steepleton), Dorset	Dor	Figure 8.2.4
ID 542	Cowleaze (Winterbourne Steepleton), Dorset	Dor	Figure 8.2.4
ID 543	Cowleaze (Winterbourne Steepleton), Dorset	Dor	Figure 8.2.4

In nine cases, all except one of the large flat buttons of Type 6a, distinct central raised knobs or nipples are present on the dome (ID 272 Net Low, Figure 5.2.6). Another example (ID 316 Rudston, Figure 5.2.6) has a raised bridge area between and around the holes, to enhance the available height for boring, and two more (ID 230 Easington, Figure 5.2.2 and ID 230 Wooler, Figure 5.2.6) have semi-circular depressions either side of the bridge, designed so that the drill could be inserted at as low an angle as possible. These three buttons are all of Type 1.

In two cases, a double set of V-perforations had been supplied (ID 202 Acklam Wold, ID 286 Little Downham). These are not to be confused with cases where a primary V-perforation has broken through at the bridge and then been replaced by a second set of holes on a different alignment. The latter scenario was noted in two cases.

DECORATION

The main aesthetic attraction of the buttons will have been the intense sheen achieved by the polishing of the conical domes. However a few buttons, all from Yorkshire, are also decorated with incised lines. Two Type 1 buttons studied have a single incised groove running around the base of the dome: Easington (ID 230, Figure 5.2.6) and Prescott's Pit (ID 231). Three more of varying Type are embellished with radial zones of decoration, infilled with closely set grooves forming a ladder or feather pattern (ID 312, ID 319, ID 415, Figure 5.2.6). In two cases, there is also a zone of ladder-filled decoration around the base of the dome (e.g. ID 319, Figure 5.2.2).

MATERIAL

Most of the buttons are made from Whitby jet. They range in colour from black and blackish-brown to rich dark brown, and the woodgrain texture of the jet is visible in 12 cases. Extensive criss-cross cracking is visible in 36 cases; this occurs usually on both the dome and the base, but in six cases such cracking was seen only on the dome. The jet identification was confirmed for six Yorkshire buttons by XRF analysis undertaken at National Museums Scotland for this project, and for five examples from Wiltshire (Bussell *et al.* 1982). Some buttons are more evenly black in colour, or tend to a dark grey or grey-brown hue. They also may display a speckled or mottled surface and a stony or compact texture. The cracking is either concentric or laminar in nature. Such items were identified visually as cannel coal or shale by Alison Sheridan or Mary Davis, and most were selected for XRF analysis, either at National Museums Scotland or by our team at the British Museum. Results showed that these buttons had been made from lignite (1 example), cannel coal (4 examples) and shale (4 examples). In addition, Bussell had previously identified four further buttons in Wessex, made from non-jet materials.

MANUFACTURE

Striations surviving from the original shaping of the buttons were commonly observed. A few, always faint, are visible on the dome (7 cases), but most often (37 instances) the striations are located on the base. These are usually multidirectional, with only six cases of unidirectional striations recorded. Sometimes the base striations are crisp (8 cases) or medium in clarity (5 cases) but most (24 instances) are faint. Striations are also visible on 11 facets; in all except one case these are diagonal, indicating that the button had been rotated and rubbed to form the facet. Rilling within the perforations was observed on all but ten of the buttons, and most of the latter were those made from non-jet materials. There is evidence for one change of drilling direction within the perforations for 22 of the buttons studied. In four cases it can be discerned that the end of the drill had been rounded in shape, while in one case the end had been sub-rectangular. Surviving sheen probably relates to the original level of polishing. Low to medium sheen and medium to high sheen occurs almost equally on both the domes and the bases, and there is a contrast between the level of sheen on the dome and base in only seven cases.

COMPLETENESS AND DAMAGE

Most of the buttons survive at or above the 95% level. One has been broken more than this in modern times, while three further examples were severely broken in antiquity but remained in use as a button or as fragments (ID 274 Dow Low, ID 476 West Monkton and ID 285 Shippea Hill). Modern damage usually occurs as flakes or chips around the outer margin of the button, or less often at the apex of the dome. More severe spalling has occurred on some buttons, especially in the Hull and East Riding Museum, where buttons have been removed from card or fabric backings to which they had been attached with adhesive; and some display substantial loss of material from criss-cross cracking and the associated 'cupping' effect.

WEAR

Ancient breaks, acquired during use, were recorded on 23 of the buttons (43%). These are usually small chips and flakes, occurring 13 times on the margin of the button and seven times on the apex of the dome.

Thread-wear was observed as smoothing of the rilling within the perforations, as softening of the perforation edges, and as distinct grooves caused by thread-pull (Figure 5.2.7). In 15 cases thread-wear occurs only at the inner margin of the perforations, adjacent to the bridge, and in only four cases is the wear located only at the outer margins. In a further 15 cases wear was noted at both the inner and outer margins of both perforations. However, in these cases, the wear on the inner bridge margins was greater than that observed on the outer edges. The overall wear patterns suggest that the buttons were indeed used

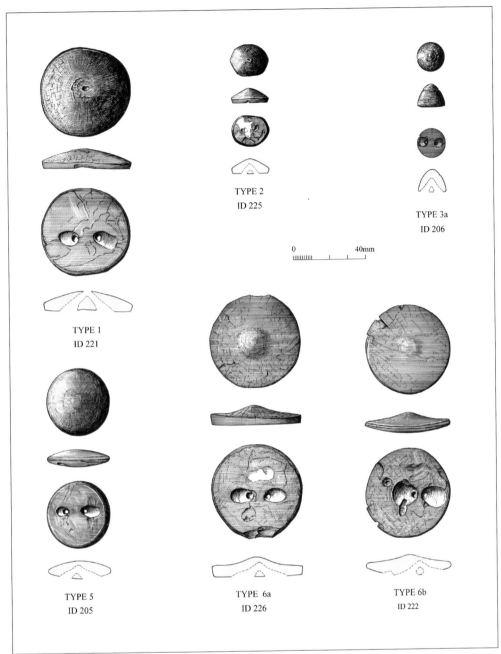

Figure 5.2.1. Examples of V-perforated button types. Type 1: ID 221 Garton Slack 161; Type 2: ID 225 Blanch 238; Type 3a: ID 206 Acklam Wold 124; Type 5: ID 205 Acklam Wold 123; Type 6a: ID 226 Kemp Howe; Type 6b: ID 222 Garton Slack 152; all East Yorkshire. (Drawings by Marion O'Neil).

as buttons, with the thread or cord pulling mainly at the sides of the central bridge. The incidence of some wear on the outer margins of the perforations may indicate that the thread used was very thick, and thus rubbed all round the inside and edge of the perforation. Alternatively the outer wear may have been caused by rubbing, either from the fabric of the garment, or from the cord loop by which the button was fastened.

Overall 24 buttons are classed as fresh or slightly worn, and 28 are moderately or very worn. (Three others could not be classified).

CONCLUSIONS

The buttons vary greatly in size and form, but all the main types have been found in association with each other (Shepherd 2009). They are very fine objects, made using a suite of similar techniques. They display high sheen on both dome and base, although polishing striations often have not been fully removed on the base. The angled drill holes have been made with a round-ended drill, usually with the drill held at one angle, but in *c.* 40% of cases the drill was re-aligned once. This changing of drill angle occurred most on buttons with low domes. Two out of three of the large Type 1 buttons come from Yorkshire or

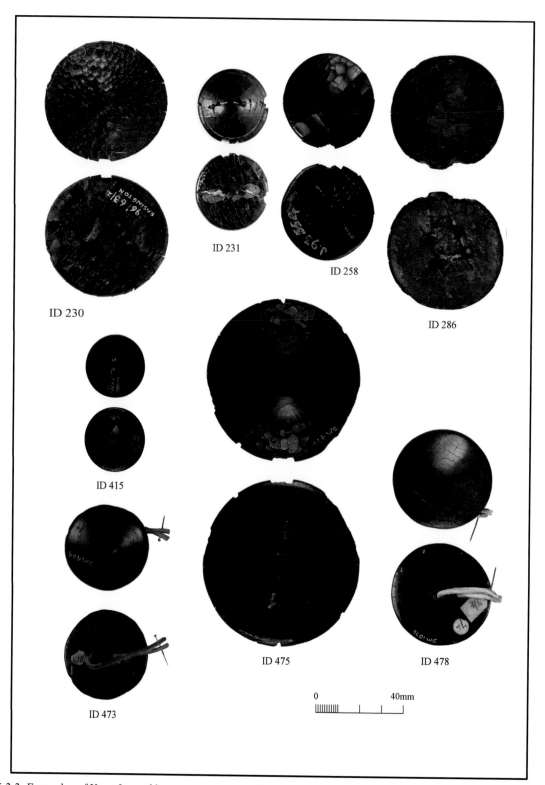

Figure 5.2.2. Examples of V-perforated buttons. Type 1: ID 230 Easington; ID 231 Prescott's Pit, Brough; ID 258 Beechenhill/ Castern; ID 286 Little Downham; ID 415 Huggate Wold; ID 473 Winterbourne Stoke G54; ID 475 Winterbourne Monkton; ID 478 Wimborne St Giles G9.

Derbyshire, and all the fancy examples, of Types 6a and 6b derive from those same counties.

Nearly all the buttons were made from Whitby jet. There are only four examples of non-jet buttons in the north

(ID 255 Middleton-on-the-Wolds, ID 415 Huggate Wold (Figure 5.2.2 and Figure 5.2.6) and two from ID 367–8 Great Tosson). Six out of the 14 buttons from Wessex are of non-jet materials and they belong to the smaller and higher

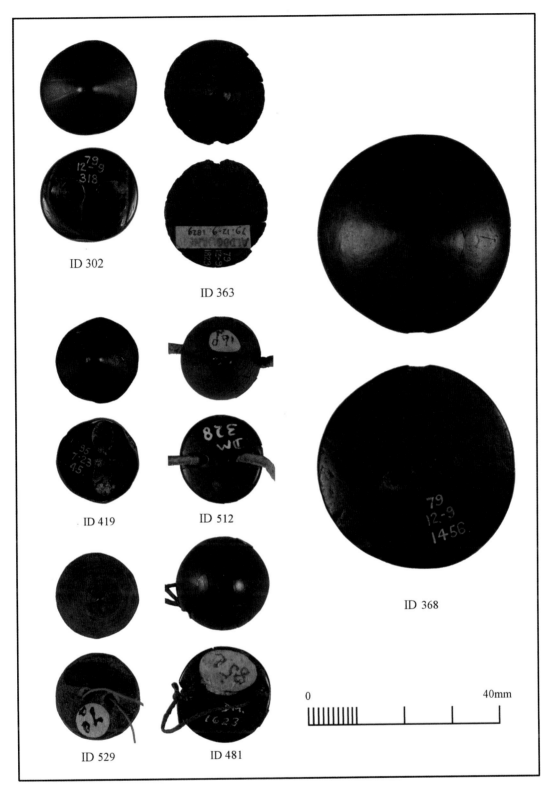

Figure 5.2.3. Examples of V-perforated buttons. Type 2: ID 302 Ganton 27, 4; ID 363 Aldbourne 280; ID 419 Wilsford G50a; ID 512 Amesbury G39; ID 529 Winterbourne Stoke G67. Type 4: ID 481 Durrington Walls. Type 5: ID 368 Great Tosson UN22, 1.

Type 2, while the two non-jet pieces from Derbyshire are of Type 1. Of the four large Yorkshire-type buttons from Wessex graves with Beakers, three are jet and one non-jet. It would seem that the large buttons came initially from Yorkshire, and that they were subsequently copied using the available local material: Kimmeridge shale. The smaller buttons in Wessex, which mostly come from graves of mature Early Bronze Age date, are mainly made from shale.

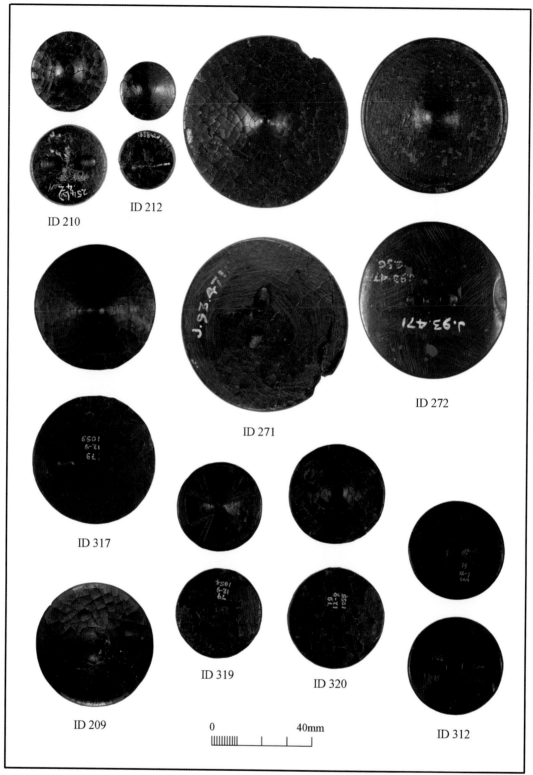

Figure 5.2.4. Examples of V-perforated buttons. Type 6a: ID 210 Hanging Grimston 55; ID 212 Painsthorpe 99; ID 271 Net Low; ID 272 Net Low; ID 317 Rudston 68, 7; ID 319 Rudston 68, 6; ID 320 Rudston 68, 6. Type 6b: ID 209 Hanging Grimston 57; ID 312 Thwing 60, 3.

Shepherd (2009) has assembled the available evidence concerning the placing of jet buttons in relation to the bodies in graves. This suggests that the large single buttons, found on the chest or below the chin, served as cloak fasteners, while some were found in lower leg positions and may have been attached to boots or leggings. Where a single button, or a pair, are associated with a jet or jet-like material pulley ring, the set may have been employed

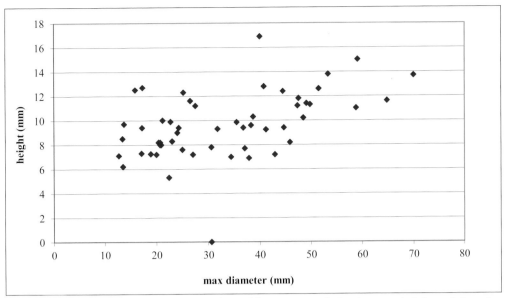

Figure 5.2.5. Jet or jet-like material V-perforated buttons: correlation between height and diameter.

to fasten a belt (but see Chapter 3.4), and other smaller buttons may have functioned as fasteners and decoration for a pouch suspended from the belt. Our study of wear patterns confirms the interpretation of buttons attached to various garments or other fabric items by a cord pulling on the central bridge between the perforations. The eccentric placing of the perforations in 40% of the buttons studied has not previously been noted or discussed. The drill holes may have been designed to occupy the upper half of the button. This would have ensured that the button would lie flat, without the upper half tending to fall forward. Such an arrangement is often found on modern brooches, where the hinged pin is fixed horizontally on the upper part of the back plate. And the overall degree of wear, and occasional re-working, of the buttons demonstrates that these were valued dress accessories with long life spans. Their value is further enhanced by the high polish applied to the raw material, and by the occasional addition of geometric decoration.

Other buttons, either small or medium in size, may occur in groups, sometimes between neck and waist, and were sets of buttons attached to inner garments. These button sets are dealt with in a separate section below (Chapter 5.3).

In many graves the jet or shale button was found as a single grave good. However there is a group of associations for the large Type 1 or Type 6a and 6b buttons which show that they were current in the later Beaker period (see above). Apart from the jet or jet-like material pulley rings (nine instances) which have been referred to above, the associations also include other special items such as daggers, made from flint (two examples) or copper alloy (two examples) and earrings (one example). Although most of the large cloak buttons derive from East Yorkshire, the occurrence of late Beaker graves with button plus other special items is roughly equal between Yorkshire and Wessex.

BONE

TYPO-CHRONOLOGY

In Britain V-perforated buttons made from animal bone are rare. There are only six examples known from England, and four of these have been studied in detail (Table 5.2.3). One, from 'North Dorset' is now lost and another from Ampleforth, Yorks was found with a Collared Urn, but is not illustrated by Longworth (1984, 249). The four studied are all small in size and high-domed, thus resembling the small buttons of central Europe which are most often made from bone. This may imply that the British bone buttons are early in date, and that some may even have been brought in from the continent. No absolute dates exist for the English examples but a domed bone button with two through perforations, from Cookston, Angus, was found with a late Beaker and is dated by radiocarbon to 2460–2045 cal BC at 2 sigma (for details see Baker *et al.* 2003, 103). This is the earliest dated perforated button from Britain, and its punctulated radial decoration resembles that on some of the bone buttons from Beaker graves in central Europe. The pair of buttons from Sutton Veny G11c (ID 920 and 921, Figure 5.2.8) were found with an awl and a lost tin bead, so these also may be relatively early. However the others, from Folkton 71, burial 15 (ID 746, Figure 5.2.8) and Bromham G2 (ID 986, Figures 5.2.6 and 5.2.8) may be from rather later grave contexts, associated respectively with a Food Vessel and the fragments of an accessory cup.

MORPHOLOGY

The four small buttons studied are all relatively high-domed. The diameters range from 13.0 to 19.7mm and the heights from 6.0 to 10.2mm. The pair of buttons from Sutton Veny are particularly small, and are very neatly made. The bridge width between the perforations varies.

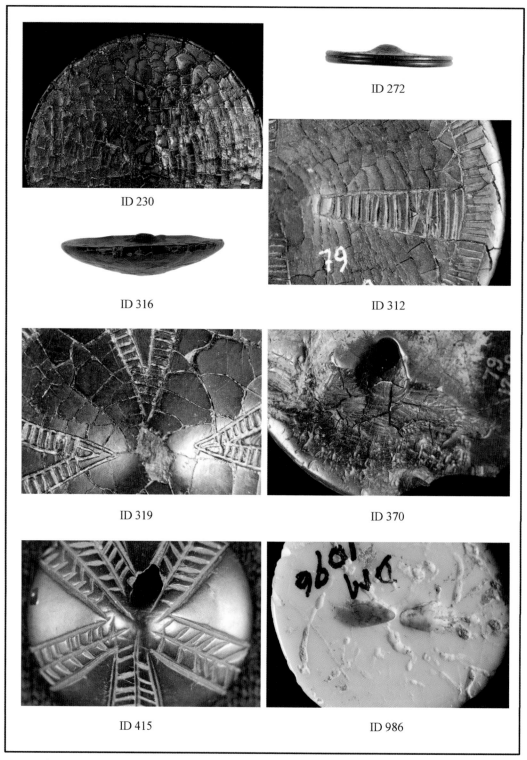

Figure 5.2.6. Details showing incised groove around base on ID 230 Easington, a raised knob or nipple on ID 272 Net Low, a raised bridge area on ID 316 Rudston 68, semi-circular depressions either side of the perforations on ID 370 Wooler, thread-wear grooves on ID 986 Bromham G2, and decoration on ID 312 Thwing 60, 3, ID 319 Rudstone 68, 6 and ID 415 Huggate Wold.

MATERIAL

Two of the buttons are made from small pieces of mammal bone, that from Folkton deriving from a medium-sized mammal and the one from Bromham from a larger animal. Of particular interest are the pair of buttons from Sutton Veny which are made from marine mammal tooth (whale/walrus) and probably from a sperm whale. The ends of the teeth have been sliced off and used to form the dome of each button.

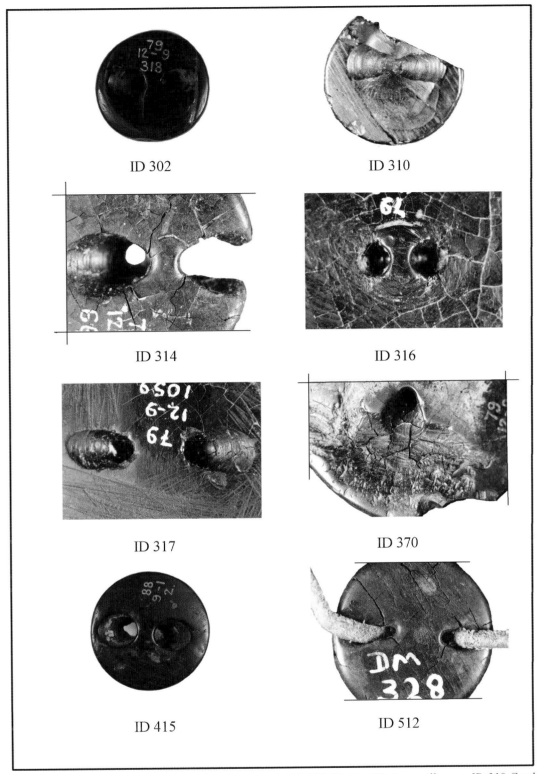

ID 302

ID 310

ID 314

ID 316

ID 317

ID 370

ID 415

ID 512

Figure 5.2.7. Details of wear: on inner edges of perforations on ID 302 Ganton 27, 4; on rilling on ID 310 Cowlam 58; on rilling and inner edge of perforations on ID 314 Rudston 61, 2; on inner edge of perforations on ID 316 Rudston 68, 7; on inner and outer edges of perforations on ID 317 Rudston 68, 7; on inner edges of perforations on ID 370 Wooler UN47, 1 and on ID 415 Huggate Wold; and inner edge of perforations on ID 512 Amesbury G39.

MANUFACTURE

All four buttons are very highly polished and this has removed most traces of shaping. However there are faint multidirectional striations visible on the base of the Folkton button and faint radial ones on the dome of one of the Sutton Veny pair. The interiors of the perforations show no signs of rilling.

COMPLETENESS AND BREAKAGE

The buttons are almost complete and in good condition. All damage is due to wear during use.

WEAR

Two buttons show damage to the apex of the dome and another has two chips acquired during ancient use. The edges of the perforations on the chipped Folkton button are relatively crisp, signifying only slight wear. However the other buttons show evidence of strong thread-wear, usually on the outer edges of the perforations. The Bromham button also has thread-wear forming a groove below the central bridge as well as double thread grooves on the outer margins of both perforations (ID 986, Figure 5.2.6). This button is classed as very worn, and the pair from Sutton Veny are worn.

CONCLUSIONS

The bone buttons are all small in size and neatly made. They are similar to buttons found in Europe and some may be actual imports. Three of them are worn and the nature of the thread-wear indicates that they may have originally been necklace buttons. The Bromham button, found in a slightly later context, appear to have had a long use life, and may have functioned as a button to fasten a garment after its original use within a necklace. The use of sperm whale tooth for the matching pair of buttons from Sutton Veny is of particular importance, as is their association with the (lost) tin tubular bead.

AMBER

TYPO-CHRONOLOGY

A total of 22 amber V-perforated buttons were studied from seven sites. However many of them were found in association with beads and display 'necklace wear': thus they will be considered in the section on composite necklaces (Chapter 8). Those discussed here are listed in Table 5.2.3. Single items include the chunky button from Kelleythorpe (ID 1347) which was found in a Beaker grave with a dagger, a Group VI bracer with gold studs and a large broken bead, also of amber. This is probably the earliest known context for an amber V-perforated button. The associated amber bead recalls that from Culduthel Mains, Inverness, also found with a late Beaker and a gold-studded Group VI bracer, although that bead is more irregular in form (Clarke *et al.* 1985, fig. 4.16). Other single V-perforated items in amber were found with a cremation at Shrewton (now lost) and a long oval piece from Acklam Wold 124. This is considered here, but may have been a necklace fastener. It was found with a jet button and jet pulley ring. The single button from Wimborne St Giles G13 (ID 1505, Figure 5.2.9) had been converted from a broken globular bead, as had one of the smaller buttons from Cowleaze (ID 1271, Figure 5.2.9). The Cowleaze

group was found with other beads and also shale buttons (see above), but as they do not display 'necklace wear' they are considered in this section. Other buttons not studied include those from Felmersham, Chalton and Winterslow (Beck and Shennan 1991, figs. 11.5.3, 11.3.4 and 11.20.1). At Felmersham and Chalton they form components of composite necklaces, while those from Winterslow (not available for study) form a group of buttons which will be considered here. The composite necklaces, some associated with amber spacer plates, would all date from the mature Early Bronze Age and, with the exception of the button from Kelleythorpe, the amber buttons will have been in currency after the main period of use of individual buttons made from jet and shale.

MORPHOLOGY

The V-perforated buttons made from amber are usually oval in shape, in contrast to those made from jet or shale which are round. Amber buttons tend to be much smaller in size, with those considered here varying in length from 12.0 to 28.6mm. They also tend to be high-domed, and this may be a reflection of the difficulty of boring the V-perforations into this raw material. The longest item, from Acklam Wold, is unusual and may have been a necklace fastener.

MATERIAL

The original colour of the glassy and translucent amber varies from bright to dark red, but is much obscured by oxidisation of all surfaces to a cream or toffee colour. It is thought that most of the amber used had been brought in from Scandinavia (Beck and Shennan 1991).

MANUFACTURE

Traces of manufacture are usually obscured by the oxidised surfaces, or by conservation coatings and adhesives. However slight traces of rilling are visible within the perforations in three cases (all Cowleaze). Two buttons had been made using half of a broken large globular bead.

COMPLETENESS AND BREAKAGE

Three buttons show major modern fractures and loss (75 to 95% present), with some breaks having been glued. All items are extremely fragile.

WEAR

Two pieces have minor chips caused by ancient use (below the oxidised surface) and one of the Cowleaze buttons had suffered major breakage in antiquity. The single buttons from Kelleythorpe and Wimborne St Giles G13 have wear on the outer margins of the perforations which might indicate that they had been used at some stage in necklaces; and of course the Kelleythorpe example was associated with one other amber bead. On the other hand, the Cowleaze

Table 5.2.3. List of bone and amber objects studied and illustrated.

Object	Site (Parish), County	Museum	Illustration
Bone			
ID 746	Folkton 71, burial 15, E. Yorks.	BM	Figure 5.2.8
ID 920	Sutton Veny G11c, Wilts.	Dev	Figure 5.2.8
ID 921	Sutton Veny G11c, Wilts.	Dev	Figure 5.2.8
ID 986	Bromham G2, Wilts.	Dev	Figure 5.2.6; Figure 5.2.8
Amber			
ID 207	Acklam Wold 124 (Acklam), E. Yorks.	Hull	Not illustrated
ID 1268	Cowleaze (Winterbourne Steepleton), Dorset	Dor	Figure 5.2.9
ID 1269	Cowleaze (Winterbourne Steepleton), Dorset	Dor	Figure 5.2.9
ID 1270	Cowleaze (Winterbourne Steepleton), Dorset	Dor	Not illustrated
ID 1271	Cowleaze (Winterbourne Steepleton), Dorset	Dor	Figure 5.2.9
ID 1374	Driffield (Kelleythorpe 2 UN101, burial 2), E. Yorks.	BM	Not illustrated
ID 1505	Wimborne St Giles G13, Dorset	Dev	Figure 5.2.9

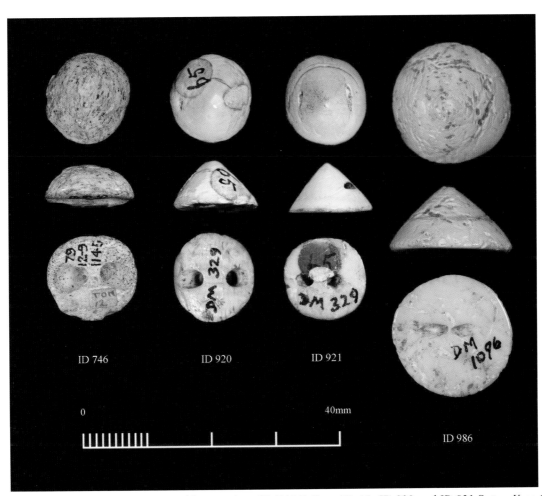

Figure 5.2.8. Examples of bone V-perforated buttons from ID 746 Folkton 71, 15; ID 920 and ID 921 Sutton Veny G11c; ID 986 Bromham G2.

buttons show wear on the inner edges of the perforations, indicating that they had been sewn on individually (Figure 5.2.9) Thus they would resemble some of the sets of jet buttons. Overall four buttons were slightly worn, two worn and one indeterminate.

CONCLUSIONS

Most of the V-perforated amber buttons are small and form components of composite necklaces or amber spacer plate necklaces. These are Early Bronze Age in date. However, one set of buttons may have been sewn onto a garment as

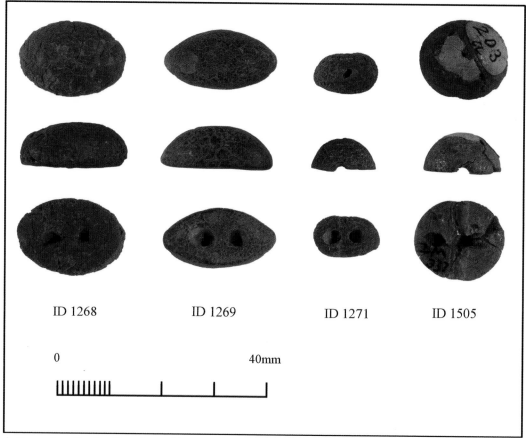

Figure 5.2.9. Examples of amber V-perforated buttons from Cowleaze (ID 1268, ID 1269 and ID 1271) and Wimborne St Giles G13 (ID 1505).

ornaments. The two items from Kelleythorpe and Acklam Wold are probably slightly earlier in date i.e. before or around 2000 cal BC. The unusual buttons from Winterslow (not available for study) may also have been a set from a garment. The group includes four square, prismatic buttons with rectangular bases (Shepherd Type 7) and 18 small round high-domed buttons (Shepherd Type 3a) along with one longer piece which possibly had been a fastener or functional button (Shepherd 2009, 360). This group was found with a secondary cremation in a Cornish urn, with a bronze class 1 razor and accessory vessel. These artefacts date from the very end of the Early Bronze Age.

STONE

Very few V-perforated buttons made from stone are known. The only one studied in detail is that contained within the button set from Butterwick (see Chapter 5.3), and another forms part of the button set from Rameldry, Fife (Baker *et al.* 2003, Ill. 3,2). A third button was found at Boscregan, Cornwall in association with a cremation, probably of a woman or child, and a set of faience and shale beads (Borlase 1885, 188–9). This was a small hemispherical button which appears to have been converted from a large globular bead 12.7mm in diameter (*ibid*, fig. C). It was made from 'a substance undetermined, but of the appearance of a concrete'.

5.3 BUTTON SETS OF JET AND JET-LIKE MATERIALS *(with Alison Sheridan)*

ID 232–44 Garton Slack VI, grave 1, burial 1, East Yorkshire, set of 13 buttons

CONTEXT

The 13 buttons (Figure 5.3.1) were found in an oval grave containing the skeleton of an adult aged 20 to 25, crouched on its right side, with head to the south; it is assumed that the grave had been covered with a scrape mound (Brewster 1980, 202–6 and 703). Brewster reports that the sex was probably female, but added that the skeleton had some male features (p. 703). The buttons lay in an untidy row, in the chest area, all with their base side upwards. A broken composite necklace comprising tubular sheet bronze beads and tiny black disc beads made from relatively low-quality jet was also found (ID 250, Chapter 7). Brewster's account of the relative positions of the buttons and necklace varies, with the caption to his fig. 90 stating that the necklace was found below the buttons, yet his description (p.205) states that the necklace had been on top; either way, he interpreted the buttons as having been attached to a garment that had been folded and laid on the corpse's chest along with the deliberately-broken necklace (Brewster 1980, 202 and figs. 89–92; Dent 1983, 10). The illustrations are listed in Table 5.3.1. The skeleton was radiocarbon-dated (see Chapter 9).

MORPHOLOGY

The buttons range in diameter from 20 to 38mm, and in height from 5.2 to 11.2mm. Most are roughly circular in plan, with ID 236–38 being roughly oval; bases are in most cases flat, but very slightly convex in ID 233, ID 237 and ID 243, and more markedly convex in ID 235 and 236. Four of the largest buttons (ID 239–41 and ID 243) have a low concavo-convex dome with a well-defined facet. ID 238 has a high, almost hipped profile, while the rest are low (or low to medium-) domed, with a continuously curving upper surface.

MATERIAL

On the basis of macroscopic examination and (in the case of ID 232–37 and ID 244) of analysis using X-ray fluorescence spectrometry (by Lore Troalen of NMS), it is clear that nine of the buttons are of Whitby jet (ID 233–34 and ID 238–244). All but one of these (ID 233) are of soft jet, as revealed in their extensive criss-cross cracking; ID 233 is probably of hard jet. The jet buttons are in various shades of a rich dark brown and blackish-brown; their fine-grained woody texture is evident in the patterning of the colour, the nature of the surface cracking and in exposed sub-surface areas. The four non-jet buttons (ID 232 and ID 235–37) are all of the same black to blackish-grey material, which is compact, 'stony' rather than 'woody' in texture, and iron-rich, and contains black-brown iron-rich inclusions. It is probably cannel coal or oil shale.

MANUFACTURE

Grinding striations on the base and dome (and facet, where one exists) are generally sparse and faint or very faint. The exception is the bases of ID 233 and ID 243; in the latter case, crisper striations occur where the convex base rises up towards the edge. Base and dome striations are multi-directional, while those on facets are mostly unidirectional (except on ID 239). Borehole rilling (in various degrees of faintness) was noted in 11 examples, and ID 232 also had gouge-like scratches running down one of the perforations. Obvious changes of drill direction were noted in seven cases, and where the shape of the drill tip could be observed at the bottom of perforations, it was rounded. Ancient flake or chip scars, caused during manufacture, were noted on five buttons; they occur variously on the dome, base, edge and next to the V-perforation. On ID 234, a small hole at the top of the dome is likely to relate to too-deep perforation drilling. Excepting ID 234 and ID 242, no pair of perforations showed obvious 'vertical' eccentricity, although 'lateral' eccentricity (i.e. with the end of one perforation lying closer to the edge than its counterpart) was noted in four instances.

ID 240, the largest button (Figure 5.3.2) displays a complex history of borehole drilling, in response to the failure of the initial bridge. It appears that a second pair of holes was used until its bridge also broke; then various abortive attempts were made to create other viable hole pairs before a final, perpendicular hole was drilled from the top of the dome. At least two different drills had been used, one with a round tip and another (seen in three drillings) apparently with a hollow tip.

Regarding surface finish, all the buttons had been polished, generally to a low or medium sheen (with the curving parts of the base of ID 243 being less polished than elsewhere). Where differing levels of sheen were noted within a button, the dome is glossier than the base.

COMPLETENESS AND DAMAGE

Apart from the wear-induced damage noted in ID 240, and the chipping and spalling caused during manufacture as noted above, the main type of damage is post-depositional loss of spalls and chips as a result of the cracking of the soft jet. The only other damage is the ancient loss of two small spalls from the top of the dome on ID 238, and the loss of inclusions from the base of ID 235, leaving small rough areas. All the buttons are essentially intact.

WEAR

All the buttons show wear, albeit to different degrees. The most heavily worn is ID 240 (Figure 5.3.2). This button is important in demonstrating the role of fabric rub in softening perforation edges, since some of the abandoned perforations have slightly softened edges (although these are still markedly crisper than in many of the buttons' 'functional' holes). That ID 240 had been used after its final,

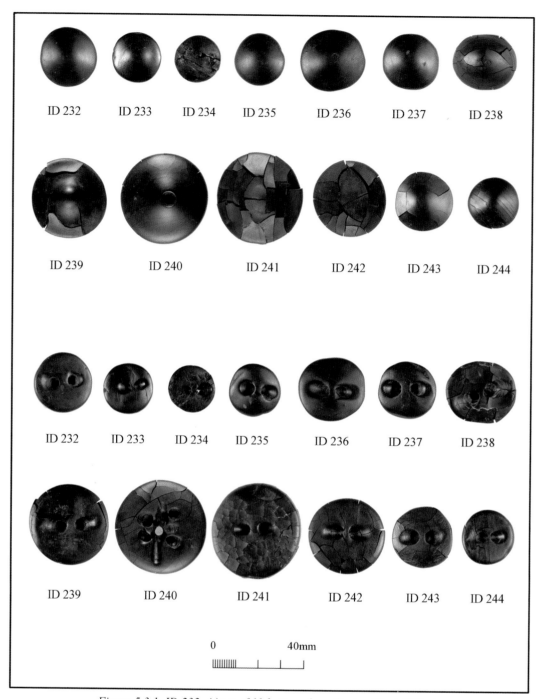

Figure 5.3.1. ID 232–44 set of 13 buttons from Garton Slack VI/1, 1.

perpendicular perforation is shown by the edge-smoothing and interior polish to this hole.

Thread-wear is manifested in the smoothing of perforation edges (all around in most cases, but more markedly to the outer edges) and the polishing of the outer part of the perforation interior (all around, including the bridge). On the large concavo-convex button ID 239 (Figure 5.3.1), the whole of the perforation interior has been thread-smoothed. ID 235 has two thread grooves running across the bridge (Figure 5.3.2); these suggest that the thread at this point had been *c.* 2.3mm thick. ID 237 has a similar, but fainter pair running across the bridge; here, the thread

was only *c.* 1.8mm thick. A similarly thin and faint thread groove was noted on ID 242. ID 232 has uneven thread-wear, with a possible thread-pull groove to the inner edge of one perforation and thread-wear to the outer edge of the opposite hole. The maximum likely thickness of a thread is *c.* 3mm, as estimated in the case of ID 233.

Probable evidence for fabric rub was noted on several buttons, occurring on the base (mostly at the bridge and around the perforations, as seen in the otherwise lightly-worn ID 243, Figure 5.3.2) and/or the apex of the dome. In each of these cases, the difference in sheen that is likely to have been caused by this is minimal. Overall, six of

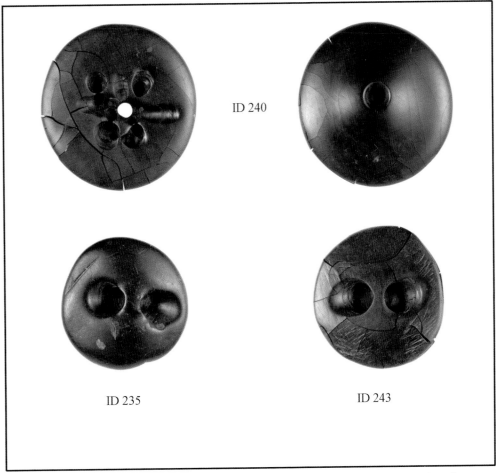

Figure 5.3.2. Garton Slack VI/1, 1: details showing complex history of drilling on ID 240, double thread groove across bridge on ID 235 and fabric rub on bridge and around perforations on ID 243 (not to scale).

the buttons are very worn, six are worn and only one is slightly worn.

CONCLUSIONS

The variability in size, shape, material and wear suggests that this group of buttons had not originated as a single set, but instead had probably been acquired at different times, before being attached to clothing (probably a jacket-like garment). It may be that the large concavo-convex buttons had been 'recycled' from an older garment; the care taken to extend the life of ID 240 – culminating in its final (and rather clumsy) perpendicular threading – demonstrates the value attached to these items. The similarity in material and degree of wear among the non-jet buttons suggests that they, too, could have come from a set (or at least had been made at the same time as each other). The fact that thread-wear has been noted all around the interior of the perforations in virtually every case indicates that the buttons had been used as functioning (toggle-like) buttons, rather than as decorative studs or as beads, at least at some point in their lives. Their spatial arrangement within the grave suggested to Brewer (1980, 204) that they might have been

attached to the garment as two rows, with no particular order in terms of size.

ID 565–69 Raunds 1, primary burial, Northamptonshire, set of five buttons

CONTEXT

A set of five buttons was found in a cache of objects near the feet of a crouched adult male in Barrow 1. The grave was then covered by a limestone cairn and a covering of cattle skulls (Harding and Healy 2007, fig. 4.6). The following text summarises observations made by Shepherd with some additions resulting from renewed study (by AW) in 2007. The illustrations are listed in Table 5.3.1.

MORPHOLOGY

There are four small buttons and one large (>25mm diameter). They range in base diameter from 18 to 26mm, with three being slightly oval in shape. The smaller buttons seem to fall into two pairs, one of diameter 18.0 to 9.1mm and the other with diameters of 22.0 to 23.5mm. All have straight-sided conical domes and flat bases. In height they vary from 7.0 to 10.6mm, but the heights do not correlate directly with size, and one of the smaller buttons is relatively high (ID 566). The oval perforations are positioned slightly eccentrically in the vertical plane on three of the buttons. Bridge width is narrow except in one case (ID 565). All possess a facet of uneven height and slightly angled outwards from the base.

MATERIAL

All the buttons are black in colour. There is no criss-cross cracking, but laminar cracking, often concentric, is visible in all cases. Visually the material displayed some of the characteristics of high-grade lignite (e.g. the lack of criss-cross cracking), but the four smaller buttons show some signs of the woody texture typical of jet. However analysis by Mary Davis using XRF and SEM techniques indicated that all the buttons were made from low-grade jet from the Whitby source.

MANUFACTURE

Faint striations from the original shaping are visible on the dome in three cases, and on four of the facets. Marked multi-directional striations occur on the base in four cases, especially towards the centre where they have not been worn away. On the remaining example the striations are uni-directional. Rilling is visible in all perforations and on two buttons two drill directions are evident in one of the holes. In all cases the surfaces of the button had been polished to a high sheen, but some flake scars, and natural imperfections within the jet have not been polished out. On button ID 567 the striations on the facet are fresh, and the lower edge of the facet cuts into the more worn striations on the base. This suggests that this facet was added at a secondary stage of working.

COMPLETENESS AND DAMAGE

The buttons are all virtually complete, with the only damage relating to loss of some material within the concentric laminar cracks.

WEAR

There is little sign of any breakage during use, but all the perforations show evidence of wear, albeit to varying degrees. This comprises softening of the edges and of the internal rilling, plus one distinct instance of thread-pull on the outer edge of one perforation on button ID 569. Most wear is on the inner edges of the perforations, at the bridge, and this suggests that they had been used as buttons, or sewn onto a garment fairly tightly. One button is very worn, two moderately worn, one slightly worn and one only scarcely used at all (ID 567). In several cases there is also fabric wear around the margins of the base.

CONCLUSIONS

The five buttons do not form a unified set. The variations in overall size may suggest that the group comprised one larger button and two smaller pairs, although the dome heights are totally variable. The large button was the most used and this piece was large enough to have originally been a single fastener for a cloak (see individual buttons section above). The other four buttons show slight to moderate use, with the wear on the perforations indicating a function as buttons or decorative studs.

Shepherd (Harding and Healy 2007, digital section) notes that the addition of the facet on button ID 567 at a secondary stage may indicate that this button was modified at the time of burial. It may have been an attempt to make this button match the other five faceted examples that were to be deposited. The four smaller buttons may have been a set which embellished a garment belonging to the deceased. But, if so, the variation in degree of wear may indicate that they had been acquired from several different sources. Size-wise there may have been two pairs represented, but the detailed wear patterns do not strengthen this possibility. Alternatively, and as the buttons were found in a cache containing many other items, some of them also exotic, it may be that the individual buttons were contributed separately by different members of the family or mourning party. However, if this did occur, then care was taken, by the addition of the facet to the one plain button, to make them look like a unified set.

ID 337–56 Hunmanby 250, burial 3, East Yorkshire, set of 20 buttons

CONTEXT

An adult inhumation was crouched on its right hand side, with head at the west, and in an oval grave. The set of 20 buttons (probably studs) (Figure 5.3.3) were located in a row from the neck to the waist. There was a bronze ring at the hips, a sherd at the feet and 'seven ribs of small ox behind hips' (Kinnes and Longworth 1985, 119, no. 250). Illustrations and cross-referencing to Kinnes and Longworth's illustrations are listed in Table 5.3.1 and Table 5.3.2.

MORPHOLOGY

All are small, conical 'buttons', with straight sides, round-pointed apices, flat bases and narrow, gently-inclined facets. All but two are high-domed, the others being medium-domed. In 13 cases the facets are themselves faceted (e.g. ID 356, Figure 5.3.4). The base is circular in three cases and slightly oval in the rest. The perforations are all oval and the bridge is narrow in five cases, medium-width in 13 cases and wide in two (e.g. ID 341, Figure 5.3.4). The maximum basal dimension ranges from 13.8 to 16.0mm – a narrow range – but the height ranges from 5.6 to 9.7mm, a difference of 4.1mm.

Table 5.3.1. List of button sets of jet and jet-like materials studied and illustrated. *Note: the finds as illustrated in Harding and Healy 2007, fig 4.7 are un-numbered. The cross-reference numbering here runs from top to bottom, i.e. ID 565 is no. 1 (top), ID 569 is no. 5 (bottom).

Object	Cross reference	Site (Parish), County	Illustration
ID 232-44		Garton Slack VI Grave 1, group, (Garton-on-the-Wolds), E. Yorks.	Figure 5.3.1; Figure 5.3.2 (ID 235, ID 240, ID 243)
ID 565	AOR 34861: Harding and Healy 2007 fig. 4.6, no 1	Raunds 1, Northants.*	Not illustrated
ID 566	AOR 34862: Harding and Healy 2007 fig. 4.6, no 2	Raunds 1, Northants.*	Not illustrated
ID 567	AOR 34863: Harding and Healy 2007 fig. 4.6, no 3	Raunds 1, Northants.*	Not illustrated
ID 568	AOR 34864: Harding and Healy 2007 fig. 4.6, no 4	Raunds 1, Northants.*	Not illustrated
ID 569	AOR 34870: Harding and Healy 2007 fig. 4.6, no 5	Raunds 1, Northants.*	Not illustrated
ID 337-56		Hunmanby 250, burial 3, E. Yorks.	Figure 5.3.3; Figure 5.3.4 (ID 341, 346, 347, 348, 356)
ID 18		Butterwick 39, burial 1, E. Yorks.	Figure 5.3.5
ID 303-307		Butterwick 39, burial 1, E. Yorks.	Figure.5.3.5

Table 5.3.2. Cross-reference table between ID numbers cited here and Kinnes and Longworth illustration (1985, 199: Hunmanby, site 250, burial 3).

Object number	Line illustration in Kinnes and Longworth 1985
ID 337	row 2, 3
ID 338	row 5, 2
ID 339	row 1, 2
ID 340	row 1, 1
ID 341	row 1, 4
ID 342	row 3, 1
ID 343	row 2, 1
ID 344	row 3, 3
ID 345	row 4, 1
ID 346	row 4, 2
ID 347	row 5, 4
ID 348	row 3, 2
ID 349	row 2, 2
ID 350	probably row 5, 1
ID 351	probably row 2, 4
ID 352	row 5, 3 or row 1, 3
ID 353	probably row 4, 3
ID 354	not identified to drawing
ID 355	not identified to drawing
ID 356	not identified to drawing

MATERIAL

Two of the buttons, ID 339 and ID 340, are a black and grey-brown, while the others are either all black (four) or mottled black-brown, with exposed sub-surfaces appearing as dark brown. In eight cases the dome is a mottled black-brown and the base is black. Eighteen of the buttons have criss-cross-cracking (mostly hairline), and in nine of these cases the cracking is concentric; ID 339 has hairline concentric cracks and laminar spalling; and ID 343 – one of the black-brown buttons – has no cracking. One shows a conchoidal fracture (ID 346, Figure 5.3.4). Sixteen of the buttons have a very fine-grained woody texture, while four – including the distinctively-coloured ID 339 and ID 340, along with ID 343 and ID 348 – appear to have a coarser woody structure, reminiscent of lignite.

Visually it appeared that while all the buttons were of jet, some may be of a lower quality, resembling lignite. Three buttons (ID 338, ID 342 and ID 344) were analysed by XRF at the British Museum (DH/MD), and a fragment from ID 343 was analysed by Dr J M Jones using reflected light microscopy. The results confirmed that the lignitic-like material was indeed jet, of a slightly lower quality than the rest; Jones remarks that the jet of ID 343 'is very cellular, showing the original plant structure'.

MANUFACTURE

Striations from shaping the buttons were noted on all 20 buttons – on the dome in 17 cases, and on the base and facet in all cases. The dome striations are faint to very faint and mostly concentric; those on the base are crisp and almost

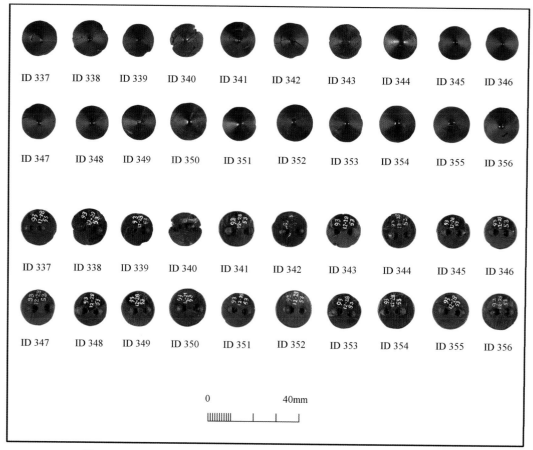

Figure 5.3.3. ID 337–356 set of 20 buttons from Hunmanby 250, burial 3.

universally unidirectional; while on the facet they range from crisp to faint and are diagonal, indicating that the button was rotated and rubbed to create the facet. In many cases, the facet is noticeably narrower in one sector; this may indicate that the same person had made the set, using a standardised range of practices. Rilling is visible in all the perforations (except in button ID 340, where glue and sediment obscure the holes), and changes of drill direction are clear, with 3 buttons having evidence for one to two repositionings, and 16 having more than two. Where the end of the perforation is visible – in 15 buttons – in all cases a round-ended drill had been used.

In almost every case, the dome had been polished to a medium to high sheen, while the base had only a low or minimal sheen. Some of the facets have a low sheen, others a medium sheen.

COMPLETENESS AND DAMAGE

Most of the buttons are over 95% complete. Ancient damage consists of the loss of small chips, 12 on the base or facet, two on the apex. A small fragment had become detached from ID 343 since its excavation; part of this was used for analysis by Dr J M Jones.

WEAR

Wear traces consist mostly of fabric rub, localised to the apices (14 cases), around the top of the facet (16 cases) and around the outer edges of the perforations on the base (all cases, e.g. ID 348, Figure 5.3.4). Elsewhere on the bases, however, the grinding striations are still crisp. Thread-wear was noted in the perforations on six buttons, and possible thread-wear on a seventh. In all cases it occurred as thread-smoothing to the outer edges of the perforations, and in four of these (including the 'possible') there was also thread-smoothing at the perforations' inner edge as well, at and near the bridge. In general, the overall degree of wear is slight. Nineteen were classified as slightly worn, and only one as worn.

CONCLUSIONS

The consistency in the buttons' shape, size, manufacture and condition strongly suggests that this was a set made by a single person. The slight variability in the quality of the material used may simply relate to what was available at the time of manufacture. The minimal degree of wear, and the localised nature of the fabric rub, suggests that these items were not used as functioning buttons, but had been attached to a garment as decorative studs; the 'nipple rub' on the dome suggests that a further garment had been worn over this one (e.g. ID 347, Figure 5.3.4). Overall, the

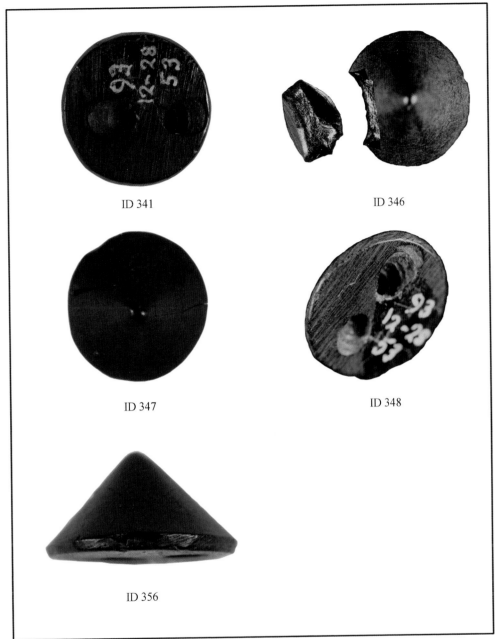

ID 341

ID 346

ID 347

ID 348

ID 356

Figure 5.3.4. Details of Hunmanby buttons showing: wide bridge on ID 341; conchoidal fracture on ID 346; nipple rub on ID 347; fabric rub on base around perforations on ID 348; faceting of the facet on ID 356.

relatively minor degree of wear suggests that these items had not been worn for very long before being buried.

ID 18 and 303–307 Butterwick 39, burial 1, East Yorkshire, set of 6 buttons

CONTEXT

An adult male burial was crouched on his left hand side, head at the north-east with dagger in hand pointing towards the chin and with a bronze axe at the hips with its haft trace extending towards the heels. The six buttons (Figure 5.3.5) lay along the chest (Kinnes and Longworth 1985,

39, 4–9; Greenwell and Rolleston 1877, 186–91). The set consists of four jet buttons, together with one made from cannel coal, and one of stone. The illustrations are listed in Table 5.3.1.

MORPHOLOGY

In shape the buttons are quite variable, with three nearly circular and three of them markedly oval in outline. The maximum diameters range from 30.4 to 49.8mm. Two of them are relatively low-domed (ID 305–7) while the stone button is much higher than any of the jet ones. Four have concavo-convex sides, but one is straight-sided (ID 307) and one has a continuously curving profile (ID 304). Two of them have a convex base (ID 305 and the stone button ID 18), but this feature does not correlate with any one form of dome profile. The perforations are all oval in shape, but the bridges vary from narrow (four examples) to medium and wide. The width of the perforations in the stone button was considerably larger, suggesting that a different style of drill was required for this harder raw material. The setting of the perforations is not always central. In two cases one perforation was located rather close to the edge of the button, and in four cases the V-perforation was placed nearer to the top of the button than to its bottom.

MATERIAL

The stone button is pale greenish-brown in colour while the rest are black. In two cases the woody texture of soft Whitby jet is visible on the base and all bar one have the criss-cross cracking which is typical of this raw material. Visually four of the buttons appeared to be made from jet, but the fifth showed some non-jet characteristics (ID 304). Two buttons were analysed using the XRF technique (DH/MD). One (ID 305) was found to be jet, while the other (ID 304) was identified as cannel coal. The stone button is made from a fine-grained probably crystalline rock. This may be a rhyolite or acid volcanoclastic rock, and, if so may derive from the Cheviots (See Appendix VI).

MANUFACTURE

All the black buttons except one (ID 305) have original polishing striations still visible on the base. These are faint and multidirectional except in the case of ID 307, where they are more marked and occur in one direction only. All have a low to medium sheen, but this is somewhat obscured by modern coatings. In most cases there is evidence for one change of direction of drilling in each perforation, but in two buttons (ID 304 and ID 306) the drill had been realigned three times. Rilling within the perforations is very faint in all except one and the stone button ID 18. Furthermore two of them had been re-bored, with the remains of two successive V-perforations. Only five chips had been incurred at the time of manufacture. One perforation in the stone button shows two changes of direction. This was probably drilled first, with the second perforation being drilled in one operation only.

The stone button is also unusual in that it is the only one to have been decorated. The decoration consists of four radial incised lines on the dome, which do not meet at the apex, and a single incised line around the outer edge of the flat base. The widths of these grooves are 1.3mm on the dome and 1.5mm on the base.

COMPLETENESS AND DAMAGE

Amongst the group as a whole 22 breaks were recorded. Of these eight were modern, and four of the buttons survive virtually complete.

WEAR

All six buttons had certainly been used, as the perforations showed indications of thread-wear with the rilling smoothed away. However this wear is located in different areas of the perforations as follows: mainly on the outer edges of the perforations in buttons ID 303, ID 305 (both successive V-perforations) and ID 307 (initial V-perforation) and mainly towards the bridge in the perforations of buttons ID 304 and ID 306. In the second V-perforation of ID 307 the thread-wear extended all round the insides of the perforations. The rilling within the perforations of the stone button did not show any signs of wear, but there was a distinct sheen visible on the apex of the dome, and this may result from fabric rub suffered during wear. Ancient damage during the use lives of the buttons occurred only on ID 305 and ID 307. In the case of ID 305 the damage related to the breaking through of the initial V-perforation, and on ID 307 there is ancient edge damage and cracking on the base. The stone bead also displays ancient large chips on its edge, indicative of a long use life.

Overall, the cannel coal button ID 304 appears to be in fresh condition, and was the newest button in the set. Jet buttons ID 303 and ID 306 were slightly worn, while the re-used buttons ID 305 and ID 307, along with the stone button, could be classified as very worn.

CONCLUSIONS

The set of V-perforated buttons was found on the chest of the skeleton and may therefore relate to the fastening, or embellishment, of one or more garments. However, in terms of material, size and shape the individual buttons vary greatly, and it can be concluded that the items were not manufactured as a set but had been gathered together from various different sources. The wear patterns suggest that the set comprises two pairs of buttons (ID 303 and ID 306; ID 305 and 307) made from jet. The latter pair is very worn, and also rebored, indicating a longer use life than for the others. The fresh cannel coal button ID 304 may have been made specially to make up the complete set prior to deposition.

Within the new set, the thread wear patterns might suggest that ID 304 and 306, the two smaller buttons, may have been sewn on tightly through their centres, as a pair, and used as functional fastening buttons. The three other jet buttons, with signs of wear on the outer edges of the perforations may have been sewn on differently, perhaps in a tight row, to perform as permanent decorative studs. The stone button would have stood out as something very different, with its pale colour and different texture, and because it was the only button bearing decoration. It also contrasts very strongly with the other buttons in terms of weight, as it weighs approximately twice as much as any of the black buttons. Perhaps this item had a slightly different function in relation to its positioning on the garments concerned. It is also interesting to note that if this button had been attached tightly, the decoration on the base would not have been visible.

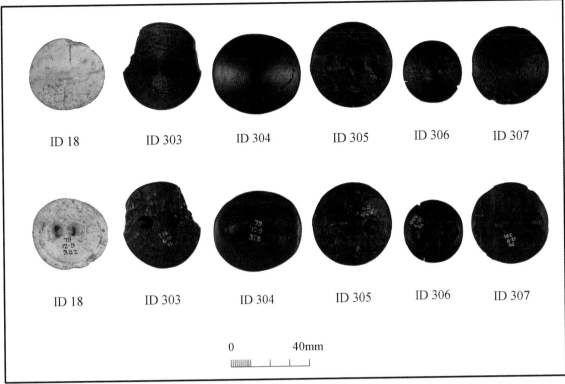

Figure 5.3.5. ID 18 and ID 303–307 set of six buttons from Butterwick 39, burial 1.

GENERAL DISCUSSION

FUNCTION

Four button sets from England have been studied in detail and have been described above (see Table 5.3.1 for list of those illustrated). Most of the buttons are made from jet, but a few are of cannel coal, and one of stone. The most uniform set is the group of 20 small buttons from Hunmanby (Figure 5.3.3). These were probably made by a single craftsman and they display equal degrees of wear. They were probably attached to an inner garment where they functioned as decorative studs rather than working buttons, and the location of some of the fabric rub on the apices suggests that a further garment was worn on top of the decorated shirt or tunic. The buttons were found in a row from neck to waist. Overall, wear traces are slight. The group of 13 buttons from Garton Slack VI, 1, grave 1 is much more variable (Figure 5.3.1). At least three groups of buttons may have been gathered together. Four small to medium-sized buttons are made from cannel coal or lignite and show similar degrees of medium to heavy wear. Four of the largest jet buttons have concavo-convex profiles and are even more worn, especially one item which displays repeated re-borings. Both these groups of buttons may have experienced use lives on previous garments. The remainder of the jet buttons are mainly small in size and exhibit slightly less wear. When combined, the 13 buttons appear to have been attached to the front of a garment in two vertical rows, of six and seven buttons respectively. The presence of thread-grooves across the bridge on four

buttons, and the fact that thread-wear occurs all around the interior of the perforations in virtually every case, indicates that the buttons had been used as functioning (toggle-like) buttons, rather than as decorative studs or as beads. This is in marked contrast to the button set from Hunmanby (see above and Figure 5.3.3) where the buttons had probably been sewn on as ornaments, and where overall wear was slight.

Smaller sets of buttons come from Raunds and Butterwick. The five buttons from Raunds were not found on the body and show varying degrees of wear. One is rather larger than the others, but not particularly so. This one is very worn and may have started out its life as a single cloak fastener. Amongst the smaller buttons, one is fresh and had its facet added just prior to deposition. Thus the set may have been put together for the burial, and indeed the individual buttons may have been contributed by different members of the funeral party. The set of six buttons from Butterwick is equally diverse, although all of these are much larger than the sets discussed so far (Figure 5.3.5). The five black buttons appear to comprise two pairs in jet, one of which had been rebored, and a fresh single button made from cannel coal. The largest button is that made from stone. This is very worn and is decorated with an incised cruciform design. Wear patterns may indicate that the two smaller buttons acted as functional fasteners, while others were permanently sewn on as decorative embellishments. All were found in the chest area of the body.

Some of the characteristics of these four button sets are summarised in Table 5.3.3, and this also includes details of

Ritual in Early Bronze Age Grave Goods

Table 5.3.3. Key characteristics of button sets from England and Scotland.

Site	County	Total	Material	Size range (mm)	Facets	Dec	Worn/ very worn	Slight to moderate wear	Fresh
Raunds	Northants	5	Jet	18–26	All	None	1	3	1
Hunmanby	E. Yorks.	20	Jet	13.8–16	All	None	-	20	-
Butterwick	E. Yorks.	6	Jet 4	30.4–49.8	No	1	2	2	-
			C.coal 1				-	-	1
			Stone 1				1	-	-
Garton Slack VI/1	E. Yorks.	13	Jet 9	20–38	4	None	5	8	-
			C.coal or lignite 4						
Harehope	Peebles	32	Jet or jet-like material	18–34; 63	?	13	-	11	21
Migdale	Sutherland	6	Jet or jet-like material	28.5–45	?	2	6	-	-
Rameldry	Fife	6	Jet 5	42.3–49.8	None	1	1	4	1
			Stone 1						
Kirkaldy	Fife	12	Jet/ lignite	12.7–20.4	A few	None	-	-	-
Ingleby Barwick	N. Yorks.	17 + 7 frags	Jet	12–18 two 'sets'	?	None	-	-	-
Street House	N. Yorks.	20	Jet	14–20 three 'sets'	11	None	2	10	-

four sets of buttons from Scotland and two from northern England, with which our data may be compared. The northern British examples are from Street House (Jelley in Vyner 1984) and Ingleby Barwick (Vyner forthcoming).

The uniform set of button from Hunmanby can best be compared with the set of small buttons from Kirkaldy (Piggott and Stewart 1958), found with a Beaker burial, although these seem to vary rather more in shape and size. No details relating to wear are available. The group of 32 buttons from Harehope are slightly more diverse (Jobey 1980; Clarke *et al.* 1985, 273–4 and fig. 5.46). The size range is very great, and a large number of them are decorated with a ladder pattern cruciform design. The buttons fall into two groups, one of them worn and one very fresh. This may indicate that two different sets of buttons, comprising 11 and 21 buttons each, were combined before or at the time of deposition. However, both sets contain buttons which are decorated in the same style. The smaller sets of five small buttons from Raunds and the six relatively large buttons from Butterwick can be compared with the sets of six buttons each from Rameldry (Sheridan in Baker *et al.* 2003) and Migdale (Clarke *et al.* 1985, 303 and fig. 4.37). The Migdale set forms part of a hoard, but the Rameldry buttons were found in front of a crouched body, albeit in disturbed positions. As at Butterwick, one of the Rameldry buttons is decorated and one is made from stone. However while at Butterwick it is the stone button that is decorated, at Rameldry the stone button is enhanced with a coloured coating and one of the jet buttons is decorated with a complex geometric design which had been infilled with tin (the Rameldry stone button is made from lizardite which may have come from a Scottish source, or perhaps from Cornwall). As at Butterwick and Raunds, one of the buttons is much fresher and may have been added to the

set at the time of deposition. The group of six buttons in the Migdale hoard all appear to be worn, but two have traces of incised decoration which had not been completed.

Overall it does appear that there seem to have been two main types of button set. Firstly, there are the large sets of small buttons, which, on the basis of our study of the Hunmanby items, may have been sewn-on decorative studs rather than functional buttons. However wear patterns on the set from Garton Slack indicate that all the buttons in that group may have been functional toggle-like fasteners. In contrast, the smaller groups of buttons contain examples which are much larger in size. Some of the components display evidence of long use lives, and some may have started their lives as single or paired cloak fasteners. Single fresh items are often added to complete a set at the time of deposition, and these may be of alternative materials such as cannel coal. Two groups contain a single button made from stone, and decorated examples tend to occur once only in a group. Use wear indicates that these smaller sets may have included some items functioning as fasteners and some as sewn-on ornaments. However the number of buttons seems to have been tightly prescribed, at five or six items per set.

The association of the Harehope buttons with a pulley ring may indicate that one of the buttons there was associated with that ring as means of fastening a belt, and others therefore may have fastened and adorned a pouch which hung from the belt (Clarke *et al.* 1985, 215). One therefore wonders whether the group from Rameldry, found in a disturbed location in front of the lower body, may also have been attached to a pouch rather than to a garment. Where the human remains could be identified the bodies concerned were found to be adult males in three cases (Raunds, Butterwick and Rameldry), but definitely

Table 5.3.4. Button arrangements in European Beaker graves (from Hajek 1957).

Page no. in Hajek 1957	Site	Total buttons	Body positions
391	Bohdalice	8	Horizontal row just below pelvis
398	Dablice	12	3 or 4 widely spaced horizontal rows across chest
400	Knezeves	12	2 vertical rows of 6 down centre of chest
402	Lysolaje	16	4 widely spaced horizontal rows across chest
408	Ragelsdorf	7	4 in tight vertical row on chest; 3 at skull

female at Garton Slack VI, 1, 1 and Ingleby Barwick (also see Shepherd 2009 for further discussion).

Sets of V-perforated buttons, usually made from bone or sometimes amber rather than of jet or jet-like materials, are known particularly from Beaker graves in central and eastern Europe (Heyd 2007, 332 and fig. 9). Amber buttons occur with males or females but the bone button sets tend to occur only with women. An illuminating set of grave plans was published by Hajek (1957) and some of the results are summarised in Table 5.3.4. The positionings tie in well with interpretations suggested for the British buttons, with some sets possibly having functioned as fastenings down the centre of a jacket or tunic, and others sewn on as rows of decorative studs. The set below the pelvis may have been attached to a pouch, or perhaps to a belt or girdle. No buttons in Britain have been found at the head, but in Table 5.3.4 one example may indicate that buttons sometimes were also used to adorn a hat or other form or special head covering. Some other examples of large sets of tiny buttons occur just below the neck and can be interpreted as elements within necklaces or decorative collars (Heyd 2007, 344 and fig. 4, lower right). It is likely that the idea of small V-perforated buttons was transferred

to Britain from the Continent, but the variety of uses in Britain seems to have been less diverse. However, the larger buttons and the use of jet are British developments, apparently linked to the fashion for cloak fasteners and, in conjunction with pulley rings, for elaborate jet belt or strap fittings (see sections on individual V-perforated buttons above and belt rings, Chapter 3.4).

CHRONOLOGY AND ASSOCIATIONS

Grave associations for the button sets include two bronze flat riveted daggers, a flanged axe, bronze awls, a decorated jet pulley ring, a reused Group VI stone bracer, sponge finger stone, flint dagger, tubular bronze beads and a jet disc bead necklace. In conjunction with the two associated finds of late style Beakers, at Raunds and Kirkaldy (Clarke 1970, no.1655), it appears that the button sets date from the later Beaker period. This is confirmed by the available radiocarbon dates (see Chapter 9). Within England the button sets can be seen to have been in use during late Beaker times and the currency of earlier forms of Food Vessel, all within the few centuries leading up to *c.* 2000 cal BC, and immediately thereafter.

5.4 EARRINGS AND TRESS RINGS

COPPER ALLOY EARRINGS

TYPO-CHRONOLOGY

Seven individual earrings were studied, belonging to four original pairs found in graves (Table 5.4.1). They fall into two distinct types: basket-shaped ornaments and open flat bands, all provided with tapered tangs. All were found in Yorkshire or the Peak District. The basket-shaped examples from Cowlam 58 (ID 1304–5; Figure 5.4.1) and Staker Hill (ID 1228) resemble the basket earrings of sheet gold found at Chilbolton, Hants (Russel 1990, fig. 7), Radley 4A, Oxon (Barclay and Halpin 1999, fig. 5.4) and Boltby

Scar, Yorkshire (Brailsford 1953, 34), as well as the two pairs found with the Amesbury Archer and the 'Companion' burial (Fitzpatrick 2011, figs. 25 and 43). However, the main 'blades' of these gold ornaments are both wider (27 to 50mm), and more tightly curled (diameters 5.0 to 6.5mm), than those of the bronze items. Also they bear scribed linear decoration of a highly prescribed format, whilst the bronze ones are much plainer. The gold ornaments are associated with early Beaker graves, several of which have been dated by radiocarbon to the mid to second half of the 3rd millennium cal BC. The grave goods associated with the bronze examples are rather later in date; a V-perforated jet button (ID 310) with the Cowlam pair is probably of the late Beaker period, and the Staker Hill example (ID 1228),

Table 5.4.1. List of earrings studied and illustrated.

Object	Site (Parish), County	Museum	Illustration
ID 1146	Garton Slack 153 (Garton-on-the-Wolds), E. Yorks.	Hull	Figure 5.4.2
ID 1147	Garton Slack 153 (Garton-on-the-Wolds), E. Yorks.	Hull	Figure 5.4.2
ID 1228	Staker Hill (Hartington Upper), Derbys.	Shef	Not illustrated
ID 1304	Cowlam 58, burial 6, E. Yorks.	BM	Figure 5.4.1
ID 1305	Cowlam 58, burial 6, E. Yorks.	BM	Figure 5.4.1
ID 1306	Goodmanham 115, burial 1, E. Yorks.	BM	Not illustrated
ID 1307	Goodmanham 115, burial 1, E. Yorks.	BM	Figure 5.4.3

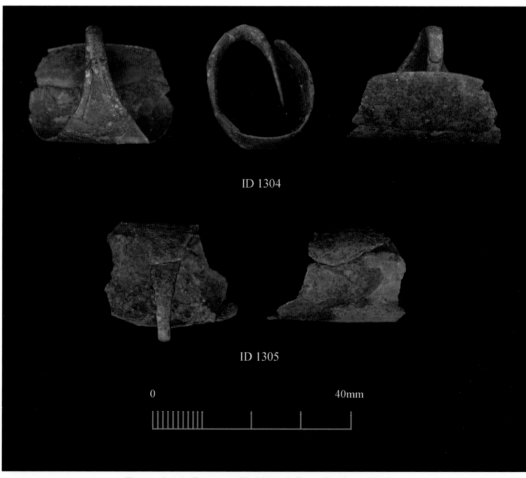

ID 1304

ID 1305

0   40mm

Figure 5.4.1. Earrings ID 1304–5 from Cowlam 58, 6.

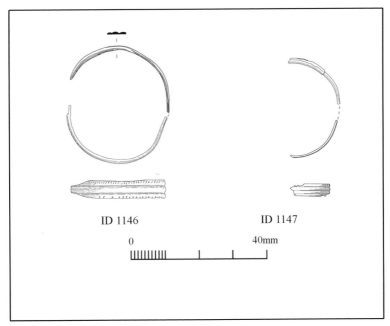

Figure 5.4.2. Earrings ID 1146–47 from Garton Slack 153. Drawings by Henry Buglass.

part of a pair when found, is from a grave containing a late necked Beaker. This later dating is further demonstrated by the radiocarbon date of 1890–1670 cal BC (at 2 sigma) for a grave with a late style Beaker, shale armlet and a single basket earring, with traces of sun-ray incised ornament, from Stanwick, Northamptonshire (Harding and Healy 2007, fig. 4.8).

The circular band variety, from Goodmanham (ID 1306–7) and Garton Slack (ID 1146–7; Figure 5.4.2) were both found with Food Vessels. The currency of such ceramics overlapped chronologically with late Beakers, so the two types of ornament may have been contemporary. However the basket ornaments may have continued the insular tradition initiated by the fashion for gold basket ornaments in the early Beaker period, while the rings were a completely new style associated with the use of Food Vessels.

MORPHOLOGY

Only two small fragments from one of the basket earrings from Staker Hill (ID 1228) survives, but its configuration suggests that the reconstruction drawing provided by Clarke (1970, fig. 910) is accurate. Both fragments are gently curved and no decoration survives. The pair from Cowlam (ID 1304–5) are 28 and 30mm wide and curled to diameters of 20.5 and 18.8mm; the sheet is 0.7 and 1.0mm thick while the tangs are 2.2 and 2.6mm thick. Both are decorated with marginal grooves which extend from the flared lower portion of the tang onto the main blade. The pairs of simple rings are roughly 30mm in diameter, although all are now squashed to irregular oval outlines. In each case however, the widths of the pair members are different: 8.1mm and 7.2mm for ID 1306–7 and 5.5mm and 4.2mm for ID 1146–47. All the rings are ribbed and

Figure 5.4.3. Detail of earring ID 1307 from Goodmanham 115, 1 showing ribbed and punched decoration.

decorated. The Goodmanham pair (ID 1306–7) has four ribs, with the five intermediate hollows filled with rows of punched impressions forming a chevron pattern, and there are U-shaped indents on the edges (Figure 5.4.3). The pair from Garton Slack (ID 1146–47; Figure 5.4.2) are incorrectly restored on a perspex mount: in fact the two larger fragments belong to one ring, and the two smaller ones to the second (as illustrated by Mortimer 1905, figs. 560–1). One ring has two grooves forming three zones; the top edge is decorated with close-set diagonal impressions and the lower with a row of almost joining oval impressions which gives the effect of running lozenges. The second ring has three grooves forming four zones; the top edge has widely-spaced diagonal impressions and the lower edge is decorated in the same way as the other ring.

MATERIAL

None of the earrings have been analysed.

MANUFACTURE

On one of the Cowlam basket earrings (ID 1304) there are faint longitudinal striations at the exterior junction of tang and blade; any such traces on the Staker Hill fragments are obscured by lacquer. Each of the Garton Slack pair of rings has faint longitudinal polishing striations surviving on the plain zones between the ribs, but any traces on the Goodmanham pair are obscured by lacquer.

COMPLETENESS AND DAMAGE

The Staker Hill basket earrings have decayed badly since excavation, but the Cowlam ones survive at the 70% and 85% level. Some of the breaks are modern, although as they are glued this is difficult to determine. Most of the band varieties have modern breaks, many of which are glued, and overall survival is poor. The most complete is ID 1146 which survives at the 95% level.

WEAR

Any wear on the Staker Hill basket fragments cannot be determined, but the Cowlam pair is classified as worn. One of this pair has ancient breaks across the tang and the edges of the blade, and the interior of ID 1304 is smoothed. On both items, the grooved decoration is very worn and there are also cracks indicative of stress across the blades in various places; these presumably result from continual bending and unbending during use. The Garton Slack pair of rings shows little obvious signs of wear and the decoration is fairly crisp: these are only slightly worn. In contrast the pair from Goodmanham have longitudinal and diagonal scratches inside the bands and ancient fatigue cracks from bending. Both members of the pair seem to have been already broken at the time of deposition and they are classified as worn.

CONCLUSIONS

The earrings are made from very thin sheet metal and are very fragile. As a result they have not survived well in the graves, or subsequently in museum collections. Two morphological types are apparent. The first is similar to early Beaker gold basket ornaments but the copper alloy examples are narrower, and found in late Beaker contexts. The other type which comprise simple flat bands with tapered ends are found with Food Vessels in Yorkshire. In terms of size and decoration the earrings are quite variable, and the members of individual pairs sometimes do not match exactly. All except one pair have been heavily used, and they may have been curated valuable items. Cracks due to metal fatigue, and some ancient lateral breaks, are evidence of continual bending and re-bending in antiquity.

By taking into account various groups of hair ornaments from Early Bronze Age Europe, Sherratt argued that the gold basket earrings were more likely to have been tress ornaments used for embellishing special hair styles, rather than earrings (Sherratt 1986;1987). The term 'basket ornaments' is thus preferred (Needham in Fitzpatrick 2011, 136). Microscopic analysis of the two pairs from Chilbolton showed wear around the edges of the tang and absence of scratches inside the 'basket' (Russel 1990, 164–6). Russel concluded that this indicated that the ornaments had in fact been earrings, with wear on the tang relating to the placing of the tang through a slit in the ear lobe. However it would seem that use of such items as hair tresses would not lead to scratching inside the curled ornament either, and the argument therefore remains inconclusive. Taking into account the similar lack of wear within the basket areas of the ornament from the Amesbury Archer and 'Companion' graves, and the fact that the tangs appeared to have been curled into place just once, Needham has argued that they may have adorned a removable headdress or collar, with the gold ornaments wrapped around cloth or braids of rope (Needham in Fitzpatrick 2011, 136–8). No traces of wear were detected microscopically on the pair from Radley 4A (Barclay and Halpin 1999, 183). One of the Cowlam copper alloy earrings (ID 1304) has scratches on both the exterior and the interior of the blade, but the inside also shows smoothing and more signs of use. In three of the cases studied in detail, the ornaments were found either side of the skull, or in the vicinity of the skull, so ornaments relating to the head are definitely implied. But whether these bronze items were inserted into the ear lobes as earrings, or employed as tress ornaments, cannot be proven on the current evidence. However, the headdress or collar hypothesis advanced by Needham is an attractive one.

5.5 DRESS PINS

GENERAL TYPO-CHRONOLOGY

A series of 36 fancy pins made from bronze or animal bone were listed by Gerloff (1975, Appendix C) and associated by her with the Wessex Culture. Many of these items have been studied in detail, and in addition further bone examples have been identified. A total of 28 items have been studied here (Table 5.5.1). Gerloff usefully divided the pins by head form into three main groups: those with crutch heads, a few with bulb heads and finally the ring-headed forms (*ibid*, 110–2). Her distribution map (*ibid*, pl. 62) demonstrates that most such pins have been found in Wessex, although there is also a significant group from East Yorkshire, the latter mainly made from bone. In functional terms, the use of such pins, which are thought to have been used to fasten items of dress, herald a significant departure from the use of buttons in the preceding Beaker and earlier Early Bronze Age period. Some of the bronze crutch-headed pins and the two bulb-headed pins have hollow heads. The hollow casting method did not come in use until the later stages of the Wessex Early Bronze Age, and the dateable associations for the various pins, which are mainly daggers of Camerton-Snowshill types, also indicate a later Early

Bronze Age date. Gerloff discussed possible continental parallels for the various pin types in detail (*ibid*, 119–123). She felt that the bronze types bore close resemblance to many examples in south Germany, northern Italy, and in particular Switzerland and Bohemia, and that the British examples may well have been imports. The bone examples were then thought to be copies of such imported types. Detailed parallels were cited for the pins from Camerton (ID 1158), Collingbourne Ducis G4 (ID 1418) and Loose Howe (ID 1329), and the unusual pins from Norton Bavant G1 (ID 1191) and another from 'South Wiltshire' were compared with two specific continental types: the petschaftkopf pins and ösenkopfnadeln of Tumulus Culture date (Gerloff 1975, 122). However, Needham, following Coles and Taylor (1971, 9), has pointed out that many of the British bronze pins do not possess exact parallels in Europe, and it may be only one or two (such as the Camerton example) that had actually been imported from the continent. Once the new form of dress attachment had been introduced, native craftsmen would quickly have been able to imitate the novel metal fastenings. Indeed the few imported pins may have come in attached to new styles of garment (Needham 2000a, 178). The ring-headed pins, mainly in silver, from the Breton dagger graves are rather different, and may have

Table 5.5.1 . List of dress pins studied and illustrated.

Object	Site (Parish), County	Museum	Illustration
Beaker-age			
ID 1061	Amesbury Archer, Wilts.	Sal	Not illustrated
ID 1330	Sewell (Totternhoe), Beds.	BM	Figure 5.5.1
ID 1370	Roundway G8, Wilts.	Dev	Figure 5.5.1
Crutch-headed			
ID 1049	Dewlish, Dorset	Dor	Figure 5.5.2
ID 1163	Priddy G3, Somerset	Brist	Figure 5.5.2
ID 1313	Snowshill 297, burial 1, Gloucs.	BM	Figure 5.5.2
ID 1393	Wilsford G23, Wilts.	Dev	Figure 5.5.2; Figure 5.5.4
ID 1484	West Overton G1, Wilts.	Dev	Figure 5.5.2
ID 1485	Milston G3 or 7, Wilts.	Dev	Figure 5.5.2; Figure 5.5.4
Bulb-headed			
ID 1158	Camerton, Timsbury G1, Somerset	Brist	Figure 5.5.1; Figure 5.5.4
ID 1498	Wimborne St Giles G33a, Dorset	Dev	Figure 5.5.1
Possibly continental			
ID 1191	Norton Bavant G1, Wilts.	Sal	Figure 5.5.1; Figure 5.5.4
ID 1192	Norton Bavant G1, Wilts.	Sal	Figure 5.5.1
Ring-headed			
ID 602	Wharram Percy 47, E. Yorks.	Hull	Figure 5.5.3
ID 606	Aldro 109 (Birdsall), E. Yorks.	Hull	Not illustrated
ID 817	Ganton (Brough) UN69, E. Yorks.	BM	Figure 5.5.3; Figure 5.5.4
ID 821	Aldbourne 283, burial 1, Wilts.	BM	Figure 5.5.3
ID 925	Wilsford G56, Wilts.	Dev	Figure 5.5.3
ID 971	Collingbourne Ducis G21c, Wilts.	Dev	Figure 5.5.3
ID 972	Wilsford G40, Wilts.	Dev	Figure 5.5.3
ID 1046	Amesbury G82, Wilts.	Sal	Figure 5.5.3
ID 1053	Dorchester Two Barrows, Dorset	Dor	Figure 5.5.3
ID 1054	Dorchester Two Barrows, Dorset	Dor	Not illustrated
ID 1056	Milborne St Andrew G16e, Dorset	Dor	Figure 5.5.3
ID 1329	Loose Howe (Rosedale), N. Yorks.	BM	Figure 5.5.3
ID 1418	Collingbourne Ducis G4, Wilts.	Dev	Figure 5.5.3; Figure 5.5.4
Shaft only			
ID 1051	Edmonsham G2, Dorset	Dor	Not illustrated
ID 1193	Shrewton G23a, Wilts.	Sal	Not illustrated

been associated with the dagger sheaths rather than with items of dress (*ibid*). In addition to the probable imported pin from Camerton, there are also a few from early graves that may have been imported. These include the cinquefoil-headed bone pin from Brough (Ganton ID 817), found with an Armorico-British Series 4 dagger (*ibid*, fig. 18). A slightly earlier horizon of pin use in England is evidenced by four items from early Beaker graves: two in copper and two in bone, and these will be considered first.

PINS FROM EARLY BEAKER GRAVES

MORPHOLOGY AND MATERIAL

Two pins made from copper, one with a racquet-shaped head from Roundway G8 (ID 1370, Figure 5.5.1) and one with a double-spiral head from Sewell (ID 1330, Figure 5.5.1) were previously thought to have been continental imports. However the possible parallels occur in graves rather later than the two English graves concerned and both may in fact be indigenous products (O'Connor 2010). The bone pin from the Amesbury Archer (ID 1061) grave has an unusual hammer-head with marked end facets which are decorated with central rectangular projections, while that from grave 4660 at Barrow Hills, Oxon has a double winged head (Barclay and Halpin 1999, fig. 4.23, WB4). The pin with the Amesbury Archer is made from the shaft of a limb bone from a large mammal, and the Barrow Hills pin also from a longbone splinter from a large mammal: cattle, red deer or possibly horse (*ibid*, 63). These two pins are very carefully executed and the wing-headed one may be an import, with a close parallel in Lower Saxony (*ibid*, 236). All very different in style, the pins vary in length from 73.5 to 145mm.

MANUFACTURE

No traces of manufacture survive on the Roundway pin, but the Sewell one (ID 1330) retains faint lateral striations on one part of the surviving spiral. Although well-polished, on the Amesbury Archer pin (ID 1061) there are clear traces of the shaping of the projection on the end of the surviving head flange.

COMPLETENESS, DAMAGE AND WEAR

None of the three pins studied survive well. All have severe damage to the heads, which occurred in antiquity and, for ID 1370, partly in modern times. The tip had also been damaged anciently in two cases. The Amesbury Archer pin has wear traces on the shaft, and the Sewell pin also shows signs of wear although the tip is intact (both categorised as worn). The tip of the Roundway pin is also intact but the overall degree of wear is indeterminate.

CONCLUSIONS

The degree of workmanship of these very early pins, taken together with their signs of use wear and the fact that three

had been broken prior to deposition, suggests that they were valuable and probably curated items.

CRUTCH-HEADED PINS

MORPHOLOGY

Four crutch-headed pins in bronze vary in length from 114.5 to 166mm, and the maximum widths of the head range between 16.1 to 21.3mm. The shafts are of circular cross section and are gently tapered to a sharp point. Two of the heads, which are of circular or oval profile, are hollow cast, with open holes at either side end, while two are solid. Both hollow cast items, and one of the solid ones are decorated (*contra* Gerloff 1975, 111). Two have zones of encircling parallel incised lines near to the side terminals of the head (ID 1485, Figure 5.5.2 and Figure 5.5.4, with six lines in each zone; ID 1484, Figure 5.5.2, with three in each zone), while that from Wilsford G23 (ID 1393, Figure 5.5.2 and Figure 5.5.4) bears an incised design of lozenges between pairs of horizontal grooves on the front and top (and originally the rear) of the head. One pin (ID 1485) also has a spiral twist in the upper two-thirds of the shaft (Figure 5.5.2). Of the two versions in bone, 132.4mm and 106mm in length, one has a plain head (ID 1049, Figure 5.5.2) but the other (ID 1163, Figure 5.5.2) is pierced by a row of three well-spaced perforations 2.4mm in diameter. The head of the latter piece is also carefully shaped with a long slightly rounded lentoid upper surface and neat end facets. The stem of the pin from Dewlish (ID 1049, Figure 5.5.2) is not twisted, as previously thought, but the broken fragment of a spirally twisted bone pin shaft from Edmonsham (ID 1051) may be related to this group of crutch-headed pins.

MATERIAL

The pin from Snowshill (ID 1313, Figure 5.5.2) is made from A plus BB metal (Peter Bray). The material of two bone pins was identified: both were made from mammalian limb bone, but one from a large mammal (ID 1049) and one from a sheep-sized animal (ID 1051).

MANUFACTURE

Two of the bronze pins were very corroded but the other two retain faint longitudinal striations on the shaft, and on ID 1313 lateral and diagonal polishing striations are also visible on the crutch head. The bone examples also have faint longitudinal striations on the shafts as well as evidence of the shaping of the heads. There are diagonal shaping marks in the neck of ID 1049, and the Priddy example (ID 1163) has marked lateral striations on the faces of the head and top of the shaft, faint lateral marks on the top and faint diagonal ones on the edge of the top facet.

COMPLETENESS AND DAMAGE

The four bronze pins are almost complete, but two modern fractures to the shafts are glued. Two of them are severely corroded. The bone ones have not survived quite as well, and there is modern damage to the tip and one perforation on ID 1163 and to the upper shaft of ID 1049.

WEAR

The heads have all been subject to ancient damage, with that from Edmonsham completely missing. There are also ancient fractures at the tips on ID 1049 and ID 1051 and the shaft of ID 1051. Although in places obscured by corrosion, traces of wear suggest that three of the bronze pins were worn or very worn. In two cases, ID 1393 and ID 1313 the crutch heads displayed extreme wear. On ID 1313 all edges of the head were well smoothed, and the complex decoration on ID 1393 had almost worn away at the two ends of the head, and particularly on one of the faces (Figure 5.5.4). This may have been the face that was against the garment and the wear thus caused by fabric rub. Two of the bone pins are also heavily worn. That from Dewlish (ID 1049) has scratches and a series of notches on the shaft, caused by use; these were the marks previously

interpreted as traces of spiral twisting. Use gloss on the head of the Priddy pin (ID 1163) continues onto the surface of the ancient break and there are multidirectional ancient scratches on the shaft. The Edmonsham shaft fragment also shows slight wear. Overall one was slightly worn, two worn, three very worn and one indeterminate.

BULB-HEADED PINS

MORPHOLOGY AND MATERIAL

Two pins with bulb heads are both made from bronze. They are hollow-cast and possess perforations, ID 1498 (Figure 5.5.1) in the top of the detached bulb head and in the case of the Camerton example (ID 1158, Figure 5.5.1) a central hole 3.5mm in diameter accompanied by a smaller angled one 2.2mm in diameter, located in the neck area at the base of the hollow bulb (Figure 5.5.4). The Camerton pin is 106.8mm long with a bulb 14mm in diameter, while the bulb of ID 1498 is 16.6mm across. The detached bulb head has a single decorative groove located

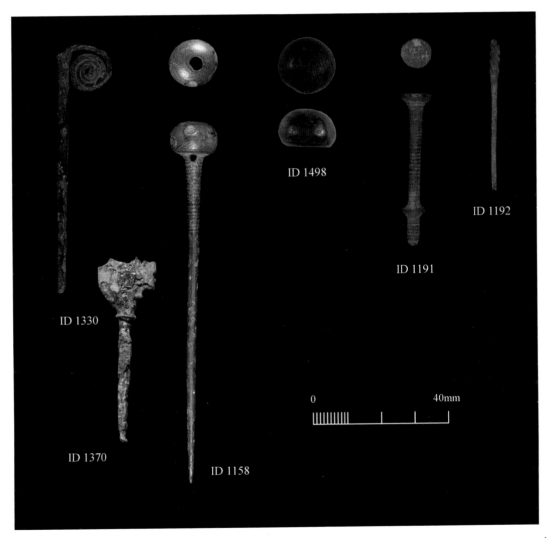

Figure 5.5.1. Beaker-age pins ID 1330 Sewell and ID 1370 Roundway; bulb-headed pins ID 1158 Camerton and ID 1498 Wimborne St Giles G33a; possible continental pins ID 1191 Norton Bavant G1 and ID 1192 Norton Bavant G1.

just above the flattened base, while the Camerton example is richly decorated. On the bulb there are three zones of diagonal incised lines with linear borders, forming a neat herringbone design, and the upper zone (to 24mm) of the shaft is embellished with bands formed from horizontal incised lines (Figure 5.5.4).

MANUFACTURE

Both bulb heads are highly polished and all traces of any striations have been removed. However on the Camerton head there is a small flaw in the casting which has not been polished over.

COMPLETENESS AND DAMAGE

Both are virtually complete, although the shaft of ID 1498, parts of which were found at the time of excavation, is now missing. There are no traces of any other modern damage.

WEAR

Both pins show signs of wear in the form of general ancient scratching, and the decoration is worn in both cases. On the head of the Camerton pin the decoration on the head has almost been worn away, especially on the side away from the basal angled perforation, presumably due to fabric rub. Both are categorised as worn.

POSSIBLE CONTINENTAL PIN FORMS

MORPHOLOGY AND MATERIAL

The upper portion of a pin from Norton Bavant G1 (ID 1191, Figure 5.5.1) has a disc head 9.7mm in diameter, and a 34mm long straight neck above a distinct angled collar of 7.5mm diameter. The main shaft below that is broken, but the remaining portion, and the neck are decorated with horizontal ribbing. The top of the head is also decorated, with an incised cross-hatch design (Figure 5.5.4). The pin can be compared closely with Tumulus Culture (Reinecke C or D) examples in Europe (see above, and Moore and Rowlands 1972, 49–50). A second shaft fragment from the same barrow (ID 1192, Figure 5.5.1) is partly spirally twisted above a square-sectioned plain zone. This is in contrast to the twisted stems of the crutch-headed pins discussed above, which have round cross sections. Square-sectioned pin shafts with spiral twisting also have Tumulus parallels in Europe (*ibid*). A third pin which may be an import from the continent is the lost disc-headed pin with

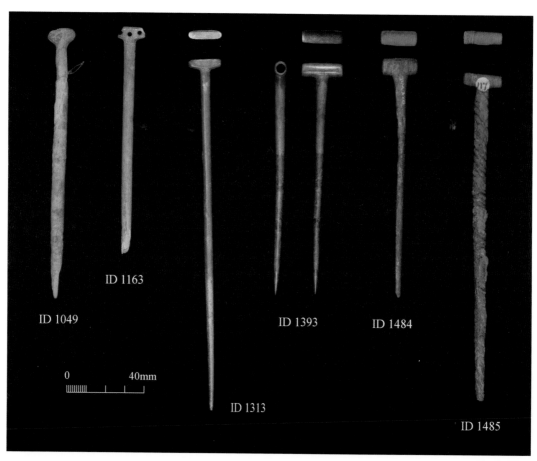

Figure 5.5.2. Crutch-headed pins: ID 1049 Dewlish G7; ID 1163 Priddy G3; ID 1313 Snowshill 297,1; ID 1393 Wilsford G23; ID 1484 West Overton G1; ID 1485 Milston G3 or 7.

herringbone decoration on the upper shaft from 'South Wiltshire' (see above).

MANUFACTURE

Neither of the pins studied shows any surviving signs of manufacture, due to corrosion.

CONDITION AND COMPLETENESS

Both pieces are fragments. The original lengths of the pins cannot be estimated, and no modern breaks are present.

WEAR

Both pins were broken in antiquity and were deposited in the grave as fragments. The decoration on the head and neck of ID 1191 is not crisp, and both pins appear to have been subject to slight wear prior to breakage.

RING-HEADED PINS

MORPHOLOGY AND MATERIAL

A total of 14 ring-headed pins can be divided into two groups: those with complex multi-ringed heads, and those with a simple single-ring head. The complex items will be described individually.

ID 817. Ganton (Brough) (Figure 5.5.3). This cinquefoil headed pin is made from the shaft of a limb bone from a large mammal. The pin is very finely finished, 61mm in length and 5mm thick, and with five conjoined rings of 10.5 to 12.2mm diameter. The holes vary in diameter from 5.2 to 6mm in diameter and are slightly hourglass in profile. The two lower lobes are decorated on front, sides and rear with radial grooves (Figure 5.5.4), while the two upper outer lobes have circumferential grooving around their outer sides. The central lobe is not decorated; the pin is worn.

ID 821. Aldbourne 283, burial 1 (Figure 5.5.3). A long pin (109mm) is 3.5mm thick, with a circular cross section and a flattened quatrefoil head 11.5mm across. The surviving lobes are 5.5 to 6.3mm in diameter and the three surviving holes are all about 3mm across. The pin is made from the shaft of a mammalian limb bone and is fresh or slightly worn.

ID 1329. Loose Howe (Figure 5.5.3). The upper portion of this bronze pin of maximum surviving length 37.5mm and surviving width 26.5 has a trefoil head 6mm thick. Two of the holes are 3.5mm and 1.5mm in diameter; the level of wear is indeterminate.

ID 1418. Collingbourne Ducis G4 (Figure 5.5.3). This bronze pin is 161mm long, and, with circular cross section of 6.2mm diameter, has a double-ringed head 36mm wide. Each ring is 14.5mm in diameter, and from each one hangs

an interlocked ring on average 10.5mm across. Between the two fixed rings there is pointillé decoration, while below the head there is a zone of incised discontinuous running chevron decoration. On the inner edges of all four rings there are incised spaced diagonal strokes (Figure 5.5.4). The pin is very worn.

The remaining pins have a single ring, and those studied are all made from bone or antler. There is one example of such a ring-headed pin in bronze, found with a Camerton type dagger, but it is lost (Amesbury G24; Gerloff 1975, pl. 48,G). The bone and antler items have been separated from the main series of bone points with perforated heads (see bone points section, Chapter 4.7) by virtue of the distinct angle that exists between the base of the ring head and the top of the shaft. The ring-headed pins vary greatly in length from 44 to 136.6mm. The heads also vary widely in diameter, and the perforations range from 5.2 to 10.2mm in diameter. None are decorated. Most of them are made from limb bone shafts from a large mammal, although in one case the size of mammal could not be estimated, and in two cases (ID 602, Figure 5.5.3 and ID 606) the pins were made from antler, one of them (ID 602) specifically from red deer antler. Interestingly, both antler items are from East Yorkshire.

MANUFACTURE

Three of the complex pins have longitudinal striations on the shaft (but not ID 1329 which is heavily consolidated). Also one of the complex bone pins (ID 821) has gouge marks surviving below one of the lobes. In six cases of the simple ring-headed pins of bone/antler faint longitudinal shaping striations are visible on the shaft. More marked striations of varying direction are present in the neck area on five examples, and traces of shaping of the head on two. Many of the items are finished to a high polish. One interesting aspect is that three of the bone pins (ID 1163, Figure 5.2.2; ID 1053, Figure 5.5.3 and ID 925, Figure 5.5.3) display a uniform dark green colour. This penetrates throughout the material and appears to be the result of deliberate colouring, presumably in imitation of bronze, either at the time of manufacture or during use.

COMPLETENESS AND DAMAGE

One complex pin (ID 821) had been through the pyre and is severely burnt. One lobe of this pin has been lost in modern times and slight modern damage or chips are also evident in four cases.

WEAR

Any wear on the Loose Howe bronze pin (ID 1329) is obscured by consolidant but the pin with hanging rings (ID 1418) shows heavy wear, with much of the decoration on the shaft almost worn away and general wear evident on the hanging rings (Figure 5.5.4). The cinquefoil bone pin (ID 817), with ancient scratching and a blunted tip also appears to be worn, while the burnt pin (ID 821) seems to have been in fresh condition when deposited. Most of the pins with single ring-heads are slightly worn, with only one classified as worn, and one as fresh. The wear traces include scratches, irregular or diagonal on shafts and tips. In only one case was any wear on the inside of the ring detected (ID 606). Overall ten pins were slightly worn (including one complex example), three were worn (including one complex pin) and one complex pin was very worn.

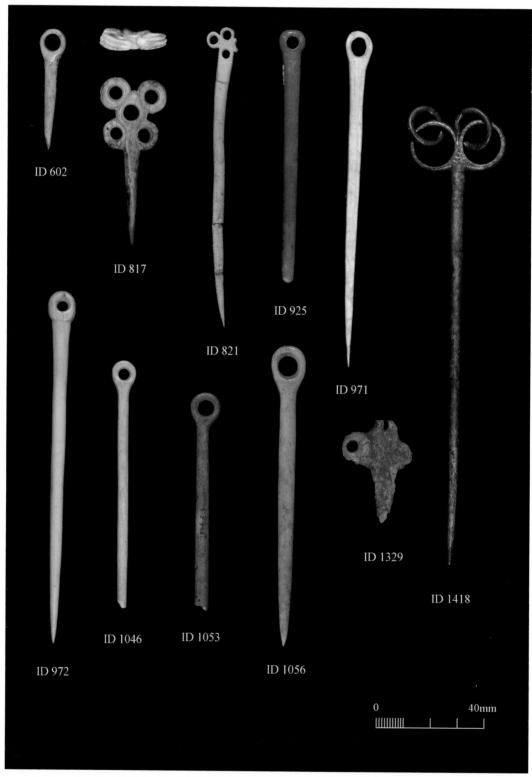

Figure 5.5.3. Ring-headed pins: ID 602 Wharram Percy 47; ID 817 Ganton (Brough) UN69; ID 821 Aldbourne 283, 1; ID 925 Wilsford G56; ID 971 Collingbourne Ducis G21c; ID 972 Wilsford G40; ID 1046 Amesbury G82; ID 1053 Dorchester Two Barrows; ID 1056 Milborne St Andrew G16e; ID 1329 Loose Howe; ID 1418 Collingbourne Ducis G4.

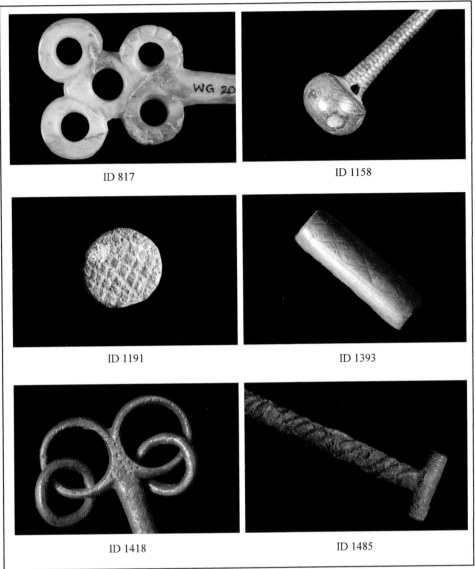

ID 817

ID 1158

ID 1191

ID 1393

ID 1418

ID 1485

Figure 5.5.4. Details: ID 817 Ganton showing decoration on lobes; ID 1158 Camerton showing neck perforation and wear; ID 1191 Norton Bavant G1 showing decorated head; ID 1393 Wilsford G23 showing incised decoration; ID 1418 Collingbourne Ducis G4 showing decoration and wear; and ID 1485 Milston G3 or 7 showing incised decoration.

CONCLUSIONS

The pins appear to have been very special items. All are very finely made and highly polished, with fancy heads, and three of the bone items seem to have been coloured in imitation of bronze. No two pins are the same in size or style; in fact they are all very different from each other and appear to have been individually produced, perhaps for specific individuals in the first instance. A few of the pins may be imports from continental Europe and others may be copies of such exotic items. The bone items are mainly made from long bones of cattle or red deer. This may relate to the size of bone required to make items of this nature, but the choice of animal for the source material may have been symbolic. In connection with this, it is interesting to note that two pins from Yorkshire are made from antler, one of them definitely from red deer.

With the exception of the two exotic pin fragments from Norton Bavant, most of the pins survive complete, or almost complete (at the 95% level or above). However, in several cases the fragile shafts or tips have broken since excavation and have been glued. Traces of wear show that all of the complex pins, the Beaker-age examples and those with bulb, crutch or complex ring heads were worn or heavily worn. This extreme wear indicates that the pins had long use lives and probably had been curated through several generations prior to deposition. In a few cases wear is present across ancient breaks, and the two fragments of exotic pins from Norton Bavant also appear to have been carefully curated items. The simple ring-headed pins of bone and antler tend to show less wear, but had been used prior to burial. It may be that these less complex items were not valued to the same extent as the fancy pins.

5.6 STUDS (with Alison Sheridan)

TYPO-CHRONOLOGY

Circular waisted studs are a little-studied category of artefact. No synthesis of the material has previously been attempted, although some of the corpus has been listed in connection with two recent finds of clay examples (Woodward 2000; Ladle and Woodward 2009; also see Sheridan forthcoming a). The two sets of wooden studs found at Whitehorse Hill, Devon were discovered too late for inclusion in the current study. Research associated with these has shown that the total of finds for Britain and Ireland now stands at 60 (Jones forthcoming). Table 5.6.2 summarises details of 43 studs from England, Wales and Ireland; their distribution shows a marked bias towards East Anglia and Yorkshire. Ten have been studied in detail (plus two replicas; Table 5.6.1). Two basic types can be distinguished: small almost cylindrical items, which have sometimes been described as toggles, and flatter pieces of more varied diameter. The examples from East Anglia and adjacent counties are all of the cylindrical variety. The studs are made from two main material types: jet and jet-like materials and fired clay.

Studs have been found with four crouched inhumations in round barrows of Early Bronze Age date: a pair at Wharram Percy 70 (ID 200–201, Figure 5.6.1), and single examples from Chippenham 5, Preshute G1a (ID 1423, Figure 5.6.2) and Cowdery's Down; further graves at Langtoft and Norton Subcourse have produced pairs of studs (for references and county attributions see Table 5.6.2). Preshute G1a is one of the richest of the Wessex Series graves in Wiltshire, known as the Manton Barrow. A fifth stud from a barrow was found in the ring ditch at Radwell (Hall and Woodward 1977). Three further examples (ID 540, Figure 5.6.2; ID 1229, Figure 5.6.2, and Gawsworth) were found in cremation deposits, two of which were contained in Early Bronze Age Collared Urns. Studs were also found with Collared Urns at Cefn Cwmwd, Gwynedd, Brenig 44, Clwyd and Raunds. While most studs have been found in funerary contexts, a remarkable set of eight – of which seven are of jet or a similar material, and one is of fired clay – were found in a Collared Urn-associated settlement at West Row Fen and it has been suggested that these, too, had been made as pairs.

In terms of chronology, it appears that most studs are likely to belong to the first quarter of the second millennium BC i.e. the Early Bronze Age, as in the case of the pair of fired clay examples from Brenig 44, Clwyd, where the cremated bone has been radiocarbon dated (see Chapter 9). With their associated radiocarbon date of 1420–1220 cal BC (see Chapter 9), the pair from Norton Subcourse stand out as being significantly later than this, even though the studs are not noticeably different from a pair of biconical studs dated to the first quarter of the millennium at Barleycroft (Chris Evans pers. comm.). The Middle Bronze Age radiocarbon date for charcoal found with the Radwell example, and the association of a toggle with urns of Middle Bronze Age style at Barton-under-Needwood also indicate that some studs had a long currency. The inherent value of this artefact type may be demonstrated further by the occurrence of two items as residual and curated pieces found in later pit fillings (at Lockington and Bestwall); at Bestwall the rest of the material in the pit was of Late Bronze Age date, which might imply survival of this piece, or the tradition, through many centuries.

MORPHOLOGY

The main dimensions of the items studied in detail, and some particulars relating to other studs from England and Wales are summarised in Table 5.6.2. The chart (Figure 5.6.3) shows that the studs vary greatly in average front diameter, and height. The items made from jet, shale or lignite fall into two groups: five which are relatively narrow and high, and three which are both larger and flatter. Within the group of clay studs, maximum diameter varies more evenly with height, and the overall size range is more restricted than within the jet and jet-like material examples. Most of the studs have slightly domed upper and lower surfaces, but two (one jet ID 449, Figure 5.6.2, and one in clay, from Lockington) have distinctive dished surfaces. In several cases the front/upper surface has a slightly higher evenly domed surface than the rear. All have a marked neck, waist or stem, and these vary quite widely in diameter from 9.6 to 22.3mm. Obviously this dimension varies according to the overall size of the stud, but it can be noted that the stem is narrowest in some of the larger jet/jet-like items, and widest on the tall cylindrical pieces. None of the studs are decorated, although all of the jet and jet-like examples, and at least some of the ceramic examples are, or were, polished.

Table 5.6.1 . List of studs studied and illustrated.

Object	Site (Parish), County	Museum	Illustration
ID 200	Wharram Percy 70, E. Yorks.	Hull	Figure 5.6.1
ID 201	Wharram Percy 70, E. Yorks.	Hull	Figure 5.6.1
ID 293	St Neots, Cambs.	Camb	Figure 5.6.2
ID 440	Fylingdales, N. Yorks.	BM	Figure 5.6.2; Figure 5.6.4
ID 441	Fylingdales, N. Yorks.	BM	Figure 5.6.2
ID 449	Nawton (Beadlam), N. Yorks.	BM	Figure 5.6.2
ID 453	Nawton (Beadlam), N. Yorks.	BM	Not illustrated
ID 540	Cowleaze B (Winterbourne Steepleton), Dorset	Dor	Figure 5.6.2
ID 1229	Stanton Moor 13J, Derbys.	Shef	Figure 5.6.2
ID 1423	Preshute G1a, Wilts.	Dev	Figure 5.6.2

Table 5.6.2. Dimensions of stud ornaments from England, Wales and Ireland (C = (bi)conical; F = flattish).

Site	County	Material	Form	Top diam. (mm)	Base diam. (mm)	Min stem (mm)	Height (mm)	Reference
Wharram Percy 70	E. Yorks.	Jet	F	21.7 by 22.0	18.4 by 18.5	12.7	15	ID 200
Wharram Percy 70	E. Yorks.	Jet	F	21.8 by 21.9	18.5 by18.7	13.5	14.5	ID 201
St Neots	Cambs.	?Lignite	C	11.0 by10.8	10.8 by 8.7	9.0 by 8.2	14.9	ID 293
Fylingdales	N. Yorks.	Jet	F	32.5 by 34.5	Same	21.2 by 23.4	16.1	ID 440
Fylingdales	N. Yorks.	Jet	F	28.6 by 29.5	Same	21.5 by 22.6	13	ID 441
Nawton, Beadlam	N. Yorks.	Jet	Concave	41.3 by 42.7	24.7 by 26.5	21.5	15.5	ID 449
Nawton, Beadlam	N. Yorks.	Jet	Concave	Absent	25.8	20.6	6.8 plus	ID 453
Cowleaze, Winterbourne Steepleton B	Dorset	Prob. jet	C	17	13.2	11.7	20.1	ID 540
Stanton Moor 13J	Derbys.	Clay	F	24.0 by 23.2	25.2	16.9	13	ID 1229
Preshute G1 (Manton Barrow)	Wilts.	Clay	F	17.5	18	10.5	12.2	ID 1423
Marshfield REPLICA	Gloucs.	'Shale'			14.7	10.2	12.6	ID 1168
Marshfield REPLICA	Gloucs.	'Shale'			15.2	11.1	13.8	ID 1169
Gawsworth	Cheshire	Clay	?					Longworth 1984, no.134
Lockington	Leics.	Clay	Bi-concave	28			13	Woodward 2000b, 56–7
Barton-under-Needwood	Staffs.	Clay	F	33			19	Martin and Allen 2001, 10–12
Brenig 44	N. Wales	Clay	F	27.5			12.3	Lynch 1993, 129–30
Brenig 44	N. Wales	Clay	F	30.3			13.5	
Bestwall	Dorset	Clay	Bi-concave	34			21	Ladle and Woodward 2009, fig. 191.1
Radwell	Beds.	Jet	C	13			12	Hall and Woodward 1977, fig. 4, K
Chippenham 5, burial F	Cambs.	'Shale'	C	13.5			21	Leaf 1940, fig 10,10
Cowdery's Down, Basingstoke	Hants.	'Jet'	C (crude)	15		11	20	Millet and James 1983
West Row Fen	Suffolk	'Jet' ×7 Clay ×1	C					Martin and Murphy 1988
Raunds, West Cotton 6	Northants.	Clay	C					Tomalin 2011, 558–9
Langtoft	Lincs.	K. shale	C					Hutton 2008
Langtoft	Lincs.	K. shale	C Perforated					Hutton 2008
Fengate	Cambs.	?	C					Evans and Appleby 2008, 178, right
Fengate	Cambs.	?						Evans and Appleby 2008, 178, left
Cefn Cwmwd	Anglesey	K. shale	C					Sheridan 2012a
Ballinchalla	Co. Mayo, Ireland	Clay	C					Mary Cahill pers. comm.
Norton Subcourse, burial 2	Norfolk	Jet	C	13.1	11.4 by 12.9	9	16.3	Sheridan forthcoming a
Norton Subcourse, Burial 2	Norfolk	Jet	C	9.1 by 9.6	8.3 by 8.5	5.2–5.4	13.6	Sheridan forthcoming a
Over barrow 12	Cambs.	Stone (white)	C					Sheridan in prep
Over barrow 2	Cambs.	K. shale	C					Sheridan in prep
Over barrow 2	Cambs.	K. shale	C					Sheridan in prep
Over barrow 2	Cambs.	K. shale	C					Sheridan in prep
Barleycroft ring-ditch 3	Cambs.	?	C					Sheridan in prep

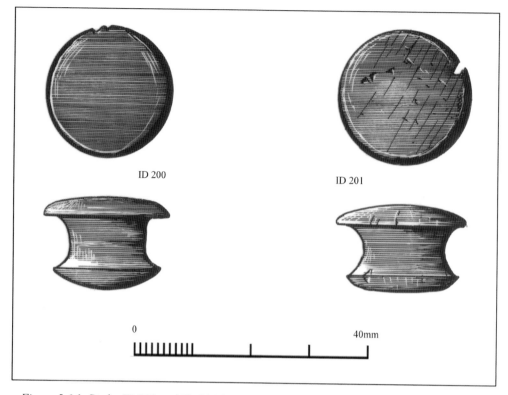

Figure 5.6.1. Studs: ID 200 and ID 201 from Wharram Percy 70. Drawings by Marion O'Neil.

In one case (Barton-under-Needwood) there is a perforation 11mm wide, extending right through the centre of the stud.

MATERIAL

Six of the jet or jet-like studs studied in detail are made from Whitby jet, and all six were found in Yorkshire. The Wharram Percy pair (ID 200–1) were identified by XRF analysis at Edinburgh, and the other four were identified visually by AS/MD. These four were characterised by woodgrain texture and the criss-cross cracking typical of jet. The cylindrical stud from St Neots (ID 293, Figure 5.6.2) appears to be made from high grade lignite (AS visual identification). The similar example from Winterbourne Steepleton (ID 540, Figure 5.6.2) was thought to be possibly made from cannel coal (XRF analysis by Pollard in Woodward 1991, 102), but visual inspection by AS indicated that the material is probably jet. The fired clay studs examined in detail vary greatly in colour, from pink-beige (ID 1229, Figure 5.6.2) and buff (Bestwall) through to dark brown/black (ID 1423, Figure 5.6.2), but all are made from very fine ceramic fabrics, always containing grog, which is sometimes accompanied by specks of mica.

MANUFACTURE

Many of the front and rear faces of the jet/jet-like studs have been polished to a high sheen. In a few cases the rear face retained a higher sheen than the front. Only two examples (ID 201 and ID 540) have polishing striations (faint diagonal) surviving on the front face. Manufacturing striations are visible, however, on the undersides of the faces in five cases: these comprise faint multidirectional or circumferential striations, or in the case of ID 440, patches of diagonal striations. The most prominent traces of manufacture survive around the necks and stems. These include faint but close-set circumferential striations (ID 201; ID 440, Figure 5.6.4; ID 441), diagonal striations (ID 540) and gouge marks on the stem of ID 200. The fired clay studs studied in detail do not display any signs of manufacture, but the fabrics are very fine and the outer surfaces polished to a high sheen. The finish is such that the clay material is disguised, and it may be that the darker pieces were intended to imitate jet or shale, while the pink one from Stanton Moor (ID 1229) may have been in imitation of amber or special stone.

COMPLETENESS AND DAMAGE

All the studs except one survive almost entire (at the 95 to 100% level); only one of the items from Nawton (ID 453) is more broken (only 55% survival). In this case one whole face is missing; and the break shows one major conchoidal fracture. Both clay studs, and four of the jet or jet-like items, have ancient marginal chips or breaks. Most major breaks are modern, including three catastrophic fractures which have been glued. One of the clay studs (ID 1229) also has modern flaking on the rear face.

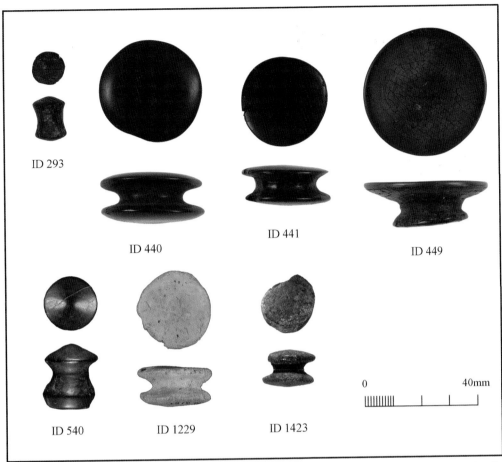

Figure 5.6.2. Studs: ID 293 St Neots; ID 440 Fylingdales; ID 441 Fylingdales; ID 449 Nawton; ID 540 Cowleaze; ID 1229 Stanton Moor 13J; ID 1423 Preshute G1.

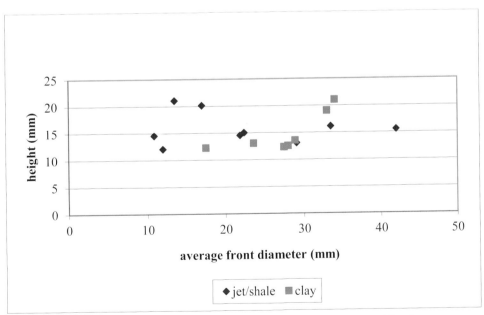

Figure 5.6.3. Studs: the relationship between front diameter and height.

WEAR

In a few cases, any wear traces have been obscured by lacquer, but the faces bear multidirectional ancient scratches and/or scuffing on four of the jet or jet-like items, e.g. ID 440, Figure 5.6.4. Scuffing on the flat undersides of the faces is also visible on ID 440 and ID 441. The most obvious, and the most common feature discerned is that the necks and stems had never been polished and in

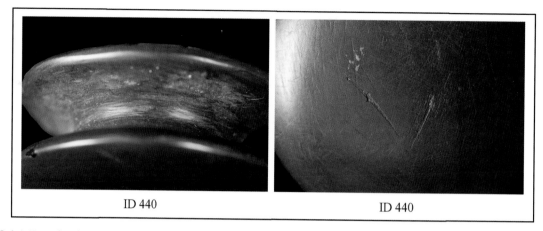

ID 440   ID 440

Figure 5.6.4. Details of ID 440 Fylingdales showing (left) circumferential striations around neck and (right) surface scuffing.

almost every case there were no traces of wear at all in this location. The only exception to this is the existence of some sporadic multidirectional ancient scratches on the stem of ID 449. Overall general wear can be categorised as 'worn' in four cases, and 'slightly worn' in a further four. Only one item, ID 453, which may have been broken during manufacture, appears to be in fresh condition.

CONCLUSIONS

This little-studied class of objects have variously been described as studs or toggles. They vary greatly in form and size, but the strong evidence of the lack of any wear in the neck or stem areas shows that none of them is likely to have functioned as a toggle. In the case of the jet/jet-like pieces in particular, if they had been used as any kind of fastener, smoothing or eradication of the traces of manufacture in the neck/stem area would undoubtedly have occurred. It seems most likely therefore that these pieces were used as

ornamental studs which were inserted into some soft part of the body tissue. In seven cases the studs were found as pairs. Ethnographic and modern parallels would suggest that such studs might have been inserted into the ear lobe, or into the upper or lower lip as labrets.

Several examples found in relation to a buried inhumation provide evidence of body placement. At Wharram Percy 70 the pair of jet studs (ID 200–201) were found 'close to the neck', and at Preshute G1, the Manton Barrow (ID1423), the clay stud was also found 'close to the neck of the skeleton; near to the chin'. The shale stud from Chippenham Barrow 5 was found 'beneath the head' and the pairs from Norton Subcourse and Langtoft were found either side of the skull. All these findings would be in accord with use of the studs as ear or (in some cases) lip ornaments. In terms of gender associations, where the sex of the deceased has been reliably identified, it has been female. The three 'male' identifications, from Cowleaze, Langtoft and Over, are all tentative rather than definitive.

5.7 BEADS (SINGLETONS)

TYPO-CHRONOLOGY

A total of 18 singleton beads were studied (Table 5.7.1); however ten of them were unstratified. The remainder of the many thousands of beads recorded occurred in groups, of one or more materials, and have been classified as necklaces (see Chapters 7 and 8). Of the eight stratified beads two are from Beaker-age graves: the Kelleythorpe amber bead ID 1348 found with a Beaker, bracer and an amber button, and the Shuttlestone/Parwich Moor jet or shale disc bead ID 259 associated with a Series 2 dagger, flat bronze axe and an animal skin. Two more were found in rich Early Bronze Age graves: ID 741 Crosby Garrett with a female cremation and infant inhumations, jet spacer plate and two bone items, and ID 1161 Wall Mead II with a knife dagger (ID 1160) and a rim sherd from an Aldbourne Cup. Two further beads were associated with Collared Urn cremation burials: ID 436 (jet bead) with a jet pendant at Hungry Bentley, and ID 540 (shale bead) with a bronze awl and bone point at Amesbury G72, while the associations at Stanton Moor 13A, ID 697 (bone bead) were unidentified urn fragments and a flint artefact. Finally, at Hepple, a jet bead of full Early Bronze Age style (ID 369) was the sole grave good associated with a cremation burial. Interestingly, most of the stratified single beads come from the Peak District or further north, with only two found stratified in barrows in Wessex.

MORPHOLOGY AND MATERIAL

Of the eight stratified beads, four are of jet or jet-like materials, two of bone, one of stone and one of amber.

Only the stratified examples are described in detail here.

ID 259. A chunky, wedge-shaped disc bead of black jet or shale, 2.3 by 7.4mm, with a perforation diameter of 2.3mm.

ID 369. A plump fusiform bead of brownish black jet (MD/DH), 25.0 by 11.2mm, with a perforation diameter of 3.2mm.

ID 436. A plump fusiform bead of black jet (MD/DH), 10.2 by 10.2, with a perforation diameter of 5.1mm.

ID 540. A chunky annular bead of dark grey-brown Kimmeridge shale (AS), 8 by 13.1mm, with perforation dimensions of 6.3 by 6.4mm.

ID 697. A segmented bead of white bone (sheep-sized limb shaft MM), 26.0 by 8.9mm, with perforation dimensions of 3.4 by 4.5mm; the bead is composed of irregular segments varying in length from 5.2mm to 8.5mm.

ID 741. A large decorated barrel bead made from antler stem (red deer MM), 39.2 by 23.0mm. The main perforation is indeterminate, but there are three perforations on the side, each 3.5 by 2.0mm. Decoration consists of a central plain band defined by single grooves; outside this band are two matching zones of steep single-lined running chevrons. There are double grooves at each outer end (Figure 5.7.1).

ID 1161. A medium fusiform bead of red-brown stone (?Pennant Sandstone: AW/DB), 17.3 by 8.5mm, with perforation dimensions 3.7mm and 4.3mm; it appears to be copying a jet bead form.

Table 5.7.1 . List of singleton beads studied and illustrated.

Object	Site (Parish), County	Museum	Illustration
Jet or jet-like materials			
ID 259	Shuttlestone/Parwich Moor, Derbys.	Shef	Not illustrated
ID 260	Lean Low (Hartington Town), Derbys.	Shef	Not illustrated
ID 277	Wigber Low (Kniveton), Derbys.	Shef	Not illustrated
ID 278	Wigber Low (Kniveton), Derbys.	Shef	Not illustrated
ID 279	Wigber Low (Kniveton), Derbys.	Shef	Not illustrated
ID 301	Heslerton 5, burial 1, E. Yorks.	BM	Not illustrated
ID 369	Hepple, Northumb.	BM	Not illustrated
ID 418	Wilsford, Lake, Wilts.	BM	Not illustrated
ID 433	Roughton Heath (Cromer), Norfolk	BM	Not illustrated
ID 436	Hungry Bentley, Derbys.	BM	Not illustrated
ID 540	Amesbury G72, Wilts.	Sal	Not illustrated
Bone			
ID 697	Stanton Moor 13A, Derbys.	Shef	Not illustrated
ID 739	Roughridge Down, Bishop Cannings G61, Wilts.	BM	Not illustrated
ID 741	Crosby Garrett 176, burial 2, Cumbria	BM	Figure 5.7.1
? Stone			
ID 418a	Wilsford Lake, Wiltshire	BM	Not illustrated
ID 1161	Wall Mead II (Timsbury), Somerset	Brist	Not illustrated
Amber			
ID 1348	Kelleythorpe UN101, burial 2, E. Yorks.	BM	Not illustrated
ID 1535	Winterbourne Stoke G38, Wilts.	Sal	Not illustrated

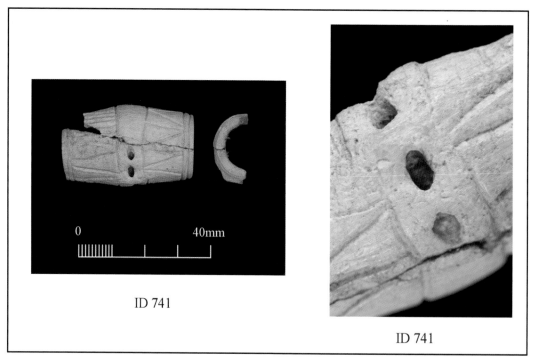

Figure 5.7.1. Bead ID 741 Crosby Garrett 176, 2, including detail of decoration and perforations.

ID 1348. A high, bun-shaped bead of orange to bright red amber, diameter 22.2mm, broken.

COMPLETENESS AND DAMAGE

Six of the beads are complete or almost complete. The other three have catastrophic breaks, ID 697 surviving at 70% and ID 741 and ID 1161 at only 40%. Two items have modern chips.

WEAR

Ancient chips occur on five beads, and the major breaks on ID 741 and ID 1161 are ancient. Damage to the burnt bone bead ID 697 however probably occurred during the cremation process. Thread-wear is apparent on three of the jet or jet-like beads, one bone bead, one of stone/shale and the one of amber. On bead ID 741 the two outer perforations have string wear on their outer edges only (Figure 5.7.1, right). ID 1535 also has traces of bead-on-bead wear. Overall six of the beads were classified as slightly worn, one as worn, and one as indeterminate.

CONCLUSIONS

Single beads occur very rarely in Chalcolithic or Early Bronze Age graves. They derive from burials of varying date, and they also vary greatly in terms of material, form and degrees of use and breakage. However none are included in the very worn category.

5.8 SPACER PLATES (SINGLETONS)

TYPO-CHRONOLOGY

Nine single spacer plates have been studied, six of jet and three of bone (Table 5.8.1). Ultimately they will have derived from spacer plate necklaces, the morphology and chronology of which are described in Chapter 7. The original necklaces will have dated probably from several centuries surrounding 2000 cal BC. The four items from East Anglia (ID 282 from Burwell Fen and IDs 1058–60 from Feltwell Fen) were found as stray finds in the fenland. The single plain example from Crosby Garrett 176, Cumbria (ID 329) was found with a female cremation burial, two infant inhumations, two bone points (ID 747 and 803) and a large fragment from a decorated bone barrel bead (ID 741, see previous section). The pair of decorated spacers from Helperthorpe (IDs 371–72) was found within a pit in a long barrow along with a perforated jet button (ID 373), while the exact location of the decorated pair from the barrow at Holwick-in-Teesdale (ID 375–76) is not known. The decorative motifs are similar to some found on later Beakers, especially those of Clarke's Southern series, and steps 5 to 7 of the Lanting and Van Der Waals classificatory system (Shepherd 1973, Ch. 5). Other single or small groups of spacer plates have been found in East Anglia: with other jet beads (fusiform or disc) at two sites within Risby parish (Martin 1976; Vatcher and Vatcher 1976), at Soham Fen (ID 391) and at Snailwell (ID 281), as well as within the composite necklace from Radwell, Bedfordshire (Hall and Woodward 1977). The Soham Fen and Snailwell necklaces are described in detail in Chapter 7.

MORPHOLOGY

ID 282 (Figure 5.8.1 and Figure 5.8.3). This is a roughly triangular terminal plate or SP1, 31.7 by 24.3mm (at wider end) by 4.5mm thick, with straight bored perforations reducing from four to three; the borings are very fine, measuring between 1.2 and 2.1mm in diameter. The decoration comprises chevron and line motifs worked in a very finely executed 'rocker' technique which produced a shallowly-incised zigzag effect (Figure 5.8.3).

ID 329 (Figure 5.8.1). This is an almost rectangular undecorated plate, probably a left-hand SP1, 33 by 18.9mm at the wider end by 5.7mm thick, with four straight bored perforations. The perforations vary in diameter from 2.2 to 3.4mm.

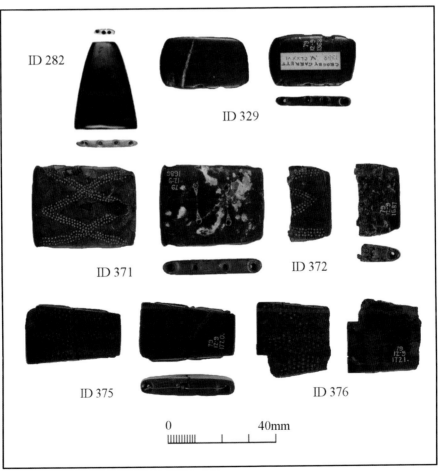

Figure 5.8.1. Singleton spacer plates of jet: ID 282 Burwell Fell; ID 329 Crosby Garrett 176, 2; ID 371–372 Helperthorpe UN95; ID 375 and 376 Holwick in Teesdale 123.

ID 371 and 372 (Figure 5.8.1). These are probably left hand and right hand plates (SP1 or 2) of width 29.7mm and 26.7mm respectively and similar thicknesses of 6.6mm. ID 372 is broken, but the length of ID 371 is 38.4mm. ID 371 has two straight bored perforations plus two elbow borings, and ID 372 was probably similar when complete. The decoration on each is similar and they both derive from the same necklace. The close-set fine pointillé design forms a pattern of running lozenges, all defined by three bands of pointillé. The punctulations are of U-profile and are up to 0.7mm wide.

ID 375 and 376 (Figure 5.8.1 and Figure 5.8.3). The left hand SP1 and SP2 are from the same necklace, each with three straight-bored perforations originally, although ID 376 is now broken. The more complete ID 375 measures 36.4 by 22.2mm and the pair are 7.9 and 7.7mm thick. The borings vary in diameter between 2.5 and 3.3mm. The decoration comprises filled running lozenges, outlined and infilled with U-profiled punctulations on average 0.75mm diameter. Those on ID 376 are slightly more variable in size (up to 0.9mm diameter) than on ID 375 and the two plates may have been made by different workers.

ID 1058–60 (Figure 5.8.2). These probably represent a left and right hand SP2 plus one left terminal plate, all from the same necklace. Dimensions are 60.2 by 22mm, 58.8 by 28mm and 38 by 23.2mm respectively. The SP2 pieces have nine reducing to six and ten reducing to six elbow perforations, while the terminal plate has three elbow perforations reducing to one. The plates vary in thickness from 6.3 to 7.2mm. The borings on the three plates are very similar and range in diameter from 2.3 to 3mm on the sides and from 2.0 to 3.5mm on the rear faces, where they are more oval in shape. The outer perforations on the lower end of the terminal plate (ID 1060) are also bored to the side, so are three-way borings. The decoration on the SP2 plates comprises a single punctulated filled lozenge set within

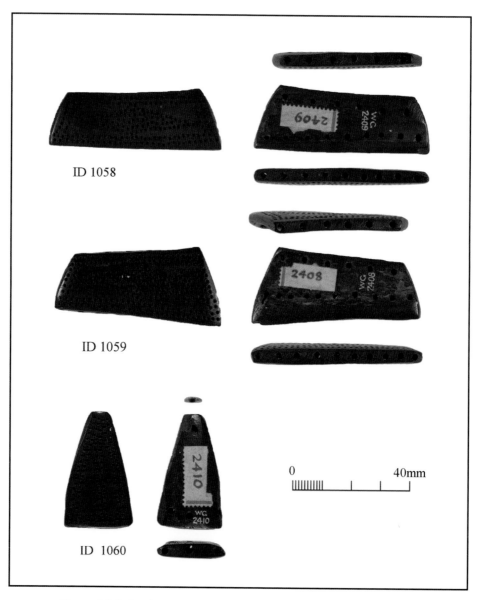

ID 1058

ID 1059

ID 1060

0   40mm

Figure 5.8.2. Singleton spacer plates of bone: ID 1058–60 Feltwell Fen.

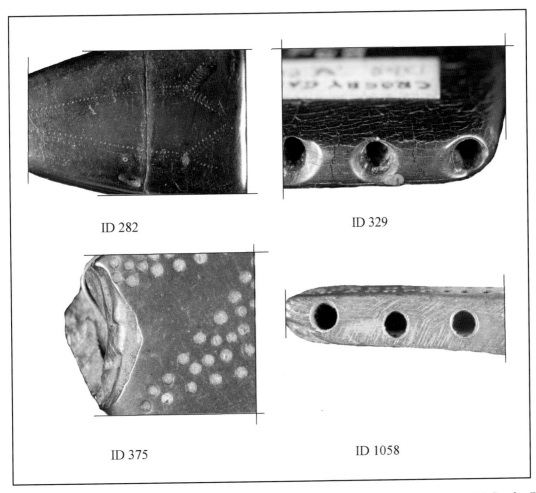

Figure 5.8.3. Details showing: incised zigzag decoration on ID 282 Burwell Fell; thread-polish on ID 329 Crosby Garrett 176, 2; decoration detail on ID 375 Holwick in Teesdale 123, and striations on ID 1058 Feltwell Fen.

Table 5.8.1. Singleton spacer plates: thread-wear (number of perforations).

Object	Site, County	Thread-polish	Ancient thread-pull	Modern thread-pull	Bead-on-bead wear	Wear	Museum	Illustrated
Jet								
ID 282	Burwell Fen, Cambs.	-	-	-	7	Slight	Cambs	Figure 5.8.1; Figure 5.8.3
ID 329	Crosby Garrett 176, burial 2, Cumbria	8	1	-	-	V. worn	BM	Figure 5.8.1; Figure 5.8.3
ID 371	Helperthorpe UN95, Feature A, E. Yorks.	-	7	-	1	V. worn	BM	Figure 5.8.1
ID 372	Helperthorpe UN95, Feature A, E. Yorks.	-	-	-	3	V. worn	BM	Figure 5.8.1
ID 375	Holwick in Teesdale UN123, u/s, N. Yorks.	-	3	-	6	V. worn	BM	Figure 5.8.1; Figure 5.8.3
ID 376	Holwick in Teesdale UN123, u/s, N. Yorks.	-	3	-	3	V. worn	BM	Figure 5.8.1
Bone								
ID 1058	Feltwell Fen, Norfolk	30	2	5	-	Slight	BM	Figure 5.8.2; Figure 5.8.3
ID 1059	Feltwell Fen, Norfolk	25	3	3	-	Slight	BM	Figure 5.8.2
ID 1060	Feltwell Fen, Norfolk	7	2	4	-	Slight	BM	Figure 5.8.2

a frame of a double row of punctulations which follows the outline of the plate. The outlines of the lozenges, and their infilling, are rather irregular. The roughly triangular terminal plate has a similar framing motif along the three edges and a further double row of punctulations down the centre. All the decoration appears to have been made with the same tool, and the punctulations are all *c.* 0.7mm in diameter.

MATERIAL

All the black spacers are characterised by brown-black colour, sometimes with woody texture, and are made from Whitby jet (AS/MD and confirmed by XRF by MD/DH for ID 371 and ID 375). The set of bone spacers were not seen by MM and the material has not been identified to species. The dark brown colour of these pieces is unusual but may result from staining in the peat from which they were recovered.

MANUFACTURE

All the spacer plates apart from ID 329 show traces of original polishing striations. These are lateral and longitudinal on ID 282, multidirectional on the rear of ID 371, longitudinal on the rear and sides of ID 376 and marked diagonal on the rest, including the set of three bone plates, ID 1058–60 (Figure 5.8.3). Gouge marks are also visible on the rear faces of ID 371 and ID 375. Clear rilling is visible within one perforation of ID 372. Sheen on the jet pieces varies from low/medium to very high, and the bone plates are well polished.

COMPLETENESS AND DAMAGE

Most of the plates are virtually complete, surviving at the 95% level or above. But one of the pieces from Helperthorpe (ID 372) is a fragment (20%) and one from Holwick-in-Teesdale (ID 376) only survives at 70%. Modern damage includes loss due to cracking on the jet items, and some tiny chips. ID 282 is broken across and has been glued, and ID 375 is also in two halves that have been wired together. The group of bone plates displays traces of thread-wear which are both of ancient and modern date (see below Table 5.8.1). This indicates that they have been restrung, presumably for display purposes, in modern times.

WEAR

The main traces of wear comprise thread-polish, smoothing, pulls and bead-on-bead wear visible at the perforations. The occurrence of such wear is summarised in Table 5.8.1. The decoration is worn, especially to one side on ID 282, and on ID 372 the decoration is also slightly worn. ID 329 is very worn and, judging from the thread- and bead-wear (Figure 5.8.3), it might have been worn both ways round during its use life. On ID 371, traces of thread-wear on the rear perforations of the two elbow borings pull towards the centre, and there are also wear grooves between them. The catastrophic breaking of ID 372 probably occurred pre-burial, but the fractured surface is not worn. The edges of the major break of ID 375 have been smoothed in antiquity. Perhaps this had been used as two separate pieces, in conjunction with the broken fragment ID 376, also from Holwick-in-Teesdale. This fragment shows orange peel surface irregularities along the broken edge and this may indicate that the plate fractured along an irregularity or crack in the parent piece of jet used. Overall all the spacer plates are worn, four of them only slightly, but five very worn.

CONCLUSIONS

All these plates which occurred singly in graves or in small groups are worn, and appear to have been heirlooms which derived originally from spacer plate necklaces. They may have been strung in necklaces, along with beads of perishable materials which have not survived, or may have been individual pieces prized for their amuletic properties. These spacer plates need to be considered alongside those within the spacer plate necklaces which are described in detail in Chapter 7. In particular it is interesting to note that the unusual 'rocker' decoration found on the single jet spacer from Burwell Fen (ID 282) is identical to that found on two spacers within the necklace from Soham Fen (ID 391) and the two terminal spacers in the Snailwell necklace (ID 281). And similar 'rocker' decoration is also found on the jet lozenge ornament from Carlton Colville, Lowestoft. It is likely that all these pieces were made by a single craftsman, and the spacer plates from Snailwell and Soham Fen may have been part of the same original necklace.

5.9 PENDANTS AND INDIVIDUAL NECKLACE FASTENERS

TYPO-CHRONOLOGY

Pendants have not previously been considered as a functional group. The raw materials are various, ranging from gold, bronze and jet and jet-like materials to amber and bone. Several of them are made from more than one of these materials and are famous Wessex Series objects; others are not so well known. Pendants tend not to occur in necklaces but are found as single items in a grave group or in small groups of similar pieces. The two largest groups are the varied selections of pendants found in two rich grave groups, Wilsford G7 and Wilsford G8, amongst the Normanton Down cemetery near Stonehenge. Other complex pendants are known from graves in the Peak District and East Yorkshire, and a series of more simple pendants are also widely spread. In Yorkshire there is also a group of what appear to be necklace fasteners, but they occur singly in graves. These may have been re-used as pendants, so are included in this section. The objects studied and their descriptions are grouped into these categories:

Table 5.9.1. List of pendants and individual necklace fasteners studied and illustrated. Note: ID 247 is part of a spacer plate necklace but all appropriate profiles are shown here. It is described in detail in Chapter 7.

Object	Site (Parish), County	Museum	Illustration
Complex Pendants			
ID 325	Hutton Buscel 157, burial 1, N. Yorks.	BM	Figure 5.9.3; Figure 5.9.4
ID 361	Aldbourne 280, burial 1, Wilts.	BM	Figure 5.9.3 Figure 5.9.4
ID 422	Copton (Pickering), N. Yorks.	BM	Figure 5.9.3
ID 435	Hungry Bentley, Derbys.	BM	Figure 5.9.3 Figure 5.9.4
ID 457	Scamridge, N. Yorks.	BM	Not illustrated
ID 485	Wilsford G7, Wilts.	Dev	Figure 5.9.3
ID 1381	Wilsford G7, Wilts.	Dev	Figure 5.9.3
ID 1383	Wilsford G7, Wilts.	Dev	Figure 5.9.3
ID 1384	Wilsford G7, Wilts.	Dev	Figure 5.9.3
ID 1388	Wilsford G7, Wilts.	Dev	Figure 5.9.2
ID 1404	Wilsford G8, Wilts.	Dev	Figure 5.9.1
ID 1406/901	Wilsford G8, Wilts.	Dev	Figure 5.9.2 Figure 5.9.4
ID 1412	Wilsford G8, Wilts.	Dev	Figure 5.9.1
ID 1413	Wilsford G8, Wilts.	Dev	Figure 5.9.1
ID 1414	Wilsford G8, Wilts.	Dev	Figure 5.9.3
ID 1415	Wilsford G8, Wilts.	Dev	Figure 5.9.3
ID 1416	Wilsford G8, Wilts.	Dev	Figure 5.9.2 Figure 5.9.4
ID 1417	Wilsford G8, Wilts.	Dev	Figure 5.9.1 Figure 5.9.4
ID 1420	Preshute G1a (Manton), Wilts.	Dev	Figure 5.9.1 Figure 5.9.4
ID 1422	Preshute G1a (Manton), Wilts.	Dev	Figure 5.9.3
ID 1473	Wilsford G47, Wilts.	Dev	Figure 5.9.3
ID 1474	Wilsford G47, Wilts.	Dev	Not illustrated
ID 1475	Wilsford G47, Wilts.	Dev	
Simple pendants			
ID 218	Painsthorpe 118 (Thixendale), E. Yorks.	Hull	Not illustrated
ID 324	Hutton Buscel 153, burial 2, N. Yorks.	BM	Figure 5.9.5; Figure 5.9.6
ID 417	Lambourn 31, Berks.	BM	Figure 5.9.5; Figure 5.9.6
ID 498	Durrington G14, Wilts.	Dev	Figure 5.9.5
ID 499	Durrington G14, Wilts.	Dev	Not illustrated
ID 500	Durrington G14, Wilts.	Dev	Not illustrated
ID 899	Wilsford G15, Wilts.	Dev	Figure 5.9.5
ID 1057	Milborne St Andrew G16e, Dorset	Dor	Figure 5.9.5
ID 1382	Wilsford G7, Wilts.	Dev	Figure 5.9.5
ID 1407	Wilsford G8, Wilts.	Dev	Figure 5.9.5
ID 1408	Wilsford G8, Wilts.	Dev	Figure 5.9.5
ID 1409	Wilsford G8, Wilts.	Dev	Figure 5.9.5
ID 1410	Wilsford G8, Wilts.	Dev	Figure 5.9.5
ID 1411	Wilsford G8, Wilts.	Dev	Figure 5.9.5; Figure 5.9.6
ID 1528	Shrewton G5j, Wilts.	Sal	Figure 5.9.5
Individual Necklace Fasteners			
ID 211	Painsthorpe 118 (Thixendale), E. Yorks.	Hull	Not illustrated
ID 217	Painsthorpe 200 (Kirby Underdale), E. Yorks.	Hull	Figure 5.9.7
ID 219	Calais Wold 29, Riggs (Thixendale), E. Yorks.	Hull	Not illustrated
ID 224	Garton Slack 81 (Kirkburn), E. Yorks.	Hull	Figure 5.9.7
ID 247	Calais Wold 13 (Bishop Wilton), E. Yorks.	Hull	Figure 5.9.7 (Drawing)
ID 321	Goodmanham 89, burial 6, E. Yorks.	BM	Figure 5.9.7

complex pendants, simple pendants and individual necklace fasteners (Table 5.9.1).

The pendants were probably made and were in use over many centuries. Those that occur as single jet or jet-like material items in the north may be the earliest, related as they appear to be to the jet disc bead and spacer plate necklaces. Radiocarbon dates suggest that these necklaces were current in the few centuries before 2000 cal BC and just thereafter. However, the fancy pendants from the grave groups in Wessex date from a rather later period, mainly during the currency of the Wessex 2 Series graves. As the items are so varied a very brief description is supplied for each example or small group. Full dimensions and further details may be found in the digital database.

COMPLEX PENDANTS

ID 1404 Wilsford G8. Figure 5.9.1. A halberd pendant of length 25mm. The tapered haft is formed from amber which is bound with a series of four bands of gold of variable width. Most of the bands are decorated with three grooves, while the top one has two grooves. The straight transverse perforation at the base is broken out and one corner of the gold is cracked: the date of these breaks is indeterminate. The very thin copper alloy blade, which is attached with two tiny pins, is also broken, undoubtedly in antiquity. The piece is heavily coated with consolidant, such that any traces of manufacture are not visible, but the pendant does appear to have been used and is categorised as slightly worn.

ID 1422 Preshute G1a. Figure 5.9.1. A halberd pendant of length 30.5mm. The tapered haft of this pendant is slightly longer, and is completely covered with gold. Some splitting (of unknown date) indicates that the core may be of copper alloy which has begun to corrode. The gold cover has been made in two hollow parts which were joined almost invisibly near the centre. The cover is decorated by 11 bands of triple grooves, with each band measuring 1 to 1.2mm (Figure 5.9.4). Two small perforations in the base belong to a tiny V-perforation. Part of the copper alloy blade is missing and again it is heavily consolidated. Any traces of manufacture are thus obscured, but the gold does display smoothed and slightly scuffed rounded edges, indicating slight wear. (Note: these two halberd pendants are considered in more detail within Chapter 6 below; brief summaries are included here for completeness)

ID 1412 Wilsford G8. Figure 5.9.1. A gold-bound amber disc of diameter 27.3 to 27.7mm. A disc of amber which is slightly convex on the upper and lower surfaces is bound in gold sheet, applied in two pieces which join around the centre of the edge facet. The gold extends around the edges and laps over the front and rear edges of the disc. On front and rear the gold sheet is decorated with two zones of four grooves, each zone 2mm wide. On the front only the innermost groove is pressed into the amber. On the edge facet there is one circumferential groove on each

piece. All grooves on both front and rear are embellished with regular punctulations. A finely pierced and obtusely angled V-perforation may have been added as a secondary feature. If so the double-sided item originally functioned as something other than a pendant. The disc is scuffed all over but the age of this damage or use wear is indeterminate. There are no breaks apart from slight loss of gold on the facet, and no obvious thread wear.

ID 1413 Wilsford G8. Figure 5.9.1. A gold-bound amber disc of diameter 27.3 to 27.5mm. In terms of construction and decoration this piece is exactly the same as the previous item, except that the amber disc is convex only on one surface. Again the V-perforation may have been secondary. The wear is indeterminate.

ID 1420 Preshute G1a. Figure 5.9.1 A gold-bound amber disc of diameter 23.5mm. This smaller flat disc of amber is bound on the facet and edges with two pieces of gold sheet, as in the case of the pair of discs from Wilsford G8. The gold is decorated on front and back with six grooves in a single zone, with punctulations within all grooves. The edge facet has only one groove, which is on the rear gold element. The obtusely angled fine V-perforation is similar also, and again may have been a secondary feature. The gold bindings have sprung apart around the mid-point of the circumference except in the area between the perforations. Within the gap there is a groove which appears to have been made deliberately and may have held a fine thread (Figure 5.9.4). If the springing occurred when the perforation was drilled, which is a distinct possibility, then the groove may have been added then, or at a later time in the life of the piece. Traces of manufacture in the form of diagonal striations survive on the gold on the edge facet, and there are no signs of any scuffing. The decorative grooves are crisp and the piece does not seem to have been much used, even though it may have been modified during its use life. The wear category is indeterminate.

ID 1417 Wilsford G8. Figure 5.9.2. A curved penannular pendant of maximum diameter 32.5mm. A copper alloy core forms a rough circle with the two terminals tapering and angled outwards. There is a shallow V-perforation at the top. On the rear the butt joint of the gold sheet is embellished with a row of punctulations on either side of the join (Figure 5.9.4). If decoration, this would hardly have been visible when the pendant was worn. When worn the tips would have projected distinctly from the body. One tip is missing and some gold is missing at the junction on the rear; the age of this damage is indeterminate. It is possible that the gold foil was added to a primary copper alloy pendant. Probably ancient scuffing is visible all over the piece and it appears to be worn.

ID 1406/901 Wilsford G8. Figure 5.9.2. A gold-encased bone pendant of maximum diameter 17.7mm. A piece of flat bone is encased on one side and on its edges by a gold sheet cover. The top of the roughly oval shaped pendant carries a crescentic indent and in the base of this there are two straight perforations (0.9mm across) which exit on the main rear surface of the bone. The edge of the bone is double-grooved to hold the gold sheet covering, with the gold indented into the grooves for adhesion, and on the gold-covered face the gold sheet is decorated with straight grooves running in two directions (seven by seven) to form a grid design. The average side of a grid square is 2mm and the grooves are less than 0.5mm wide. The design is fairly regular but distorted towards the edges. The piece of bone shows surviving sutures and comes from a mammalian skull. This could be from the parietal bone of a sheep or goat, but a human identification cannot be ruled out (MM) (Figure 5.9.4). The object is essentially complete although there is a small piece of gold missing from one area of the side facet. The age of this loss is indeterminate. On both sides of the front of the pendant the decoration on the gold is partly worn, and the object appears to have been well used. It is possible that the bone pendant was the original piece, with a possibly more even surface displayed on the front, and that this important object was later partly encased in gold, with the significant bone fragment hidden in the back of the final version. The object is worn.

ID 1388 Wilsford G7. Figure 5.9.2. A gold-covered shale sphere of diameter 13.7mm. Two hemispherical hollow gold sheet elements completely encase a sphere of jet or shale which is not visible for study. There is a single groove either side of the butted joint and the outer holes (*c.* 1mm diameter) for a fine V-perforation are placed either side of the joint. The object is complete but heavily scuffed and worn, probably in antiquity. One perforation is damaged but this may be due to thread damage during display in the modern era. The object is worn.

ID 1381 Wilsford G7 and ID 1414–16 Wilsford G8. Figures 5.9.3. These are four shield-shaped amber pendants with fairly straight vertical profiles. The broken example from G7 would have had a straight top surface, the others are more gently curved. All are perforated straight through from side to side near the top. They are all decorated with shallow horizontal grooves, providing a corrugated effect. That from G7 has 11 grooves, those from G8 seven grooves (two examples) and nine grooves. The grooves on the G7 example are narrower, at 0.2 to 0.3mm wide, than those on the G8 ones which are about 1mm wide. The G7 pendant is made from mid-orange amber, oxidised to pale toffee, while those from G8 are of bright red amber oxidised to dark opaque toffee. In all cases the perforation edges are fairly crisp, but the pendants have been used, and can be categorised as slightly worn. Patches of a green substance occur on two of the G8 pendants, including one area within a perforation. These may derive from copper alloy, possibly a wire used in original threading. The three pendants from G8 may have been strung as a graduated set of three, with ID 1415 the larger central item.

ID 1383 Wilsford G7. Figure 5.9.3 A disc-shaped amber pendant of diameter 21.5mm. The circular disc is of amber with almost flat surfaces and a roughly rectangular cross section which carries a fine relatively steeply angled V-perforation at the top. The original colour of the amber is not visible. The perforations are roughly rectangular, but have suffered modern damage such that any wear traces have been destroyed. The wear is indeterminate.

ID 1384 Wilsford G7 and ID 1473–74 (Figure 5.9.3), *ID 1475 Wilsford G47.* These are four conical amber pendants with diameters 15.4 to 17.5mm. They are similar to the one just described (ID 1383) except that they have a steep conical profile and a vertical base facet with a rounded upper edge. The perforations are drilled into this facet. The amber used is bright to dark red in colour, but oxidised to brown or cream hues. Two of the pendants from Wilsford G47 have been broken since excavation. The perforations show slight to very slight wear at their edges, and on one item from G47 there are green metal deposits inside the perforations. The G47 pendants are from the same find as the amber necklace elements housed in the British Museum (ID 1360). The perforations in these pendants would not allow them to sit neatly in a spacer plate necklace, so they have been described separately in this section. Three have slight wear visible, but wear on the fourth ID 1475 is indeterminate.

ID 485 Wilsford G7. Figure 5.9.3. An axe-shaped jet pendant of length 15.2mm. This is a very neatly crafted pendant in the form of a double-bladed axe, with a regular long oval long cross section. The rich blackish brown woody texture, hairline criss-cross cracking and chemical analysis by Bussell (no. 5) show that the material is Whitby jet. The piece is complete and sheen from slight wear is visible on all four sharp corners (the interior of the perforation is not visible due to the method of display). The object is slightly worn.

ID 361 Aldbourne 280. Figure 5.9.3. An oval jet pendant with projection and maximum diameter 32.2mm. The pendant is slightly oval from top to bottom, the ring is rounded on the outside and cut to a point on the interior. The side-to-side straight perforation is housed in an integral upper projection. Although visually expected to be cannel coal, chemical analysis (MD/DH) indicated shale. Striations surviving from the method of manufacture are visible on the outer and inner faces of the ring, and on the shoulders and top of the upper projection (Figure 5.9.4). Smoothing at the upper margin of the perforation on both sides suggests slight wear.

ID 435 Hungry Bentley. Figure 5.9.3. A triple-looped jet pendant of maximum length 43.6mm. This highly accomplished piece comprises three conjoined rings below a projection which carries a 5.5mm wide side-to-side straight perforation. Colour and the nature of the criss-

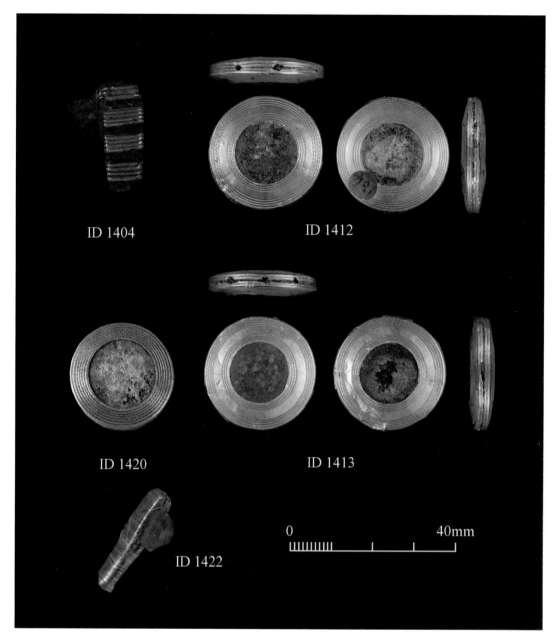

Figure 5.9.1. Complex pendants: ID 1404 Wilsford G8; ID 1412 Wilsford G8; ID 1413 Wilsford G8; ID 1420 Preshute G1a; ID 1422 Preshute G1a.

cross cracking suggest that the material is hard jet. On most surfaces all traces of manufacture have been well polished out but on the top and bottom surfaces there are faint irregular striations in the indented areas (Figure 5.9.4), and rilling within the three large rings is also visible. There is wear to the upper margin of the top perforation, and also to the lower edges of each of the three main rings. This may suggest that further elements had been suspended from these rings. The object is worn.

ID 422 (Copton Barrow, near Pickering). Figure 5.9.3. A low-domed pendant with a flat base of diameter 20.3mm and height 8.6mm. There is a deep facet which has a concave profile and contains three to five grooves, which are much damaged. Similar concentric fine grooves, three

in number, occur around the outer edge of the dome. A V-perforation pierces the facet. The brown-black material is soft jet, with low sheen all over. The bridge of the V-perforation is broken out and there are further breaks around the margin of the base and around the perforations. Related to severe criss-cross cracking all this damage is modern. The decoration on the dome and facet all shows signs of wear, and the best-surviving perforation shows strong thread-wear towards the margin of the dome above. The pendant is classified as worn, and may have been a copy of Wessex items such as ID 1384 above.

ID 325 Hutton Buscel 157. Figure 5.9.3. A domed and decorated jet pendant of diameter 17.1mm. Unevenly circular in shape this pendant has a high gently curved

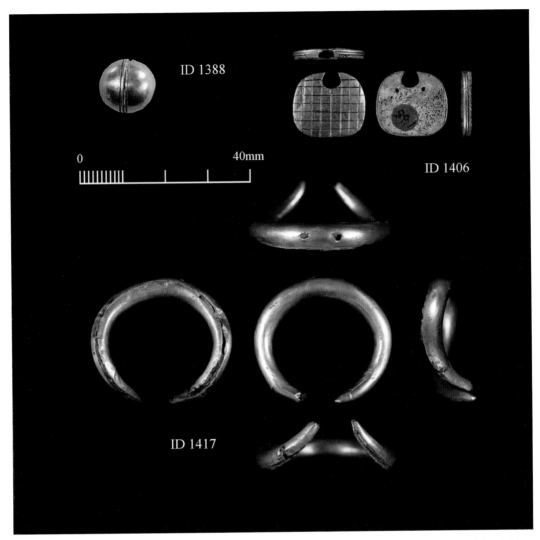

Figure 5.9.2. Complex pendants: ID 1388 Wilsford G7; ID 1406 Wilsford G8; ID 1417 Wilsford G8.

dome and an elbow perforation running from the base to an indented marginal facet (Figure 5.9.4). The upper face is decorated with a single incised circle, diameter 9.6mm, around the top, and a row of nine rough incised triangles around the edge. Black and smooth in texture, chemical analysis confirmed the material identification as jet (MD/DH). The dome is very worn by smoothing and the decoration is almost worn away. Also the perforations are strongly smoothed and exhibit extreme thread-pulls. The object is very worn.

ID 457 Scamridge. A curved pendant of length 38.1mm. This rather roughly carved piece has a strongly indented profile and a large hourglass perforation with visible rilling. The black woody texture and extreme criss-cross cracking indicate that the material is jet. Strong wear has occurred to two grooves on the outer face and within the hollowed inner face. Also the perforation shows extensive use with a strong thread-pull on one side. The object is very worn.

SIMPLE PENDANTS

ID 218 Painsthorpe 118. A lozenge shaped jet pendant of length 43.5mm. Flat in vertical section but with a slight thickening towards the base, the pendant has a single off-centre hourglass perforation near the top. Surface characteristics and the woody texture indicate that it is made from a minimally modified jet pebble. The surfaces are slightly worn and the perforation shows minor smoothing. The object is slightly worn.

ID 324 Hutton Buscel 153. Figure 5.9.5. A triangular shale pendant of length 33.5mm. This unfinished piece is roughly triangular in shape, with a small straight perforation near the top. The brownish-black stony material was analysed and identified as shale (MD/DH). All faces have marked multi-directional shaping striations (Figure 5.9.6), and the edges of the perforation are crisp. The object was never used: it was probably designed to be a pendant, but there is the slight possibility that it was the roughout for a terminal spacer plate. Its condition is fresh.

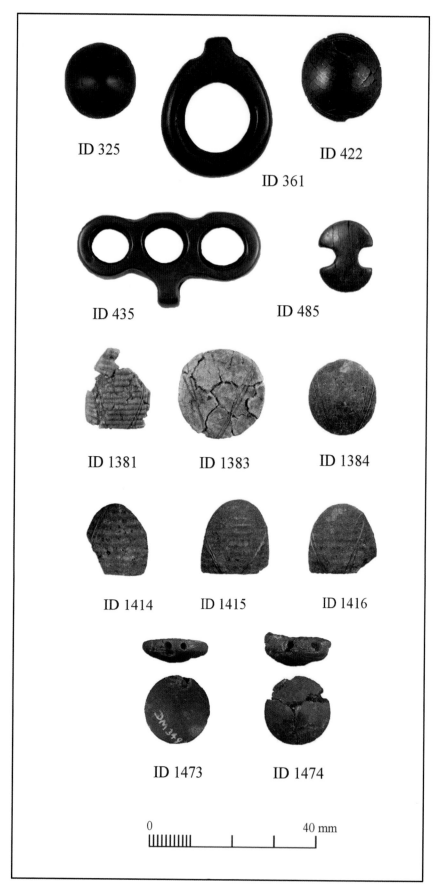

Figure 5.9.3. Complex pendants: ID 325 Hutton Buscel 157, 1; ID 361 Aldbourne 280, 1; ID 422 Copton, Pickering; ID 435 Hungry Bentley; ID 485 Wilsford G8; ID 1381 Wilsford G7; ID 1383 Wilsford G7; ID 1384 Wilsford G7; ID 1414 Wilsford G8; ID 1415 Wilsford G8; ID 1416 Wilsford G8; ID 1473 Wilsford G47; ID 1474 Wilsford G47.

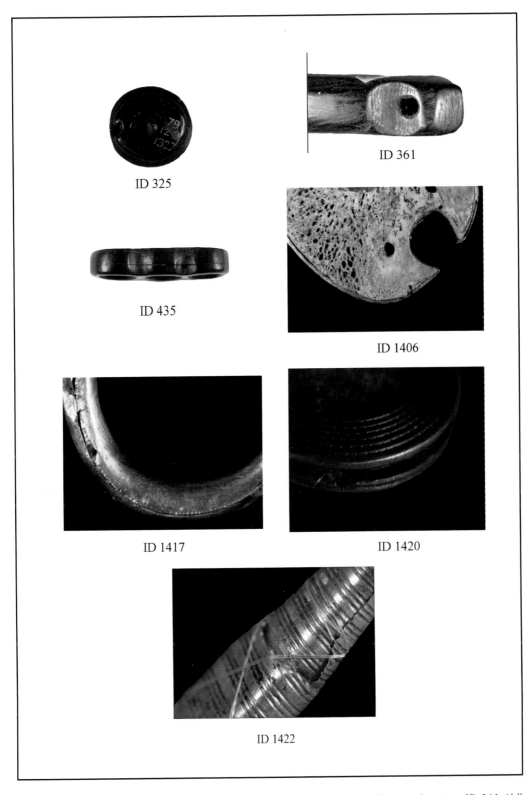

Figure 5.9.4. Details of complex pendants: ID 325 Hutton Buscel 157, 1 showing elbow perforation; ID 361 Aldbourne 280, 1 showing striations; ID 435 Hungry Bentley showing striations; ID 1406 Wilsford G8 showing back; ID 1417 Wilsford G8 showing decoration; ID 1420 Preshute G1a showing possible groove for thread; ID 1422 Preshute G1a showing fissure.

ID 417 Lambourn 31. Figure 5.9.5. A rectangular jet pendant of length 19mm. This neatly formed piece has a rectangular section and a straight perforation near the top. The black colour, cracking and chemical analysis (MD/DH) indicate identification as jet. It is polished to a high sheen. There is extreme smoothing at the top margin of the perforation on both sides (Figure 5.9.6), and the piece is therefore classified as worn.

ID 1528 Shrewton G5j. Figure 5.9.5. A teardrop amber pendant of length 13.5mm. The original form of this pendant is not known as it had broken across the two arms in antiquity. Following the fracture both arms were re-polished and the piece could have been suspended from the wider loop, which may originally have been the base. The original amber was bright orange, now oxidised to light toffee. The inside surfaces of the large hole are all smoothed, particularly towards the base; the latter may be related to use wear following the major fracture and re-working of the piece. The object is worn.

ID 498 (Figure 5.9.5), *ID 499–500 Durrington G14.* Three shale pestle pendants of lengths 15.7 to 17.2mm. Circular in cross section and with bowed projections at both top and bottom, these pendants are perforated straight through from side to side near the top. Dark grey-brown and speckled, with a fibrous stony texture, the material is identified as Kimmeridge shale (Bussell nos. 13–15). All are slightly damaged by ancient chips and the perforations show edge smoothing indicating slight wear. Two are longer than the third so they may have functioned as a graduated set.

ID 1407–11 Wilsford G8. Figure 5.9.5. Five amber pestle pendants of lengths 13 to 24mm. Four of the pendants are oval in cross section and with bowed projections at the base only. The fifth piece is the core from a similar pendant, broken in antiquity. All are perforated straight through from side to side near the top (Figure 9.5.6). The original colour of the amber is variable, ranging from mid and dark orange to dark red. No traces of manufacture or wear are visible and the degree of wear is indeterminate. Colour and variation in size and shape indicate that they do not appear to have been designed as an integrated graduated set.

ID 1382 Wilsford G7. Figure 5.9.5. A trapezoidal amber pendant which is broken. This is the lower portion of a thin pendant which has fractured across the perforation in antiquity. Originally pale orange in colour, there are no traces of manufacture and the surviving edges of the hole are fairly crisp, indicating slight wear.

ID 899 Wilsford G15. Figure 5.9.5. A triangular bone pendant of length 33.6mm. A thin and flat pendant with a single hourglass perforation placed eccentrically near the angled top. Pale cream in colour the material is a fragment of bone from a large mammal. The vertical edges are sharp and not polished, and it may be that the piece was never finished, or perhaps was cut down from a larger object. The

perforation edges are crisp and the piece appears to have been unused. The object is in fresh condition. The outline of this piece may be imitating the shape of a dagger blade.

ID 1057 Milborne St Andrew G16e. Figure 5.9.5. A circular probable fossil (initially thought to have been bone) of average diameter 32mm and 10.1mm high. It is roughly pierced through the centre and may have been used as a pendant. The hourglass perforation is oval in shape, with smooth inner surfaces. There are no traces of manufacture or wear and the wear category is indeterminate.

INDIVIDUAL NECKLACE FASTENERS

Five jet fasteners from Yorkshire were found as individual items. Their main features are summarised in Table 5.9.2. Those illustrated are shown in Figure 5.9.7. The morphology of such items is shown in Figure 5.9.8 which illustrates a similar fastener from a necklace (ID 247 Calais Wold 13; see Chapter 7). Identification of the first four items as jet was undertaken visually by AS. ID 321 was chemically analysed and identified as low quality jet (MD/DH).

The through perforation on ID 217 may have been a secondary addition. This fact, taken in conjunction with the relatively high degrees of wear encountered among these fasteners, does support the idea that they had been re-used, in a second use life, as pendants. The fasteners that have been found in association with necklaces present a greater variety of shapes (see Chapter 7), so it seems that the triangular forms were particularly valued subsequently as potential pendants.

CONCLUSIONS

The pendants described above are highly variable in terms of shape, general morphology and the raw materials employed. Where decorated the motifs are linear and sharp geometric outline shapes, such as the triangle or trapezium seem to have been preferred. Thus these objects seem to have been highly individual and probably were personalised. In several cases the pendant had been modified for extended or later use, and this includes the series of re-used necklace fasteners. Interestingly, it was triangular shaped fasteners that were selected for this specific purpose. Overall analysis of use wear (see Table 5.9.3) shows that almost all the pendants show wear, which is sometimes heavy. The necklace fasteners are particularly worn (with only one out of five in the slightly worn category), while the other pendants have a greater tendency to be fresh or slightly worn (13 out of the 23 complex pendants, and seven out of the 15 simple examples).

One strong characteristic of the pendants is miniaturisation. Several of the more complex items copy tool or other forms. The exotic composite halberd pendants are copying a tool type which is not known to occur in England or Wales, although it does occur in Europe and

Figure 5.9.5. Simple pendants: ID 324 Hutton Buscel 153, 2; ID 417 Lambourn 31; ID 498 Durrington G14; ID 899 Wilsford G15; ID 1057 Milborne St Andrew G16e; ID 1382 Wilsford G7; ID 1407–1411 Wilsford G8; ID 1528 Shrewton G5j.

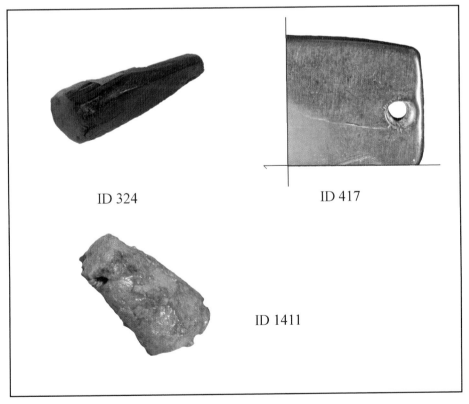

Figure 5.9.6. Details of simple pendants: ID 324 Hutton Buscel 153, 2 showing striations; ID 417 Lambourn 31 showing smoothing around perforation; ID 1411 Wilsford G8 showing location of perforation.

Table 5.9.2. Individual jet necklace fasteners: key features.

ID	L (mm)	Shape	Base	Perfs.	Traces of manufacture	Wear traces	Wear category
211	32.6	High triangular	Flat, narrow rectangular	Single through	Polished out	Thread-polish at perf.	Worn
217	51.4	Low triangular	Flat, narrow, boat-shaped	2 sets V-perf in base; single through	Longitudinal striations near ends of base	Thread-polish in all perfs.	Worn
219	22.6+ broken	Low triangular	Flat, narrow	1 set V-perf	None	Thread-polish and -wear	Very worn
224	31.7	High triangular	Flat, narrow, boat-shaped	2 sets V-perf	Longitudinal striations all over base	Slight thread-polish and -wear	Slightly worn
321	19.5	Triangular, deep	Facet with rounded edges	Single side to side at top	Longitudinal striations on front, rear, sides and base	Side facets not crisp; perf.-wear at top	Worn

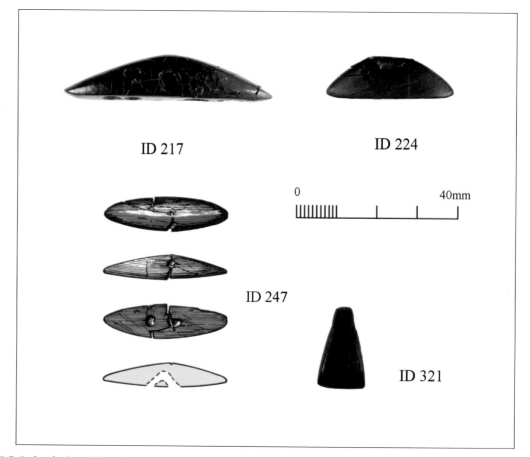

Figure 5.9.7. Individual necklace fasteners: ID 217 Painsthorpe 200; ID 224 Garton Slack 81; ID 247 Calais Wold 13 (drawing by Marion O'Neil); ID 321 Goodmanham 89, 6.

Ireland (Harbison 1969; also see Chapter 6). And the jet double-axe pendant appears to be copying a battle-axe of the Scotsburn or Crichie groups, concentrated in Ireland and northern Britain (Roe 1966). The curved copper alloy pendant with gold cover is often termed an 'ingot pendant' referring to its similarity to bronze ingots known in Europe. However it seems more likely that it is intended to illustrate a pair of horns, presumably of cattle, or even the tusks of a pig or boar. When worn the curved points would have projected significantly from the human body. It has been

suggested by Thomas (1966) that the gold-covered bone pendant may be a miniature representation of a gold lunula. This similarity is not very exact and it can alternatively be suggested that it may well represent the animal from which the bone material was derived. This may have been an important cult creature, or, if human, the remnant from an ancestor. Such a human memento may have been passed down a kin line, or may have been recovered from an earlier burial and revered as a magical ancestral relic.

It has already been noted that many of the most complex

Table 5.9.3. Pendants: degree of use wear.

Type	Fresh	Slight wear	Moderate wear	Heavy wear	Indeterminate	Total
Complex	-	13	5	2	3	23
Simple	2	5	2	-	6	15
Fastener	-	1	3	1	-	5
Totals	**2**	**19**	**10**	**3**	**9**	**43**

pendants come from graves adjacent to Stonehenge. Furthermore it can be suggested that some were made by particular schools of craftsmen. The way the materials are joined in the two halberd pendants, and the third one known from Hengistbury Head (Clarke *et al.* 1985) strongly suggests that they may have been made by the same person, and the groups of three grooves on the gold mounts of the two studied in detail might confirm this hypothesis. Similarly, it is possible to suggest that the three gold-bound amber discs were also made by one craftsman, or a group of specialists (Coles and Taylor 1971; Taylor 2004 and Taylor in Clarke *et al.* 1985, 186–7). The defining characteristic is the rows of punctulations within the grooved decoration. However the Preshute G1a example is rather smaller in size and the amber disc is flatter. It appears to have been mounted slightly differently and is less worn than the pair from Wilsford G8.

Most of the pendants from Early Bronze Age graves in England have been studied, either in this section or within the necklace descriptions. For instance the intriguingly shaped pestle pendants are also represented in two large amber necklaces (ID 1111–26 Little Cressingham and ID 1360 Wilsford-cum-Lake; Chapter 7) and also, in shale, in a composite necklace (ID 1330–31 Shrewton 5J; Chapter 8). And a further example which is slightly more teardrop-shaped forms one element in the composite necklace from Radwell (Hall and Woodward 1977, fig. 4, E). However there are a few other individual items which are worthy of note. These include the fragment of a circular amber pendant from Ringlemere, Kent (Needham *et al.* 2006, fig. 24d); this bears resemblance to the circular pendant from Wilsford G7 (ID 1383), but the grooving of the sides is better paralleled in Brittany (*ibid*, 41). There is an unusual jet or lignite pendant from Ashville, Abingdon which appears to represent an axe with crescentic blade (Balkwill 1978, fig. 26, 5). This falls into our category of miniature weapon pendants. Also of particular interest are various examples of fragments from spacer plates, made from both amber and jet, which have been employed in a secondary life as pendants in necklaces of varying type. These will be considered in the appropriate necklace sections.

5.10 DECORATED ORNAMENTS OF COPPER ALLOY (Stuart Needham with the authors)

BRONZE NECK OR HEAD ORNAMENT

ID 1152 Garton Slack 107 (Garton-on-the-Wolds), East Yorkshire; Hull and East Riding Museum

CONTEXT

The three items were found in a secondary oval grave (E) under a round barrow (Mortimer 1905, 230–232, fig. 589). The grave contained the skeleton of an adult aged about 50, crouched on its left side, with head to east. The copper or bronze band and rods (*ibid*, fig. 591; Britton 1963, 280, fig. 14, 281) were found immediately beneath a dagger of series 2 (*ibid*, fig. 590; ID 1151, Figure 3.1.5), which lay behind ('to the right of') the skull, with point facing east.

MORPHOLOGY

This consists of three pieces of bronze/copper of similar, but not exactly comparable diameters found together and presumed to interlink as a single composite ornament.

ID 1152A (Figure 5.10.1 and Figure 5.10.2d). This is an approximately parallel-sided band (13.2 to 14.2mm wide where intact) curved to form approximately 58% of a full circle. Damage makes it difficult to ascertain whether the curvature was originally constant. The maximum diameter is estimated at 150mm (142mm on current mount). The band is *c.* 0.7mm thick in centre and 0.5mm along most of the edges which are rounded to squared in section. It tapers towards the terminals to a width of 10.0mm over the last 20mm (terminal 1) and to width of 8.8mm over the last 40mm (terminal 2). The latter terminal has a complete oval perforation (4.1 by 3.1mm) whereas on terminal 1 the presumed equivalent hole has broken across the middle (4.5mm across) and this has been replaced by a second, smaller perforation (diameter 2.4 to 2.6mm) inset along the axis. A significant part of the band has a concave section facing outwards – probably due to the punching of the decoration.

ID 1152B (Figure 5.10.2). The inner rod (mostly mounted on perspex) comprises two terminals (lengths 19.5 and 10.5mm) and three mid-sections (lengths 90, 44.5, and 28mm). The diameters of the two longest fragments are 120 and 140mm. The rod is of rectangular section, thickness 1.0 to 1.5mm and width 2.0 to 2.2mm. The longer terminal is curly, like a pig's tail (2.0 by 1.5mm at the end); the shorter one is a simpler, more gentle curve in profile, but still skewed to one side in face view (end 2.1 by 1.2mm). There is no decoration, contrary to the depiction in Mortimer (1905).

ID 1152C (Figure 5.10.2). The outer rod (mounted on perspex), comprises two terminal fragments (lengths 57 and 26mm) and four mid-sections, two of which join (lengths

50, 13.5 and 12mm). The rod, again of rectangular section, is thinner than the inner rod (0.7 to 1.2mm; thinnest away from the terminals; width 2.2 to 2.5mm) and consistently describes a slacker curvature (the diameters of the two longest fragments are 170 and 185mm). The longer terminal fragment has only part of a tightly hooked end surviving (2.0 by 1.0mm at break), but a full crook is present on the shorter one, the terminal being thinned wedge fashion (1.2 by 0.3mm) (Figure 5.10.2b).

DECORATION

ID 1152A (Figure 5.10.2). The band bears a sequence of eight lozenges (lengths 14 to 16mm; widths 4.5 to 5.5mm) spaced fairly evenly around the circuit, each being formed of four straight strokes which do not necessarily meet at the apices; the first and last lozenge are represented by just one end of the motif expanding towards their respective perforations. The lozenges are linked together by four parallel grooves which split into two pairs bifurcating around each lozenge in turn. The overall design is not especially neatly executed and the spacing of grooves is most variable around the lozenges, from 1 to 2.5mm, the inner spaces generally being the narrower. The outer margins of the band throughout its whole length are milled – a continuous row of transverse punched strokes; the milling contracts where the grooves expand to accommodate the lozenges. There are also traces of transverse strokes within most lozenges (nos. 2–5) and even, occasionally, between linear grooves. All grooves and punched strokes are about 0.5mm wide.

ID 1152C (Figure 5.10.2b). The outer face was neatly milled with transverse strokes throughout, reaching almost to the hooked turns.

MATERIAL

The items are of copper/bronze (no analysis was undertaken) and have probably been lacquered. ID 1152A has a blackish-green patina spotted with brighter green, ID 1152B is mid- to dark green, partly pocked and etched, and ID 1152C has blackish-green to brown patina.

MANUFACTURE

The secondary perforation in terminal 1 of the band is punched from the front producing mini-lipping at the back.

The faint traces of transverse grooves within the string-of-lozenges design suggest two phases of decoration: a simple continuous row of closely set transverse lines crossing the whole band width, followed by the superimposition of the string of lozenges. These need not have been separated much in time, but suggest a change in intended design. The linear grooves are irregular under magnification, perhaps due to coarse reaming out after punching. Extremely fine wavy fissures on parts of the sides of the outer rod (1152C) are likely to be by-products of folding and forging to create the rod.

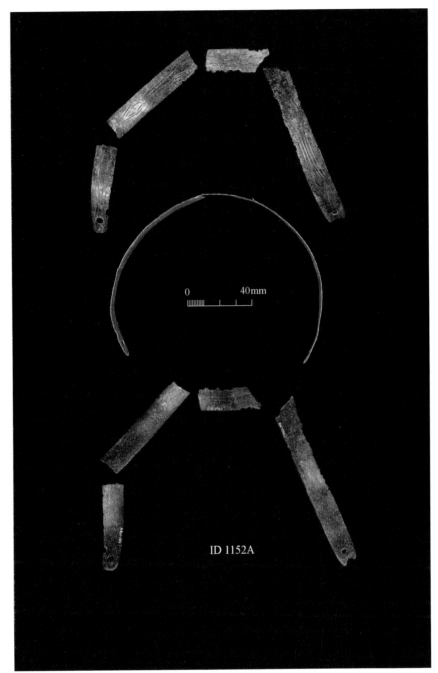

Figure 5.10.1. ID 1152A Garton Slack 107 showing exterior (top), side (middle), and interior (bottom) views.

COMPLETENESS AND DAMAGE

ID 1152A is 97% present. The loss was ancient and the band is now in four joining segments, presumably due to post-depositional damage; a corner at one break is upturned. There is also a series of subtle bends and, while some could be due to adjustments to fit the wearer, those closest to either terminal are more pronounced and are likely damage. Limited areas have been rubbed to a brighter golden colour, some being associated with fine scratches and are doubtless modern. There is limited corrosion damage, but corrosion chipping probably accounts for frequent edge notches. ID 1152B is *c.* 90% present, in five fragments, and ID 1152C is *c.* 60% present, in six fragments.

WEAR

ID 1152A. The notch at the end of terminal 1 was almost certainly a broken perforation originally similar to that in terminal 2 (as recognised by Mortimer 1905, 232); both have rather uneven edges under magnification and have well flattened lips. This explains the shorter distance of taper towards that terminal as well as it being broader. The break is ancient and punching of the replacement hole suggests that the object was required to function in the same fashion after breakage. The secondary perforation itself is ragged in shape and externally bevelled by wear, and much of the inner lip has been worn away; wear has also affected the adjacent grooves.

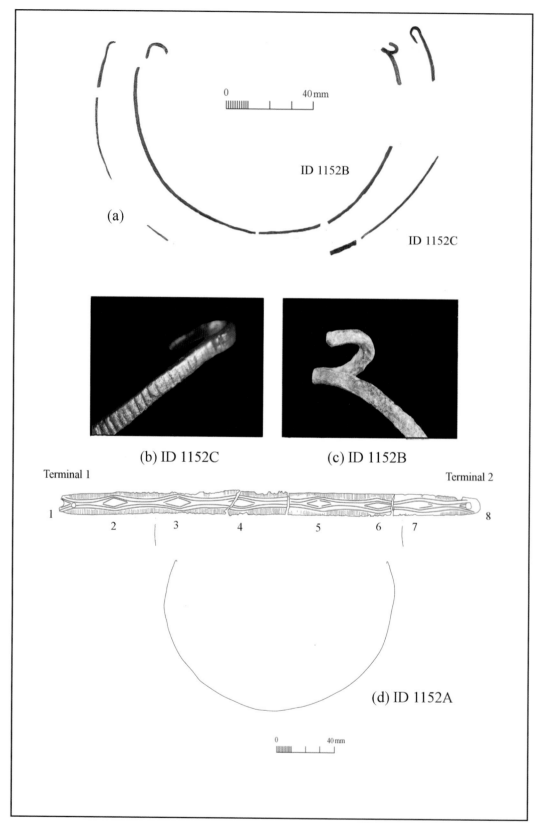

Figure 5.10.2. (a) ID 1152B and ID 1152C Garton Slack 107 as currently displayed with ID 1152B on the inside; (b) details of decoration on ID 1152C; (c) details of hook end of ID 1152B; (d) drawing of decoration on ID 1152A by Henry Buglass. The numbers on the drawing are the lozenge numbers mentioned in the text.

There is also significant wear around terminal 2: the grooves of part-lozenge 8 seem to disappear in a mass of mini gougings and striations, while lozenge 7 and the milling around it have been all but effaced. It is unclear whether this is due to wear or more deliberate effacing; the linear grooves survive better. There is a worn zone of milling on one margin near the middle of the band (lozenge 4).

ID 1152B. There is a possible minor constriction from wear just after the first tight bend of the pig-tail terminal. The other terminal fragment is thinnest at its break, potentially therefore thinned by wear around the crook, leading to stress and fracture.

ID 1152C. Parts of the milled face on the outer rod have been rubbed almost smooth, probably due to ancient wear. The complete terminal has slight bevelling of the innermost angle in the crook, again probably due to wear. Overall, this composite ornament is classified as very worn.

CONCLUSIONS

The design of this ornament is at present unique and even the band component is only matched in occasional, undecorated bands of sheet gold which lack any context. Although it cannot be absolutely certain, the three components are best interpreted as belonging together, the hooked ends of the rods being hooked into the terminal perforations in the band. Such a loose articulation between the three parts could explain the heavy wear around those perforations, although signs of reciprocal wear on the hooks are slighter. The fragmented condition of the rods makes it difficult to know whether their apparently different diameters were consistent throughout their circuits and this impedes detailed reconstruction; either rod could have curved in more tightly towards its ends.

Mortimer (1905, 232, pl. LXXIX, fig. 591) showed the three components running in parallel and he conjectured that they may have been the handle for a wooden vessel, presumably drawing on finds from later contexts. Britton (1963, 281) recognised the band's stylistic similarities with some Early Bronze Age armlets and observed that the length would be acceptable for an overlapped bracelet, but he also noted that the curvature was too open. A more obvious identification now is a composite neck-ring or headband, but if it had been the intention to run the strands in parallel the mode of linking them together seems unnecessarily awkward. The alternative is that one or both rods served to complete the ring by running around the back of the neck or head; the hook-and-eye linkages would facilitate dressing and removal. The fact that the larger diameter rod has milling, to match the margins of the band, might suggest that it hung to the front of the wearer as a supplementary appendage to the band. In this arrangement it is noteworthy that the pig-tail terminal, which would best act as a hinge, is on the plainer, presumed back-linking rod.

A further variant arrangement is worth mention: the plain 'inner' rod again completing the circuit of the band, but the 'outer' rod running in an arc at 90° to the plane of that circuit; thus together they would form a broadly hemispherical frame such as might sit over a cap or directly on a head (the shape of the rods does not seem suited to one having passed under the chin). Diameters are consonant with such a function, but this interpretation begs the question as to why it would be necessary to link the three arcs by means of hook-and-eyes, and preference is therefore given to the neck adornment option.

Consideration of the decorative design usually focuses on the lozenge motif in isolation, comparing it to similar motifs on Beaker pottery. However, the manner in which the eight lozenges are strung together is rather reminiscent of a string of lozenge-shaped fusiform beads of the type frequently made of jet and similar materials. These are thought to have sometimes been strung for bracelets (A. Sheridan pers. comm.), but their predominant use in necklaces would allow the Garton Slack neckring to be a straightforward skeuomorph. In this context it is noteworthy that rather different skeuomorphs, embossed in sheet bronze and sheet gold, represent lozenge beads on armlets (Group 3) from Melfort, Masterton, Lockington and Whitfield (Needham 2000a). Again, strings of lozenge beads are amongst the myriad of beads embossed into the Mold gold cape (Needham 2000c, 44). Milling is another feature found on Group 3 armlets of the Early Bronze Age (Needham 2000b, 31, table 2).

COPPER OR BRONZE ARMLET

ID 1379 Amesbury G41, Wiltshire; Wiltshire Heritage Museum

TYPO-CHRONOLGY

The Early Bronze Age armlets of Britain have recently been reassessed by Needham, in relation to the finding of the two gold examples at Lockington, Leicestershire (Needham 2000b, 29–38). This example from Amesbury G41 (Figure 5.10.3) belongs to his Group 1 (*ibid*, Appendix 1, no.3). These are always of copper or bronze (not gold) and are flat penannular bands of thin sheet metal. The band can be broad or narrow and is often decorated, usually with longitudinal punched lines in combination with geometric infill patterns. Such armlets contrast with the thick copper or bronze bar armlets of Group 2, and with the Group 3 ribbed armlets, which also occur in gold. Within Group 1, ID 1379 belongs to the broader sub-group, and at the larger margin of variation in terms of diameter (*ibid*, table 2 and fig. 22). Group 1 armlets are found mainly in southern or middle England, with one outlier from Yorkshire and two in Scotland (*ibid*, fig. 23), while those of Group 2 come mainly from Scotland and the north. Armlets occur with late Beakers, Food Vessels and jet ornaments, and probably

Figure 5.10.3. Copper or bronze armlet ID 1379 Amesbury G41, also showing detail of decoration.

date between *c.* 2200–1700 cal BC. Armlets of Group 1 were probably the earliest in Britain.

Deposited with one of four primary inhumations comprising two adults and two children, the armlet was found encircling the arm of one of the children.

MORPHOLOGY

The armlet comprises a parallel-sided band measuring 209.3 by 37.2mm. The curvature, as currently displayed, is very uneven, with the diameter ranging from 60 to 69.9mm. If originally roughly circular in form, the diameter would have been around 62mm. The thickness is fairly even at 1.5mm.

DECORATION

The outer face of the band is decorated all over with a scheme of five groove bands, with incised decoration filling the four zones thus defined (Figure 5.10.3). Each groove band includes two parallel grooves each of average width 1.3mm: they are fairly wide, shallow and U-shaped. The groove bands vary in width from 3 to 3.6mm. The four wider zones between the groove bands are infilled with closely-set narrow vertical grooves spaced approximately 0.5mm apart, and at each end of each zone the decoration is terminated with an open triangle with the point facing the terminals of the bracelet. These zones vary in width between 5.4 and 6mm.

MATERIAL

The metal, which has not been analysed, is of greenish hue with a reddish tinge and appears to have been lacquered.

MANUFACTURE

Although lacquered, it seems that the outer surface was originally highly polished; the inner face less so. The item could not be removed from fixed display for study under the microscope, but it is probable that all traces of manufacture had been polished out on both faces.

COMPLETENESS AND DAMAGE

When found the armlet was trodden on by the labourers and broken into three pieces (Hoare 1812, 160). It is now in five pieces, with four major fractures through the band, and there is also some loss at the side margins. It is 97% present. All breaks are thus modern, but the piece has been carefully repaired for display. The current curvature probably does not reflect accurately the original configuration of the armlet (see above).

WEAR

Slight differential smoothing of the decorated surfaces is visible. This shows especially within the zones of vertical incisions. The piece is classified as slightly worn.

6. ITEMS OF PERSONAL ADORNMENTS II: GOLD AND THE REGALIA FROM BUSH BARROW

6.1 GOLD OBJECTS (by Stuart Needham and the main authors)

The various objects in this chapter are listed in terms of their context of discovery for ease of discussion and cross-reference. The objects studied and illustrated are listed in Table 6.1.1.

6.1.1 MERE G6A, WILTSHIRE

Id 1376 Gold Sheet Disc
References: Hoare 1812, 44, pl. II; Thurnam 1871, 527, fig. 218; Annable and Simpson 1964, no. 94; Case 1977, no. 12; Taylor 1980, 87 Wt. 11.

CONTEXT AND ASSOCIATIONS

This is one of two discs originally found, although their positions in the grave are not recorded. The lost disc was evidently identical in design (Hoare 1812, pl. II). They were found with the crouched inhumation of 'a large man' and, by his right side, the skeleton of a younger person, possibly female. The burials were contained within a long grave under a low bowl barrow on Mere Down. A Beaker vessel was found close to the bodies. To the left side of the man were a Series 1 copper dagger (ID 1377, Figure 3.1.3) and a stone bracer (lost; Woodward and Hunter 2012, 170). There was also a bone spatula (ID 1071, Figure 4.5.1), the position of which was not recorded.

Table 6.1.1. List of gold objects studied and illustrated.

Object	Site, County	Museum	Illustration
ID 492	Upton Lovell G2e, Wilts.	Dev	Figure 6.1.6
ID 1107	Little Cressingham, Norfolk	Norwich	Figure 6.1.2; Figure 6.1.4
ID 1108A	Little Cressingham, Norfolk	Norwich	Figure 6.1.3; Figure 6.1.4
ID 1108B	Little Cressingham, Norfolk	Norwich	Figure 6.1.3; Figure 6.1.4
ID 1109	Little Cressingham, Norfolk	Norwich	Figure 6.1.3; Figure 6.1.4
ID 1110	Little Cressingham, Norfolk	Norwich	Figure 6.1.3; Figure 6.1.4
ID 1376	Mere G6a, Wilts.	Dev	Figure 6.1.1
ID 1404	Wilsford G8, Wilts.	Dev	Figure 6.1.8; Figure 5.9.1
ID 1405	Wilsford G8, Wilts.	Dev	Figure 6.1.8
ID 1422	Manton Barrow, Preshute G2a, Wilts.	Dev	Figure 6.1.8; Figure 5.9.1
ID 1443	Upton Lovell G2e, Wilts.	Dev	Figure 6.1.7
ID 1447	Upton Lovell G2e, Wilts.	Dev	Figure 6.1.6
ID 1448	Upton Lovell G2e, Wilts.	Dev	Figure 6.1.6
ID 1449	Upton Lovell G2e, Wilts.	Dev	Figure 6.1.5
ID 1450	Upton Lovell G2e, Wilts.	Dev	Figure 6.1.6
ID 1570	Wilsford-cum-Lake G47, 48 or 49, Wilts.	BM	Figure 6.1.1
ID 1571	Wilsford-cum-Lake G47, 48 or 49, Wilts.	BM	Figure 6.1.1
ID 1572	Wilsford-cum-Lake G47, 48 or 49, Wilts.	BM	Figure 6.1.1
ID 1573	Wilsford-cum-Lake G47, 48 or 49, Wilts.	BM	Figure 6.1.1
ID 1239	Winterborne St Martin G31 (Clandon), Dorset	Dor	Not illustrated (see Needham and Woodward 2008, fig.4)
Accessory cup	Winterborne St Martin G31 (Clandon), Dorset	Dor	Not illustrated
Collared Urn	Winterborne St Martin G31 (Clandon), Dorset	Dor	Not illustrated
Gold plaque	Winterborne St Martin G31 (Clandon), Dorset	Dor	Figure 6.1.9
Jet mace-head	Winterborne St Martin G31 (Clandon), Dorset	Dor	Figure 6.1.9
Amber cup	Winterborne St Martin G31 (Clandon), Dorset	Dor	Figure 6.1.9

MORPHOLOGY

This is a simple yet poorly shaped, near-circular (27.6 by 26.3mm) disc of sheet gold, probably less than 0.2mm thick; its weight is 0.81g (Figure 6.1.1). At the centre is a pair of fairly neat perforations (diameters 1mm) pierced from the 'front' and creating upstanding lips at the back (Figure 6.1.1d).

DECORATION

The edge is outlined by a single light groove, <1mm wide, forming a band (1.7 to 2.6mm wide) within which is a row of closely spaced punctulations (<1mm diameter) impressed from the back (Figure 6.1.1c). The circular field within the decorated margin holds a free-floating, centrally placed cruciform motif (20.0 by 17.0mm), each arm (width *c.* 2.5mm) comprising a 'ladder' – two lines infilled with transverse strokes (Figure 6.1.1c). The arms tend to expand a little outwards, but neither their alignments nor widths are very regular; the outlining grooves are up to 0.6mm wide, deeper than that at the margin (but still less than 1mm); in contrast to all the other motifs, the ladder rungs were impressed from the front (repoussé decoration raised from both sides; Taylor 1980, 23).

MATERIAL

The sheet has a bright gold coloured front; the back is of a redder gold.

MANUFACTURE

Both faces appear to be polished, the front more highly. Spacing of the dots is irregular with no sign of repeating pattern from a stamp, but the outlining groove is made up of repeating strokes *c.* 8mm in length. These sometimes overlap at junctions and each is gently curved with sharp profile, perhaps impressed with a flint blade or sharp bone edge. The associated 'spatula' of bone (ID 1071) has a chisel-like edge of comparable width, but in its current state it is not straight enough in plan and does not have the curve in end-view. Some of the punctulations have just pierced through the sheet and one is double-struck. The central perforations interrupt the decoration and were formed secondarily (Figure 6.1.1d).

COMPLETENESS AND DAMAGE

The sheet is 100% present, with a tiny tear in one edge.

WEAR

The object shows random multi-directional striations on both faces (Figure 6.1.1c and Figure 6.1.1d) and a few scratches on the front; it is classified as worn. The area on the front immediately around the perforations is rather disfigured under magnification, perhaps due to contact with a small 'clamping' boss through which the stitching was passed; this could explain why there is no apparent tug-wear on the holes through the gold.

CONCLUSIONS

This type of centrally perforated disc has frequently been found as matched pairs. It is uncontroversial to accept that they were stitched to a garment, either as non-functional badges, or to serve as buttons (Case 1977). In the latter case the gold sheet would be a cover stuck onto a more robust core object. Given that this disc appears to have been used, the lack of more than minimal edge damage favours a stout backing, perhaps one which extended beyond the rim of the gold disc. Gluing onto a backing could explain the different colour of the rear face. The possible evidence for a central boss on the front adds a new component to the image of these early discs in use; the gold face may thus have been both encircled by exposed wood, leather or bone of the backing object and also punctuated in the middle by a similar material to prevent the thread or thong pulling through the wafer-thin gold. This hypothetical composite button could suggest a prototype for the conical buttons of mature Beaker culture, especially those with a rather flat face and pimpled centre (type 6a; Shepherd 2009, fig. 2).

The associations in the grave suggest a Chalcolithic date, probably early in the period (Association Group Ia – Needham 2012, 16, table 1.6). The simplicity of the design contrasts with some more elaborate cruciform-decorated discs, which are likely to be later developments. The somewhat sloppy execution of both base shape and decoration is not uncommon on the earliest gold-work from Britain (Eogan 1994, 18).

6.1.2 WILSFORD-CUM-LAKE G47, 49 or 50, DUKE'S BARROW 20, WILTSHIRE

CONTEXT AND ASSOCIATIONS

The four gold objects were found in a barrow excavated by E. Duke in 1807. The barrow was one of five barrows, two of them bell barrows, opened by Duke. Duke's barrow 20 contained a possibly primary inhumation associated with an amber spacer plate necklace (ID 1360, Figure 7.3.1 and Figure 7.3.2), the four gold discs, an accessory cup, a bronze awl (not studied) and, perhaps, faience beads. It should be noted that the attributions of Duke's finds to individual barrows are not always certain. The objects were described by the excavator as 'gold rings to the ears' of a skeleton (Duke mss; Goddard 1907–8, 586); however, they were fortunately illustrated as discs rather than 'rings' by Hoare shortly after discovery. The position given, at the ears, need not be taken too literally since the description is scant, but the implication is that these gold ornaments (or some of them) were above the shoulders, and one possibility is that they were terminals for the amber necklace.

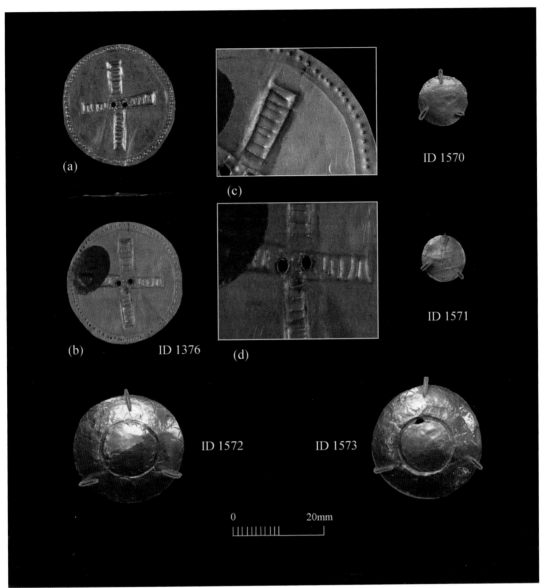

Figure 6.1.1. Mere G6a, Wiltshire ID 1376 gold sheet disc showing: front (a) and rear (b) with details showing (c) punctulations and impressed ladder rung and (d) central perforations; Wilsford-cum-Lake G47, 49 or 50 ID 1570 and ID 1571 gold sheet discs; Wilsford-cum-Lake G47, 49 or 50 ID 1572 and ID 1573 domed button covers. The four Wilsford-cum-Lake objects were photographed mounted.

ID 1570 [55D] and ID 1571 [55C] Pair of Gold Sheet Discs
References: Hoare 1812, 213, pl. XXXI; Taylor 1980, 47, 88 Wt. 36, pl. 26h-i.

MORPHOLOGY

These are very thin discs, near circular: ID 1570 is 11.8 by 11.4mm and ID 1571 is 10.8 by 10.7mm; the thickness of each is estimated to be less than 0.05mm (Figure 6.1.1). Although seemingly flat, there are hints that both may have been very slightly convex towards the front.

DECORATION

Both discs have a ring of minute and close-set punctulations immediately inside the rim, punched from the rear. Viewed close up, the alignment and spacing of the dots is rather irregular.

MATERIAL

The (presumed) front faces are of burnished gold, but neither is very bright coloured and ID 1570 is quite dull; both are a browner gold on the rear. Analysis: 1895 7–23 55c: gold 86.6%, silver 13.0%, copper 0.5%; 1895 7–23 55d: gold 85.3%, silver 13.9%, copper 0.8% (La Niece 2011, 139 table 23 – EDX on abraded metal).

MANUFACTURE

The impressing of the punctulations has frequently caused tiny pin-prick perforations through the sheet.

COMPLETENESS AND DAMAGE

Both items are 100% present.

WEAR

The decoration on ID 1571 is fairly crisp under low magnification, but that on ID 1570 seems distinctly more worn. Both have some minor buckling, but again ID 1570 seems to have suffered the greater wear resulting in more dents and scratches. Both were classified as slightly worn.

CONCLUSIONS

These are rather unimpressive little discs, small and minimally decorated. They have no means of attachment so, if in their original form, they would need to have been fixed to a backing with adhesive; this might explain the different colour of their backs. It is, however, intriguing that these discs are almost exactly the size of the central groove-defined roundels of the associated larger pair (ID 1572 and ID 1573). This suggests two possibilities: (i) that they are neatly cut down from similar larger ornaments having edge grips, or (ii) that they were stuck onto the middle of a larger disc of another (probably perishable) material, e.g. polished wood or leather, to create more impressive two-tone ornaments which contrasted with the other pair.

Simple, small discs like these are not otherwise known from firmly dated contexts, but parallels worth citing are from Lough Gur, Co Limerick (Case 1977, no. 14), and Longbridge Deverill, Wiltshire (Varndell – TAR 1998–9, 10 no. 2). The latter repeats the marginal ring of dots seen on these Lake examples, as also do two larger 'sun-discs' from Banc Tynddol, Cwmystwyth, Ceredigion (Timberlake 2009, 104, fig. 7.7) and Kirk Andreas, Isle of Man (Taylor 1980, 81), and various basket ornaments (Needham 2011).

ID 1572 [55B] and ID 1573 [55A] Pair of Gold Sheet Domed Button Covers

MORPHOLOGY

Two circular sheet covers are less than 0.1mm thick with small turned edges to grip the core object. ID 1572 measures 25.9 by 25.3mm and ID 1573 measures 26.0 by 25.9mm (Figure 6.1.1). Despite buckled surfaces, it is clear that they always had gently domed profiles; the current depth in profile is about 4.8mm in each case of which about 4.0mm is domed face; the angle between face and side is moderately crisp. Beyond a shallow side (0.8mm), the rear grips turn inwards by between 0.7 and 1.3mm.

DECORATION

A single 0.7mm wide groove defines a central roundel on each (diameters 12.5mm and 12.2mm); this is flanked inside and outside by a running zigzag made of fine strokes 0.4mm wide. A further, more strongly drawn zigzag outlines the perimeter of the face, and yet another runs round the side of the grip; the last comprises deeper incisions, 0.5mm wide, and the strokes are shorter and correspondingly more spaced, thus creating a broken zigzag.

MATERIAL

The gold is burnished on the front faces. Analysis: 1895 7–23 55a: gold 91.0%, silver 8.7%, copper 0.3%; 1895 7–23 55b: gold 90.0%, silver 9.7%, copper 0.3% (La Niece 2011, 139 table 23 – EDX on abraded metal).

MANUFACTURE

There are tiny crimps at intervals around the rear grips. A perforation just inside the ring-groove of ID 1573 has extremely thin edges and may be an area over-thinned during manufacture which made it particularly susceptible to wear during use.

If the decoration was lightly pressed rather than drawn, it would appear that three tools of different lengths were used: about 1.2mm long for the innermost face zigzag, about 2.0mm for the middle and outermost face zigzags, and about 0.7mm for that on the side; this last is constrained by the field available.

COMPLETENESS AND DAMAGE

ID 1572 is 100% present and ID 1573 is 95% present, a small segment of the margin being missing; this damage had already occurred before Crocker illustrated it, as had a split across much of a diameter across ID 1572. There are some strong scratches which are probably post-recovery.

WEAR

Both button covers are rather badly disfigured with scratches and mini-puckering. While the decoration on ID 1572 is still fairly crisp, every corresponding element of decoration on ID 1573 is more worn; only the slightest trace remains of the innermost ring. This heavy wear may account for the perforation (see above, manufacture). One cover is classified as slightly worn and the other as very worn.

CONCLUSIONS

The most obvious function for this pair is as covers for gently domed 'buttons', the cores of which we can assume would have had provision for attachment, most likely a V-boring. Taylor (1980, 47) recognised that they were worn and there is little doubt from the wear pattern that one had experienced considerable rubbing. The wear was focussed on the centre of the dome on ID 1573, but this is less evident on ID 1572; furthermore, it is possible that even the marginal zigzags suffered some rubbing if the contrast with the side decoration is a result of wear rather than the initial depths of impression. It is intriguing that both disc pairs have one more worn than the other and this might suggest some consistently asymmetric element of costume, coiffure *etc*, that affected one side of the body and not the other (for example, a bound plait of hair drawn only to one side).

Dating these four gold ornaments relies on their intrinsic characteristics and their association with the amber ornament suite. Traditionally, they have been seen as belonging to the Wessex linear goldwork tradition (e.g. Taylor 1980, 47). However, aside from general comparisons (see overall discussion below), there is little specific comparison with the classic Wessex goldwork. Gently domed button covers are in fact best paralleled at Barnhill, Angus, although the styling there is different. Lake is one of the very few large (potentially complete) sets of amber beads making up a spacer-plate necklace (see Chapter 7). While these have normally been linked to the 'Wessex' grave series, there is no reason why the spacer-plate necklace in amber should not have emerged a little earlier given the dating of jet examples, and gold lunulae, from Period 2 onwards. An early, 'proto-Wessex', date for the group might also be argued for the simpler pair of discs; in their current form they best relate to the discs well known among Beaker goldwork, although this simple form need not have been short-lived. The possibility of a different background and/or a different date of manufacture for the two pairs comes from metal analysis (La Niece 2011); each pair is reasonably consistent, but the smaller discs contain higher levels of both silver and copper.

6.1.3 LITTLE CRESSINGHAM, NORFOLK

CONTEXT AND ASSOCIATIONS

A short time before 1849 a remarkable Bronze Age inhumation grave was found in a field formerly called Hills Field in the parish of Little Cressingham, Norfolk. It was found through chance by a labourer digging in the field but Barton was able to determine that the burial had occupied an off-centre location within a heavily ploughed round barrow (Barton 1852, 1). It may, therefore, have been a secondary interment. The barrow belongs to a group of six barrows and a single ring ditch, located on a slight slope flanking the outer margin of a large meander of the River Blackwater. The body was arranged in a crouched position with head to the south. It is not stated whether the body was lying on its right or left side. The skeleton has not survived, and may well have never been removed from the grave. Barton recorded that the skeleton was that of a male 'of about average height'. The man 'had passed the meridian of life; and his teeth were much worn, but good' (*ibid*, 2). A dagger and a knife (ID 1105 and ID

1106, Figure 3.1.8) were found by his side, and a gold plate (ID 1107), described below, upon the breast. A piece of decorated gold (ID 1110) was found on one side, while the locations of the remains of three other items of gold, referred to as boxes (ID 1108A, ID 1108B and ID 1109), were not recorded in detail. A large number of amber beads were found scattered about the neck, but many of them were broken. This necklace (ID 999) is illustrated in Figure 7.3.9 and Figure 7.3.10. The objects were illustrated by Barton (1952), Piggott (1938, fig. 22) and Gerloff (1975, pl. 46.F), while a set of watercolour paintings, executed by Frederick Sandys not long after the excavation, and housed in Norwich Castle Museum, were published by Clarke *et al.* in 1985 (fig. 7.27).

ID 1107 Gold Sheet Rectangular Plaque
References: Thurnam 1871, 528, fig. 219; Piggott 1938, 93, fig. 22.4; Rainbird Clarke 1960, pl.14; Norfolk Museum Service 1977, fig. 8; Taylor 1980, 84 Nf. 13, pl. 26a–b.

MORPHOLOGY (Studied mounted on perspex)

As the plaque is fixed to a perspex backing plate it was not possible to measure its thickness or weight. The cover is nearly rectangular (maximum length 92.5mm; width 60.0 to 62.0mm), although the corners are not sharp right-angles and the plan is now very slightly rhombic, probably due to buckling (Figure 6.1.2 and Figure 6.1.4). Narrow turns on each side are currently variable in profile – rolled, crushed or distorted; however, there is consistent evidence that the face/side junction was originally fairly angular and that there was a second angular turn between 1.0 and 1.5mm behind. It may be deduced that they originally gripped the sides of a core-object, the sides of which were flat and up to 1.5mm across, the gold sheet just lapping around onto the back (Figure 6.1.2b). Localised hollowing of the sides is due to damage rather than the impression of a side groove. Given slack metal within the face, it is possible that it was originally very slightly domed.

DECORATION

The face is decorated with six concentric rectangular frames (numbered 1–6 from centre outwards), each formed of a triple-groove band with a further, single-groove frame outlining the edge; groove widths mostly lie between 0.5 and 1.0mm (Figure 6.1.2d). These frames reduce in length and width fairly evenly rather than proportionally, hence they become more elongated inwards. The innermost rectangle is split longitudinally by an axial triple-groove band, thus forming a buckle-like design. On the long edges the outermost frame is so close to the single groove that it effectively becomes a quadruple groove, but along the short edges there is a blank field in between.

Many of the grooves are filled with continuous rows of small pin-pricks, or punctulations (Figure 6.1.2d). There is a pattern governing which grooves were punctulated

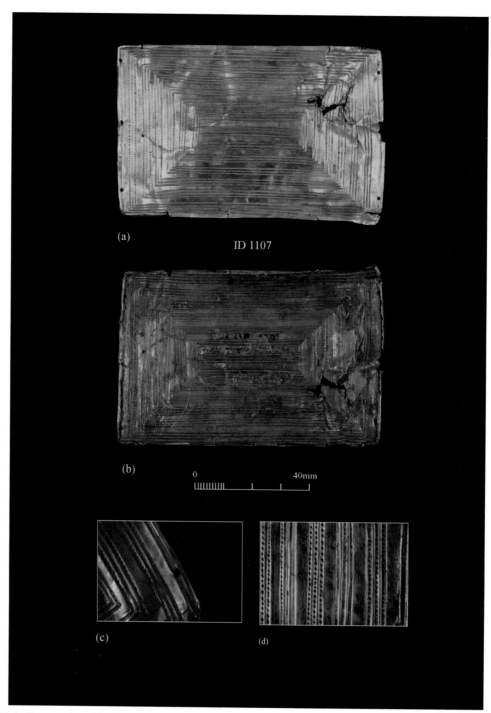

Figure 6.1.2. Little Cressingham ID 1107 rectangular gold sheet plaque showing (a) front view, (b) rear view (through perspex), (c) detail of folded edge and perforation from front, (d) groove bands, punctulations and striations.

(recognised by Clarke *et al.* 1985, 276): on the short axes the outer and inner grooves in each band are consistently punctulated, leaving the middle groove plain; on the long axes the format alternates between either all three grooves punctulated (central band, frames 2, 4 and 6), or none punctulated (frames 1, 3 and 5), except that there appears to have been a mistake in frame 5 where one outer groove was punctulated. The outer (single) groove is punctulated on the long axes only except for two dots straying round a corner into one short axis.

PERFORATIONS

Both ends of the plaque have three tiny perforations on the line of the edge-defining groove (Figure 6.1.2c), although only half of the middle hole survives at one end where a segment is missing. The intact holes are consistently about 1.2mm in diameter, their shape circular or sub-circular. Some display micro-lipping around edges which seems insufficient to have been caused by simple piercing and there was probably some associated rotary action; one is partly closed by a flap which has been pushed back inwards. Under magnification the sides of the perforations show brighter metal than that surrounding, but since they are described as being present immediately after discovery (Barton 1852), they must be ancient. In four cases the rear grip partly or wholly overlapped the front perforation and had become indented by the piercing tool. In one instance the rear indent is offset inwards relative to the front perforation and this probably indicates that crushing of the edge grip in this sector took place after the perforations were made, again supporting their ancient origin.

MATERIAL

The material is mainly of bright-coloured gold with small patches showing a coppery sheen. Analysis: silver 45%, copper 0.27%, tin 0.015% (balance gold) (Hartmann 1982, no. 2435; Taylor 1980, 140 no. 98).

MANUFACTURE

Two corners have crimps and overlaps at the back where the two side returns impinge on one another; the other two had been cut diagonally prior to turning the sides, thus avoiding overlap. The long-axis groove bands show a strong tendency (ten of twelve runs) towards being slightly concave, the maximum offset from a straight line ranging up to 1.5mm. Only one long-axis run is effectively straight, while another is a little wavy. This systematic but not very obvious deviation from the straight lines that would seem to have been intended is not easily explained. They cannot be due to the compression of a simple domed face rising from a flat plane, as has been argued for the Bush Barrow and Clandon Barrow lozenges (Kinnes *et al.* 1989; Needham and Woodward 2008, 13–17), because this results in bowing in the opposite direction – convex rather than concave. This does not rule out some other subtle shaping, which would be supported by the current undulating nature of the sheet. Alternatively the bowed lines might derive from a slightly curved aid (ruler) used for laying them out, especially since the central band is also slightly curved. The single grooves on the short ends are actually marginally convex, but most on the shorter axis are either more-or-less straight or damaged.

The groove bands generally meet neatly at their right-angled junction; only rarely is there a minimal over-run. It would therefore appear that the design was well planned and marked out on the sheet prior to execution. To the naked eye the punctulated grooves look neatly rouletted, but under magnification the punctulations are erratically spaced and aligned and evidently individually impressed rather than using a repeating comb-stamp. A few dots, including a row of seven in one groove, have actually pierced the sheet metal (noted previously by Taylor 1985, 154). They were formed with a very fine, but nevertheless blunt-ended tool, likely to have been of bone or wood; the rather variable prick diameters, ranging up to 0.4mm, would correlate with depth of impression. One of the rear grip indents caused when the end perforations were made

is clearly of smaller diameter than the front hole, as would be expected.

Striations abound on the flat surfaces of the face, predominantly aligned parallel to the adjacent grooves (Figure 6.1.2d), although there are also small groups of diagonal ones locally, especially near the major tear; the former are almost certainly ancient.

COMPLETENESS AND DAMAGE

The plaque is virtually complete, lacking only a tiny segment from the middle of one end; this was already missing in Sandys' watercolour sketch (Clarke *et al.* 1985, fig. 7.27) and, as it split the middle perforation, one possible cause of the tear would have been removal of the gold sheet cover from its backing in antiquity. However, this explanation would imply that the object was no longer attached to the deceased's clothing despite its reported position on the body.

The plaque has suffered a lot of damage: the whole surface is variably buckled, there is a ragged tear towards one corner, several fine internal cracks and a series of edge tears mainly < 3mm long. The large tear is flanked by pronounced buckling and this has pulled the nearest corner inwards; its edges and surrounding defects are bright, suggesting damage perhaps during excavation. Elsewhere one longer invasive split has opened up causing splaying of the adjacent corner; this split appears to have parted at a lap in the gold sheet which had presumably been closed by hammer-welding during initial beating out. One corner has been lifted about 2mm above the general plane of the plaque. Along part of one long edge a linear strip had formerly been detached, but is now restored. Some fine scratches exposing brighter gold cut across striated zones and are probably modern damage, as are minor gougings, of which one at least cuts through coppery patina.

WEAR

There is no definitive evidence for use wear, but some multidirectional striations may be ancient and the overall impression gained is that this was not by any means a pristine object at the time of burial. Overall the object can be classified as slightly worn.

CONCLUSIONS

As would be expected, this sheet gold plaque covered a core object of wood or some other perishable material. The core object evidently had sides between 1.0 and 1.5mm thick around which the cover wrapped, extending onto the back. It is likely, but not easily demonstrated from geometric principles, that the core object was not a simple flat form. The rectangular form of the plaque might owe something to a derivation from bracers (Taylor 2005, 322; Woodward and Hunter 2011, Ch 4); there is, for example, a superficial similarity to the contemporary 'bracer-ornaments' of Brittany (Needham 2000a, 165, fig.

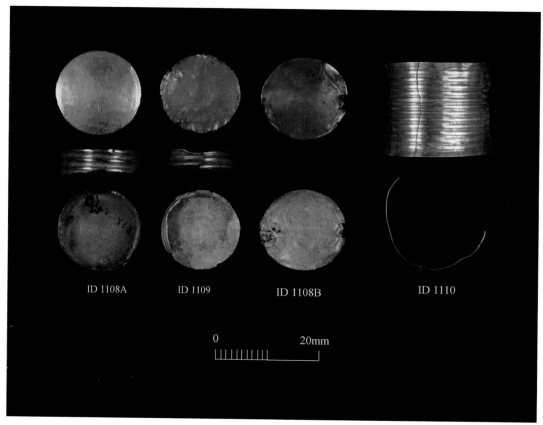

Figure 6.1.3. Little Cressingham ID 1108A, ID 1108B and ID 1109 gold sheet cap-ends; ID 1110 gold sheet corrugated band.

6, 17–19), although the intense decoration is not present on those continental pieces.

Clarke's suggestion (1970, 231) that this and the Upton Lovell parallel were derivative Aunjetitz cuff-bands is untenable, as Piggott recognised (1973, 368) – unfurling a tightly curled form would result in unmistakable tears and/or distortions. Moreover, it was found 'upon the breast' of the skeleton, although there is admittedly some latitude in explaining this position given the lack of a burial plan. The main mode of attachment of the composite object is uncertain, but was probably in the back of the core. It cannot be determined whether the end perforations were original or secondary (but still ancient) additions, but since they did not pierce through the rear grip, they would only seem able to have fixed the cover to the core; in order to fix the whole object to costume, the holes would need to be re-bored at a slant, thus missing the rear turn of gold. They do not show any encircling impressions that might arise from stud-like fixings; instead they may have held either thin rivets/pins which had minimally expanded heads, or fine threads. Thread running from one hole to the next might well sit neatly within the linking groove, but this would mean the central holes, which are no larger than the others, had to take two threads.

Taylor regarded the Little Cressingham plaque as being a less accomplished piece than much of the Wessex linear goldwork which she attributes to a 'master craftsman'

(1980, 46; 1985, 184, 187). Poor execution is primarily a feature of the punctulations and is barely apparent to the naked eye. The somewhat variable if slight curvature of the linear grooves might also be put down to less skilled crafting, assuming it is not a function of subsequent distortions of the original morphology. Even so, making allowance for all the subsequent damage and possible compression of a non-flat form, this would have been a fine looking ornament with a regular, well conceived and controlled design.

ID 1108A Gold Sheet Cap-End or 'Box'
References: Piggott 1938, 93, fig. 22.5; Norfolk Museum Service 1977, fig. 9; Taylor 1980, 84 Nf. 14, pl. 26c.

MORPHOLOGY

This is a squat cylindrical cap-end with very slightly convex face (diameter 17.1 to 17.3mm; projection *c.* 0.5mm) and corrugated sides (intact width 4.5 to 4.8mm) (Figure 6.1.3 and Figure 6.1.4). The face/side junction is a sub-angular rib. The side continues in an even, sinuous profile with two full furrows and ribs and part of a third furrow. The diameter of the mouth is 16.3 to 17.0mm (the latter due to distortion) and the rim is rounded or, in places, feathers out. The thickness at crack edges is 0.1mm; the weight is 0.61g.

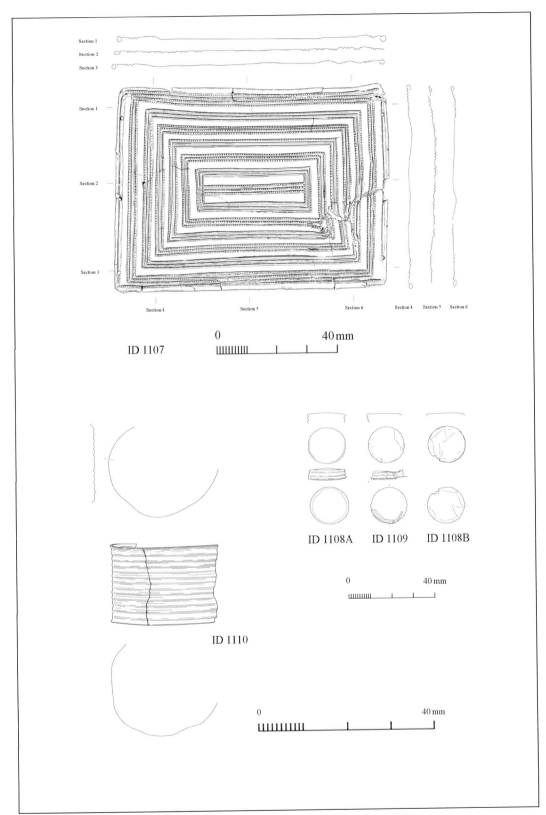

Figure 6.1.4. Drawings of objects from Little Cressingham: ID 1107 rectangular gold sheet plaque; ID 1108A, ID 1108B and ID 1109 gold sheet cap ends; ID 1110 gold sheet corrugated band. Drawings by Henry Buglass.

MATERIAL

The object has an exterior colour of yellow-gold with tiny spots of reddish patina especially in the furrows. The interior is of dull gold with a speckled black deposit in the inner face/side angle, possibly a remnant of adhesive.

MANUFACTURE

There are a few very light creases and pockmarks in the face; a slight lap of gold at a microscopic tear in the rim was perhaps caused during manufacture. Striations are aligned along the furrows externally and concentrically on the face. There are also faint concentric ones inside the face.

COMPLETENESS AND DAMAGE

Although undulating, the rim does not seem to be broken and the object is therefore 100% present.

WEAR

There are small notches along the rim, one being associated with an inward bend. There is also a crack running transversely across the side creating a mini-cusp at the face. Random scratches, both single and multiple, are apparent on the face exterior, and mini-indentations are mostly due to use wear. Overall this object is designated as worn.

ID 1108B Gold Sheet Cap-End or 'Box'
Reference: Taylor 1980, 84 Nf. 15.

MORPHOLOGY

This is a circular disc with a slightly dished face (diameter 17.0 to 17.2mm; thickness 0.2mm; weight 0.27g); the edge shows the beginning of a turn in places and there may originally have been sides all round (Figure 6.1.3 and Figure 6.1.4).

MATERIAL

The reverse is of dull gold, whereas the external face is brighter. The former has darker coloration towards edges (as 1108A). Analysis: silver *c.* 20%, copper 0.84%, tin 0.059% (Hartmann 1982, no. 2434; Taylor 1980, 140 no. 99).

MANUFACTURE

The reverse bears fine concentric ridge/groove features *c.* 0.5mm in from the edge; these are barely discernible on the front and may be imprints taken from the core object as the sheet was burnished onto it. There are many fine scratches across the front face which are likely to be ancient.

COMPLETENESS AND DAMAGE

In addition to a marked notch, the edges are rather denticulated under magnification, possibly the result of tearing along an angle where the sheet was over-thinned. On this basis the object is incomplete, but it is not possible to estimate the percentage lost empirically. There are some modern minor scratches.

WEAR

This object displays moderate wear.

ID 1109 Gold Sheet Cap-End or 'Box'
Reference: Taylor 1980, 84 Nf. 16.

MORPHOLOGY

This is a squat cylindrical cover with an essentially flat face (excepting damage) and a rounded junction with corrugated sides (diameter 16.4 to 16.8mm) (Figure 6.1.3 and Figure 6.1.4). There is a maximum of three ribs and two furrows present on the sides (maximum width 4.4mm), the rib bordering the face being slightly more pronounced than the others. The rim around the mouth is rounded. The thickness is ≤ 0.5mm and the weight 0.31g.

MATERIAL

The interior is of dull gold with widespread fine-speckled blackish and coppery coloration; the external face is of brighter gold.

MANUFACTURE

There are flaws in the surface which are visible under a microscope; there is also some minor puckering. The concentric striations are possibly from the original finishing.

COMPLETENESS AND DAMAGE

The object is 70% present with the whole of the face and almost half of the sides surviving. The latter comprises two fragments which join one another but are not necessarily positioned correctly in relation to the face. Nevertheless, under magnification traces of a turn can be seen around the face disc, indicating that it did have sides.

WEAR

A dent in the face close to one side and an associated scratch are likely to be recent damage. There are also other micro-dents, some struck from inside, and many fine, multidirectional scratches on the exterior. Some of these look fresh, but most are probably ancient. Parts of the sides have been crushed concertina fashion. Overall the object is designated as worn.

CONCLUSIONS (1108A, 1108B, 1109)

These objects have normally been described in the past as 'boxes' (Barton 1852; Thurnam 1871, 526, 528; Taylor 1980, 47; Clarke *et al.* 1985, 276), a description reinforced by the Sandys' depiction of two pairs, one butted together, the other opened up (Clarke *et al.* 1985, fig. 7.27). This contemporary depiction, however, immediately exposes a problem since it is not easily reconciled with Barton's statement that 'by far the most curious objects were a small box and the remains of two others…'. If, for Barton, a 'box' involved a pair of these cap-ends, then the 'remains of two others' suggests fragments that obviously came from at least three more cap-ends – a minimum total of five would have to have been found, two of which have since gone missing. More likely Barton used 'box' to refer just to a single cap-end – i.e. it was an open box – and that his total of three are indeed the three still extant, especially since these also match his description of their condition. Yet Sandys illustrates four in total, all of them seemingly complete; it may be that, having recognised that two of them could be butted together at their open ends to form a closed box, he surmised there should have been a fourth to complement cap-end 3. Although his depictions are generally faithful, it is worth noting that he added non-existent perforations to one of the long sides of the rectangular plaque.

Acceptance that these formed 'boxes', closed or open, combined with a lack of evidence for perforations led Taylor to rule out possible functions as clothing fasteners or pendants (1980, 47). However, the 'box' terminology is misleading since these could never have functioned as hollow objects and must have had a core, most likely a solid object of wood. Moreover, we cannot be sure that the core objects did not project beyond the gold mounts. It is possible that two cap-ends with similar diameters decoratively closed off two ends of a longer cylindrical core-object such as a staff (see also discussion for the Upton Lovell cap-ends below, ID 1447 and ID 1448), but this does leave the third example unsatisfactorily unexplained. The neatly corrugated sides of these covers were clearly intended to be visible, so they would have furnished cylindrical projections on a larger object or, more simply, covered the front of three separate disc-shaped ornaments. Stylistic comparisons can be made with the amber disc-pendants which have both gently bowed faces and corrugated sides, and some of which also have gold-bound edges (ID 1412, ID 1413 and ID 1420; see Chapter 5.9; Needham *et al.* 2006, 40–1). The Little Cressingham objects were of smaller diameter than these amber/gold parallels; they also lack evidence of side perforations, but could alternatively have been mounted or strung by means of rear perforations or loops in the presumed wooden support. As disc-ornaments, they could have been either free-strung (necklace terminals or pendants) or stitched to a garment (as buttons or purely ornamental studs). Despite these small-ornament possibilities, their use as embellishments on the ends of staffs should not be ruled out, not least because it has the virtue of explaining why the sides of the objects are more ornate than the ends. Although there is some modern-looking damage, the mass of fine scratches and some dents suggest a fair degree of ancient wear.

ID 1110 Gold Sheet Corrugated Band
References: Piggott 1938, 93 fig. 22.6; Norfolk Museums Service 1977, 32, fig. 10; Taylor 1980, 84 Nf. 12, pl. 26c.

MORPHOLOGY (Studied mounted on perspex)
Part of a round or oval band (width 17.7 to 17.9mm; thickness 0.2 to 0.3mm), but no terminal survives and it is not known whether the shape was annular or penannular (Figure 6.1.3 and Figure 6.1.4). The band has 12 evenly spaced corrugations of sinuous cross-section; the curvature of the furrows is a little tighter than that of ribs. Both rims are everted flanges (by *c.* 30°), thin (0.3 to 0.4mm) and neatly finished, varying from rounded to flat. Allowing for distortion, two segments and the ends of the third suggest a diameter of about 20mm (*cf* current restoration of 25.5mm maximum diameter). The remainder of the third segment is much less curved, perhaps due to opening up during breakage.

MATERIAL
It is of a brighter gold colour than the associated goldwork; there are tiny reddish or sporadically dark brown patches in the furrows. Analysis: silver *c.* 20%, copper 0.09%, tin 0.016% (Hartmann 1982, no. 2436; Taylor 1980, 140 no. 100).

MANUFACTURE
The rims have consistent micro-lipping along the inner edges surviving from light pressure shaping. The upper one also has external lipping partially pressed back to the surface. Striations along the ridges and furrows are likely to be from finishing and/or cleaning.

COMPLETENESS AND DAMAGE
The object survives much as depicted soon after discovery by Sandys (Clarke *et al.* 1985, fig. 7.27): around 60–70% is probably extant comprising three segments joining at two points; the remaining two irregular breaks would not join together if closed up. Most fractured ends have minor bends or flattening alongside, thus distorting the original curvature. There are further slight crimps and flattening within two of the segments, while the third has an invasive crack from one rim.

WEAR
Overall, there is very little wear, and the object is classified as slightly worn. A few short diagonal to transverse scratches may be ancient.

CONCLUSIONS
The original suggestion made by Barton (1852) was that this was an 'armilla'. Thurnam (1871, 528) followed this interpretation suggesting that it would have had 'lapped' terminals despite its evident fragmentary state at (or soon after) discovery; he compared it with the Cuxwold armlet and a fragment in the Mountfield hoard (probably of Middle Bronze Age date). Much later, a more neutral

terminology, 'strip', was adopted in the Norwich Castle Museum catalogue (Norfolk Museums Service 1977, 32), whilst others suggested that it belonged to a small group of corrugated gold sheet hilt or pommel mounts, otherwise known from Scotland and Ireland (Gerloff 1975, 75; Clarke *et al.* 1985, 276). Taylor listed it as a 'hilt mounting', but did not discuss this attribution (Taylor 1980, 49, 84 Nf. 12). The piece is significantly deeper than the other hilt mounts known and the currently oval shape may be due to distortion. The best estimate of original diameter (20mm) is rather small for a pommel, but would be comfortable for the mid-handle of a dagger or other implement. A new dagger find from Forteviot, Perth and Kinross (Noble and Brophy 2011, 798) shows that its corrugated hilt-band actually sits just under the pommel piece. However, the evidence from the hilt-bands and surviving pommels alike is for distinctly oval-sectioned handles on British Early Bronze Age daggers and knives, whereas the Little Cressingham piece could only have furnished a near-circular handle. An alternative is that it could have furnished the shaft of a rod or staff. However, there would be complications in getting it flush with a shaft if placed in the middle, rather than at one end; the following section develops this possibility. If the mount had been in a position that suffered handling, it had evidently seen relatively little use.

LITTLE CRESSINGHAM GROUP: OVERALL CONCLUSIONS

An interpretation as costume fittings has been considered for four of the five gold objects, a conclusion least controversial for the large plaque described as having been at the breast of the skeleton. The three cylindrical covers have been traditionally called 'boxes' with the implication that two components together formed a closed, unfixed object, like a counter or gaming piece. However, they were more likely covers, or cap-ends for three similar core objects; the objects could have been variations on the well established themes of V-bored buttons, terminals and pendants, in which case these might have been the functioning closures for a cloak or other garment on which the plaque served more as a badge of office. However, since the front of the supposed buttons is plain, this may favour the alternative interpretation that they furnished the ends of staffs.

The fifth object (ID 1110) is difficult to construe in relation to costume, or indeed to the array of amber beads and pendants (ID 1111–26, Chapter 7). There are also obstacles to interpreting it as a mount for the handle of either the dagger or the knife in the grave. However, it may be that it helps explain the odd number of cap-ends; its estimated original diameter is only a little larger than those of the cap-ends and it is not inconceivable that a staff might expand very slightly towards one end. The fact that the band is not closed off could suggest that the staff projected through it; this could have provided a tenon on which to mount something else, for example, a mace-head. Bearing in mind the use of gold-covered

studs on the Clandon mace-head and Ashbee's (1967, 30) more speculative suggestion for the gold cones from Hengistbury Head, it would be appealing to see the three cap-ends as embellishing cylindrical bosses on a mace-head; however, this does need to be considered also in the light of the close parallels from Upton Lovell (ID 1447A and B, 1448A and B).

Reconstruction in a mace or similar hafted implement might explain the freshness of the corrugated band relative to the cap-ends if it was in a protected area immediately under the head. If, on the other hand its lack of wear was due to it being a more recently manufactured object, the time lag need only have been a matter of years or decades, rather than generations, but it would be of note that the corrugated form of the cap-end sides was perpetuated in the band, which at the same time perpetuated the earlier begun tradition of corrugated bands around dagger pommels.

Since the accuracy of Hartmann's gold analyses has been questioned (Warner *et al.* 2009), it may not be sensible to make too much of the published results, except to note that there is a massive difference, presumably qualitatively correct, in the silver context of the rectangular plaque relative to the other two analysed pieces. In fact the former would appear to have one of the highest silver contexts recorded for British Bronze Age goldwork. Nevertheless, there is growing evidence for the exploitation of a new, silver-rich gold source from about 2000 BC onwards, a source likely to have been in Britain (Ehser *et al.* 2011; Needham 2012).

6.1.4 UPTON LOVELL G2e, WILTSHIRE

CONTEXT AND ASSOCIATIONS

The gold items described here were found with a secondary burial, probably a cremation, under a bowl barrow known as 'The Golden Barrow' (Hoare 1812, 98 and pls. X–XI). The barrow is located in a low-lying position on the northern bank of the River Wylye. A small pile of burnt bones was found in a shallow pit, with a heap of ashes and small fragments of burnt bones nearby. A cluster of gold and amber objects was located two feet (*c.* 610mm) from the pile of burnt human bones. As well as the gold items, there were the remains of an amber spacer plate necklace (ID 1444, Figure 7.3.4 and Figure 7.3.5). Also present were a grape cup, two urns (one lost) and an awl (ID 1442, Figure 4.6.4).

ID 1449 Gold Sheet Rectangular Plaque
References: Cunnington 1806, pl. VII, 4; Annable and Simpson 1964, no. 232; Taylor 1980, 87 Wt. 26, pl. 23d; Clarke *et al.* 1985, 279 no. 100.4, pl. 4.57.

MORPHOLOGY (On fibreglass backing)

The plaque is sub-rectangular with bowed long sides; the two intact corners are somewhat rounded and the short side in between is roughly straight (Figure 6.1.5). The length is reconstructed to have been 156.5mm; maximum width is 74.5mm; width of intact end 68mm. The sheet is extremely thin (<0.1mm) with a weight of 15.84g, most of which will be due to the modern backing.

Because the edges are irregular from damage, the line of the decorative frame gives the best indication of precise shape (see below). All the edges were turned sharply to form a very narrow side, 0.8 to 1.0mm across, and then turned again as a rear grip, 1.0 to 1.5mm wide (Figure 6.1.5a and 6.1.5b). On the latter there are consistent hints of a groove or furrow, presumably the impression of a feature just inside the edge of the rear of the core object. Overall the long profile is very slightly bowed, while the cross profile has a slightly raised kick along the medial line. There is in fact a crack along part of this line and it is possible that the crease-cum-crack was caused by tensions due to the flattening of a formerly domed or weakly keeled face. Many slight undulations might likewise be due to compression, although it is always possible that some localised stretching would have occurred due to pressure points in the burial environment.

A tiny hole perforates each of the two intact corners – presumably there were two more at the opposite end. They are not neatly circular (diameters of 1.7 and 2.0mm).

DECORATION

The face is divided by quadruple-groove bands into three panels: a large central one and a much narrower one at either end. The central panel is divided longitudinally by further quadruple-groove bands into nine strip-fields; each field carries three well spaced triple-groove chevrons, alternate ones pointing in opposite directions. The chevrons all line up across the strip-fields. The two end panels are each filled with a dense lattice of grooves (Figure 6.1.5b). The three panels together are framed by a quadruple-groove band and then, right on the edges of the object, is a cable-effect border formed of a continuous row of diagonal incisions. The groove band is marginally convex for most of the long sides, but there is a distinct, albeit obtuse angle at the junction with the intact end panel, thus making the latter trapeze-shaped (Figure 6.1.5b). The groove band along the short side here is also marginally bowed (offset *c.* 1mm).

MATERIAL

The plaque is of bright gold colour. There is no published analysis.

MANUFACTURE

There are masses of very fine striations set on varied alignments, longitudinal, transverse and diagonal – not necessarily all ancient. These give a well-polished surface. The perforations were pierced from the front.

None of the longitudinal groove bands are absolutely straight, instead being a little wavy – some of this cannot be attributed to damage. There are occasional over-runs of

grooves into adjacent decorative elements (Figure 6.1.5b), but in general they butt up to one another very well, this being especially true of the chevrons. Most grooves have neat V-sections with widths of 0.2 to 0.3mm, but the lattices were probably scribed with a more round-ended tool producing grooves of width 0.1 to 0.2mm. Both tools, however, have been applied with sensitivity, presumably against a flexible backing, such that none have torn the extremely thin gold sheet. The spacing of the close-set grooves in the lattice panels is regular to the naked eye (though there are some deviations under microscope) and may have been achieved with some form of spacing aid; they could conceivably have been made using a 'comb' with very widely spaced and fine teeth; such an instrument would have to have been kept absolutely orthogonal to the plaque while being dragged diagonally; in such a process two corners would still be blank and would need to be filled with individually drawn lines. There are 'ghosts' of some lattice lines extending onto the marginal groove band implying that the former were executed before the latter and the over-runs were not fully erased.

COMPLETENESS AND DAMAGE

Approximately 90% of the object is extant and in several fragments. Seven or more pieces towards the incomplete end seem to have been separate prior to conservation; this is reinforced by Cunnington's (1806) original depiction which, although somewhat stylised, shows only the major portion, a little over half the object. The side grips have suffered more loss, around 60% remaining; they are variably crushed which, combined with two dents and several short invasive edge tears, results in slightly irregular edges. There are other major tears which have not detached fragments and a badly puckered zone which includes some stronger dents – there is no differentiation in colour, though it is possible that some of the damage occurred at the time of excavation.

WEAR

The decoration shows significant wear locally, at the extremities of the intact lattice panel and at the ends of some longitudinal groove bands. Some random fine scratches may also result from use. Overall this item is classified as very worn (Figure 6.1.5c).

CONCLUSIONS

The plaque almost certainly covered a backing, or core object, of wood or some other perishable material. The face was most likely gently domed. The cover wrapped around the narrow sides and extended a little onto the rear where it may have seated into a light groove. Further fastening was achieved by a tiny pin, peg or thread in each corner; since no traces survive it must be presumed that these also were of organic material. These corner fixings may also have threaded through to a garment to help keep the

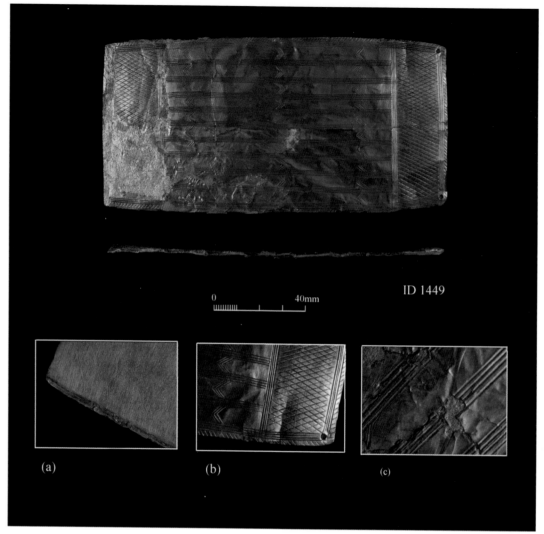

Figure 6.1.5. Upton Lovell G2e: ID 1449 gold sheet rectangular plaque on fibreglass mount with details showing (a) folded edge, (b) end decoration and (c) wear and damage.

ornament from rotating or falling forward, but they may have been additional to a main fixing, such as a V-boring, in the rear of the core object. There is evidence that there was persistent rubbing of certain spots on the object's face showing that it did see active use.

One aspect of the design of this piece has hitherto gone unremarked. The triptych-like decorative scheme is actually subtly mirrored in the outline shape, there being a distinct if subtle change in the line of the long sides (preserved best in the outlining groove band) at the panel junction. If we exclude the slight bowing of the central panel's sides, thought to be due to compression (above), the whole object would still be slightly barrel-shaped, thus deviating from the more rectangular shape of the Little Cressingham plaque. Furthermore, the two have very different proportions (width/length 48% and 67% respectively) and, by the time we add in their individual decoration concepts and the use of quadruple rather than triple grooves for the main structural lines, it is clear that the two are quite different renderings of a common model. This echoes the distinctions drawn between the two large

lozenge plaques from Bush Barrow and Clandon (Needham and Woodward 2008, 21).

Some damage may have been ancient, but it is probable that the object was buried intact because detaching the cover from the core, especially if resin-bonded, would undoubtedly have led to greater distortions.

ID 1450 Conical Pendant or Button

References: Cunnington 1806, pl. VII, 1; Annable and Simpson 1964, no. 233; Taylor 1980, 87 Wt. 23, pls. 24b and d; Clarke *et al.* 1985, 279 no. 100.5, pl. 4.57.

MORPHOLOGY

The gold sheet entirely covers a solid conical core object of shale (ID 492), the 'front' and 'back' being two separate pieces (Figure 6.1.6). The conical profile of the front has slightly convex faces meeting in an acutely angled apex. The circular disc forming the back is essentially flat in the central, decorated part, but its perimeter is gently chamfered so that overall it is convex. The overall height of the cone is 30.0mm, maximum diameter 46.5mm and thickness of the gold sheet <<0.1mm. The weight of the cone is 6.10g; the weight of the flat 'back' (including fibreglass support) is 2.74g.

DECORATION

Described resting on its flattish 'back', the lower half of the cone is encircled by three evenly spaced groove bands, a double groove at the base and two triple grooves; the grooves are 0.2 to 0.3mm wide. The lower of the fields created in between is decorated with a simple zigzag line of narrower groove dimension (0.1mm wide); the upper field is plain.

The disc has a plain band around the circumference, but a large central zone encircled by a single groove is filled with a dense multiple cruciform design made up of triple-groove bands. At its heart is a simple cruciform, but each quadrant contains a series of three chevrons respecting its orthogonal lines and reducing in size outwards.

PERFORATIONS

There are two perforations in the back, both very ragged with a tear running off. It is likely that they were somewhat oblong (3.5 by 1.5mm) and that the lips from piercing were partly pushed back into place. A further small perforation in the side of the cone breaks through the middle groove band; it is slightly oval and the maximum dimension is 1.7mm.

MATERIAL

The object is of a bright gold colour. There is no published analysis.

MANUFACTURE

Most grooves are strongly indented and U-profiled, but the zigzag was executed with a lighter touch and thinner tool. Under magnification the zigzag is not especially neat; the strokes are often not straight and do not consistently meet neighbouring ones. All the decoration is matched closely on the shale/jet core object (Figure 6.1.6), making allowance for the distortion from cracking (Hoare 1812, 99; Clarke *et al.* 1985, 279). The underlying decoration on the core object must have been executed prior to sheathing, since inscribing the shale/jet would be impossible without totally tearing the thin gold sheet. This leaves at least two possibilities: firstly, that the visible decoration on the gold was a close mimic of that underneath perhaps through reference to a pattern; or, secondly, that in the process of burnishing the gold sheet onto its core it was possible to pick up enough of a 'rubbing' of the underlying design to allow a stylus to be drawn fairly accurately into those grooves. The latter option certainly seems feasible for such thin sheet, but it would have the interesting ramification that the gold in the decorated zones rested directly on the shale/jet, without any

intervening resin float. A third hypothetical possibility is that there was a non-adhesive float between, and that the mounted gold was decorated leaving an impression in it; the gold cover was then removed and the core object inscribed along the impressions left before final re-assembly. This would seem to be a curious procedure, but it is anyway difficult to comprehend why it was necessary to have the core object decorated unless the gold cover was a secondary addition. However, a two-phase interpretation is not given support by the core, which shows no obvious wear (below).

Extremely fine striations are scattered across the whole surface with no obvious prevailing alignment.

COMPLETENESS AND DAMAGE

The object is 100% present; four cracks run up the cone from its rim, while there is a tiny split at the apex, potentially caused by the conflation of an organic float between gold sheet and shale core.

WEAR

It has generally a rather worn appearance. Both components have many dents, buckles and scratches; only occasionally are they brighter in colour and thus possibly modern. The overall wear category is moderately worn.

ID 492 Conical Pendant or Button: Shale or Jet Core

MORPHOLOGY AND DECORATION

The shale core originally was exactly the same shape as the gold cover, although, due to the extensive cracking, the current dimensions are slightly larger: maximum diameter 48.2 by 47.1mm. It weighs 34.5g. The scheme of decoration reflects that described for the gold cone exactly (Figure 6.1.6).

PERFORATIONS

The oval perforations measure 4.4 by 2.8mm and 4 by 3mm. Thus they are larger than the perforations in the gold. The angles of drilling, where visible, are shallow, and the internal surfaces are smooth, not rilled.

MATERIAL

The blackish brown material has a woody, almost laminar, texture. Classed as non-jet by Bussell (no. 1), AS considered that the material was possibly jet, or very high quality woody shale.

MANUFACTURE

On the base, the bounding circle was scribed first, as it is cut by internal lines in places, and all the base decoration

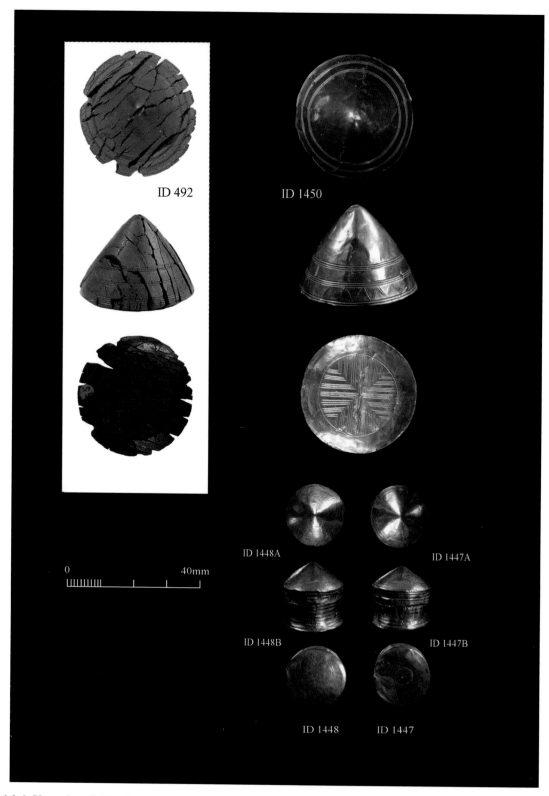

ID 492

ID 1450

ID 1448A

ID 1447A

ID 1448B

ID 1447B

ID 1448   ID 1447

0   40mm

Figure 6.1.6. Upton Lovell G2e:ID 1450 conical pendant or button with ID 492 shale core; ID 1447 and ID 1448 gold sheet cap ends. ID 1447A and ID 1448A are currently reconstructed butted up to ID 1447B and ID 1448B respectively, probably incorrectly.

was scribed with a single narrow tool, providing lines of maximum width 0.3mm. On the sides of the cone the zigzags were inscribed after the line bands. Here the lines are 0.1 to 0.2mm wide, with the same tool having been used. The degree of workmanship is highly skilled.

COMPLETENESS AND DAMAGE

The core is considerably enlarged and distorted owing to the extreme, deep and sprung criss-cross cracking and to extensive lamination. There are traces of conservation coating and brush marks, especially near the apex of the dome. The object is 90% complete, with modern loss within the cracking, as well as many modern chips.

WEAR

Slightly higher sheen is visible towards the apex. This may be where the core rubbed against the gold, or could be a patch of modern consolidant. Any thread wear within or around the perforations could not be detected owing to the presence of the many modern chips. The object is classified as fresh.

CONCLUSIONS (ID 1450 and ID 492)

This is one of only three known gold-covered objects of pronounced conical shape (see also ID 1405 below). Superficially it appears to be an aggrandised button with exaggerated profile and intensely decorated, but still retaining in its 'back' the V-bored perforation of its conical button progenitors. This derivation is highly plausible given temporal juxtaposition, but it may now be argued that the function or orientation had changed significantly. Firstly, the perforations are insubstantial and would not hold such a relatively heavy example in the usual orientation of standard buttons. More persuasive though is the intense decoration of the 'back', presumably intended to be seen; by contrast, decoration on the conical 'front' is simple and is absent from close to the apex, which may therefore have been least visible in normal use.

Three possible interpretations may be considered: (i) that the object was tightly stitched or wired to a stiff material simply as a decorative stud; the cruciform design would have been hidden from view; (ii) a radical alternative is that the object was freely suspended by its perforations as a pendant, rather plumb-bob like; this would set off to good effect the intense decoration on the 'back', now the top; (iii) a variation on this pendant idea would instead see the button serving as a downward hanging toggle, thereby retaining the clothes-fastening function of its precursors, yet having a new orientation. Such a device for securing, for example, a cape would be captivating as it sat on the breast of the subject. An alternative use as a fastener would be on the end of a belt.

Cruciform and saltire designs are commonplace in Early Bronze Age decorative schemes, including on the bases of various pots. In detail, this Upton Lovell complex cruciform design with inset chevrons is closely allied to that in the central panel of the Clandon lozenge plaque. These may have been developed from occasional gold-sheet discs ('sun-discs') on which a chevron motif has been inserted into each of the quadrants defined by the cruciform (Case 1977, nos. 1, 22 and 23; finds from Ballyshannon, Co.

Donegal, and (pair) Tedavnet, Co. Monaghan), although there is obviously a geographical gap here.

ID 1447A Gold Sheet Cap-End or 'Box'

References: Cunnington 1806, pl. VII, 3; Annable and Simpson 1964, no. 231; Taylor 1980, 87 Wt. 24; Clarke *et al.* 1985, 279 no. 100.3, pl. 4.57.

MORPHOLOGY AND DECORATION

This is generally assumed to cover a single object with ID 1147B and has been restored thus; the detail at the junction line is thus partly obscured. It bears a squat cylindrical sheet cover with conical front and corrugated sides of diameter 24.0 to 24.9mm, and height 20.5mm (illustrated as reconstructed with ID 1447B in Figure 6.1.6). In profile the cone is crisp but with an obtuse apex; the sides comprise a maximum of five corrugations rather variable in profile, perhaps largely due to damage, but the rib bordering the front is more pronounced. The sides end in a thin, wavy rim. There are faint traces of four concentric grooves inside the edge of the conical face (Figure 6.1.6).

MATERIAL

This is especially bright gold. There is no published analysis.

MANUFACTURE

The object shows masses of very fine striations, mainly but not exclusively concentric.

COMPLETENESS AND DAMAGE

95% of the object is present; occasional cracks run down the sides from the front angle and meet a concentric split, possibly running all round and thus separating the last two to three corrugations from the rest; their relative position is probably restored correctly.

WEAR

There is extensive wear of the face grooves, all being faint and the innermost one being almost erased. The miscellaneous scratches and dents look ancient, and it is classified as very worn.

ID 1447B Gold Sheet Cap-End or 'Box'

References: Cunnington 1806, pl. VII, 2; Annable and Simpson 1964, no. 231; Taylor 1980, 87 Wt. 24; Clarke *et al.* 1985, 279 no. 100.3, pl. 4.57.

Table 6.1.2. Dimensions of gold beads ID 1443.1–11.

Object	Length (mm)	Maximum diameters (mm)				
		End 1	Middle	End 2	Perf. 1	Perf. 2
ID 1443.1	10.7	7.7	7.3	7.9	1.7	1.5
ID 1443.2	10.6	8.1	7.6	8.3	0.8	0.8
ID 1443.3	9.9	8.0	7.7	8.2	1.5	1.8
ID 1443.4	10.5	7.7	7.3	7.7	1.3	1.0
ID 1443.5	10.7	7.7	7.2	7.6	1.7	1.5
ID 1443.6	10.7	8.0	7.7	8.0	1.3	1.3
ID 1443.7	10.3	7.6	7.4	7.8	1.3	1.5
ID 1443.8	10.0	8.0	7.4	7.8	1.5	1.4
ID 1443.9	10.6	8.3	7.7	8.1	1.3	1.1
ID 1443.10	10.8	8.3	7.9	8.1	1.2	1.2
ID 1443.11	9.3	7.9	7.2	8.0	1.2	1.1

MORPHOLOGY

It is generally assumed to be a single object with ID 1147A and has been restored as such but in a manner which partly obscures detail at the junction (Figure 6.1.6). This cover is cylindrical with fairly flat, but slightly undulating front of 24.2 to 25.5mm diameter; the sides have an overall concave profile meeting the face in an acute angle and they comprise six to seven corrugations (severe damage inhibits exact count). There are two perforations through the sides, neither of them very neat. One close to the face angle is only 0.5mm across and was pierced from inside, so may be modern. The other is larger (2mm), sub-triangular, and further towards the rim of the mouth; it was not obviously intended as a functional hole.

MATERIAL

The object is gold coloured.

MANUFACTURE

There are very fine scratches around the mouth which might have been associated with trimming it to shape.

COMPLETENESS AND DAMAGE

The object is 100% present. Occasional cracks run down the sides from the front angle.

WEAR

Miscellaneous scratches and dents look ancient. The corrugations close to the face are in best condition (but still damaged), but they quickly become distorted and ironed out due to subsequent pressures; this is likely to result from persistent pressure during use, but it also implies that the core object was not corrugated and that there was a compressible float in between. It is classed as very worn.

ID 1448A Gold Sheet Cap-End or 'Box'

References: Cunnington 1806; Annable and Simpson 1964,

no. 231; Taylor 1980, 87 Wt. 25; Clarke *et al.* 1985, 279 no. 100.2, pl. 4.57.

MORPHOLOGY AND DECORATION

This is generally assumed to cover a single object with ID 1148B and has been restored thus; however, only limited stretches meet at the butt joint (*c.* 40%) because of loss to this component (illustrated reconstructed with ID 1448B in Figure 6.1.6). The diameter varies between 24.3 and 24.8mm, and the height, together with that of ID 1148B is 20.2mm. It has a very similar form to that of 1447A, the sides having between three and four corrugations of rather variable profile; this may in part be due to damage, but one of the short segments reaching the rim of the mouth has a very sharply defined and narrow groove instead of a sinuous corrugation. This looks to be undistorted and would seem to indicate a definite change in profile for the encircling feature just inside the rim. There are very slight hints of concentric grooves inset from edge (*cf* 1447A), but so faint as to be difficult to enumerate.

MATERIAL

The face is brighter than the sides.

MANUFACTURE

There are many fine striations with no prevailing alignments.

COMPLETENESS AND DAMAGE

The object is 90% present (less if none actually reaches original rim), all of the loss being from the sides; cracks run up the sides and onto the edge of the face at intervals; these are sometimes linked by encircling cracks resulting in detached and missing fragments.

WEAR

Overall it is very worn, especially given the state of presumed decoration. There is considerable minor puckering and random scratches, much of which is likely to be ancient damage.

ID 1448B Gold Sheet Cap-End or 'Box'

References: Cunnington 1806; Annable and Simpson 1964, no. 231; Taylor 1980, 87 Wt. 25; Clarke *et al.* 1985, 279 no. 100.2, pl. 4.57.

MORPHOLOGY

This is generally assumed to cover a single object with ID 1148A and has been restored thus (Figure 6.1.6). It has a cylindrical cover with slightly convex face of diameter 24.2 to 25mm; the sides have an overall concave profile meeting the face in an acute angle and they comprise up to nine corrugations. The sides end in a thin, fairly straight rim with occasional minor irregularities.

MATERIAL

The face is of brighter gold than the sides.

MANUFACTURE

There are occasional cut marks discernible along the rim. There are many fine striations with no prevailing alignment.

COMPLETENESS AND DAMAGE

The object is 100% present. There are occasional cracks invading from the rim, one reaching as far as the side/face angle.

WEAR

Overall, the object is very worn. There is considerable minor puckering and random scratches which are most likely to be ancient damage. In 50% of the circuit most corrugations (not those close to the face) are partially smoothed out.

CONCLUSIONS (ID 1447A, ID 1447B, ID 1448A and ID 1448B)

Cunnington (1806) had deduced that these four cap-ends 'covered the ends of staves', but more latterly the established view has been that they belonged to two sets, each forming a 'box' (but note Taylor 2005, 322). If 'boxes' are the correct reconstruction, they would best compare with a series of jet or shale 'collar-stud' ornaments (see Chapter 5.6), which sometimes match in having one conical and one flatter end; however, the Upton Lovell ornaments are of larger diameter. The substantial wear around the waist of both composite objects might suggest that a thong or cord gripped this point, perhaps thus creating a toggle over which a loop could be passed. However, great care

was expended in forming the delicately corrugated sides which would have been largely hidden from view in this mode of use.

There are subtleties of form which might suggest they do not butt together in pairs: the lines of the respective complementary rims, in so far as damage allows to be judged, do not closely correspond; there is also a mismatch in the slope of the sides at the meeting point and the tantalising evidence of a narrower groove at the rim of one cone-faced cover (ID 1448A). These differences might be explained by there being a gap between the two components in which the core object was exposed, for example, Cunnington's staves; such a construction would echo in larger scale that of the associated beads with their central tube and two cap-ends.

Given the discussion for the Little Cressingham parallels, serious consideration must also be given to these being the covers for four separate button cores, two in one style and two in another. On this interpretation, attachment to a garment would most likely have been via perforations in the back of the core and it would be natural to assume that the buttonhole or loop would mainly chafe on the stitches behind. Either as buttons or stave-ends, the extensive wear of the side corrugations of the two flat-faced examples would not be readily explained.

ID 1443.1 – ID 1443.11 Eleven Gold-Sheet Covered Clindrical Beads/Pendants

References: Cunnington 1806, pl. VII, 5; Annable and Simpson 1964, no. 226; Taylor 1980, 87 Wt. 27, pl. 23g; Clarke *et al.* 1985, 279 no. 100.1, pl. 4.57.

MORPHOLOGY

The group consists of eleven (originally 13) cylindrical beads all similar in form with just small variations in dimensions (Figure 6.1.7; Table 6.1.2). A rolled strip forms the body and two neatly flanged cap-ends cover either open end; this mode of construction results in the ends being fractionally larger in diameter than the middle sections. The ends are flat or marginally dished.

DECORATION

There is a double punctulated groove at either end of all beads but one (ID 1443.3), on which one groove appears to have been omitted at one end. The dots are around 0.5mm in diameter and some are sub-triangular under magnification. The spacing is fairly even given the minute scale at which the decoration was being executed. Although described here as decoration, these dots may have been functional in helping to crimp the cap-ends onto the rolled cylinder.

PERFORATIONS

Each bead has two tiny perforations on the same side, inset

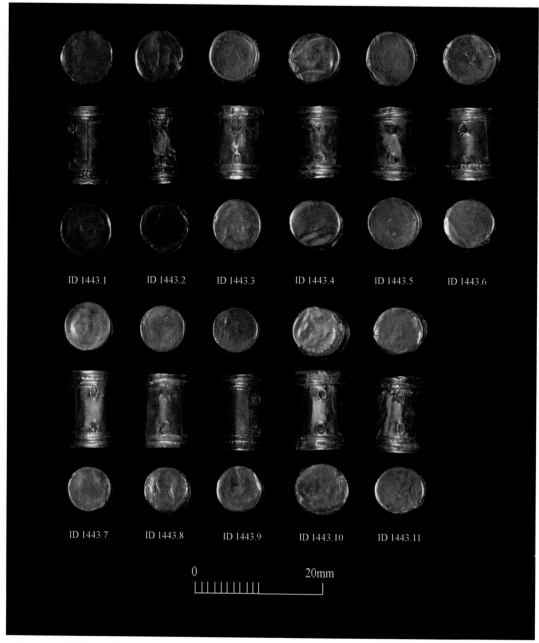

Figure 6.1.7. Upton Lovell G2e: ID 1443.1 – ID 1443.11 gold sheet-covered cylindrical beads/pendants.

from either end and varying in maximum dimension by just over a factor of two. They are often oval, being aligned with the bead's long axis. The dimensions are summarised in Table 6.1.2.

MATERIAL

The beads are gold coloured. There is no published analysis. A light grey core material, conceivably a 'white' metal in corroded state rather than soil or consolidant, is exposed through cracks in ID1443.4 and may also be apparent through some perforations.

MANUFACTURE

Striations are predominantly around the cylinders, although they are also present on the ends. The external ends of the rolled strip making the cylinders are normally transverse, but three are slightly oblique (ID 1443.5, ID 1443.9 and ID 1443.11); cut marks are discernible alongside that for ID 1443.1 and ID 1443.9, those on the latter being aligned obliquely. The side flanges of the cap-ends normally span both grooves, but only the first is reached on one or both ends of ID 1443.3 and ID 1443.6.

COMPLETENESS AND DAMAGE

Given their small size and fragility, these items are

in remarkably good condition and largely complete, presumably because their cores gave long-term support; ID 1443.8 and ID 1443.10 have tiny bits of their cap-ends missing. Traces of adhesive bear witness to some restoration. On three beads the perforations through the inner lap of the rolled sheet making the cylinders have become misaligned with those in the outer lap and can thus be out of sight (ID 1443.1, ID 1443.5 and ID 1443.8); this suggests contraction of the cylinders subsequent to use, presumably due to partial decay or contraction of the internal core. Most have tiny cracks in one or both cap ends.

WEAR

Overall the beads are designated as worn. The ends frequently bear mini-dents, scratches and undulations; the cylinders often have intermittent creases. The punctulations at one end of ID 1443.5 have almost become erased.

CONCLUSIONS

The most obvious mode of use sees these objects strung in series on a single thread, their long axes aligned on the thread. Unlike true beads, these would have hung below the thread, more like pendants. However, another possibility is that each bead was stitched individually to a garment; these could be on any alignment, for instance if vertical they would form a row of 'drums'. In this mode they could, for example, be attached to a strip to make a choker. These delicate ornaments might be less prone to damage mounted thus, than if they were hanging free as beads.

6.1.5 WILSFORD G8, WILTSHIRE

CONTEXT AND ASSOCIATIONS

The objects were found with a primary cremation on the old ground surface below a bell barrow within the Normanton Down barrow group. The other grave goods comprised a group of beads and ornaments made from gold, amber, bronze, Kimmeridge shale and bone (ID 1412, ID 1413, ID 1417, ID 901/1406, ID 1407–11 and ID 1414–16; all on Figure 8.5.2).

ID 1405 Conical Pendant or Button

References: Hoare 1812, 201–2, pl. XXV, 1; Annable and Simpson 1964, no. 181; Taylor 1980, 88 Wt. 33, pl. 24a.

MORPHOLOGY

The gold sheet entirely encases a solid conical core object of shale-like material; the 'front' and 'back' are two separate pieces but are currently fixed to the core, which is therefore invisible (Figure 6.1.8). The profile of the conical front has gently convex faces meeting in an acutely angled apex (height 33.6mm); the back is near circular (diameter 40.7 by 42.0mm), slightly concave and its edge is turned around the rim of the front cover; this turn is up to 2mm deep, duplicates the basal groove of the lowest groove band of the cone and just tucks into the second groove. The combined weight is 32.75g.

DECORATION

Described as if resting on its flat 'back', the lower half of the cone is encircled by four almost evenly spaced (two at 2.5mm, one at 3.0mm) groove bands, each of four grooves. The grooves are neat, narrow and spaced less than 1mm apart; all are punctulated with rather evenly spaced dots. The base has three concentric quadruple-groove bands, again evenly punctulated, surrounding a plain field of *c.* 16mm diameter, the outermost one lying just inside the rim. Again the spacing is not quite regular (3.0 and 3.2mm) and the outer band is wider (2.5mm) than the other two (2.0mm).

PERFORATIONS

A pair of diametrically opposed perforations (1.7 by 1.2 and 1.7 by 1.6mm), spaced 13.5mm apart, pierces the back just inside the line of the inner groove band; they are irregular in shape and the edge lips have been partially pushed back and, elsewhere, crumpled (Figure 6.1.8). Corresponding perforations through the core are not visible, presumably due to misalignment in the restoration.

MATERIAL

The object is a very glossy gold colour. Previous analysis of the core object demonstrated it to be 'non-jet' (Pollard *et al.* 1981, table 5, VI; Bussell *et al.* 1982, no. 6).

MANUFACTURE

The edges of the rear disc were neatly lapped around the rim of the conical front. The small-scale precision of the decoration is noteworthy, as too is the careful replication of the basal grooves at the junction of the two gold sheet components. The surface has minor puckering in various places; some close to the rim of the cone may derive from burnishing it onto the core. The many fine striations are likely to be from polishing.

The fact that the underlying core (not currently viewable) was apparently decorated identically to the gold cover is intriguing. Possible methods of replicating the decoration have been discussed above for the close parallel from Upton Lovell, ID 1450.

COMPLETENESS AND DAMAGE

The object is 95% present. A crease in the gold sheet runs between the two perforations; it is not obviously due to thread stress during use and may instead be a consequence of the collapse of a surface that was originally slightly convex. A major crack runs diametrically across the cone, crossing the apex and splitting this component into two; small portions are missing from the join. There is no significant distortion alongside, so it appears not to be a break due to severe crushing in the ground. There are small tears around the rim of the disc and this has resulted in the loss of three segments of the turned flange.

WEAR

There are random scuff marks and slight pulls in the perforations towards one another (Figure 6.1.8). These indicate a moderate degree of wear. It is therefore classified as worn.

CONCLUSIONS

The questions surrounding function are essentially those for the parallel object from Upton Lovell G2e (ID 1450, Figure 6.1.6). The derivation from conical 'buttons' need not mean there was no change in function or orientation. Although the 'back' decoration of this conical ornament is less complex than that of Upton Lovell, it is nevertheless present and attractive. Likewise, the apex end of the cone is left undecorated, these two points together suggesting that it was the apex of the object that was normally away from view. The favoured interpretation is therefore that the ornament hung vertically from its suspension thread, either as a pendant or a dangling toggle.

The third known conical object of this type comes from a grave at Portsdown, Hampshire (Ashbee 1967). A lignite core is covered by a conical 'front' sheet of gold and if a disc had originally covered the 'back', it had been detached before burial. The back is gently convex with the normal V-bored perforation. Unlike the Upton Lovell and Wilsford G8 examples, the face decoration continues close to the apex of the cone and there is no decoration on the base of the lignite core. Nevertheless, most of the decoration comprises evenly spaced single encircling lines, whereas the only component of more intense decoration is a quadruple groove band at the base of the cone. Most of the grooves are punctulated.

ID 1404 Halberd Pendant

References: Hoare 1812, 201, pl. XXV, 4; Annable and Simpson 1964, no.180; Taylor 1980, 87 Wt. 30, pl. 23e.

MORPHOLOGY (Studied attached to display board)

The shaft (length 25.1mm) is of sub-rectangular section, made from a single piece of amber which tapers slightly towards the butt end; the maximum width of the haft is 10.5mm and the thickness 5mm (Figure 6.1.8; also Chapter 5, Figure 5.9.1). The remains of a thin flat blade of copper alloy projects at right angles, and only a little more of the broken edge was present when the object was illustrated for Colt Hoare. The blade is inserted into a slot within the amber haft, and is held in place by two tiny copper/alloy rivets, the ends of which lie flush with the surface of the amber.

DECORATION

The shaft is encircled by four separate gold bands (Figure 6.1.8), three of which contain three grooves, while that above the blade has only two. All the grooves are very shallow. The bands vary in width, in sequence from butt upwards: 4.0mm, 3.2mm, 3.5mm and 3.0mm. The intervening spaces vary between 1.8mm and 2mm in width.

PERFORATION

The butt end of the amber haft had been perforated through the narrow sides, i.e. from front to back. The perforation is broken out, but the diameter would originally have been *c*. 1.5mm and there is a trace of copper alloy staining at one end which may suggest it had a wire ring attachment.

MATERIAL

This is of composite material. The pendant is of orange-red amber wrapped with bands of polished gold sheet; the copper/alloy blade is bright bluish-green but coated with conservation lacquer. Analysis of the gold: silver *c*. 17%, copper 0.56%, tin 0.013% (Hartmann 1982, no. 2040; Taylor 1980, 139 no. 97).

MANUFACTURE

No polishing striations are visible on the blade, the surface of which is obscured by conservation materials. Neither are any visible on the gold bands (no inspection under microscope was possible). The decorated gold bands are carefully executed, with no obvious signs of the joining process; and the blade riveting is both neat and unobtrusive.

COMPLETENESS AND DAMAGE

The perforated end of the haft was severely damaged, possibly in antiquity, but this is not certain. It appears that only the stump of the metal blade survives, the tip already being absent immediately after excavation and conceivably missed by the excavators. Overall *c*. 90% of the amber haft survives, and perhaps *c*. 50% of the metal blade.

WEAR

The surviving edges of the metal blade appear to be intact and sharp, and overall the object appears to have been only slightly worn.

CONCLUSIONS

(see below)

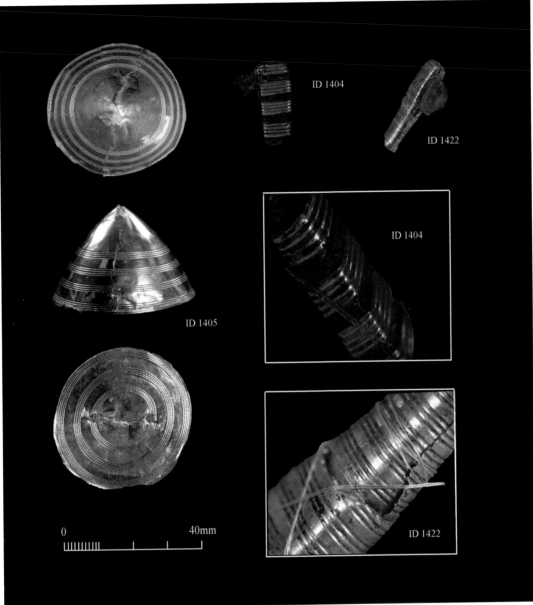

Figure 6.1.8. Wilsford G8 conical pendant ID 1405 and halberd pendant ID 1404, including detail of decoration; Manton Barrow halberd pendant ID 1422 including detail of decoration, main transverse join and longitudinal split.

6.1.6 MANTON BARROW, PRESHUTE G1a, WILTSHIRE

CONTEXT AND ASSOCIATIONS

The halberd pendant was found with the primary crouched inhumation of a 'female of considerable age', lying on her left side with head to the south-east, in an isolated and low-lying bowl barrow. The burial, excavated in 1906, had been placed on the old ground surface. Remains and impressions of more than one type of cloth suggest that the body had been wrapped prior to burial, while traces of wood supported the head. The grave goods were found in two main groups (see sketch in Cunnington 1908). Most of the beads and ornaments, including the halberd pendant, were found 'in a little heap' located above and behind the head. Other items in this group included a Series 7 knife (ID 1430) with an amber pommel (ID 1429), a disc bead necklace (ID 491, Figure 7.1.9), a gold-covered amber disc (ID 1420), a gold-bound shale bead (ID 489), a fossil bead (ID 1425) and amber beads (ID 1431–33) (for the disc and beads see Figure 8.5.1). A second group of objects, comprising a second knife, the three awls (ID 1426–28), a fluted shale bead (ID 490) and two beads of stone (ID 1421 and ID 1424), was found at the feet of the body (these beads are illustrated in Figure 8.5.1). In front of the chin area was a single clay stud (ID 1423, Figure 5.6.2). A grape cup was found behind the lower neck, and a second accessory vessel a little distance behind this. A Collared Urn found nine feet from the primary inhumation may or may not have been associated with the burial (Longworth 1985, 288, no. 169 and pl. 189e).

ID 1422 Halberd Pendant

References: Cunnington 1907–8, 8–9 no. 6, pl; Annable and Simpson 1964, no. 200; Taylor 1980, 87 Wt. 10.

MORPHOLOGY (Studied attached to display board)

The shaft (length 30.5mm) is of sub-rectangular section with a small flattened beading around the butt end (8.1 by 5.5mm); from the lower end it swells slightly asymmetrically towards the blade grip (width 9.6mm), where there is a slight indentation (Figure 6.1.8; also Chapter 5, Figure 5.9.1). The thin blade (length 14.2mm and width 10.4mm) projects orthogonally, at first parallel sided then tapering abruptly and asymmetrically. However, the tapered part seems to be modern restoration since the blade was found with a squat rectangular shape (Cunnington 1907–8, pl. no. 6). The gold cover is made of two slightly overlapping sockets (see Manufacture below).

DECORATION

The whole of the shaft is encircled by eleven evenly spaced triple-groove bands, each band between 1 and 1.2mm wide, the gaps between being narrower; the grooves are *c.* 0.25mm wide.

PERFORATIONS

There are two tiny perforations (diameter 0.5mm and 4.0mm apart) through the butt end, presumably linked internally by a V-boring.

MATERIAL

This is of composite materials: the shaft has a polished gold sheet cover; the bright green copper/alloy blade is covered by a skin of possibly conservation material. The excavator presumed that the core was of wood, but no indications were noted in this study. Analysis of the gold: silver *c.* 5–10%, copper 0.64%, tin 0.009% (Hartmann 1982, no. 2039; Taylor 1980, 139 no. 94).

MANUFACTURE

There are no obvious striations. The gold cover is constructed in two halves: the butt end and blade end of the shaft each comprise a hollow sub-rectangular tube closed at one end. Minor loss of the rim of the blade-end tube exposes the neat rim of the butt-end tube which it otherwise overlaps; the latter has an extremely narrow groove outlining the rim. Both shaft halves have longitudinal 'splits' which are slightly irregular lines, but there is no associated distortion of profiles to suggest they resulted from crushing, so they may be re-opened butt-joints formed during turning the sheet into a socket (Figure 6.1.8). The decoration is extremely neatly executed, given its minute scale; it must have been added after the cover was in place around the core.

COMPLETENESS AND DAMAGE

98% of the gold cover is present, although the surviving proportion of the blade is uncertain. Cunnington could see no evidence that it was broken, despite its stumpy proportions (1907–8, 8), but the restoration prevents re-assessment. The longitudinal split in the gold cover has been forced apart close to the blade, perhaps due to corrosion expansion. There is some puckering around the suspension holes.

WEAR

The object is slightly worn and shows light scuffing of the rounded edges of the gold cover.

CONCLUSIONS (HALBERD PENDANTS ID 1404 AND 1422)

These are two of three known 'halberd' ornaments and both have surviving shaft butts with double perforations showing that they were suspended upside down. Although both are damaged, probably at least partly post-burial, neither seems to have experienced heavy use.

The shafts are a little different in material construction (Piggott 1938, 84): that from Wilsford G8 (ID 1404) has an amber shaft with gold restricted to four groove-decorated bands, whereas the Manton piece has a continuous gold cover encircled by eleven groove-bands; the third example, from Hengistbury Head (Clarke *et al.* 1985, pl. 4.55, cat. no. 96), is different again – simply an amber shaft without any gold or decoration. The blade of the Hengistbury Head example is intact and triangular, perhaps suggesting that the two studied examples did originally have blades tapering to a tip (as indeed seen on halberds). The two groove-decorated examples have long been recognised as miniature imitations of the metal-shafted and metal-bound halberds of the northern Aunjetitz zone in Germany and Poland (Piggott 1938, 84–5; 1973, 361; for examples in zone of use see Wüstemann 1995). Although halberds were well known in the British Isles, there is no evidence that any of the insular examples had other than wooden hafts. Moreover, they had gone out of use somewhat before these miniatures were being made (Needham 2004, 231–3).

The implications of the imitation in diminutive of a weapon type in use in a remote region are profound, more so since such diminutives are not known in the home region itself. In fact, their mode of construction is entirely in keeping with that of many other ornaments in southern central England and more sporadically elsewhere in Britain. One suggestion is that they were significant mementos of a homeland for high status individuals married into households in Britain, but they must have been made locally rather than being brought in by incomers (Needham 2008, 324–5).

6.1.7 CLANDON BARROW, WINTERBORNE St MARTIN G31, CLANDON, DORSET

References: Drew and Piggott 1936; Needham and Woodward 2008.

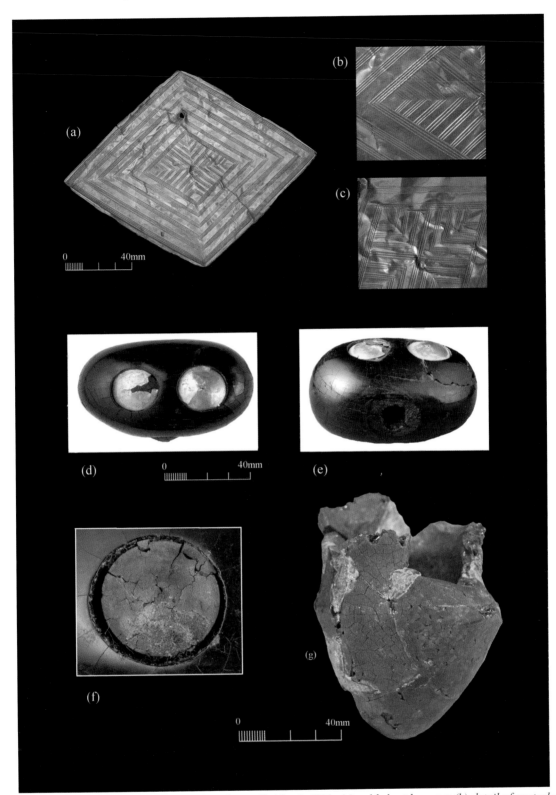

Figure 6.1.9. Objects from Clandon Barrow, Winterborne St Martin G31: (a) gold sheet lozenge; (b) detail of central panel of gold sheet lozenge; (c) buckling of central panel of gold sheet lozenge; (d) jet mace-head with gold-covered shale studs; (e) jet mace-head showing shaft-hole and unpolished shaft seating; (f) Kimmeridge shale stud within jet mace-head; (g) amber cup showing lower stub of handle to right.

The rich assemblage of finery from Clandon Barrow has been published previously by the project (Needham and Woodward 2008). Full description and discussion of the objects discovered may be found in that report. For the sake of completeness, brief descriptions are supplied below and, with the exception of the dagger and ceramic vessels, the items are illustrated in Figure 6.1.9. The objects were studied during the pilot project and so, apart from the dagger, have not been ascribed ID numbers within the present research.

CONTEXT

The six artefacts were found by Edward Cunnington during partial excavation of the centre of a large bowl barrow (Winterborne St Martin G31, Dorset) near Maiden Castle (Drew and Piggott 1936). The objects were found in a secondary position: over, within and beneath a cairn of flints, more than half way up the core of the barrow mound. No human remains were present.

Ribbed dagger
A Series 4 mid-ribbed dagger of Armorico-British B type (ID 1239; Needham and Woodward 2008, fig. 4). This shows extensive corrosion damage, thus leaving the degree of ancient wear indeterminate.

Accessory cup and Collared Urn
A slotted accessory cup with complex but very worn geometric decoration. Also a Collared Urn had been placed a little above the flint cairn (Needham and Woodward 2008, figs. 14 and 16).

Gold plaque cover
A sheet gold lozenge plaque cover bearing a dense geometric design (Figures 6.1.9a to Figure 6.1.9c; Needham and Woodward 2008, fig. 8). This is a diamond-shaped sheet displaying distinct buckling and puckering; the cover turns sharply around narrow edges, each carrying a single groove. As with the similar large lozenge from Bush Barrow it seems likely that the face was originally slightly domed.

Jet mace-head
A jet mace-head with gold-covered shale studs (Figure 6.1.9d to Figure 6.1.9f; Needham and Woodward 2008, fig. 11). A large ovoid block or pebble of polished Whitby jet with a subtriangular shaft-hole through its centre. Five studs made from Kimmeridge shale were inserted into a series of sockets, possibly as a secondary embellishment; two are on each side, and one on the top, immediately above the shaft-hole. In three cases, gold sheet covers for these slightly conical studs survive. Slight wear was only visible on the base around the shaft-hole mouth.

Amber cup
An amber cup (Figure 6.1.9g; Needham and Woodward 2008, fig. 13). The broken and scattered fragments appear to represent *c.* 75% of a carinated cup with concave neck and a minimally flattened conical base; only the stumps of a strap handle survive. On the side opposite the handle there is a large crescentic notch below the carination, which may have functioned as a finger furrow for the person holding the vessel. The excavator believed the vessel was already fragmentary when deposited and it is possible that it was broken as part of a depositional ritual.

6.2 THE REGALIA FROM WILSFORD G5, WILTSHIRE (BUSH BARROW) *(by Stuart Needham and the main authors)*

This famous grave group was found in association with the inhumation burial of a large male, placed north to south on the old ground surface beneath a bowl barrow within the Normanton Down barrow group (Hoare 1812, 202–5 and pls. XXVI and XXVII).

A recent reassessment of the original records relating to the excavation of Bush Barrow by Cunnington and Colt Hoare in 1808 has led to the suggestion that the skeleton had not been extended, but was in fact a crouched inhumation with head at the south (Lawson 2007, fig. 7.20). This realisation has inspired a new consideration of the placement of the various grave goods in relation to the body, and a summary of the implications and new reconstructions of some of the items was published to celebrate the bicentenary of the original excavation (Needham *et al.* 2010). That summary was based on a full analysis of the individual objects which is presented for the first time below. The revised reconstruction plan of the skeleton and artefact positions may be found in Figure 6.2.7. The list of items studied and illustrated here is shown in Table 6.2.1.

ID 1402 (Smaller) Gold Sheet Lozenge Plaque Cover

References: Hoare 1812, pl. XXVII, 5; Annable and Simpson 1964, no. 177; Taylor 1980, 87 Wt. 5; Kinnes *et al.* 1988, 29–30, figs. 3–4.

GRAVE CONTEXT

This was apparently found with the group of objects to the 'right' side of the body, including bone shaft mounts (ID 855–56, ID 894–96), stone mace-head (ID 1400) and small bone rings; now thought most likely to be behind a crouched inhumation lying on its left side (see Figure 6.2.7).

MORPHOLOGY (Studied on perspex mount)

This is a fairly neat lozenge-shaped gold sheet cover, 31.5 by 19.3mm, with turned edges creating a side up to 1.8mm deep, beyond which there is a tiny further turn to 'grip' the back of the core object; the sides bear a single groove (Figure 6.2.1a–b). It weighs 0.89g (including perspex). A fine beading survives on parts of the edge and this is likely to be an original feature. Immediately inside the beading, the face tends to be hollowed as far as a slight positive inflection running parallel to and a little outside the outermost groove (present on the three better preserved sides). A further inflection running along the long axis is not especially neat, but since there is no distortion of the neat turns at the corners it terminates at, it is unlikely to be the result of damage after decay of the core object.

DECORATION

Three neat lozenges, each of a single V-profiled groove (average width 0.25mm), echo the overall shape and divide it into four concentric fields. The outermost field is 2.5mm wide (on axes parallel to the sides), those between grooves average 1.8mm and the central space is roughly double that dimension.

MATERIAL

The object is of gold with a high polish. Tiny specks of coppery looking material on the back (under perspex) are of unknown origin.

MANUFACTURE

The folds are lapped at the back of the corners. The decoration was inscribed from the front with a stylus, each diagonal being a single stroke; there are two small overruns at one of the obtuse junctions of each of the outer and middle grooves. There are very faint longitudinal striations.

COMPLETENESS AND DAMAGE

The object is 98% present. The sides in particular are rather ragged and were more so before British Museum conservation in 1977 (Kinnes *et al.* 1988, 30). There are a series of tiny tears, one running along the face/side angle, plus localised crushing and a minor section missing. The

Table 6.2.1. List of regalia objects from Wilsford G5 studied and illustrated.

Object	Site, County	Museum	Illustration
ID 855-6	Wilsford G5 (Bush Barrow), Wilts.	Dev	Figure 6.2.5
ID 894-6	Wilsford G5 (Bush Barrow), Wilts.	Dev	Figure 6.2.5
ID 1394	Wilsford G5 (Bush Barrow), Wilts.	Dev	Figure 6.2.1
ID 1395	Wilsford G5 (Bush Barrow), Wilts.	Dev	Figure 6.2.4
ID 1397A	Wilsford G5 (Bush Barrow), Wilts.	Dev	Figure 6.2.7
ID 1398	Wilsford G5 (Bush Barrow), Wilts.	Dev	Figure 6.2.7
ID 1399A-B	Wilsford G5 (Bush Barrow), Wilts.	Dev	Not illustrated
ID 1399C	Wilsford G5 (Bush Barrow), Wilts.	Dev	Figure 6.2.7
ID 1399D	Wilsford G5 (Bush Barrow), Wilts.	Dev	Figure 6.2.7
ID 1400	Wilsford G5 (Bush Barrow), Wilts.	Dev	Figure 6.2.5; Figure 6.2.6
ID 1401	Wilsford G5 (Bush Barrow), Wilts.	Dev	Figure 6.2.2; Figure 6.2.3
ID 1402	Wilsford G5 (Bush Barrow), Wilts.	Dev	Figure 6.2.1

face is generally gently buckled and small areas are more puckered. A fold running across one acute apex and into a tear at either end must have happened after the core object had been detached or had decayed; it is not shown in the original published engraving (Hoare 1812, pl. XXVII) and thus might be subsequent damage.

WEAR

The object is slightly worn: the grooves are still crisply defined, but a series of fine random scratches could largely be from ancient wear.

CONCLUSIONS

An attempt was made in the 1980s study to understand the original morphology of this piece. The central crease, although not especially neat, is deduced to be an original longitudinal arris which was later distorted during compression. In addition, it would seem that the outer margin of the face was very lightly furrowed before meeting the side in a fine beading (Kinnes *et al.* 1988, 30, fig. 4). This reconstructed morphology differs from that for the larger lozenge plaques and indeed the parallel in jet from Carlton Colville, Lowestoft. It is considered possible that this small lozenge was mounted on the shaft of the mace-head (see discussion below for the bone zigzag mounts, ID 894–96).

ID 1394 (Larger) Gold Sheet Lozenge Plaque Cover

References: Hoare 1812, 204, pl. XXVI; Taylor 1980, 87 Wt. 6, pl. 25c; Kinnes *et al.* 1988; 25–29, pls. 1–3.

GRAVE CONTEXT

The object is described as being located 'immediately on the breastbone...', (see Figure 6.2.7).

MORPHOLOGY

A lozenge-shaped face measures 185.5 by 157mm on the main axes (Figure 6.2.1c-g). The edges are folded back round three angles, the first two forming a square-edged side between 3.4 and 4.0mm wide and the final turn giving a very small flange which presumably tucked into a groove at the back of the presumed wooden core-object. The sides are also moulded with a single longitudinal furrow which would have given further purchase between cover and core. At the corners the folds are lapped (Figure 6.2.1e).

Prior to the 1985 restoration, the whole of the face was buckled to varying degrees (Kinnes *et al.* 1988, pl. 1), so there was slack metal within the plane of the edge-frame. The restoration took out all the major undulations resulting in a gently domed profile *c.* 10mm high; many minor undulations and imperfections were left untouched (Figure 6.2.1c and f).

DECORATION

The face is divided into concentric fields by a series of four lozenge frames of reducing size, each comprising a quadruple groove-band (bands between 2.5 and 3.5mm wide, grooves *c.* 0.7mm wide). The grooves have a sub-V profile. The intervals between groove-bands are very regular – as an example, one gap only varies between 11.5 and 12.1mm. The central field is slightly less than twice this dimension and is subdivided by a lattice formed of two lines on each axis (grooves 0.4 to 0.5mm wide), creating nine equal lozenges. The middle two fields are plain, but the outermost one has an extremely regular zigzag design running round all four sides. Each zigzag angle is close to a right-angle; at the obtuse apices of the full object, the craftsman has been able to use the same line to start the two meeting zigzags, whereas at the acute apices two separate lines slightly diverge from one another.

PERFORATIONS

Two perforations, one at each of the acute corners on the long axis, were present at the time of excavation; they are rather ragged and different in size (maximum 1.3 and 1.0mm; Figure 6.2.1g).

MATERIAL

The front is of bright polished gold; the rear is a more matt gold colour.

MANUFACTURE

The apical laps are partially worked out on the sides with minor crimps still showing, but seem to be unworked on the rear folds (Figure 6.2.1e). The front has multi-directional striations all over the surface, probably a mixture of original finishing and later use wear/polishing; not all of these are necessarily ancient. There is a tendency for some triangles within the zigzag zone to be polished in opposite directions, possibly to enhance the decorative effect through their alternating reflective properties (Figure 6.2.1f).

CONDITION AND FRAGMENTATION

100% of the object is present. There are a few small tears across the sides, possibly due to tension arising from compression of the original form.

WEAR

The decoration is still very crisp. Two small mini-puckered areas lie immediately around the perforations (Figure 6.2.1g); they comprise a series of well defined indentations relative to the buckling elsewhere and are consistent with damage caused either by pressure on 'heads' attached via the perforations (for example a stud head or knot), or by an attempt to prise up such heads in order perhaps to remove or sever them. On either interpretation these features suggest

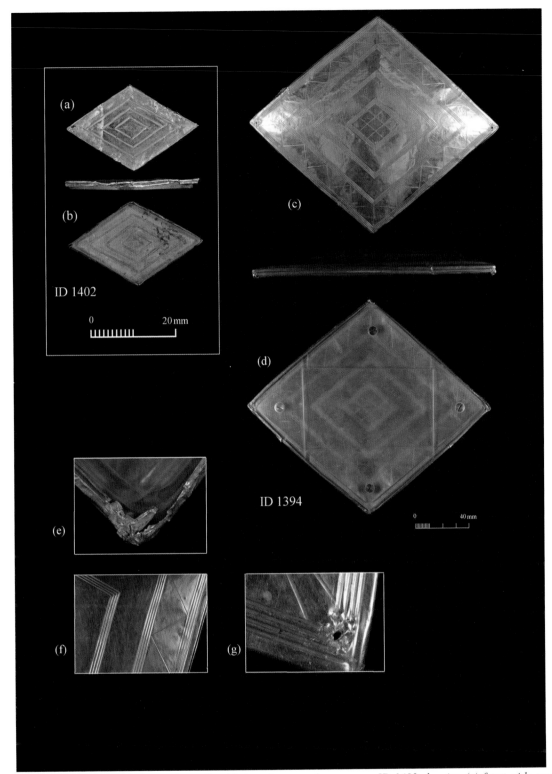

Figure 6.2.1. Wilsford G5 (Bush Barrow) small gold sheet lozenge plaque cover ID 1402 showing (a) front, side and (b) rear (through perspex); ID 1394 large gold sheet lozenge plaque cover showing (c) front and side, (d) rear and details of (e) lapped corners, (f) undulations and decoration and (g) perforation with surrounding puckering.

that the plaque had been put into service. Also some of the striations may represent use wear rather than original polishing. The lozenge is classified as slightly worn.

CONCLUSIONS

The detailed design is quite different from that of the closest parallel, that from Clandon Barrow (Needham and Woodward 2008, 18; Figure 6.1.9 above). The domed profile, while controversial at the time of restoration, has much support from comparable objects (*ibid*, 18).

The perforations are paralleled on the two rectangular plaques (ID 1107 and ID 1449), but are still difficult to explain; they would hardly be necessary to pin the cover to the core-object so close to the edges with their good grip all round. It might be argued that they were secondary fixings, but that would imply that the edge grip was no longer fulfilling its purpose and yet there is no evidence for it having become ineffective. One alternative is that they were designed to accommodate ornamental stud-form embellishments. Studs made of metal should have survived, so either they would have been detached prior to burial or they were actually made of polished wood which has decayed. Although the smaller Carlton Colville lozenge of jet has pairs of perforations close to the shorter axis apices, these ones on the Bush Barrow lozenge seem too insubstantial to have been the main means of attaching it to a garment and it is most likely that the core object (presumably of wood, since bone would have survived) was V-bored at the back to provide the main attachment. However, such a large ornament held by one or two thongs near the centre may have swung awkwardly, and it is therefore possible that further stays were provided at the acute apices to improve stability. In this arrangement the lozenge could not have functioned easily as a button.

The zigzag decoration required careful planning. It is evident that the designer wished to keep all the zigzags the same – a series of isosceles triangles of constant base dimension. These triangles were designed then to meet at the obtuse apices in a single line, but this made it inevitable that two diverging lines would result at the acute apices. More impressive is the fact that the five contiguous zigzags together give exactly the same length as the groove-band on the inner side; there is no mismatch. This required the spacing between the flanking groove-bands to be in a given proportion relative to the length of the inner one and doubtless required a certain amount of trialling, templating and previous experience.

Thom *et al.* (1988) have argued that the proportions of the lozenge, along with many internal points in the decorative scheme, were very carefully contrived in order that it could function as an alidade for marking out a 16-epoch year. Their theory is ingenious and it must be said that it is an intriguing coincidence that the acute angles of the lozenge groove-bands are approximately 81°, which is effectively the difference between the two solstice alignments in the Stonehenge area. While it is conceivable that the proportions chosen for the lozenge plaque were somehow derived from the key solar alignments that were central in observations at Stonehenge, it may be noted that the three other known lozenge plaques, including the smaller one at Bush Barrow itself, have different angles (average angles 62°, 71°, 75°); the four together give the sort of spread one would expect if wishing to create a diamond shape that was neither too square, nor too elongate.

The internal divisions suggested by Thom *et al.* are even more likely to have arisen by coincidence and are dismissed

by Ruggles as fitting 'arbitrary theories to a convenient subset of the available data and … completely untestable' (1999, 248 footnotes 188 and 189). These particular alignments depend on the division of the sides into four and this may be, fortuitously, the number of zigzags that looked best to the designer. Moreover, as Thom *et al.* themselves conceded (1988, 501) the set of alignments identified break the '16-epoch' year into non-uniform segments – ½, 1, 2, 4, 6, 7, 7 ½, 8, 8½, 9, 10, 12, 14, 15, 15½, 16 – which certainly obscures any simple partitioning of the year (one 'epoch' represents about 22.75 days). As for the potential lunar alignments suggested by the same authors, one can only ask, why embody a record of them in such a bizarre way by linking up points occurring on *different* lozenge frames, rather than laying out or denoting actual radiating lines along the desired alignments.

ID 1401 Gold Sheet Belt-Hook Cover

References: Hoare 1812, pl. XXVII, 1; Annable and Simpson 1964, no. 176; Taylor 1980, 87 Wt. 4, pl. 25 d, e and g; Kinnes *et al.* 1988, 30–38, pls. 4 and 5.

GRAVE CONTEXT

This is almost certainly the 'curious article of gold which I conceive had once ornamented the case of the Dagger' noted by Cunnington close to the daggers (Cunnington mss. X, 9). Although he went on to describe it as a 'thin plate of gold neatly ornamented and in high preservation', without mentioning the hook, it is much more likely this refers to the belt-hook (*pace* Annable and Simpson 1964, 46) than the small lozenge (otherwise unmentioned by Cunnington and placed by Hoare elsewhere in the grave) (see Figure 6.2.7).

MORPHOLOGY (Mounted on perspex and described with the hook pointing downwards)

The object consists of two separate gold-sheet components, one covering a back-plate, the other covering a hook which projects through an aperture in the former (Figure 6.2.2 and Figure 6.2.3). Overall the object and perspex backing weigh 39.8g. The back-plate is trapeze-shaped (maximum length 78mm, width at top 58mm, and width at bottom 71mm) except that the edges are not straight: the sides are gently convex, the top and bottom concave. The sides are all turned through two 90° angles, thus gripping the sides of a core object and extending onto the back, where a single groove gave further keying immediately inside the margin. The face is very gently domed and this is reflected in the convex front profile of the sides; vestigial chines come in from the corners. The sides, top and bottom have maximum breadths of 4.3, 4.7, 5.7 and 4.3mm respectively, whereas breadths at the corners range between 3.3 and 4.6mm. Five neat and tiny holes (*c.* 0.5mm diameter) perforate the rear grip flange (Figure 6.2.2b and d), four of them being at the corners and the fifth only 7mm from one corner. Towards

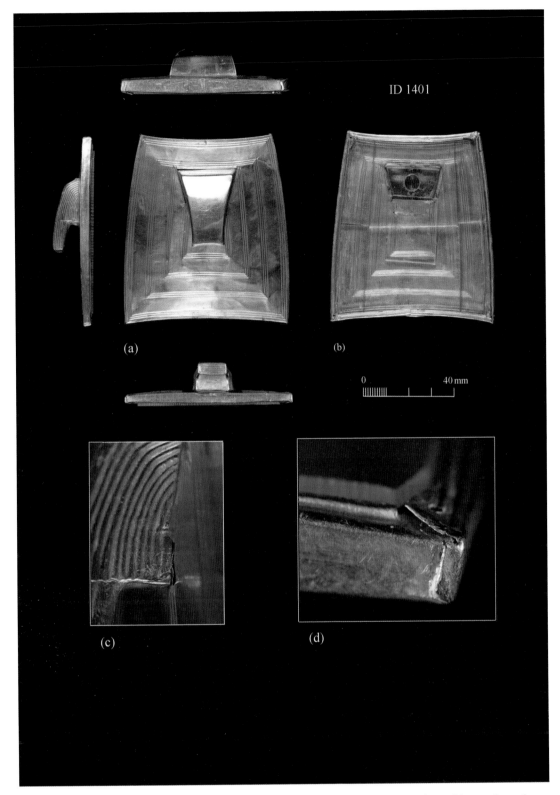

ID 1401

Figure 6.2.2. Wilsford G5 (Bush Barrow) gold sheet belt hook cover ID 1401 showing (a) front, (b) rear through perspex mount and details of (c) hook/back-plate junction and side grooving, and (d) corner construction.

the top of the back-plate is an aperture for the hook, also trapeze-shaped, but tapering in the opposite direction; the edges of the aperture have been neatened and strengthened by doubling back small lips of the gold sheet.

The hook (length 30.5mm and maximum width 26.0mm)

has a tongue gracefully tapering to a slightly concave squared end (width 13.5mm). The face is smoothly convex in profile, but gives way to its upper surface at an obtuse bevel; the underside has a near right-angled profile. The maximum projection from the back-plate is 12.5mm and the

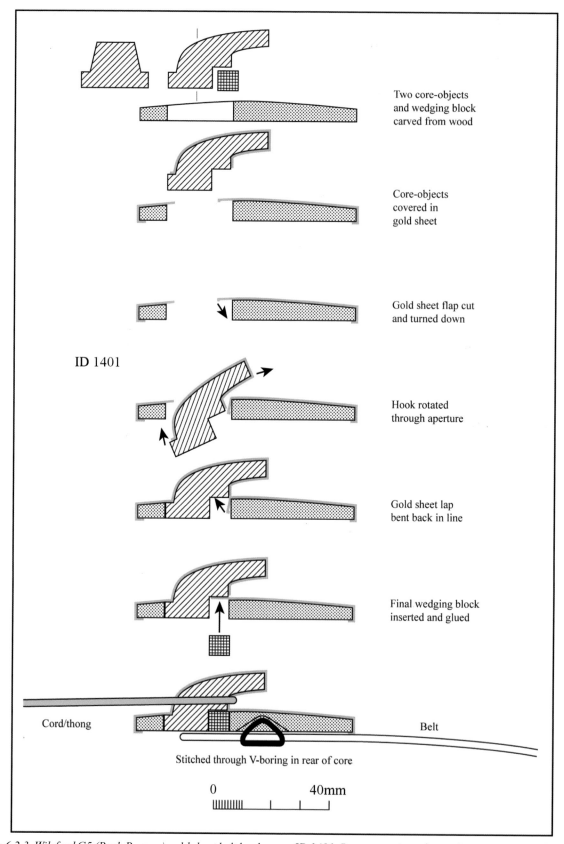

Two core-objects
and wedging block
carved from wood

Core-objects
covered in
gold sheet

Gold sheet flap cut
and turned down

ID 1401

Hook rotated
through aperture

Gold sheet lap
bent back in line

Final wedging block
inserted and glued

Cord/thong   Belt

Stitched through V-boring in rear of core

0   40mm

Figure 6.2.3. Wilsford G5 (Bush Barrow) gold sheet belt hook cover ID 1401. Reconstruction of manufacture sequence. Drawings by Stuart Needham.

maximum clearance beneath is 6mm, narrowing to about 4.5mm in the crook. The top and sides of the hook's base have small flanges turned outwards through 90°; these seem to have been designed to lap under the respective edges of the back-plate aperture so that the break between the two components was less obvious (Figure 6.2.2b).

DECORATION

The face is partitioned by four sub-trapeze frames, each a triple-groove band. The two outer bands are concentric with the edges echoing their concave-convex lines. The other two, however, have only three sides which become straighter towards the middle: the third band from the edge is appended to the top side of the second band, where it brackets the top of the aperture; the fourth is appended to the base of the aperture. All grooves have a sub-V profile. The hook has nine and eleven grooves along its left and right sides respectively, four of which interlink around the flat end of the hook. These grooves are so closely set as to give the appearance of sinuous corrugations.

MATERIAL

The face is of bright polished gold; the rear is matt gold.

MANUFACTURE

The overlaps at the rear of the corners have not been worked out (Figure 6.2.2d). By contrast, the laps on the underside of the hook have been hammer-welded together, but subsequent coarse grinding marks were left, presumably because they would not have been visible (Kinnes *et al.* 1988, pl. 5a). The back-plate grooves are generally well butted up at corners, but just occasionally over-run by a fraction.

Understanding the mode of assembly is made difficult by the fact that the aperture in the back-plate is bordered on the lower side by an additional flap which had evidently been folded back at some stage during construction before being restored to its original position in the plane of the main face (Figure 6.2.2b). This flap was then re-hammered back into position, only partially hammer-welding the side cuts (Figure 6.2.2c), and the decoration was blurred locally in the process. A proposed reconstruction of the manufacturing technique is illustrated in Figure 6.2.3 and discussed further below, although variations may work equally well. The single rear attachment shown might have led to the hook being skewed under tension and this could have been mitigated by having two fixings, one perhaps through the base of the hook's core.

Masses of light striations occur on both longitudinal and transverse axes. These are sometimes superimposed, but the prevailing direction is that of the flanking grooves.

COMPLETENESS AND DAMAGE

The object is 100% present. Much of the surface is gently undulating, there being a more marked crease to the left of the hook. There are also scratches, dents and other minor disfigurements of uncertain age (for a fuller description see Kinnes *et al.* 1988, 38).

WEAR

The decoration appears not to have suffered significant rubbing. In contrast, the external angles of the hook are a little 'soft', as if rounded by wear, while the underside was more heavily smoothed after the coarse grinding and also features wide shallow diagonal scratches. Further coarse grinding is still evident on the sides of the hook, but it is not very obvious amongst the corrugations. Small tears or creases issue from each of the corners of the back-plate aperture (not the cuts creating the flap). These seem unlikely to have been caused by the hook being pulled through the aperture after excavation because this would have straightened out the small flanges on the hook. Instead, they might perhaps have been due to some movement of the hook component if it began to loosen with use.

CONCLUSIONS

There are strong arguments against regarding the two components as being intended to be constantly separated, as in a functioning hook-and-eye system (*pace* Thomas 1966, 8). Instead, the two components derived from the mode of assembly and an attempt has previously been made by the writer to explain the sequence (Kinnes *et al.* 1988). There, the flap in the back-plate, which was restored to its original position before final union, was seen as a mistake, but this view deserves revision. The craftsman may have intended initially to rotate the hook through the aperture at its desired (i.e. final) size, but in practice it would have quickly been discovered that the bend of the hook was too thick on its diagonal to pass through the aperture in the core object; this probably explains why the flap looks like a second thought. The revised plan also required the back-plate core to be cut back a little and the gap then to be filled by a wedging block (Figure 6.2.3).

Cunnington's original supposition was that this object ornamented the sheath of the dagger, presumably because it was found nearby; more latterly it has been referred to as a 'belt-hook', but few have been explicit about how it might have functioned. The high craftsmanship and attractive appearance of the front makes it highly unlikely that more than a small portion would have been hidden from view in general use. One possibility is that it was an entirely ornamental plaque, merely symbolising its functional antecedents. However, the significant smoothing of the hook, particularly its underside, argues for use which chafed there and yet left little obvious wear elsewhere. These observations

Table 6.2.2. Wood fragments containing gold wire studs ID 1395.

Fragment	Length (longitudinal axis) (mm)	Width (across face) (mm)	Breadth (side profile) (mm)	Notes
1	13	20.5	7	3 longitudinal fractures: 2 right through, one possibly not
2	14.5	15.5	6	Single longitudinal fracture
3	12.5	7.5	6.5	Wrongly orientated in modern mount
4	5.5	3	>1.5	-
5	5.0	5.5	2.5	-
6	3.5	2.5	2.5	-
7	4.0	2.5	2.0	-

make it unlikely that the object hooked a sheath either to the front of a belt or tucked behind it. Instead, they suggest that a simple loop of cord or thong, or a hoop of wood or bone, passed around the hook; this could have either fastened two ends of a belt or strap, or simply suspended an article such as a pouch. The absence of clear wear across the 'top' edge of the back-plate is one impediment to this hypothesis, but might perhaps be explained if the tension exerted by the loop slightly tilted the whole hook-and-back-plate away from the plane of their interconnection (Figure 6.2.3). In any functional arrangement, it must be assumed that the back-plate was secured to garment or strap by means of a V-bored or similar perforation(s) in the back of the core object. Two of the bone parallels have through-perforations for attachment, but there is a V-boring in the rear of the quadrangular plaque of cannel coal from the Law, Fife, that seems to mimic the back-plate of a Bush Barrow type belt-hook (Sheridan 2007a).

ID 1395 Gold Wire Studded Dagger Hilt

References: Hoare 1812, 204, pl. XXVII, 2; Annable and Simpson 1964, no. 169; Taylor 1980, 87 Wt. 3; Corfield 2012.

GRAVE CONTEXT

The object is recorded as being located 'near the right arm', along with two dagger blades and a gold ornament; most recently reconstructed as immediately in front of the torso of a crouched individual (Needham *et al.* 2010). Cunnington was unequivocal that it had belonged to the 'dagger' (flat blade, ID 1395, Figure 3.1.6), not the longer 'spearhead' (midribbed blade, ID 1396, Figure 3.1.7) (see Figure 6.2.7).

MORPHOLOGY

The remains of this hilt comprise several gold-studded wood fragments and a large number of separate minute gold wire studs (Figure 6.2.4); even the largest piece of wood is only a small proportion of the whole hilt and this makes it difficult to ascertain the fidelity of Philip Crocker's original illustration (Crocker mss.; Hoare 1812, pl. XXVII, 2),

particularly since a different proportion of the whole design is shown surviving in the original watercolour relative to the published woodcut. The latter is presumed to have been derived from the former and the more fragmented decorative pattern there may have been intended to show that there was an element of reconstruction involved. There are likely to be problems of differential shrinkage, displacement of some studs and differential loss of the studded surface, these all adding to the difficulty of interpreting the original form. The lengths of detached studs vary between 0.5 and 1.5mm, although most are 0.8 to 1.2mm, and diameters are around 0.25mm (Corfield 2012). The dimensions of the hilt fragments are given in Table 6.2.2.

The five most informative fragments (numbered 1 to 5 on Figure 6.2.4a) are currently mounted on a modern wooden backing shaped like a hilt. This emphasises how little now survives. The largest, (no. 1), comprises four separate pieces joined together, but discontinuity in design and edge shapes suggest they may not all have butted up to one another exactly as reconstituted. Nevertheless, they are likely to have been near-contiguous and all have wire studs across the top surface as well as most of the front surface. The top surface is convex in side profile (Figure 6.2.4b) and there are also elements of convexity across the face which suggest either a less flat hilt than shown by Crocker, or that these fragments come from near the side. The wood grain runs vertically – probably from front to back. The top has no strident patterning in the studs, although they are set in neat diagonal rows; the front shows the 'vandyke' pattern (Figure 6.2.4c) made legendary by Crocker's illustration. Two zigzag bands, each comprising four rows of studs, run horizontally; the upper indents are filled by triangular fields of studs, while the lower have small triangular voids before, apparently, a horizontal band again four studs broad. Above the zigzag motif is another horizontal band, three studs wide, and above this a very fragmented field of studs in the position where Crocker shows a running chevron band. It is just possible, with the eye of faith, to discern one or two chevrons. It may be that some of the chevron row has crumbled away since 1808, for the underlying wood is exposed and some studs are clearly displaced. To judge from the intact surfaces, the whole zone was saturated with studs; this meant that the pattern had to be brought out through relief using small steps between bands of studs.

The other large portion, (no. 2), has unfortunately lost

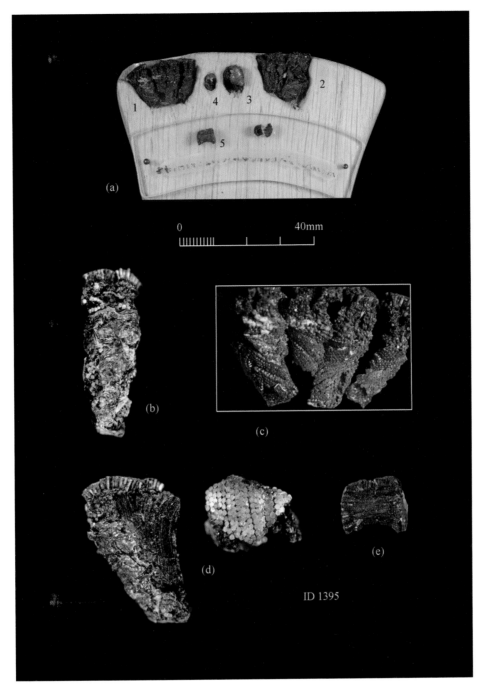

Figure 6.2.4. Wilsford G5 (Bush Barrow) gold wire studded dagger hilt ID 1395 showing (a) museum reconstruction of hilt and numbered fragments of stud groups. Details show: (b) vertical profile of no. 1; (c) 'vandyke' pattern on convex face of no. 1; (d) profile and top, convex surface of no. 3; (e) cross section and wood grain on no.5 (details not to consistent scale).

most of its surface, and hence most of the wire studding. Fragment no. 3, like fragment no. 1, has studding surviving on both top and face, the latter partly covered with crud (Figure 6.2.4d). More importantly, the latter surface is tightly curved in cross-section, almost certainly deriving from the corner of the pommel, although there is a tiny amount of loss here (top left side in Figure 6.2.4d). From the projected lines of respective surfaces, it would seem that the sides of the pommel were well flared, as in Crocker's illustration and well matched in contemporary surviving pommels of bone. The portion of pommel top extant is

actually double-bowed with a gentle cusp between. If this is not due to distortion it would suggest a line other than a simple curve – perhaps a gently lobate line.

Fragment no. 5 has an important sub-square cross section of which three faces retain *in-situ* wire studs, all perpendicular to their respective faces (Figure 6.2.4e). The thickness of 5.5mm between parallel decorated faces combined with the alignment of wood grain relative to other fragments place fragment no. 5 on one side of the hilt or pommel, rather than across the top. The side is in fact slightly concave.

MATERIAL

The object is of wood and gold, sometimes dulled by a coating of ?shellac. The wood species has not been determined. In addition, there are four or more tiny pieces of copper/alloy in amongst the loose studs (discovered by Mike Corfield). Analysis of the gold: Hartmann 1982, Au 2038: silver *c.* 9%, copper 0.48% (rel. gold), tin 0.006% (rel. gold).

MANUFACTURE

Methods of manufacture are evaluated in detail by Corfield (2012). He has calculated the density of studs to be in excess of a thousand per centimetre and the pseudo-pommel alone could have consumed in the region of 60,000 to 70,000 studs! The studs are round in section, relatively consistent in diameter, *c.* 0.25mm, and cut from block-twisted wire. The inner ends (which would have been hidden from view) are fairly crudely chopped through by a pincer-cut action. The outer ends have near flat, slightly expanded 'heads' (0.02 to 0.04mm wider than the shafts), doubtless formed by tamping the upper cut end; the degree of expansion is again surprisingly uniform given the minuteness of the articles. The studs were set so closely in the hilt that the lips of one row frequently overlap those of the adjacent row; where this occurs it indicates the sequence of insertion.

It is difficult to be sure how the studs were set into the hilt. Most certain is that the holes were pre-drilled; examples of now empty holes of this calibre can be seen on the hilt remnant attached to the dagger blade (ID 1395), and again on the Winterbourne Stoke G5 hilt remains (Annable and Simpson 1964, no. 266, and plate). Further support now comes from Corfield's discovery of two broken tips of copper/bronze bradawls amongst the mass of loose studs; these are only 0.5mm long and 0.2mm in diameter with wedge-tapered ends; these had presumably broken off during the boring of holes and remained embedded in the wooden hilt. Initial logic would suggest the formation of the heads is a result of them being tapped into the holes, but Corfield argues that would have given rise to much less consistency in head form and size, so he inclines towards the pins each having been shaped to give them their heads prior to insertion. The main difficulty with this hypothesis is that of handling such minute objects, many thousands of them in succession. Corfield envisages the key work could only have been achieved by an exceptionally short-sighted person. Since the holes were pre-drilled and the studs preformed there would not necessarily be a tight fit and use of an adhesive is invoked, for which there is some parallel evidence (Corfield 2012).

One of the two remaining pieces of copper or bronze may relate to a mistake during manufacture, or a later repair. It has a long oval flat top with four descending projections, like a comb. Three of the projections are of similar length, descending *c.* 1mm beneath the flat surface, while the fourth is more stumpy. The overall length is *c.* 2mm and the four projections, given gaps between, are therefore of very similar dimensions and spacing to the gold

wire studs. It seems possible that during initial production, or later, the top surface of wood across four contiguous drilled holes splintered out and the consequent conjoined hole was then filled with a droplet of molten copper/bronze as a means of repair.

COMPLETENESS AND DAMAGE

Very little of the hilt survives today, probably less than 5%. Crocker showed rather more, perhaps 25–30% from the pommel top downwards. Cunnington's narrative left little doubt that the hilt had been badly broken before it was recognised what had been disturbed.

WEAR

The level of wear is indeterminate.

CONCLUSIONS

Despite the large number of studs surviving, and Cunnington's fear that they had overlooked an even larger number, there is no reason to suppose that the main field of gold ornamentation was more extensive than the deep zone shown by Crocker at the top of the hilt. This, in effect, distinguishes a pseudo-pommel from the grip. Less certain is the extent of encrustation around the shoulders; there was certainly a single line of studs outlining the omega hilt-line surviving on the blade's hilt-plate, but no clear evidence for the band of saturated studding shown in Thurnam's reconstruction (1870, pl. XXXV fig. 1; Thurnam is known to have made various errors and assumptions regarding the details of specific objects).

The band of running chevrons on the pseudo-pommel (if Crocker's depiction is faithful) recalls the impressed design around the lip of the gold-covered pommel from Weymouth G8 (ID 1238, see Chapter 3.2, Figure 3.2.6; Taylor 1970), but the two are otherwise very different in proportions despite both being associated with Armorico-British (Series 3A) daggers.

The upper hilt as depicted by Crocker is broad (85mm at pommel, 55mm at break) compared to contemporary hilts; this might suggest a degree of extrapolation from material more fragmentary than depicted, but since this is such an exceptional hilt anyway, there could be grounds for non-conformity. It was, moreover, the handle for a dagger imported from Brittany (Piggott 1973, 358; Needham 2000, 180), whence the gold studding technique itself almost certainly emanates. Corfield has shown that none of the known parallels there match the complexity of design seen at Bush Barrow (discounting the unsubstantiated reconstruction for one from Mouden Bras – possibly based on Bush Barrow itself), so it is possible that this was an enhancement of the more regular skills, either by a Breton artisan under new patronage, or by a British apprentice who came to surpass even the skills developed over time in the source area. However, most of the Breton finds were even more fragmentary than that from Bush Barrow and there is evidence for some having dense fields of studding (especially Mouden Bras and Saint Fiacre) or having geometric patterns including a chevron at one site (Crugruel, Saint-Fiacre, Kernonen, Tanwedou; see Corfield 2012 for details), so the key elements of technical sophistication seen at Bush Barrow certainly existed in the presumed source area. The prevailing design themes to emerge from the Breton fragments are (i) simple horizontal lines, most often single and frequently outlining the hilt-line, and (ii) a ring of studs encircling a copper/bronze rivet. The former design is known on the Bush Barrow dagger considered here and there is probably another with a line of drilled holes from Winterbourne Stoke G5 (Annable and Simpson 1964, no. 266 and plate), while Corfield has found the latter to be present on the second Bush Barrow dagger (ID 1396).

There is little doubt that the cross-section of the hilt would have been rather elongate, probably with gently bowed faces and (in part?) flattened or lightly hollowed sides; this differs a little from the rather rectangular looking section depicted by Crocker. If the flat copper blade (ID 1395) was indeed the one associated with this hilt, its rivets indicate an elliptical cross-section at this low position. The hilt would have flared significantly towards a pommel with flattish top and rounded corners. In terms of the pre-existing British dagger series, the relative breadth of the handle might owe something to the fairly broad hilts sometimes documented for Type Milston daggers (Series 2C) and it is worth the passing speculation that the bronze rivet studded hilts sometimes present on that type, now potentially recognised at Bush Barrow itself (ID 1397), could have been a stimulus for the technique of gold wire studding in neighbouring Brittany. A further connection here is that the stud-ringed rivets found on Breton dagger hilts seem to imitate or be imitated by dot rings on the Milston dagger itself (Hoare 1812, pl. XXIII).

ID 885–86, ID 894–96 Bone Denticulated Shaft Mounts

References: Hoare 1812, 204, pl. XXVII, 4; Annable and Simpson 1964, no. 174; Clarke *et al.* 1985, pl. 4.42, 280.

GRAVE CONTEXT

The objects are recorded as being located '....on the right side of the skeleton', with the stone mace-head (ID 1400) and small bone rings; now thought most likely to be behind a crouched inhumation lying on its left side (see Figure 6.2.7).

MORPHOLOGY

Five tubular mounts with one or both ends denticulated are currently mounted at intervals along a modern wooden shaft (Figure 6.2.5). All are either incomplete or reconstructed from fragments and their original diameters are not always easy to estimate, not least because they may have been oval as a result of the morphology of the bone shafts from which they were carved.

Two terminal mounts are denticulated at one end only, the other end being flat; they both had six teeth (although Crocker's illustration only shows five; Hoare 1812, pl. XXVII) and probably similar diameters originally. The complete example (ID 886; Table 6.2.3) is oval externally and circular internally (9.5mm); the incomplete one (ID 885) is currently restored with a long-axis external diameter of 23.3mm and an internal diameter of 12mm. They differ in detailed profile: the untoothed end of the longer one (ID 886) is shaped into a gently bulbous moulding, whereas ID 885 is shorter and expands gradually from the tooth ends to the butt; the butt end itself is slightly in-sloped giving an acute external angle.

The three medial mounts appear to have been similar to one another and were longer and of larger diameters (estimated original diameter *c.* 25mm, Table 6.2.3) than the terminals. Profiles are generally parallel-sided, but can in places be slightly bowed due to thinning towards the tooth ends. The marked denticulation of the two ends is out of phase and the indents almost reach the mid-line of each tube, the overall effect being to create continuous and pronounced zigzag rings. Unlike the terminals, there were only five teeth per end, hence five full zigzags around the circuit. The bases of each triangular tooth seem to have been rather consistent (maximum 13.2mm). Where tooth ends are undamaged, they are acute angles (ID 895, ID 896), whereas the tips are squared off on the terminal piece ID 886 and on one tooth of ID 885. There is a very neat small perforation (diameter *c.* 1mm) through the centre of the base of one tooth on ID 895 (Figure 6.2.5); there is no sign of any stain from copper/alloy.

Table 6.2.3. Wilsford G5 bone denticulated mounts: key dimensions.

ID	Number	Length (mm)	External diameter (as restored) (mm)	Thickness (mm)	Tooth tips surviving		Length from indent to opposite tip (mm)
					Top	Bottom	
886	1 (terminal)	19.5	20.2 by 17.9	4.0	6	-	n/a
894	2 (medial)	47–49	26.9	*c.* 3	4	4	26.5–27
895	3 (medial)	43.5	*c.* 25.5	*c.* 3	1	2	27
896	4 (medial)	> 32.5 (*c.* 40)	*c.* 28	*c.* 3	0	0	-
885	5 (terminal)	14.7	23.3	*c.* 2.5	-	4	n/a

MATERIAL

The mounts are of animal bone. The terminal mounts (ID 885–86) are of medium mammal limb shaft; the medial mounts (ID 894–96) are of large mammal limb shaft, each of different thickness, hence different bone species were used.

ID 885 and ID 886 are light greeny-brown; ID 894–96 have off-white matt surfaces with some dark specks and stains; in addition ID 896 has a little green coloration at one end. It would be difficult to account for the consistent green tinge of the terminal pieces by the accidental contact with bronze (this would have to have been wrapped all round) and it is therefore more likely the result of some deliberate treatment (possibly heat treatment) to give them a distinctive colour.

MANUFACTURE

A lining of cancellous tissue is still visible on the inside of most mounts, this being a remnant of the original bone interior that was otherwise reamed out to create the sockets. The terminal of ID 886 is highly polished (possibly lacquered), that of ID 885 less so, while the medial mounts are rather matt, but still smooth. Narrow longitudinal furrows on part of ID 896 are probably original whittle marks not fully polished out. Otherwise though, there are no marking out lines and no over-cuts in evidence, which combined with the regularity of triangle proportions suggests well-planned design and execution.

COMPLETENESS AND DAMAGE

ID 886 consists of three fragments and is 100% present; ID 894 is 85% present but with no intact tooth ends; ID 895 is 40% present and comprises two non-joining fragments and two intact teeth; ID 896 is 75% present, and ID 885 is 65% present and comprises two joining fragments. It also has four complete teeth and there is nibble-damage all round the external lip of the butt.

WEAR

The items are fresh or slightly worn: the body angles are generally very crisp suggesting either little wear, or protection from wear. However, the acute tip ends of the medial mounts show slight rounding under magnification; it is unclear whether this occurred during original shaping or subsequent use wear; likewise there is minor damage around the lip of ID 885.

CONCLUSIONS

These are amongst the most celebrated of 'Wessex culture' objects, not because of the use of a rare/exotic material, but because of their uniqueness in Britain and the oft-cited rare parallel from shaft grave Iota at Mycenae (Piggott 1973, 363; Harding 1990, 150, fig. 10.4; Clarke *et al.* 1985, 126). In terms of function, there is little doubt that they were mounts to furnish one or more shafts, but two more

specific questions arise because of their reported location in the grave – they were apparently found as a group with the ellipsoidal mace-head (ID 1400, Figure 6.2.6) but also with '…a great many small rings of Bones which were broken to pieces'. The non-recovery of these rings does not inspire confidence that all fragments of the zigzag mounts would have been recovered, so it would be unwise to draw any conclusions from their state of fragmentation. The two questions are, firstly, do all five mounts belong to a single shaft? Secondly, did they ornament the shaft for the mace-head, as generally assumed (e.g. Piggott 1938, 3 fig. 3.7, 87)? Later, Piggott followed by others veered away from this association (e.g. Piggott 1973, 363; Clarke *et al.* 1985, 115, 280).

The difference in character between the terminal and medial mounts – in terms of diameter, surface finish and number of teeth – may encourage the view that these were produced as two separate sets, possibly therefore for two different objects. There is though a practical reason for some of the differences; the centre mounts are not long enough or strong enough to hold together butt-jointed segments of shaft without further aids (such as rivets or dowels), so they are most likely to have been slid onto the middle of a shaft, thus initially standing proud of the shaft's surface. In contrast, it would have been practicable to flush-mount the terminals, involving the careful cutting of complementary toothed rebates in the shaft ends. Fitting both flush-mounted and proud-mounted examples on a single shaft would necessitate different diameters and thus perhaps different bone types. Having said this, the mismatch between six teeth and five teeth is strange if all mounts had been produced together as a single design. This does not rule out all five mounts having furnished a single shaft at the time of burial, but it may suggest they are not the product of a unitary design from the outset.

Pursuing the single object hypothesis, and allowing that the restored diameters of the medial mounts may be a little large, it is possible that all five furnished a single shaft with a diameter of around 17 to 20mm. This arrangement (effectively as in the modern reconstruction) without further components is not aesthetically pleasing (to the modern eye at least). The only way of melding the medial mounts better into the shaft (and also protecting their vulnerable apices) would be to infill the indentations, and perhaps the whole interval between mounts, with either a paste that set hard, or individually shaped pieces of wood, rather like marquetry. Indeed, unless the mounts were butted up against other components, a rather unfortunate sandwich of cancellous tissue and dense bone would have been visible at the edges of the teeth. The 'marquetry' infills would give a pleasing bi-material contrast, but there would then have to have been a marked contraction towards both terminals if the flush-mount effect was to be maintained throughout the composite object. Such a composition would work better if the medial mounts were concentrated near the middle, rather than being spread at regular intervals along a shaft as hitherto portrayed, thereby allowing a longer distance for the taper towards the terminals (Figure

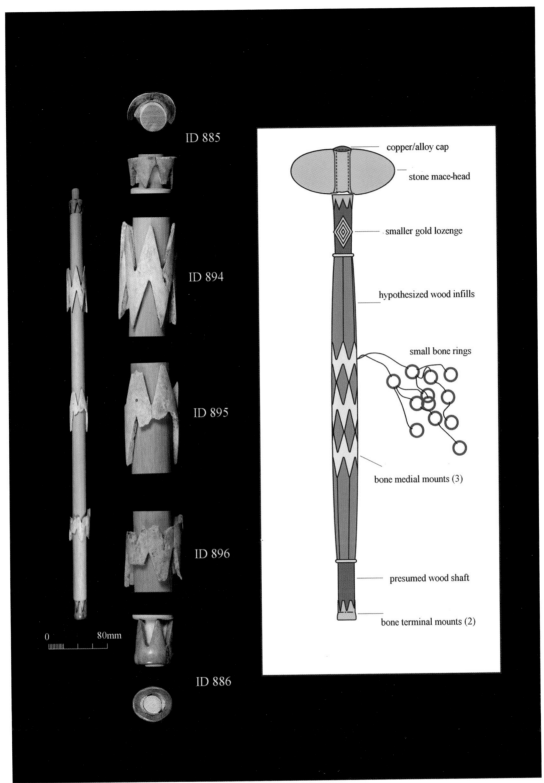

Figure 6.2.5. Wilsford G5 (Bush Barrow) bone denticulated shaft-mounts ID 885–6 and ID 894–6 shown (left) as in museum display with details, and (right) as reinterpreted in Needham et al. 2010, 23. Drawing by Stuart Needham.

6.2.5). It is unlikely that the medial mounts were tightly interlocked with one another since their denticulations are of different amplitudes. They are usually conceived as spaced with complementary zigzag bands in between. An alternative, however, is that they were butted up apex to apex; this would create a string of diamond shaped infills between each pair of medial mounts. Hypothetically, even the terminals could have been surface mounted, their teeth subsequently being complemented by the other material, but this seems unlikely because of the mismatch between their six teeth and the five of the nearest medial mount. The optimum reconstruction for a single shaft is therefore as shown in Figure 6.2.5, the marquetry being butted against a simple ring top and bottom, though it might equally be feathered out or stepped at these points.

Turning now to the question of whether the mace-head was supported on this shaft, it is first worth noting that neither of the 'terminal mounts' need strictly speaking be actual terminals. This is recognised in the current reconstruction which has a narrowed prong of the shaft projecting through the end aperture of one terminal (ID 885). An extension might therefore have provided the support for the perforated mace-head; the diameter of the rod beyond ID 885 would have been a maximum of 12mm in diameter, which is smaller than the minimum diameter of the mace-head itself, 15mm. However, thin wedges have occasionally been found with shaft-hole implements evidently used to secure the shaft, so we cannot assume that shafts would tightly fit the corresponding holes.

A further question, more tricky because none survive, is whether the 'many small rings' belonged with any of the associated gear. That no fragments were saved rather suggests they were much more fragile than the zigzag mounts, having suffered decay and/or severe fragmentation during excavation. Without information on their diameters, form and quantity, introducing them to any reconstruction must be highly speculative; two tentative possibilities are offered in Figure 6.2.5. Firstly, rings similar in diameter to the mounts could have been used to terminate the hypothesised in-fill plaques of wood. Secondly, a mass of small rings could have been dangles, much like a flail. In this context, attention may be drawn to the otherwise unexplained perforation in medial mount ID 895; this single delicate hole would hardly serve to fix mount to shaft and perhaps instead held a peg or thread.

Overall then, there are a number of disparities which leave some doubt as to whether the five bone shaft mounts and mace-head belonged to a single composite object. However, if this *had been* the initial design, it must be acknowledged that it was ambitious and perhaps experimental on the part of the craftworker with the consequent potential for minor design mistakes to arise. The possibility that one set of mounts was made at a different time from the other suggests either that two or more instruments were represented in this cache in the grave, or that the full set only came together over time. In particular, the medial mounts and associated marquetry could have been later additions resulting in the thickening and greater ornamentation of an existing shaft.

The zigzag mounts are important, regardless of specific interpretation, in reiterating a motif present in two other objects in the Bush Barrow grave group – the gold lozenge plaque and the gold-wire studded dagger hilt. There are also plenty of immediate antecedents for the motif, particularly on Beaker pottery, so there is no need to invoke outside inspiration for the zigzag design (Harding 1990, 148; Needham 2000, 177), and neither does the technology involved merit the need for external stimulus. One interesting effect of the hypothesised apical butting of the medial mounts is the creation of two strings of diamonds

running circumferentially around the mid-shaft; these too could be derived from Beaker decoration and are of course echoed in the two lozenge-shaped gold plaques. In this context it may not be without coincidence then that the small plaque (ID 1402) was reported to have been found somewhere close to the bone mounts and mace-head (Hoare 1812, 204). It is not of the correct dimensions to have slotted neatly between the medial mounts, but since its width is comparable to the diameter of the terminals it may perhaps have been an ensign mounted higher on the shaft, beneath the mace-head itself; it could not have curled around the shaft and would have to have been tangentially mounted and conceivably slotted into a recess (Figure 6.2.1a–b).

ID 1400 Perforated Stone Mace-Head

References: Hoare 1812, 204, pl. XXVII, 3; Annable and Simpson 1964, no. 175; Roe 1979, 30, 34, fig. 10, D.

GRAVE CONTEXT

The object is recorded as being located '....on the right side of the skeleton...', with the bone shaft mounts (ID 885–86 and ID 894–96) and small bone rings. This is now thought most likely to be behind a crouched inhumation lying on its left side (see Figure 6.2.7).

MORPHOLOGY

This is represented by a symmetrical ellipsoidal block, length 103.2mm, width 46.0mm and depth 43.7mm (Figure 6.2.6; also see Figure 6.2.5). The perforation is central (within 0.5mm) and its intact half is virtually cylindrical, expanding minimally from the middle (*c.* 15mm diameter) to the aperture (*c.* 16mm), where there is a chamfer opening up to 18mm diameter. Traces of copper/alloy are intermittent on the chamfer (*c.* 50% covered) and just outside it; they were noted by Cunnington and Hoare (Hoare 1812, 204; Figure 6.2.6a) and are presumably the remains of a bronze ring or cap-end.

MATERIAL

Lithologically the object is of Coralline limestone. It is an orange (light brown 5YR 4/6 on the Geological Society of America rock-colour chart) colonial fossil with no internal structures set in a carbonate matrix with abundant discrete <1mm diameter black crystals (?magnetite). The fossil comprises pink dolomite and the matrix is ?calcite. The fossil has been identified as *Amphipora ramosa*. This is Middle Devonian in age. In terms of provenance, the closest Middle Devonian limestones crop out in the Plymouth, Torquay and Chudleigh areas of Devon. However the mace-head may have been formed from a beach pebble, derived from anywhere along the south coast (R. Ixer pers. comm.). The copper/alloy traces have not been analysed. There is also a speck of copper/alloy one-sixth the length from one end.

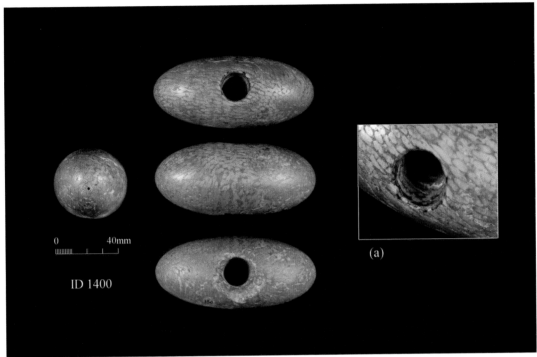

Figure 6.2.6. Wilsford G5 (Bush Barrow) perforated stone mace-head ID 1400 and detail (a) showing copper alloy staining.

MANUFACTURE

The mace-head is highly polished, but riddled with structural fissures between the individual worm-like fossils. No striations from the finishing were noted on the exterior, but occasional rotational grooves are present within the perforation and there are rotational striations on the top aperture chamfer (where not concealed by bronze traces).

COMPLETION AND DAMAGE

The object is 97% present; the loss is from the lower half of the perforation which has bad chipping around three sides, some chips having cleaved away along fissures. It is mostly weathered or dirty, but there are limited areas with fresh red-ochre colour. This might suggest significant damage in antiquity, but given the coarse-structured limestone, it was possibly due to decay along lines of structural weakness in the burial environment.

WEAR

The object is slightly worn. There are tiny 'spalls' at one end, but these are no more dense than interstitial cracks elsewhere on the surface due to the rock type. However, there is some variation in the smoothness of the surface which may result from wear.

CONCLUSIONS

Cunnington's manuscript account (mss. X, 9) stated that the 'neat ornament of brass on the top' was fastened to the handle 'by a brass pin'. It is not possible to be certain whether this 'pin' survives in the Stourhead collection in Devizes Museum. One possibility is the wire hook, ID 1399D (Figure 6.2.7), which might perhaps have been sunk through a double perforation in the top of the 'brass ornament', rather like a staple. Cunnington's primary account said that 'it had a handle of wood' and this has often been taken to mean that he detected traces of wood in the grave; however, it is a highly ambiguous statement which could just as likely indicate that he deduced from the perforation and the *absence* of a handle that it would have been of wood. The complex question of the haft in relation to the other objects found close by is dealt with under the bone shaft mounts (ID 885 *et al.,* see above).

Ellipsoidal and other centrally-perforated mace-heads have recently been re-considered in relation to the Clandon example, which is often cited as a close parallel to this example (Needham and Woodward 2007, 24–7). The main point to be re-emphasised here is that the general class is rather rare in the south compared to both further north in Britain, especially Yorkshire and beyond, and northern Ireland. A number occur with burials in these areas.

ID 1397A Group Of 33 Copper Alloy Rivets – ?Rivet-Studded Dagger Hilt

References: Hoare 1812, 203; Annable and Simpson 1964, no. 171 (28 rivets illustrated).

GRAVE CONTEXT

The rivets are recorded as being located in a group with

fragments of bronze and wood (ID 1399): 'About Eighteen Inches South of the head …a large quantity of Brass rivets intermixed with wood and some thin bits of Brass nearly decomposed, these articles covered a space of 12 Inches or more,…' (Cunnington mss. X, 9) (see Figure 6.2.7).

MORPHOLOGY (Mounted on perspex backing)

The perspex fixing inhibited inspection of both ends (Figure 6.2.7). The individual rivets are numbered left to right (top row 1–18, bottom row 19–33). The key dimensions and features are listed in Table 6.2.4. The shanks are basically round in section and expand to heads which, where well preserved are flat, or in just two cases slightly dished. The heads vary in their orientation, either transverse to the shank's axis or oblique, sometimes parallel to the opposing head, sometimes in a slightly converging plane. One other recurrent feature is a light groove (or occasionally ridge) encircling the middle of most shanks; these are often off-centre.

Table 6.2.4. Group of rivets ID 1397A: features of the rivet set.

No.	Diam. Outer head (mm)	Diam. Centre (mm)	Diam. Inner head (mm)	Length (mm)	Groove	Head orientations
1	3.7	2.6	4.2	5.8	Off-central	Parallel
2	4.5	3.1	5.4	5.9	Off-central	Parallel
3	Lost	2.8	3.0	7.0	-	?Parallel
4	3.8	3.0	2.9(+)	5.4	-	Outer strongly oblique
5	4.2	3.0	4.8	5.4	Off-central	Parallel
6	3.8	2.9	4.0	5.5	-	Oblique, especially outer
7	4.5	2.7	4.0	5.5	Off-central	Parallel (one dished)
8	4.5	2.9	4.6	5.6	Central	Both oblique, parallel
9	3.2(+)	2.5	4.2	5.7	-	?Parallel
10	4.3	3.0	5.2	5.2	Central	Both oblique, parallel
11	3.9	2.8	4.4	5.5	-	Near parallel
12	5.0	2.9	4.8	6.6	Off-central	Parallel (one dished)
13	4.0	2.7	3.0(+)	4.7	-	Near parallel
14	4.5	2.9	-	6.0	-	Outer oblique
15	5.0	2.7	3.2(+)	6.0	-	Parallel
16	4.0	2.9	5.0	5.4	Central ledge	Both oblique, parallel
17	4.4	2.6	2.8	5.0	Off-central	Parallel
18	4.0	2.7	3.0	7.1	Off-central rib	Near parallel
19	-	2.2	-	-	-	*Tiny stump only*
20	2.7(+)	2.8	4.1	5.5(+)	-	Inner oblique
21	3.6	3.0	6.0	3.5	-	Parallel
22	3.8	2.8	4.3	6.0	?Off-central	Both slightly oblique, parallel
23	3.8	2.7	4.5	5.1	-	Slightly converging
24	4.6	2.7	3.0(?+)	5.1	-	?Slightly oblique
25	3.0(+)	2.5	4.2	5.8	Central (hint of)	Both oblique, parallel
26	4.5	2.8	4.6	6.0	Central	Near parallel
27	5.0	3.0	4.6	5.4	-	Slightly converging
28	3.9	2.9	4.3	5.5	Central ridge	Near parallel
29	3.8	2.2	3.2(+)	5.5	Central	Slightly converging
30	3.0	2.5	Lost	5.0(+)	-	-
31	4.5	2.2	-	3.0(+)	-	*Half or more missing*
32	-	-	-	-	-	*Flake only on mount*
33	-	2.5	-	-	-	*Flake only on mount*

Table 6.2.5. Comparisons between rivet-studded daggers.

Object	Site	Rivet length (mm)	Outlier lengths (mm)	Central diameter (outliers) (mm)	Number of rivets through hilt (including those fixing blade)	Number of pommel fixings
ID 1397A	Wilsford G5	4.7 – 7.1	3.5	2.5 – 3.0	31 (29 excluding 'flakes')	?2 rivets
-	Ferry Fryston	7.4 – 10.0	5.8, 6.6	3.1 – 3.8 (4.2, 4.5)	21	2 long studs
ID 1378	Milston G51 (Figure 3.1.4)	c. 10	-	c. 2.5	30	2 rivets
ID 1206	Net Low, Eaton and Alsop (Figure 3.2.2)	?	-	c. 3	30	2 long studs
ID 1151	Garton Slack 107, Garton-on-the-Wolds (Figure 3.1.5)	c. 7 – 11	-	3.2 – 3.7	39	2 rivets
-	Leicester	c. 7.5 – 10	-	c. 3	17 (minimum)	2 rivets

The intact lengths vary between 3.5 and 7.1mm, but the great majority are more concentrated in the range 5 to 6mm. Most shanks have a fairly consistent diameter at the centre, between 2.5 and 3.1mm; just two are more slender (nos. 29 and 31).

MATERIAL

The rivets are of copper/alloy. One has been analysed and shown to be of unalloyed copper (unpublished list of analyses conducted under the auspices of the late Humphrey Case – his no. 268): Sn 0.08–0.10%, As 0.006–0.007%, Pb 0.03–0.04%, Bi <0.001%, Ni 0.10–0.15%, Ag 0.10–0.15%, Zn 0.002–0.003%; Sb, Co, Fe and Au may have been sought but not been detected. The surfaces are textured to a powdery corroded green.

MANUFACTURE

The central grooves seem unlikely to be a deliberate feature of the rivets and may instead derive from their clenching, once in position through the object. This might suggest the presence of a central thin plate of a material more resistant than the sandwiching materials. The alternative is that these features were somehow created by differential corrosion, again being due to a distinct layer or interface in the middle of the assembly.

COMPLETENESS AND DAMAGE

Eighteen of the rivets appear to be complete (100%) and a further seven have probably only lost a part of one head (*c.* 95%); four are lacking evidence for one head (*c.* 90%) and the remaining four are small fragments (nos. 19 and 31) or mere flakes from one head (nos. 32 and 33).

WEAR

The extent of wear is indeterminate.

CONCLUSIONS

There has been little consensus on the interpretation of this group of rivets and accompanying remains; ideas have included the remains of a wooden shield (Hoare 1812, 203), a helmet (Annable and Simpson 1964, 23; Grinsell nd, 34; Megaw and Simpson 1979, 212 – presumably because the head was nearest) or an alidade (Thom *et al.* 1988, 493) in each case the object being rivet-studded. None of these are particularly convincing; neither shields nor helmets are yet documented this early in the Bronze Age. Double-headed rivets do imply a clamping function rather than simply ornamental studding.

A much more satisfactory identification can be found in five daggers from other sites in Britain whose hilts were gripped by a dense pattern of rivets. Four are early finds

(Gerloff 1975, nos. 57–59, 67) and a fifth, from Ferry Fryston, Yorkshire, has recently provided the opportunity for a fresh appraisal of the group and its closest relatives (Needham 2007). There can be no certainty that all rivets were recovered for the early excavated finds, Bush Barrow included, but in general terms these hilts stand apart from the vast majority of daggers which only have at most a handful of rivets clamping the hilt plates and blade. Comparative numbers (as surviving) and dimensions of rivets are shown in Table 6.2.5, which also shows that pommels were attached by either two rivets or two longitudinal long-shanked studs. The pommel rivets tend to be slighter than their counterparts through the hilt, thus providing a possible explanation for the two more slender Bush Barrow rivets (nos. 29 and 31). It should be noted that the Bush Barrow rivets are shorter overall than any of the parallels, implying a thinner hilt; the reconstructed profile (Figure 6.2.7) is not however implausible. Only one of the rivets has been analysed, but being of unalloyed copper if might suggest a transitional Chalcolithic/Period 2 date unless the softer metal was specifically chosen for the rivet studding.

Where evidence survives for the arrangement of hilt-stud rivets they may be in either three or four columns, splaying as they approach the blade. Various arrangements have been tried for the Bush Barrow set taking stock of possible variations in rivet length from side to side of the hilt and along its length. Obviously, with uncertainty as to the exact number of rivets originally, reconstruction can only be tentative, but an arrangement of four columns ending in an arc of seven for the blade fixing is plausible: the three longest rivets (6.6 to 7.1mm) would be in the line closest to the pommel where the hilt was thickest; the next longest (eight between 5.7 and 6.0mm) would form a block in the centre of the hilt, with slightly shorter ones (5.4 to 5.6mm) to either side. Still shorter rivets (5.0 to 5.2mm) are suggested to have gripped the blade in an arc with the very shortest at the shoulders (3.5 and 4.7mm).

Once the rivets are seen in this light it becomes possible to re-interpret the wood and bronze 'plate' fragment (for details see ID 1399 below). The latter could well be a fragment of a flat bronze dagger of Series 2, which is entirely appropriate for a rivet-studded hilt; indeed, there is a possible rivet-hole edge. The wood fragments would be most likely to be remains of wooden sheath plates.

The implications of identifying a Series 2 rivet-studded dagger in close proximity to the main grave in Bush Barrow are profound and considered in detail elsewhere (Needham *et al.* 2010). They either give an archaic element to the grave assemblage or indicate the presence of an earlier burial disturbed by the well-furnished one.

ID 1399A–C Wood And Bronze/Copper Fragments

References: Hoare 1812, 203; Annable and Simpson 1964, 46.

GRAVE CONTEXT

The context is the same as for rivets ID 1397 (see Figure 6.2.7).

MORPHOLOGY (Mounted on perspex backing)

There are two fragments of wood (ID 1399A and ID 1399B) and a third fragment, referred to by Annable and Simpson as wood, but in fact corroded bronze or copper (ID 1399C) (Figure 6.2.7).

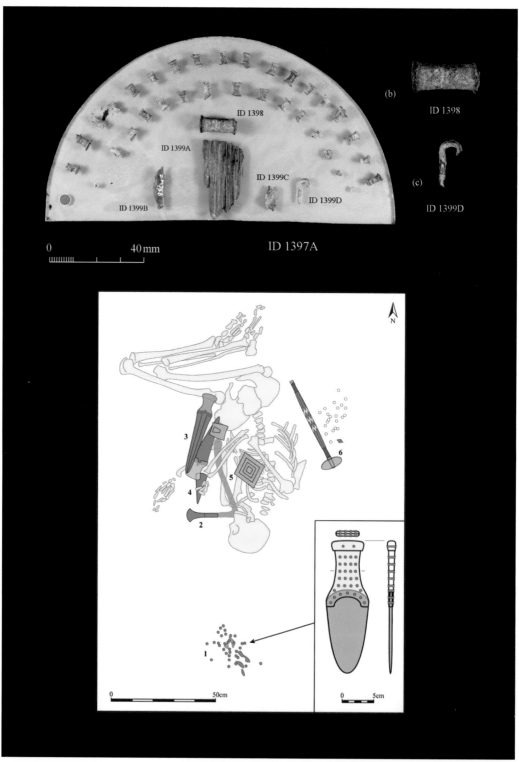

Figure 6.2.7. Wilsford G5 (Bush Barrow). Top: 33 copper/alloy rivets ID 1397A (top row, left to right nos. 1–18; bottom row, left to right nos. 19–33), large bronze rivet ID 1398, wood fragments ID 1399A–B, copper/alloy ?dagger fragment ID 1399C and copper/alloy crooked wire shank ID 1399D; details of (b) ID 1398 and (c) ID 1399D. Bottom: reconstruction of bronze and wood pieces as a studded hilt dagger and in relation to burial, from Needham et al. 2010, 11. Drawing by Stuart Needham.

ID 1399A is the largest – 33mm long, 19.5mm wide and *c.* 3.5mm thick – a flat splint of wood with two roughly parallel edges, being fractures along the grain, and with an irregular pointed end. The final edge is convex and, although a little ragged, is potentially an original shaped edge. About 5mm in from this edge are two tiny but neat perforations (diameter *c.* 0.4mm), piercing right through – they do not look recent and were perhaps stitch holes. ID 1399B is a much smaller, elongate fragment of wood – length 18mm, width 5.2mm. In cross section one face and one side are roughly flat and might be original.

ID 1399C is a flat copper/bronze fragment – 11mm long, 6mm wide and *c.* 2mm thick – none of the edges are especially neat, but one gently convex side is also a little thinner and could be part of the butt of a flat dagger (Figure 6.2.7). Part of one end is smoothly concave and might be a fragment of a rivet hole, but the lack of a patinated surface precludes certainty.

MATERIAL

Both fragments ID 1399A and ID 1399B are of unidentified wood species. ID 1399C is of copper/alloy of which there has been no analysis. The core is pallid green, with a skin of darker green in which wood or horn grain is preserved.

MANUFACTURE

Under magnification the holes in ID 1399A appear to have been drilled. They suggest the wood belonged to a composite-material object and this would be consistent with contemporary dagger sheaths.

COMPLETION AND DAMAGE

In all three cases the extent of fragmentation is indeterminate.

WEAR

The level of wear is indeterminate.

CONCLUSIONS

Given the intervening history, it is impossible to be sure that these wood and metal remnants were those originally associated with the rivet set (ID 1397), but the small piece of metal corresponds with Cunnington's original description of 'some thin bits of Brass nearly decomposed'; his account suggests more than one was found. These can readily be interpreted as the remains of a badly decayed or fragmented dagger blade; in this context the splints of wood could well be components of a sheath of the composite sort well attested for Early Bronze Age daggers in graves. This ties in well with the interpretation of the associated rivets as furnishings for a complex hilt (ID 1397A).

ID 1398 Bronze Rivet

Reference : Annable and Simpson 1964, no. 172.

GRAVE CONTEXT

There is no recorded context.

MORPHOLOGY (Mounted on perspex backing)

This is a fairly large rivet (length 16.5mm) with a thick, round-sectioned shank (diameter 6.0mm) and expanded heads (7.7, 7.3mm) (Figure 6.2.7b). The caps are marginally convex. There is a very slight constriction in the middle of the shank.

MATERIAL

The rivet is of copper/bronze. The surface is textured varied green with brown-green areas at the shank middle. An analysis drill-hole has been made in one end and a corresponding entry appears on an unpublished list of analyses conducted under the auspices of the late Humphrey Case (his no. 267): Sn 12.50%, As 0.40%, Sb 0.20–0.30%, Pb 0.15–0.20%, Bi 0.02–0.03%, Ni 0.15–0.20%, Ag 0.20–0.25%, Zn 0.02–0.03%; Co, Fe and Au may have been sought but not been detected.

MANUFACTURE

The central constriction is unlikely to be intentional and more likely to be an incidental product of production or fitting, for example, if the rivet was clenched (causing compression) while the middle was within a more resistant material than the rest of shank. This could suggest the rivet passed through thin metal, such as a dagger butt, sandwiched between organic layers.

COMPLETION AND DAMAGE

98% of the rivet is present. There is corrosion loss of small parts of lip of one head.

WEAR

The level of wear is indeterminate.

CONCLUSIONS

This rivet is currently mounted alongside rivet set (ID 1397) on the perspex board, but being much longer it clearly did not clasp the same component and it would be difficult to incorporate it in a rivet-studded dagger such as reconstructed above. It does, however, look like a standard rivet for certain types of Early Bronze Age dagger; in particular it matches many rivets among Series 2 and Series

5 daggers, but curiously not those of daggers contemporary with the main Bush Barrow assemblage. Moreover, the analysed composition is entirely in keeping with the majority composition found in Camerton-Snowshill daggers and contemporary metalwork. Since the rivet is not mentioned specifically by Cunnington or Hoare (it cannot sensibly be seen as the 'pin' fixing the bronze fitting on top of the mace-head), there must be a possibility that it is in fact from another burial altogether and had become associated with the Bush Barrow assemblage early in its post-recovery history.

ID 1399D Bronze/Copper Crooked Wire Shank

Reference: Annable and Simpson 1964, no. 173.

GRAVE CONTEXT

There is no recorded context.

MORPHOLOGY (Mounted on perspex backing)

This comprises a piece of wire or thin rod, with a straight stretch leading into a tight original bend, which turns 190° before being broken (Figure 6.2.7c). The wire has a square section around the crook, giving way to a sub-D section for the straight extension which also tapers fractionally. The extant length is 11.0mm, the width across the crook 5.1mm and the maximum thickness 1.5mm (the breadth is similar but not measurable).

MATERIAL

The shank has a varied green 'dusty' surface with a tendency towards lamination. It is stated to be bronze in Annable and Simpson, but there is no known analysis.

MANUFACTURE

The bend is very neat and tight (internal diameter *c.* 2.5mm) presumably the wire having been turned around a thin rod-like object, such as an awl.

COMPLETENESS AND DAMAGE

The proportion present is unknown. Both ends are modern breaks revealing unpatinated grey metal.

WEAR

The level of wear is indeterminate.

CONCLUSIONS

The slight tapering of the straight stretch could suggest that this was a pin or other shanked object. For a dress pin, the shank would need to have been much longer, moreover the wire is rather insubstantial by comparison with contemporary pins and no parallels are known for a crooked head at this date. Alternatively it may be a damaged fixing pin/stud, such as that mentioned by Cunnington as securing a bronze fitting to the top of the mace shaft; in this case it could either have had two tapering shanks rather like a staple, or have been passed laterally through a perforation with the ends turned to prevent it slipping out.

However, it is equally possible that this is a fragment from a larger wire ornament or fitting, the crook being either a terminal or an 180° turn midway along a doubled-back bracelet or ring. A rare example of tightly curled terminals occurs on the Garton Slack 107 ornament (ID 1142, see Chapter 5.10), where the tighter crook is *c.* 5mm across, very comparable to the Bush Barrow piece. Doubled-back wire ornaments are not yet known in the British Early Bronze Age, but are familiar on the *Noppenringe* of the Straubing culture (and more widely in the Aunjetitz world). On *Noppenringe* the doubling back of the wire is normally so tight that there is no gap at all between the two strands; however, some then have a second wire running alongside and turning around the bend in the first (e.g. Hundt 1958, pl. 9 nos. 7, 8, 24–26, *inter alia*) – these have radii of turn very similar to the Bush Barrow fragment. No firm identification can be offered for the obvious reason of how little has survived.

6.3 DISCUSSION: REAPPRAISING 'WESSEX' GOLDWORK (by Stuart Needham)

BACKGROUND

Most of the goldwork in this research programme is from Wessex, a region long celebrated for yielding a series of gold-bearing graves. Early syntheses of the Wessex gold include that by Stuart Piggott in his seminal paper on *The Early Bronze Age in Wessex* (1938, 77–80), but it was Joan Taylor who first described in any detail the characteristics and qualities of the fine array of gold artefacts (1980, 45–50). Further publications have followed, the most recent ones bringing into discussion some newly obtained compositional analyses (Taylor 1985, 186–7; 1994, 48–51; 1999; 2004; 2005). For Taylor, the Wessex gold represents the 'culmination of Early Bronze Age linear sheetwork' (1980, 45).

It has thus come to be accepted that a group of objects in 'Wessex' graves, mainly but not exclusively from the region itself, are strongly interlinked by various combinations of decorative motifs, design, technology and functions. The present writer has previously applied the term *Wessex linear goldworking tradition* to this group (Needham 2000c), but both its coherence and its specificity in regional or cultural terms deserve re-examination. The numerical imbalance of gold finds from Wessex graves relative to other regions has often led to the Wessex assemblage being seen not only as the natural focus for consideration of stylistic interconnections, but also as the inspirational force behind developments in other regions. However, this implicit notion of *ex-Wessex lux* has been questioned (Needham 2000b, 46; 2000c) and the present study gives a further opportunity to review aspects of the 'Wessex' tradition in relation to the broader repertoire of goldworking in the earlier half of the second millennium BC. This review will touch on various aspects: the uses gold was put to, technical accomplishments, the degree of design coherence, and the transmission of knowledge through time and across space. A summary of the longer term development of goldworking also allows the placing of one earlier object studied – the Mere disc (ID 1376, Figure 6.1.1).

As is to be expected of the material, gold is used almost exclusively for ornamentation during the early metal age; its practical use is obviously limited, but gold can be used to make vessels and was so, occasionally, towards the end of our insular sequence. 'Ornamentation' itself simplifies a wider range of uses including body ornaments, costume fasteners, appliqués and decorative furnishings for other objects. All of these modes of use can be interpreted from the full range of Chalcolithic and Early Bronze Age goldwork. The last mode of use is certain only in the case of dagger hilt-bands and pommel embellishments, but may possibly also be seen in baton/shaft fittings – one interpretation of the Upton Lovell and Little Cressingham cap-ends and the Bush Barrow small lozenge (ID 1447–48, Figure 6.1.6; ID 1108–9, Figure 6.1.3 and ID 1402, Figure 6.2.1). Even these uses of gold might be construed as

primarily serving to enhance personal adornment (and thus potentially signifying status), although maces and similar regalia could equally have had more 'collective' religious-cum-ceremonial connotations, as has been suggested elsewhere for lunulae (Taylor 1999, 110) or precious cups (Needham *et al.* 2006, 69–72, 81).

Gold metalwork arrived in Britain at much the same time as copper metalwork, having been introduced with Beaker cultural traditions around 2450/2400 BC. As far as archaeological chronologies allow us to determine, there is no perceptible time-lapse between the introduction of goldwork and the actual working of gold in Britain, and it may be that the know-how to work this material came with the first Beaker incomers (Needham 2011a). The burial contexts involved in this project take us down to the end of the Early Bronze Age, *c.* 1500 BC, so we are looking at the evolution of a craft skill over a considerable period of time, almost a millennium, yet interpretation has to be based on comparatively rare finds. Even the amalgamated gold in 17 'Wessex culture' graves constitutes a very small amount in terms of weight, possibly as little as 100g (a point also acknowledged by Taylor 1999, 111).

Archaeological representation is therefore extremely low; in part this is due to the scarceness of the raw material, but it can easily be compounded by consequent greater retention of gold in circulation relative to the more common metals of copper or bronze (Needham 2007b, 285–6; *cf* Taylor's view that recycling was minimal during this period, 1999, 110). Such an underlying rubric focuses ever greater attention on the particular reasons that led to gold being deposited in perpetuity in certain contexts at certain times. The corollary is that we must be acutely aware of the possibility that some contemporary types of gold artefact may still remain hidden from our view. Certainly, the level of skill exhibited in many gold objects spread throughout the period would argue for goldsmiths having extensive experience drawn from both passed down knowledge and their own productions. This implies continuity of practice and a reasonable level of productivity belied by numbers of finds.

During this long period, gold was exclusively worked into sheet (Taylor 1985, 183–4), which Taylor sees as being determined by 'social preference' rather than a dearth of raw material or any technical limitations (*ibid*, 1999, 110; also 1994, 53). Nevertheless, a variety of specific forming methods were used to create equally diverse object types. One of the most frequent modes of use, by far the dominant one for the study-corpus, is its application as a cover to backings/supports of other materials – often seemingly wood, but bone, leather, amber, shale, jet and copper/alloy can also be documented or surmised. Such backings/supports can be termed collectively *core objects*.

EARLY DEVELOPMENTS

Goldwork of the pioneering Beaker phase in Britain, termed by George Eogan as *primary Bell Beaker goldwork* (Eogan 1994, 13–18), takes the form of three small and simple sheet-gold ornament types: 'flat' discs sometimes called 'sun-discs', curled basket-shaped ornaments (for shorthand, *basket ornaments*) and coiled tubular beads (see also Taylor 1994, 52–7). The Mere object (ID 1376, Figure 6.1.1) belongs to the first type and should be one of the earliest, probably dating to the early Chalcolithic, around the 24th century BC. Although the discs and basket ornaments have some parallels on the Continent and may owe their ultimate origins to introduced ideas, it is striking that with rare exceptions the British and Irish finds are of insular styles. Indeed, it is not impossible that basket ornaments were first devised in Britain by pioneer Beaker communities drawing inspiration from slightly different spirally coiled ornaments with one spatulate terminal in central Europe (Needham 2011a). Similarly, although there are occasional gold discs on the Continent that appear to be more or less contemporary, there is currently no evidence for the prior emergence of the distinctive cruciform-decorated discs which are predominant in Ireland and Britain; moreover, the similarly decorated racquet-headed copper pins of central Europe are too late to be prototypes (*pace* Taylor 1994, 44). It is likely that this style of disc in gold at least was an insular innovation, although we cannot rule out transfer from discs in another medium (note, for example, the cruciform decorated bone disc from a Beaker grave at Cookston, Angus (Coutts 1971)).

The first diversification in the use of gold seems to occur in the later Chalcolithic: its application being to cover the studs which attached stone bracers to a backing or garment (e.g. Woodward and Hunter 2011, 80). The stud covers are only known on three bracers. Although it is a very minimal and technologically undemanding use of the material, the effect of gold-studding the attractive polished stone is nevertheless striking. These finds raise another important point: while the basket ornaments were probably wrapped around hair tresses or, alternatively, some element of costume (Needham 2011a, 136–7), and the discs were flat covers (although possibly with a central knob formed of an organic fixing – see ID 1376 above), the bracer stud covers for the first time moulded sheet gold onto a three-dimensional form. This was to set in train a long sequence of this mode of use which was developed to its apogee in some 'Wessex' objects.

Basket ornaments in gold (as opposed to those in bronze, which occur in later contexts; Bradley 2011 and Chapter 5.4 above) may not have outlasted the Chalcolithic and, for Britain, this may have been the case also for flat discs. Meanwhile in Ireland some diversity in the decorative style of discs (Case 1977; Cahill 2006, 268–72) suggests there could have been a more prolonged sequence of development, though this is difficult to document in detail given the paucity of cross-associations. One rare association between a pair of cruciform-decorated discs and a classical style lunula, found at Coggalbeg, Co Roscommon (Kelly and Cahill 2010), suggests that relatively simple designs continued in use until after lunulae first emerged, perhaps around the transition from the Chalcolithic to the Early Bronze Age, *c.* 2200 BC. Discs with more 'developed' decoration may be later still (Cahill 2006, 268–72).

Lunulae essentially continue 'flat' sheet-gold techniques, but they are much larger ornaments than hitherto, a development presumably made possible by the discovery and systematic exploitation of a reliable gold source, or sources, such as those in the Mourne Mountains suggested recently by Warner *et al.* (2009). Although produced in a 'flat-working' technology, it is nevertheless clear from the deportment of many lunulae that they would have fallen in a gentle, non-planar curve around a human collar or a matching life-size form (for example, an idol – e.g. Taylor 1999, 110). The terminal plates can also sometimes be twisted out of the flat plane. These limited elements of three-dimensionality, like that of the curled basket ornaments and the coiled beads, should not, however, be confused with two other forms that dominate the later Early Bronze Age sequence in Britain – sheet-goldwork in the round and the sheet-gold covers already introduced above and most relevant here.

SHEET-GOLD COVERS

Most post-Chalcolithic goldwork in Britain can be described as *sheet-gold covers*. The sheet is almost always thin, sometimes incredibly thin (often termed 'foil'). The covers were applied to a variety of forms and are correspondingly diverse in the technical sophistication required. Where sheet-covers fold round curving edges or over the sharp apices of cones, crimps and creases would inevitably form and these needed to be erased by careful planishing. On the other hand, where adjacent straight edges met at an angle, as on the quadrangular plaques, with careful cutting overlaps could be restricted to the unseen rear.

The simplest examples are front covers for objects that are almost invariably domed or contoured to some degree. They range from small circular caps, such as at Lake (ID 1570–71, Figure 6.1.1), to the large quadrangular plaques (ID 1107, Figure 6.1.2; ID 1449, Figure 6.1.5; ID 1394, Figure 6.2.1). In several instances, however, two shaped covers are brought together at a 'seam', thus partly or totally encasing the core object. Some are matching pairs of well-developed domes or cones, united to encase spherical or biconical beads (e.g. Wilsford G7 ID 1388, Figure 5.9.2), or the rim of the gold-bound amber discs (Wilsford G8 ID 1412 and ID 1413, Figure 5.9.1); others are asymmetric sets, as on the deep conical pendants (ID 1405, Figure 6.1.8; ID 1450, Figure 6.1.6) where the second component is more or less flat to cover the 'back'. Another asymmetric pairing is seen in the Ridgeway 7 pommel cover (Taylor 1970a; 1980, 80 Do 15, pl. 27 a–e; ID 1238, Figure 3.2.6) where the construction and shaping is more complex; the underside of this assembly would probably need to have been applied to the pommel core, to which it was secured by a row of gold pins, before the pommel was mounted on its handle.

One other two-part construction, the Bush Barrow belt-hook (ID 1401, Figure 6.2.2 and Figure 6.2.3) is entirely different. Here there is no rear cover and the second component is needed instead to cope with the prominent projection of the hook from a gently convex back-plate.

This complex morphology would be extremely difficult to cover in a single process; indeed, covering the hook part alone was quite a tricky job involving much folding and lapping. The major laps were kept to the underside, out of direct sight in the assembled object, and they were not fully worked out.

There are further variants within this sheet-cover milieu requiring technological finesse, both unbroken annular bands such as dagger hilt-bands (e.g. Henshall 1968), or socketed forms, such as the cap-ends or the two halves of the Manton halberd pendant (ID 1108–10; Figure 6.1.3 and Figure 6.1.4; ID 1422, Figure 6.1.8; ID 1447–48, Figure 6.1.6). Depending on precise morphology, some of these could have been preformed, having been raised from small blocks of gold, before being slid over the core object. Detail such as corrugated profiles or groove decoration could have been added *in situ*, especially if there was a float of pitch or resin in between (e.g. Taylor 1970a), or traced from features already present in the underlying core. The alternative is for the sheet or strip to have been wrapped around the core object, the overlap then being burnish-welded to conceal the join (Taylor 1985, 184), but there is little discernible evidence for this process – only perhaps the re-opened split on the Manton halberd pendant.

Although edge grooves are present on some plaques and smaller pendants, these may have originated mainly to help the cover to grip the core object; they do not have the impact of the multiple corrugations that were created on the annular bands and cap-ends. The close-set multiple grooving on the hook of the Bush Barrow belt-hook, however, may be an attempt to mimic true corrugations. The technique of corrugating hilt-bands may not have started before mid Period 2 (*c.* 2100/2050 BC) and probably continued into Period 3 (1950 – 1750/1700 BC) to judge from the similar object at Little Cressingham and the radiocarbon date associated with the example from Topped Mountain, Co. Fermanagh (Brindley 2007, 85). It has been suggested, however, that these simple corrugated forms may have sown the seed for 'free-standing' three-dimensional objects stiffened with ribs and bosses – what has been defined elsewhere as the *embossed goldworking tradition* (Needham 2000c).

Although concurrent with the Wessex linear goldwork, the embossed tradition employed a different set of technical skills to different ends, while the two also have mutually exclusive geographical distributions (Needham 2000c, 50). Embossed goldwork tends to involve thicker sheet metal which is self-supporting if necessary (as in the cups); even so, in most cases (armlets, capes) they were undoubtedly given a backing, although this would have been added to an essentially complete object. In terms of decorative techniques, the traditions are partly defined by their very different emphases: a focus on impressed line-work and pointillé (sometimes combined to give *punctulated* lines) on the 'Wessex linear' objects, and the employment of pronounced ribs, corrugations and bosses on the embossed objects.

WESSEX AND THE GOLDWORK REPERTOIRE OF THE EARLY SECOND MILLENNIUM

For Taylor, a number of gold objects in some of the more spectacular of 'Wessex' grave groups are linked so closely together by technical execution and choice of motifs that they can be attributed to a single craftsman, the 'Wessex Master Craftsman' (Taylor 1980, 46–7; 1985, 186; 2004; 2005). Such a specific link in terms of production means rather tight constraints on the period of production, namely the practising lifetime of the craftsman in question – '.... A period of at most 40–50 years' (Taylor 1980, 47). Subsequently this was refined to 'about thirty years for the deposition of *all* the gold objects' (Taylor 1999, 112; my italics). This view had been prefigured in Coles and Taylor's (1971) much earlier 'minimal view' of Wessex graves. The claim that new analyses of some Wessex gold (using laser-ablation induction-coupled plasma mass spectrometry) support the pre-established stylistic links and therefore also the proposed short currency (Taylor 1999; 2004; 2005) is impossible to evaluate on current evidence. The actual figures obtained from the analyses have yet to be published, and it remains unclear whether the values and their dispersions amongst the handful of Wessex objects presented are typical or not of those found within contemporary goldwork at large. There is the added complication as to how they might relate to natural variations in the source or sources contributing to the gold stock in circulation at the time.

There are undeniably a few cases for which the execution of a given decorative element – notably the punctulated quadruple-groove bands – has strikingly similar qualities and one should not exclude the possibility that occasional objects that have come down to us might have been manufactured by the same hand, especially when other traits of the objects reinforce the connections. However, overstating the 'minimal view' can obscure the likely reality that craft skills could be faithfully maintained within a tightly knit goldworking 'school', or tradition (Needham 2000c, 56–7). This latter model does require that goldworking was continually perpetuated in a region over longer durations than envisaged by Taylor, but this is unproblematic given the prediction of low-visibility outlined above.

Decoration has loomed large in discussions of 'Wessex' and contemporary goldwork, but taken in isolation it poses difficulties. When not simply outlining edges or encircling shafts, decoration is 'geometric' throughout the early metal age. Moreover, certain specific themes or motifs recur over a long time-span: multiple-groove bands are present on some of the earliest basket ornaments as well as on 'Wessex linear' goldwork; chevrons, zigzags and triangles can occur on 'sun-discs', lunulae and later sheet-cover types; dot-rows are also employed frequently and throughout the sequence, although an important variation beginning around the turn of the millennium is the placing of dots within grooves (*punctulation*). It is worth noting their simultaneous use in a different way in the embossed tradition, to outline the embossed features (*pointillé outlining*). With such long-running themes, the concept of a 'Wessex linear tradition' defined empirically on the basis of decoration becomes problematic. Virtually all of the more complex decorative designs known are unique in detail and some are quite inventive. This in itself does not have to imply production by varied craftworkers or craft schools; it may simply mean that individualistic creativity was valued. Nevertheless, there may be some differences in design concepts that betray distinct ideas about creating such individualistic pieces.

Given these uncertainties, it may be instructive to map out the full spectrum of sheet-gold covers and their interrelationships for the earlier half of the second millennium BC in terms of broad form-cum-functional categories (Figure 6.3.1). Key prototypes, or stimuli, for certain gold forms are also shown in the diagram. The categories defined cannot be guaranteed all to be strictly equivalent in functional terms for the obvious reason that functions are often ambiguous; so, for example, the shallow cones may not all have been used in the same way. Similarly, categories such as cylindrical bead covers, spherical bead covers or pommel embellishments may group together different technical approaches. Nevertheless, the diagram helps elucidate the complex interconnections between

grave groups in terms of morphological categories. So, for example, the Upton Lovell assemblage is at the intersection of four categories (and in addition *shallow conical covers* are represented on two of the cap-ends).

There are rather few associations relative to number of types; this makes it difficult to be sure whether any internal groupings might relate to craft-tradition or, alternatively, have some other significance. However, the map does set certain finds a little apart, for example, the Lake and Broughty Ferry domed discs, even though these are only subtly different from the shallower of the conical covers. Similarly, the group of finds interconnecting with Bush Barrow is only linked to the main grouping (in terms of goldwork) by the Clandon find. It may be noted that all four British associations in this sector include daggers, partly predetermined by the pommel embellishment category, and it is possible that this reflects a broad gender division within the full spectrum; only one other find – Little Cressingham – includes a dagger. This too stands a little apart, only being linked to the complex web of interrelationships via Upton Lovell (although note that its amber types provide a bridge with the Lake grave group, see ID 1444).

It is also useful to consider decorative trends in relation to this form-cum-function map; they are presented here in terms of the level of design sophistication. This classification does

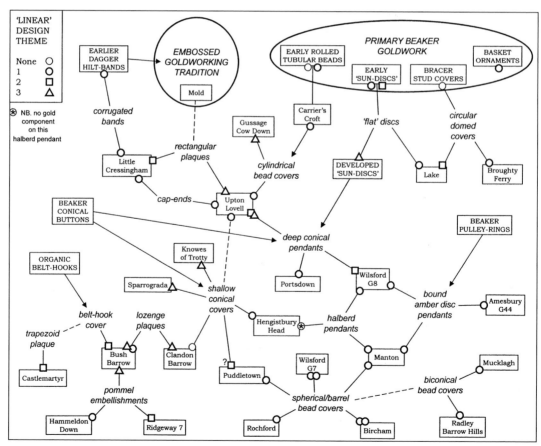

Figure 6.3.1. Map of form-cum-function relationships amongst goldwork of the earlier half of the second millennium BC in Britain and Ireland. One related silver find is included (Gussage Cow Down). Key stylistic stimuli are also indicated. A few objects of uncertain character, or not readily related to others, are excluded.

not cover the quality of execution. Given the individuality already emphasised, the classification of design (as opposed to component motifs) must be kept fairly general:

Design theme 1: Designs using only *simple rows*, usually just as outlining devices, but sometimes as simple dividers – lines, line-bands, dot-rows, or occasionally rows of short strokes; despite the lack of elaboration in concept, these designs are often extremely fine and proficiently executed, and they can serve well in emphasising the morphology of the objects. The fine corrugations seen on some types of object (e.g. ID 1108–10, Figure 6.1.3 and ID 1447–48, Figure 6.1.6) can also be treated as 'simple rows', just achieved in another technique.

Design theme 2: Designs that can be described as *simple geometric*; they elaborate a little on the simple rows in various ways: simple stroke in-fills of parallel or diagonal lines (Mere disc ID 1376, Figure 6.1.1, and other early discs); the addition of simple 'fringe' motifs (Lake domed covers, ID 1572–73, Figure 6.1.1); concentrically repeating elements of diminishing size (Bush Barrow belt-hook, ID 1401, Figure 6.2.2).

Design theme 3: Designs with more *complex geometric* forms, for which rather more forethought had to go into the spatial relationship of the design elements; these are almost always individual creations. There are only a modest number of examples, but in addition to the well-known 'Wessex' pieces from Upton Lovell, Bush Barrow and Clandon Barrow, there are the covers from the Knowes of Trotty and Sparrograda, the most elaborately decorated 'sun-discs', and the only silver cover, from Gussage Cow Down.

The correlation between these decoration categories and object types is shown in Figure 6.3.1; beads and other small objects (such as the halberd pendants, or bound amber bead pendants) mostly have simple-row decoration. It is obvious that size constrains the ability to diversify the design, yet relatively simple outlining can nevertheless enhance the impact of small gold components. Simple geometric decoration is widely distributed in relation to goldwork forms, and complex geometric decoration is likewise not confined to any particular zone of the map of inter-relationships. Conversely, some object forms show a mix of decorative themes – even true of the seemingly homogeneous type of deep conical pendants.

Turning briefly to morphology, it can be seen from this map of relationships that many of the defined categories are not regionally restricted. This is the case for circular domed covers, shallow conical covers and the various bead shapes – biconical, cylindrical and spherical/barrel; although the last variety is only known from southern England, two of the five finds are from East Anglia. Likewise, the two examples of cap-ends are split between Wessex and East Anglia, and the same is true of the two formal rectangular plaques, while a probable third, cut from a larger object of embossed gold, comes from Mold, north-east Wales (Needham 2012a, 229–30 and fig. 10). The question may even be asked of the lozenge plaques given the recent discovery of a jet example at Carlton Colville,

Suffolk, and possibly a portion of an amber example from Heathrow Terminal 5, west London (Pitts 2007; Sheridan 2010, 127). This still leaves the question as to whether *gold* lozenges were Wessex specific, but finds elsewhere are currently too few. It is clear then that much of the goldwork of this period is not strongly regionalised and to give it the appellation 'Wessex gold' merely acknowledges the benevolent conditions of survival and recovery there.

On this basis, it may be a mistake to perpetuate the notion of Wessex goldwork, other than for a tightly circumscribed group of types and decorative designs. This is best comprised of three specialised pendant types – deep conical, bound amber disc and halberd. Apart from their restricted distributions in central southern England, these types are also linked by the intricate composition of gold and other exotic materials. Other pendant and bead types featuring such compositions may also be specific to the region, for, although some gold finds elsewhere (including bead covers) were associated with amber and/or shale beads, the different materials were not evidently used compositely. Similarly, although there are occasional parallels for the amber disc pendants outside Wessex, these lack the gold binding of three Wessex finds (Needham *et al.* 2006, 40–1).

In terms of larger ornaments, some are unique – the Ridgeway pommel cover, the Bush Barrow belt-hook cover – and others are divergent in style. For example, both proportions and design differentiate the Bush Barrow and Clandon lozenges (Needham and Woodward 2008, 18–21), and the same is true of the Upton Lovell and Little Cressingham rectangular plaques. Little Cressingham echoes the concentric line-bands of the Wessex plaques and belt-hook, and although its execution looks divergent (Taylor 1980, 46; 1985, 187), this in itself need not eliminate it from the same craft tradition. However, the Upton Lovell example follows a quite distinct design principle, if anything reflecting the complex decorative panels on some contemporary (Period 3) bronze axe-heads or some copper/bronze armlets of Group 1 (Clarke 1970, 230–1, 396–7 figs 942–946; Needham 2000b, 29–30, 35–7). In addition to the main schema, it is unusual in its cable-effect edging. The corrugated cap-ends at these two sites plus the corrugated band at Little Cressingham have technical-cum-stylistic links to the dagger hilt-bands, which are overtly non-Wessex: five examples are now known from Scotland, one from Ireland. Amongst the Upton Lovell gold assemblage, that only leaves the deep conical pendant as firmly attributable to a Wessex-specific tradition.

To define a Wessex goldworking tradition – or rather, a multi-material craft-working tradition – in the narrow terms set out does not exclude some other objects, either the simple or the unique, having also been produced under the aegis of the same craftworkers. However, associations between different goldwork types do not necessarily help identify these. As we have seen above, it is possible to view the Upton Lovell assemblage as representing diverse styles, techniques and influences. Likewise, the gold wire-studded pommel at Bush Barrow, undoubtedly of Armorican inspiration if not manufacture, illustrates the association of very distinct goldworking techniques and perhaps therefore traditions within a single grave group. Most other types and styles are either sufficiently individual or too unspecific to be attributed to either Wessex or any other tradition on the current rather sparse dataset.

CONCLUSIONS

All the known goldwork of the Chalcolithic and Early Bronze Age falls within the broad umbrella of sheet-goldwork. Yet as gold-working developed after the primary Beaker phase, not only did it come to be applied in quite diverse ways to cover a wide variety of forms, but it was also made to count visually in different ways; this was especially important when the gold available was extremely limited in amount. Visual impact might be categorised as follows:

- Sheer opulence, in terms of both large surface area and rich contouring – this is a particular feature of embossed goldwork, which often made use of a goodly amount of the raw material
- Striking geometric linear designs serving to zone large flat or continuously curved reflective surfaces – seen in varied formats on lunulae, plaques, deep cones, a belt-hook and a pommel cover (design themes 2 and 3 are represented)
- Saturation decoration to micro-contour a surface, thus making it continuously rippled, hatched or stippled – this can be seen on certain discs, cones, plaques and beads (among design themes 2 and 3). Examples are the Sparrograda (Ballydehob) disc or shallow cone and the Knockane (Castlemartyr) trapezoid plaque (Cahill 2006, 269–72), and the Knowes of Trotty shallow cones (Clarke *et al.* 1985, 113 pl. 4.39); the roundel within the 'back' of the Upton Lovell conical pendant (ID 1450, Figure 6.1.6) is also densely filled. 'Saturation' is also achieved using an entirely different technique on the Bush Barrow wire-studded pommel
- An emphasis on intricacy: either fine traced decoration (lines and dots), or small corrugations giving simple but pleasing contouring, all of these occurring on small items, while in Wessex the gold was frequently combined with other exotic or attractive materials, thus enhancing colour and texture contrasts – halberd pendants, amber disc pendants, bead covers, conical and domed covers, hilt-bands and cap-ends (primarily design theme 1). Taylor (1999, 112) remarks that these include some of the most exquisitely executed pieces of goldwork in the whole European Bronze Age.

Although the sheet-cover technique which dominates the above discussion was at times developed to sophisticated levels amongst so-called 'Wessex' goldwork, the basic technique was evidently widespread and of early origins, and it should not in itself be seen as having any particular cultural or regional connotations. The whole of the sheet-cover repertoire seems to have been drawn from three Chalcolithic types – tubular beads, sun-discs and bracer stud-covers – and the Period 2 dagger hilt-bands (Figure 6.3.1). The latter may have had only a limited impact on later sheet-cover morphologies, but instead stimulated the parallel mode of embossed goldwork. No stylistic contribution can be attributed to the impressive ornaments known as lunulae, setting aside rather generic forms of geometric ornament which had wide currency in the early metal age, both here and in continental Europe (e.g. Taylor 1985, 183). Meanwhile basket ornaments underwent a media transfer from gold to bronze at around the Chalcolithic/earliest Bronze Age transition and this may help explain their lack of impact on subsequent developments in goldworking.

The evidence amassed in this project and elsewhere suggests that virtually none, if any, of the sheet-gold covers were totally flat after the primary Beaker phase. In an age of mature utilisation of the resource, there seems to have been widespread appreciation that subtle three-dimensionality gave the object more 'body' because of the way light played across its surface (Needham 2000c, 54–5). In this respect the sheet-cover repertoire was exploiting the same advantageous properties of the material as is seen, in rather more blatant fashion, in the embossed tradition.

While there are clearly some qualitative aspects of selected pieces of goldwork that may draw them together and provide a core 'Wessex' tradition, the analysis of functional/morphological categories and decorative design sophistication shows this to bleed out into the wider repertoire of early second millennium goldwork. As such, it is difficult to delimit a meaningful Wessex tradition, especially since finds from the Wessex region are likely still to be greatly over-represented relative to most other regions. The best evidence for a genuine regional tradition lies in the range of specialised composite material beads and pendants, where intricacy and, in some cases also, ancestral symbolic references are further markers. For the remainder of the goldwork discussed here, it is probably prudent for the present to retain a looser definition, such as the *sheet-gold cover tradition*, to avoid the potentially false connotations implicit in the 'Wessex' label.

7. NECKLACES I: DISC BEADS AND SPACER PLATE NECKLACES

7.1 DISC BEAD NECKLACES (by Alison Sheridan and the main authors)

A list of items studied and illustrated is shown in Table 7.1.1. Entries are ordered in ID sequence of study: East Yorkshire; the Peak District; Wessex, and other regions. The necklaces vary considerably in size and, although it was desirable to illustrate them at a consistent scale for comparative purposes (Figures 7.1.1– 7.1.12), this was not always possible. Nor was it always possible to retain colour accuracy when taking close-up images. Jet and jet/like materials analysis codes: B=Gill Bussell; MD/DH=Mary Davis/Duncan Hook; AS/MD=Alison Sheridan/Mary Davis.

7.1.1 EAST YORKSHIRE

ID 246 Garrowby Wold 64, Painsthorpe (Kirby Underdale), East Yorkshire

References: Mortimer 1905, 137–8, fig. 362; Sheppard 1900, 32; 1929, 49.

COMPOSITION

This single-strand necklace comprises two fusiform beads and, when found, 204 complete disc beads plus 'a few broken discs'. Mortimer (1905, 138) reported that, in addition, a few smaller disc beads may have escaped detection, despite sieving of the clayey soil matrix in which they were found. The current total of disc beads is 203 (although it is uncertain whether any of the fragments are also still extant). The arrangement of beads is apparently unchanged from that shown in Mortimer's figure 362, with the missing disc bead presumably having been lost from among the smallest disc beads at the back of the necklace (i.e. towards the top of Figure 7.1.1). No fastener was found, so either an organic fastener, or else some other method of securing the necklace, had been used. (That the necklace had indeed been fastened when the body was interred is suggested by the clustering of the beads in the neck area, indicating that it was worn on the body).

CONTEXT AND ASSOCIATIONS

The necklace was discovered in an oval rock-cut grave under the centre of a round mound. It was found 'in the clayey soil just above the neck' of an unburnt, decayed contracted skeleton of an adult, on its right side, with head to east. Mortimer stated that the remains were those of a female, but whether this identification was on the basis of the grave goods, or on osteological examination,

Table 7.1.1. List of disc bead necklaces studied and illustrated.

Object	Site (Parish), County	Museum	Illustration
ID 246	Garrowby Wold 64, Painsthorpe (Kirby Underdale), E. Yorks.	Hull	Figure 7.1.1
ID 245, ID 250	Garton Slack 75, E. Yorks.	Hull	Figure 7.1.2
ID 251	Garton Slack VI, burial 1, E. Yorks.	Hull	Figure 7.1.3
ID 252	Garton Slack 29, burial D, E. Yorks.	Hull	Figure 7.1.4
ID 308	Weaverthorpe 44, burial 2, E. Yorks.	BM	Figure 7.1.5
ID 322	Goodmanham 121, burial 6, E. Yorks.	BM	Figure 7.1.6
ID 366	Folkton 245, burial 8, E. Yorks.	BM	Figure 7.1.7
ID 470	Winterbourne Stoke G47, Wilts.	Sal	Figure 7.1.8
ID 491	Preshute G1a, Manton, Wilts.	Dev	Figure 7.1.9
ID 517	Wilsford G39, Wilts.	Dev	Figure 7.1.10
ID 334	Eglingham 200, burial 3, Northumberland	BM	Figure 7.1.11
ID 434	Beggar's Haven/ Devil's Dyke (Poynings), E. Sussex	BM	Figure 7.1.12

is unknown; the former is suspected. A tanged, single-pointed awl of copper or copper alloy was also found, but its location in the grave is not stated. A 'portion of the leg of an animal' had been placed near the skeleton. Under the skeleton, and in the floor of the grave, was a circular hole containing calcined human bones.

MORPHOLOGY

The two fusiform beads are slender to medium girth, with the larger (shown on the left in Figure 7.1.1) being 20.7mm long, 6.7 to 7.3mm in maximum diameter, and with a perforation 3.6mm in diameter. In cross section it is a rounded D-shape. Both ends slope, in opposite directions. Because the necklace could not be removed from its mounted display for examination, it was not possible to examine the shape of the ends in more detail.

The smaller fusiform bead measures 19.2mm long, 6.7 to 7.1mm in maximum diameter and has a relatively wide perforation, 4.9mm wide; it is more of an elongated, flattish-sided 'D' in cross-section than the other fusiform bead. Like its partner, it has sloping, divergent ends.

The disc beads are graded in size, with the smallest strung at the back and the largest at the front (which may well correspond to their original overall arrangement). In external diameter the largest is 7.7mm and the smallest 3.9mm. They range in thickness from 1.1 to 2.85mm. The outer edges are almost all squared off (with just a few having a slightly sloping edge) and most of the beads are parallel-sided. It was not possible to examine the beads in detail, although it appears that the perforation had been central. Mortimer remarked that the disc beads 'are very circular, evenly cut, and truly bored, obviously by metal tools' (1905, 138). The diameter of the perforation, measured in one of the beads between the two fusiform beads, is 2.7mm, and this seems to be typical (to judge from other beads whose perforations are visible).

The overall length of the necklace, as currently strung, is *c.* 365mm; the missing disc bead would have added 1–2mm to this length. This would equate to the modern 'choker' length for a necklace, lying fairly high on the neck but not as tightly as a 'collar'-type necklace.

MATERIAL

Both the fusiform beads are black and dark brown, the smaller of the two having a larger area of dark brown. The larger bead has incipient hairline criss-cross cracking, and both have a fine-grained woody texture. These features are consistent with the material being jet. The disc beads all seem to be of a compact, blackish-grey material; the presence of consolidant makes them appear blacker in parts. Their texture appears stony; this, and the colour, suggests that they are not of jet.

Both the fusiform beads, plus the three disc beads strung between the fusiforms and a small number of the small disc beads at the back of the necklace, were subjected to compositional analysis using X-ray fluorescence spectrometry at the National Museums Scotland Conservation and Analytical Research laboratory in February 2007; the analyst was Lore Troalen. Calcium, probably deriving from the adjacent bones, was found on all the analysed beads. Both the fusiform beads were found to have the 'relatively' high zirconium, low iron content typical of good quality Whitby jet, with one having slightly more titanium than the other. The disc beads had little to minimal zirconium and medium or high iron. This, together with the stony texture of the disc beads, could indicate the use of a non-jet material, perhaps cannel coal or oil shale. This need not mean that the disc beads had not been made around Whitby, however, since oil shale resembling cannel coal is known to occur on the coast around Whitby (Bussell 1976, 72).

MANUFACTURE

The fact that the beads could not be separated out for detailed examination means that only basic information about their manufacture could be recorded. That said, there are no obvious signs of faceting or of grinding striations on the fusiform beads. Their divergent ends could have been a deliberate design feature. Both had been polished, although the original degree of sheen is hard to determine owing to the presence of a thin coating of consolidant which adds to the sheen. It is assumed that they had been perforated from both ends.

There are no obvious tool marks on the disc beads. While their outer edges had been ground smooth, they do not appear to have been polished; the partial sheen seen on many of the beads is once more due to the presence of consolidant. It was not possible to determine whether they had been individually perforated.

COMPLETENESS AND DAMAGE

With the exception of the few broken disc beads referred to by Mortimer (which could have been broken during excavation), the beads appear to be complete and in good condition.

WEAR

While the disc beads show no obvious signs of wear, both of the fusiform beads had clearly seen some wear before deposition (and arguably before being added to the necklace). Thread-smoothing of the perforation was noted in the smaller fusiform bead, and some bead-on-bead wear was noted on both; at one end of the larger bead, this wear seems to have been caused by grinding against another fusiform bead, while the wear at the other end is consistent with grinding from a disc bead. The smaller bead seems to have slight disc bead wear at both ends.

The overall degree of wear is shown on Table 7.1.2. The state of wear of the disc beads is described as indeterminate because in most cases it was not possible to examine the perforation; where it could be seen, however, there were no obvious signs of wear and so these beads could arguably be attributed to the fresh/slight wear category. As noted

Figure 7.1.1. ID 246 Garrowby Wold 64, Painsthorpe. Photograph: National Museums Scotland.

with other necklaces, disc beads often do not show wear, and so it can be hard to assess the duration of their use.

CONCLUSIONS

The two different bead shapes, materials and degrees of wear suggest that the fusiform beads had previously seen use elsewhere, most probably in a spacer plate necklace, before being added to the disc bead necklace. The apparent wear on the fusiform beads from rubbing against disc beads suggests that the necklace had been worn for some time with the fusiform beads present before its interment, although the length of time is hard to determine.

ID 245 and ID 250 Garton Slack barrow 75, (Garton-on-the-Wolds), East Yorkshire

References: Sheppard 1900, 40 and fig. 13; Mortimer 1905, 222–3 and figs 569a (No. 2) and 575a; Sheppard 1929, 80.

COMPOSITION

This is a single-strand disc bead necklace which, when found, comprised 168 disc beads (according to the illustration published in Sheppard 1900 and Mortimer 1905) and a triangular fastener. Today 133 complete and

fragmentary beads survive in the Hull and East Riding Museum, with an additional bead having been removed for neutron activation analysis by Gill Bussell in 1975 or 1976; the fastener (and possibly the 34 outstanding disc beads) appears to have gone missing by 1929 when Sheppard published his last Catalogue of the Mortimer Collection. The complete beads have been removed from a sheet of card, on which they had previously been stored, and were re-strung by the compiler of this record (AS) (Figure 7.1.2).

CONTEXT AND ASSOCIATIONS

The necklace was found in the neck area of the contracted skeleton of an adult woman, lying on her left side, with head to the west, and buried around half-way down the fill of a shaft grave, centrally located under a large round barrow. This individual lay some distance above the primary interment (a contracted skeleton), and below a subsequent interment (of cremated human remains). At her feet lay a heap of cremated human remains. A bronze awl in its wooden handle (ID 1149, Figure 4.6.3) was found behind her shoulders, and a Vase Food Vessel stood upright in front of her head. The sex of the individual has been confirmed within the last five years through osteological examination carried out for the Beaker People Project (Mandy Jay pers. comm.).

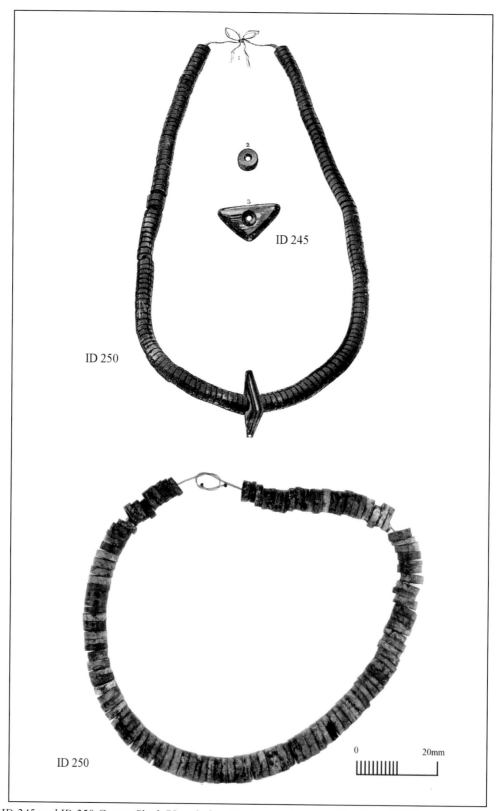

Figure 7.1.2. ID 245 and ID 250 Garton Slack 75 including (top) engraving from Mortimer (1905) which shows (now lost) ID 245 triangular fastener.

MORPHOLOGY

The disc beads are circular, chunky, and relatively uniform in size, ranging in diameter from 5.2 to 6.8mm and in thickness from 1.0 to 2.0mm. With but two exceptions (which are slightly wedge-shaped), the sides are parallel. In most cases the outer edge is straight and perpendicular to the flat sides, but in a few cases the edge tapers slightly. The perforations, which range in diameter between 2.7

and 2.9mm, are central and perpendicular (see below for the direction of drilling). If one multiplies the average thickness of the beads (1.85mm) by the number of beads shown in Mortimer's illustration (168), the original length of the strand would have been around 311mm: not quite long enough to fit comfortably around an adult female's neck without some bead-free thread, and probably worn as a choker-style necklace.

Information about the fastener (ID 245) was obtained from examining the illustration published by Sheppard (1900, fig. 13) and Mortimer (1905, fig. 575; see Figure 7.1.2, top). It was fairly thin (*c.* 3.5mm) and triangular in plan (*c.* 24mm long and *c.* 13.5mm wide), with narrow, gently rounded edges and a central perforation.

MATERIAL

The material of the disc beads is black, with a grey tinge, although numerous beads have a pale grey to creamy-coloured sediment adhering. It is also compact; a few beads show hairline laminar cracking. Where one bead had broken, its interior is black, with a shiny conchoidal fracture – a characteristic of jet. One bead had been analysed by Bussell in 1975 or 1976, using neutron activation analysis (Bussell 1976, 54, table 11 (where it is described incorrectly as 'two halves of biconical bead'), 65, table 21, 66, table 22 and 79). She found it to be 'extremely similar in all [its] characteristic elements to the petrographically defined [raw jet samples]' (1976, 79). Analysis of a fragment of another bead, by Dr J.M. Jones using oil immersion reflected light microscopy and reflectance measurement, led to the same conclusion, and Dr Jones was able to add that the jet used had not been of very high quality, that it matched the jet used for the other Garton Slack disc beads (from Area VI, grave 1 and Area 29, burial D), and that it may have come from the same source. XRF analysis of the same fragment, by Lore Troalen at NMS, did not pick up the zirconium that had been found through NAA in the other bead, but did show clear calcium contamination, either from proximity to the skeleton, or from chalk rubble in the grave fill, or both. The absence of the fastener means that its material cannot be identified, but by analogy with most other triangular fasteners from disc bead necklaces, it is highly likely to be jet.

MANUFACTURE

Only two disc beads have striations running across their flat sides, probably resulting from grinding. In 104 cases the perforation is hourglass-shaped, indicating that the beads had been individually perforated; the junction between the two halves of the hourglass is sharp, and its location is sometimes mid-way through the bead, sometimes not. In 13 cases, the perforation is V-shaped, indicating that it had been drilled mostly or entirely from one side. Several beads have broad rilling, indicating that a bow- or pump-drill had been used; in some cases the rilling is crisp, in others, less so. The outer edge of the beads is smooth but matt.

COMPLETENESS AND DAMAGE

The necklace is likely to have been complete, and seems to have been in good condition, when buried. If Mortimer's illustration of the necklace accurately portrays the original number of beads present (168) and their condition when found, then the fragmentation of some beads will have occurred at some time after the necklace arrived at the Mortimer Museum in Driffield. The loss of 34 beads, and the removal of one other by Bussell for compositional analysis, has already been noted; in addition, part of one of the bead fragments was mounted for reflectance microscopy.

WEAR

Unusually for disc beads, thread-smoothing (and, in a few cases, polish) was noted in the interior of the perforation in some beads, usually just over a half of the circumference. In addition, some have very slight signs of bead-on-bead wear, in the form of localised areas of polish on their flat surfaces. The degree of wear can be described overall as slight (Table 7.1.2). No obvious wear is shown on the engraving of the triangular fastener but, in its absence, its condition can only be described as indeterminate.

CONCLUSIONS

This necklace belongs to a group of necklaces that feature tiny disc beads that are either fairly uniform in diameter, or minimally graded. It is of 'choker' type, and although it had clearly seen some wear, it may not have been very old when buried.

ID 251 Garton Slack, Area VI, grave 1, burial 1, East Yorkshire

References: Brewster 1980, 202–6 and figs. 89–92; Dent 1983, 10; further information from. J. Montgomery pers. comm.

COMPOSITION

This single-strand necklace is reported (by Brewster, the excavator) to have consisted of 180 disc beads, 6 tubular sheet copper alloy beads and one boat-shaped fastener. The copper alloy beads were found at what would have been the front of the necklace, separated from each other by two disc beads apiece (Figure 7.1.3). In the museum there are actually 243 disc beads, plus fragments of several more, labelled as coming from this grave and it seems likely that Brewster's total of '180' had been an estimate (and a considerable underestimate, at that). Forty-three beads were studied in detail for the current project.

CONTEXT AND ASSOCIATIONS

The necklace comes from an oval grave that is assumed to have been covered 'with a scrape mound, probably with an inner capping mound of chalk gravel' (Brewster 1980, 203). Inside the grave was the skeleton of an adult, aged 20–25, identified as probably female but with some male features (see below), crouched on the right side, with head to south and resting on 'a pillow of white gravel' (*ibid*). The necklace was found in front of the chest area, lying in such a way as to suggest that it had been deliberately broken then laid out 'as an extended wavy line as if for display' (Brewster 1980, 205). A set of 13 V-perforated buttons (ID 232–244; Figure 5.3.1) was also found in the same area, lying in an untidy row, with their bases uppermost; Brewster interpreted this as evidence that they had been attached to a garment that had been folded and deposited in the grave in front of the chest. Brewster's account of the relative positions of the necklace and buttons varies: his figure 90 states that the necklace was found below the buttons, but in his description (p. 205) he clearly states that [the necklace] 'must have been laid on top of the garment'; it is assumed that the latter is the correct version. A haematite nodule is present among the material from this grave in the museum, but was not mentioned by Brewster and is likely to represent an accidental addition to the assemblage during its life in the museum. Normally such nodules are assumed to be part of fire-making kits, and are associated with males.

The sex of the skeleton was assessed by Jean Dawes for Brewster, and the note of her identification (in Brewster 1980, 703) is as follows:

'This skeleton was probably that of a woman, though the skull was heavy and had certain apparently male features. She had been between 20 and 25 years old and 155cm in height. There was probably some degree of underbite. There was a slight right maxillary torus and a marked bony projection on each humerus above the deltoid tuberosity at the insertion of the latissimus dorsi. The latter suggests a great deal of habitual heavy muscular effort of the arms. The teeth were all present and healthy though the lower left third molar was much reduced in size. There was very slight calculus and slight periodontal disease.'

The sex of the individual has been confirmed as female within the last five years through osteological examination carried out for the Beaker People Project (J. Montgomery, pers. comm.). That project also assessed the age as 'middle adult.'. The skeleton was radiocarbon-dated (in 2008) to 2299–2057 cal BC (see Chapter 9).

MORPHOLOGY

The overall shape of this single-strand necklace has been described above. The fastener was found immediately adjacent to the disc beads, as if the necklace had been deposited in a fastened state (albeit deliberately broken at the front). It is hard to assess the overall length of the necklace as the beads are stored in an unstrung condition, and some are fragmentary. As drawn in Brewster's slightly schematic figure 92 (Brewster 1980), the overall length is

shown as *c*. 740mm (including gaps between the beads) – making it long enough to extend to mid-chest level on an adult. This tallies with the estimated length of *c*. 750 mm, based on an assumed average disc bead thickness of 2.5mm, and average bronze bead length of 25mm.

The disc beads are small and of relatively uniform diameter, ranging (in the set examined in detail) between 3.5 and 4.6mm in diameter and between 0.9 and 2.8mm in thickness (Figure 7.1.3, inset). They are circular in plan and mostly parallel-sided in profile, with some being slightly wedge-shaped. In most cases the edge is straight and perpendicular to the flat sides, although at least two of the beads (including a relatively thick specimen) have a slightly tapering edge and in at least one, the edge is slightly convex. The perforation is central and perpendicular, ranging in diameter between 1.5 and 2.3mm.

The fastener is boat-shaped. In plan it is a long, narrow oval with round-pointed ends, 19.7mm long, 6.7mm wide and 6.6mm thick. In profile it is roughly triangular (scalene), with a minimally convex base and a rounded apex. It has been perforated through this base, from either side at its widest point, by two perforations forming a very shallow 'V' (Figure 7.1.3, top right). One of these is larger than the other, extending 3.5mm across the base as opposed to just 2.8mm on the other side. The bridge between the perforations is very narrow, at just 1.8mm.

Only three of the six tubular copper alloy beads were examined and the current whereabouts of the others is unclear. These have each been made by bending a thin sheet of copper alloy until the two ends overlap slightly; one is 25.3mm long and 4.9 to 5.4mm in diameter and another is 24.5mm long and 5.2 to 5.6mm in diameter. The third bead is in two fragments, the largest of which is *c*. 15mm long. The metal ranges in thickness between 0.2 and *c*. 0.4mm. The shape of the ends varies, with one having ragged ends, probably from corrosion. Two have small holes in their sides; some of these probably relate to corrosion, although at least one seems to have been deliberately made with a diameter of *c*. 0.4mm. Given the difference in diameter between the metal and the disc beads, the former are likely to have had a wooden core.

MATERIAL

The disc beads are mostly of a black, very slightly laminar material, their black colour intensified by the consolidant with which they have been coated. Three beads stored with the tubular bead found under the pelvis (and possibly found with it) are a dull brown-grey, with a white sediment on their surface. Some beads have transverse cracking. XRF analysis of five of the black and brown-grey beads at NMS by Lore Troalen revealed that they have a relatively high iron content and the ones stored with the bronze bead have a high copper content, from their proximity to the bead. They also have a high calcium content, probably from their proximity to the skeleton. A fragment of a disc bead was also analysed by Dr J.M. Jones using oil immersion reflected light microscopy and reflectance measurement.

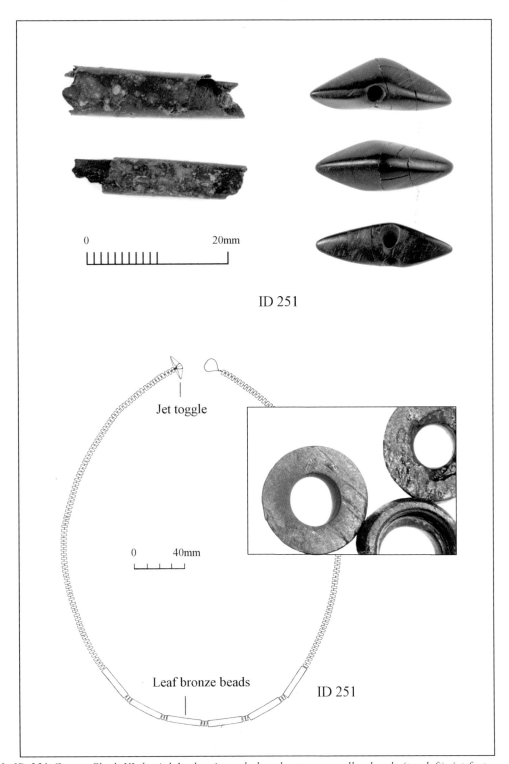

Figure 7.1.3. ID 251 Garton Slack VI, burial 1, showing tubular sheet copper alloy beads (top left), jet fastener (top right), drawing of necklace (from Brewster 1980), and inset showing detail of striations on disc beads.

Dr Jones concluded that they are of relatively low-quality jet. The high iron content may well relate to the presence of pyrites in the jet, or to the former proximity of pyrites.

The fastener is of a compact, black and dark brown material which macroscopically appears to be jet, possibly of soft jet (to judge from the surface criss-cross cracking:

Figure 7.1.3). XRF analysis at NMS confirmed that it is indeed of jet.

Semi-quantitative XRF analysis of the surface of two of the copper alloy beads confirmed the presence of copper and tin, and also the presence of arsenic. This kind of analysis cannot be used to infer the likely source of the copper alloy.

MANUFACTURE

Some of the disc beads that were examined under a microscope have striations running across their flat sides, presumably from grinding them flat (Figure 7.1.3, inset). The perforations are mostly parallel-sided, although three beads have a Y-shaped perforation, suggesting drilling from one side. On one thick bead the perforation is a rounded Y-shape, and the end of the bead at the top of the 'Y' has rounded ends. These beads with Y-shaped perforations could mark the entry of a drill bit into columnar or cigar-shaped roughouts. One bead has faint diagonal nibble striations on its outer edge, probably made to effect a slight convexity of the edge. The outer edge is smooth and matt on some beads, while on others it has a low sheen (ignoring any change in finish caused by the application of consolidant).

The basic shape of the fastener had been achieved through grinding, traces of which survive as striations on the underside (i.e. the inner side, when worn), and on one side of the upper surface (see Figure 7.1.3). The diameter of the drill used to perforate the holes may have been around 2.6mm; it has left faint circumferential rilling. The upper surface had been polished to a high sheen, the underside slightly less so.

The method of manufacture of the copper alloy beads has been described above. The original shape of the sheets will have been roughly rectangular in most cases, but one of the beads illustrated by Brewster (1980, fig. 91.18) seems to have had one curved end. The surfaces had been smooth and had probably been polished; when new, the beads would have been a golden colour.

COMPLETENESS AND DAMAGE

The large number of beads present suggests that the necklace had been complete when deposited. Given the discrepancy between Brewster's total of 180 beads and the observed presence of 243 beads plus fragments of others, however, it is impossible to tell whether any beads had been lost since excavation; the fragmentation of some beads may have occurred during and/or after excavation. The fastener is intact and undamaged.

There are a few signs of ancient damage to some of the disc beads, with chipping to the borehole noted in at least one case and chipping to the outer edge noted in two others. The former will have been caused during the drilling of the hole; whether the latter had also resulted from the manufacture process is harder to tell, but is possible.

The copper alloy bead found in two pieces under the pelvis may be around 70% present; the others are likely to be around 95% complete, with corrosion accounting for the loss of the remaining 5%.

WEAR

No obvious traces of wear were noted on the disc beads, and the fact that striations were observed on the flat sides of several beads indicates that there had not been enough bead-on-bead rotational wear to abrade these. They are classified as slightly worn (Table 7.1.2). There is slight thread-wear on the fastener, in the form of smoothing to the inner edge of the bridge; smoothing to the outer edge of the larger perforation (Figure 7.1.3) and along this perforation, and smoothing of the rilling inside the perforation. Against this is the fact that some of the grinding striations on the underside of the fastener and on one side have survived, along with traces of the rilling in the perforations. The fact that the copper alloy beads are corroded makes it hard to assess the kind and degree of wear on them.

CONCLUSIONS

This necklace belongs to a group of single-strand necklaces (of varying lengths) featuring large numbers of tiny disc beads, which are either fairly uniform in diameter – as here – or which are graded slightly. A close parallel, albeit without tubular sheet bronze beads and with many more disc beads, was found elsewhere in the Garton Slack cemetery at 29, burial D (ID 252), while a shorter disc bead necklace featuring beads that are slightly larger was found at Garton Slack 75 (ID 245, 250).

In contrast to the buttons from the Garton Slack VI, burial 1 grave, some of which show signs of very heavy wear, the necklace does not seem to have been very old when buried. The evidence comes mainly from the fastener, since disc beads tend not to show signs of wear in any case, and as noted above the corrosion to the metal beads makes it hard to assess their degree of wear. If it is assumed that the fastener is the original fastener for the necklace, then the degree of wear is slight. The narrowness of the bridge makes the fastener very fragile, and the fact that it has not broken indicates that it had not been stressed. The fastener has been very skilfully made, as it is difficult to make such shallow perforations without breaking the bridge. The shallowness of the perforations, and the fact that they run across the base, is unusual for a fastener; most boat-shaped fasteners have deeper V-perforations, in line with the long axis of the fastener.

As regards the gender associations of this type of necklace, where skeletons have been reliably sexed, they seem predominantly to be female, although the Chalcolithic example from Chilbolton, Hampshore (Russel 1990) had been found with a male.

ID 252 Garton Slack Area 29, grave 1, burial D, East Yorkshire

References: Brewster 1980, 581 and figs. 412, 414 and 415; Dent 1983, 10.

COMPOSITION

This is a long, single-strand disc bead necklace with a triangular fastener (Figure 7.1.4a). The number of disc beads was reported by Brewster, the excavator, to be 750 but only 722 complete disc beads (plus fragments of at least nine more) were seen and it is suspected that, as with the necklace from Garton Slack Area 6, grave 1, Brewster's figure had just been an estimate. The beads were examined in batches of 50.

CONTEXT AND ASSOCIATIONS

The necklace was associated with the contracted skeleton of an adult female around 35 years old, buried on her right side with head to the south, in a large, irregularly-shaped grave pit along with four other individuals, spaced apart in the pit. The necklace was found close to the left shoulder and near the back of the head, and so had probably been worn around the neck of the corpse. A bronze awl was found close to the beads and fastener, and Brewster has interpreted its presence here (1980, fig. 415) as having been used to secure the loop at the end of the thread, preventing beads from slipping past its end. The skeleton was radiocarbon-dated (in 2008) to 2140–1950 cal BC (see Chapter 9).

MORPHOLOGY

The disc beads are tiny, circular (except in one case where the bead is slightly oval) and very subtly graded in size so that the smallest ones are nearest the ends of the strand. The diameters range from 3.0 to 3.6mm, and the thickness from 0.5 to 2.3mm. The sides are mostly parallel, with

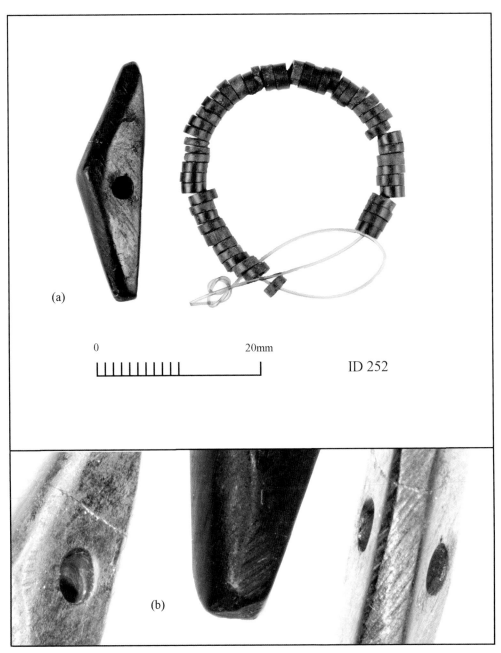

Figure 7.1.4. ID 252 Garton Slack 29, burial D showing (a) a selection of the c. 731 disc beads recorded plus the fastener, (b) details of striations and the perforation on the fastener.

occasional examples being slightly wedge-shaped, and the outer edge is straight and perpendicular to the flat sides. The perforation is central, perpendicular and mostly parallel-sided, ranging in diameter from 1.3 to 2.2mm, and is fairly wide in relation to the overall diameter of the beads. The estimated overall length of the necklace (excluding the fastener) is *c.* 950mm, making it long enough to extend to just above the waist of the woman with whom it had been buried, if worn as a simple long strand.

The fastener is a narrow, scalene-triangular plate, with rounded apices and narrow flattish edges; in profile it broadens towards the apex between the two longest sides, and its upper edge is slightly convex with a gentle ridge at its mid-point. The length is 28.0mm, the height 7.6mm and the maximum thickness is 5.4mm. It has a single, minimally diagonal transverse perforation at mid-length, just below mid-height. At its narrowest the perforation is 2.3mm across, and at its widest, 2.9mm.

MATERIAL

The disc beads are of a black, slightly laminar material with a slight greyish tinge and a 'stony' rather than 'woody' texture that does not macroscopically look very much like jet. One has a brownish, probably iron-rich natural inclusion. X-ray fluorescence (XRF) spectrometric analysis of three beads (at NMS, by Lore Troalen) revealed that there was very little zirconium and low iron, and it also revealed the presence of appreciable amounts of calcium (probably from contact with the skeleton) and copper (probably from the beads' proximity to the bronze awl). Analysis of a small fragment of one bead by Dr J.M. Jones using oil immersion reflected light microscopy and reflectance measurement confirmed that the material is indeed jet, albeit of not very good quality.

The fastener is black, but shows dark brown patches under strong light, and is compact. XRF analysis by Lore Troalen at NMS confirmed that it is of jet. It may be of hard jet.

MANUFACTURE

Many of the disc beads have striations, usually unidirectional, running across their flat sides: these probably relate to their grinding. A minority have nibble striations running across the outer parts of their outer edge. A smaller minority have striations running right across their edge, and in one case a criss-cross pattern of striations was noted. While edge striations are normally found on beads with slightly convex edges, that is not the case here and it is not clear whether their presence here relates instead to preparing beads for separation from a columnar roughout. The perforation is, in most cases, parallel-sided but a few have Y-shaped perforations (as if they had been at the end of the column) and a very few have hourglass perforations indicating that they had been individually drilled from both sides. Broad rilling was noted in the perforation on a few beads. The outer edge had been smoothed (although not enough to erase the striations where these were noted) but left matt

in many cases; with others, the edge had been polished to a low to medium sheen.

That the fastener had been ground into shape is indicated by unidirectional striations along its narrow underside (i.e. the longest edge) and along one other edge, and also by the presence of the gentle keel at its top (Figure 7.1.4b). This indicates where the direction of grinding had changed. The perforation had been bored from both sides, with a ledge two-thirds of the way through indicating the junction between the boreholes. The drill has left internal circumferential rilling, indicating the use of a bow- (or similar) drill. The surfaces had been smoothed (although not enough to erase the striations on two edges) and polished to a low to medium sheen.

COMPLETENESS AND DAMAGE

The large number of beads present suggests that the necklace had been complete when buried. As with the necklace from Garton Slack Area VI, grave 1, the discrepancy between the current total of 722 beads (plus fragments of at least nine more) and Brewster's figure of 750 beads makes it impossible to know whether any beads had been lost since excavation. The fragmentation of a few beads may well have occurred after the necklace had been lifted from the grave. Ancient damage, observed in a few cases, consists of chipping around the borehole (resulting from its drilling) and around the outer edge (again, probably relating to the manufacture process). At some point post-excavation the fastener had broken around a third of the way along, and has been well re-joined. It is complete.

WEAR

There is no obvious evidence for wear on the disc beads. The outer edge of the perforation is generally crisp, and there is no sign of rotary bead-on-bead wear. There is minimal wear on the fastener, limited to one area of thread-polish and edge-smoothing to the perforation on one side; otherwise the ends of the perforation are crisp. Overall, the necklace would fall within the category of slightly worn (Table 7.1.2).

CONCLUSIONS

This necklace shares several features in common with the example from Garton Slack Area VI, grave 1 (ID 251), including the use of the same grade of jet for the disc beads; it may be that this slightly low quality jet had been chosen because of the ease with which it could be shaped into disc beads. Like other necklaces of this type, it does not appear to have been worn for long before burial.

ID 308 Weaverthorpe barrow 44, burial 2, East Yorkshire

Reference: Kinnes and Longworth 1985, 47, no.44.

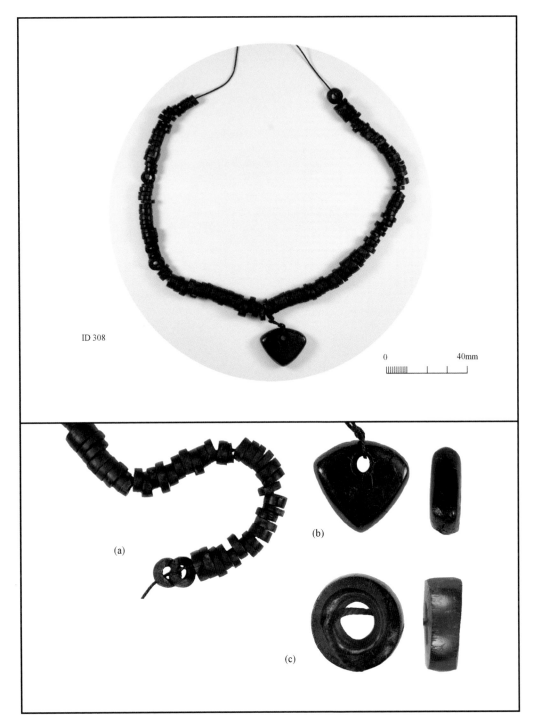

ID 308

0   40mm

Figure 7.1.5. ID 308 Weaverthorpe showing details of (a) both parallel-sided and wedge-shaped beads, (b) fastener exhibiting grinding striations on its edge, and (c) wedge-shaped bead with hour-glass perforation, rilling and nibble striations.

COMPOSITION

The necklace comprises 118 disc beads (of which 114 are currently strung) plus a fastener (Figure 7.1.5). Three of the beads were studied in detail; the rest were examined less closely, not least because all seemed to form a homogeneous set in terms of material and manufacture.

CONTEXT AND ASSOCIATIONS

The necklace was found at the neck of the contracted skeleton of an adult female, buried in a shallow grave under the centre of a round barrow. She had been laid on her right with her head towards the east. A pot described by the excavator, Canon Greenwell, as a 'Food Vessel' lay behind the head; its current whereabouts are not known.

MORPHOLOGY

The beads are circular and mostly parallel-sided (Figure 7.1.5a), with a few being wedge-shaped (Figure 7.1.5c). Their outer edge ranges from straight to slightly convex, and in some cases slopes very gently. They are generally small and many have a chunky appearance. Graded in size, they range in diameter from 4.9 to 8.6mm and in thickness from 1.4 to 5.3mm. They had almost certainly been arranged with the smallest beads towards the back and the largest at the front, although that arrangement is not followed in the current stringing. The perforation is mostly central and hourglass-shaped (Figure 7.1.5c), with generally crisp edges; perforation diameter ranges from 2.4 to 3.5mm.

The fastener is sub-triangular, with convex edges; it is roughly rectangular in vertical section, with rounded top and bottom (Figure 7.1.5b). There is no obvious front or back side. The length is 17.5mm, the width 21.4mm and thickness 6.6mm. Midway along the most convex edge is a single perpendicular hourglass perforation, 14.2mm wide on one side and 4.8mm on the other.

MATERIAL

The beads all appear to be of the same material: a compact black and mottled black-brown material (predominantly brown in two cases), with laminar cracking in some beads (Figure 7.1.5a) and criss-cross cracking in at least one case. Three beads studied in detail have a fine-grained woody texture. From visual inspection all the beads appear to be probably of jet, albeit not the same jet as that used for the fastener. However, XRF analysis of one bead in 2007 (MD/DH) indicated that it has a high iron content. In texture this bead does not resemble cannel coal, so the possibility that the material is a slightly laminar, high-iron jet cannot be excluded, especially given that similar material had been identified as a poor-quality jet in two necklaces from Garton Slack (ID 251 and 252).

The colour of the fastener is black, but brownish in the perforation and elsewhere where the sub-surface has been exposed. There is irregular criss-cross cracking which is deeper on one side than on the other, and with some loss of spalls due to this cracking on that side. A woody texture is visible in spall scars. Visual identification (high confidence: AS/MD) suggests it to be of soft jet. No analysis was undertaken.

MANUFACTURE

Many beads have tiny transverse nibble striations around their outer edge (Figure 7.1.5c) and, in contrast to some other necklaces' disc beads, it does not appear that this scoring had been undertaken to make the edge convex. The hourglass shape of the perforation indicates that the beads had been individually drilled, and there is clear circumferential rilling in all of the closely-examined beads (Figure 7.1.7c). The beads' outer edge had been polished, in some cases to a medium sheen, in others to a low sheen; the presence of a coating of consolidant obscures the degree of sheen in many of the beads.

Grinding striations are evident on the edges of the fastener; these are mostly uni-directional and some are quite deep (Figure 7.1.5b). There are almost gouge-like grooves at one point on one edge. The perforation shows circumferential rilling. The fastener has been polished to a low to medium sheen, higher on the broad sides than on the edges, although this has been partly obscured by consolidant.

COMPLETENESS AND DAMAGE

Four beads are fragmentary, and all of the complete beads have been coated with a consolidant, which obscures details such as wear traces. There are no signs of ancient damage. One small ancient spall is evident at one edge of the perforation in the fastener; otherwise minor loss of spalls from one side is due to cracking. The fastener has been coated with a consolidant.

WEAR

Thread-wear was noted in two of the three beads studied in detail. One has thread-polish to one side of the perforation, together with smoothing of the edges of the perforation at this point. The other has similar perforation-edge smoothing at one point. No obvious bead-on-bead wear was detected. The overall degree of wear was slight to medium (Table 7.1.2). Thread-smoothing is evident within the perforation towards the edge of the fastener. There is also minor thread-pull wear on both flat surfaces above the perforation. The overall degree of wear is slight to medium.

CONCLUSIONS

The estimated overall length of *c.* 340mm is sufficient for this to have been worn as a 'choker' type necklace. This necklace falls within the category of small, chunky, size-graded disc bead necklaces. The shape of the fastener is not exactly paralleled elsewhere but variability in fastener shape is a feature of disc bead necklaces, especially in northern England.

The wear traces show that the necklace had been worn before burial, although not for long enough to produce heavy wear. The slight difference in the texture of the material used for the beads and the fastener makes sense in terms of selecting material that can readily be shaped into disc beads; a piece of soft jet has been used for the fastener, in common with those seen on many other disc-bead necklaces.

ID 322 Goodmanham barrow 121, burial 6, East Yorkshire

References: Greenwell and Rolleston 1877, 329–31; Kinnes and Longworth 1985, 89, no. 121, burial 6, 3.

COMPOSITION

The necklace comprised 124 small disc beads (of which 123 were seen during this study; the whereabouts of the 124th are unknown) and one mitriform object, described by Kinnes and Longworth as a pendant but probably a fastener (Figure 7.1.6). The necklace was not de-strung for examination or analysis. While all of the disc beads were inspected under a microscope, only four (namely the largest, smallest, thinnest and thickest) were recorded in detail, but these seemed to be a representative sub-set.

CONTEXT AND ASSOCIATIONS

The necklace was associated with the contracted skeleton of an adolescent lying on its right side, with head to west-north-west, at the base of a central grave (orientated south-south-east/north-north-west) under an oval barrow. Mention of 'chalk fill with basal wood lining' (Kinnes and Longworth 1985, 89) suggests the possible former presence of a wooden grave chamber, or at least a woodlined grave. The necklace was found 'in place' (thus presumably in the neck area). Lumps of 'a yellowish substance', probably ochre, were found near the body.

MORPHOLOGY

The disc beads are small and subtly graded in size, ranging in diameter from 4.4 to 6.6mm, and slightly chunky, ranging in thickness between 1.7 and 2.7mm. The perforations are mostly central but in some cases slightly eccentric, ranging in diameter from 2.4 to 3.8mm. The beads are almost all neatly circular, and their flat sides are mostly parallel; a few markedly wedge-shaped beads are present. Their edge is perpendicular to the flat surfaces, and either straight or in some cases minimally convex.

The fastener is mitriform, its shape made by cutting two V-shaped segments from a chunky, minimally wedge-shaped disc (Figure 7.1.6b). The diameter ranges between 14.7 and 16.7mm. The maximum thickness is 6.7mm, thinning slightly towards the cut segment. It has a central, hourglass-shaped perforation 2.8mm wide at its narrowest point and 8.7mm at its widest (on one side).

MATERIAL

Macroscopically, the material for all the components appears to be jet (AS/MD). In colour, the beads are blackish-brown, with some appearing mostly brown, others mostly black; the fastener is also blackish-brown but browner than the disc beads. In texture, many of the disc beads have slight or more marked wood grain. In terms of surface condition, several of the beads have hairline laminar cracks, while the fastener has deep radial cracks and extensive hairline criss-cross cracking, with some loss of tiny chips from where the deep cracks have sprung apart. This suggests that soft jet had been used, at least for the fastener.

The fastener and one of the beads were analysed at the British Museum (MD/DH) by XRF. The fastener was found to be of jet, but possibly of a low quality, given its iron content (assessed as 'medium'). A high calcium reading probably derives from the fastener's proximity to the skeleton. The analysed bead was found to be possibly of lignite, or else poor quality jet, with only a trace amount of zirconium and a slight to medium iron content (zirconium being one of the indicator elements for jet). By analogy with other disc bead necklaces (e.g. from Garton Slack, ID 245/250 and 251), it is likely that this is low grade jet. While the analysed disc bead did not have any calcium contamination, it did register a trace presence of copper and a medium presence of tin; this may well relate to the use of a bronze drill bit to create the perforation.

MANUFACTURE

Two of the disc beads are not truly circular in plan but have traces of the facets that would have been prepared in their initial roughing-out; one of these can be seen just right of the centre in Figure 7.1.6a. Several beads have nibbling – short transverse striations – on their edge, and this is just visible as faint lines on a few of the beads in Figure 7.1.6a (around 10 beads to the right of the faceted example). As discussed in Chapter 7.3 and as borne out by the edge shape of the beads in question, it may be that these striations related to the creation of a slightly convex edge. The subsequent polishing of the edge (to a low to medium sheen) has failed to remove these marks. Where it has been possible to inspect the perforation, it seems to have been drilled from one side, although with the largest bead there are hints that it might have been perforated from both sides. Rilling, suggesting the use of a bow-drill, was noted in the interior of the perforation on several beads and, as indicated above, the compositional analysis of one bead suggests the probable use of a bronze drill bit.

The outer edge of the fastener has faint faceting from its process of manufacture, and there are multidirectional striations that are quite deep and gouge-like. This may indicate the use of a knife to shape the fastener and, in particular, to cut the V-segments. Polishing has smoothed over the cuts around the edge but the ones in the V-cuts have been left clearly visible, with just minimal polishing. There are no manufacturing striations on the flat surfaces, one of which has a low sheen, the other a medium sheen. The perforation has been drilled from both sides and there are traces of circumferential rilling. On one side the drill may have been re-positioned as its hole is less neatly executed than on the other side.

COMPLETENESS AND DAMAGE

The disc beads are intact, except for one ancient spall scar noted on the thinnest bead (probably resulting from the manufacturing process). The loss of tiny chips from the fastener, due to the cracks having sprung, makes it 99% complete but it would have been complete when deposited.

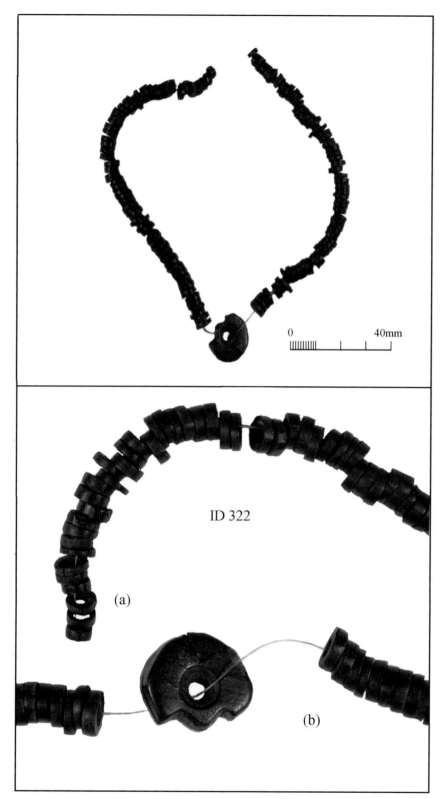

Figure 7.1.6. ID 322 Goodmanham showing details of (a) faint nibble striations visible on a few of the beads, and (b) detail of fastener.

WEAR

The edges of the perforations on the disc beads are generally crisp, but slight thread-wear to one area of the perforation (in the form of the smoothing of the edge) was noted on three of the four beads that were subjected to particularly close scrutiny. All four of these beads had slight polish on the high points of their flat surfaces, indicating bead-on-bead wear which is assumed to have taken place before the necklace's burial. This indicates that the necklace had been worn, though not necessarily for a long time, prior to burial. The fastener has slight traces of thread-smoothing over one part of its perforation. This has smoothed the rilling on one side and at the narrowest point of the perforation and also indicates that the necklace had seen some use, although it is not heavily worn. Given that the four disc beads that were recorded in detail are representative of all the beads, the overall wear can be summarised as slight (Table 7.1.2).

CONCLUSIONS

This necklace, which was probably not very old when buried, belongs to a group of disc bead necklaces characterised by small, sometimes chunky beads which are either of uniform diameter or which are subtly graded in size. The beads are generally somewhat thicker than those found in necklaces featuring larger disc beads that are more markedly graded in diameter. The necklace has been very well made and it is clear that the disc beads had been made as a set. The choice of a low grade jet for their manufacture may well have been deliberate, as its slightly laminar structure will have facilitated the detachment of individual beads from a cylindrical roughout (if this had indeed been the method used).

ID 366 Folkton barrow 245 ('Bording Dale'), burial 8, East Yorkshire

References: Excavations Annual Report 1969; Kinnes and Longworth 1985, 116, no. 245, burial 8, 8.

COMPOSITION

According to Kinnes and Longworth (1985, 116, no. 245, burial 8, 8), the necklace comprised 160 disc beads, but 163 were counted during this study, 91 of which are strung together and accompanied by a card label that reads 'Bordingdale Barrow 1 TR VI Sect Q_2 + R_2 Grave III Jet beads 91' (Figure 7.1.7a). The remaining 72 are strung on a separate string (Figure 7.1.7b). Four beads from each of the two sets of beads were recorded in detail, but all were examined under a microscope.

CONTEXT AND ASSOCIATIONS

The necklace was found in the neck area of a contracted skeleton of an adolescent (also described by Kinnes and Longworth as a 'child'), lying on the right side with head to the west, in an east-west orientated grave, south-west of centre under a round barrow believed to be the same barrow as the one excavated by Canon Greenwell in 1889. It was excavated by T.C.M. Brewster in 1969. Two All-Over-Cord Beakers were found at the shoulder; the skull and fragments of post-cranial bones of an infant were also present. A broken bone belt ring (ID 750, Figure 3.4.1) was found in the lower part of the grave fill, along with a flint scraper and two flint flakes.

MORPHOLOGY

The beads are small and of fairly uniform diameter, ranging between 4.5 and 6.3mm. They are mostly chunky, varying widely in thickness between 1.3 and 6.4mm. Assuming an average thickness of 3mm, when strung as a single strand (extending nearly 500mm) the necklace would have hung down to a few centimetres below the collarbone; in modern necklace terminology, it would count as 'Princess' length, somewhat longer than the 'choker' length represented by several other disc bead necklaces. The perforations are mostly central and perpendicular, ranging in diameter from 1.5 to 4.2mm. The beads are circular in plan; most are parallel-sided, but quite a high proportion are slightly or markedly wedge-shaped (Figure 7.1.7c). The shape of the edge varies from straight and perpendicular to the flat sides, to slightly convex. In a few cases it slopes and in one case, a particularly thick bead, it is even slightly concave.

MATERIAL

Macroscopically the material appears to be jet in every case (AS/MD). In colour the beads range from black to blackish-brown. Wood grain was visible in a couple of cases, and, where present, the laminar cracking follows the line of the wood grain. One bead from the 72-bead strand has a shiny conchoidal flake scar – a classic indicator of jet. Another characteristic of jet, an 'orange peel'-like hollow, was noted on one of the beads in the labelled strand. On the 72-bead strand, one bead has a natural inclusion of a quartz grain. Analysis at the British Museum (MD/DH), using XRF, confirmed the identification as jet. Given the relatively minor amount of cracking, it is likely that hard jet had been used.

MANUFACTURE

A distinctive feature of this necklace is the presence of a significant minority of beads in each strand (nine, in the case of the labelled strand) bearing very clear transverse nibble striations on their edge (Figure 7.1.7d and e). While this nibbling has been noted on disc beads in several other necklaces (e.g. ID 322 Goodmanham), the Folkton necklace offers by far the clearest expression of this feature and indeed it may well be that the beads in question had been added to the necklace, since the quality of their manufacture is lower than that seen on the remainder of the beads. Since all the beads in question have convex outer surfaces, it seems likely that the nibbling had been undertaken to create this convexity. The nibbling traces had not been polished away and these beads have a much less glossy edge than the other beads. Furthermore, their perforation is significantly narrower than that of the other beads, confirming the suspicion that they had been made by a different person.

That the perforation in most of the beads in the necklace had been drilled from both sides is indicated by the (usually asymmetrical) hourglass shape of some of the perforations. The drill bit had also been re-positioned in several cases

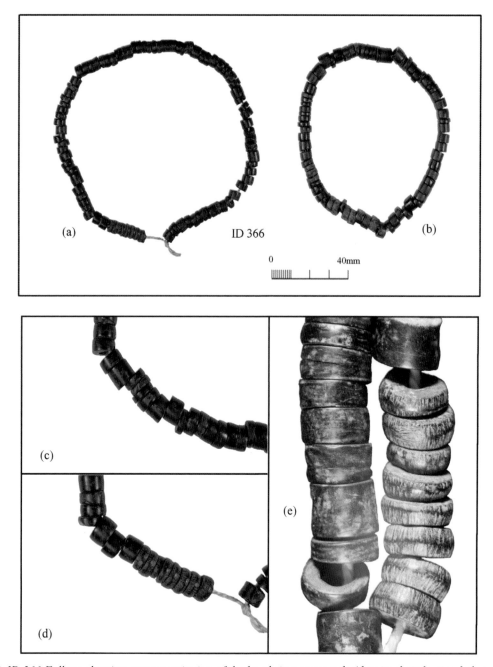

Figure 7.1.7. ID 366 Folkton showing current stringing of the beads in two strands (despite their having belonged to a single necklace originally): (a) the strand labelled 'Bordingdale Barrow', and (b) the remaining disc beads. Details show: (c) both circular and wedge-shaped beads; (d) clear manufacturing nibble striations on the eight beads at the end of the strand, and (e) closer view of nibble striations.

– sometimes on each side of the bead (as clearly seen in the thickest of the beads in the labelled strand). The perforation is, in most cases, relatively wide and where there have been mis-bores, the end of the bit is revealed to have been rounded. Circumferential rilling was noted inside the perforation on many beads indicating the use of a bow- or pump-action drill. With the exception of the nibbled beads described above, the edge of the beads had been polished to a medium or high sheen.

COMPLETENESS AND DAMAGE

One of the beads in the 72-bead strand has part of one side missing; this represents ancient damage during manufacture and probably relates to the fact that a quartz grain is naturally embedded (see above). Otherwise there is very minor ancient chipping to one or two beads. It is likely that the necklace is complete, unless there had been an organic fastener (see below).

Table 7.1.2. Wear on selected necklace items.

Object no.	Type	Fresh/slight wear	Worn	Very worn	Indet.	Total
ID 246	Fusiform	-	2	-	-	2
	Disc	-	-	-	203	203
ID 250	Disc	133	-	-	-	133
ID 245	Fastener	-	-	-	1	1
ID 251	Disc	243	-	-	-	243
	Copper tubular	-	-	-	6	6
ID 252	Disc	731	-	-	-	731
	Fastener	1	-	-	-	1
ID 308	Disc	118	-	-	-	118
	Fastener	1	-	-	-	1
ID 322	Disc	123	-	-	-	123
	Fastener	1	-	-	-	1
ID 366	Disc	-	163	-	-	163
ID 470.1-37	Disc	37+	-	-	-	37+
ID 491	Disc	-	-	-	144	144
ID 517	Disc	12	-	-	-	12
ID 334	Fusiform	-	6	2	-	8
	Disc	92	-	-	-	92
ID 434	Disc	-	-	-	14	14
	Copper tubular	-	-	-	5+	5+

WEAR

The beads that have the nibble striations do not show obvious signs of wear other than perhaps wear-polish on the highest part of their edge, but on several of the other beads there is clear evidence for thread- and/or bead-on-bead wear. The thread-wear takes the form of smoothing of the edge of the perforation and, in those cases where the perforation narrows, smoothing of the narrowest part of the perforation. The bead-on-bead wear takes the form of slight polish to the flat sides. In terms of overall wear, and bearing in mind the variation between the beads, the necklace can be classed as moderately worn.

CONCLUSIONS

This necklace belongs to a group of necklaces made from small, usually fairly chunky disc beads that vary little in their diameter. The absence of a fastener could mean either that the necklace had been secured by simply tying the thread (a parallel for which is offered by a disc bead necklace from Barns Farm, Fife: Watkins 1982, 67 and pl. 6), or else that an organic fastener had been used and had decayed completely.

As noted above, the fact that a few beads differ from the rest in being less highly polished, in having nibble striations and comparatively narrow perforations and in appearing less worn than some of the others, suggests that these may have been added to the necklace after the rest of the beads had been made as a single set.

7.1.2 WESSEX

ID 470. 1–37 Winterbourne Stoke G47, Greenlands Farm, Wiltshire

References: Gingell 1988, 58–63; Beck and Shennan 1991, 182.

COMPOSITION

This is a composite necklace, comprising 30 complete or near-complete disc beads of Kimmeridge shale, plus fragments of at least eight further disc beads of the same material, along with two large fusiform beads of amber (confusingly described as 'oblate' in Gingell 1988), and two small oblate (fat annular) beads of amber. The disc beads are illustrated in their storage layout in Figure 7.1.8; the four amber beads are discussed in detail in Chapter 8.2.1, and illustrated in Figure 8.2.1.

CONTEXT AND ASSOCIATIONS

The necklace derives from a 'central' (actually slightly eccentric) grave under a large disc barrow, associated with the cremated remains of an adult, at least 25 years old, of indeterminate sex, plus a Series 5 dagger (ID 1183, Figure 3.1.9), bronze awl (ID 1176, Figure 6.4.2) and traces of twined coarse grass or rushes, possibly representing matting. Two microscopic fragments, one of silver, the other gold, were found during sieving of a 'brown substance from the base of the cremation centre', originally thought to be a leather bag but found to consist instead of charcoal, soil particles, chalk and bone.

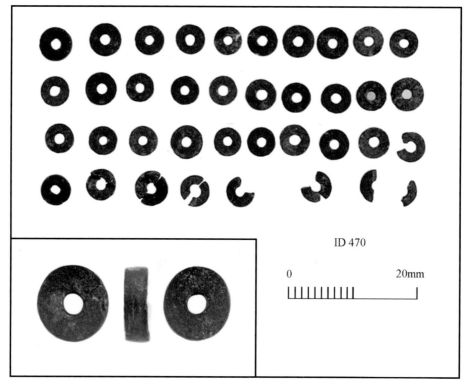

Figure 7.1.8. ID 470 Winterbourne Stoke G47 showing the shale disc beads in their storage layout together with detail of an individual, parallel-sided bead. Note that its outer edges are actually straighter than they appear in the specific lighting of this image. See Figure 8.2.1 for the amber beads from this necklace.

MORPHOLOGY

The shale disc beads are all circular in profile, thin, and of fairly consistent external diameter (4.7 to 5.5mm), thickness (0.8 to 2.0mm), and perforation diameter (1.4 to 2.0mm) (Figure 7.1.8). Just under half are parallel-sided, the rest being slightly wedge-shaped; the edge is neatly squared off and perpendicular to the flat surfaces in each case. The borehole is perpendicular and central in some beads, slightly eccentric in others; in most cases it is funnel-shaped, but in three cases it is parallel-sided.

MATERIAL

The beads are all of a compact laminar material, of a speckled black and dark brown colour (varying between beads in the dominance of black and brown), with a stony texture. Macroscopically it appears to be of Kimmeridge shale (AS).

MANUFACTURE

There are no striations on the flat sides of the disc beads to indicate the manner of shaping the beads, but the funnel shape of the borehole in most beads indicates that the beads were individually perforated, from one side. The prevalence of chipping around the borehole suggests that the person drilling the hole might not have made a small starter hole at the other side, to prevent chipping

as the drill bit penetrated the far surface. In one bead, an internal ledge indicates where the drill was repositioned. The interior of the borehole is smooth. The outer edge had not been polished.

COMPLETENESS AND DAMAGE

These are fragile and vary in their degree of completeness from 100% to <5%. The more complete examples have been treated with a consolidant, possibly carbowax. All, or virtually all the beads have ancient chipping or spalling to one or both sides, usually around the borehole and sometimes extending from there to the edge; this is likely to have occurred during their perforation. The beads are matt all over (except for a very slight sheen on the flat surface of many beads).

WEAR

It is unclear whether the smoothness of the borehole in the disc beads is due to thread-wear, but the edges of the borehole are crisp. The only sign suggesting wear is a slight sheen on the flat surface of many of the beads, possibly caused by bead-on-bead wear.

CONCLUSIONS

Overall, the dominant impression of the disc beads is of

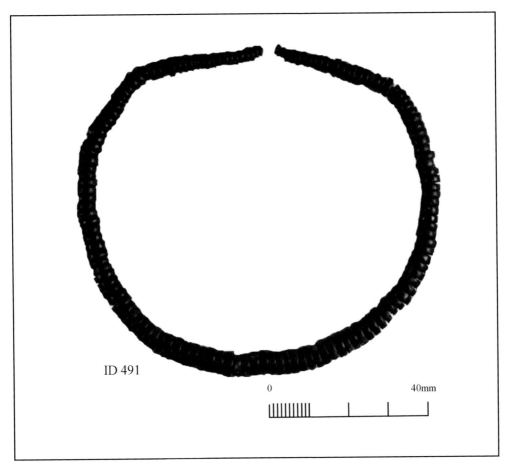

ID 491

0   40mm

Figure 7.1.9. ID 491 Preshute G1a (Manton). See Figure 8.5.1 for the amber and encrinite beads from this necklace.

little use and slight wear, although wear was recorded in detail for only 20 examples. Little wear was recorded on the associated amber fusiform examples (Chapter 8.2.1).

ID 491 The Manton Barrow, Preshute G1a, Wiltshire

References: Cunnington 1908; Piggott 1938, 105; Grinsell 1957, 187–8; Annable and Simpson 1964, no. 203; Gerloff 1975, no. 241; Pollard *et al.* 1981, table 5; Bussell *et al.* 1982, 29; Beck and Shennan 1991, 167.

COMPOSITION

This is a single-strand necklace comprising150 disc beads, of which 144 are strung in the museum display and are made of ?lignite (Bussell *et al.* 1982), plus a stem joint of a fossil encrinite, used as a bead (but not strung on the necklace in the display), and five 'small much decayed amber beads' (Figure 7.1.9). As with the Winterbourne Stoke G47 necklace (ID 470), this is actually a composite necklace, although it differs from most such necklaces in being dominated by one type of bead, of one material. The amber and encrinite beads are considered in Chapter 8.5.1; see also Figure 8.5.1.

CONTEXT AND ASSOCIATIONS

The necklace was found in a primary grave under a bowl barrow, lying 'in a little heap', *c.* 15–20cm from the head of the contracted skeleton of an 'aged female', lying on her left side, orientated south-east to north-west. Her head was to the south-east and was bent towards her chest. Elsewhere in the grave were found a halberd pendant of bronze and gold (ID 1422, Figure 5.9.1), found beside a biconical gold-bound bead probably of shale and a gold-bound amber disc pendant (ID 1420, Figure 5.9.1); a fired clay stud (probably a labret or an ear stud; ID 1423, Figure 5.6.2); a fluted bead of ?lignite, found beside a chalk bead and quoit-like ring bead of ?steatite ('some pinkish substance resembling soft stone'); two knife-daggers (ID 1430 and lost), one with an amber pommel (ID 1429); fragments of three bronze awls (ID 1426–8); a grape cup and a second accessory vessel; remains and impressions of woven cloth, of more than one type; traces of wood, found around the head, and a deposit of clayey soil containing decayed fragments of bone (see also Chapter 8.5.1 where the non-disc beads are described).

MORPHOLOGY

As the necklace is tightly strung, it was decided to record in detail only the largest, smallest, thinnest and fattest beads.

The photograph (Figure 7.1.9) gives an overall impression of the necklace as currently strung (without its non-?lignite elements). The disc beads are tiny and graded in diameter between 2.8 and 6.3mm; they range in thickness between 1.0 and 2.9mm, and the borehole diameter is 1mm. When laid together they form a strand *c.* 290mm long, and the necklace would originally have been just over 300mm long, not long enough to encircle an adult female neck (for which a circumference of *c.* 360mm would be normal) without a stretch of 'blank' thread at the back. In theory the beads could have been worn as a bracelet, although they would have had to be wrapped around the wrist; it is assumed that they had been worn instead as a 'choker'-type necklace. In plan the beads are circular to sub-circular and mostly parallel-sided, with a slightly convex edge. In a few cases the edge slopes slightly. The borehole is perpendicular, narrow, neatly executed and slightly eccentric, and in the two beads where its shape is clearly visible, it is parallel-sided.

MATERIAL

The beads are clearly all of the same material (AS): a compact, black to black-grey, non-jet material that takes a satiny sheen, which Bussell (Bussell *et al.* 1982, B9) tentatively identified as '?lignite' on the basis of XRF compositional analysis, later confirmed by Pollard *et al.* (1981). One bead has a hairline laminar crack. The material is the same as that used for the fluted bead.

MANUFACTURE

The fact that this necklace could not be dismantled for examination, and that it was not examined under a microscope, limits the amount that can be said. No obvious striations were noted upon macroscopic inspection. The very slight curvature of the edge of some beads suggests that they were individually shaped after being made into their circular shape. One bead has a markedly rounded side-edge junction. The shape of the perforation makes it hard to determine whether the beads had been individually perforated, or drilled while on a hypothetical roughout block. The outer edge of the beads had been polished to a low to medium satiny sheen; two beads have a slightly higher sheen.

COMPLETENESS AND DAMAGE

The condition of the six missing beads could not be determined, but the 144 on the string are all either complete, or nearly so, missing only tiny chips from their outer edge. It was not noted whether they had been treated with consolidant.

WEAR

Given that the flat sides and perforations of most of the beads could not be seen, the degree of wear must be recorded as indeterminate.

CONCLUSIONS

Little can be concluded about the age of this necklace when buried, other than to say that the disc beads had clearly all belonged to a single necklace, rather than being acquired piecemeal.

ID 517 Wilsford G39, Wiltshire

References: Hoare 1810, 210; Annable and Simpson 1964, no. 480; Bussell *et al.* 1982, 31, no.71.

COMPOSITION

The necklace consists of 12 disc beads, although 15 were noted by Annable and Simpson (1964, no. 480) and, according to Colt Hoare's original description, 20–30 were originally found (Hoare 1810, 210) (Figure 7.1.10).

CONTEXT AND ASSOCIATIONS

The necklace was found in a grave – possibly in a primary position – under a bowl barrow; it accompanied cremated remains and a bone pin (lost).

MORPHOLOGY

The disc beads are small and circular in plan, of fairly uniform external diameter (6.0 to 6.4mm) and thickness (1.4 to 2.3mm), and have a perforation diameter of 2.4 to 3.0mm. Half are parallel-sided, the rest being slightly wedge-shaped. The outer edge is minimally convex in nine beads, and angled in the remaining three. The perforation is central and perpendicular; its shape varies from parallel-sided (six beads) to V-shaped (five beads) and hourglass-shaped (one bead). The outer edge is matt, as are the flat surfaces.

MATERIAL

Superficially, all the beads appear to have been made of the same blackish (or black-brown) compact, slightly laminar material whose fracture surfaces are dull and non-conchoidal. However, several beads are slightly speckled, a feature noted on Kimmeridge shale (AS), and on some beads the surface has cracked in a criss-cross pattern. On one bead a slightly woody texture is visible in a chip scar. This may therefore suggest the use of more than one material. The beads were analysed by Gill Bussell, using XRF, and reported to be of jet (Bussell *et al.* 1982, no. 71; it is not known whether all the beads were analysed). However, if this identification is correct, then this is not good quality jet; it is reminiscent of the low-grade jet used to make some of the tiny disc beads in north-east England (e.g. at Garton Slack VI, ID 251). It may have come from the Whitby area. However, given that Bussell *et al.*'s identification of the Amesbury G39 items as 'jet' has been revised in the light of further XRF analysis by Mark Pollard,

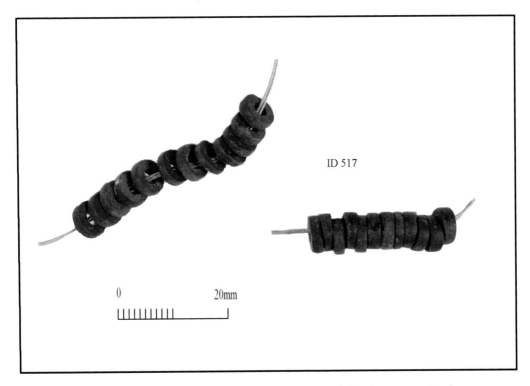

Figure 7.1.10. ID 517 Wilsford G39 showing views of the 12 surviving beads.

as 'Kimmeridge shale' (quoted in Woodward 1991, 102–3), then it would arguably be worth re-analysing these beads to check whether they, too, might be of Kimmeridge shale (despite the criss-cross cracking, and the slightly woody texture of one bead). The Kimmeridge jet deposits should be re-examined as well, to determine whether material resembling this can be found among those deposits. For the moment, then, the material identification should be restricted to 'jet?' (or 'jet-like'), with the proviso that future analysis may reveal that it is really Kimmeridge shale, or a mixture of Kimmeridge shale and jet.

MANUFACTURE

The minimally convex shape of the edge of most beads suggests that they had been individually shaped, although whether they had originally been detached from a cylindrical roughout block or not is harder to determine. Evidence that might support such an interpretation comes from the fact that one bead has a slightly faceted shape in side view, and another has one deeply-dished side: these features could conceivably indicate that these had been the end beads on such a roughout block. According to the borehole shape, however, the beads (or at least some of them) were individually perforated: the V-shaped boreholes indicate that the drilling was done from one side (with perhaps a starter hole on the other side, to prevent chipping around the borehole), while the hourglass-shaped perforation shows that that bead was drilled from both sides. Faint rilling marks, noted in the perforations of four beads, indicate the use of a bow- or pump-action drill. The outer edge was not polished.

COMPLETENESS AND DAMAGE

The beads are all between 97 and 100% complete. Damage consists of ancient chipping to the borehole, noted in eight beads, plus additional ancient chipping or spalling from the edge, noted on six beads. The beads had been consolidated.

WEAR

The edges of the perforation are crisp, although there are traces of slight thread-polish to the inside of the perforation, just inside the end, in all but two of the beads. In once case the perforation interior is obscured by consolidant. Slight bead-on-bead wear in the form of slight polish at the highest part of the surface was noted on five beads. Overall the degree of wear can be described as slight (Table 7.1.2).

CONCLUSIONS

It appears that the necklace had seen some wear before its burial. It is hard to assess how long the necklace had been worn since disc beads tend to display wear marks less than fusiform beads.

7.1.3 OTHER REGIONS

ID 334 Eglingham (Blawearie) barrow 200, burial 3, Northumberland

References: Greenwell 1868, 203–4; Greenwell and Rolleston 1877, 418–21; Kinnes and Longworth 1985, 103, no. 200, burial 3, 2.

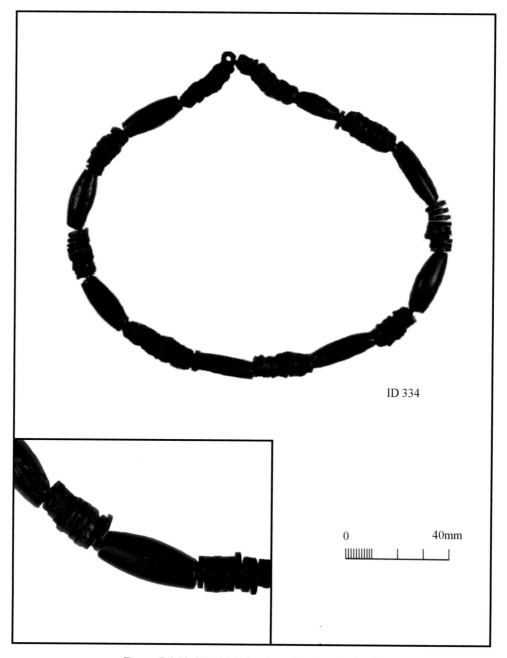

ID 334

0   40mm

Figure 7.1.11. ID 334 Eglingham, Northumberland.

COMPOSITION

This is a disc and fusiform bead necklace, comprising eight fusiform and 92 disc beads (Figure 7.1.11).

CONTEXT AND ASSOCIATIONS

The necklace was found in the northern corner of a disturbed, non-central cist under a round cairn. Also present in the cist were a flint knife and possible traces of a decayed skeleton. Given the necklace's position, it is likely to have been worn by the corpse when interred, and suggests that the corpse had been laid on the left side, with the head to the north.

MORPHOLOGY

The disc beads are thin and slightly graded in size, ranging in diameter from 4.4 to 8.7mm and in thickness from 1.1 to 1.6mm. They are currently strung in groups between the fusiform beads, with each group itself graded (to a certain extent) so that the widest beads are in the centre, echoing the shape of the fusiform beads (Figure 7.1.11, detail). Whether this corresponds at all with the original arrangement of the beads, or the arrangement when found, is unknown. The beads are neatly circular, their flat sides parallel and their edge straight and perpendicular to their flat sides in most cases. The perforation is also perpendicular and, in most cases, central; it ranges in diameter between 1.9 and 2.5mm. The beads are a blackish-grey colour.

The fusiform beads range in length from 17.2 to 24.2mm, and in maximum diameter from 7.2 to 8.2mm; one is relatively slender, the others, of medium-thickness to plump. In mid-point cross section the beads range from squashed circular to a rounded D-shape. Their ends are slightly angled in four cases, are rounded in most cases, and squared off in one. Their colour varies from black to dark brown, with both colours present in most of the beads.

MATERIAL

The disc beads are all of the same, compact-laminar non-jet material, identified from macro- and microscopic examination as cannel coal or shale (AS/MD). XRF analysis of two disc beads by MD/DH at the British Museum confirmed that they are likely to be of shale.

The fusiform beads were identified macro- and microscopically as all being of jet (with one possible exception), on the basis of their colour, texture and pattern of cracking (AS/MD). Wood grain was visible in four beads and criss-cross cracking was observed on all the beads except one which instead showed hairline longitudinal cracking. Some beads also had concentric cracking. The cracking was extensive and deep in three beads, with cupping and/or loss of surface in the case of three others; this suggests that the jet used had been of the soft variety. One bead was analysed using XRF and its composition is consistent with low-quality jet, with a medium iron content (MD/DH).

MANUFACTURE

The disc beads appear to have been perforated individually; several have hour-glass perforations, while others had been perforated mostly or wholly from one side. Faint rilling was noted on the interior of the largest bead. It was not possible to inspect every perforation as the necklace remained strung. One bead has striations on one of its flat surfaces, probably resulting from the manufacture process.

The fusiform beads generally do not show any manufacture traces; faint striations are mostly likely to be brush strokes from the application of a consolidant, although on one example some slightly clearer, diagonal striations (and possible gouge-marks) around the middle of the bead may well relate to its manufacture. Where the interior of the perforation was visible, no traces of rilling were observed.

COMPLETENESS AND DAMAGE

The beads range in completeness between 95% and 100%, the damaged beads all being fusiform. Ancient damage includes the loss of a large chip from near the end of one fusiform bead. Post-excavation damage consists of the loss of part of one end of two beads, and surface losses through cracking. All the fusiform beads have been coated with a consolidant, and one also has glue in its perforation at one end. Despite the coating, it was possible to tell that most of the beads had been polished to a medium sheen (or, at least, that the sheen had survived to a medium level); one bead showed areas of high sheen. The outer edge of the disc beads had been polished to a low sheen.

WEAR

Virtually no wear was noted on the disc beads, other than a circumferential groove worn into one side of one bead that may have been caused by a piece of grit being trapped between two beads. The perforations have crisp edges (Table 7.1.2).

In contrast, the fusiform beads show moderate wear in six cases, and moderate to heavy wear in the remaining two. In every case where the interior of the perforation was visible, thread-wear had removed any traces of rilling that might originally have been present. The interior is smooth. The edges of the perforations had been smoothed, probably through thread-wear in nearly every case, and one bead has a thread-pull groove at one end. Bead-on-bead wear was noted in five beads, taking the form of grinding to the outside of the end. It is possible that the angularity of the ends of one bead and the mid-point concavity of the ends of another is due, at least in part, to bead-on-bead wear.

CONCLUSIONS

While disc beads are generally less susceptible to use wear than beads of other shapes, the contrast between the condition of the disc and the fusiform beads, and the difference in the number of each type of bead present, make it most likely that the fusiform beads had been recycled from an old and worn spacer plate necklace, and added to the disc beads to form a disc and fusiform bead necklace. The disc beads may not have been worn for long (if at all) when the fusiform beads were added. The size and thinness of the disc beads link this necklace to others (with or without fusiform beads) that feature thin, graded-size disc (or 'washer') beads; such necklaces are mostly (or exclusively) found in northern England and Scotland. Examples include those from Almondbank, Perth and Kinross (Close-Brooks and Shepherd 1997).

ID 434 Beggar's Haven (Devil's Dyke), Poynings, East Sussex

References: Grinsell 1930, 39; Clarke 1970, no. 991, 302, fig. 167; Kinnes 1985 (Series A, no. 10).

COMPOSITION

The necklace comprises at least five tubular sheet copper beads (in nine fragments), formerly with a wooden backing (of which three fragments survive), plus 14 tiny disc beads of jet, some fragmentary (Figure 7.1.2). The copper beads were not studied in detail.

Figure 7.1.12. ID 434 Devil's Dyke (Beggar's Haven), East Sussex showing disc beads at top and four of the tubular sheet copper beads at bottom.

CONTEXT AND ASSOCIATIONS

It was found in 1887, circumstances unknown. According to Kinnes (1985), the beads are recorded as 'around the neck of the skeleton' (BM Register 1890). This was a 'contracted (?female) skeleton', claimed on unknown evidence (Grinsell 1930, 39), with 'no recorded barrows in area'. The necklace is associated with a Beaker of Clarke's W/MR type, or a Mid-carinated Beaker according to Needham's scheme (2005; see also Clarke 1970, no. 991, 302, fig. 167).

MORPHOLOGY

The disc beads are tiny, and of fairly homogeneous diameter (ranging between 3.8 and 4.6mm), but varying in thickness from 1.3 to 2.9mm. In profile some are parallel-sided, others slightly or markedly wedge-shaped. The outer edge is minimally or slightly convex. The borehole is broad in comparison to the overall diameter (ranging between 1.9 and 2.25mm in diameter). It is located centrally in most beads (slightly eccentric in at least one case), perpendicular, and mostly parallel-sided, although one bead has slight signs of an hourglass-shaped borehole.

MATERIAL

The same material had been used to make all the disc beads. It is black, with pale grey sediment ingrained in its surface; where the subsurface has been revealed through fragmentation or chipping, the fracture surfaces are black, conchoidal and shiny. This, and the slightly criss-cross laminar cracking of the fat bead at one end of the thread, led to the suspicion that the beads are of jet (AS/MD), and this was confirmed through oil immersion reflected light microscopy and reflectance measurement of one of the small fragments by Dr J.M. Jones. He reported that it was of good quality jet. Prior to this, two beads were also analysed non-destructively, through XRF, by MD/DH in the British Museum. They concluded that it was ?jet. The results from the reflectance microscopy examination leave no doubt as to the identification as jet.

MANUFACTURE

The slight convexity of the outer edge of several of the beads, together with faint traces of short nibble striations on this surface, noted on two of the beads (including the widest bead, fourth from the left on Figure 7.1.12), suggests that the beads had been individually shaped. The fact that the widest bead has a perforation that had probably been drilled from both sides suggests that the beads may all been drilled individually, although the parallel-sidedness of the borehole in most beads suggests that any trace of the drill's point of entry had been ground off, and that they may mostly have been drilled from one side. In terms of surface finish, the outer edges range from matt to having a low to medium sheen; it is unclear whether they had originally been polished to a higher sheen.

COMPLETENESS AND DAMAGE

Ten of the beads are complete; the eleventh bead is complete but in five fragments, having disintegrated during examination (and after photography: it is the second from the left in the photograph (Figure 7.1.12). The twelfth is nearly complete but in four fragments (not shown on Figure 7.1.12) and since used for analysis by Dr J M Jones); the thirteenth is around 66% complete; and the fourteenth

in two fragments, is just over 66% complete. The beads' fragility made it impossible to examine all of the threaded beads closely. Three of the threaded beads have chip scars. On one, this runs from the outer edge of one flat surface and is probably ancient; on the other two, the chips had been lost from the edge, possibly in the relatively recent past.

WEAR

As indicated above, it was not possible to examine the threaded beads in detail, although it was noted that there was no thread-smoothing to the borehole, and no obvious bead-on-bead wear, where this could be observed. The most prudent way to describe the degree of wear is indeterminate; like all disc beads, it may be that these had been worn for some time, but that the wear had not left any obvious signs (Table 7.1.2).

CONCLUSIONS

This necklace constitutes one of the earliest of the Chalcolithic and Early Bronze Age composite necklaces. Confirmation of the disc beads' material as jet means that this is also one of the earliest, if not the earliest, evidence for the use of jet during the British Chalcolithic.

7.2 SPACER PLATE NECKLACES OF JET AND JET-LIKE MATERIALS *(by Alison Sheridan and the main authors)*

A list of items studied and illustrated is shown in Table 7.2.1. The necklaces vary considerably in size and, although it was desirable to illustrate them at a consistent scale for comparative purposes (Figure 7.2.1 to Figure 7.2.19), this was not always possible. Nor was it always possible to retain colour accuracy when taking close-up images. Note that the use of the term 'button' to describe the conical, V-perforated objects found in several of these necklaces should not be taken to imply that they had necessarily been used as buttons before being incorporated into the necklaces; while this may be the case in some instances, others could have been made as beads. The term 'button' is simply used as shorthand. Detailed measurements of certain dimensions relating to these necklaces, including perforation diameters, are tabulated in Appendix VII where some fuller descriptions of spacer plates are also held.

7.2.1 EAST YORKSHIRE

ID 247 Calais (Callis) Wold 13, Bishop Wilton, East Yorkshire

References: Jewitt 1870; Mortimer 1905, 164–6 and pl. LIII, fig. 418a; Sheppard 1929, 58 (no. 418a), 141.

COMPOSITION

The necklace consists of six strands at its front; when found it comprised two terminal plates, two boat-shaped V-perforated buttons, 10 circular to oval V-perforated buttons, 35 fusiform beads, one tubular bead and 573 tiny disc beads, making a total number of 623 components. Figure 7.2.1 shows Mortimer's original photograph (Mortimer 1905, fig. 418a) together with a photograph of the necklace as currently strung. Now, two of the round V-perforated buttons and 18 of the tiny disc beads are missing, so the overall number of surviving components is 603.

This can be regarded as a variant form of spacer plate necklace, lacking spacer plates but having multiple-bored terminal plates, along with other elements that are commonly found in spacer plate necklaces in northern England. Mortimer's arrangement of the components (which he admitted was conjectural) may well be correct in showing the V-perforated components lying behind the terminal plates. Where the original arrangement may have differed from his, however, is in the positioning of the two boat-shaped ornaments and in the relative positioning of the different kinds of bead (Figure 7.2.1; see also Chapter 5, Figure 5.9.7 for drawings). By analogy with other necklaces, the boat-shaped components may have formed part of a fastening mechanism. Normally they are found singly, and are thought to have articulated with a loop in the thread, but it may be that a more elaborate thread-loop arrangement was used here, so that the two pieces could lie side by side and at right-angles to the rest of the necklace. They will henceforth be referred to as 'boat-shaped fasteners'. Regarding the relative positions of the beads below the terminal plates it may be that, by analogy with a necklace from Masterton, Fife (Henshall and Wallace 1964, fig. 2), the fusiform and tubular beads had been clustered towards the front of the necklace, with

Table 7.2.1. List of spacer plate necklaces of jet and jet-like materials studied and illustrated.

Object	Site (Parish), County	Museum	Illustration
ID 247	Calais Wold 13 (Bishop Wilton), E.Yorks.	Hull	Figure 7.2.1
			Figure 7.2.2
ID 249	Middleton-on-the-Wolds, E. Yorks.	Hull	Figure 7.2.3
ID 266	Cow Low (Green Fairfield), Derbys.	Shef	Figure 7.2.4
ID 267	Cow Low (Green Fairfield), Derbys.	Shef	Figure 7.2.5
			Figure 7.2.6
ID 268	Hill Head, Hasling House (Hartington Upper), Derbys.	Shef	Figure 7.2.7
			Figure 7.2.8
ID 269	Middleton Moor (Middleton and Smerrill), Derbys.	Shef	Figure 7.2.9
			Figure 7.2.10
			Figure 7.2.11
ID 270	Grindlow (Over Haddon), Derbys.	Shef	Figure 7.2.12
			Figure 7.2.13
ID 273	Windle Nook (Wormhill), Derbys.	Shef	Figure 7.2.14
			Figure 7.2.15
ID 264/5	NW of Pickering, N. Yorks.	Shef	Figure 7.2.16
ID 281	Snailwell C, Cambs.	Camb	Figure 7.2.17
ID 282	Burwell Fen, Cambs.	Camb	Figure 7.2.17
ID 379-90	Pockley, N.Yorks.	BM	Figure 7.2.18
ID 391	Soham Fen, Cambs.	BM	Figure 2.1.19

the disc beads extending between them and the terminal plates. Indeed, the spacing of the holes along the bottom of the terminal plates would accommodate six disc beads comfortably.

The necklace had been partially re-strung since Mortimer's book was published (Figure 7.2.1, bottom), so that one of the boat-shaped fasteners and all of the surviving round and oval buttons are omitted from the current reconstruction, being stored separately.

CONTEXT AND ASSOCIATIONS

The necklace was found under the central area of a round barrow. It was thought by Mortimer to belong to a primary, ground-level interment of which no trace other than a 'film of dark matter' survived (Mortimer 1905, 166), although other finds from the barrow excavation (namely fine, leaf-shaped flint arrowheads and 'javelin heads') make it clear that there had been earlier, Early to Middle Neolithic activity at the site (*ibid*, 164 and figs. 413–16). The position of the beads found in an area 'covering a little more than a square yard of the old land surface' led Mortimer to conclude that 'they had been placed round the neck of a body' (*ibid*, 166). No other grave goods were found, although the presence of traces of copper on the necklace suggests that a small artefact of copper or copper alloy, such as an awl, may well have been present. Note also that, during a previous investigation of the barrow, Mortimer's workmen had found one V-perforated, slightly oval-based button while infilling their trench cut through the same part of the barrow (*ibid*, fig. 418). Comparable in shape and size to the buttons on the necklace, it could have come from the necklace. Since it was not inspected by the team, it will not be described here.

MORPHOLOGY

The terminal plates form a very similar, but not identical pair, each with a rounded apex (Figure 7.2.2). The left-hand terminal (TL) has an indentation caused by wear on its apex; its outer edge is gently convex, and its inner edge is minimally concave. The lower edge is straight and missing its inner corner. Both of the outer edges of the right hand plate (TR) are very slightly convex and rounded; its lower edge is straight and squared-off. The two terminal plates are very similar in size, with TL being 41mm long at its mid-point, 28mm (extrapolated) at its widest point and 5.8mm thick, while the corresponding measurements for TR are 41 by 28 by 6.6mm. In both, the perforations are all elbow-bored, with a single hole at the apex end and six holes at the lower end; the holes on the back surface are obscured by thread, and it was not possible to measure the holes on the TL due to the tightness of the stringing. However, on the lower edge of TR the holes range from 3.0 by 2.5mm to 2.4 by 2.0mm. Both plates are decorated on their upper (exterior) surface with a pointillé design featuring an increasing number (one to three) of double-line rows extending from the apex to the bottom, framed by a line running around the exterior of the design and separated

by transverse lines. There are minor differences: the TL plate has one and a half double-line rows in its central part rather than two, and the TR has a third transverse row towards the apex. However, these plates were clearly designed as a pair.

The boat-shaped fasteners have elliptical bases and fairly steep sides terminating in a rounded ridge. The apex on the example that is currently strung on the necklace is slightly asymmetrical. To distinguish the two, the example that is not on the necklace is denoted ID 247.9 (Figure 7.2.2; see also Figure 5.9.7). It measures 31.4 by 8.9 by 6.1mm (L by W by H) compared to 38.9 by 7.0 by 10.8mm for the strung example. The perforations measure 3.5 by 2.7mm and 3.8 by 2.6mm with a bridge width of 2.8mm. The perforations on the strung example measure 2.5 by 3.2mm and 2.3 by 3.2mm with a bridge width of 3.7mm.

The eight surviving buttons (Figure 7.2.2) are mostly approximately circular in plan, with domes that vary from medium-height to tall and from rounded to pointed; two (ID 247.6 and ID 247.8) have sloping facets between the dome and the base, and three others (ID 247.1, ID 247.2 and ID 247.4) have partial facets. One (ID 247.7) differs from the rest in having a markedly oval base shape and a low, rounded dome. The principal characteristics of the buttons are summarised in Appendix VII, Table 1.

To judge from Mortimer's photograph, the two missing buttons fall within the shape range of the others; one (the rear left example on Mortimer's fig. 418a) had been smaller than the rest.

The fusiform beads vary in length from 11.0 to 24.5mm and in maximum thickness from 5.5 to 8.5mm; in shape they range from long and slender to short and squat, and in cross section from roughly circular, to slightly D-shaped, with five having two flattish sides (Figure 7.2.1). These flattish examples may originally have lain adjacent to a spacer plate on a spacer plate necklace. The diameter of the longitudinal perforation ranges between 2.0 and 4.1mm. The four beads with the widest perforation are also the smallest, all being below 13.5mm in length. The ends are generally gently squared off and in some cases are perpendicular to the bead's long axis; in most cases, however, one or both ends slope, and in the latter cases the ends mostly slope away from each other. Such ends (and indeed body) shapes are characteristic of fusiform beads found in spacer plate necklaces.

The tubular bead is 13.9mm long and 4.8mm in thickness and has a narrow perforation, 1.8mm in diameter (Figure 7.2.1, innermost strand, second non-disc bead along). It is cylindrical in profile and circular in cross section, with squared-off, perpendicular ends. The tiny disc beads are circular in plan and mostly parallel-sided with a straight (as opposed to convex) outer edge (Figure 7.2.1). They are markedly uniform in diameter (4.2 to 4.3mm) but vary in thickness from *c.* 0.4 to 3.6mm; the perforation is narrow (*c.* 2.5mm), central, and perpendicular.

MATERIAL

Macroscopically, all the components, except the tiny disc

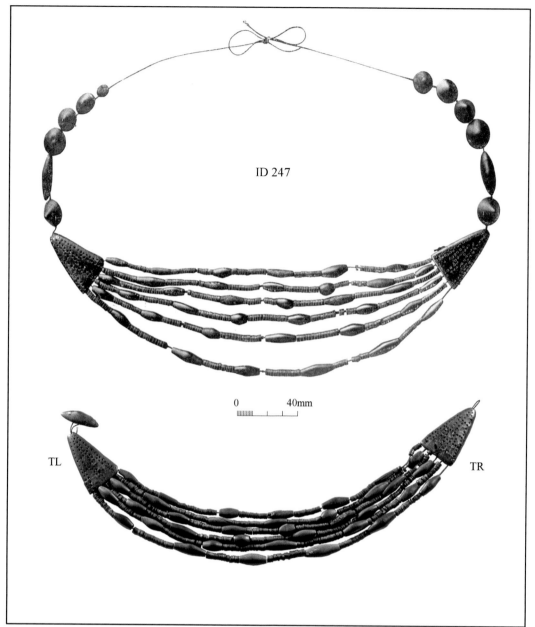

ID 247

0   40mm

TL

TR

Figure 7.2.1. ID 247 Calais Wold showing (top) reproduction of Mortimer's 1905 illustration and (bottom) the current strung configuration (courtesy of National Museums Scotland).

beads and the tubular bead, show obvious signs of being made from jet, with both soft and hard varieties present (the former showing extensive and/or deep cracking) (AS). The terminal plates, fasteners and the buttons are a deep brown and black colour, and the fusiform beads range from a rich brown to blackish colour. Where present, the cracking pattern is characteristic of jet (i.e. criss-cross and oval). A fine-woody texture is particularly clearly visible where the surface is brown, and is also clear on the bottom of button ID 247.6 (Figure 7.2.2) and on one of the brown fusiform beads, where part of the surface had spalled off. Other characteristic features are the presence of quartz grains (a commonly-found jet inclusion) in one of the fusiform beads, and of a natural oval hollow on the underside of the

unattached fastener (Figure 7.2.2). A similar hollow exists on the dome of button ID 247.5 (Figure 7.2.2).

As for the other components, the tubular bead is blackish grey and the tiny disc beads are mostly black or dark grey, although several include dark brown areas. The material for both the tubular bead and the disc beads is compact and not obviously woody (although this was not checked under a microscope). A couple of beads have incipient laminar cracking, and a laminar structure has been exploited for forming the individual beads.

Both of the fasteners and all of the buttons, together with the left-hand terminal plate, three fusiform beads and two groups of tiny disc beads, were compositionally analysed using X-ray fluorescence spectrometry, by Lore Troalen of

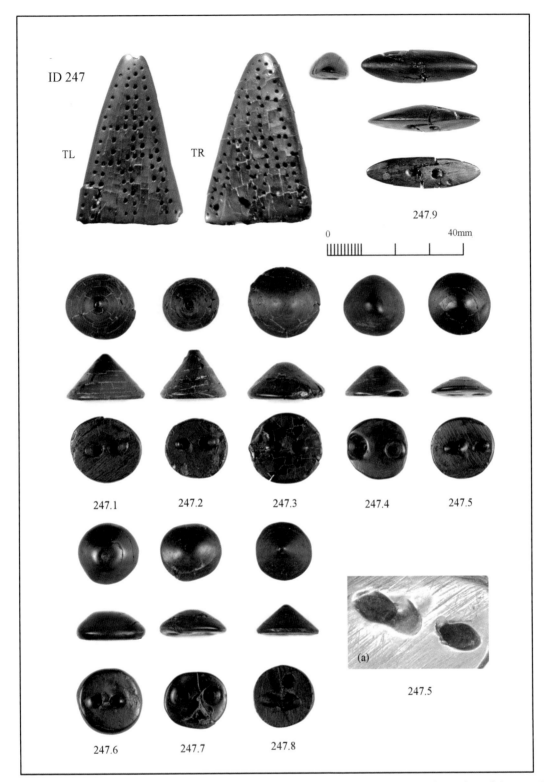

Figure 7.2.2. ID 247 Calais Wold showing the two terminal plates (TL and TR), detail of the boat-shaped fastener ID 247.9 illustrating striations and drilling technique, and the eight surviving buttons. Inset (a) shows details of the striations and drilling on button ID 247.5.

National Museums Scotland, with samples of raw Whitby jet and of cannel coal used as *comparanda*. This confirmed that the elements macroscopically identified as being of jet were indeed of this material. The analysis also revealed some compositional variability in the jet, which probably relates to inclusions and confirms the view that several different pieces of parent material were used to make the various jet components. Thus, buttons ID 247.2 and ID

247.8 and the boat-shaped fastener currently attached to the necklace have a relatively high iron content which may relate to the proximity to pyritic inclusions in the parent material; the fusiform bead closest to the TL on the innermost strand has an appreciable germanium content. Button ID 247.5 has a high zinc content, and variable amounts of yttrium were present in one of the analysed fusiform beads, in the unattached boat-shaped fastener, and in buttons ID 247.2, ID 247.6 and ID 247.8. Extraneous compositional elements noted on some of the components are calcium, which will probably have derived from the bones of the skeleton (thereby confirming Mortimer's suggestion that the necklace had been around the neck of the deceased), and copper, which may suggest the former presence of a small object of copper or copper alloy in the vicinity of the necklace.

Analysis of the tiny disc beads showed that they did indeed differ in their composition from the other analysed components, but the presence of zirconium indicates that jet cannot be ruled out as a raw material; this is consistent with the brown colour of some of the beads. As elsewhere (e.g. Garton Slack VI, 1, ID 251), a lower grade of jet had probably been used to make the beads. Other characteristics of these disc beads are the presence of yttrium and (in some) of appreciable amounts of iron; calcium was also noted, again probably from the associated body, and with one group of disc beads there was an appreciable level of copper.

MANUFACTURE

Very few traces relating to the original shaping of the terminal plates are visible, partly because they had probably been polished away and partly because much of the rear of the plates is obscured by thread. The borehole interiors are similarly obscured. There are a few faint striations running along the perforated lower edge of the TR plate. Three accidental holes on the upper (front) surface of the TR, close to its lower edge, may have resulted from drilling too close to that surface when creating the elbow-boreholes. At the apex of the TR, a small hollow beside the borehole may mark where drilling had started before the drill was repositioned, and on the back of the plate, a flake scar adjacent to the top perforation may relate to damage during drilling, or else (more probably) to spalling through pressure from the necklace thread. The pointillé decoration, with its maximum diameter of just over 1mm, had been made with a narrow pointed object, possibly an awl; the traces of a creamy material spotted in the base of several punctulations may be the last remains of a deliberate infill intended to highlight the design, as has been seen on spacer plate necklaces elsewhere. There are no signs of guide-lines for the design. The decoration had probably been made after the terminal plates had been polished. In common with the buttons and fasteners, the underside of each of the terminal plates has a higher sheen than the upper surface. This could be a product of post-depositional, partial dulling of the surfaces that had not been in direct contact with the corpse: the whole of the surface (except the perforated lower edge) may originally have been polished to a high sheen.

There are also few traces relating to the initial shaping of the boat-shaped fasteners; here, this is because they had mostly been polished away. A few faint longitudinal striations are present running along the flat side of the fastener that is currently attached to the necklace. More numerous, and multidirectional faint striations are present on the same surface of the other fastener (ID 247.9, Figure 7.2.2). Regarding the perforations, no rilling is present; the slightly uneven outline of the right hand perforation in 247.9 (Figure 7.2.2) may indicate that the drill was presented twice, once to start the hole, and then to drill diagonally. The underside of the fasteners preserves the high sheen that had probably formerly covered the whole of both fasteners.

Various manufacture details are visible on some of the buttons (Figure 7.2.2). The conical examples (ID 247.1, ID 247.2 and ID 247.8) have fairly crisp multi-directional grinding striations on their lower, flat surfaces, and also have crisp diagonal striations on their facets; faint striations on the dome were noted on ID 247.8. Button ID 247.5 also has clear multi-directional striations on its underside, including where the surface slopes up (see Figure 7.2.2a), and fainter striations were noted on the underside of ID 247.3, ID 247.4 and ID 247.7. The truncated shape of the dome on ID 247.6 may well relate to the loss of the tip of the cone during manufacture. Rather than discarding the object, the maker smoothed over the fracture surface. As regards the V-borings, rilling in one or more perforation was noted in every button except ID 247.3 and ID 247.5, and in ID 247.6 and ID 247.7 it is faint. Evidence for the repositioning of the drill (from vertical to diagonal) was noted in ID 247.1–5 and ID 247.7, and evidence that the drill bit tip had been gently pointed is clear from ID 247.4, ID 247.7 and ID 247.8. However, the same bit does not seem to have been used for these three buttons. The width of the tip, in ID 247.4, is *c.* 1.7mm. Chipping during drilling was noted on ID 247.2, ID 247.5 and arguably also ID 247.6; and in ID 247.8 not only had there been chipping, but it is likely that the bridge between the perforations was broken during manufacture, necessitating the drilling of a third perforation. A curving hollow on the base of ID 247.8 may indicate where an impurity in the raw material had been removed, the perforations have avoided this area. With ID 247.7 the drilling had gone too close to the top of the button, breaking through the surface.

The degree of sheen on the buttons relates to several factors: the initial degree of polish; the subsequent gain of sheen through wear, and the subsequent partial loss of sheen post-depositionally. Generally the underside has a higher sheen than the dome.

There are no obvious manufacture traces (e.g. grinding striations or faceting traces) on the fusiform beads, except for faint traces of faceting on one of the short, squat beads indicating that these had been polished away. It was not possible to inspect the interior of most of the beads for signs of rilling. Only one bead showed any obvious manufacture traces, exhibiting two unpolished scars on one side, one possibly a gouge-mark relating to the removal of impurities in the jet. One other fusiform bead has an incompletely polished chip at one end, and another has a worn chip scar at the same position, but it is impossible to tell whether the damage had occurred during manufacture or wear. All the fusiform beads had been polished, but the degree of sheen varies between beads, from very low to high; most have a medium sheen.

There are no signs of the shaping process visible on the cylindrical bead, and it was not possible to inspect the interior of the perforation. However, it is clear from the bead's shape that its ends were ground flat, perpendicular to the long axis. The surface is smooth and has a low sheen; given the nature of the raw material, it might never have had a higher sheen.

Evidence suggesting how the disc beads may have been made is provided by a run of beads on the outermost strand, between the fusiform beads at the left end of the necklace. Here, the closely-interlocking individual elements suggest that their original respective positions have been maintained from when they were either detached from a cylindrical parent roughout, or else ground into shape as a set of roughout beads. It was not possible to inspect the perforations to check for any traces of rilling or to see whether the boreholes had been drilled from both sides. As for polish, while the edge of the disc beads had been carefully smoothed, it may never have been polished to a high sheen; the degree of smoothing ranges from matt (i.e. no sheen) to moderate.

COMPLETENESS AND DAMAGE

The components are mostly in good condition, although many of the soft jet items had suffered from the effects of cracking. There is some cupping on the upper surfaces of the terminal plates, some 'springing' along crack lines (e.g. on button ID 247.1), and some loss of chips (e.g. on at least two fusiform beads). Both the fasteners, the left terminal plate, button ID 247.7 and two fusiform beads had broken, or lost fragments, along crack lines since being excavated. These had been repaired, either with glue or with a black waxy material; the same black material is present as a consolidant on button ID 247.3 and on the underside of the right terminal plate. Despite this, and despite showing varying degrees of wear, the components are almost all complete, or very nearly so. The exceptions are one of the disc beads, where around a third of the circumference is missing, and one of the fusiform beads, which had disintegrated and lost much of one side before being repaired using the black material. In addition, two of the fusiform beads (the first on the right in the third strand, and the third from the right in the sixth strand, counting out from the innermost strand) had lost part of one side due to laminar spalling along natural grain planes in antiquity.

Ancient damage in the form of chipping during drilling has been noted above, along with the fracturing of a bridge

on button ID 247.8, the loss of the tip of button ID 247.6 and the accidental puncturing of the upper surface of the right terminal plate and of the apex of button ID 247.7, probably during hole-drilling. Other ancient damage through wear is detailed below.

WEAR

Assessment of the degree and type of wear was affected by the fact that the strung components are fairly tightly strung. It is for this reason, together with the fact that disc beads tend not to show wear as much as other components, that the amount of wear on the disc beads is given in Table 7.2.2 as mostly indeterminate. That said, the degree of wear on the terminal plates, and on a few of the fusiform beads, falls between the 'fresh or slight' and 'worn' categories; and the degree of wear on one of the buttons (ID 247.7) falls between the 'worn' and 'very worn' wear categories.

Although the interiors of the boreholes of the terminal plates are mostly obscured by thread, it is clear that there had been some slight thread-smoothing to the edges of the boreholes. There is also some thread-pull wear. On the TR plate this occurs along its lower edge, the outermost hole (i.e. on the longest strand) having traces of thread-pull towards the centre of the plate, and it may be that thread-pull had also been responsible for the loss of a chip from the corner at this point, on the upper surface (Figure 7.2.2). At the upper end of that plate, on the back, thread-pull had worn a hollow leading down from the borehole, and may also have caused the loss of a flake from the edge of the perforation. (It was at this point that all six threads would have converged). On the TL plate, the ancient loss of the corner at the innermost strand could have been due to thread-pull, and at the top end, there is wear to both ends of the elbow-boring, again probably due to thread-pull, although rubbing from an adjacent button may have been partly responsible for the U-shaped hollow at the apex of the plate (Figure 7.2.2). At the lower ends of both plates, no obvious traces of bead-on-plate grinding were evident, although close examination was not possible. The decorated surface of each plate showed some rub-wear which has affected some of the punctulations close to the apices; this wear may be due to rubbing by a garment.

Both boat-shaped fasteners show both thread-wear and some rub-wear. On both the thread has smoothed the edge of the perforations, especially to their outer sides (Figure 7.2.2), and it may be that some of the smoothing of the perforated surface, and some of its sheen relates to rubbing against the skin (or a garment) in addition to deliberate polishing. It must be admitted that the pattern of thread-wear is not what would be expected from use as fasteners where greater wear to the inner side of each perforation would be expected. This could mean that they had previously been used in another way, and/or that they had been strung as beads rather than as fasteners.

The buttons show variable degrees of thread-wear and rub-wear with the conical buttons showing the least amount of wear overall. With these, the edges of the perforations are relatively crisp (e.g. on ID 247.8: Figure 7.2.2) and there is very little rub-wear. In contrast, the other buttons show thread-smoothing around the perforation edge, and thread-pull towards the outside of the perforations which would accord with their use as necklace beads. These buttons also show varying degrees of rub-wear, mostly on the base where the surface is highest (e.g. ID 247.4 and ID 247.7, Figure 7.2.2). On ID 247.4 the highest point of the dome has a higher sheen than the rest of the dome, and this may be due to rub-wear against a garment. Similarly, the smoothing of the edge of the accidental perforation at the top of the dome on ID 247.7 may be due to rub-wear. Overall, this is the most heavily worn button.

While it was difficult to examine the perforation edges of the fusiform beads, it is clear that only a few beads show obvious signs of thread-wear or bead-on-bead wear. The latter include one of the short, squat beads (around the middle of the third strand on Figure 7.2.1). Here, there is clear thread-polish to one end, and bead-on-bead wear at the other end, where the end of an adjacent bead has ground and polished that end, giving the bead an asymmetrical profile. A large hole along one side might also have resulted from wear. Another of the squat beads (in the second strand, third fusiform bead from right) has thread-polish to both ends. As for the other beads, there are two cases where thread-pull had damaged one end: on the third bead from the right in the innermost strand, there is a thread-pull groove (at the opposite end from where a chip had been lost in the relatively recent past), while the second bead from the right in the second strand has a chip missing from one end, probably due to thread-pull. In two other cases where chips are missing from one end (the second bead from the left in the third strand, and the third bead on the right in the fourth strand) it is unclear whether the chipping occurred through wear or, as noted above, during manufacture.

The cylindrical bead showed no obvious signs of wear, although it was not possible to inspect the edge of the perforation. As far as the disc beads are concerned, as noted above, it was difficult to check for signs of wear, although slight smoothing of the perforation edge was noted on seven examples.

CONCLUSIONS

The only observation that can be made with confidence is that the terminal plates had been manufactured as a pair, and that the necklace had seen some wear before it was buried. Beyond that it is likely that the various components were obtained from different sources. The fusiform beads show signs of having come from at least one pre-existing spacer plate necklace; it may well be that the short, squat examples with wide perforations (and in at least one case marginally more wear than most of the other fusiform beads) had belonged to a different parent necklace from the rest. By contrast, the tiny disc beads may have been made when the present necklace was assembled, to fill the gaps between the fusiform beads and the terminal plates

(as suggested above). The tubular bead, which seems to be of the same material as the disc beads, may have been made at the same time and been designed for the same purpose. As a pseudo-fusiform bead, it could have lain beside the fusiform beads. The cylindrical bead looks as though it could have been a preform for a set of disc beads (if indeed disc beads had been made in this way), albeit slightly broader than the examples in the necklace. The V-perforated components show differing degrees of wear: the most markedly conical examples have the least wear, and possibly having being made for the necklace, and the more heavily-worn examples having seen service elsewhere (probably as beads) before being incorporated into the necklace. Therefore, the necklace appears to be a combination of some components that were specifically produced, and other components that were gathered from other necklaces.

If worn according to the layout proposed by Mortimer, then excluding any bead-free thread (and allowing for the missing components), the necklace would have had an overall length of *c.* 670mm, allowing it to have lain between the collarbone and the breast, assuming that it had indeed been worn by a woman (as seems likely by analogy with necklaces from reliably-sexed skeletons). In terms of modern necklace lengths, it lies between 'matinée' and 'opera' lengths.

ID 249 Middleton-on-the-Wolds, East Yorkshire

References: Mortimer 1905, 353–4 and fig. 1017; Sheppard 1929, 106 (no. 1017).

COMPOSITION

This spacer plate necklace currently comprises two terminal plates and five spacer plates, plus one spacer plate and 26 fusiform beads that were made in the 20th century to form a 'reconstructed' necklace for display. The 20th-century spacer plate is the one adjacent to the right terminal plate on Mortimer's illustration (reproduced here as Figure 7.2.3a) – in other words, the 'Sp 1 R' plate. In the current museum display, this plate is represented by a photograph; it appears that the reconstruction made for Mortimer is no longer extant. In the store there is an undecorated and unperforated substitute, probably made when the current display was being prepared but not used as a large piece had broken off it during manufacture (Paula Gentil pers. comm.). The number of strands increases from three (between the terminal plates and the adjacent spacer plates) to four. The necklace is firmly attached to a backboard in the museum and could not be removed for examination without major disruption to the display (Figure 7.2.3b). For this reason, the recording could not be as thorough as with most other artefacts.

CONTEXT AND ASSOCIATIONS

The remains were found in 1901, at a depth of 3 feet

(around 900mm) when digging for sand in a garden. They were associated with an unburnt contracted skeleton whose current whereabouts is unknown and about which no further details exist. Mortimer records (1905, 353–4) that 'With the skeleton were found seven large flat pieces of jet, evidently part of a necklace, a restoration of which is given in fig. 1017. One of the broad pieces and all the smaller beads shown in the illustration were not found, having probably been overlooked by the workmen'.

MORPHOLOGY

The individual plates are cross-referenced on Mortimer's illustration where TL is the left hand terminal and TR is the right hand terminal. The other plates are numbered, prefixed by 'Sp' (for 'spacer') and suffixed by L or R (left or right respectively) (Figure 7.2.3a). As noted above, there is no Sp 1 R plate.

TL and TR are fairly long, with TR being broader and thicker than TL. The inner edge of each (i.e. the edge facing the wearer's head) is fairly straight while the outer edge is curving. Both have a transverse perforation close to their apex, plus three elbow-bored holes at their broader end, the perforations exiting at the back of the plates. Neither is decorated. The spacer plates are all trapezoidal, increasing in size towards the front (centre) of the necklace. Their inner and outer (i.e. unperforated) edges are rounded, while the perforated edges are squared off (but are not all straight: those of Sp 3 L, for example, bow out slightly). Their outer edges are gently convex, their inner edges slightly less so. There is no neat symmetry in the size and shape of the plates between the left and right sides of the necklace: for example, Sp 2 R is broader than Sp 2 L. The dimensions of individual plates are listed in Appendix VII, Table 2, insofar as it was possible to measure them *in situ*. All the spacer plates except Sp 3 R (which is elbow bored) are through-perforated, with Sp 1 L (and presumably also the missing Sp 1 R) involving a Y-boring in order to increase the number of strands from three to four.

All the spacer plates are decorated with a pointillé design, and there are hints (e.g. in Sp 1 L and Sp 2 L) of the presence of whitish material in the base of the dots. However, without being able to examine this microscopically, it is unclear whether this represents sediment from the grave, or material – perhaps polishing material – that had been deliberately left in to highlight the design. While four of the plates have a design featuring a central lozenge flanked by two isosceles triangles (with the latter being dot-filled in the case of Sp 2 R: Figure 7.2.3e), the narrower Sp 1 L has a different design, featuring two opposing triangles, resembling a bow tie.

MATERIAL

The colour (black and rich dark brown), texture (fine-grained woody, as visible in some cases) and condition of the plates (see below) leave no doubt that the material of all of the plates is jet (AS). The uncracked condition of Sp 1 L suggests that it is likely to be hard jet, and the minimally-cracked condition of Sp 3 R suggests that this, too, may be of hard jet (Figure 7.2.3e). Conversely, the extensive surface cracking of the other plates suggests that they are of soft jet (Figure 7.2.3c).

MANUFACTURE

The circumstances under which the necklace was recorded meant that it was not possible to check for manufacturing traces microscopically, so some may well have been missed. Shallow striations between perforations (from the grinding of the plate edge) were noted on the left edges of Sp 2 L, Sp 3 R and Sp 2 R. No guide lines for the pointillé decoration were visible, while the decoration itself had been made using a round-tipped tool, possibly an awl. The plates had been polished; all now have a low to medium sheen, although the degree of sheen may well originally have been higher.

COMPLETENESS AND DAMAGE

The TL plate is in the worst condition, with extensive surface criss-cross cracking and cupping (Figure 7.2.3c), and some consequent loss of spalls, on its upper surface; it was not possible to see its underside clearly. One of the elbow-borings had been broken through, although it was not possible to determine whether this damage had been due to ancient wear.

The Sp 1 L plate is in good condition, with only a little hairline cracking to its upper (decorated) and lower surfaces. Sp 2 L and Sp 3 L are in worse condition, with extensive criss-cross cracking and some cupping on their upper surface; their underside, however, is not noticeably cracked. The underside of Sp 2 R and Sp 3 R also seems to be uncracked, while the upper surface of Sp 2 R has hairline criss-cross cracking. This pattern of differential degradation suggests that the underside of the necklace had been protected, probably by being in contact with the deceased's skin or garment. However, the TR plate has extensive criss-cross cracking on both its upper and lower surfaces. Sp 2 R has a long spall missing from its upper surface, close to one perforated edge, and this may represent ancient damage. Sp 2 L also has a long spall scar on its upper surface, plus a rounder spall scar, and these may have resulted from the surface cracking. The only other damage that was noted is the fact that the innermost and outermost boreholes of Sp 3 L had perforated the plate's upper surface (Figure 7.2.3d). The position of the holes corresponds to where the boreholes from each end of the plate are likely to have met, and suggests that the perforations had been drilled too close to the surface. The drill may have broken through the surface during manufacture.

The overall degree of completeness of the necklace depends on whether Mortimer's suggestion that there had been an additional spacer plate and 26 fusiform beads was correct. If so, then the surviving portion represents around 60–70% of the necklace. Given that this necklace is of a

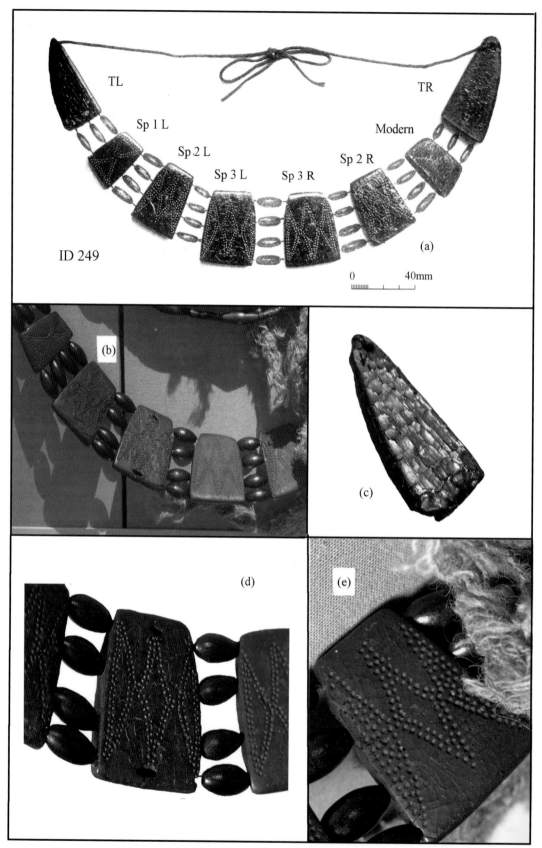

Figure 7.2.3. ID 249 Middleton-on-the-Wolds: (a) reproduction of Mortimer's 1905 illustration with annotations; (b) current (2010) museum display with Sp 1 L at top left and Sp 2 R at bottom right; (c) detail of TL showing heavy surface cracking and cupping; (d) detail of Sp 3 L showing decoration and front surface broken by perforations, and (e) detail of Sp 2 R showing decoration. Note: as with the Sp 1 R plate, all the fusiform beads are of 20th-century date.

type where there had not been much increase in the number of strands, and where there are numerous spacer plates, it is likely that Mortimer was correct.

WEAR

Some clear signs of wear were noted on some, but not all, of the plates. The breaking-through of one of the elbow-boreholes on TL has been noted, along with the uncertainty as to whether this had resulted from wear. The transverse hole near the upper end of TL does, however, show signs of ancient thread-pull wear, to its upper edge on the underside of the plate, where the thread would have pulled towards the back of the neck. Some thread-pull wear was also noted on the corresponding hole of TR, and all three of its perforations along its bottom edge also show thread-wear, especially the outermost hole. The aforementioned holes on the upper surface of Sp 3 L have slightly smooth edges, as though they had undergone some wear.

One of the holes on Sp 1 L, the outermost hole on the edge closest to the adjacent terminal plate, has thread-wear and this was also noted to the ends of the holes of Sp 2 L, particularly on the innermost and outermost holes. On the innermost hole the thread has pulled towards the underside of the plate. Such wear may relate to the plate having rested on the collarbone. Finally, one of the elbow-bored holes on the underside of Sp 3 R (either the innermost hole or the outermost) has a thread-groove worn into its inner edge.

The overall degree of wear can be said to be variable, from slight to worn (perhaps heavier in the case of the terminal plates) and is recorded in Table 7.2.2.

CONCLUSIONS

If, as argued above, Mortimer was indeed correct in postulating that there had been only a single row of fusiform beads between the plates, then the estimated maximum circumference of the necklace (estimating an average length of 15mm for each of the outermost beads, and extrapolating the width of the missing plate) amounts to nearly 400mm, not counting any space between the apices of the terminal plates. This would encircle an adult's neck as a fairly tight, choker-length necklace, and this is consistent with the observed pattern of wear, even if the apices of the terminal plates had not actually abutted each other when in use. Regarding its overall design, this necklace is comparable to others that deviate from the 'lunula-like' format in having more or fewer than the normal set of six plates, and in which the number of strands increases slightly, or not at all (e.g. Cow Low ID 266 and Blindmill, Aberdeenshire: Stuart 1866).

That this necklace was not new when buried is clear from the degree of wear seen on some of the plates. That it may have acquired pieces during its life is suggested by the facts that that the two terminal plates are not only undecorated (unlike the other plates) but also that they differ from each other in size and shape. However, neither this nor the difference in decoration between Sp 1 L and

the other extant decorated plates is sufficient to prove that the components had not been made as a set.

7.2.2 PEAK DISTRICT

ID 266 Cow Low, Green Fairfield, Derbyshire

References: Bateman 1848, 91–5; Howarth 1899, 57; Vine 1982, 62.

COMPOSITION

This two-strand spacer plate necklace comprises two terminal plates, two spacer plates and 42 fusiform beads (Figure 7.2.4). There is some confusion as to whether or not a globular bead may also have belonged to this necklace (below), since the Bateman Collection Catalogue entry (Howarth 1899, 57) is ambiguous and there is a good chance that it had not been associated. The bead will therefore be described separately.

CONTEXT AND ASSOCIATIONS

The necklace is from a cist in a secondary position in a round barrow. It is one of two necklaces to have been found in the cist (the other being ID 267) and, since the two necklaces have separate museum registration numbers, it is assumed that they had been spatially distinct from each other within the cist. The two necklaces are described and discussed separately here. Inside the cist was found the contracted skeleton of an adult, whose sex Bateman reported to be female, along with 'a fine instrument of calcined flint, of the circular-ended form' (Howarth 1899, 57). The relationship of the two necklaces to this individual is described, somewhat vaguely, by Bateman as '...the bones of a female in the usual contracted position, with which were two sets of Kimmeridge coal beads (one hundred and seventeen in number)...' (*ibid*). Bateman noted that a few fusiform beads 'lay on the outside of the cist, where was part of the skeleton of a child, to whom possibly one set of beads might belong, or, what is more probable, that they were disturbed at the time of the construction of [another cist]' (*ibid*). It is therefore unclear whether one of the two Cow Low necklaces had originally accompanied a child, whose remains were disturbed by the insertion of the later cist. It remains a possibility; and of the two necklaces, ID 266, the smaller example, seems most likely to have been associated with the child.

A globular bead which shares the same museum registration number as this necklace is the subject of some confusion (Figure 7.2.4b). It is mentioned in Howarth's catalogue heading '1 Necklace of Kimeridge coal [sic] – comprising 42 cylindrical beads, *one globular bead*, [italics added] and four flat ornaments rather triangular in shape. Found with a secondary interment in Cowlow barrow, near Buxton' (*ibid*), although Bateman's account, published below this heading, is different. Bateman states that the overall number of 'beads' in the two necklaces

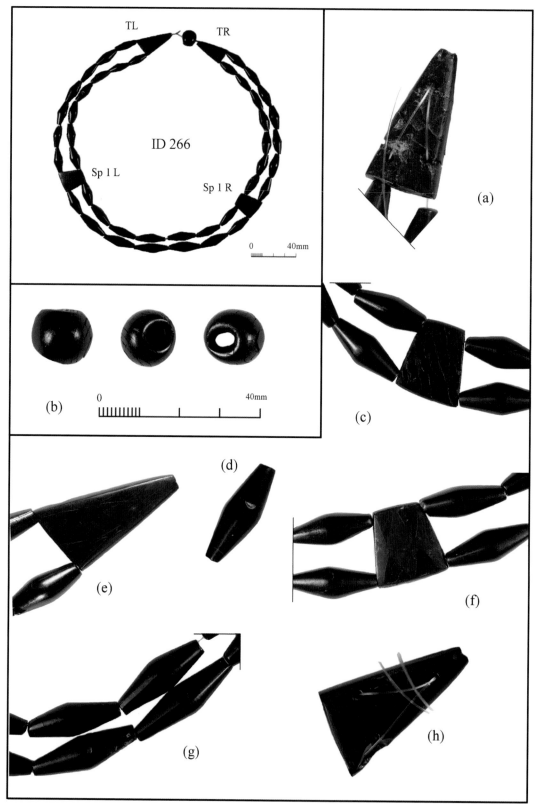

Figure 7.2.4. ID 266 Cow Low showing reconstructed necklace (complete with non-associated globular bead), with details (not to scale): (a) boreholes on the back of the right-hand terminal; (b) the globular bead; (c) criss-cross cracking on spacer plate Sp 1 R; (d) dimple on one of the fusiform beads; (e) decoration on left terminal plate; (f) decoration on spacer plate Sp 1 L, showing the clear two-tone colouration caused by deliberate partial dulling; (g) faceting on fusiform beads, and (h) large chip scar on the back of the left terminal plate.

is 117 – a total that corresponds to the number of extant components *without* counting the globular bead. That this bead had not been part of either necklace is suggested by Bateman's later statement (appearing in Howarth 1899, 58–9) that 'In various parts of the tumulus, but not in situations where they could be allotted with certainty to any of the interments, were found a scattered deposit of burnt bones, *a bead of Kimmeridge coal, of more globular form than the others, much worn* [italics added];…' Such a description fits the bead in question.

MORPHOLOGY

All four plates are trapezoidal and flat, with the terminal plates narrowing considerably to their apices; in each case the perforated edges are straight and fairly crisply squared off, and the other edges are rounded. The outer edges of the terminal plates are very slightly convex, as are the edges of the spacer plates. The right hand terminal plate is markedly narrower than its counterpart on the left, and it seems to have been narrowed (see below, manufacture). Each terminal plate has a single elbow-bored hole towards its upper, narrow end and two elbow-bored holes close to its lower end (with traces of a further, broken hole on the right terminal: see below and Figure 7.2.4a). The elbow borings open to the underside of the plates. The spacer plates each have two through-perforations. The perforations at the broad end of each terminal plate, and in the spacer plates, are all very close to the plates' rounded edges. Dimensions of the plates are shown in Appendix VII, Table 3. All the plates are decorated on their upper faces, with a subtle geometric design featuring triangles and diamond shapes; see below for details.

The fusiform beads (Figure 7.2.4) are fairly plump to plump, with many being slightly angular, and many are slightly flattish over part of their circumference. They range in length from 18.0 to 32.0mm and in width from 6.6 by 6.9mm to 10.1 by 10.1mm; their perforation diameters range between 2.2 and 2.6mm. Their ends are mostly gently squared off and either perpendicular to the long axis or minimally angled (with one end of the shortest bead more markedly angled, possibly through wear). Like the plates, the beads give the impression of belonging to a consistent set, rather than comprising a mixture of components from more than one parent necklace.

The overall length of the necklace from left terminal tip to right terminal tip is *c.* 610mm which would equate to a 'matinée' length (*c.* 24 inches) in terms of modern necklace categories. In other words, it would extend slightly below the collarbone, whether it be worn by a child or an adult.

MATERIAL

Macroscopically, all the plates are clearly of jet (AS). This is indicated by their colour (a rich dark brown to blackish-brown, made darker by the presence of a coating of consolidant or lacquer), by a deliberate two-tone blackish

and brown variegation on their upper surfaces, and by the criss-cross cracking seen on all the plates except the left terminal (Figure 7.2.4c). It is also clear from the fine-grained woody texture seen in the exposed subsurface of the right terminal plate, and by the presence of an oval dimple (a natural irregularity seen in jet) on the outer edge of spacer plate Sp 1 L and the inner edge of Sp 1 R. (This is not to be confused with deliberately- and accidentally-created dimples that are sometimes seen in jet fusiform beads.) The cracking is more marked on the underside of the plates, and the underside of the right terminal is darker than the decorated upper surface. The presence of the cracking on all but one of the plates suggests the use of soft jet (albeit less prone to cracking than a lot of soft jet, including that used for the plates in the other Cow Low necklace, ID 267). The consistency in colour, condition and texture among these three plates suggests that they may well have been made from the same parent piece of raw material. The exception, the left terminal, is not cracked and had probably been made of hard jet.

The fusiform beads are all black and macroscopically look to be of hard jet. Cracking, where present, is minimal and hairline, in criss-cross and oval shapes. Chip scars tend to be shiny and conchoidal and where the sub-surface has been revealed, it is fine-grained and woody in appearance. Six beads have the oval 'dimple' feature as noted above (Figure 7.2.4d) and, with one possible exception, these probably relate to natural irregularities or to accidental spalling rather than to deliberate shaping. All these features are characteristic of jet.

Two sets of analyses have been applied to components of this necklace. During the 1970s, Bussell analysed the composition of fragments from two of the fusiform beads using neutron activation analysis (NAA; Bussell 1976), and for the present study a tiny detached chip from a fusiform bead was mounted, polished and examined by Dr J.M. Jones by oil immersion reflected light microscopy and reflectance measurement. As the chip had been lying loose, it was impossible to determine from which bead it had originated. While the latter was shown to be of good quality jet, the beads analysed by Bussell did not have classic jet compositional signatures. She commented that their low lanthanum and scandium and high iron content were features shared by the specimens of cannel coal from north-east Yorkshire which were included in her programme of analysis, although they differed from these cannel coals in having exceptionally high levels of cobalt and lower lanthanum levels (Bussell 1976, 79. Note that Bussell later qualified her use of the term cannel coal by saying that the material could actually be Jet Rock oil-shales, or else soft jet, unless it was genuinely cannel coal that had been missed by the Geological Survey: *ibid*, 91). Elsewhere *(ibid*, 71) she noted that the level of scandium in jet could be very variable. Since work by Jones has shown that some jet can be high in iron (and since Bussell did not analyse a wide range of jet samples), the likelihood that all the beads are indeed of jet must be considered.

MANUFACTURE

Manufacturing traces in the form of shallow grinding striations were noted on all the plates, even though the presence of a coating of consolidant or lacquer on the right terminal plate has obscured some of these. Most of the striations are on the perforated edges of the left terminal plate and of both the spacer plates; some are unidirectional, others multidirectional. Further striations were noted on the upper and lower surfaces, and unperforated sides, of the left terminal plate.

The boring of the perforations in the plates had been carried out neatly, but the positioning of the lower holes close to the long edges had created problems for the terminal plates, since in both cases the holes on the outer side had broken through (Figure 7.2.4h). With the right hand terminal plate, the remains of a broken outer perforation are clearly visible and it appears that the plate had been narrowed along much of its length, and re-drilled. This would explain why this plate is *c.* 4mm narrower than its counterpart on the left.

The decoration on the upper surfaces of the plates is subtle and hard to see, as the colour distinction between the brown areas and the black areas is less marked than it would originally have been. There are very shallow and slightly rough-looking scratches, forming a geometric design on each of the plates. With the terminal plates the design consists of two triangles extending from the lower, broader edge and two long diamond shapes extending towards the upper, narrow edge (Figure 7.2.4e); on the spacer plates it consists of two sets of two opposed triangles extending from the inner and outer edges, their apices facing each other but not touching. The area inside the triangles and diamonds is blackish, while the rest of the upper surface is a deep brown. This is most clearly seen on spacer Sp 1 L (Figure 7.2.4f). The effect would have been achieved by first polishing the surface to a high sheen to bring out the black in the jet, then carefully dulling selected areas to bring out the dark brown colour of the jet's sub-surface (Redvers-Jones pers. comm.). Whether the scratch marks had been made beforehand to act as guidelines, or added afterwards, to highlight the boundary between the areas of different colour, is uncertain although the latter is indeed a plausible explanation. It is clear, in any case, that the selective dulling had been most skilfully executed.

The fusiform beads show manufacturing traces in the form of frequent remains of faceting towards the ends (Figure 7.2.4g), diagonal faint grinding striations towards each end, and other grinding striations elsewhere. Some beads also have traces of rilling in their borehole. They show that a consistent method of manufacture had been used. The beads had been polished to a high sheen, although its appearance has been enhanced by the application of consolidant or lacquer.

COMPLETENESS AND DAMAGE

The ancient damage and repair to the right terminal plate has already been noted. Other ancient damage to the plates comprises the loss of a large chip on the underside of the left terminal plate, leading from the perforation near the outer edge (Figure 7.2.4h); this was caused by thread-pull to a vulnerable area. Similar damage exists at the borehole on the upper, narrow edge of both terminal plates (Figure 7.2.4a), and a large spall had become detached next to the borehole on the underside of the right terminal plate, close to its outer edge. Spacer plate Sp 1 R has a large chip missing at the upper borehole on the right edge and a smaller spall missing from the underside at the opposite corner, and Sp 1 L has a small chip scar in a similar position. In most cases this damage will have been caused by thread-pull, but the last chip could have resulted from the drilling process. Damage to the upper surface of the right hand terminal plate that may be recent is the loss of a large chip, its long edge corresponding to a crack-line.

Several of the beads appear to have been damaged since their discovery, with some having been broken, or having lost chips, and then having been glued back together. A few beads had been chipped in antiquity. Damage is otherwise in the form of thread- or bead-on-bead wear (see below). Traces of probable 'Blu-Tack' were noted on a couple of the beads.

WEAR

The loss of parts of each terminal plate due to thread-pull to vulnerable areas has already been noted; in addition, there is a shallow thread-pull groove on the underside of the left hand terminal plate extending from the upper (narrow) end towards the outer edge, terminating at the upper borehole with a distinct nick, and terminating at the lower borehole with the loss of surface. The plate would nevertheless still have been usable. There is also thread-smoothing to the boreholes on this plate, and angled bead-on-plate wear towards the outer edge on its lower (broad) end. With the right hand terminal plate, the failure of the outermost borehole due to thread-pull had necessitated the re-shaping and re-boring of the plate, and this has obliterated part of the design on the upper surface. There had been thread-pull wear to both ends of the perforation at the upper (narrow) end, with loss of a chip on the edge, and polish to the perforation on the underside. The loss of a spall beside the borehole towards the outer edge may well also have resulted from thread pressure. There was no other obvious wear to the boreholes near the bottom (broad) edge, so it may be that the necklace was not worn for very long after the plate had been re-shaped.

The spacer plates show a lesser degree of wear, although the chipping and spalling around the boreholes on Sp 1 R may well be due to thread-pull, and some thread-polish to the interior of one of the perforations was noted. The left hand borehole near the outer edge of this plate also has some shallow bead-on-plate grinding wear. Similar bead-on-plate wear was noted at three of the four hole ends on spacer Sp 1 L (including both the ends towards the outer edge), and there was also thread-smoothing and polishing to both hole ends on the right side and to the outermost hole end on the left side.

The beads also showed thread-wear in the form of smoothing to the interior of the borehole, smoothing of the inner edge of the borehole, and chipping – or in a few cases, more marked angling – to one or both ends, from bead-on-bead wear. The overall degree of wear is shown in Table 7.2.2.

CONCLUSIONS

This necklace may well have been complete and have contained all its original components when buried. It falls within the category of spacer plate necklaces that deviate from the lunula-like format since it has only two spacer plates and only two strands. Like the other necklace in the cist (ID 267), it had been skilfully made, using very good quality material. It had clearly been worn for long enough for the terminal plates and a few of the beads to show signs of heavy wear, and for the right hand plate to have required re-shaping and re-boring.

Despite being a smaller necklace than ID 267 and lacking a jet fastener, ID 266 shares such marked similarities with it in terms of raw material, style of manufacture, bead shape and plate decoration that it could well have been made by the same person or group of people. The presence of these two necklaces in the cist raises the question of whether they had both belonged to the woman buried in the cist, or whether they may have been worn by related females of high status, perhaps a mother and daughter, with the smaller necklace being deposited as a grave good – be it associated with the child's skeleton or not – that symbolised the close bond between the two. The fact that its plates are relatively small and slender in comparison with those from many other spacer plate necklaces might lend support to the latter hypothesis.

The significance of this necklace, in terms of the rarity of its decorative technique, the possibility that it had been made by the same hand/s as ID 267 and the possibility that it had been made for a young person, is discussed further in Chapter 7.3.

The globular bead from Cow Low

This is globular in plan and roughly teardrop-shaped in profile, with a large, oval, eccentric hourglass perforation. The length is 15.0mm, the width 14.7mm and the thickness 7.7 to 12.4mm. The perforation measures 7.45 by 4.0mm. There is no obvious front or back surface to this bead. Macroscopically, the material is soft jet: the bead is black, with deep and extensive criss-cross cracking. The bead had been carefully smoothed so that any traces of manufacture had been removed, although there are gouge-like marks running part of the way around the edge of the perforation on one side. It is unclear why these marks are present. The bead has a high sheen, and although to some extent this is due to the presence of consolidant or lacquer, it is likely that it had originally been polished to a high sheen. The bead is complete and sound apart from the deep cracking. There is thread-polish around the inside of the perforation and

probable thread-smoothing to the edge of the perforation; overall, the degree of wear could be described as moderate.

ID 267 Cow Low, Green Fairfield, Derbyshire

References: Bateman 1848, 91–5; Howarth 1899, 57; Vine 1982, 62.

COMPOSITION

This spacer plate necklace, possibly complete, comprises one triangular fastener, two terminal plates, two pairs of spacer plates and 64 fusiform beads (rather than 40, as Bateman had erroneously stated; he seems to have counted only the beads lying behind the terminal plates in the reconstruction shown in Figure 7.2.5 even though he correctly gave the overall number of components in ID 266 and 267 as 117). The current arrangement of the components is almost certain to be Bateman's and is incorrect, for three reasons. First, the two largest spacer plates have been strung with their outermost edges facing inwards (so that what currently appears as the right hand plate should have been on the left hand side), and the terminal plates also need to be switched around, for the same reason. Second, the two other spacer plates are strung with their decorated surfaces on the underside of the necklace, suggesting that Bateman had not spotted the subtle decoration on all the plates. Finally, if the necklace had been strung in the conventional Early Bronze Age manner, the fusiform beads currently lying between the fastener and the terminal plates would instead have lain between the innermost pair of spacer plates.

CONTEXT AND ASSOCIATIONS

This is the larger of two jet spacer plate necklaces found in 1846 in a cist in a secondary position in a round barrow, the other being ID 266. Details of the cist's contents have already been presented in the entry for ID 266; as noted there, it may be that ID 267 had belonged with the adult female while the smaller necklace ID 266 had belonged with a child.

MORPHOLOGY

The fastener is flat, triangular with rounded corners, and has a narrow transverse perforation close to its longest edge; it is 29.3mm long, 12.7mm wide and 6.4mm in maximum thickness. The perforation diameter is 2.5mm.

The characteristics of the terminal and spacer plates are summarised in Appendix VII, Table 4. (See also Figure 7.2.6a–d). Sp 1 refers to the pair that would have been uppermost on the necklace (i.e. lying on or above the collarbone), and Sp 2 refers to the larger pair that would have lain lower down at the front of the necklace. L and R refer to the left and right sides as currently strung. All the plates have squared-off perforated edges and rounded unperforated edges, and all are flat (or flattish) and slightly

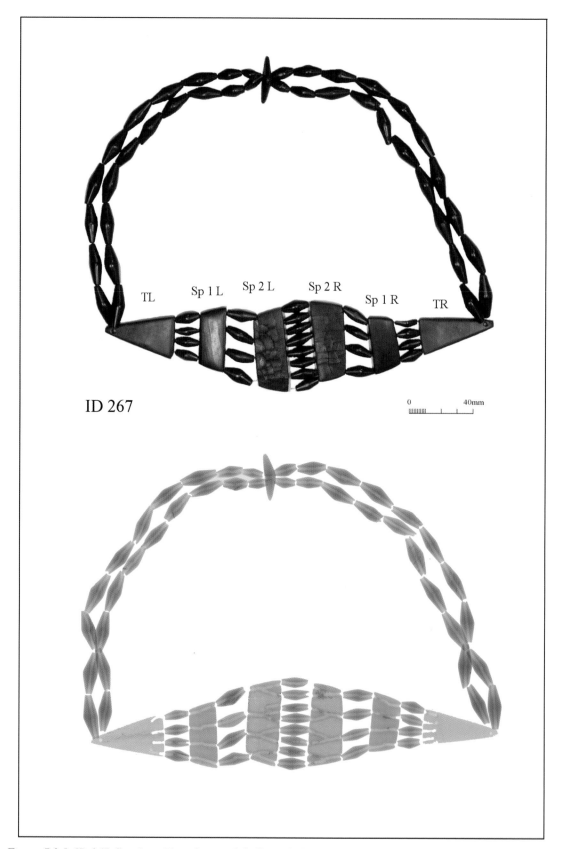

Figure 7.2.5. ID 267 Cow Low. Top: showing labelling of plates; bottom: X-ray (National Museums Scotland).

asymmetrical. As is the case with the other Cow Low necklace (ID 266), all the plates are relatively thin. The terminal plates (TL and TR) are isosceles triangles with squared-off apices (slanting on TR) and fairly straight sides; each has a single transverse hole near its apex and four elbow-bored holes along its wider edge. Both Sp 1 plates

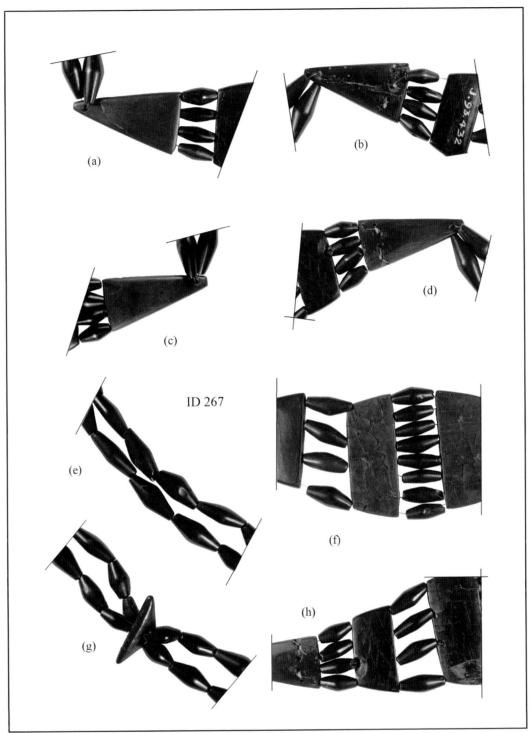

Figure 7.2.6. ID 267 Cow Low. Details showing: (a) TL front with faint incised triangular decoration; (b) TL back; (c) TR front with faint incised triangles; (d) TR back with multi-directional striations; (e) sloping ends of fusiform beads and dimple on one bead; (f) extensive cracking on plates; (g) fastener with criss-cross cracking, and (h) surface loss on Sp 1 R and incised diamond-shaped design.

have four through-bored holes and both Sp 2 plates have Y-borings that increase the number of holes from four to eight. All the plates are decorated with a faint geometric design on their upper surface; as noted above, two of the spacer plates have been strung into the necklace with these decorated faces pointing downwards.

The evidence indicating the original 'sidedness' of the terminal and Sp 2 plates is based on the direction of the thread-wear on the uppermost holes of the terminal plates, and on the fact that one unperforated edge of each of the Sp 2 plates is longer than the other. (The longer edge would originally have lain on the lower edge of the necklace).

The spacer plates are all trapezoidal with straight perforated edges and minimally-convex unperforated edges.

The fusiform beads (Figure 7.2.6a–h), like those in the other Cow Low necklace, are medium to plump in girth. Many are slightly angular in appearance; and many are flattish over part of their circumference, forming one or two flattish sides. Some or all of the 13 beads with two flattish sides had probably been designed to lie next to the Sp 2 plates, where eight beads would have had to be accommodated beside each of the plates. They range in length from 13.2 to 27.8mm and in maximum girth from 5.6 by 7.0mm to 9.3 by 9.85mm. Their ends are mostly squared off and roughly perpendicular. Apart from damaged examples, a few have one slightly sloping end, and one has two sloping ends (Figure 7.2.6e). A few have a cupped end, although it is unclear whether this relates to their drilling. Sixteen of the beads have one or more dimple feature, at various positions (Figure 7.2.6e). In one such case (labelled as bead 32 in the original notes) the multiple small hollows are clearly a natural, 'orange peel' surface irregularity, as seen in many jet objects, whereas on other beads some of the larger dimples had probably been a deliberate design feature to allow beads in adjacent strands to nestle tightly, while others may relate to accidental flaking during manufacture. Similar dimples had been noted on the fusiform beads from the other Cow Low necklace (ID 266).

MATERIAL

Macroscopically, all the components appear to be of jet, mostly hard jet, although the extensive cracking seen on the largest pair of spacer plates suggests that soft jet had been used for these (Figure 7.2.6f) (AS). All but one of the fusiform beads are black (with the exception being a black-brown), with a compact, very fine-grained woody texture. The blackness may have been enhanced slightly by the presence of a thin coating of consolidant/lacquer on some of the necklace components.

The fastener is blackish-brown on one side and a rich dark brown on the other, and has criss-cross cracking (Figure 7.2.6g). The plates range in colour from black (in the case of Sp 1 L) to a rich dark brown mottled with black-brown (in the case of Sp 2 R). A fine-grained woody texture was noted in the fusiform beads and in TR, Sp 1 R and Sp 2 L, and an area of matt, woody sub-surface has been exposed on the back of Sp 2 R where a spall had come off. Other features characteristic of jet include the aforementioned fine 'orange peel' surface irregularities seen on one bead (plus similar but longer hollows seen on the TL) and shiny conchoidal flake scars, seen on several beads.

Three sets of analyses have been applied to components of this necklace. During the 1970s, Bussell analysed fragments of a spacer plate and of a fusiform bead using neutron activation analysis (NAA), plus a further fusiform bead and a 'V-perforated endpiece' (presumably a terminal plate, although neither these nor the fastener is V-bored) using X-ray fluorescence spectrometry (XRF; Bussell 1976, 53, 63, 64, 79, 85, 92). She concluded that all of the items except one of the beads were of jet; the other had a high iron reading that was interpreted to indicate cannel coal or bituminous shale. (See above regarding Bussell's discussion of north-east Yorkshire cannel coal.) In 2007, Dr J.M. Jones analysed a tiny chip that had been lying loose among the components of the necklace, using oil immersion reflected light microscopy and reflectance measurement, and also found it to be of jet. Later in December 2007 Lore Troalen of National Museums Scotland analysed eight fusiform beads, the fastener and the TL using XRF. The fastener, the TL and six of the beads were found to be of jet with a composition that matched that of reference samples of Whitby jet. The remaining two beads were found to contain very little zirconium and a relatively high level of iron, even though macro- and microscopically they appear identical to the other beads; indeed, in one case (bead 20) slightly wavy woodgrain lines are visible. A similar compositional phenomenon had been noted by Bussell in her NAA analysis of two beads from the other Cow Low necklace (*ibid*, 79). However, since it is known that the iron content (and indeed zirconium content) of jet can vary, it is quite possible that the beads in question had indeed been made of jet, but with a high iron content due to proximity to pyrite inclusions. This would account for their jet-like texture. All the components analysed by Lore Troalen also produced a high calcium signature, which may well relate to their having been in contact with (or at least proximity to) the skeleton.

MANUFACTURE

Grinding striations were noted on all components except for the fastener and one of the fusiform beads. On the plates these are most commonly faint lines on the perforated edges, running either along or across them and clearly having been produced prior to perforation drilling, but the underside of Sp 2 R has numerous, multidirectional, fairly crisp striations, and there are also multidirectional striations (plus some gentle faceting) on the underside of TR, along with faint striations on one unperforated edge of TL and on both unperforated edges of Sp 2 R. On the fusiform beads the striations are mostly longitudinal, found towards the ends, but on 44 of the beads they are also found at the beads' mid-point, and in a very few cases they are also visible on the ends; they range from faint to crisp. Other signs of the initial shaping of the beads are the faceting, sometimes faint, sometimes obvious, seen on all but two of the fusiform beads.

A clear indication that the beads and plates had been drilled from both sides to create longitudinal perforations is provided by the X-ray (Figure 7.2.5). This image also shows an abortive borehole on Sp 2 L and its replacement in the adjacent Y-boring; the person who perforated the plate had evidently realised that the former was at the wrong angle to meet the long limb of the 'Y' that had already been drilled from the opposite end of the plate. Notwithstanding this fault, the drilling had been done skilfully and neatly. The relative consistency of the borehole diameters (including on the fastener) may indicate that the same drill had been used throughout. Rilling was noted on many of the beads (except where the perforation interior was obscured by tight stringing) and ranges from faint to crisp. The fastener may have been drilled from both sides; its sides are parallel.

All the components had been polished, possibly to a high sheen, although the degree of sheen visible today may have been affected by the application of a thin coating of clear consolidant or lacquer, which may have enhanced the sheen slightly, combined with a probable post-depositional dulling of the outer surfaces of the plates. The beads have a uniform high sheen. With most of the plates and the fastener a different degree of sheen was noted on different sides, with the back having (or retaining) a high sheen while the front has a medium sheen; this is probably due to natural, post-depositional dulling of the polish on the side facing out. Plates Sp 1 L and Sp 2 L have a more consistent level of polish, except on the unperforated edges of Sp 2 L, which have a lower sheen than the rest of the plate.

Regarding the decoration on the plates, this consists of a geometric design defined by shallow scratched lines; whether there had also been any selective dulling of areas of the design to create a two-tone, black and brown colouration, as had been noted in ID 266, is hard to tell but there are perhaps hints of this on the right terminal (Figure 7.2.6c). All that can be seen of the decoration on the left terminal is three triangles opening towards the lower perforated edge (Figure 7.2.6a), whereas on the right terminal the corresponding Vs are part of a design featuring rows of triangles (Figure 7.2.6c). The design on the spacer plates features rows of lozenges, terminating in triangles (Figure 7.2.6g); it is nearly imperceptible on the largest pair of plates, due to surface cracking. The narrowness (<0.2mm) and shallowness of the scratched lines indicates that a very narrow point or blade had been used to create them, and such is the similarity of the markings between ID 267 and ID 266 that it may be that the same tool had been used to create the designs. These lines (Figure 7.2.6a, c and h) resemble the guide lines made in preparation for the creation of a punctulated design that have been noted on some other decorated jet spacer plates. However, the evidence from the smaller Cow Low necklace suggests that we may not be dealing with guide lines for a design that was unfinished. On that necklace there are signs that selected areas within the design had had their polish deliberately dulled, to create a colour difference between the browner sub-surface thus exposed and the blacker, polished surface (see also Figure 7.2.4f); the lines may have been added after the dulling process, to accentuate the design. It may be that a similar decorative technique had been used for the plates on ID 267, but here any two-tone effect is much harder to spot, not least because of the extensive surface cracking and cupping on the Sp 2 plates.

COMPLETENESS AND DAMAGE

While the individual components are all complete or nearly

so, with the least complete being a fusiform bead where 20% had been lost from chipping, there is evidence for post-excavation damage to the ends of many of the beads, probably due to over-tight stringing for museum display. (This was also noted on the smaller Cow Low necklace.) Two beads had been broken and glued together, and it appears that the loss of one corner of Sp 2 L could also have been caused through over-tight stringing in the museum.

Surface degradation in the form of extensive criss-cross cracking, with some cupping, is evident on both the Sp 2 plates, and hairline criss-cross cracking, mostly superficial, was noted on the fastener, on the undecorated side of Sp 1 R and Sp 1 L and on virtually all of the beads. The TL has a few straight and curving hairline cracks.

Ancient damage was noted, both from the manufacture process and from wear. The former includes a deep chip missing from the underside of TR, plus a chip scar adjacent to the transverse hole on the back of the same terminal plate. The latter chipping may have occurred during the drilling process. A small spall had become detached from the decorated face of Sp 2 R during manufacture as had various small chips and spalls from several fusiform beads (although some of this loss may have occurred during subsequent wear, due to thread-pull). The narrowness of the jet used for the plates had clearly made the areas around the boreholes susceptible to surface loss, especially from thread-pull. This had probably caused the loss of a spall from the decorated surface of Sp 1 R (Figure 7.2.6h), extending from one of the boreholes, and of two spalls from the underside of Sp 2 R, extending from two holes. (The holes along the narrow edge of that plate had been drilled close to the underside of the plate). A similar loss, of one corner of the back of the TL (Figure 7.2.6b), could have resulted from either ancient or modern thread-pull. The loss of a spall from the adjacent elbow-boring on the back of the same plate will have occurred either during drilling, or else during wear, through pressure from the thread.

WEAR

The degree of wear is summarised in Table 7.2.2 and the distribution of the type of wear (i.e. thread-wear and bead-on-plate wear) among the components is summarised in Appendix VII, Table 5; essentially 23 out of the 71 components, or just under a third, show signs of moderate or heavy wear while the remainder show no or only slight wear. The bead polish and/or grinding noted around many of the holes is consistent with wear from the end of fusiform beads.

CONCLUSIONS

Despite the use of both soft and hard jet, the consistency of the design and manufacture of the components (and indeed of the ancient wear traces) strongly suggests that they had been made and used together. Even where one of the fusiform beads (No. 47 in the record notes) differs from the rest in being a rich dark brown colour rather than black, this does not mean that it had not been made as part of the original set; some of the plates include this colour of jet.

The necklace may well have been complete when deposited. Even though most complete jet spacer plate necklaces had been made using significantly more than the 64 fusiform beads found here, the Cow Low set would have formed a perfectly adequate necklace, with the central eight strands each containing six beads (if strung as a conventional spacer plate necklace). The overall increase in strands from the back to the front of the necklace is from four (between the terminals and Sp 1 plates, and between the Sp 1 and Sp 2 plates) and eight (between the Sp 2 plates).

The most striking characteristic of this necklace is its close similarity to the other spacer plate necklace found at Cow Low (ID 266), the key difference being that the latter had only two strands and fewer fusiform beads (42, as opposed to 64). In material and style of manufacture, however, the necklaces are virtually identical and it is tempting to speculate that they may have been made for, and belonged to, two generations of elite females. One cannot be certain whether the child bones found outside the cist had belonged to an interment in the cist which had been subsequently disturbed, but this is a distinct possibility. Like the smaller necklace (ID 266), ID 267 had seen some use before it was deposited in the cist, but clearly not heavy wear overall; those fusiform beads whose degree of wear is described as 'very worn' have wear relating to tight stringing in antiquity, where the pressure from the thread and/or adjacent beads had caused some chipping and/or grinding. (The recent chipping due to over-tight stringing in the museum is not counted in the assessment of wear.)

ID 268 Hill Head (Hasling House), Hartington Upper, Derbyshire

References: Bateman 1861, 66–7; Howarth 1899, 60–1; Bussell 1976, 53, 85, 92; Vine 1982, 404, no. 938; Shepherd 2009.

COMPOSITION

This spacer plate necklace comprises one left terminal plate with perforations for three strands of beads, a pair of upper spacer plates (each bored to increase the number of strands from three to four), a pair of 'four to eight' lower spacer plates, 47 fusiform beads, nine tiny disc beads, and 12 V-perforated buttons. (See Figure 7.2.7, which includes an X-ray image of the plates and associated beads). When found there had been six further fusiform beads and two more disc beads, bringing the total of components to 81. The plates are all undecorated. A painted wooden right hand terminal plate was added during the 19th century, along with metal plates at either end of the damaged right-hand upper spacer plate (Sp 1 R) and at the broad end of the lower right-hand spacer plate (Sp 2 R). There is no record of the necklace having had a fastener, although it may have had one of perishable organic material. Bateman remarked that it was likely that 'many more of the small flat beads

[i.e. the disc beads] would have been found if the tumulus had not been before disturbed'.

CONTEXT AND ASSOCIATIONS

The components were found scattered over 'an area of many feet' under a previously-opened and greatly denuded round barrow, 'around twelve yards' across' (Bateman 1861, 66–7). The necklace will have been associated with one of three or four skeletons whose remains had been disturbed by the earlier exploration.

MORPHOLOGY

The left terminal plate (TL) is of a roughly trapezoidal D shape, of length 40.0mm, width 24.1mm and thickness 7.4mm (Figure 7.2.8a and b). Its outer edge curves out more markedly than its inner and it has squared-off perforated ends, gently rounded sides, a flattish inner surface and a slightly convex outer surface. It has one elbow-bored hole at its upper end (for the thread loop that either held, or looped around, the fastener) and three elbow-bored holes at its lower end. The other plates are all trapezoidal, with similar shaped ends and sides, and flattish surfaces (e.g. Figure 7.2.8c and d). With the exception of Sp 1 R, all are through-bored, with the increase in the perforations from the plates' shorter to longer edges being achieved by adding elbow-boreholes between the through-borings (e.g. Sp 2 R, Figure 7.2.8d; also X-ray Figure 7.2.7). The holes in Sp 1 R had all been elbow-bored (Figure 7.2.8e; also X-ray Figure 7.2.7). The dimensions are shown in Appendix VII, Table 6.

The morphology of the fusiform beads varies according to their material (see below), with the single shale bead and those of the inferior quality black jet being slenderer and less tapered than those made of the better quality jet; some are virtually cylindrical (Figure 7.2.8f, bottom bead). The chunky-looking bead of shale adjacent to TL measures 10.9 by 7.5mm with a perforation diameter of 2.6mm, and the black jet examples range in length from 9.2 to 21mm and in maximum diameter/width from 4.2 to 7.3mm. The boreholes range from 2.2 to 3.5mm. Eleven of the black jet beads are flattish on two sides and could originally have been made to lie close together immediately adjacent to the longer edge of the lower spacer plates. The fusiform beads are made of better quality jet and tend to be larger, fatter and more tapered; two stand out as being larger than the rest and these had probably originated in a different necklace. These are both around 21mm long, the fattest being 11mm in maximum width; they are the second and third beads counting up from the modern TR in Figure 7.2.7. The rest of the fusiform beads are of good quality jet and range in length from 13.1 to 25mm and in maximum diameter/width from 6.0 to 9.2mm, with perforation diameters from 2.4 to 3.9mm.

The disc beads are of a uniform size and shape, with external diameters ranging from 3.5 to 4.2mm, thicknesses from 1.0 to 1.9mm and perforation diameters from 1.9 to 2.7mm. All are neatly circular; six are minimally wedge-shaped in profile, the others parallel-sided, and all but one have a central perforation (Figures 7.2.8f).

The buttons are fairly small, ranging in diameter from 12.2 to 17mm and in height from 5.1mm (low-domed) to 7.7mm (high-domed) (Figure 7.2.7 and 7.2.8g). The dome shape ranges from a continuous curve to a marked cone. According to Shepherd (2009), six fall within his Type 2, the others in Type 2a. All but three are roughly circular in plan, the others being sub-rectangular with rounded corners. All are flat-based; five have a narrow facet at the base-dome junction. The perforation diameters and spacing vary, with two of the sub-rectangular buttons having relatively small perforations (no larger than 2.6mm in one case), contrasting with one of the low-domed circular buttons, with perforations over 5mm in diameter.

MATERIAL

Macro- and microscopically it appears that the plates, disc beads and one of the fusiform beads are of cannel coal or shale, black in colour (dark grey in the disc beads) and polished to a low to medium sheen. Some of the disc beads are matt. The buttons and 17 of the fusiform beads appear to be of a high quality jet, rich brown or brown and black and polished to a high sheen. The remaining beads are of a different and blacker kind of jet, compact and with a fine woody texture but with a low sheen and arguably of inferior quality (AS). Compositional analysis had previously been undertaken by Bussell (1976) using neutron activation analysis to examine two spacer plates, one fusiform bead and three disc beads, and X-ray fluorescence spectrometry (XRF) to analyse a further spacer plate and two fusiform beads. Additional XRF analysis was undertaken in 2007 by Lore Troalen, National Museums Scotland, and this covered all the plates (including the Victorian terminal), four fusiform beads and two buttons. The X-raying was also undertaken by Lore Troalen. The analytical results agreed with Bussell's earlier findings and confirmed the macro/microscopic identifications. Regarding the non-jet material, Bussell had observed that it has compositional features in common both with Swine Sty cannel coal and with Kimmeridge shale, and suggested that it was probably a bituminous shale from the Jet Rock of north-east Yorkshire. One of the disc beads (not analysed) is light grey at its edge but dark grey elsewhere, prompting speculation that it might have been made of a light-coloured material, coated in antiquity to make it resemble jet or shale.

MANUFACTURE (X-ray Figure 7.2.7)

Faint grinding striations are visible at each end of the terminal plate (with those at the top end slightly deeper than those on the bottom) and also on each of the perforated edges of Sp 1 L, on the longer of the perforated edges of Sp 1 R, on both perforated edges of Sp 2 L, on the shorter of the perforated edges and on the underside of Sp 2 R, on seven of the fusiform beads, and on the base of nine of the buttons (Figure 7.2.8g). A tenth button has crisper striations on its base. Striations were also noted on four of the button facets.

Faint rilling marks were noted in the perforations of five of the buttons and a change of slope, indicating a repositioning of the drill, was noted in the perforations in four, possibly five cases. The fusiform beads had been drilled from either end, and this was also the case with the through-perforations on the plates. The elbow-borings had been drilled from the edge and the back of the plate. With the disc beads, in most cases the perforations are parallel-sided and it is not possible to tell whether they had been individually drilled. However, in one case the presence of one angled end may indicate where the drill had entered from one side, and in another, both sides of the bead taper in towards the perforation.

One of the fusiform beads has two shallow gouge marks where an inclusion in the jet had been gouged out; further gouge marks were noted on three of the buttons, and in one case the mark is adjacent to a crystalline inclusion which had been left *in situ*. Two of the fusiform beads have traces of the faceting left from their initial shaping.

COMPLETENESS AND DAMAGE

Overall, the necklace lacks its original right terminal plate and perhaps its fastener (and probably many of its fusiform and disc beads) and there is damage to the corners of Sp 2 L (Figure 7.2.8d), Sp 2 R (Figure 7.2.8c) and Sp 1 R; over a quarter of Sp 1 R had chipped off in antiquity (Figure 7.2.8e). The upper surface of Sp 1 L has extensive laminar spalling, and the terminal plate had split along a lamination plane. There is also a deep laminar crack on the back of Sp 2 L (Figure 7.2.8d).

Damage resulting from manufacture is clear on the underside of Sp 1 L, where the drilling of the elbow-bore hole had created a large shallow chip. This, together with thread-pull from one end of one of the through-perforations, led to the spalling-off of much of the underside. It may well be that the elbow-boring of Sp 1 R had led to the loss of much of this plate, weakening an already poor-quality piece of laminar shale. Manufacture damage is also visible on some of the buttons: in one case the drill had broken through the upper surface, and with the others, there is minor chipping to the edge of the perforations.

Damage resulting from wear was noted on the plates and on several of the fusiform beads. Recent damage was noted on Sp 1 R where fragments had become detached and been badly glued back (Figure 7.2.8e). Fourteen of the fusiform beads also have recent damage: in most cases the beads had been broken and the pieces badly glued together, but there was also end damage that could have resulted from the way that the necklace had been re-strung for display. The loss of a large chip from one of the buttons may also have occurred since the excavation. On another button there has been some spalling and chipping as a result of the cracking of the jet.

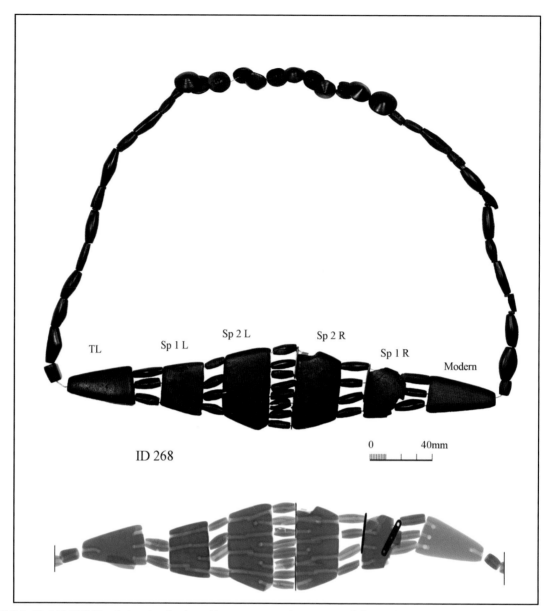

Figure 7.2.7. ID 268 Hill Head showing (top) necklace as currently strung and (bottom) X-ray of plates and associated beads (National Museums Scotland).

WEAR

The various necklace components exhibit differential wear, as detailed in Table 7.2.2; the nature of wear to the plates and spacers is shown in Appendix VII, Table 7. The wear to the fusiform beads consists of thread-smoothing, polishing and chipping due to thread-pull and bead-on-bead wear, leading to shallow to deep grooving where the end of one bead has ground into the end of the adjacent bead at an angle.

In general, the buttons are noticeably less worn than the fusiform beads and plates. The wear consists mostly of thread-smoothing and polish to the perforations, with the smoothing most marked on the outer edges in all but one case – the exception having most wear to the inner edge of the perforations. Some probable 'garment or skin rub'

wear to the base of the buttons was noted in six cases. As for the disc beads, it is always hard to detect signs of wear, and no obvious signs were noted in this case.

CONCLUSIONS

This necklace was old when buried, and apparently lacking its right terminal plate (although it could have had an organic plate that decomposed completely, or else the plate had been removed or destroyed during the initial exploration of the barrow). The variation in raw material, shape and degree of wear of its various components indicates that they are an amalgam of parts from different necklaces, with the shale components (or at least the old, mostly heavily worn shale plates) coming from one necklace, the compact dark

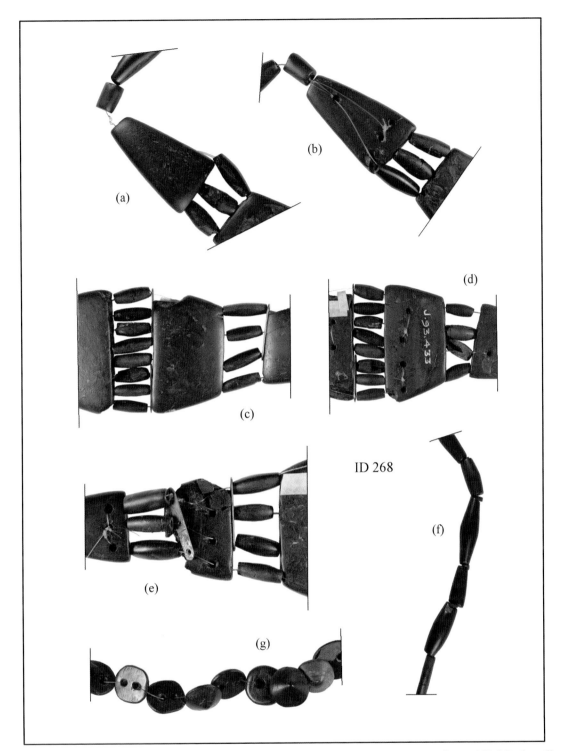

Figure 7.2.8. ID 268 Hill Head. Details showing: (a) front of TL plate: (b) rear of TL plate; (c) front of SP 2 R plate illustrating damage; (d) rear of SP 2 L plate illustrating damage; (e) rear of Sp 1 R with lost corner, damage and glueing; (f) selection of fusiform beads and disc beads; (g) buttons, also illustrating manufacturing striations. Details not to consistent scale.

jet fusiform beads coming from another, the buttons and 15 of the fusiform beads of good quality jet coming from a third, and two further fusiform beads of the same kind of jet probably coming from a fourth.

ID 269 Middleton Moor, Middleton and Smerrill, Derbyshire

References: Jewitt 1850; Bateman 1861, 24–6; Davis and Thurnam 1865; Howarth 1899, 61–2; Bussell 1976, chapters 11 and 12; Vine 1982, 404, no. 937; Shepherd 2009, 357, no. 13, a–j.

COMPOSITION

This collection of beads, plates and buttons may well have been buried as a necklace but cannot be arranged into a conventional spacer plate necklace design (Figures 7.2.9–11; Figure 7.2.10 is a watercolour by Jewitt, in Museums Sheffield, showing the various components). There are currently 407 components (including a Victorian narrow spacer plate) but Bateman's account mentions 420, so 14 tiny disc beads are now missing. It has varying numbers of strands (up to seven) according to the variously-bored spacer and terminal plates and is currently strung according to the arrangement shown in Bateman's publication (1861, 24–6). This arrangement is undoubtedly wrong, not least since Bateman failed to recognise the presence of a triangular fastener. While the original arrangement of the components cannot be ascertained, if there had been the intention to make the assemblage appear like a lunula-like spacer plate necklace then the fastener should have been at the back, next to two of the terminal plates, and more of the fusiform beads should have lain between the spacer plates than are shown in its current arrangement.

The currently extant components are as follows (excluding the Victorian spacer plate no. 66; numbers as per Figure 7.2.9):

- No. 69. One flat triangular fastener (Figure 7.2.11a).
- Nos. 65, 72 and 73. Three terminal plates, with differing numbers of boreholes along their lower edge (Figure 7.2.11b–d).
- Nos. 67 and 68. Two narrow spacer plates of black material (no. 67, Figure 7.2.11a).
- No. 71. One bone spacer plate (Figure 7.2.11e).
- No. 70. One fragment of a spacer plate, re-used as a bead (Figure 7.2.11a).
- Nos. 1–10 and no. 31. Ten complete (or near-complete) V- perforated buttons, plus one fragmentary example, used as beads (front views Figure 7.2.11f–g; back views Figure 7.2.11h–i).
- 53 fusiform beads (Nos. 11–30, 32–64; Figure 7.2.9).
- Nos. 74–406. 334 tiny disc beads (out of the original total of 348) (Figure 7.2.9 and Figure 7.2.11c, e and j).

CONTEXT AND ASSOCIATIONS

The necklace was recovered from a 'rude cist or enclosure', comprising several slabs and boulders set on edge, under a very small, low barrow near Arbor Low henge near the boundary of Middleton Moor in the direction of Parcelly Hay (Bateman 1861, 24). The 'cist' contained the remains of an adult female lying on her left side, legs flexed, plus a child of around four years above her, behind her shoulders. The necklace is reported to have been found around the woman's neck, but while it may well have been on her neck when she was buried, it will have disaggregated when the thread decayed. The adult skeleton has recently been studied and radiocarbon dated for the *Beaker People Project* (2010–1772 cal BC; see Chapter 9). While the most recent

osteological identification as to sex has concluded that the individual might have been male, both Bateman and Davis and Thurnam were adamant that the sex had been female. The individual's age (stated by Bateman to be 'about 40' 1861, 264) has been confirmed as 'middle adult'.

MORPHOLOGY

The reference numbers correspond with those shown on the illustration (Figure 7.2.9). The Victorian piece (spacer plate no. 66) is not included in the following discussion.

The fastener (no. 69; Figure 7.2.11a) is 30.5mm long, 16.5mm wide and 4.7mm in maximum thickness. It is flattish with a slender D-/rounded-triangular shape, with one long straight edge and one continuously curving edge, both rounded. Two spalls had broken off from the junction between the straight and the curving edge in prehistory, and wear to the straight edge has left it a little uneven. The perforation is roughly central and transverse, running through the flattish sides.

Details of the terminal and spacer plates (nos. 65, 67, 68, 70–73, of which no. 70 is a fragmentary spacer plate reused as a bead) are summarised in Appendix VII, Table 8, with perforation numbering corresponding to the sketches in the original record sheets. See also Figure 7.2.11a–e.

Eight of the ten complete or near-complete buttons (nos. 1–10; Figure 7.2.11f–i) have a roundish base; nos. 2 and 3 have (or had been) oval-based, and the base of no. 2 is slightly convex. One (no. 7) is low-domed (height 4.2mm). Three, plus the fragment (no. 31), had been high-domed (maximum height 10.1mm), and the rest, medium-domed. No. 1 has an upright facet at the wall-base junction. The smallest button (excluding the fragment), no. 6, measures 15.2 to 16.1mm at its base; the largest, no. 3, 18.5 to 22.9mm. Even though Shepherd had classed all the buttons as his Type 2, there is clearly some variability.

The fusiform beads (nos. 11–30, 32–64; Figure 7.2.9) range from slender (e.g. no. 23) to plump (e.g. no. 64), with ends that are perpendicular to the long axis in some cases (e.g. no. 39), slanted (in the same or different directions, e.g. nos. 13 and 51 respectively), or perpendicular at one end and slanted at the other (e.g. no. 24). At least two (nos. 53 and 56) have two flat sides and could originally have been designed to sit below a lower spacer plate. Many have had their original shape considerably modified through bead-on-bead wear. The beads range in length from 9.3 to 24.7mm (although in several cases the length has been shortened through wear); the diameter/thickness range is 5.2 to 9.4mm, and the perforation diameter range is 1.7 to 3.2mm.

The tiny disc beads (nos. 74–406; Figure 7.2.11c) are circular in plan and straight-edged, with a central perforation. They range in outer diameter from 3.4 to 5.1mm, and in thickness from 0.6 to 3.2mm. (It was not possible to measure the diameter of the perforation). Some 45 are wedge-shaped in profile, while the others have parallel flat sides. The outer edge of many of the beads has been polished to a medium sheen.

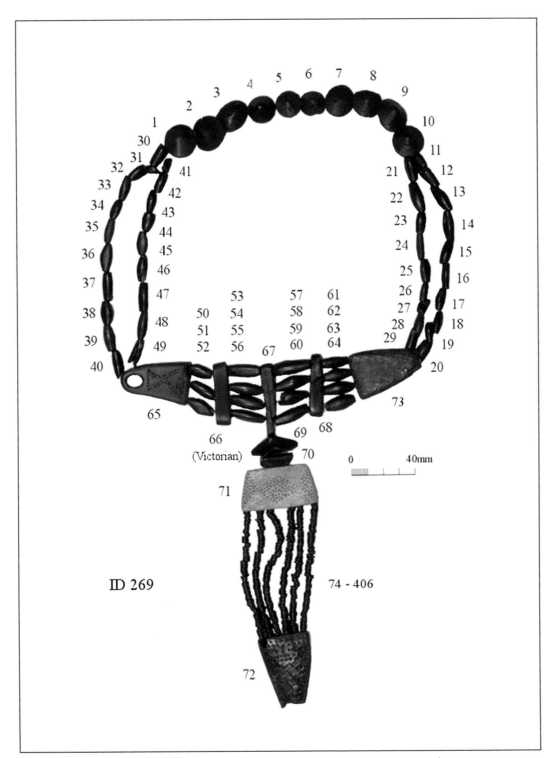

Figure 7.2.9. ID 269 Middleton Moor necklace showing numbering used in text.

MATERIAL

Identification of the material has been by macro- and microscopic examination; by neutron activation analysis of five components (by Bussell), and by X-ray fluorescence spectrometry (XRF) of one of the decorated terminal plates (Bussell 1976, 53, 78, 79, 85, 92). Reflectance microscopy was also undertaken by Dr J. M. Jones on a tiny detached speck (unlocated as to component) and on a detached chip

from one of the narrow spacer plates (no. 68). The latter had been accidentally glued in the past to an adjacent fusiform bead (no. 62).

Four, possibly five materials appear to be present, including the mammal bone from which the largest of the spacer plates had been made. (The species of this bone was not determined during the project). From macro- and microscopic examination it appears that all ten of the

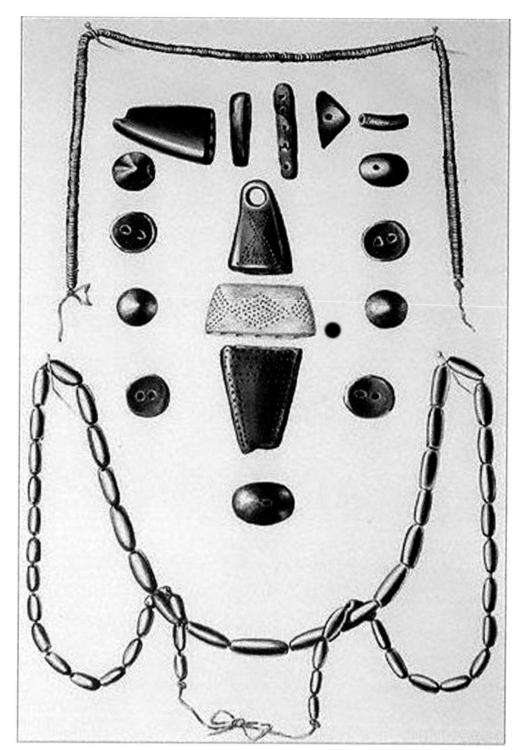

Figure 7.2.10. ID 269 Middleton Moor, early watercolour of components by Jewitt, courtesy of Museums Sheffield.

complete/substantially complete buttons are of jet, as are all three of the terminal plates, the fragment of a spacer plate reused as a bead, plus seven out of the 53 fusiform beads (AS/AW). Its colour ranges from a rich chocolate brown (as seen in the terminal plate, no. 65 (Figure 7.2.11b) to blackish, with some pieces being a variegated dark brown/black-brown colouration Figure 7.2.11f–i). Both hard and soft jet are present, the latter showing extensive criss-cross cracking (plus some concentric cracking, on some buttons).

The eleventh button, the fastener, the narrow spacer plates (excluding the Victorian piece), the remaining fusiform beads and the tiny disc beads are of cannel coal or shale, of a blackish-grey or black colour. Some of the components of this material show laminar cracking.

The various analyses confirm these observations. The tiny speck of material identified by Dr J. M. Jones (which is likely to have been detached from one of the cracked, fragile components) was confirmed as being of good

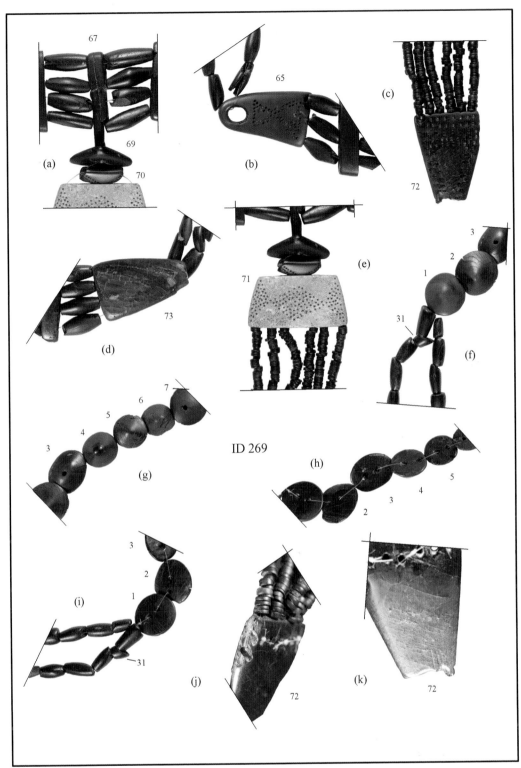

Figure 7.2.11. ID 269 Middleton Moor. Details showing: (a) triangular fastener (no. 69), spacer plate reused as bead (no. 70) and narrow spacer plate (no. 67); (b–d) terminal plates nos. 65, 72 and 73 exhibiting different numbers of boreholes, also disc beads; (e) bone spacer plate (no. 71) and disc beads; (f–i) V-perforated buttons including fragmentary example used as bead (no. 31); (j) break and abandonment of perforation in terminal (no. 72) and disc beads, and (k) fractured lower end of terminal (no. 72) inhibiting further stringing.

quality Whitby jet. The chip from the narrow spacer plate was confirmed as being of cannel coal, with a vitrinite reflectance value of 0.6; it might derive from any of the northern British coalfields (pers. comm. Dr J. M. Jones). As for the components analysed by Bussell, two were tiny disc beads, and the material of one (her sample 456.7) was identified as 'resembling Kimmeridge shale in all characteristic elements', while the other was identified as being similar to a cannel coal (Bussell 1976, 78–9). Material resembling Kimmeridge shale may well be bituminous oil shale from the Jet Rock of north-east Yorkshire (*ibid*, 92). A third sample was a fragment of one of the narrow spacer plates – it is uncertain whether this was the same plate as analysed by Dr J. M. Jones, but it is likely – and its material was found to be cannel coal. The remaining two samples were one longitudinal segment of a fusiform bead, plus a fragment of another; both must have been from among the beads macro/microscopically identified in the current project as being of cannel coal, as they are described as being dull and black. Bussell concluded that both were 'extremely unusual' compositionally, and could not be matched with her analysed raw material samples of jet, cannel coals and shales. However, some kind of cannel coal or shale is implied by their texture and colour. Finally, the results of the XRF analysis of the decorated terminal plate concluded that it was probably of jet. Thus, the necklace contains components of bone, Whitby jet, cannel coal, Kimmeridge shale-like oil shale, and an unusual material (but probably in the cannel coal/shale family). Had all the dull black fusiform beads been analysed, it would have become clear whether the two examined by Bussell had a typical composition. The Whitby jet and North Yorkshire oil shale components would have travelled across the Pennines; whether the cannel coal (and indeed bone) components had come from North Yorkshire or closer to the findspot cannot be determined.

MANUFACTURE

In the case of the fastener (no. 69), its perforation had been drilled from both sides and is nearly perpendicular; there are traces of rilling in the borehole on both sides.

With the terminal and spacer plates, faint grinding striations were evident on both perforated edges of no. 73 (faint), more marked striations were seen on the bottom edge of no. 65, and very faint striations were seen on one of the perforated edges of no. 68; others were seen at various points on the front and back surfaces of no. 72. As regards their perforations, the large transverse perforation at the top of no. 65 had been drilled from both sides, as had the smaller (and probably non-original) perforation at the top of no. 72. There is ancient chipping around the top hole of no. 65. There had clearly been problems with the seventh perforation along the lower, outer edge of no. 72: there are traces of an aborted drill hole on the back, and further up, a diagonal replacement hole had been drilled, but this may have led to the whole of the corner breaking off and the abandonment of the seventh perforation (Figure 7.2.11j). No rilling marks were noted in any of the perforations except for the exposed seventh perforation on no. 72. A slight funnelling to the outer parts of three holes on the right hand edge of plate no. 67, and to two holes on the left hand side of plate no. 68, relates either to the hole-boring process or to bead-on-plate wear. The same is true of some of the holes on no. 73.

Regarding the decoration on the spacer plates, the tools used to make the punctulated decoration tapered to a rounded point. Variation in the width of the punctulations makes it clear that different tools had been used on each of the plates. No guidelines were noted on any of the designs. The white material in no. 65, and the yellow material in nos. 70 and 72, constitutes the last traces of material probably used both to polish the plates and to highlight the design. Other features relating to the manufacture of the spacer plates consist of two oval gouge marks on the curving side of no. 70, the spacer plate that had been converted into a bead. The reshaping, using this gouge, had carefully avoided all but the endmost perforation.

With the buttons, faint, multi-directional grinding striations were noted on the base of nos. 1, 2, 8 and 10, and very faint, vertical striations were noted on the dome of nos. 1 and 2. The perforations had probably been drilled in two stages; any rilling made by the drill had been totally or largely worn away. In two cases (nos. 3 and 7), one of the perforations had broken through the dome. The bridge between the perforations is mostly of medium width to wide.

Time constraints meant that the fusiform beads could not be individually examined under a microscope, but none showed obvious faceting or manufacturing striations.

As far as could be discerned from the tiny disc beads whose interior surfaces could be seen, the perforations are parallel-sided. It is unclear whether they had been perforated individually, but if they had been, then they would have been drilled wholly or mainly from one side, to judge from the shape of the borehole.

COMPLETENESS AND DAMAGE

In addition to those components that are incomplete due to heavy wear (see below), several components show signs of ancient damage. The end of terminal plate no. 72 had broken off in antiquity and its fracture surface had subsequently become worn: a short groove adjacent to the fracture surface on the underside of the plate may relate to an abandoned attempt to create an anchor for a thread to continue its stringing (Figure 7.2.11j). This piece had also lost part of one lower corner, and an attempt seems to have been made, then abandoned, to replace the seventh borehole that had been truncated by the loss (see above and Figure 7.2.11j). Overall, the plate had lost around 15%, leaving *c*. 85% extant. The fragmentary button (no. 31), reused as a bead, had lost much more of its body in antiquity, with only around 30% being present. Similarly, the old spacer plate (no. 70), reused as a bead, is less than 20% of its original size. As for the narrow spacer plates, no. 67 is 75–80% complete (with the loss of a large fragment occurring in antiquity), while no. 68 is 96% present (with the detachment of the small fragment having occurred post-excavation). Ancient damage was responsible for the loss of surface around one borehole on terminal plate no. 65. On the fastener, two spalls from each of the acute-angled corners had become detached, through use, in antiquity. More modern damage is suggested by the fact that one of the narrow spacer plates (no. 67) had been broken and glued.

The fact that the fastener and most of the plates have a higher sheen on their underside (presumably the side touching the body) than on their upper side suggests that they had all originally been polished to the degree seen on the underside, with the micro-environment of the grave causing dulling to the upper surface.

WEAR

The overall degree of wear noted on the various components is shown in Table 7.2.2 (including the bone spacer plate but excluding the Victorian spacer plate, and grouping the terminal plates with the spacer plates). Over 50% of the components whose wear could be assessed show signs of heavy wear. As for the tiny disc beads, since they are fairly tightly strung, it was hard to inspect their interior surfaces for signs of wear. From superficial inspection it is likely that they have light to moderate wear; in any case, disc beads tend to wear less than fusiform beads.

Both thread-wear and bead-on-bead wear (plus some possible bead-on-plate wear) is also present. The fastener (no. 69) shows thread-smoothing all around the perforation, with polish on the edges of the rilling and at the centre point of the hole. Also, there is a broad thread-wear groove on the straight edge of the fastener which corresponds to the position of an old, worn spall scar (also likely to relate to thread-wear, from the pressure of the tight thread causing a spall to pop off). Old spall scars at the corners on one side are not due to thread-wear, but probably due to general wear. A detailed analysis of wear on the spacer plates is shown in Appendix VII, Table 9.

All the buttons have thread-smoothing, especially to the outer edge of the perforations, plus thread-polish that runs at least half way down the perforations. (The innermost area is obscured by the thread). This lateral wear is characteristic of the wear seen on necklace buttons. At least some of the polish on the flat side of the buttons is likely to have resulted from wear, with the buttons rubbing against a garment or against skin.

All kinds of thread-wear and bead-on-bead wear were noted on the fusiform beads, with the degree of wear being heavy in *c.* 50% of cases. The difficulty of ascertaining the degree (and kind) of wear to the tiny disc beads has been noted above.

CONCLUSIONS

This necklace had clearly been an heirloom item when buried as it constitutes the gathered-up remains of at least six necklaces – to judge from the variability in borehole numbers, the decoration on the terminal and spacer plates, and the shape of the terminal and spacer plates. It also includes a significant proportion of heavily worn components, as well as a variety of materials. As noted above, its beads and plates could not have been strung as a conventional spacer plate necklace and it is unclear exactly

how (or indeed whether) they had been strung, although some suggestions are offered above. No matches between any of the plates in this necklace and those seen in other spacer plate necklaces have been found.

The radiocarbon date for the associated skeleton is in line with the conclusion that many of the necklace components were old when buried: since we know (from dated Scottish examples) that some spacer plate necklaces had been made during the last two centuries of the third millennium BC, parts of the Middleton Moor necklace could theoretically have been centuries old when buried.

ID 270 (including ID 256 and ID 257) Grindlow, Over Haddon, Derbyshire

References: Bateman 1861, 46–8; Howarth 1899, 62–4; Bussell 1976, 53, 63, 64, 79, 80, 85, 91–2; Vine 1982, 404 (nos. 939–40); Shepherd 2009, 356 (no. 13).

COMPOSITION

This is a three-strand spacer plate necklace (Figure 7.2.12). When found it was described by Bateman as comprising seven spacer plates of jet and one of bone, together with 26 fusiform ('cylindrical') beads and 39 buttons ('conical studs'), making a total of 73 components (Bateman 1861, 46–8; see also Howarth 1899, 62–4 and Vine 1982, 404, nos. 939–40). In his published illustration of the strung necklace, a woodcut by Jewitt (in Bateman 1861; Figure 7.2.12, top), the bone spacer plate is not shown, and only 36 buttons are shown. Today there are 36 buttons, although two (ID 256 and ID 257) are stored separately from the necklace. Unless three buttons went missing at an early stage or were deliberately omitted from Jewitt's engraving, the possibility that Bateman mistakenly wrote '39' for '36' must be borne in mind. As currently strung, the necklace follows Bateman's arrangement (Figure 7.2.12).

CONTEXT AND ASSOCIATIONS

The necklace was found in a primary grave, possibly rock-cut ('on the rock a little below the natural surface': Bateman 1861, 47) and under a round barrow five feet (*c.* 1.5m) high at its summit. It was associated with one of three contracted skeletons and accompanied by 'one or two rude instruments of flint' (*ibid*). According to Bateman, two of the three skeletons were female, and the necklace was associated with one of these. The account refers to the bodies being covered with stone and, above that, with earth. No formal cist structure is mentioned.

MORPHOLOGY

The spacer plates comprise six decorated jet plates, one undecorated jet plate and a decorated bone plate (Figure 7.2.12 and Figure 7.2.13a–f). The six decorated jet plates are all flat and slightly trapezoidal, with gently squared-off outer and inner edges and more sharply squared-off

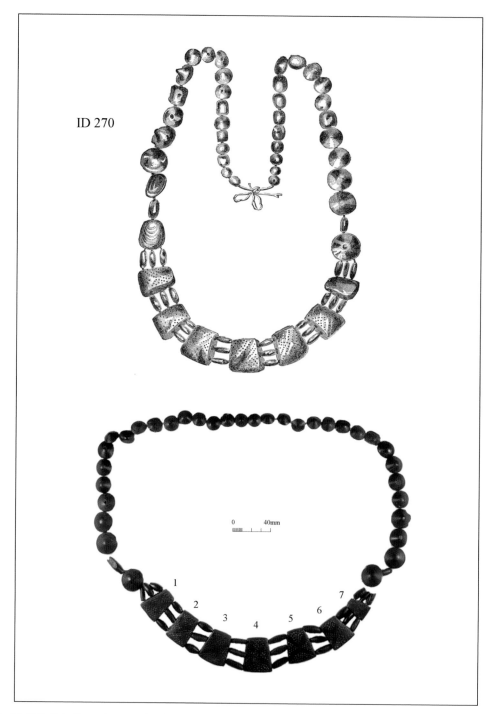

ID 270

Figure 7.2.12. ID 270 Grindlow showing (top) Jewitt woodcut of 1861 and (bottom) necklace as currently strung. Note: the bone spacer plate is not shown.

perforated edges (Figure 7.2.12, with examples in Figure 7.2.13a–c). They each have three sets of elbow-borings and are of roughly similar size to each other. Their dimensions, along with those of the other spacer plates, are summarised in Appendix VII, Table 10. They are decorated on their outer surface with a saltire design, created by filling triangular areas with punctulations and leaving a blank cross-shaped area between them. The maximum diameter of the punctulations is *c.* 1.4mm. Creamy-white material in

some of the punctulations may be a deliberate inlay, used to pick out the design.

The undecorated spacer plate (Figure 7.2.13d) is smaller than the decorated plates, and more markedly trapezoidal. It has three through-bored perforations. It is flat, with gently squared off outer and inner edges and more markedly squared-off perforated edges.

The bone spacer plate (not illustrated) is narrow, minimally trapezoidal, and significantly wider than all

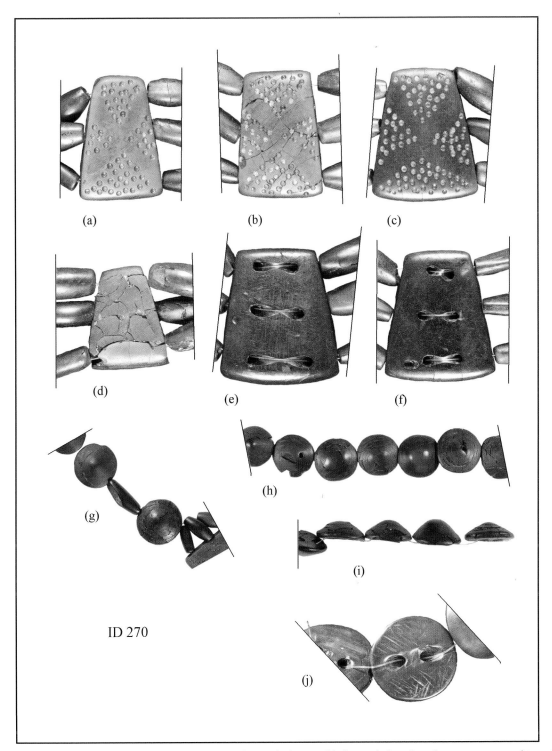

Figure 7.2.13. ID 270 Grindlow. Details showing: (a) front of plate 1; (b) front of plate 2 with criss-cross cracking; (c) front of plate 5; (d) front of plate 7 with criss-cross cracking; (e) rear of plate 3 with striations, oval hollow (top right) and elbow-borings including an abortive hole (bottom left); (f) rear of plate 5 with oval hollow and elbow borings; (g) buttons and bead from which part of the surface had spalled off to reveal woody subsurface; (h) and (i) selection of buttons of different heights and angularity of domes, and (i) grinding striations on bases of buttons.

of the jet plates. It had been through-perforated using Y-perforations to increase the number of holes from three on the narrower edge to nine on the broader edge, suggesting that it had originally been one of a pair of lower plates at the front of a spacer plate necklace (i.e. a

Sp 2 plate), and a very slight asymmetry in plan suggests that this had probably been a right hand spacer plate. One corner of the longer side has been worn away through bead-wear. The underside has a slight concavity relating to the natural shape of the bone. The upper, decorated side is flattish, the unperforated edges have been gently squared off, and the perforated edges are more sharply squared off. The upper surface has been decorated with three rows of punctulations; the widest punctulation is *c.* 1.1mm across.

The 26 fusifom beads (Figure 7.2.12) range in profile from near-cylindrical to plump, and only one is slightly angular. In cross-section they range from circular, to rounded-triangular, D-shaped and oval. Five have two flat sides, as if made to lie immediately beside a Sp 2 plate with multiple, close-set borings, a feature that would not be necessary for use with the three-hole plates in the Grindlow necklace. Some beads have ends that are perpendicular to the long axis; with others, one or both ends is/are angled (Figure 7.2.13g), usually slanting in opposite directions but in one case, both slanting in the same direction. The ends are generally gently squared off or gently pointed. One bead has one cupped end. The lengths range from 13.5 to 22.3mm, and the maximum widths from 5.8 by 5.0mm to 8.2 by 7.9mm; the longest bead is also the broadest. The perforation diameter ranges from 2.1 to 5.9mm, with most beads having holes in the range of 2.5 to 3.5mm.

The 36 extant buttons vary in size and in the height and angularity of their dome (Figure 7.2.13h–i). Sixteen are circular in plan, 15 range from sub-circular to roughly oval, and five are sub-rectangular. Fourteen have a facet (either rounded or angular) between the dome and the base, in most cases angled towards the base. The maximum width of the base ranges from 14.1 to 23.7mm, and the height ranges from 4.5 to 9.6mm. The maximum size of the boreholes ranges from 2.25 to 8.9mm, and the width of the bridge between them ranges from *c.* 1.8 to 5.3mm. Details of the button dimensions are given in Appendix VII, Table 11.

Shepherd classified all of the buttons as his Type 2 (Hunmanby type); these are small and sharply conical, with a flat, round base (Shepherd 2009, 356 no. 13) – and indeed this fits the description of some. However, the more gently-domed examples fit better within his Type 4.

MATERIAL

Macroscopically, the six decorated spacer plates show every appearance of being made of jet, mostly hard jet, to judge from the relatively slight degree of cracking on plates 1, 3, 4 and 6 (AS; see Figure 7.2.12 for the numbering of the plates). On their front (decorated) surface they range from a mid-brown to a variegated blackish-brown colour, while on their back they are a darker blackish-brown. A fine woody texture is visible, especially where a small part of the surface had spalled off in antiquity on plate 4; the rear of this plate also has a natural depression, showing the lighter brown, matt, woody sub-surface. Plates 3 and 5 each have a small oval hollow on their back (Figure 7.2.13e–f); such hollows are sometimes found as natural irregularities in jet. The front surface of plate 2 has fairly extensive criss-cross cracking, suggesting that the plate may have been made from soft jet (Figure 7.2.13b). Plate 5 also has some similar cracking. Hairline criss-cross cracking was noted on plates 1, 3, 4 and 6; as noted above, these

are likely to have been made from hard jet. It may be that more than one of the plates had been made from the same parent piece of jet.

Spacer plate 7 is undecorated (Figure 7.2.13d) and also seems to be of jet, probably soft jet, to judge from the extensive criss-cross cracking (with some cupping). Its outer surface is a rich dark brown and blackish-brown; the back is more blackish-brown. The fine-woody texture is visible in a spall scar on the back of the plate, and there is a conchoidal chip scar. The decorated bone spacer plate is assumed to be of terrestrial mammal bone, possibly a rib or scapula; the undulation of its underside may provide a clue. Unfortunately, it was not possible to include this artefact as part of the animal bone study undertaken with other material in the project.

Macroscopically, 20 of the fusiform beads appear to be of jet, mostly probably hard jet, while six seem to be of cannel coal (AS). The former are various shades of colour from a rich dark brown to black-brown and have a fine-woody texture. Where there is cracking, it is criss-cross or concentric. The woody texture is particularly clear where spalls had fallen off along the grain of the jet (Figure 7.2.13g). By contrast, the suspected cannel coal beads are all black and have a stony texture. Compositional analysis of a longitudinal section of one of the fusiform beads (probably a piece that had already spalled off, or was removed along a grain plane) using neutron activation analysis (NAA) confirmed that this bead was indeed of jet (Bussell 1976, 53, 63, 64 and 79; her sample no. 456.8).

Macroscopically, 27 of the buttons appear to be of jet, some of hard jet, some of soft jet; nine have features more characteristic of cannel coal (AS). The distinguishing features are the same as those shown by the fusiform beads, and a good example of the contrast in colour, texture and condition is illustrated in Figure 7.2.13g and h). Bussell analysed one button using NAA, and found it to be a cannel coal closely comparable in composition with the north-east Yorkshire cannel coal samples that had been collected from the Whitby area (Bussell 1976, 53, 63, 64, 79, 80; her sample no. 456.13. See, however, Bussell 1976, 91 for the possibility that the material may actually be Jet Rock oil-shale). She also compositionally analysed either the same button or a second, using X-ray fluorescence spectrometry (*ibid*, 85) and the results were consistent with an identification as cannel coal. It is not clear whether one or two buttons were analysed, or indeed which one(s). However, they are probably not the two that are currently stored separately from the necklace, since these macroscopically appear to be jet. Two buttons macroscopically identified as cannel coal have chip scars that could conceivably represent sample scars.

One additional analysis was carried out, by Dr J.M. Jones, on a tiny detached speck of material, whose original location on the necklace could not be ascertained; it could be from a button. Using reflectance microscopy, Dr Jones concluded that it was probably a strange form of jet (pers. comm.), full of bubbles or pyrite specks (and showing as red due to the iron from the pyrite).

MANUFACTURE

The six decorated jet plates show a marked consistency in their technique and style of manufacture. All have faint longitudinal grinding striations along both of their perforated ends and multidirectional striations on their undecorated rear surfaces (Figure 7.2.12e). In some cases these are fairly crisp. A drill bit that could have been as narrow as 2.6mm had been used to create their elbow-borings. These holes were not drilled at right-angles, but instead the perforation from the rear was drilled as a steep diagonal, perhaps to minimise the extent to which the thread would stand proud of the back of the plate. It is unclear as to why the decision was made to elbow-bore, rather than through-bore, when the plates were sufficiently thick to permit the latter. It could relate to the confidence of the maker, who evidently did not want to risk splitting the jet. Plate 5 has an aborted drill hole on its back which may have been abandoned as it was felt to be too close to the edge (Figure 7.2.13f). This shows clearly that the drilling had been a two-stage process: an initial vertical 'starter hole' followed by a diagonal perforation. The bottom of the drill hole is rounded and flattish, and 2.5mm wide. No trace of rilling was seen in any of the boreholes. The front, back and unperforated sides had been polished, probably to a high sheen. (See below regarding probable post-depositional partial dulling.) The punctulated decoration could have been created by the tip of an awl, no wider than 1.6mm. The saltire design had been created without the aid of any guide-lines. As noted above, traces of a creamy-coloured material in the punctulations may well represent a substance that had been deliberately left in the hollows to accentuate the design.

The undecorated jet spacer plate has some faint multidirectional striations along one perforated side, and had been polished to at least a medium sheen. It is assumed that the through-perforations had been drilled from both ends of the plate. No signs of any rilling were noted.

The bone spacer plate had been made from a broad, flat bone. The application of lacquer to the surface has obscured any grinding striations that may have existed; the horizontal lines along the three-hole edge are the natural texture of the bone. It is likewise hard to establish what had been the original degree of polish. The process of drilling is clear from the three-hole edge where the width of each perforation shows that the drill had been presented at least twice to create the diagonal boreholes. The third hole in each set may have been drilled from the other side of the plate, meeting up with these V-borings. The drill bit may have had a diameter of *c.* 2.7mm. No rilling was noted in the holes. The punctulated decoration had been made using a round-tipped tool *c.* 1.1mm across. There are no signs of any guide-lines, and the three lines of punctulations are uneven.

Traces of the initial shaping of the fusiform beads are only visible in three cases: as the remains of faceting on one end of one; as faint mid-point grinding striations on another, and as very faint diagonal striations near one end of a third. The perforations had been drilled from both ends, as revealed by a mis-bore on one example where the drill had perforated one side of the bead. It may be that the cupping of the end of one bead relates to the drilling process, rather than to subsequent wear. While the angling of one or both ends of some beads may have been an original design feature, in some cases it was exacerbated or caused by wear. All the beads had been polished, perhaps originally to a high sheen.

Grinding striations (either unidirectional or multidirectional) were noted on the base of 21 of the buttons. In most cases these are faint, but in one or two cases, they are slightly crisper (e.g. Figure 7.2.13j). Striations were also noted on four of the facets and on one, or possibly two, of the domes. Drilling of the perforations had probably mostly been a two-stage process, with a vertical 'starter hole' followed by a diagonal perforation. Evidence in support of this comes, for example, from one button where much of the perforated surface had spalled away to leave the bottom of a vertically-bored hole just 1.2mm wide. Elsewhere, a change of slope is clearly visible. Some buttons show no signs of drill repositioning, and on one example the drill may have been repositioned twice while creating one of the holes. Faint rilling was noted in the holes of only three buttons. The drill had accidentally perforated the dome of two buttons. In a further example the relatively broad width of the outer part of the perforations raises the question as to whether this button may have been re-bored (or initially bored with a wide drill bit). All the jet buttons had been polished, possibly initially to a high sheen (although see below regarding probable post-depositional dulling). The cannel coal examples have a much lower sheen and may never have been polished, with one exception which has a medium to high sheen on its dome. The relatively high sheen seen on the apex of one button could be due to wear.

COMPLETENESS AND DAMAGE

One characteristic common to many of the jet components is that the back (i.e. the side which would have been closest to the skin) has a higher sheen, and darker colour, than the front. This was noted on three of the fusiform beads as well as on many of the plates and buttons. It suggests that, in common with many other jet objects in this study, natural, post-depositional dulling (and some surface colour change) had occurred within the micro-environment of the grave.

Except for signs of wear and of some cracking (with minor surface spalling to plate 5), the decorated jet spacer plates are in relatively good condition and are complete, or virtually so. There is ancient spalling, probably caused during manufacture, to the back and to one perforated edge of plate 1, and on plate 2 the punctulation process may have detached a spall from the front surface. In addition, there is minor chipping to some of the perforations on the back of plate 2, probably caused during manufacture. Two scratches on the back may represent either ancient or more recent damage. On plate 4 the elbow boring has broken through the front surface close to one corner, and there is ancient chipping to the adjacent lateral perforation, along with other minor chipping, probably caused through wear. Plate 5 has minor chipping to one perforation, plus a slightly larger loss of the upper surface through wear to one of the lateral perforations. On plate 6, one of the perforations on the back is larger than it should be, due to a mis-alignment of the two drillings that constitute the elbow-boring; thread-wear has caused some of the outer surface to spall off. There is also minor chipping (from the drilling process) to another hole on the back, and some loss of spalls due to surface cracking.

The undecorated jet spacer plate has lost some spalls through surface cracking, and thread-pull (plus bead pressure) to one of the holes has caused part of the surface to chip away. The bone spacer plate shows no obvious sign of damage; the apparent loss of one corner may simply reflect the original outer edge shape of the bone.

Ancient damage to the fusiform beads consists mostly of use-wear damage, including the loss of one end of four beads and the hole in another caused by the aforementioned mis-bore during manufacture. There are also signs of more recent, post-depositional damage to five or six beads, in the form of minor chipping to the ends, and the loss of chips and spalls through cracking of the jet. Two of the beads have traces of glue, which may have been applied as a consolidant.

While most of the buttons are complete or virtually so, there is evidence for both ancient damage (during manufacture and wear) and more recent damage. Ancient damage includes chipping to boreholes during their drilling and the loss of spalls and chips from the outer surface, most notably on one example where there are several chip scars around the edge of the base. Some of the more recent (post-excavation) damage is due to the process of cracking, but some relates to the necklace's display history. ID 257 has glue and backing material on its underside and lacks the bridge between the perforations; this suggests that it had been stuck to a back-board and, when it was pulled off, the bridge came away. The same may be true of another example, where the bridge had come away and been re-fitted using a black waxy consolidant. On another, the bridge had come away and been replaced by a blob of the same waxy consolidant. The addition of a strip of white fabric to the underside of ID 256 had also probably been an attempt to repair damage; there are also recent chips around its outer surface. Scratches running down one of the perforations in three other examples also look to be post-depositional damage. On a further button, an attempt had been made to consolidate the fracture surfaces after the loss of part of one side, probably along crack-lines; there are also traces of glue in the perforations of another.

WEAR

Levels of wear in the different components are summarised in Table 7.2.2, from which it is clear that 47 of the 70 components, including all of the spacer plates, have moderate or heavy wear; in particular, the decorated jet spacer plates all show signs of heavy wear. All have marked thread-pull wear on their back, where the thread has worn grooves between the holes, particularly on the inner and outer strands. There is also a thread-wear groove, pulling towards the front of plate 2, and the thread had also worn away whatever rilling may originally have existed in all of the boreholes. There are traces of bead-on-plate wear on all these plates, in the form of polish and, in some cases, the grinding of hollows. Again, the wear is most marked at the holes on the inner and outer strands. The diameter of the bead wear is consistent with grinding by the ends of fusiform beads. On plate 4, a combination of bead-wear and thread-pull has detached a sizeable chip from the plate's front surface at its innermost left-hand corner, and a smaller chip from the adjacent hole.

The undecorated jet spacer plate is also heavily worn. The thread had polished smooth the interior of the boreholes, and there is heavy bead grinding wear to all of the holes. A combination of bead pressure and thread-pull had detached a chip from the upper surface, at the outermost left hand borehole.

The bone spacer plate shows a moderate to heavy degree of wear, with thread-polish to the boreholes, thread-smoothing to parts of the edges of most boreholes along the long side, and some thread-pull wear. Along the narrower of the perforated edges, the thread in two of the holes has pulled towards the third (outermost) hole, while along the broader edge, the four holes on either side of the central hole have paired thread-pull wear, where the strands had pulled towards each other. There has also been some bead grinding at the outermost holes on the long edge; in one case this had worn away part of the corner of the plate. At the same end of the plate, there has been some rub-wear to the pointillé decoration.

While only ten of the 26 fusiform beads show a moderate or high degree of wear, there are signs of thread-wear in the form of borehole polish in all the beads, and in most cases the thread has also smoothed the edges of the perforations. The more serious wear all relates to bead-on-bead (and possibly some bead-on-plate) wear, and takes the form of heavy abrasion (which has caused or exacerbated the slope of one or both ends) and the chipping-off of part of one end. Less heavy bead-on-bead wear features some abrasion and polish to one or both ends.

As far as the buttons are concerned, despite variability in the degree of wear, in all those cases where the boreholes are visible, there is thread-wear to their outer edges (in the form of edge-smoothing and polish) that demonstrates that these items had been worn as components of the necklace. In some cases only the outer edges show any wear; in a few cases, the thread-softening extends all round the perforations. On one button there are two probable narrow thread-grooves on one borehole, running across the hole; other possible thread-grooves were noted on three others. Thread-wear that is mainly on the inner edges of the perforations was noted on another. Other signs of thread-wear include the fact that traces of rilling were noted on only three of the buttons; in every other case, the thread had probably worn it smooth, and in several cases there is thread-polish to part of the borehole interior. On one, the bridge between the boreholes is very thin-walled, again probably due (at least in part) to thread-wear; on another there is a hollow running across the bridge. This may be a thread-wear hollow, and could perhaps indicate the former presence of a knot at this point (which, in turn, might suggest that this button had been used as a fastener). Rub-wear, caused by rubbing against a garment or skin was probably partly or mainly responsible for the polish seen on the bases of the jet buttons and on the high points of the bases of some of the cannel coal examples.

CONCLUSIONS

This assemblage of components, which varies in design, material and degree of wear, clearly comprises material that had not originally belonged together, and raises the question of whether the items had indeed all been strung together as a necklace in the grave. If they had been, and if the arrangement had been as in Bateman's reconstruction, then this necklace would have lain significantly lower on the chest than other spacer plate necklaces. That the buttons had indeed been used as necklace components is suggested by their thread-wear pattern. If they had been threaded in a double strand, rather than singly as is currently the case, the necklace would not have been much longer than a more conventional spacer plate necklace, such as the larger of the examples from Cow Low, Derbyshire (ID 267). The Grindlow necklace contains the largest number of buttons of any Early Bronze Age necklace of jet and similar materials.

It is unclear as to whether the bone spacer plate had been attached to the necklace since its arrangement of boreholes does not match that of the jet plates. Alternative possibilities are that it had been placed separately in the grave, as an isolated offering, or had been used as a somewhat ungainly fastener, or else had formed part of a second necklace, all of organic material, and all decayed. That said, there are parallels for the (presumed) stringing together of diverse components (e.g. at Middleton Moor, Derbyshire ID 269).

The groupings of components that can be discerned are as follows:

- The six decorated spacer plates, consistent in their design and manufacture and all showing signs of fairly heavy wear.
- The undecorated, and heavily worn, spacer plate.
- The bone spacer plate (whose 3 to 9 boring does not correspond to the number of boreholes in the other spacer plates).
- The fusiform beads (which could mostly have originated in a single necklace set, despite variation in the degree of wear; the presence of some beads of cannel coal might indicate that these had been added to the set of beads).
- The jet buttons (which might be subdivided between those with minimal wear and those with more marked wear; other subdivisions, by shape, can be suggested).
- The cannel coal buttons.

One possible scenario (but not the only one) for the evolution of this assemblage prior to its deposition in the grave is as follows:

- The decorated spacer plates will have constituted the main portion of a three-strand necklace, perhaps together with some of the buttons and along with fusiform beads (but not necessarily the fusiform beads that are currently present). By analogy with other spacer plate necklaces, this example had also probably included a pair of terminal plates.
- The fusiform beads are likely to have started out in a larger spacer plate necklace, given the presence of several flat-sided beads (whose shape would not have been necessary for the current, three-strand necklace). The cannel coal beads may have been added to that set as individual jet beads broke. At some point, the fusiform beads were united with the decorated spacer plates. (There are enough present to have accommodated an additional spacer plate, as well as two terminal plates).
- Having lost its terminal plates (and possibly a spacer plate and a few fusiform beads), the remains of the necklace were supplemented by an undecorated spacer plate from a different necklace; by the bone spacer plate from another necklace; and by some or all of the buttons. There had probably been more than one episode of button acquisition, given the variability in their size, design and material.

Comparanda for the Grindlow necklace, including for the use of bone for making spacer plates, are discussed in Chapter 7.3. The fact that the material used for at least one of the cannel coal components had probably originated in the Whitby area is significant, since it is a reminder that not all the cannel coal found in jet-like jewellery needs to have come from locations far from the source of jet. This finding contrasts with that for Hill Head, where cannel coal from the Peak District is suspected to have been used (Bussell 1976, 78).

ID 273 Windle Nook (Wind Low) Wormhill, Derbyshire

References: Bateman 1847, 234–5; 1848, 88–89; Jewitt 1850, B.37; 1870, fig. 172; Howarth 1899, 59–60; Shepherd 2009, 357 (no. 19a–b).

COMPOSITION

When found, this spacer plate necklace comprised two terminal plates and two pairs of spacer plates of bone, along with two V-perforated buttons and 76 fusiform beads of jet or jet-like material. Jewitt's watercolour of 1850 (Figure 7.2.14, top) shows the necklace as originally strung (by or for Bateman); by the time an engraving was published by Howarth in 1899, one of the largest of the bone spacer plates had been replaced by a replica bone plate, which is still there today (Figure 7.2.14 and Figure 7.2.15a). It is unclear whether the original plate survives. The current stringing, which follows the 1899 version, is certainly not true to its original Early Bronze Age arrangement, whereby the fusiform beads will probably all have lain between the terminal and spacer plates, with the eight strands at the front each having seven beads, and in some cases eight. The wear pattern on the fusiform beads is consistent with such an arrangement. It is unclear whether the two buttons will have fulfilled the role of fasteners at the back of the necklace (since usually only one fastener was used) but this is not impossible.

CONTEXT AND ASSOCIATIONS

The necklace was found on 12th August 1846, when opening a low round barrow. Bateman's account (as reported in Howarth 1899, 59–60) is not entirely clear, but it implies that the necklace had been associated with the contracted skeleton of what he concluded to be a woman, found a few inches above the floor of a large cist measuring nearly 1.8 by 1.2m. According to Bateman, the deposition of this individual had disturbed the previously deposited remains of two adults, two children, cremated bones, animal bones, potsherds and flints; subsequently, the cist's contents had been disturbed by treasure hunters.

MORPHOLOGY

In the following descriptions, some details are missing or imprecise because the necklace has been tightly strung and fixed firmly to a backboard; most of the plates have been fixed to metal supports (Figure 7.2.15a), hindering inspection and measurement of some features.

The terminal and spacer plates (Figures 7.2.15a and d) are all slender, flattish and fairly thin, with gently squared-off unperforated edges and more crisply squared-off perforated edges. All are decorated on their upper (front) surface with a zigzag motif defined by punctulations, each up to *c.* 1mm in diameter. The terminal plates (Figure 7.2.14 and Figure 7.2.15d–e) approximate to isosceles triangles in shape, with three elbow-bored holes at their broader end (i.e. towards the front of the necklace) and a double transverse perforation at the upper end of the TL plate (Figure 7.2.15b). The TR plate had probably also had a double transverse perforation, but only one hole survives as the end of the plate had broken off (Figure 7.2.15e). The long sides of the TL plate are fairly straight, with the inner side being minimally convex; both long sides of the TR plate are slightly concave. The spacer plates are trapezoidal, with fairly straight outer edges. The number of perforations increases from three to four in the smaller Sp 1 plates and from four to eight in the larger Sp 2 plate(s). The perforations may have been elbow-bored, but without X-raying the necklace it is hard to be certain of this. The dimensions of the plates, excluding the Victorian replica Sp 2 L, are listed in Appendix VII, Table 12.

The button on the left side of the necklace in Figure 7.2.14 is irregular and almost sub-rectangular in plan, with a rounded, low to medium-height dome and a base that is mostly flattish, but with parts that curve up to the rounded junction with the dome (Figure 7.2.15b). The perforations are not clearly visible as the object is firmly fixed to the backboard. The base measures 13.6 by *c.* 16.0mm and the maximum height is *c.* 5.1mm. The right hand button (Figure 7.2.14 and Figure 7.2.15e) is circular in plan, with a low but slightly more peaked dome and a flattish base. Once more, the perforations are not clearly visible. The base diameter is *c.* 16.5mm and the height *c.* 5.6mm. In Shepherd's classification, both are Type 2 buttons.

The fusiform beads (Figure 7.2.14 and Figure 7.2.15) show a variety in length, width and profile that is characteristic of fusiform beads from spacer plate necklaces. None has a particularly angular shape and, in profile, most fall within the 'slender' to 'medium' categories. The ends of the beads are perpendicular to the long axis in some cases, but more frequently one, or both, slope to a greater or lesser degree. One bead has two oval dimples around its mid-point. The shortest bead is 5.8mm long (Figure 7.2.14 and Figure 7.2.15c, located in the upper row, second bead from left), and the longest is 26.5mm (Figure 7.2.14 and Figure 7.2.15b, located next to the button above the left terminal plate). Most range between 18 and 23mm in length. The maximum width ranges from 5.2 to 8.7mm, and the perforation diameter ranges between *c.* 1.9mm and 3.4mm. In cross section most of the beads are circular and a few are slightly D-shaped, but 18 have two flattish sides. Beads of this flat-sided shape are known from other spacer plate necklaces to have been designed to lie immediately adjacent to the longest edge of the Sp 2 plates. Sixteen of these beads may well have occupied that position in the original stringing of this necklace.

MATERIAL

Macroscopically, it appears that the material used for the terminal and spacer plates is terrestrial mammal bone (rather than whalebone, antler or marine ivory). It is compact and very slightly laminar, and the thinness of the plates probably reflects the maximum thickness of such bone before the spongy inner part of the bone was reached. It was unfortunately not possible to include these plates in the animal bone analysis, but it is clear that the shape of the plates and the presence of a slight 'grain' in the bone offer clues as to which bone, from which mammal, had been used.

The left-hand button (Figure 7.2.15b) is of a black, compact material that has taken a high surface polish and is significantly glossier than the other button; the sub-surface texture, exposed in small spall scars, appears slightly stony, rather than woody. While jet cannot be ruled out as a raw material, the object could equally be of cannel coal or oil shale (AS). No compositional analysis has been undertaken. In contrast, the right hand button (Figure 7.2.15e) has macroscopic characteristics of jet. It is black and black-brown, with a fine-woody texture; there is concentric cracking on the dome and criss-cross cracking on both the dome and the base, with some springing and consequent loss of chips. Like all the other components of the necklace, it has not been analysed.

Macroscopically the fusiform beads all appear to be of jet, of good quality and mostly of hard jet, to judge from the relative paucity of cracking. The beads are a rich dark brown to blackish-brown, and have a fine-woody texture. Where cracking occurs it follows a concentric or criss-cross pattern, characteristic of jet. Additional diagnostic features include the occasional presence of dull, matt brown areas. Confirmation of the identification of the material as jet is provided by Gill Bussell's analysis of two of the fusiform beads (Bussell 1976, table 28).

MANUFACTURE

No obvious grinding striations were noted on any of the components, nor was it possible to examine the necklace under a microscope to check for fainter traces.

The terminal and spacer plates must have been cut from a bone and any cancellous bone ground away, although no traces remain of this process (and in any case the underside of the plates, probably the inner surface of the bone, cannot be seen). Regarding the method of perforation, it is clear that the holes along the bottom (wide) end of the terminal plates had been elbow-bored (Figure 7.2.15a and Figure 7.2.15d), and it is likely that this method had also been used on the spacer plates, to judge from the small circular holes on the upper surface of all the surviving spacer plates (Figure 7.2.15a and Figure 7.2.15d). These could have been caused by the drill coming too close to the outer surface when the holes on the underside were being bored (but see below regarding Sp 1 L). In addition, the holes towards the top (narrow) ends of the terminal plates had been drilled transversely through the bone, as had an additional hole, drilled through the upper surface of the left terminal when its outer corner had broken off through wear (Figure 7.2.15a). It may be that the neat hole through the upper surface, at the mid-point of Sp 1 L's narrow edge (Figure 7.2.15a), had also been a repair hole rather than the result of over-drilling from the underside.

Regarding the decoration, there are no signs of any faint guide lines (except on the Victorian replica of Sp 2 L). Triangular areas of pointillé design, made with a narrow, sharp tool such as a narrow awl, define undecorated zigzags. On TL the undecorated zone is a chevron, whereas on TR it is a true zigzag. On both terminal plates the design stops short of the transverse perforations. The same tool seems to have been used to decorate all the plates. It is likely that the first punctulations to have been drilled were those that define the edge of the undecorated zone (Figure 7.2.15d).

The plates had probably been polished prior to decoration (except perhaps on their perforated edges), although some of the sheen currently visible may be due to wear, possible from rubbing against a garment.

As far as the buttons are concerned, while the perforations could not be examined, it is clear that a small hole close to the top of the dome on the right-hand example

(Figure 7.2.15e) relates to the accidental perforation of the surface during the drilling of the V-perforation. While both buttons had been polished (at least on their domes), the degree of sheen on the left hand example is significantly higher than on its partner, and the former's sheen may well have become dulled post-depositionally.

The fusiform beads show no trace of the faceting that had been involved in their initial shaping; this had been smoothed away. Regarding the perforations, it is assumed that they had been drilled from both ends, in common with their counterparts from other necklaces. The angling of one or both ends, seen on many of the beads, may well have been a deliberate design feature to allow the beads to sit snugly in an arc. In some cases the angling has been accentuated through bead-on-bead grinding or chipping. The beads had all been polished, and the degree of sheen varies from low to high, with most lying in the 'medium' category. Variation in the degree of sheen within a single bead was noted in a few cases, including one of the beads between Sp 1 R and Sp 2 R (Figure 7.2.15d), where one side (of a rich dark brown colour) has low to no sheen, while the other side (a darker, blackish-brown) has a high sheen. This feature, noted in many other examples of jet jewellery, may relate to differential post-depositional dulling, with the side nearest the skin retaining the higher sheen.

COMPLETENESS AND DAMAGE

In general, the plates are in a relatively poor condition, while the buttons and most of the beads are in a better, more complete state. Parts of all the spacer plates are missing, with Sp 1 L being only *c.* 60% to 70% present; there has also been some loss of surface from around the perforations on the terminal and spacer plates, and the tip of TR is missing. All this damage had occurred in antiquity. Ancient damage to the buttons occurred during manufacture and consists of the accidental perforation of the dome of the right-hand button, plus the loss of a large chip from the side of the left-hand button, along with the loss of two tiny spalls from its dome. The cracking and resultant loss of tiny chips from the right-hand button has been noted, and this could have occurred post-depositionally. There is also a curving hairline crack across the dome on the left-hand button.

There are signs of both ancient and more recent damage to the fusiform beads. The former relates to thread- and bead-on-bead wear. The latter consists mainly of dulling to the ends of the beads that are closest to the spacer plates (and, more particularly, to the Victorian metal supports for the spacer plates). In addition, dulling around the mid-point of at least two of the beads that are currently strung between the largest spacer plates (Figure 7.2.14) may well have resulted from recent rotational abrasion. The loss of a large part of one side of three beads (e.g. bottom left bead on Figure 7.2.15b) has also probably occurred since excavation and follows planes of weakness in the jet. One of the fusiform beads has a small patch of blue material, resembling 'Blu-Tack', near one end.

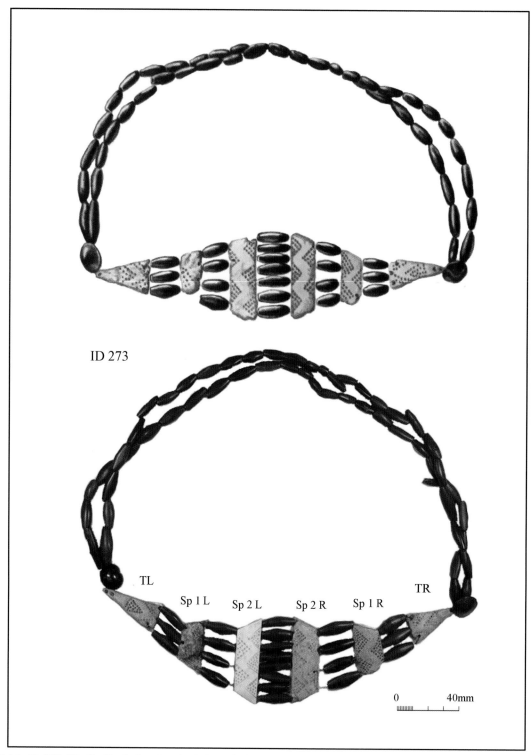

Figure 7.2.14. ID 273 Windle Nook showing (top) Jewitt's 1850 watercolour, courtesy of Museums Sheffield and (bottom) the necklace as currently strung.

WEAR

The overall degree of wear is shown in Table 7.2.2. The terminal and spacer plates all show a considerable amount of wear, mostly resulting from thread-pull, with some bead-on-plate wear as well. This has led to the enlargement of the upper edge of the holes (e.g. Figure 7.2.15a), and

on the left terminal plate an entire corner had broken off, necessitating the re-boring of the plate transversely (Figure 7.2.14). As noted above, the adjacent Sp 1 L may also have had one of its holes re-bored transversely. The loss of the tip of the right terminal plate, of the two outer corners of Sp 1 R (Figure 7.2.14), of two corners of Sp 2 R (Figure

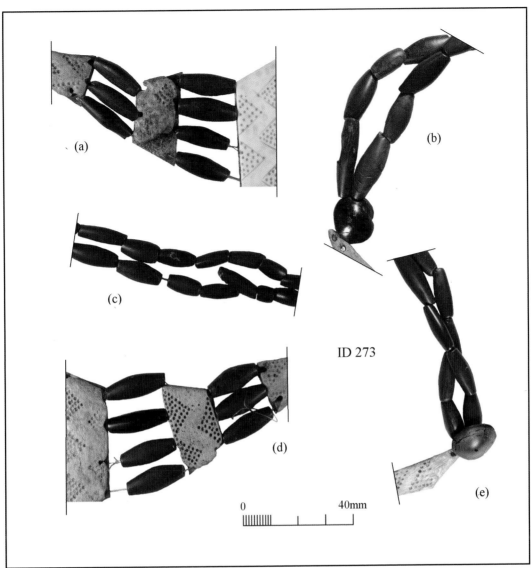

Figure 7.2.15. ID 273 Windle Nook. Details showing: (a) the poor condition of and metal mounting for Sp 1 L, and Victorian replacement Sp 2 L plate (at right); (b) button beside TL, perforations at top of TL, and adjacent fusiform beads; (c) variation in fusiform bead length and colour; (d) bone plates Sp 2 R, Sp 1 R and part of TR, and (e) button beside TR, apex of TR and adjacent fusiform beads.

7.2.15d) and of much of Sp 1 L (Figure 7.2.15a), had all probably been the result of thread-pull and bead-on-plate pressure. Where the interior of the boreholes is visible, it is clear that these had been worn smooth by the thread. There is also rub-wear to the decoration on all of the plates (Figure 7.2.15) although on Sp 1 R it is limited to just a few punctulations close to the damaged corner. It is assumed that the rub-wear had resulted from the friction of a garment against the decorated surface.

Since the underside of the buttons could not be seen, it was impossible to assess the degree and kind of wear, but the fact that the edge of the hole on the dome of the right-hand button had been worn smooth suggests that this item was not new when buried.

While it was not possible to inspect the interior of the perforations in the fusiform beads for thread-wear, it is clear that many beads show bead-on-bead wear, to a greater or lesser degree. Examples include a smoothing of the junction between the end and the side of the bead seen on the second bead from the button on the left hand strand (Figure 7.2.15e), and the uneven profile of the end, where an adjacent bead had worn a hollow as it ground against the bead at an angle on the outermost bead between the terminal and Sp 1 L (Figure 7.2.15a). Bead-on-bead wear may also have contributed to the degree to which one or both ends slope; and, together with thread-pull pressure, it was probably responsible for chipping to the end/s of at least seven beads (e.g. on the bead next to the button on the upper strand, Figure 7.2.15b). One bead with a particularly asymmetrical profile may well have lost one end and had the fracture surface ground smooth through wear, and three others, all of which taper less than the other beads, might

Ritual in Early Bronze Age Grave Goods

*Table 7.2.2. Levels of wear on individual components of the spacer plate necklaces discussed in section 7.2. * On ID 273 it is assumed that the sixth plate (the missing Sp 2 L plate that had been replaced by a Victorian replica) had also been heavily worn. ** This includes examples that show slight to moderate wear; without being able to inspect the perforations closely, it is impossible to be more precise.*

Object no.	Type	Fresh/slight wear	Worn	Very worn	Indet.	Total
ID 247	Terminal plates	2	-	-	-	2
	Boat-shaped fasteners	-	2	-	-	2
	Buttons	3	5	-	-	8
	Fusiform	34	1	-	-	35
	Cylindrical	1	-	-	-	1
	Disc	7	-	-	548	555
ID 249	Terminal plates	-	2	-	-	2
	Spacer plates	2	3	-	-	5
ID 266	Terminal and spacer plates	1	1	2	-	4
	Fusiforms	23	14	4	1	42
ID 267	Fastener	1	-	-	-	1
	Terminal and spacer plates	5	1	-	-	6
	Fusiforms	42	16	6	-	64
ID 268	Terminal and spacer plates	-	1	4	-	5
	Fusiforms	21	15	10	1	47
	Discs	9	-	-	-	9
	Buttons	4	8	-	-	12
ID 269	Fastener	-	-	1	-	1
	Terminal and spacer plates	-	1	6	-	7
	Buttons	-	5	6	-	11
	Fusiforms	-	26	27	-	53
	Discs	-	-	-	334	334
ID 270	Spacer plates	-	1	7	-	8
	Fusiform beads	16	3	7	-	26
	Buttons	7	26	3	-	36
ID 273	Terminal and spacer plates	-	-	5*	-	5
	Fusiforms	-	72**	4	-	76
	Buttons	-	-	-	2	2
ID 264-5	Spacer plates	2	-	-	1	3
	Fusiforms	14	-	-	1	15
	Buttons	8	-	-	4	12
ID 281	Fusiforms	1	2	1	-	4
	Discs	-	-	-	24	24
	Terminal plates	-	-	2	-	2
ID 282	Terminal plate	-	1	-	-	1
ID 379-90	Spacer plate	-	1	-	-	1
	Fusiform	1	-	-	-	1
	Buttons	5	-	-	-	5
	Fastener	2	-	-	-	2
	Pendant	1	-	-	-	1
	Disc	298 + 27 frags	-	-	-	325
ID 391	Fastener	1	-	-	-	1
	Spacer plates	-	2	-	-	2
	Discs	19	-	-	-	19
	Fusiform	1	-	-	-	1
	Biconical	5	-	-	-	5
	Oblate	-	1	-	-	1

also have been truncated and re-shaped through wear. These include the shortest bead in the necklace. These four beads are recorded in Table 7.2.2 as very worn.

CONCLUSIONS

This appears to be a complete necklace, albeit one with fewer fusiform beads than are known from many spacer plate necklaces found further to the north. Its current stringing implies that it had lain low on the chest, but as explained above it is much more likely that all the fusiform beads had been strung between the plates, so that the necklace would have lain closer to the neck. In the shape and size of the plates, the maximum number of strands (eight) and the number of fusiform beads (76, compared with 64), it bears a striking resemblance to the larger of the two jet spacer plate necklaces from Cow Low (ID 266 and ID 267), just over 6km away as the crow flies. Indeed, it could have been designed to emulate that necklace. Another similar necklace in the area, although with longer spacer plates, is known from Hill Head (ID 268), again a few kilometres from Windle Nook.

The bone plates had clearly been made as a set. The fusiform beads show a consistency in design, material and style of manufacture that suggests that they, too, had been made as a set, although whether they had been made to accompany the bone plates or had had a previous life in another spacer plate necklace is unknown. The buttons, which differ from each other in shape and possibly also in material, need not have belonged to either set of components originally. The heavy wear to the plates shows that the necklace had been worn for some time before it was buried. How long that had been is hard to tell, however, since it may be that bone is more susceptible to wear than jet. The condition of the fusiform beads indicates that they, too, had been worn for some time, and this might also be true of the buttons. The use of bone for the plates suggests that the owner had not been able to obtain plates of jet, a more precious material. The use of bone for spacer plates is discussed further in Chapter 7.3.

7.2.3 OTHER REGIONS

ID 264 barrow 'in the neighbourhood of Pickering', and ID 265, one of a pair of barrows 6 miles NW of Pickering (probably the same barrow), North Yorkshire

References: Bateman 1861, 228, 239; Howarth 1899, 188.

COMPOSITION

These pieces belong to a two-strand jet spacer plate necklace, comprising three complete and fragmentary spacer plates (two in ID 264, one in ID 265), 15 complete and fragmentary fusiform beads (two in ID 264, 13 in ID 265) and 12 complete and fragmentary V-perforated buttons (one in ID 264, 11 in ID 265) (Figure 7.2.16). The close similarity between the material in ID 264 (Museums Sheffield, part of registration number J93-582) and ID 265 (J93-583) leaves little doubt that the components had originally belonged together in a single necklace, and for that reason the objects are described together here. The

beads and buttons from ID 265 that are currently strung together are shown in Figure 7.2.16a with details in Figure 7.2.16c and Figure 7.2.16d; the spacer plates are illustrated in Figure 7.2.16b.

CONTEXT AND ASSOCIATIONS

It seems likely that all the components had come from the same barrow. Bateman describes the discovery of ID 265 on 28th May 1851 by a Mr Ruddock, who investigated a pair of twin barrows six miles NW of Pickering 'on account of a [previous] casual discovery of jet ornaments within them' (Bateman 1861, 228). On opening the first barrow, measuring 46 yards (*c.* 42m) in circumference and four feet (*c.* 1.22m) high and constructed of sand, 'The trench, begun at the north side, had only advanced about two feet from the surface when a variety of jet beads was found, sufficient to compose a very pretty necklace, comprising a rectangular centre-piece, ornamented with a saltire made by small holes drilled a little way in; thirteen long beads, and nine [sic] cone-shaped studs' (*ibid*). A few pages later, Bateman explains that Mr Ruddock's sudden death prevented him from preparing notes of his later discoveries, but Bateman lists, under finds 'From barrows in the neighbourhood of Pickering, opened in 1854 and 1855', 'part of a fine jet necklace, consisting of a conical stud, two cylindrical beads, and two flat dividing plates, each ornamented with a saltire in punctures...' (*ibid*, 239). The entry for J93-582 in Howarth's Catalogue of the Bateman Collection lists 'Two cylindrical [i.e. fusiform] beads and 6 other jet ornaments – From tumuli [sic], near Pickering, 1855.', implying that material from more than one barrow is included in J93-582 (Howarth 1899, 188). Three of these 'ornaments' (or four, if one counts the two fragments of one spacer plate as two separate objects) are listed above along with the fusiform beads. Two other objects were noted by the present project team among the J93-582 material: one appears to be a roughout (unperforated) for a spacer plate or trapezoidal fastener, while the other is a small perforated block of jet, possibly a pendant. If the Catalogue is correct in stating that the J93-582 material came from more than one barrow, then the presence of these objects along with the pieces from the necklace need not imply that they had been found with them; they will not be described further here.

The necklace components found in May 1851 were not associated with human remains or other material, although when the trench was diverted towards the west part of the barrow, a child's skull and other disturbed human bones were found. It is not known what became of the jet objects that had been found prior to Ruddock's excavation. One cannot rule out the possibility that he acquired them and that they became part of J93-582, rather than being found during excavations in 1855, although this cannot be proven.

MORPHOLOGY

The three spacer plates are very similar in shape and size,

although they differ in their condition (see below). They are rectangular, with a flat underside, slightly domed top, straight perforated edges and gently convex unperforated edges, with crisp junctions between all the surfaces. Each has two through-drilled perforations running along its long axis. The upper surface of each is decorated with a pointillé saltire design, featuring a relatively large central punctulation and limbs comprising two smaller punctulations. The dimensions are shown in Appendix VII, Table 13; see also Figure 7.2.16b.

All but one of the fusiform beads are fat, the exception (represented by two fragments) being slender. The fat beads range in length from *c.* 16.6 to *c.* 28.5mm and in width from 8.7 to 12.2mm. Not enough of the slender bead survives to assess its maximum width. In cross section the fat beads are round, and in profile they taper fairly evenly to straight or slightly angled ends. The longitudinal borehole varies from being central to noticeably eccentric (Figure 7.2.16d).

The buttons are high-domed, with a pointed apex, gently convex dome and flat circular base; five have a narrow or minimal facet (bevel) between the dome and the base (Figure 7.2.16c). The perforations are obscured by glue in several cases, but where visible they appear to be mostly symmetrically-positioned, oval, and with a bridge ranging up to 4.0mm in width. The diameters range from *c.* 13.2 to *c.* 20.0mm, and the heights (where surviving intact), from 6.1 to 8.8mm. According to Shepherd's typology (2009), they fall within his Type 2, the commonest type of button to have been found with spacer plate necklaces, and are listed as entries 101 and 102 in his Catalogue (although the museum Registration Numbers are transposed and the presence of bevels in five examples is not noted there: Shepherd 2009, 363).

MATERIAL

Macroscopically, in all cases the material appears to be jet, as revealed by one or more of the following characteristics in each case: woody texture, colour (notwithstanding the darkening caused by the presence of lacquer in many cases), criss-cross cracking and shiny conchoidal fracture (AS). The complete spacer plate in ID 265 has a particularly distinctive woody texture, shown as wavy ripples on the top and underside (Figure 7.2.16b); the same feature is also present, but less noticeable, on the most incomplete spacer plate in ID 264. All the spacer plates are a rich, variegated black and dark brown colour, characteristic of jet, and despite the damage to the most incomplete example, their general condition suggests that they had been made using hard jet, in contrast to the beads and many of the buttons, which appear (from their degree of cracking) to have been made from soft jet. Four of the buttons differ from the other components in being a dull, greyish-black colour; some of these have a distinctive finely-crazed surface on their dome. It may well be that slightly lower-quality jet was used for these buttons than the jet used for the beads and plates; and it may be that a particular block of jet was used to make at least two of the spacer plates, if not all three.

One fragment from a fat fusiform bead was analysed using oil immersion reflected light microscopy and reflectance measurement by Dr J. M. Jones, who concluded that the material was jet, not of the best quality, but probably from Whitby. White material was noted as a deliberate infill in the punctulations of the most complete spacer plate (ID 265).

MANUFACTURE

The presence of lacquer on most pieces, and of glue on some, makes it hard to assess the original degree of polish and has obscured details such as boreholes on some of the buttons. Nevertheless, faint manufacturing striations were noted near the end/s of several beads, and traces of faceting remained on four fusiform beads. The perforations in the beads and spacer plates are very likely to have been drilled from both ends; ancient chipping to one or both ends of the borehole was noted in three fusiform beads, and to one end of one borehole in the ID 265 spacer plate. The difference in size of the punctulated decoration on the spacer plates seems to have been achieved by enlarging the central hole, which had probably initially been drilled using the same tool as that used for the other punctulations. The process of enlargement can be seen clearly in the more complete of the ID 264 spacer plates. Regarding the buttons, faint multi-directional striations were noted on the bases of five examples, and marked striations on the base of one. Most of the button boreholes showed no signs of rilling; one perforation has a shouldered profile, showing that the drill had been re-positioned.

Despite the fact that lacquer has obscured the original degree of polish, it seems likely that the spacer plates, fusiform beads and many of the buttons had originally been polished to a high or medium sheen. The four greyish-black buttons had probably had a low to medium sheen, and one seems to have been matt or polished to a low sheen.

COMPLETENESS AND DAMAGE

Many of the components show evidence for post-excavation damage in the form of missing fragments, and many have glue on one side and/or where attempts to re-fit detached fragments had been made in the past. (The glue has become discoloured to a brown colour). Most, if not all, of this damage is likely to be due to the fact that the necklace had been strung during the 19th century with copper or bronze wire (a fragment of which survives in one perforation of the most incomplete spacer plate), and subsequently re-strung with linen thread; it may well have been glued to a back-board when re-strung. Furthermore, the application of lacquer to most of the components has obscured the original degree of polish, has made them appear blacker that they may originally have been, and has obscured some details of wear. The most incomplete spacer plate is the most extensively damaged; it had broken twice along one of the perforations, and has one detached but conjoining fragment.

That said, most of the components are missing less than

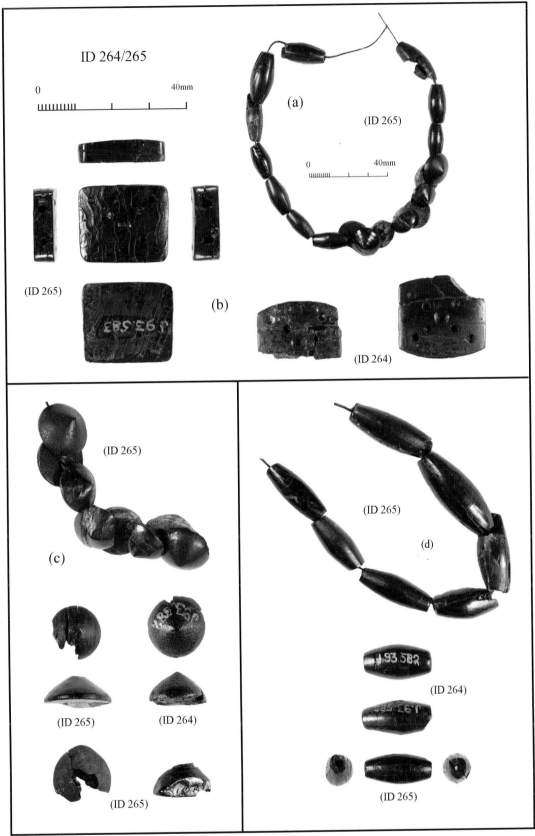

Figure 7.2.16. ID 264/265 'In the neighbourhood of Pickering' showing: (a) the strung components as currently displayed; (b) spacer plates; (c) details of buttons, and (d) details of fusiform beads.

10% of their body. Ancient damage is limited to minor chipping, flaking and spalling of several beads and to two of the spacer plates (the third being in such poor condition, due to post-excavation damage, that it is impossible to assess ancient damage). Criss-cross and/or laminar cracking is present on most of the beads and buttons, and the complete and near-complete spacer plates have hairline cracking.

WEAR

The presence of glue and/or lacquer has, in many cases, obscured the areas where evidence for wear would be discerned. However, where it could be investigated, the evidence indicates that the spacer plates have no obvious thread-wear and no bead-on-plate wear. Similarly, the fusiform beads have no obvious signs of thread-wear (other than damage caused by the use of metal wire in the museum) and no bead-on-bead wear. Where the end/s of some beads are angled, this does not appear to be the result of wear (with one possible exception). Wear to the buttons is slight and mostly consists of thread-polish to the perforations; in most cases, however, the edges of the perforations have remained crisp. Only on one button was there smoothing of the edge of the perforations through wear, and this was to the outside of one perforation (which is consistent with necklace wear, where the thread pulls to the outer edge of the perforations). There is no evidence to suggest that any of the buttons had previously been used as buttons (i.e. fasteners) before their use as beads in the necklace. Overall it appears that this necklace had not been worn long enough for noticeable wear to develop; nor is there significant difference between the degree of wear seen in the different components. The wear (excluding recent wear) is summarised in Table 7.2.2.

CONCLUSIONS

The circumstances of discovery of ID 265, and the uncertainty concerning the discovery of ID 264, make it difficult to judge whether we are dealing with a necklace that had been buried with an individual and subsequently disturbed, or whether it had been deposited on its own in the upper part of the barrow. Similarly, it is impossible to tell whether or not it had been complete when deposited; and whether the different components (i.e. plates, beads and buttons) had been brought together at different times to form the necklace, or else made as a single set. Several conclusions can be drawn: that it had been a two-strand necklace, not worn for long before deposition; that two, if not all of the spacer plates had been made from a piece of good quality hard jet with distinctive annual growth rings that appear as projecting wavy lines; that the beads and some of the buttons had been made of soft jet, and that a few of the buttons appear to have been made using a lower-quality jet. The presence of white infill in the decoration of one of the spacer plates is a feature noted in several other jet spacer plate necklaces; analysis by Mary Davis has concluded that, in some cases, its main constituent had been barium sulphate, and in others, burnt bone (of indeterminate species: Sheridan and Davis 2002).

For a discussion of the *comparanda* for this necklace, see Chapter 7.3.

ID 281 Snailwell, barrow C, Cambridgeshire
Reference: Lethbridge 1949, 35, fig. 4 and pl. VIII.

COMPOSITION

This consists of a fragment of a spacer plate necklace, comprising two decorated terminal plates (with the decoration being scarcely visible in one case), four fusiform beads, and 24 out of the 25 disc beads that were found when the site was excavated in 1940 (Figure 7.2.17a and Figure 7.2.17b). The disc beads are currently strung separately More components may originally have been present; the interment had been disturbed.

CONTEXT AND ASSOCIATIONS

The necklace was associated with the contracted skeleton of a child, lying on its right side under a round barrow. There were no other grave goods. According to Lethbridge's very brief description, the body 'had probably lain on the old turf line' within the north-west quadrant of the barrow's footprint 'inside a rough post-circle' (Lethbridge 1949, 35). His plan, however, implies that the body had lain in a grave (*ibid*, fig. 4, 1NH 1). The remains had been disturbed, by rabbits and/or people, and the components of the necklace were found scattered around.

MORPHOLOGY

The terminal plates had originally been of similar shape and size (and quite possibly similarly decorated), although the loss of two large fragments from one of the plates in antiquity, along with surface degradation of that plate through cracking and cupping, has obscured the similarities. To distinguish between the two, the terms 'intact' and 'damaged' will be used.

The plates are trapezoidal and slightly asymmetrical in plan, with straight sides; the perforated edges had been gently squared off, while the sides had been rounded. On the intact plate, the fact that one side is longer and more splaying than the other suggests that this had probably been the right hand terminal plate. The dimensions are shown in Appendix VII, Table 14.

This intact plate has three boreholes at its squared-off, narrow upper end (Figure 7.2.17e) and four holes (plus an abortive fifth) at its broader end (Figure 7.2.17d). The increase from three to four perforations had been achieved through drilling a Y-perforation. The abortive hole is on the outer end of the row of holes, corresponding to an intended outermost (i.e. lowest) strand on the necklace. On the upper surface there is a design, executed in a 'rocker' technique, featuring two Y-shaped lines, extending from the upper end of the plate and diverging towards its lower end. This design echoes, but does not precisely match, the pattern of boreholes.

The condition of the damaged plate makes it hard to make out the decoration and to assess the original number of boreholes. Regarding the decoration, Lethbridge had mentioned that both plates had 'dotted ornament' (*ibid*, 35), but since he excavated the necklace the cracking of the surface, which is visible on his published photograph (*ibid*, fig. 4), has become worse, with some cupping of the surface, and the application of lacquer/consolidant to counteract this has obscured fine detail. Consequently, only a short stretch of very faint decoration can be made out, although it appears to have been executed in the same 'rocker' style as seen on the other plate, and the design may also have been similar. As regards the number of perforations, it is likely that the top had only had three, but the loss of a large fragment from the bottom right hand corner makes it impossible to tell whether there had originally been three or four holes (plus an abortive hole). However, the fact that the shape of the hole in the fracture surface is oval suggests that there may indeed have been four functioning holes along the bottom, with the boring at this side of the plate being a long Y-boring. It may be significant that the abortive borehole at one end of the bottom edge corresponds (in a strung position) to that seen on the intact plate; this supports the idea that the two plates had been made as a matching pair, albeit using different pieces of parent jet material (as detailed below).

The fusiform beads range in length from 12.5 to 20.0mm and in maximum girth from 5.0 to 5.7mm, with their longitudinal perforation ranging in diameter from 1.8 to 2.8mm. In shape they range from slender to medium, according to the descriptive scheme used for all of the fusiform beads in this project. Two of the beads have one angled end (probably caused through wear, as noted below) and the next to longest bead had lost two chips from its ends, making them angled (Figure 7.2.17a and c).

The disc beads (Figure 7.2.17b) are slightly graded in size, ranging in diameter from 5.3 to 7.5mm and in thickness from 1.0 to 2.1mm, and have a fairly narrow central perforation. Determining the perforation diameter was hindered by the presence of thread and the fact that they are tightly strung, but the beads at either end of the thread have perforations of 1.4 and 1.9mm. Some beads are parallel-sided, others slightly wedge-shaped.

MATERIAL

The terminal plates and fusiform beads appear macroscopically to be of jet, with the heavily cracked damaged terminal plate being of soft jet (AS). The intact plate is a black and black-brown colour and has a fine-woody texture, with superficial criss-cross cracking. The damaged plate is black, with deep criss-cross cracking and some cupping within the network of cracks. The fusiform beads are black and have curving laminar cracks that follow the original woodgrain of the jet.

The disc beads range in colour from black to black-brown and dark greyish; fine laminar cracking, parallel to the beads' flat surfaces, was noted in at least two cases. The question of whether these beads are of jet or of cannel coal or shale can only be addressed through compositional analysis. Given the limited scope for examining their flat surfaces, it was not possible to make a confident guess based on macroscopic inspection.

MANUFACTURE

Identification of manufacture traces was hampered by the fact that all the pieces had been coated with a lacquer/consolidant and that the disc beads are tightly strung. Nevertheless, the absence of obvious grinding striations from the terminal plates and fusiform beads (with the possible exception of some very faint striations along the bottom end of the intact plate, Figure 7.2.17d) attests to the worn state of these components. No striations were noted on the flat sides of the disc beads at each end of the string. Similarly, with the fusiform beads, no traces remained of the facets that had formed part of their shaping process.

Where the interior of the perforations is visible, there is no sign of rilling. The perforations on both the plates and the fusiform beads will have been drilled from both ends. One of the fusiform beads has a small hole on its side near one end, and this may have resulted from the drill proceeding too close to the surface of the bead. The presence of an aborted drill hole on each of the terminal plates has already been noted and suggests a change of plan during the manufacture of the necklace. The regular spacing of the boreholes makes it clear that the original intention had indeed been to have five strands issuing from the terminal plates – a relatively large number of strands by comparison with other spacer plate necklaces. (The number of boreholes issuing from the top end of each plate is also unusually large).

As regards the degree of polish on each of the components, the presence of lacquer/consolidant will have enhanced the sheen. That said, there is a difference in the degree of sheen on the front and back of the intact terminal plate, with the back having the higher sheen. It may be that the whole of the plate had originally been polished to a high sheen and that the exposed side had lost some of this over time. The damaged plate has a uniform medium sheen, and the fusiform beads have a medium to high sheen. The disc beads have a low sheen on their edge. Where their flat surfaces are visible, these are either matt or have a low to medium sheen.

The technique used to create the 'rocker' decoration on the plates is very unusual. While Beck, discussing the identical decoration on the Burwell Fen terminal plate (ID 282), had speculated that it had been made using a curving punch (Beck 1928, 57), in the opinion of contemporary Whitby jetworker Hal Redvers-Jones (who has replicated this style of decoration) it had actually been executed by freehand scribing, by a very steady and skilled individual. The ends of each curve had been accentuated and deepened by a twist of the scribing tool.

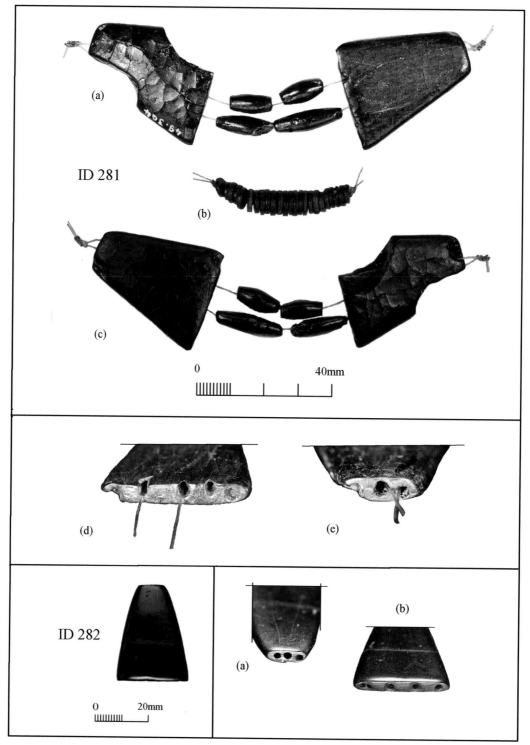

Figure 7.2.17. ID 281 Snailwell (top) and ID 282 Burwell Fen (bottom). Top: details showing: (a) front view of two terminal plates and four fusiform beads (note faint decoration on both plates); (b) disc beads; (c) back view of terminal plates and beads; (d) detail showing faint striations along the bottom end of the intact plate as well as evidence of thread-smoothing, thread-pull damage and 'haloes' from bead-on-plate wear. Also shows the abortive drill hole at the right end, and (e) detail showing thread-pull damage to hole on the left and shallow groove from thread-wear between that hole and the central perforation. Bottom: ID 282 Burwell Fen, showing decoration and fracture line across plate and (a) perforations at top and (b) perforations at bottom. The abortive perforation is on the far left; see also where the drill has perforated the upper surface, a little way in from this.

COMPLETENESS AND DAMAGE

Overall, the necklace is very far from complete. Compared with a complete classic lunula-like jet spacer plate necklace, it is lacking two pairs of spacer plates, a fastener, and around a hundred fusiform beads. Notwithstanding the fact that the interment had been disturbed, the balance of probability is that the necklace had been substantially incomplete when deposited irrespective of whether or not it had started out as a 'classic example'.

Regarding its individual components, only 70% of the damaged terminal plate is present, two large fragments having been lost from its corners in antiquity. The other terminal has chips missing as a result of ancient thread-wear (and possibly bead-wear in the case of damage to its lower holes). Two of the fusiform beads had lost chips in antiquity, again through wear. The disc beads all appear to be complete but close inspection for signs of damage was hindered by the fact that they are all coated with lacquer/consolidant and are strung tightly.

WEAR

The intact terminal plate has thread-smoothing to all its perforations, plus thread-pull that has resulted in the chipping away of the surface at both ends of the plate (Figure 7.2.17d and Figure 7.2.17e). Along the bottom, one thread has pulled towards the back of the plate, detaching a chip from the corner of the plate, while three have pulled towards the front, in one case detaching a small chip. These three perforations had been drilled very close to the front of the plate. Furthermore, there are hints of possible bead-wear, from the end of fusiform beads, around two of the perforations on this bottom edge: this appears as faint 'haloes' on Figure 7.2.1d. Along the top edge, the thread has worn a shallow groove between the centre hole and the chipped hole (Figure 7.2.10e). This indicates that the necklace had been re-strung at this point, to compensate for the damage to the end hole. The decoration on the intact plate is fairly faint and has been worn towards the upper and lower ends of the plate; that on the damaged plate is near-invisible, partly due to wear.

With the damaged terminal plate, it is unclear whether the loss of two large fragments had been related to thread-pull, but the degree of loss seems excessive for this to have been the cause. However, there is evidence for thread-pull having caused chipping at the upper edge, with the pull towards the back of the plate. Along the bottom edge, one of the holes shows slight thread-pull towards the centre. No obvious bead-on-plate grinding wear was noted. The fracture surfaces where the two large fragments had been broken off are worn, demonstrating that the plate had been used in its damaged state.

With the fusiform beads, there has been thread-smoothing to the ends of the perforations. The angling of one end on two of the beads, and the chipping of both ends of a third, had probably been caused by bead-on-bead wear. As for the disc beads, the only visible sign of wear was possible thread-pull on one bead; otherwise, the presence of lacquer/consolidant, and the tightness of their threading, made it hard to inspect the beads for signs of wear. The overall degree of wear on all the items is summarised in Table 7.2.2.

CONCLUSIONS

This necklace is substantially incomplete, even allowing for some loss of components due to disturbance, and its terminal plates and fusiform beads were clearly old and worn when deposited. Whether the disc beads were also old is harder to determine, since such beads tend not to show wear as much as fusiform beads and plates. As for whether the components derive from more than one parent necklace, the similarities between the terminal plates, despite the difference in the physical state of the damaged piece, suggest that these had been made as a set. The fusiform beads had clearly been used in a spacer plate necklace, but whether they had originally belonged to the same necklace as the terminal plates is unclear. Similarly, it is unclear whether the disc beads had been added from a different necklace, or had formed part of the original design. While disc beads had not formed part of the design of the earliest jet spacer plate necklaces, by the time the Snailwell plates were made it may be that they formed part of the original design, alongside fusiform beads. This point is discussed more fully in Chapter 7.3, along with the regionally-specific *comparanda* for this necklace, including for its distinctive decoration.

ID 282 Burwell Fen, Cambridgeshire

References: Anon. 1854; Fox 1923, 55; Beck 1928, 57 and fig. 44; Craw 1929, 186; Fowler 1932, 362 and note 3; Salzman 1938, 271 and fig. 15; Lethbridge 1949, 35, note 1.

COMPOSITION

The necklace survives as a single terminal plate (possibly right hand) from a spacer plate necklace.

CONTEXT AND ASSOCIATIONS

The item was found in peat prior to 1854. Accounts differ, but according to the 1854 *Cambridge Antiquarian Society Report XIV* (Anon. 1854), which records the acquisition of this object from the collection of the late Isaiah Deck, a complete necklace is believed to have been found: 'A piece of ornamented jet from Burwell Fen. It is believed that Mr Litchfield has the remaining part of a necklace to which this belonged' (E. Litchfield was a collector). Fox (1923, 55) and Craw (1929, 186) refer back to the *Report*, but later publications refer to the spacer plate as having been an isolated find in the peat. Fowler (1932, 362) speculated that it may have been associated with a body like several other bodies that had been found in the Fens (*cf* Roberts 1998).

MORPHOLOGY

The plate is trapezoidal and virtually symmetrical with very slightly convex, rounded sides and fairly crisply squared-off perforated ends (Figure 7.2.17, bottom). It is impossible to tell whether this had been a right hand or left hand terminal plate. Its length is 31.7mm, maximum width 24.3mm and maximum thickness *c.* 4.5mm. The perforations are relatively small with diameters ranging between 1.3 and 2.0mm. These had been through-bored and must have involved one Y-boring. There are three perforations along the top edge (Figure 7.2.17 bottom, a) and four functioning holes along the bottom edge, plus a fifth hole – the hole closest to one edge, and forming a twin with its near neighbour – which is suspected to have been abortive. This last hole which, like its closely-set neighbour, is narrower than the others (Figure 7.2.17 bottom, b) may well be related to an accidental hole on the front surface just under half way up the body where the drill had broken through the surface of the plate. This pattern of boreholes matches that seen on the Snailwell terminal plates.

The front surface is decorated with a linear design executed by the 'rocker' technique featuring two long Y-shaped lines extending from the upper (narrow) edge of the plate to the bottom edge. Flanking these, and very faint, are two further, straight lines. The latter are shown more clearly than they actually appear in Salzman 1938 (fig. 16); a less accurate rendition, and one showing just one of the straight lines, is offered by Beck (1928, fig. 44).

MATERIAL

Macroscopically, the material appears to be jet. It is a variegated black and black-brown on its front surface, and on the back there is a shallow conchoidal flake scar. The absence of cracking suggests that hard, rather than soft jet had been used (AS).

MANUFACTURE

The fact that the plate had been glued to a sheet of clear perspex means that it was not possible to examine the back in much detail. Nevertheless, it was possible to observe grinding striations, of varying degrees of faintness, running across the top and bottom edges of the plate. It is also clear that the grinding preceded the hole-drilling. The latter must have proceeded from both ends of the plate and had broken through the front surface at one point. No rilling was noted inside the holes.

The 'rocker' the decorative technique has been discussed in the entry for the Snailwell necklace (ID 281) in this section and will have been achieved by controlled, highly skilled scribing. As for the degree of polish, the front and sides have a uniform, very high sheen, while the perforated edges are unpolished. The degree of polish on the back of the plate could not be ascertained.

COMPLETENESS AND DAMAGE

The plate is complete but for a small chip where the drill had penetrated through the front surface, and a shallow spall at the back, extending to the top. Both losses had happened in antiquity, and probably both during manufacture. More recently, the plate had snapped in two just below its half-way point at some point after its discovery and the two

parts had been glued back together (Figure 7.2.17 bottom, a and b). There are also some shallow superficial scratches on the front surface.

WEAR

Overall, the plate shows a moderate degree of wear. Thread-wear is minor with the edges of the perforations remaining fairly crisp, but there is clear bead-on-plate wear in the form of hollows, ground by the ends of fusiform beads, around all the holes on the lower edge (Figure 7.2.17 bottom, b). (The bead-wear around the double perforation on the left hand side encompasses both of the holes, confirming that there had been four strands of fusiform beads issuing from the bottom of the plate). Furthermore, parts of the decoration had been abraded to varying degrees with the outermost straight lines rendered nearly imperceptible through wear. Faint traces of the upper ends of those lines are visible on Figure 7.2.17 bottom, a. The bottom ends of the Y-shaped lines have also been heavily worn. This wear had also softened the edges of the hole on the front surface.

CONCLUSIONS

This terminal plate had clearly seen some use before its deposition in the peat. The most remarkable aspect of this object is the fact that its unusual and distinctive style of decoration is matched on a pair of terminal plates found at Snailwell, Cambridgeshire (ID 281) *c.* 8 km away, on a pair of spacer plates found at Soham Fen, Cambridgeshire (ID 391) *c.* 9 km away, and on a lozenge-shaped ornament (a probable skeuomorph of the large gold lozenge from Bush Barrow, Wiltshire) found at Carlton Colville, Suffolk (Pitts 2007). All these items are of jet and, as discussed in Chapter 7.3, this remarkable similarity (which also extends to the matched borehole pattern between the Snailwell and Burwell Fen terminal plates) suggests that they may well be the work of a single individual probably based in East Anglia.

ID 379–390 Pockley (Oxclose Farm), barrow 2, North Yorkshire

References: Pacitto unpublished TS (1970); Smith 1994, 111, NYM 89; Shepherd 2009, 363; (additional information from Ian Kinnes pers. comm.).

COMPOSITION

The composition of the necklace is unclear since accounts vary and since virtually all of the pieces were scattered over the old ground surface. The items of jet or jet-like material from this barrow comprise:

- 298 small disc beads plus 27 fragments of same; 297 beads are threaded on two strands (ID 384), with 65 on one and 232 on the other. There is also a single disc bead (ID 387). The strand of 65 beads is associated with 6 of the fragments and the 232 beads with the remaining 21 fragments. According to Kinnes (pers. comm.) the threading of these beads onto two strands is likely to have been done by (or for) Pacitto and may relate to spatial groupings; there is otherwise no difference between the beads in each strand. The smaller strand is illustrated here (Figure 7.2.18a).

- one spacer plate, undecorated (ID 386, Figure 7.2.18b).
- one fusiform bead (ID 381, Figure 7.2.18c).
- two V-perforated fasteners or pendants (ID 389, Figure 7.2.18d, and ID 380).
- one through-perforated pendant or fastener (ID 390).
- one probable roughout for a pendant (not numbered).
- five V-perforated buttons (ID 379, ID 382–3, ID 385, Figure 7.2.18e, and ID 388).

Of these, it is unclear whether the buttons and fasteners/pendants had belonged to the necklace; the probable pendant roughout cannot have belonged and is not discussed in any detail here.

CONTEXT AND ASSOCIATIONS

All the material comes from a severely plough-damaged barrow. Most of the items were found scattered over an area under 1m in diameter on the level of the old ground surface below the barrow in its south-west quadrant, to the north of burial 2. According to the Pacitto typescript the barrow contained no skeletal remains and no grave goods. Two items are reported to have come from the filling of burial 2 (*ibid*), and are also reported by Smith as being in the 'the fill of a pit in the SW quadrant' (1994, 111, NYM 89). The labelling in the British Museum has one of the V-perforated fasteners and one of the buttons as coming from burial 4, although the Pacitto typescript states that there were no grave goods from burial 4. A further source of confusion arises from the fact that the Pacitto typescript refers to the discovery of 'some 200 tiny drum shaped beads with single perforations [there being in fact over 300 present], several spacer plates [there being only one present] and a conical button [there being five present]'; in the opinion of Ian Kinnes (pers. comm.), Pacitto had accidentally mis-reported these finds. As a final source of confusion, Shepherd's reference to the buttons incorrectly states that they were associated with the small cist, in the north-west quadrant that was only large enough for an infant and which contained a Food Vessel (Shepherd 2009, 363).

MORPHOLOGY

The disc beads are all small, neatly circular, and relatively uniform in their diameter (3.9 to 5.1mm) and thickness (1.1 to 2.4mm). The vast majority are parallel-sided, with only a very few that are slightly wedge-shaped in profile. The outer edge is straight and perpendicular to the flat sides. The perforation is central and perpendicular, and ranges from 1.5 to 2.5mm in diameter. They are all black; some have dark brown sediment from their burial context adhering to their surface (and indeed sealed in by the consolidant used to coat them). If all the complete and fragmentary

disc beads were laid in a line, it would be around 640mm long but if, as seems likely from the spacer plate boreholes, they had been deployed as five strands, the length of each strand would have been a fraction of this. The fusiform bead is fairly short (13mm in length) and plump (8.3mm in maximum breadth), with a central longitudinal perforation 2.3mm in diameter (Figure 7.2.18c). This had been drilled from both ends, meeting at a slight off-set. The ends are rounded and angled, each sloping in the same direction, and in cross section the bead is oval. An irregular ridge runs around the bead's fattest point, giving it a slightly biconical appearance. It is black, with hints of blackish-brown.

The spacer plate is a fairly narrow rectangle in plan, with rounded top and bottom edges, flattish front and back surfaces and squared-off perforated edges (Figure 7.2.18b). Its length is 28.0mm, width 11.75mm, and maximum thickness 6.0mm. It has five through-perforated boreholes, neatly drilled from both ends, with the perforation diameters (at their narrowest point) ranging from 2.2 to 2.6mm. It is black-brown in colour.

Both V-perforated fasteners are roughly oval in plan and very slightly wedge-shaped in profile. The smaller one (ID 380) has a diameter ranging between 10.8 and 12.3mm and is 8.1mm thick at its thickest point. ID 389 is 19.5 by 15.8 by 11.2mm in its respective dimensions (Figure 7.2.18d). The V-perforation on ID 380 features narrow holes 3.5mm in their maximum width, with a narrow bridge just under 2mm wide between them. On ID 389 the perforations have been drilled at a broader angle and they are wider (up to 7.5mm wide in one case) with a bridge 8.1mm wide between them. ID 380 is black but has brown sediment in its many surface irregularites; ID 389 is black-brown, but lighter on one side than the other.

The through-perforated fastener is irregular in shape, roughly pear-shaped in plan and unevenly rectangular in profile, and looks to be a perforated pebble. It is 17.2mm long, 10.5mm wide and 8.2mm thick with a perforation 2.3mm wide at its narrowest point and 5.0mm wide at its widest (on one side of the pendant). It is light grey to black.

All the V-perforated buttons are fairly consistent in shape, being circular in plan, medium- to high-domed in profile, and with a more or less clearly-defined bevel immediately above their base. According to Shepherd's classification (2009), they count as Type 2(B) (although in Shepherd 2009, only two are listed as having a bevel). ID 382, ID 385 and ID 388 have (or had) a pointed apex. Their dimensions and colours are shown in Appendix VII, Table 15.

MATERIAL

It is clear, macroscopically, that there is variability in the material. Analysis has confirmed that it is jet (although the through-perforated pendant ID 390 was not analysed and there is a question mark over whether it is of jet). The un-numbered ?pendant roughout was not recorded in detail or analysed, although on initial rapid macroscopic inspection it appeared to be of jet, possibly of high quality.

The best-quality jet is represented in spacer plate ID

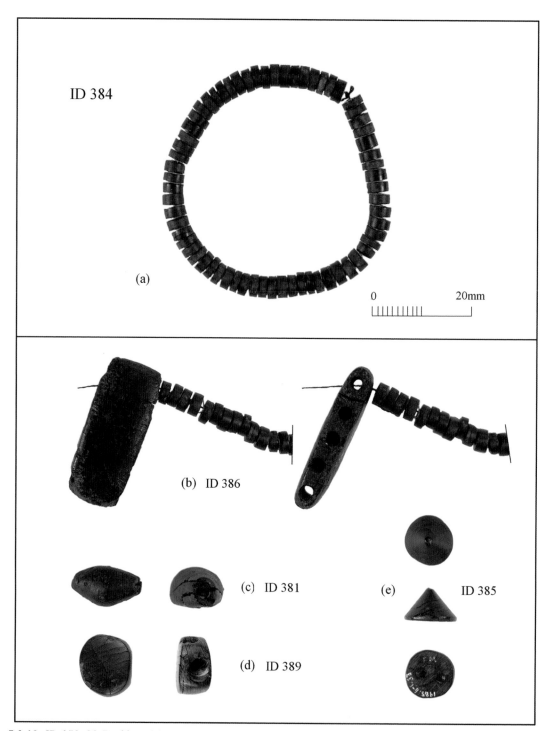

Figure 7.2.18. ID 379–90 Pockley: (a) ID 384, the smaller of the two strings of disc beads, containing 65 beads; (b) details (not to scale) of spacer plate ID 386 showing outer surface and perforations; (c) detail of fusiform bead ID 381; (d) detail of fastener ID 389, and (e) detail of V-perforated button ID 385.

386 (Figure 7.2.18b) and in the V-perforated fastener ID 389 (Figure 7.2.18d) (AS/MD). Both objects have criss-cross cracking (more marked in the fastener than in the spacer plate, including some incipient cupping indicating the use of soft jet) and had been polished to a high sheen. ID 386 has a thin vein of whitish spar, a natural inclusion seen in some jet. Both may well have been beach pebbles. On ID 386 the presence of 'orange peel' natural hollows

may represent traces of the pebble's original outer surface, while the slight irregularity in ID 389's shape may echo the pebble's original shape.

At the other end of the spectrum, several objects, including the button ID 379, have a more fibrous (woody) or even slightly grainy texture and many surface irregularities, and have not been polished to any more than a low sheen (probably because the raw material had not been capable of taking a high polish). Where the surface had cracked, the cracks are criss-cross (in the case of ID 379); concentric (ID 382) or 'wandering' (ID 383 and ID 388); the fusiform bead (ID 381) has laminar cracking. Compositional analysis of three such items (ID 379, ID 380 and ID 382) at the British Museum by X-ray fluorescence spectrometry (MD/DH) revealed that they have a high to very high iron content and are low in zirconium. Analysis of a tiny detached fragment from ID 379 by Dr J.M. Jones using oil immersion reflected light microscopy and reflectance measurement led to the conclusion that this had been pyrite-rich jet from which much of the pyrite had oxidised away. The items that fall within this low-quality jet category are ID 379–83 and ID 388.

In between these lie the disc beads (ID 384 and ID 387) and the button ID 385 (Figure 7.2.18e); they are of a compact, black/black-brown jet, with hairline criss-cross and concentric cracking on the button and with some hairline laminar cracking on the beads. Analysis of a fragment of one of the beads by Dr J.M. Jones revealed that it was jet of average quality (pers. comm.). The presence of two small 'orange peel' hollows on the bevel of button ID 385 suggests that here was the outer edge of the parent pebble of jet.

MANUFACTURE

Where visible, the flat surfaces of most of the disc beads have fairly crisp striations running across them. These are likely to relate to the grinding flat of these surfaces and indicate their individual shaping, at least as far as achieving a parallel-sided shape is concerned. The perforations are almost all parallel-sided (rather than hourglass- or Y-shaped) and suggest drilling from one direction. However, two beads have a slightly Y-shaped perforation and a rounded junction between the perforation and the flat surface, suggesting that here are traces of where the drill had entered the bead (or a columnar roughout for several beads). It is unclear whether the beads had all been shaped and drilled individually, or made by detaching them from a columnar roughout. If the former, then this implies that the drill's entry traces have been ground away and that their relatively uniform diameter had been achieved by roll-grinding the beads. The outer edge of the beads had been smoothed, but not polished.

The presence of an irregular ridge running around the broadest part of the single fusiform bead relates to its shaping by the grinding of a faceted roughout, smoothing one half and then the other. Faint circumferential rilling inside the perforation suggests the use of a bow- (or similar) drill. The surface had been polished to a low sheen.

On the spacer plate gouge marks, made by a toothed tool, on the 'front' surface and on one of the rounded edges probably relate to the removal of natural inclusions in the jet (Figure 7.2.18b). There are faint and irregular striations, from the grinding of the plate, on the front and back of the plate, but not on its perforated edges. The perforations had been drilled neatly from each end of the plate and are parallel-sided. No rilling is visible. The front and back surfaces and the rounded edges have a high sheen, and

while this is partly due to the consolidant used to coat the plate, nevertheless there seems to have been a differential degree of polish on these surfaces and on the perforated edges, the latter having a low to medium sheen only.

As far as the V-perforated fasteners are concerned, ID 380 has a slightly facetted edge, reflecting the way it had been shaped, and there are patches of faint circumferential striations that relate to the grinding of the edge. The back of the fastener has one patch of faint diagonal striations from grinding. The V-perforation had been made by a single episode of drilling from each end, using a drill with a round-tipped bit. Circumferential rilling is present in the right hand perforation. The surface is uneven (due to the loss of pyrite inclusions) and matt. In contrast, ID 389 had been polished to at least a medium sheen. There are faint diagonal striations on the edge, especially in the area around the bridge, and there is circumferential rilling in the interior of both perforations. The drill bit used to make the V-perforations had been relatively broad and round-tipped; there is no sign that the drill had been repositioned during the creation of the V-perforation.

The only manufacturing traces visible on the through-perforated fastener or pendant are from the perforation which had been drilled from either side (and which may have caused a large flake to become detached). Otherwise, the object appears to be an unmodified, irregularly-shaped pebble. No note was taken of the manufacturing traces on the ?pendant roughout.

Faint diagonal or multidirectional striations were noted on the bevel facet of all five V-perforated buttons, and uni- or multidirectional grinding striations were noted on the base of ID 382, ID 383, ID 385 and ID 388. They are particularly crisp on ID 385 (Figure 7.2.18e). The perforations were made using a round-ended drill, and in ID 382, where the apex had been lost, a central hole shows that the V-perforation had been at a steep angle. Evidence for both single-stage drilling, and drilling featuring a change of direction, was noted, and chipping around the perforations (as in ID 385) suggests damage during drilling. The presence of consolidant has obscured traces of rilling, although faint traces were noted in ID 385.

COMPLETENESS AND DAMAGE

Most of the items appear to have been coated with a consolidant. The presence of 27 fragments of disc beads indicates that not all the beads are complete or indeed present. The excavation took place during challenging conditions, and although the soil was sieved, it is possible that some further fragments or beads had formerly been present. Similarly, the fusiform bead is only 55% complete, having broken longitudinally along a laminar plane in antiquity; one end had become detached during or after excavation.

The spacer plate is 95% complete. A long chip is missing from two perforations on the left hand edge. On the right hand edge, extending to the front surface, sizeable chips are missing from either end. This is ancient damage and may relate to the plate's use. There has also been loss of a tiny flake from a deep crack between two of the perforations at an indeterminate date (Figure 7.2.18b).

The V-perforated fastener ID 389 has no missing parts, while fastener ID 380 has slight spalling of its surface (of an indeterminate age) and a flake missing from one side which appears to be an ancient loss. Overall 98% of the original object is present. Similarly the through-perforated fastener or pendant is nearly complete (*c.* 97%), lacking only a large flake that may have become detached during manufacture. The roughout is more fragmentary, but no details of the degree of incompleteness were recorded.

The V-perforated buttons range in completeness between 55% and 99%, with damage ranging from the loss of part of the apex in ID 385 (Figure 7.2.18e), to loss of just under half of the button upon (or since) excavation. The loss of part or all of the apex (in the case of ID 385 and 388) may have occurred in antiquity.

WEAR

The degree of wear of all the objects is summarised in Table 7.2.2. Essentially, the only item to show more than the slightest degree of wear is the spacer plate. The wear on the beads (including the fusiform bead) falls into the category of 'fresh' or 'slight'. If the interpretation of the two disc beads with slightly Y-shaped perforations is correct (see above), and this feature relates to their manufacture (as seems likely) and not to heavy thread-wear, then the disc beads show no obvious signs of wear at all. This is borne out by the fairly crisp striations seen on the flat surfaces of many beads. It is unclear whether the angled shape of the ends of the fusiform bead was an original design feature or was partly or wholly due to wear. Signs of wear consist of a slight smoothing to the outer edges of the perforation and a thread-pull groove to one end.

There is a moderate degree of wear on the spacer plate. There is a bead-ground hollow, 4.5mm across, on one perforation on the right hand perforated edge, and there is thread-polish all along the perforations. While there is only a minor amount of thread-smoothing of perforation ends, thread-pull hollowing was noted in four holes. In three cases, the pull was to the back of the plate; with the fourth, it is to the front. As noted above, it is possible that chipping along the perforated edges relates to use.

Of the V-perforated fasteners, ID 380 shows virtually no traces of wear, the only signs being the minimal smoothing to the inner edge of one of the perforations. Its condition is therefore fresh. ID 389 has thread-smoothing to the inner edge of both perforations, and comes under the category 'slightly worn'. There were no obvious signs of wear on the through-perforated fastener or pendant (ID 390). Similarly, although the presence of consolidant has obscured details on the V-perforated buttons, it appears that they fall within the categories 'fresh' and 'slightly worn', the wear consisting of the slight smoothing to the outer edge of one or both perforations. The manufacturing striations on ID 385 are particularly crisp (Figure 7.2.18e).

CONCLUSIONS

The fact that the finds had been scattered, and that confusion surrounds the account of their discovery, makes it hard to assess how the objects had originally been configured and thus how many discrete items of jewellery are represented. It is difficult to determine whether they had originally been in a grave or (as Pacitto's report implies) had not been interred with human remains, but simply deposited under the barrow. With regard to the necklace, the presence of a spacer plate raises the possibility that the disc beads had been strung in five strands. The spacing of the perforations in the spacer plate are such that five strands of disc beads could indeed have been accommodated (Figure 7.2.18b). The bead-on-plate wear is not inconsistent with rubbing by one of the larger disc beads, although it could equally have been caused by a fusiform bead. However, if arranged in this way, with equal numbers of disc beads on either side of the plate, each of the ten lengths of beads would only amount to *c.* 32mm. An alternative interpretation is that the spacer plate and fusiform bead had been collected from a spacer plate necklace and kept as a separate entity, with the disc beads being strung in a single, long (*c.* 640mm long) strand which would have extended to mid-chest level on an adult. Moreover, the presence of two V-perforated objects, assumed to be fasteners, is unusual. Normally with disc-bead necklaces there is only one fastener. In addition, it is unclear whether the somewhat crude through-perforated pendant, and the V-perforated buttons, would have formed part of the necklace. Although there is slight wear to the outer edge of the perforations on four of the buttons, this does not prove that they had been used as necklace beads. The use-wear evidence suggests that none of these artefacts had been worn for very long before burial. Comparatively speaking, the spacer plate is the most worn object. The variability in the quality of the jet used confirms that several different pieces of jet had been used to make the items.

ID 391 Soham Fen, Cambridgeshire

References: Fox 1923, 55; Craw 1929, 186; Salzman 1938, 271; Lethbridge 1932, 362; Roberts 1988, 191–2.

COMPOSITION

This is an incomplete spacer plate necklace (Figure 7.2.19a) comprising an unusually-shaped, squat biconical object interpreted as a fastener, a pair of decorated spacer plates, 19 disc beads, one fusiform bead, five biconical beads and a squat oblate bead.

CONTEXT AND ASSOCIATIONS

The necklace was found before 1850 in peat at the south-eastern edge of the Fens near Soham Fen (Roberts 1988, 191). It was associated with the skeleton of an adult female as well as cremated remains. An alleged, and chronologically implausible association with a 'socketed chisel-like axe of late type' (Fox 1923, 55) can be discounted. The discovery constitutes one of a number of finds of human remains in the Fens, including several from Soham Fen (Roberts 1988). While Fox had argued that these were victims of accidental deaths by drowning (1923, 55; followed by Lethbridge 1932), it is more likely that some, including the present example, represent the deliberate funerary deposition of bodies.

MORPHOLOGY

The numbering used to identify the individual components corresponds to that shown in Figure 7.2.19a. The object that is most likely to have been a fastener (no. 1, Figure 7.2.19b) is a slightly squashed circle in plan and a squat bicone in profile with a rounded junction between the two cones and a narrow V-perforation drilled below the apex on one side. It measures *c.* 24mm in diameter and 14.1mm in height. The perforations measure 1.7 by 2.1mm and 1.9 by 2.1mm in diameter respectively.

The spacer plates (nos. 2–3, Figure 7.2.19c–d) are very similar to each other, each being rectangular with straight, crisply squared-off perforated edges and gently convex, rounded unperforated edges. Plate no. 2 measures 26.7 by 17.7 by 4.4mm; plate no. 3 measures 27.8 by 19.4 by 4.0mm. Each has four through-bored perforations varying in diameter between 1.5 and 1.7mm. It is impossible to tell which plate had originally been intended to lie on the left hand side, and which on the right.

The 19 disc beads (nos. 11–29, Figure 7.2.19a and Figure 7.2.19e) are circular in plan and parallel-sided (although one is very slightly wedge-shaped), with central narrow perforations that are perpendicular in all but one case and a slightly bevelled, minimally convex outer edge. They are slightly graded in size, their external diameter ranging from 5.1 to 8.2mm. In maximum thickness they range between 1.2 and 2.0mm.

The fusiform bead (no. 10, Figure 7.2.19f) is slender, fairly symmetrical in profile and a slightly squashed circle in section, with two flattish sides and a central longitudinal perforation. One of the flattish sides has a concave oval depression at mid-point, and there is a smaller, flatter oval facet at the corresponding point on the other side of the bead. The ends of the bead are roughly perpendicular, with one being squared off and the other more rounded. The bead is 21.0mm long (making it the longest bead in the necklace), 6.2mm in greatest width, and the perforation is 1.7mm in diameter.

The five biconical beads (nos. 5–9, Figure 7.2.19a, h and i) range from medium to plump in profile, and in cross section from roughly circular (no. 9) to rounded-triangular (no. 7), with squared-off ends that are perpendicular in some cases and very slightly sloping in others. Bead no. 7 could be regarded either as a biconical bead or as a plump fusiform bead. The broadest part of the beads is well defined but rounded and falls, in most cases, mid-way along the bead; in nos. 6 and 9 it 'wanders' around the mid-point. The longitudinal perforation is usually centrally placed but is slightly eccentric at one end of no. 6. In length the

beads range from 14.1mm (no. 7) to 15.8mm (no. 9), and in maximum width from 7.2mm (nos. 5 and 7) to 9.3mm (no. 9). The perforation diameter ranges from 1.4mm (no. 8) to 1.5mm (all the other beads).

The oblate bead (no. 4, Figure 7.2.19g) is roughly circular in plan and squat, slightly wedge-shaped in profile, with a convex outer edge that tapers towards the broad, circular, near-perpendicular perforation. Its maximum diameter is 10.2mm and maximum thickness is 6.5mm. The perforation diameter ranges between 5.0 and 5.8mm.

MATERIAL

Macroscopically, in every case except possibly the oblate bead (no. 10), the material appears to be jet and the fact that cracking is absent in most cases, and present only as incipient hairline criss-cross cracking in others (including on spacer plate no. 2), suggests that hard jet has been used (AS). All pieces are black, although there are also hints of dark brown on many of the components, especially where the subsurface has been exposed (through bead-wear, in the case of the spacer plates). On spacer plate no. 2 the undecorated side is a darker black than the decorated side. A fine, woody texture was noted in the fastener, spacer plates, disc beads and two of the biconical beads. A few small surface irregularities on the broadest part of the fastener (Figure 7.2.19b) resemble the 'orange peel' hollows seen on other jet objects, and may indicate the outer edge of the parent material (although such cavities are also known to occur within the body of jet). Clearly a fairly thick piece of jet had been used to create the fastener. By contrast, it is likely that a narrow piece of jet had been used to make the fusiform bead no. 10; this will have constrained the shape of the bead. 'Orange peel' hollows were also noted on the lower surface of spacer plate no. 2.

The oblate bead (no. 4) has some features that point towards the material being jet; these include tiny 'orange peel' hollows at either end of the perforation, and the presence of a shiny conchoidal spall scar beside the perforation at one end. The bead is black and of a compact material. Compositional analysis at the British Museum, using X-ray fluorescence spectrometry (MD/DH), revealed a high iron content and no zirconium. Compositionally then, the material appears closer to shale than to jet.

MANUFACTURE

On the fastener, no striations or faceting from the initial shaping were noted, although there is a very faint, shallow gouge-like mark close to the perforations and beside the painted registration number (Figure 7.2.19j). Whether this had related to the removal of a surface irregularity is unknown. The slight flattening of the edge of the fastener where surface irregularities exist may relate to attempts to grind them flat. The V-perforation had been neatly executed with a narrow drill, but the change of slope of both perforations shows that the drill had been repositioned once, and faint rilling from the drilling is visible on the left

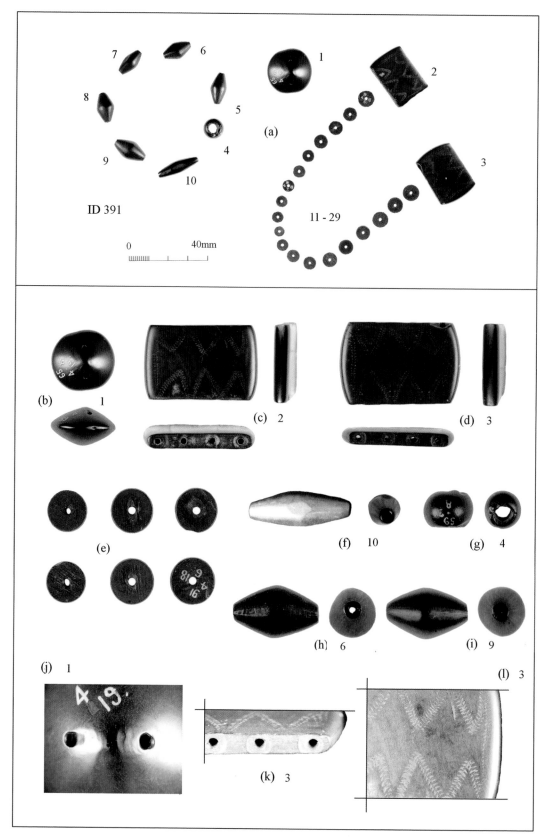

Figure 7.2.19. ID 391 Soham Fen: (a) individually numbered necklace components; (b) detail of fastener (no. 1); (c) and (d) detail of spacer plates (no. 2 and 3 respectively), showing bead-on-plate wear and very faint striations; (e) selection of disc beads showing faint striations; (f) detail of fusiform bead (no. 10) showing faceting and striations; (g) detail of oblate bead (no. 4); (h) and (i) detail of biconical beads (no. 6 and 9 respectively); (j) detail of perforations in fastener (no. 1); note also the shallow gouge mark beside the '4' on the label; (k) detail of end of spacer plate (no. 3) showing bead-on-plate wear and faint striations, and (l) detail of 'rocker' decoration on spacer plate (no. 3). Note: detailed images are not at consistent scales.

hand perforation (Figure 7.2.19j). The fastener had been polished all over. The perforated side has a high sheen, and the other side has a medium to high sheen.

There are very faint striations on the back of spacer plate no. 2, and these run across a very shallow hollow which is a natural surface irregularity in the jet. Similar striations were noted running across the back of spacer plate no. 3. There are also a few very faint striations running along part of one of the perforated edges on plate no. 2, and similar striations along both perforated edges of no. 3 (Figure 7.2.19d and k). The two plates are so similar in thickness and texture as to suggest that they may have originated in the same parent piece of jet. The perforations through both the plates had been very neatly drilled from both ends; they are straight-sided, with no splaying at the ends. Faint rilling was noted inside all the perforations on no. 2 (except for one which was clogged with sediment) and also inside one of the perforations on no. 1. Both plates had been polished, but the degree of sheen varies due to differential polish, possibly to wear, and to probable post-depositional dulling. The perforated edges range from matt (no. 2) to a low to medium sheen (no. 3), and the fact that the backs of the plates have a higher sheen than the front may be due to a combination of wear (leading to a natural polishing of the side nearest the skin/garment) and natural post-depositional dulling of the outermost surface. Both plates are decorated on their front surface with a design, executed by the 'rocker' technique (Figure 7.2.19l), featuring a continuous line running across the plate close to each end and zigzagging its way along the length of the plate.

All the disc beads have faint striations either from sawing or, more probably grinding, on one or both flat surfaces (Figure 7.2.19e), and in all but two cases there are nibble marks (faint transverse striations) at one or both sides of the outer, bevelled edge. These marks relate to the creation of the beads' slightly convex outer edge. In some cases the perforation is parallel-sided, in others slightly V-shaped, and in 12 cases fine rilling (in various degrees of faintness) is visible inside the perforation. A universal feature is a slight step near one end of the perforation accompanied by chipping to the surface adjacent to that end. This suggests that the drilling had mostly been effected from one side with a starter hole having been made on the other side. The outer edge had been polished to a medium to high sheen, and the flat surfaces had also been polished to a low sheen. These beads had been skilfully made.

The fusiform bead exhibits clear faceting, and faint unidirectional striations towards each end, representing traces left by its initial shaping (Figure 7.2.19f). The oval hollow on one of the flattish sides, and of an oval facet on another side, seem to be deliberate design features undertaken so that the bead would sit in a dense formation alongside other fusiform beads. It may be that this had originally been one of the beads immediately adjacent to a spacer plate. The perforation had almost certainly been drilled from both ends, and rilling is visible in the perforation. Excepting the facets, the exterior has a high sheen.

Four of the biconical beads have faint faceting, and all have faint unilinear striations towards one or both ends (Figure 7.2.19h and i). The narrow perforations have almost certainly been drilled from both ends, and rilling is visible in the perforation in four cases with the fifth having consolidant/lacquer obscuring the perforation's interior. The same drill seems to have been used to perforate all five beads and possibly also to the disc beads where the perforations are of a comparable diameter and quality. All the beads have a medium sheen; on no. 6, the sheen is lower where the woody texture of the jet is clearest.

There are no facets, striations or rilling on the oblate bead and it is hard to tell whether the perforation had been drilled from both sides. Its sides are straight. The surface has a high sheen, higher than that seen on the other components.

COMPLETENESS AND DAMAGE

All the components are complete or virtually complete. There is minor modern damage, in the form of small scratches on three of the biconical beads. Ancient damage is in the form of spalls or chips, most of which will have been detached during manufacture (as in the case of the spalls around disc bead perforations). Smoothing of the edge of some of the scars (as in biconical beads no. 7 and no. 9, the oblate bead and both spacer plates) suggests that the maker had tried to smooth these over, or else they have been worn smooth.

WEAR

The degree of wear on the individual components is summarised in Table 7.2.2 where it can be seen that wear to the oblate bead and the spacer plates is greater than on the other components. The nature of the wear is described in detail in Appendix VII, Table 16. Regarding the bead-on-plate wear, the diameter of the hollows suggests that the wear is from the fusiform beads, rather than from the biconical, oblate or disc beads, all of which have ends that are broader than the hollows.

CONCLUSIONS

With the exception of the oblate bead, all the components are likely to have been made as parts of the same necklace, such is the consistency and quality of the raw material and the style of, and skilfulness shown in, their manufacture. The disc beads, unusually for such beads, have been made from jet and are exceptionally fine examples of this bead type. That the necklace had formally comprised at least 15 more fusiform beads is indicated by the bead-wear on the spacer plates, and the presence of the oval hollow and facet on fusiform bead no. 10 is consistent with that bead having been designed to nestle closely against other strands of fusiform beads. It is also clear that the necklace had seen some wear on the basis of the bead-wear to the spacer plates, but it need not have been very old when buried.

The fact that this necklace bears the same style of manufacture and the same distinctive decoration as the finds from Snailwell (ID 281) and Burwell Fen (ID 282), and indeed that the components from two of these findspots could have originated as the same necklace, is discussed in Chapter 7.3. As regards the oblate bead, which stands out as being different in several respects from the rest of the Soham Fen necklace, two possible explanations offer themselves. The first is that this was a bead from a different necklace, incorporated in the Soham Fen necklace in prehistory. The second is that it may have become associated accidentally with the Soham Fen necklace in the British Museum during the 19th century, having been found in the same fen; its registration date, 1859, is different from that of the other components (whose registration dates range from 1865 to 1891). Unless there is documentation in the British Museum that could shed further light on the matter, this possibility cannot be ruled out.

7.3 DISCUSSION OF DISC BEAD AND SPACER PLATE NECKLACES OF JET AND JET-LIKE MATERIALS *(by Alison Sheridan)*

INTRODUCTION

The two types of necklace made from jet and jet-like materials described in this chapter – the single-strand necklaces that consist wholly or mainly of disc beads (Chapter 7.1), and the multi-strand necklaces whose strands are separated by spacer plates (Chapter 7.2) – represent two different, but chronologically overlapping design traditions. The origin of the former can be found in Continental Beaker jewellery and dress accessories of the mid-third millennium BC; the origin of the latter (*contra* Frieman 2012) lies in the gold lunulae which seem to have emerged in Ireland around the 22nd century BC. (Spacer plate necklaces made of amber are dealt with separately in Chapter 7.4.)

The variability in the necklaces that we see today has resulted from several processes, including 'style drift' from an initial design canon and the accretion, loss, and mixing of individual components during the use life of a necklace. The latter process accounts, for example, for the presence of fusiform beads in some disc bead necklaces (e.g. ID 246 Garrowby Wold). The presence of disc beads in some spacer plate necklaces could, in some cases, be due to the addition of beads from a disc bead necklace (as may be the case with ID 281 Snailwell, for example); in other cases, the disc beads could have formed an integral part of the initial design (e.g. at ID 247 Calais Wold or ID 391 Soham Fen) and represent a sharing of a design idea across the two traditions. To complicate the narrative yet further, elements of both necklace types (namely fusiform and disc beads) can also be found in composite necklaces (as described in Chapter 8). It is clear that some of these – such as the old and worn fusiform beads from Hay Top Hill, Derbyshire (ID 275) – had originated in old necklaces of the type/s discussed here, while others will have been new when worn in composite jewellery. This was evidently the case with the hundreds of disc beads of jet and white shell, recently discovered in a Beaker-associated grave at Great Cornard, Suffolk and radiocarbon-dated to the last quarter of the third millennium BC (Mo Muldowney pers. comm.). These had been strung, zebra-like, in an elaborate necklace or chest ornament that also included several amber beads and plates. Furthermore, like the Great Cornard example, the disc bead necklaces that incorporate tubular sheet metal beads (e.g. ID 434 Devil's Dyke and ID 251 Garton Slack VI, grave 1, burial 1) actually constitute early versions of composite necklaces. They are discussed here, rather than in Chapter 8, because of their explanatory role in the development of disc bead necklaces. A final complication surrounds the uncertainty over whether all the disc bead necklaces that incorporated tubular sheet metal beads had actually been worn as necklaces, rather than as sewn-on dress accessories. This point will be returned to below.

In order to clarify this complex picture, this discussion will start with a consideration of the origin and development of the two traditions before dealing with contexts and

associations, raw materials, aspects of manufacture (including the organisation and location of production) and life histories. The discussion will not be restricted to the 25 necklaces described in detail in Chapter 7.1 and Chapter 7.2, but will draw on the broader set of disc bead and spacer plate necklaces made of jet and jet-like materials that have been found in Britain and Ireland, and on the results of research by Alison Sheridan and Mary Davis, undertaken since the 1990s as a long-term National Museums Scotland research project (e.g. Sheridan and Davis 1998; 2002; 2008).

ORIGINS AND DEVELOPMENT OF THE TWO TRADITIONS

Disc bead necklaces (and dress accessories)

As indicated above, disc bead and spacer plate necklaces originated in different places at different times. The earlier of the two is the disc bead tradition, which appears to be one of several novelties associated with the use of Beaker pottery to be introduced to Britain from mainland Europe during the third quarter of the third millennium. Continental examples include representations of single-strand disc bead necklaces on the Bell Beaker period funerary stelae from Petit-Chasseur, Sion, Switzerland (Harrison and Heyd 2007, 158, 170–1, fig. 20) where they appear on both male and female stelae (Corboud and Curdy 2009), and disc beads from Bell Beaker contexts in the Mediterranean, where they are mostly made of shell (*ibid*, 171). They are not, however, a widespread element of Bell Beaker material culture and indeed it was not until the Early Bronze Age (*c.* 2000–1800 BC; possibly just before 2000 BC at Straubing in Bavaria: Hundt 1958) that the use of tiny disc beads – and tightly-coiled metal beads that resemble rows of disc beads – became popular in central and west-central Europe (as in the Franzhausen I cemetery, Austria: Neugebauer and Neugebauer 1997, e.g. 589). In these contexts they are often associated with tubular sheet metal beads and at Petit-Chasseur, in a grave dating to this period (grave 3, 2200–1800 BC), some of the tiny disc beads may well have been deployed alongside (and interspersed with) such beads as a sewn-on decorative border to a garment, while others may have been worn in a necklace (Rast-Eicher 2012, fig. 19.5).

The earliest dated disc bead necklace from Britain is that from a richly-equipped Bell Beaker-associated grave at Chilbolton, Hampshire (Russel 1990; Needham 2012b, 10). It consists of 55 tiny (3.3 to 4 mm diameter) disc beads, probably of Kimmeridge shale, together with a tubular sheet gold bead; the latter, and 20% of the former, were found near the skull, suggesting their deployment as a necklace. This was associated with the unburnt remains (contracted skeleton) of a man in his late twenties, a European-style, Low-carinated Beaker, two pairs of gold basket-shaped hair ornaments, a flint strike-a-light and marcasite nodule for making fire, a tanged copper dagger, an antler spatula and several flint flakes. The skeleton was recently radiocarbon dated, for the Beaker People Project, to 2570–2300 cal

BC (see Chapter 9); this supersedes a date determined during the late 1980s and confirms that the grave belongs to the Chalcolithic period. A similar disc bead necklace, which may have been roughly contemporary, was found at Beggar's Haven (Devil's Dyke), East Sussex (ID 434); of this, 14 tiny jet disc beads and fragments of at least five tubular sheet copper beads survive, alongside three fragments of wooden stiffeners for the latter. This was associated with a Beaker of Clarke's Wessex/Middle Rhine (Needham's Mid-carinated) type. Here, although the beads are recorded as having been found 'around the neck of the skeleton', the presence of a side perforation in one of the metal bead fragments suggests that we might be dealing with a sewn-on decorative border to a garment, rather than a necklace. At the very least, it suggests that the tubular beads had probably been sewn onto a garment at some point during their use life. (Deployment of similar beads and other sheet metal ornaments (of copper alloy) as appliqué decoration on an item of headgear, from a later, Early Bronze Age hoard at Migdale, Highland, has been suggested on the same grounds: Haveman and Sheridan 2006, 124–5). A further early example of a necklace featuring tiny disc beads (probably of lignite) plus tubular sheet gold beads, along with large amber ornaments that may or may not have formed part of the same object, is known from a recent Beaker-associated find at Horton, Berkshire (http://www.wessexarch.co.uk/blogs/news/2013/04/19/beaker-burial; accessed July 2013). As at Beggar's Haven and Migdale, the metal beads have side perforations, suggesting that they had also been sewn onto something during their use life.

Two other disc bead ornaments that may date to the Chalcolithic period are known to the authors. One is a necklace that was associated with an adolescent, two All-Over-Cord (AOC) Beakers, a 'tanged' bone belt ring (Figure 3.4.1), a flint scraper fragment and two flint flakes at Folkton, East Yorkshire, possibly in barrow 245 (ID 366); if this really was barrow 245, this is the same barrow as the one associated with the 'Folkton drums' grave. While it is known that the currency of AOC Beakers was not restricted to the third quarter of the third millennium, but extended into the fourth, nevertheless the form of the belt ring is one that is associated elsewhere with early Beakers. Therefore, this grave may well date to *c.* 2450–2200 BC. The other probably Chalcolithic disc bead ornament was found associated with the contracted skeleton of an adult female and a Low-carinated Beaker at Tarrant Hinton, Dorset (Graham 2006). Twenty-nine tiny beads, reportedly (and probably) of shale and measuring 4mm in diameter, were found in the pelvic region, in a position suggesting that they had been strung. Whether these had been from a belt is impossible to determine.

The use of disc beads (and of jet and jet-like jewellery in general) seems to have increased dramatically at the beginning of the Early Bronze Age, during the 22nd to 19th century BC, and this increase in popularity was accompanied by a diversification in the use and design of disc beads and an expansion in their geographical distribution, extending from Kent to Inverness and including eastern Ireland. Most of the disc bead necklaces studied in the current project belong to this period. To simplify a complicated picture, during this earliest Bronze Age we can discern the following uses:

1   Continuing use of tiny, uniform-diameter disc beads alongside tubular sheet metal beads in composite necklaces (and possibly also as appliqué dress accessories – see below).

2   Use of tiny, uniform-diameter disc beads, either on their own or accompanied by fusiform beads (probably reused from spacer plate necklaces), for choker-length necklaces, one much longer single-strand necklace and – in at least one case – a belt.

3   Use (and, in some cases, re-use) of tiny, uniform-diameter disc beads in spacer plate and composite necklaces.

4   Use of disc beads that are subtly graded in size, mostly to make choker-length necklaces. In some cases (as at ID 246 Garrowby Wold) some of the beads are under 5mm in diameter; in others (e.g. ID 245 and ID 250 Garton Slack 75) they are slightly over 5mm (here, 5.2 to 6.8mm). In northern Britain there are over 30 examples of disc bead necklaces where the beads are somewhat larger and thinner (which has given rise to their description as 'washer beads'); one such example was found at Barbush Quarry, Dunblane, Stirling, with the beads ranging between 9.0 and 11.3mm in diameter (Sheridan and Davis 2001; see also Sheridan and Davis 2002). Sometimes fusiform beads, probably reused from spacer plate necklaces, are also present, as at Garrowby Wold 64, East Yorkshire (ID 246, Figure 7.1.1) and Eglingham, Northumberland (ID 334, Figure 7.1.11). In these cases the necklaces are often referred to as 'disc-and-fusiform bead necklaces'.

Fasteners are often, but not always found with these items, and they are most commonly flat and triangular, with a central transverse perforation (Figure 7.1.4), or boat-shaped and V-perforated (Figure 7.1.3). In Yorkshire there is an interesting diversity in the fasteners associated with some choker-length disc bead necklaces (e.g. ID 308 Weaverthorpe, Figure 7.1.5; ID 322 Goodmanham, Figure 7.1.6, and ID 380 and ID 389 Pockley) and it may well be that this was used to individualise the otherwise similar-looking, and almost certainly contemporary, necklaces.

As for the disc-and-tubular metal bead items referred to above, there are three examples that fall within the Early Bronze Age: ID 251 Garton Slack VI, grave 1, burial 1, East Yorkshire; Ingleby Barwick, North Yorkshire (Blaise Vyner, pers. comm.), and Waterhall Farm (grave II), Chippenham, Cambridgeshire (Martin 1976, 48). At Garton Slack, the position of the tubular beads and disc beads suggests that these had indeed formed a necklace, and its excavator may be correct in arguing that it had been deliberately pulled apart when deposited in the grave, and laid down, in a sinuous strand, above what may have been a folded garment adorned with V-perforated jet and

?cannel coal buttons (ID 232–44; Brewster 1980, 202–6 and figs. 89–92). At least two of the copper alloy beads have perforations in their side, so once more these might have been used previously as appliqué dress accessories. The young adult skeleton, probably female, associated with the artefacts has been radiocarbon dated to 2300–2060 cal BC (see Chapter 9). At Ingleby Barwick, a richly-equipped grave for a young to middle-aged woman produced a similar assemblage of numerous tiny disc beads (of jet), along with one fusiform bead of low-quality jet, one bead of ?chalk, at least 45 tubular sheet bronze beads, one bronze bangle, 17 small V-perforated jet buttons and a fragment of what had probably been a copper alloy awl (plus worked flint items). Almost all of these were found on the upper part of the torso (with the bangle on one arm). The excavator felt that the metal and jet beads need not have been deployed together, in a necklace, since the metal beads were found above, and extending over a slightly larger area, than the jet beads. (There were possible traces of wooden stiffeners inside some of the metal beads.) The V-perforated buttons may have been attached to a garment, as decorative studs (see Chapter 5.6). The Ingleby Barwick skeleton has produced a radiocarbon date of 2030–1900 cal BC (see Chapter 9). (The author is grateful to Blaise Vyner for allowing this information to be used here). Finally, at Chippenham, a single tiny disc bead (of 'low grade [cannel] coal') and a single fragment of copper/copper alloy tubular bead were found in a grave that had contained the successively-deposited remains of at least four women (two relatively old, one aged around 20–30) plus an infant and a baby (Martin 1976). It was not possible to be sure whether the beads had been associated with the earliest of these interments, but if this was the case, then the disturbance caused by successive depositions may well have removed more beads. A long-necked Beaker (of Clarke's S2 or S3 type) was found in the grave and this should, on current reckoning, date to around 2000 BC (Needham 2005; Gibson 2008, table 1/8, fig. 1/32). Bones from one of the disarticulated individuals produced a radiocarbon date of 3520±70 BP (HAR-3880, 2040–1660 cal BC at 95.4%), but this individual could have post-dated the woman associated with the beads.

It is not intended to discuss all the other categories of Early Bronze Age disc bead ornaments in similar detail here. Suffice it to note that the examples of items belonging to category 2 above include a disc-and-fusiform bead choker-length necklace with triangular fastener found at Oldbridge, County Meath, in eastern Ireland (Ó Ríordáin and Waddell 1993, 161); the associated Bowl Food Vessel is of a type of pottery dated to 2160–1930/20 BC (Brindley 2007, 328). It appears that this necklace, like the category 4 washer bead disc bead necklace found with a Bowl Food Vessel in the Mound of the Hostages (burial 19), Tara, County Meath (O'Sullivan 2005, 107–12, fig. 104, plate 7) represents the adoption of a style of jewellery – or even the importation of necklaces – from contacts with Britain at this time. Examples of choker-length necklaces consisting wholly of tiny disc beads include one from Monkton,

Kent (Sheridan and Davis 2008) which, to judge from a grave containing a long-necked, Clarke's S2 Beaker found abutting (and respecting) the necklace grave, may date to around 2000 BC (Gibson 2008, table 1/8, fig. 1/32). The long necklace referred to in category 2 above is that from a woman's grave at Garton Slack 29 (burial D), East Yorkshire (ID 252). It consists of 731 (750, according to the excavator) tiny disc beads of relatively poor quality jet plus a triangular jet fastener; the associated skeleton has been radiocarbon dated to 2140–1950 cal BC (see Chapter 9). The belt comes from a female cist grave at Culduthel, on the outskirts of Inverness, and it is clear from the initial description of its discovery, with the beads found below and above the skeleton's waist, that it had indeed been worn as a belt rather than as a necklace (Low 1929, 218–9). It comprises over 538 tiny disc beads, plus six larger washer beads, 18 fusiform beads and a V-perforated, boat-shaped fastener. The washer and fusiform beads had probably been reused from necklaces. The skeleton has been radiocarbon dated to 2200–1980 cal BC (see Chapter 9).

The use of tiny disc beads in spacer plate necklaces will be discussed below, under 'spacer plate necklaces'; see also Chapter 7.4.3 for a discussion of the amber washer beads in the Shaw Cairn necklace, which was contemporary with the disc bead ornaments discussed above.

It is clear that disc bead jewellery continued to be used through the first half of the second millennium, especially in Wessex. In addition to examples in jet and jet-like materials – both of tiny, chunky disc beads and of thinner, sometimes slightly larger washer beads – examples of the tiny disc beads in amber are known (e.g. in the composite necklace from ID 540 Net Down, barrow 5j, Shrewton, Wiltshire, and in a composite necklace from Cossington, Leicestershire; Sheridan 2008). The jet and jet-like examples that definitely or arguably belong to the first quarter of the second millennium – acknowledging some chronological overlap with the material discussed above – include the single-material disc bead necklace ID 517 from Wilsford G39 (Lake H5), Wiltshire (Figure 7.1.10); the single-material probable bracelet of minuscule (2.0 to 2.6mm diameter) Kimmeridge shale beads from Roundway, Wiltshire (unpublished report by Sheridan and Davis), and the composite necklaces from the Manton barrow (ID 491, Figure 7.1.9), Wiltshire, and Whitehorse Hill, Devon (Jones forthcoming) – the latter's date being confirmed by radiocarbon dating. Further examples that are likely to date to this period include the composite necklaces found at Upton Pyne, Devon (Kirwan 1872); Ports Down (Southwick 7), Hampshire (Corney *et al.* 1969; Gerloff 1975, 259; Beck and Shennan 1991, 170–1, fig. 11.12.7, the necklace being accompanied by a gold-covered shale cone); and Stockbridge Down, Hampshire (Stone and Hill 1940). The Manton necklace is dealt with in this chapter, rather than with the composite necklaces discussed in Chapter 8, because the tiny lignite(?) disc beads dominate, comprising 144 of the 150 beads present.

The use of disc beads (both of jet/jet-like materials and of amber) continued through the second quarter of the second millennium, as demonstrated by examples of tiny disc beads of Kimmeridge shale in the composite necklace from Solstice Park, Amesbury, Wiltshire (Sheridan forthcoming b) and in the composite necklace from Winterbourne Stoke G47, Wiltshire (ID 470, Figure 7.1.8). The former is associated with a radiocarbon date (from cremated bone) of 1610–1430 cal BC (see Chapter 9), and the latter can be dated to this period on the basis of its associated Series 5 dagger (see Chapter 3.1). Examples of the use of amber disc beads during this period include the necklace found at Boscombe Down, Wiltshire (Barclay 2010), which is associated with a radiocarbon date of 1600–1430 cal BC (see Chapter 9).

Overall, therefore, it appears that the use of tiny disc beads of jet and jet-like materials had a very long currency, with the radiocarbon dates suggesting that it may have lasted up to a millennium; Bayesian modelling may be able to refine the chronological picture. A much later, and obviously unrelated, use of tiny jet disc beads is known from Roman contexts, both in Britain (e.g. at Catterick and York, Yorkshire: Wilson 2002, Allason-Jones 1996) and abroad (e.g. Cologne: Allason-Jones 1996, fig. 12).

Spacer plate necklaces

While the use of disc bead ornaments is attested from the third quarter of the third millennium, the earliest spacer plate necklaces of jet or jet-like material do not seem to have appeared before 2200 BC, to judge from the available radiocarbon dating evidence. (See also Chapter 9). The reason for this is that these necklaces have a different origin from the disc bead necklaces discussed above, and to some extent this is reflected in the different (but overlapping) distribution patterns of the two necklace types, with almost all of the jet/jet-like spacer plate necklaces being found north of the Wash (see Figure 12.4). Despite recent claims to the contrary (Frieman 2012), spacer plate necklaces emerged as a faithful copy, or skeuomorph, of the gold lunulae that were popular in late third millennium Ireland (Taylor 1970b; 1980; Eogan 1994; Cahill 2005). This is clear from the designs of the earliest spacer plate necklaces, where the makers have replicated not only the overall shape of a lunula (by means of increasing the number of bead strands from the back to the front), but also, in some cases, the decoration that is present on the horns of many lunulae (as seen, for example, on the spacer plate necklace found at Mount Stuart, Bute: Sheridan 2013, fig. 4.9, left). The dating of lunulae leaves much to be desired, since there is only one directly dated example, found with its alder carrying case at Crossdoney, County Cavan; the case produced a radiocarbon date of 3800±50 BP (GrA-13982, 2460–2050 cal BC at 95.4%; Cahill 2006). However, recent improvements in the dating of the Beaker pottery that shares the same design motifs as lunulae (Taylor 1970; 1980) have produced a (Bayesian-modelled) 'window of probability' for the period of motif-sharing of *c.* 2360 to *c.* 2070 cal BC (Curtis and Wilkin 2012, 240). This chronological picture allows for a period – not necessarily very long – when lunulae were in use, before being copied in jet. The

most probable scenario for the invention of jet/jet-like spacer plate necklaces is that the Early Bronze Age elite in Scotland, having seen (and in a few cases, possessed) gold lunulae, commissioned copies in jet from Whitby-based specialist jetworkers. (There is plentiful independent evidence for the existence of links between Scotland and Yorkshire around this time, and indeed in earlier times as well: Sheridan 2012b). The Scottish elite might also have had a few lunulae made in Scotland; but here is not the place to discuss this complex topic (Sheridan 2014), or the reasons for choosing jet as an alternative, precious, special raw material.

While the dating of jet/jet-like spacer plate necklaces also needs to be underpinned by many more radiocarbon dates than presently exist there is, however, enough evidence to indicate (a) that most are likely to have been made between *c.* 2200 and *c.* 2000/1900 BC, with only a very few being made later, probably between *c.* 2000/1900 and 1800 BC; and (b) that individual components of some spacer plate necklaces were in use over a long time, possibly up to half a millennium. This, together with the fact that the people who made these necklaces did not slavishly and conservatively adhere to a single design template over the currency of this necklace type, accounts for the variability that can be seen in the examples that survive.

The 'classic', earliest form of the spacer plate necklace of jet/jet-like materials, which is most commonly found in Scotland (Sheridan and Davis 2002), consists of a fastener (often of flat, triangular form); two terminal plates; two pairs of spacer plates; and up to 139, but usually closer to 100, fusiform beads whose shape and size varied according to their position on the necklace, for example at East Kinwhirrie, Angus (Figure 7.3.1). The maximum number of strands, at the front of the necklace, is ten (at Inchmarnock: Sheridan 2013, fig. 4.9, right); seven or eight is the commonest number. Between the pairs of spacer plates, the number of strands is most often four or five; and between the 'upper' spacer plates and terminal plates there are most often four strands. The plates could be undecorated or decorated. Tightly strung (as can be inferred from the pattern of bead and plate wear), these necklaces would have sat high and fairly rigid on the neck, just as lunulae would have done.

Of the spacer plate necklaces studied in the current project, those from Cow Low (ID 267, Figure 7.2.5), Windle Nook (ID 273, Figure 7.2.14) and Hill Head (ID 268, Figure 7.2.7), all in Derbyshire, come closest to this classic form, even though the terminal and spacer plates of the Windle Nook necklace are of bone, not jet, and Hill Head includes several buttons used as beads – a characteristic of many spacer plate necklaces in Yorkshire and the Peak District. (Furthermore, as argued in the detailed description in Chapter 7.2 above the current form of Hill Head results from several changes over the course of its use life). It is important to note that the current configuration of the components in these, and in several other of the spacer plate necklaces studied in the project, is most unlikely to correspond to their original configuration;

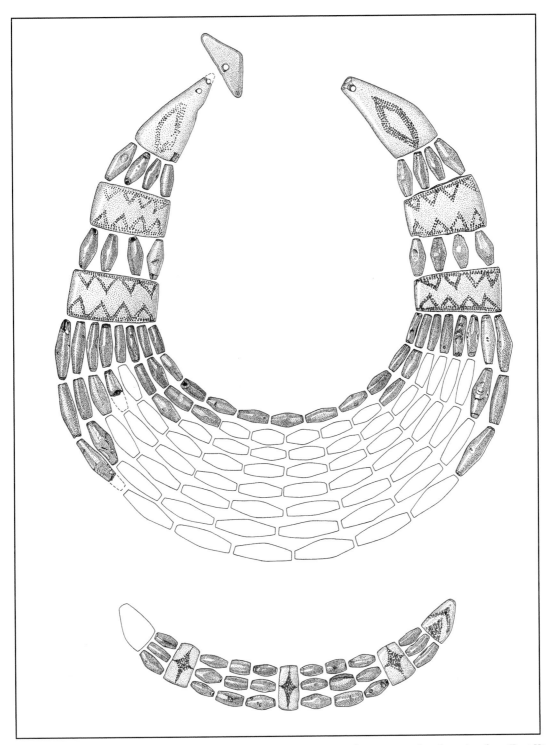

Figure 7.3.1. Example of a 'classic' lunula-like spacer plate necklace, plus matching spacer plate bracelet, from East Kinwhirrie, Angus. All items are of jet. The strung width of the necklace as illustrated is 230mm. Note that this reconstruction has probably slightly over estimated the number of beads per strand at the front of the necklace, making it look even less crescentic than it would have been. Drawing by Helen Jackson.

we are mostly dealing with the reconstructions made by the Victorian antiquaries Mortimer and Bateman. When originally made, the Cow Low necklace would have had a 4-4-8 arrangement of strands, with most of the beads lying between the pair of largest spacer plates; the arrangement

for Windle Nook would have been 3-4-8, and that for Hill Head 3-4-8.

Among the spacer plate necklaces that most closely resemble lunulae, then, there is variability in the number of strands and beads, and in whether plates are decorated or

Table 7.3.1. List of components of jet/jet-like spacer plate necklaces discussed in Chapter 7.2.

ID no.	Terminal plates	Spacer plates	Buttons	Fusiform beads	Disc beads	Fast-eners[3]	Other	Total[5]	Est. max. no. of strands[6]
247	2	-	10	35	573	2	1	623	6
249	2	5	-	-	-	-	-	7	4
264/ 265	-	3	12	15	-	-	-	30	2
266	2	2	-	42	-	-	-	46	2
267	2	4	-	64	-	1	-	71	8
268	1	4	12	53	11	-	-	81	8
269	3	2(1)	11	53	348	1	1	419 (1)	7
270	-	7(1)	36[2]	26	-	-	-	69 (1)	9 (in bone plate; otherwise 3)
273	(2)[1]	(4)	2	76	-	-	-	78(6)	8
379-390	-	1	5	1	298+ 27 frags	?3[4]	-	308+ beads in frags	5
281	2	-	-	4	25	-	-	31	4
282	1	-	-	-	-	-	-	1	4
391	-	2	-	1	19	1	6	29	4

Notes:

1. Figures in parenthesis denote number of bone components and are in addition to the total for the non-bone components.
2. See text regarding the number of buttons originally present.
3. The items labelled 'fasteners' include boat-shaped, V-perforated objects that are assumed to have been used as fasteners.
4. See text for details.
5. These totals include objects recorded at the time and since lost, hence there are minor discrepancies between this table and Table 7.2.2 which denotes levels of wear on surviving items.
6. The figure for the maximum number of strands relates to the largest number of holes present in any of the terminal or spacer plates. It does not mean that the necklace necessarily had that many strands, since some plates that had been incorporated from different necklaces have far more perforations than the other plates in the necklace.

not; there is also variability in the technique of decoration and in the motifs used, and a regionally specific use of buttons as beads in northern England. Other spacer plate necklaces deviate from the lunula-like design more markedly, and in various ways. In some cases, this deviation occurred from their moment of manufacture (and could be termed 'style drift'); in some cases, it is due to the life history of the necklaces in question, whereby the elements present at the time of their deposition may bear little relationship to the necklaces' original composition. As regards style drift, this is manifested in the following ways (both among the necklaces examined in the project, and more widely):

1 Having fewer or more plates than the standard total of six.
2 No increase, or only a modest increase, in the number of strands from the back to the front – involving spacer plates that are squarish, rectangular or squat-trapezoidal (i.e. with different proportions from the trapezoidal plates in the lunula-like necklaces).
3 Fewer fusiform beads than in the lunula-like examples.
4 Inclusion of disc beads and/or buttons.

The necklace from Calais Wold 13, East Yorkshire (ID 247, Figure 7.2.1 and Figure 7.2.2) combines all of these characteristics. It comprises just two plates (both terminal plates), has six strands between these plates, has only 35 fusiform beads (plus one tubular bead), and incorporates large numbers of tiny disc beads and several buttons (and not one, but two boat-shaped V-perforated buttons, at least one of which is likely to have been a fastener). The necklace from Middleton-on-the-Wolds, Derbyshire (ID 249, Figure 7.2.3) had seven plates when found (with Mortimer arguing that an eighth – the Sp 1 R plate, shown as a museum reconstruction in Figure 7.2.3 – must have been overlooked by the diggers), and four strands for most of its length, decreasing to three between the terminal plates and adjacent plates. While the 26 fusiform beads present today are 20th-century reconstructions, the originals having been left behind by Mortimer's workmen, it may be that there never were any more beads than this. The necklace from Grindlow, Derbyshire (ID 270, Figures 7.2.12 and 7.2.13) has evidently undergone changes since its manufacture, but in its original state it will have differed from the lunula-like necklaces in having only three strands, probably more than six decorated plates (if terminal plates had originally been present), many fewer fusiform beads (even allowing for some possible losses over its use life), and buttons used as beads (although at least some had probably been added subsequently). The smaller of the two necklaces from Cow Low (ID 266, Figure 7.2.4) has only four plates (including two terminal plates), only two strands and only

42 fusiform beads; and the fragmentary necklace found 'in the neighbourhood of Pickering', North Yorkshire (ID 264/265, Figure 7.2.16) had also just two strands. That from Pockley, North Yorkshire (ID 379–90, Figure 7.2.18) apparently consists mostly of tiny disc beads, arranged in five strands; while that from Soham Fen, Cambridgeshire (ID 391, Figure 7.2.19) incorporated disc beads as well as fusiform beads in its original design. (See Table 7.3.1 for a summary of the composition of the spacer plate necklaces examined in the project).

This variability in necklace design is echoed elsewhere. For example, a necklace from Blindmill (also known as Blinmill and Blindmills), Aberdeenshire, resembles the Grindlow necklace in having eight plates (including a pair of terminal plates), just three strands, and only 20 fusiform beads (plus, intriguingly, two amber beads: Stuart 1866). Another from Pen y Bonc, Anglesey, has long, concave-sided terminal plates and narrow spacer plates, with the perforations in a 5-9-9 arrangement (Sheridan and Davis 1998; Burrow 2011, 138–9). Elsewhere in Wales, a necklace found in a cairn at Llong, near Mold, consisted mostly of numerous small disc beads, one narrow spacer plate with five boreholes (implying a five-strand necklace) and four fusiform beads (Sheridan and Davis 1998; Burrow 2011, 140–1; now restrung as a five-strand necklace).

It is not intended to discuss in detail the various biographies of necklaces that resulted in the diverse assemblages of components that have survived today (e.g. at Middleton Moor, Derbyshire (ID 269, Figures 7.2.9 to 7.2.11), since this has already been covered in Chapter 7.2 and is touched upon again below; suffice it to note once more that the current arrangement of these components owes more to antiquarian opinion and museum practice than to prehistoric reality. Examples in addition to those studied in the project include the finds from Radwell 1, Bedfordshire (Hall and Woodward 1977; Woodward 2002) and from Melfort, Argyll and Bute; in the latter case, components from four or five different necklaces had been buried together in a cist (Sheridan and Davis 2002, 823). Sometimes, the 'end of the road' for a spacer plate necklace consisted of the deposition of a single plate, as may be the case with a single terminal plate, old and worn, of cannel coal or shale, found in 2010 at Boughton Monchelsea, Kent (http://finds.org.uk/database/artefacts/record/id/403072; accessed July 2013). An intriguing case where it has been possible to identify the fate of an individual necklace or two concerns the finds from Burwell Fen (ID 282, Figure 7.2.17), Soham Fen (ID 391, Figure 7.2.19) and Snailwell (ID 281, Figure 7.2.17), all in Cambridgeshire; this will be discussed below.

As regards the chronology of manufacture and use of spacer plate necklaces (and parts thereof), the *floruit* appears to lie between the 22nd and 20th/19th centuries BC. There is, however, some evidence from East Anglia to suggest that one or two necklaces in this region were probably made within the first quarter of the second millennium. These are represented by the aforementioned finds from Cambridgeshire, and as noted below, what

sets them apart from all other spacer plate necklaces is their distinctive 'rocker' decoration – a distinctive motif and technique shared with the jet lozenge from Carlton Colville, Suffolk (Pitts 2007). If, as seems likely, the latter is a skeuomorph of the Wessex 1 gold lozenges found at Bush Barrow, Wiltshire and Clandon, Dorset, and if the necklaces and lozenge were made by the same hand, then on current reckoning about the date when Wessex 1 material was made (Needham *et al.* 2010), these will have been made between 2000 and 1750 BC, and possibly towards the beginning of that time range. It should be noted here that there is evidence suggesting the continued manufacture of fusiform beads – as opposed to spacer plate necklaces – into the second quarter of the second millennium, as has been argued, for example, in the case of the aforementioned composite necklace from Solstice Park, Amesbury, Wiltshire.

As for how long spacer plate necklaces or their components continued to be used, late examples include the aforementioned collection of mostly old and worn necklace parts from Middleton Moor, Derbyshire (ID 269, Figures 7.2.9 to 7.2.11) which includes terminal plates from three different necklaces and which, overall, comprises parts of at least six necklaces. The unburnt bones of the associated adult female have recently been radiocarbon-dated (for the Beaker People Project) to 2010–1770 cal BC (see Chapter 9). Another second-millennium example is the varied assortment of necklace components from Radwell ring ditch 1, Bedfordshire, which were found in a Collared Urn, accompanying the cremated remains of an adult woman and man. The bone pommel that accompanied the remains is of Class 3 that dates to Needham's Periods 3 and 4, i.e. *c*. 2050–1500 BC (see Chapter 3.2); a similarly-shaped pommel had been found in the Manton grave discussed above (Needham 2011b, 386–88 and table SS3.1; http://www.english-heritage.org.uk/content/publications/publicationsNew/archaeology/neolithic-and-bronze-age-landscape-vol2/raundsareaproj2-ss3.pdf; accessed July 2013). Further east, in East Anglia, unburnt bone from the contracted skeleton of an adult woman buried at Barrow Bottom, Risby, Suffolk, along with a necklace comprising two terminal plates, one 4–5-bored spacer plate, 43 fusiform beads, 105 disc beads and a tubular sheet copper/alloy bead (Martin 1976), has been radiocarbon-dated to 1900–1740 cal BC (see Chapter 9 and Gerloff 2004, 84). Other finds from this grave include a small, empty, inverted Collared Urn. (Note that the excavator's suggestion that some of the beads may have belonged to a bracelet is weakened by the fact that there had been considerable (and probably post-depositional) scattering of the necklace beads). The Barrow Bottom necklace could have been contemporary with the aforementioned Cambridgeshire finds, and it is quite likely that another spacer plate necklace found *c*. 3 km away at Risby (on Poor's Heath; Vatcher and Vatcher 1976) had also been deposited during the first quarter of the second millennium. Comprising one spacer plate, four fusiform beads and a disc bead, this was found among and near the disturbed remains of a young adult of indeterminate sex, aged 18 to 20, buried in a contracted position and post-dating the probable tree-trunk coffin grave of an adult male. Examination of both of the Risby finds would be useful to determine whether parts of the same necklace may be represented.

A final clue as to the longevity of use of components deriving from jet/jet-like spacer plate necklaces comes from the old and worn fusiform beads that have been found in composite necklaces, as discussed in Chapter 8.6. It is unfortunate that none of the examples studied in this project (namely ID 509 Wilsford G3; ID 513–4 Amesbury G39; ID 494–6 Upton Lovell G2a, Wiltshire; ID 402–3 and ID 411 Oxsettle Bottom, Sussex, and ID 275 Hay Top Hill, Derbyshire) has been radiocarbon dated. However, the battle-axes found in the Upton Lovell G2a ('shaman's') grave are of types known to date to between *c.* 1800 BC and *c.* 1550 BC: Sheridan 2007e, fig. 14.10), and it is known that the use of the quoit-shaped faience ornaments as seen in the Oxsettle necklace extended into the second quarter of the second millennium (e.g. at Longniddry, East Lothian: Sheridan and Shortland 2004, illus. 21.1).

CONTEXTS AND ASSOCIATIONS

Some idea of the contexts and associations of disc bead and spacer plate necklaces – both with regard to the 25 examples studied in the project, and more generally – has already been provided above (see also Table 7.3.2 and Table 7.3.3). It is unfortunate that most of the necklaces studied in the project come from 19th-century antiquarian investigations, with all their attendant uncertainties – e.g. over the sex of the deceased which, in some cases, may well have been assumed to be female from the presence of ornaments, rather than on the basis of osteological examination.

The necklaces studied in the project, like virtually all of their counterparts elsewhere, are definitely or probably from funerary contexts. This could indeed be the case with the stray find from Burwell Fen (ID 282), where an entire spacer plate necklace is rumoured to have been found in peat at some time before 1854; that fact that another spacer plate necklace found in peat at Soham Fen (ID 391), just 9 km away, had been associated with the skeleton of an adult woman raises the possibility that the Burwell Fen find had also accompanied human remains. Even where a necklace has definitely not been deposited with human remains, as is the case with the aforementioned spacer plate necklace from Llong, Clwyd, there is a connection with funerary activity: here the necklace was found in the body of an Early Bronze Age cairn, under which was the contracted skeleton of an adult woman; there can be arguably little doubt that the necklace and the woman had been associated in life (Burrow 2011, 140–1).

The commonest funerary rite associated with both necklace types is inhumation of the body, in a contracted (crouched) position, although in a few instances – as with the disc bead necklaces from Winterbourne Stoke G47 (ID 470) and Wilsford G39 (ID 517), both in Wiltshire –

the body had been cremated. The earliest dated example of the practice of cremation associated with the use of either necklace type is that from Easter Essendy, Perth and Kinross, where a jet spacer plate necklace was found in a cist alongside one of two sets of cremated remains of adults, of indeterminate sex (Thoms 1980). The individuals have been radiocarbon-dated to 3710±35 BP (GrA-32131, 2210–1980 cal BC at 95.4%) and 3630±35 BP (GrA-32133, 2140–1890 cal BC at 95.4%) respectively, the former date obtained from the bones associated with the necklace (Sheridan 2006). The earliest example of cremated remains being associated with a disc bead necklace comes from the filling of an Early Neolithic passage tomb at Achnacreebeag, Argyll and Bute, where cremated bone that is likely to have been associated with one or more Beakers has been dated to 2190–1920 cal BC (see Chapter 9). However, the Wiltshire examples are later than this, with Winterbourne Stoke G47 attributable to the second quarter of the second millennium, as noted above.

The form of the grave varies. In some cases, for example at Calais Wold 13, East Yorkshire (ID 247), it appears that the deceased had been laid on the old ground surface, while in many others, for example at Garton Slack Area VI, grave 1, East Yorkshire (ID 251) a grave pit had been dug, sometimes through solid rock as at Garrowby Wold 64, East Yorkshire (ID 246). At Garton Slack 75, East Yorkshire (ID 245 and ID 250), the individual had been buried in the fill of a shaft grave. A wood lining in the grave was noted at Goodmanham 121, East Yorkshire (ID 322) and some kind of wooden structure was also noted around the head in the Manton barrow, Wiltshire (ID 491) although its nature is unclear. The use of stone, either as a simple grave pit lining, as at Middleton Moor, Derbyshire (ID 269), or as a cist, as at Cow Low, Derbyshire (ID 266–7), is a characteristic feature of some Peak District graves; and virtually all Scottish graves associated with either type of necklace are cists. Interment within the watery context of the Cambridgeshire Fens has already been noted; the absence of contextual detail is particularly regrettable here (*cf* Roberts 1998). As for cremated remains associated with disc bead necklaces, at Winterbourne Stoke G47 (ID 470), these seem to have been contained, along with the grave goods, in a skin bag inside the grave pit.

In many, but by no means all cases, the graves had been covered by a barrow or cairn, with the barrow being round but varying in its shape and size: Winterbourne G47, for example, had been a large disc barrow (Gingell 1988, 58), whereas most of the Yorkshire barrows had been plain round mounds, some incorporating stone in their make-up. In most cases the interments with necklaces had been the primary, and often the sole, interment associated with the mound; exceptions include the Cow Low cist, which was secondary. The presence of more than one individual in the grave has been noted with seven, possibly nine of the studied necklaces, and further examples from elsewhere are known (e.g. Easter Essendy, as mentioned above). At Middleton Moor, Derbyshire (ID 269) and possibly also at Cow Low, Derbyshire (ID 266–7), an adult female was

*Table 7.3.2. Contexts and associations of the disc-head necklaces described in Chapter 7. * The use of italics indicates that the grounds for identifying the sex are unknown. Key: I = inhumation of unburnt remains; C = deposit of cremated remains. Age: Ad = adult, Adol = adolescent. Attitude: Cont. = Contracted (crouched); Dist = disturbed.*

ID no.	Findspot	Context	Associated human remains				Associated artefacts			Comments
			I/C	Sex*	Age	Attitude	Pottery	Metal	Other	
246	Garrowby Wold (Painsthorpe) barrow 64, E. Yorks.	Oval rock-cut grave under centre of round barrow	I	*F*	Ad	Cont. on R, E–W, head to E	-	Bronze awl	-	Necklace found just above the neck. Age estimate based on length of tibia (12.5"/ 32 cm long). 'Portion of the leg of an animal' beside body. Cremated remains in hole under skeleton. No other interments.
245 + 250	Garton Slack barrow 75, E. Yorks.	Half way down oval shaft grave under centre of round barrow	I	F	Ad	Cont. on L, E–W, head to W	Vase Food Vessel	Bronze awl in wooden handle	-	Necklace found in neck area; pot in front of head. Heap of cremated remains at foot. Secondary to interment of contracted adult male. Mortimer does not state whether shaft was rock-cut but this seems likely.
251	Garton Slack Area VI, grave 1, burial 1, E. Yorks.	Oval grave under mound (presumably round)	I	Prob F	Ad, 20–25	Cont. on R, head to S	-	-	13 V-perforated buttons of jet and cannel coal/oil shale	Head rested on 'pillow of white gravel'. Osteologist concluded that 'skeleton was probably that of a woman, though the skull was heavy and had certain apparently male features'. C14 date for skeleton: 3781±31 BP (OxA-V-2279-34, 2300–2050 cal BC at 95.4%). Necklace found on top of buttons in chest area; Brewster argued that buttons represented a folded garment, and the necklace had been broken and laid on top of the garment. Haematite nodule present in museum among material supposedly from this grave, but is not mentioned by Brewster and may not have come from this grave. No other interments associated with this mound.

ID no.	Findspot	Context	Associated human remains				Associated artefacts			Comments
			I/C	Sex*	Age	Attitude	Pottery	Metal	Other	
252	Garton Slack Area 29, burial D, E. Yorks.	Large, multiple grave	I	F	Ad, c. 35	Cont. on R, roughly N–S (NNE–SSW), head roughly to S (SSW)	-	Bronze awl	-	Necklace probably worn: found close to L shoulder and near back of head. Four other contracted inhumations in same large pit; this was the only one with any grave goods. Brewster interpreted the awl as having been used to secure the thread loop at one end of the necklace, but this was not necessarily the case. C14 date for skeleton: 3668±32 BP (OxA-V-2279-33, 2140–1950 cal BC at 95.4%).
308	Weaverthorpe barrow 44, burial 2, E. Yorks.	Shallow grave under centre of round barrow	I	F	Ad	Cont. on R, head to E	Food Vessel (not preserved)	-	-	Individual described as 'wearing' the necklace. Three other interments under barrow.
322	Goodmanham barrow 121, burial 6, E. Yorks.	Central, wood-lined grave, under oval barrow	I	Indet	Adol	Cont. on R, roughly E–W (SSE–NNW), head roughly to N (WNW)	-	-	Lumps of 'yellowish substance', probably ochre, near body	Unclear whether wood lining had been part of a grave chamber. Necklace found 'in place' (i.e. presumably in neck area).
366	Folkton barrow ?245, burial 8, E. Yorks.	Grave under round barrow, SW of centre	I	Indet	Adol; also infant	Cont. on R, E–W, head to W	2 All-Over-Cord beakers	-	Broken bone belt-ring (ID 750); flint scraper fragment and 2 flint flakes	Necklace found in neck area. Presence of belt ring in lower grave fill suggests adolescent likely to have been male. If the barrow excavated by Brewster was indeed barrow 245, this is the one associated with the 'Folkton drums' grave and six other interments.
470	Winterbourne Stoke G47, Wilts.	Grave under large disc barrow; 'central' (actually slightly eccentric)	C	Indet	Ad, at least 25	-	-	Series 5B2 'dagger'; bronze awl; 2 microscopic fragments of silver and gold	Traces of twined coarse grass or rushes, possibly matting	Barrow form suggests that the individual may have been female, and this is not contradicted by the presence of the unusual 'dagger'; the sex of the cremated remains could not be identified. Objects must have been kept apart from the body during its cremation.

ID no.	Findspot	Context	Associated human remains				Associated artefacts			Comments
			I/C	Sex*	Age	Attitude	Pottery	Metal	Other	
491	Preshute G1a, Manton, Wilts.	Primary grave under bowl barrow	I	F	Ad, 'of considerable age'	Cont, on L, SE–NW, head to SE and bent forward to chest	2 accessory vessels including one grape cup	Knife-dagger with amber pommel and wooden hilt; knife-dagger blade; 3 bronze awls; gold-bound amber disc; miniature halberd with gold shaft and bronze blade; gold-bound shale biconical bead	Fluted ?lignite bead; stone ring-bead; chalk or chalk-like bead; fired clay stud, probably a labret. Impressions of 2 textiles: coarsely-woven, probably linen, shroud-like, and finely-woven. Traces of wood in head area. 'Clayey soil full of [fragments of] bones' in front of skeleton	Composite necklace deposited in a little heap behind head. Identifications of the ?lignite and shale beads by Pollard *et al.* (1981; see also Bussell *et al.* 1982).
517	Wilsford G39, Wilts.	Grave under bowl barrow	C	No info	No info	-	-	-	Bone pin (lost)	Possibly primary grave.
334	Eglingham 200, burial 3, Northumberland	Cist under round cairn, non-central	I	-	-	Cont. may have been on L, head to N; cist orientated SE–NW	-	-	Flint knife	Skeleton decayed. Necklace in N corner of cist, suggesting that it had been worn (and implying the body position). Three other interments under cairn.
434	Beggar's Haven (Devil's Dyke). East Sussex	No information	?	No info	No info	See comment	No info	No info	No info	Found 1887, circumstances unknown; necklace 'around the neck of the skeleton' (British Museum Register 1890); 'contracted (?) female skeleton' claimed on unknown evidence (Grinsell 1930, 39, quoted in Kinnes 1985).

Table 7.3.3. *Contexts and associations of the spacer plate necklaces described in Chapter 7. * The use of italics indicates that the grounds for identifying the sex are unknown. Key: I =
inhumation of unburnt remains; C = deposit of cremated remains. Age: Ad = adult, Ch = child. Attitude: Cont. = Contracted (crouched); Dist = disturbed.*

| ID no. | Findspot | Context | Associated human remains | | | | Associated artefacts | | | Comments |
			I/C	Sex*	Age	Attitude	Pottery	Metal	Other	
247	Calais Wold 13, E. Yorks.	On ground surface under centre of round barrow	[I]	-	-	-	-	-	-	'The beads occurred on a film of dark matter, and – though there was no trace of bone – their position seemed to favour the idea that they had been placed round the neck of a body, the primary interment, which had entirely decayed.' (Mortimer 1905, 166). Barrow also contained secondary interments (cremated remains, urned and un-urned).
249	Middleton-on-the-Wolds, E. Yorks.	Found c. 900 mm below ground surface while digging for sand in a garden	I	-	-	Cont.	-	-	-	-
266	Cow Low, Derbyshire	In cist in secondary position in round barrow	I	*F*	Ad	Cont.	-	-	1. 'A fine instrument of calcined flint, of the circular-ended form' (Howarth 1899, 57); 2. Second necklace (see below)	Cist may originally have held the skeleton of a child and the smaller spacer plate necklace ID 267; seems to have been disturbed when another cist was constructed above, and partly overlying, this cist.
267	Cow Low, Derbyshire	Most of necklace found in cist where ID 266 found; a few beads found outside	I	-	Ch	[Dist]	-	-	See above, ID 266	Association with child is assumed but seems likely, given probable disturbance of cist. The beads found outside the cist were found with part of the child's skeleton.
268	Hill Head, Hasling House, Derbyshire	Necklace components scattered under a previously-opened round barrow	[I]	-	See com-ment	[Dist]	-	-	-	Will have been associated with one of three or four skeletons disturbed during a previous opening of the barrow.

ID no.	Findspot	Context	Associated human remains				Associated artefacts			Comments
			I/C	Sex*	Age	Attitude	Pottery	Metal	Other	
269	Middleton Moor, Derbyshire	'Rude cist or enclosure' (slab- and boulder-lined hollow) under round barrow	I	F	Ad, c. 40	Cont. on L	-	-	-	Accompanied by remains of child of *c.* 4 years, found slightly above and behind head of woman. Necklace reported to have been found 'around' the woman's neck. Woman C14-dated to 3550±30 BP (GU-19920, 2010–1770 cal BC at 95.4%).
270	Grindlow, Derbyshire	Grave, possibly rock-cut, under round barrow	I	See comment	Presumably Ad	Cont.	-	-	'One or two rude instruments of flint' (Bateman 1861, 47)	Associated with one of three contracted skeletons in the grave, two of whom were female. Absence of reference to the age of the skeletons suggests that they are likely to have been adult (as Bateman normally noted where children were present). There had also been a secondary interment in the barrow.
273	Windle Nook, Derbyshire	In large cist under round barrow	I	F	Ad	Cont.	-	-	-	A secondary interment, found a few inches above the cist floor. Deposition of this individual had disturbed the remains of 2 adults, 2 children, cremated bones, animal bones, sherds and flints in the cist.
264/ 265	NW of Pickering, North Yorkshire	From a disturbed barrow	-	-	-	-	-	-	-	Likely to have been from a grave; original excavator died without publishing find, so details unclear. See Catalogue entry for more information.
281	Snailwell C, Cambridgeshire	Grave(?) on old ground surface under round barrow, not central; this and other graves surrounded by pre-barrow post ring	I	-	Ch	Cont. on R, roughly N–S (NNW–SSE), head roughly S (SSE)	-	-	-	Lethbridge's account (1949) is ambiguous regarding the form of the interment: he states that it had probably been 'on the old turf line', but his plan (fig. 4) clearly indicates a cut grave. The interment had been badly disturbed by rabbits or treasure-hunters. Two other graves with contracted skeletons (one adult, one child) and two deposits of cremated remains found under barrow. Components of the old and fragmentary necklace found scattered.
282	Burwell Fen, Cambridgeshire	Found in peat	-	-	-	-	-	-	-	Found before 1854; no further details, other than suggestion that a complete necklace had been found.
379– 390	Pockley, North Yorks.	From severely plough-damaged barrow	-	-	-	-	-	-	-	Most of the components found scattered over an area under 1m in diameter on old land surface below barrow in its SW quadrant, to the N of burial 2. No skeletal remains found in/under the barrow.
391	Soham Fen, Cambridgeshire	Found in peat	I	F	Ad	-	-	-	-	Associated with cremated remains. Found before 1850.

accompanied by a child, suggesting a probably familial relationship. At Cow Low the adult female was found in the cist and the disturbed, partial remains of a child's skeleton were found outside the cist along with some beads from one of the necklaces. Bateman suggested that the smaller of the two necklaces might originally have been associated with the child, with the cist being disturbed by the subsequent insertion of a further cist nearby. In three examples, at Garrowby Wold 64, East Yorkshire (ID 246), Garton Slack 75 East Yorkshire (ID 245 and ID 250) and Soham Fen, Cambridgeshire (ID 391), the unburnt skeletons of putatively female adults were accompanied by deposits of cremated remains. At Folkton, East Yorkshire (ID 366 and ID 750), an adolescent was buried with an infant. At Grindlow, Derbyshire (ID 256–7 and ID 270), two women and one other person had been buried inside a probably rock-cut grave, with the spacer plate necklace being associated with one of the women; and at Garton Slack 29, East Yorkshire (ID 252), the adult woman buried wearing a necklace was one of five contracted individuals found in a large and irregularly-shaped grave pit.

While the sex of the individuals associated with disc bead and spacer plate necklaces has often been inferred, rather than demonstrated, in cases where the remains have been reliably sexed, they have been found to be female in virtually every case. Among the 25 necklaces studied, only five are associated with reliably-sexed individuals (ID 269 Middleton Moor; ID 251, ID 252, ID 245 with ID 250 Garton Slack VI, 29 and 75; ID 491 Manton) and all are female, although the woman from Garton Slack VI was described as having a 'heavy' skull and some male features. The only positively identified male to be associated with a jet/jet-like necklace is the 20 to 30 year old individual from Chilbolton, Hampshire (Russel 1990), whose Kimmeridge shale and gold disc bead necklace is the earliest example of this type to be found in Britain. This echoes Continental practice where, to judge from the stelae at Petit-Chasseur, Sion and as noted above, both male and female figures are shown wearing disc bead necklaces. Given the presence of a Continental-style tanged bone belt ring (ID 750; Figure 3.4.1) – a male accoutrement – in the grave at Folkton ?245 (ID 366), it may be that the adolescent buried here with a disc bead necklace and two All-Over-Cord Beakers had also been male. A later example of where a disc bead necklace has been associated with a male – albeit with beads made of amber, rather than of jet or jet-like material – is the aforementioned individual from Boscombe Down, Wiltshire, radiocarbon-dated to *c.* 1500 BC (Barclay 2010). It should be noted, however, that this individual was only 14 to 15 years old, and it can sometimes be hard to reach a definitive sex identification with skeletons of that age.

Regarding the age of the individuals associated with either necklace type, most are adults, and at Manton (ID 491) the woman had reached a considerable age. Where ages of the adults have been estimated, most fall within the 20 to 40 range. A few adolescents are, however, represented, including the aforementioned individual from Folkton (ID 366); and the cist at Cow Low provides a rare example of

where a necklace may have been associated with a child. Here, a 'normal'-sized, lunula-shaped spacer plate necklace was associated with an adult, putatively female, while the second necklace, with smaller plates and fewer beads, may have been associated with the child whose disturbed remains were found outside the cist. One other example of a child-sized necklace is known from Barns Farm, Dalgety, Fife, where a pair of similarly diminutive spacer plates was found in a small cist along with the remains of a juvenile aged around 11 or 12 (plus some adult remains: Watkins 1982, 67–8; 91; 104; fig. 18). Finally, parts of an adult-sized necklace were associated with the body of a child at Snailwell, Cambridgeshire (ID 281); the particular life history of this necklace is discussed below.

As regards the position of the necklace when buried, numerous accounts refer to components being found around the neck, or in the neck area, implying that the necklaces had been worn on the deceased's body. However, there are a few examples where this was definitely not the case. The disc-and-tubular copper alloy bead necklace from Garton Slack VI (ID 251) may well have been deliberately broken and laid down on top of a folded garment on the woman's chest, while the shale and amber disc bead necklace at Manton had been placed 'in a little heap' behind the woman's head. The examples found with cremated remains had obviously been kept apart from the body as it was cremated, then reunited, probably being deposited in a bag along with the bones in the case of Winterbourne Stoke G47 (ID 470). In some instances, however, it is difficult to assess the original position of the necklace, such is the degree of post-depositional disturbance.

The presence of other grave goods is not a particularly common occurrence – with the presence of the necklace usually sufficing to mark its owner out as being special – although, as noted above regarding the Chilbolton assemblage and as is clear at Manton, in some cases necklaces come from artefact-rich graves, underlining the deceased's special status. Regarding ceramic finds, these range chronologically from early-style Beakers (e.g. at Chilbolton, Beggar's Haven and Folkton 245) to accessory vessels (at Manton), a small Collared Urn (at Barrow Bottom, Risby, Suffolk: Martin 1976) and a Cordoned Urn (if one counts the single washer disc bead found at Fence's Farm, North Ayrshire: Edwards 1928. The Trevisker Urn from Solstice Park, Amesbury, is excluded as the associated disc beads were part of a multi-material composite necklace). Food Vessels are, however, the commonest ceramic association, being represented among the 25 studied assemblages at Garton Slack 75 (ID 245 and ID 250) and Weaverthorpe 44 (ID 308) and featuring regularly among Scottish finds of both types of necklace (e.g. at Almondbank, Perth and Kinross: Close-Brooks and Shepherd 1997). Beakers other than the early types are also attested in Scotland, including a late-style 'Beaker/Food Vessel hybrid' at Stoneykirk, Dumfries and Galloway (Mann 1902).

Copper alloy awls appear to be the commonest metal find to be associated with jet and jet-like necklaces, and this accords with the impression that these necklaces were principally worn by women (see Chapter 4.6; Thomas and Ellwood 2005). Series 7 knife-daggers – a type of object found in both female and male graves – have also been found (e.g. at Manton), and the unusual 'dagger' found at Winterbourne Stoke G47 need not be taken as an indication that the deceased had been male, since it could have been a female possession. Flint objects, including plano-convex knives, are occasionally found. Some indication of the contents of the more artefact-rich graves has been offered above and in Table 7.3.2 and Table 7.3.3; notable objects include the two pairs of gold basket-shaped ornaments from Chilbolton, the button-decorated garments from Garton Slack VI and Ingleby Barwick, the array of precious ornaments (including a gold-bound amber disc and a miniature halberd) from the Manton grave, and the fragments of gold and silver from Winterbourne Stoke G47. Overall, the overwhelming impression given by the graves containing disc bead and spacer plate necklaces of jet and jet-like materials is that their occupants had been accorded a special status in society.

RAW MATERIALS

The range of raw materials used to make disc bead and spacer plate necklaces considered in this chapter encompasses jet, lignite, cannel coal, organic-rich shale (including Kimmeridge shale) and probably also material intermediate between cannel coal and shale. (Other materials such as albertite, known to have been used elsewhere, as in a button from Isbister, Orkney (Shepherd 2009, 341), were not encountered during this project). While all these materials have been formed by the alteration of a parent material, that material and the specific formation process vary. Jet originated as logs of wood of the *araucaria* family (which includes the monkey puzzle tree) which became impregnated with liquid hydrocarbons, while lignite started as a wider range of organic material (including wood, leaves and charcoal of various species) and cannel coal originated as plant debris (including spores) mixed with inorganic sediment. Shale is compacted mud or clay with a low organic content, turned to rock by pressure or heat. (The geological literature on this subject is large; see, for example, Tomkieiff 1954 and Allason-Jones and Jones 2001).

Distinguishing between these materials without undertaking destructive analysis – a key consideration when dealing with archaeological artefacts – involves a combination of macro- and microscopic examination (to examine colour, texture and composition), touch (to assess warmth and density) and compositional analysis (Davis 1993). Various non- and minimally-destructive techniques of compositional analysis exist, each with their benefits and limitations. For example, research by Siobhan Watts and Mark Pollard has shown that the minimally-destructive technique of Fourier Transform Infrared Spectroscopy (FTIR) has been found to be better at discriminating between jet and lignite than other techniques

such as neutron activation analysis (NAA), although exact matching of archaeological specimens to geological samples is hampered by post-depositional oxidation of the artefacts (http://irug.org/documents/5Watts.pdf; accessed August 3013). A useful assessment of the utility of different analytical techniques is provided by Hunter *et al.* 1993.

The current project applied macro- and microscopic examination (and touch) to all the jet and jet-like objects, and it was able to make use of the analytical results for many of the items from Yorkshire, Derbyshire and southern England that had previously been obtained by Gill Bussell and colleagues during the 1970s and early 1980s (Bussell 1976; Pollard *et al.* 1981; Bussell *et al.* 1982). Bussell had initially used NAA, but switched to X-ray fluorescence spectrometry (XRF) when she realised that this offered a more rapid, effective technique that was also more flexible as regards sample size.

The technique of XRF was also used to undertake fresh compositional analysis, specifically for the project. Through the kind offices of the British Museum's Department of Scientific Research, 66 items from that museum's collection were analysed by Mary Davis along with Duncan Hook of the British Museum, principally to check the identifications of suspected non-jet objects but also to verify some jet identifications. Further XRF analysis, on 74 jet and jet-like objects from Derbyshire and Yorkshire (along with a few other objects), was carried out using the National Museums' Scotland XRF equipment, the analyses being undertaken by Lore Troalen. In addition, two necklaces (ID 267 Cow Low, and ID 268 Hill Head) were X-rayed at NMS by Lore Troalen, and photomicroscopy of several objects was also undertaken there by AS.

The final technique employed by the project was that of reflected light oil immersion microscopy and reflectance measurement – that is, the detailed investigation of the botanical components of the material and of the degree of alteration of that plant material, as shown by its reflectance at normal incidence under oil immersion (Allason-Jones and Jones 1994; 2001). Sixteen artefacts, mostly from Yorkshire and Derbyshire but including southern English items from Bloxworth, Tan Hill and Beggar's Haven, were kindly analysed for the project by Dr John Michael (Mick) Jones, who sadly died before the project was completed. The technique is minimally destructive, but was applied to minute fragments that were already detached. It is particularly well suited to the characterisation and sourcing of cannel coals and shales (as well as to jets and lignites), and a major advantage was that Dr Jones had access to the National Coal Board collection of reference samples.

A list of all the analyses is presented in Appendix V, together with details of instrument settings and summary listings of the results. In several cases, different analytical methods were applied to the same object or necklace, with the results complementing each other and confirming or clarifying the identification. By combining the analytical results with those of macro- and microscopic and tactile examination, it was possible to make raw material identifications with a reasonable degree of confidence. A few areas of uncertainty remain, particularly with regard to differentiating between poor quality jet and lignite and to characterising materials that are intermediate between cannel coals and shales through XRF or NAA analysis. Identifying the sources of non-jet materials other than by oil-immersion reflected light microscopy and reflectance measurement (or by a more destructive technique) is also problematic, given their widespread natural distribution. Kimmeridge shale, for example, does not just outcrop in Kimmeridge Bay but can be found in a broad band to north Yorkshire, with occasional outcrops elsewhere (Allason-Jones and Jones 2001, 236) – even though the distribution of artefacts made from this material points towards the Dorset outcrop as being the most probable source area that was exploited. It was also clear, from the results of Dr Jones' analyses of relatively poor quality, high-iron jet as used for some tiny disc beads, that there is greater variability in the jet used in prehistory than had previously been assumed. (See also below and *cf* Muller 1980 on compositional variability in Whitby jet). The authors concur with Gill Bussell that further analysis of the jet and jet-like material that can be found in the Whitby area is needed.

Table 7.3.4, adapted from Davis 1993, table 1, summarises the main characteristics that were used to distinguish between the materials (and see Pollard *et al.* 1981 and Hunter *et al.* 1993 for discussion of the variable discriminatory power of different chemical elements). It should be noted that in addition to recording the composition of the raw materials, the XRF analyses also revealed compositional characteristics that reflected the objects' depositional environment (and possibly also their manufacture technique). High levels of copper could generally be accounted for by the proximity of the item to copper alloy objects, while high levels of calcium could derive from contact with human bones (although this is not the only possible source of enhanced calcium: burial in a calcareous environment, and the use of rottenstone as a polishing medium, could also raise calcium levels).

As suggested above, the pinpointing of source areas for the various materials is not always a straightforward matter. This is because the distribution and abundance of the raw materials varies widely, with jet being considerably rarer than the other materials, while cannel coals and shales are relatively widespread (and harder to source using NAA and XRF). The Jurassic deposits on the coast around Whitby in North Yorkshire, and in the Eskdale valleys slightly inland from there, constitute the largest source of jet in Britain (Bussell 1976, 87–91 and fig. 9), and even though other, more minor British sources of jet are known (including at Kimmeridge in Dorset: Watts *et al.* 1997), there is no proof that these were used. Indeed in some cases, jet from these minor sources (e.g. Eathie, Highland) is clearly unsuitable for working into artefacts. Given that there is a significant concentration of prehistoric jet artefacts in Yorkshire (plus some Early Bronze Age working debris and tools), and that the compositional range of the analysed jet artefacts provides an acceptable match with that of Whitby jet, it seems reasonable to conclude that if an object is of jet, the origin of the raw material is most likely to have been the deposits in and near the Whitby area. (It would be possible to check, non-destructively, whether any Kimmeridge jet had been used, by applying FTIR which can distinguish between Kimmeridge jet and Whitby jet: *cf* Watts *et al.* 1997).

Within the Whitby area, various grades of jet are known, with the main distinction being between 'hard' and 'soft' jet, the former having been formed in saline, anaerobic conditions, and occurring in the Jet Rock series at the base of the Jurassic strata, and the latter formed in more freshwater and aerobic conditions, and occurring in the overlying Bituminous Shales (Bussell 1976, 87; Rayner and Hemingway 1974, 174). Both hard and soft jet can be found not only where they outcrop but also on the shore, having been weathered out during storms and rolled around by the sea. Soft jet tends to be brittle and prone to cracking far more than the hard jet. In addition, hard jet can vary in its iron content, due to the fact that pyritic inclusions may be present in variable quantities; and jet can also vary in its texture, depending on where in the outcrop it had originated. In many cases, the woody structure of the parent material is clearly visible, microscopically and sometimes macroscopically; the spacer plates from 'NW of Pickering' (ID 264 and ID 265, Figure 7.2.16) offer a particularly vivid example of the latter, with the wavy texture of the compressed woodgrain standing out in relief.

A complex picture of material use has emerged from our, and others', research. Several materials were used to make the earliest necklaces, i.e. the Chalcolithic disc bead necklaces. Jet (probably hard jet) was used for the examples ID 434 Beggar's Haven, Sussex and ID 366 Folkton, East Yorkshire; Kimmeridge shale for the one from Chilbolton, Hampshire; and lignite for the Horton, Berkshire necklace. Assuming that the Kimmeridge shale had indeed come from Kimmeridge, this means that it had travelled almost 80 kilometres as the crow flies, while the jet in the Beggar's Haven necklace, assuming it is from Whitby, will have travelled around 400 kilometres.

Diversity in material use is also clear from the Early Bronze Age, but there is also some patterning. Regarding disc bead necklaces, jet continued to be used (e.g. for the example from Monkton, Kent), and a particular type of Whitby jet which is texturally inferior but well suited to the manufacture of tiny disc beads had been used to make the three necklaces from Garton Slack VI, 29 and 75, East Yorkshire (ID 251, ID 252 and ID 245 with ID 250). Various shales and cannel coals were also used, especially in Scotland, where most disc beads are of these materials; the laminar texture of shale lends itself well to the manufacture of disc beads, especially of the thin washer type. Even though shales and cannel coals can be tricky to source, the evidence indicates that materials from various sources were used: in northern Scotland, for example, the presence of a probable bead roughout at Lairg in Highland (Sheridan *et al.* 1998), and of a 'necklace' of 118 disc beads, of which only six were perforated, in a cist at Dunrobin Park, Highland (Callander 1916, 238), suggest the use of locally-available materials in this shale-rich region. For northern England, Bussell's results suggested the probable use of the bituminous shales found in the Jet Rock around Whitby to make the disc beads in the spacer plate necklaces found at Hill Head (ID 268) and Middleton Moor (ID 269), Derbyshire (Bussell 1976, 92). Similar material may have been used to make the disc beads from Garrowby Wold (ID 246), although the use of oil immersion reflected light microscopy and reflectance measurement to check the identification is recommended. In southern England, in addition to jet, the use of Kimmeridge shale (e.g. for ID 470 Winterbourne Stoke G47, Wiltshire) and probably lignite (for ID 491 Manton, Wiltshire), is attested. While the disc beads in many of these necklaces are of non-jet materials, nevertheless where fasteners exist, these are usually made of jet (as, for example, at Barbush Quarry, Stirling: Sheridan and Davis 2001).

With spacer plate necklaces, it appears that the overwhelming majority started their lives as being made from Whitby jet, with other, more locally available materials being added subsequently when individual components broke (or when embellishments were added). Only two spacer plate necklaces which were made entirely from non-jet materials (other than amber, of course) have been encountered: these are from Burgie Lodge, Moray (Sheridan and Davis 2002, 823) and Pitkennedy, Angus. Both are from areas rich in 'jet substitute' materials, namely oil shale and cannel coal respectively, and it seems that local craft workers emulated the imported Whitby jet necklaces that were relatively common in these areas. (A third non-jet necklace, from 'Yirdies', South Lanarkshire, is suspected to be an early 20th-century fake). In addition to these, the necklace from Pen y Bonc, Anglesey, with its oddly-shaped plates, is almost entirely of non-jet materials (with only one fusiform bead plus the button fastener being of jet: Sheridan and Davis 1998); the same is the case for the Llong necklace (Burrow 2011, 140–1), where macro- and microscopic examination, and compositional analysis, suggests that the only jet components are the four fusiform beads. (Despite containing a spacer plate, the Llong necklace would however better be described as a disc bead necklace).

The use of non-jet materials to make substitutes for broken components in spacer plate necklaces is widely attested. Gill Bussell's analyses indicated that the oil shale that outcrops in direct association with jet in the Jet Rock layer around Whitby had been used, being present for example in the array of diverse components that make up the necklace ID 268 Hill Head, Derbyshire (Bussell 1976, 92) and in a disc bead from Barrow Bottom, Risby, Suffolk (Bussell in Martin 1976). It appears, from Bussell's research, that among this oil shale is material that closely resembles cannel coal (and had sometimes been described as such), and this seems to have been used as well, appearing for example in one of the buttons in the necklace ID 270 Grindlow, Derbyshire. Derbyshire cannel coal seems to have been used to make at least one (and probably all) of the narrow spacer plates in the materially-

diverse necklace ID 269 Middleton Moor, Derbyshire; in the same necklace are two fusiform beads, probably in the cannel coal/shale spectrum of materials, that defied precise identification (Bussell 1976, 79). The use of locally- or regionally-available substitute materials is also attested in Scotland, for example on Bute and Inchmarnock (Sheridan 2013).

It was not only jet-like stone that was used as a substitute for jet: animal bone was used to make spacer plates in the necklaces from Middleton Moor, Derbyshire (ID 269, Figures 7.2.9 to 7.2.11), Grindlow, Derbyshire; Windle Nook, Derbyshire (ID 273, Figures 7.2.14 to 15); Feltwell Fen, Cambridgeshire (ID 1058–60, Figure 5.8.2) and Barton Mills, Suffolk (Vatcher and Vatcher 1976, 274). Animal bone was also used for the fastener of the simple disc-and-fusiform (and button) necklace from Hay Top Hill, Derbyshire (ID 275, Figure 8.2.1). It is likely that the Grindlow plate had originally belonged to a different necklace, since its 3-9 borehole pattern is at odds with the 3-3 pattern of the jet spacer plates.

MANUFACTURE AND THE NATURE OF PRODUCTION

This section will consider the *chaîne opératoire* of manufacture, the tools used, and the location and organisation of necklace production (and repair). Discussion of the first two aspects draws on the experience of Hal Redvers-Jones, one of the last two traditional Whitby jetworkers; on the experimental work by Iain Clark and Kate Verkooijen (Verkooijen and Sheridan forthcoming); and from Ian Shepherd's research on jetworking (Shepherd 1981; 1985). Since much of the detail has already been published (e.g. in Shepherd 1981 and 1985 and Sheridan and Davis 2002), only a summary will be given.

As a general principle, when making a spacer plate, fusiform bead, button or fastener of whatever material, the maker is most likely to have selected a piece of parent material that is not significantly larger than the finished object, to minimise the amount of shaping required. That said, there are some assemblages of components (as with the fusiform beads in the two Cow Low necklaces, ID 266–67, for example) where the consistency of material is such that the use of one or more sizeable blocks of hard jet to create several items can be suggested. Cutting, using a flint knife or saw, has been shown experimentally to work and the discovery of several saws in Early Bronze Age barrows in Yorkshire (e.g. at Towthorpe 242: Mortimer 1905, 43) confirms the existence of such tools. Indeed, C.S. Greaves used a Bronze Age flint saw to cut jet (Greaves 1872, quoted in Shepherd 1981). Grinding against an abrasive stone such as sandstone is the main method used to shape objects, and this leaves characteristic striations that can be uni- or multidirectional. The use of a toothed gouge to remove quartz, alum or pyrites embedded in the surface of jet is attested, for example on a fusiform bead from ID 268 Hill Head. As for the shaping of fusiform beads, this involved the grinding of sloping facets on a cylindrical or

Table 7.3.4. Criteria used in the current project to distinguish between the materials used to make the Chalcolithic and Early Bronze Age jet and jet-like objects. (See also Davis 1993 for further criteria that can be used in non-destructive analyses).

	Jet	Lignite	Cannel coal	Shale
Colour	Black and/or dark brown, occasionally slightly lighter brown. Where polished, surface can be black while the subsurface is dark brown. Low-quality jet can be black with a dark-grey tinge.	Blackish-brown but can also be black, mid to dark brown and grey.	Black	Naturally occurs in various colours including red and even green, but as encountered in the current project, black, dark grey and (in the case of Kimmeridge shale) blackish-grey with a hint of dark brown; can be slightly speckled.
Texture (as revealed through macro- and binocular microscopic inspection)	Can have a visibly woody texture, sometimes fine-grained, sometimes slightly coarser-grained; visible microscopically if not also macroscopically. Sometimes highlighted by colour differentiation (black to dark brown) following wood grain. Low-grade jet can have a 'stony' appearance.	Can have a coarse-grained woody or fibrous texture; lignite with a high degree of bitumen impregnation can resemble jet.	Stony	Stony
Feel	Warm to the touch; light.	Slightly warm to the touch; light.	Generally cold to the touch; slightly heavier than jet or lignite.	Cold or slightly warm to the touch; weight similar to cannel coal.
Degradation characteristics	Cracking can be sinuous-linear, criss-cross, oval and laminar. Advanced cases have springing along cracks, surface cupping, and loss of chips or spalls. Signs of degradation most obvious in soft jet; hard jet objects often show no, or minimal, degradation.	Can resemble jet, with more pronounced cracks along wood grain.	Laminar cracking; occasionally short curving cracks. Often shows no signs of degradation.	Laminar cracking, but some Kimmeridge shale can have criss-cross cracking as well, and springing and cupping, like jet (as seen in some Roman and Iron Age artefacts; not encountered in the present project). Often shows no signs of degradation.
Fracture characteristics	Conchoidal, shiny	Non-conchoidal, dull (except with high-bitumen lignite which can be shiny and conchoidal).	Can be conchoidal (non-shiny), or flattish (along lamination plane), or slightly angular.	Mostly non-conchoidal (and dull) but can be shallow-conchoidal and (in high-bitumen specimens) shiny; usually flattish (along lamination plane) or slightly angular.
Surface polish characteristics	Both hard and soft jet can take a brilliant sheen.	No higher than medium sheen and usually matt or low-sheen.	Satiny, not glossy, sheen; some cannel coal artefacts have a high sheen, but many have a low to medium sheen and some are matt.	Generally as cannel coal, although some Kimmeridge shale is capable of taking a high-gloss sheen (as seen in some Roman artefacts, but not in any of the artefacts studied in the present project).
Principal diagnostic compositional elements using XRF (see note 3)	Iron: in most cases, low (Pollard *et al.* 1981 quoted mostly < 800 ppm), but can be high if pyrites present, or had been nearby; high iron noted in some low-grade jet. Zirconium: relatively high; and where there is a high zirconium peak, the strontium level is very low. Vanadium: relatively high. (Pollard *et al.* 1981 cited >30–50 ppm). Zinc: where present in high amounts (>40 ppm), characteristic of some jet; where present in low amounts, can be indistinguishable from other materials. Other XRF evidence: Rayleigh/Compton peak relatively high in comparison to other peaks (reflecting high organic content).	Iron: higher than jet. (Pollard *et al.* 1981 cite figures of c. 1600–1800 ppm for geological samples, and up to 3000 ppm for artefacts considered as possible candidates for lignite). Zirconium: can be as high as jet, but ranges to very low. Vanadium: Comparable to jet. Zinc: can be present in low amounts. Other XRF evidence: relative height of Rayleigh/Compton peak in comparison to other peaks intermediate between jet and shale. Lignite tends to contain more impurities than jet.	Iron: high, but not as high as shale, with shaley cannels and canneloid shales having intermediate amounts between cannel coal and shale. Pollard *et al.* 1981 cited > 5000 ppm for cannel coal. Hunter *et al.* 1993 noted that one of their geological cannel coal specimens (plus one oil shale specimen) had low iron, but not as low as in jet. Zirconium: low or absent. Vanadium: generally low or absent. Zinc: can be present in low amounts. Other XRF evidence: relative height of Rayleigh/Compton peak in comparison to other peaks intermediate between jet and shale.	Iron: very high. Pollard *et al.* 1981 cite figures up to 12500 ppm. Zirconium: low or absent. Vanadium: low or absent. Zinc: can be present in low amounts. Other XRF evidence: Rayleigh/Compton peak relatively low in comparison to other peaks (reflecting high inorganic content), and underlying curve from 0–40 keV flatter than in other materials.

	Jet	Lignite	Cannel coal	Shale
X-ray characteristics (see note 4)	Low density; can see inclusions where present (it may be that low-grade jet is slightly denser, but none was X-rayed in this project).	Similar to jet but denser	Medium-density	High density
Reflected light microscopy and reflectance characteristics	Cell structure of the wood visible; pyrite inclusions (or voids left by dissolved pyrites) can also be seen where present. Reflectance: 0.17–0.25% (= range observed for British jet).	Cell structure of the plant material from which the lignite formed is visible. Reflectance: 0.2–0.4%.	Characterised by algae, spores and macerals (organic-origin components). Reflectance: 0.4–0.7%.	Characterised by suites of clay minerals, plant spores, microfossils and macerals, which vary between different shales. Reflectance: up to 1.5%; mostly between 0.6% and 1.5% but some shale can be as low as 0.34% (Allason-Jones and Jones 1994, 269).
Other	May contain occasional mineral inclusions (although these were normally removed by the jet-worker): quartz grains, alum crystals, pyrites.	Can contain pyrites, fine-grained clay minerals and other mineral inclusions; these are normally only visible through thin-section or scanning electron microscopy.	Can contain various inorganic inclusions including fine-grained clay minerals, although these are normally only visible through thin-section or scanning electron microscopy.	Clay minerals as a dominant component. Can contains various other inorganic inclusions, such as quartz (sand) grains, pyrite, and calcium-rich material – most of which may only be visible through thin-section or scanning electron microscopy.

Notes:

1. Within each 'family' of materials, there is textural and compositional variation. This table does not attempt to characterise all the variability that can be discerned within and between the materials in question, or to offer a comprehensive guide to the ways in which the materials can be differentiated, but instead focuses on the criteria used for the present project. For further criteria used in non-destructive and minimally-destructive analyses, see Davis 1993, Hunter *et al.* 1993 and Watts and Pollard (http://irug.org/documents/5Watts.pdf; accessed August 3013).

2. It is suspected that materials intermediate between cannel coals and shales (i.e. shaley cannels and canneloid shales) had been used in a few cases, but distinguishing between these without using reflectance microscopy or more destructive methods is difficult.

3. The diagnostic criteria as determined by Bussell using neutron activation analysis (NAA, Bussell 1976) are not included here, partly because they add little to what can be detected using XRF and partly because there were issues surrounding the use of the quantitative (parts per million) data, as explained in Pollard *et al.* 1981 (150–151). The only diagnostic elements covered by the NAA analyses, but not the XRF analyses as undertaken for this project, are potassium and phosphorus – although concentrations of the latter can be affected by post-depositional contamination from skeletal material. With potassium Bussell found that jet and lignite have low quantities, cannel coals have moderate amounts (overlapping at their lower end with the jets and lignites) and shales have high quantities, with Kimmeridge shale not containing less than 1100 ppm. (North East Yorkshire cannel coals also contain high potassium levels). With the XRF results, Bussell was able to obtain quantitative results by using standards, but with the analyses undertaken at the BM and NMS, the results are expressed qualitatively and are based on visual comparison of the peak intensities relative to the Rayleigh peak. See also Hunter *et al.* 1993 for information on the discriminatory potential of other elements, for a discussion of the interpretation of XRF results, and for the use of results normalised against either the Rayleigh or the Compton peak.

4. The density (which appears as differing degrees of opacity and intensity of white when viewed as a conventional X-ray, or black when viewed in 'negative') relates to the relative proportions of organic and inorganic material in the object. There is a need to take into account the thickness of the analysed artefacts when comparing X-ray images for different materials. The X-ray of the Hill Head necklace (ID 268, Figure 7.2.7) shows the contrast between the jet and non-jet elements well; for further examples, see Hunter *et al.* 1993.

squarish piece of material, rather like knife-sharpening a pencil, followed by the grinding smooth of the edges of these facets. Sometimes the facet edges are still visible (as with some of the beads from the Cow Low necklaces, e.g. ID 266, Figure 7.2.4g). The ends of these beads could be tapered or squared off, and either perpendicular to the long axis, or sloping.

Perforation is likely to have occurred after the initial roughing-out stage but before the fine shaping, since this is the stage with the highest risk of breakage. While a flint point could have been used to create the V-perforations in buttons (Shepherd 1981; 2009), in the opinion of Hal Redvers-Jones the narrower perforations in fusiform beads and plates are more likely to have been created using a metal-tipped drill bit, its end hammered into a diamond shape (Sheridan and Davis 2002, 823). Drilling would have proceeded from both ends and was probably done using a bow- or pump-drill, turned slowly so as to avoid heat-related cracking; this process left the characteristic rilling seen in many holes. The perforation of spacer and terminal plates varied, with the technically-demanding Y-perforation being used in many cases to increase the number of boreholes – as can be seen in the X-ray of the Cow Low necklace (ID 267, Figure 7.2.5). However, in some cases the simpler but riskier technique of elbow-boring was used, as in the Hill Head necklace (ID 268, Figure 7.2.7). By drilling through the back of the plate as well as the end, this created localised weakness which, when combined with thread-pull, sometimes led to the loss of spalls or fragments (as was the case with both upper spacer plates of the Hill Head necklace). Returning to the perforation of buttons, it is clear that in many cases the drill had been repositioned during the process, to achieve the desired angle. Ian Shepherd's suggestion that an initial pair of vertical 'starter borings' had been made was borne out in several cases.

Polishing would have been effected using abrasive materials of increasing fineness, as described by Shepherd (1981), with jet dust paste being used in the final stages and with calcium-rich rottenstone a candidate for the penultimate stage. Different materials would be susceptible to taking differing degrees of sheen, with hard jet capable of taking the most brilliant sheen. Soft jet and some cannel coal can take a moderate to high sheen, as can Kimmeridge shale, although most shale beads tend to be matt, or have a low sheen. Some subsequent loss of sheen in the micro-environment of the grave was noted, with the outer faces of what would have been highly-polished jet components becoming dulled while the side closest to the body retained its higher sheen. This was noted, for example, in the necklace from Calais Wold, East Yorkshire (ID 247).

The decoration that is found on the outer surface of many plates would have been created after the polishing stage. Punctulation, probably using a metal awl, is the commonest method, with the designs being geometric and often featuring triangles, lozenges, saltires or zigzags. Sometimes faint scratched guidelines are visible (e.g. at East Kinwhirrie, Angus: Sheridan 1998), and sometimes

the punctulations had been filled with a whitish or cream-coloured paste, analysis of which by Mary Davis has been shown to consist of barium sulphate or calcined bone in an organic binder. This would have accentuated the design. An unusual and subtle decorative method is attested on both the Cow Low necklaces' plates: here, selective dulling of specific areas would have brought out the brown sub-surface of the jet, contrasting with the black of the polished areas. There are shallow scratched lines outlining the geometric design, but whether these had been incised prior to the dulling, or afterwards, to outline the brown areas, is unclear. The only other jet jewellery to have been decorated using selective dulling is the tin-inlaid V-perforated button from Rameldry Farm, Fife (Sheridan and Davis 2003).

As for precisely how disc beads were manufactured – whether by separating them from a cylindrical or cigar-shaped roughout block, or individually shaping thin pieces of material, the more labour-intensive method – has been the subject of much discussion, speculation and experimentation. The non-laminar nature of good quality jet means that it is not susceptible to splitting, and sawing is wasteful of raw material. This suggests that jet beads were probably individually shaped and individually perforated, reaching their final form by grinding (and in some cases, polishing) a set of roughout beads, strung together after perforation. There is indeed plentiful evidence for individual perforation from both sides, with the creation of a small starter perforation on one side helping to prevent spalling as the drill approached from the other side of the bead. As with fusiform beads and spacer plates, the drilling could have been effected using a narrow metal drill bit. There is also evidence, from some beads, for grinding the broad surfaces flat (or slightly wedge-shaped, in some cases); although this grinding could equally have been a stage in the 'detached from preform' method.

Whether any non-jet disc beads were also individually shaped, rather than being split or sawn from a solid preform, has been the subject of much speculation. While many beads had clearly been drilled individually, two pieces of evidence had initially led to the suspicion that the solid preform method had been used – although in both cases the team revised their opinion. The first is the cigar-shaped, grooved object from Stanhope, Durham (ID 456, Figure 4.14.1), which was originally suspected to be an abandoned roughout for thin, washer-shaped disc beads. However, close re-examination of this object by Kate Verkooijen concluded that this was unlikely, and the realisation that this object is, in fact, a reused Roman lathe-turned knife-handle means that it is irrelevant to the question of Chalcolithic and Early Bronze Age disc beads, as noted in Chapter 4.14. The second piece of evidence is the presence of transverse scratches ('nibble striations' or 'nibbling') on the narrow, outer edge of some disc beads; this is shown most clearly on the disc beads that seem to represent secondary additions to the disc bead necklace from Folkton barrow ?245 (ID 366, Figure 7.1.7). It was originally thought that these incisions had been scratched on a solid preform to facilitate sawing or splitting, but it was subsequently realised that they had instead been scratched onto individual beads to help achieve a convex, as opposed to flat, bead edge. In spite of these findings, one cannot rule out the possibility that some disc beads had indeed been made by detaching them from a solid block. Either way, a considerable amount of effort had gone into the manufacture of these modest-looking beads.

Some indication of the arrangement of components in disc bead and spacer plate necklaces has already been given above; this can be deduced not only from the variability in the size and shape of components, but also from wear patterns (i.e. from thread-wear, from bead-on-bead wear and from bead-on-plate wear). Thus, with disc bead necklaces in which the beads are graded in size, in virtually every case it seems that the smaller beads would be towards the back. The only clear exception comes from a disc-and-fusiform bead necklace from Almondbank, Perth and Kinross, where the disc beads had been grouped in size-graded clusters to resemble the fusiform beads (Close-Brooks and Shepherd 1997). With the lunula-like spacer plate necklaces, there is a general increase in bead size from the innermost to the outermost strand; the beads immediately below the lowest spacer plate are often slender and flattish on two sides; and the beads would be arranged with their broadest point nesting against the narrow parts of beads in adjacent strands, so as to create the impression of a solid expanse of jet. These necklaces would have been tightly strung, using a narrow, organic thread, possibly of sinew or plant material; woollen thread is unlikely to have been used as it would have been too elastic. Threading of a spacer plate necklace would have started from the front of the necklace, as it is easier to send the thread upwards through a Y-perforated plate than downwards. At one end, all the strands would have been threaded through a fastener and firmly knotted; at the other, a loop would have been created, and again firmly knotted. The loose ends could have been threaded back through the terminal plates.

It should be clear from the foregoing that the manufacture of both necklace types required time and skill, with a lunula-like spacer plate necklace taking many hundreds of hours. As pointed out by Hal Redvers-Jones, however, some less demanding tasks such as grinding and polishing may have been carried out by less-skilled workers (e.g. assistants, apprentices or children), while the riskier process of perforating fusiform beads and plates would have required skill and experience. There is strong evidence to suggest the existence of specialist jetworkers based in the Whitby area, probably working as individuals (plus helpers) who interacted and shared know-how, rather than operating on a workshop or factory basis. This evidence comes not only from the consistency of design and manufacturing technique among widely-dispersed necklaces (especially as far as the lunula-like necklaces are concerned), but also from the presence of jetworking tools in the Whitby area (as mentioned above), and of unfinished pieces, including the probable pendant roughout found at Pockley, North Yorkshire (ID 459, Figure 4.14.1) and the probable spacer plate roughout found in one of the barrows 'NW of

Pickering' (ID 264). That there had been variability in the skill of the Whitby-based jetworkers is suggested by the variability in plate-drilling techniques, as detailed above.

That not all specialist (or highly-skilled) jetworkers were based in the Whitby area, however, is suggested by the evidence from the Cambridgeshire Fens. Here, exceptionally, the work of a single hand can arguably be detected in the necklace components found at Soham Fen (ID 391), Snailwell C (ID 281) and Burwell Fen (ID 282), which share a distinctive style of decoration not found in northern Britain. This 'rocker' decoration, probably executed freehand with considerable skill (Redvers-Jones pers. comm.) rather than with a curving punch (Beck 1928, 57), has also been noted by one of the authors (AS) on the aforementioned lozenge-shaped ornament from Carlton Colville, Suffolk (Pitts 2007), and it suggests the existence of a highly-skilled East Anglian-based craft worker. It also implies that some jet was probably travelling between Yorkshire and East Anglia in raw material form; it is questionable whether the requisite amounts of top-quality hard jet could have been gathered through beachcombing on the East Anglian coast (*cf* Roberts 1998, 192). The only other example of where the work of a single hand can be identified is in the two Cow Low, Derbyshire, necklaces (ID 266–7, Figure 7.2.4 to Figure 7.2.6), which share so many characteristics in common, despite differences in their overall design, that it seems unlikely that they had been made by different people.

The work of other skilled individuals, not based in the Whitby area, can be seen in the wholly or mostly non-jet spacer plate necklaces from Burgie Lodge, Moray, Pitkennedy, Angus and Pen y Bonc, Anglesey. Some of the non-jet necklace components made as substitutes for broken jet components – or as embellishments, as in the case of the Inchmarnock necklace (Sheridan 2013) – have also been competently made. However, some non-jet components, and indeed at least one jet component, had clearly been made by lesser-skilled individuals, as is the case, for instance, with the crudely-perforated right terminal plate (strung as a left terminal plate) of jet from Middleton Moor, Derbyshire (ID 269; Figure 7.2.9 to Figure 7.2.11).

The question of how the manufacture of disc bead necklaces had been organised is harder to answer. Some, including the three from Garton Slack, had probably been made by Whitby-based specialists, while some non-jet examples (e.g. the aforementioned Lairg and Dunrobin necklaces) were probably made by local craft workers. Whether there had been any specialist production of non-jet disc bead necklaces, with certain individuals creating more than one necklace, is a question that requires further research.

LIFE HISTORIES OF THE NECKLACES

The biographies of each of the necklaces are presented in Chapter 7.1 and Chapter 7.2 so will not be repeated here; suffice it to note that some necklaces, particularly of disc bead type, had probably not been worn for long when they were buried, while others, particularly of spacer plate type, had undergone significant wear and/or modification over the course of their lifetimes. (See Table 7.2.2 for a summary of wear traces among the spacer plate necklaces studied in the project). It is clear that, in many cases, the compositional modification had not been done simply to replace components that had broken or been lost (although this undoubtedly also occurred); with necklaces such as that from Middleton Moor (ID 269), for example, the accretion of components had resulted in assemblages that could not form a 'conventional' spacer plate necklace shape, irrespective of how they were strung together. With this particular example, radiocarbon-dated to 2010–1770 cal BC (see Chapter 9), some of the components could have been centuries old when buried. Earlier examples of the accretion of parts from several necklaces include those from Melfort and Inchmarnock, both Argyll and Bute (Clarke *et al.* 1985, fig. 5.48 and Sheridan 2013). In both cases, parts from over four necklaces are present (not two in the case of Melfort, as stated in Clarke *et al.* 1985) and, as with the Middleton Moor example, the Melfort components could not be strung to make a coherent, conventional design of necklace. In such cases it may be that the presence of tangible links to other people and other generations was what mattered, rather than reproducing a conventional necklace design. With the Inchmarnock necklace, however, it has been argued elsewhere that a deliberate process of aggrandisement had occurred, with the components from several necklaces (plus some newly-made fusiform beads) being worked into a coherent, lunula-like design as part of a process of competitive conspicuous consumption (Sheridan 2013).

In the current project, as in the longer-term National Museums Scotland 'jet' project, particular attention has been paid to tracing the fate of individual necklaces that had become fragmented. This approach has paid off since it appears that most of the necklace components found in the Cambridgeshire Fens at Snailwell C (ID 281) and Soham Fen (ID 391), some 8km away, may well have come from the same original necklace, since they share the same distinctive 'rocker' decoration and distinctive style of manufacture, and constitute complementary parts of a necklace. (With the Snailwell necklace, the fusiform beads had probably been acquired from a different necklace). As noted above, the same design is present on the surviving terminal plate from Burwell Fen, some 8km from Snailwell and 9km from Soham Fen; it is rumoured that an entire necklace had been found here and, if that is so, it had probably been made by the same person as the maker of the Snailwell/Soham Fen necklace. The degree of consistency in manufacture is illustrated by the fact that the Burwell Fen terminal is only 4mm narrower than the Snailwell terminal plates at its longest end, and has two more lines of 'rocker' decoration.

This discovery about the linkage between the Snailwell and Soham Fen necklace parts – the former found with a child, and in an old and worn condition, the latter with an adult woman, and in a much less worn condition – raises the question about the relationship between the individuals in question: had they been related? If the bones from Soham Fen can be found, then perhaps a DNA testing could show whether there was a familial relationship. It may be that other linked necklace parts exist; the evidence from the partial necklaces found at Barrow Bottom and Poor's Heath, Risby, Suffolk, with their complementary components, is suggestive (Martin 1976; Vatcher and Vatcher 1976), with the two findspots being separated by just *c.* 3km. Furthermore, the fusiform beads in the Snailwell necklace resemble those found as a bracelet associated with a young adult female at Southery Fen, Norfolk, around 24km away (Lethbridge *et al.* 1932; Roberts 1998, 191 and fig. 3); while the biconical beads found in the Poor's Heath, Risby grave are reminiscent of those in the Soham Fen necklace, just under 20km away. Further research would, however, be necessary to investigate whether these apparent links are genuine.

It is hoped that the detailed overview presented here demonstrates how much information can be obtained by adopting a 'forensic' approach to the study of jet and jet-like jewellery.

7.4 AMBER NECKLACES (by the main authors and David Bukach)

A list of items studied and illustrated is shown in Table 7.4.1. The necklaces vary considerably in size and, although it was desirable to illustrate them at a consistent scale for comparative purposes (Figure 7.4.1 to Figure 7.4.9), this was not always possible. Nor was it always possible to retain colour accuracy when taking close-up images of amber: the refractive qualities of the material are such that there is an inevitable compromise between illustrating particular features and maintaining colour consistency. Detailed measurements of certain dimensions, including perforations, are tabulated in Appendix VII, Tables 17–19.

7.4.1 WESSEX

ID 1360 Wilsford-cum-Lake G47, 49 or 50, Wiltshire

References: Hoare 1812, 212–3; Piggott 1938, pl. X; Grinsell 1957, 198; Beck and Shennan 1991, 179 and figs. 11.17 and 11.18.

COMPOSITION

The necklace currently comprises 11 spacer or terminal plates, 10 pestle pendants, 17 fusiform beads, 49 globular beads, four annular beads and 11 V-perforated buttons. All the plates and many of the beads and pendants are on display, but the buttons, annular beads, a few of the fusiform beads and one globular bead are in store at the British Museum. Also recorded as coming from the same barrow is a group of three amber pendants housed in the Wiltshire Heritage Museum, Devizes (Annable and Simpson 1964, 54, no. 343). Due to the uncertainty of the association these items have been described separately in the section covering pendants (ID 1472–4, Figure 5.9.3), and are not included in the discussions below.

CONTEXT AND ASSOCIATIONS

The necklace elements were found in a barrow excavated by E. Duke (Hoare 1812, 212–3). The barrow was one of five barrows, two of them bell barrows, opened by Duke in 1806. Duke's barrow 20 contained a possibly primary inhumation burial associated with the amber necklace, four gold discs (ID 1570–73, Figure 6.1.1), an accessory cup, a bronze awl (not studied) and perhaps faience beads. Seven

of the pestle pendants, the gold discs and the accessory cup are illustrated by Hoare (1812, Pl. XXXI). However it should be noted that the attributions of Duke's finds to individual barrows are uncertain, and the amber items may in fact have been recovered from more than one barrow and/or grave.

MORPHOLOGY

Eleven surviving plates include five terminal plates and six spacer plates of relatively great width (Figure 7.4.1). As they were sewn tightly to the textile-covered display board it proved very difficult to measure the perforations, and no details could be viewed under the microscope. However the perforated edges were studied in detail using hand lenses. The dimensions of the plates, which are given in Appendix VII, Table 17, indicate immediately that the plates comprise three distinct pairs of spacer plates plus one extra, and two pairs of terminal plates. It can also be seen that one of the pairs of terminal plates is much wider (measured between the edges bearing perforations) than the very narrow spacer plates. Plate thickness varies from 5.5 to 8.4mm. The plates appear to belong to two distinct groups: three pairs of large spacer plates which probably were associated with the pair of larger terminal plates, and a single smaller and less rectangular spacer (no. 10) which, on the basis of the borehole patterns, is more likely to have been associated with the smaller pair of terminal plates (nos. 9 and 11). This group of three plates all possess four through-bored perforations. They may have been part of a bracelet or, alternatively, these three plates may relate to a different necklace, perhaps found in a separate grave.

The lower edges of all plates are gently curved while the upper edges are straight. All perforations in the terminal plates are through-bored. Each spacer plate has two through-bored perforations which are placed near to the top and bottom margins, while in between these there is a series of contiguous shallow V-perforations running down each long side edge (see Figure 7.4.2). The borings would have provided an attractive decorative effect when the amber was new and translucent. In many cases the edge V-perforations have broken out, such that only the apex of the V survives. However it was possible to measure the diameter of perforations, both of the main borings and of the V-perforations, in many cases. The data are summarised in Appendix VII, Table 17. The diameters of the main bore holes vary between 1.1 and 2.6mm, while those of the generally smaller borings for the V-perforations (only measureable at an angle) vary between 1.5 and 5.4mm.

Table 7.4.1. List of amber necklaces studied and illustrated.

Object	Site (Parish), County	Museum	Illustration
ID 1360	Wilsford-cum-Lake G47, 49 or 50, Wilts.	BM	Figure 7.3.1; Figure 7.3.2
ID 1444	Upton Lovell G2e, Wilts.	Dev	Figure 7.3.4; Figure 7.3.5
ID 1496	Wimborne St Giles G9, Dorset	Dev	Figure 7.3.7; Figure 7.3.8
ID 999	Little Cressingham, Norfolk	Norwich	Figure 7.3.9; Figure 7.3.10

Figure 7.4.1. ID 1360 Wilsford-cum-Lake G47, 49 or 50 showing: necklace as on display with details of certain plates and perforations below (numbered as per display); (a) details of three fusiform beads; (b) details of four globular beads and (c) details of two pestle pendants. Note: the items are not to consistent scale.

The boreholes in the three plates that possibly belong to a bracelet (nos. 9, 10 and 11) tend to be slightly narrower.

It is possible that the six larger spacer plates and the two larger terminal plates belonged to a necklace that supported just two strands of beads, utilising the upper and lower through-bored perforations. However, the terminal

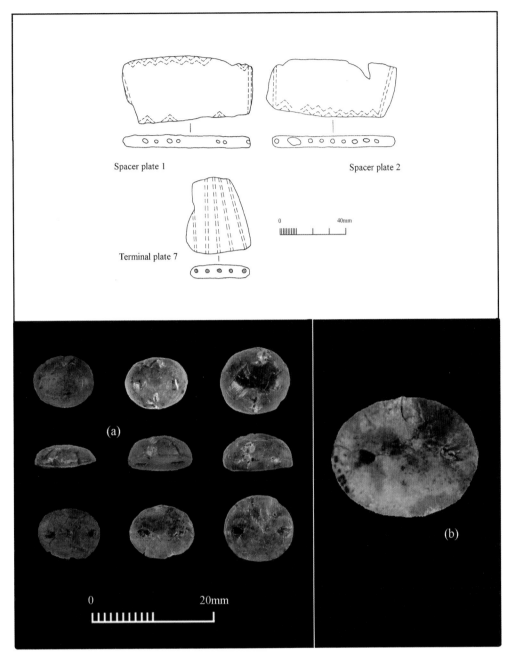

Figure 7.4.2. ID 1360 Wilsford-cum-Lake G47, 49 or 50 showing at top details of perforations and borings in spacer plates (after Beck and Shennan 1991; drawing by Peter Woodward), below (a) details of three V-perforated buttons, and (b) enlargement of necklace wear patterning on the base of one V-perforated button.

plates possess five through-bored perforations, and unless the three inner perforations were merely decorative, this suggests that some at least of the necklace had more than two strands. The possibility that the V-perforations located on the long sides of the spacer plates had been utilised to support further strings of beads was therefore investigated during the detailed study. The disposition of the overall number of possible attachment points, including the marginal through-perforations, does suggest that they may have been designed to support particular numbers of strings. Thus the proposed attachment points increase from five to six in the outer spacer plates (nos. 5 and 6),

from six to ten attachment points in the next pair of spacer plates (nos. 3 and 4), and, finally, there are ten potential attachment points on each side of the two largest spacer plates (nos. 1 and 2). The various stringing possibilities can also be considered in relation to the evidence for wear, which will be discussed below.

Of the ten pestle pendants, six are almost complete with their horizontal perforation near the top surviving. All pendants have a tapering outline with ovoid section and flat sides. The tops are rounded and the basal bowing is also gently rounded in each case (Figure 7.4.1c). The complete pieces vary in length from 21.0 to 29.2mm, and measureable perforations lie between 1.5 and 2.0mm in diameter. One piece is significantly larger, and may have formed a central focus for the group, but the rest do not seem to have been designed as matching pairs in a graduated sequence (see dimensions plotted in Figure 7.4.3). Many of the pieces have a lower width of *c*. 15mm, with only two forming a smaller pair. There is greater variation in depth (front to back), with five deeper examples and five thinner. The thicker ones also have a more rounded cross-section, and two of these appear to have been crafted more precisely; it is, therefore, possible that the ten pestle pendants were derived from two different original sets.

The 17 fusiform beads are all of medium plumpness, standardised at around 9mm in height (Figure 7.4.1a). In length they vary between 10.8 and 17.0mm and in maximum diameter between 6.5 and 10.4mm. The fairly narrow perforations vary between 1.2 and 2.8mm in diameter. All have squared off ends, but some have angled ends, designed to sit within a curve on the string. Three also display flattened sides, which would allow them to fit snugly against beads in an adjacent string. The variation in length shows an even gradation, although with slightly fewer beads at the larger end of the range.

A total of 49 globular beads could be divided visually into three groups according to overall shape: globular (Figure 7.4.1b); squashed globular, and oblate (globular with flattened ends). The oblate and squashed bead shapes were designed with flattened sides, in order that the beads would fit tightly against each other in the necklace. A plot of the major dimensions for the members of these three groups of bead (in archive) showed that all shapes occur within the same, fairly considerable, size ranges. However among the squashed globular beads no particularly large, or particularly small, examples are represented. The lengths vary from 9.3 to 17.1mm and widths from 8.5 to 19.3mm. The diameters of the small perforations measure between 1.4 and 2.2mm. Four annular beads, one of them comprising three fragments only are smaller in diameter than the smallest globular beads (range 6.3 to 8.7mm). The perforations however are much larger, between 2.0 and 4.1mm across.

All ten of the loose V-perforated buttons have a neat oval base, between 10.2 and 12.1mm in length, and a medium to high, gently curved dome (3.8 to 5.5mm high). In each case a pair of neatly drilled and widely spaced oval perforations is located symmetrically on the base (Figure 7.4.2). They form a very uniform set. One larger oval item, measuring 27.1 by 21.9mm and 14.3mm high, is sewn tightly to the display board. It may also be a button but the underside could not be viewed.

MATERIAL

The four widest spacers are made from very dark red amber whose surfaces have oxidised to a light toffee colour. All the other plates are made from bright red amber, with variable oxidation colouration. Most are of mid toffee hues, but the pair of smaller terminal plates (9 and 11) have markedly paler, creamy surfaces. These are the terminals that probably belonged to an associated bracelet (see above). The pestle pendants are all made from dark red amber while the surfaces have oxidised to a light toffee colour. Similarly the fusiform beads and annular beads are of rich red amber, while the original colour of the amber used for the globular beads is obscured by creamy oxidisation. The V-perforated buttons are all of bright red amber, the surfaces of which are oxidised to a light toffee hue.

MANUFACTURE

Due to the heavy oxidation of most pieces, and the fact that the items sewn to the display board could not be studied under the microscope, no traces of manufacture are visible. The buttons, which are stored as individual items, could be studied in more detail. No traces of manufacture are visible on the coated surfaces, but rilling within the perforations is visible on four buttons.

COMPLETENESS AND DAMAGE

Crazed cracking is present on all outer oxidised surfaces of the spacer and terminal plates. All pieces except one (terminal 8) show evidence of post-depositional damage in the form of fractures to the edges, and in one case the surface, of the plates. The breakage of top surfaces, and some loss of the oxidised surfaces, all appear to be modern. In three cases the top has broken away across the drill hole while a further three have their upper portions completely missing (75% to 80% complete). The fusiform beads survive between the 60% and 100% levels, with several breaks occurring at the ends, all in modern times. Three have oxidisation which is slightly less cracked. Most of the globular beads are complete or virtually complete, with only four displaying end breaks, which appear to be modern. All four annular beads have become chipped or broken in modern times. Most of the buttons are complete, but three display major breaks (50 to 60% present) and some have chipping, all of which appears to be modern. The surfaces are obscured by thick conservation coatings, with visible brush strokes.

WEAR

General wear is shown in Table 7.4.2. In five cases the plates have one or more corners showing evidence of ancient damage where the end of the top or bottom through-perforation has been pulled by threads and broken out. This may well have been the case for many more of the corners, but these instances have been obscured by modern damage. It must be borne in mind that the plates had been strung using the through-bored perforations in at least two previous museum display configurations (see Piggott 1938, Pl. X and unpublished British Museum X-ray), and this may account for much of the modern damage. The incidence of survival of original stretches of plate margins is of interest. The narrower margins, adjacent to

Table 7.4.2. Wear on selected necklace items.

Object no.	Type	Fresh/slight wear	Worn	Very worn	Indet.	Total
ID 999	Pestle pendant	3	7	-	-	10
	Fusiform	4	-	-	-	4
	Annular	5	-	-	-	5
	Disc	23	3	-	2	28
ID 1360	Spacer	1	5	5	-	11
	Pestle pendant	3	-	-	7	10
	Fusiform	9	3	-	5	17
	Globular	21	16	-	12	49
	Annular	-	-	-	4	4
	Button	5	3	-	3	11
ID 1444	Spacer	-	1	5	-	6
	Fusiform	2	-	-	6	8
	Globular	-	-	-	3	3
	Squashed globular	-	44	-	290	334
	Annular	-	-	-	5	5
ID 1496	Spacer	1	1	-	7	9
	Fusiform	-	-	-	3	3
	Globular	-	-	-	1	1
	Squashed globular	2	-	-	5	7
	Button	3	-	-	-	3

the through-bored perforations, are usually better preserved than the longer margins bearing the V-perforations. If the V-perforations were purely decorative, one might expect these longer margins to have survived better than those adjoining the through-perforations. The fact that they are severely damaged may indicate that the V-perforations had at some stage been used to support strings of beads, and that the weight of the beads had caused the V-perforations to break out.

As noted previously, few of the total number of perforations have survived intact, but amongst them various cases of thread-wear were observed, and one example of bead-on-bead wear. The majority of the incidences of thread-wear and ancient damage on the spacer plates relate to the ends of the marginal through-bored perforations. This suggests that these perforations had supported two strands of beads for a lengthy period of time. In the case of the terminal plates half of the observed cases of thread-wear relate to the outer boreholes (i.e. at the corners) while the others relate to the intermediate boreholes, both on the upper (narrow) and lower (wider) margins (see Figure 7.4.1, details 7 and 9). This suggests that, at least at some stage of use, all five perforations were in use, and that five strings of beads had been supported in this area of the necklace. Although the longer sides of the spacer plates are very damaged it was also possible to discern possible thread-pull in boreholes relating to the V-perforations in four cases. Overall there is therefore some evidence which suggests that strings of beads had been supported in the V-perforations. Overall most pairs of plates are classified as very worn (3 with 4, 5 with 6), or worn. The pair of

lighter coloured terminal plates (9 with 11), which may have belonged to a bracelet or separate necklace, are however slightly less worn.

Traces of wear were not often visible on the pestle pendants, but include two cases of crisp edges to the perforation while the broken-out perforation showed smoothing at one end of the drill-hole. This suggests minimal to slight wear. Four of the fusiform beads have crisp perforations, subjected to only slight wear, while three other beads show evidence of distinct thread-wear. Among the globular beads edges to the perforations are crisp in 13 cases, but show softening in six cases and evidence of slight or strong thread-pull in 14 cases. There are also eight instances of clear bead-on-bead wear.

With regard to the annular beads which have a large central hole, wear traces are not easily visible, but some softening of the inner edges was noted. Softening of the perforation edges occurs on four buttons, and slight or strong thread-wear occurs on seven examples. In six cases the thread-wear is situated at the outer edges of the perforations (e.g. Figure 7.4.2b), and in only one case has the thread pulled on the sides of the bridge. The wear varied from slight (five cases) to moderate and worn (three cases); examples are illustrated in Figure 7.4.2.

CONCLUSIONS

The spacer plates form three pairs plus two pairs of terminals and a single extra spacer plate. The three main pairs of spacers are of similar material and design and appear to form an original set. Both pairs of terminals differ

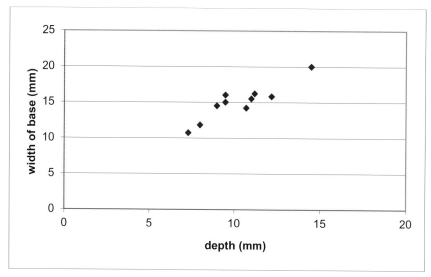

Figure 7.4.3. ID 1360 Wilsford-cum-Lake G47, 49 or 50: dimensions of all amber pestle pendants.

from these in material and/or degree of wear, and one pair of terminals (7 with 8) displays a lesser degree of finish at manufacture. As mentioned above, the pair of smaller terminal plates (9 with 11), which is slightly different in colour, and the small broken spacer plate (10) may derive from a bracelet, or from a separate necklace perhaps from a different grave. An idea of the original layout of the spacers within the necklace is probably better portrayed in the former display arrangement, as shown in Piggott's photograph (1938, pl. X), than in the modern display depicted here in Figure 7.4.1. Aspects of the morphology of the plates and evidence for wear, as discussed above, may indicate that in an original necklace design strands of beads may have been supported by the small V-perforations, as well as by the marginal through-bored perforations. In such a scenario, it can be deduced that there could have been up to ten strings of beads within the necklace. However, the ends of the through-bored perforations, at the corners of the plates, display extreme wear, and it may be that, following the breaking out of many of the small V-perforations, the necklace was re-strung with just two strands of beads.

It is possible that the ten pestle pendants were derived from two different original sets. However, the material was the same, and it was not possible to detect any variations in the degree of use as most of the perforations were absent, or too damaged for any thread-wear to be visible. Although there is slight variation in visible wear traces on the fusiform beads, there is nothing to suggest that these beads might not have formed a single original set. However the presence of the flattened beads, and those with angled ends, may indicate that they may be derived from a necklace that possessed rather more fusiform beads than this (i.e. one with several strands of fusiform beads that fitted neatly one above each other). In contrast, the globular beads display much more variation. The differences in visible wear are the first indication that the beads may have derived from more than one source. The larger beads appear to be more regular in shape and form a clear set, while the

smaller beads are much more variable in shape. Also four small beads are particularly regular and flattened. There is no obvious correlation between these bead groups and degree of wear, but the oblate beads do tend to display a high degree of wear, with no crisp perforations recorded. This may indicate that the globular beads may have come originally from two or more different original necklaces. These beads are truly spherical in shape and are not reminiscent of the squashed globular beads found within other spacer plate necklaces (e.g. ID 1444 Upton Lovell G2e, see below). The few annular beads are anomalous in the context of the overall bead group, and may be sole survivors from some previous necklace.

The set of eleven buttons is highly uniform, and they were manufactured to a high level of craftsmanship. The patterns of wear show that the set had definitely been in use, and probably for some time, while the location of the thread-wear equates to Shepherd's class of 'necklace wear' (Shepherd 2009). This may mean that the buttons did form part of the one or more necklaces represented in this find group. The larger high-domed oval item, sewn onto the display board, may be a single much larger V-perforated button, but the underside is not visible for study. In the arrangement of selected necklace items within a former display this piece seems to have been placed as a fastener (Piggott 1938, pl. X), and this may indeed have been its function.

It is immediately apparent that all the amber items in this group could not have belonged to one necklace, and that various sets of beads and spacers may originally have formed parts of earlier necklaces. Firstly it seems extremely likely that, if not the remnants from a different spacer plate necklace, the smaller pair of terminal plates and the single small broken spacer plate derive from a bracelet. This could have formed part of a matching set of jewellery along with the main spacer plate necklace, similar to the set in jet known from East Kinwhirrie, Angus, Scotland (Sheridan and Davis 2002, fig. 1; Figure 7.3.1). Some of the smaller beads may belong to this bracelet. The remainder of the terminals and spacers appear to form a uniform set from a large spacer plate necklace. The beads usually associated with such necklaces are of squashed globular and oblate form (*cf* the necklace from Upton Lovell G2e ID 1444, see below) and these are certainly present in this group (12 squashed globular and 10 oblate). However, most of the globular beads are truly globular (spherical) in shape (25 examples), a form that is not commonly found within other spacer plate necklaces. The total number of globular beads surviving (49, two of them of indeterminate shape) would be totally inadequate to string between the spacer plates, if the necklace had possessed ten strands at the front (as discussed above). However they may have been sufficient in number to have been placed between the spacers in a two-strand version of the necklace. Furthermore, the fact that so few beads have survived from the grave lends support to the idea that a two-strand necklace was a later simplification of an earlier multi-stranded version.

Fusiform beads can also be associated with spacer plate necklaces made from amber and may well have formed part of the overall design of such ornaments. Unfortunately, no complete necklaces survive, either in Britain or on the continent. The total number of fusiform beads from Wilsford-cum-Lake is again low (17), but they appear to form a single set and they may have formed one or more rows, possibly at the centre of the necklace, or have been placed next to the terminal plates. The four annular beads, and indeed the pestle pendants, are unlikely to have been components of a spacer plate necklace. Both these forms occur as elements of the composite amber necklace from Little Cressingham (ID 999, see below) and it may be that the pestle pendants and annular beads had formed part of a similar smaller necklace deposited at Wilsford-cum-Lake. It is possible that the ten pestle pendants were derived from two different original sets. However, the material was the same, and it was not possible to detect any variations in the degree of use as most of the perforations were absent, or too damaged for any thread-wear to be visible. The single large oval possible button may have functioned as a necklace fastener.

Finally, the group of ten small V-perforated buttons form a remarkably uniform set, and the use wear indicates that they had been used in a necklace. They may have been employed within a separate necklace, along with the pestle pendants. Another possibility is that they formed the rear area of the main spacer plate necklace, in the same way that rows of necklace buttons appear to have functioned within some of the large jet necklaces from the Peak District (see Chapter 7.2). The two sets of gold discs may have been covers for further gently domed buttons (Chapter 6.1.2). These may have been designed to be sewn onto garments or could possibly have been strung within one of the amber necklaces represented in this finds assemblage. Unfortunately the excavation records are confused and it may be that several different necklaces, from two or more different graves or barrows, are represented in the overall group.

ID 1444 Upton Lovell G2e (The Golden Barrow), Wiltshire

References: Hoare 1812, 98, pls. X–XI; Annable and Simpson 1964, 48 and 103; Beck and Shennan 1991, 175 and fig. 11.15, 1.

COMPOSITION

The surviving necklace elements comprise one terminal plate and five spacer plates, along with 334 beads, mainly squashed globular in form, all of which have been sewn on to a textile-covered board for display purposes. In store there are a further 13 beads: nine fusiform; three globular, and one annular. The current stringing is shown on Figure 7.4.4 with the individual plates numbered 1 to 6. Originally a total of 'about 1000' beads was discovered.

CONTEXT AND ASSOCIATIONS

The beads and spacer plates were found near a probable secondary cremation burial beneath a bowl barrow (Hoare 1812, 98, pls. X–XI; Annable and Simpson 1964, 48 and 103). The bowl barrow was excavated by Cunnington in 1803 and also in 1807, and it is unclear whether the finds from those two investigations, discovered close to each other, had come from one or two secondary graves (Clarke *et al.* 1985, 279). The objects were found about 2 feet (*c.* 0.6m) away from the cremated remains. The finds from the 1803 excavation comprised several amber spacer plates and 'over 1000' amber beads, together with a grape cup and several sheet gold ornaments: 13 drum-shaped gold beads (ID 1443, Figure 6.1.7), a conical shale pendant or button covered with gold sheet (ID 1450/492, Figure 6.1.6), a gold rectangular plate (ID 1449, Figure 6.1.5) and four small gold sheet cap-ends (ID 1447A–B and ID 1448A–B, Figure 6.1.6). The finds from the 1807 investigation comprised further amber beads (from the same or from a second necklace), plus a Collared Urn containing a smaller, plain pot (probably an accessory vessel), a bronze awl (ID 1442, Figure 4.6.4) and a small flat bronze knife (ID 1446).

MORPHOLOGY

The six spacer plates, as displayed, comprise one terminal plate and five spacers (Figure 7.4.4a–h). However two of these spacers comprise two separate fragments which were glued together, and thus the original number of pieces was eight. Unfortunately none of the plates was drawn at the time of discovery. Most of the plates are broken along two or more margins and it is difficult to assess the original presence of any paired plates. If these six spacer plates have been joined correctly (which appears to be the case) then they represent two terminal plates and two sets of spacers. This matches the scheme of plates found with many of the classic jet necklaces. Obviously, the full complement of plates and terminals from a functioning necklace do not all necessarily survive, and it seems possible that the elements found in the grave did not comprise an entire spacer plate

Figure 7.4.4. ID 1444 Upton Lovell G2e. The top part of the illustration shows the necklace as currently mounted with the plates numbered for this project. Detailed images below show: (a) plate 1; (b) plate 6 exhibiting wear around perforations; (c) plate 4; (d) plate 4 with main and V-perforated drill holes of different sizes; (e) plate 3; (f); plate 2 possibly an amalgamation of fragments of different plates on the basis of colour; (g) and (h) plate 5 exhibiting wear around perforations on both sides.

necklace. There is only one terminal plate, and the plate located at the left hand end of the necklace (plate 6), as reconstructed for display, is in fact a fragment from a spacer plate. These points will be discussed further below.

Each plate possesses a series of parallel through-perforations, while the terminal plate (plate 1) has splayed through-perforations (Appendix VII, Table 18). Between these perforations, on the upper and lower (perforated) margins, there are shallow V-perforations. When the amber was new and translucent the bore holes and V-perforations would have formed attractive patterns on the faces of the spacers (see Figure 7.4.5). In many cases these V-perforations have broken out, such that only the apex of the V survives. The fact that the apex or portions of the

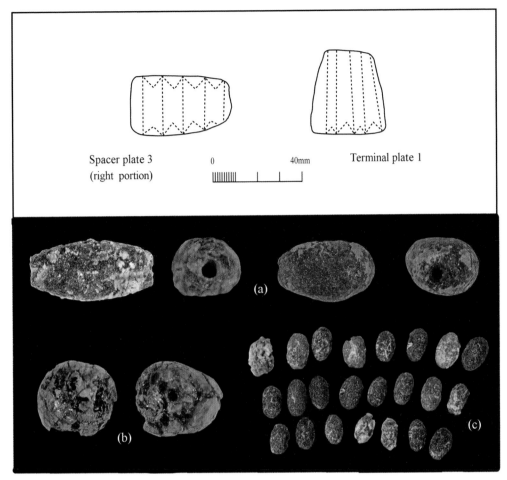

Figure 7.4.5. ID 1444 Upton Lovell G2e showing at top details of perforations and borings in plates (after Annable and Simpson 1964; drawing by Peter Woodward), and below (a) detail of examples of fusiform beads; (b) detail of example of globular bead, and (c) detail of examples of squashed globular beads Note: the items are not to consistent scale.

V-perforations survive indicates that the perforated margins have broken only to a limited degree, with maximum loss of only a few millimetres. However, the inner and outer sides of the spacer plates, which originally would have been solid, have all broken along the line of a through-perforation. Only in the case of the tapered terminal plate do the inner and outer curved margins, as well as the lower perforated edge, survive. Thus pairing of plates according to the surviving number of through-perforations cannot be attempted. Nor does a consideration of plate length (perforation to perforation) aid interpretation as the lengths all fall between 21.0 and 23.1mm. Thus all the plates seem to have had similar lengths (perforation to perforation measurement), although their widths may have varied. The presumably accurate join of the two fragments forming plate 3 (Figure 7.4.4e) shows that this plate was 52.7mm wide plus at least *c.* 5mm to make up the outer sides of the two broken through perforations; indeed, it may have been considerably wider. There is a hint, therefore, that originally these spacer plates were wide and shallow and similar in principle to those found in the necklace from Wilsford-cum-Lake (ID 1360, see above). The diameters of the perforations are remarkably uniform amongst the

various plates (see Appendix VII, Table 18). The through-perforations vary from 1.5 to 3.7mm in diameter, but most are between 1.5 and 1.9mm across. The holes bored to form the V-perforations are finer, varying between 1.1 and 1.9mm in diameter. Figure 7.4.4d shows the differing sizes of the main and V-perforated drill holes of different sizes on plate 4.

Of the *c.* 1000 beads found at the time of excavation, a total of 334 survive and are mounted within the displayed necklace. The beads vary in size, material and colour (Figure 7.4.5c). The mounted beads are all of similar shape, each being of even slightly elongated globular form, but with the perforated sides distinctly flattened. The flattening of the sides was achieved so that the beads would sit closely and snugly together when strung. This form of bead is generally termed 'squashed globular'. The length, width and perforation diameters were recorded for all surviving beads. The length and width appeared to be positively correlated, so presentation of a single dimension can provide a good impression of the variation in bead size. The dimension chosen was the length, measured from perforation to perforation (Figure 7.4.6). It can be seen from the bar chart that bead size was fairly evenly graduated, although there are far more beads in the medium size range, with 58% of them measuring between 3.6 and 5mm in length. Perforation diameters range from 1.2mm to a maximum of 2.7mm but most fall between 1.4 and 1.6mm.

A small number of beads which were not of squashed globular shape have not been incorporated within the necklace as currently displayed and are curated in store. However these beads were strung in the previously displayed array, as illustrated, for example, by Annable and Simpson (1964, 103 no. 227) and photographed in Clarke *et al.* (1985, fig. 4.51). It should be noted that the few black fusiform beads of jet or jet-like material which were mounted in this first display version of the necklace are thought not to have derived from this burial (Annable and Simpson 1964, 48).

A total of eight fusiform beads and one fragment have survived. The eight beads vary in length from 11.0 to 23.5mm with perforation diameters ranging between 1.5 and 2.5mm (Figure 7.4.5a). In overall shape there is a fair degree of variation, with three being slender in profile (one of these is the fragmentary bead), one plump and five of medium plumpness. Three beads are of true globular shape, as opposed to the squashed globular variety described above (Figure 7.4.5b). Their measured maximum diameters are 9.0mm, 9.3mm and 13.1mm and their perforations vary in diameter between 1.5 and 2mm. Finally a total of five surviving beads are of flattened annular or disc form. A measurable example was 5.5mm in diameter, with a perforation diameter of 3mm.

MATERIAL

Four spacers, including the single terminal plate, are of dark red amber. Three fragments vary more in colour: plate 5 (mid to dark red) and the two portions glued together as plate 2 (dark red-brown and dark orange). This may indicate that these two fragments are not in fact from the same original plate (Figure 7.4.4f). The variation in colour may suggest that the plates derived from more than one original spacer plate necklaces, although it may be that amber of slightly different colours had been deliberately chosen to provide attractive contrasts within a single necklace.

The 334 squashed globular beads vary in colour and degree of oxidisation. The original colour of most beads (69%) was dark red, with 21% originally light red and the minority (10%) a very dark red. Five of the fusiform beads are of dark orange amber and four are of bright orange amber. Two of the truly globular beads are of bright orange amber, and one was dark red. The annular beads are of light or dark red amber with slightly oxidised surfaces.

MANUFACTURE

Apart from the size of the drill holes, no traces of manufacturing technique or polishing are visible on the spacer plates and terminal plate. And, owing to the degree of oxidisation, and the fact that most of the beads are sewn tightly onto a textile-covered display board, no traces of manufacture or polishing are visible on these either.

COMPLETENESS AND DAMAGE

The flat faces of the plates are characterised by dimpled partially oxidised surfaces and minor crazed cracking, whilst the cream coloured oxidation is most evident inside the drill holes. Modern damage includes the catastrophic breaks across plates 2 and 3 (although these could not be examined due to the modern joining), damage to corners (plates 1, 5 and 6) and a degree of damage to the margins in plates 1 and 2. The squashed globular beads possess varying degrees of surface oxidisation, usually light toffee in colour but occasionally dark cream. Most show only slight oxidisation, but 27 (8%) are heavily oxidised and 57 (17%) have moderately oxidised surfaces. There are very few traces of modern damage to the beads. All nine fusiform beads have surfaces which have oxidised to a mid-toffee colour. No obviously modern breaks were detected. All three truly globular beads have surfaces which are oxidised to a mid-toffee colour. Various chips are present on the ends and sides of different beads, but whether these had occurred in ancient or modern times could not be discerned. Amongst the annular beads the age of one catastrophic break is indeterminate.

WEAR

The general level of wear on the plates and beads is summarised in Table 7.4.2. Ancient damage is apparent on all plates apart from terminal plate 1. This involved severe breaks to nearly all the outer and inner margins of each spacer plate, and often along the perforated margins as well. Although the perforated margins were almost always damaged along at least part of their length, and many of the decorative V-perforations broken out, a large number of the perforations appear to display slight softening and loss around their margins, for example plate 5 (Figure 7.4.4g–h) and plate 6 (Figure 7.4.4b). This wear seems to be ancient, and not the result of modern stringing employed previously in the museum display.

This suggests that the plates had experienced thread-wear whilst employed *in their damaged state*. In other words, the broken plates had been re-used after the original perforated margins had been damaged. Overall, all the spacer plates are classified as very worn, while the single terminal plate is worn. Amongst the squashed globular beads breaks were recorded for a total of 44 beads (13% of the total). It seemed that these were ancient in origin and they would not have impeded the stringing of the beads within a necklace. Owing to the nature of mounting upon the display board it was not possible to assess the degree of any surviving thread-wear within or around the perforations. Turning to the other loose small beads, in most cases the degree of any wear could not be detected, but two fusiform beads display evidence of slight thread-wear at the perforations.

CONCLUSIONS

The necklace as found appears to have incorporated a set

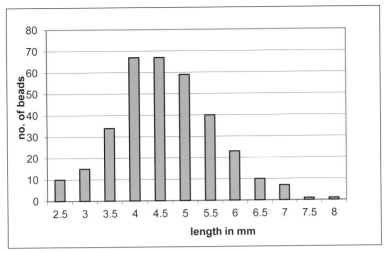

Figure 7.4.6. ID 1444 Upton Lovell G2e. Squashed globular beads: variation in length (measured from perforation to perforation).

of spacer plates which were already fragmented, with all their outer and inner margins broken in antiquity. Originally the plates may have possessed between six and more than nine through-perforations. These may have been arranged as three pairs below the terminal plates, and have supported, at the centre of the original necklace, at least ten strings of small beads. However, as found, the fragmentary spacer plates which had been broken in antiquity, probably supported far fewer strands of the squashed globular beads within a 'secondary' necklace.

If a second terminal plate was really missing from the excavated assemblage, then the surviving terminal (1) may in fact have functioned as a spacer plate. Thus, the damaged plates could perhaps originally have functioned within the 'secondary' necklace as three pairs: 2 with 3 as the widest, with seven and nine through-perforations surviving, arranged below the other four, which have between five and six through-perforations surviving. The arrangement that has been used within the reconstruction of the necklace on display differs slightly from such a scheme, with spacers 2 and 4 transposed (see Figure 7.4.4). However, variation in the colour of the fragments conjoined to form plate 2 may indicate that these fragments derived from two different original spacer plates. In this case, more pairs of spacers may originally have been included within the necklace. It was not possible to check whether the glued breaks were ancient or modern, but it is assumed that the conservator would only have joined breaks which fitted tightly, thus indicating that these breaks had been modern (i.e. had occurred at the time of excavation or subsequently, rather than in the Early Bronze Age). However, if these breaks *were* ancient then it may be that a total of seven fragmentary spacer plates and one terminal plate were originally represented. In this case, the original number of plates might have matched those within the necklace from Wilsford-cum-Lake (ID 1360, see above) with its three sets of spacers and pair of terminal plates. The plates as they survive exhibit ancient breaks on all outer and inner margins. Thus, within the final format of the necklace during the Bronze Age, the plates possessed

fewer functional bore holes than indicated in Appendix VII, Table 18. The numbers of functional bore holes for the plates within the necklace as it was deposited are as follows: terminal plate 1 five to six perforations; plates 2 (as glued) and 4 five to five perforations; plate 3 (as glued) seven to seven perforations; plate 5 four to four perforations; and plate 6 three to three perforations. Thus, in its final format the spacers probably supported only five strands of small beads, perhaps reducing to three strands towards the rear of the necklace.

The current mounted version of the necklace employs all the spacers and most of the small beads (334 squashed globular beads) to provide an impression of *c.* 60% to 70% of an original necklace formation. However the total number of beads found at the time of excavation was 'about 1000'. This suggests either that the original necklace was of a different format than that represented in the display, or that more than one necklace was represented in the burial. A larger necklace would either have incorporated more strings in one or more sections between adjacent spacers, or the zones between spacers might have been longer. As discussed above, the functional bore holes in the plates of the final 'secondary' necklace vary from three to six. If the maximum number of strands was six, then the necklace must have been longer, and so perhaps there were in fact three sets of spacer plates, plus terminals, within the final design. If the number of strands was five, then there would have been up to 200 beads within each strand and no increase of strands towards the centre of the necklace. Such an arrangement was originally devised for the first display array at the museum, which formed the basis for the illustration in Annable and Simpson (1964, 103). However this formation only includes the surviving squashed globular beads, which may only represent *c.* 30 to 40% of those found in the grave. Perhaps some of the squashed globulars, surviving from the original multi-stranded necklace, were subsequently strung as separate items, either as simple, shorter necklaces, to be worn in association with the 'secondary' spacer plate necklace, or as one or more bracelets? No doubt as the outer boreholes on the plates gradually broke out during use the necklace would have undergone many processes of modification and redesign, and its overall life span may have been extensive.

The variations in colour of the spacer and terminal plates may suggest that they derived from more than one original spacer plate necklaces, although it seems more likely that amber of slightly different colours had been deliberately chosen to provide attractive contrasts within a single necklace. The plates were mostly of dark red amber, as were the majority (69%) of the small squashed globular beads. However some of these were of lighter or darker red amber, while the fusiform beads and two of the truly globular beads were more orange in hue. This may indicate that the few beads of varying shape had in fact derived from one or more necklaces that were different from those which had provided the squashed globular beads and the spacers. Thus, overall the beads may have originally come from three or even more original necklaces of varying form.

The presence of ancient breaks on most of the margins of the spacer plates, and on 13% of the squashed globular beads, suggests that the necklace elements had been in circulation for a long time before they were deposited in the grave. Owing to the nature of the display mounting it was not possible to view the perforations of the small beads in detail, and therefore the degree of any thread-wear present could not be assessed. However two of the loose fusiform beads did show signs of slight thread-wear when viewed under the microscope. The plates were more informative. In their edge-damaged state, each plate had then been subjected to further use wear, demonstrated by slight thread softening of the amber around some of the already damaged through-perforations. Overall the necklace can be classified as very worn.

ID 1496 Wimborne St Giles G8, Dorset

References: Cunnington MSS, iii, 11–12; Annable and Simpson 1964, 407–13; Beck and Shennan 1991, 180 and fig. 11.19, 1.

COMPOSITION

The surviving elements of the necklace comprise nine spacer plates, many of them fragmentary, eleven beads of varying shape and three V-perforated buttons (Figure 7.4.7).

CONTEXT AND ASSOCIATIONS

Finds of amber were made within both tumps of a twin disc barrow. According to Cunnington (Cunnington MSS, iii, 11–12) the north-west tump produced about 100 beads and a Series 7 knife (ID 1497), while further amber items and an Aldbourne Cup were found in the eastern tump. The spacer plates and beads from the two tumps cannot now be separated. Surviving in the museum are nine spacer plates, or fragments thereof, and eleven beads. Of the nine spacer plates illustrated by Beck and Shennan, one is now broken into two pieces, and one could not be located. Also boxed as coming from Wimborne St Giles are three broken V-perforated buttons. These are illustrated by Beck and Shennan as having derived from Wimborne St Giles G6 (*ibid*, fig. 11.19.4), but previous records indicate that the amber items from that barrow are lost (Piggott 1938, 102; Grinsell 1959, 169). Although the provenance of these buttons is not proven, they are included in this entry for the sake of completeness.

MORPHOLOGY

All the surviving plates appear to have possessed three through-bored perforations originally (Appendix VII, Table 19). The two well-preserved plates (1 and 2), and a third large fragment (not seen), are neatly formed rectangular blocks measuring 32.0 by 21mm with slightly tapered edges; they are on average 6.0mm thick. The three through-perforations are widely spaced, but with the two outer ones placed fairly near to the inner and outer margins of the plate. Both inner and outer margins are gently curved to a similar degree. Between the through-perforations there are very deeply pierced V-perforations, which would have formed a visible decorative geometric design when the plates were freshly made (see Figure 7.4.8). One piece (plate 8), of roughly triangular shape and with angled perforations, would definitely have functioned as a terminal plate, and the five other fragments, probably from a total of four other plates, which also display non-parallel through-perforations, may have come from terminal plates, or other tapering plates from the side areas of a necklace. All these pieces were also decorated with V-perforations between the through-perforations, but these V-perforations are much narrower, and less deep than those present on the rectangular plates. All were also rather thinner, with thicknesses ranging between 4.4 and 4.8mm. The perforations in all cases were very fine and neatly bored, ranging in diameter from 1.3mm to about 1.9mm when originally executed.

The beads are shown in Figure 7.4.7j. All three fusiform beads are medium plump in form and are fairly standardised in size, measuring 12.5 by 7.2mm, 12.2 by 7.5mm and 11.8 by 7.1mm. The diameters of the perforations range from 2.3 to 2.5mm (for example, see Figure 7.4.7m). One globular bead is truly spherical, with a maximum diameter of 8.9mm and perforation diameter of 1.9mm (Figure 7.4.7k). The other seven beads are of squashed globular form. All are slightly elongated with the perforated sides distinctly flattened. Their diameters range from 6.1 to 9.1mm and thickness (perforation to perforation) varies from 2.8 to 5.5mm. The diameters of the perforations range between 1.5 and 2.1mm. The largest is shown on Figure 7.4.7n and the smallest on Figure 7.4.7l. The three V-perforated buttons have oval bases, but due to damage none of the base dimensions could be measured (not illustrated). The dome heights range from low (7.2mm) to high (9.9mm). The boreholes for the basal V-perforations are fairly closely spaced and vary in diameter from 1.5 to 2.8mm.

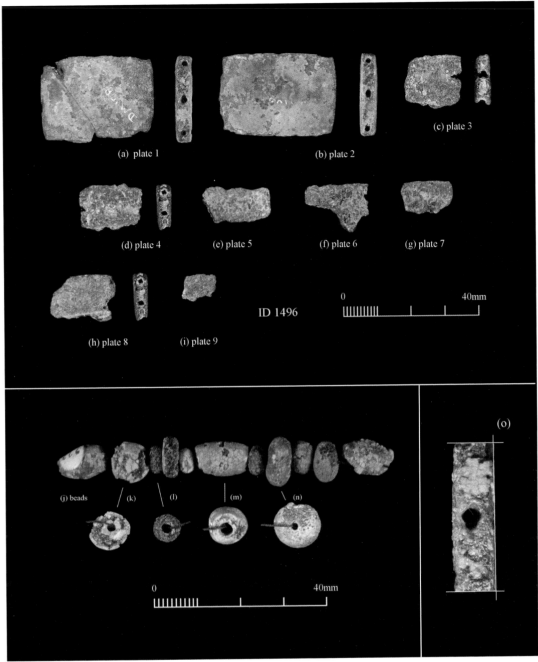

Figure 7.4.7. ID 1496 Wimborne St Giles G8 showing: (a) plate 1; (b) plate 2; (c) plate 3; (d) plate 4; (e) plate 5; (f) plate 6; (g) plate 7; (h) plate 8; (i) plate 9; (j) strung beads; (k) profile of globular bead; (l) profile of smallest squashed globular bead; (m) profile of fusiform bead; (n) profile of largest squashed globular bead; (o) thread-wear on plate 1.

MATERIAL

Most of the plates are of bright orange amber, but plate numbers 5 and 7 are darker orange in colour. The various beads also vary in colour. They range from light orange (one fusiform, one squashed globular) to dark orange (one fusiform, the globular bead and three squashed globulars), bright red (one fusiform) and dark red (one squashed globular). Two further squashed globular beads were completely oxidised, and the original colour of the amber

could not be deduced. Of the V-perforated buttons, two were originally bright red, and one of them dark red in colour.

MANUFACTURE

No traces of polishing striations or other evidence for manufacture could be detected on any of the components. The perforations within the spacer and terminal plates were studied under the microscope but no traces of rilling were evident. Any details of the perforations within the beads

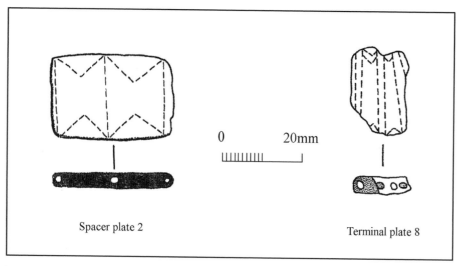

Figure 7.4.8. ID 1496 Wimborne St Giles G8 showing details of perforations and borings in plates (after Beck and Shennan 1991; drawing by Peter Woodward).

could not be examined as they have been strung in modern times and could not be viewed under the microscope.

COMPLETENESS AND DAMAGE

The surfaces of the spacer and terminal plates are all oxidised to a yellowy-cream colour, especially within the cracks. Most of the beads and buttons have extensive oxidisation of dark cream or light brown hue. The degree of completeness of most of the plate fragments cannot be determined, but the three rectangular spacers viewed survive at the 95% and 100% levels. The fusiform beads are 70% to 90% complete while most of the globular beads survive at the 90% to 100% level, with only one squashed globular at the 70% level. The V-perforated buttons display greater damage and survive only at the 35%, 40% and 50% levels. Spacer plate 2 is complete, but plate 1 has broken right across and is now glued together. There are missing fragments adjacent to this break, which appears to be modern. The other plate fragments are all broken along three or four or their margins, and the age of the breaks is indeterminate. Most of the beads display chips, especially at the ends, but whether such damage was ancient or more recent could not be determined. However, the major damage to the buttons appears to be recent in origin.

WEAR

The general level of wear on the plates and beads is summarised in Table 7.4.2. As discussed above, it was not possible to determine whether any of the breaks observed on the plates or beads were ancient. Due to the degree of oxidation it was not possible to detect any signs of ancient wear on the surfaces of the plates. However, one instance of thread-wear was noted, at either end of the central perforation of plate 1 (Figure 7.4.7o). Any wear traces on the fusiform and spherical globular beads were

obscured by oxidation products, but two of the squashed globular beads have evidence of thread-wear within one perforation. The bases of the V-perforated buttons are less oxidised and wear was visible in the form of smoothing around the outer edges of all the perforations. This wear was categorised as slight.

CONCLUSIONS

The plates form two distinct groups, in terms of their general morphology and thickness. They may derive from two different necklaces, one employing the rectangular plates with widely spaced through-bored perforations and the other utilising the plates with the more closely spaced and slightly splayed perforations. The size of the decorative V-perforations also varies between the two groups, with those on the rectangular plates being particularly large. If two such necklaces are represented, both would have had three strands of beads. If all the plates were from a single three-strand necklace the three rectangular plates may have been centrally placed, with at least one pair of trapezoidal plates located between those three and a pair of more triangular-shaped terminal plates. Alternatively the trapezoidal plates may include pairs of terminal plates from two different necklaces. The fusiform beads are fairly uniform in size, shape and original colour and may have been part of an original set. The spherical bead is a singleton, whilst the small group of squashed globular beads are of the form and size of those typically found within spacer plate necklaces. The nature of the wear on the three buttons is typical of 'necklace wear' as defined by Shepherd, and so these elements could well have formed part of a necklace.

The morphology and original colours of the various plates indicates that more than one necklace may be represented. The various sets of beads and buttons may derive from a single necklace, or from two or more original necklaces. As it is not possible to separate the sets of beads that were recovered from the two tumps of the disc barrow, and as many of the original hundred or so beads found are now lost, it is unfortunately not possible to reach any definite conclusion. However the most likely interpretation might be that two spacer plate necklaces are represented, one of which may have been recovered from each tump of the barrow.

7.4.2 OTHER REGIONS

ID 999 Little Cressingham, Norfolk

References: Barton 1852; Piggott 1938, fig. 22; Gerloff 1975, pl. 46.7; Clarke *et al.* 1985, fig. 4.29 and 275–6; Beck and Shennan 1991, fig. 11.8.

COMPOSITION

The surviving 47 amber elements of the necklace comprise nine pestle-shaped pendants and the upper fragment of a tenth example (ID 1117–25A), five annular beads (ID 1112A–C and 1126A–B), four beads of fusiform type (ID 1113–16) and 28 disc beads (ID 1111.1–28) (Figure 7.4.9 and Figure 7.4.10).

CONTEXT AND ASSOCIATIONS

A short time before 1849 a remarkable Bronze Age inhumation grave was found in a field formerly called Hills Field in the parish of Little Cressingham, Norfolk. It was found through chance by a labourer digging in the field but Barton was able to determine that the burial had occupied an off-centre location within a heavily ploughed round barrow (Barton 1852, 1). It may, therefore, have been a secondary interment. The barrow belongs to a group of six barrows and a single ring ditch, located on a slight slope flanking the outer margin of a large meander of the River Blackwater. The body was arranged in a contracted position with head to the south. It is not stated whether the body was lying on its right or left side. The skeleton has not survived, and may well have never been removed from the grave. Barton recorded that the skeleton was that of a male 'of about average height'. The man 'had passed the meridian of life; and his teeth were much worn, but good' (*ibid*, 2). Two daggers (ID 1105 and ID 1106, Figure 3.1.8) were found by his side, and a gold plate (ID 1107, Figure 6.1.2) upon the breast. A piece of decorated gold (ID 1110, Figure 6.1.3) was found on one side, while the locations of the remains of three other items of gold, referred to as 'boxes' (ID 1108A, ID 1108B and ID 1109, Figure 6.1.3), were not recorded in detail. A large number of beads were found scattered about the neck, but many of them were broken. The surviving total of 47 beads and pendants is hardly a 'large number' and so it seems likely that some beads were lost before the group was purchased by the museum in 1950. The objects were illustrated by Barton (1952), Piggott (1938, fig. 22), Gerloff (1975, pl.

46.F) and Beck and Shennan (1991, fig. 11.8), while a set of watercolour paintings, executed by Frederick Sandys not long after the excavation and housed in Norwich Castle Museum, were published by Clarke *et al.* in 1985 (fig. 7.27).

MORPHOLOGY

The ten elongated pendants are drawn in Figure 7.4.10 (excluding the fragmentary example); they are trapezoidal in shape with marked and regular basal bowing. An enlarged example is shown in Figure 7.4.9c. Of oval cross section they are rather wider than deep, and with gently rounded surfaces. They vary in length from 21.6 to 34.5mm, while the maximum width ranges from 15.0 to 22.7mm. They are from 12.0 to 18.5mm thick, from front to back. The lower facets are neatly bevelled and rounded, while the top surfaces are flat, with relatively sharp margins. Each pendant is perforated with a single borehole running from side to side. The top margins of these boreholes are located from 1.0 to 1.8mm below the top surface of the pendant, and the perforations vary in diameter from 1.2 to 3.5mm. The main dimensions are presented in Figure 7.4.11, and this shows that the largest pendant (ID 1117) stands out from the others and may have been located at the centre of the necklace. The two next largest (ID 1118 and ID 1119) form a reasonable pair in terms of size and shape, although the remaining four complete pendants do not form clearly matched pairs. However, overall the gentle grading of pendant size is pleasing to the eye (see Figure 7.4.9).

The four fusiform beads ID 1113–16 (Figure 7.4.9a and Figure 7.4.10) all taper towards their perforated ends, but one is of medium form and three chunky in shape. They are of variable size, ranging from 9.5 to 12.4mm in length and between 6.5 and 8.4mm in average diameter. All four are roughly square or rectangular in cross-section and the perforation diameters range from 2.2 to 4.1mm. The three complete annular beads (ID 1112A, ID 1112B and ID 1112C; Figure 7.4.9b and Figure 7.4.10), and large fragments from at least two more examples, mainly have rounded profiles but one (ID 1112C) has a V-shaped hoop section. They range in diameter from 11.0 to 16mm, and in thickness from 4.0 to 6mm. The diameters of the perforations vary from 5.0 to 8mm. Of the 28 surviving disc beads under the heading of ID 1111, seven numbered examples are illustrated in Figure 7.4.10 and a further seven (unnumbered) in Figure 7.4.9d. They are small flat beads of 6 to 8.5mm maximum diameter and 2.4 to 4mm thick. All possess rectangular profiles with sharply-defined edges. The diameters of the perforations range from 2.0 to 2.6mm but most fall between 2.0 and 2.2mm.

MATERIAL

In all cases, the original colour of the amber employed could be discerned. The pestle pendants and the annular beads are all of dark red amber. Two of the fusiform beads are also dark red, but the other two are dark brown in

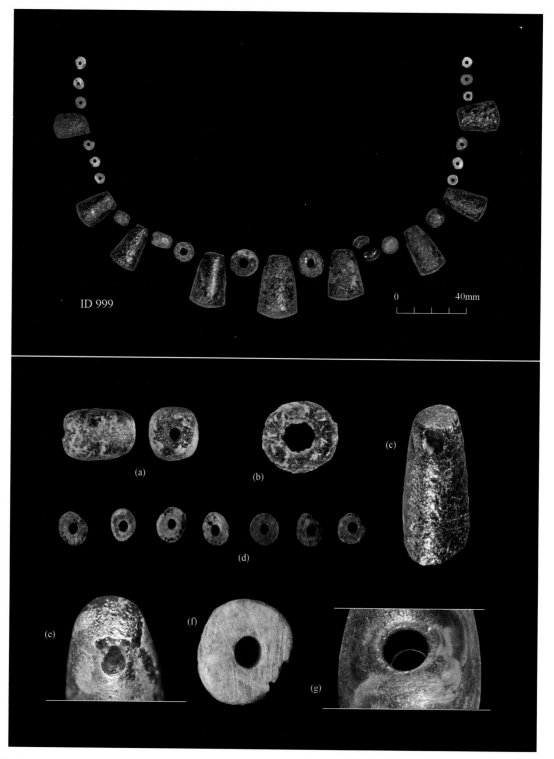

Figure 7.4.9. ID 999 Little Cressingham showing (top) one possible arrangement of necklace and (bottom) details of selected items. Details: (a) ID 1113 fusiform bead; (b) ID 1112A annular bead; (c) ID 1121 pestle pendant; (d) ID 1111 selection of disc beads; (e) ID 1120 pestle pendant showing rilling and thread wear; (f) ID 1111 (no. 11) disc bead showing striations; (g) ID 1115 fusiform bead showing softening of the perforation through use. Note: the items are not to consistent scale.

colour, opaque and grainy. The 28 disc beads are much more variable in original colour. Three only are red, seven orange, six buff, six orange to buff, three red to buff and three orange to red.

MANUFACTURE

In many cases no traces of manufacture survived or these had been obscured by oxidisation of the surfaces. However in one instance, the interior of the borehole of a pestle

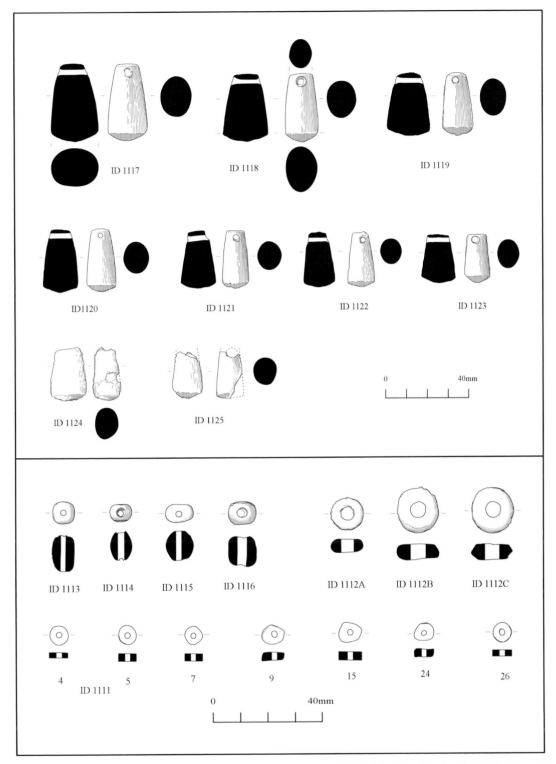

Figure 7.4.10. ID 999 Little Cressingham: ID 1117–25 pestle pendants; ID 1113–16 fusiform beads; ID 1112A–C annular beads; ID 1111, selection of disc beads. Drawings by Henry Buglass.

pendant displays traces of rilling (Figure 7.4.9e). The boreholes of five pestle pendants showed evidence, in the form of internal ridges or ledges, that the holes had been bored from both sides. There is evidence that one of the fusiform beads had also been perforated from both ends.

Many of the disc beads have surviving saw marks and/or polishing striations on their flat upper and/or lower surfaces. Most of these striations are unidirectional and marked and are present on one (seven beads) or both faces (a further seven beads). In four cases marked multidirectional

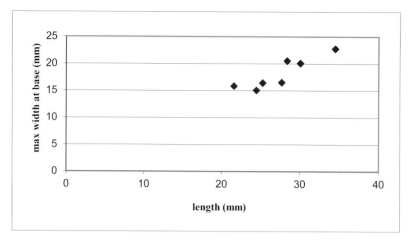

Figure 7.4.11. ID 999 Little Cressingham. Whole pestle pendants: major dimensions.

striations are present on one side (Figure 7.4.3f), and there are single further instances of faint unidirectional striations and a combination of unidirectional and multidirectional marks. All the disc beads are neatly made with the perforations often bored from one side only such that in section the boreholes are sometimes slightly funnel-shaped (17 examples). Others, with straight boreholes may have been bored from both sides, as undoubtedly were five examples with a perforation of hourglass section.

COMPLETENESS AND DAMAGE

Most of the items display traces of oxidised surfaces which are mainly buff in colour. In April 1984, presumably in preparation for the loan to the *Symbols of Power* exhibition at the then named National Museum of Antiquities of Scotland in Edinburgh, the amber necklace was consolidated for display (Norfolk Museum Service Conservation Department records). This was necessary as the surfaces of the amber items were 'very sugary and rapidly being lost'. Most of the pestle pendants are complete, but one survives only at the 90% level and two are fragments (60% and 10% only surviving). There are three complete annular beads and *c.* 25% of two others. Two fusiform beads are complete, with the others surviving at the 90% and 95% levels. Only one of the disc beads survives completely undamaged. However eleven are 90% present or more. Seven survive at the 80% to 85% level, and another seven at the 70% to 75% level. Only one bead is severely broken with only 50% surviving. Only one of the pestle pendants, the 10% top fragment, appears to have been damaged in modern times. The age of the breaks relating to the damaged annular beads cannot be determined, but two of the fusiform beads display modern chips or flaking. Much of the damage to the disc beads appears to be modern. This comprises chips to the outer edges in 18 cases and occasional damage to the edge of the perforation or one of the flat surfaces.

WEAR

The general level of wear on the plates and beads is summarised in Table 7.4.2. The top and rear of one of the pestle pendants (ID 1125) were apparently damaged in antiquity, and one of the complete pendants has an ancient chip next to one of the perforations. Evidence for wear mainly consists of thread-wear. This is always located at the top edge of the perforations, is moderate or heavy, and may occur in one or both of the perforations (see ID 1120, Figure 7.4.9e). As a result seven pendants are classed as worn and three as slightly worn. The fusiform beads have no ancient breaks, but in all four cases the edges of one or both of the perforations have been softened through use (see ID 1115, Figure 7.4.9g). They are classified as slightly worn. The annular beads also display no evidence of ancient breaks; the edges of the perforations are slightly sharper, but again they are categorised as slightly worn. Nine out of the 28 disc beads appear to have been damaged in antiquity. Six have old chips on outer edges and three have flakes missing from the outer sides. Where the condition of the edges of the perforations could be assessed, 12 beads have sharp edges with no signs of wear, 11 show some softening and three display distinct softening around one of the perforations only. Where overall condition could be determined most of the beads (23) seem to be in fresh condition, and three slightly worn.

CONCLUSIONS

The cultural context of the grave group, and its importance within the Early Bronze Age of Britain, was emphasised by Piggott who marked it out as one of the key graves belonging to the extension of his newly defined 'Wessex Culture' in the regions beyond Wessex itself (Piggott 1938, 92–3 and fig. 22). However the composition of the necklace is unusual and, in the absence of any spacer plates, V-perforated buttons or any squashed globular beads of the kind typically found within the amber spacer plate necklaces, it cannot be compared directly with the other three examples described in this section. The only strong parallel is between the graduated set of pestle pendants and the members of one or two similar sets within the assemblage from Wilsford-cum-Lake G47, 49 or 50 (ID 1360, see above). The large annular beads are unusual and the overall collection of beads of varying shape and size is notable. The original record of a 'large number' of beads does suggest that many items may have been lost, but it seems likely that most of the more substantial items have survived and it may have been further small disc beads that have disappeared.

The grouping of small numbers of beads of varying styles indicates that the different sets of beads and pendants may originally have derived from various previous necklaces and may have been obtained from different sources. This suggestion is further reinforced by the result of our detailed study of the materials employed and traces of use wear detected. The pestle pendants and annular beads are made from very uniform dark red amber. The materials used for the fusiform beads are either red or grainy brown, and the disc beads display a very wide range of colours and colour combinations. This may suggest that the different groups of beads were made from different sets of material, and possibly by different craftspeople. A further contrast is provided by the use-wear data. The pendants and larger beads all display signs of slight or moderate wear, but many of the disc beads appear to be in fresh or almost fresh condition. It would seem that the fine set of pestle pendants, and perhaps the large annular beads, was supplemented by small numbers of fusiform beads from one or more other sources, and finally strung in association with a large set of small, and possibly newly manufactured, disc beads.

As noted by Taylor (1980, 45) the small concentration of rich 'Wessex' finds in Norfolk may be related to the occurrence of amber washed up on the northern East Anglian shores. However this cannot be proved (Lawson 1984, 153) and it may be that all the amber used to produce ornaments in the Early Bronze Age of Britain may have been imported from the Baltic region.

7.4.3 GENERAL DISCUSSION (with Alison Sheridan)

Four amber necklaces were studied in detail: the spacer plate necklaces from Upton Lovell G2e, Wilsford-cum-Lake and Wimborne St Giles G8, all in Wessex, and the single-strand necklace featuring pestle-shaped and other amber beads from Little Cressingham, Norfolk. These constitute all the surviving necklaces from Wessex and East Anglia that comprise a relatively large number of components. This section will refer to some other finds of amber necklaces from England, including examples which are lost and known only from antiquarian descriptions, and also a recently-found spacer plate necklace from Shaw Cairn, Greater Manchester, which pre-dates the Wessex amber spacer plate necklaces (Sheridan 2010a; Hearle

2011). The main necklaces that feature in the discussion are listed in Table 7.4.3.

CONTEXTS, DATING AND ASSOCIATIONS

The four necklaces studied in detail all derive from burial contexts which were excavated by antiquaries during the first half of the 19th century, and uncertainties regarding details of context and association surround three of these. Of the two necklaces excavated by Cunnington, both associated with cremated remains, one (ID 1444 Upton Lovell G2e) comes from a bowl barrow that he excavated in 1803 and also in 1807, and it is unclear whether the finds from those two investigations, discovered close to each other, had come from one or two secondary graves (see Chapter 7.4 above). The components of the other necklace excavated by Cunnington (ID 1496 Wimborne St Giles G8) had been associated with primary deposits of cremated remains within both tumps of a disc barrow; unfortunately it is not possible to separate the finds from the two tumps. Uncertainty also surrounds the context details of the necklace components from a bowl barrow at Lake (ID 1360). Excavated by Reverend Duke in 1806, the objects were probably found with an inhumation that may have been primary, but the context details are not secure; indeed, it is not known whether the barrow was barrow G47, G49 or G50, and there is even a possibility that finds from two graves had been mixed together. However, the Little Cressingham necklace was found with a relatively well-recorded primary or secondary crouched inhumation, whose sex was reported to be male (see below).

While none of these four necklaces has been associated with a radiocarbon date, all can arguably be attributed to the first quarter of the second millennium BC (as regards both their manufacture and their deposition). The grave good assemblages of which they form a part belong within the Wessex 1 series of rich graves, and although there is only one radiocarbon date for a Wessex 1 grave within Wessex itself – from a tree-trunk coffin at West Overton (Needham *et al.* 2010) – a vital clue to the date of the spacer plate necklaces comes from the Knowes of Trotty, Orkney. Here, fragments of an old, worn amber spacer plate necklace of identical type to the southern English examples (and almost certainly acquired in Wessex) have been associated with a radiocarbon date of 2030–1770 cal BC (at 95.4% probability; see Chapter 9) obtained from the associated cremated bone. Such a date is closely comparable with that obtained for the Wessex 1 grave at West Overton (SUERC-26203 (GU-19959), 2020–1770 cal BC at 95.4% probability, from unburnt human bone). It is also comparable with the date of 3625±35 BP (SUERC-33965, 2130–1890 cal BC at 95.4% probability, from unburnt human bone) recently obtained from a Wessex 1 grave containing a Series 3A Armorico-British dagger at Cockley Cley, Norfolk (Sheridan *et al.* 2010); and among the other dates relevant to the dating of the Wessex 1 series of rich graves are the two obtained from cremated bone at Breach Farm, Glamorgan, where four bronze axeheads of the same type as the one found at West Overton, Bush Barrow and Ridgeway 7 were among the grave goods: 3520±60 BP (GrA-19964) and 3530±60 BP (GrA-20601), both calibrating to 2030–1690 cal BC at 95.4% probability. As for the date of the Little Cressingham grave, this is informed by the presence of the Series 4A Armorico-British dagger. To judge from the available dating evidence for this dagger type, the currency for its use lies between *c.* 1950 and 1750/1700 BC (see Chapter 3.1), but a date towards the beginning of this range is perhaps suggested by the sharing of amber pestle-shaped pendants with the Lake assemblage (although see above for reservations about the Lake material).

As for the sex of the individuals associated with these necklaces, this has only been determined in one case (Little Cressingham). The 19th-century identification of a man was probably correct, to judge from associations elsewhere with daggers. As for the others, there is a reasonable likelihood, on the basis of sexed graves elsewhere, that they had been female (Garwood 2011 *cf* Gerloff 1975); the only way to check would be to re-excavate the graves in question. All the studied necklaces come from richly-furnished graves, with those from Lake, Upton Lovell and Little Cressingham containing fine gold objects belonging to the sheet gold-cover tradition. The presence of a Series 4A bronze-bladed dagger in the Little Cressingham grave has already been noted; in addition there was a smaller-bladed object, either a small dagger or (more probably) a knife. Similar Series 7 blades were found in the Wimborne St Giles G8 grave and at Upton Lovell; this type of object has been found in both male and female graves (Needham pers. comm.). The presence of awls at Lake and Upton Lovell G2e (1807 find) lends support to the suggestion that these had probably been female graves, since the dominant sex association of this artefact type in Early Bronze Age graves is female (see Chapter 4.6 and Chapter 11). As for ceramic associations, the uncertainty as to whether the Collared Urn and the probable accessory vessel found inside it at Upton Lovell in 1807 belonged to the same grave as the 1803 finds has already been mentioned. However, the grape cup from Upton Lovell was associated with the spacer plate necklace. Other accessory vessels are associated with the necklaces from Lake and Wimborne St Giles G8, with the Aldbourne Cup from the latter site being found in the eastern tump of this twin-tump disc barrow. Two accessory vessels were reportedly found in the Lake grave.

These four necklaces belong to the heyday of amber use in Britain. Amber had been used, in a minor way, from as early as the Early to Middle Neolithic (e.g. at Greenbrae, Aberdeenshire: Clarke *et al.* 1985, fig. 3.38) but, with the sole exception of the aforementioned necklace from Shaw Cairn, amber does not appear to have been used in appreciable amounts until the beginning of the second millennium BC. The upswing in amber use at this time relates to the strategies used by the elites of southern England, particularly Wessex, to outdo elites elsewhere in their conspicuous consumption of precious and special materials. Using raw amber that appears to have been imported directly from

Denmark (where artefactual evidence, including an imported segmented faience bead, exists for links with Wessex), the elite in Wessex used specialist craftworkers to create spacer plate necklaces that were bigger and 'better' than the pre-existing spacer plate necklaces of jet and jet-like materials that had been particularly popular in northern Britain for the previous one to two centuries. These amber necklaces have spacer plates that are generally larger than most of the jet examples, and the largest examples contained many more beads than their counterparts in jet – even allowing for a degree of hyperbole in Hoare's estimate of the original number of beads in the Upton Lovell G2e necklace. (For statistics, see Table 7.4.3 and note that since, in some excavation records, it is noted that many small beads were lost at the time of recovery, we are undoubtedly missing large numbers of the beads that would have been strung between the spacers within the necklaces). It should be noted, however, that the Shaw Cairn amber spacer plate necklace does not belong to this Wessex 1 series necklace group, but instead is an earlier creation, contemporary with the late third millennium Early Bronze Age *floruit* of jet/jet-like spacer plate necklace manufacturing and constituting a faithful replica of one variant of that type of necklace in northern England. (It had rectangular spacer plates and was a two-strand necklace, featuring both fusiform and disc-shaped beads). Having probably been buried on an unburnt body, represented only by a stain on the floor of the cist, it is associated with a radiocarbon date of 2190–1940 cal BC at 95.4% probability (see Chapter 9). As there is no evidence for direct links to Scandinavia at this time, the amber used to make this necklace is arguably more likely to have been collected from the East Anglian (or possibly Yorkshire) coast than to have been imported from Denmark.

As for the amber jewellery whose manufacture dates to the first quarter of the second millennium, Wessex-style spacer plate necklaces, and re-used components thereof, are known from a handful of findspots, some far-flung (as at the Knowes of Trotty in Orkney, Mold in north Wales (in the form of beads that probably derive from one such necklace), Exloo in the Netherlands (likewise, as beads), and even the Shaft Graves of Mycenae (Sheridan *et al.* 2003; Needham 2012; Haveman and Sheridan 2006; Harding 1984, 68–79). Within Wessex, the lost spacer plate necklace from Kingston Deverill barrow G5, Wiltshire (Hoare 1812, plate III) comprised over 50 components when deposited, while the lost example from Amesbury barrow G44, Wiltshire (Stukeley 1740, 44, tab. xxxii) may have been a composite necklace, since the amber spacer plates were reportedly found alongside beads of faience and shale (see Table 8.6.2). Both these examples were associated with cremated remains, the latter within a Collared Urn and associated with a bronze awl and a 'knife-dagger'; the sex of the deceased is assumed to be female. The amber spacer plates and beads from Amesbury G44 may have been reused from an earlier spacer plate necklace. At Beaulieu (VI, Hampshire) and Radwell (I, Bedfordshire), we are probably dealing with further examples of reused components from spacer plate necklaces. The former, which

Table 7.4.3. List of components of amber spacer plate and other necklaces featuring relatively large amounts of amber (ID 999 Little Cressingham; ID 1360 Wilsford-cum-Lake; ID 1444 Upton Lovell G2e Golden Barrow; ID 1496 Wimborne St Giles G8).

ID no. or site	Pestle pend-ants	Plates	Butt-ons	Fusi. beads	Disc beads	Glob. beads	Squashed glob. beads	Ann. beads	Fastener	Est. max. no. of strands
ID 999	10	-	-	4	28	-	-	5	-	1
ID 1360	10	11	10	17	-	37	12	4	1	10 then 2
ID 1444	-	6	-	8	-	3	334	5	-	9+ then 5
ID 1496	-	9	3	3	-	1	7	-	-	3
Shaw Cairn	-	2	-	14	65+	-	-	-	1	2
Kingston Deverill G5	-	6	2	>40 beads, various forms					-	>6
Amesbury G44	-	3+	-	1+	-	1+	4+	-	-	?
Radwell I	1	1 or more	1	12+	-	-	-	-	-	?3
Beaulieu VI	-	1	-	-	-	21	-	-	-	1 or 2
Whitehill Road	-	-	-	-	21	-	-	-	-	1
Boscombe Down	-	-	-	-	90	-	-	-	-	1

was probably associated with an unburnt body, featured a fragment of a spacer plate, together with 21 beads that had almost certainly originated in a large, Wessex-style spacer plate necklace (Piggott 1943, fig. 10 and pl. 7), while the latter, found with the cremated remains of two individuals, possibly a man and a woman, was a composite necklace (Hall and Woodward 1977). As at Beaulieu, the amber spacer plate (or plates) consisted only of fragments; these fragments were associated with at least 12 fusiform beads, one pestle-shaped pendant and one 'button' of amber, plus a spacer plate, around 15 fusiform beads and around 94 disc beads of jet or jet-like material. The cremated bones have not been radiocarbon dated, although a date within the 1900–1600 BC range is suspected.

The Little Cressingham necklace illustrates the fact that not all the early second millennium amber jewellery consisted of spacer plate necklaces; see Beck and Shennan 1991 for a review of other types of Early (and Middle) Bronze Age amber jewellery, and see below for discussion of the various bead forms in use (note that this discussion does not purport to be an exhaustive review of all the amber in use during the first half of the second millennium BC). Amber disc beads, of the kind seen in the Little Cressingham necklace (and in smaller versions), are known to have been used both for disc-bead necklaces and in composite necklaces, with the currency extending into the second quarter of the second millennium. A probable necklace of tiny amber disc beads from Boscombe Down, Wiltshire, associated with the unburnt remains of a 14 to

15 year old juvenile, possibly male, has been radiocarbon-dated to 3225±25 BP (NZA-32497, 1610–1430 cal BC at 95.4% probability; Barclay 2010), while a necklace comprising 20 disc beads plus a 'circular bead with lentoid cross-section' found at Whitehill Road, Kent, is associated with a radiocarbon date of 3273±30 BP (NZA-22740, 1630–1460 cal BC at 95.4% probability (Garwood 2011, fig. 3.60 and 144). This was associated with the flexed skeleton of an adult, probably female, under a round barrow. Examples of tiny disc beads (and/or of fusiform beads) of amber from composite necklaces include the recently-discovered example from Whitehorse Hill, Devon (featuring both bead shapes, plus a further shape in amber), radiocarbon-dated to *c.* 1900–1700 BC (Jones forthcoming) and one from Solstice Park, Amesbury, Wiltshire (featuring both bead shapes plus a plano-convex bead and three V-perforated 'buttons'), radiocarbon-dated to 1620–1430 cal BC at 95.4% probability (Sheridan forthcoming b; and see Chapter 9). Both these examples were associated with cremated remains, the latter of indeterminate sex, the former currently being analysed.

One final example of a necklace with amber beads to be discussed here is that found with cremated bones, in a decorated cinerary urn, at South Chard, Tatworth, Somerset (Gray 1917, 116). This comprises 30 beads, squashed-spherical and oval in plan, and including examples that are biconvex and hexagonal in section. With lengths ranging between 15 and 24mm these are much larger than any of the truly globular beads associated with the spacer plate necklaces, and the style of the urn would indicate a date within the Middle Bronze Age.

COMPOSITION VARIATION

Overall design

The occurrence of the various plate and bead types in the four amber necklaces studied in detail, and within the other amber necklaces from England discussed above, is listed in Table 7.4.3, and the components are discussed further below. The Wessex-style amber spacer plate necklaces, when complete, comprised several sets of plates (including a pair of terminal plates), together with a variable number of beads, mostly of squashed globular form. Fusiform beads also occur, albeit in relatively small numbers, and other bead forms sometimes incorporated in these necklaces are globular beads of true spherical shape, and annular or ring-shaped beads. Pestle-shaped pendants of amber are among the 'Lake' assemblage at the British Museum but, as noted above, it is unclear whether they had originally formed part of the spacer plate necklace, or belonged to a different necklace from a separate grave. Pestle-shaped amber pendants also are present in composite necklaces at Radwell and Wilsford G8 (see below), but the former clearly features re-used components from older necklaces, so one cannot say whether these pendants were ever part of the original composition of the Wessex-style amber spacer plate necklaces. Tubular sheet gold beads formed part of the funerary assemblage at Upton Lovell G2e (Figure 6.1.7), but it is not known whether they had formed part of the amber necklace, or had been a separate, all-gold second necklace; the latter remains a distinct possibility. Disc beads are not found in Wessex-type amber spacer plate necklaces, although they do occur in the earlier, non-Wessex type spacer plate necklace from Shaw Cairn. The number of strings of beads in the Wessex-type spacer plate necklaces seems to vary widely, although the incompleteness of the spacer plates makes exact calculation of the number of strands difficult. (See Table 7.4.3 final column). This is discussed further below. As for the non-spacer plate type necklaces discussed above, pestle-shaped pendants are an important element of the Little Cressingham necklace, along with chunky disc beads, while necklaces made entirely or mainly of the latter type of amber bead are known (e.g. from Boscombe Down). The following sections will review each of the elements represented in the four analysed necklaces.

Plates

If one sets to one side the necklace from Shaw Cairn which, as noted above, pre-dates and does not belong to the Wessex series of amber spacer plate necklaces, the relationship between the plates in the 'jet' series and the 'Wessex amber' series can generally be portrayed as one of aggrandisement. The Wessex amber plates tend to be significantly wider (up to 77mm wide), and some have a much larger number of boreholes, than their 'jet' ancestors. However, whether all the boreholes had been used to support bead strands is a question that will be considered below. The ancestry of the

Wessex amber plates in the 'jet' plates seems clear, with the trapezoidal shape of the plates in the necklaces from Lake (Figure 7.4.1 and Figure 7.4.2) and from Kingston Deverill G5 (Hoare 1812, pl. III) echoing the commonest shape of 'jet' plates. The more rectangular shape of the plates in the necklaces from Upton Lovell G2e (Figure 7.4.4 and Figure 7.4.5), Amesbury G44 (Stukeley 1740, tab. xxxii) and Wimborne St Giles G8 (Figure 7.4.7 and Figure 7.4.8) is a feature that can be paralleled among a few 'jet' spacer plate necklaces (e.g. ID 264/265 NW of Pickering, Figure 7.2.16, which is particularly similar to the Wimborne St Giles G8 rectangular examples). Similarly, the presence, at Lake, of a larger number of plates than the usual set of six (i.e. two terminal plates plus two pairs of spacer plates) can be paralleled in the jet necklace from Middleton-on-the-Wolds, East Riding of Yorkshire (ID 249, Figure 7.2.3). Whether the presence of a set of smaller plates among the Lake material indicates that we are dealing with a necklace-plus-bracelet 'parure', analogous to that seen in a few jet examples (e.g. at East Kinwhirrie, Angus, Scotland: Sheridan 1998), or is the result of the aforementioned possible mixing of material from more than one grave, is unclear.

The question of how many strands were involved in the Wessex-style necklaces is not always easy to determine, partly due to the poor current state of the plates and partly because it is uncertain whether all the perforations had supported strands of beads. Since the amber would have been translucent when new, there would have been a strong decorative element to the perforations, as is clear, for example, from the V-perforations running between (and joining with) the through-perforations on the necklaces from Upton Lovell G2e and Wimborne St Giles G8. With the Lake necklace, the six large spacer plates have variable numbers of V-perforations at their edges, running between two through-perforations, and it is unclear whether any of these V-perforations had been anything other than decorative. However, since the terminal plates each have five through-bored perforations, then unless these were mostly decorative, they imply that at least part of the necklace possessed more than two strands. Also some wear evidence, discussed in detail above (Chapter 7.4.1), does indicate that all five perforations in the terminal plates were strung, and that at least some of the V-perforations may have supported strings of beads at some stage in the life of the necklace. If all of the V-perforations had accommodated bead strands then the maximum possible number of strands in this necklace would have been ten. Wear evidence also indicates that the marginal through-perforations had been subjected to long use and it is possible that the necklace went through at least two different design histories. Firstly a multi-strand version may have included up to ten strands of beads, using both the through-perforations and the V-perforations as string attachments, while at a later stage, when the V-perforations had broken out, a two-strand necklace may have been supported within the marginal through-perforations only. The Upton Lovell G2e necklace also appears to have been in use for a long period of time.

It may have started off as a multi-strand necklace with strands of beads supported by spacer plates with up to 9 (or more) through-perforations. Following breakage of the plates along the lines of some of the through-perforations, and damage to the perforated margins, further wear around the perforations suggests that the now smaller plates were used to support a probably five-strand necklace. With other necklaces, however, the number of strands is smaller. The Wimborne St Giles G8 necklace, or necklaces, seems to have had only three, while the smaller plates from Lake, possibly belonging to a bracelet, each have four.

The use of perforations as a form of decoration differentiates the Wessex amber spacer plates from their earlier 'jet' counterparts, and this difference is undoubtedly due to the fact that amber is translucent, whereas 'jet' is not. With the 'jet' spacer plate necklaces, the complex Y-borings seen in some plates had been functional, as a means of increasing the number of strands running through this opaque material; decoration was achieved by drilling punctulated designs into their outer surface, or else selectively dulling that surface (as with the two Cow Low necklaces, ID 266–7, Figure 7.2.4 and Figure 7.2.5). The style of decoration seen on the amber plates is specific to Wessex, and the design, known as the 'basic pattern', proved highly popular, with examples having been exchanged or traded into Europe, with a few travelling as far as Greece (Harding and Hughes-Brock 1974; Woodward 2002, 1044–5).

Before leaving plates, it should be noted that one object published as a fragment of an amber spacer plate, from Heathrow Terminal 5 runway, is in fact not a spacer plate at all, but rather part of a skeuomorph of the sheet gold lozenges as seen, for example, at Bush Barrow and as copied in jet at Carlton Colville, Suffolk (Sheridan 2010b).

Globular and squashed globular beads

Globular beads are the commonest element of the Wessex-style amber spacer plate necklaces, occurring in two distinct styles. The more numerous type comprises small beads with flattened, perforated sides, designed to sit snugly together in the rows of beads strung between spacer plates. The largest surviving set comes from Upton Lovell G2e, but they are also present at Lake and at Wimborne St Giles G8. In addition they occur as heirloom elements within various composite necklaces, as will be described in Chapter 8. These squashed globular beads range in length (i.e. from one end of the perforation to the other) from 2.5 to 8.0mm and have perforation diameters ranging between 1.5 and 2.7mm. The other style of globular beads represented in the amber necklaces comprises those of truly spherical shape. These are much larger than the squashed globular beads, with diameters ranging between 8.9 and 17.1mm, but the boreholes are still relatively narrow, with diameters of 1.5 to 2.0mm. These larger globular beads are present in the surviving sets of beads from all three of the Wessex amber spacer plate necklaces studied, and at Lake there are a large number (37 extant). This suggests that these necklaces may have included some strings of these larger beads among the strings of squashed globulars. Alternatively the larger globular beads may have been strung separately as a smaller necklace that fitted above the spacer plate necklace.

A necklace formed mainly from roughly spherical beads was found near the centre of a barrow at Beaulieu, Hampshire (Piggott 1943, pl. VII). The globular beads, which were associated with a fragment of an amber spacer plate, range in diameter from *c.* 8.0 to 18mm, so are similar in size to the groups of truly globular beads from the necklaces studied in detail above. A group of 30 beads varying in diameter from 7.5 to 30mm was found at South Chard, Tatworth, Somerset (Gray 1917, 116). These larger beads are flatter in form and some have bi-convex or hexagonal cross-sections. Associated with a decorated urn, this necklace is likely to be Middle Bronze Age in date. The largest bead in the necklace from Whitehill Road, Kent is of a similar flattened form, and this necklace also has a relatively late date (see above).

Fusiform beads

All of the amber necklaces studied include small numbers of fusiform beads. They occur in various forms: mostly medium-plump, but plump and slender examples are also in evidence. They vary in length from 9.5 to 23.5mm, with boreholes 1.5 to 4.1mm in diameter. The size ranges are similar within all the necklaces except that some larger examples are present at Upton Lovell G2e. The fusiform beads in the earlier Shaw Cairn amber necklace also fall within a similar size range. At Lake some of the beads have squared-off ends, some of which are angled, while at Little Cressingham all four beads display markedly square or rectangular cross sections. Such features echo the range of shapes of fusiform bead found in the jet and jet-like spacer plate necklaces, with various beads designed specifically to fit within different areas in relation to the plates, or within different strands of the necklace. As so few amber necklaces have been recovered by excavation, it seems necessary to consider whether any of the amber spacer plate necklaces might originally have included strands of fusiform beads, similar to those characteristic of the jet and jet-like necklaces. The small numbers of fusiform beads that are present in the amber necklaces from Lake, Upton Lovell G2e and Wimborne St Giles G8 may have been remnants from one or more such hypothetical necklaces, or they may just have been copies of jet or jet-like beads which were employed in small numbers. The amber fusiform beads may have been included as one or more strands within the amber necklaces or, as was suggested for the large truly globular beads, they may have been strung separately as an additional single-strand necklace that could be worn in conjunction with the spacer plate necklace.

Annular beads

Like the pestle-shaped pendants, annular beads do not occur in jet and jet-like spacer plate necklaces. They have been found in small numbers within the Lake, Upton Lovell G2e and Little Cressingham necklaces. In terms of size they are not standardised, with those from Upton Lovell G2e being the smallest (diameter 5.5mm), the Little Cressingham ones the largest (diameters 11 to 16mm) and those from Lake falling in between. The size of the hole also varies considerably, with diameters ranging from 3 to 8mm.

Disc beads
Disc beads do not occur within the Wessex-style amber spacer plate necklaces, but are well represented within the necklace from Little Cressingham. They also form a major component within the earlier necklace from Shaw Cairn. The Little Cressingham disc beads range in diameter from 6.0 to 8.5mm, while those from Shaw Cairn show a slightly larger size range with diameters between 5.8 and 10.1mm. The Little Cressingham examples are slightly thicker, but the borehole diameters (*c.* 2.0 to 2.6mm) are similar within both necklaces. Amber disc beads constitute the sole component of the recently-excavated necklace from Boscombe Down. The 90 constituent chunky beads are smaller than those from Little Cressingham or Shaw Cairn, with diameters ranging from 3.4 to 5.2mm (Barclay and Sheridan pers. comm.). These belong to the tradition of tiny disc beads that appeared during the mid to late third millennium BC (see the example from Devil's Dyke, in jet: ID 434, Figure 7.1.12). As noted above, the tradition was long-lived, with various occurrences of amber disc beads occurring within composite necklaces of the later Early Bronze Age. The best examples which include large numbers of amber disc beads are those from Shrewton G5J (see Chapter 8.3 and Green and Rollo-Smith 1984, fig. 28) and Easton Down, Hampshire (Fasham *et al.* 1989, fig. 103). The Boscombe Down burial is dated by radiocarbon to the early phase of the Middle Bronze Age (see above), and another disc bead necklace of comparable date is that from Whitehill Road, Kent, which includes 21 or more disc beads ranging from 8 to 12mm in diameter (Garwood 2011, fig. 3.60).

Pestle-shaped pendants
The pestle-shaped pendants from Lake and Little Cressingham are all of very similar shape and the size ranges are roughly equivalent: lengths between 21.0 and 29.2mm at Lake and 21.6 and 34.5mm at Little Cressingham. The nature of the perforations is also the same, although the range of borehole diameters is slightly larger for the Little Cressingham examples. The pendants appear to have been made as distinct graduated sets, and at Lake the members of two original sets, with different ranges of thickness, may be represented. A group of five amber pestle pendants from Wilsford G8 (ID 1407–11, Figure 5.9.5) are all smaller than those from Lake and Little Cressingham, although they are similar in shape and possess comparable boreholes. One of them (ID 1409) survives only as a broken core but the other four range in length from 15 to 24mm; they do not appear to represent a graduated set. The only other English assemblage that contains a pestle pendant of amber is the composite necklace from Radwell I (Hall and Woodward 1977, fig. 4, E). This example is also small, with a length of *c.* 15mm. The group of three pestle pendants made from

Kimmeridge shale, from Durrington G14 (one of which, ID 498, is illustrated in Figure 5.9.5) may have functioned as a set, with lengths of 17.2, 17.0 and 16.0mm. The pair of lignite pestle-shaped toggles from Shrewton G5J (ID 1330–1, Figure 8.3.1) are of similar length at 17.3 and 16.9mm, but are more circular, rather than oval, in cross section. Otherwise there are a few amber pendants from Brittany that can be compared with the English finds. These comprise a set of 11 from the tomb at Kernonen at Plouvorn (Briard 1984, fig. 85 and 138–140). However, most of these are trapezoidal in outline, much flatter than the English examples, and bored from front to back rather than from side to side. One pendant is 16mm long and of chunky rectangular cross section (*ibid,* fig. 85, 4), but once again it is perforated from front to back, and it does not possess the basal bowing characteristic of the English pendants.

Buttons
V-perforated oval buttons occur in the assemblages from Lake and Wimborne St Giles G8, although the contextual integrity is poor in both cases. The nature of the wear within the perforations suggests that the buttons had been strung in necklaces. The buttons from Lake form a very uniform set of medium to high-domed examples, with lengths ranging from 10.2 to 12.1mm. The damaged buttons, probably from Wimborne St Giles, are not measureable but the domes were rather higher than within the set from Lake. Buttons are common elements within some of the jet and jet-like spacer plate necklaces. However these amber buttons are oval, whereas the jet and jet-like necklace buttons tend to be circular; the amber examples also tend to possess higher domes.

RAW MATERIAL AND MANUFACTURE
As noted above, following one or two unusual precedents, amber came to be used in comparatively large amounts in southern England from the inception of the Wessex series graves, from about the turn of the second millennium BC. Analysis has shown that all the amber is Baltic in origin (Beck and Shennan 1991), and therefore, compositionally, it is impossible to distinguish between amber that had been imported directly from Scandinavia, and amber that had washed up on the East Anglian coast. As argued above, it is likely that at least some of the amber found in rich Wessex series graves had been imported directly from the amber-rich area of north-west Jutland; this is suggested by the presence of a Wessex-style segmented faience bead at Fjallerslev, and by amber beads in the form of Wessex-style grooved biconical beads at Fly and Serritslev, all in this part of Denmark (Sheridan and Shortland 2004). The types of bead and plate found in the Wessex series graves are all specific to Britain and were most probably manufactured by local specialist amber workers located in the Wessex region.

As regards the question of whether people had deliberately selected amber of particular colours, the fact that all amber tends to darken over time means that one cannot be certain whether the colours evident now had been the original colours. However, given that a variety of colours is represented among the jewellery, and that raw amber can occur in different colours depending on the degree of its oxidation since its initial emergence from the ground, then it is not impossible that there had indeed been some colour choice during the Early Bronze Age. Amongst the necklaces studied in detail there is a clear preponderance of dark or bright red components. This includes most of the terminal and spacer plates from Lake and Upton Lovell G2e, all other elements from Lake, most of the globular beads at Upton Lovell G2e, the buttons from Wimborne St Giles G8 and pestle pendants and annular beads at Little Cressingham. (A similar duality of colour had been noted in the Shaw Cairn necklace: Sheridan 2010a). At Upton Lovell G2e some of the globular beads were originally light red, while the fusiforms were mainly orange. Also orange are the plates and some of the beads at Wimborne St Giles G8. Most variable are the beads from Little Cressingham, where some of the fusiforms are dark brown and the disc beads display a wide range of colours. There are at least three possible explanations for this variability in colour: firstly, it may be a case of deliberate colour selection to provide a visual contrast, as suggested above; second, it may simply reflect the colour of whatever parent blocks and pebbles of amber were available at the time of manufacture; and thirdly, it might reflect the practice of handing down heirloom pieces.

Owing to the degree of degradation of amber and the oxidation of the surfaces, together with the fact that the two major necklaces are sewn down onto backing sheets for display, it has not proved possible to detect many traces of manufacture. Amongst the loose items, the buttons from Lake retain traces of rilling within the boreholes on four items. The beads and pendants within the necklace from Little Cressingham could be studied individually under the microscope. In five cases there is evidence that the boreholes in the pendants had been bored from both sides, and one retains traces of rilling from the passage of the drill bit. Many of the disc beads retain saw marks and/ or polishing striations, and it can be deduced that most of them were bored from one side only, with a few bored from both sides.

LIFE HISTORIES

One of the main results of our study of the amber necklaces has been the discovery that almost all the elements show evidence of wear, inviting one to consider whether the components of each necklace had been gathered together from different sources, or from previous necklaces. Wear is particularly common on the terminal and spacer plates. This consists of ancient damage to the margins of the plates and the breaking out of through-borings, especially at the corners and sides of individual plates. In spite of the heavy oxidation of many pieces, which has produced a crumbly, opaque, butterscotch-coloured crust, it also proved possible to detect traces of thread-wear and bead-

on-plate wear in a significant number of incidences. The plates from Upton Lovell G2e are of particular interest as it was noted that wear around individual perforations had occurred subsequent to major damage of the plate edge. Thus these plates had been subject to further use in their broken condition. Variable wear on the plates from Lake also suggested that they may have been employed in two different ways during the life of the necklace. The pestle pendants from Lake and Little Cressingham show signs of wear in the form of ancient chip- and thread-wear within the boreholes. Many of the beads also display evidence of wear, although this more often resulted from slight wear only. Least worn are the disc beads from Little Cressingham, but if these had been strung tightly, traces of wear may not have developed during use. The V-perforated buttons were seen to be slightly worn or worn, and the location of the wear around the boreholes indicates that the buttons had indeed been strung on necklaces, and not used as garment fastenings.

A differing life history can be deduced for each of the necklaces studied. The Little Cressingham necklace contains pestle pendants and annular beads which, on the evidence of colour and degree of wear, may belong to a set. To these the disc beads, which are of more varied material, and many of which are in fresher condition, may have been added at a later date. The small number of fusiform beads are varied in form and their squared cross sections indicate that they once may have been strung in a spacer plate necklace. Thus the necklace may be a compilation of elements from at least three different sources. The association of all the necklace elements from Wimborne St Giles G8 is not secure. However the plates, fusiform beads and squashed globulars may have belonged together as a single necklace, or perhaps two necklaces, as noted above. The fragmentary buttons, if indeed from this barrow, may also have been part of an original design. The finds from Lake may represent the remains from a bracelet along with one or more necklaces (although see above concerning the possible mixing of finds from two graves). The necklace spacers are a good matching set, and although worn, in some cases to a high degree, most of the original margins are still present, at least in part. Wear evidence indicates that originally up to ten strings of beads may have been supported at the front of the necklace, while later a two-strand necklace may have used the marginal through-perforations only. The squashed globular beads appear to go with the plates, while the uniform set of fusiform beads and the truly globular beads may have been strung in strands between the spacers, or may have been employed in separate single-strand necklaces. The true globular beads may themselves have been derived from two different sources, or previous necklaces. The pestle pendants and annular beads seem to be rather different and maybe formed part of a separate necklace, similar to that from Little Cressingham. Finally the uniform set of eleven necklace buttons may have been strung with the pestle pendants, or perhaps formed a zone towards the rear of the main necklace. Once again, the uncertainty surrounding the

Lake material's origin makes it hard to be certain whether all had come from the same grave.

Most of the amber finds from Upton Lovell G2e do seem to belong to a single necklace. However the spacers are very worn and broken and in their final form would only have supported five strands of beads at the front. Originally the spacers would have supported nine or more strings of beads at the front. The total number of squashed globular beads found during excavation (even if 'about 1000' was an exaggeration) could not have been encompassed within the final five-strand necklace, unless it had been extremely long. Alternatively it may be that more than one necklace was represented with the burial and that further spacer fragments were lost or disintegrated at the time of excavation. A further possibility is that some of the beads were strung as supplementary bracelets. The small numbers of beads of other forms (i.e. fusiform, true globular, and annular) are of varying colours and may be heirlooms from previous necklaces, although any signs of heavy wear are not visible. They may have been incorporated within the main spacer plate necklace, or within accompanying smaller strings of beads or bracelets. That amber spacer plates were revered and reused beyond their original function within crescentic necklaces is well illustrated by the presence of broken fragments of plates incorporated within the string of globular beads from Beaulieu and within the composite necklace from Radwell. The small squashed globular beads from spacer plate necklaces were also retained in small numbers and reused in composite necklaces of the later Early Bronze Age. Such beads occur within five necklaces containing small numbers of amber beads of variable shape (see Chapter 8.1) and within three composite necklaces (Chapter 8.2 and 8.3).

The main conclusions to be drawn are threefold. Firstly the generally accepted idea of the 'classic' Wessex amber spacer plate necklace, as depicted in the published drawings (which are mainly based on that within Annable and Simpson 1964, 103), and as indicated by the current array of beads within the display at Devizes, is probably oversimplified and unrealistic. From the results of our studies it seems possible that the strands of beads between the spacers may have included strings of fusiform beads and possibly true globular beads of larger size, as well as the strings of tiny squashed globular beads. Also there may have been zones of necklace buttons placed perhaps towards the rear of the necklace beyond the terminal plates. This would mirror the design concepts of some of the jet and jet-like necklaces from northern and middle England, as described above in Chapter 7.2. Secondly our analysis of the spacer plates within the necklaces from Lake and Upton Lovell G2e indicates that each necklace may have been re-designed, at least once, as the plates gradually became more damaged and broken. Finally our studies have deduced that each necklace may have been compiled from varying sets of plates and beads that may have derived in part from previous older necklaces. Thus heirloom items may have been incorporated in much the same way that they were within many of the necklaces made from jet and jet-like materials.

8. NECKLACES II: SIMPLE AND COMPOSITE NECKLACES

All the complete or near-complete necklaces studied, comprising large numbers of individual elements, have been described in Chapter 7. The remainder of the necklaces studied within the project are described in this chapter. Most of the entries relate to small groups of beads and other ornaments made from varying raw materials; such groups are termed 'composite necklaces'. However some of these smaller sets of beads and ornaments include items made only from one material. This is usually jet or jet-like material, although a few examples include beads made only from amber, bone, fossil or stone. These one-material groups are termed 'simple necklaces with components of variable shape' and will be considered in the first section of this chapter. Although the term necklace is used throughout it is possible that some of the beads and ornaments may not have been strung together, but may have been sewn onto garments or suspended individually. Such interpretation may apply particularly in the case of pendants. It is generally assumed that the sets of beads were strung as single-strand necklaces, as opposed to bracelets.

Detailed measurements of certain dimensions relating to a number of necklaces in Chapter 8.1 and Chapter 8.2 are tabulated in Appendix VII.

Jet and jet-like materials analysis codes: B=Bussell; D/H=Davis/Hook; AS/MD=Alison Sheridan/Mary Davis. Stone and fossil bead materials were identified by Rob Ixer, bone items by Mark Maltby. Faience descriptions are by Alison Sheridan.

8.1 SIMPLE NECKLACES WITH COMPONENTS OF VARIABLE SHAPE
(with Alison Sheridan)

A list of items studied and illustrated is shown in Table 8.1.1.

8.1.1 JET AND JET-LIKE MATERIALS

ID 497–500 Durrington G14, Wiltshire

References: Hoare 1812, 167; Annable and Simpson 1964, 51 and 56, nos. 274–7.

Table 8.1.1. List of simple and composite necklaces studied and illustrated.

Object	Site (Parish), County	Museum	Illustration
ID 323	Egton 124, burial 1, N. Yorks.	BM	Figure 8.1.2
ID 326–28	Hutton Buscel 157, burial 1, N. Yorks.	BM	Figure 8.1.2
ID 330–32	Ford 186, burial 3, Northumberland	BM	Figure 8.1.2
ID 357	Fylingdales 271, burial 1, N. Yorks.	BM	Figure 8.1.3
ID 392–94	Stranghow Moor (Lockwood), Redcar and Cleveland	BM	Figure 8.1.4
ID 451–52, 454–55, 458	Nawton, Pinderdale Wood (Beadlam), N. Yorks.	BM	Figure 8.1.4
ID 497–500	Durrington G14, Wilts.	Dev	Figure 8.1.1
ID 530–33	Wilsford G32, Wilts.	Dev	Figure 8.1.1
ID 537–38	Avebury G13c, Wilts.	Dev	Figure 8.1.1
ID 1340–45	Aldbourne 276, burial 3, Wilts.	BM	Figure 8.1.5
ID 1458–63	Winterbourne Stoke G14, Wilts.	Dev	Figure 8.1.5
ID 1520.1–17, 1521	Norton Bavant G1, Wilts.	Sal	Figure 8.1.6
ID 1536–37	Amesbury G70, Wilts.	Sal	Figure 8.1.7
ID 1538–43	Amesbury G71, Wilts.	Sal	Figure 8.1.8
ID 1544–50, 1552	Wilsford Shaft G33a, Wilts.	Sal	Figure 8.1.6
ID 734–37	Folkton	BM	Figure 8.1.7
ID 743A	Bedford	BM	Not illustrated
ID 743B	Kempston	BM	Figure 8.1.8

COMPOSITION

The necklace comprises three shale pestle-shaped pendants and one jet bead (Figure 8.1.1, top).

CONTEXT AND ASSOCIATIONS

It was found in a saucer barrow on Durrington Down, probably with a secondary inhumation burial. The beads were located near to the neck of the burial.

MORPHOLOGY AND MATERIAL

Half of a large globular bead (ID 497) (B16: AS) measures 18.4 by 22.8mm with a perforation diameter of 3.3mm. There are also three pestle pendants of Kimmeridge shale (ID 498–500) (B13-15; AS), see pendants section for details (Chapter 5.9). The string length is estimated at 51mm.

MANUFACTURE

The surface of the bead bears multidirectional faint striations.

COMPLETENESS AND DAMAGE

The three pendants are virtually complete, but the bead is broken in half, and chipped, in antiquity. Surviving at 60% it could still have been strung, albeit with some difficulty.

WEAR

Chips on the pendants are all ancient, and some smoothing of the perforation edges in each case indicates slight wear. The bead had been used before it broke, and the broken surface also shows signs of wear. It also is classified as slightly worn.

CONCLUSIONS

This is a very unusual combination of items, and includes a carefully curated and re-used broken piece.

ID 530–33 Wilsford G32, Wiltshire
Reference: Hoare 1812, 206.

COMPOSITION

The necklace consists of four items: an annular bead and three fusiform beads (Figure 8.1.1, middle).

CONTEXT AND ASSOCIATIONS

It derives from a bowl barrow in a zone south of the Normanton barrow group. The necklace was found with a primary cremation burial located next to a circular cist.

MORPHOLOGY AND MATERIAL

ID 530 is a large wedge-shaped annular bead of Kimmeridge shale (B33; AS) measuring 9.2 by 19.4mm with a perforation diameter of 8.9mm, ID 531 is a medium fusiform bead of Kimmeridge shale (B34; AS) measuring 21.7 by 9mm with a perforation diameter of 3mm, ID 532 is a medium to plump fusiform bead of Kimmeridge shale (B35; AS) measuring 21.1 by 9.6mm with a perforation diameter of 2.7mm, and ID 533 is a plump flattened fusiform bead of Kimmeridge shale (B36; AS) measuring 19.9 by 9.4mm with a perforation diameter of 3mm. The strung length is estimated at 72mm.

MANUFACTURE

The three fusiform beads have traces of faceting towards their ends (e.g. ID 533, Figure 8.1.1).

COMPLETENESS AND DAMAGE

ID 532–3 are complete, and the other items show slight modern damage.

WEAR

The annular bead has some small ancient chips inside the hoop. Thread-wear is present on all items, with definite pulls on the fusiform beads (e.g. ID 531, Figure 8.1.1). ID 530 is classified as slightly worn, the others as worn.

CONCLUSIONS

The fusiform beads form a set, probably derived from a spacer plate necklace. They are copying the shapes of the beads in a classic jet spacer plate necklace that sit below spacer plate 2. These beads appear to indicate that there may have been at least one spacer plate necklace in Wessex made from Kimmeridge shale, unless of course these were local replacements for damaged areas within an imported jet spacer plate necklace.

ID 537–38 Avebury G13c, Wiltshire
Reference: Hoare 1821, 91–2; pl. X.

COMPOSITION

The necklace comprises a pair of flat shale rings, together with a perforated 'jet' ornament which is lost (Figure 8.1.1, bottom).

CONTEXT AND ASSOCIATIONS

The necklace was found with a primary cremation burial in a bowl barrow within the Fox Covert Group.

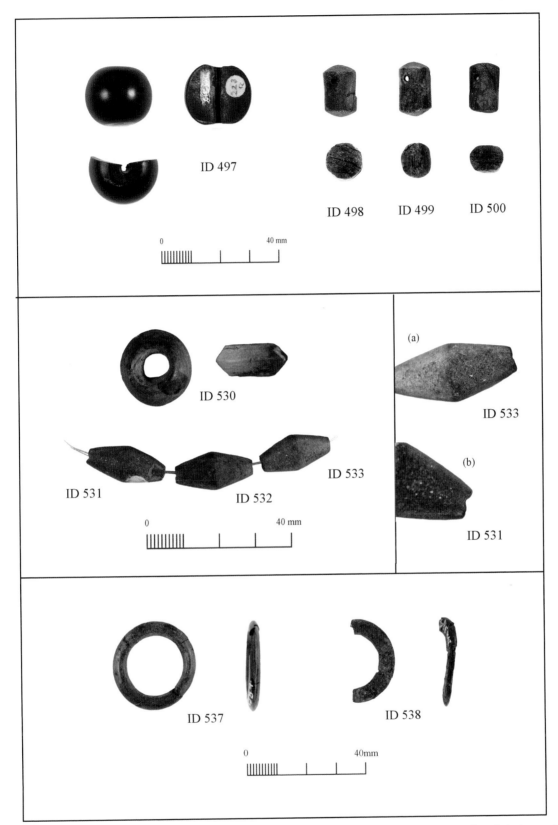

Figure 8.1.1. Simple necklaces of jet and jet-like materials. ID 497–500 Durrington G14 jet bead and shale pendants; ID 530–533 Wilsford G32 with details of (a) faceting and (b) thread-pull; ID 537–38 Avebury G13c shale rings.

MORPHOLOGY AND MATERIAL

ID 537 is a flat ring of Kimmeridge shale (AS) with a hoop section tapering sharply to the exterior and interior. The diameter is 25.9mm, the thickness 3.5mm, and the hoop width 4.7mm. ID 538 is also a flat ring of Kimmeridge shale (AS) with a hoop section tapering to the exterior only. The diameter is 28.1mm, the thickness 2.2mm, and the hoop width 5.6mm. The strung length would be a minimum of 54mm if the rings were strung flat.

MANUFACTURE

Knife cuts are visible inside both hoops.

COMPLETENESS AND DAMAGE

ID 537 is almost complete but with modern spalls and glued breaks (90%), but ID 538 is severely broken and with half of the depth missing (25% only survives). All the damage is modern.

WEAR

No obvious wear is visible and the wear category is indeterminate.

CONCLUSIONS

The variation in cross section indicates that the rings are not a matching pair.

ID 323 Egton (William Howe), North Yorkshire

References: Evans 1897, fig. 379; Greenwell 1865, 112–3, fig. 2; Greenwell and Rolleston 1877, 334–5, fig. 137; Kinnes and Longworth 1985, 89, no. 124, burial 1, 1.

COMPOSITION

This necklace comprises 14 long, slender fusiform beads and one straight-sided, square-sectioned bead (Figure 8.1.2, top).

CONTEXT AND ASSOCIATIONS

The necklace was found among the cremated remains of an adult, lying on the old ground surface under a round cairn, 4m off its centre. A secondary deposit of cremated remains, found 0.9m higher up, was associated with a Vase Food Vessel. A flint flake was found among the stones of the cairn.

MORPHOLOGY AND MATERIAL

The fusiform beads range in length from 25.6 to 45.1mm, and in maximum width from 5.0mm to 6.9mm. In cross section at their widest point they range from squashed circular (Figure 8.1.2b) and oval to D-shaped. In every case their ends have been squared off (Figure 8.1.2a–c). The diameter of the longitudinal borehole ranges from 2.0 to 3.0mm, and in two cases the hole is markedly eccentric. The beads' colour ranges from black to dark brown, with most being blackish brown and some mottled black and dark brown. The straight-sided, square-sectioned bead is 30mm long and 5.0 by 4.9mm in width and thickness, with a longitudinal borehole 2.3mm in diameter, centrally-

positioned at one end but eccentric at the other. Its ends are squared-off and perpendicular to the bead's long axis. Laid end to end, the beads' overall length comes to 479.5mm; this would make a necklace that would lie on the breastbone of an adult.

All the beads showed visual characteristics of jet (AS/MD). This identification was confirmed by XRF analysis of two of the beads, one brown and one black (MD/DH).

MANUFACTURE

Notwithstanding the presence of one bead with a markedly different cross section (square) from the others, the consistency in the beads' shape and perforation (and condition) strongly suggest that this is a set of beads made by the same hand, or in the same workshop. Facets from the shaping of the fusiform beads were observed (in some cases, faintly) on all of the fusiform beads (e.g. Figure 8.1.2c). Manufacturing striations were noted on 12 beads including the square-sectioned example; on this, and on one of the fusiform beads, they are crisp whereas on the others they are faint. On two faces of the square-sectioned bead are gouge marks made by a narrow, toothed tool likely to have been used to remove mineral inclusions in the jet; one other bead showed signs of having had inclusions removed. Where the interior of the borehole was visible, faint rilling was observed in two beads.

It may well be that the straight-sided, square-sectioned bead is actually an unfinished fusiform bead that had been polished and treated as a finished bead, since the process of manufacturing fusiform beads had probably involved grinding a perforated, square-sectioned roughout into shape.

COMPLETENESS AND DAMAGE

The beads range in completeness from 95% to 100%, with the least complete examples having lost one end, either in antiquity or more recently. Most beads have a medium sheen achieved through polishing; three have a high sheen. Traces of consolidant were noted on most beads (including, in four cases, a white waxy substance, probably carbowax). In many cases it did not seem to cover the whole bead; it had not significantly affected the overall degree of sheen although it did make it difficult to detect faint striations in some cases. The beads show no sign of heat damage so must have been kept separate from the body until the cremated remains had cooled down.

WEAR

Thread-wear in the form of smoothing of the interior of the perforation at its ends was observed in all but one of the beads. Thread-smoothing of the edges of the perforations was observed in 12 beads, mostly to a minimal degree and sometimes only at one end. Shallow thread-wear grooves were noted in four beads. There was no bead-on-bead wear. Overall, the degree of wear ranged from slightly worn to moderately worn.

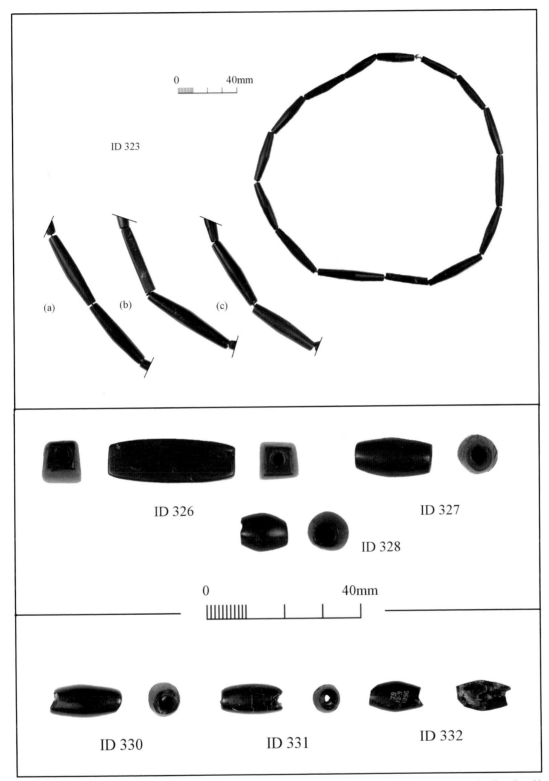

Figure 8.1.2. Simple necklaces of jet and jet-like materials. ID 323 Egton 124 details showing squared-off ends of beads, also (a) and (c) faceting, and (b) the square-sectioned bead (above the letter b). ID 326–28 Hutton Buscel 157 squarish-sectioned bead (ID 326) and thread-wear on all examples. ID 330–32 Ford 186: note the thread-pull on all the beads and the junction of drilling from both ends, visible in the exposed borehole of ID 332.

CONCLUSIONS

This necklace appears not to have seen lengthy use before its burial. With the possible exception of the square-sectioned bead, the consistency of the beads indicates that they had been made as a set and were not recycled components from an old spacer plate necklace; the slight difference in wear between the beads could possibly be explained by their position on the necklace when worn.

The shape of the square-sectioned bead is that of a fusiform bead roughout although, as noted above, the fact that it has been polished indicates the intention of treating it as a finished bead. Its stylistic similarities with the other beads in the necklace strengthens the suggestion that the beads had all been made as a set. This is also corroborated by the fact that the beads are all relatively long, longer than what is normally encountered in a spacer plate necklace; indeed, the longest bead may be the longest jet fusiform bead known from Early Bronze Age Britain and Ireland. The square-sectioned bead is paralleled at Hutton Buscel (ID 326), around 28km to the south-east.

ID 326–28 Hutton Buscel (barrow 157), North Yorkshire

References: Greenwell 1865, 247–9; Greenwell and Rolleston 1877, 365–9; Kinnes and Longworth 1985, 95, no. 157 burial 1, 4–6.

COMPOSITION

The necklace consists of one squareish-sectioned bead and two fusiform beads (Figure 8.1.2, middle). It may be that a V-perforated object, probably made from a worn V-perforated jet button, had also belonged to the necklace, either as a pendant or as a fastener (Figure 5.8.3 and Figure 5.9.4).

CONTEXT AND ASSOCIATIONS

The beads were found among a deposit of cremated bone on the original surface of a round barrow beneath a subsequent addition to the mound. Also present was the V-perforated jet object, along with an accessory vessel and fragments of a bronze awl.

MORPHOLOGY AND MATERIAL

ID 326 is a fairly long, squareish-sectioned bead with minimally convex sides, 29.5mm in length, 9.2mm in breadth and 8.6mm wide, with a relatively narrow, slightly eccentric longitudinal perforation, 2.7mm in diameter. The ends are squared off. ID 327 is a fusiform bead that is near-cylindrical and has a circular cross section. It is 19mm long with a maximum diameter of 9.6mm, and has a slightly eccentric longitudinal perforation 4.0mm in diameter. The ends taper. ID 328 is a fairly plump, asymmetrical fusiform bead, at its fattest close to one end; it is 11.0mm long and of 9.0mm maximum breadth, with a slightly asymmetrical longitudinal perforation 4.0mm in diameter. One end tapers and the other is gently squared off.

Two of the beads, ID 326 and ID 327, have the appearance of soft jet (AS/MD). XRF analysis of both these beads (MD/DH) confirmed the material as jet. In contrast, bead ID 328 is black and slightly 'stony' in appearance, and is likely to be of cannel coal or shale (AS/MD).

MANUFACTURE

The cross section shape of ID 326 suggests that this bead had been shaped by grinding, allowing each of the four sides to develop as flat surfaces; all traces of the grinding process had been polished away, and the surfaces have a medium sheen. The borehole had been drilled from both ends, and there is no rilling in the hole. ID 327 has faint, irregular striations running across each of its flat ends. Its borehole had been drilled from both ends and there is no rilling. ID 328 has similar faint, irregular striations across one end, and it appears that the borehole had been drilled from one end (although a 'starter' hole may have existed at the other end to prevent damage during drilling). There is no rilling.

COMPLETENESS AND DAMAGE

ID 326 is 99% complete, with one chip missing from one of the long sides; this damage is ancient. The other beads are complete but for thread-pull hollows; ID 328 had broken across its body, and had been glued together, this damage probably having been sustained after the bead joined the museum collection. The necklace had not passed through the pyre with the body, as otherwise it would have been consumed in the flames.

WEAR

All the beads show a moderate amount of wear (Figure 8.1.2, middle). ID 326 has thread-smoothing all around the edge of the perforation at both ends, and at one end, bead-on-bead wear in the form of a 'step' ground into one side. ID 327 has thread-smoothing around the perforation edge at both ends, and a marked thread-pull groove at one end. ID 328 has thread-smoothing all around the perforation edge at one end and thread-pull to one side at the other end. All three beads are classified as moderately worn.

CONCLUSIONS

These beads may represent the old and worn remnants of a larger necklace, the amount and kind of wear indicating that they had once been strung, probably tightly, along with additional beads. As noted above, the V-perforated object found with them could have been a pendant or a fastener for the necklace. The most likely origin for the fusiform beads (ID 327 and ID 328) is a spacer plate necklace. The long, square-sectioned bead finds a close parallel at Egton (ID 323), around 28km to the north-west; as there, this may have been a roughout for a fusiform bead which, instead of being ground into the fusiform shape, was polished and used as a finished bead.

ID 330–32 Ford (barrow 186), Northumberland

References: Greenwell and Rolleston 1877, 406, 407; Kinnes and Longworth 1985, 100, 186, burial 3, 3–5.

COMPOSITION

The necklace consists of three fusiform beads, of which two are near-cylindrical (Figure 8.1.2, bottom). A fragment of a V-perforated button of jet or jet-like material (Chapter 5.2 not illustrated, ID 333) was found with the beads and may have formed part of the necklace, as a pendant or a fastener.

CONTEXT AND ASSOCIATIONS

The necklace was found among or above the cremated human remains of an adult female, in a Collared Urn that had been deposited upright on the old ground surface and covered with a round barrow; it was found under the centre of the barrow. Also present, in addition to the broken V-perforated button and Collared Urn, was a burnt fragment of worked flint.

MORPHOLOGY AND MATERIAL

ID 330 is a slender, near-cylindrical bead, circular in cross-section and with one end slightly angled; it is 18.2mm long, 7.5mm in maximum diameter and has a longitudinal, symmetrically-placed perforation 3.5mm in diameter. The ends are gently squared off and slope. ID 331 is also slender and even more cylindrical and circular in cross section. One end is missing. The surviving length is 16.0mm. The maximum diameter is 5.2mm and the perforation diameter 2.6mm. One end of the perforation is slightly eccentric. The surviving end tapers to a point. ID 332 is more obviously fusiform in shape and circular in cross section. Half of one side, and one end, is missing. The surviving length is 14mm, the maximum diameter 8.3mm and the perforation diameter 3.0mm. The surviving end is gently squared off. All the beads are brownish-black.

Macro- and microscopically, ID 331 and ID 332 appear to be jet, while ID 330 seems to be of cannel coal (AS/MD). This was confirmed by XRF analysis of beads ID 330 and ID 332 (MD/DH).

MANUFACTURE

No traces from the shaping of the beads are visible, although in all cases it is clear that the perforation has been drilled from each end. In ID 332, where the borehole has been exposed, the junction between the two drillings can clearly be seen (Figure 8.1.2). There is no rilling in the perforations. All three beads have a low surface sheen, although on ID 330 this is hard to see clearly through the lacquer/consolidant coating the bead.

COMPLETENESS AND DAMAGE

All have suffered damage since their discovery, with the loss of a large part of ID 332, of one end of ID 331 and of a long chip from ID 330 (although the last had been glued back in position); the percentage presence is 40%, 80–85% and 95% respectively. There is also glue on ID 331, and both glue and lacquer (or similar consolidant) on ID 330.

The only sign of ancient damage is the loss of chips from one end of ID 330. The only sign of cracking is hairline criss-cross cracking all over ID 331. The necklace had not passed through the cremation pyre with the body.

WEAR

ID 330 has thread-smoothing all around each end of the perforation and thread-pull to one side at either end. This had probably weakened the bead, as this is where the long chip had subsequently become detached. ID 331 has slight thread-smoothing all round the surviving end. ID 332 has the same on its surviving end, and also a narrow zone of thread wear at this end. ID 331 is slightly worn and the other two beads display moderate wear.

CONCLUSIONS

These beads are likely to represent the last, and old, remains of a necklace, probably of spacer plate type. This is suggested by their shape and by the level of wear which is consistent with their former stringing in sufficient number, and sufficiently tightly, to result in thread-wear. If the beads had started their life in a spacer plate necklace, they could have been well over a century old, and possibly several centuries old, when deposited.

ID 357 Fylingdales (barrow 271), North Yorkshire

References: Greenwell 1890, 41–2; Kinnes and Longworth 1985, 124–5 (no. 271, burial 1, 2); Longworth 1984, 74, 75, 244, Pl. 161i, no. 1142–3.

COMPOSITION

The necklace comprises three fusiform beads, and eight complete and one fragmentary squat beads of shapes ranging from sub-biconical to sub-globular (Figure 8.1.3).

CONTEXT AND ASSOCIATIONS

The beads were found among the cremated remains of an adult (descibed as '?female' by Kinnes and Longworth, 124) in an inverted Collared Urn under a round barrow 4.9m from its centre. The grave was in a secondary position 0.4m above the old ground surface.

MORPHOLOGY AND MATERIAL

The three fusiform beads are slender, ranging in length between 17.4 and 26.3mm and in girth between 6.9 and 8.3mm, with relatively wide boreholes, between 3.2 and 3.9mm in diameter. One is rounded-triangular in cross section, the others circular and oval. Two have gently squared-off ends, while those on the third are tapered to a point. The other beads are all squat and range in shape from roughly biconical with a rounded ridge to oblate and

Figure 8.1.3. Simple necklaces of jet and jet-like materials. ID 357 Fylingdales 271, including fragmentary bead (top, centre).

sub-globular; at least one could be described as 'squat fusiform'. In length they range from 5.9 to 8.5mm, and in maximum diameter from 6.8 to 8.0mm, with perforation diameters ranging from 2.3 to 4.1mm.

In every case the beads macroscopically appear to be jet (AS/MD). Compositional analysis of one bead using XRF (MD/DH) confirmed the identification of the material as

jet. It may be that the beads with hairline cracking are of hard jet, while more deeply-cracked beads are of soft jet.

MANUFACTURE

Faint faceting traces were noted on one fusiform bead and on three other beads, while grinding striations are present on all of the squat beads (being fairly crisp in one case) and one of the fusiform beads. The borehole had probably been drilled from both ends of each bead; faint rilling was also noted in three cases. The beads had been polished, but their present appearance partly relates to the presence of patches of consolidant on all the beads. Some variation in the degree of sheen around individual beads may relate to partial post-depositional dulling.

COMPLETENESS AND DAMAGE

With one exception, where less than half the bead is present, the beads are complete or virtually so and are in good condition. Three have minor chipping, some ancient, some recent. The necklace had not passed through the cremation pyre with the body.

WEAR

In most cases, the degree of wear can be described as 'slight' and consists of thread-smoothing of the interior of the borehole. The sheen at the end of two of the beads, and ancient chipping to one end of one bead, could conceivably be due to bead-on-bead wear.

CONCLUSIONS

The overall impression is that these beads are not heavily worn and might not have been very old when buried. The size and shape of the fusiform beads – towards the upper end of the size range for such beads – suggests that they need not represent heirlooms from an older spacer plate necklace; instead they may have been made at or around the same time as the other beads.

ID 392–94 Stranghow Moor, Lockwood, Redcar and Cleveland

Reference: unpublished.

COMPOSITION

The necklace consists of one fusiform bead and two squat biconical beads (Figure 8.1.4).

CONTEXT AND ASSOCIATIONS

No details of context could be discovered.

MORPHOLOGY AND MATERIAL

ID 392 is a gently-tapering fusiform bead, fairly plump, 12.0mm long, with a maximum diameter of 8.5mm and borehole diameter of 4.6mm. The other beads are squat biconical in shape, with a clear ridge which, on ID 393, lies to one side of the bead's mid-point (Figure 8.1.4, top). ID 393 measures 9.2mm in length with a maximum

diameter of 11.5mm and borehole diameter between 6.8 and 3.5mm. ID 394 measures 10.3mm in length with a maximum diameter of 11.0mm; its borehole diameter ranges between 4.1 and 6.1mm.

All three beads macroscopically appear to be jet (AS/MD); this identification was confirmed through XRF analysis (MD/DH). The biconical beads have no or minimal cracking and could be of hard jet, while the fusiform bead has all-over hairline criss-cross cracking and may be of soft jet.

MANUFACTURE

ID 392 has no manufacturing traces on its surface. The hole had been perforated from both ends and has no rilling. The biconical beads both have faint concentric striations running around their exterior. ID 393 has a parallel-sided perforation and had been drilled from both ends; some rilling is visible but much of the hole is obscured by sediment. Rilling is clearly visible in the funnel-shaped borehole of ID 394. All three beads had been polished and have a medium sheen, although ID 393 has not been fully polished.

COMPLETENESS AND DAMAGE

ID 392 has some loss of surface at one end and along the body, some of this damage being modern, some of indeterminate age: 95% of the bead is present. ID 393 has slight, ancient chipping to one end. 98% of the bead is present. ID 394 is complete.

WEAR

There is thread-smoothing of the perforations in all three beads, slight in the case of ID 394. This bead also has a strong thread-pull hollow at a point where the wire that currently holds the bead in position sits (although the thread-pull has not been caused by the wire). Notwithstanding this thread-pull, overall the degree of wear to all of the beads can be classed as slight.

CONCLUSIONS

The fusiform bead differs in several respects from the biconical beads and may well be older than them. It is of a shape and size that is not inconsistent with its having been used previously as part of a spacer plate necklace. It may therefore represent an heirloom. The biconical beads, by contrast, are of a type that was popular after 2000 BC.

ID 451–52, ID 454–55 and ID 458 Nawton, Pinderdale Wood, Beadlam, North Yorkshire

References: Hayes 1963, Appendix A (iii), fig. 2.1–6; Smith 1994, 110 (NYM 88) and Pl. 23, 2–6.

COMPOSITION

The necklace consists of five fusiform beads (Figure 8.1.4, bottom).

CONTEXT AND ASSOCIATIONS

The beads were recovered from under the centre of a stony round mound, associated with the unburnt remains of an adolescent, possibly a female. Also with the burial were a pair of large jet studs (ID 449, Figure 5.6.2 and ID 453) and an eccentrically-perforated ring, pendant or fastener, also of jet (ID 450, Figure 4.14.2); the latter may have formed part of the necklace. A further fusiform bead was found on the mound many years later.

MORPHOLOGY AND MATERIAL

The beads are medium to plump fusiform, ranging in length from 13mm (ID 454) to 25.1mm (ID 451) and in maximum diameter from 8.3mm (ID 454) to 9.7mm (ID 452, ID 458). They are all roughly circular in cross section. The ends of ID 458 are perpendicular to the long axis, while one end of ID 451, ID 454 and ID 455, and both ends of ID 452, slope slightly. The ends of all but one of the beads are squared off. On ID 452, the outer surface tapers to a point. The longitudinal perforation is slightly eccentrically positioned in all the beads except ID 452, where, despite half of the bead being missing, it is likely to have been roughly central. The perforation diameter ranges from 2.5mm (ID 458) to 3.8mm (ID 451).

Macroscopically all five beads appear to be of jet (AS/MD), with the extensive and/or deep criss-cross cracking seen on ID 451 and 454 suggesting the use of soft jet. Beads ID 451 and ID 452 were analysed using XRF (MD/DH). The high iron content in both beads, and the low zirconium content of ID 452, caused the analysts to query whether the material is jet but, given the beads' macroscopic characteristics and the fact that some jet can have a high iron content thanks to the presence of (or proximity to) pyrite inclusions, it was concluded that the material is likely to be a high-iron jet. The presence of mercury traces on all the analysed Nawton objects is due to post-excavation contamination.

MANUFACTURE

Faceting traces, from the shaping of the fusiform beads, are present on ID 455, and faint grinding striations were noted near one or both ends of ID 451, ID 452, ID 454 and ID 455 (Figure 8.1.4), and on one end of ID 451 and ID 458. The perforations had been drilled from both ends, as is clearly demonstrated by ID 452 which had split lengthways (Figure 8.1.4). Here the mid-point junction between the two holes is clearly visible, as is faint rilling.

Bead ID 451 has several ancient chip scars on its surface which probably relate to chipping during manufacture. It is unclear, however, whether all of the surface irregularities are chip scars. Some might represent the natural 'orange peel' texture noted on some jet. On ID 452, a large and old chip scar at one end may have been caused during manufacture. All the beads had been polished with ID 452, ID 454 and ID 458 having a low sheen and ID 451 and ID 455 having a medium sheen.

COMPLETENESS AND DAMAGE

With the exception of ID 452 which had split lengthways, possibly in antiquity, and of which only around 40% survives) and ID 454, which is missing 10% in the form of ancient flake loss and recent chip loss, the beads are effectively complete. The ancient chipping to the surface of ID 451 and ID 452 has been noted.

WEAR

The beads show a variable degree of wear, with ID 455 and ID 458 showing minimal wear in the form of slight thread-smoothing of the ends of the perforations, a feature noted on all the beads. ID 451 has bead-on-bead wear at both ends, leaving it irregularly shaped (Figure 8.1.4). Probable bead-on-bead wear was also noted around part of one end of ID 454. There is thread-polish to the one surviving perforation end of ID 452, and the edge of the ancient chip scar is slightly worn. Overall three beads display slight wear, and two are worn.

CONCLUSIONS

These beads are characteristic of the fusiform beads as seen in spacer plate necklaces, and indeed could have originated as parts of one or more such necklace. It may be that ID 451 and 454, both of soft jet and showing the most wear, and possibly also ID 452, had originally come from a different set of beads from the others.

8.1.2 AMBER

ID 1340–45 Aldbourne 276, burial 3, Aldbourne, Wiltshire

References: Greenwell 1890, 46–8; Kinnes and Longworth 1985, 125–6.

COMPOSITION

The necklace consists of a group of six amber beads (Figure 8.1.5, top).

CONTEXT AND ASSOCIATIONS

The necklace was discovered with a primary adult inhumation in the central grave of a bell barrow within the Four Barrows group. It was found with a perforated bone point (ID 815, Figure 4.7.2) and an accessory cup. The bone point may have functioned as a pendant.

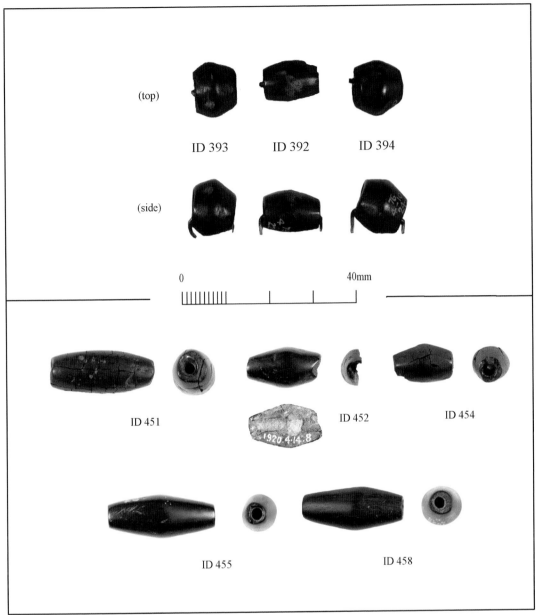

Figure 8.1.4. Simple necklaces of jet and jet-like materials. ID 392–94 Stranghow Moor: off-centre ridge in ID 393. ID 451–52, ID 454–55 and ID 458 Nawton: bead-on-bead wear on ID 451; grinding striations on ID 455. The fractured bead ID 452 indicates how the object was drilled from both ends.

MORPHOLOGY AND MATERIAL

ID 1340 and ID 1341 are two cylindrical beads of unknown original colour, one of them tapered. The lengths are 8.5 and 9.8mm, the widths 8.7 and 9.8mm, and the perforation diameters 3 and 2.7mm respectively. ID 1342 and ID 1343 are two cylindrical beads of bright red amber. The lengths are 7.8 and 9.8mm, the widths 10.9 and 11.1mm, and the perforation diameters 2.4 and 2.6mm respectively. ID 1344 and ID 1345 comprise a broken fusiform bead of dark red amber and non-joining fragments from a second. The surviving length is 10.7mm, the width 8mm, and the perforation diameter 2mm. The strung length is 135mm minimum, excluding the bone point.

MANUFACTURE

Beads ID 1340 and ID 1341 are made from two halves of a tapered amber pendant. The cut surfaces display unidirectional faint striations which are saw marks (Figure 8.1.5 inset). The surviving part of the original cross perforation of the pendant is softened; this demonstrated that the pendant had been used and worn prior to its breakage and conversion to the two beads. Otherwise no traces of manufacture are visible.

COMPLETENESS AND DAMAGE

The two modified beads are complete. The others show

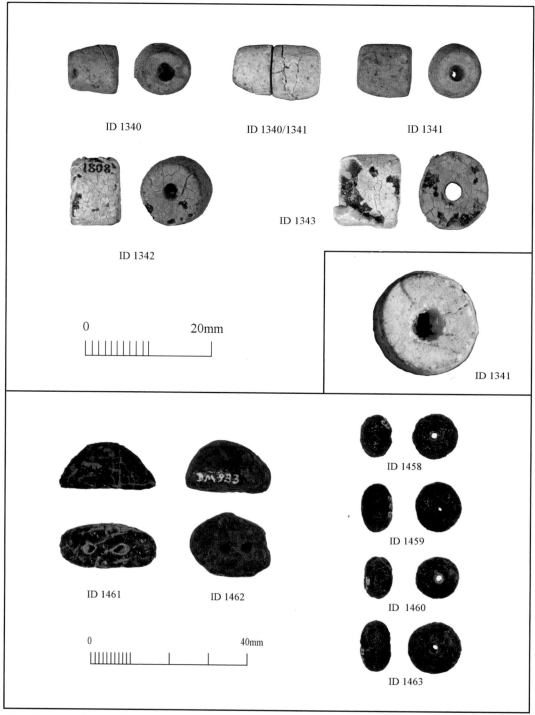

Figure 8.1.5. Simple amber necklaces. ID 1340–45 Aldbourne 276: ID 1340 and ID 1341 made from a single pendant (reconstructed at top centre) on which the saw marks are evident on ID 1341 (inset). ID 1458–63 Winterbourne Stoke G14.

varying degrees of breakage, including major breaks and chips all of which are modern.

WEAR

Thread-wear is absent on bead ID 1342 and indeterminate on ID 1344 and ID 1345. The other two show signs of

softening of the edges of the perforations and are classified as slightly worn (ID 1343) and worn (ID 1340).

CONCLUSIONS

The amber beads are of two distinct forms, both of full Early Bronze Age type and not derived from an amber spacer plate necklace. The use of a broken pendant as raw material for two of the beads is of particular interest.

ID 1458–63 Winterbourne Stoke G14, Wiltshire

Reference: Hoare 1812, 123; Annable and Simpson 1964, 51 and 107, nos. 292–8.

COMPOSITION

The necklace comprises a total of six amber items including two V-perforated ornaments and four beads (Figure 8.1.5, bottom).

CONTEXT AND ASSOCIATIONS

The items were found in a disc barrow within the Winterbourne Stoke barrow group. Two V-perforated buttons and one bead (ID 1463) were found with a primary cremation burial beneath the central tump, along with an accessory vessel. The other three beads came from a cremation burial found beneath the second tump. Thus two necklaces or groups of ornaments are represented.

MORPHOLOGY AND MATERIAL

ID 1461 is an elongated V-perforated button or fastener of dark red amber, the cross section tapering inwards towards the base. The dimensions are 23.9 by 11.6mm, and the perforation diameters 1.0 and 3.3mm. ID 1462 is a V-perforated oval button of dark red amber measuring 21.1 by 13.2mm, with both perforation diameters 2.6mm. ID 1458, ID 1459, ID 1460 and ID 1463 are four squashed globular beads of dark red amber. Their lengths range from 7.0 to 8mm, their widths from 11.0 to 12.6mm and their perforation diameters from 2.5 to 3mm. The strung lengths are 63mm for the central tump finds and 23mm for the beads from the second tump.

MANUFACTURE

The V-perforated items both have rilling within the perforations.

COMPLETENESS AND DAMAGE

All items are complete apart from button ID 1462 which has some modern chips, and one of the beads (ID 1460).

WEAR

The significant chip on the side of bead ID 1460 (95% present) is ancient damage. Thread-wear is visible in all items except ID 1460. All are classified as slightly worn, apart from ID 1463, which has stronger thread-wear and is worn. Wear on the perforations of the oval ornament (ID 1461) is towards the bridge only, indicating that this item may have functioned as a fastener, rather than having been strung within the necklace.

CONCLUSIONS

All these amber items are of the same original colour, and they may have been recycled from a single source. That source may have been an amber spacer plate necklace. The squashed globular beads are the right shape for such a necklace, although in size they lie at the larger end of the range. Also, oval V-perforated buttons occur in association with some spacer plate necklaces (see Chapter 7.3).

ID 1520.1–17 and ID 1521 Norton Bavant G1, Wiltshire

References: Colt Hoare 1812, 70; Beck and Shennan 1991, fig. 11.9, 2.

COMPOSITION

The necklace comprises a group of amber items including one large ring, a broken pendant and 16 beads. There were originally about 50 beads (Figure 8.1.6, top).

CONTEXT AND ASSOCIATIONS

The necklace was found with a primary cremation burial in a possible saucer barrow, located within Scratchbury Iron Age hillfort. Also among the goods were the tips of a dagger (ID 1190) and fragments from two exotic bronze dress pins (ID 1191 and ID 1192, both in Figure 5.5.1). The presence of a faience bead is also a slight possibility (Moore and Rowlands 1972, 49).

MORPHOLOGY AND MATERIAL

ID 1520.1 is a ring of bright red amber of diameter 34.3mm, thickness 8.1mm, and with an internal diameter of 15.5mm. ID 1520.2–3, 13 and 15 are four wedge-shaped disc beads of dark red, bright red and orange (x2) amber. Their lengths range from 3.4 to 4.3mm, their widths 5.8 to 7.7mm, and perforation diameters 1.8 to 2.8mm. ID 1520.4 and 5 are two plump disc beads of bright and medium red amber measuring 3.7 by 6.5mm and 3.8 by 7.4mm, and with perforation diameters 2.7 and 1.7mm respectively. ID 1520.6, 8–12 and 14 are seven squashed globular beads of medium red (x7) and dark red (x5) amber. Their lengths vary from 6.0 to 9.1mm, their widths from 8.6 to 14.2mm and perforation diameters from 1.5 to 3mm. ID 1520.16 and 1521 are two slender disc beads of bright red and medium orange amber measuring 2.7 by 5.2mm and 2.8 by 5.3mm, with perforation diameters 2.5 and 1.5mm respectively. ID 1520.17 is a V-perforated tear-drop shaped pendant of bright red amber measuring 9.8 by 11.4mm with perforation diameters of 7.0mm. ID 1521 is a slender disc bead of medium orange amber with ancient oxidisation,

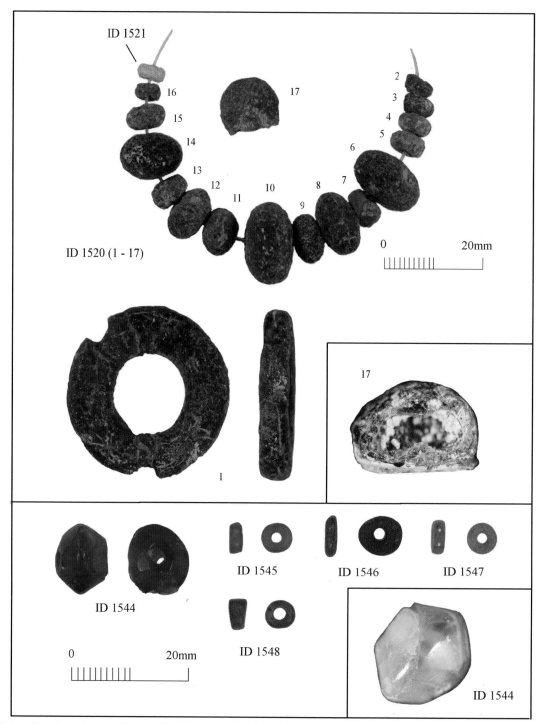

Figure 8.1.6. Simple amber necklaces. ID 1520 and ID 1521 Norton Bavant G1 also showing deeply angled V-perforation of pendant 17 (inset). ID 1544–48 Wilsford G33a also showing high ridge polish on ID 1544 (inset, under different lighting conditions).

giving the impression of white colour (previously published as chalk). The strung length of the surviving beads plus pendant is 167mm.

MANUFACTURE

No traces remain. The broken pendant had a very steeply-angled V-perforation (Figure 8.1.6 inset).

COMPLETENESS AND DAMAGE

All items are entire or almost so apart from six items which survive below the 98% level. Of these, seven have modern chips or side breaks. The top of the pendant has also been broken away in modern times.

WEAR

Ancient chipping occurs on six beads. The large ring has some wear at its narrowest point. Thread-wear is visible on 14 beads, with distinct thread-pulls in two cases. Wear on the pendant is indeterminate. Otherwise all the items can be classified as slightly worn, apart from two beads, one globular (ID 1520.6) and one annular (ID 1520.7), which are worn.

CONCLUSIONS

The amber items include a great variety of original colours and forms. One of the beads was oxidised in antiquity to a white colour, and may be from a very different source from the other items, and chosen deliberately for colour contrast. The larger beads at least, of squashed globular type, are all medium to dark red in colour and may have come originally from a spacer plate necklace, although they fall in the larger size range of such beads. The smaller beads are more irregular in shape, more damaged and occur in a wider range of colours: orange to bright red and medium red. These may have come from a different source. Of particular interest is the fact that this group was associated not only with bronze dress pin fragments, but also a Series 7 knife (or part of one).

ID 1544–50 and ID 1552 Wilsford G33a (Wilsford Shaft), Wiltshire

Reference: Ashbee *et al.* 1989, figs. 43–4, 2–7.

COMPOSITION AND CONTEXT

The necklace consists of a group of seven amber beads (Figure 8.1.6, bottom).

CONTEXT AND ASSOCIATIONS

Barrow G33a, which had been thought to be a pond barrow, turned out on excavation to be a shaft 1.8m wide and *c.* 30m deep (Ashbee *et al.* 1989, fig. 7). Other finds retrieved from the primary fill layers include a set of perforated bone points (Figure 4.7.7), a bone needle (Figure 4.7.7) and sherds of unidentified pottery.

MORPHOLOGY AND MATERIAL

ID 1544 is a plump biconical bead of bright orange amber measuring 8.5 by 11.0mm with perforation diameter 1.8mm. ID 1545, ID 1546 and ID 1547 are three slender annular beads of light to mid orange amber of lengths 1.7 to 2.1mm, widths 5.2 to 7.2mm, and perforation diameters 1.7 to 2mm. ID 1548 is a wedge-shaped annular bead of dark orange amber measuring 3.0 by 5.3mm, and with a perforation diameter of 2.7mm. ID 1549 is a very slender annular bead of bright orange amber measuring 3.3 by 5.7mm, and with a perforation diameter of 2mm. ID 1550

is a fragment of annular bead of bright orange amber (not illustrated in Ashbee *et al.* 1989). ID 1551 consists of fragments of a perforated shell disc, possibly the ?fossil bead noted by Ashbee *et al.* (1989, fig. 43, 7); this was found on the dump and is not included in the group. The strung length is 23mm.

MANUFACTURE

Unidirectional faint polishing striations are visible on the perforated surfaces of ID 1544 and ID 1545; there is high ridge polish on ID 1544 (Figure 8.1.6 inset).

COMPLETENESS AND DAMAGE

The beads are particularly well preserved, with little oxidisation, and are still translucent. Five of them however are chipped or broken. Most of the damage is modern, but there are smoothed chips on the side of ID 1545 and tiny ancient chips on ID 1547.

WEAR

Apart from the ancient damage just mentioned, traces of wear comprise thread-wear on all the beads apart from ID 1549. In four cases this wear included strong thread-pulls. Overall the three beads were classified as slightly worn and three as worn (one indeterminate).

CONCLUSIONS

This small group of beads includes a variety of types, none of which were of forms that might originally have occurred in spacer plate necklaces.

8.1.3 BONE

ID 734–37 Folkton 71, burial 6, Folkton, East Yorkshire

References: Greenwell and Rolleston 1877, 274–9; Kinnes and Longworth 1985, 78–9, 4–7.

COMPOSITION

The necklace consists of set of four bone beads (Figure 8.1.7, top).

CONTEXT AND ASSOCIATIONS

The beads were found with a Food Vessel and a bronze awl (ID 1287, Figure 4.6.1). Burial 6 within this round barrow was an adult female cremation burial, contracted on the right and with head to west-northwest; it was surrounded by chalk slabs. The burial was found in an oval grave, along with two other burials. The Food Vessel was at the face, the three decorated bone beads at the elbow, the plain bead and the awl 'below the hips'.

MORPHOLOGY AND MATERIAL

All four beads are rectangular in shape with lentoid cross section, and are light brown in colour. They are made from segments taken from the distal shaft of sheep/goat tibia (M. Maltby). In Figure 8.1.7 the images of a modern sheep tibia demonstrate how such beads could have been cut from the bone (experimental work by Sheila Hamilton-Dyer). Where decorated, the decoration comprises a positive geometric design formed of polished bone, and defined by other areas where the polish has been cut away. ID 734 measures 14.0 by 13.2 by 8.7mm, with perforation diameters 7.0 by 5.5mm and 5.0 by 4mm and is not decorated. ID 735 measures 15.5 by 12.5 by 8.8mm, with perforation diameters 5.8 by 3.5mm and 4.6 by 3.5mm. It is decorated with a positive four-rayed star on the front and 'spool' design on the rear. ID 736 measures 15.0 by 12.7 by 8.5mm, with perforation diameters 5.2 by 3.5mm and 4.6 by 3.2mm. It is decorated with a positive four-rayed star on both front and rear. ID 737 measures 14.4 by 13 by 9.3mm, with perforation diameters 5.8 by 4.5 and 5.3 by 3.7mm. The decoration consists of a positive lozenge with concave sides on the front and four separate rectangles defined by a negative straight cross on the rear. The strung length is 59mm.

MANUFACTURE

All four beads have surviving polishing striations. These are multidirectional on front, ends and rear surfaces on ID 735, ID 736 and ID 737, but diagonal on the ends and rear only in the case of ID 734. Prior to decoration the faces were highly polished, enhancing the natural smooth surface of the bone.

COMPLETENESS AND DAMAGE

All are complete.

WEAR

There are various ancient surface scratches, and all except ID 736 have visible thread-wear. They are all classed as slightly worn.

CONCLUSIONS

This is an unusual set of ornaments, but can be matched by a similar set found by Edward Duke with a cremation burial at Wilsford-cum-Lake, Wiltshire. Four small bone tablets (not beads) had perhaps been cut from one piece of bone. Three of them are decorated with star-shaped or lozenge designs, the underside being a mirror image of the face (Burl 1979, 208 and pl. 92). Burl observed that no wear was apparent and noted that William Cunnington thought that they might have been used in the process of divination.

8.1.4 FOSSIL

ID 1536–37 Amesbury G70, Wiltshire
Reference: Christie 1964, 30–45.

COMPOSITION

The necklace consists of a pair of fossil beads (Figure 8.1.7, bottom).

CONTEXT AND ASSOCIATIONS

The beads are associated with a barrow. The barrow contained a central cremation burial in a deep pit. One bead was found in the barrow ditch and the other in the turf stack over the cremation pit. This latter bead, along with large sherds from Collared Urns, may have been disturbed from the central burial during robbing of unknown date.

MORPHOLOGY AND MATERIAL

ID 1536 is a globular bead, dark cream in colour measuring 13.7 by 15mm with perforation diameters of 4.0 and 1.5mm. ID 1537 is a wedge-shaped globular bead, also dark cream in colour measuring 11.6 by 12.3mm with perforation diameters of 4.1 and 4.8mm. Both are natural near-spherical fossils of *Porosphaera glubulacia* (Christie 1964, 36: identified by Kenneth Oakley; the perforation occurs naturally in these fossils). The strung length is 25mm.

MANUFACTURE

ID 1536 has an additional aborted perforation on one side (Figure 8.1.7 inset). The naturally rough surfaces have not been polished.

COMPLETENESS AND DAMAGE

Both are complete.

WEAR

Thread-wear occurs in perforations on both beads and they are classified as slightly worn.

CONCLUSIONS

One, and possibly both of the beads may have been associated originally with the central cremation burial.

ID 1538–43 Amesbury G71, Wiltshire
Reference: Christie 1967, 349.

COMPOSITION

The necklace consists of a series of six fossil beads found

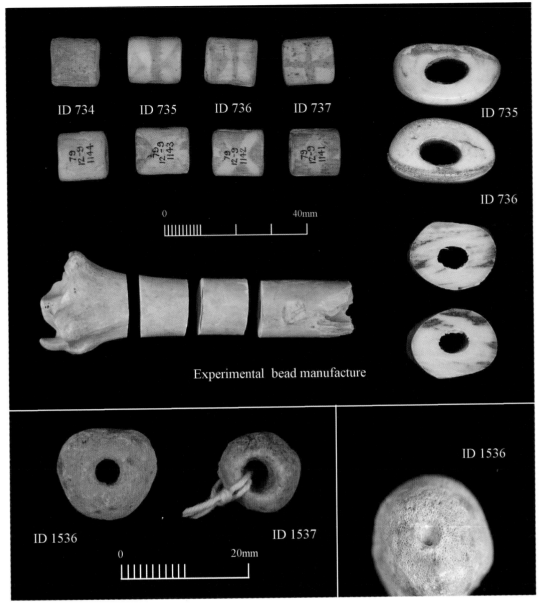

Figure 8.1.7. Simple bone necklace. ID 734–37 Folkton with modern experimental version from a sheep tibia for comparison. Simple fossil necklace. ID 1536–37 Amesbury G70 including detail of aborted perforation on ID 1536 (inset).

scattered in various secondary contexts, but probably forming a set (Figure 8.1.8, top).

CONTEXT AND ASSOCIATIONS

One bead was found with adult inhumation Burial 1, three in the soil of the associated platform and one from the top of the upper turf stack (all Phase III); the sixth bead was found in the fill of the barrow ditch.

MORPHOLOGY AND MATERIAL

ID 1538 and ID 1542 are two ovoid globular, off-white, beads measuring 7.5 by 7.7mm and 8.7 by 9.2 by 7.9mm with perforation diameters 2.4 and 3.3mm respectively.

ID 1539, ID 1540, ID 1541 and ID 1543 are globular, off-white, beads with lengths from 5.9 to 9.3mm, widths from 7.1 to 10.3mm, and perforation diameters from 2.7 to 4.7mm. All are natural near-spherical fossils of *Porosphaera glubulacia* (Christie 1967). The strung length is 48mm.

MANUFACTURE

The natural surfaces are rough and apparently unmodified (Figure 8.1.8 inset).

COMPLETENESS AND DAMAGE

All are complete.

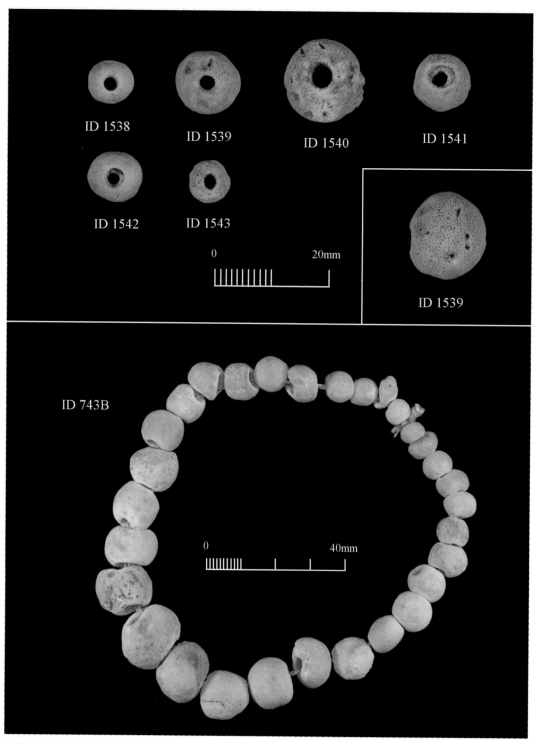

Figure 8.1.8. Simple fossil necklace. ID 1538–43 Amesbury G71 also showing detail of fossil surface on ID 1539 (inset). Simple stone necklace. ID 743B Kempston.

WEAR

All the beads display some softening of the margins of one or both perforations and they are classified as slightly worn.

CONCLUSIONS

Although found scattered, these beads probably formed a set, perhaps originally associated with one of the burials within this complex cemetery barrow. However one of the beads is rather darker in colour (ID 1540) and possesses a more pock-marked surface: this one may not belong to the set.

8.1.5 STONE

ID 743A Bedford, Bedfordshire
Reference: unpublished.

COMPOSITION

This comprises a set of 49 stone beads. The set was previously listed in the British Museum as bone.

CONTEXT AND ASSOCIATIONS

The context is unknown.

MORPHOLOGY AND MATERIAL

The individual beads are globular to oblate in shape. They vary in length from 5.0 to 18.0mm, in width from 4.0 to 14.0mm and the perforation diameters vary from 2.0 to 7.0mm (approximate measurements). They are made from dusky yellow fine-grained oolitic limestone (R. Ixer). The strung length was not determined.

MANUFACTURE

The surfaces of the beads are rough and eroded, so the degree of any original polish cannot be determined. There are two beads with possible aborted additional borings.

COMPLETENESS AND DAMAGE

The beads are very eroded, but essentially complete.

WEAR

Thread-polish is present within the perforations on three beads, and thread-wear and thread-pulls are common. There is also extreme bead-on-bead wear on all beads. They are therefore classified as very worn.

CONCLUSIONS

The rock type is available from Dorset to Hampshire, so they would have been imported to the area. The context unfortunately is not known.

ID 743B Kempston, Bedfordshire
Reference: unpublished.

COMPOSITION

The necklace consists of a set of 30 stone beads (Figure 8.1.8, bottom).

CONTEXT AND ASSOCIATIONS

The context is unknown.

MORPHOLOGY AND MATERIAL

No measurements were taken. The material is dusky yellow fine-grained oolitic limestone (R. Ixer).

MANUFACTURE

No traces were recorded.

COMPLETENESS AND DAMAGE

All are complete.

WEAR

Wear was not recorded.

8.2 COMPOSITE NECKLACES WITH TWO MATERIALS *(with Alison Sheridan)*

The entries are arranged in groups according to the combinations of raw materials employed. Necklaces containing disc beads are described first. A list of items studied and illustrated is shown in Table 8.2.1.

8.2.1 JET AND JET-LIKE DISC BEADS AND AMBER

ID 470. 1–37 Winterbourne Stoke G47, (Greenlands Farm), Wiltshire

References: Gingell 1988, 58–63; Beck and Shennan 1991, 182.

COMPOSITION

The necklace consists of thirty complete or near-complete disc beads of Kimmeridge shale, plus fragments of at least eight further disc beads of the same material, along with two large fusiform beads of amber (confusingly described as 'oblate' in Gingell 1988, 58–63), and two small oblate (fat annular) beads of amber (Figure 8.2.1, top, a–e). The disc beads are described and discussed in Chapter 7.1.2, so will ot be covered here.

CONTEXT AND ASSOCIATIONS

The necklace derives from a 'central' grave under a large disc barrow, associated with cremated remains of an adult, at least 25 years old, of indeterminate sex, plus a Series 5 dagger (ID 1183, Figure 3.1.9), a bronze awl (ID 1176, Figure 4.6.2) and traces of twined coarse grass or rushes, possibly representing matting. Two microscopic fragments, one of silver and the other gold, were found during sieving of a 'brown substance from the base of the cremation centre' (Gingell 1988, 63), originally thought to be an animal skin bag but found to be of charcoal, soil particles, chalk and bone.

MORPHOLOGY AND MATERIAL

The disc beads are illustrated in Figure 7.1.8 and Figure 8.2.1a–b; see Chapter 7.1.2 for further details. The two large fusiform beads of amber measure 27.3 and 24.4mm in length, 8.7 to 10.8mm and 10.5 to 12.4mm in their diameter, and have borehole diameters ranging between 1.8 and 1.9mm, and between 1.5 and 1.7mm respectively (ID 470.38–39) (Figure 8.2.1c–d). The larger of the two (ID 470.38) is an uneven, roughly fusiform shape, neither slender nor plump, with a squashed-circular cross section and tapering, flattish ends (of which one is markedly inclined). The borehole is slightly asymmetrically-placed. The smaller fusiform bead (ID 470.39) is plump and more obviously fusiform, with an irregular, slightly angular cross section shape and gently squared off ends (of which one is markedly inclined). As with the longer bead, the borehole is slightly asymmetrically-placed.

Of the two smaller amber beads, the complete small oblate bead is plump, roughly circular in plan and convex-sided in profile, with a central narrow borehole (ID 470.40) (Figure 8.2.1e). The length is 4.8mm, the maximum diameter 6.3mm, and the borehole diameter varies between 1.4 and 1.5mm. The other bead is incomplete and, probably of similar shape, but less plump; it has a roughly central narrow perforation of length 2.6 mm with surviving diameter 5.9 mm and a borehole diameter of 1.7 mm.

Laid end to end, the amber beads would have occupied an estimated length of 59mm. The overall length of the necklace is hard to assess, since it is not known how many more shale disc beads might have been present originally, but the extant disc beads bring the strung length of the necklace to just over 100mm.

Table 8.2.1. List of composite necklaces with two materials studied and illustrated.

Object	Site (Parish), County	Museum	Illustration
ID 248	Calais Wold 114, E. Yorks.	Hull	Figure 8.2.5
ID 275	Hay Top, nr. Monsal Dale, Derbys.	Sheff	Figure 8.2.1
ID 364-66; ID 742.1–10	Aldbourne 285 (G12), burial 1, Wilts.	BM	Figure 8.2.7
ID 427–32	Tan Hill, Bishops Cannings G46, Wilts.	BM	Figure 8.2.6
ID 442–48	Bloxworth G4a, Dorset	BM	Figure 8.2.5
ID 470	Winterbourne Stoke G47, Wilts.	Sal	Figure 8.2.1
ID 494–96; ID 878	Upton Lovell G2a (shaman), Wilts.	Dev	Figure 8.2.7
ID 501–2	Wilsford G16, Wilts.	Dev	Figure 8.2.3
ID 1466–68	"		Not illustrated
ID 503–504	Durrington G47, Wilts.	Dev	Figure 8.2.6
ID 510–11	Winterbourne Stoke G68, Wilts.	Dev	Figure 8.2.6
ID 512–14; ID 1504.1–14	Amesbury G39, Wilts.	Dev	Figure 8.2.3
ID 541–45; ID 1272–73;	Cowleaze (Winterbourne Steepleton), Dorset	Dor	Figure 8.2.4
ID 1268–69; ID 12 71–73;	"		"
ID 1275–77	"		"
ID 853–70; ID 1469	South Newton G1, Wilts.	Dev	Figure 8.2.8
ID 871–76	Warminster G10, Wilts.	Dev	Figure 8.2.8
ID 1165–67	Marshfield G5, Gloucs.	Bris	Figure 8.2.4
ID 1507A.1–21; ID 1507B	Winterbourne Stoke G64a, Wilts.	Dev	Figure 8.2.2

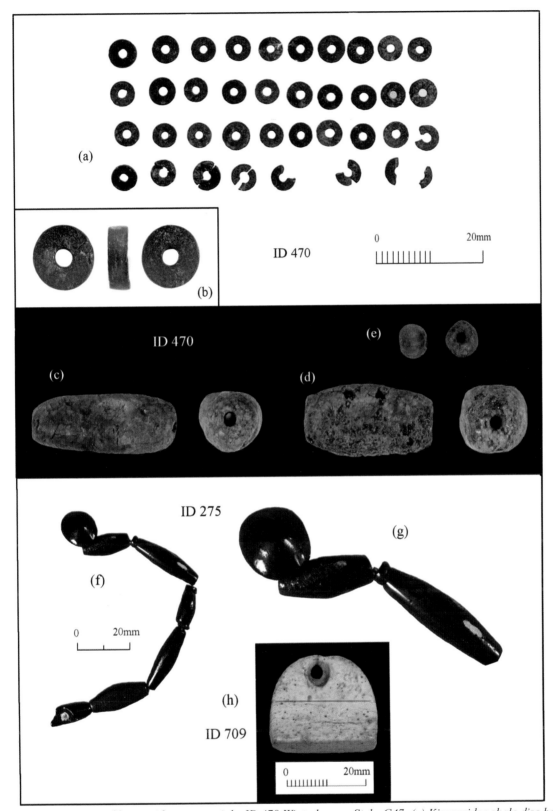

Figure 8.2.1. Composite necklaces with two materials. ID 470 Winterbourne Stoke G47: (a) Kimmeridge shale disc beads, see also Figure 7.1.8; (b) detailed views of representative disc bead; (c) ID 470.38 amber fusiform bead; (d) ID 470.39 amber fusiform bead; (e) ID 470.40 amber oblate bead. ID 275 Hay Top: (f) jet necklace; (g) detail of necklace; (h) associated bone pendant or fastener (ID 709).

Both the fusiform beads and one of the oblate beads are of a dark red amber, oxidised to a mid toffee colour; the other oblate bead is a bright red, oxidised to a light toffee colour. The process of oxidation has led to crazing of the surface of all the amber beads, and although they are now opaque they would originally have been translucent.

MANUFACTURE

The longer of the two amber fusiform beads shows no diagnostic features relating to manufacture. There are no striations and it is unclear whether the perforation had been drilled from both ends (although given the bead's length, this is highly likely) and the borehole interior is smooth. The other fusiform bead has faint, unidirectional striations on one (flat) end, and the borehole has rilling; it is unclear whether it had been drilled from both ends, but again this is likely.

The smaller amber beads have no striations; the complete bead has rilling in the borehole and evidence that it had been drilled from both ends. The smaller bead has a smooth borehole and it is not possible to tell whether it had been drilled from both ends. The oxidised condition of all the beads makes it hard to determine whether the beads had been polished, but there are hints of a low to medium sheen on both the fusiform beads, and a low sheen on the complete oblate bead.

COMPLETENESS AND DAMAGE

Both the fusiform beads and one of the oblate beads are complete; the other (ID 470.41) is 70% present. The latter has modern fracture scars, and it may well have broken during or since excavation.

WEAR

The larger of the fusiform beads appears worn, with thread-pull wear and slight smoothing of the edge of the borehole at one end, and slight thread-smoothing of the borehole edge at the other, inclined end. There may be some bead-on-bead wear at the inclined end. The other fusiform bead has only slight wear, with slight thread-smoothing to the borehole edge at one end. The complete oblate bead has thread-smoothed borehole edges and is slightly worn; the other oblate bead has no surviving borehole edges.

CONCLUSIONS

The fusiform beads are particularly large, and appear to be a mature Early Bronze Age type. They are considerably larger than the set of fusiform beads allegedly found with the amber spacer plate necklace from Wilsford-cum-Lake (ID 1360, Figure 7.3.1 and see Chapter 7.4.1 for a discussion of the ID 1360 finds). The oblate beads may however derive from an amber spacer plate necklace.

8.2.2 JET AND JET-LIKE BEADS, BUTTONS AND DISC BEADS, AND BONE

ID 275 Hay Top, near Monsal Dale, Derbyshire

References: Bateman 1861, 74–5; Davis and Thurnam 1865; Howarth 1899, 178; Shepherd 2009, 357, No. 14.

COMPOSITION

This necklace (Figure 8.2.1, bottom, f–h) comprises six fusiform beads, three tiny disc beads, one V-perforated button and what appears (from Davis and Thurnam's 1865 engraving) to be a fragment of a second button, plus an unusually-shaped bone object, possibly a pendant or, more probably, a fastener (ID 709, Figure 8.2.1h). Of these, the object resembling a fragmentary V-perforated button is no longer present. The items are fixed firmly to a base board and had been lacquered, so it was not possible to record this necklace in as much detail as other items.

CONTEXT AND ASSOCIATIONS

According to Bateman's description the necklace was recovered from a secondary interment in (under) the centre of a flat-topped barrow on the summit of a hill called Hay Top. The burial contained the remains of several individuals. Davis and Thurnam's plan of the barrow shows a contracted skeleton of an adult, on its left side; the sex was deemed to be female from the slenderness of the bones. Associated objects are recorded as 'several flints, including three thick arrow-points, and a curious bone ornament, with a hole for suspension round the neck' (Howarth 1899, 178), the latter found at the neck of the skeleton. The other items listed above were less clearly associated due to the presence of disarticulated bones in the vicinity but they had probably belonged with the bone object. The presence of arrowheads (if Bateman's account is correct) would not be typical for a female grave.

MORPHOLOGY AND MATERIAL

The six fusiform beads (Figure 8.2.1f–g) are slender, and vary in length from 11.0 to 23.6mm, in thickness from 6.5 to 8.35mm and in their perforation diameters from 1.7 to 2.7mm. In cross section they vary from squashed-circular to having one or two flattish sides; the ends are perpendicular to the long axis on two beads, and on the others one or both ends are angled. Three of the beads have squared-off ends; one has rounded ends; and one has a combination of both end shapes (Figure 8.2.1f–g). The tiny disc beads (visible between the top four fusiform beads in Figure 8.2.1f) are of fairly consistent size, with diameters ranging between 3.8 and 4.3mm, and thicknesses between 1.0 and 2.0mm. The outer edge of one bead is minimally convex, and is flat on the others. The button measures 12.5 by 13.3mm and is 5.0mm in height with a bridge diameter of *c.* 2.9mm; it has a roughly circular flat base and a medium-height dome, in the form of a continuous curve, with no facet. The perforations are slightly oval, with a relatively wide bridge. Together, these objects have a strung length of 127mm.

The colour, texture and surface condition of the fusiform beads and button is consistent with the material being jet (AS). The button is black and there are no obvious signs of surface cracking. One of the fusiform beads is black, one a rich dark brown, and the others a combination of the two colours – all features typical of jet beads. All the fusiform beads and the button could have been made from hard jet. It is not possible to judge whether the tiny disc beads are of jet without microscopic examination; one shows slight laminar cracking.

The bone pendant or fastener (ID 709) is evenly bell-shaped in profile and rectangular in cross section (Figure 8.2.1h). The flat base is markedly expanded on both sides and all the angles are slightly rounded off. The object is 21.5mm high, 27.4mm wide at the base and 5.2mm thick at the top. The single perforation near to the top has an hour-glass section; the external diameter is 6.9mm and the narrowest diameter 2.8mm. The hard creamy-white material was initially thought to have been unusual, and possibly ivory. However Sonia O'Connor confirmed through microscopic study that the bone was not cetacean (see Appendix IV, Figures 8a and 8b). The source is therefore a large mammal bone.

MANUFACTURE

The only manufacturing traces noted on the beads and button are a slight faceting of the long fusiform bead next to the damaged bead at the end of the strand, and incompletely polished-out spall scars on two of the fusiform beads. The beads and button may have been polished to a high sheen, but the presence of lacquer coating makes this hard to verify. All surfaces of the bone pendant or fastener had been carefully polished, removing all grinding striations. The perforation had been drilled from both sides and rilling is visible within it.

COMPLETENESS AND DAMAGE

The components are generally in good condition, with the button, the disc beads and four of the fusiform beads being complete and undamaged (save for minor spalling to two of the fusiform beads, suffered during manufacture and not completely polished away, and for the surface cracking to four of the fusiform beads as noted above). The degree of completeness of the fusiform bead adjacent to the button was recorded as 97%. The fusiform bead at the other end of the string – shown as a complete bead in Jewitt's engraving as published in *Crania Britannica* (Davis and Thurnam 1865) – actually lacks around half of its body on one side, and the abraded fracture surface indicates that it had broken in antiquity. This bead also has an ancient spall scar at one end.

No damage is visible on the bone pendant or fastener and the piece is complete.

WEAR

The only evidence noted was possible thread-wear to one end of one fusiform bead and smoothing of the fracture surfaces of the damaged fusiform bead. Whether the angling of the ends noted on some of the fusiform beads had been due to wear, or was an original design feature, is uncertain.

The rear surface of the bone fastener or pendant could not be examined. However the front surface has faint irregular and widely spaced striations running from top to bottom. There are also faint sporadic transverse scratches on the flat base. Immediately above the perforation and running across the top facet are marked transverse scratches suggestive of string- or thong-wear. The item is classified as slightly worn.

CONCLUSIONS

This small collection of components – which had presumably been worn as a single-strand necklace – presents the appearance of having been amassed from other necklaces, with the fusiform beads being of characteristic shape and size for those found in spacer plate necklaces. Their consistent slenderness, and the fact that several have squared-off ends, suggests that they could have belonged to the same 'parent' necklace. The very flat long bead is of a shape that suggests that it could originally have been positioned immediately below a spacer plate, where the necessity to accommodate multiple strands of beads meant that beads had to be flattish. The small fusiform bead could have belonged to the innermost strand of a spacer plate necklace. The tiny disc beads are of a type known from plain, ?single-strand disc bead necklaces (e.g. ID 245, ID 250, ID 251 and ID 252 Garton Slack; Chapter 7.1) and from multiple-strand necklaces of various designs (e.g. ID 247 Calais Wold, Chapter 7.2). All the jet beads and buttons could have come from previous necklaces and may well represent 'heirloom' items.

The bone object (Figure 8.2.1h) could have been made as a distinctively-shaped fastener to secure the necklace and as such is comparable with the unusual-shaped jet fasteners found, for example, at ID 379–90 Pockley (Chapter 7.2). Alternatively, it could have been a pendant. It is a very well-made and attractive object, and no parallels for its shape are known to the authors.

8.2.3 FOSSIL AND FIRED CLAY DISC BEADS

ID 1507A.1–21 and ID 1507B Winterbourne Stoke G64a, Wiltshire

References: Hoare 1812, 114 and pl.XIII; Cunnington MSS, xi, 30; Annable and Simpson 1964, 61 and 116, no. 481.

COMPOSITION

The material comprised 51 beads, 48 being of clay (of which 21 survived in 1964) and three fossil beads. A further 22 beads, formed from fossil shells were found separately (Figure 8.2.2).

CONTEXT AND ASSOCIATIONS

A circular flat barrow within the Coniger Group contained a double cist. No details of any human burial were recorded.

The set of 51 beads was recovered from the smaller of the two cists; the fossil necklace was found in the larger cist associated with a sheep burial and small bronze dagger (now lost).

MORPHOLOGY AND MATERIAL

A total of the 17 complete clay disc beads and some small fragments now survive; they are made from fine clay with no inclusions and are brown in colour (ID 1507A 1–18). In length they vary from 3.0 to 3.8mm, although most are in the region of 3.3 to 3.5mm. The width varies from 5.0 to 5.7mm and the perforation diameters range between 0.1 and 1.8mm (Figure 8.2.2b). The three fossil beads (ID 1507A 19–21) are formed from segments of the stem of fossil encrinites; they are buff in colour, of lengths 1.8, 2.0 and 2.3mm, widths 5.7, 6.5 and 6.7mm, and perforation diameters 1.8, 1.5 and 2.0mm respectively (Figure 8.2.2c). A total of 22 pieces of *Dentalium* shell survive (ID 1507B). Surviving lengths vary from 4.8 to 24mm but all are broken. The strung length for the clay and fossil encrinite beads is 118mm minimum (Figure 8.2.2b and Figure 8.2.2c), while the original strung length for the *Dentalium* necklace is indeterminate (Figure 8.2.2a and Figure 8.2.2d).

MANUFACTURE

In general the fired clay beads are fairly uniform in shape and size, with neatly squared off edges. No traces of finishing are visible due to conservation lacquer.

COMPLETENESS AND DAMAGE

The three fossil beads are complete, but the clay disc beads are often damaged. Only one is complete with the others surviving between the 60% and 95% levels. Damage consists of chips on the sides, but these are of indeterminate age. The shell beads are very broken up, and many are glued together; 17 are broken at both ends and 5 at the upper, wider end only.

WEAR

Thread-wear is visible on 12 of the clay disc beads, and in five cases this consists of distinct thread-pulls. Overall seven were classed as slightly worn and a further five are worn (plus five indeterminate). Wear on fossil encrinite beads is difficult to assess, but one has possible thread-wear and can be classified as worn. Wear on the fossil shell beads does not appear to be excessive, apart from the fractures, some of which may well be ancient.

CONCLUSIONS

These unusual necklaces include the only examples of fired clay beads known from the groups studied. In form and colour they may have been designed to imitate a disc bead necklace made from shale or jet.

8.2.4 JET AND JET-LIKE MATERIALS AND AMBER

ID 501–2 and ID 1466–68 Wilsford G16, Wiltshire

References: Hoare 1812, 200; Annable and Simpson 1964, 52 and 107, nos. 308–12.

COMPOSITION

The material consists of a total of six beads, two of shale and four of amber (one now lost).

CONTEXT AND ASSOCIATIONS

Within the double bell barrow located in the Normanton Down Group, the beads were associated with a primary cremation burial under the east mound. There was also a small ceramic cup but this is lost.

MORPHOLOGY AND MATERIAL

There are two squashed oblate beads (ID 501 and ID 502, Figure 8.2.3, top left) of shale, possibly Kimmeridge shale (B17 and B18; AS). They have neatly incised close radial line decoration. They measure 6.4 by 9mm and 10.7 by 12.4mm, with perforation diameters 2.3 and 2.8mm respectively. The biconical bead of dark red amber measures 14 by 15mm; the perforation diameter is 3.2mm. The squashed globular bead of dark red amber (ID 1467) measures 11.0 by 12.6mm, with the perforation diameter 2.8mm. The fusiform bead of bright red amber (ID 1468) measures 13.2 by 9.7mm, with the perforation diameter 2.0mm. The strung length is a minimum of 55mm.

MANUFACTURE

The shale beads are very neatly made, undoubtedly by the same person. The outer profiles are evenly D-shaped. The decoration is similar on each, but on ID 501 there are two concentric incised guide lines around each perforation, while on ID 502 there are three. All grooves are *c.* 0.2mm in width. The biconical amber bead ID 1466 is also decorated, with two concentric incised lines at each perforated end.

COMPLETENESS AND DAMAGE

ID 501 is complete and the other shale bead, together with the biconical and globular amber beads, are almost complete. ID 1466 has a modern chip and the fusiform amber bead ID 1468 is severely broken at one end (60% present) in modern times.

WEAR

Shale bead ID 502 and two of the amber beads have minor ancient chips. All the beads except ID 1468, where degree of wear was indeterminate, display thread-wear and in the case of ID 502 this includes thread-pull and bead-on-bead

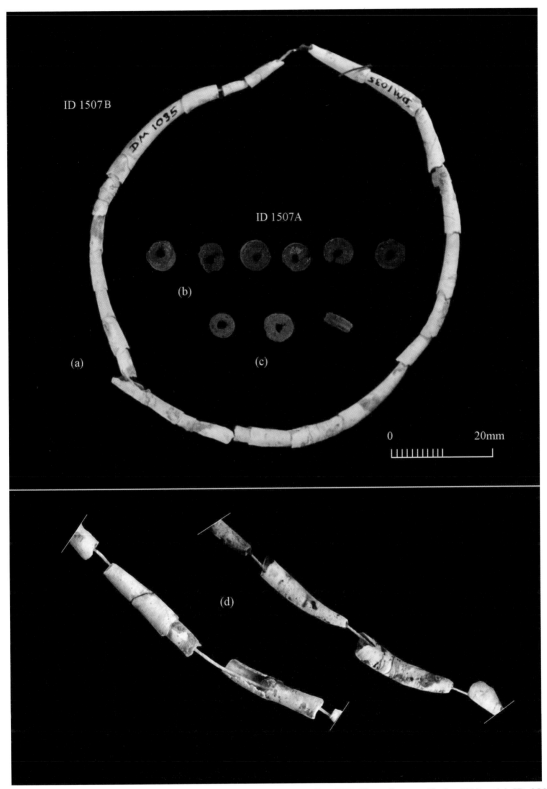

Figure 8.2.2. Composite necklaces with two materials. ID 1507A and 1507B Winterbourne Stoke G64a: (a) ID 1507B shell necklace; (b) selection of ID 1507A fired clay beads; (c) ID 1507A fossil beads; (d) details of elements of the shell necklace.

wear. In this respect, the two shale beads are very worn, and two amber beads are only slightly worn. The decoration of the two shale beads is partly worn away in each case (Figure 8.2.3).

CONCLUSIONS

This is a small but varied group of fancy beads. Fusiform amber beads are fairly unusual and the biconical amber bead is a rare type; furthermore it is also decorated. The very fine radially decorated shale beads are also a rare type, and it would appear that the decoration may be imitating the patterns found on fossil ammonites.

ID 512–14 and ID 1504.1–14 Amesbury G39, Wiltshire

References: Hoare 1812, 159; Annable and Simpson 1964, 60 and 116, nos. 467–72.

COMPOSITION

The material consists of a total of 17 objects comprising two jet beads, 13 amber beads, an amber fastener and a V-perforated jet button. Five further beads of unknown type or material are lost.

CONTEXT AND ASSOCIATIONS

The objects were found with a primary cremation burial under a bowl barrow located west of the New King Barrows.

MORPHOLOGY AND MATERIAL

The V-perforated button of jet (ID 512, Figure 8.2.3, top right and bottom) has a maximum diameter of 17.3mm and is of height 12.7mm. The button is black to brown in colour, high-domed with straight sides and a lightly convex base (also see Figure 5.2.3 and Figure 5.2.7). The squat fusiform bead of jet (ID 513, Figure 8.2.3) measures 12.1 by 12.8mm and has a perforation diameter of 3mm. The slender fusiform bead of jet (ID 514; Figure 8.2.3) measures 7.5 by 6.3mm and has a perforation diameter of 2.1mm.

Of the 12 squashed amber globular beads (ID 1504), four are bright red, five are dark red, and three are of indeterminate original colour (Figure 8.2.3a). Their thicknesses range from 7.9 to 11.4mm and their maximum widths from 7.8 to 10.2mm. The perforation diameters range from 1.5 to 2.3mm. There is also a further fragment of a fusiform bead of indeterminate colour and not measurable apart from the perforation diameter of 1.7mm (not illustrated). The conical fastener (Figure 8.2.3b–c) has a flat base and a single perforation straight through the sides of the cone; it is not V-perforated. The diameter is 10.5mm, the height 6.0mm, and the perforation diameter 1.8mm. The overall strung length is 147mm, including the button but excluding the fastener.

The V-perforated button (ID 512) and the two fusiform beads (ID 513 and ID 514) have both been identified as being of jet (B12, B10 and B11 respectively; AS).

MANUFACTURE

Longitudinal faint striations are visible on the faces of the two fusiform jet beads and on the base of the jet button. Rilling is visible within the perforations of nine globular amber beads, the fusiform amber bead and the perforation of the conical amber fastener.

COMPLETENESS AND DAMAGE

All items except the fusiform amber bead (70% present) are complete or almost complete. Modern loss includes chips on the jet button and one fusiform jet bead (ID 513), on two globular amber buttons and on the margins of the amber fastener.

WEAR

The fragmentary globular amber bead and the fusiform amber bead appear to have been broken on the side and end respectively in antiquity. The jet button perforations show strong wear on both inner and outer margins of the perforations (ID 512, Figure 8.2.3). This may indicate that the button had functioned as a button or toggle initially and then later on as a 'necklace button'. Both jet beads (ID 513 and ID 514, Figure 8.2.3) also have thread-wear, and also bead-on-bead wear. All are classified as very worn. The amber fastener displays thread-wear and bead-on-bead wear and is worn (ID 1504, Figure 8.2.3c). Amongst the amber beads nine show thread-wear; five are classified as worn and seven as slightly worn (one is indeterminate).

CONCLUSIONS

This interesting group includes an unusual small fastener of amber and also a single very worn jet button which may have been mounted as a central piece in the necklace. The two jet fusiform beads are probably recycled from a spacer plate necklace, and specifically from the inner strand. In contrast, the amber beads are chunky and rounded in form and are not similar to the beads found in amber spacer plate necklaces. They are also rather larger than standard spacer plate squashed globular beads; however a series of such beads were found as part of the group from Wilsford-cum-Lake which includes a series of spacer plates (see Figure 7.3.1).

ID 541–45 and ID 1272–77 Winterbourne Steepleton, Dorset

Reference: Woodward 1991, fig. 5, 5–19.

COMPOSITION

The material consists of a total of 15 items of shale and amber, comprising three V-perforated buttons in shale (ID 541–43) and four in amber (ID 1268–71), two shale beads (ID 544 and ID 545) and six amber beads (ID 1272–77) (Figure 8.2.4, top).

CONTEXT AND ASSOCIATIONS

The beads and buttons were found with Cremation C, within Enclosure C next to a bowl barrow (Woodward 1991, fig. 31). The enclosure was interpreted as a saucer barrow (*ibid*, 60). The cremation burial had been placed in the base of a pit (1240) *c*.1.20m wide and 0.60m deep and

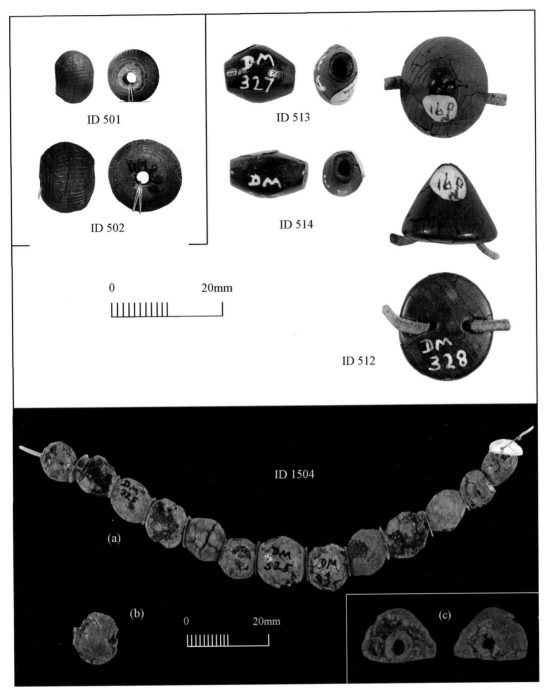

Figure 8.2.3. Composite necklaces with two materials. ID 501–2 Wilsford G16: shale oblate beads with decoration. Amesbury G39: ID 512 jet button; ID 513 squat fusiform jet bead; ID 514 slender fusiform jet bead; ID 1504 (a) amber necklace, (b) amber fastener, (c) detail of perforations on amber fastener.

the human remains and ornaments were covered by a small cairn (1098) of flints and pieces of sarsen (*ibid*, fig. 34).

MORPHOLOGY AND MATERIAL

The three shale buttons (ID 541–43) measure 12.7 by 12.2mm, 13.5 by 13mm and 12.1 by 11.8mm respectively. The two with surviving apices are high-domed, with heights of 7.1 and 6.2mm. The four amber buttons are oval in shape, measuring 20 by 13.5mm (ID 1268), 20 by 10.3mm (ID 1269), 16.5 by 13.6mm (ID 1370) and 12 by 7.2mm (ID

1271). They are or medium height with rounded upper surfaces (see also Figure 5.2.9).

The two annular beads (ID 544 and ID 545) measure 5.8 by 10mm and 2.5 by 3.0mm with perforation diameters 2.5 and 3.0mm respectively. The three squashed amber globular beads (ID 1272–74) are dull to bright orange in colour, of length 2.5 to 5.1mm, width 6.9 to 7.7mm and with perforation diameters 1.1 and 1.8mm. There are also three squashed globular beads in dark red amber (ID 1275–77), length 2.0 to 5.3mm, widths 5.3 to 7.3mm and perforation diameters 2 to 2.5mm. The strung length is approximately

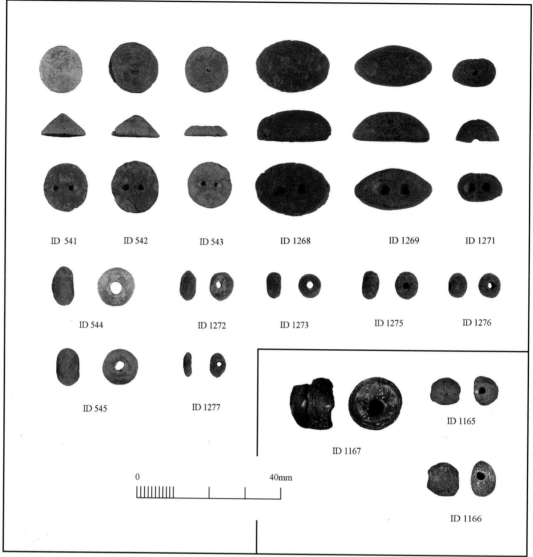

Figure 8.2.4. Composite necklaces with two materials. Winterbourne Steepleton: ID 541–43 shale buttons; ID 1268, ID 1269 and ID 1271 amber buttons; ID 544 and ID 545 shale beads; ID 1272, ID 1273, ID 1275, ID 1276 and ID 1277 amber beads. Marshfield G5: ID 1167 shale bead; ID 1165 and ID 1166 amber beads.

36mm. The three black buttons and the two annular beads (ID 544 and ID 545) are of Kimmeridge shale (AS, *contra* Pollard, in Woodward 1991, 102).

MANUFACTURE

No traces of manufacture survive on the beads. Both holes in each V-perforation of the shale buttons show one change in drill direction, and three of the four amber buttons have slight traces of rilling surviving in the perforations. ID 1271 is made from the broken portion of a large globular bead.

COMPLETENESS AND DAMAGE

Shale buttons ID 541 and ID 542 are almost complete, and the latter has one modern chip. ID 543 has a catastrophic modern break and survives at the 60% level only. Three

of the amber buttons are complete, or almost so, while ID 1270 has a major ancient break and is only 75% present. All the beads are complete apart from one (ID 1277) which has a small ancient break at the margin.

WEAR

Two of the shale buttons display wear on the outer edges of the perforations, indicating 'necklace wear', but ID 541 has wear at the inner and outer margins of the perforations. This item may have functioned as a toggle prior to use in a necklace. It is classified as worn, whilst ID 542 and ID 543 are only slightly worn. All three show signs of fabric rub on the flat base. Wear to the perforations of the three better-preserved amber buttons occurs only on the inner margins. This suggests that these items were employed as toggles or garment fasteners, and not as elements within a necklace. ID

1268 is worn, ID 1269 and ID 1270 slightly worn, and wear on broken ID 1270 is indeterminate. Thread-wear is visible on seven out of the eight beads (ID 1274 is indeterminate), and in four cases includes distinct thread-pulls. Overall three are classed as slightly worn and four as worn.

CONCLUSIONS

It seems that all three shale buttons could have been strung in a necklace, although one of them may have been used as a garment fastener before, or indeed after, that usage. In contrast, three at least of the amber buttons probably functioned as toggles or garment fasteners. One of them was made from a broken portion of a pre-existing large globular bead. The amber beads appear to have been obtained from two different sources in terms of colour, but are variable in terms of both shape and size. It is probable that all of them derive from amber spacer plate necklaces.

ID 1165–67 Marshfield G5, Gloucestershire

Reference: Grinsell 1968, 38 and fig. 9, nos. 56a(i) and (ii).

COMPOSITION

The necklace consists of a total of three beads, two of amber and one of shale (ID 1165–67, Figure 8.2.4, bottom right).

CONTEXT AND ASSOCIATIONS

The beads were found with a probably female cremation burial under a round barrow. They were associated with a pair of shale studs (replicas only survive: ID 1168 and ID 1169, Chapter 5.6) and a copper alloy awl (ID 1170, Chapter 4.6).

MORPHOLOGY AND MATERIAL

The jet-like biconical bead (ID 1167) measures 12.3 by 14.0mm with a perforation diameter of 9.8mm. The plump fusiform bead of amber (ID 1165) is dark orange, 8.0 by 6.6mm, with perforation diameters 2.0 and 1.3mm. The flattened ovoid bead of dark red amber (ID 1166) measures 8.5 by 8.3 by 6.2mm with a perforation diameter of 3.1mm. The strung length is approximately 29mm. The jet-like biconical bead (ID 1167) is of shale on the basis of its stony texture and laminar fracturing; it exhibits no criss-cross cracking or brown colouration.

MANUFACTURE

There are faint circumferential polishing striations towards one perforation on the shale bead, but no traces survive on the amber items.

COMPLETENESS AND DAMAGE

The shale bead is only 75% present but all the damage,

at both ends and around the body, is modern. The amber bead ID 1166 is complete but ID 1165, at 80%, has one side broken away in antiquity.

WEAR

One of the amber beads was damaged in antiquity (above). Due to damage to the ends of the shale bead, and the degraded surfaces of the amber items any traces of thread-wear could not be detected. Wear on the shale bead could be estimated as slightly worn, but in the case of the amber beads it was indeterminate.

CONCLUSIONS

This small collection of three very different beads is of particular interest from this region. They all appear to be mature Early Bronze Age types, and their association with the pair of shale studs is of particular note. It is one of the few cases of studs having been found in association with beads.

8.2.5 JET AND JET-LIKE MATERIALS AND FAIENCE

ID 248 Calais Wold 114, East Yorkshire

References: Mortimer 1905, 169 and fig. 426; Longworth 1984, 734, pl. 100a; Sheridan and Shortland 2004, fig. 21.1; Brindley 2007, 309–10, 313–5.

COMPOSITION

The necklace comprises nine beads of jet – Mortimer described them as being of 'jet and Kimeridge [sic] coal' – and one or two of faience (Figure 8.2.5, top). Only one faience bead exists now and Mortimer's published illustration shows only one, although his account refers to two. This may be an error, as Mortimer is known to have included incorrect information elsewhere in his book.

CONTEXT AND ASSOCIATIONS

The material was found accompanying cremated human remains in an upright Collared Urn at the base of a round barrow. The urn was one of two, found 'rather south-east of centre', each containing the cremated remains of an adult. The necklace had clearly not been on the corpse in the pyre, as the beads show no sign of heat damage. There remains some uncertainty as to which of the two Collared Urns was the one associated with the beads.

MORPHOLOGY AND MATERIAL

One of the jet beads is of short fusiform shape, while the others can be described as 'squat biconical', with curving rather than crisply faceted sides. The profile of the latter varies, with two approximating to an oblate shape, and

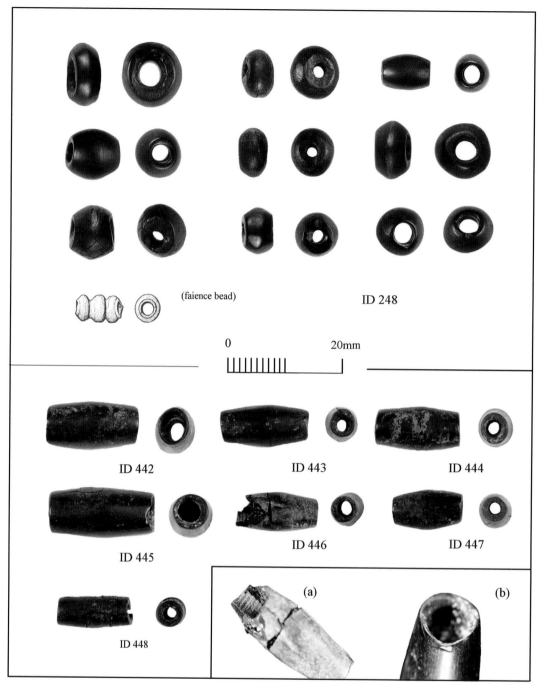

Figure 8.2.5. Composite necklaces with two materials. ID 248 Calais Wold 114: nine jet beads and a faience bead (drawing by Marion O'Neil). ID 442–48 Bloxworth: jet beads. Inset: (a) ID 446 exhibiting borehole rilling; (b) ID 445 wear caused by thread-pull.

the width of the boreholes in comparison to the beads' maximum diameter bead varies. Most of the ends are gently squared off; two are slightly dished. The length varies between 5.7 and 9.9mm (with the short fusiform bead being 9.1mm long), the diameter between 7.0 and 12.3mm, and the diameter of the borehole between 2.3 and 5.2mm. The strung length would have been 71mm.

Macroscopically, these beads appear to be of jet: their black colour, showing as black-brown under strong light, is typical, as is the fine woody texture visible on most of

the beads and the pattern of criss-cross cracking seen on all of them in various degrees of severity. Compositional analysis of all the beads using XRF (at NMS by Lore Troalen) has provided further confirmation; the jet will almost certainly have come from the Whitby area, not far from Calais Wold.

The faience bead is incomplete and segmented, of length 7.9mm, diameter 4.8mm and borehole diameter 2.3mm. The surface is a pale turquoise, darker towards one end, and is mostly matt, with numerous shallow pits formed through gassing-off during the bead's firing. Part of the surface has spalled off to reveal a pale blue subsurface, and it is clear from the fracture surfaces that this colour extends through the core. Fine-grained sand, probably crushed, had been used. At one point on the subsurface there is a tiny area of coppery red colour. This bead was analysed by Katherine Eremin (formerly of NMS) using electron microprobe compositional analysis. The high silica content relates to the fact that quartz (sand) is the main constituent, and the presence of copper relates to the use of a material containing copper as the glaze colourant.

MANUFACTURE

All the jet beads had been polished to a low sheen. Faint striations were noted on one end of several beads and on both ends of one example. One retains traces of the faceting that had been part of its initial shaping. The use of a bow- or pump-action drill to perforate at least some of the beads is suggested by the rilling observed in the boreholes of three beads, and the chipping around the borehole seen on two examples probably resulted from the drilling process. The shape of the borehole varies between beads; some were clearly drilled from both ends.

Although the interior surface of the hole of the faience bead shows no corrugation, it is clear that this would have been made by wrapping faience paste around a piece of straw or other organic material, then rolling this tube of faience paste against a 'butter pat'-shaped former to create the segments (Sheridan and Shortland 2004). It is unclear whether the glaze had been applied to, or integrated with, the paste.

COMPLETENESS AND DAMAGE

The jet beads are all complete but for the odd missing chip or spall, all representing ancient damage, some (or all) of it occurring during manufacture. One bead suggests that an attempt had been made to file smooth a shallow spall scar on one end.

The faience bead is incomplete, with just three segments present. Its current state matches Mortimer's illustration, and, given that the fracture surfaces at either end appear to be relatively fresh, it would seem that breakage had occurred during excavation.

WEAR

In general, the jet beads are not heavily worn. They all have thread-polishing of the borehole, either towards its ends or all along, but in general the edges of the boreholes had not been smoothed by the thread, and there are no obvious signs of bead-on-bead wear; grinding striations survive on the end/s of several of the beads. It is harder to detect signs of wear to the faience bead.

CONCLUSIONS

The use-wear evidence suggests that this necklace had probably not been worn for long before burial. However, since the beads on this composite necklace had probably not been tightly strung (unless there had been additional organic beads that have not survived) then the wearing of the necklace need not have produced obvious signs of wear. The use of this type of necklace, along with the shape of the jet beads and the inclusion of the segmented faience bead, indicates a sharing of practice with southern England, particularly Wessex; it seems likely that its owner was emulating a Wessex fashion.

ID 427–432 Tan Hill, Bishops Cannings G46, Wiltshire

Reference: Thurnam 1860, 324–5; 1871, 509–10, fig. 200.

COMPOSITION

The necklace comprises five fairly plump fusiform beads (ID 427–31) and a pendant or fastener of wedge-shaped trapezoidal form (ID 432, Figure 8.2.6, top). There was also a segmented faience bead (not illustrated).

CONTEXT AND ASSOCIATIONS

The necklace was found with a possibly primary deposit of cremated remains beneath Thurnam's bowl barrow 15. Thurnam recorded the finding of burnt bones 'apparently of a female or young person' at a depth of three and a half feet. The basis for the sex identification was not specified. Note that Thurnam referred only to three beads of jet (plus the 'pendant') rather than the five beads that are present and are shown in his engraving (Thurnam 1871, fig. 200). That illustration omits the faience bead.

MORPHOLOGY AND MATERIAL

Four of the five fusiform beads (ID 427–30) are symmetrical in profile and are of consistent size, ranging between 15.8 and 15.9mm in length and 9.6 to 9.9mm in maximum diameter (Figure 8.2.6a–b). The fifth (ID 431) is slightly asymmetrical and smaller (12.0 by 9.2mm). ID 427–28 and ID 430 are round in cross section, ID 429 is flattish on one side, and ID 431 is slightly oval. All the beads have gently squared-off ends, perpendicular to the beads' long axis except for ID 430, where they splay very slightly. The longitudinal perforation is centrally positioned. The pendant or fastener (ID 432) is approximately trapezoidal in plan, with a slightly convex narrow top edge and faceted sides and a fairly straight, broader lower edge (Figure 8.2.6c–d). It is wedge-shaped in profile, tapering to the lower edge and roughly rectangular in cross section, but wider at one side. The length is 18.3mm, the width at the base is 12.3mm, and the maximum thickness is 6.3mm.

A narrow borehole 2.2mm in diameter runs through the narrow side close to the top edge. The strung length, excluding the pendant or fastener, is 75mm.

All the components are of the same material, identifiable as jet by its colour, woody texture, warmth to the touch, criss-cross pattern of cracking, conchoidal flake scars and (on the fastener/pendant) 'orange peel' surface irregularities. The cracked condition indicates soft jet. The identification as jet was confirmed through XRF analysis of one fusiform bead (ID 428) (MD/DH) and through oil immersion reflected light microscopy and reflectance measurement, by Dr J M Jones, of a minute fragment that had probably originated in bead ID 428.

The faience bead formerly had five segments (Thurnam 1871, fig. 186; note that Thurnam's caption to this illustration is misleading) but now exists as a three-segment piece, 10.4mm long and 5.1mm in diameter, plus a detached segment and three small fragments. It is roughly cylindrical, with fairly broad, flattish segments. One side of the bead, where the glaze is concentrated, is a dark turquoise colour and has a low sheen; elsewhere the whitish, yellowish-buff and grey-buff core colour shows through, and the surface is matt.

MANUFACTURE

The jet items could not be removed from their modern display thread for detailed inspection. However, none of the fusiform beads showed any traces of the facets that had been part of their initial shaping, but faint striations from the grinding process were noted on ID 429 and on ID 431. A hole on the side of ID 429 indicates that the borehole had been drilled from both ends. All the beads had been polished to a high sheen. Faint striations from grinding were noted on the top, narrow surface of the pendant or fastener, running across it. Irregularities on its surface suggest that this object had probably been made from a small pebble of jet, collected from the beach around Whitby, with some of its original surface contours and features being preserved. The object has a medium to high surface sheen.

The faience bead had been shaped by rolling the tube of paste against a grooved 'butter pat' former, to create evenly-shaped ridges and hollows. The presence of a glaze drip running along the interior indicates that the glaze had been applied to the bead, rather than being mixed in with the paste.

COMPLETENESS AND DAMAGE

The fusiform beads are all virtually complete, the missing chips having been lost since excavation due to the process of cracking. Criss-cross, longitudinal and concentric cracking, to various degrees of severity, was noted on all the beads, with some springing. On ID 429, one side is markedly less cracked and also darker in colour than the other. Two of the beads (ID 427 and ID 430) showed signs of having been coated with a consolidant. Around 90% of the pendant or fastener is present; there is an ancient break beside

the borehole on one side, with further loss from this area (including part of the wall around the borehole) since the time of Thurnam's illustration. There is also major spalling to one face since excavation. There are traces suggesting the presence of a thin surface coating of consolidant.

WEAR

Inspection of all the items was hindered by the presence of modern thread, but it was possible to discern a little thread-polish to the interior of the borehole close to the ends in beads ID 428, ID 429, ID 430 and ID 431. Minimal thread-smoothing of the edge of the borehole was evident at one or both ends of ID 428, ID 429 and ID 430. One possible thread-pull groove was noted at one end of ID 431. On ID 429 the fracture surface, where the drill had penetrated through the bead's wall, had been worn smooth. No obvious bead-on-bead wear was noted. Some thread-polish was noted in the interior of the pendant or fastener ID 432, and the surviving end of the borehole shows a little thread-smoothing. Overall wear on the beads is provisionally classified as worn, and that on the pendant or fastener as slightly worn.

CONCLUSIONS

The general consistency in the shape and in details of manufacture of the fusiform beads (e.g. their gently squared-off ends) suggests that they had been made together as a set, or as part of a larger necklace. The apparent difference in the degree of wear between the beads and the pendant or fastener could be taken to indicate that the beads had been 'recycled' from a spacer plate necklace, with the pendant or fastener as a subsequent addition. It is uncertain whether this object would have lain at the front of the necklace, as a pendant, or at the back, as a fastener; its lateral perforation ensured that it would lie flat, with maximum visual impact, whichever way it was deployed. The overall form of this necklace, comprising a few beads and a pendant or fastener, suggests a date in the early second millennium, perhaps around 1750 cal BC.

ID 442–48 Bloxworth Down, Barrow 4a, Dorset

References: Warne 1866, Pt. II, 13; Payne 1892, 22, no. 67; Abercromby 1907, fig. 197; Longworth 1984, 182 no. 372; Longworth and Haith 1992, 157 and pls. 5–6.

COMPOSITION

This necklace, reportedly comprising '20 jet and shell [sic] beads', was found in 1854 (Henry Durden, quoted in Longworth and Haith 1992, 157), although only 12 beads are mentioned in Payne's catalogue of the Durden Collection (1892, 22) (Figure 8.2.5). Today the British Museum has only ten complete or near-complete beads (of which seven are of jet and three are segmented faience beads), along with a glass phial containing several fragments of one or more segmented faience beads. It is likely that this phial contains parts of the additional beads shown in Abercromby's illustration of 1907.

CONTEXT AND ASSOCIATIONS

The beads were found with a fragmentary 'pair of tweezers' (ID 767, Figure 4.8.1) of bone, a fragment of a bone pin, and cremated bones, in an inverted Collared Urn (Longworth 1984, 182, no. 372). This was the primary grave, the urn being deposited in a pit cut into the natural chalk, under the centre of a disc barrow; the barrow had also contained several secondary inhumations. The bone objects were not burnt.

MORPHOLOGY AND MATERIAL

The seven jet beads (Figure 8.2.5, bottom) range in shape from virtually cylindrical (in the case of ID 448) to slender fusiform (ID 442–46) and medium-girth fusiform (ID 447), with cross sections ranging from circular (ID 444 and ID 448) to squashed-circular (ID 442 and ID 445–47) and angular squashed-circular (ID 443). In most cases, the ends are squared off, with ID 442 and 445 each having one cupped end. The ends are perpendicular to the long axis in ID 444 and 445, and very slightly angled on the others. In length they range from 12.6mm (ID 447) to 15.8mm (ID 442); the narrowest is the cylindrical bead ID 448 (4.8 by 5.0mm), and the thickest, ID 447 (6.7mm). The longitudinal borehole is centrally positioned in all cases but one (ID 447), where it is slightly eccentric and its diameter ranges between 2.2 and 3.6mm.

The three surviving faience beads (not illustrated) are, like the fragments, segmented. The longest, at 16.8mm, has eight segments but had nine when Abercromby's 1907 photograph was taken, and had been incomplete even then; the others each have six segments and are incomplete, with one 10.8mm long and the other 11.3mm long. In diameter they range between 4.3 and 4.7mm, with wide longitudinal holes between 2.6 and *c.* 3.1mm in diameter; all are roughly circular in cross section and all have segments that are evenly defined around the bead's circumference. One of the missing beads seems to taper towards one end and to have indistinct segments.

It is clear, both from macro- and microscopic examination and from compositional analysis (by XRF; MD/DH) of ID 444, ID 446 and ID 448, that the dark-coloured beads are definitely not of amber (*contra* many earlier writers). In colour they are mostly blackish and black-brown, or dark brown to black-brown. ID 446 is a grey and blackish-brown, with a hint of red-brown, while ID 448 is a rusty brown colour where the subsurface is exposed. A wood grain texture was noted on all but one of the beads, as was criss-cross cracking. All these features are characteristic of jet and this identification was confirmed by the XRF analysis of ID 444 and ID 446 (MD/DH). ID 448 was found to have a high iron and low zirconium content, features normally found on cannel coal or shale, although its woody texture and crack pattern suggested that the material could be a low grade, high-iron jet. This was confirmed through further analysis of a minuscule detached chip probably from this bead, undertaken by Dr J.M. Jones using oil immersion reflected light microscopy and reflectance measurement. This confirmed the material as iron-rich, pyritic jet. His analysis of another chip, probably from ID 446, confirmed its material as jet.

The faience beads had also previously been mis-identified, as of shell. The core colour of the faience is pale buff and whitish. The glaze is of variable thickness and discontinuous; in places, it is a bright turquoise, elsewhere pale turquoise; inside the longest bead is a glaze drip that is greenish. Where the glaze is thickest and most glassy, it has a low sheen.

MANUFACTURE

Facet traces from the shaping of the fusiform beads were noted as faint or very faint features in ID 442 and ID 445–47, and as a marked feature in ID 443. Faint or very faint striations were noted towards one or both ends of beads ID 443 and ID 445, at the centre of ID 443, ID 446 and ID 447, and on the facets on ID 447. The borehole had been drilled from both ends in every case, with a mis-alignment in ID 442; fairly crisp rilling is visible where part of the end had broken away on ID 446 (Figure 8.2.5 inset a), and fainter rilling was noted in all the other beads.

It may be that the cupped ends noted in ID 442 and ID 445 relate to the drilling of the borehole, and that the squared-off ends noted on the other beads were produced by grinding the ends after drilling, to remove this cupping. The beads had all been polished, but degree of sheen varies and is affected by the presence of a coating of consolidant on most of the beads. Furthermore, the degree of sheen may have decreased over time. It varies from low (e.g. ID 446) to medium to high (e.g. ID 442).

Evidence for the method of manufacture of the faience beads is offered by the shape of the segments, which indicates that they had been made by rolling the unfired bead against a former shaped like a 'butter pat', and by the variable thickness and the distribution of the glaze (including a drip on the interior of the longest surviving bead), which indicates that the glaze had been applied.

COMPLETENESS AND DAMAGE

Five out of the seven of the jet beads are complete or virtually so, while ID 446 is missing much of one end, having been broken and its pieces refitted, and ID 448 is missing around 5%, from the loss of chips. ID 448 had broken into three main pieces and had been glued together. In every case this damage has occurred since the beads were excavated; no definite ancient damage (other than wear) was observed. It is clear that none of these beads had been on the pyre with the deceased, as otherwise they would have been consumed in the flames.

Being made of a fragile, glassy material, the faience beads have suffered a greater degree of 20th-century damage, as shown by the loss of one segment from the longest bead, and by the small size of the fragments in the phial. Some ancient damage is indicated by ancient fracture surfaces at one end of two of the beads. The glaze is crazed; this is a common feature of weathered glaze. The faience beads show no obvious signs of having been burnt on the pyre.

Most of the jet and faience beads have traces of a yellow-white accretion, probably calcium carbonate precipitated from the groundwater or else particles of the cremated remains among which they had lain.

WEAR

The jet beads do not show signs of heavy wear, although they were not new when buried. There is some probable thread-smoothing to the interior of the borehole (except in ID 446, where the rilling is crisp), and slight thread-smoothing of one or both ends of the borehole in all the beads. There is a broad thread-pull groove at one end of ID 445 (Figure 8.2.5 inset b). Bead-on-bead wear was noted on ID 442, ID 443 and ID 445. Three are classified as slightly worn, and four as worn.

Assessing use wear on faience beads is hard, because they tend not to abrade like jet and jet-like materials. The fact that two of the beads have ancient fracture surfaces at one end could, however, suggest wear-damage, although this is not the only possibility.

CONCLUSIONS

As with all composite necklaces, this ensemble of beads will have been brought together from different sources. However, it is possible that at least six of the seven dark-coloured beads had originally been made as part of a set: this is suggested, for example, by the shared distinctive profiles of ID 444 and ID 446. While they have clearly seen some wear, they are not heavily worn, as might be expected had they been old, 'heirloom' objects from an old spacer plate necklace. It may be that they were not substantially older than the faience beads when they were buried. As noted above, it is harder to assess wear on faience beads. The consistency in shape and manufacture of the extant faience beads could be taken to indicate that they, too, had been made as part of a set, although whether the oddly-shaped missing bead had originally belonged to that set is debatable.

ID 503–4 Durrington G47, Wiltshire
References: Hoare 1812, 168; Annable and Simpson 1964, 53 and 108, nos. 334–6.

COMPOSITION

The necklace comprises two shale rings and a faience bead (Figure 8.2.6, centre).

CONTEXT AND ASSOCIATIONS

The objects were found with a probably primary cremation burial under a bowl barrow located north of the east end of the Stonehenge Cursus.

MORPHOLOGY AND MATERIAL

One ring (ID 503) is in the form of a D-shaped hoop tapering to the outer margins; it has an external diameter of 23.8mm, internal diameter of 16.2mm, and is of thickness 4mm. The width of the hoop is 4.1mm. The other ring (ID 504) has a lentoid hoop section; the external diameter is 24.3mm, the internal diameter is 16.0mm, and the thickness is 2.9mm. The width of the hoop is 4.4mm. Both rings have been identified as being of Kimmeridge shale (B63 and B64 respectively; AS). The faience bead is 7.0mm long and consists of four surviving segments. If the rings were strung flat, the overall strung length is 55.0mm.

MANUFACTURE

There are no manufacturing traces visible.

COMPLETENESS AND DAMAGE

One ring (ID 503) is almost complete, with just a few modern chips; the other (ID 504) has major modern breaks which are glued, as well as ancient damage, and survives at 75% only.

WEAR

One of the rings displays a large and ancient spall, thus it would seem that the rings had suffered some use. No wear traces are visible and the overall wear categories are indeterminate.

CONCLUSIONS

Flat rings of this type can occur in groups without any other items, so do not necessarily signify the presence of a necklace. However in this case the associated faience bead suggests that they were strung as elements of a necklace. The rings are not a matching pair in terms of their hoop sections.

ID 510–11 and ID 1499–1502 and faience
Winterbourne Stoke G68, Wiltshire

References: Hoare 1812, 114–5; Annable and Simpson 1964, 60 and 115, nos. 455–61.

COMPOSITION

The necklace comprises two shale rings and four faience beads (Figure 8.2.6, bottom).

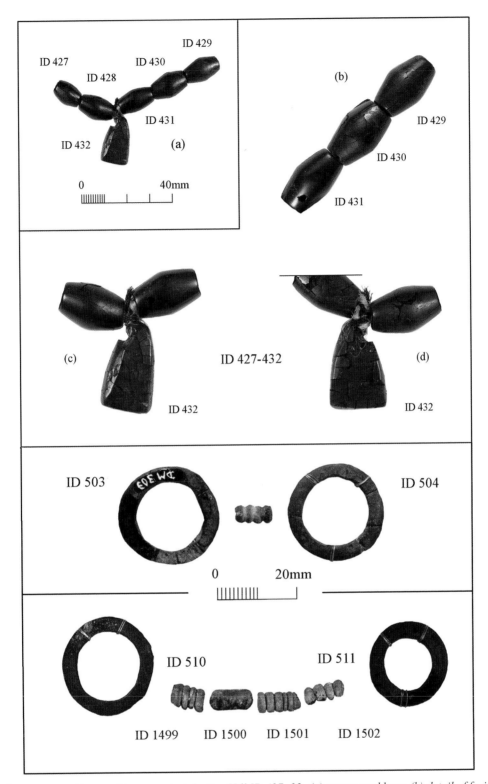

Figure 8.2.6. Composite necklaces with two materials. Tan Hill ID 427–32: (a) strung necklace; (b) detail of fusiform beads ID 429–31; (c) and (d) details of both sides of pendant/fastener ID 432. ID 503 and ID 504 Durrington G47: pair of shale rings and segmented faience bead. ID 442–48 and ID 1499–1502 Winterbourne Stoke G68: pair of shale rings and four segmented faience beads.

CONTEXT AND ASSOCIATIONS

The finds were associated with a primary cremation burial in a disc barrow within the Coniger Group. Hoare records that all had been placed beneath an inverted urn (now lost). Three shale beads and a large bead of amber, all lost, may also have been associated with this grave group.

MORPHOLOGY AND MATERIAL

One ring (ID 510) has a rectangular hoop cross section, an external diameter of 23.3mm and a thickness of 3.8mm. The hoop has a width of 3.9mm. The other ring (ID 511) has a D-shaped cross section with a slightly curved inner face. The exterior diameter is 20.2mm and the thickness 4.3mm. The hoop width is 3.9mm. Both rings have been identified as being of Kimmeridge shale (B25 and B26 respectively; AS). Of the four faience beads (ID 1499–1502) three have four segments surviving, and one has six segments. Their lengths are *c.* 7.5, 8, 11 and 12mm respectively. If the rings were strung flat, the overall strung length is 82.0mm.

MANUFACTURE

There are no manufacturing traces visible.

COMPLETENESS AND DAMAGE

ID 511 is complete but ID 510 has a large modern spall (90% present).

WEAR

Wear on ID 510 is indeterminate but ID 511 has traces of polish inside the hoop and a zone of fabric rub on one section of the outer margin of the hoop. This ring is classified as slightly worn.

CONCLUSIONS

Although the cross sections do not match, in terms of hoop width and thickness the two shale rings form a fairly uniform pair. However one is definitely larger than the other.

8.2.6 JET AND JET-LIKE MATERIALS AND STONE

ID 364–65 and 742.1–10 Aldbourne 285 (G12), Wiltshire

References: Greenwell 1890, 56–7; Kinnes and Longworth 1985, barrow 285, burial 1 (the beads recorded there as bone are in fact made from stone, and that recorded as shell is actually of chalk).

COMPOSITION

The necklace comprises a total of 13 beads: one of jet, one of cannel coal or shale and 11 of stone (Figure 8.2.7, top).

CONTEXT AND ASSOCIATIONS

The beads were associated with an adult cremation deposit within the central grave of a round barrow. They were found amongst the burnt bones whilst a decorated accessory cup,

and sherds from a second cup, had been placed on top of the bones.

MORPHOLOGY AND MATERIAL

The black bead (ID 364) is a medium fusiform bead of jet (D/H) measuring 11.7 by 7.0mm with a perforation diameter of 2.3mm (Figure 8.2.7a–b). The plump annular bead (ID 365) is of cannel coal or shale (D/H) measuring 6.7 by 10.9mm with an hourglass perforation of minimum diameter 2.6mm. (Figure 8.2.7a–c). The third bead (ID 742.11) is a biconical bead of white chalk (R. Ixer) (Figure 8.2.7b).

The stone beads (ID 742.1–10) comprise 10 beads of yellow-grey silicious sinter (R. Ixer), originally polished. Six are biconical (ID 742.2, 4, 7–10) ranging in length from 8.4 to 11.2mm and width from 11.2 to 12.2mm; perforation diameters lie between 3.3 to 8mm. Three are subconical and slightly larger (ID 742.1, 3, 6) ranging in length from 9.4 to 12.3mm and width 10.2 to 13.2mm; perforation diameters lie between 3.7 to 7mm. The single ridged biconical bead measuring 9.6 by 11mm with a perforation diameter of 3.7mm. The chalk bead (ID 742.11) measures 9.0 by 10.0mm with perforation diameters of 3.1 and 3.5mm. The strung length is 128mm.

MANUFACTURE

No obvious traces survive.

COMPLETENESS AND DAMAGE

The two jet and jet-like beads survive at 80% and 98% with all damage due to modern chips. The stone beads are almost complete (99% present) but in this case the slight occasional chipping was suffered in antiquity.

WEAR

The ancient chipping indicates that the stone beads had suffered considerable wear. The two black beads both have thread-smoothing and are classified as worn (see ID 365, Figure 8.2.7c). Amongst the stone beads, seven display thread-wear, sometimes including definite thread-pulls or nicks, and two further beads have bead-on-bead wear at one or both ends. In only one case (ID 742.10) did the edges of the perforation appear to be relatively sharp. The stone beads are all classed as very worn.

CONCLUSIONS

This is an unusual combination of raw materials, with the two black beads providing strong contrast of colour and texture with the pale cream and white of the stone beads. The silicious sinter may have been obtained fairly locally in southern England. The single ridged biconical stone bead is unusual, and appear to be a copy of a faience bead type.

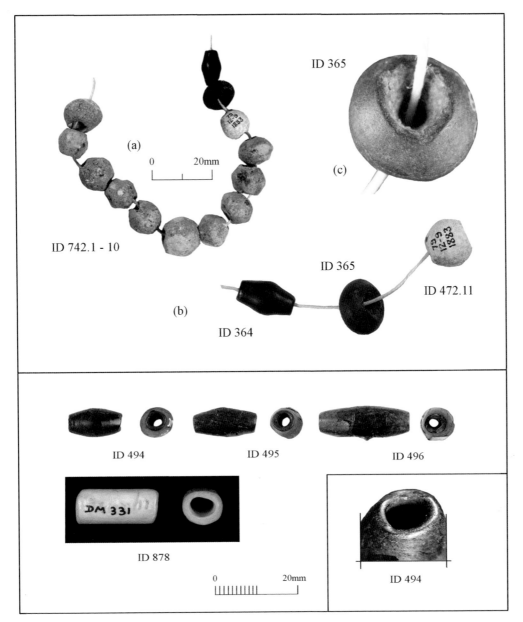

Figure 8.2.7. Composite necklaces with two materials. ID 364–65 and ID 742.1–10 Aldbourne 285, G12: (a) full necklace; (b) detail of jet and jet-like beads ID 364, ID 365 and chalk bead ID 472.11; (c) detail of thread-smoothing on ID 365. Upton Lovell G2a (shaman): three jet beads ID 494–96; the bone bead ID 878; detail of bead-on-bead wear on ID 494 (inset).

8.2.7 JET AND JET-LIKE MATERIALS AND BONE

ID 494–96 and 878 Upton Lovell G2a (shaman), Wiltshire

References: Hoare 1812, 75–6 and pls. V to VII 9 (but beads not illustrated); Annable and Simpson 1964, 49–50 and 108, nos. 242–62.

COMPOSITION

The necklace comprises a group of three jet beads and one bead of bone (Figure 8.2.7, bottom).

CONTEXT AND ASSOCIATIONS

Two primary inhumation burials under a bowl barrow comprised an extended, probably male, skeleton in the base of the grave and a partially overlapping much smaller skeleton, possibly female 'in a sitting posture' i.e. contracted. It cannot be certain which objects were originally associated with each burial and Hoare himself recorded that it was impossible to separate the objects appropriate to each burial. However, many of the items were recorded as having been located in particular areas of the lower skeleton: notably the stone items (not studied), the sets of perforated bone points (ID 930–70, Figure 4.7.9 and Figure 4.7.13) and the boar tusks (ID 850–52, Figure 5.1.1).A jet belt ring (ID 433; B22) was found with the

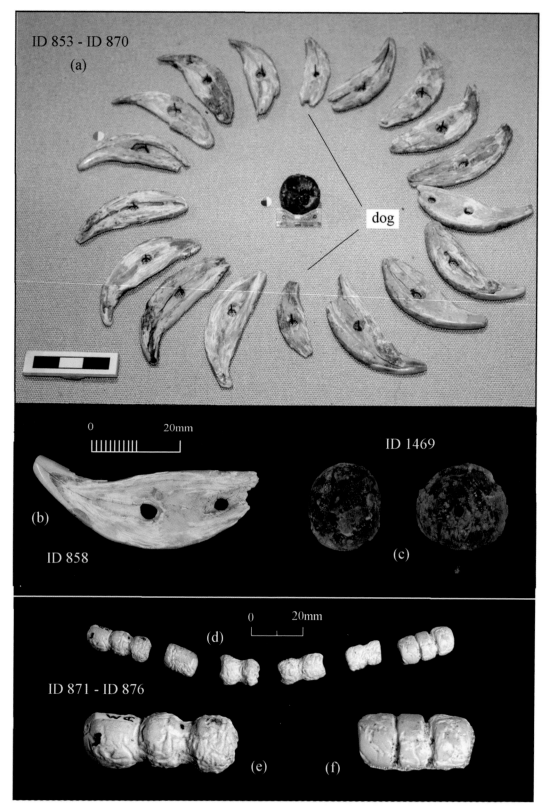

Figure 8.2.8. Composite necklaces with two materials. ID 853–70 and ID 1469 South Newton G1: (a) displayed assemblage (the dog teeth are indicated); (b) detail of wolf tooth with double perforation, grinding and enamel at tip; (c) detail of amber bead ID 1469. ID 871–76 Warminster G10: (d) six bone beads; (e) detail of smoothly curved segments on ID 871; (f) detail of grooves on ID 876.

lower skeleton, after collapse of part of the upper skeleton, so it may be that this item had originally been deposited with the contracted individual. The position of the bronze awl (ID 1452, Figure 4.6.2) and of the beads of jet and bone unfortunately was not recorded.

MORPHOLOGY AND MATERIAL

The black beads comprised a slightly plump fusiform bead of jet (ID 494; B19; AS) measuring 3.6 by 7.8mm with a perforation diameter of 3.4mm and two medium fusiform beads of jet (ID 495–96; B20 and 21; AS) measuring 15.4 by 7.8mm and 21.7 by 9.2 by 7.8mm with perforations diameters 3.8 and 3.5mm respectively. The bone bead is cylindrical in shape (ID 878, Figure 8.2.7), cream in colour and made from the distal shaft of a sheep/goat tibia (M. Maltby). It measures 19 by 8.5mm with perforation diameters 5.5 and 4mm. The strung length is 70mm.

MANUFACTURE

The plump fusiform jet bead (ID 494) has multidirectional faint polishing striations on the surfaces, and ID 496 has faint circumferential striations visible. The bone bead was polished all over, and longitudinal faint striations are visible all over.

COMPLETENESS AND DAMAGE

All of the beads are complete, or nearly so, with some slight loss or modern chips and spalls on the three jet beads.

WEAR

The three jet beads all have visible thread-wear, ID 495 has end-polish and the other two display bead-on-bead wear (e.g. ID 494, Figure 8.2.7 inset). All are very worn. The bone bead also has visible thread-wear and is classified as worn.

CONCLUSIONS

This small group of beads from an important grave are significant in their variety of colour, and heavy degree of wear. The form of the jet beads suggests that they were all recycled from a jet spacer plate necklace; they would have derived from different strands, with ID 494 having come from the innermost strand.

8.2.8 AMBER AND BONE

ID 853–70 and ID 1469 South Newton G1, Wiltshire

References: Hoare 1812, 214; Annable and Simpson 1964, 53 and 107, nos. 316–21; Thomas 1954, 315–7.

COMPOSITION

The collection comprises one amber bead and 18 pierced tooth beads (Figure 8.2.8, top and centre, a).

CONTEXT AND ASSOCIATIONS

The beads were found with a primary inhumation burial beneath an isolated bowl barrow located on a hill top. The burial had been disturbed prior to Hoare's investigation by an earlier antiquary. Some of the bones were stained green, suggesting that one or more items of bronze had originally been present.

MORPHOLOGY AND MATERIAL

The amber bead (ID 1469) is a large globular bead of dark red amber measuring 16 by 15.7mm with a perforation diameter of 1.5mm (Figure 8.2.8c). Two of the tooth beads (ID 853 and ID 862) are made from the canine teeth of dog (M. Maltby); they measure 37.8 by 3.0mm and 34.6 by 3.5mm with perforation diameters 2.8 and 3.5mm respectively (arrowed on Figure 8.2.8a). The other 16 beads (ID 854–61 and ID 863–70) are made from the canine teeth of wolf (M. Maltby); their average size is 50.3 by 4.9mm, and average perforation diameter 4.6mm. The overall strung length is 96mm.

MANUFACTURE

Each tooth bead is made from half of a split tooth. There are grinding marks on both sides of each, and only a little original enamel survives, mainly towards the tips (tip only in 12 cases; tip and towards the centre in three cases; towards the centre only in a further three). Two beads have a double perforation (e.g. ID 858, Figure 8.2.8b). The perforation is circular on the two dog tooth beads and on eight of the wolf teeth examples. On the other eight wolf tooth beads, the perforations are oval in shape. The beads appear to have been designed to be tightly strung side by side with the tooth points projecting to the front.

COMPLETENESS AND DAMAGE

The amber bead is complete, as are the two beads made from dog's teeth. The other tooth beads survive at the 90 to 95% level, with most damage probably being modern.

WEAR

Wear on the amber bead is indeterminate. Wear at the perforation was only visible on one wolf tooth bead and bead-on-bead wear on another. If tightly strung, thread-wear may have been minimal, and the overall impression during study was that the tooth beads are all worn.

CONCLUSIONS

This necklace is unique. Thomas (1954, 316) was of the opinion that the amber bead and possible dagger may have been associated with the disturbed inhumation and that the tooth necklace may have derived from an earlier disturbed burial. However, this appears to be special pleading. Cornwall was able to pair off four sets of upper and lower canines from adult wolves, some very old (*ibid*).

8.2.9 BONE AND FOSSIL

ID 871–76 Warminster G10

References: Hoare 1812, 67–8; Thomas 1954, 314–5; Annable and Simpson 1964, 51 and 106, nos. 279–84.

COMPOSITION

The necklace comprises six bone beads and a fossil shell (Figure 8.2.8, bottom).

CONTEXT AND ASSOCIATIONS

The beads were found with a pair of inhumation burials, apparently of a woman and child, and a cremation burial under a bowl barrow with outer bank on Cop Head Hill (also called Cop Heap Hill). All three burials were located in a single grave north of centre within the barrow. The fossil sea shell was probably associated with the child skeleton and the bone beads were found with the cremation burial. It is possible that the inhumations were subsequent to the cremation which may have been the primary burial. Thomas (1954, 315) considered that all the beads were associated.

MORPHOLOGY AND MATERIAL

The beads are tightly strung on a display board, and thus the full dimensions could not be obtained (Figure 8.2.8d).

Two of the cylindrical beads (ID 871 and ID 876, both detailed in Figure 8.2.8e–f) each have three segments with lengths of 26.2 and 22.5mm respectively, and similar perforation diameters of 4.2mm. Three further cylindrical beads (ID 873–75) have two segments with lengths of 16.4, 18.4 and 14.6mm respectively. The perforations are not visible. One bead (ID 872) has a single segment and is of length 13.3mm; the perforations are not visible. The beads are all made from the distal shaft of sheep/goat tibia. The fossil (not illustrated) is a sea-shell, a phasianellid from Jurassic deposits which occur north, south and west of Devizes (Thomas 1954, 315). The strung length is 112mm.

MANUFACTURE

The beads were originally polished to a low sheen and are white in colour. Some of the segments are defined by grooves (Figure 8.2.8f), others have been more carefully finished such that the segments appear smoothly curved (Figure 8.2.8e).

COMPLETENESS AND DAMAGE

All of the items are 100% present, except ID 874 which had a modern break at one end.

WEAR

The perforations appear to be fairly crisp and the beads are therefore classified as slightly worn.

CONCLUSIONS

The beads appear to be imitating the form of segmented faience beads.

8.3 COMPOSITE NECKLACES WITH THREE MATERIALS

The entries are described in groups according to the combinations of raw materials employed. A list of items studied and illustrated is shown in Table 8.3.1.

8.3.1 JET AND JET-LIKE MATERIALS, AMBER AND SHELL

ID 464–5, ID 1331, ID 1526, ID 1527.1–6 and ID 1568 Shrewton G5j, Wiltshire

Reference: Green and Rollo-Smith 1984, fig. 28.

COMPOSITION

A total of 11 beads survive; these comprise four of a jet or jet-like material (one now lost), one of shell and six of amber (Figure 8.3.1, top). There were also '45 or more' small amber disc beads, of which only two survive for study.

CONTEXT AND ASSOCIATIONS

The necklace was found with a secondary interment (no. 3) within pit 3 beneath a probable bell barrow (Green and Rollo-Smith 1984, 273–5 and fig. 10). Pit 3 had probably been cut through the chalk capping of the pre-existing mound. The burial comprised a contracted inhumation of an elderly woman. The beads were found around the neck, as if within a necklace which had been tightly worn. The body had been covered with a cairn of flints.

MORPHOLOGY AND MATERIAL

Of the four jet or jet-like beads two are of plump fusiform type (ID 464–5, one lost) and are both of ?lignite (ID 464: Bussell *et al.* 1982, 31; AS). The surviving bead measures

25.3 by 9.1mm with a perforation diameter of 2.3mm. Two are pestle-shaped toggle beads. One (ID 1568) is probably of lignite (Bussell *et al.* 1982, 31; AS) and measures 17.3 by 11.3mm with perforation diameters of 3.8 and 3.7mm. It has a waisted shape with basal bowing and a slightly raised top; the geometric incised decoration shown in the published illustration (Green and Rollo-Smith 1984, fig. 28) is now almost invisible. The other (ID 1331) is also of lignite (Bussell *et al.* 1982, 31; AS) and measures 16.9 by 12.2mm with perforation diameters of 2.8 and 3.2mm. Both beads are of similar shape and decoration. Traces of the cross motif on the top of ID 1331 are still visible.

Of the six amber beads three are of medium annular type (ID 1527.1, Figure 8.3.1; ID 1527.2 and 6) and are of bright orange amber; their thicknesses range from 2.8 to 3.1mm, widths from 4.3 to 7.2mm, and perforations 1.4 to 1.9mm. Two further amber beads are wedged-shaped (ID 1527.3, Figure 8.3.1; ID 1527.5); one is dark red, the other of indeterminate colour. They measure 4.2 by 7.5mm and 3.8 by 5.8mm, with perforation diameters of 2.4 and 0.7mm respectively. The final amber bead (ID 1527.4) is of plump annular type and of indeterminate original colour. It measures 3.2 by 6.2mm with a perforation diameter of 2.7mm.

The shell bead (ID 1526, Figure 8.3.1) is of *Littorina littoralis/L.obcusata* and is of natural shape with an irregular perforation with broken edges. The original colour is likely to have been orange/red; it measures 13.1 by 10.4mm with a perforation diameter of 3.2 by 4.2mm.

The overall strung length using the larger beads only would be *c.* 97mm. By incorporating the 45 small amber disc beads (estimated at *c.* 90mm), this would extend to an estimate of 187mm.

MANUFACTURE

The only traces of manufacture visible are rilling within

Table 8.3.1.. List of composite necklaces with three materials studied and illustrated.

Object	Site (Parish), County	Museum	Illustration
ID 398–409, 411–12	Oxsettle Bottom, Mount Caburn , E. Sussex	BM	Figure 8.3.2
ID 1349–50	"		Figure 8.3.2
ID 410, 1351–52	"		Not illustrated
ID 464, 1330, 1331, 1526	Shrewton G5j, Wilts.	Sal	Figure 8.3.1
ID 1527.1, 1527.3	"		Figure 8.3.1
ID 465, 1527.2, 4, 5, 6	"		Not illustrated
ID 505–7.1–9, 1472.1–11	Upton Lovell G1, Wilts.	Dev	Figure 8.3.3
ID 509.1–6, 1492.1–11	Wilsford G3, Wilts.	Dev	Figure 8.3.1
ID 1493–94	"		Figure 8.3.1
ID 519–20, 1511–1511A	Collingbourne Kingston G8, Wilts.	Dev	Figure 8.3.3
ID 539, 1510	"		Not illustrated
ID 524–29	Winterbourne Stoke G67, Wilts.	Dev	Figure 8.3.4
ID 879–80	Winterbourne Stoke G8, Wilts.	Dev	Figure 8.3.4
ID 1443–44	Upton Lovell G2e, Wilts.	Dev	See Chapters 6 and 7
ID 1488	Wilsford G42, Wilts.	Dev	Figure 8.3.4
ID 1495.1–12	Amesbury G48, Wilts.	Dev	Figure 8.3.4
ID 1513–14A	Wilsford G46, Wilts.	Dev	Figure 8.3.4

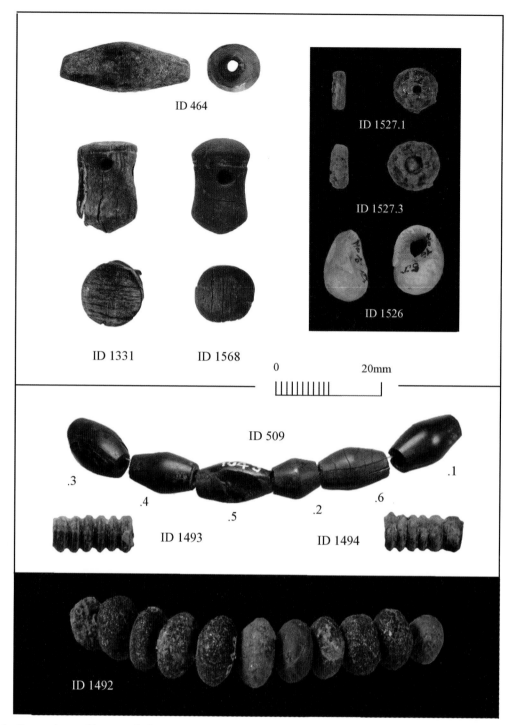

Figure 8.3.1. Composite necklaces with three materials. ID 464–5, ID 1331, ID 1526–7 and ID 1568 Shrewton G5j showing: ID 464 ?lignite fusiform bead; ID 1331 and ID 1568 two ?lignite pestle toggles with ID 1331 exhibiting traces of decoration on top and cracked base; ID 1527.1 medium annular amber bead; ID 1527.3 wedge-shaped amber bead; ID 1526 shell bead. ID 509.1–6, ID 1492, 1–11 and ID 1493–4 Wilsford G3 showing ID 509 jet beads; ID 1492 amber beads numbered 1–11 from left to right; ID 1493–94 faience beads.

the perforations of the surviving fusiform ?lignite bead and two of the amber beads.

COMPLETENESS AND DAMAGE

All the beads are complete apart from the fusiform ?lignite

example, one amber bead and one of the pestle beads (ID 1331) which has a modern crack at the base.

WEAR

Ancient damage includes a chip (or possible thread-pull)

on one end of the fusiform ?lignite bead, a major break on one side of one of the surviving amber beads (ID 1527.4) and a lesser break on the side of pestle bead ID 1331. The fusiform ?lignite bead displays strong thread- and bead-on-bead wear and is classified as worn. The shell bead and all the surviving beads of amber show slight thread-smoothing and/or wear and are slightly worn. The two pestle beads/toggles have visible thread-wear which is positioned at the sides, thus indicating that these items were tightly strung as beads, and not loosely as pendants. They are both very worn.

CONCLUSIONS

The variation in shape and size of the beads, and the strong contrast between the black and red items, would have formed a striking ensemble. Neither the fusiform beads nor the amber annular and disc beads are of types that would have derived from spacer plate necklaces, and all are of forms that may have been made specifically during the mature Early Bronze Age. The pestle beads are very unusual and appear to be rough copies of the pestle pendants of amber, like those found in the Little Cressingham necklace, and occasionally elsewhere in shale e.g. Durrington G14. The source of the lignite, which did not appear to be Kimmeridge shale, is not known, but the shell will have derived from the coast. The excavator recorded the layout of the beads below the neck of the body, and they were arranged as in his published illustration, with the large central fusiform flanked by the two pestle beads and then the smaller fusiform on the left and the shell bead on the right; all interspersed with varying numbers of the smaller amber beads.

8.3.2 GOLD, AMBER AND JET AND JET-LIKE MATERIALS

ID 1443 and ID 1444 Upton Lovell G2e, Wiltshire

References: Hoare 1812, 98 and pls. X–XI; Annable and Simpson 1964, 48 and 103, nos. 225–33.

COMPOSITION

The group comprised three elements: a set of 13 cylindrical gold 'beads', two of which are lost (ID 1443, Figure 6.1.7), an amber spacer plate necklace (ID 1444, Figure 7.3.4 and Figure 7.3.5) and a gold-covered conical pendant or button of shale (ID 492/1450, Figure 6.1.6). This entry is a cross-reference only as these items are discussed and illustrated elsewhere. (For full details see Chapter 6 or Chapter 7 respectively). It should be noted that the few black fusiform beads of jet or jet-like material, which were mounted in an early display version of the amber necklace, are thought not to have derived from this burial (Annable and Simpson 1964, 48).

CONTEXT AND ASSOCIATIONS

The objects were found near a cremation beneath a barrow which came to be known as 'The Golden Barrow'. It is located in a low-lying position on the northern bank of the River Wylye. The bowl barrow was excavated by Cunnington in 1803 and also in 1807, and it is unclear whether the finds from those two investigations, discovered close to each other, had come from one or two secondary graves (Clarke *et al.* 1985, 279). The objects were found about 2 feet (*c.* 0.6m) away from the cremated remains. The finds from the 1803 excavation comprised several amber spacer plates and 'over 1000' amber beads, the 13 cylindrical gold beads, the conical shale button covered with gold sheet, a gold rectangular plate (ID 1449, Figure 6.1.5) and four small gold sheet cap-ends (ID 1447A–B and ID 1448A–B, Figure 6.1.6), together with a grape cup. The finds from the 1807 investigation comprised further amber beads (from the same or from a different necklace), plus a Collared Urn containing a smaller, plain pot (probably an accessory vessel), a bronze awl (ID 1442, Figure 4.6.4) and a small flat bronze knife (ID 1446).

CONCLUSIONS

The largest component of this group is the amber spacer plate necklace. The gold 'beads', which are perforated on the sides rather than the ends, may have been strung as a row of pendants, or, possibly more likely, were sewn onto a garment as ornaments (see Chapter 6.1.4). The decorated gold-covered cone may have functioned as a pendant. It is unlikely to have been attached as a button, as the complex decoration on the flat surface would have been hidden from view. Suspended from the flat surface it may have been used as a pendant or a downward hanging toggle (see Chapter 6.1.4). Thus this unique group of items cannot be classified as a composite necklace as such, but the ornaments can be perceived as a set of jewellery and ornaments, along with the rectangular gold plate, which, like the gold 'beads', may have been sewn onto a garment. All the elements display high degrees of use wear.

8.3.3 JET AND JET-LIKE MATERIALS, AMBER AND FAIENCE

ID 398–413 and ID 1349–52 Oxteddle (Oxsettle) Bottom, Mount Caburn, East Sussex

References: Horsfield 1824, 47–8; Curwen 1954, 168 and fig. 46; Longworth 1984, 197, no. 562, pl. 197e.

COMPOSITION

The set of beads and ornaments comprises a total of 25 items, including four items of faience, four amber beads and 17 pieces of jet or jet-like materials (Figure 8.3.2). One of the chunky annular beads was not seen and may be lost.

CONTEXT AND ASSOCIATIONS

The group also includes a decorated bronze overlapping ring (not seen), a fragment of bone pin and a broken boar's tusk (both lost). The finds resulted from the antiquarian excavation of a bowl barrow on the slope of the hill to the north-east of Oxsettle Bottom. All items were found unburnt with a cremation burial within an inverted Collared Urn. This urn was one of a pair which was found either side of an extended inhumation burial (Horsfield 1824, pl. V). However, as Curwen suggests, this inhumation burial was probably a secondary burial of Saxon date.

MORPHOLOGY AND MATERIALS

The jet and jet-like components exhibit a range of different forms. There is a jet-like circular ring (ID 398) of Kimmeridge shale (D/H); it has flat sides and rounded edges with a diameter of 24.3mm and thickness 3.9mm. It has four transverse perforations close to the inner edge of the hoop, unevenly spaced; three of these had broken through to the hoop's edge. The perforations range in diameter from 2.4 to 3.9mm, as measured on one surface. ID 399 is a squashed-circular ring, possibly of cannel coal (D/H), with flat sides and rounded edges, of diameter 24mm and thickness 5.8mm. A narrow incised groove runs around the mid-point of the outer edge, and through this a V-perforation had been drilled. There is an abortive drill-hole for a further perforation elsewhere on the circumference. Both of the arms of the V-perforation had been mis-bored, the drill breaking through the flat surface on the back to produce small holes. One of these holes looks to have been enlarged by drilling from the flat surface. ID 400 and ID 402 are both fusiform beads of jet (ID 400 D/H, ID 402 AS/MD) measuring 19 by 11.5mm (plump) and 19.2 by 7.1mm (slender) with perforation diameters of 3.6 and 3.2mm respectively. ID 401, ID 403 and ID 411 are fusiform beads of Kimmeridge shale (AS/MD; ID 411 D/H) measuring 14.6 by 10.7mm (plump), 17.2 by 7.8mm (slender) and 12.0 by 8.3mm (plump). The perforation diameters range from 2.5 to 3.9mm. One object (ID 404) is a conical grooved ornament, resembling a button, but without any perforation. It is roughly circular in plan, with a medium-height dome terminating in a broad vertical facet. A single incised groove runs around the facet. The base is flat with a diameter of 27.3mm, and height 10.1mm. The ornament would probably have been attached to the necklace by a thread running around the groove.

ID 405 is a roughly circular quoit-shaped ring, possibly of cannel coal (D/H), with a D-shaped hoop section; the ring has a profile which is very slightly wedge-shaped, a diameter of 22.6mm and a thickness of 5mm. ID 406 is a small irregularly-circular ring of Kimmeridge shale (D/H), with roughly rectangular hoop section (with gently curving outer edge), a diameter of 17.3mm, and a thickness of 3.9mm. ID 407 is a small, roughly circular quoit-shaped ring of Kimmeridge shale (D/H). It has a triangular hoop section; in profile it is parallel-sided with rounded outer edge. The diameter is 17.5mm and the

thickness 4.5mm. There are three chunky annular beads (ID 408–9 and ID 413). ID 409 is of jet (AS/MD), the others are of Kimmeridge shale (D/H) plus one not seen, and suspected to be lost. All are oval in plan: ID 408 is slightly wedge-shaped in profile, while the others are roughly parallel-sided, with rounded ends. The lengths range from 4.4 to 6.3mm, the widths from 8.5 to 9.9mm, and the perforation diameters from 4.1 to 5.5mm. There are two squat biconical beads of jet (ID 410 AS/MD; ID 412 D/H). ID 410 comprises three fragments of a squat biconical bead; it is probable that Curwen drew just one fragment, making it appear as a fusiform bead (1954, fig. 46, bottom line, penultimate from the right corner), but it is clear from reassembling the fragments that it had actually resembled ID 412, the intact squat biconical bead. The diameters are 11.0 and 8.9mm, the width of ID 412 is 12.0mm, and the perforation diameters 2.5 and 4.8mm respectively.

Note on material: ID 399, the grooved V-perforated ring and ID 405, the larger of the quoit-shaped rings, are blacker and were found analytically to have a higher iron content, similar to that of cannel coal. They may, however, represent an iron-rich variant of Kimmeridge shale.

There are two chunky annular beads of dark and bright red amber (ID 1349 and ID 1350) measuring 6.3 by 10.8 by 10.5mm and 3.3 by 6.1 by 5.8mm, and with perforation diameters of 3.5 and 1.5mm respectively. There are also fragments from two fusiform beads, both in dark red amber (ID 1351 and ID 1352); these were not measureable.

The four faience items (not illustrated) comprise one quoit pendant and three segmented beads, of which one is complete and two survive as fragments. The quoit pendant is of slightly irregular circular shape, with a perforated lug for suspension; including the lug, the diameter is 30.0mm, and excluding the lug, 28.2mm. The hoop is an elongated and symmetrical triangle, with a fairly sharp outer edge and minimally convex long sides; its thickness ranges from 5.2mm to 5.6mm (at the lug) and its width is *c.* 10mm. The main hole is large, concentric and not quite perpendicular, and has a diameter of 16.3 to17.6mm; that of the hole in the lug is 3.6mm. The complete segmented bead has five segments and curves noticeably; it is 14.6mm long and has a diameter of 4.1mm and hole diameter of 2.5mm. One of the fragmentary segmented beads survives as two main fragments. The largest fragment is 12.3mm long, with a diameter of 3.5mm and a hole diameter of 2.5mm. Overall there are five segments but as only one end is an original end, it will have had more. The other fragmentary segmented bead is represented by a small, two-segment fragment, broken at both ends and missing some of its wall. The bead had been a fairly broad, squashed cylinder; it survives to a length of 6.5mm, with a maximum diameter of 5.6mm and hole diameter of 3.0mm.

The overall length of the necklace, if strung flat, is estimated at 322mm.

MANUFACTURE

Only in three cases were any traces of the manufacture

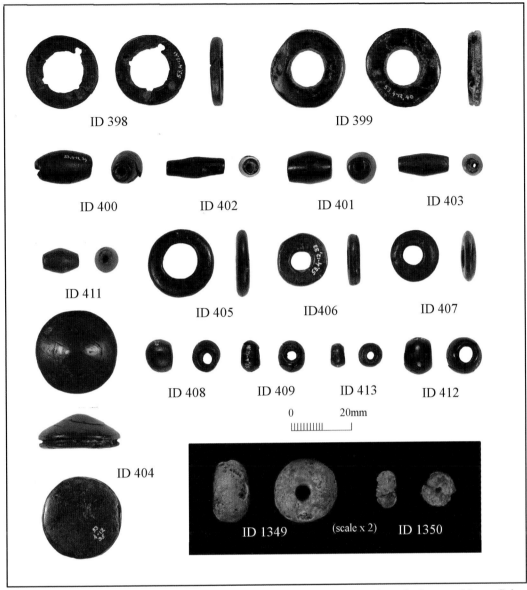

Figure 8.3.2. Composite necklaces with three materials. ID 398–413, ID 1349–52 Oxsettle Bottom, Mount Caburn: ID 398 shale ring; ID 399 ?cannel coal ring with perforations; ID 400 and ID 402 jet fusiform beads; ID 401, ID 403 and ID 411 shale fusiform beads with ID 411 showing thread-wear; ID 404 shale conical ornament; ID 405 ?cannel coal quoit ring; ID 406 shale ring; ID 407 shale quoit ring; ID 408 shale annular bead; ID 409 jet annular bead; ID 413 shale annular bead; ID 412 jet biconical bead; ID 1349–50 amber annular beads.

process visible; with the others, the coating of consolidant has obscured any traces that may have existed. On ID 399, the grooved V-perforated ring, faint diagonal striations are visible on the back. On the conical object ID 404, faint multidirectional striations are visible on the base, especially around a surface irregularity where an attempt had been made to smooth it. On fusiform bead ID 402, a step in the interior of the perforation indicates the junction between drillings from either end.

The lug of the faience quoit pendant had clearly been applied to the hoop, and perforated after its attachment. Glaze is present over the whole of the surface. It is various shades of green-blue, from medium to pale. The segments

of the complete faience bead had been formed by rolling the paste tube against a 'butter pat'-like former, resulting in continuous ridges and hollows. The surface colour varies from a dark green-blue on one side to a slightly paler shade on the other; this colour had penetrated through to the interior. The glaze had clearly been applied, as demonstrated by the presence of a glaze drip along the interior. The fragmentary segmented beads had also been formed by rolling the paste tube against a 'butter pat'-like former, resulting in continuous ridges and hollows. The glaze colours are medium to dark turquoise and pale turquoise respectively, and in both cases the glaze had probably been applied.

COMPLETENESS AND DAMAGE

All the items have been coated with consolidant, and in the case of ID 398 this has sealed some pale-coloured sediment in two of the perforations. Apart from the faience beads, the least complete piece is the fragmentary jet biconical bead, of which around 70% is present. Otherwise, over 95% is present in each case. Four beads of jet-like materials and all those of amber have modern damage. The faience pendant is complete and undamaged, as is one of the faience beads.

WEAR

The nature and degree of wear varies, with the most heavily worn items being the perforated ring ID 398, the grooved V-perforated ring ID 399, and one of the jet fusiform beads ID 402. The next-heavily worn items are the conical object ID 404 and the large quoit-shaped ring ID 405. All three rings, and all except one of the beads made from jet and shale exhibit thread-wear in or around their perforations. Three of them also have evidence of thread-pull (ID 402, ID 403 and ID 413). Only one bead, the crushed biconical bead ID 410, has crisp perforation edges surviving. Wear on the amber beads was difficult to discern, but in the case of ID 1359 it was possible to note that the edges of one perforation were smoothed through wear. Overall seven of the items studied are slightly worn, eight are worn, two very worn and three indeterminate.

CONCLUSIONS

From the original description it appears that all these items, including the other grave goods, had been found inside the Collared Urn along with the cremated bones. Clearly none had been through the pyre, as otherwise most would have been destroyed; but there is no information about their specific disposition. The question arises as to whether they had formed an ensemble, as a single piece of composite jewellery (e.g. necklace) or dress accessory, or whether they had belonged to more than one object. The range of object shapes is reminiscent of that found on some other composite jewellery (such as Amesbury Solstice Park; Sheridan forthcoming b), although the imperforate conical object is without close parallel. The differential degree of wear suggests that some items had probably been used longer than others. It is the largest objects (plus one fusiform jet bead) that show the heaviest wear.

The jet fusiform beads were probably recycled from old jet spacer plate necklaces, and at least one of the amber beads probably was derived from an amber spacer plate necklace. These worn items contrast with the black biconical beads which were relatively new when deposited. The ring with four perforations (ID 398) may have originally functioned as a kind of spacer, for separating out four different strands of beads on the chest. However it could not have been employed as such in the final ensemble as all four perforations had already broken out. The non-perforated conical item (ID 404) must have been fixed by binding running around the marginal groove, and the wear

observed is consistent with this interpretation. The ring with V-perforation (ID 399) is definitely not a belt ring. It is unclear why the external groove was needed as well as the perforation, but this arrangement does imply that the ring lay flat within the stringing. The faience quoit pendant is similar in size and cross section to the ring from Shrewton 5L (Figure 8.4.1), although that does not possess the perforated suspension lug.

ID 505–507.1–7 and 1472.1–11 and faience Upton Lovell G1, Wiltshire

References: Hoare 1812, 76 and pl. IX; Annable and ApSimon 1964, 54 and 108, 340–2.

COMPOSITION

The maximum number of beads recorded by Hoare is 8 of shale, 27 of amber and 16 of faience, plus two shale rings, giving a total of 53 items. Of these the following survive for study: two rings, nine shale beads, 11 amber beads and ten faience beads (Figure 8.3.3a).

CONTEXT AND ASSOCIATIONS

The necklace was found with a primary cremation burial within a bell barrow.

MORPHOLOGY AND MATERIALS

Objects of jet-like materials include two rings of shale, one (ID 505, Figure 8.3.3b; B37; AS) with a D-shaped hoop section which tapers to the outer margin. The diameter is 20.6mm, thickness 3.6mm and the diameter inside the hoop 9.8mm. The other, ID 506 (B38; AS), is a ring with rounded rectangular hoop section; it measures 20 by 18mm, is 3.5mm thick and the diameter within the hoop is 10.9mm. There are five squat biconical beads of jet (ID 507.1–3 and 8–9, e.g. Figure 8.3.3c; (B43–45 and B46–47; AS) varying in length from 6.0 to 8mm and width 7.5 to 8.75mm. The perforation diameters range between 4.0 to 4.2mm. ID 507.4 is a flat rhomboidal bead of jet (B39; AS) measuring 14.9 by 10.75mm with a perforation diameter of 2.9mm (Figure 8.3.3d). Three medium fusiform beads of jet (ID 507.5–7, e.g. Figure 8.3.3e; B40–42; AS) vary in length from 14.6 to 18.5mm and width 7 to 9.3mm. Their perforation diameters range from 2.4 to 4.2mm.

The amber beads include three slender annular examples (ID 1472.1–2, 7, e.g. Figure 8.3.3b), 1–2 dark orange and 7 dark red in original colour. They vary in length from 3.0 to 3.8mm and in thickness 5.8 to 6.7mm. The perforation diameters range between 1.5 to 3mm. There are six medium annular beads (ID 1472.3, 5, 8–11, e.g. Figure 8.3.3e), three of which are dark orange and three dark red. They vary in length from 3.5 to 4.8mm and in thickness from 7.0 to 7.5mm. The perforation diameters range between 1.5 and 2.5mm. ID 1472.4 (Figure 8.3.3d) is a plump wedge-shaped bead, dark red, measuring 6.0 by

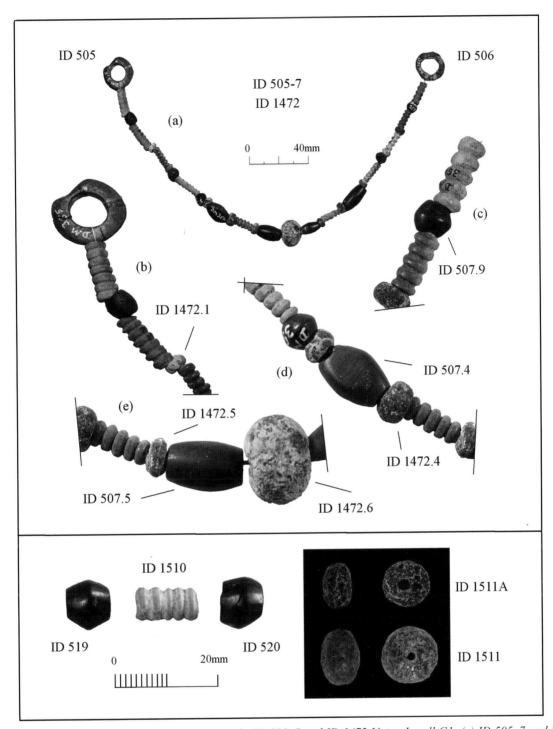

Figure 8.3.3. Composite necklaces with three materials. ID 505–7 and ID 1472 Upton Lovell G1: (a) ID 505–7 and ID 1472 whole necklace; (b) details of ID 505 left hand shale ring and ID 1472.1 slender annular amber bead; (c) details of ID 507.9 jet squat biconical bead and faience beads; (d) details of ID 507.4 jet flat rhomboidal bead and ID 1472.4 plump wedge-shaped amber bead; (e) details of ID 507.5 jet fusiform bead, ID 1472.5 medium annular amber bead and ID 1472.6 squashed globular amber bead (note: details not to consistent scale). ID 519–20, ID 539, ID 1510–11A Collingbourne Kingston G8: ID 519–20 jet biconical beads; ID 1510 faience bead; ID 1511–11A amber beads.

8.8mm with a perforation diameter of 3mm. ID 1472.6 is a squashed globular bead, dark orange, measuring 13.0 by 6.5mm with a perforation diameter of 4mm (Figure 8.3.3e). There are also ten segmented beads of faience; these were not measured. Due to the loss of many beads the strung length is indeterminate.

MANUFACTURE

One shale ring (ID 506) has faint lateral striations within the hoop, and two of the jet fusiform beads (ID 507.5 and ID 507.7) show hints of longitudinal faint faceting towards their ends.

COMPLETENESS AND DAMAGE

All but four of the surviving beads, and one of the rings are complete, although both rings have several glued breaks. The latter breaks are modern, as are chips on one of the amber beads. Other minor chips, on amber or jet beads, are of indeterminate age. One of the rings has an ancient spall.

WEAR

Both shale rings display a slight area of concavity on the hoop which is smoothed. This may indicate where the rings were strung so as to lie flat against the body. In some cases wear on the beads could not be determined owing to the tight modern stringing on the display. However, four jet beads have thread-polish (ID 507.5, 6, 8 and 9) and one displays bead-on-bead wear (ID 507.5). Five amber beads also have thread-polish (ID 1472.4, 6, 8, 9 and 11) while three others have crisp edges to the perforations (ID 507.3, 7 and 10). Overall, where wear could be categorised, two are fresh to slightly worn (both amber), 11 are slightly worn, and five worn. None show heavy wear.

CONCLUSIONS

The four raw materials employed provide pleasing colour contrasts between the black, blue and red items. Jet was used as well as shale and there were two main colours of amber represented. The shapes of the beads are also very varied. Although very few of the items show ancient damage the degree of wear is highly variable, and individual elements were probably obtained from a variety of sources, such as earlier necklaces. However the jet beads were not derived from earlier spacer plate necklaces, as they are of the type made *de novo* in the full Early Bronze Age. And the amber beads, again very variable in size and form, are not of the type used in amber spacer plate necklaces.

ID 509.1–6, 1492.1–11 and 1493–94 Wilsford G3, Wiltshire

References: Hoare 1812, 205; Annable and Simpson 1964, 57 and 112, nos. 390–5.

COMPOSITION

The necklace contains 19 items comprising six jet beads, 11 amber beads and two faience beads (Figure 8.3.1, bottom).

CONTEXT AND ASSOCIATIONS

The beads were found with a primary cremation burial within a disc barrow in the Normanton Group. The burial was contained in a small circular pit.

MORPHOLOGY AND MATERIALS

The jet beads (ID 509.1–6, Figure 8.3.1) comprise two medium fusiform beads (ID 509.1 and 3; B65 and B67;

AS) of lengths 14.2 and 14.5mm, widths 8.4 and 2.9mm and perforation diameters both of 2.9mm. There is a plump fusiform bead (ID 509.2; B66; AS) measuring 9.0 by 6.9mm with a perforation diameter of 2.8mm, and three slender fusiform beads (ID 509.4–6; B68-70; AS) of lengths 12.8 to 14.3mm, widths 7.1 to 7.7mm and perforation diameters 2.4 to 2.9mm. All eleven amber beads (numbered ID 1492.1–11, from left to right in Figure 8.3.1) are of squashed globular type; all are dark red except for nos. 4, 7–8 and 10 which are bright red in original colour. The thicknesses vary from 5.0 to 7.4mm, widths from 8.4 to 11.7mm and perforation diameters 1.2 to 3.5mm. The two faience beads are segmented, each with six segments; the longer is 18.0mm. The overall strung length is 360mm.

MANUFACTURE

Faint traces of faceting were found towards the ends of three of the fusiform jet beads, but no signs of manufacture are visible on the amber items.

COMPLETENESS AND DAMAGE

All the amber beads are complete, plus two of the jet examples. The other four jet beads have chips, spalls and one break, but all these are modern.

WEAR

Two of the jet beads show minimal thread-polish (ID 509.2 and 4) and the rest have slight thread-polish and bead-on-bead wear. However in four cases the beads are almost pristine and were categorised as fresh. The other two are slightly worn. Amongst the amber beads, wear was sometimes indeterminate, but in six cases the edges of the perforations are fairly crisp, denoting slight wear only. Thus overall the beads appear to be fresh or only slightly worn.

CONCLUSIONS

The strong contrast between the black, red and blue elements of this necklace would once again have been very striking, although the forms of the beads belonging to each of the three materials is fairly uniform. The jet beads are a single set, made by one hand and with a fairly consistent degree of wear (some of the thread-wear may be recent, due to stringing during display). They were probably recycled from a jet spacer plate necklace and, judging by their small size, from the inner strand of such a necklace. They are similar to those from Upton Lovell G2a (Figure 8.2.7 lower), but are less worn. The amber beads are very tightly strung in the modern display. However it is possible to discern that they are all of similar shape and form. There is some gradation in size but all probably derive from one or more amber spacer plate necklaces. Colour is fairly consistent between bright and dark red so they may all have come from a single original necklace.

ID 519–20, ID 539, ID 1510 and ID 1511–1511A Collingbourne Kingston G8, Wiltshire

References: Annable and Simpson 1964, 64 and 119, 515–8; Longworth 1984, no. 1673, pl. 186c; Thomas 2005, fig. 54, K1–K7.

COMPOSITION

The necklace comprises a total of six beads of which three are of jet, two of amber and one of faience (Figure 8.3.3, bottom) along with a toggle-shaped pendant, probably of jet (not seen).

CONTEXT AND ASSOCIATIONS

The objects were found in association with a Collared Urn within a secondary cremation burial in a bell barrow within the group on Snail Down. The centre of the mound had been investigated by Cunnington, and the barrow was later fully excavated by Thomas in the 1950s (2005, fig. 9). The burial concerned is Thomas' Secondary Burial 1 (*ibid*, 37–8 and fig. 13). The upright Collared Urn had been placed within a small pit and was covered by a cairn of flints. Within the urn were cremated remains, possibly of a child and probably contained within a bag of perishable material. The beads were found near the base of the bone pile, while the toggle pendant had been placed within the flint cairn.

MORPHOLOGY AND MATERIALS

Of the three jet beads two were squat biconical in form (ID 519–20; B60 and B61; AS) and measured 8.5 by 8mm and 8.4 by 8mm with perforation diameters 2.8 and 2.5mm respectively. The third was a broad annular bead (ID 539; B62; AS) measuring 5.5 by 6.6mm with a perforation diameter of 4.2mm (not illustrated). The two amber beads were of medium annular type (ID 1511 and ID 1511A), of dark orange and dark red amber respectively, measuring 6.5 by 10.8mm and 5.5 by 9mm, and with perforation diameters 1.5 and 2.5mm. The single faience bead (ID 1510) is 12.0mm in length formed in five segments. The strung length is likely to be 46mm.

MANUFACTURE

The annular jet bead and one of the biconical ones (ID 520) have faint longitudinal striations on both ends and the exterior respectively.

COMPLETENESS AND DAMAGE

One jet and one amber bead are complete and further jet and amber beads have modern spalling or chips. The annular bead only survives at 70%, with a large modern break on one side.

WEAR

No ancient damage is visible. Thread-wear is detectable on one biconical jet bead (ID 519), the annular jet bead and on one of the amber beads (ID 1511A). Overall three beads are worn (ID 519, ID 539 and ID 1511A), while the other biconical jet bead is fresh (ID 520).

CONCLUSIONS

This small black, red and blue necklace contains beads of varying shapes. The amber ones may have derived from an original spacer plate necklace. However the jet beads are of non-spacer plate necklace type, having been made afresh in the mature Early Bronze Age period. One of the biconical jet beads (ID 520) is very fresh and may have been made specifically for this set.

ID 524–29 and faience Winterbourne Stoke G67, Wiltshire

Reference: Colt Hoare 1812, 114 and pl. XIII.

COMPOSITION

The total of 11 items comprises five flat shale rings, one shale V-perforated button, one amber bead and three beads of faience; there is also a shale bead which is lost (Figure 8.3.4, top).

CONTEXT AND ASSOCIATIONS

The objects were found with a probably primary cremation burial within a disc barrow. The cremated remains had been wrapped in a linen cloth, and with them were found the rings, the button and the beads. The wrapped items were covered by an inverted urn (lost).

MORPHOLOGY AND MATERIALS

Of the five flat shale rings ID 524 is of Kimmeridge shale (B27; AS); the diameter is 25.3mm, thickness 4.8mm and the width of the hoop is 6.9mm. The hoop section is tapered to the interior and exterior, but more so to the exterior. There is one small neat perforation of diameter 1.7mm, for suspension. ID 525, also of Kimmeridge shale (B28; AS), has a diameter of 22.3mm; the thickness is 3.4mm and the width of the hoop is 4.9mm. The hoop section is tapered to the exterior only. ID 526, of Kimmeridge shale (B29; AS), is 27mm in diameter, 4.2mm thick and the hoop is 5mm wide. The hoop section is tapered to the interior only, and the exterior face is gently curved. ID 527, also of Kimmeridge shale (B30; AS), has a diameter of 26.2mm, is 4.9mm thick and the width of the hoop is 4.7mm. The hoop section tapers evenly to the interior and exterior. This ring has a fine incipient hole, presumably designed for suspension, which has been drilled twice but the hoop has not been perforated; the drillhole diameter is 1.25mm. The final flat ring is also of Kimmeridge shale (ID 528; B31; AS); it has a hoop section tapered to the interior with an exterior curved face. The diameter is 27mm, the thickness 5.4mm, and the hoop width 4.7mm.

The V-perforated button is of Kimmeridge shale (ID 529; B32; AS). It is high-domed with a diameter of 17.1mm and height 9.2mm (see also Chapter 5.2, Figure 5.2.3). The globular amber bead (not studied) measures 17.0 by 16mm. One of the faience beads has four segments, the other has three. Their lengths were not recorded. The strung length is likely to have been 128mm minimum (based on the rings only as the button does not show 'necklace wear', see below).

MANUFACTURE

All five rings have tool marks visible inside the hoop, all made with a similar broad knife. The shale button has faint horizontal polishing striations on the facet at its base.

COMPLETENESS AND DAMAGE

The rings are almost complete. Four of them have minor chips, but all are modern except for one on ID 527. The button is entire, but broken across and glued.

WEAR

No obvious wear is visible within the hoops of the five rings. However there is possible fabric wear on both flat surfaces of ID 525 and ID 526 and on one surface of ID 528. Overall assessment of wear could not be determined, although it was thought that ID 524 was fairly fresh. The button has marked thread-wear on the inner sides of the perforations, indicating that it had been used as a button or stud, and had not been strung in a necklace; the base also displays fabric rub, but overall it seemed fresh to slightly worn.

CONCLUSIONS

The grouping of five rings and only four beads in this group is unusual. From consideration of the dimensions and cross-section descriptions for the five rings it can be suggested that they comprise two pairs (ID 524/527 and ID 526/528) and one single ring (ID 525). The first pair exhibits perforations for suspension, although this was unfinished in one of them, and the single ring is rather smaller in size. The shale button is a copy of an Early Bronze Age jet high-domed form, and all the shale items may not have been very old when buried.

8.3.4 AMBER, FAIENCE AND STONE

ID 1495 Amesbury G48, Wiltshire

Reference: Hoare 1812, 162–3; Annable and Simpson 1964, 57 and 112, nos. 399–405.

COMPOSITION

The necklace consists of 14 surviving items: nine amber beads; two beads of stone, two faience beads and an amber ring (Figure 8.3.4, centre left). A further bead of 'transparent horn-like substance' was recorded by Hoare (lost).

CONTEXT AND ASSOCIATIONS

The beads were found with a primary cremation burial within a bowl barrow with outer bank within the Cursus Group.

MORPHOLOGY AND MATERIAL

Eight of the nine annular amber beads are of squashed globular type (ID 1495.2, 5–11). All are all dark orange in colour with lengths varying from 4.2 to 5.8mm and thicknesses from 8.5 to 10mm. The perforation diameters vary between 2.2 and 2.7mm but many are indeterminate. The remaining amber bead is of thin annular type (ID 1495.3), dark orange in colour and measuring 4.5 by 7.5mm with a very fine perforation. ID 1495.12 is a dark orange amber ring measuring 23.5 by 5.5mm with an internal diameter of 9.0mm.

The two stone beads are made from a uniform fine-grained rock (R. Ixer). Both are of wedge-shaped annular form. One (ID 1495.1) is grey to pink in colour with a matt surface measuring 7.0 by 12.7mm with a perforation diameter of 7.0mm; the other (ID 1495.4) is grey-green in colour and measures 3.5 by 4.8 by 9.5mm with a perforation diameter of 9.5mm. The two faience beads are both segmented; one is broken and has five segments, the other four segments. If the amber ring was strung flat the strung length is 106mm.

MANUFACTURE

No traces of manufacture are visible.

COMPLETENESS AND DAMAGE

All items are complete apart from the amber ring (at 80%), where all outer edges have been eroded by modern breakdown of the oxidised surfaces, and one amber bead with a modern break on one side (70% survival).

WEAR

Traces of wear are seldom visible on amber items such as these, but the two stone beads have thread-wear and are classified as worn.

CONCLUSIONS

The variety of beads employed would have provided colour contrasts between the red amber and the blue faience. The stone beads, one of pink and one of grey-green rock may have been selected to reflect this same colour contrast. The

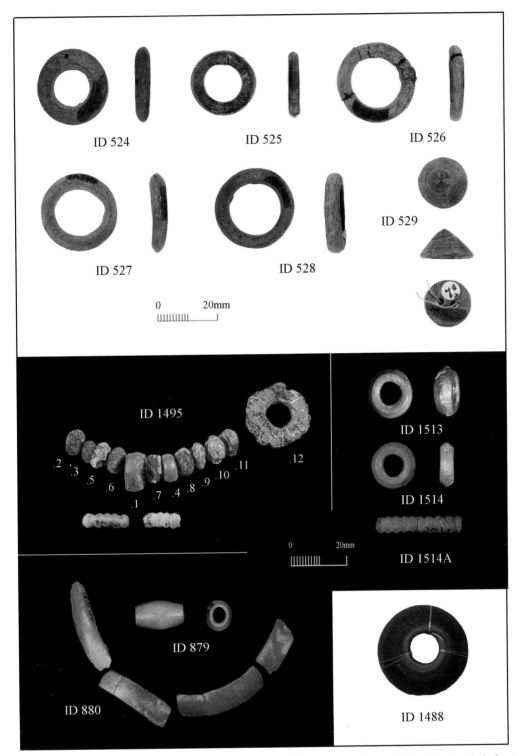

Figure 8.3.4. Composite necklaces with three materials. ID 524–29 Winterbourne Stoke G67: ID 524–28 shale rings; ID 529 shale button. ID 1495 Amesbury G48: necklace of nine amber beads, two stone beads, amber ring and two faience beads. ID 1513–14A Wilsford G46 showing two stone beads and segmented faience bead. ID 879–80 Winterbourne Stoke G8 showing bone bead and beaver tooth. ID 1488 Wilsford G42 showing glass bead.

amber beads are mainly of a single type and are of the kind used in known amber spacer plate necklaces. They were probably recycled from one or more such necklaces, with the constancy of colour maybe indicating that they came from the same spacer plate necklace.

ID 1513–1514A Wilsford G46, Wiltshire

References: Hoare 1812, 211 and pl. XXX, 6 and 7; Annable and Simpson 1964, 54 and 108, nos. 337–9.

COMPOSITION

A total of three beads survive, two of stone and one of faience (Figure 8.3.4, centre right).

CONTEXT AND ASSOCIATIONS

The beads were found with a primary cremation burial within the south-east mound of two confluent barrows within the Lake Group. Originally found were also three further faience beads, two amber beads and a bronze awl (all lost).

MORPHOLOGY AND MATERIALS

Of the two stone beads one is an annular bead of red/pink laminated mudstone, from Devon or southwest Wales (ID 1513; R Ixer); it has a matt surface and measures 5.8 by 14.6mm with a perforation diameter of 6.7mm. The other stone bead (ID 1514) is biconical of buff/brown slate or shale from an unknown source (R Ixer); it also has a matt surface and measures 11.2 by 13.3mm with a perforation diameter of 7.3mm. The faience bead (ID 1514A) is of ten segments and is of length 28.0mm. The strung length is a minimum of 45mm.

MANUFACTURE

ID 1513 is neatly shaped with a distinct ridge around the outer margin, and both stone beads have visible rilling within the perforations.

COMPLETENESS AND DAMAGE

Both stone beads survive at 100%.

WEAR

Some softening of the surfaces within the perforation is visible on both stone beads, and they are classified as slightly worn.

CONCLUSIONS

The number of faience beads present and the strong shapes and colours of the stone beads mark this out as an unusual group. It is unfortunate that the amber beads are lost.

8.3.5 RED GLASS, STONE AND FOSSIL

ID 1488 Wilsford G42, Wiltshire

References: Hoare 1812, 210 and pl. XXX, 3 and 4; Annable and Simpson 1964, 56, no. 364, not illustrated; Guido *et al.* 1984, pls. 8 and 9.

COMPOSITION

This consists of a single large bead of red glass (Figure 8.3.4, bottom right). Also found were a bronze awl (ID 1487), bronze dagger, an 'ivory' bead (actually a fossil sponge) and 'haematites' (all are lost except the awl).

CONTEXT AND ASSOCIATIONS

The objects accompanied a primary cremation within a bell barrow within the Lake Group.

MORPHOLOGY AND MATERIALS

The glass bead (ID 1488) is a large symmetric annular bead of dark pinky red to black glass measuring 12.2 by 33mm with a perforation diameter of 10.5mm. The strung length is 12mm.

MANUFACTURE

Traces of the technique of spiral winding, with at least five turns, are very apparent, partly defined by lines which are black in colour. The red colour is due to the presence of copper (Guido *et al.* 1984).

COMPLETENESS AND DAMAGE

The glass bead is complete.

WEAR

Wear is indeterminate as the material is so hard. Microscopic analysis by Guido *et al.* (1984, 247) demonstrated nil wear.

CONCLUSIONS

This is a very early instance of the use of real glass, as opposed to faience.

8.3.6 STONE, FOSSIL AND BONE

ID 879–80 Winterbourne Stoke G8, Wiltshire

References: Hoare 1812, 124; Annable and Simpson 1964, 52 and 107, nos. 300–5.

COMPOSITION

The surviving group includes one bone bead and a beaver tooth (Figure 8.3.4, bottom left).

CONTEXT AND ASSOCIATIONS

The objects were found with a primary inhumation burial beneath a bowl barrow within the Winterbourne Stoke Crossroads Group. Also surviving from the grave group are a grape cup, two simple whetstones (ID 51–52, Figure 4.4.1) and a bronze awl (ID 1464, Figure 4.6.6). Other items found were a second cup, another bone bead, a fossil *Rhynconella* (scallop) and a piece of stalactite (all now lost). The accessory cups, beaver tooth, bone beads and whetstones were found on the right side of the head of the skeleton. And close by were the awl, fossil shell and piece of stalactite.

MORPHOLOGY AND MATERIALS

The bone bead is biconical (ID 879), buff and highly polished, and made from the distal shaft of a sheep/goat tibia (M. Maltby). It measures 15.5 by 10.8mm and has a perforation diameter of 5mm. The tooth (ID 880) is an incisor tooth of mature beaver (M. Maltby) and of a natural red-brown colour (see Chapter 5.1); the length is indeterminate, the width 9.0mm and the thickness 3.5mm. As only one bead survives the strength length is a minimum of 15.5mm.

MANUFACTURE

The beaver tooth shows no signs of modification, and on the surviving bead any traces of manufacture are all polished out.

COMPLETENESS AND DAMAGE

The bead is complete, and the tooth is almost complete. It is however in six pieces, four of which have been glued together. This represents modern damage.

WEAR

Any wear traces on the bone bead are obscured by lacquer but it appears to be in fresh condition. There are no non-natural signs of wear on the beaver tooth that would indicate use as a tool. Its overall wear category is indeterminate.

CONCLUSIONS

This represents a very interesting group of varied materials; it is unfortunate that several of the items are lost and so not available for detailed study.

8.4 COMPOSITE NECKLACES WITH FOUR MATERIALS

The entries are described according to the combinations of raw materials employed. A list of items studied and illustrated is shown in Table 8.4.1.

8.4.1 GOLD, JET AND JET-LIKE MATERIALS, AMBER AND FOSSIL

ID 484–86, ID 487/1387, ID 1381–86 and ID 1388 Wilsford G7, Wiltshire

References: Hoare 1812, 202 and pl. XXV; Longworth 1985, 289, no. 1716 and pl. 10a; Annable and Simpson 1964, 44 and 98, nos. 147–58.

COMPOSITION

The items comprise a total of ten ornaments: a group of six pendants (four of amber, a further probably shale pendant but surviving as a gold cover only, and one of jet), together with one gold-covered shale bead, one shale bead and two fossil beads (Figure 8.4.1, top).

CONTEXT AND ASSOCIATIONS

All the grave goods were found with a primary inhumation burial under a bowl barrow in the Normanton Down Group (Hoare erroneously described the site as a bell barrow). The grave was very shallow and the body had been laid with the head to the west. In addition to the ornaments the grave contained a grape cup and a Collared Urn. The Collared Urn had been placed at the feet of the body, but the location of the other objects was not recorded by Hoare.

MORPHOLOGY AND MATERIALS

There are two gold objects: a spherical gold pendant cover in two sections (ID 1388), and ID 487/1387 which is a large spherical bead of ?lignite (B4; AS) with a gold cover decorated with zones of four very narrow grooves at each perforation and four at the belly. It measures 18.0 by 18.3mm with a perforation diameter of 3.5mm (*c.* 4.5 in the shale). There are five other pendants: ID 485 is an axe-shaped pendant of jet, and ID 1381–84 are four pendants of amber. Two of these are trapezoidal and two are circular with V-perforations. Details of all these pendants can be found in Chapter 5.9 where they are also illustrated (Figure 5.9.2, Figure 5.9.3 and Figure 5.9.5).

There are also two ribbed oblate beads of Kimmeridge shale (ID 484 and ID 486; B2; AS and B3; AS) measuring 7.9 by 11.1mm and 8.4 by 10.4mm, and with perforation diameters 4.3 and 4.6mm respectively. ID 1385 and ID 1386 are two cylindrical fossil encrinite beads, one with six ossicles and the other with four; they measure 9.2 by 10.2mm and 9.3 by 11.3mm, with perforation diameters 4.0 and 6.5mm respectively. The overall strung length is estimated as 156mm.

MANUFACTURE

Discussion on pendants is contained in Chapter 5.9. The gold on the bead ID 487/1387 is well polished and its shale core has some unidirectional concentric very faint striations near the centre zone.

COMPLETENESS AND DAMAGE

All the items are complete or have very minor modern damage, with the exception of two amber pendants (ID 1381–82), which have more extensive modern damage; one of these (ID 1382) also has some damage which is probably ancient.

WEAR

The gold/shale and ribbed shale beads both show thread-polishing. The former has distinct thread-pull on the gold, and one of the shale beads also has possible bead-on-bead wear. Both gold items are defined as worn; one of the ribbed shale beads is very worn, the jet axe-shaped pendant (ID 485) is fresh to slightly worn, as are three of the amber pendants and the other ribbed shale bead (ID 486). Wear on the fourth amber pendant and on the two fossil beads is indeterminate. Overall, where wear can be determined, six items are fresh or slightly worn, two are worn and one very worn.

CONCLUSIONS

The gold-covered shale bead appears to have been made by the same craftsman as the gold cone cover from Upton Lovell G2e (ID 1450, Figure 6.1.6). This unique collection of highly varied and exotic objects includes a wide range of raw materials. The axe-shaped pendant made from Whitby jet is particularly notable. The items were found to display strong variation in their degree of wear, and this suggests that they had been gathered together from many

Table 8.4.1. List of composite necklaces with four materials studied and illustrated.

Object	Site (Parish), County	Museum	Illustration
ID 23, 300, 759	Langton 2, burial 2, E.Yorks.	BM	Figure 8.4.2
ID 460–63, 1040, 1523	Winterslow G21, Wilts.	Sal	Figure 8.4.2
ID 1524–25	"		Not illustrated
ID 466–68, 1529–33	Shrewton G5L, Wilts.	Sal	Figure 8.4.1
ID 484–87, 1381–88	Wilsford G7, Wilts.	Dev	Figure 8.4.1

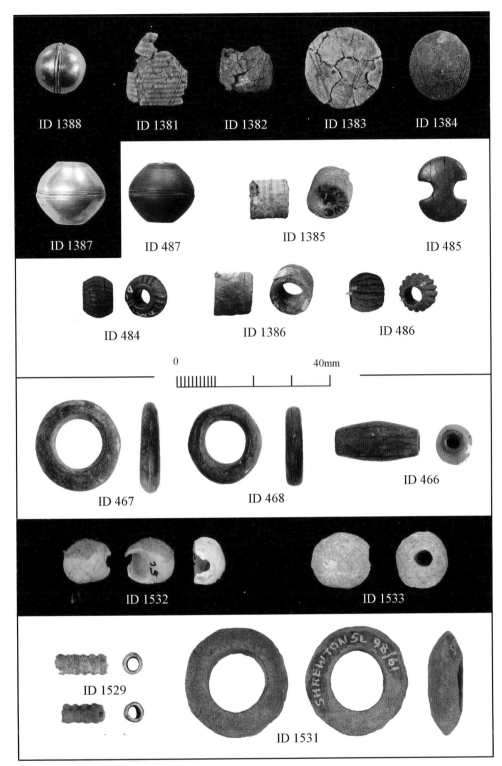

Figure 8.4.1. Composite necklaces with four materials. ID 484–86, ID 487/1387, ID 1388, ID 1381–86 Wilsford G7: ID 484 and ID 486 shale ribbed oblate beads; ID 485 jet pendant; ID 487/1387 gold/shale bead; ID 1338 gold pendant; ID 1381–84 amber pendants; ID 1385–86 fossil beads. ID 466–68, 1529–33 Shrewton G5L: ID 466 fusiform ?lignite bead; ID 467–68 shale rings; ID 1529 faience segmented bead; ID 1531 faience quoit; ID 1532 shell bead; ID 1533 stone bead.

different sources, and that some were of heirloom status. The objects with evidence of most wear are the two gold pieces and one of the ribbed shale beads.

8.4.2 JET AND JET-LIKE MATERIALS, FAIENCE, STONE AND SHELL

ID 466–68, ID 1529–33 Shrewton G5L, Wiltshire

Reference: Green and Rollo-Smith 1984, fig. 29.

COMPOSITION

The eight items comprise two shale rings, one ?lignite bead, one shell bead, one stone bead, two faience beads and one faience ring (Figure 8.4.1, bottom).

CONTEXT AND ASSOCIATIONS

The group was found in a bowl barrow with an inner turf mound within the Net Down Group. The beads were associated with a probably secondary cremation burial, interment 2, in Pit 2 (Green and Rollo-Smith 1984, 279–80 and fig. 13). In the base of the pit, above a thin layer of ash and charcoal, the cremated remains of a young female had been placed in an organic container. It appeared that this container had been secured with the string of beads. The pit had been sealed with a chalk capping.

MORPHOLOGY AND MATERIALS

There are two rings of Kimmeridge shale (ID 467; Bussell *et al.* 1982, 31; AS, and ID 468; Bussell *et al.* 1982, 31; AS). The former has a tapered internal cross section; the diameter is 21.4mm, thickness 5.9mm and internal diameter 11.4mm; the latter has a D-shaped hoop with a diameter of 18.6mm, thickness 4.6mm and internal diameter 10.2mm. ID 466 is a plump fusiform bead of ?lignite (Bussell *et al.* 1982, 31; AS) measuring 21.2 by 9.6mm and with a perforation diameter of 4.2mm. The faience quoit bead ID 1531 is large, with an external diameter of 27.3 to 27.5mm and a thickness of 7.6 to 8.2mm (AS). Its triangular-sectioned hoop is *c.* 6.3 mm wide and the diameter of the hole is 14.2 to 15.0mm; although it may have lain flat and pendant-like on the composite necklace of which it formed a part; the hoop is not perforated, nor does it have any added loop to aid its suspension as a pendant, as seen on some other quoit-shaped objects of faience (e.g. Oxteddle Bottom, Chapter 8.3). The hoop is straight-sided and has quite crisply defined apices. The upper surface is an intense greenish-turquoise with patches of brownish-buff core showing through while the lower surface is predominantly brownish-buff, with some greenish-turquoise patches. The segmented bead ID 1529 consists of two fragments, one with six segments and part of a seventh, the other with four segments and hints of a fifth. Only one original end seems to be present, on the smaller of the two fragments. It is clear that both fragments had originally formed part of a long bead with 12 or more segments (as shown in Green and Rollo-Smith 1984, fig. 29). A second long segmented faience bead, shown on that illustration as having been of similar length to ID 1529, had been crushed too badly during burial to be retrieved. The dimensions of the two fragments are as follows, respectively: length: 13.25mm and 10.55mm (implying an overall length of at least 23.8mm); outer diameter 4.7 to 4.9mm and 4.5 to 4.6mm; hole diameter 3.4 to 3.6mm.

ID 1532 is a shell bead, *Littorina littoralis/L. obcusata*, and originally would have been red in colour. Its natural shape is 12.3 by 9.7mm with a perforation diameter of 2.9mm. ID 1533 is a globular stone bead of limestone (R.

Ixer), buff in colour, measuring 12.8 by 2.2mm and with perforation diameters of 4.5 and 2.7mm. The maximum strung length is *c.* 160mm, if the rings were strung flat.

MANUFACTURE

The shale rings shows traces of knife shaping within the hoops and one (ID 467) also has traces on the outer facet of the hoop. Both are not exactly circular but are formed in a series of six chords. The fusiform bead has visible faceting on the body and faint traces of rilling within the perforation, while the stone bead displays strong rilling in the perforation. The glaze on the faience quoit bead had clearly been applied to the bead's core, with more ending on the upper surface than on the lower. The segments of the surviving segmented faience bead had been formed by rolling the paste tube against a 'butter pat'-like former, resulting in continuous ridges and hollows. The bright turquoise surface colour varies in its intensity from one side of the bead to the other, and there are patches that are almost glassy, due to the fusion of the individual quartz grains. The glaze had been applied.

COMPLETENESS AND DAMAGE

All the items are complete apart from the shell bead which has broken between the edge and the perforation in modern times.

WEAR

One shale ring (ID 467) shows thread-wear and this indicates that the ring may have been strung tightly in a flat position. The other ring shows probable fabric rub on one face, which indicates that it also had been worn flat. The ?lignite and stone beads both exhibit thread-wear, while the shell bead has a crisp perforation. All items were classified as slightly worn, except for the shell bead which may have been fresh.

CONCLUSIONS

The necklace group is highly varied in terms of raw material employed, colour, texture and artefact type. All the items were entire when placed in the grave, but where use wear could be detected it indicated slight wear during use. The shell bead was fresher, and may have been added later; it derives from the seashore, as would the raw material for the two shale rings. The large fusiform bead of ?lignite is from a different source, and is a form typical of the mature Early Bronze Age (*c.* 18th century cal BC).

The excavator deduced the original stringing order as follows (despite the items being found crushed) from left as facing the chest of the person: two segmented faience beads; shale ring; faience quoit; shale ring; lignite fusiform bead; shell bead, and stone bead (Green and Rollo-Smith 1984, 311). If this is correct the stringing was therefore markedly asymmetric in character.

8.4.3 JET AND JET-LIKE MATERIALS, AMBER, FAIENCE AND BONE

ID 460–63, ID 1040 and ID 1523–25 Winterslow G21 (Easton Down), Wiltshire

Reference: Stone 1932; Longworth 1985, 291, no. 1739 and pl. 149e.

COMPOSITION

A total of eight items was found comprising four beads of jet or shale, three amber beads and one faience bead (Figure 8.4.2, top).

CONTEXT AND ASSOCIATIONS

The objects were found with a cremation burial contained within a Collared Urn which was lying on its side. The urn had been packed round with ashes in a small pit. The burial was one of seven cremations covered by a long cairn of flints located on Easton Down. The site was excavated by J. F. S. Stone. The group also included a bone pin ID 1040, and all the items were associated with the Collared Urn (Longworth 1984, no.1742, pl.149e).

MORPHOLOGY AND MATERIALS

ID 460 and ID 461 are plump biconical beads of jet (Bussell *et al.* 1982, 31; AS) measuring 13.2 by 8.9mm and 13.3 by 10.8mm, and with perforation diameters 3.2 and 3.8mm respectively. ID 463 and 462 are both short biconical beads of jet and possibly shale respectively (Bussell *et al.* 1982, 31; AS) measuring 6.3 by 8mm and 6.9 by 6.4mm with perforation diameters of 3.4 and 3.8mm. The amber bead (ID 1523) is of plump fusiform type, light orange in colour, and measures 15.7 by 9.0mm with a perforation diameter of 2.3mm. Only fragments survive from two very small amber beads (ID 1524 and ID 1525) and no surfaces or perforations are visible under the microscope. The segmented faience bead (AS; not illustrated) is thin-walled and not definitely complete, with six segments. It is 13.5mm long, 5.2mm in diameter, and has a slightly elliptical and slightly eccentric hole measuring 3.1 by 2.7mm.

The strung length is a minimum of 13mm, excluding the small broken amber beads, and the bone point (ID 1040) which may have functioned as a pendant.

MANUFACTURE

No obvious traces of manufacture are visible on the jet, jet-like and amber beads, and no rilling is present within the perforations of any of these beads. The segments of the faience bead had been formed by rolling the paste tube against a 'butter pat'-like former, resulting in continuous ridges and hollows.. The bead's surface, which is matt, is mostly a light, slightly greenish blue colour, while the core is creamy with green-blue tinges.

COMPLETENESS AND DAMAGE

Apart from the fragmented smaller amber beads, all the items are almost complete, at 96% survival or above. Damage that includes chips and breaks right across is usually modern, except in the case of the large amber bead.

WEAR

The fusiform amber bead had been broken at one end during use, and displays strong thread-pulls. Two of the biconical jet beads show wear: thread-wear in ID 461, and bead-on-bead wear on ID 463. In contrast, the third jet bead ID 460 shows no wear, while any wear on ID 462 is indeterminate due to masking by consolidant. Overall, ID 460 was categorised as fresh, ID 463 as slightly worn, ID 461 as worn and ID 1523 (the amber fusiform) as very worn. The other items were indeterminate in terms of wear category.

CONCLUSIONS

This small group of beads is remarkably varied, both in terms of the number of raw materials used, and the types of beads represented. Two of the beads (ID 461 and ID 463) are of good jet, while ID 460 and ID 462 are probably of jet but are from a different source. These were selected, or made afresh, to match in with ID 461 and 463. The degree of wear relating to the individual items is also extremely variable: one each of fresh, slightly worn, worn and very worn. This further indicates that the different beads had been obtained from very different sources, and possibly over a period of time.

8.4.4 JET AND JET-LIKE MATERIALS, BONE, FOSSIL AND SHELL

ID 23, ID 300 and ID 759 Langton 2, burial 2, East Yorkshire

References: Greenwell and Rolleston 1877, 136–140; Kinnes and Longworth 1985, 32, barrow 2, burial 2.

COMPOSITION

The total of ten items comprises one jet bead, one fossil bead, two shell beads, three shells, one fossil, one tooth bead and one tusk ornament. The jet bead (ID 300), the tusk (ID 759 and the fossil (ID 23) were all examined (Figure 8.4.2, bottom); the other items were not seen.

CONTEXT AND ASSOCIATIONS

The objects were found with the secondary contracted inhumation burial of an adult woman. The burial was laid on its right side with the head to the south-west; it was located 0.2 m above the old ground surface 4.5m south-east from the centre of the barrow. All the finds were grouped at the waist of the body. Also in the grave were three bronze awls (ID 1280 and ID 1281, both Figure 4.6.2 and ID 1282).

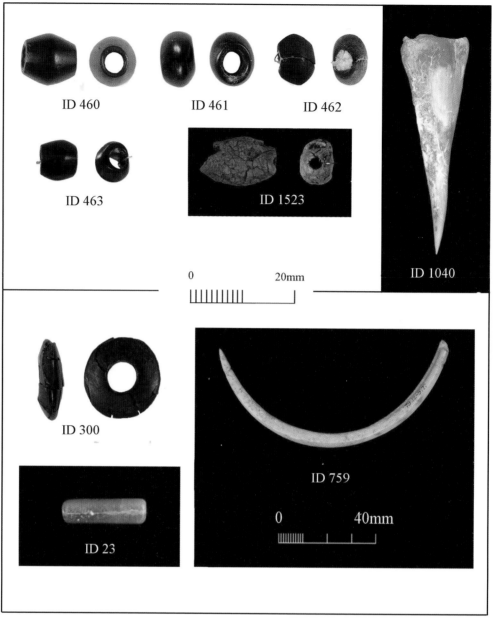

Figure 8.4.2. Composite necklaces with four materials. ID 460–63, ID 1040 and ID 1523–25 Winterslow G21: ID 460 and ID 461 plump biconical jet beads; ID 462 and ID 463 short biconical beads of jet and ?lignite respectively; ID 1523 plump fusiform amber bead; ID 1040 bone point. ID 23, ID 300 and ID 79 Langton 2, burial 2: ID 23 fossil bead; ID 759 tusk; ID 300 annular jet bead.

MORPHOLOGY AND MATERIALS

ID 300 is a slender, annular bead of jet (AS/MD) with a cross section tapering to the outer margin; it measures 14.8 by 4.4mm with a perforation diameter of 6.0mm. The tooth (ID 759) is a pig canine from a mandible (M. Maltby) and is cream with a polished surface; it measures 94.0 by 5.7mm, and has been cut down from the outer margin of a large tusk (see also Figures 5.1.1 and 5.1.2). A series of grooves at the wider end would have facilitated suspension by threads or sinews; it also has a single groove across the tip. There is also a tooth bead (root only and species not identified) measuring 15.0 by 11.0mm. The fossil (ID 23)

is a solid length of belemnite (R. Ixer), shiny and orange-brown in colour, and measuring 17.3 by 5.2mm. One of the shell beads, *Littorina obtusata*, has a longitudinal perforation near the base; the original colour would have been orange-red (not studied). The second shell bead is a fragment of *Dentalium* (*Antalis entalis*), comprising a small cylinder with a natural longitudinal perforation (not studied). The three shells are cowrie shells, *Trivia arctica*; none were perforated. The fossil fish vertebra has a central perforation, but the species is unidentifiable (not studied). The strung length is *c.* 39mm, plus four items which are not stringable.

MANUFACTURE

No traces of manufacture are discernible except in the cutting down of the tusk ornament.

COMPLETENESS AND DAMAGE

All items are complete apart from the tooth bead. The date of the damage to this bead was not determined. The tusk ornament has a split toward the root (wider) end which is partly modern and partly ancient.

WEAR

The jet bead was worn, with smoothing to the interior rilling. The tusk showed scuffing marks on surviving enamel, and the mounting grooves have wear-polish within the grooves and are slightly worn. The other items were not conducive to wear categorisation.

CONCLUSIONS

The variety of object types and raw materials employed is remarkable. However, only six out of the ten items could have been strung in a necklace. The jet bead is a later type, belonging to the mature Early Bronze Age, being a skeuomorph of a quoit-shaped faience bead.

8.5 COMPOSITE NECKLACES WITH FIVE MATERIALS

The entries are described according to the combinations of raw materials employed. A list of items studied and illustrated is shown in Table 8.5.1.

8.5.1 GOLD, JET AND JET-LIKE MATERIALS, AMBER, STONE AND FOSSIL

ID 489–91, ID 1420–22, ID 1424–25 and ID 1431–33 The Manton Barrow (Preshute G1a), Wiltshire

References: Cunnington 1908; Annable and Simpson 1964, 47 and 101, nos. 195–210; Lawson 2007, fig. 7.27.

COMPOSITION

The group consists of ten items: two pendants made from combinations of gold, amber and bronze, a bead of shale with gold, a shale bead, two stone beads, a fossil bead and three amber beads (Figure 8.5.1). There were also other ornaments: a further amber bead (lost); a shale disc bead necklace ID 491 (see Chapter 7.1.9, also Figure 8.5.1); a fired clay stud (ID 1423, Figure 5.6.2); two Series 7 knifes (one ID 1430, the other with an amber pommel ID 1429 now lost); three awls (ID 1426–28); a grape cup, and a further accessory vessel.

CONTEXT AND ASSOCIATIONS

The necklace was found with the primary contracted inhumation burial of a 'female of considerable age', lying on her left side with head to the south-east, in an isolated and low-lying bowl barrow. The burial, excavated in 1906, had been placed on the old ground surface. Remains and impressions of more than one type of cloth suggest that the body had been wrapped prior to burial, while traces of wood supported the head. The grave goods were found in two main groups (see sketch in Cunnington 1908). Most of the necklace items were found 'in a little heap' located above and behind the head. This group included the disc bead necklace, halberd pendant, gold-covered amber disc, the gold-bound shale bead, fossil bead and amber beads. Also in this area were the Series 7 knife with its amber pommel, while the clay stud was found near the chin.

A second group of objects, comprising the second dagger, the three awls, fluted shale bead and two beads of stone, was found at the feet of the body. The grape cup

was found behind the lower neck, and a second accessory vessel a little distance behind this. A Collared Urn found nine feet from the primary inhumation may or may not have been associated with the burial (Longworth 1985, 288, no. 169 and pl. 189e).

MORPHOLOGY AND MATERIALS

ID 489 is a plump barrel bead of ?lignite (B8; AS) with gold bands; it measures 14.9 by 14.7mm with a perforation diameter of 5.7mm. Gold combinations are also present in the gold-bound amber disc (ID 1420) and the halberd pendant (ID 1422) (see Chapter 5.9 and Chapter 6.1.6 for descriptions; also see Figure 5.9.1 and Figure 6.1.8). Kimmeridge shale was additionally used for ID 490, a squat ribbed biconical bead (B7; AS) measuring 6.5 by 12.1mm with a perforation diameter of 5.4mm. There are two stone beads: one, a chunky globular bead with sharp angles (ID 1421) is made of light grey siltstone (siliceous sediment) (R. Ixer) and measures 7.8 by 10mm with a perforation diameter of 2.7mm; the other (ID 1424) is a flat annular bead of pinky-red laminated mudstone (from Wales or the south-west; R. Ixer) measuring 4.0 by 12.2mm with a perforation diameter of 6.0mm. The fossil bead (ID 1425) is formed from one ossicle of an encrinite measuring 2.9 by 5.4mm with a perforation diameter of 2.4mm. Of the three amber beads, two are annular (ID 1431 and ID 1433), dark and bright red in colour, measuring 2.0 by 3.3mm and 2.0 by 4.6mm with perforation diameters 1.3 and 1.6mm respectively; the third (ID 1432) is a squashed globular bead with its original colour obscured, measuring 2.9 by 3.6mm and with a perforation diameter of 0.6mm. The strung length excluding the disc bead necklace is 43mm.

The necklace (ID 491, Figure 7.1.9 and Figure 8.5.1) is composed of tiny disc beads graded in diameter between 2.8 and 6.3mm; they range in thickness between 1.0 and 2.9mm, and the borehole diameter is 1mm. When laid together they form a strand *c.* 290mm long, and the necklace would originally have been just over 300mm long, not long enough to encircle an adult female neck (for which a circumference of *c.* 360mm would be normal) without a stretch of 'blank' thread at the back. In theory the beads could have been worn as a bracelet, although they would have had to be wrapped around the wrist; it is assumed that they had been worn instead as a necklace. In plan the beads are circular to sub-circular and mostly parallel-sided, with a slightly convex edge. The borehole is perpendicular, narrow, neatly executed and slightly eccentric, and in the two beads where its shape is clearly

Table 8.5.1. List of composite necklaces with five materials studied and illustrated.

Object	Site (Parish), County	Museum	Illustration
ID 24–25, 360–63, 1346	Aldbourne 280 (G6), burial 1, Wilts.	BM	Figure 8.5.3
ID 364–65	"		Not illustrated
ID 489–91, 1420–22, 1424–25, ID 1431–33	Manton Barrow (Preshute G1a), Wilts.	Dev	Figure 8.5.1
	"		
ID 1404–17	Wilsford G8, Wilts.	Dev	Figure 8.5.2

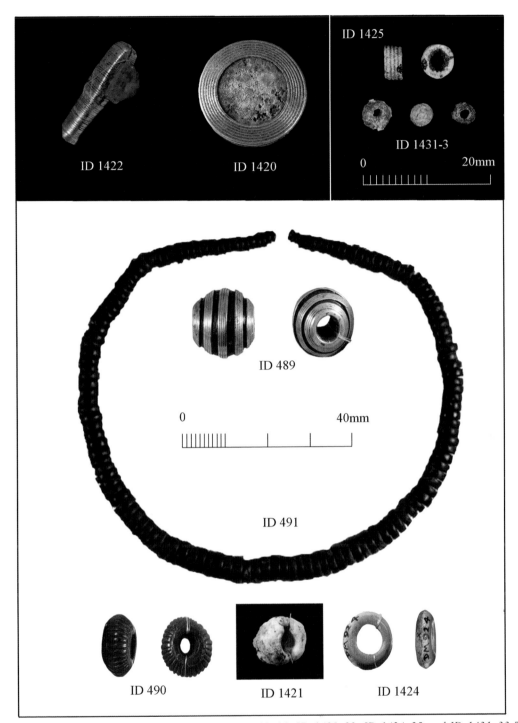

Figure 8.5.1. Composite necklaces with five materials. ID 489–91, ID 1420–22, ID 1424–25 and ID 1431–33 The Manton Barrow, Preshute G1. At the head of the burial: ID 1422 gold-bound halberd pendant; ID 1420 gold-bound amber disc; ID 491 disc bead necklace; ID 489 gold-bound shale barrel-shaped bead; ID 1425 fossil bead; ID 1431–33 amber beads. At the foot of the burial: ID 490 ribbed shale biconical bead; ID 1421 stone globular bead; ID 1424 pinky-red stone annular bead.

visible, it is parallel-sided. The beads are clearly all of the same material (B9; AS): a compact, black to black-grey, non-jet material that takes a satiny sheen, which Bussell *et al.* (1982, 29) tentatively identified as '?lignite' on the basis of XRF compositional analysis, later confirmed by Pollard *et al.* (1981). One bead has a hairline laminar crack. The material is the same as that used for the fluted bead.

MANUFACTURE

No manufacturing traces survive.

COMPLETENESS AND DAMAGE

All nine items survive complete, and all the disc beads studied are complete, or nearly so.

WEAR

Where wear traces can be seen the degree of wear is mainly slight only. This applies to the ribbed shale bead (with smoothed edges to the perforations and a possible thread-nick), one stone bead (ID 1424) and to the gold-bound amber disc. The other stone bead is very worn. In marked contrast, the gold-bound barrel bead is fresh. The degree of wear for the disc bead necklace could not be determined.

CONCLUSIONS

This group is unusually associated with knives, and also with a series of awls. The ornaments are very varied (Figure 8.5.1), and the degrees of wear also range widely. The decoration of the ribbed shale bead appears to imitate the segments found on an ammonite fossil.

It is particularly interesting to note that the unusual material used for the gold-bound bead ID 489 is matched by that employed for the cores of the gold-covered spherical bead from Wilsford G7 (ID 487/1387; see above) and the conical pendant or button from Upton Lovell G2e (ID 492/1450; see Chapter 6.1). This may indicate that these pieces were made by the same craftsperson.

8.5.2 GOLD, JET AND JET-LIKE MATERIALS, BRONZE, AMBER AND BONE

ID 1404–17 Wilsford G8, Wiltshire

References: Hoare 1812, 201–2 and pl. XXV; Annable and Simpson 1964, 46 and 100, nos. 179–192.

COMPOSITION

The necklace comprises 14 items, all of which are pendants and are described in detail in the pendants section (Chapter 5.9 and Figure 5.9.1 to Figure 5.9.5) and in Chapter 6.1.5 (Figure 6.1.8). Six are made from combinations of gold, amber, bronze, shale and/or bone, and the other eight are of amber (Figure 8.5.2).

CONTEXT AND ASSOCIATIONS

The objects were found with a primary cremation burial on the old ground surface below a bell barrow within the Normanton Down Group. They were found with a perforated wall cup.

MORPHOLOGY AND MATERIALS

ID 1404 is a halberd pendant of gold, bronze and amber; ID 1417 is a horned pendant of gold and bronze; ID 1405/488 is a gold-covered shale cone; ID 1412–13 are two gold-bound amber disc pendants, and ID 1406/901 is a gold pendant encasing a bone disc. There are also eight objects which are solely of amber: five pestle-shaped pendants (ID 1407–11) and three shield-shaped pendants (ID 1414–16).

The strung length is estimated at *c.* 206mm, excluding the gold-covered cone.

MANUFACTURE

Evidence of manufacturing is recorded in the pendants section (Chapter 5.9) and in Chapter 6.1.5.

COMPLETENESS AND DAMAGE

Seven items are complete or nearly so. The less complete items are all of amber, including the halberd pendant. The age of the breaks cannot usually be determined, but one modern and one possible ancient break are visible.

WEAR

Wear traces on five of the amber pendants and the two gold-bound amber discs could not be determined. Otherwise four items show slight wear and three (ID 1406 the gold/bone pendant, ID 1417 the gold/bronze horned pendant, and ID 488/1405 the gold-covered cone) can be described as worn.

CONCLUSIONS

This group is unusual not only for its wide range of highly exotic materials, material combinations and forms, but because it is one of the very few groups that contains no beads at all.

8.5.3 JET AND JET-LIKE MATERIALS, AMBER, FAIENCE, STONE AND FOSSIL

ID 24–5, ID 360–65 and ID 1346 Aldbourne 280, burial 1 (G6), Wiltshire

References: Greenwell 1881; Greenwell 1890, 50–53; Kinnes and Longworth 1985, 126–7.

COMPOSITION

The necklace comprises 14 items: one cannel coal or shale ring; a shale pendant; a shale button; three beads of jet or shale; two amber beads; three faience beads; a fossil bead and an unperforated fossil (Figure 8.5.3). An additional polished stone was not studied.

CONTEXT AND ASSOCIATIONS

The objects were found with a probably primary cremation deposit located at the centre of a barrow with a core of sarsens. The bones had been laid on the remains of wood in an area that had been deturfed. The barrow site is located south-west of Four Barrows. It also contained small dagger fragments (not numbered), awl fragments (ID 1291A and B) and two Aldbourne Cups.

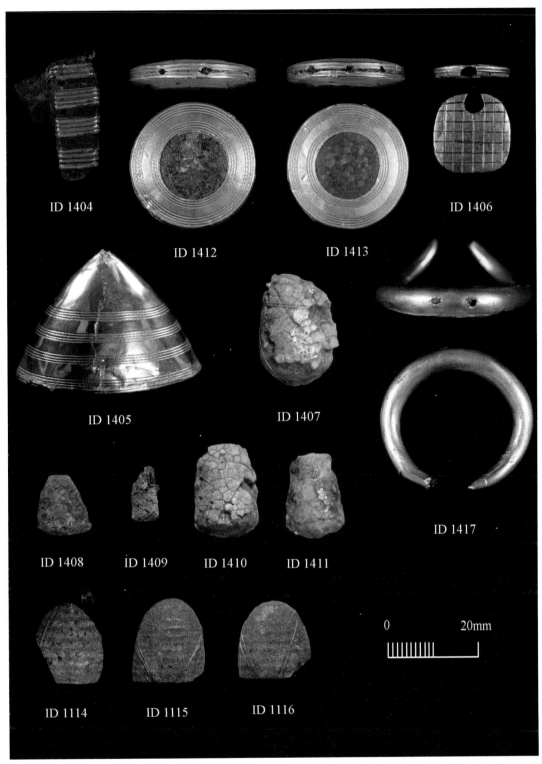

Figure 8.5.2. Composite necklaces with five materials. ID 1404–17 Wilsford G8: ID 1404 gold-bound halberd; ID 1405 gold-covered shale cone; ID 1406 gold-covered bone disc; ID 1407–11 five pestle-shaped amber pendants; ID 1412–13 two gold-bound amber discs; ID 1414–16 three shield-shaped amber pendants; ID 1417 horned pendant of gold and bronze.

MORPHOLOGY AND MATERIAL

The oval ring (ID 360) of cannel coal or shale (D/H) has a slightly tapered vertical profile, a diameter of 42.4mm and thickness 8.4mm. The outer edge is D-shaped and gently rounded. The oval pendant (ID 361) is of shale (D/H), of maximum diameter 32.2mm and thickness 6.2mm, with a projection housing a lateral perforation of diameter 1.5mm. The hoop is of D-shaped section with an internal ridge (also see pendant section Chapter 5.9). The V-perforated button (ID 363) is high-domed and of shale (AS/MD) with

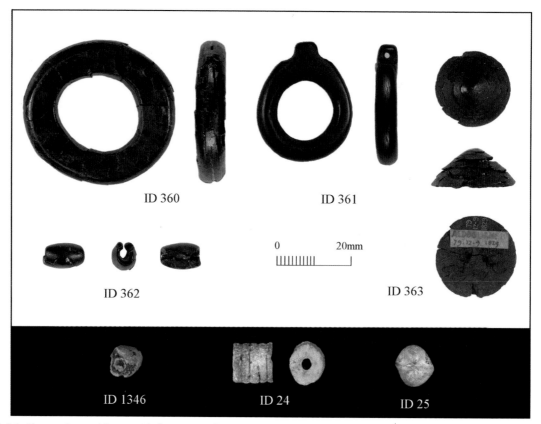

Figure 8.5.3. Composite necklaces with five materials. ID 24–5, ID 360–63 and ID 1346 Aldbourne G6: ID 24 fossil bead; ID 25 fossil; ID 360 shale ring; ID 361 shale pendant; ID 362 jet fusiform bead; ID 363 shale V-perforated button; ID 1346 part of amber fusiform bead showing bright red interior.

a diameter of 21.2mm (also see Chapter 5.2 and Figure 5.2.3). The two medium fusiform beads (ID 362 and ID 364) are both of jet (AS/MD; D/H) measuring 11.8 by 7.4mm and 11.7 by 7.0mm, with perforation diameters of 2.5 and 2.3mm respectively. The squat globular bead (ID 365) is of cannel coal or shale (D/H) and measures 6.7 by 10.9mm with a minimum perforation diameter of 2.6mm.

One of the two amber beads survives, but only as the centre portion of a fusiform shape (ID 1346); the colour is bright red and the surviving diameter is 8.5mm showing a perforation diameter of 2.3mm. The fossil bead (ID 24) is a rough surfaced mid-brown cylindrical encrinite portion with five ossicles and measures 11.6 by 9.5mm with a perforation diameter of 2.8mm. ID 25 is a solid fossil bivalve measuring 13.5 by 13.3mm and is light greenish-brown in colour. The final object, a stone, is a pebble of polished haematite measuring 9.0 by 8.0 by 5.0mm and was not studied. One segmented faience bead, out of the three originally found, survives (AS; not illustrated); the others had gone missing between 1936 (when they are shown in a photograph in Beck and Stone's publication on faience: Beck and Stone 1936, pl. LXIII, fig. 1.8) and 1985 (when the assemblage from this barrow was re-published by Kinnes and Longworth). However, it is clear from the published photograph that the missing beads are similar to the survivor. The surviving bead is probably complete, although damage to both ends makes it hard to be certain.

It has five segments and is 11.3mm long, with a maximum diameter of 4.5mm and a hole diameter of 3.3mm. The strung length is estimated at 97mm.

MANUFACTURE

Only two of the non-faience items retain any traces of manufacture. The shale ring (ID 360) has longitudinal shaping striations inside the ring, and the pendant (ID 361) has shaping marks on all surfaces of the ring and lateral irregular striations around the shoulders and top projection.

The segments of the surviving faience bead are broad, shallow and flat-topped, and had clearly been formed by rolling the paste tube against a 'butter pat'-like former, resulting in continuous ridges and hollows. The segments are a medium turquoise colour, with one particularly intense patch near one end. The glaze had probably been applied.

COMPLETENESS AND DAMAGE

Many of the objects are complete, but the three jet and jet-like beads and the amber bead have all suffered modern damage; they survive between the 60% and 98% levels. The faience bead is also broken at one end. Each segment of the encrinite bead is an ossicle and the bead may be 'as found'.

WEAR

None of the items has ancient breaks. The ring (ID 360) shows softening all round the inside of the hoop, and the upper edge of the perforation on the pendant (ID 361) also shows use; both are categorised as slightly worn. Wear on the button, the fossils and the amber bead is indeterminate but all three jet and jet-like beads have visible thread-wear and are classified as worn.

CONCLUSIONS

The object group is highly varied in terms of raw material employed, colour, texture and artefact type (Figure 8.5.3). All the items were entire when placed in the grave, but where use wear could be detected it indicated slight or medium wear during use. The squat globular cannel coal or shale bead (ID 365) is a copy of a faience bead type, and the fossil encrinite may also have been selected as it resembles the shape of a segmented faience bead. The large ring (ID 360) is typical of a group of flattish simple rings that are found in graves of the later Early Bronze Age period (*c.* 1750–1500 cal BC). The fossils are exotic to the region and may have been obtained from beaches on the south coast.

8.6 DISCUSSION

This discussion includes consideration of the 34 necklaces studied in detail in Chapter 8.2 to 8.5 above, together with the data relating to 47 other such necklaces, gathered from published or archival sources. The site details and references for these additional composite necklaces are listed in Table 8.6.1. All 81 necklaces, along with the 18 simple necklaces with components of variable shape described in Chapter 8.1, are mapped in Chapter 12 (Figure 12.8).

Table 8.6.1. Composite necklaces from England: examples additional to those studied (listed in alphabetical order of county).

Site	County	Reference
Radwell 1	Beds.	Hall and Woodward 1977, pl. 2
Stonea, Wimbleton	Cambs.	Potter 1977, fig. 6
Boscregan	Cornwall	Borlase 1879
Abney Moor	Derbys.	Beck and Shennan 1991, 145 and fig. 11.1, 2
North Molton	Devon	Fox and Stone 1951
Upton Pyne	Devon	Kirwan 1872
Puddletown Hundred	Dorset	Thurnam 1872, 530
Thomas Hardye School (Dorchester)	Dorset	Gardiner *et al.* 2007, fig. 11, 15–18
Winterbourne St Martin G5a	Dorset	Sydenham 1844, pl. 17c
Wimborne St Giles G6	Dorset	Hoare 1812, 238
Wimborne St Giles G8 (SE tump)	Dorset	Hoare 1812, 238
Wimborne St Giles G33a	Dorset	Hoare 1812, 243
Little Chesterford	Essex	Collins 1980, fig. 5
Rochford	Essex	Lawson *et al.* 1981, fig. page 63
Chalton	Hants.	Longworth 1984, 202; Beck and Shennan 1991, 151–2 and fig. 11, 11.3, 4
Easton Lane (Winchester)	Hants.	Fasham *et al.* 1989, fig. 103
Hengistbury Head	Hants.	Clarke *et al.* 1985, fig. 4.55
Portsdown (Southwick)	Hants.	Gerloff 1975, 259
Stockbridge Down	Hants.	Stone and Hill 1940, fig. 2, 1–11
Kentucky Farm, Pilling	Lancs.	Lancs. HER no. 1876; Edwards 2007, 232
Cossington	Leics.	Sheridan 2008a, fig. 73
Caistor St Edmund	Norfolk	Bamford and Ashwin 2000, fig. 72
Ashville (Abingdon)	Oxon.	Parrington 1978, fig. 26.4
Barrow Hills barrow 16 (Radley)	Oxon.	Barclay and Halpin 1999, fig. 5.12
Stanton Harcourt XVI, 1	Oxon.	Barclay *et al.* 1995, fig. 52, 5a–c
Ashen Hill (Chewton Mendip G11)	Somerset	Scarth 1859, 148–9
Chilcompton 2016	Somerset	Sheridan in prep.
Rowbarrow (Shipham G2)	Somerset	Grinsell 1971, 118–9
Tynings East (Cheddar G5)	Somerset	Taylor 1950, 128–9
Todmorden A	W. Yorks.	Longworth 1984, 280, no.1607
Todmorden B	W. Yorks.	Longworth 1984, 280, no.1610
New Barn Down (Amesbury G61a)	Wilts.	Ashbee 1985, fig. 39.7
Solstice Park (Amesbury)	Wilts.	Sheridan 2008b, 59; Sheridan forthcoming b
Amesbury G44 (E mound)	Wilts.	Stukeley 1740, 44; Hoare 1812, 161–2
Amesbury G54	Wilts.	Beck and Shennan 1991, fig. 11.1.6
Avebury G23d	Wilts.	Stukeley 1743, 44
Avebury G55	Wilts.	Smith 1965, fig. 3, 3–6
Collingbourne Kingston G5	Wilts.	Thomas 2005, fig. 54, K9–11
Collingbourne Kingston G8	Wilts.	Thomas 2005, fig. 54, K1–7
Collingbourne Ducis G12	Wilts.	Lukis 1867, 91
East Knoyle G1	Wilts.	Hoare 1812, 49
Ablington (Figheldean G12)	Wilts.	Hawley 1910, 622–3
Kingston Deverill G5	Wilts.	Hoare 1812, 46
Kingston Deverill G9	Wilts.	Hoare 1812, 45–6
Maiden Bradley G5	Wilts.	Hoare 1812, 47
Wilsford G72	Wilts.	Hoare 1812, 207
Winterbourne Stoke G9	Wilts.	Hoare 1812, 124–5

MATERIAL

The nature, significance and dating of composite necklaces in Britain has been discussed recently by Sheridan (2007b; 2008 and forthcoming). By definition a composite necklace or ornament set comprises items made from more than one material. The materials employed include gold, copper alloy, amber, jet and jet-like materials, bone, stone, fired clay, faience, fossil, shell and minerals. These materials are often unusual and exotic, and were sourced from faraway places. Thus the amber found in early second millennium composite necklaces most probably came from Denmark and was worked up by Wessex-based specialists, while jet from around Whitby in Yorkshire and shale from Kimmeridge Bay in Dorset also travelled considerable distances. Both amber and jet possess electrostatic properties which would have been perceived as special and magical materials. Some of the stone used for bead-making is also exotic, and shells and minerals were derived from coastal locations and from the depths of inland caves. Other minerals were those associated with the making of fire (haematite). The fossils selected may also have been imbued with magical power as they appeared to copy in stone the forms of plants and animals (e.g. 'tusk shells'), or to imitate the form of segmented beads. Gold and copper alloy were prized materials, while faience was an entirely new material, made using a process that was probably kept secret. Most of the faience beads in these necklaces are of the segmented variety, and most of these had been shaped by rolling the faience tube against a grooved former shaped like a traditional 'butter pat' tool; as argued elsewhere, this technique of manufacture is characteristic of Wessex, where most had probably been made (Sheridan and Shortland 2004). The variety of materials selected will also have provided strong contrasts in colour, with shades of black, white, red and blue being especially preferred. The acquisition of the raw materials from faraway and sometimes liminal or otherwise auspicious locations would in itself have involved cosmological overtones, as will the use of components that had been passed down through the generations (Helms 1988 and 1993; Needham 2000; and see below).

The relative occurrence of different raw materials within composite necklaces is shown in Table 8.6.2. This table provides data relating to the 34 necklaces studied in detail in the present project, together with those for 47 other such necklaces, gathered from published and archival sources. The entries are organised in terms of the number of different raw materials included in each necklace, starting with those containing two materials. Large necklaces present in the grave, such as a set of shale disc beads or an amber spacer plate necklace, are not included in the overall counts, but are noted in the second column. From the table it can be seen that the most commonly occurring elements in the necklaces are items made from amber and jet or jet-like materiuals. The next most common material is faience, followed by beads made from fossils, although the latter figure is enhanced by the inclusion of two necklaces made up of a large number of fossil beads. The figure for fired clay is also a distorted one, as it includes one necklace (from

Winterbourne Stoke G64a) where the components include 48 fired clay disc beads, while the similar total for beads of bone and teeth is more realistic. The objects which occur less often in the necklaces are those of shell, and items which combine various materials with elements of gold.

MORPHOLOGY

Shapes

Another key characteristic of composite necklaces is the presence of beads or ornaments in a variety of forms and shapes. Beads may be cylindrical, fusiform, biconical, disc, globular or oblate in shape and other ornaments include flat rings, as well as pendants of various sizes and form. The different items were probably strung to form particular and possibly symmetrical patterns within each necklace. The order of stringing has survived and been recorded in very few cases, notably at Cossington, Leicestershire, where five beads at the centre of the necklace were found *in situ*, and the layout of the entire string of 13 beads could be reconstructed (Sheridan 2008a, fig. 73). The original stringing order of a few other necklaces has also been attempted, as for Shrewton 5j and 5L (Green and Rollo-Smith 1984, figs. 28 and 29), Upton Lovell G1 (on the display board at the Wiltshire Heritage Museum, Devizes), and rather more fancifully, the complex necklace from Radwell, Bedfordshire (Hall and Woodward 1977, pl. 2). Most of the necklaces include a relatively small number of beads or other pierced ornaments. It seems therefore that generally the beads had been threaded on a single string. However in one case, that of Radwell (mentioned above), the presence of a large number of small beads, together with fragments of spacer plates that may still have functioned as such, suggests that several strands may have been involved.

Mimicry

Many of the beads used were chosen and manufactured or finished to imitate the appearance of other special items. Thus, as noted above, segments from naturally perforated fossil encrinite stems resemble segmented beads. Other beads, made usually from jet or shale, were decorated with ribbing possibly imitating the configuration of fossil ammonites. The form of segmented faience beads was copied in bone, and faience quoit ornaments were imitated in jet or shale. On the other hand, some faience beads were made as copies of biconical beads which were more often made from jet or shale. Many of the fusiform beads, of jet, shale or amber, were copies of the slightly earlier versions of fusiform beads that formed the components of jet spacer necklaces, but they tended to be both larger and plumper. Finally there is evidence that some beads of more mundane materials were coated, either with gold sheet, or with a black coating in imitation of jet or shale (as at Solstice Park, Amesbury; Sheridan forthcoming b). Alongside the standard bead forms, and the mimics just discussed, some entirely new types were also devised. Alongside a variety of chunky pendants there were also sharply biconical beads, beads with marked grooved or ribbed decoration, and squashed bun-shaped or chunky disc beads in amber.

RECYCLING AND HEIRLOOMS

As well as the standard bead forms, the mimics and the new types discussed above, the necklaces and sets also include many items which had been recycled and reused from earlier necklaces. Such beads mainly comprise fusiform beads derived from jet spacer plate necklaces of classic form, and squashed globular beads from amber spacer plate necklaces. Occasionally fragments of spacer plates, either in jet or amber, are also incorporated (e.g. Beaulieu, Hampshire: Piggott 1943 and Radwell, Bedfordshire: Hall and Woodward 1977). Such items would have been prized heirlooms, probably passed down through several generations and deriving from an unknown total number of original necklaces manufactured up to several centuries earlier. Beads of differing shape and material may also have been exchanged between contemporary relations or other social contacts. It has been suggested that the faience beads in the necklace from Solstice Park, Amesbury, Wiltshire may have come from seven different 'parent' necklaces (Sheridan 2008b, Sheridan forthcoming b). This topic will be further discussed in Chapter 10.

DATING AND ASSOCIATIONS

While the use of more than one material in a necklace is attested in Britain from as early as the Neolithic (at Greenbrae, Aberdeenshire; Kenworthy 1977), the origin of the Chalcolithic and Early Bronze Age tradition of wearing composite jewellery lies in Continental Beaker-associated practice. The earliest British examples of this tradition date to the third quarter of the third millennium BC (i.e. the Chalcolithic period). A necklace comprising tiny shale disc beads plus one tubular sheet gold bead, found with an early Low-carinated Beaker, at Chilbolton, Hampshire (Russel 1990, figs. 4 and 7,17), has been radiocarbon-dated (from the unburnt remains of the associated adult male) to 2570–2300 cal BC (see Chapter 9). A second composite necklace, comprising numerous tiny shale disc beads and a small number of tubular sheet copper beads, found with a Mid-carinated Beaker at Beggar's Haven, East Sussex (ID 434), is also probably of Chalcolithic date. The Beggar's Haven necklace, along with a slightly later example comprising tiny disc beads along with tubular sheet bronze beads found at Garton Slack (VI, burial 1, ID 251), East Yorkshire, are illustrated and described in Chapter 7.1.

Most composite necklaces and ornament sets date from the first half of the second millennium BC. (For more details see Chapter 9). This currency spans the Wessex Series 1 and Wessex Series 2 graves. It is apparent that most derive from cremation burials of the Wessex Series 2 graves, but some also occur in graves of Series 1. Faience is known to have been in use from the 20th century cal BC (Sheridan and Shortland 2004), but it does not seem to occur in the composite necklaces found in Wessex Series 1 graves.

Where ceramic vessels are present in graves which contain composite necklaces they tend to be either Collared Urns or accessory vessels. The latter often comprise special forms such as Grape Cups, Aldbourne Cups or Slotted Cups. A very common association is a copper alloy awl, or indeed a set of awls, and other objects include daggers of Series 5 and 7, studs and special items made from gold.

Distribution

Most of the composite necklaces have been found in the Wessex region (see map in Chapter 12, Figure 12.8). However there are examples from many other areas of the country, including the south-west, Sussex, the upper Thames valley, Bedfordshire, Leicestershire, East Anglia and Yorkshire, and also from further afield, as at Tara in eastern Ireland (Sheridan *et al.* 2013) and at Exloo in the Netherlands (Haveman and Sheridan 2006). In these last two necklaces, elements had been added in their countries of discovery. Sheridan has suggested that the tradition became particularly popular in Wessex, and that some of the outlying examples may represent 'emulation' of the Wessex idea (and/or actual exports from Wessex with subsequent embellishments); a connection with the trade in tin partly explains the distribution pattern (Sheridan 2008a, 84 and table 8; Haveman and Sheridan 2006).

Age and sex

A list of 27 necklaces of this type was provided by Gerloff (1975, Appendix 7), who termed them 'Female burials of the Wessex Culture'. However the recorded evidence of age and sex of the individuals interred with composite necklaces is slight, and this gender attribution should not automatically be assumed. Female remains have been confirmed in only four cases: Shrewton 5L and 5j, Preshute 1a (the Manton Barrow: an elderly individual) and Solstice Park, Amesbury. The body at Boscregan was either a young woman or a child, and at Portsdown two individuals probably comprised a man and a woman. Two male associations are known: an older man at Bedd Branwen grave H (Anglesey, Wales) and a youth of 14 to 15 years at Tara, Co Meath (Ireland; Sheridan *et al.* 2013). The male association of the Chilbolton necklace should also be noted. Thus the gender attribution for these necklace graves is by no means clear-cut. However, against this it can be noted that faience, which occurs in 41 of the composite necklaces listed in Table 8.6.2, is a material that is usually associated with the graves of women (Sheridan and Shortland 2004).

ANALYSIS

The occurrence of different raw materials in the necklaces studied, and within other published examples, is listed in Table 8.6.2 and summarised above. Table 8.6.3 shows the relationship between the number of raw materials present per necklace and the actual raw materials used in the individual necklaces. From this table it can be seen that gold items, or composite objects which include gold, occur mainly in necklaces that contain three different materials or more; the same applies to the occurrences of seashells. Furthermore, when the number of necklaces analysed is taken into account it can be concluded that none of the

Table 8.6.2. Composite necklaces: numbers of elements by material (necklaces not studied, as listed in Table 8.6.1, in italic; gold combination denotes objects which combine gold with other materials; jet or jet-like materials, amber; bone and/or copper alloy; beads in column 2 are not included in the total; in the totals >1 denotes that the actual number is unknown and is counted as 2).

Site	Necklace	Gold Combination /red glass	Jet/ jet-like	Amber	Faience	Bone	Stone	Fossil	Shell	Clay	Total	Strung length (mm)
Two materials												
Winterbourne Stoke G47	shale disc ×37+			4							4	4
Hay Top			11			1					12	112+
Winterbourne Stoke G64a								25		48	73	118
Wilsford G16			2	4							6	55
Amesbury G39			3	14							17	147
Winterbourne Steepleton			5	10							15	36
Marshfield G5			1	2							3	29
Calais Wold 114			9		1 or 2						10–11	71
Tan Hill (Bishops Cannings G46)			6		1						7	75
Bloxworth G4a			7		6						13	139
Durrington G47			2		1						3	55
Winterbourne Stoke G68			2		4						6	82
Aldbourne 285, burial 1			2				11				13	128
Upton Lovell G2a			3			1					4	70
South Newton G1				1		18					19	96
Warminster G10						6		1			7	112
Stonea, Wimblington			17	11							28	
Wimborne St Giles G6			>1	>1	>1						4+	
Little Chesterford					1	4					5	
Rochford		3									3	
Easton Lane, Winchester			3	27							30	
Pilling			many	1	4						many	
Ashen Hill, Chewton Mendip G11				5							6	
Todmorden A			>1			>1					8+	
Todmorden B			9	5							14	
Amesbury G54				7	3						10	
Avebury G23d				>1	>1						4+	
Avebury G55							1	3			4	
Collingbourne Kingston G5				2					1		3	
Collingbourne Ducis G12			2	5							7	
East Knoyle G1			>1	>1							4+	
Ablington (Figheldean G12)			5		8						13	
Maiden Bradley G5			1	>1							4+	
Winterbourne Stoke G9			>1	>1							4+	
Three materials												
Shrewton G5j	amber disc ×45+		4	7					1		12	c.97
Upton Lovell G2e	amber spacer plate necklace	17									17	
Oxsettle Bottom			18	4	2						24	289
Upton Lovell G1			10	27	16						53	
Wilsford G3			6	11	2						19	360
Collingbourne Kingston G8			4	2	1						7	46
Winterbourne Stoke G67			7	1	3						11	128

Site (and notes)										Total
Amesbury G48			10	2			2		14	106
Wilsford G46			2	4			2		8	45
Wilsford G42						1	1		3	12+
Winterbourne Stoke G8				1	3	1			5	16
Abney Moor (red glass bead)	2		>1						5	4+
Puddletown Hundred (2+)										2+
Wimborne St Giles G8 (SE)	>1	>1	>1	>1	>1			1	6+	6+
Wimborne St Giles G33a	>1	>1	>1						6+	6+
Winterbourne St Martin G5a				6	1				8	8
Radwell (shale disc ×94)	16	15			1				32	32
Boscregan	2+			12		2	2		16+	16+
North Molton	9	1		8					18	18
Upton Pyne (shale disc ×50)	3					1		1	5	5
Chalton	1	6		7					14	14
Portsdown (shale disc ×107)	1		16						17	17
Stockbridge Down (shale disc ×125)	4			4					11	11
Cossington	2		10	1		3	3		13	13
Caistor St Edmund	4		2	3					9	9
Ashville, Abingdon	2		1		1				4	4
Barrow Hills 16, Radley	10	3		1					14	14
Stanton Harcourt XVI, 1	1	1							3	3
Chilcompton 2016	3	1		1	1				5	5
Rowbarrow (Shipham G2)	'Beads of various colours'			1 or more					indet	indet
Tynings East, Cheddar G5	7		>1						9	9
Kingston Deverill G9	>1	>1	>1						6+	6+
Wilsford G72	>1	>1	>1						6+	6+

Four materials

Site (and notes)										Total
Wilsford G7	2	2	4			2			10	156
Shrewton G5L	3	3			1				8	160
Winterslow G21	4	3	1	1				1	9	13
Langton 2, burial 2	1	1		2		2		5	10	39
Thomas Hardye School (shale disc × c.130)		1			42			4	47	
Hengistbury Head	2		4		1				7	
Amesbury G44 (East)	1	>1	>1	1					7+	
Solstice Park, Amesbury (shale disc ×58)	7	22	7	>1					43	
Collingbourne Kingston G8	4	1	10	1		4			7	
Kingston Deverill G5	>1	40+	>1	>1	2	1	2		46+	

Five materials

Site (and notes)										Total
Preshute G1a (Manton) (shale disc ×150)	3	1	4			2	2		11	43
Wilsford G8	6	8	8				1		14	206
Aldbourne G6	6	2	2	3	1	2			14	97

Six materials

Site (and notes)										Total
Amesbury G61a	-	3	3	2	1	1	1	2	10	
Totals	**38**	**253**	**332**	**142**	**47**	**33**	**83**	**15**	**49**	**994**

Table 8.6.3. Composite necklaces: the occurrence of raw materials according to the number of materials present in the necklace or ornament set. The numbers in the materials columns indicate the total of components of each material in all the necklaces in question.

Number of materials	Number of necklaces	Gold	Jet/ jet-like	Amber	Faience	Bone	Stone	Fossil	Shell	Fired clay
Five	4	9	7	17	5	1	4	4	2	-
Four	9	4	10	11	4	3	1	4	6	-
Three	22	5	21	76	18	6	5	46	10	-
Two	13	3	97	105	33	32	12	29	1	47

Table 8.6.4. Composite necklaces: the degree of wear in relation to the number of materials represented (data taken from Tables 10.12 and 10.13).

Number of materials	Fresh or slightly worn	Worn	Very worn	Worn or very worn	Indeterminate
Four to five	29	8	3	11	34
Three	45	17	4	21	57
Two	44	47	19	66	27
Totals	**118**	**72**	**26**	**98**	**118**

Table 8.6.5. Composite necklaces: variations in 'strung length' in relation to the number of materials represented.

Number of materials	Up to 50mm	51 to 100mm	101 to 200mm	Over 200mm
Four to five	3	1	2	1
Three	3	-	2	3
Two	3	6	4	-
One	4	3	3	-
Totals	**13**	**10**	**11**	**4**

materials occurs at a constant level within all the necklaces. One feature is that items of jet or jet-like materials, amber and faience occur relatively more often in the necklaces which contain only two different materials. To a lesser extent the same can be said for elements made from bone and stone, while, in contrast, fossil beads occur relatively more often in necklaces of three materials. One overall pattern that can be deduced is that in all the necklaces, elements made from amber and jet or jet-like materials are the most common. Otherwise it seems that the only real distinction is that, as noted above, gold items are less common in necklaces with fewer than three materials.

The categorisation of the necklace beads according to the degree of overall wear observed is summarised in Chapter 10 (Table 10.12 and Table 10.13) and here in Table 8.6.4. In many cases the incidence of wear could not be determined, due to breakage, the presence of conservation lacquer or oxidisation of the surfaces. However, in 216 cases this was possible, and the results show that very many (55%) of the beads were only slightly worn. However in a significant number of cases, the individual beads were worn (33%) or very worn (12%). Many of the latter will have been heirloom items (see above and also Chapter 10). There was often variation in the patterns of wear amongst the beads of a single necklace. Usually there were only two categories represented, and usually these were slightly worn, and worn. However, in five cases all three wear categories were present in a single necklace (Tables

10.12 and 10.13). The relative degrees of wear in relation to the number of raw materials represented in each necklace is shown in Table 8.6.4. It can be concluded from these figures that in necklaces containing three to five different raw materials, fresh or slightly worn items outnumber those which are worn or very worn. But in the case of necklaces with only two raw materials represented the situation is reversed: more items are worn or very worn, compared to fewer fresh or slightly worn elements. This may indicate that the necklaces with fewer raw materials were 'further down the line', either socially or chronologically. The people who put these necklaces together had access to fewer of the exotic gold items, and also they used a higher proportion of worn and very worn, potentially old and recycled heirloom items. In chronological terms any further argument is impeded by the small number of radiocarbon dates that have been obtained so far. The necklaces which include items of gold, and which, it might be argued, were put together during the currency of the Wessex 1 series of graves in the first quarter of the second millennium, do tend to contain more items which are fresh or only slightly worn (see Table 10.13: Wilsford G7, Preshute G1a and Wilsford G8). Unfortunately none of the necklaces well-dated by radiocarbon to the second quarter of the second millennium were studied in detail during the project, so comparable wear data for these is not available.

Another aspect of variation amongst the composite necklaces is overall size. This can be assessed by consideration of the total number of surviving items in each necklace, and these data are listed in Table 8.6.2. Excluding the jet or jet-like disc bead elements the number of items in the necklaces studied in detail varies from 3 to 73 items, but most contain ten or fewer items, followed by those with between 11 and 20 items. Very few of the necklaces have more beads than this. As mentioned above, it is likely that most of the necklaces involved a single strand of beads only. It is felt therefore that a better measure of the size of each necklace might be the computation of the 'strung length'. This comprises the total of the lengths of the beads and pendants recorded, where length is the distance between the two perforations. This statistic is recorded, for the necklaces studied in detail, in Table 8.6.2. Further analysis of these measurements is summarised in Table 8.6.5, where the occurrence of ranges of 'strung length' is shown in relation to the numbers of raw materials represented in the necklaces. The figures seem to show some interesting patterns. Firstly, it can be observed that the necklaces containing the larger ranges of raw materials (three to six materials) include several of those with strung lengths of over 100mm, and all of those which are over 200mm. The necklaces containing

only one or two materials have shorter strung lengths, with the highest incidence for two materials falling in the 51 to 100mm range, and the highest figure for those of one material in the up to 50mm category. This may imply that the more valuable necklaces in terms of exotic materials represented were also more valuable in terms of size, i.e. they were longer. It may also mean that when the more simple necklaces, with one or two materials, and a higher incidence of worn and very worn heirlooms items (see above) were being put together, fewer items were in fact available. This may have been a chronological trend (which cannot be tested due to the small number of absolute dates available at present), or may have been a social phenomenon. It is however an intriguing pattern. A further point that needs to be emphasised when considering necklace size or length is that there may well have been additional perishable elements, especially of organic materials such as wood or animal skin, which have not survived in the graves. Certainly the stringing material, no examples of which have survived, must have been perishable, perhaps of sinew or a textile thread. All we can say, from measuring the diameters of all the thread-holes, is that the thread must have been very fine.

9. CHRONOLOGY

INTRODUCTION

The grave goods project was not intended to provide a comprehensive description and discussion of all artefact types current within the Chalcolithic and Early Bronze Age periods in England; nor was it proposed to present an exhaustive study of all the available dating evidence for the various artefact categories. However, the topic of chronology does relate particularly to one of the main aims of the project. This theme encompasses the need to compare the results obtained from grave assemblages dating from the Beaker period with those obtained from graves of mature Early Bronze Age date. As explained in Chapter 1, the purpose of such a comparison is to determine whether key aspects of the material, such as artefact function or the occurrence of heirloom items, varied through time, and to what extent characteristics of the Early Bronze Age grave assemblages had their origin within the Beaker tradition.

The chronological aspects need to be considered by employing absolute dating evidence in the form of radiocarbon determinations alongside the evidence of associations within graves with artefact types which have well-researched typological and chronological trajectories. Such artefact types mainly comprise copper and bronze daggers/knives and the various classes of pottery vessels: notably Beakers, Food Vessels and Collared Urns. For the Early Bronze Age in England the number of radiocarbon dates available is not large. However, the corpus of determinations relating to Beaker graves has

been substantially increased in recent years as a result of new research included within the Beaker People Project. We are very grateful to Professor Parker Pearson and his team for allowing the use of selected high precision (AMS) radiocarbon dates from that project within the analysis presented below. It should be noted that the period of currency of the earlier styles of Beaker is sometimes termed the Chalcolithic (see Allen *et al.* 2012). A useful summary of dating for the Chalcolithic and Early Bronze Age periods, in terms of Periods 1 to 4, has been published recently by Needham (2010, table 1), and slightly modified extracts from his table are reproduced here as Table 9.1.

Following a brief summary and tabulation of the current state of chronological knowledge relating to the dagger/ knife series and the major classes of pottery, a summary of the dating evidence for each of the artefact categories studied within the grave goods project is presented. This is divided into consideration of those object categories which occur only within Beaker assemblages, followed by those which occur only within grave groups of mature Early Bronze Age date. Finally, the discussion addresses those artefact categories which occur within both periods. Within each chronological group the object categories are considered in the same order as their presentation within Chapters 3 to 8 above. The chronological arguments are not always simple. Obviously there will be overlaps of object types between any two major chronological periods within prehistory, and the divide between the Beaker and

Table 9.1. Summary chronology for the southern British Chalcolithic and Early Bronze Age (based on Needham 2010, table 1).

Period	Date range (cal BC)	Main burial traditions	Simple description
1 Chalcolithic	2450–2200/2150	Beaker styles up to 'fission horizon'	Early Beaker
2 EBA	2200/2150–1950	Later Beaker styles, Food Vessels, Series 2 flat daggers	Climax Beaker
3 EBA	1950–1750/1700	Food Vessels, Urns, 'Wessex 1', Series 3 and 4 daggers (Bush Barrow types)	Early Urn
4 EBA	1750/1700–1550/1500	Urns, 'Wessex 2', Series 5 daggers (Camerton-Snowshill)	Middle Urn

Early Bronze Age periods is my no means clear-cut. Some Beakers belonging to the later styles were current within the Early Bronze Age, and, even more pertinent, the known currency of several object categories spans the potential chronological dividing line between the two periods. This applies particularly to items of jet or jet-like materials, such as buttons and certain forms of necklace. It will be necessary to place such categories on one side of the divide or the other in order that the broad-brush comparisons required by the project can be attempted. The radiocarbon dates cited have all been calibrated using OxCal v. 4.1 (http://c14.arch.ox.ac.uk/; Bronk Ramsey 2009) and are quoted at the two sigma (95.4%) level of probability.

CHRONOLOGICAL DIVISIONS

Daggers/knives

A revised chronology for the British dagger series has been formulated by Needham and is presented above in Chapter 3.1 and Appendix 1 (CD). This chronology is based on radiocarbon dating and an assessment of the co-occurrences within grave groups with other artefacts for which date ranges are available. The results are summarised here. It can be noted that the number of radiocarbon determinations available for Series 3, 4 and 5 dagger graves are rather few, but dating evidence from grave and hoard associations is more abundant.

Series 1: Tanged daggers/knives (copper)
Early group: Early Chalcolithic, *c.* 2450/2400–2300 cal BC.
Late group: Later Chalcolithic, *c.* 2300–2200/2150 cal BC.
Transitional types: Chalcolithic/Early Bronze Age *c.* 2200–2100 cal BC.

Series 2: Butt-rivetted flat daggers (bronze)
Overall range: 2200/2150–1950/1900 cal BC.
Sub series 2F1 and 2C: 2200–2050 cal BC.
Sub series 2D, 2E and 2F2: 2150–1950 cal BC.
Sub series 2A, 2B and 2F3: 2100–1900 cal BC.

Series 3: Thin lenticular-section daggers (includes Gerloff's 'Armorico-British A' daggers of Wessex Series 1 graves)

Range *c.* 1950–1750/1700 cal BC (with a few items dated earlier than *c.* 1950).

Series 4: Ribbed flat-bladed daggers (includes some of Gerloff's 'Armorico-British B' daggers of Wessex Series 1 graves)

Range *c.* 1950–1750/1700 cal BC (with a few items dated earlier than *c.*1950).

Series 5: Thick-bladed daggers (including many of Gerloff's 'Camerton-Snowshill' daggers of Wessex Series 2 graves)

Range *c.* 1750/1700–1500 cal BC.

Beakers

Absolute dating evidence for the various styles of Beakers as initially defined by Needham (2005) has recently been assembled by Healy (2012). Using Bayesian statistics she has been able to define a new series of date ranges (*ibid*, table 10.2). Two different models were employed, one of which (Beaker model 2) omitted some earlier and less accurate determinations (*ibid*, 156). It is the dates relating to this model 2 that are summarised here. The date ranges quoted are posterior density estimates which habitually are shown in italic.

Beaker model 2 (England) Beakers start date cal BC: *2490–2340 (95% probability).*
Beaker model 2 (England) Beakers end date cal BC: *1880–1740 (95% probability).*

Needham's 'fission horizon', which marks the beginning of the varied later and local styles of Beaker is dated by him to *c.* 2250–2150 cal BC (Needham 2005, fig. 13). The date ranges of Beaker styles, both early and late, have been modelled by Healy (2012, table 10.3 and figs. 10.5a, 10.5j and 10.5k). A summary for England, again using Healy's model 2, and with all posterior density estimates quoted at 95% probability, is as follows:

Low-carinated Beakers
Start: *2470–2330 cal BC.* End: *2210–2030 cal BC.*

Mid-carinated Beakers (includes Needham's original classes of 'weak-carinated' and 'tall mid-carinated')
Start: *2440–2220 cal BC.* End: *1990–1780 cal BC.*

Long-necked Beakers
Start: *2340–2320 cal BC (1%)* or *2310–2120 cal BC (94%).* End: *1940–1790 cal BC.*

S-profile Beakers
Start: *2450–2290 cal BC.* End: *1920–1770 cal BC.*

Early Bronze Age pottery

Far fewer radiocarbon determinations are available for the classes of pottery that became current during the mature Early Bronze Age, and no recent summary covering those for the whole of England has been published. However an overview of the dates from northern England and Wales was included by Brindley in her discussion of a detailed treatment of the dates for Food Vessels in Ireland (Brindley 2007, 321). The general results, termed 'preliminary calibrated date ranges' (PCDR) for northern England and Wales are as follows:

Beakers: 2450/2400–1950 cal BC.
Food Vessels: not clear (for Ireland: *c.* 2020–1740 cal BC: *ibid*, 328).
Collared Urns: 1900–1700 cal BC.
Cordoned Urns: 1750–1500 cal BC.

The evidence for the chronological spans of the different Series of daggers and pottery styles presented above is summarised in diagrammatic form in Table 9.2. The next step is to decide on an approximate dividing line between the Beaker and Early Bronze Age periods that could be employed within the project analyses. In effect this involves combining the four Periods listed in Table 9.1 into two major periods. Taking into account the date ranges suggested by Needham, and shown in column 2 of Table 9.1, and the more detailed spans for daggers and pottery based largely on new considerations of the available radiocarbon determinations, it has been decided to take the dividing line as the beginning of the second millennium cal BC i.e. *c.* 2000 cal BC. This suggested dividing line is indicated on Table 9.2. On this basis the chronological aspects of each of the individual object categories studied within the project can now be discussed in brief, starting with those which occurred only in the Beaker period i.e. before or around 2000 cal BC. Radiocarbon determinations that relate to non-ceramic and non-dagger grave goods have mainly been obtained as a part of the Beaker People Project; these are listed in Table 9.3 and cross-referenced below as 'BPP' numbers. Other radiocarbon dates (cited in the lists below as 'Other dates') tend to have been obtained much earlier on, and are far less accurate. Such dates will be quoted where relevant, but the listings are not exhaustive. Certain dates which were obtained a long time ago, often on unidentified charcoal, are indicated as such. Section numbers relating to Chapters 3 to 8 above are added in brackets after each object category heading. For most categories an overall date range, based on the radiocarbon dates cited, is presented. The dates within these overall ranges have been rounded to the nearest ten years.

CHALCOLITHIC GRAVE GOODS

(Note: in this and the following sections overall date ranges simply show the range of the dates cited; they are not posterior density estimates).

Daggers/knives (Chapter 3.1)

Daggers of Series 1 all fall before 2000 cal BC, as do most of those belonging to Series 2 (see Table 9.2). For the purpose of analysis, all Series 2 daggers and their associated grave goods have been placed within the Beaker period.

Stone bracers

Bracers are found in Beaker graves containing vessels which belong to early and later styles. Just a few fragmentary and relict items, often re-worked as pendants, derive from Early Bronze Age burials associated with urns. Full discussion of associations and radiocarbon dating may be found in Woodward and Hunter 2011, Ch. 7.

C14 dates
BPP numbers (Table 9.3): 130 (Roundway G8); 162 (Hemp Knoll); 187 (Thomas Hardye School); 241 (Raunds 1); 301 (Amesbury Archer).

Belt and pulley rings (Chapter 3.4)

Classes I to IV are all found in Beaker graves, associated with Beaker vessels of both early and later styles. Classes I and II are the earliest. Belt and pulley rings are associated with daggers of Series 1 and 2, stone bracers of early (amphibolite, red and black) and later (Group VI) types. The later Classes III and IV are also associated with flint daggers, barbed-and-tanged arrowheads, V-perforated buttons of jet or jet-like materials, an awl and sponge finger stones. One worn Class I ring from an Early Bronze Age grave (Upton Lovell G2a: shaman) may have been an heirloom.

C14 dates
BPP numbers (Table 9.3): 61 (Acklam Wold 124, burial 4); 241 (Raunds 1); 301 (Amesbury Archer).

Overall date range: 2470–1940 cal BC.

Sponge finger stones (Chapter 4.1)

These are associated with later style necked Beakers, pulley rings of jet or jet-like materials and V-perforated buttons, one Series 2 dagger, a flint dagger, one spatula and two heirloom bracers.

C14 dates
BPP number (Table 9.3): 241 (Raunds 1).
Other date: Gravelly Guy UB-3122 3709±35 BP (2203–1981 cal BC) (Lambrick and Allen 2004).

Overall date range: 2200–1940 cal BC.

Buttons of jet or jet-like materials (Chapter 5.3)

Associations include Series 2 daggers, disc bead necklaces, tubular sheet bronze beads, a late style Beaker, a flint dagger, a re-worked stone bracer (Group VI), sponge finger stones, an amber belt ring, a bronze ring and a bronze axe of Migdale type.

C14 dates
BPP numbers (Table 9.3): 241 (Raunds 1); 317 (Garton Slack VI, 1, burial 1).
Other dates: Rameldry (Scotland) GU-9574 3725±40 BP (2279–1982 cal BC) (Baker *et al.* 2003); Migdale (Scotland) OxA-4659 3655±75 BP (2281–1779 cal BC) (Baker *et al.* 2003); Ingleby Barwick UB-4174 3609±24 BP (2030–1899 cal BC) (Vyner pers. comm.).

Overall date range: 2300–1780 cal BC.

EARLY BRONZE AGE GRAVE GOODS

Daggers/knives (Chapter 3.1)

Daggers of Series 3, 4 and 5 all fall after 2000 cal BC (see Table 9.2).

Belt hooks (Chapter 3.3)

Belt hooks are associated with Collared Urns, Food Vessels,

Table 9.2. Approximate chronological spans for daggers and pottery types. Beaker styles: LC low-carinated, MC mid-carinated, LN long-necked, SP S-profiled. Early Bronze Age ceramics: FV Food Vessel, CU Collared Urn, CorU Cordoned Urn. The shaded zone at 2000 cal BC defines the division between the 'Beaker period' and 'Early Bronze Age' period employed in the project.

Date cal BC	Dagger Series					Beaker styles				EBA ceramics		
	S1	S2	S3	S4	S5	LC	MC	LN	SP	FV	CU	CorU
2500												
2450												
2400	█					▒						
2350	█					▒	▒		▒			
2300	█					▒	▒		▒			
2250	█					▒	▒	▒	▒			
2200	█					▒	▒	▒	▒			
2150	█	█				▒	▒	▒	▒			
2100	█	█					▒	▒	▒			
2050		█					▒	▒	▒			
2000	(division)											
1950		█	█	█				▒	▒	▒		
1900			█	█					▒	▒	▒	
1850			█						▒	▒	▒	
1800			█							▒	▒	
1750			█							▒	▒	▒
1700			█		█						▒	▒
1650					█							▒
1600					█							▒
1550					█							▒
1500					█							▒

an accessory vessel, stone battle-axes, daggers of Series 3 and 4, a jet bead, bone pins or toggles and a bone pendant.

C14 dates

Other dates: Norton Bavant Borrow Pit BM-2909 3410±35 BP (1872–1619 cal BC) (Sheridan 2007, 114); Stanbury, weighted mean OxA-18361 and SUERC-16360 3554±23 BP (1972–1777 cal BC) (Richardson and Vyner 2011, 50); Bargrennan (Scotland) GU-13906 3475±35 BP (1890–1692 cal BC) (Sheridan 2007, 114); Fan Foel (Wales) average of 2 GrA 3525±28 BP (1934–1756 cal BC) (Sheridan 2007, 114).

Overall date range: 1930–1620 cal BC.

Grooved stones (Chapter 4.2)

These objects are associated with a Series 5 dagger, small knives of Series 7, bronze axes and the pronged object from Wilsford G58, plus undateable equipment made from bone and antler. There are no ceramic associations in England, but the pair from Breach Farm, Glamorgan (Wales) is associated with an accessory vessel.

Perforated stones (Chapter 4.3)

Associations include daggers of Series 4 and 5, battle-axes, accessory cups, dress pins, bone tweezers, a bone belt hook and a wind instrument. Flat perforated stones occur throughout the Early Bronze Age, while those with square sections occur only with the later daggers of Series 5, and in one case with a Collared Urn.

C14 dates
Other dates: Edmonsham BM-708 3069±45 BP (1435–1212 cal BC) (Burleigh *et al.* 1976, 29–30: an old date on charred human bone); Hove BM-682 3189±36 BP (1526–1405 cal BC) (Burleigh *et al.* 1976, 27) (an old date on unidentified charcoal from coffin); Norton Bavant Borrow Pit BM-2909 3410±35 BP (1872–1619 cal BC) (Sheridan 2007, 114).

Overall date range: 1870–1210 cal BC.

Worked stones without perforations (Chapter 4.4)
These are associated with a Series 5 dagger, awls, beads, an accessory cup and bone equipment.

Bone tweezers (Chapter 4.8)
Associations include daggers, usually of Series 5, perforated stones, bone dress pins and beads of various materials.

C14 dates
Other dates: Edmonsham BM-708 3069±45 BP (1435–1212 cal BC) (Burleigh *et al.* 1976, 29–30: an old date on charred human bone); Barrow Hills, Radley, Barrow 1 OxA-1886 3520±70 (2035–1668 cal BC) (Barclay and Halpin 1999, 307).

Overall date range: 2040–1210 cal BC.

Bone tubes (wind instruments) (Chapter 4.9)
These items are found with a Collared Urn, a Cordoned Urn, bone points and in three rich Early Bronze Age graves. These include Wilsford G23 with daggers/knives of Series 4 and 7, a bronze dress pin and a perforated stone.

C14 dates
Other date: Eaglestone Flat, Curbar OxA-3245 3430±90 BP (1961–1513 cal BC) (Barnatt 1994, 304).

Bone plates (Chapter 4.10)
Four derive from rich Early Bronze Age grave groups in Wessex. Associations include a Series 7 knife, bronze axes, a battle-axe, perforated and grooved stones, and bone points.

Antler handles (Chapter 4.12.1)
These occur in rich Early Bronze Age graves, associated with daggers/knives of Series 3, 5 and 7, a bronze axe, a battle-axe, grooved stones, spatulae, bone plates and other Early Bronze Age object types.

Studs (Chapter 5.6)
Associations are mainly with Collared Urns, plus one rich Wessex grave: the Manton Barrow (Preshute G1a). In East Anglia and the Midlands studs continue to be deposited in graves of Middle Bronze Age, or even Late Bronze Age date.

C14 dates
Other dates: Brenig 44 (Wales) GRA-22970 3550±50

BP (2024–1750 cal BC) (Brindley 2007, 365); Norton Subcourse, Norfolk Beta-299801 3060±40 BP (1426–1213 cal BC) (Sheridan forthcoming); Radwell HAR-1420 3000±90 BP (1441–980 cal BC) (Hall and Woodward 1977) (an old date on unidentified charcoal).

Overall date range: 2020–980 cal BC.

Single spacer plates (Chapter 5.8)
These are associated with a composite necklace, bone points and one small jet button. They derive from spacer plate necklaces made from jet or jet-like materials (see below).

Pendants and individual necklace fasteners (Chapter 5.9)
The jet items from northern England are probably the earliest, dating from *c.* 2000 cal BC onwards. Many of the more complex pendants occur in rich graves of the Wessex Series, especially those belonging to the later phase of the Early Bronze Age. Associations include a Collared Urn, accessory cups and bronze awls.

Gold objects and the regalia from Bush Barrow (Chapters 6.1 and 6.2)
With the exception of the decorated gold disc from Beaker grave Mere G6a, the gold objects derive from rich graves of the Early Bronze Age. Associations include daggers of Series 3 and 4, a bronze axe of Type Willerby, a Collared Urn, accessory cup, amber necklaces and bronze awls.

Spacer plate necklaces of jet or jet-like materials (Chapter 7.2)
Usually found alone in graves in England, evidence from Scotland, together with the few available radiocarbon dates, suggests that these necklaces were current in a few centuries either side of 2000 cal BC. Although some may have been made before 2000 cal BC, for the purpose of analysis in this project all are treated as dating from the Early Bronze Age period.

C14 dates
BPP number (Table 9.3): 202 (Middleton Moor).
Other dates: Easter Essendy cremation 1 (Scotland) GrA-32131 3710±35 BP (2204–1981 cal BC) (Sheridan pers. comm.); Inchmarnock cist 3 (Scotland) GrA-34345 3635±35 BP (2133–1902 cal BC) (Sheridan pers. comm.); Almondbank cist VII (Scotland) SRR-591 3517±BP (2008–1695 cal BC) (Sheridan pers. comm.); Scalpsie (Scotland) SUERC-37704 (GU23930) 3730±30 BP (2267–2032 cal BC) (Sheridan pers. comm.); Cnip, Lewis (Scotland) SUERC, modelled dates for phase of deposition: *start 1795–1695 cal BC (95.4%); end 1745–1650 cal BC (95.4%)* (Sheridan pers. comm.); Risby, Barrow Bottom (elements from an older necklace) GrA-11358 3495±30 BP (1900–1740 cal BC) (Longworth 1984, no. 1516, pl. 20c).

Overall date range: 2270–1650 cal BC.

Spacer plate and large necklaces of amber (Chapter 7.3) Dateable associations include daggers/knives of Series 4 and 7, a Collared Urn and an accessory vessel. The amber necklaces are probably rather later than the spacer plate necklaces of jet or jet-like materials, from which they appear to be derived.

C14 dates
Other dates: Shaw Cairn (a relatively early date for a necklace with spacers and fusiforms, copying a jet spacer plate necklace) SUERC-26852 3665±35 BP (2187–1941 cal BC); Knowes of Trotty, Orkney (Scotland) (old fragment from spacer plate necklace) GrA-34776 3575±35 BP (2029–1779 cal BC) (Sheridan and Bradley 2007, 220).

Overall date range: 2190–1780 cal BC.

Composite necklaces and ornament sets (Chapter 8) Composite necklaces are usually found alone with burials, but there are some associated grave goods. These include Collared Urns, accessory vessels, a Wessex Biconical Urn (of the latest Early Bronze Age), daggers/knives of Series 5 and 7, gold objects, a tusk ornament, studs and, especially, bronze awls. All available radiocarbon dates have been listed by Sheridan (in Gardiner *et al.* 2007, table 9); only those for England are cited below. Absolute dating indicates a long currency.

C14 dates
Snail Down, Collingbourne Kingston G8 GU-5302 3440±90 BP (2020–1520 cal BC); Barrow Hills, Radley, barrow 16, pit E GrA-26608 3455±40 BP (1889–1669 cal BC); Amesbury G61a GrA-24853 3365±40 BP (1746–1531 cal BC); Little Chesterford GrA-28632 3310±35 BP (1683–1509 cal BC); Amesbury (Solstice Park) GrA-22371 3240±40 BP (1612–1433 cal BC).

Overall date range: 1890–1430 cal BC.

GRAVE GOODS FOUND IN BOTH THE BEAKER AND EARLY BRONZE AGE PERIODS

Pommels (Chapter 3.2)
According to associations with Beakers and daggers of Series 1 and 2, pommels of Classes 1 and 2 belong within the Beaker period. One example of a Class 4 pommel may date from the Beaker period, but most of them, along with those of Classes 3 and 5, are Early Bronze Age in date. Class 3 are often associated with Collared Urns and one with a Series 5 dagger, while those of Class 5 occur with Early Bronze Age daggers.

C14 dates
BPP number (Table 9.3): 147 (Shrewton G5k).

Bone and antler spatulae (Chapter 4.5)
The majority derive from Beaker-age graves, in association with Beakers of both early and later styles and with barbed-and-tanged arrowheads. They often occur in particularly well-furnished Beaker graves such as Amesbury Archer, Gravelly Guy, Mere G6a and Raunds 1. Just a few graves are cremations which are associated with Early Bronze Age object types such as grooved stones and bone points.

C14 dates
BPP numbers (Table 9.3): 198 (Green Low); 241 (Raunds 1); 301 (Amesbury Archer).
Other dates: Gravelly Guy UB-3122 3709±35 BP (2203–1981 cal BC) (Lambrick and Allen 2004); Chilbolton OxA-1072 3740±80 BP (2457–1940 cal BC) (Needham 2005, 185); Amesbury G51, burial A BM-287 3738±90 BP (2459–1926 cal BC) (Ashbee 1976, 24); Barrow Hills, Radley ring ditch 201, 203 BM-2700 3360±50 BP (1768–1517 cal BC) (Barclay and Halpin 1999, 308); Barrow Hills, Radley 4660 BM-2704 3650±50 BP (2193–1893 cal BC) (Barclay and Halpin 1999, 305).

Overall date range: 2470–1520 cal BC.

Metal awls (Chapter 4.6)
Group 1 awls, double-pointed with central swelling, are often made from copper and occur in Beaker graves, usually associated with later style Beakers. However a few are found with Collared Urns or Food Vessels. The single-pointed awls of Groups 2 and 3 are Early Bronze Age in date. Those of Groups 2A/B and 2C tend to occur with Collared Urns; those of Group 2D with Food Vessels. They also occur in rich Early Bronze Age contexts, such as the Manton Barrow (Preshute G1a) where a set of awls are associated with necklaces and a stud. For purposes of analysis Group 1 awls associated with Beaker vessels are treated as Beaker-age and the rest as belonging to the Early Bronze Age.

C14 dates
BPP numbers (Table 9.3): 121 (Garton Slack 75, burial 1); 210 (Bee Low).
Other dates: Cowleaze B, cremation 2, Winterbourne Steepleton HAR-5620 3120±120 (1668–1048 cal BC) (Woodward 1991: with a shale stud); Barrow Hills, Radley Barrow 12, 607 BM-2699 3720±60 BP (2294–1946 cal BC) (Barclay and Halpin 1999, 307: Group 1 awl with a Beaker); Barrow Hills, Radley Barrow ring ditch 201, 203 BM-2700 3360±50 BP (1768–1517) (*ibid*, 308: with a late Beaker); Barrow Hills, Radley ring ditch 801, 802 OxA-1888 3470±70 BP (1973–1616 cal BC) (*ibid*, 308: Early Bronze Age grave).

Overall date range: Beaker 2290–1520 cal BC; Early Bronze Age 1970–1050 cal BC (for further Early Bronze Age radiocarbon dates see Needham 1999, 190–1, table 7.8).

Bone points (Chapter 4.7)
Only four of the grave groups studied containing bone points are of Beaker date, and these objects are larger and

more varied in shape than the main series. Most derive from Early Bronze Age graves, often in association with Collared Urns. They also occur with Food Vessels, Series 5 daggers, beads of jet or jet-like materials or amber, and bronze awls. Other associations are very diverse, including battle-axes, bronze axes, bone belt hooks, tweezers and dress pins, as well as perforated and grooved stones.

C14 dates
BPP numbers (Table 9.3): 61 (Acklam Wold 124, burial 4); 198 (Green Low); 205 (Galley Low); 215 (Mouse Low). Other date: Norton Bavant Borrow Pit BM-2909 3410±35 BP (1872–1619 cal BC).

Overall date range: Beaker 2330–1880 cal BC; Early Bronze Age 1870–1620 cal BC.

Bone toggles (Chapter 4.11)
Toggles mostly derive from rich Beaker graves and are often associated with stone bracers. However two occur with Food Vessels, one with an accessory cup and battle-axe, and one is from a probably Early Bronze Age cremation, associated with an heirloom pendant made from a bracer fragment. In analysis the contexts of different dates are treated separately.

C14 dates
BPP numbers (Table 9.3): 162 (Hemp Knoll); 187 (Thomas Hardye School); 313 (Sewell).

Overall date range (Beaker): 2460–2150 cal BC.

Copper alloy axes (Chapter 4.13.1)
The axe-heads are mainly of Type Willerby, dating from the Early Bronze Age period. However two of those studied are associated with Series 2 daggers and thus fall within the Beaker period.

C14 dates
BPP number (Table 9.3): 213 (with Series 2 dagger) (Shuttlestone, Parwich Moor).

Tusks and teeth (Chapter 5.1)
Tusks and teeth occur in graves of Neolithic, Beaker and Early Bronze Age date. In Early Bronze Age graves they are found with Food Vessels, beads and other Early Bronze Age ornament types. In analysis, items of Beaker and Early Bronze Age date are treated separately.

C14 dates
BPP number (Table 9.3): (Beaker-age graves) 295 (Amesbury Archer Companion); 301 (Amesbury Archer); 241 (Raunds 1).

Overall date range (Beaker only): 2470–1940 cal BC.

V-perforated buttons of jet or jet-like materials, amber and bone (Chapter 5.2)
Most buttons derive from Beaker-age graves, associated with Beaker vessels of mainly later styles, Series 1 and 2 daggers, flint daggers and pulley rings of jet or jet-like materials. A few are found in Early Bronze Age graves, and these tend to be smaller in size. Two such buttons are associated with Food Vessels and four from the Wessex region are associated with other goods of mature Early Bronze Age style. In project analysis the buttons of the two periods are treated separately, according to their contexts.

C14 dates
BPP numbers (Table 9.3): (Beaker-age graves) 61 (Acklam Wold 124, burial 4); 101 (Painsthorpe Wold); 108 (Garton Slack 152, burial 5); 113 (Garton Slack 152, burial 4).

Overall date range (Beaker only): 2330–1920 cal BC.

Earrings and tress rings (Chapter 5.4)
Basket-shaped ornaments of gold occur with early Beakers, while the similar items studied, but made of copper alloy, are associated with late style Beakers and a V-perforated button.

C14 dates
BPP numbers (Table 9.3): 295 (Amesbury Archer Companion); 301 (Amesbury Archer).
Other date: Barrow Hills, Radley 4A OxA-4356 3880±90 BP (2580–2043 cal BC) (Barclay and Halpin 1999, 307).

Overall date range: 2650–2040 cal BC.

Earrings in the form of pennanular flat bands are later and, with Food Vessel associations, belong to the Early Bronze Age period.

Dress pins of metal and bone (Chapter 5.5)
Four pins studied were found with Beakers, spanning the early and later stages of the Beaker period. Most dress pins, however, are of Early Bronze Age date. Associations include daggers, mainly of Series 5, within the later Early Bronze Age and many were found within rich grave groups within the Wessex region. A few items date from an earlier stage within the Early Bronze Age, including one associated with a Series 4 dagger.

C14 dates (Beaker period)
BPP number (Table 9.3): 130 (Roundway G8); 313 (Sewell).
Other date: Barrow Hills, Radley 4660 BM-2704 3650±50 BP (2193–1893 cal BC) (Barclay and Halpin 1999, 305).

C14 dates (Early Bronze Age period)
Other dates: Edmonsham BM-708 3069±45 BP (1435–1212 cal BC) (Burleigh *et al.* 1976, 29–30) (an old date on charred human bone); Barrow Hills, Radley, Barrow 1 OxA-1886 3520±70 (2035–1668 cal BC) (Barclay and Halpin 1999, 307).

Overall date ranges: Beaker 2460–1890 cal BC; Early Bronze Age 2040–1210 cal BC.

Table 9.3. Radiocarbon dates from the Beaker People Project (BPP) and other recent projects: relating to selected object types (courtesy of Mike Parker Pearson, Alison Sheridan, Mandy Jay and the Beaker People Project). M = Mortimer 1905; G = Gerloff 1975; A&S = Annable and Simpson 1964; J93 numbers denote accession numbers within the Bateman Collection at Sheffield Museum.

BPP SK No.	Site/burial	Object	Leverhulme ID No.	Reference	C14 dates: Lab no.	Date BP	Date cal BC, 1 sigma and 2 sigma (bold), using OxCal v.4.1
61	Acklam Wold 124, burial 4	Jet button	ID 206	M fig. 212	OxA-V-2197-50	3774 ±36	2279–2140 **2333–2041**
		Amber button/fastener	ID 207	M fig. 213			
		Jet pulley ring	ID 208	M fig. 216			
		Bone pin	ID 618	M fig. 215			
81	Aldro 116, burial 2	Series 2 bronze dagger	ID 1133	M fig. 98 G50	OxA-V-2199-43	3679 ±32	2134–2024 **2191–1962**
96	Garrowby Wold 32, burial 4	Series 2B bronze dagger	ID 1141	M fig. 391 G43	OxA-V-2199-33	3729±29	2197–2045 **2205–2033**
101	Painsthorpe Wold 200	Bone pommel	ID 711	M fig. 391			
		Jet button	ID 215	M fig. 288	OxA-V-2199-34	3719±27	2194–2041 **2200–2033**
		Jet button	ID 216	M fig. 289			
		Jet fastener	ID 217	M fig. 290			
108	Garton Slack 152, burial 5, sk 20	Jet button	ID 222	M fig. 556	OxA-V-2199-37	3764±28	2272–2138 **2287–2049**
		Flint dagger and knife	-	M figs. 555, 557			
113	Garton Slack 152, burial 4	Jet button	ID 222	M fig. 556	OxA-V-2199-41	3643±30	2112–1954 **2134–1922**
121	Garton Slack 75, burial 1	Bronze awl	ID 1149	M fig. 572	SUERC-26157 (GU-19915)	3600±30	2016–1913 **2032–1887**
130	Roundway G8	Amphibolite bracer	ID 28	A&S 61	OxA-V-2228-40	3734±30	2198–2050 **2271–2033**
		Series 1A1 tanged dagger	ID 1371	A&S 62			
		Copper dress pin	ID 1370	A&S 59			
147	Shrewton 5k, primary	Series 1B copper dagger	ID 1180	Green and Rollo-Smith 1984	OxA-V-2232-37 (supersedes BM-3017: 3900±40)	3871±30	2456–2294 **2466–2212**
162	Hemp Knoll	Bone pommel	ID 1018	"	OxA-V-2271-34 (supersedes two dates done long time ago, on charcoal)	3834±29	2341–2206 **2458–2200**
		Group VI bracer	ID 7	Robertson-Mackay 1980			
		Bone ring/toggle	ID 721				
187	Thomas Hardye School 1643	Amphibolite bracer	ID 67	Gardiner et al. 2007	NZA-23745 (not a BPP date)	3856±30	2452–2234 **2462–2208**
		Series 1 dagger	(lost)				
		Bone toggle	-				
190	Stakor Hill, Hartington Upper (J93.922)	Bronze earring	ID 1228	J93.549	SUERC-26163 (GU-19918)	3680±30	2134–2026 **2191–1965**
198	Green Low, Alsop Moor (J93.909)	Bone spatulae × 3	ID 670–72	J93.427	SUERC-26164 (GU-19919)	3660±30	2128–1977 **2136–1950**
		Bone point	ID 699	J93.426			
210	Bee Low, cist 1 (J93.944)	Bronze awl	-		SUERC-31855 (GU-22612)	3720±30	2195–2041 **2202–2031**
202	Middleton Moor, Middleton and Smerrill (J93.942)	Necklace of jet or jet-like material	ID 269	J93.434	SUERC-26165 (GU-19920)	3550±30	1945–1784 **2010–1772**

BPP SK No.	Site/burial	Object	Leverhulme ID No.	Reference	C14 dates: Lab no.	Date BP	Date cal BC, 1 sigma and 2 sigma (bold), using OxCal v.4.1
205	Galley Low, Brassington (J93.920)	Perforated bone point	ID 658	J93.419	SUERC-26166 (GU-19921)	3590±30	2008–1900 **2030–1882**
213	Parwich Moor, Shuttlestone (J93.948)	Series 2F3 bronze dagger	ID 1205	Gerloff 54 J93.448	SUERC-26172 (GU-19924)	3680±30	2134–2026 **2191–1965**
215	Mouse Low, Deepdale (J93.914)	Jet disc bead Bone points × 2	ID 259 ID 686 and ID 687	J93.562 J93.417	SUERC-26174 (GU-19926)	3610±30	2021–1930 **2111–1888**
241	Raunds barrow 1, Irthlingborough, skeleton 6410	Group VI bracer Set of jet buttons Sponge finger stone Chalk finger stone Amber belt ring	ID 116 ID 565–69 ID 117 ID 125 ID 1565	Harding and Healy 2007, fig. 4.6 " "	UB-3148 (not a BPP date)	3681±47	2138–1981 **2201–1940**
295	Amesbury Archer Companion (Boscombe Down, Skeleton 1236, Burial 1238)	Boar's tusk Gold basket ornaments	ID 1069 -	Fitzpatrick 2011, figs. 25–26	OxA-13562 (not a BPP date)	3829±38	2343–2203 **2459–2147**
301	Amesbury Archer (Boscombe Down, Skeleton 50875)	Stone bracers × 2 Shale belt ring Antler spatulae × 3 Boar's tusks × 4 Bone pin Series 1 daggers × 3 Gold basket ornaments	ID 56–57 ID 471 ID 1062–64 ID 1065–68 ID 1061 - -	Fitzpatrick 2011, fig. 28 " " " "	OxA-13541 (not a BPP date)	3895±32	2462–2346 **2471–2290**
313	Sewell, Totternhoe	Amphibolite bracer Bone toggle Copper pin	ID 12 ID 722 ID 1330	Clarke 1970, pl. 3	SUERC-26194 (GU-19940)	3830±30	2338–2205 **2458–2152**
317	Garton Slack VI, grave 1, burial 1	Set of 13 buttons of jet or jet-like materials Necklace of tiny disc beads of jet or jet-like materials and tubular sheet bronze beads	ID 232–44 ID 251	Brewster 1981 (fiche)	OxA-V-2279-34 (date not BPP; funded privately; supersedes earlier date)	3781±31	2281–2142 **2299–2057**
318	Garton Slack Area 29 grave 1 ('D')	Disc bead necklace of jet or jet-like materials with triangular fastener	ID 252	Brewster 1980	OxA-2279-33 R (date not BPP; funded privately)	3668±32	2130–1980 **2140–1950**

Disc bead necklaces (Chapter 7.1)
A few necklaces of tiny disc beads made from jet or jet-like materials plus sheet metal (copper or gold) tubular beads are known from Beaker graves. The associated Beakers are of relatively early styles, while the necklace from Garton Slack Area VI, grave 1 is associated with a set of jet buttons.

C14 dates (Beaker period)
BPP number (Table 9.3): 317 (Garton Slack Area VI, grave 1).
Other dates: Chilbolton OxA-V-2271-35 3935±32 BP (2570–2300 cal BC) (Needham 2012, Appendix 1); Achnacreebeag (Scotland) GrA-26543 3660±40 BP (2190–1926 cal BC) (Sheridan 2007c).

In the Early Bronze Age period disc bead necklaces become more common and associations include jet buttons, awls, a Food Vessel, a bone pin and jet beads. In the Wessex region there are further associations of beads and pendants made from various materials, accessory cups, a clay stud, amber pommel and a Series 7 knife. Overall dating suggests that disc bead necklaces were mainly current around the turn of the second millennium cal BC.

C14 dates (Early Bronze Age period)
BPP number (Table 9.3): 318 (Garton Slack 29, grave D).
Other dates: Ingleby Barwick UB-4174 3609±24 BP (2030–1899 cal BC) (Vyner pers. comm.); Barns Farm, cist 4 (Scotland) with a hybrid Beaker/Food Vessel SUERC-2866 3530±35 BP (1949–1751 cal BC) (Sheridan 2007); Culduthel (Scotland: a belt) with an awl OxA-V-2166-45 S-EVA 1130 3697±33 BP (2199–1978) (Sheridan *et al.* 2006, 200); Almondbank cist VII (Scotland) (re-used disc beads in disc and fusiform bead necklace) SRR-591 3517±BP (2008–1695 cal BC) (Sheridan pers. comm.); Boscombe Down (amber disc bead necklace) NZA-32497 3225±25 BP (1602–1432 cal BC) (Wessex Archaeology).

Overall date ranges: Beaker period 2460–1930 cal BC; Early Bronze Age period 2200–1430 cal BC.

CONCLUSIONS

In order that comparisons can be made between the objects found in graves belonging to the Beaker and Early Bronze Age traditions it has been necessary to consider the dating evidence for each category of objects studied. This dating evidence comprises absolute dating derived from the available radiocarbon determinations together with evidence from grave associations. The aim has been to date each grave group to one or other major tradition such that each group could be assigned either to the project Beaker site database or to the Early Bronze Age site database. In grave groups where diagnostic ceramic vessels or well dated items such as daggers or copper alloy axes are present assignation to tradition proved relatively simple. Where such items are not present, it has usually been possible to ascribe any grave group to the appropriate tradition

on the basis of radiocarbon dating, and/or by reference to recurring associations of similar objects elsewhere with dateable vessels or daggers. The dating evidence for each object category has been presented above according to whether each category dates mainly from the Beaker period, the Early Bronze Age period or belongs within both traditions. Here, for easy reference, this evidence is summarised according to the arrangement of the object category descriptions in Chapters 3 to 8 (Table 9.4).

As explained above it was decided to define the division between the Beaker and Early Bronze Age periods, as employed in this project, at roughly 2000 cal BC (see Table 9.2). Inevitably some problems of attribution arose, and systematic solutions to such problems needed to be devised. Mention of a few such problems will illustrate the strategy. Series 2 tanged riveted daggers occur mainly before 2000 cal BC, but some occur later than this (see Table 9.2). However, within the project all graves containing Series 2 daggers have been ascribed to the Beaker site database. Similarly, although radiocarbon dating evidence demonstrates that some graves containing large V-perforated buttons of jet or jet-like materials occurred after 2000 cal BC, all such graves have been ascribed to the Beaker site database. The major issues relate to object categories that usually, or often, occur in graves which do not contain pottery vessels, daggers or other easily dated items. Such categories include most of the necklaces, and also copper alloy awls. Disc bead necklaces composed of tiny beads occur in the Beaker period, and early within that time span. If they were found with a Beaker then they have been ascribed to the Beaker site database; however the majority of disc bead necklaces are listed in the Early Bronze Age database. From the available radiocarbon dates it is known that spacer plate necklaces of jet or jet-like materials were current in a few centuries both before and after 2000 cal BC. However, for the purpose of analysis in this project, all such necklace graves have been ascribed to the Early Bronze Age database. For these necklace categories a more suitable chronological divide might have been *c.* 2200 cal BC, which correlates with the end of the Chalcolithic (early Beaker) period, and Needham's 'fission horizon' associated with the rise of many localised and varied traditions of Beaker pottery. However, for most of the object categories studied in this project, the *c.* 2000 cal BC divide seems to be more relevant, and so this was chosen for all the categories. The most difficult issue has arisen in the case of awls, which are often found alone in graves. If found with a Beaker, awl graves have been ascribed to the Beaker site database, and if found with other items of obviously Early Bronze Age date, the graves have been placed in the Early Bronze Age site database. Graves with an awl only, of any type later than Group 1, have been ascribed to the Early Bronze Age site database.

Probably the most significant issue to address is the fact that late Beakers overlap in currency with Early Bronze Age ceramic types for a couple of centuries, from *c.* 2025 cal BC through to *c.* 1825 cal BC (see Table 9.2). There is also a problem relating to the dating of Food Vessels. This class

Table 9.4. Dating of object categories to project period, in Chapter order. Radiocarbon date ranges are based on the dates cited in this chapter only. Bkr = Beaker.

Chapter	Object category	Project period		C14 date range cal BC (95.4% probability)
		Beaker	Early Bronze Age	
3.1	Daggers/knives	Series 1 and 2	Series 3, 4 and 5	see Table 9.2
3.2	Pommels	Class 1 and 2	Classes 3, 4 and 5	n/a
3.3	Belt hooks	-	all	1930–1620
3.4	Belt and pulley rings	all	-	2470–1940
4.1	Sponge finger stones	all	-	2200–1940
4.2	Grooved stones	-	all	no dates
4.3	Perforated stones	-	all	1870–1210
4.5	Bone/antler spatula	majority	few	2470–1520
4.6	Copper alloy awls	Group 1	Groups 2 and 3	Bkr: 2290–1520 EBA: 1970–1050
4.7	Bone points	few	majority	Bkr: 2330–1820 EBA: 1870–1620
4.8	Bone tweezers	-	all	2040–1210
4.9	Bone tubes	-	all	1960–1510
4.10	Bone plates	-	all	no dates
4.11	Bone toggles	majority	few	Bkr: 2460–2150
4.12.1	Antler handles	-	all	no dates
4.13.1	Copper alloy axes	some	some	no dates
5.1	Tusks and teeth	some	some	Bkr: 2470–1940
5.2	V-perforated buttons	most	few	Bkr: 2330–1920
5.3	Button sets	all		2300–1780
5.4	Earrings/tress rings	basket	band	Bkr: 2650–2040
5.5	Dress pins	few	majority	Bkr: 2460–1890 EBA: 2040–1210
5.6	Studs	-	all	2020–980
5.8	Single spacer plates	-	all	no dates
5.9	Pendants and single necklace fasteners	-	all	no dates
6.1	Gold objects	-	all	no dates
6.2	Regalia from Bush Barrow	-	all	no dates
7.1	Disc bead necklaces	few	majority	Bkr: 2460–1930 EBA: 2200–1430
7.2	Spacer plate necklaces of jet or jet-like materials	-	all	2270–1650
7.3	Spacer plate and large necklaces of amber	-	all	2190–1780
8.2–5	Composite necklaces	-	all	1890–1430

of pottery is rare in southern England but is more prominent in northern England. Radiocarbon dates from England are few and it is necessary to rely on determinations from Scotland and Ireland. In these countries Food Vessels were well developed before 2000 cal BC, but in southern England they may have started a little later. At face value, such observations might lead one to doubt the validity of dividing grave goods material into two separate traditions termed Beaker and Early Bronze Age. However, within the present project this chronological issue is less of a problem.

This is because the project is attempting to compare the grave goods associated with the two main *traditions,* not two closely defined chronological periods. Thus the main purpose of the project is an exploration of any patterns of continuity or contrasts between the grave goods found in Beaker-style graves and those associated with Food Vessels, Collared Urns and other styles of urn. And this ties in with the significant change from butt-riveted flat daggers of Series 2 to the more developed dagger types of Series 3, 4 and 5.

10. OBJECT LIFE STORIES

(with David Bukach)

INTRODUCTION

Archaeologists recognise that the deposition of objects in burial contexts represents only the final stage of an object's complete life history. Rather than simply reading objects as indicators of archaeological cultures or as chronological markers, objects are seen to pass through a series of stages before becoming a part of the archaeological record. Varying sequences of technological procedures (*chaines operatoires*) are followed by variations in use (and often re-use), discard (and sometimes recycling), and final deposition (Lemonnier 1980; Leroi-Gourhan 1943; Mauss 1947). Furthermore, each of these processes is ultimately grounded in social relations and interaction and, as an object passes through each stage, it acquires meaning and symbolism through the performance of these relations. Specific criteria can be established to explore evidence for the curation of objects as heirlooms in material deposition in grave contexts through the British Chalcolithic and Early Bronze Age.

There have been relatively few instances of detailed study of fragmentation and heirlooms in studies of Early Bronze Age Britain (Jones 2002; Woodward 2002; Sheridan and Davis 2002). There has, however, been significant research within other contexts which help to inform analysis conducted here. On the whole, emphasis of past research has been on understanding the underlying social processes behind the fragmentation of pottery and ceramic objects (e.g. Chapman 2000). A particular issue that emerges is the lack of consistent terminology to describe objects with potentially long life histories; for example, commonly used terms such as 'heirloom' and 'relic' require more careful consideration. In particular, there are important distinctions between 'heirloom' and 'relic', both of which have symbolic and religious dimensions. 'Heirloom' is most frequently defined as an object which has passed down through one or more generations through family members, while 'relic' is normally a personal item of religious significance retained and preserved for the purposes of veneration (Woodward 2002). As analytic terms, both are problematic as each is intrinsically interpretive, imposing a model of either religious or social organisation on the

archaeological record. In response to this issue, Chapman and Gaydarska (2007) have developed a more general concept referred to as 'enchainment'. This views the object as embedded (or 'enchained') within a complex web of social interaction and relationships of meaning, aspects of which the object acquires throughout its life history. This goes some way towards removing specific religious overtones inherent in the terms 'heirlooms' and 'relic', although 'enchainment' inevitably replaces these with explicitly theoretical ones, particularly notions of objects and social agency. In order to maintain an objective view as possible at this stage, the term 'heirloom' is still used here, except that a narrower definition is employed as referring to an object which has been identified as having been either circulated, exchanged, used and/or curated over an extensive period of time, probably spanning more than one generation. The identification of an heirloom on this basis therefore relies on examining evidence for its use over time and evidence for its fragmentation into smaller entities that may have been retained for future exchange and curation.

This chapter is devoted to presenting specific lines of evidence which demonstrate the presence of heirlooms in Beaker and Early Bronze Age British contexts; it considers object use wear between and within sites, followed by an exploration of evidence for the fragmentation of grave objects. Both approaches compare results from Beaker and Early Bronze Age contexts as well as identifying any spatial patterns.

In order to identify potential heirlooms in the archaeological record, a number of criteria were considered. These were based on the comparison of results from a systematic categorisation of the overall condition of all objects studied in this project. Overall condition was determined on the basis of observed use wear and fragmentation, and consists of three categories, varying between slight use ('fresh' or 'slightly worn') to moderate use ('worn') and finally heavy use ('very worn'). The following criteria were established:

- *Variation in condition between similar objects*: an heirloom object is more likely to be in a very worn condition compared to a similar object that is not an heirloom.

- *Variation in condition within an assemblage:* an heirloom is likely to have a comparatively more heavily worn condition than associated objects within the same grave assemblage.

- *Objects in child or adolescent burials:* objects from a grave containing a child or adolescent which display a worn or very worn overall condition are less likely to be related to use wear from use by that individual than the same objects found in an adult or mature adult grave.

- *Fragmented objects:* an heirloom is likely to be more highly fragmented (or incomplete) than a non-heirloom object.

In the case of analysis of Beaker graves, sites were selected from a database of all identified well-furnished graves from across England. For the Early Bronze Age, sites were selected from a database of three key Early Bronze Age regions in England, namely East Yorkshire, the Peak District and Wessex, plus a few key well-furnished grave groups from elsewhere in England.

It has been observed that selected Early Bronze Age necklaces are in fact composed of individual components which were themselves part of other, perhaps older necklaces (Woodward 2002; Sheridan and Davis 2002; Sheridan 2008). Thus, the process of removing a bead from one necklace (or several necklaces) to form a different necklace is not only a process of retaining some necklace components as heirlooms, but also represents a process of fragmentation of an original whole necklace. Necklaces are defined here as at least two or more individual components (beads, pendants, rings or similar) identified as part of a set based on contextual data. They are therefore a special class of multiple object requiring a slightly different approach. For necklaces the following additional criteria can be identified:

- heirloom necklace components will be comparatively more heavily worn than other components within the same necklace.

- heirloom necklace components may display shape characteristics which, differ from other components within the same necklace.

- a necklace composed of one or more heirlooms may display less overall design symmetry.

The first point requires an analysis of variation between necklace components along the same lines as the first object variation criterion proposed above, except that the scale has been reduced from the grave assemblage as a whole to the necklace itself. In basic terms, the second and third points suggest that a necklace manufactured as part of an original set will have components similar in shape and design characteristics. This can be measured through bead outline and section shape and in other morphological characteristics such as perforation size and overall object dimensions. In addition, necklace components manufactured as a set will display what can be referred to as symmetry in bead design.

In other words, it is assumed that the shape and size of necklace components along either side of a necklace are designed to be symmetric in appearance.

In the case of both fragmentation and overall condition, the context of deposition is of critical importance. In response to methodological concerns in past fragmentation analyses, Chapman and Gaydarska (2007) have emphasised the importance of ensuring fragmentation studies are conducted using data obtained from fully excavated sites and/or closed contexts. Thus, only in a closed context can the absence of whole objects be confidently attributed to social action rather than post-depositional processes or missing data. Similarly, observations of object condition can only be considered reflective of its age when obtained from a closed context. Burial data is particularly useful as it can be reasonably assumed that a single grave represents a single closed context. As a result, all examination undertaken here includes only those objects which have been identified by antiquarian or modern sources as having been associated with an inhumation or cremation deposit. All fragmentation analysis has been further restricted to inhumations only, and is discussed in greater detail later in the chapter.

VARIATION IN CONDITION BETWEEN SIMILAR OBJECTS

The first task was to investigate whether any particular artefact categories are likely to have been employed as heirlooms. The evidence for use wear for all artefact categories except for necklaces is summarised in Table 10.1 (Beaker) and Table 10.2 (Early Bronze Age). Where a single category dates from both periods (e.g. V-perforated buttons, bone points or dress pins) the evidence has been split according to the probable date of each grave concerned. All relevant wear data has been included, and thus in the Early Bronze Age list (Table 10.2) the totals include records for some key grave groups that occur outside the three main regional study areas, i.e. outside East Yorkshire, the Peak District and Wessex. Total records for slightly worn or fresh, worn and very worn condition are listed for each artefact category, along with the number of items studied where wear condition could not be determined. The final columns provide a quantitative estimate of the overall degree of wear for each artefact category. This has been calculated by dividing the total number of worn and very worn items by the total number of determinate items for each category. If the total number of items in any one category is less than ten this estimate is deemed to be less significant and has therefore been enclosed in brackets. Categories which show most wear (60–100% worn or very worn) are shown in bold, while the entries shown in italic are those categories where most items were fresh or slightly worn (<30% worn or very worn). The remainder show medium wear.

In the Beaker period the artefact categories that display most wear, and are therefore most likely to have functioned as heirlooms, are Series 1 dagger/knives, pommels, belt

Table 10.1. Beaker object categories: the occurrence of levels of wear in all objects studied. Entries in bold italic show most wear (60–100% worn or very worn), entries in italic are slightly worn or fresh (<30% worn or very worn) and the remainder show medium wear.

Object type	Material	Fresh/slightly worn	Worn	Very worn	Indet wear	Total	W or VW/total determinate objects %
Dagger/knife Series 1	***Copper/bronze***	*3*	*4*	*1*	*2*	*10*	*63%*
Dagger/knife Series 2	*Bronze*	*21*	*4*	*1*	*3*	*29*	*19%*
Pommel (Class 1 and 2)	***Bone/ivory***	*-*	*4*	*5*	*-*	*9*	*(100%)*
Belt ring/pulley object	***Bone, amber, jet and jet-like materials***	*5*	*5*	*7*	*3*	*20*	*71%*
Bracer	Stone	35	22	1	1	59	40%
Sponge finger stone	***Stone***	*1*	*7*	*2*	*-*	*10*	*90%*
Spatula	***Bone/antler***	*1*	*10*	*1*	*1*	*13*	*92%*
Awl (Group 1)	*Copper/bronze*	*6*	*2*	*-*	*6*	*14*	*25%*
Bone point	*Bone/antler*	*4*	*1*	*-*	*1*	*6*	*(20%)*
Toggle	**Bone/antler**	*1*	*-*	*2*	*-*	*3*	*(66%)*
Tusk	*Tooth*	*4*	*-*	*-*	*2*	*6*	*(0%)*
V-perforated button	Jet and jet-like materials, amber	19	18	5	1	43	55%
Buttons from sets (× 2)	Jet and jet-like materials, stone	6	2	3	-	11	45%
Earring	***Bronze***	*-*	*2*	*-*	*2*	*4*	*(100%)*
Dress pin	***Copper, bronze, bone***	*-*	*2*	*-*	*1*	*3*	*(100%)*
Single bead	*Amber*	*1*	*-*	*-*	*-*	*1*	*(0%)*
Gold ornament	***Gold***	*-*	*1*	*-*	*-*	*1*	*(100%)*

rings and pulley objects, sponge finger stones and spatulae (see bold rows in Table 10.1). Other categories where heirlooms may have been common, but where less than ten items were studied, are pommels, toggles, earrings, dress pins and the single gold ornament. The artefact categories which show least wear are Series 2 dagger/knives and Group 1 awls, and possibly bone points. On the other hand, V-perforated buttons, whether found singly, as pairs or in sets, show medium wear.

Turning to the Early Bronze Age evidence (Table 10.2), it can be seen that the artefact categories that display most wear, and thus may have functioned as heirlooms, are pommels, perforated stones, spatulae and complex dress pins. Categories with less than ten items studied which may also fall into this bracket are grooved stones, worked stones, handles and tools, antlers and earrings. The artefact categories which show least wear are awls, bone points, tweezers, bone plates, tusks, ring-headed dress pins and single beads. The remaining categories show medium wear: dagger/knives, bone tubes, V-perforated buttons, studs, single spacer plates, pendants and gold ornaments.

The evidence for both periods is compared in Table 10.3. This lists the artefact categories which have high heirloom potential (60–100% items worn or very worn), and lesser heirloom potential (30–59% items worn or very worn) for each of the two periods. Where a single artefact category occurs in both periods there is remarkable consistency

within the data. Thus, in both periods, pommels, spatulae, earrings and complex dress pins score high values, while V-perforated buttons score medium values. There are two cases where the values differ: Beaker period tanged daggers, and gold ornaments. The former are more worn than the later classes of dagger, a difference which may relate to the heirloom status of the Series 1 daggers, or to the softer nature of their copper material (see Chapter 3.1). With regard to the gold items, determinate wear was only recorded for one Beaker item and the score for the Early Bronze Age gold ornaments is 58% which lies only just below the defining score for objects of high heirloom potential.

It could be argued that objects designed to be used as tools might well accrue heavy wear from use within a single lifetime, and thus worn tools might not have actually functioned as heirlooms. This argument might apply to the sponge finger stones (probably used in leather working), the spatulae (used for the pressure flaking of flint), grooved and worked stones, and the bone tools. The main categories of high heirloom potential would then be the pommels, belt rings, toggles and other ornaments, plus the bone and antler handles and, probably, the gold ornaments. These are mainly items of dress or ornament, and most of the categories in the list of artefact types of lesser heirloom potential are also items of adornment, or are items with ritual connotations such as the bone tubes.

Table 10.2. Early Bronze Age non-necklace object categories: the occurrence of levels of wear in all objects studied. Entries in bold italic show most wear (60–100% worn or very worn), entries in italic are slightly worn or fresh (<30% worn or very worn) and the remainder show medium wear.

Object type	Material	Fresh/ slightly worn	Worn	Very worn	Indet wear	Total	W or VW/total determinate objects %
Dagger/knife Series 3	Bronze	6	1	2	-	9	33%
Dagger/knife Series 4	Bronze	6	4	-	2	12	40%
Dagger/knife Series 5	Bronze	19	9	1	1	30	34%
Dagger/knife Series 6 and 7	Bronze	17	10	3	19	49	43%
Pommel (Class 3 to 5)	***Bone/antler, ivory, gold***	*1*	*3*	*4*	*1*	*9*	***88%***
Belt hook	Bone, gold, bronze	5	1	3	1	10	44%
Grooved stone	***Stone***	*2*	*5*	*1*	-	*8*	***(75%)***
Perforated stone	***Stone***	*5*	*9*	*3*	-	*17*	***71%***
Worked stones	***Stone***	-	*2*	*4*	-	*6*	***(100%)***
Spatula	***Bone/antler***	*3*	*5*	*2*	*2*	*12*	***70%***
Awl	*Bronze*	*18*	*2*	-	*13*	*33*	*10%*
Point	*Bone*	*123*	*38*	*3*	*27*	*191*	*25%*
Tweezers	*Bone*	*7*	*1*	*2*	-	*10*	*30%*
Tube	Bone	3	3	1	-	7	(57%)
Plate	*Bone*	*3*	*1*	-	-	*4*	*(25%)*
Toggle	Bone	2	-	-	1	3	(33%)
Handle	***Bone***	-	*3*	*2*	-	*5*	***(100%)***
Tool	***Bone***	-	*2*	*3*	*2*	*7*	***(100%)***
Antler	***Antler***	*2*	*2*	*1*	*1*	*6*	***(60%)***
Axe/pronged object	Bronze	2	1	1	1	5	(50%)
Tusk	*Tooth*	*10*	*2*	-	*7*	*19*	*17%*
V-perforated button	Jet and jet-like materials, amber, bone	8	8	2	2	20	56%
Button from sets (× 2)	Jet and jet-like materials	21	6	6	-	33	36%
Earring	***Bronze***	*2*	*4*	-	*2*	*8*	***(67%)***
Dress pin: complex	***Bronze, bone***	*3*	*4*	*3*	*1*	*11*	***70%***
Dress pin: ring-head	*Bone /antler*	*10*	*3*	*1*	-	*14*	*29%*
Stud	Jet and jet-like materials, clay	5	4	-	1	10	44%
Single bead	*Jet and jet-like materials, bone, amber, stone*	*11*	*4*	-	*1*	*16*	*27%*
Single spacer plate	Jet and jet-like materials	4	-	5	-	9	56%
Pendant	Jet and jet-like materials, bone, amber, gold, bronze	18	7	2	11	38	33%
Neckring and bracelet	Bronze	1	-	1	-	2	(50%)
Gold ornament	Gold	8	5	6	-	19	58%

VARIATION IN CONDITION WITHIN AN ASSEMBLAGE

The second analysis conducted was the identification of variation in overall condition between objects within the same grave assemblage. Sites were selected on the basis of having at least two objects with identified overall condition from a grave context, and were observed for both Beaker and Early Bronze Age sites. In addition, any site containing components of known necklaces from a grave context were included and examined separately. At a basic level, it is assumed that objects from the same grave context will have similar condition characteristics. Thus, any object whose overall condition varies significantly from other associated items is potentially an heirloom. This discussion mainly addresses items which are more heavily worn than associated objects. Thus, a site which displays only minimal use wear variation between two objects and whose overall condition is expected based on the average condition scores discussed in the previous section would possess low potential for the presence of

Table 10.3. Artefact categories of high and lesser heirloom potential.

Artefact category	Beaker	EBA
High heirloom potential (60–100% worn or very worn)		
Series 1 dagger/knife	63%	(lesser potential)
Pommel	(100%)	88%
Belt ring/pulley object	71%	-
Sponge finger stone	90%	-
Spatula	92%	70%
Toggle	66%	-
Earring	(100%)	(67%)
Complex dress pin	(100%)	70%
Gold ornament	(100%)	(lesser potential)
Grooved stone	-	(75%)
Worked stone	-	(100%)
Handle	-	(100%)
Tool	-	(100%)
Lesser heirloom potential (30–59% worn or very worn)		
V-perforated button	55%	56%
Buttons in sets	45%	36%
Bracer	40%	-
Dagger/knife	(higher potential)	33% to 40%
Belt hook	-	44%
Bone tube	-	(57%)
Stud	-	44%
Single spacer plate	-	(56%)
Pendant	-	33%
Gold ornament	(higher potential)	58%

heirlooms. Medium potential are sites which show a higher degree of variation between objects and their expected condition scores, while high potential sites contain objects whose condition is clearly at odds with associated objects and/or expected scores. On the whole, variation in overall condition for a given assemblage was far easier to identify when it consisted of three or more objects. Grave groups containing non-necklace items are considered first, followed by graves containing both necklace and non-necklace items and finally the necklace grave data.

Grave groups containing non-necklace items only

Using the parameters outlined above, wear evidence for the items included in 37 non-necklace Beaker grave groups is listed in Table 10.4. As previously, the number of items where the degree of wear could not be determined is also listed, as well as the number of items not analysed. This final column relates mainly to items of pottery (usually a Beaker) or of flint, both of which are categories of object which were not studied during the project as a whole. The groups which are most likely to contain heirloom items are those which contain items of highly variable wear condition i.e. fresh/slightly worn, worn and very worn objects, or those displaying a marked contrast in wear condition i.e. fresh/slightly worn objects along with very worn items. Within Table 10.4 groups containing objects of all three wear categories (four examples) are shown in bold, while

those with contrasting fresh/slightly worn and very worn items (eight examples) are shown in italic.

Heirloom potential is most evident on the basis of observed wear condition which is unusual for given object types. For example, at Acklam Wold 124, although the presence of a heavily worn belt ring/pulley object is not unusual, the fact that it is alongside two V-perforated buttons which show only slight wear is significant. Across all grave contexts, V-perforated buttons are highly likely to have been worn, which is not the case here. As all items are pieces of dress equipment, it therefore seems likely that the belt ring/pulley object is an older object. A similar pattern is evident at Kelleythorpe UN101, 2. The dagger displays clear signs of wear, while all other object types in the grave assemblage, including those expected to be more heavily worn (i.e. V-perforated button and bead), show little signs of wear. A grave with items of highly variable wear is Winterbourne Monkton, with a fresh or slightly worn pulley ring, and a pair of buttons, one of which is worn, and the other, the possible heirloom, very worn. Other graves demonstrating highly variable wear records are those with large numbers of goods. Only a proportion of the goods from the grave of the Amesbury Archer were studied in this project, but wear variation is high, with one of the bracers, a spatula and possibly the cushion stone having been heirlooms. The situation is complex in this case as many of the artefacts were deposited in separate and distinct caches. Indeed some of the items may have been offerings from mourners rather than associated with the individual buried. However the extreme wear status of some of the items could still indicate heirloom status. At Raunds 1, not only are two sponge finger stones with very different conditions present (one worn, one fresh), but alongside this is the only instance of a very worn and reworked bracer from a bracer context. Also the set of buttons includes two in a fresh or slightly worn condition and one which was very worn. This button, and the bracer, may well have been heirloom items, as was the tusk (not seen in the project) which, according to the radiocarbon date, was between 420 and 990 years old when deposited (Harding and Healy 2007, 254–5).

A summary of the combinations of wear categories represented within this suite of 37 Beaker graves is provided below in Table 10.6. From this it can be seen that the most common association was between items showing slight and moderate wear (35%), but 22% of the graves contained the combination of fresh/slightly worn and very worn items, indicative of the presence of one or more heirlooms, and 10% contained items displaying all three wear categories. Thus a total of 12 graves (32%) out of the 37 are likely to have contained heirlooms.

Using the parameters and format outlined above, wear evidence for the items included in 47 non-necklace Early Bronze Age grave groups is listed in Table 10.5. Once again, the final column relates mainly to items of pottery or flint, which were not studied within the project. However, this time, as there is more variation in the vessel types represented, the actual items not analysed are listed.

Table 10.4. Beaker grave groups with two or more items studied: occurrence of objects by wear category (items not analysed were mainly pottery i.e. Beakers or flint artefacts). Objects covering all three wear categories are in bold, those with contrastingly fresh/slightly worn and very worn items are in italic.

Site	Region/ county	Fresh/ slightly worn	Worn	Very worn	Indet wear	Items not analysed
Melton Quarry	*E.Yorks.*	*Bracer*	-	*Bone belt ring*	-	*1*
Acklam Wold M124	*E.Yorks.*	*Jet button* *Amber button* *Bone point*	-	*Jet pulley ring*	-	*4*
Butterwick 39, 1	*E.Yorks.*	*Axe head* *Dagger* *Awl* *Jet buttons ×2* *Cannel coal buttons ×1*	-	*Jet button* *×2* *Stone button*	-	*1*
Cowlam 58, 6	E.Yorks.	-	Earrings ×2	-	-	-
Kelleythorpe UN101, 2	E.Yorks.	Bracer Amber bead Amber button	Dagger	-	-	1
Helperthorpe 49, 6	E.Yorks.	-	Pommel	Dagger	-	-
Painsthorpe Wold M99	E.Yorks.	-	Jet button	Jet button	-	-
Rudston 68, 6	E.Yorks.	Dagger	Sponge finger Jet pulley ring Jet buttons ×2	-	-	2
Rudston 68, 7	E.Yorks.	-	Jet buttons ×2	-	-	2
Thwing 60, 3	E.Yorks.	-	Jet button Jet pulley ring	-	-	-
Garrowby Wold M32	E.Yorks.	Dagger	Pommel	-	-	-
Green Low	Peak	Bone point	Spatulae × 3	-	-	6
Net Low	Peak	Dagger Jet button	Jet button	-	-	1
Staker Hill	Peak	Bone point	Bone point	-	-	-
Gospel Hillocks	Peak	Cannel coal button	Cannel coal button	-	-	-
Kenslow	Peak	Bone ornaments ×7	-	-	-	1
Ribden Low	Peak	Spatula	Spatula	-	-	6
Mouse Low	Peak	-	Spatulae ×2	-	-	6
Dow Low	Peak	Dagger	Jet button	-	-	2
Amesbury Archer	**Wessex**	**Spatula Bracer Shale ring Tusk ×3**	**Bracer Bone pin Spatula**	**Cushion stone**	**2**	**many**
Hemp Knoll	Wessex	Bone toggle	Bracer	-	-	2
Mere G6a	Wessex	Bracer	Dagger Gold disc Spatula	-	-	2
Milston G51	*Wessex*	*Dagger*	-	*Pommel*	-	*-*
Roundway G8	Wessex	Bracer	Dagger	-	1	2
Shrewton G5k	*Wessex*	*Dagger*	-	*Pommel*	-	*2*
West Overton G6b	Wessex	-	Sponge finger ×2 Spatula	-	-	2+
Winterbourne Monkton	**Wessex**	**Jet pulley ring**	**Jet button**	**Jet button**	-	**2**
Winterbourne Stoke G54	Wessex	-	Sponge finger ×2 Shale button	Shale pulley ring	-	2
Wimborne St Giles G9	Wessex	-	Jet button Shale pulley ring, Awl	-	1	6
Durrington Walls	**Wessex**	**Whetstone**	**Whetstone Jet button Sponge finger**	**Shale pulley ring**	-	**1**
Sewell	Beds.	Bracer	Copper alloy dress pin	-	1	1
Barnack	*Cambs.*	*Bracer* *Bone toggle*	-	*Dagger*	-	*1*
Little Downham	Cambs.	-	Jet button	Jet pulley ring	-	3
Tring	*Herts.*	*Bracer*	-	*Jet pulley ring*	-	*4*
Sittingbourne	*Kent*	*Bracer*	-	*Bone belt ring*	*1*	*-*
Raunds 1	**Northants.**	**Sponge finger Jet buttons ×2**	**Sponge finger Jet button**	**Bracer Jet button**	**1**	**many**
Pyecombe	E.Sussex	-	Bracer	Pommel	-	2

Table 10.5. Early Bronze Age non-necklace grave groups with two or more items studied: occurrence of objects by wear category (M denotes Mortimer). Objects covering all three wear categories are in bold, those with contrastingly fresh/slightly worn and very worn items are in italic.

Site	Region/county	Fresh/slightly worn	Worn	Very worn	Indet wear	Items not analysed
Goodmanham 115, 1	E.Yorks.	-	Earring ×2	-	Awl	Food Vessel
Hunmanby 250, 3	E.Yorks.	Jet buttons ×20	-	-	-	Copper alloy ring
Brough UN69, 1	E.Yorks.	-	Dagger Bone dress pin	-	-	-
Wharram Percy M70	E.Yorks.	Jet studs ×2	-	-	-	-
Aldro M113	E.Yorks.	Bone point ×4	Bone point ×2	-	-	Flint ×3
Acklam M123	E.Yorks.	Jet buttons ×2	-	-	-	Jet button ×2 (not seen)
Garton M153	E.Yorks.	Earring ×2	-	-	-	Food Vessel Flint Fossil
Painsthorpe M200	**E.Yorks.**	**Jet fastener**	**Jet button**	**Jet button**	**-**	**Bone object**
Galley Low	*Peak*	*Bone point*	*-*	*Pommel*	*-*	*Food Vessel Urn ×2*
Hungry Bentley	Peak	Jet bead	Jet pendant	-	-	Collared Urn Flint Jet button ×2
Stanton Moor 1926	*Peak*	*Bone point ×2*	*-*	*Pommel*	*Dagger*	*Collared Urn*
Stanshope Pasture	Peak	Bone point ×2	-	-	-	Flint
Little Lea 3, Castern	Peak	-	Bone point ×2	-	-	Flint
Throwley Moor	**Peak**	**Bone point**	**Bone point Awl**	**Bone tube**	**-**	**Battle-axe**
Top Low	*Peak*	*Bone point ×1*	*-*	*Bone point ×1*	*-*	*-*
Aldbourne G8	Wessex	Dagger Bone point	-	-	-	-
Aldbourne G11	Wessex	Bone point ×2	-	-	-	Flint arrowhead
Aldbourne G13, 1	**Wessex**	**Tweezers**	**Bracer Bone point**	**Perforated stone**	**-**	**Shell**
Amesbury G4	Wessex	Dagger	Awl	-	-	-
Amesbury G85	Wessex	Dagger	Pommel	-	-	Flint scraper
Bishops Cannings G61	Wessex	-	Bone point	-	Bone point	-
Collingbourne Ducis G4	Wessex	Dagger	Dress pin	-	-	Accessory cup sherds
Figheldean G25c	*Wessex*	*Dagger ×2 Tusk ×3*	*-*	*Antler*	*Antler ×2*	*Sherds*
Roundway G5b	Wessex	Grooved stone Spatula	Grooved stone Bone handle	-	Dagger Spatula	Flint arrowhead Flint ×2
Norton Bavant Borrow Pit	**Wessex**	**Dagger**	**Perforated stone Bone point**	**Belt hook**	**Dagger**	**Accessory cup**
Sutton Veny G11c	Wessex	Awl	V-perforated bone button ×2	-	-	Tin bead (lost)
Winterbourne Stoke G4	Wessex	Dagger Pommel Tweezers	Dagger	-	Sheet bronze fragments	Bone point
Wilsford G5 (Bush Barrow)	Wessex	Dagger Gold lozenge ×2 Gold belt hook Bone mounts ×5	Dagger Stone macehead Pommel with gold pins	-	Dagger (lost)	-
Wilsford G23	Wessex	Dagger Dress pin Bone tube	Perforated stone	-	-	-
Wilsford G43	Wessex	Dagger	Perforated stone	-	-	-
Wilsford G56	Wessex	Tweezers	Dagger ×2	-	Dress pin	Bone point

Wilsford G58	Wessex	Tusk Bone tube	Grooved stone Antler handle Bone plate	Pronged object	Copper alloy axe head	Stone Battle-axe
Wilsford G60B	Wessex	Dagger Bone plate	Perforated stone Worked stone	-	Bone tool	Flint ×2
Winterbourne Stoke G5	Wessex	Dagger ×2	Bone handle	-	Awl	Handled vessel Fossil wood
Winterbourne Stoke G28	Wessex	Awl	Bone awl handle	-	-	Collared Urn
Winterbourne Stoke G66	Wessex	-	Dagger Pommel	-	-	Collared Urn
Wilsford G16	Wessex	Bone pendant Bone belt Hook	-	-	-	-
Dewlish G7	*Wessex*	*Dagger Perforated stone*	-	*Bone dress pin Tweezers*	-	-
Edmonsham G2	Wessex	Dagger Perforated stone Bone dress pin	Tweezers	-	-	-
Weymouth G8, 3	Wessex	Dagger	-	Dagger	Dagger	Gold pommel Copper alloy axe head
Weymouth G8, 1	*Wessex*	*Dagger*	-	*Bone pommel*	-	-
Wimborne St Giles G19	Wessex	Bone point ×2	-	-	-	-
Wimborne St Giles G20	Wessex	Dagger Bone point	-	-	-	Linen Urn Bone pendant
Winterbourne Steepleton B, cremation 2	*Wessex*	*Awl*	-	*Jet stud*	-	-
Winterborne St Martin G31 (Clandon Barrow)	Wessex	Jet/shale/gold mace-head	Gold plaque Amber cup	-	Dagger	Accessory cup
Timsbury G1 (Camerton Barrow)	Somerset	Dagger	Dress pin Perforated stone	-	-	Accessory cup
Priddy G3 (Green Barrow)	*Somerset*	*Dagger*	-	*Bone dress pin*	-	-

Table 10.6. Combinations of wear categories for non-necklace items within Beaker and Early Bronze Age (non-necklace) grave groups.

Wear categories	Beaker graves	%	EBA non-necklace graves	%	EBA non-necklace + necklace graves	%	Total	%
Fresh/slight wear only	1	3%	10	21%	4	40%	15	16%
Worn only	6	16%	5	11%	1	10%	12	13%
Very worn only	none	0%	none	0%	none	0%	none	0%
Fresh/slight + worn	13	35%	19	40%	3	30%	35	37%
Fresh/slight + very worn	8	22%	8	17%	1	10%	17	18%
Worn + very worn	5	14%	none	none	none	0%	5	5%
Fresh/slight + worn + very worn	4	10%	5	11%	1	10%	10	11%
Total number of graves	**37**	**100%**	**47**	**100%**	**10**	**100%**	**94**	**100%**

As before, the grave groups which are most likely to contain heirloom items are shown in bold or italic text: those containing objects of all three wear categories (five examples) in bold, and those with contrasting fresh/slightly worn and very worn items (eight examples) in italic.

Although the total number of high potential sites is too numerous to highlight individually, a few of the most important results can be explored in more detail. The group from Aldbourne G13 includes fresh tweezers, a worn bone point, worn re-worked stone bracer and a very worn perforated stone whetstone pendant. This indicates that the bracer and perforated whetstone were most probably heirloom items. At Wilsford G58 a slightly worn tusk and the bone tube (probably a sound instrument) were associated with a worn grooved stone, antler handle and bone plate and the very worn bronze pronged object. The latter piece, and the antler handle and bone plate may well have been heirlooms. The group from Norton Bavant Borrow Pit contains a fresh dagger, worn perforated whetstone pendant and bone point and a very worn belt hook. The accessory cup was also fresh, and it would appear that the belt hook and perforated whetstone may have been heirloom items. Amongst the groups with fresh/slightly worn items contrasting with worn artefacts, the combination of fresh or slightly worn dagger and worn or very worn pommel is notable (see Amesbury G85 and Weymouth G8, 1). Dewlish G7 consists of an unusual combination of objects of varying wear. Most notable is the presence of a very worn and fragmentary set of bone tweezers and dress pin associated with a grooved dagger with near fresh pointillé decoration and little or no signs of having been used and/or sharpened. Similarly, at Priddy G3 a fresh or slightly worn dagger was associated with a very worn, and re-worked, bone dress pin.

Although the assemblage from Bush Barrow (Wilsford G5) does not contain any recorded examples of heavily worn items, the combination of fresh or slightly worn and worn items appears to be significant. In the case of the two surviving daggers, one shows clear signs of wear, while the other does not. In addition, the copper alloy axe is also clearly worn. In the case of the gold objects, although the two lozenges and belt hook only appear to be slightly worn, the gold-pinned pommel from the worn dagger is heavily worn. Lastly, the mace-head (ID 1400), a stone object and therefore slow to wear, is also worn. But the bone mounts, which probably adorned the shaft of the mace, are only slightly worn. Hence, a range of important and rare object types are widely variable in overall condition, with one of the daggers and the stone mace-head likely to have been curated as heirlooms.

A summary of the combinations of wear categories represented within these 47 Early Bronze Age graves is provided in Table 10.6. From this it can be seen that the most common association is between items showing slight and moderate wear (40%), but 17% of the graves contain the combination of fresh/slightly worn and very worn items, indicative of the presence of one or more heirlooms, and 11% contain items displaying all three wear categories. Thus a total of 13 graves (28%) out of the 47 are most likely to have contained heirlooms.

Early Bronze Age grave groups containing non-necklace items alongside necklaces

Using the same analytical parameters, a series of ten grave groups which contain non-necklace items alongside necklaces can be defined and these are listed in Table 10.7. These groups are all of Early Bronze Age date.

The wear condition of the necklace elements is discussed below. In most cases the non-necklace items are few in number within each group, and it is notable that many necklaces were found alone within graves. Some instances of possible heirlooms can however be highlighted. There is one example of a grave containing items falling within

all three wear categories and one group with items of fresh, slightly worn and very worn condition. At Upton Lovell G2e (The Golden Barrow) a fresh bronze awl is associated with the worn gold-covered cone and very worn gold plaque and cap ends or 'boxes'. The latter gold items appear to have been older than the awl and cone and may well have been heirlooms. Similarly, at Little Cressingham there was a variation in wear condition amongst the various gold items, and the cap ends or 'boxes' from this grave may have been heirlooms. Within the group containing fresh and very worn items, Winterbourne Stoke G8, the very worn pieces are worked stones. These probably functioned as whetstones, tools which may have suffered extreme wear during a single lifetime, and may not have been heirlooms. A summary of the combinations of wear categories represented within these 11 Early Bronze Age graves is provided in Table 10.6. Amongst these graves 10% of the non-necklace elements display a combination of all three wear categories and a further 10% have the combination of fresh/slightly worn and very worn items. Thus a total of two of these graves (20%) are most likely to have contained heirlooms.

In order to compare the occurrence of possible heirlooms within the Beaker and Early Bronze Age periods, the incidence of different wear categories and combinations for the grave groups with two or more items with recorded wear condition is summarised in Table 10.6. There are no graves with very worn items only, and those with worn plus very worn items only occur in the Beaker period. Graves with fresh/slightly worn or worn only elements do occur throughout, although fresh only items are rare in the Beaker period. As argued above, the combination most likely to indicate the presence of heirlooms are the fresh/slight wear plus very worn or fresh/slight plus worn plus very worn categories. The graves containing objects of all three wear categories occur consistently between the two periods, while those with fresh/slight and very worn items are slightly more common in the Beaker period (Figure 10.1). The most common combination however is that of fresh/slightly worn and worn items. Such graves are slightly more common in the Early Bronze Age period, and, as noted above, may also have included some objects which were of heirloom status. The most remarkable feature of these statistics, however, is that the practice of depositing heirlooms in graves appears to have been common in both periods. Not only was the practice highly evident already in the Beaker period, but also the level of incidence of non-necklace heirloom deposition seems to have stayed relatively stable throughout the two periods.

Early Bronze Age graves containing necklaces

The incidence of variations in wear amongst the beads belonging to necklaces has been recorded and discussed fully in Chapters 7 and 8. Here the data relating to the different classes of necklace are summarised in a series of tables. The main classes of necklace are the same as those

Table 10.7. Early Bronze Age grave groups containing necklace and non-necklace items, with two or more items studied: occurrence of objects by wear category (M denotes Mortimer). The necklace elements are listed in Tables 10.8 to 10.13.

Site	Region /county	Fresh/ slightly worn	Worn	Very worn	Indet wear	Items not analysed
Folkton 71, 6	E.Yorks.	Awl	-	-	-	Food Vessel Flint scraper
Aldbourne 276, 3 (G1)	Wessex	Bone point	-	-	-	Accessory cup Flint
Scratchbury, Norton Bavant G1	Wessex	Dress pin ×2	-	-	Knife-dagger	Faience
Preshute G1a (Manton Barrow)	Wessex	-	-	-	Dagger Amber pommel Awl ×3	Dagger Accessory cup ×2
Upton Lovell G2a (shaman)	Wessex	Bone point ×37 Tusk ×3 Awl	Jet belt ring Grooved stone Bone point ×1	-	-	19 (mainly flint or stone)
Upton Lovell G2e (Golden Barrow)	**Wessex**	**Awl Shale cone core**	**Gold covered cone**	**Gold plaque Gold 'boxes' ×4**	**Dagger**	**Collared Urn Accessory cup ×2**
Wilsford G47, 49 or 50	Wessex	Gold disc ×3	Gold disc ×1 Jet button	-	-	Awl Faience Bone/stone ?beads
Winterbourne Stoke G8	*Wessex*	*Awl*	-	*Worked stone ×2*	*Beaver tooth*	*Accessory cup ×2 Misc. stone ×2*
Winterbourne Stoke G47	Wessex	Dagger Awl	-	-	-	-
Bloxworth G4a	Wessex		Tweezers	-	Bone pendant	Collared Urn
Little Cressingham	Norfolk	Gold plaque Gold band	Gold 'boxes' ×3	-	-	-

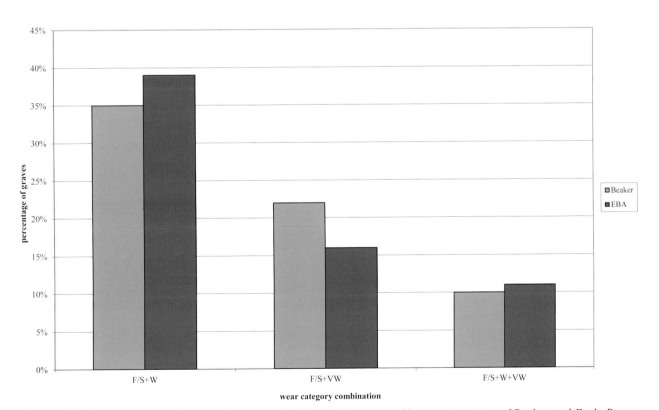

Figure 10.1. The occurrence of wear category combinations within non-necklace grave groups of Beaker and Early Bronze Age date.

defined in Chapters 7 and 8. The starting point is with those necklaces which are made up from large numbers of small disc beads of jet or jet-like materials; the occurrence of wear categories relating to these is shown in Table 10.8.

In most cases it proved possible to determine that the level of wear was slight (although this was sometimes deduced from detailed study of a small sample of the total beads represented). Although the 203 disc beads from Painsthorpe M64 are entered as indeterminate, it is probable that they also were slightly worn. In two cases, such necklaces also include tubular sheet beads of copper or copper alloy, and one of these, from Devils's Dyke, certainly dated from the Beaker period. There was little variation amongst the disc beads of jet or jet-like materials within any one necklace, and it can be concluded that these necklaces were made as sets of beads, and were not worn on the body for any length of time. However, occasionally older beads of different shapes had been incorporated into the necklaces as heirloom items. Thus at Painsthorpe M64, two fusiform beads (one slightly worn and one worn) would have derived from an older spacer plate necklace. Six worn and two very worn fusiform beads in the necklace from Eglingham 200, 3 would have been acquired from a similar source. In Wessex, the disc beads from Winterbourne Stoke G47 are associated with four amber beads, three of which are slightly or moderately worn, and at Preshute G1a, the Manton Barrow, there are also beads and pendants of various other materials which display varying degrees of wear (see Table 10.13 below).

The earliest spacer plate necklaces made from jet and jet-like materials are those that copy gold lunulae and these occur mainly in Scotland. Some however occur in northern England and the Peak District. Other English examples include complex combinations of spacer plates, fusiform beads, disc beads and V-perforated necklace buttons, and these may be later in date. Full descriptions have been provided in Chapter 7. A summary of the occurrence of wear categories for the necklaces studied is given in Table 10.9.

The totals indicate that most beads were fresh or slightly worn. However, if the disc beads from Pockley are excluded, the most common category becomes those beads which are moderately worn. There is also a significant occurrence of heavily worn items. This suggests that many of the beads, plates and buttons may have been re-used as heirloom items in necklaces which were re-worked through time. Spacer plates and terminal plates tend to be particularly worn and appear to have been re-used several times. They also occur as single items in graves, even when broken, indicating that these highly valued items may have continued their use lives as amulets or charms (see Chapter 5.8). The more symmetrical, and possibly earlier necklaces, such as the two from Cow Low and that from Middleton-on-the-Wolds, tend to have more beads which are fresh or only slightly worn. The necklace from Hill Head, which has a balanced set of spacer plates, many fusiform beads and just a few buttons, has a more even representation of worn and unworn elements. In contrast, amongst the necklaces with many buttons (Grind Low and Middleton

Moor) and that with spacers made from bone (Windle Nook) the incidence of worn and very worn items is much higher. Such necklaces appear to contain many potential heirloom items and this is particularly well illustrated by the assemblage of elements from Middleton Moor, with its unevenly matched spacer and terminal plates, several of which had been modified for re-use. This last necklace contained no fresh or slightly worn items, and the majority are heavily worn. On the other hand, the small sets of necklace items including spacer plates from East Anglia seem to be relatively late and made by a local craftsman. These groups (Snailwell C and Soham Fen) contain fresh or slightly worn pieces, and a lower incidence of worn or very worn items which might have been heirlooms.

A second group of spacer plate or other complex necklaces are made from amber. The surfaces of amber beads are often oxidised to a great extent and have sometimes been treated with consolidant. This means that it is often very difficult (or impossible) to assess the degree of wear, and many beads are therefore recorded as having indeterminate wear. However, the wear data that is available from the project is summarised in Table 10.10.

The composition of the four necklaces studied is highly varied (see Chapter 7 for full details), and the wear categories within the different components of each necklace also vary. The two necklaces with most elements surviving, those from Lake and Upton Lovell, both have sets of spacer plates which are very worn, and apparently re-worked. In the case of Lake these are associated with smaller beads which, where the level of wear could be detected, are fresh or slightly worn. This suggests that the spacer plates may have been older heirloom items. At Upton Lovell the globular beads that could be studied in terms of wear are moderately worn, but once again the re-worked spacer plates may have been heirlooms, as also may have been the small numbers of beads of other shapes. The degree of wear on the items from Wimborne St Giles G9 could not be determined in many cases, but examples of globular beads, V-perforated buttons and one of the spacer plates are all fresh or slightly worn, and no pieces stand out as possible heirlooms in this case. For the set of beads and pendants from Little Cressingham, many more items showed visible signs of wear condition. Once again, many of the individual pieces were slightly worn, or indeed in fresh condition. This suggests that the necklace was put together as a set of new elements, although it is just possible that some of the pestle pendants had been used previously.

There are 15 simple necklaces with components of variable shape that have relevant recorded wear data and these are listed in Table 10.11. Full descriptions may be found in Chapter 8. Most of these groups of beads are small, often containing less than five items. The beads are usually fresh or slightly worn, although a significant number are worn. None however show heavy wear. Three materials are represented: amber, bone and, especially, jet (and jet-like materials). Types of bead include fusiform, annular and globular, and other items such as fasteners or pendants (Tan Hill; Norton Bavant G1), rings (Avebury

Table 10.8. Disc bead necklaces: occurrence of levels of wear (* denotes presence of tubular sheet copper alloy beads; ** denotes association with beads of other materials, which are listed in Tables 10.12 and 10.13).

ID number	Site	Region/ county	Fresh/ slightly worn	Worn	Very worn	Indet wear	Total beads
ID 251	Garton Slack VI, 1*	E.Yorks.	243	-	-	6	249
ID 434	Devil's Dyke*	Sussex		-	-	19	19
ID 246	Painsthorpe M64	E.Yorks.	1	1	-	203	205
ID 250; ID 245	Garton Slack 75	E.Yorks.	133	-	-	1	134
ID 252	Garton Slack 29, D	E.Yorks.	732	-	-	-	732
ID 308	Weaverthorpe 44, burial 2	E.Yorks.	119	-	-	-	119
ID 322	Goodmanham 121, burial 6	E.Yorks.	124	-	-	-	124
ID 366	Folkton 245, burial 8	E.Yorks.	-	163	-	-	163
ID 334	Eglingham 200, burial 3	Northumb.	92	6	2	-	100
ID 470	Winterbourne Stoke G47 **	Wessex	37+	-	-	-	37+
ID 491	Preshute G1a ** (Manton Barrow)	Wessex	-	-	-	144	144
ID 517	Wilsford G39	Wessex	12	-	-	-	12
Totals			**1493**	**170**	**2**	**373**	**2038**

Table 10.9. Spacer plate necklaces of jet or jet-like materials: occurrence of levels of wear (*325 beads in this necklace are disc beads; **334 beads are disc beads).

ID number	Site	Region/ county	Fresh/ slightly worn	Worn	Very worn	Indet wear	Total beads
ID 247	Calais Wold 13	E.Yorks.	47	8	-	548	603
ID 249	Middleton-on-the-Wolds	E.Yorks.	2	5	-	-	7
ID 264	NW of Pickering	N.Yorks.	24	-	-	6	30
ID 379–89	Pockley*	E.Yorks.	334	1	-	-	335
ID 266	Cow Low	Peak	24	15	6	1	46
ID 267	Cow Low	Peak	48	17	6	-	71
ID 268	Hill Head	Peak	34	24	14	1	73
ID 269	Middleton Moor	Peak	-	32	40	334**	406
ID 270, ID 256 and ID 257	Grind Low	Peak	23	30	17	-	70
ID 273	Windle Nook	Peak	-	72	9	2	83
ID 281	Snailwell C	Cambs.	1	2	3	24	30
ID 391	Soham Fen	Cambs.	26	3	-	-	29
Totals			**563**	**290**	**95**	**916**	**1783**

G13c; Norton Bavant G1) and a button (Winterbourne Stoke G14, 1) are also represented. There are no groups which contain the combinations of wear categories that might indicate heirloom potential (i.e. fresh or slightly worn items associated with very worn items), or the combination of all three wear categories. However, the form of many of the beads indicates the presence of heirlooms. Within the necklaces of jet and jet-like materials, such beads are fusiform in shape and derived from earlier spacer plate necklaces. These occur in six of the necklaces listed, and of the 20 such fusiform beads studied, 15 are worn and only five slightly worn. This evidence also contributes to the likelihood of their heirloom status. Amongst the five amber necklace groups, three contain squashed globular beads of the type found in the large amber spacer plate necklaces, and these also are probably heirlooms. And, once again, most of these beads are worn rather than slightly worn. In strong contrast to these small groups of beads, other small necklace grave groups contain items of mature Early Bronze Age type which probably were made *de novo* for these necklaces. These groups tend to contain larger

numbers of beads (up to 12), as well as other forms such as pendants, rings and buttons (see above). They include the necklaces from Durrington G14, Avebury G13c, Egton 124, 1, Fylingdales 271, 1, Aldbourne 276, 3 and the bone beads from Folkton 71, 6. Of the 45 beads with recorded wear category contained in this group of *de novo* necklaces 38 are fresh or slightly worn, and only seven are worn. This serves to confirm the fresher condition of the items in these necklaces, and the lack of heirloom items compared with the group of necklaces containing beads recycled from spacer plate necklaces discussed above. The overall counts (see totals row in Table 10.11) show that most of the beads in these necklaces are fresh or slightly worn. A significant number are worn, but none were recorded as being very worn.

The next to be considered are the grave groups containing composite necklaces. Such necklaces are characterised by the presence of beads or other ornaments made from differing materials, and in various sizes and shapes. For analysis purposes here, they have been divided into necklaces containing beads of two materials only, and

Table 10.10. Spacer plate and other large necklaces of amber: occurrence of levels of wear.

ID number	Site/objects	Region/ county	Fresh/ slightly worn	Worn	Very worn	Indet wear	Total beads
ID 1360	Wilsford-cum-Lake	Wessex					
	Spacer plate		1	5	5	-	11
	Pestle pendant		3	-	-	7	10
	Globular		21	16	-	12	49
	Fusiform		9	3	-	5	17
	Annular		-	-	-	4	4
	V-perf. button		5	3	-	3	11
	Total		**39**	**27**	**5**	**31**	**102**
ID 1444	Upton Lovell G2e	Wessex					
	Spacer plate		-	1	5	-	6
	Globular		-	44	-	293	337
	Fusiform		2	-	-	6	8
	Annular/other		-	-	-	5	5
	Total		**2**	**45**	**5**	**304**	**356**
ID 1496	Wimborne St Giles G9	Wessex					
	Spacer plate		1	1	-	7	9
	Globular		2	-	-	6	8
	Fusiform		-	-	-	3	3
	V-perf. button		3	-	-	-	3
	Total		**6**	**1**	**-**	**16**	**23**
ID 1111–1126	Little Cressingham	Norfolk					
	Pestle pendant		3	7	-	-	10
	Fusiform		4	-	-	-	4
	Annular		5	-	-	-	5
	Disc		23	3	-	2	28
	Total		**35**	**10**	**-**	**2**	**47**
Totals			**82**	**83**	**10**	**353**	**528**

then those containing more than two materials. Fifteen grave groups which contain composite necklaces with two materials are listed in Table 10.12. Full descriptions may be found in Chapter 8. For the first time, it can be noted that most of the examples come from Wessex, rather than from Yorkshire. Most of the beads are made from jet, jet-like materials or amber, but stone, fossil, fired clay, teeth and bone are also represented. In four graves (Calais Wold 114; Bloxworth G4a; Durrington G47; Winterbourne Stoke G68) segmented faience beads are also present. Faience was not studied as part of the project as a whole, but use wear evidence on faience beads is very difficult to assess and would seldom have contributed to our present discussion. Using the criteria previously employed there are two groups which are likely to have contained heirlooms: Amesbury G39 which includes items of all three wear categories, and Wilsford G16 with beads in fresh/slightly worn and very worn condition. In addition there are five groups which include fusiform beads of jet or jet-like materials, or squashed globular amber beads of types indicating recycling from earlier spacer plate necklaces. Three of these include jet or shale fusiforms (Hay Top; Amesbury G39 ; Upton Lovell G2a); in the last two cases the beads concerned are very worn. Two groups contain probably recycled squashed globular beads of amber (Winterbourne Stoke G47; Winterbourne Steepleton). All these beads are probably heirloom items. Other groups contain beads of mature Early Bronze Age type. Such groups include Wilsford G16, Calais Wold 114 and Bloxworth G4a.

However, some of the beads in these groups are very worn and may in fact be heirlooms from earlier composite necklaces. The overall counts (see totals row in Table 10.12) show that there are roughly equal proportions of beads which are fresh/slightly worn and worn, while less than about half as many are very worn.

Sixteen grave groups which contain composite necklaces with three, four or five different materials are listed in Table 10.13. Once again, it can be noted that most of the examples come from the south, rather than from Yorkshire. Most of the beads are made from jet or jet-like materials or amber, but stone, fossil, shell, teeth and bone are also represented. Many more of these necklaces also contain segmented faience beads (seven out of the 16); indeed these account for many of the items where wear condition could not be determined. The other major characteristic of this group of necklaces is that they tend to contain elements of highly variable shape. As well as beads of various types there are pendants of many different shapes and sizes and also flat rings, and all these forms occur in various different raw materials: amber; jet, shale or lignite, and faience. The pendants include some more complex items made from two or more materials including gold and copper alloy. One group, Wilsford G8, contains only pendants, with no beads represented at all. Full descriptions of all these necklaces and ornament sets may be found in Chapter 8. Using the criteria previously employed there are five groups which are likely to have contained heirlooms. Four include items within all three wear categories: Shrewton G5j; Oxsettle

Table 10.11. Simple necklaces with components of variable shape: occurrence of levels of wear.

ID number	Material	Site	Region/ county	Fresh/ slightly worn	Worn	Very worn	Indet wear	Total beads
ID 497–500	Jet and shale	Durrington G14	Wessex	4	-	-	-	4
ID 530–33	Shale	Wilsford G32	Wessex	1	3	-	-	4
ID 537–38	Shale	Avebury G13c	Wessex	-	-	-	3	3
ID 323	Jet	Egton 124, burial 1	N.Yorks.	12	3	-	-	15
ID 326–28	Jet and cannel coal or shale	Hutton Buscel 157, burial 1	N.Yorks.	-	3	-	-	3
ID 357	Jet	Fylingdales 271, burial 1	N.Yorks.	12	-	-	-	12
ID 392–94	Jet	Stranghow Moor	N.Yorks.	3	-	-	-	3
ID 451–52, ID 455 and ID 458	Jet	Nawton	N.Yorks.	3	2	-	-	5
ID 330–32	Jet and cannel coal	Ford 186, burial 3	Northumb.	1	2	-	-	3
ID 1340–45	Amber	Aldbourne 276, burial 3	Wessex	1	1	-	2	4
ID 1461–63	Amber	Winterbourne Stoke G14, 1 (central)	Wessex	2	1	-	-	3
ID 1458–60	Amber	Winterbourne Stoke G14, 2	Wessex	3	-	-	-	3
ID 1520.1–17 and ID 1521	Amber	Norton Bavant G1	Wessex	14	2	-	2	18
ID 1544–50 and ID 1552	Amber	Wilsford G33a	Wessex	3	3	-	1	7
ID 734–37	Bone	Folkton 71, burial 6	E.Yorks.	4	-	-	-	4
Totals				63	20	-	8	91

Bottom; Wilsford G7 and Winterslow G21, while the fifth grave group, Preshute G1a (Manton Barrow) includes items which are only slightly worn and one which is very worn. Interestingly, amongst the beads there are hardly any instances of items that might have been recycled from spacer plate necklaces. The main examples are the jet and amber beads from Wilsford G3, which all appear to be of spacer plate necklace form. However they are mainly fresh or only slightly worn, so do not appear to have been very old when incorporated within the composite necklace. Most of the beads, as well as the flat rings and various shapes of pendant, are of de novo mature Early Bronze Age type.

The two necklaces from Shrewton barrows provide an interesting contrast. All the beads and rings in the necklace from barrow G5L are fresh or only slightly worn, suggesting that the necklace may have been assembled for a single individual. However that from Shrewton G5j includes toggle pendants and a fusiform bead, all of lignite, which are worn or very worn, and appear to be heirlooms. Another necklace where mainly fresh/slightly worn elements may have been assembled during a single lifetime if that from Upton Lovell G1, although the three worn items (two jet beads and one of amber) may be heirlooms. Also at the Manton Barrow (Preshute G1a) most of the beads and the gold-bound amber pendants are fresh or slightly worn, with only one very worn item, the stone bead, possibly incorporated as an heirloom. The group of beads and pendants from Wilsford G7 includes items displaying variable wear condition. Most are fresh or slightly worn, but the two objects incorporating gold are worn, and the ribbed shale bead very worn. These latter

three items may be heirlooms. At Wilsford G8 however, none of the determinate items are very worn, but the three worn items: the horned gold pendant, gold-covered cone, and gold and bone pendant are all worn. Once again, the objects incorporating gold may be heirlooms; however, the halberd pendant from this grave, which also incorporates gold, appears to be fresh or only slightly worn.

Perhaps the best example of a group incorporating heirloom items is the complex mixture of object types, in at least four raw materials, from Oxsettle Bottom, East Sussex. The wear condition of the faience quoit pendant and surviving segmented faience bead, as well as for three of the amber beads could not be determined. There are seven slightly worn items, all beads, including two of jet, four shale and one in amber. However most of the pieces are worn or very worn and may be heirloom items. There are two worn shale beads, and single jet beads which are worn and very worn, but most of the more worn items are unusual forms: four rings made from shale and cannel coal, and a non-perforated cone ornament of shale. The most worn piece is one of the rings which had four through-perforations originally but these had broken out and the ring was re-used in a different way in the final ensemble. The two jet fusiform beads, one slightly worn and one very worn, derive from earlier spacer plate necklaces, and at least one of the amber beads also will have come originally from a spacer plate necklace. The overall counts (see totals row in Table 10.13) show that a large proportion of the beads, rings and pendants included in these necklaces are fresh or only slightly worn. Far fewer are worn, and very few are classified as very worn.

Table 10.12. Composite necklaces with two materials: occurrence of levels of wear (in same order as descriptions in Chapter 8).

ID number	Site	Region/ county	Fresh/ slightly worn	Worn	Very worn	Indet wear	Total Beads
ID 427–31	Tan Hill	Wessex	1	5	-	-	6
ID 470	Winterbourne Stoke G47	Wessex	2	1	-	1	4
ID 275	Hay Top	Peak	3	-	-	8	11
ID 1507A.1–21 and ID 1507B	Winterbourne Stoke G64a	Wessex	7	6	-	(60)	13 (73)
ID 501–502 and ID 1466–1468	*Wilsford G16*	*Wessex*	2	-	2	2	6
ID 512–14 and ID 1504.1–14	**Amesbury G39**	**Wessex**	7	6	3	1	17
ID 544–45, ID 1272.4 and ID 1272.5–7	Winterbourne Steepleton	Wessex	3	4	-	1	8
ID 248	Calais Wold 114	E.Yorks.	9	-	-	1	10
ID 442–48	Bloxworth G4a	Wessex	3	4	-	3	10
ID 503–504	Durrington G47	Wessex	-	-	-	3	3
ID 510–11	Winterbourne Stoke G68	Wessex	1	-	-	5	6
ID 364–65 and ID 742.1–10	Aldbourne 285, burial 1 (G12)	Wessex	-	2	11	-	13
ID 494–96 and ID 878	Upton Lovell G2a	Wessex	-	1	3	-	4
ID 853–70 and ID 1469	South Newton G1	Wessex	-	18	-	1	19
ID 871–76	Warminster G10	Wessex	6	-	-	1	7
Totals			**44**	**47**	**19**	**27**	**137**

Table 10.13. Composite necklaces with three, four or five materials: occurrence of levels of wear (in same order as descriptions in Chapter 8; for ID numbers see Chapter 8).

Site	Region/ county	Fresh/ slightly worn	Worn	Very worn	Indet wear	Total beads
Three materials						
Shrewton G5j	**Wessex**	7	1	2	1	**11 studied**
Oxsettle Bottom	**E.Sussex**	7	8	2	5	**22**
Upton Lovell G1	Wessex	13	3	-	16	32 studied
Wilsford G3	Wessex	12	-	-	7	19
Collingbourne Kingston G8	Wessex	1	3	-	2	6
Winterbourne Stoke G67	Wessex	2	-	-	9	11
Amesbury G48	Wessex	-	2	-	12	14
Wilsford G46	Wessex	2	-	-	1	3
Winterbourne Stoke G8	Wessex	1	-	-	4	5
Four materials						
Langton 2, burial 2	E.Yorks.	1	1	-	8	10
Wilsford G7	**Wessex**	5	2	1	3	**11**
Shrewton G5L	Wessex	8	-	-	1	9
Winterslow G21	**Wessex**	2	1	1	4	**8**
Five materials						
Preshute G1a (Manton)	*Wessex*	7	-	*1*	2	*10*
Wilsford G8	Wessex	4	3	-	7	14
Aldbourne 280, burial 1 (G6)	Wessex	2	1	-	9	12
Totals		**74**	**25**	**7**	**90**	**196**

Table 10.14. Early Bronze Age necklaces in graves: the occurrence of determinate wear condition.

Type of necklace	Fresh/slightly worn	%	Worn	%	Very worn	%	Total determinate beads
Disc bead	1489	90%	170	10%	2	-	1661
Spacer plate of jet or jet-like materials	563	65%	210	24%	95	11%	868
Amber spacer plate	80	45%	72	40%	26	15%	178
Simple necklaces with components of variable shape	64	72%	25	28%	-	-	89
Composite, 2 materials	43	42%	42	40%	19	18%	104
Composite, 3, 4 or 5 materials	74	70%	25	24%	7	6%	106

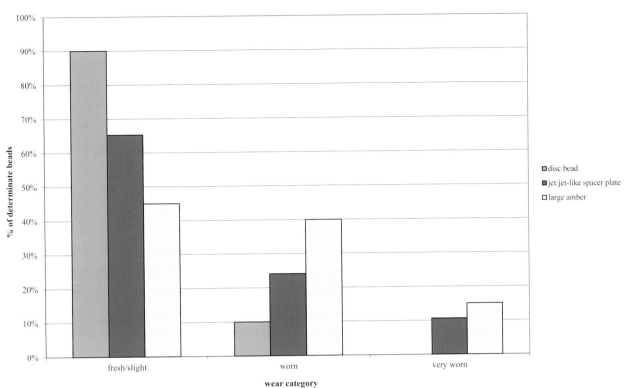

Figure 10.2. Necklaces with large numbers of beads: the percentage occurrence of wear categories.

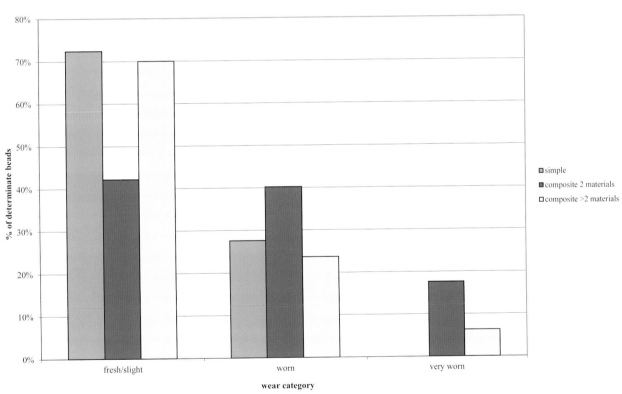

Figure 10.3. Necklaces with small numbers of beads: the percentage occurrence of wear categories.

The occurrence of wear categories amongst all the types of necklace defined is listed in Table 10.14, and the percentage occurrences are summarised in two histograms (Figure 10.2 and Figure 10.3). The necklaces which contain many beads of a single raw material, and with components of relatively uniform types are included in Figure 10.2. The necklace group showing least wear of all are those made up from jet or shale disc beads. There are no very worn items recorded, and heirloom items are probably not present, or only very rare. The spacer plate necklaces of jet and jet-like materials also show a high percentage of unworn beads, but heirloom elements are often present alongside these. These heirlooms are often the spacer plates themselves. Within a total of 42 plates with recorded wear condition, 21 are very worn and 13 moderately worn; thus they appear to have been re-used and sometimes modified within different necklaces. The spacer plate and other complex necklaces made from amber generally include more worn items. None of the few surviving examples seem to be original compositions, and the vast majority of the spacer plates (16 out of 19 where wear could be determined) appear to be heirlooms recycled from earlier necklaces.

The percentages of use wear occurrence for the smaller necklace types are shown in Figure 10.3. These necklaces contain either components of a single material, but of different shapes, or a mixture of beads and ornaments of differing forms and raw materials. It can be seen that all three necklace types display a wide range of wear conditions. The simple necklaces with beads of one material include many fresh or slightly worn items, although many of the beads had been recycled from spacer plate necklaces of jet, jet-like materials or amber. Amongst the composite necklaces with components of two raw materials there are relatively more worn or heavily worn items which probably have heirloom status. Once again, these heirlooms are often beads recycled from earlier spacer plate necklaces. This trend is not repeated however for the composite necklaces with items of more than two raw materials. In these necklaces there are relatively more fresh or slightly worn beads or ornaments. This may reflect the greater employment of new beads or ornaments belonging to mature Early Bronze Age types within these necklaces, and the lesser occurrence of recycled beads from spacer plate necklaces.

OBJECTS IN CHILD OR ADOLESCENT BURIALS

The third question to be explored using overall object condition is related to the presence of worn and very worn objects associated with child and adolescent burials. As a group this refers to all graves containing a burial of at least one individual under 18 years of age. In general, this has achieved mixed results. With regards to Beaker graves of children or adolescents, only three sites have analysed objects with an identifiable overall condition. Of these, only a single non-necklace object had a worn or very worn condition. Uneventfully, this consists of a single worn spatula from an adolescent male burial (Smerril Moor, Derbyshire). There is also a disc bead necklace with worn elements from the grave of a child at Folkton 245, 8, East Yorkshire. For Early Bronze Age sites, there is a larger sub-sample of sites, consisting of a total of 22 sites with objects with identifiable overall conditions, three of which are necklaces. Of these, eight sites were identified as having either worn or heavily worn items, one of which was a necklace site.

On the basis of observed wear against expected wear for object types and on specific wear characteristics on relevant objects, two sites have a high potential for heirloom presence. One of the most significant is the shale bead from Collingbourne Ducis G16, which is also the only object found in association with a child burial. There is evidence for strong thread-pull on the object, and this is also a relatively rare circumstance of a single bead not found as a component of a necklace. The worn amber and jet beads from Collingbourne Kingston G8 are also significant, given a further jet bead from the necklace found in association showed no use wear. Thus, the necklace appears to have been a mix of old and new objects alongside a child burial.

Although this approach has only identified four sites in total, at least two of the sites are highly indicative of an unusual pattern of object deposition in grave contexts. It seems highly unlikely that either the worn beads from Collingbourne Ducis G16 or the necklace components from Collingbourne Kingston G8 would be the result of wear during the life of the person they were ultimately deposited with. The presence of a single bead with the child burial at Collingbourne Ducis G16 is also highly indicative of some level of necklace fragmentation taking place, where an existing worn necklace was fragmented so that a bead could be deposited with the child.

FRAGMENTED OBJECTS

Although a number of fragmented objects have already been mentioned, a systematic approach to identifying all relevant fragmented objects can indicate further examples of potential heirloom objects. As with analysis of use-wear condition, only sites with a clear grave context were selected for analysis. In addition, only objects associated with inhumations were selected. In the case of cremated remains, although some may have been cremated *in situ*, many were likely to have been moved from the place of cremation to grave. Therefore, any objects burnt alongside the body may well have been fragmented due to heat and may not have been transported whole to the grave. In addition, few antiquarian excavators retained cremated remains, and any material intermixed with these remains will have been lost. This is a particular problem with fragmented bone objects whose fragments might not have been differentiated from fragments of human bone. Some objects were clearly added to deposits of cremated bone after the burning process but it has not always been possible to distinguish between burnt and unburnt items. Thus, only highly fragmented objects recorded in association with inhumations have been considered here. Fragmentation of necklaces is also explored, and evidence of fragmentation in this case includes the removal and re-organisation of whole components in addition to breakage of individual objects. For the purpose of the present analysis 'highly fragmented' objects have been defined on the basis of the presence of fractures and breaks identified as having taken place prior to final deposition and which have removed at least 20% of the original object.

By definition, fragmentation of a single object will result in at least two new objects, an original and a new fragment (or fragments). One, both (or even potentially neither) objects may remain in circulation after the act. Fragmentation can also arise when an object breaks because of prolonged and/or intensive use, resulting in both a heavily worn as well as fragmentary object. Although this fragmentation may not be deliberate, it still suggests that although broken, the object has sufficient importance to be retained or to be refashioned into an object with a new function. In many cases, the identification of very worn objects above has already identified fragmented objects which have continued in circulation after their deliberate or accidental fragmentation. On the other hand, a fragmented object displaying little wear is less straightforward, as it either represents a deliberate break grounded in social processes, or, more mundanely, the disposal of a broken object which is no longer functional. Further examination of the specific details of these objects is therefore necessary. In any case, either condition, that of a heavily worn and fragmented object, or that of an only slightly worn and fragmented object, when viewed in a closed context of an inhumation, potentially imparts some greater significance to the object. It was either too precious to discard after breakage, or its breakage could impart meaning into the new fragments. Thus, severe fragmentation (defined as being under 80% of original object present) marks out an object as having a high potential as an heirloom. Examples of specific object types are discussed below. A total of ten non-necklace Beaker-age and 22 non-necklace Early Bronze Age objects (from 10 sites) were identified as severely fragmented and are listed in Table 10.15. Of the ten identified non-necklace Beaker-age severely fragmented objects from inhumation contexts, seven are significant when specific details of each are examined more closely.

Beaker-age bracers

The bracer from Wellington Quarry, Herefordshire, is one of the most highly fragmented examples (Woodward and Hunter 2011, 140). Only a corner of the Wellington Quarry bracer remains, representing less than a quarter of the original piece. Examining the fractured surfaces of the bracer, however, there are no signs of re-working or smoothing. Thus, after fragmentation, the fragment was retained as it was, essentially as a non-functional fragment, until eventual deposition in a burial context. This is in sharp contrast to the bracer from Raunds 1, Northamptonshire, where there are clear signs of re-fashioning after fragmentation. Specifically, the main break across the width of the bracer has been polished and smoothed to form a new end, while one of the original perforations, broken sometime after manufacture was partially smoothed. In addition, there are two pairs of flakes on either side, at approximately the mid-point of the rear of the piece. The flakes themselves have a worn appearance and have clearly been smoothed, perhaps by string- or similar wear, and would suggest that the bracer

was re-hafted after breakage for use as a different object, perhaps as a tool.

Daggers and pommels

Pommels, frequently found heavily worn, are occasionally severely fragmented, including the Beaker-age whalebone pommel from Shrewton G5k. The top surface, the surface regularly on display, is very smooth from prolonged use. The tang or haft, however, shows less overall use, although one of the perforations used to attach the pommel to the dagger hilt has been broken and re-fashioned. This may suggest that the pommel broke from its dagger, or perhaps was removed from an original dagger and re-fashioned to attach to a new one. The latter would suggest that pommels had special significance, perhaps even more so than the daggers to which they belonged, and were thus important enough to retain and use for long periods (as evidenced by overall condition) and to be recycled as part of a new dagger and pommel set. The Beaker-age dagger from Shuttlestone, Derbyshire is also unusual as a significant portion of the blade leading to tip has been fractured off. The remaining tip, which represents a significant portion of the original dagger, was not found in the grave. Thus, either this missing fragment was retained as an heirloom after the dagger here was deposited in the grave, or *vice versa*. The Beaker-age dagger from Scamridge, North Yorkshire, on the other hand, has both severe damage to the hilt, resulting in the separation of rivets from the dagger, as well as two large fractures across the centre of the blade. These breaks appear to have occurred prior to deposition, and would suggest the dagger was severely broken but still retained for a period. Interestingly, the dagger itself shows little sign of actual wear and only slight signs of polishing and/ or re-sharpening. Thus, although broken and functionally useless, it may have remained in circulation for a time.

The Early Bronze Age whalebone pommel from Amesbury G85, Wiltshire is both heavily worn and fragmented. There is considerable damage to one side as well as to the base of the pommel. Nonetheless, it was found in association with an only slightly worn dagger. This suggests that the pommel either is an older piece attached to the dagger, or that the dagger itself was used largely for display only, and that the pommel received greater wear by virtue of being the only part of the dagger in a position to receive wear from nearby garments or handling.

Copper alloys

In the case of the Early Bronze Age decorated copper alloy earrings from Goodmanham 115,1, East Yorkshire, nearly half of one of the original earrings was missing at the time of deposition. There is considerable cracking running laterally along the piece, which would suggest regular use as an earring, receiving stress from repeated dressing and removal from the ear. The fragment that survives does not appear to remain functional, and was therefore placed in the grave after it had been broken. In the case of the copper

Table 10.15. List of all Beaker period and Early Bronze Age non-necklace objects displaying signs of severe fragmentation (80% or less of object surviving when deposited).

Site	Period	Object type	Material	Over 50% of object present?	Condition
Wellington Quarry, Marden, Herefordshire	Beaker	Bracer	Stone	No	Slightly worn
Raunds 1, Northants.	Beaker	Bracer	Stone	No	Very worn
Hemp Knoll, Wiltshire	Beaker	Toggle	Bone	No	Slightly worn
Folkton 245, burial 8, E. Yorkshire	Beaker	Belt ring/pulley object	Bone	Yes	Slightly worn
Shrewton G5k, Wiltshire	Beaker	Pommel	Bone	Yes	Very worn
Shuttlestone, Derbyshire	Beaker	Dagger/knife	Copper alloy	Yes	Slightly worn
Scamridge, N. Yorkshire	Beaker	Dagger/knife	Copper alloy	Yes	Slightly worn
Rudston 62, burial 4, E. Yorkshire	Beaker	Awl	Copper alloy	Yes	Indeterminate
Ferry Fryson 161, burial 9, W. Yorkshire	Beaker	Awl	Copper alloy	Yes	Indeterminate
Sewell, Bedfordshire	Beaker	Dress pin	Copper alloy	Yes	
Etton 82, burial 2, E. Yorkshire	EBA	Point	Bone	Yes?	Indeterminate
Bloxworth G4a, Dorset	EBA	Misc. object (pendant?)	Bone	No	Indeterminate
Norton Bavant Borrow Pit, Wiltshire	EBA	Belt hook	Bone	Yes	Very worn
Norton Bavant Borrow Pit, Wiltshire	EBA	Dagger/knife	Copper alloy	Yes	Indeterminate
Amesbury G85, Wiltshire	EBA	Pommel	Bone	Yes	Worn
Langton 2, burial 2, E. Yorkshire	EBA	Awl	Copper alloy	Yes?	Indeterminate
Goodmanham 115, burial 1, E. Yorkshire	EBA	Earring	Copper alloy	No	Worn
Preshute G1a, Wiltshire	EBA	Awl	Copper alloy	No?	Indeterminate
West Overton G1, Wiltshire	EBA	Dress pin	Copper alloy	Yes	Worn
Upton Lovell G1a, Wiltshire	EBA	Collection of points found in burial in association with adult male ('shaman' burial)	Bone	Number of points 80% or less = 13 of 50 analysed	Nearly all slightly worn

alloy dress pin from West Overton G1, there is a fracture across the lower part of the shaft resulting in a missing portion. As this fracture appears to be ancient, the pin may not have been usable as a dress pin after the event, or if used, the fragmentary nature of the object would be apparent, as was the case with the similar Beaker-age dress pin from Sewell, Bedfordshire.

This pin from Sewell, Bedfordshire is significant due to the nature of its missing components. Both a large portion of the lower shaft and decorated head are missing. Originally, the dress pin would have consisted of a head composed of two opposed spirals of bent metal, one of which is now missing. The fracture which caused the bottom half of the pin to be removed is not fresh, and therefore is likely to have occurred at some time before final deposition. Although this may not have resulted in the end of its use as a dress pin, such a break would have made use more difficult. The break at the head is similarly ancient, and would mean that if worn, the missing portion would have been obvious to anyone viewing the pin. Again, the item appears to have been significant enough to have been worn after fragmentation. Finally, although the missing portion of

the head of the pin may have been the result of general wear and tear (the object was overall quite worn), the possibility of the deliberate fragmentation of a distinctive decorative element such as this from the original piece should not be discounted. As an individual item, the decorative spiral portion of the original dress pin would have represented an easily identified synecdoche for the original.

Bone objects

The decorated Beaker-age bone toggle from Hemp Knoll, Wiltshire had been broken in half at some point in antiquity and, despite this, had continued in use. Although not displaying strong signs of extensive use wear, nearly all surfaces are polished, including the fractured surfaces which have a smooth appearance suggesting that breakage had occurred significantly before final deposition.

The Early Bronze Age bone points from Upton Lovell G1a deserve special attention as a collection of points from a single site where a significant proportion of objects are highly fragmented. A total of 49 bone points were found at various positions on the remains of an adult male and

13 of them (26%) display severe fragmentation. All the fragmented points have missing tips, and despite the high proportion of fragmented points none have any significant use wear. It has been suggested that these points formed fringes for a garment, worn by a shaman or other ceremonial figure. Given that these points are not tools, it is difficult to explain the cause of such widespread fragmentation within the collection. It seems more likely that the points were broken either deliberately or were broken over the course of a long period of regular display. Thus, fragmentation is linked either to special significance of the points or to their long curation as heirlooms.

Necklaces

Unlike single objects, which if fragmented may result in a non-functional object, individual beads can easily be moved from necklace to necklace without damaging the integrity of an individual bead. Thus, fragmentation can occur in a number of ways, including either through the removal of selected beads, the re-organisation of components taken from different necklaces, the addition of later beads to an existing bead set, or the re-fashioning and re-use of worn and/or broken beads into new necklaces. Thus, there is a much wider set of parameters by which potential heirlooms within a necklace can be identified than with individual objects.

Although not all of these processes may be recognisable in the archaeological record, there are observable patterns which can be used to detect fragmentation in necklaces. As already seen, differences in patterns of use wear have already resulted in the identification of several necklaces which are likely to have consisted of components of different ages brought together from several older necklaces. Yet to be explored, however, are the final two criteria proposed which are specific to necklaces, namely that: (1) heirloom necklace component(s) will be shaped differently from other components in the necklace (morphological variation) and (2) a necklace with heirloom components will display poor overall design symmetry (symmetry variation). Both morphology and symmetry will be considered in tandem. Looking at variation in Early Bronze Age necklace component shape and symmetry simultaneously, there are numerous cases where this variation appears to be significant. Furthermore, these variations can be further supported by observed wear patterns and fragmentation. All relevant necklaces have been considered in detail in Chapters 7 and 8. Here a few examples will be described in detail in order to illustrate the relevant points.

At Langton 2, 2, all three beads, which were found at the waist of an adult female, have both a different shape and composition. In addition, all three beads vary in overall condition, from fresh (fossil bead) to worn (jet bead) (Chapter 8, Figure 8.4.2). The necklace at Durrington G14 consists of three pestle pendants and a single oblate-shaped bead, found in place around the neck (Chapter 8, Figure 8.1.1). Although all four beads are only slightly worn the oblong bead, in addition to being a different shape, shows

clear signs of having a complex use life. The bead itself has been cut approximately in half such that the original perforation at the centre is visible in cross section, and the cut surface worked smooth. Thus, at some point the bead was broken or deliberately fragmented and then re-fashioned into a new bead.

At Preshute G1a, a complex collection of necklace components of varying shape and size are present (Chapter 7, Figure 7.1.9; Chapter 8, Figure 8.5.1). A range of different shapes and bead composition are present, including a barrel-shaped gold-ribbed shale bead, a gold-bound amber disc, a halberd pendant of gold and bronze, a fossil encrinite bead, two annular amber beads, a globular amber bead, a biconical shale bead shaped after a fossil ammonite, an annular stone bead, a globular stone bead and 150 shale disc beads. Three beads were found at the feet of the elderly female inhumation, while the remaining seven beads and the 150 disc beads were found behind the head. Looking more closely, if the relative size of some of the beads of similar shape are compared, further differences emerge. In the case of the annular beads of amber and stone, the two annular amber beads are different sizes, while the annular stone bead has a perforation much larger than the annular amber beads. When considered alongside the single beads of widely different shape already present, it is difficult to see how these beads could be strung together to form a single necklace of symmetrical design. In addition, it has already been shown that the globular stone bead is more heavily worn than the other necklace components. Thus, on grounds of wear, shape and symmetry, it is likely that these components were not originally strung as a single necklace.

At Wilsford G7, there is a similar pattern of highly mismatched necklace components (Chapter 8, Figure 8.4.1). Although the necklace position was not recorded, a total of 11 items was recovered in association with a primary inhumation burial in a shallow cist. The surviving necklace consists of four amber pendants, two decorated shale beads shaped like fossil ammonites, an axe-shaped jet pendant, a biconical gold-covered shale bead with ribbed decoration and finally a spherical gold-covered bead. The four amber pendants are significant as they vary considerably in both size and shape. In addition, one of them is highly fragmented, with an ancient break which has destroyed the perforations. Given the nature of the break, the object could not easily have been strung as a necklace component and as such may not have been a component of the necklace by the time of final deposition. None of the other components match the shapes of the four amber pendants, and there is no evident symmetry in design using any of the components, amber or otherwise. For example, although there are two gold-covered beads present, one is much larger than the other, their decorative patterns are different, one is oblate and the other spherical, and finally their method of suspension is completely different, with one having been strung through the top of the bead rather than straight through the middle. Although the decorated shale beads are both shaped after fossil ammonites, one has more heavy wear in the form of thread softening at perforation edges and in the form of increased polishing-out of decorated surfaces.

At Shrewton G5j, a composite necklace was found around the neck of a mature female inhumation (Chapter 8, Figure 8.3.1). There are a total of 11 surviving beads including two decorated pestle-shaped ?lignite toggle beads, one fusiform ?lignite bead, six annular amber beads (of an original total of about 50), a single shell bead of *Littorina littoralis* and an amber pendant. Significant variation in overall condition has already been identified, with the pestle-shaped and fusiform beads and the amber pendant exhibiting greater wear than the other annular beads. The examined annular beads and the shell bead show only slight signs of smoothing around perforation edges. However, one amber bead has what appears to be an ancient major break on one side, resulting in a significantly smaller bead than at manufacture. Thus, it is possible that the fusiform and pestle-shaped toggle beads are older objects, along with at least one annular amber bead. Additionally, although both are decorated, the design on each of the two pestle-shaped toggle beads differs. One has a triple band of grooves on the upper side below the top surface, while the other has only a single band. The top of the latter bead bears two intersecting bands of closely-packed grooves forming a cruciform pattern, while the top of the other bead has a more complex pattern of intersecting wide bands forming a cruciform shape but which intersects off-centre on the top surface. The difference in decorative design may suggest that the two objects were not originally part of a set within the necklace observed at final deposition. Although wear patterns and decorative characteristics amongst analysed beads differs, the necklace, if in fact re-organised using new components as is suggested, still possesses a symmetrical necklace arrangement. Although the beads had been disturbed they appear to have been worn immediately below the neck of a middle-aged woman, possibly arranged in the order illustrated in the excavation report (Green and Rollo-Smith 1984, fig. 28). The larger lignite bead was flanked by the pair of pestle pendants and then by the other fusiform bead and shell, with various numbers of the small amber beads interspersed between them.

Using undisturbed inhumations, it is clear that a significant proportion of the necklaces recovered from Early Bronze Age burial contexts have characteristics which suggest their circulation within a complex process of manufacture, assembly, use, fragmentation, re-assembly, and then deposition. If we were to include evidence for fragmentation in necklaces from cremation contexts then we can see that many other necklaces are likely to have undergone similar processes as those emphasised here.

Individual beads

Another end result of the process of fragmentation and re-assembly of necklace components is the deposition of individual beads which have been separated from all other beads from the original or re-assembled necklaces. Thus, the presence of an individual bead in a closed grave context, namely undisturbed inhumations, can also reflect a high heirloom potential.

Single sites from the Beaker period have an individual bead or a pommel without a dagger. A total of six sites have been identified from the Early Bronze Age, five with beads and a sixth with a pommel. The first Early Bronze Age site is Rudston 63, burial 10, East Yorkshire, where a single fossil ammonite bead fragment was found in front of the face of an adult male inhumation. Also found in front of the face was a Food Vessel and a barbed and tanged arrowhead. At Sherburn 106, burial 1 a single clay bead was found in association with a grave containing up to 15 inhumations. The only other objects present included a bone point and a flint arrowhead, the latter found inside a skull of one of the bodies. At Idmiston G25e, Wiltshire a cylindrical bead of unspecified composition was found associated with a child inhumation, and perhaps an urn of unspecified type. A single stone bead or ring was found at Warminster G13, Wiltshire in association with a double inhumation burial with no other finds. At Shuttlestone, Derbyshire a jet or jet-like bead was found at the head of a Beaker-age mature male inhumation burial. Also associated with the inhumation was a copper alloy dagger, an axe of unspecified composition, and organic material including animal skins and ferns. The dagger is notable as it has already been identified above as severely fragmented.

Perhaps the best Early Bronze Age example is from Collingbourne Ducis G16, Wiltshire where a single biconical jet or jet-like bead was found near the breast of a child inhumation, in association with a handled cup. Overall, the condition of the bead is worn, with thread-smoothing within the perforation and a slight thread-pull groove on one side. Most importantly, there is considerable sheen around both perforations, caused by bead-on-bead wear. It is also important to note that this site has already been identified as having high heirloom potential, as it was a site with a worn object in association with a child burial.

At Galley Low, Derbyshire, a pommel was found at the head of an inhumation, in association with two urns of unspecified type and a Food Vessel. Although the pommel surfaces are partially obscured by lacquer and erosion, there is extensive polishing wear across the top and sides, resulting in a very worn overall condition. This overall condition follows a similar pattern to other pommels from both Beaker and Early Bronze Age contexts, and the presence of a heavily worn pommel in a closed context without an accompanying dagger represents one of the best examples of an heirloom object in our study.

CONCLUSIONS

This chapter has investigated the evidence for the existence of heirlooms within grave groups of Beaker and Early Bronze Age date. For the purpose of this analysis the term heirloom has been defined as an object which has been identified as having been either circulated, exchanged, used and/or curated over an extensive period of time, probably spanning more than one generation. The identification of heirlooms therefore relies on examining evidence for use of objects over time and evidence for their fragmentation into smaller entities that may have been retained for future exchange and curation. A series of criteria have been investigated, and the main results are summarised below.

- *an heirloom is more likely to be in a very worn condition than a non-heirloom object*

In the Beaker period the artefact categories that display most wear, and are therefore most likely to have functioned as heirlooms are Series 1 daggers, pommels, belt rings/pulley objects and sponge finger stones. Other categories where heirlooms may have been common are pommels, toggles, earrings, dress pins and the single gold ornament. In the Early Bronze Age the artefact categories that display most wear are pommels, perforated stones, spatulae and complex dress pins. Categories which may also fall into this bracket are grooved stones, worked stones, handles and tools, antlers and earrings and, probably, gold ornaments. Thus, in both periods, pommels, spatulae, earrings and complex dress pins have high heirloom potential, while V-perforated buttons display medium potential. It could be argued that objects designed to be used as tools might well accrue heavy wear from use within a single lifetime, and thus worn tools might not have actually functioned as heirlooms. This argument might apply to the sponge finger stones, the spatulae, grooved and worked stones, and the bone tools. The main categories of high heirloom potential would then be the pommels, belt rings, toggles and other ornaments, plus the bone and antler handles and, probably, the gold ornaments.

- *an heirloom is likely to have a comparatively more heavily worn condition than associated objects within the same grave assemblage*

Suitable wear data is available for 37 Beaker graves containing non-necklace objects and 47 of Early Bronze Age date. Within the Beaker sample, 22% of the graves contained the combination of fresh/slightly worn and very worn items, indicative of the presence of one or more heirlooms, and 10% contained items displaying all three wear categories. Thus a total of 12 graves (32%) out of the 37 are likely to have contained heirlooms. Amongst the Early Bronze Age graves, 17% of the graves contained the combination of fresh/slightly worn and very worn items, indicative of the presence of one or more heirlooms, and 11% contained items displaying all three wear categories. Thus a total of 13 graves (28%) out of the 47 are most likely to have contained heirlooms. In a further ten Early Bronze Age grave groups which contain both non-necklace items and necklaces, 10% of the non-necklace elements display a combination of all three wear categories and a further 10% have the combination of fresh/slightly worn and very worn items. Thus a total of two of these graves (20%) are most likely to have contained heirlooms. The graves containing objects of all three wear categories occur consistently between the two periods, while those with fresh/slight and very worn items are slightly more common

in the Beaker period. Thus the practice of depositing heirlooms in graves appears to have been common in both periods. Not only was the practice highly evident already in the Beaker period, but also the level of incidence of non-necklace heirloom deposition seems to have stayed relatively stable throughout the two periods.

- *heirloom necklace component(s) will be comparatively more heavily worn than other components within the same necklace*

The incidence of variations in wear amongst the beads belonging to necklaces has been recorded and discussed fully in Chapters 7 and 8. In this chapter the data relating to the different classes of necklace has been summarised in a series of tables. Data relating to a total of 74 have been considered. The necklaces showing least wear of all are those made up from jet or jet-like disc beads. There are no very worn items recorded, and heirloom items are probably not present, or are only very rare. The spacer plate necklaces of jet or jet-like materials also show a high percentage of unworn beads, but heirloom elements are often present alongside these. These heirlooms are often the spacer plates themselves. The spacer plate and other complex necklaces made from amber generally include more worn items. None of the few surviving examples seem to be original compositions, and the vast majority of the spacer plates appear to be heirlooms recycled from earlier necklaces.

The smaller necklace types contain either components of a single material, but of different shapes, or a mixture of beads and ornaments of differing forms and raw materials. These necklace types display a wide range of wear conditions. The simple necklaces with beads of one material only include many fresh or slightly worn items, although many of the beads had been recycled from spacer plate necklaces of jet, jet-like materials or amber. Amongst the composite necklaces with components of two raw materials there are relatively more worn or heavily worn items which probably have heirloom status. Once again, these heirlooms are often beads recycled from earlier spacer plate necklaces. This trend is not repeated however for the composite necklaces with items of more than two raw materials. In these necklaces there are relatively more fresh or slightly worn beads or ornaments. This may reflect the greater employment of new beads or ornaments belonging to mature Early Bronze Age types within these necklaces, and the lesser occurrence of recycled beads from spacer plate necklaces.

- *objects from a grave containing a child or adolescent which display a worn or very worn overall condition are less likely to be related to use wear from use by that individual than the same objects found in an adult or mature adult grave*

Although this approach has only identified four sites in total, at least two of the sites are highly indicative of an unusual pattern of object deposition in grave contexts. It seems highly unlikely that either the worn beads from

Collingbourne Ducis G16 or the necklace components from Collingbourne Kingston G8 would be the result of wear during the life of the person they were ultimately deposited with. The presence of a single bead with the child burial at Collingbourne Ducis G16 is also highly indicative of some level of necklace fragmentation taking place, where an existing worn necklace was fragmented so that a bead could be deposited with the child.

- *an heirloom is likely to be more highly fragmented (or incomplete) than a non-heirloom object*

For the purpose of the present analysis highly fragmented objects have been defined on the basis of the presence of fractures and breaks identified as having taken place prior to final deposition and which have removed at least 20% of the original object. Of the ten identified non-necklace Beaker period severely fragmented objects from inhumation contexts, seven are significant when specific details of each are examined more closely. Of the 22 identified highly fragmented objects from ten inhumation contexts in the Early Bronze Age, four cases proved to be significant when specific details were examined.

- *heirloom necklace component(s) may display shape characteristics which differ from other components within the same necklace*
- *a necklace composed of one or more heirlooms may display less overall design symmetry*

Looking at variation in Early Bronze Age necklace component shape and symmetry simultaneously, there are numerous cases where this variation appears to be significant. The evidence for five necklaces has been treated in detail in this chapter and relevant details for other necklaces may be found in Chapters 7 and 8. There are also six instances of worn single beads found as goods in Early Bronze Age graves and these also provide firm evidence for the presence of heirlooms.

As a result it can be seen that the evidence examined in relation to each of the various criteria proposed has shown clear and extensive evidence for the existence of the deposition of heirlooms within the grave assemblages studied. And it is clear that the practice of venerating old, and sometimes refurbished, items in this way was already well established in the Beaker period. However in terms of regional variation, the data suggests the practice across all regions throughout both periods was not universal. In the case of our main three regions (East Yorkshire, the Peak District and Wessex), although the total percentage of sites with potential heirlooms remains fairly stable, the practice in the Peak District is considerably more uncommon in the Beaker period. This disparity is not maintained into the Early Bronze Age, however, although total absolute site numbers are low for the Peak District region. Wessex sites maintain high values in comparison to other regions throughout both periods, and this is probably due to the fact that a significant number of the fragmented necklaces examined come from this region.

Of particular note is that in many cases, pommels are nearly always more heavily worn than their accompanying daggers. A total of seven out of ten total sites with analysed pommels and daggers with identifiable overall conditions have pommels that are more heavily worn than daggers. At a further two sites the overall wear is the same. This supports the notion that daggers with pommels were objects of display rather than for regular use. Given a number of daggers have evidence for sheaths, it seems likely that the pommel received the most regular wear as the only part of the dagger regularly handled and rubbed against the body or clothing. In addition, a small number of pommels are also orphaned from their original dagger, and at least some pommels were also refitted to more than one dagger over the course of their use life.

Although the presence of worn objects alongside child and adolescent burials has been considered, the opposite condition, the presence of fresh and slightly worn objects alongside mature burials deserves a brief mention. Contrary to the curation of objects as heirlooms, this would suggest the manufacture of some objects specifically for deposition within the grave. A total of seven Beaker and eight Early Bronze Age sites have slightly worn objects alongside a mature burial, representing a total of 26 objects. However, only a few of these objects have conditions which are unexpected for their object type, a condition which would suggest a high potential for having been manufactured for deposition. The exceptions are two slightly worn V-perforated buttons from a mature male Beaker inhumation at Acklam Wold 124, interment 4, East Yorkshire, two further slightly worn V-perforated buttons from a mature Early Bronze Age male inhumation from Acklam Wold 123, East Yorkshire, and a slightly worn bone tool from a mature female inhumation from Garton-on-the-Wolds 162, interment 3, East Yorkshire. At this stage and given these parameters, it is difficult to suggest that there was a widespread practice of object manufacture for grave deposition. Indeed, in terms of analysed objects, a total of only 26 Beaker and 14 Early Bronze Age objects and four necklaces come from mature graves.

It is worth pointing out, however, that there are a number of factors which act to limit the evidence derived from analysis in this chapter. First and foremost, the composition of an object has an important role in determining the rate and visibility of use wear. For example, jet is overall a soft material, and wear will appear sooner on jet objects than objects of much harder material such as stone. Thus, a bracer or whetstone which displays significant use wear can reasonably be considered very heavily used in comparison against a heavily worn jet object. In addition, the surface of some material types is not conducive to preservation of surface patterns of use wear. This was most common amongst object of amber and copper alloy, both of which suffer from surface oxidisation which obscures wear patterns. Thus, object surface condition was an important factor in limiting the total number of available sites for heirloom analysis. As already outlined, the act of cremation appears to have included the burning of some grave objects, resulting in the obscuring of surface wear and potentially damaging an object such that a heavier wear classification and/or greater fragmentation might be imposed than was actually the case.

Analysis here has worked to mitigate these issues in a number of different ways. The first method has been to consider expected use wear values for all object types, which reflects the expected wear based on object function as well as composition. Although this was beyond the scope of the project, supplementing this approach by conducting a detailed observation of use wear on experimental reproductions of objects in different compositions, and by recording the differences in rate of use wear, would have provided further data for comparative analysis.

11. OBJECT FUNCTION

(with David Bukach)

MORPHOLOGY, MATERIAL AND MANUFACTURE

The relationship between object function and morphology is usually a very simple and direct one, with the shape and size of the item designed with a particular practical function in mind. Thus beads will be relatively small, perforated and usually rounded in shape, spacer plates flat, buttons round and perforated, dress pins long, narrow and pointed, pendants flat and with a single perforation near the top, daggers long, tapering and pointed and spatulae long, flat and narrow. How such categories of object could be made however would depend very much on the choice of material or materials employed.

Raw materials

The occurrence of the use of different raw materials for the manufacture of objects belonging to various categories is summarised in Table 11.1, and some observations on the use of each material can be made. It can immediately be seen from this table that some raw materials were used for many more object types than others, and also that certain object categories employed a wide range of materials. The categories that used most variation in materials were composite necklaces (and individual beads), and pendants, followed by V-perforated buttons and button sets, pommels and belt hooks, rings and pulleys. A further series of categories employed two different raw materials only: including dress pins, earrings/tress rings, fasteners and studs. Of particular interest are the items that combined two or more raw materials in a single object: various pendants and the gold-covered shale cones. In general it can be noted that items of personal adornment tend to employ a wider range of materials per category than other items of personal equipment. In the latter grouping, many categories are made from one raw material only, and that is most often stone or animal bone. Table 11.1 also demonstrates that the raw materials used for the greatest number of object categories were animal bone and jet and similar jet-like materials, followed by bronze, stone and amber.

Metal

Gold and copper alloy were the best materials for making objects of complex shape, such as daggers or complicated pins, or items that need to be particularly thin, such as earrings/hair tresses or bracelets. In addition the medium lends itself to the production of fine decoration, either incorporated in a casting or through repoussé or engraved working by hand. Copper alloy was also used to make items which needed a particularly fine, and relatively long-lasting point, such as the awls.

Jet and jet-like materials

Jet, shale, lignite and cannel coal are relatively soft materials which could be shaped, perforated and polished. These materials were therefore ideal for the production of rings, all kinds of beads, spacer plates, pendants, studs and objects with V-perforations such as the buttons and cones. Although the high sheen of polished jet and jet-like materials is decorative in itself, the materials also lend themselves to incised decoration, which occurs on certain classes of item (see below).

Amber

Like jet and similar jet-like materials, amber could be worked into various shapes and could be perforated and polished with relative ease. It was used for a similar range of items of personal adornment: rings, beads, spacer plates and V-perforated buttons. Incised decoration is very rare, but the transparent nature of the original material meant that decorative effects could be achieved through patterns of drilling within flat spacer plates.

Stone

The varieties of stone selected were chosen both for their ease of working, and for their texture and colour. Thus foliation characteristics were important, as well as a degree of hardness that would allow perforation by hand to be achieved. Stone beads are fairly rare, but form important components in some necklaces; there is also one decorated V-perforated button. Stone is also used for fine items which would have been partly decorative as well as functional,

Table 11.1. The occurrence of raw materials within object categories.

Category	Bronze	Gold	Jet and jet-like material	Amber	Stone	Bone	Fossil/ shell	Clay	Faience	Total
Equipment										
Dagger/knife	*									1
Pommel		*		*		*				3
Sponge finger stone					*					1
Grooved stone					*					1
Perforated stone					*					1
Spatula						*				1
Awl	*									1
Bone point						*				1
Tweezers						*				1
Bone tube						*				1
Bone plate						*				1
Toggle						*				1
Handle/tool						*				1
Antler						*				1
Bronze axe	*									1
Personal adornment										
Bracer		*			*					2
Belt hook	*	*				*				3
Belt/pulley ring			*	*		*				3
Tusk/tooth						*				1
V-perf. button			*	*	*	*				4
Button set			*	*	*					3
Earring	*	*								2
Dress pin	*					*				2
Stud			*					*		2
Single bead			*	*	*	*				4
Pendant	*	*	*	*		*				5
Neckring/ bracelet	*		*							2
Special item	*	*	*							3
Necklace	*	*	*	*	*	*	*	*	*	9
Fastener			*			*				2
Spacer plate			*	*		*				3
Totals	**10**	**7**	**11**	**8**	**8**	**19**	**1**	**2**	**1**	**67**

such as bracers and some of the perforated whetstones. Otherwise stone was used mainly for whetstones and grooved stones of a more directly functional nature.

Animal bone/antler
This range of raw materials was used amongst a very wide range of object categories; it reflects the great variety of shapes and textures of bones, teeth and antler available for use, and the relative softness of the material which can be cut and worked fairly easily. Bone was used for items of personal adornment, ranging from beads, dress pins, fasteners, spacer plates, toggles, belt hooks, pendants and a few V-perforated buttons. However most bone objects fall into the group of other personal equipment: points, spatulae, modified tusks and teeth, pommels, tweezers, handles and tools, tubes, plates and slightly modified antlers.

Flint
Flint can be made, relatively easily, into very fine and thin artefacts, such as the barbed-and-tanged arrowheads and flint daggers, which are the categories recorded in the present study.

Fired clay
Ceramic materials were used for a small number of items of personal adornment, such as beads and studs. Most clay items are pottery vessels. Clay is by its nature a highly malleable and versatile raw material, which can be formed into a very wide variety of shapes, and also is conducive to many techniques of decoration.

Other materials
A few further materials were used particularly for the manufacture of beads, or use as amulets. These included natural materials such as fossils, sea and fresh water shells, and also faience. Fossils and shells may possess natural perforations or have been perforated intentionally for use as beads. Faience beads were made from a particularly special material which was fairly difficult to produce; it was employed for special forms of beads and pendants, which could be shaped prior to firing by hand, or moulded around a perishable former such as a stick.

Colour

Many of the grave goods were brightly coloured, shiny and lustrous and this trend increased from the Beaker period through to the mature Early Bronze Age. It seems highly probable that, apart from purely aesthetic considerations, these bright colours may also have possessed symbolic power. Thus colour may have been closely related to the specific function of an object. This aspect of Early Bronze Age grave goods has been discussed fully in recent years (Woodward 2000, 111–3; Jones 2002; Sheridan and Shortland 2003). The most preferred colour appears to have been golden or silver; this would have been represented by all items of metalwork, such as daggers, pins and awls, in their original state, as well as the special ornaments made from gold itself. Red and black were also commonly represented. Red items included ornaments made from amber as well as certain beads and bracers made from carefully selected red stones and nodules of haematite, which may have been used to colour clothing or human skin. The colour black relates mainly to items made from jet or jet-like materials or, once again, stone tools or other equipment made from specific black or very dark grey stone. In contrast to the red and black items, many other pieces were white or cream in colour. These included myriad beads, rings and other ornaments or tools made from bone, shell and fossils, or from chalk and other white stones. Brown was another common colour, usually characteristic of objects made from stone, such as battle-axes, or antler.

Against the juxtapositions of red/gold and black/white colour schemes, one further colour would have stood out. This was the bright turquoise blue of the faience beads: the result of a truly dramatic technical development during the mature Early Bronze Age period (Sheridan and Shortland 2004). The selection of special green and blue-tinged rocks had been evidenced since the Neolithic, notably by the use of the green jadeitite and Langdale tuff rocks for the manufacture of axe heads (Sheridan 2007d; Bradley and Edmonds 1993). Many of these undoubtedly possessed symbolic importance, and this trend was continued into the Beaker period with the use of a distinctly blue-tinged amphibolite-rich rock for a series of bracers (Woodward and Hunter 2011). It is not possible to know what exactly the different colours might have symbolised in the Early Bronze Age. However, in many different human societies around the world the colour red is associated with blood and danger, flesh and fertility and black with darkness and death. White often denotes bones, hardness and light but can also be connected to human milk. Thus white may signify female against red which denotes male. However, in many Early Bronze Age graves red and white objects occur together, so any such simple system is unlikely to apply in any rigid manner to the data considered in this volume. For Iron Age Britain it has been suggested that the colour of red enamel was associated with males, and the blue of glass beads with females (Giles 2008, 72–3), so it is interesting to note that the gender associations for blue faience beads in Britain are almost exclusively female (Sheridan and Shortland 2004, 267). Unfortunately, many

Early Bronze Age graves contain beads of both blue and red materials, so a simple gender correlation cannot be discerned for our subject material.

Physical properties

Several of the materials that came to be used more often in the Early Bronze Age period possessed physical properties that may have been perceived to be magical in quality (Shepherd 1985, 204; Woodward 2000, 109–111; Sheridan and Shortland 2003). Such magical qualities may have enhanced the function of special items of dress as well as objects used in ritual enactments. The brightness and shine of gold, and of newly-made bronze objects, would have been highly distinctive and impressive to the eye, and the very means of production of bronze and of faience, using high temperature methods, will have appeared to be a magical process. Amber and jet were special substances in a quite different way, due to their property of static electricity. When rubbed with certain materials such as textiles or fur, significant electrostatic energy is released. In addition, jet and amber can be burnt as a form of incense. It is also believed that amber possesses therapeutic properties. Hippocrates recommended amber oil as a stimulant, for the relief of asthma, or as liniment for chest complaints, and Dr Joan Evans recorded that, in 1922 Mayfair, amber necklaces were still being sold as curatives for croup, whooping cough and asthma (Woodward 2000, 109). Applications such as these may also have been appreciated in prehistory.

Decoration

A further important and informative aspect of object morphology is the incidence and nature of applied decoration. Items which do not carry decoration mainly belong within the categories of personal equipment rather than items of adornment, and include all types of whetstone, sponge finger stones, copper alloy awls, bone points and spatulae, tubes, bone plates, bone tools and handles. Toggles also are seldom decorated. Decoration occurs mainly on items of personal adornment and is invariably linear or geometric in nature, and usually incised. Such designs occur on gold hair tresses and sheet plates, copper alloy earrings, selected V-perforated buttons, spacer plates, gold-covered cones, dress pins, occasional tusk ornaments, many forms of pendant, occasional beads, and belt and pulley rings made from jet or jet-like materials. Simple outlining linear decoration is also sometimes found on items of other personal equipment, such as the gold pommel and some of the sets of tweezers. The most complex decorative schemes, which often incorporate lozenges infilled with pointillé or punctulated shading, are found on spacer plates of jet and jet-like materials or bone, whilst the accompanying necklace beads are usually plain and depend on their high sheen for their visual impact. Sometimes decoration appears to be skeuomorphic in nature. For instance, there are beads with finely ribbed decoration which appears to copy the ribs on fossil encrinites, which were also employed as beads, or the ribbing on ammonites. However most of the linear and geometric motifs and designs were those that had been used to decorate Beaker vessels. Some of the earliest items with complex decoration were the spacer plates within necklaces made from Whitby jet, and these were current in the north of England from before *c.* 2000 cal BC, well within the currency of the later styles of Beaker. These stylistic links, and the relationships between jet spacer necklaces and gold lunulae, were fully discussed by Shepherd (1973, Chapter 5; 1985, 214).

Most items found in Beaker graves tend to be undecorated, although the gold earrings, some buttons and pulley rings are exceptions to this pattern. In the mature Early Bronze Age there is an explosion of decorative craftsmanship, especially on items of personal adornment. This is visible not least on daggers, where the decoration is rather different from the styles already described and is the subject of more detailed discussion here. Use of elaborate moulds allowed the production of sets of grooves following the blade outline as well as mid-ribs of complex cross section, which would have served a decorative as well as functional purpose. Some of the groove sets were ogival in shape, and provide the only examples of curvilinear decoration within the Early Bronze Age repertoire. Some daggers of Series 5 were also embellished with pointillé decoration, and this provides a stylistic link to the filled triangles and lozenges found on other items, as discussed above. Advances in bronze technology also led to the first occurrences of some very special techniques which incorporated a decorative aspect, namely the twisting of shaft and bars, and the production of interlocking rings.

Daggers (with Stuart Needham; see also Chapter 3.1)
There is one category of objects where varying details of morphology may inform the question of functionality, and this is daggers, knives and razors. There is much uncertainty about the significance and validity of the bipartite division into 'daggers' and 'knife-daggers' (or 'knives'). A further complication arises from the potential function of smaller blades being either knives or razors, or both. The dagger/knife conundrum lies partly in whether there is a real dimensional or style break between the two categories. Any divisions on the lines of dimension or style are unlikely to be consistent over all phases of these implements; with a span of roughly nine centuries it is highly unlikely that expressions of intended functional differentiation would be unchanging. The validity of any differentiation is therefore best considered for each phase-group in its own right. Neither category need have had a single function, and the functional range of the two might even have overlapped. A second question often posed concerns the effectiveness of many blades, including some normally called daggers, as real daggers.

Series 1: Tanged flat blade (copper)
The lengths vary widely. It appears that only a small minority of the implements were daggers, the majority being knives.

Series 2: Butt-riveted flat blade
These blades are usually referred to as daggers, despite the fact that many are not particularly long and have relatively obtuse tips. Nevertheless, this label is valuable in distinguishing them from the contemporary but smaller butt-riveted 'knife-daggers'.

Series 3: Butt-riveted, lenticular section blade (Armorico-British and related forms)
Many are fairly long implements and, combined with their acute shape, they can be usefully described as 'daggers'. No small-sized implements mimic this style, so there is evidently no 'knife-dagger' equivalent.

Series 4: Butt-riveted, ribbed flat blade
As for Series 3, the great majority of these are eminently suitable to function as daggers. There are a number of butt-riveted 'knife-daggers' with midribs of varying character which could, arguably, be diminutives related to this series.

Series 5: Butt-riveted thick blade
The Camerton-Snowshill daggers (5D) are stout blades with a wide size range and are not apparently suited to a stabbing function. Occasional small-sized blades have points of resemblance, but only one has all the key attributes to suggest it is a diminutive Camerton-Snowshill blade. However, some other variants (5C2 and 5E1) are consistently long. Many of these also taper quickly to slender lower blades and thus begin to look like effective stabbing weapons.

Series 6 and Series 7: Tanged and Butt-riveted small blade implements
The classification of small blades is highly problematic. They can be relatively easily divided into those with riveted butts, hafted in the manner of the larger daggers, and those with tangs, with or without a securing rivet. The full set of labels that has been applied in the past is: knives, knife-daggers, razors, or razor-knives. One group tends to be associated with very fine edges – these implements are generally accepted as capable of shaving, and are usually called 'tanged razors'. Other Series 6 blades are more substantial in the mid-blade zone and could have served well as knives, in some cases also having a sharp tip for piercing.

It can be concluded that all the small blades (of Series 6 and 7), probably those of Series 1 and a proportion of the other dagger types may have functioned as knives rather than as stabbing weapons. Some recent research has suggested that many Early Bronze Age daggers in northern Europe as a whole may have been used to slaughter cattle or other livestock, rather than functioning as weapons to kill human adversaries. Thus they may be perceived as implements employed in ritual sacrifice, and symbols of high office, rather than daggers wielded in combat (Skak-Nielsen 2009). The fact that use wear studies in the current project have recorded examples of blades which have been consistently sharpened on one side only (see below) might add weight to such an interpretation.

Manufacture

Apart from the topics of basic shaping of objects, and the application of decoration, which have been covered in the previous sections, the other main aspect of manufacture which may relate to object function is fineness of craftsmanship. Consideration of this aspect needs to include discussion of surface finish, the manufacture of perforations, the employment of novel techniques and the overall complexity of manufacture amongst the different object categories defined.

It can be observed that amongst many of the categories studied, a highly polished surface finish was both desired and achieved. This applied to polished items of bronze, the careful polishing of objects of jet, amber and stone, all of which were usually more finely finished on the front surfaces, and to the original surfaces of the specially produced glassy blue faience. Some bone materials were naturally shiny, and some bone items were deliberately polished as well. However certain other materials, notably tusks, teeth and antler, and also fossils were retained with their natural surfaces, which presumably were valued for their symbolic content. As so many of the objects made were intended for adornment of the body, they needed to be perforated in order to facilitate attachment, whether within necklaces or to garments, belts, headdresses or other items of costume. The technology of perforating raw materials therefore became extremely important and specific techniques were developed to produce suitable drill holes in jet, jet-like materials, amber, stone and bone. The tools used were probably of flint, but different tool sets would have been used for the different materials. Detailed descriptions and discussion of the techniques that may have been used for the polishing and drilling of amber and jet have been provided by Shepherd (1985, 205–210) and Sheridan *et al.* (2003).

The relative value of an item in functional terms may have been related to the time taken to produce the item by the craftsmen or team of craftsmen. To assess any differences between the time taken to manufacture different single objects a substantial programme of experimental work would need to be undertaken. Such a programme did not fall within the remit of the current project. However a few preliminary observations on this topic can be advanced. The degree of non-functional use of any object may be related to the overall complexity of its manufacture. Following this premise, the working of different raw materials may be broken down into three possible groups as follows:

Complex manufacture: high temperature processes for bronze (especially two-piece moulds for some daggers) and faience; twisting of bronze rods; interlocking bronze rings; very fine decoration e.g. on gold plates; the production of small items incorporating several different raw materials.

Manufacture of medium complexity: cold working, drilling and decoration of items made from jet and jet-like materials or amber; shaping and decoration of more simple gold items.

Simple manufacture: cold shaping, and occasional decoration, of bone/ivory/teeth/antler items; shaping, polishing and perforation of carefully selected stone materials.

From this simple categorisation it can be concluded that there may well have been a relationship with the complexity of manufacture and the non-utilitarian function of any of the objects studied.

USE WEAR
Equipment

Daggers/knives (Chapter 3.1)

For most Series, overall wear was categorised as slightly worn in many cases. This statistic was roughly similar for blades belonging to Series 4, 5 and 7. However, the Beaker-age Series 1 (tanged copper) daggers appeared to be overall more worn, while those of Series 3 displayed a higher level of slight wear, and for the flat riveted daggers of Series 2, 81% of those where wear could be determined are only slightly worn.

Most traces of use wear related to general wear on the blade surfaces and thus to length of use. Variations in wear on the blade edges and points were not apparent, although sometimes one blade edge had been used and/ or resharpened more often than the other edge. It has not been possible therefore to determine whether the points were more worn than the blade edges, i.e. whether the items had been used primarily as knives or razors, or as thrusting implements or weapons. However, the presence of sharpening of a single edge of the blade may indicate that they were used primarily as knives designed for cutting rather than for stabbing. Wear on the mid-rib, and on decoration in that location, may relate to the repeated drawing of the blade from a scabbard, or have resulted from fabric rub.

Pommels (Chapter 3.2)

Almost all those studied are worn or very worn, with a high complement of examples in the very worn category. In addition to this, in six cases there was evidence that ancient breaks or other damage had been smoothed out, polished over or otherwise reworked. And in most of these cases the modification of the tang or lower slot may have related to the need to fit the pommel to a subsequent dagger. Thus they show signs of extreme wear and often were re-used. In other words, the pommels themselves may have been more valuable than the metal knife and dagger blades to which they were attached. Finds of pommels still attached to blades confirm that these objects were designed to function as decorative terminals to hilts, but it has been demonstrated that pommels were sometimes converted for use on a series of two or more subsequent blades, and also that individual pommels (without the dagger) were sometimes deposited as independent valuables.

Sponge finger stones (Chapter 4.1)

All the sponge finger stones made from hard rock have been used extensively, and they seem to have functioned as tools. Usually one end was used in a repetitive smoothing or polishing action, and it may be that some of the polish on the surfaces also resulted from such use. It has been suggested that such tools had been used in leather working (Smith and Simpson 1966, 134), and our detailed studies would confirm such a hypothesis. Certainly the stones had been held in one hand and worn down relatively slightly against a fairly soft material, and had not been used for whetting metal. The shape of the working end is reminiscent of some tools still used by cobblers in the finishing of leather boots and shoes, although a more general purpose in the treating of leather for garments, bags or pouches and/or containers may be indicated for these prehistoric examples. In two cases the stones occurred as pairs in the grave. The chalk piece is totally fresh and may have been made as a replica item for deposition in the grave.

Grooved stones (Chapter 4.2)

These objects have previously been interpreted as arrowshaft-straighteners. However this seems unlikely as the grooves are very shallow, and certainly not semi-circular in profile. Also, if the arrowshafts in use were in the order of 7 to 10mm in diameter, as surviving examples might imply (Clark 1963, 74), then the grooves on these stones would be over-large for the purpose. Grooved stones are, in fact, rarely associated with flint arrowheads and instead tend to occur in well-furnished graves which contain metal items alongside other unusual pieces of equipment made from bone or antler. The specific shape does suggest that they were designed for a particular purpose, logically for reducing the surfaces of longitudinal shafts, probably made from wood or bone. They could have been used to trim thicker shafts for other implements, such as mace-heads or battle-axes. Some of the grooves are not completely straight, and it may be that stones with such grooves were employed in the general production of various tools and equipment made from bone or wood. Such tools may have been for animal skin working (Moore and Rowlands 1972, 45), or even functioned as multi-purpose tools and rubbers.

Perforated stones (Chapter 4.3)

Our studies have shown that in all cases there are in fact clear indications of use, and it is probable that these items had been used, to varying degrees, in the whetting of metal blades. However, in many cases the choice of imported stone and the fine degree of finish indicates that some of these objects could also have been valued as decorative items.

Stones without perforations (Chapter 4.4)

The patterns of wear on these items, and the rocks used, suggest that most of the pieces were hones used in the whetting of metal blades. One piece however (ID 59) appears to be a polisher, possibly used in the finishing of pottery vessels or animal skin.

Spatulae (Chapter 4.5)

The distal ends, which are usually rounded or tapered in shape, show most traces of use wear. This comprises mainly close-set and fairly regular striae or shallow grooves, but only in one case did the grooves resemble the transverse/lateral marks described for the Easton Lane spatulae (Fasham *et al.* 1989, 104). However, the overall use wear evidence does seem to be in support of the pressure flaking function postulated for the group of such artefacts from Easton Lane, Winchester. Interpretations as netting tools, components for bows (which would not have shown use wear) or pot modelling tools can safely be ruled out, and the marks are probably too distinct to have been the result of burnishing leather.

Awls (Chapter 4.6)

The question of possible function was discussed in detail by Thomas (2005, 222). The female associations suggest a use in some domestic craft and it has often been proposed that awls were used to pierce leather prior to sewing, or in decoration by pricking or scoring. However, as Thomas pointed out, the points are rather too fine for such purposes. Our use wear studies show little signs of wear towards the points, and many of the points are in fact pristine. If used for piercing, then the material pierced must have been very soft, and thus the suggestion of use in tattooing or scarification (Woodward 2000, 115; Thomas 2005, 222), in which the points would have been employed to pierce human flesh, is an attractive one. In four cases studied the awls occurred in sets of awls of slightly differing sizes.

Bone points (Chapter 4.7)

Most of the points were polished to a fine degree, while only very few were decorated. Ancient breaks occur at both tip and head and relate to use in antiquity. Most wear traces were located at the perforations, and are indicative of cord- or thread-wear. This probably indicates that the points were suspended, maybe on a necklace or girdle, or fastened to a garment or headdress. In only very few cases were any wear traces at or near the tip indicative of use as a tool, and in most cases these were of Beaker-age rather than of mature Early Bronze Age date. Overall the traces of wear are fairly slight, with 75% of points where a level of wear could be determined falling in the fresh or slightly worn categories. It was therefore concluded that most of the points were not used as tools but for some other purpose, presumably as items of adornment. Such functions could have included hair pins, head ornaments or headdresses, or embellishments for clothing and costume.

The use of bone points in adornment of the body or costume is particularly well demonstrated by consideration of the points that were found in groups within individual graves. Four main sets of items contain an array of points which are slightly graduated in length, as if they had been designed as decorative sets. The evidence of the location of string- or cord-wear recorded within the perforations on many of the points suggests that in many cases the points were not strung simply so that they hung from a position at the top of the object. The occurrence of cord-wear at positions either side of the top (top right or top left) is fairly common, and it also occurs at the sides of some perforations, or even towards the base. This may indicate that the points were attached or loosely sewn into exact locations on items of dress or costume. These may have included headdresses, as discussed above, or garments of varying type.

Evidence for a special garment was obtained from the 'shaman' grave at Upton Lovell G2a, where the points occurred in two locations on the body: more than three dozen at the feet and a further two dozen 'near the breast'. Piggott (1962) suggested that these bone items had functioned as the elements of ornamental fringes, sewn on to one or more special garments.

Tweezers (Chapter 4.8)

Thomas (1966) pointed out that these items were probably not tweezers, as the arms are too inflexible for depilatory use. Also there is no sign of particular wear at the tips of the arms that might have been expected if they had been used regularly to remove hair from the chin, eyebrows or elsewhere on the human body. Although all had been used, the various perforations only show evidence of strong thread- or string-wear in one case. However in the larger holes, a free-moving string is unlikely to have formed such wear traces. The perforations may have been employed to facilitate suspension from a belt or the neck, or may have held strings, or perhaps thongs, of a more practical nature, used in securing another item, or for encircling a bun of human hair. Thomas (*ibid*) suggested that they may have been special clips, used perhaps to display ritual feathers, cloth, or even a scalp. Alternatively, as indicated above, they may have been used to secure a special hairstyle. The tweezers are often found in association with a special bone pin and the two artefact types seem to have functioned as a particular 'set' of equipment.

Bone tubes (Chapter 4.9)

All examples except the 'flute' from Wilsford G23 are made from the same animal bone and have one perforation or none. These may have functioned as simple whistles, with those lacking holes cross-blown. The finely made longer tube from Aldro 52 also has a notch which may have served to hold an additional acoustic device such as a reed. The Wilsford G23 'flute' has two surviving holes. All items except this 'flute' show evidence of ancient damage which is indicative of use. This damage includes some major breaks, but mainly comprises chips and nicks, often around the upper margin. Traces of use in the form of ancient scratches and scuffs are visible in four cases. On two tubes such wear was greater on the front side, and in one case use sheen was most prominent towards the wider end. On the Wilsford G23 'flute' the major break lies at the point where the thumb and first finger of the left hand would have rested, so therefore this may have been a worn and weakened location.

Bone plates (Chapter 4.10)

Wear is not heavy, and the perforations in particular show no obvious signs of use for strings or cordage. The lack of thread-wear in the perforations argues against an interpretation as spacer plates for necklaces, the suggestion that was made by Thomas (1954). Also they are not at all similar to the spacer plates in bone known from East Anglia. It is difficult to see how the plates could have functioned in a necklace, and none of them are associated with beads of any kind. The lack of wear at the perforations would also rule out their use as belt fasteners or for any heavy use as tools. The plates are very thin and one of them was embellished with further fastenings in the form of contrasting copper wire. Although Thomas thought that an interpretation as wristguards was unlikely, it could be that these plates were intended to be fixed, like stone bracers, to leather or textile as ornaments for the lower arm. Or they may have been fixed elsewhere on the body.

Toggles (Chapter 4.11)

Of a total of eight examples known from Beaker-age bracer graves, the position in relation to the body was recorded in five cases (Woodward and Hunter 2011). Three times the toggle was placed on the left side of the body: once at the thigh, once at the left elbow and once at the left arm. Another was positioned on the chest. It therefore seems unlikely that these toggles functioned as belt fasteners. Instead they were all situated in a zone that would have been close to the bracer, which in all these cases was situated on the left lower arm. It seems possible therefore that the toggles may have possessed a specific function that was related to the use of the stone bracers.

The two toggles from Food Vessel graves also seem to have been special pieces of equipment. That from Kelleythorpe was found with a ball of metal and a strip of metal and wood. The metal was described as iron by the excavator (Londesborough 1851), but may well have been of some alloy or mineral. All the items were found in the hand of one of the two skeletons in the grave. The similar toggle and a second perforated bag-shaped toggle from Garton Slack 162 were found beside the skull of the burial of a child. Composite pieces of equipment may be implied.

Antler handles (Chapter 4.12)

All were much-used and some much-modified during their use life, and thus they appear to have been important and valuable items.

Bone tools (Chapter 4.12)

All were well-used, being classified, where the wear pattern was determinable, as either worn or very worn.

Antlers (Chapter 4.12)

Piggott (1962) originally suggested that antlers with no signs of use as tools may have formed part of cult headdresses. Moore and Rowlands (1972, 48) thought that the fact that the ends of some of the tines on the antlers from Ablington show wear and polishing indicated possible use as tools in some craft process. However, our detailed microscopic study suggests that there is no relevant use wear to support this idea, and that the polishing was achieved in order to enhance the appearance of the antlers. The shaping of the base areas would not be necessary for a tool, as it is unlikely that such large items would ever have been hafted, and this shaping may rather have been designed to facilitate the mounting of the antlers in some kind of head gear made primarily from perishable materials such as cloth or animal skin.

Axe (Chapter 4.13)

Use wear on bronze axes is not often visible, and no overall study of this aspect for the numerous axes from hoards has yet been attempted. It is usually assumed that axes were used as cutting tools, especially for woodworking.

Pronged object (Chapter 4.13)

Previous interpretations of this unique object from Wilsford G58 include function as a standard mount (Smith 1921; Ashbee and ApSimon 1954), exotic vessel handle (Grinsell 1957, 212), horse goad (Piggott 1973, 361) and flesh-hook (dismissed in Needham and Bowman 2005, 117). The flanged-and-riveted tang suggests that the instrument was mounted at the end of a handle or shaft. While it would have made an impressive standard mount, the wear pattern does not support such a function. Piggott's goad hypothesis is more appealing; the rings would have rattled whenever it was brought down on the animal's rump and soon the beast (perhaps draught ox rather than horse) would have associated noise with action. However, it is clear from the wear pattern in the aperture that when the object was in motion, the prongs were not pointing upward as would be expected of a goad. It may be presumed that this was a ceremonial or ritual version of instruments more generally made in perishable materials and thus it may no longer have literally served the original function of the prototype.

Working debris of jet and jet-like materials (Chapter 4.14)

This group of items comprises pieces of raw material or partly finished objects. However, all exhibit ancient wear to varying degrees, so were probably handled and used as amulets after breakage or conversion.

Spindle object plus fossil (Chapter 4.14)

A finely made jet object from Garton Slack 153, cylindrical in form and with a series of circumferential rounded ribs appears to be a copy of the section of ammonite fossil with which it was found. Both probably functioned as amulets.

Personal adornment

Bracers

Detailed information relating to use wear detected on Beaker-age stone bracers has been published by Woodward and Hunter (2011, Ch. 6). It proved very difficult to detect traces of ancient wear on the surfaces, but it proved possible to ascribe overall categories of wear. More were fresh or slightly worn (56% of a total of 62 bracers), with a lesser quantity of worn or very worn examples (42%; with 2% indeterminate). More traces of wear were detected within or around the perforations. Many bracers had been broken, and quite often the pieces were reworked to form pendants or amulets. The function of bracers is best informed by their placement on the body (see below). Many were placed on the outer or leading face of the arm, rather than in the inner wrist area, suggesting that these exotic and unusually coloured objects may have functioned as valuable decorative embellishments to the arm, either in the context of archery or falconry.

Belt hooks (Chapter 3.3)

It has always been assumed that the hooks functioned as belt fasteners, and Sheridan (2007a, fig. A3.3) has shown how they may have been sewn horizontally into one end of a belt, and hooked over a metal ring which was attached to the other end. Metal stains on two of the hooks studied in this project would also fit in with such a reconstruction, but the metal staining on ID 1014 (Norton Bavant) occurs on the rear and inner edges of the back plate only. However, the finding of the remains of the metal hook attached to the corrosion products of the sheath of the larger dagger from Wilsford G23 (ID 1391) may suggest a different interpretation. It may be that the hooks were attached vertically into the front of a sheath of scabbard, with the hook providing anchorage for a narrow thong or cord which provided attachment to the belt above. Much ancient damage on the burnt examples results from the hooks having passed through the cremation pyre, and there are ancient small chips on two unburnt items. Evidence of wear is highly variable, and one piece has sharp edges and pristine decoration, indicating that it is a fresh and unused item. Three hooks have obvious wear traces within the angle of the hook, in two cases extreme. And the edges and interior surfaces of the gold hook from Bush Barrow also show definite signs of use. The outer edge of the perforation on one hook also shows strong wear traces. In three cases the decoration also shows signs of considerable wear.

Belt rings/pulley objects (Chapter 3.4)

Although it has long been assumed that the Beaker-age rings were used to fasten belts of perishable substances such as leather or textile, such a function does need to be confirmed. In the case of the Class I rings, use wear may have occurred generally all around the ring, but in the case of those with fixed fastening points, one might expect to detect more localised signs of wear. Most wear in all cases is evident around the V-perforations or other perforations supplied for attachment to the putative belt. This is often extreme. However, one might also expect to find traces of wear and fabric rub from the end of the belt that was strung through the ring, either in the zone directly opposite the fastening perforations, or, if the belt was tied in the manner suggested by Clarke (1970, fig. 144) at the top and bottom of the ring. In spite of our intensive microscopic study, very few traces of such wear have been detected. In only one case is wear opposite the perforations present. Another shows extreme wear on one side, but it is at the top or bottom only, not the area opposite the perforations. In four cases there is evidence of wear to the hoop all around its circumference which may imply general wear from a belt end which was placed in varying detailed positions during the life of the ring. A further slight problem with the belt ring interpretation is that, however the belt was slotted through the ring, much of the valuable, and sometimes intensively decorated, hoop would have been obscured by the belt. Perhaps an alternative interpretation involving use as a hanging ornament or badge, perhaps suspended *from* a belt, or upon a special costume, should also be considered. Similar problems apply to the Class I bone rings of magnifying glass form. Whilst the pattern of use wear on two pieces might be consistent with usage as a belt ring, that detected on the inner segments of both hoops on a third example could not. An alternative interpretation for these rings, as a bow stringer, has previously been suggested (Barclay *et al.* 1995, 99), and in this connection, it is interesting to note the occurrence of these early belt rings with archery-related equipment such as stone bracers and fancy arrowheads.

Simple rings (jet and jet-like materials) (Chapter 4.14)

Four rings, of inferior workmanship and of later date when compared with the series of Beaker-age belt rings, may have functioned as ornaments or fasteners. There is no wear evidence to indicate use as belt rings, although such use may not have caused strong wear unless the ring was in a fixed position on the belt. They are also larger, and much thicker, that the series of flat rings, often made from Kimmeridge shale, which are found within composite necklaces in the Wessex region.

Tusks/teeth (Chapter 5.1)

Our detailed analysis shows that only eight out of the 36 items studied have been sharpened by human enhancement

of the distal pointed end. However there are very few traces of use wear, and in only three cases is wear that *might* have been caused by using the tusk as a tool visible. We suggest that the previous overarching interpretations of tusks as blades or tools are incorrect, and that most, and maybe all, of the tusks were in fact designed to perform as ornaments. Further evidence can be cited in favour of this hypothesis. Firstly, two of the Early Bronze Age tusks are designed as pendants, and two Neolithic ones had been cut across deliberately at the proximal end and one of them perforated. A further Neolithic example has also been cut across and perforated centrally. Altogether four of the tusks studied, in addition to the two pendants, have surviving perforations. The fact that the edges of these perforations are not worn suggests that they did not hang by a string from a belt, as might have been the case if they functioned as tools. The only groove at a perforation is at an angle, and this may indicate that the tusk was sewn onto a garment such that the tusk lay in a particular chosen position. We know that the perforated tusks with the burial at Upton Lovell G2a were found on the legs, and that, in association with a large number of perforated bone points, these probably served to decorate an elaborate costume (see above). In general the little wear that was observed under the microscope comprises general scuffing and smoothing which is probably due to fabric rub, so this also adds to the ornamental interpretation. It can be concluded that the tusks functioned mainly as ornaments, both in the Early Neolithic and Beaker/Early Bronze Age periods.

Beaver teeth (Chapter 5.1)

There is no evidence that beaver teeth were used as wood-working tools. They seem to be in pristine condition, although sometimes have been cut down at the proximal, root end. Their distinctive colour may have been of great significance, and they tend to be found with groups of other highly coloured beads or small items of natural origin. Thus their function may have been more symbolic in nature, and they may have been employed as amulets.

Canine teeth (Chapter 5.1)

Within the set of seven items from Kenslow, each piece comprises half of a canine tooth from large dog or wolf which has been split axially to provide a crescent-shaped object with plano-convex profile. In terms of wear, most of the perforations have fairly sharp edges but overall the pieces do seem to have been used and they can be categorised as slightly worn. It is difficult to see how the crescents could have been strung in a necklace, and there is no differential wear at the perforations which might have supported such an interpretation. It seems likely that they were sewn permanently onto a garment as ornaments, in a similar way to some of the sets of buttons made from jet and jet-like materials. In contrast, the set of 18 dog and wolf teeth from South Newton G1 could have been strung as a necklace.

V-perforated buttons (Chapter 5.2)

Our study of wear patterns has identified strong evidence for a cord pulling on the central bridge between the perforations. This serves to confirm an interpretation involving buttons attached to various garments or other fabric items. The overall degree of wear, and occasional re-working, of the buttons demonstrates that these were valued dress accessories with long life spans. Where a single button, or a pair, are associated with a pulley ring of jet or jet-like material, the set may have been employed to fasten a belt, and other smaller buttons may have functioned as fasteners and decoration for a pouch suspended from the belt. Three of the few V-perforated buttons made from bone are worn and the nature of the thread-wear indicates that they may have originally been necklace buttons. The Bromham bone button, found in a slightly later context, appears to have had a long use life, and may have functioned as a button to fasten a garment after its original use within a necklace. Most of the V-perforated amber buttons are small and form components of composite necklaces or amber spacer plate necklaces. However, one set of buttons may have been sewn onto a garment as ornaments.

Button sets (Chapter 5.3)

Four button sets from England have been studied in detail. Most of the buttons are made from jet, but a few are of cannel coal, and one of stone. The most uniform set is the group of 20 small buttons from Hunmanby. These were probably made by a single craftsperson and they display equal, but slight, degrees of wear. They were probably attached to an inner garment where they functioned as decorative studs rather than working buttons, and the location of some of the fabric rub on the apices suggests that a further garment was worn on top of the decorated shirt or tunic. The buttons were found in a row from neck to waist. The group of 13 buttons from Garton Slack VI, grave 1 is much more variable. At least three groups of buttons may have been gathered together. Four small to medium-sized buttons are made from cannel coal or lignite and show similar degrees of medium to heavy wear. Four of the largest jet buttons have concavo-convex profiles and are even more worn, especially one item which displays repeated re-borings. These eight buttons may have experienced use lives on previous garments. The remainder of the jet buttons are mainly small in size and exhibit slightly less wear. When combined, the 13 buttons appear to have been attached to the front of a garment in two vertical rows, of six and seven buttons respectively. The presence of thread-grooves across the bridge on four buttons, and the fact that thread-wear occurs all around the interior of the perforations in virtually every case, indicates that the buttons had been used as functioning (toggle-like) buttons, rather than as decorative studs or as beads. This is in marked contrast to the button set from Hunmanby (see above) where the buttons had probably been sewn on as ornaments, and where overall wear was slight.

Smaller sets of buttons come from Raunds and Butterwick. The five buttons from Raunds were not found on the body and show varying degrees of wear. One is rather larger than the others, but not particularly so. This one is very worn and may have started out its life as a single cloak fastener. Amongst the smaller buttons, one is fresh and had its facet added just prior to deposition. Thus the set may have been put together for the burial, and indeed the individual buttons may have been contributed by different member of the funeral party. The set of six buttons from Butterwick is equally diverse, although all of these are much larger than buttons in the sets discussed so far. The five black buttons appear to comprise two pairs in jet, one of which had been rebored, and a fresh single button made from cannel coal. The largest button is that made from stone. This is very worn and is decorated with an incised cruciform design. Wear patterns may indicate that the two smaller buttons acted as functional fasteners, while others were permanently sewn on as decorative embellishments. All were found in the chest area of the body.

Earrings and basket ornaments (Chapter 5.4)

By taking into account various groups of hair ornaments from Early Bronze Age Europe, Sherratt argued that the gold basket earrings were more likely to have been tress ornaments used for embellishing special hair styles, rather than earrings (Sherratt 1986; 1987). The term basket ornaments is thus preferred (Needham 2011, 136). Microscopic analysis of the two pairs from Chilbolton showed wear around the edges of the tang and absence of scratches inside the 'basket' (Russel 1990, 164–6). Russel concluded that this indicated that the ornaments had in fact been earrings, with wear on the tang relating to the placing of the tang through a slit in the ear lobe. However it would seem that use of such items as hair tresses would not lead to scratching inside the curled ornament either, and the argument therefore remains inconclusive. No traces of wear were detected microscopically on the pair from Radley 4A (Barclay and Halpin 1999, 183). Taking into account the similar lack of wear within the basket areas of the ornaments from the Amesbury Archer and 'Companion' graves, and the fact that the tangs appeared to have been curled into place just once, Needham has argued that they may have adorned a removable headdress or collar, with the gold ornaments wrapped around cloth or braids of rope (Needham 2011, 136–8). One of the Cowlam copper alloy earrings (ID 1304) has scratches on both the exterior and the interior of the blade, but the inside also shows smoothing and more signs of use. In three of the cases studied in detail, the ornaments were found either side of the skull, or in the vicinity of the skull, so ornaments relating to the head are definitely implied. But whether these bronze items were inserted into the ear lobes as earrings, or employed as tress or headdress ornaments, cannot be proven on the current use wear evidence.

Dress pins (Chapter 5.5)

Traces of wear show that all of the complex pins: the Beaker-age examples and those with bulb, crutch or complex ringed heads were worn or heavily worn. The simple ring-headed pins of bone and antler tend to show less wear, but had been used prior to burial. It may be that these less complex items were not valued to the same extent as the fancy pins. Wear of the decoration on some of the heads indicates fabric rub, thus suggesting that the pins were indeed employed to fasten and/or embellish garments. Some pins continued in use after breakage or damage, indicating that these items were valued highly.

Studs (Chapter 5.6)

This little studied class of objects have variously been described as studs or toggles. They vary greatly in form and size, but the strong evidence of the lack of any wear in the neck or stem areas, shows that none of them are likely to have functioned as toggles. In the case of the jet and jet-like pieces in particular, if they had been used as any kind of fastener, smoothing or eradication of the traces of manufacture in the neck/stem area would undoubtedly have occurred. It seems most likely therefore that these pieces were used as ornamental studs which were inserted into some soft part of the body tissue. Ethnographic and modern parallels would suggest that such studs might have been inserted into the ear lobe, or into the upper or lower lip as labrets.

Pendants (Chapter 5.9)

The pendants are highly variable in terms of shape, general morphology and the raw materials employed. In several cases the pendant has been modified for extended or later use, and this includes the series of re-used necklace fasteners. Overall analyses of use wear show that almost all the pendants exhibit wear, and this is often heavy. As well as wear to the decoration or surfaces, which could be due to fabric rub, varying degrees of thread-wear within the perforations indicate that these objects were indeed strung as individual pendants or as components within necklaces.

Neckring and armlet (Chapter 5.10)

The bronze decorated strip from Garton Slack 107 was associated with two curved rods with curled terminals. Both the original perforations at the ends of the strip show wear, and one was replaced following breakage. The lozenge decoration also displays wear, both near to the terminals and at a zone near the middle of the band. The crooks of the curved rods are worn within the curls, and the milled decoration on the outer rod is worn almost smooth. The hooked ends of the rods presumably fitted into the perforations at the ends of the decorated flat band. The original curvatures cannot now be determined, but the rods may have sat behind the neck, with the decorated band to the front, or the rods may have been placed separately over the back of the head, with the band lying on the forehead.

The bronze armlet from Amesbury G41 possesses a diameter suitable for adornment of the arm, although the restored diameter may not reflect accurately the original size of the piece. It was found on the arm of an adult inhumation. The decoration shows slight wear.

Special items of gold (Chapter 6.1 and Chapter 6.2)

Of the four large decorated gold sheet plaques known, two were found on the chest of inhumation burials, and they are thought to have been attached to the front of ceremonial garments. All would have been supported by cores, probably made from wood, and these could have been V-perforated to enable fastening to a tunic or other element of costume. The rectangular plaque from Little Cressingham is slightly worn, with some ancient striations, while the slightly barrel-shaped example from Upton Lovell G2e has many scratches and extensive wear to the decoration; it is thus classified as very worn. The large lozenge from Wilsford G5 (Bush Barrow) has indentations around the two perforations and some striations, suggesting slight wear. The small decorated gold sheet lozenge from Bush Barrow again would have been mounted originally on a wooden core with a flat back. It was found in association with the stone mace-head and bone shaft mount, and it is now suggested that this piece may have ornamented the wooden shaft of the mace. This lozenge is slightly worn, with some ancient scratches, and the bone zigzag mounts and stone mace-head have also been classified as slightly worn.

A series of gold sheet discs were probably covers for buttons. The surviving member of the pair from Mere G6a lacks edge damage. This suggests that it was mounted as a button on a stout backing of wood or bone; and the absence of tug-wear on the central pair of holes, and pressure-wear around them, may indicate that the holes held a small 'clamping boss', again of wood or bone, through which the stitching would have passed. The disc is worn, with multidirectional ancient striations on both faces.

Four gold sheet discs from Wilsford-cum-Lake G47, 49 or 50, found with the remains of a large amber spacer plate necklace, form two pairs, one of them flat and the other domed. All were probably mounted on organic backings which would have held a V-perforation. Thus they could have functioned as the covers for buttons. Three show signs of slight wear, while the decoration on one of the domed examples is very worn. All four were found near the ears, and certainly above the shoulders. They may have been strung towards the ends of the spacer plate necklace. A series of seven small circular objects with corrugated sides and one open end have previously been interpreted as cap-ends for wooden staves, or, in use as pairs to form closed 'boxes'. Three from Little Cressingham possess almost flat faces, and, with ancient cracks and indentations, are moderately worn. The four from Upton Lovell G2e, which have been restored as two conjoining pairs, have conical faces. They are all very worn, with visible puckering, scratches, dents and distortions to the corrugations. All seven items were more probably covers for organic cores, with V-perforations originally placed in the rear centre of the core. Such items could have functioned as buttons or as ornamental studs. Unfortunately, the position of these finds in relation to the body at Little Cressingham was not recorded.

The set of eleven gold sheet-covered cylindrical beads from Upton Lovell G2e are a unique find. Each bead has two tiny perforations on the same side, so, unlike beads, they would have hung below the thread, more like pendants. Or they may have been stitched individually to a garment, or to a choker made from cloth or leather. The presence of mini-dents, ancient scratches and creases suggests that their condition is worn. The corrugated gold sheet band from Little Cressingham originally was thought to be an armlet or perhaps a pommel mount. The estimated original diameter is rather small for a pommel, but may have fitted a mid-handle position on a dagger or other implement. It shows slight wear.

Two large decorated cones of shale covered in gold sheet each possess a V-perforation in the centre of the flat 'base'. The one from Upton Lovell G2e exhibits moderate wear and that from Wilsford G8 is also worn, with random scuff marks and slight pull in the perforation margins. The location of the decoration, which is especially concentrated on the flat 'base' suggests that these items were suspended point downwards, unlike the earlier series of V-perforated buttons in jet or jet-like materials. The cones may have functioned as pendants or downward-hanging toggles on clothing such as a cape, or have been employed as plumb-bobs in ritual activities.

Beads/necklaces (Chapter 7 and Chapter 8)

The almost ubiquitous incidence of thread-wear, and fairly common occurrence of bead-on-bead wear, demonstrates that beads were usually strung together to form necklaces, or occasionally bracelets. No stringing materials survive but it is likely that these were naturally occurring and perishable substances such as flax, other plant fibres or animal sinews.

Necklace buttons (Chapter 7 and Chapter 8)

Small buttons found as components of complex necklaces of jet and jet-like material show distinctive wear patterns which demonstrate that they were indeed strung within the necklace. This wear comprises thread-smoothing, polish and sometimes pull traces on the *outer* edges of the set of perforations.

Single spacer plates (Chapter 5.8)

These are found as single items, pairs, or in one case a set of three. In the total absence of beads from the grave groups concerned it seems unlikely that the spacers were being employed within necklaces. This conclusion is borne out

by the fact that several were broken in antiquity, and some display wear on the broken surfaces. It would seem likely that the spacers were important pieces in their own right, made from fine raw materials and often bearing complex decoration. As such they may have functioned as amulets.

PLACEMENT OF OBJECTS WITH THE BODY

This and the following two chapter sections are based on the information relating to grave groups recorded in the project site databases only. For the Beaker period the site database includes all well-furnished graves in England, arranged within four geographical groups: East Yorkshire; the Peak District (Derbyshire and Staffordshire); Wessex (Dorset and Wiltshire) and the rest of the country. For the Early Bronze Age period the site database covers only the three main concentrations in East Yorkshire, the Peak District and Wessex (see Chapter 2). Although the sets of data for the two period divisions are therefore not strictly comparable, many informative patterns may be deduced, the main aim being to compare such patterns between the Beaker and Early Bronze Age traditions. It should be noted that the site databases contain all well-furnished graves recorded in the published literature or in Historic Environment Records (HERs) and include many more objects than were studied in detail during the project. For both Beaker and Early Bronze Age contexts, sites were selected for analysis on the basis of the presence of at least one item of special interest, namely: copper alloy objects including daggers and awls; selected flint objects including daggers, barbed and tanged arrowheads and plano-convex knives; accessory cups; stone bracers and whetstones, including sponge finger stones, and personal adornments and regalia composed of bone, amber, jet, and stone. Discussion here relates to the placement of particular categories of object in relation to the body in inhumation graves as well as to the practice of placing objects in bags and caches (particularly in the Beaker period), and of the significance of objects in, or associated with, cremation burials.

Perhaps the most significant contextual clue to the function of an object, at least at time of deposition, is the position of the object on the body within an inhumation burial. For the Beaker period, when inhumation burial was the norm, this includes nearly all relevant areas and object types (Table 11.2). For the Early Bronze Age, there are some object types where position data is unavailable due to the greater incidence of cremation burial. However, differences of object presence between inhumation and cremation burials are informative, as well as showing significant trends (Table 11.3).

Within the Early Bronze Age there are object types with significant frequencies in inhumation contexts. Food Vessels appear mostly in inhumation contexts, and, as will be seen later, are largely restricted to the East Yorkshire region. On the other hand, tweezers and perforated stones, accessory cups, dress pins and Collared Urns appear mostly in cremation contexts. This is due partly to the

Table 11.2. Presence of Beaker object types within inhumation/cremation contexts, by number of graves.

Object type	Inhumation	Cremation	Total
Barbed/tanged arrowhead	22	1	22
Awl	21	0	21
Battle-axe	6	0	6
Bead	6	1	7
Beaker	101	0	101
Beaker (sherds only)	7	1	8
Belt ring/pulley object	20	0	20
Bracelet	3	0	3
Bracer	26	1	27
Button set	3	0	3
Button, unspecified type	6	0	6
Dagger/knife	57	0	57
Disc – gold	2	0	2
Dress pin	4	0	4
Earring/tress ring	7	0	7
Flint flake	30	0	30
Flint dagger	13	1	14
Flint knife	20	0	20
Flint, unspecified type	10	1	11
Iron pyrite nodule	6	0	6
Misc. bone/antler	3	0	3
Misc. bone	10	1	11
Misc. copper/bronze	4	1	5
Misc. flint implement	11	0	11
Misc. stone	12	0	12
Misc. shell/fossil	3	0	3
Necklace	2	0	2
Plano-convex knife	3	0	3
Point	17	0	17
Pommel	10	0	10
Spatula	16	1	17
Scraper	8	0	8
Sponge finger stone	7	0	7
Toggle	4	0	4
Tusk/tooth	5	0	5
V-perforated button	25	1	26

chronological spans of different object types, with those occurring mainly in cremation burials being the later types. Potential patterns relating to object body positions are best considered by examining object type in turn, and by pointing out any notable differences between Beaker and Early Bronze Age contexts, as well as any differences in regional patterns of deposition where appropriate. Object categories with sufficient numbers of recorded instances of body placement can be discussed in detail. Due to their highly variable morphologies, miscellaneous objects of jet and jet-like materials, bone, antler, stone, and shell/fossil have been excluded from this analysis.

A total of 29 object types are discussed here; these have been divided into three groups for discussion purposes: the first relates to articles of personal equipment (11), notably daggers and points, the second contains objects considered to be items of personal adornment, including buttons and necklaces (14) and the third (smaller) group considers pottery (4). With the exception of pottery, which is only discussed as an associated item, the various categories are reviewed in the same order as they appear in Chapters 3 to 6 above.

Personal equipment

There is a total of 11 object types.

> Daggers/knives
> Sponge finger stones
> Grooved stones
> Spatulae
> Awls
> Bone points
> Bone tubes and plates
> Toggles
> Flint daggers
> Barbed and tanged arrowheads
> Battle axes

Daggers/knives

A total of 46 Beaker graves contain at least one dagger/knife with positioning data. Overall, Beaker daggers are placed quite variably around the body, although there is a clear trend to place the dagger at the arms or hands or at the chest. Across all regions, 19 graves have daggers placed near the arms, including eight which are in position within or near the hands (Acklam Wold 205; Butterwick

Table 11.3. Presence of Early Bronze Age object types within inhumation/cremation contexts, by number of graves.

Object type	Inhumation	Cremation	Total	% inhum.	% crem.
Accessory cup	11	27	**38**	29	71
Accessory cup (sherd)	0	8	**8**	0	100
Antler	1	2	**3**	33	67
Barbed/tanged arrowhead	4	0	**4**	100	0
Arrowhead – unspecified type	1	4	**5**	20	80
Awl	29	53	**82**	35	65
Axe – copper/bronze	1	2	**3**	33	67
Battle-axe	9	7	**16**	56	44
Bead (individual)	6	8	**14**	43	57
Beaker	1	1	**2**	50	50
Belt hook	2	2	**4**	50	50
Belt ring/pulley object	1	4	**5**	20	80
Bone handle	2	1	**3**	67	33
Bone tool	3	1	**4**	75	25
Bracelet	1	0	**1**	100	0
Bracer	0	1	**1**	0	100
Button set	2	2	**4**	50	50
Button – unspecified type	4	3	**7**	57	43
Collared Urn	3	42	**45**	7	93
Dagger/knife	28	77	**105**	27	73
Disc	0	1	**1**	0	100
Dress pin	2	11	**13**	15	85
Earring	2	0	**2**	100	0
End piece	1	0	**1**	100	0
Fastener	4	0	**4**	100	0
Flint flake	15	12	**27**	56	44
Flint knife	12	10	**22**	55	45
Food Vessel	24	9	**33**	73	27
Grooved whetstone	3	1	**4**	75	25
Iron pyrite nodule	0	2	**2**	0	100
Objects of jet and jet-like materials	1	0	**1**	100	0
Working debris of jet and jet-like materials	2	0	**2**	100	0
Mace-head	2	0	**2**	100	0
Misc. amber	0	1	**1**	0	100
Misc. bone/antler	2	8	**10**	20	80
Misc. bone	7	6	**13**	54	46
Misc. copper/bronze	4	4	**8**	50	50
Misc. flint implement	3	3	**6**	50	50
Misc. gold	3	3	**6**	50	50
Misc. jet and jet like-material	0	3	**3**	0	100
Misc. stone	10	3	**13**	77	23
Mount	1	0	**1**	100	0
Misc. shell/fossil	3	1	**4**	75	25
Necklace	30	56	**86**	35	65
Other whetstone	2	1	**3**	67	33
Pendant	0	5	**5**	0	100
Perforated stone	0	11	**11**	0	100
Plano-convex knife	1	0	**1**	100	0
Plate	2	2	**4**	50	50
Point	36	63	**99**	36	64
Pommel	5	6	**11**	45	55
Ring copper/bronze	1	0	**1**	100	0
Spatula	2	1	**3**	67	33
Scraper	10	0	**10**	100	0
Stud	2	2	**4**	50	50
Toggle	3	0	**3**	100	0
Tube	1	3	**4**	25	75
Tusk/tooth	11	3	**14**	79	21
Tweezers	0	14	**14**	0%	100
Urn – unspecified type	4	34	**38**	11	89
Vessel – unspecified type	6	3	**9**	67	33
V-perforated button	6	4	**10**	60	40

Table 11.4. Body positions of Beaker daggers/knives across all regions, by number of daggers/knives.

Position	E. Yorkshire	Peak District	Wessex	Other	Totals
Near head, in front or behind	2	3	5	2	**12**
Near chest or shoulders, in front or behind	2	4	1	4	**11**
Near pelvis, including behind and 'at side'	1	0	2	3	**6**
At arms, including in hand	3	6	5	5	**19**
At feet or legs	0	0	1	0	**1**
Total	**8**	**13**	**14**	**14**	**49**

Table 11.5. Body positions of Early Bronze Age daggers/knives across all regions, by number of daggers/knives.

Position	E. Yorkshire	Peak District	Wessex	Totals
Near head, in front or behind	0	0	7	**7**
Near chest or shoulders, in front or behind	1	0	2	**3**
Near pelvis, including behind and 'at side'	2	0	0	**2**
At arms, including in hand	1	0	4	**5**
At feet or legs	2	0	3	**5**
Total	**6**	**0**	**16**	**22**

39, 1; Helperthorpe 49, 6; Middleton Moor; Roundway G8; Dorchester XII; Scamridge; Ferry Fryston 2245), while at a further five graves they are placed in front of the chest. Of the remaining sites, many are placed at the head, either in front or behind (12 graves), at the back or behind the shoulders (three graves), or at or behind the waist (six graves). Only a single grave, the Amesbury Archer, contains a dagger placed at the feet, where it is recorded as having been in a bag with other objects. It is also one of three daggers found with this burial, the others having been placed behind the back and in front of the face. Thus, although Beaker daggers are found in a range of positions (Table 11.4), on the whole they are found near the arms or in and around the upper body. Early Bronze Age graves show some significant changes in body position, although this is largely confined to Wessex daggers due to the large number of examples from this region. Of the 22 inhumations with daggers with recorded body positions, 16 graves are from Wessex, several of which are graves containing more than one dagger (Preshute G1a; Norton Bavant Borrow Pit; Wilsford G5: Bush Barrow; Winterbourne Stoke G5). At Wessex sites there appears to be a greater emphasis towards placing the dagger near the head, particularly behind the head (Table 11.5). A total of five graves contain daggers behind the head, compared to none in the Beaker period, all of which are from Wessex. In fact, at Wessex sites more daggers are found behind the head than at the arms or hands. Daggers/knives are also found more frequently at the legs or feet in the Early Bronze Age, including two graves from East Yorkshire (Blanch 2; Towthorpe 139) and three graves from Wessex (Preshute G1a; Wilsford G58; Winterbourne Stoke G5).

Sponge finger stones
These only occur in Beaker contexts. A total of five graves contain positioning data, including three sites with two sponge finger stones (West Overton G6b; Winterbourne Stoke G54; Raunds 1). At three sites they are recorded

at or near the feet, including at Gravelly Guy, where an example was found in a cluster containing a spatula, flint scraper and bracer. As with other object types found near the feet, this may suggest their use as a tool.

Grooved stones
Only three Early Bronze Age graves contain grooved stones, two of which were placed at the feet of the interment (Upton Lovell G2a; Wilsford G58). This may be indicative of their use as a tool, placed at the feet in the same way as barbed and tanged arrowheads.

Spatulae
Eleven spatulae are recorded with positions in Beaker graves. Of these, three graves have spatulae behind the back or at the shoulder (Green Low; Amesbury G51; West Overton G6b), three are near the feet (Raunds; Radley 4660; Gravelly Guy), and three near the pelvis (Haddon Fields; Easton Lane pit 1017; Radley 201). The placement behind the back is interesting, as awls are also frequently recorded in this position. Placement at the feet in several contexts may also be indicative of their use as a tool, alongside other object types found in this position. Only two graves from the Early Bronze Age have recorded positions for spatulae, one lying at the side (Painsthorpe Wold 4) and one lying near the legs (Huggate Wold 249).

Awls
A total of 17 Beaker graves and 20 Early Bronze Age graves contain awls with positioning data. As a whole, body position of awls across both periods is amongst the most variable of any object type observed, with awls in positions across most of the body (Table 11.6). Despite this wide variation, a number of awls appear to occupy locations where other tools are found, namely near the feet and behind the shoulder and back. A total of ten Beaker and Early Bronze Age graves contain awls placed at either the shoulder or behind the back or pelvis, while eight sites

Table 11.6. Recorded positions of Beaker and Early Bronze Age awls, by number of awls.

Position	Beaker awls	Site	EBA awls	Site
Near or at head	4	Garton Slack 163 Amesbury G51 Frampton G5 Gravelly Guy	9	Goodmanham 103,1 Goodmanham 112, 2 Goodmanham 115, 1 Garton Slack 29 Bee Low (4 awls) Winterbourne Stoke G8
Chest or shoulders	4	Rudston 62, 4 Huggate and Warter 254 Minninglow West Overton G6b	5	Rudston 62, 1 Etton 79, 2 Garton Slack 75 Waggon Low Winterbourne Stoke G5
At arm/hand	2	Butterwick 39, 1 Cassington, Tolley's Pit 10	4	Garrowby Wold 101 Garton Slack 137 Garton Slack 156 Huggate and Warter 249
Near waist/pelvis	3	Aldro 116 Rudston 62, 4 Haddon Fields	4	Langton 2, 2 (3 awls) Folkton 71, 6
Near feet/legs	5	Thickthorn Down Wimborne St Giles G9 Lambourn G19 Radley 201 Ferry Fryston161, 9	5	Garton Slack 75 Garton Slack 152 Preshute G1a (3 awls)
Total	**18**		**27**	

have awls at or near the feet or legs. Thus, nearly half of awls from both periods (18 of 38, 47%) are found in these three positions (i.e. shoulder, legs, pelvis).

Bone points

This is perhaps the most interesting object type as it shows clear patterns which differ across both time and space. A total of 10 Beaker period graves with points with recorded positions have been identified. In six of these graves points were placed at or near the side or pelvis (Acklam Wold 124; Green Low; Staker Hill; Amesbury G40; Easton Lane pit 1071; Radley 201), occurring in this position across all four Beaker regions. This is in contrast to the Early Bronze Age, where numerous points were located near the head or shoulders. Of a total of 27 Early Bronze Age graves, 16 had points near the head, including eight behind or above the head and eight in front of the head, at its side or near the head. In the remaining graves, three had points at the back or behind the shoulders, four had points near the hips or pelvis (Rudston 61, 6; Folkton 245, 1; Hanging Grimston 12; Acklam Wold 124), and a further three at the legs or feet (Weaverthorpe 44, 1; Painsthorpe Wold 98; Upton Lovell G2a). The final bone point was found in front of the neck (Etton 82, 2).

One site, at Upton Lovell G2a, Wiltshire, is unusual as it contains a total of 42 points from a single male inhumation. These lay in front of the legs and on the chest of the individual. Only two Beaker graves had points behind or near the head (Amesbury G51; Hasting Hill). Given this pattern, there would appear to be a clear shift in overall bone point positioning on the body between the two traditions, from placement near the pelvis or waist, to an association with the head. This appears to occur both in

East Yorkshire and Wessex, although three Early Bronze Age graves from East Yorkshire have points found near the pelvis. Unfortunately, no points with positions are recorded in the Peak District. In terms of the points associated with the head and shoulder, it is likely that many points in the Early Bronze Age were used as hair pins. The position of a majority of Beaker points at or near the pelvis or waist is more difficult to interpret. These may have acted as a pin to secure a garment at the waist, or conversely may have been tools placed at the waist for easy access. Only three of these points have been analysed in detail by this project (Green Low and two from Staker Hill). All three are rather crude bone points, and would appear to have been tools rather than objects for display.

Bone tubes and plates

Most of the bone tubes and plates, recorded from graves in Wessex only, were found in cremation burials. However one example of each category was found at the feet of the burial Wilsford G58. They occurred in a group which also contained other objects: a battle-axe; a grooved stone; a tusk; a bronze axe head and a pronged object, also of bronze.

Toggles

A total of four Beaker and two Early Bronze Age graves with toggles have body positions recorded. Overall their position during both periods is variable. Two Beaker toggles (Thomas Hardye School 1004; Lambourn) and one Early Bronze Age example (Kelleythorpe UN101, 1) have been found near the arm or hand. One Beaker toggle was found at the thigh (Hemp Knoll), another at the chest (Sewell), while two toggles were at the left side of the head in the Early

Bronze Age grave at Garton Slack 162. The positioning of some toggles amongst the arms is difficult to interpret, and the overall variation in toggle shape makes a single function for this group unlikely.

Flint daggers

A total of 8 Beaker graves have recorded positions for flint daggers, all in the Beaker period. Of these, they occur at or near the feet in four graves (Garton Slack 152; Somerford Keynes 121; Raunds 1; Raunds 6). This is different from Beaker Period copper alloy daggers/knives which tend to occur on the upper body, either near the head, near the chest or back, at the pelvis, or at the arms/hands. Although the total number of flint daggers is small, the observed pattern of placement does not support the idea of producing flint daggers that acted as symbolic copies of copper alloy daggers. If this were the case, it would have been expected that flint daggers were placed in similar positions on the body as copper alloy daggers.

Barbed and tanged arrowheads

A total of 13 barbed and tanged arrowheads from Beaker contexts are recorded with positioning data. Of these, six graves have arrowheads placed at the knees or feet (Winterslow G3; Thomas Hardye School 1004; Wimborne St Giles G9; Lambourn G31; Tring; Radley 4660) and three graves have arrowheads positioned at the pelvis (Amesbury Archer; Easton Lane pit 1071; Stanton Harcourt XXI, 1a). Two arrowheads are recorded near the head (Mouse Low; Roundway G8). Two further arrowheads were found near the chest and spine respectively and were the likely cause of death of the interred (Stonehenge ditch; Radley 201). In general, these positions suggest the inclusion of barbed and tanged arrowheads in groups as part of a tool kit at or near the feet, or as a tool at the waist. In the case of Early Bronze Age graves with barbed and tanged arrowheads, only three graves have position data, all three of which are in different positions, one near the face (Rudston 63, 10), one in front of the chest (Figheldean G26), and one near the knees (Conygar Hill).

Battle-axes

A total of five Beaker and six Early Bronze Age graves contain battle-axes with positioning data. In the Beaker period battle-axes are placed at either the head (Garton Slack 37; Durrington G67) or torso (Carder Low; Parsley Hay; East Kennet G1c). Early Bronze Age battle-axes are similarly placed, although one grave contained a battle-axe at the feet (Wilsford G58). Interestingly, the emphasis in placement towards the upper body is in contrast to other stone objects such as grooved whetstones and sponge finger stones, which, as seen above, tend to have been placed near the legs or feet in most cases.

Personal adornment

There is a total of 14 object types.

Bracers
Belt hook
Belt rings/pulley objects
Tusks and teeth
V-perforated buttons
Button sets
Earrings
Dress pins
Studs
Individual beads (not part of a necklace)
Pendants and individual necklace fasteners
Bracelets
Necklaces
Special objects of gold

Bracers

Stone bracers are usually found in relation to the lower arm bones; six instances on the outside of the arm, and four times on the inside. Nine out of the 12 well-recorded instances were found on the left arm, indicating that most archers (or falconers) may have been right-handed (Woodward and Hunter 2011, 104).

Belt hooks

Most belt hooks have been found in cremation burials, but two derive from inhumations. The gold belt hook from Bush Barrow (Wilsford G5) was found near to the two large daggers (Needham *et al.* 2010, fig. 3) while the example in bone from Norton Bavant Borrow Pit was found in a group of objects located behind the head and shoulders. There is thus no body placement information to confirm a function as belt fastener, although the use wear evidence (see above and Chapter 3.3) is relevant here.

Belt rings/pulley objects

In the case of belt rings/pulley objects, body position is variable. Of 11 Beaker graves, five contain belt rings/pulley objects at the feet or knees (Rudston 61, 2; Amesbury Archer; Winterbourne Stoke G54; Tring; Raunds 1), three in the region of the upper leg or waist (Acklam Wold 124; Wimborne St Giles G9; Stanton Harcourt XXI, 1), one near the right arm (Thwing 60, 3), one at the shoulder (Ferry Fryston 2245), and one at the chest (Rudston 68, 6). As suggested with some other object types, it is difficult to interpret the function of objects placed away from the body, particularly when located at or below the feet. It is likely that these are objects placed in the grave separately from the body, and may represent activity by mourners during the process of burial. Discounting the four objects from the region of the feet, it appears that the object was sometimes placed at or near the waist, confirming that at least some may have functioned as a kind of belt ring. However, as two others have been found on the chest or at the shoulder, some belt ring/pulley objects may have been used to suspend or hold a garment around the shoulder, or were suspended as ornaments in their own right. A single Early Bronze Age belt/ring pulley object was recorded at the feet of a male inhumation at (Upton Lovell G2a).

Tusks and teeth

A total of four Beaker and nine Early Bronze Age graves have recorded positions for tusks or teeth. For Beaker sites the pattern is unclear, with objects appearing near the hands (Scamridge), near the breast (Longbridge Deverill G3b), near the feet (Raunds 1), behind the back (two tusks with the Amesbury Archer) and in front of the face (two further tusks from the same grave). For the Early Bronze Age the picture is equally mixed, with three graves with tusk/teeth at the chest or pelvis (Folkton 70, 13; Painsthorpe Wold 98; Garrowby Wold 101), four at various positions around the head (Folkton 70, 13; Goodmanham 117, 1; Garton Slack 40; Bailey Hill), and three at the feet or legs (Stonesteads; Upton Lovell G2a; Wilsford G58).

V-perforated buttons

A total of 16 Beaker period and five Early Bronze Age graves have been identified with recorded positions for V-perforated buttons of all compositions. We note that for the present analysis the generally smaller buttons found within necklace deposits (and displaying different wear patterns) are not included. Broadly speaking, during the Beaker period, V-perforated buttons are found near the torso in 13 of 17 cases. Within this basic position, however, there is considerable variation. Buttons from two sites are found at or near the pelvis (a pair at Acklam Wold 124; Wimborne St Giles G9), while three are found near the arms (Rudston 61, 2; Thwing 60, 3; the pair from Net Low). Although the remaining are found near the chest, two buttons from Rudston 68, 7 are behind the back, and two sites have buttons at the shoulder (Castern; Lambourn 31). A single example is found resting on the breast bone at Hanging Grimston 55. There are also two instances of buttons having been found near the feet or legs (Acklam Wold 123 and the pair from Painsthorpe Wold 200). The buttons found near the feet and legs may have been employed in the fastening of footwear or leggings. In the case of Early Bronze Age graves with V-perforated buttons, two are positioned near the chest or neck (Ganton 27, 4; Folkton 71, 15). Tentatively, this may suggest that Early Bronze Age V-perforated buttons had a more restricted use associated with fastening a garment near the chest only.

Button sets

Two Early Bronze Age (Hunmanby 250, 3; Garton Slack burial 1) and two Beaker graves (Butterwick 39, 1; Raunds 1) have recorded positions for button sets. The set from Raunds was found with other objects in a group deposited near the feet. In the other three cases the buttons are recorded as being on or near the chest. At Hunmanby the buttons were placed in a row from the neck to the waist, while at Garton Slack the buttons were placed in pairs and resting on the chest; and at Butterwick they were 'along the chest'. Thus, it is highly likely these objects formed sets of buttons or decorative studs for a garment worn on the upper body.

This information relating to V-perforated buttons and button sets, along with further data from outside our detailed English study areas, and from Scotland, has been discussed in detail by Shepherd (2009). He concluded that four forms of dress may be represented: a cloak or loose outer garment fastened by one or two large buttons, a more tightly-buttoned garment such as a shirt or tunic requiring a set of small buttons, a similar tunic but of heavier fabric requiring a set of larger buttons and, finally, foot-wrappings or leggings fastened with buttons. Other body positioning and close association with unusual finds such as strike-a-lights and iron pyrites suggests that some buttons, or sets of buttons, were used to fasten and decorate pouches, worn at the waist (*ibid*, 346–7).

Earrings

Nearly all recorded positions for copper alloy or gold earrings and basket-shaped ornaments are consistent with having been worn in the region of the ear. Of six Beaker graves, five have such ornaments positioned at the side of the head. At Cowlam 58, 6 they are specifically recorded at having been placed at the temporal of the skull, while at Staker Hill they are positioned at the mastoid bones. Similarly, both Early Bronze Age graves record the earrings at the side of the head (Goodmanham; Garton Slack 153). Only the Amesbury Archer gold ornaments are found elsewhere, in a possible 'bag' or cache at the knees.

Dress pins

A total of four Beaker period and two Early Bronze Age graves containing dress pins have recorded body positioning, including both copper alloy and bone examples. Of the Beaker dress pins, one was found near the top of the skull (at Radley 4660), another at the arm (Amesbury Archer), a third in front of the chest (Roundway G8), and a fourth near the upper left arm (Sewell). In the Early Bronze Age, one copper alloy pin was found at the shoulder (Brough UN69, 1), while another was recorded near the head (West Overton G1). In the case of the two dress pins found close to the head, it is possible that these were used as hair pins, while the dress pins found at the shoulder and close to the arms may have fastened garments.

Studs

Many finds of studs are associated with cremations, but a pair of small jet studs were found either side of the skull in the neck area of the body at Wharram Percy 70. At Manton (Preshute G1a) however a single clay stud was found in front of the face in the chin area. This last example may have functioned therefore as a lip stud, or labret. Outside the project study areas, further examples of studs, sometimes in pairs, have been found in lower skull or neck positions within inhumations at Cowdery's Down, Hampshire (Millet and James 1983), at Fengate, Cambridgeshire (Evans and Appleby 2008) and in a series of more recently excavated graves in East Anglia (Sheridan forthcoming a). These finds, along with the pair from Wharram Percy 70, indicate that the studs most often functioned as ear studs.

Individual beads

Individual beads appear to have a similar pattern of body position as necklaces across the Beaker period and Early Bronze Age. Of four Beaker graves with individual beads with body position data, three have beads positioned near the neck and skull (Kelleythorpe UN101, 2; Shuttlestone; Chilbolton gold bead). These would be consistent with having been worn around the neck. Single beads from Early Bronze Age inhumations are from disturbed contexts (Crosby Garrett 176, 2; Wall Mead II) and otherwise were included in cremation burials.

Pendants and individual necklace fasteners

Early Bronze Age pendants, made from various materials, mainly derive from cremation burials, but in two cases they are recorded as having been on or around the neck of an inhumation (Durrington G14; Shrewton G5j). They are often associated with beads and appear to have formed elements within necklaces.

A total of four graves have recorded positions for individual fasteners of all compositions, again all from Early Bronze Age contexts. All four fasteners are found in East Yorkshire, two of them are positioned behind the head or neck (Goodmanham 89, 6; Painsthorpe Wold 118), one on the chest (Garton Slack 81), and one near the feet (Painsthorpe Wold 200). The presence of three objects near the head, chest and neck area is suggestive of a use related to fastening a garment around the neck or as a pendant, although again the total number of fasteners available for study is small.

Bracelets

A total of three Beaker period graves have recorded positions for copper alloy bracelets, all of which occur on the arm or wrist (Bardon; Somerford Keynes 1007; Raunds secondary in long barrow). Although a single Early Bronze Age bracelet from Castern is recorded at the pelvis rather than the arm or wrist, that from Amesbury G41was worn around the arm. It is likely that these were worn as either armlets or bracelets over both periods.

Necklaces

A total of three Beaker Period and 16 Early Bronze Age graves with necklaces were recorded with body positions, and consist of jet and jet-like materials, copper alloy, amber, faience, gold and composite necklaces. In the case of the

Beaker necklaces, all graves (Folkton 245, 8; Beggar's Haven; Ditchling Road) contained necklaces found around the neck of the deceased. Of the relevant Early Bronze Age sites, 13 contained necklaces in and around the neck or head including at least eight sites with necklaces specifically recorded as having been found around the neck (Weaverthorpe 44, 2; Goodmanham 121, 6; Garton Slack 29, 5; Garton Slack 75; Garrowby Wold 64; Middleton Moor; Shrewton G5j; Winterbourne Stoke G9). Two further necklaces were found at the waist or elbow (Langton 2, 2; Folkton 71, 6), and components of another necklace were recorded at the feet (Preshute G1a). In the case of the latter (Manton Barrow) the necklace components may belong to a necklace found above and behind the head of the inhumation, and were found beside a dagger and three awls. Thus, nearly all necklaces were worn as such, with a small number either placed alongside, perhaps as part of a cache of objects.

Special objects of gold

Among the special items of gold for which details of body placement are recorded, the most important are probably the two sheet gold plaques which occurred 'at the breast' at Little Cressingham and 'immediately on the breastbone' at Bush Barrow (Wilsford G5). These plaques, attached to their organic backings, were probably fixed to garments of textile or leather. Most of the other gold items derive from cremation burials, but the smaller gold lozenge from Bush Barrow was found behind the body, along with elements of the mace, and the four gold discs from Wilsford G47, 49 or 50 were found near the ears, and certainly above the shoulders. They may have been attached near to the upper terminals of the amber spacer plate necklace from this same burial.

Pottery

Body positions for a total of four pottery types have been examined.

 Beakers
 Accessory cups
 Collared Urns
 Food Vessels

It needs to be remembered that this data refers only to vessels found in graves with other associated grave goods, as defined within the remit of this project, and may or may

Table 11.7. Body positions of Beakers across all regions, by number of Beakers (including fragmentary beakers).

Position	E. Yorkshire	Peak District	Wessex	Other	Totals
Near head, in front or above	2	1	3	4	**10**
Near head, behind	4	0	1	2	**7**
Near chest, including in front	0	1	0	1	**2**
Behind back or by shoulders	3	3	2	5	**13**
Near pelvis, including behind	1	0	1	2	**4**
Near arms	0	0	1	2	**3**
At feet or legs	5	0	12	17	**34**
Total	**15**	**5**	**20**	**33**	**73**

Table 11.8. Beaker body placement: those in graves with significant grave goods compared with all Beakers ('all Beakers' data from Clarke 1970, 455).

Position	With significant grave goods	%	All Beakers	%
In front of head, above head or near chest	12	16	45	25
Behind head, shoulders or back	20	27	65	36
At feet or legs	34	47	69	39
Other positions	7	10	-	-
Totals	**73**	**100**	**179**	**100**

not relate to the proportions of different body placement positions relevant to these classes of pottery as a whole.

Beakers

A total of 73 graves contain a Beaker with positioning data. In examining Beaker placements there are significant differences between regions (Table 11.7). Although placement at the feet or legs is by far the most common practice (17 sites), Wessex has a comparatively restricted range of Beaker positions. Only nine of 21 Beaker graves contain Beakers away from the feet, and all of these are in different positions on the body. These include single graves with Beakers behind the head, above the head, at the chest, behind the back, at the shoulders and at the arms. This differs from East Yorkshire, where placement at the feet is closely matched by placement near or behind the head. Although there are only a total of five Peak District graves with Beaker position data, it is interesting to note that none are at the feet. Thus, as with Bronze Age daggers/knives, the placement of Beakers seems to represent a complex combination of expressions of burial practice at both the regional and wider level.

For Beakers, statistics for the body placement available for all vessels recorded up to 1970 are available (Clarke 1970, 455), and so it is possible to compare these general patterns with that obtained here for Beakers occurring in well-furnished graves only. The results of such a comparison are summarised in Table 11.8. There do not seem to be any major differences, although it may be that the higher incidence of Beakers placed at the feet or near legs in the well-furnished graves may be significant.

Accessory cups

Accessory cups are exclusively found in Early Bronze Age graves, and a total of eight sites have recorded positioning data. Of these graves, six cups are positioned in the head area, including two at the side, one at the neck, and one in front of the head. A further cup was inserted in the mouth of the inhumation at Garton Slack 40, displacing the jaw.

Collared Urns

Very few Collared Urns are found within inhumation burials, with only three graves containing relevant position data. Of these, each is placed in a different location, including one behind the hips, one at the crown of the head and one at the feet.

Food Vessels

As with accessory cups, Food Vessels are only found in Early Bronze Age contexts, and include a total of 23 graves with positioning data. There is a strong regional bias in results, as only three graves occur outside East Yorkshire, one in the Peak District and the remaining two in Wessex. Of the 20 East Yorkshire graves, 11 are found in front of the head. A further four graves have Food Vessels behind the head, and two above the head. Only four Food Vessels from East Yorkshire were found away from the head, including two near the shoulders, one at the chest and one near the hands.

Therefore, there appears to be a clear pattern of placement of Food Vessels near the head, particularly in front of the head or face. As with earlier Beaker body placements from East Yorkshire, there appears to be an emphasis in placing pottery vessels near the head in this region, although Beaker examples tend to be placed behind rather than in front of the head. Although very few numbers of Food Vessels occur in inhumations outside East Yorkshire, it is interesting to note that both graves from Wessex have Food Vessels by the knees rather than near the head.

Bags and caches

A number of objects appear to have been placed in specific tight groups at different points at the side or feet of the body, particularly in Beaker contexts. Most of the examples of such caches relate to graves which have been excavated under modern conditions, with careful record of the exact placement of all the grave goods A total of 12 Beaker and 7 Early Bronze Age sites have evidence for the deposition of grave goods in caches (Table 11.9 and Table 11.10). Necklaces were excluded as cache objects unless accompanied by another object type. In the case of Beaker caches, a common element in all 14 caches (from 12 sites) is the presence of at least one flint flake or scraper, commonly either a flake, a knife or barbed and tanged arrowheads, with three caches containing barbed and tanged arrowheads only. Other items present include sponge finger stones, awls, and spatulae. In three cases, at Raunds, Northamptonshire, Gravelly Guy, Oxfordshire and in the Amesbury Archer grave bracers are also present. The bracer at Raunds is highly fragmented, having one end missing and reworked into a smooth edge, and may suggest that at the time it was deposited it was being used as a stone tool. Although the Raunds and the Amesbury Archer graves both include a belt ring, and in the case of Amesbury Archer gold ornaments, the frequency of flint implements and other potential tools suggest that the character of caches is strongly associate with tool kits.

Table 11.9. Beaker sites identified as containing potential object caches.

Site	Cache summary
Acklam Wold 124, interment 4 (Mortimer), E. Yorks.	Inhumation: flint dagger under hand, further flint knife and implement found underneath dagger
Rudston 62, burial 4 (Greenwell), E. Yorks.	Inhumation: two flint flakes at chest, awl under flints, flint knife nearby
Mouse Low, Grindon, Staffordshire	Inhumation: two bone spatulae (ID 686 and ID 687) and two barbed and tanged arrowheads inside Beaker
Amesbury Archer, Wiltshire	Inhumation: three caches
	Cache 1. In front of head: copper dagger/knife, antler spatula, antler strip, 2 tusks, perforated oyster shell, worked flints, iron pyrites nodule
	Cache 2. Behind head and shoulder: 2 tusks, cushion stone, worked flints
	Cache 3. A looser group of objects in possible bag in front of knees: bracer (ID 56), copper dagger/knife, shale belt ring (ID 471), 2 gold basket-shaped ornaments, antler strip, worked flint
Thomas Hardye School, site 1004, grave 1643, Dorset	Inhumation: three barbed and tanged arrowheads in a group behind feet
Raunds, barrow 1, Northamptonshire	Inhumation: cluster of several objects beyond the feet, including a bracer (ID 116), 2 sponge finger stones (ID 117 and ID 125), an amber belt ring (ID 1565), set of 5 jet buttons, three bone spatulae, a tusk, a flint dagger, 3 flint scrapers, 6 flint flakes and a misc. stone
Ferry Fryston 2245, W. Yorks.	Inhumation: Beaker, bracer (ID 73), flint borer and flake in cluster beyond feet
Raunds, barrow 6, Northamptonshire	Inhumation: flint dagger, button of jet or jet-like material and flint flake below feet
Radley, ring ditch 201, central grave 203, Oxfordshire	Inhumation: 5 barbed and tanged arrowheads in cluster behind right foot
Barrow Hills, flat grave 4660, Oxfordshire	Inhumation: barbed and tanged arrowhead and two flint flakes at feet
Gravelly Guy, ring ditch 4004, Stanton Harcourt, Oxfordshire	Inhumation: a bracer (ID 74), sponge finger stone, antler spatula, 2 flint scrapers, and 7 barbed and tanged arrowheads in cluster near feet
Linch Hill, field XXI, ring ditch 1a, Stanton Harcourt, Oxfordshire	Inhumation: 7 barbed and tanged arrowheads in a tight cluster below the pelvis

Table 11.10. Early Bonze Age sites identified as containing potential object caches.

Site	Cache summary
Rudston 61, burial 6 (Greenwell), E. Yorks.	Inhumation: 3 flint flakes, a flint scraper and a bone point (ID 784) behind hips, point laying on flints
Garton Slack 65, interment 1 (Mortimer), E. Yorks.	Inhumation: awl (ID 1149) and flint flake together, close to left knee
Painsthorpe Wold 98, grave C (Mortimer), E. Yorks.	Inhumation: 2 flint knives, a beaver tooth, and flint flake in front of chest, one flint knife resting on flake
Garton Slack 137, E of centre (Mortimer), E. Yorks.	Inhumation: flint flake and awl, awl resting on flint
Amesbury G96a, Wiltshire	Cremation: cluster of objects resting against Collared Urn, including a composite necklace and awl
Preshute G1a, Wiltshire	Inhumation: 3 awls (ID 1426–8), beads and a dagger/knife at feet, awls close behind dagger/knife
Norton Bavant Borrow Pit, Sutton Veny, Wiltshire	Inhumation: 2 daggers/knives, one on top of one another (ID 1179 and ID 1187) and a grooved whetstone underneath daggers (ID 60), all behind head

For the Early Bronze Age period the identification of caches is more difficult. As many of the burials were cremations, the placing of any grave goods in a group close to the cremated human remains tended to be the norm. However, occasionally the deposition of a cache of objects can be suggested, and there are also a few examples associated with inhumation burials. Once again, the caches tend to contain items that may have comprised tool kits. Although they less frequently contain flints, instead awls, bone points, and whetstones are common features. Daggers/knives are also present in two caches. Thus, Early Bronze Age caches are similarly oriented towards tools, but associated with daggers/knives rather than bracers. It seems possible that these caches may be kits associated with the production and use of weapons or symbolically linked with warfare. In the Beaker period it appears that some caches are linked with archery and/or hunting and

flint tool production, given the prevalence of barbed and tanged arrowheads, while during the Early Bronze Age they are linked with metal blades, employed either in warfare or animal sacrifice.

Cremations

Examining cremation data introduces a number of problems when considering the function of objects. These include damage from the cremation fire which impacts on the ability to identify aspects of morphology and wear (and hence heirloom potential), and absence of any information on positioning in relation to the body prior to deposition. Nonetheless, some interesting patterns can be considered using a limited range of object types.

Object associations can occur in four basic locations in relation to both urned and unurned cremations: either

Table 11.11. Early Bronze Age cremation graves with both burnt and unburnt objects.

Site	Burnt object(s)	Unburnt object(s)	Uncertain
Stanton Moor 1926, Derbyshire	Bone pommel (ID 663)	Bone points x 2 (ID 661 and ID 662)	Dagger/knife (ID 1216), Collared Urn
Throwley Moor, Waterhouses, Staffordshire	Bone points x 3 (ID 669, ID 710 and ID 712)	Bone point (ID 664) Bone tube (ID 666)	Awl (ID 1232), Battle-axe, flints
Aldbourne G13, Wiltshire	Bone point (ID 813)	Bone tweezers (ID 766)	Bracer (ID 14), Perforated stone (ID 19)
Winterslow G21, Wiltshire	Bone point (ID 1040)	Composite necklace of jet, jet-like material and amber (ID 460–3 and ID 1523–5)	Collared Urn

Table 11.12. Early Bronze Age inhumation graves containing a burnt object.

Site	Period	Burnt object
Rudston 63, burial 3, (Greenwell), E. Yorks.	Early Bronze Age	Bone point (ID 783)
Wharram Percy 121 (Mortimer), E. Yorks.	Early Bronze Age	Bone point (ID 623)

Table 11.13. Objects placed on top of Early Bronze Age cremations, by number of objects.

Object types	East Yorkshire	Wessex
Awls	1	2
Accessory cup (whole only)	1	1
Daggers/knife	1	9
Bone points	1	3
Bead (individual)	1	1
Necklace	0	4

amongst or mixed within the cremation; at the top of the cremation; at the base of the deposit, or placed beside or nearby. In the case of urned cremations, objects either in, on or beneath a cremation will also be either inside or underneath an inverted urn. There is clearly a choice being made at various stages of the cremation process about where objects are to be placed. Some are burnt with the cremation, and some are placed with the cremated remains subsequently. A number are also seen to be separated from the cremated remains (pyre goods) and placed alongside with the unburnt objects (grave goods). Also, some cremations have been recorded as being placed within bags or cloths, perhaps with an object such as a point or pin holding the bag closed. These object types should appear more frequently at the top of cremations after the cloth, animal skin or similar material holding the cremation has decomposed.

Many objects associated with cremation graves can be identified as not having passed through the cremation fire, notably bone objects and, to a lesser extent, objects of copper alloy. Additionally, it would not be expected that objects of amber or jet would survive the high temperatures associated with the cremation of a human body. If these factors are considered, a total of over 142 of 250 (57%) of all Early Bronze Age cremation graves contain objects of bone, antler, tooth, amber, jet and jet-like materials and faience which by virtue of observation or composition are unburnt. A total of 27 bone objects from 27 sites have been identified as burnt. A total of seven objects of stone and copper alloy have also been recorded as burnt, including three stone battle-axes, two awls, a copper alloy dagger/

knife and a copper alloy implement. In most cases, objects identified as burnt were found alongside pottery and/or flint objects only. However, four graves contained burnt bone objects alongside objects likely to have remained unburnt (Table 11.11). Interestingly, the opposite also occurs, with two burnt objects occurring within Early Bronze Age inhumations (Table 11.12), and this may suggest that a few burnt objects were re-circulated. Thus, complexity in the process of object deposition in cremation practice is confirmed, with at least some tentative evidence for burning of objects along with the cremation, and others added to the burial deposit afterwards.

In examining the position of object types likely to have been used to fasten bags or cloths containing cremations, dress pins, awls, points, tusk/teeth and daggers/knives were selected as potential candidates. Objects used as fasteners should occur in greater frequency at the top of cremations. Unfortunately, many sources only list the presence of objects as 'with' the cremation, and from this it is impossible to attribute the object to a position either within, on top of, or beside the urn using this data. As such there are many sites where positioning data cannot be extracted. On this basis, there is no available data on tusk/ tooth position, and very few examples for dress pins. As a whole, there may be evidence for the practice of using bone points or daggers as fasteners for cremation bags, but only as a significant practice in Wessex contexts (Table 11.13).

AGE AND SEX

A further element which can provide insight into burial

Table 11.14. Total number of Beaker and Early Bronze Age graves with either male or female interments, divided by regions.

Period	Region	Male only	Female only	Male and female	Total
Beaker	East Yorkshire	13 (76%)	4 (24%)	0	17
	Peak District	8 (89%)	1 (11%)	0	9
	Wessex	13 (88%)	1(6%)	1 (6%)	15
	Other	27 (77%)	8 (23%)	0	35
All Beaker		**61 (80%)**	**14 (19%)**	**1 (1%)**	**76**
EBA	East Yorkshire	19 (37%)	32 (63%)	0	51
	Peak District	5 (45%)	6 (55%)	0	11
	Wessex	15 (52%)	13 (45%)	1 (3%)	29
All EBA		**39 (43%)**	**51 (56%)**	**1 (1%)**	**91**

Table 11.15. Frequency of selected object types found with males in Beaker period graves, sorted from largest to smallest by grave frequency (minimum 2 instances, n=62).

Object type	Number				Total
	E. Yorks.	Peak	Wessex	Other	
Dagger/knife	4	3	7	8	**22**
Barbed/tanged arrowhead	0	2	4	8	**14**
Bracer	0	0	6	8	**14**
Spatula	0	4	4	6	**14**
Flint dagger	2	2	0	5	**9**
Point	2	1	2	4	**9**
Awl	1	1	3	3	**8**
V-perforated button	6	0	0	1	**7**
Belt ring/pulley object	3	0	2	1	**6**
Pommel	1	0	2	3	**6**
Sponge finger stone	1	0	1	3	**5**
Iron pyrite nodule	3	1	0	1	**5**
Dress pin	0	0	2	2	**4**
Toggle	0	0	2	2	**4**
Earring/tress ring	0	0	1	2	**3**
Bead	0	1	0	1	**2**
Plano-convex knife	0	2	0	0	**2**
Tusk/tooth	0	0	1	1	**2**
Button set	1	0	0	1	**2**

practice is the relationship between the age and sex of the interred and the associated objects. Patterns of association in specific object types across sex and age parameters can provide evidence for differences in social function, such as rank or status as well as illuminate roles and meaning related to gender. The aim is to examine available age and sex evidence in order to identify any relevant patterns of difference in grave object deposition between Beaker and Early Bronze Age contexts, as well as any variations detected between the three main project regions: East Yorkshire, the Peak District, and Wessex. Evidence for differences in grave object associations based on sex will be presented first, followed by those related to the age of the individual.

At the outset it is important to assess the validity of the data compiled for human remains associated with grave goods covered by the project. The majority of sites were excavated in the 19th century by antiquarian scholars, and in many cases human remains were not retained for

deposit in museum collections. Furthermore, some later scholars synthesising these results throughout the first half of the 20th century have made identifications of sex based largely on object associations rather than on actual skeletal observations. It has therefore been necessary to develop a system to rate the accuracy of different age and sex characteristics for all sites used in this chapter and throughout the volume. Four categories were devised, listed in descending levels of reliability.

The most reliable data comes from excavation reports which include a human bone report, frequently from a named specialist (Category 1, including 29% of sites of all periods and regions with either age or sex data). Although this consists largely of modern excavation reports from the 1950s onwards, several earlier sources fulfil this requirement. A very small number of sites excavated using modern archaeological methods had age and sex data but no specific bone report, and these were considered to be the next most reliable (Category 2, 2%). The largest number

Table 11.16. Frequency of selected object types found with females in Beaker period graves, sorted from largest to smallest by grave frequency (minimum 1 instance, n=15).

Object type	Composition	Number				Total
		E. Yorks.	Peak	Wessex	Other	
Awl	Copper/bronze	2	0	1	3	**6**
Earring/tress ring	Copper/bronze	1	1	0	1	**3**
Bead	All types	0	0	0	2	**2**
Bracelet	All types	0	0	0	2	**2**
Dagger/knife	Copper/bronze	0	0	0	1	**1**
Belt ring/pulley object	All types	1	0	0	0	**1**
Bracer	Stone	0	0	1	0	**1**
V-perforated button	All types	0	0	0	1	**1**

of sites are those with data taken from antiquarian sources and which are widely recognised as having reliable or fairly reliable age and sex classifications (Category 3, 60%). Primarily, this includes the published work of Greenwell (summarised in Kinnes and Longworth 1985), Hoare (1812), Mortimer (1905), and Bateman (1848; 1861). The final group contains those whose data could not be reliably considered (Category 4, 10%). In all cases of antiquarian identifications, data from original accounts was obtained where possible, and this resulted in significantly reducing the total number of unreliable information. All analysis has been restricted to the first three categories of data, namely reliable antiquarian sources and data from modern excavations. All sites included in the project database were selected on the basis of the presence of one or more non-pottery and non-flint object types, with the exception of flint daggers and barbed and tanged arrowheads, which were included if accompanied by a non-flint/Beaker object. Pottery values were only included if accompanied by these other object types.

Objects associations with males versus females

In total, 76 Beaker and 91 Early Bronze Age graves have a reliable sex identification attributed, according to the parameters outlined above. Their regional distribution is summarised in Table 11.14. In the case of the Wessex region, one site from each period contained a multiple grave with identified individuals of different sex. Interestingly, across all analysed regions there is a shift in frequency from predominantly male burials in the Beaker period (80% across all regions), to a majority of female burials in the Early Bronze Age (56% across all regions). The most dramatic shift is in East Yorkshire, where almost two thirds of Early Bronze Age graves are female.

Across all regions, there are also differences in the types of objects which appear most frequently in male as opposed to female graves. Values for Beaker object types outside East Yorkshire, the Peak District and Wessex are included in total numbers from all regions; however, due to their wide geographic range they are not incorporated into discussions regarding regional differences. Based on total numbers of objects present, the commonest Beaker period male grave good is a dagger/knife, occurring in 22 graves, or 35% of male Beaker sites (Table 11.15). This is followed by barbed and tanged arrowheads (23%), bracers

(23%), spatulae (23%), flint daggers (15%) and bone points (15%). Female Beaker graves, however, display significant differences. The most common object type in Beaker female graves is an awl, occurring in 40% of all identified graves (Table 11.16). Although awls are present in male Beaker graves across all regions, their frequency is much lower (13%). Other grave good frequencies for Beaker females are uncertain due to the small total number of identified female Beaker graves, but they include copper alloy earrings (20%), individual beads (13%), and bracelets (13%).

When grave assemblages are compared by individual region, significant differences also emerge between male graves across different regions. In order to confirm that observed differences in regional frequency of specific object types in graves of identified sex were not a function of sampling bias, the total frequency of all objects from known inhumations or cremations regardless of skeletal characteristics was also calculated (Table 11.17 and Table 11.18). This highlights any significant differences between frequencies in graves irrespective of sexing data. However, when this data is introduced a number of observations can be made; in particular male Beaker grave assemblages from East Yorkshire differ markedly from those from Wessex and the Peak District (Table 11.19 and Table 11.20). For example, V-perforated buttons occur in nearly half of male Beaker graves in East Yorkshire (46%). None are present in identified male Wessex or Peak District graves, and if unidentified interments are taken into account there is still a significant majority of V-perforated buttons from East Yorkshire over other contexts. Although total object numbers are small, belt ring/pulley objects, also a feature of male Beaker graves from East Yorkshire (23%), are less common elsewhere. Surprisingly, although bracers have a wide distribution across Britain during the Beaker period, of those in grave assemblages with identified sex data, none occur in East Yorkshire or the Peak District. If all graves, regardless of skeletal data, are taken into account this patterns still holds, with 10 of 12 bracers from Wessex, the Peak District or East Yorkshire occurring in Wessex graves.

Although male East Yorkshire graves are distinctive, there are clearer parallels between male Beaker grave assemblages in the Peak District and Wessex. Daggers/ knives, spatulae and barbed and tanged arrowheads occur frequently in both these regions, with the most significant difference being the aforementioned presence of bracers exclusively within Wessex graves with sex data. Also

Table 11.17. Frequency of selected object types found in Beaker period graves, regardless of skeletal data (minimum 2 instances).

Object type	Number				Totals
	E. Yorks. graves (39)	Peak graves (34)	Wessex graves (35)	Other graves (54)	(162)
Barbed/tanged arrowhead	0	3	8	12	23
Awl	5	3	6	7	21
Bead	1	1	0	4	6
Belt ring/pulley object	7	0	7	6	20
Bracer	2	0	10	15	27
Button set	2	0	0	1	3
Button, unspecified morphology	3	2	0	1	6
Dagger/knife	8	17	16	16	57
Disc, gold	0	0	2	1	3
Dress pin	0	0	2	2	4
Earring, copper/bronze	1	1	1	4	7
Flint dagger	4	2	1	6	13
Iron pyrite nodule	4	1	0	1	6
Plano-convex knife	0	2	1	0	3
Point	6	3	4	4	17
Pommel	3	0	3	4	10
Spatula	0	6	4	7	17
Sponge finger stone	1	0	3	3	7
Toggle	0	0	2	2	4
Tusk/tooth	0	1	2	2	5
V-perforated button	14	4	4	4	26

Table 11.18. Frequency of selected object types found in Early Bronze Age graves, regardless of skeletal data, by number of graves (minimum 2 instances).

Object type	Number			Totals
	E. Yorks. graves (114)	Peak graves (63)	Wessex graves (223)	(400)
Accessory cup	4	3	37	44
Awl	19	14	49	82
Barbed/tanged arrowhead	1	0	3	4
Battle-axe	7	3	6	16
Bead	4	4	7	15
Belt hook	1	0	3	4
Belt ring/pulley object	0	0	5	5
Button, unspecified type	3	2	2	7
Collared Urn	10	16	19	45
Dagger/knife	9	9	87	105
Dress pin	4	0	9	13
Earring, copper/bronze	2	0	0	2
Fastener	4	0	0	4
Food Vessel	25	3	5	33
Grooved stone	0	0	4	4
Mace-head	1	0	1	2
Misc. gold	0	0	5	5
Necklace	10	10	66	86
Perforated stone	0	0	11	11
Plate, bone	0	0	4	4
Point	41	24	34	99
Pommel	0	3	8	11
Spatula	2	0	1	3
Stud	1	1	2	4
Tube, bone	1	1	2	4
Tusk/tooth	7	4	4	15
V-perforated button	5	0	5	10

of note is the regional distribution of barbed and tanged arrowheads within identified male Beaker graves. None are present in male East Yorkshire grave assemblages, even if grave sites without skeletal data are considered.

It should be emphasised that all frequencies listed here, including those sites without skeletal data, are based on more narrow parameters in that flint daggers and barbed and tanged arrowheads have been recorded only if other

Table 11.19. Most frequent object types for Beaker males and females across all regions, listed in order of frequency according to number of graves present. Objects common to both groups in italics.

Male graves (n=62)	Number of objects	Female graves (n=15)	Number of Objects
Dagger/knife	22	*Awl*	6
Barbed and tanged arrowhead	14	Copper alloy earrings	3
Bracer	14	Individual beads	2
Spatula	14	Bracelets	2
Flint dagger	9		
Bone point	9		
Awl	8		
V-perforated button	7		

Table 11.20. Most frequent object types for Beaker males by region, listed in order of frequency according to number of graves present. Objects common to more than one group in italics.

Male graves, E. Yorkshire (n=13)	Number of objects	Male graves, Peak District (n=8)	Number of objects	Male graves, Wessex (n=14)	Number of objects
V-perforated button	6	*Spatula*	4	*Dagger/knife*	7
Dagger/knife	4	*Dagger/knife*	3	Bracer	6
Belt ring/pulley	3	*Barbed/tanged arrowhead*	2	*Barbed/tanged arrowhead*	4
Iron pyrite nodule	3				
Bone point	2	Flint dagger	2	*Spatula*	4
Flint dagger	2	Plano-convex knife	2	Awl	3

important objects were also present. Thus, results for flint material is not representative of all sites of the period. The lack of barbed and tanged arrowheads in East Yorkshire is not necessarily indicative of the lack of arrowheads of this type across the region, but rather the lack of arrowheads found in association with other non-pottery and non-flint objects. Due to the small total number of female graves in the Beaker period, reliable conclusions regarding regional differences were not possible.

For Early Bronze Age graves, the association of daggers/knives for males and awls for females established in the Beaker period continues when considered across all regions, but with the exception of the Peak District where the total number of identified male graves is too low to draw reliable conclusions. Across all sites, daggers/knives occur in 35% of all male graves (Table 11.21), followed by bone points (20%), Food Vessels (15%), tusk/teeth (13%), and battle-axes (13%). V-perforated buttons are present in 10% of all male Early Bronze Age graves and, as with Beaker assemblages, remain exclusive to East Yorkshire. Female graves across all regions most frequently contain awls, as in the Beaker period (38%), followed by necklaces (31%), bone points (21%), and Food Vessels (15%) (Table 11.22). Firstly, we can see the addition of new object types, particularly new pottery forms, bone and tooth objects, battle-axes and necklaces, alongside a longer tradition of objects from the Beaker period, namely awls, and V-perforated buttons. Secondly, it is clear that the types of objects continue to differ between male and female graves. Most notable is the strong association between female graves and necklaces, which occur only infrequently in male graves (10%). Alongside this, however, bone points and tusk/teeth become regular features in graves of both sexes, such that their function across both sexes must be similar.

If Early Bronze Age object frequencies by sex are considered by region, further patterns of difference emerge (Table 11.23 and Table 11.24). As with the Beaker period, male graves from East Yorkshire contain elements less frequent in Wessex male grave contexts. Perhaps the most striking are Food Vessels which occur almost exclusively in East Yorkshire graves, both male and female. The lone Wessex example is Sutton Veny G4a, Wiltshire, where a Food Vessel was found at the knees of a male inhumation alongside a dagger/knife and an accessory cup. The combination of a Food Vessel, common in East Yorkshire and an accessory cup, common to Wessex, in the same context is unique. However, it should be noted that other Food Vessels from graves without skeletal data are present in both the Peak District and Wessex. Nonetheless, three quarters of all identified Food Vessel graves are from East Yorkshire. V-perforated buttons also remain common to male East Yorkshire graves, although the same number of V-perforated buttons occur at a number of Early Bronze Age Wessex graves without skeletal data. In the case of male Wessex burials, three sites include necklaces, while there are no examples of male graves with necklaces in East Yorkshire. Finally, although daggers/knives continue to remain important in male graves in both regions through the Early Bronze Age, in Wessex they seem to take on new importance. In Wessex, daggers/knives occur in 56% of male graves, while in East Yorkshire they occur in just over 21%. If all graves regardless of skeletal data are considered, this ratio becomes more pronounced, with a total of 81% of all Early Bronze Age graves with daggers/knives occurring in Wessex.

Unlike the Beaker period, there are sufficient Early Bronze Age female graves to compare differences between female grave from Wessex and East Yorkshire. Overall,

Table 11.21. Frequency of selected object types found with males in Early Bronze Age graves, sorted from largest to smallest by grave frequency (minimum 2 instances).

Object type	Number			Total
	E. Yorks.	Peak	Wessex	
Dagger/knife	4	1	9	**14**
Point	3	1	4	**8**
Food Vessel	5	0	1	**6**
Battle axe	3	0	2	**5**
Tusk/tooth	2	1	2	**5**
Collared Urn	1	2	1	**4**
V-perforated button	4	0	0	**4**
Necklace	0	1	2	**3**
Awl	1	1	1	**3**
Grooved stone	0	0	3	**3**
Accessory cup	0	0	2	**2**
Perforated stone	0	0	2	**2**
Belt hook	0	0	2	**2**
Mace-head	1	0	1	**2**
Misc. gold	0	0	2	**2**
Plate, bone	0	0	2	**2**

Table 11.22. Frequency of selected object types found with females in Early Bronze Age graves, sorted from largest to smallest by grave frequency (minimum 2 instances).

Object type	Number			Total
	E. Yorks.	Peak	Wessex	
Awl	14	0	6	**20**
Necklace	8	5	3	**16**
Point	11	0	0	**11**
Food Vessel	8	0	0	**8**
Dagger/knife	0	0	4	**4**
Collared Urn	2	0	1	**3**
Accessory cup	1	0	2	**3**
Tusk/tooth	2	1	0	**3**
Bead	0	1	1	**2**
Fastener	2	0	0	**2**

Table 11.23. Most frequent Early Bronze Age object types for males and females across all regions, listed in order of frequency according to number of graves present. Objects common to both in italics.

Male graves (n=40)	Number of objects	Female graves (n=52)	Number of objects
Dagger/knife	14	Necklace	16
Bone point	8	Awl	20
Food Vessel	6	*Bone point*	11
Battle-axe	5	*Food Vessel*	8
Tusk/tooth	5	*Dagger/knife*	4
V-perforated button	4		
Collared Urn	4		

Table 11.24. Most frequent object types for Early Bronze Age males and females by region and sex, listed in order of frequency according to number of graves present.

Region	Male graves	Number of objects	Female graves	Number of objects
East	Food Vessel	5	Awl	14
Yorkshire	Dagger/knife	4	Bone point	11
	V-perforated button	4	Necklace	8
(Male n=19	Bone point	3	Food Vessel	8
Female n=32)	Battle-axe	3		
Wessex	Dagger/knife	9	Awl	6
	Bone point	4	Dagger/knife	4
(Male n=16	Grooved stone	3	Necklace	3
Female n=16)			Accessory cup	2

Table 11.25. Number of Beaker graves with age and sex data used in analysis, by number of graves with relationships analysed in italics.

Region	Child		Youth		Adult		Mature		Notes
	male	female	male	female	male	female	male	female	
E. Yorkshire	0	0	0	0	*6*	2	*5*	2	No child and youth sites for analysis; too few female graves for comparison
Peak	0	0	1	0	1	0	5	0	Too few sites with age or sex for comparison
Wessex	0	0	0	0	*10*	1	*3*	0	No child and youth sites for analysis; too few female graves for comparison
Other	0	0	0	0	*20*	5	*5*	2	Too few child and youth sites for analysis; too few female graves for comparison
Total	**0**	**0**	**1**	**0**	**37**	**8**	**18**	**4**	

Table 11.26. Number of Early Bronze Age graves with age and sex data used in analysis, by number of graves with relationships analysed in italics.

Region	Child		Youth		Adult		Mature		Notes
	male	female	male	female	male	female	male	female	
E. Yorkshire	1	0	2	6	*9*	*17*	*6*	6	Too few child and youth sites for comparison
Peak	0	0	0	0	2	2	3	0	Too few sites with age or sex for comparison
Wessex	0	1	1	2	8	*6*	1	*3*	Too few child and youth sites for analysis; too few mature male graves for comparison
Total	**1**	**1**	**3**	**8**	**19**	**25**	**10**	**9**	

the differences are equally dramatic as male graves, with few similar objects between assemblages. For example, although awls and necklaces are similarly common in both regions, bone points are considerably rarer in female Wessex graves. As with male graves, Food Vessels are only found in East Yorkshire. Finally, although strongly linked to male graves, daggers/knives are still found in 29% of female Wessex graves and are absent from the other regions.

Object association by age group

In terms of understanding patterns of object association on the basis of age, age data was divided into four categories: (a) child – any individual under 12 years of age, (2) youth – any individual between 12 and 18 years of age, (3) adult – any individual between 19 and 40 years of age, and (4) mature – any individual over 40 years old. In total, 67 Beaker and 85 Early Bronze Age graves with age data were selected for analysis.

Given the observed differences within types of grave good on the basis of sex and region already identified, the best approach might be to explore age, sex and region in tandem in order to establish relevant differences. The limitation of this approach is that the total numbers of many age and sex categories within each region are too small to reach meaningful conclusions. In the case of Beaker graves, analysis is limited to comparison of adult and mature graves from Wessex and East Yorkshire, and to a lesser extent the Peak District (Table 11.25 and Table 11.26). Although

Beaker graves from other areas are not normally examined in detail in other parts of this chapter, the large number of sites available for analysis requires some comment. Comparisons reveal that most object types common in adult male Beaker graves are also common in mature graves, and there is little to suggest differentiation of grave object deposition between adults and mature graves (Table 11.27, Table 11.28 and Table 11.29). A notable exception, however, are pommels, which are more common in mature graves, with one example from Helperthorpe 49, burial 6 (Greenwell), East Yorkshire and three examples from other counties (Foxley Farm, Eynsham 15, Oxfordshire; Gravelly Guy 4004, Oxfordshire; Pyecombe, East Sussex). A further example from Garton Slack 107, grave E (Mortimer), East Yorkshire could also be added, occurring in a mature grave of unknown sex. As has been noted previously, many pommels are in a very worn state, and their presence in mature graves is an important factor in considering the practice of keeping heirlooms (see Chapter 10).

In the case of the Early Bronze Age, the total number of child and youth graves is also too few for meaningful comparison. However, objects from both male and female adult and mature graves from East Yorkshire can be compared, as well as mature female graves from Wessex (Table 11.30, Table 11.31 and Table 11.32). As with Beaker graves, in all three comparisons (East Yorkshire adult versus mature male graves, East Yorkshire adult versus mature female graves, and Wessex adult versus mature female graves), most object types common in adult graves are also

Table 11.27. Comparison of frequency of object types from Beaker adult and mature graves from East Yorkshire, by number of graves. Objects common to more than one group in italics.

East Yorkshire adult male (n=6)	Number of graves	East Yorkshire mature male *(n=5)*	Number of graves
V-perforated button	3	*V-perforated button*	2
Belt ring/pulley object	2	Flint dagger	2
Dagger/knife	2	*Dagger/knife*	1
Iron pyrite nodule	2	*Belt ring/pulley object*	1
		Pommel	1
		Bone point	1
		Iron pyrite nodule	1

Table 11.28. Comparison of frequency of object types from Beaker adult and mature graves from Wessex, by number of graves. Object types common to both age groups in italics.

Wessex adult male (n=10)	Number of graves	Wessex mature male (n=3)	Number of graves
Dagger/knife	5	*Dagger/knife*	2
Bracer	4	*Barbed/tanged arrowhead*	1
Barbed/tanged arrowhead	3	*Spatula*	1
Spatula	2	Sponge finger stone	1
Awl	2	*Awl*	1
Bone point	2	*Bracer*	1
Toggle	2	Dress pin	1
Pommel	2		
Belt ring/pulley object	2		

Table 11.29. Comparison of frequency of object types from Beaker adult and mature graves from other counties, by number of graves. Object types common to both groups in italics.

Other counties adult male (n=20)	Number of graves	Other counties mature male (n=6)	Number of graves
Barbed/tanged arrowhead	7	*Dagger/knife*	5
Bracer	6	Pommel	3
Flint dagger	4	*Spatula*	2
Spatula	4	*Bracer*	2
Dagger/knife	4	*Barbed/tanged arrowhead*	2
Bone point	3		

Table 11.30. Comparison of frequency of object types from Early Bronze Age male adult and mature graves from East Yorkshire, by number of graves. Object types common to both groups in italics.

East Yorkshire adult male (n=9)	Number of graves	East Yorkshire mature male (n=6)	Number of graves
Dagger/knife	2	Food Vessel	3
Battle-axe	2	*Dagger/knife*	2
V-perforated button	2	Barbed/tanged arrowhead	2

Table 11.31. Comparison of frequency of object types from Early Bronze Age female adult and mature graves from East Yorkshire, by number of graves. Object types common to both groups in italics.

East Yorkshire adult female (n=17)	Number of graves	East Yorkshire mature female (n=6)	Number of graves
Awl	8	*Awl*	2
Necklace	6	*Bone point*	2
Bone point	6	Collared Urn	1
Food Vessel	5	*Food Vessel*	1
		Fastener	1

Table 11.32. Comparison of frequency of object types from Early Bronze Age female adult and mature graves from Wessex, by number of graves. Object types common to both groups in italics.

Wessex adult female (n=6)	Number of graves	Wessex mature female (n=3)	Number of graves
Dagger/knife	2	*Necklace*	2
Awl	1	*Awl*	2
Necklace	1	*Dagger/knife*	1
Accessory cup	1	Pommel	1
Iron pyrite nodule	1	Stud	1
		Accessory cup	1
		Other whetstone	1

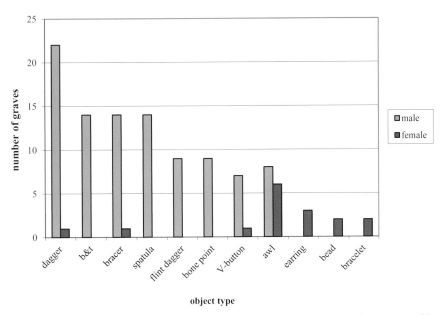

Figure 11.1. Beaker burials: the occurrence of selected object types according to sex of burial.

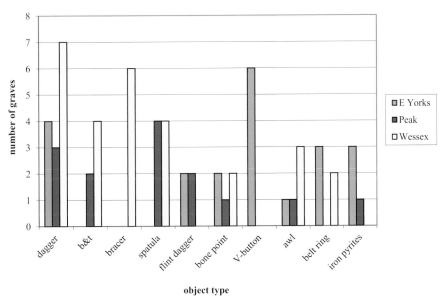

Figure 11.2. Male Beaker burials: the occurrence of selected object types by region.

common in mature graves. Perhaps the most significant exception is the lack of necklaces in mature female graves from East Yorkshire. Although there are only three mature graves available for comparison, it is unusual that no necklaces are present given the significant proportion of adult female graves with necklaces.

Age and sex summary

The results indicate that in terms of object deposition in grave contexts in the Beaker and Early Bronze Age, the selection of grave goods was influenced by at least three different criteria, namely gender, region and period.

The main conclusions relating to gender may be summarised as follows:

- Well-furnished Beaker graves are more often male, whilst in the Early Bronze Age the gender division was more equal.

- In the Beaker period there is a clear gender division within the object types included in graves (Figure 11.1). Males are accompanied by a wider range of items, especially daggers, barbed and tanged arrowheads, bracers, spatulae, flint daggers, bone points, V-perforated buttons and awls, while females have only awls, or in a few cases earrings, beads or bracelet.

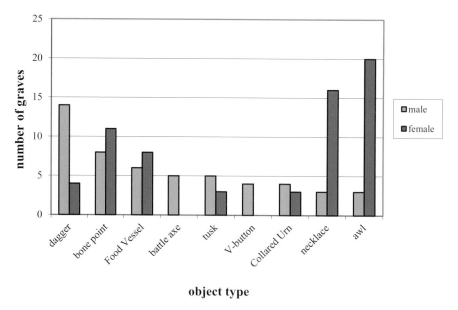

Figure 11.3. Early Bronze Age burials: the occurrence of selected object types by sex.

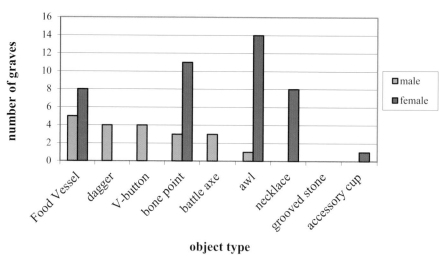

Figure 11.4. Early Bronze Age burials: the occurrence of selected object types by sex in the East Yorkshire region.

- Some regional differences amongst the male Beaker graves can be distinguished (Figure 11.2). Daggers are found in all three regions, as also are bone points and awls at lower levels. However V-perforated buttons are more common in East Yorkshire, bracers in Wessex, belt rings in East Yorkshire and Wessex, and arrowheads and spatulae in Wessex and the Peak District.
- In the Early Bronze Age the gender pattern of daggers with males and awls with females continues from the Beaker period (Figure 11.3). Food Vessels, bone points, tusks and Collared Urns also occur with both men and women.
- Early Bronze Age battle-axes and V-perforated buttons occur with men, while a smaller range of goods associated with women are dominated by necklaces (Figure 11.3).

- Once again some regional differences can be discerned (Figure 11.4 and Figure 11.5). In East Yorkshire V-perforated buttons, daggers and battle-axes occur in male graves, while necklaces are found with females. However in Wessex, necklaces occur in graves of both men and women, and there is a noted predominance of daggers, which also occur in graves of both sexes.

The long currency of daggers/knives in male assemblages in all regions, and in both Beaker and Early Bronze Age contexts, suggests that daggers held primary importance in expressing male roles and/or identity across Britain at this time. Similarly, awls can be viewed as central to female roles at this wider scale. This is highly significant as it suggests that, symbolically at least, there were clear differences in the roles of both women and men in Beaker and Bronze Age society across Britain. In addition, within

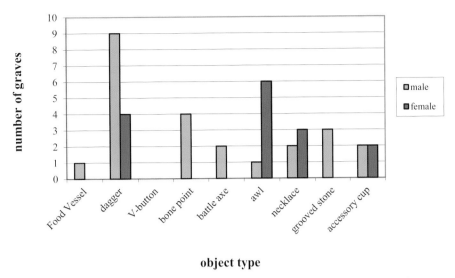

object type

Figure 11.5. Early Bronze Age burials: the occurrence of selected object types by sex in the Wessex region.

this wider scale of gender-based object association are patterns of similarity and difference which are contingent on time and place. Some objects, most notably bracers, barbed and tanged arrowheads, flint daggers, sponge finger stones and spatulae, do not remain important into the Early Bronze Age. These are replaced by an increased emphasis on bone points, necklaces and pottery forms such as Food Vessels and accessory cups. Additionally, many objects from East Yorkshire such as V-perforated buttons, belt ring/pulley objects and Food Vessels are used to express meaning, social roles, and identity at a more local, regional level. Necklaces, common in female Wessex Early Bronze Age graves, can be viewed in a similar manner. This would indicate that although many object types occur across all regions, the selection of some object types as relevant to the expression of gender, identity and social meaning is fundamentally negotiated at the regional level in both the Beaker period and in the Early Bronze Age.

Finally, it is difficult to see differences in the pace or scale of change in male versus female graves between the Beaker and Early Bronze Age periods, although arguably the small numbers of some object types often limits the usefulness of the results. This is potentially highly significant as it suggests that many of the patterns outlined above are evident from the outset of the Beaker period and are maintained throughout the Early Bronze Age. This applies particularly to the placing of daggers/ knives in adult and mature male graves. Although the types of objects change through time, it is less clear that there are substantial changes in underlying social processes and structure. In addition, there appears to be little available evidence for difference between object types deposited in adult versus mature graves in either the Beaker or Early Bronze Age, with the exception of pommels for Beaker period males from 'other regions' and Early Bronze Age necklaces for Wessex females. Thus, although there appears

to be differences in the nature of inclusion of grave goods in terms of gender, this is not often demonstrable in terms of age. Although it may be possible that differences did exist between adult and younger graves, the sample size of youth and child graves simply is too small to allow the establishment of any relationship.

ASSOCIATIONS

A final approach in exploring object function is the examination of patterns of associations between objects within individual grave assemblages. One aspect of this, namely the occurrence of caches, has already been discussed above, and has demonstrated how certain object types commonly found in association with other object types within a grave might be more easily interpreted. This section pursues other levels of relationship and explores patterns of associations between all recorded object types available.

Graves and objects were selected for analysis from the Beaker and Early Bronze Age periods where objects were in clear association with either an interred individual or group of individuals. As in previous sections, analysis divided the material into Beaker and Early Bronze Age contexts as well as between the key regions of East Yorkshire, the Peak District and Wessex; it included all graves which contained at least one non-flint and non-pottery object in association with the interment. The previous sections on age, sex and position of objects on the body have clearly shown that there are relationships between object types and the sex of the interred as well as differences in object frequencies by region. Associations between object types, and their changing patterns over time and space, can also provide clues to social practice and meaning, including, for example, the identity and social role of the deceased, evidence for ranking or social stratification, or aspects of burial ceremony and practice.

Table 11.33. Selected Beaker Period object types from all inhumation or cremation contexts, by number of sites.

Object type	Composition	Number				Total (157)
		E. Yorks graves (36)	Peak graves (35)	Wessex graves (34)	Other graves (52)	
Dagger/knife	Copper/bronze	11	17	12	11	**51**
Bracer	Stone	3	0	10	12	**25**
Barbed/tanged arrowhead	Flint	0	3	10	11	**24**
V-perforated button	All types	12	3	4	5	**24**
Awl	Copper/bronze	6	4	6	6	**22**
Belt ring/pulley object	All types	8	0	6	5	**19**
Spatula	All types	0	6	4	7	**17**
Point	Bone	6	2	3	4	**15**
Flint dagger	Flint	5	2	1	6	**14**
Individual bead	All types	3	1	0	3	**7**
Sponge finger stone	Stone	1	0	3	3	**7**

Method

There are a number of object types which occur only rarely in graves and, as previously, these have been excluded from the analysis. Only object types which occur in the greatest number of graves are used, but these also now include a wider range of flint objects, including scrapers, flakes and other implements. Objects believed to be related are discussed together as groups. Associations have been identified on the basis of two sets of relationships. The first is based on frequency of associations within each object type, where an object is considered to have either a strong, weak or no association. A strong association is defined as an association with another object with a frequency of 50% or more, while a weak association is one with a frequency of 25 to 49%. In both cases there must be at least two instances for an association to be considered valid. The second parameter compares the relative strength of association between two related objects, defining the association as *mutual* if each has the same strength of relationship, or *uneven* if they do not. Associations can also be defined using the strongest association present only, such that an uneven weak association means one object association is weak while the corresponding association is not present. Similarly, a strong uneven association means one association is strong, while the corresponding association is weak or not present. There is a distinction made between an *association* and a *relationship*. An association is any result where a significant number of sites contain the same sets of objects; a meaningful association is an inferred relationship between object types which is more likely to have been based on actual patterns of burial practice in the past.

Object associations during the Beaker Period

In the case of Beaker object types, a total of 11 object types were selected for further analysis (Table 11.33).

East Yorkshire

Several relationships can be identified from Beaker grave object associations in East Yorkshire, although the total number of sites in some cases is rather low (Table 11.34). These include uneven associations between: (1) belt ring/pulley objects and V-perforated buttons, (2) belt ring/pulley objects and bracers and daggers/knives, (3) bracers and daggers/knives, (4) flint daggers and V-perforated buttons, and finally (5) flint daggers and bone points. In the case of belt ring/pulley objects and V-perforated buttons the relationship is uneven, with belt ring/pulley objects strongly associated with V-perforated buttons but V-perforated buttons are only weakly associated in return, occurring together in four of 12 sites (33%) where V-perforated buttons are recorded. Belt ring/pulley objects also have a weak and uneven association with both bracers and daggers/knives. In the case of bracers, they are strongly associated with belt ring/pulley objects, although there are only three sites available for comparison. Bracers also have a strong and uneven relationship with daggers/knives. Daggers/knives, however, only appear alongside bracers, belt rings/pulley objects or V-perforated buttons less than 20% of the time. Daggers/knives are most frequently found in graves without other object types. Flint daggers, on the other hand have an uneven association with V-perforated buttons, to which they are strongly associated, and a mutual weak association with bone points. Although associations between many of these objects are overlapping and complex some conclusions can be made. Daggers/knives, when associated with other objects, can appear along with a wide variety of object types, and therefore appear initially not to be clearly linked with any particular object types. There does appear to be a link between belt ring/pulley objects and V-perforated buttons in East Yorkshire, which likely relates to their both having functioned as dress equipment. If these inter-relationships are expressed visually (Figure 11.6), it suggests that there may have been a suite of four key objects which were part of an interchangeable package, namely belt ring/pulley objects, V-perforated buttons, bracers, and dagger/knives, which all have some co-associations. Flint daggers could be included, but their

Table 11.34. Relationship matrix for selected Beaker object types from East Yorkshire, by number and frequency in graves.

	Awl	Bead	Belt ring/pulley object	Bracer	Dagger/ knife	Flint dagger	Bone point	V-perf. button	**Total**
Awl		0	0	0	1 (16%)	0	0	0	**6**
Bead	0		0	1 (33%)	1 (33%)	0	0	1 (33%)	**3**
Belt ring/pulley	0	0		2 (25%)	2 (25%)	0	0	4 (50%)	**8**
Bracer	0	1 (33%)	1 (33%)		2 (66%)	0	0	1 (33%)	**3**
Dagger/ knife	1 (9%)	1 (9%)	2 (18%)	2 (18%)		0	0	2 (18%)	**11**
Flint dagger	0	0	1 (20%)	0	0		2 (40%)	3 (60%)	**5**
Bone point	0	0	1 (16%)	0	0	0		1 (16%)	**6**
V-perf. button	0	1 (8%)	4 (33%)	0	0	3 (25%)	0		**12**

association with bone points, suggests their presence within a different object set.

Peak District
Owing to the small number of available sites, attributing relationships between objects in the Peak District during the Beaker period has been less successful. Only a single relationship can be identified, a mutually strong association between spatulae and barbed and tanged arrowheads (Table 11.35). A strong mutual association, however, is significant and suggests that spatulae may have been used in the manufacture and/or maintenance of barbed and tanged arrowheads (this ties in with the use wear evidence, see above). However a strong association between spatulae and barbed and tanged arrowheads is not maintained in Beaker period Wessex.

Wessex
A number of relationships can be identified for Beaker period Wessex on the basis of the following associations: (1) awls with spatulae, (2) barbed and tanged arrowheads with bracers, dagger/knives and belt ring/pulley objects, (3) belt ring/pulley objects with V-perforated buttons, (4) spatulae with bracers and dagger/knives, and (5) sponge finger stones with belt ring/pulley objects and V-perforated buttons (Table 11.36). On the whole, awls are not strongly associated with any object type, with the exception of a weak and uneven association with spatulae. Spatulae, on the other hand are more strongly associated with awls and also have strong associations with daggers/knives and bracers. Awls appear with nearly all other object types in Table 11.36, suggesting that awls could be placed alongside any suite of objects without significant restriction.

As in East Yorkshire, there appears to be an association between daggers/knives, bracers and belt/ring pulley objects, although the associations are stronger and include barbed and tanged arrowheads. Barbed and tanged arrowheads have a strong mutual association with both daggers and bracers and therefore would seem to represent part of a suite of grave objects in Beaker period Wessex. Belt ring/pulley objects also appear to be associated, having a strong uneven association with barbed and tanged arrowheads. However, they do not seem to form part of a clear set of largely mutual and strong associations evident between daggers/knives, barbed and tanged arrowheads and bracers. Belt ring/ pulley objects have only a weak and uneven association with daggers and no clear association with bracers. This contrasts with East Yorkshire where there were greater co-associations between belt ring/pulley objects, bracers and dagger/knives. There is also a similar association between belt ring/pulley objects and V-perforated buttons in Wessex and East Yorkshire, although in the case of Wessex sponge finger stones also appear alongside them, rather than flint daggers which do not feature. Spatulae have both a strong and uneven association with bracers and dagger/knives as well as a strong and uneven association with awls. Again although the total number of sites available is rather small and the associations between object types overlapping, two suites of object types can be suggested (Figure 11.7). The first suite is dagger/knives, bracers and barbed and tanged arrowheads, which form a cohesive group of strong associations. Spatulae also appear to be linked with this group, although have other associations. The second group consists of belt ring/pulley objects and V-perforated buttons, and to a slightly lesser extent sponge finger stones.

Object associations during the Early Bronze Age
In the case of Early Bronze Age object types a total of 15 objects types were selected for further analysis, based

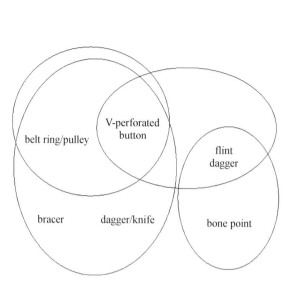

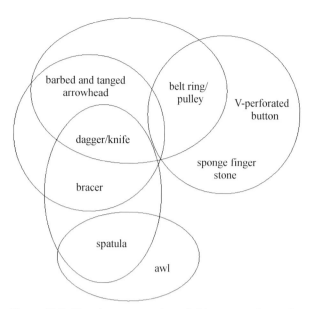

Figure 11.6. Visual representation of object type relationships in Beaker period East Yorkshire.

Figure 11.7. Visual representation of object type relationships in Beaker period Wessex.

Table 11.35. Relationship matrix for selected Beaker object types from the Peak District, by number and frequency in graves.

	Awl	Barbed and tanged arrowhead	Dagger/knife	Spatula	V-perf. button	**Total**
Awl		0	1 (16%)	1 (16%)	0	**6**
Barbed and tanged arrowhead	0		0	3 (100%)	0	**3**
Dagger/knife	1 (9%)	0		0	2 (18%)	**11**
Spatula	1 (16%)	3 (50%)	0%		0	**6**
V-perf. button	0	0	1 (33%)	0		**3**

on the total number of graves present in which the object type occurred. Table 11.37 lists these objects and their total frequency, by region.

East Yorkshire
In the case of East Yorkshire, few convincing associations could be identified for the Early Bronze Age. Potential associations include: (1) accessory cup and Collared Urns, (2) awls, necklaces and Food Vessels, (3) tusk/teeth and Food Vessels, (4) Collared Urns and bone points, and (5) tusk/teeth with bone points (Table 11.38). Accessory cups have a strong and uneven association with Collared Urns. As smaller vessels, they may be linked specifically with the deposition of Collared Urns in Early Bronze Age graves. Accessory cups only rarely accompany Food Vessels in all regions. Finally, Collared Urns have a weak uneven association with bone points. Associations with Food Vessels, bone points and dagger/knives are unlikely

to be significant, however, due to the fact that there are no interrelationships between objects associated with these object types and that all are common types to East Yorkshire graves. This is particularly the case with bone points which appear in 44 of 125 total sites. Notably, bone points and dagger/knives are most frequently found alone, without other object types. Thus, the most meaningful associations in East Yorkshire at this time are those between accessory cups and Collared Urns as well as those between awls, necklaces and perhaps Food Vessels.

Peak District
For the Peak District, there are several strong associations, largely between Collared Urns and other object types, namely accessory cups, dagger/knives and bone points (Table 11.39). Each has a strong and uneven association with Collared Urns, although in the case of accessory cups there are only three Peak District sites. However,

Table 11.36. Relationship matrix for selected Beaker object types from Wessex, by number and frequency in graves.

	Awl	Barbed and tanged arrowhead	Belt ring/pulley object	Bracer	Dagger/knife	Bone point	Spatula	Sponge finger stone	V-perf. button	Total
Awl		1 (16%)	1 (16%)	0	1 (16%)	1 (16%)	2 (33%)	1 (16%)	1 (16%)	**6**
Barbed and tanged arrowhead	1(10%)		3 (30%)	5 (50%)	6 (60%)	0	1 (10%)	0%	1 (10%)	**10**
Belt ring/pulley object	1(16%)	3 (50%)		1 (16%)	2 (33%)	0	1 (16%)	1 (16%)	3 (50%)	**6**
Bracer	0	5 (50%)	1 (10%)		5 (50%)	0	2 (20%)	0	0	**10**
Dagger/knife	1 (8%)	6 (50%)	2 (16%)	4 (33%)		1 (8%)	2 (16%)	0	1 (8%)	**12**
Bone point	1 (33%)	0	0	0	1 (33%)		1 (33%)	0	0	**3**
Spatula	2 (50%)	1 (25%)	1 (25%)	2 (50%)	2 (50%)	1 (25%)		1 (25%)	0	**4**
Sponge finger stone	1 (33%)	0	2 (66%)	0	0	0	1 (33%)		2 (66%)	**3**
V-perf. button	1 (25%)	1 (25%)	4 (100%)	0	1 (25%)	0	0	2 (50%)		**4**

Table 11.37. Selected Early Bronze Age object types from all inhumation or cremation contexts, by number of sites.

Object type	Composition	Number			Total
		E. Yorks graves (125)	Peak graves (60)	Wessex graves (227)	**(412)**
Dagger/knife	Copper/bronze	14	9	92	**115**
Point	Bone	44	24	35	**103**
Necklace	All types	11	10	63	**84**
Awl	Copper/bronze	18	7	49	**74**
Accessory cup	Pottery	8	3	37	**48**
Collared Urn	Pottery	11	15	20	**46**
Food Vessel	Pottery	25	3	5	**33**
Individual bead	All types	4	4	23	**31**
Tusk/tooth	Tusk/tooth	8	4	4	**16**
Dress pin	All types	4	0	10	**14**
Battle-axe	Stone	7	3	4	**14**
Tweezers	Bone	0	2	12	**14**
Perforated stone	Stone	0	0	11	**11**
V-perforated button	All types	5	1	5	**11**
Misc. gold	Gold	0	0	7	**7**

there are no clear associations between accessory cups, dagger/knives or bone points, and thus a distinctive suite of objects related to Collared Urns is not evident. The only exception may be bone points, which have a weak to strong association with Collared Urns both in the Peak District and East Yorkshire.

A further association of note is between necklaces with awls and Food Vessels, although the total number of Food Vessels is rather low (Figure 11.8). Necklaces have a mutual weak association with awls, while Food Vessels have a strong and uneven association with necklaces. There appears to be no clear association between awls and Food Vessels. Food Vessels also have a strong and uneven association with bone points. From these associations, it seems likely that there is a relationship between necklaces and awls, with a possible link with Food Vessels. In

addition, there is a relationship between accessory cups and Collared Urns which is distinct from necklaces and awls (Figure 11.8). Other object types may be related to Collared Urns, but the relationships are less certain, namely bone points and dagger/knives.

Wessex

Owing to the larger number of identified sites and object types in Wessex, object associations are more numerous and complex. On the basis of shared associations, three relationships can be suggested: (1) awls with necklaces and accessory cups, and perhaps dagger/knives and Collared Urns, (2) V-perforated buttons with awls and accessory cups, (3) dress pins with dagger/knives, and (4) perforated stones with daggers/knives (Figure 11.9).

In the case of the first proposed relationship, it can be

Table 11.38. Relationship matrix for selected Early Bronze Age object types from East Yorkshire, by number and frequency in graves.

	Accessory cup	Awl	Battle-axe	Bead	Collared Urn	Dagger/knife	Dress pin	Food Vessel	Necklace	Point	Tusk/tooth	V-perforated button	Total	Without other objects
Accessory cup	■	1 (12%)	0	0	4 (50%)	3 (37%)	0	0	1 (12%)	1 (12%)	1 (12%)	0	**8**	0
Awl	1 (5%)	■	0	0	1 (5%)	0	0	7 (39%)	5 (28%)	2 (11%)	1 (5%)	0	**18**	3 (17%)
Battle-axe	0	0	■	0	1 (14%)	1 (14%)	0	0	0	3 (43%)	0	0	**7**	1 (14%)
Bead	0	0	0	■	1 (25%)	0	0	1 (25%)	0	1 (25%)	0	0	**4**	1 (25%)
Collared Urn	4 (36%)	1 (9%)	0	1 (9%)	■	1 (9%)	0	0	1 (9%)	5 (45%)	0	0	**11**	0
Dagger/knife	3 (21%)	0	2 (14%)	0	1 (7%)	■	1 (7%)	0	0	1 (7%)	0	0	**14**	4 (28%)
Dress pin	0	0	0	0	0	1(25%)	■	0	0	0	0	0	**4**	1 (25%)
Food Vessel	0	7 (28%)	1 (4%)	1 (4%)	0	0	1 (4%)	■	3 (12%)	4 (16%)	3 (12%)	1 (4%)	**25**	0
Necklace	1 (9%)	5 (45%)	0	0	2 (18%)	0	0	3 (27%)	■	2 (18%)	0	0	**11**	1 (9%)
Point	1 (2%)	2 (4%)	3 (7%)	1 (2%)	6 (13%)	1 (2%)	0	4 (9%)	2 (4%)	■	2 (4%)	0	**44**	15 (34%)
Tusk/tooth	1 (12%)	1 (12%)	0	0	0	0	0	3 (37%)	0	2 (25%)	■	0	**8**	3 (37%)
V-perforated button	0	0	0	0	0	0	0	1 (25%)	0	0	0	■	**5**	0

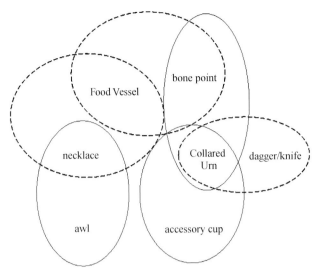

Figure 11.8. Visual representation of object type relationships in the Peak District in the Early Bronze Age (relationships depicted with solid lines, uncertain or weak relationships depicted with dotted lines).

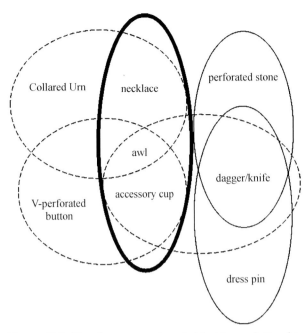

Figure 11.9. Visual representation of object type relationships in Wessex in the Early Bronze Age (relationships depicted with solid lines, uncertain or weak relationships depicted with dotted lines).

seen that awls have a weak mutual association with both necklaces and accessory cups, while accessory cups have an uneven strong association with necklaces (Table 11.40). Thus, all three object types are linked by associations with one another to at least some degree. Both accessory cups and awls have a weak uneven association with dagger/ knives, while no clear association exists between dagger/ knives and necklaces. In the case of Collared Urns, they have a weak mutual association with awls and a weak uneven association with necklaces. V-perforated buttons also have a weak association with awls and accessory cups, although the total number of buttons is quite small.

Both dress pins and perforated stones have a strong uneven association with dagger/knives. In the case of dress pins, the association is very strong, with nine of ten Wessex examples occurring alongside dagger/knives. Given the disparity in overall number of sites in which these object types occur in relation with daggers, it is clear that although the presence of dagger/knives is relevant to the deposition of dress pins and perforated stones in graves, these objects do not play a strong role in understanding the deposition of dagger/knives themselves across all sites. Overall the associations point towards a central relationship between necklaces, awls and accessory cups to which other object types are occasionally added. In addition there are relationships between dagger/knives and perforated stones and dagger/knives and dress pins which are functioning largely outside this central relationship (Figure 11.9).

Object associations discussion

Analysis here will demonstrate differences between the deposition of grave goods across all regions and between the Beaker period and the Early Bronze Age. In the case of the Beaker contexts, although similar object types are

found in each region, it can be seen that they are configured into different relationships (Table 11.41). This can be seen in the relationships between dagger/knives and other object types across regions. In East Yorkshire dagger/knives tend to be found alongside bracers and belt ring pulley/objects. In Wessex, although the same relationship exists between dagger/knives and bracers as in East Yorkshire, dagger/ knives can also be seen to have relationships with spatulae, belt ring/pulley objects and barbed and tanged arrowheads. Another good example is V-perforated buttons, which appear in both Wessex and East Yorkshire, but in different relationships. In East Yorkshire they are generally found with belt ring/pulley objects or flint daggers. In Wessex, they are again found with belt ring/pulley objects but also with sponge finger stones. Thus, there are grave object relationships which make reference to both regional as well as to wider burial practice.

This pattern continues into the Early Bronze Age, although the objects in question have changed significantly (Table 11.42). For example, awls and necklaces have a significant relationship across all three regions. In East Yorkshire and the Peak District there is a suggestion of a relationship between these object types and Food Vessels. In contrast, in Wessex where Food Vessels are uncommon, awls and necklaces are related to accessory cups. Although Collared Urns and accessory cups are also found together in both East Yorkshire and the Peak District, Collared Urns in the Peak District are related to bone points which is not a feature within East Yorkshire. In Wessex, neither relationship can be identified, and if there is any relationship between Collared Urns and other

Table 11.39. Relationship matrix for selected Early Bronze Age object types from the Peak District, by number and frequency in graves.

	Accessory cup	Awl	Battle-axe	Bead	Collared Urn	Dagger/knife	Food Vessel	Necklace	Point	Tusk/tooth	**Total**	Without other objects
Accessory cup		1 (33%)	0	0	3 (100%)	0	0	1 (33%)	0	0	**3**	0
Awl	1 (5%)		0	0	2 (11%)	0	0	0	1 (5%)	1 (5%)	**18**	2 (11%)
Battle-axe	0	0		0	0	0	0	0	0	1 (33%)	**3**	2 (66%)
Bead	0	1 (25%)	0		2 (50%)	0	0	0	0	0	**4**	2 (50%)
Collared Urn	2 (13%)	1 (6%)	0	2 (13%)		5 (33%)	0	2 (13%)	8 (53%)	0	**15**	0
Dagger/knife	0	0	0	0	5 (55%)		0	1 (11%)	2 (22%)	0	**9**	5?
Food Vessel	0	0	0	0	0	0		0	2 (66%)	1 (33%)	**3**	0
Necklace	1 (9%)	5 (45%)	0	0	2 (18%)	0	3 (27%)		2 (18%)	0	**11**	1 (9%)
Point	0	1 (4%)	0	0	7 (29%)	2 (8%)	0	1 (4%)		0	**24**	6 (25%)
Tusk/tooth	0	1 (25%)	1 (25%)	0	0	0	1 (25%)	0	0		**4**	0

Table 11.40. Relationship matrix for selected Early Bronze Age object types from Wessex, by number and frequency in graves.

	Accessory cup	Awl	Battle-axe	Bead	Collared Urn	Dagger/knife	Dress pin	Food Vessel	Misc. gold	Necklace	Perf. stone	Point	Tusk/tooth	Tweezer	V-perforated button	Total	Without other objects
Accessory cup	■	18 (48%)	0	2 (5%)	5 (13%)	9 (24%)	2 (5%)	1 (3%)	4 (11%)	20 (54%)	0	6 (16%)	0	0	2 (5%)	**37**	0
Awl	18 (36%)	■	1 (2%)	3 (6%)	7 (14%)	12 (24%)	1 (2%)	1 (2%)	3 (6%)	23 (47%)	0	3 (6%)	1 (2%)	0	2 (4%)	**49**	9 (18%)
Battle-axe	0	1 (25%)	■	0	0	1 (25%)	0	0	0	1 (25%)	0	1 (25%)	1 (25%)	0	0	**4**	1 (25%)
Bead	8 (35%)	8 (35%)	0	■	4 (17%)	4 (17%)	1 (4%)	0	0	16 (69%)	0	3 (13%)	0	1 (4%)	0	**23**	2 (8%)
Collared Urn	5 (15%)	7 (35%)	0	4 (20%)	■	4 (20%)	0	0	2 (10%)	8 (40%)	1 (5%)	3 (15%)	0	2 (10%)	0	**20**	1 (5%)
Dagger/knife	10 (11%)	12 (13%)	1 (1%)	0	4 (4%)	■	9 (10%)	2 (2%)	3 (3%)	10 (11%)	6 (6%)	8 (8%)	3 (3%)	4 (4%)	0	**92**	25 (27%)
Dress pin	2 (20%)	1 (10%)	0	0	0	9 (90%)	■	0	0	2	2 (20%)	1 (10%)	0	1 (10%)	0	**10**	0
Food Vessel	1 (20%)	1 (20%)	0	0	0	2 (40%)	0	■	0	2 (40%)	0	0	0	0	0	**5**	0
Misc. gold	4 (57%)	2 (28%)	0	0	2 (28%)	3 (43%)	0	0	■	5 (71%)	0	0	0	0	1 (14%)	**7**	0
Necklace	18 (28%)	22 (35%)	1 (1%)	0	7 (11%)	8 (12%)	2 (3%)	2 (3%)	5 (8%)	■	0	4 (6%)	1 (1%)	1 (1%)	1 (1%)	**63**	21 (33%)
Perforated stone	0	0	0	0	1 (9%)	6 (54%)	2 (18%)	0	0	0	■	3 (27%)	0	3	0	**11**	3 (27%)
Point	6 (17%)	3 (8%)	1 (3%)	2 (5%)	3 (8%)	8 (23%)	1 (3%)	0	0	3 (8%)	3 (8%)	■	1 (3%)	5 (14%)	0	**35**	7 (20%)
Tusk/tooth	0	0	1 (25%)	0	0	3 (75%)	0	0	0	1 (25%)	0	1 (25%)	■	0	0	**4**	0
Tweezers	0	0	0	0	2 (16%)	4 (33%)	1 (8%)	0	0	2 (16%)	3 (25%)	5 (41%)	0	■	0	**12**	1 (8%)
V-perforated button	2 (40%)	2 (40%)	0	0	0	0	0	0	0	1 (20%)	0	0	0	0	■	**5**	2 (40%)

Table 11.41. Comparison of key object relationships between regions in the Beaker period.

East Yorkshire relationships	Peak District relationships	Wessex relationships
Belt ring/pulley object + bracer + dagger Belt ring/pulley object + V-perforated button Flint dagger + V-perforated button Flint dagger + bone point	Barbed and tanged arrowhead + spatula	Bracer + dagger/knife + barbed and tanged arrowhead Bracer + dagger + spatula Belt ring/pulley object + barbed and tanged arrowhead + dagger/knife Belt ring/pulley object + sponge finger stone + V-perforated button Awl + spatula

Table 11.42. Comparison of key object relationships between regions in the Early Bronze Age.

East Yorkshire relationships	Peak District relationships	Wessex relationships
Awl + necklace (+ Food Vessel) Collared Urn + accessory cup	Awl + necklace (+ Food Vessel) Collared Urn + accessory cup Collared Urn + bone point	Awl + necklace + accessory cup Dagger/knife + dress pin Dagger/knife + perforated stone

Table 11.43. Sex of interment compared with identified Beaker object relationships.

Relationship	Region	No. of sites w/sex data	Site	Gender
Belt ring/pulley object + bracer + dagger/knife	East Yorkshire	1	Rudston 68, burial 6 (Greenwell)	M
Belt ring/pulley object + V-perforated button	East Yorkshire	2	Acklam Wold Group 124, interment 4 (Mortimer) Rudston 68, burial 6 (Greenwell) Rudston 61, burial 2 (Greenwell)	M M M
Flint dagger + V-perforated button	East Yorkshire	2	Acklam Wold Group 124, interment 4 (Mortimer) Garton Slack Group 163, interment 2 (Mortimer)	M M
Flint dagger + bone point	East Yorkshire	1	Acklam Wold Group 124, interment 4 (Mortimer)	M
Barbed and tanged arrowhead + spatula	Peak District	2	Green Low, Eaton and Alsop, Derbyshire Mouse Low, Grindon, Staffordshire	M M
Bracer + dagger/knife + barbed and tanged arrowhead	Wessex	3	Amesbury Archer, Wiltshire Roundway G8, Wiltshire Thomas Hardye School, Dorchester 1004, grave 1643	M M M
Bracer + dagger + spatula	Wessex	1	Amesbury Archer, Wiltshire	M
Belt ring/pulley object + barbed and tanged arrowhead + dagger/knife	Wessex	1	Amesbury Archer, Wiltshire	M
Belt ring/pulley object + sponge finger stone + V-perforated button	Wessex	0	n/a	n/a
Awl + spatula	Wessex	1	Amesbury G51, burial A, Wiltshire	M

Table 11.44. Sex of interment compared with identified Early Bronze Age object relationships.

Relationship	Region(s)	No. of sites w/sex data	Site	Gender
Awl + necklace (+ Food Vessel)	East Yorkshire and Peak District	5	Langton 2, burial 2 (Greenwell) Folkton 71, burial 6 (Greenwell) Garrowby Wold Group 64 (Mortimer) Garton Slack Group 75, interment 2 (Mortimer) Garton Slack barrow 29, burial 5	F F F F F
Collared Urn + accessory cup	East Yorkshire and Peak District	2	Blanch Group 194 (Mortimer) Blackheath Barrow, Todmorden, West Yorkshire	F F
Collared Urn + bone point	Peak District	3	Stanton Moor 1926, Derbyshire Stanton Moor barrow 17A, Derbyshire Horse Pastures, Beeley, Derbyshire	F M M
Awl + necklace + accessory cup	Wessex	2	Collingbourne Kingston G6, burial 1, Wiltshire (awl + accessory cup only) Manton Barrow, Preshute G1a, Wiltshire	F F
Dagger/knife + dress pin	Wessex	0	n/a	n/a
Dagger/knife + perforated stone	Wessex	1	Edmonsham G2, Dorset	M

Table 11.45. Comparison of tools-to-grave ratio of selected object types from the Beaker period (ratio of graves to instances of flint object types other than daggers and arrowheads plus instances of sponge finger stones and spatulae).

Object type	Material	Graves total	Total tool type instances	Tools-to-graves ratio
Sponge finger stone	Stone	7	13	**1.86**
Flint dagger	Flint	14	26	**1.86**
Spatula	All types	17	23	**1.35**
Awl	Copper alloy	22	24	**1.09**
Belt ring/pulley object	All types	19	20	**1.05**
V-perforated button	All types	24	25	**1.04**
Barbed/tanged arrowhead	Flint	24	23	**0.96**
Bead, individual, non-necklace	All types	7	6	**0.86**
Point	Bone	17	14	**0.82**
Bracer	Stone	26	14	**0.54**
Dagger/knife	Copper alloy	52	18	**0.35**

object types it is instead with awls. Finally, in Wessex the relationships between daggers/knives and dress pins and dagger/knives and perforated stones are not evident in either East Yorkshire or the Peak District. Again, two scales of practice are taking place, one which sees necklaces and awls as having an important relationship across all regions, and another which sees this relationship embedded within regional burial practice.

As seen in the previous section, several object types are found most frequently in association with male or female burials. Female-oriented objects included awls and necklaces, while male-oriented objects include dagger/knives and barbed and tanged arrowheads. Although the total number of sites which display the relationships outlined above and which contain reliable skeletal data is very small, some very tentative patterns can be considered. In the Beaker period, nearly all identified relationships are associated with males (Table 11.43). In no case are there object relationships identified as specifically female, although this is unsurprising given the small total number of identified well-furnished female graves in the Beaker period. For the Early Bronze Age, the relationship between awls and necklaces is confirmed as female-oriented, with all graves with skeletal data and both object types present occurring in female graves (Table 11.44). Evidence for gender associations within other object type relationships is patchy, with some suggestion that Collared Urns with accessory cups are female-oriented and dagger/knives with perforated stones are male oriented. The only case where both sexes are included occurs in the Collared Urns with bone points relationship. However, given the very small number of examples of skeletal data for these relationships, the definition of many of these patterns should be regarded as preliminary. What it does suggest, however, is that alongside regional differences in burial practice, notions of gender were also expressed through grave object deposition in graves.

Given the wide range of object types and the incomplete nature of much of the grave data, the identification of patterns of relationships between multiple variables

is difficult to interpret. Despite compiling a record of 569 graves across both the Beaker and Early Bronze Age periods, after inappropriate graves or graves with incomplete data have been removed, and graves have been divided by time period, by gender and region, the final comparative subsample is often very small. Thus, although patterns can be suggested, the strength of association and the basis for conclusions must at times be speculative.

Finally, some suggestion of object type function requires consideration. On the whole, the object relationships discussed above appear to be more strongly linked with social practice than with object function, particularly given the identification of regional as well as gender differences in object relationships. One potential route to suggesting function, at least at a very basic level, is to compare object types against other material which is likely to have been used as a tool. The most obvious candidates for comparison are flint tools which occur in both Beaker and Early Bronze Age graves across all regions. To these can be added a number of other object types, namely spatulae, whetstones and sponge finger stones. Thus, for both Beaker and Early Bronze Age graves, the total number of instances of these object types alongside other selected object types can be compared. For this purpose, across both periods, flint objects include all flint other than flint daggers and barbed and tanged arrowheads. For Beaker graves alone instances of spatulae and sponge finger stones could be added to the flint totals. For Early Bronze Age graves alone flint instances were added to instances of whetstones (grooved and other whetstones) and spatulae. In order to emphasise graves which contain more than one tool type, instances of each tool type were added together and expressed as a ratio against the total number of sites for a given object type. Results of this approach are presented in Table 11.45 and Table 11.46 below.

Here data from all regions were combined on the basis that the same object types would have had the same functional purpose across all regions, even if their social meaning might vary. By necessity, this analysis also

Table 11.46. Comparison of tools-to-grave ratio of selected object types from the Early Bronze Age (ratio of graves to instances of flint object types other than daggers and arrowheads plus instances of whetstones and spatulae).

Object type	Material	Graves total	Total tool type instances	Tools-to-graves ratio
Tusk/tooth	Tusk/tooth	16	9	**0.56**
Food Vessel	Pottery	35	19	**0.54**
Battle-axe	Stone	14	6	**0.43**
Point	Bone	102	39	**0.38**
V-perforated button	All types	11	3	**0.27**
Perforated stone	Stone	11	3	**0.27**
Collared Urn	Pottery	50	12	**0.24**
Dress pin	All types	15	3	**0.20**
Awl	Copper alloy	73	13	**0.18**
Bead, individual, non-necklace	All types	32	5	**0.16**
Dagger/knife	Copper alloy	111	18	**0.16**
Pommel	All types	14	2	**0.14**
Accessory cup	Pottery	49	6	**0.12**
Necklace	All types	84	8	**0.10**
Tweezers	Bone	13	0	**0.00**
Miscellaneous gold	Gold	7	0	**0.00**
Button set	All types	4	0	**0.00**

assumes that the presence of objects of flint and simple bone tools was consistently recorded across all regions. It is likely that at least some antiquarian sources chose not to emphasise these object types in the description of grave goods, perhaps favouring objects believed to be of greater value or importance. However, some key sources, namely those graves recorded by Greenwell, Hoare and Mortimer in fact regularly refer to the presence of objects of flint, and thus a reasonable level of consistency of recording of flint in most graves can be assumed.

For the Beaker period, the results strongly suggest the use of sponge finger stones and spatulae as tools as both object types have a high ratio compared to other tool types (Table 11.45). Unsurprisingly, awls also are found in association with tool types. The lowest ratios are clearly associated with dagger/knives and bracers, and may suggest their function as objects of display rather than as part of tool sets. On the other hand, bone points have a fairly low ratio, and this may reflect their function both as tools and also as objects of adornment. The ratios associated with belt ring/pulley objects and individual beads are surprising: ratios for both should be comparable to other objects of display and adornment, and their higher association with tool types is difficult to explain using this approach.

Nonetheless, a general pattern of co-association of object types used as tools is apparent, alongside a corresponding lack of association with other selected object types.

This pattern continues in the Early Bronze Age, although the ratios are smaller due to the fact that flint is found less frequently in graves during this period (Table 11.46). There is a significant collection of objects with very low ratios, including button sets, gold objects, tweezers, necklaces, pommels and dagger/knives. As many of these object types would be expected to be objects of display and adornment, their low ratios are perhaps to be expected. As with the Beaker period, dagger/knives are not linked with tool types, and this would again suggest a function related to display rather than use as a tool. Awls also have a low ratio which is counter to expectations. However, during the Early Bronze Age awls have a significant relationship with necklaces and are frequently found in female graves; these relationships may be more important than association with other tool types. Bone points have a comparatively higher ratio than other object types, and might suggest their continuing use as both tools and as personal adornments. Lastly, a high ratio for battle-axes is also interesting, and may reflect their dual role as both objects of personal display and as more mundane implements.

12. REGIONAL VARIATION

INTRODUCTION

One of the original aims of the project was to define 'rich' graves belonging to the Wessex Culture. The less loaded term of 'well furnished' was developed, and in order to test how such a definition might be achieved site databases listing various criteria for all graves of Beaker and Early Bronze Age date containing particular classes and combinations of grave good were compiled. There are three main questions to be addressed. First, do the so-called Wessex Series graves really stand out, and if so, by which criteria? Second, within the corpus of well-furnished graves can any regional variations be detected? And finally, how do any patterns discerned for the Early Bronze Age relate to the nature and distribution of well-furnished graves of the Beaker tradition?

The site databases were compiled using existing *corpora*, the antiquarian accounts, Historic Environment Records (HERs), and county journals for finds from *c.*1970 onwards. As explained in Chapter 2 the preparation of detailed site databases for the Early Bronze Age period covered our three detailed study areas of East Yorkshire (the Wolds), the Peak District and Wessex only, while for the Beaker period time allowed the compilation of a full database for all the well-furnished graves in England. In order that a balanced analysis could be achieved in the present chapter, a less detailed listing of well-furnished Early Bronze Age graves outside the three detailed study areas was also prepared. This list relied heavily on data obtained from HERs and concentrated on objects present rather than details of the burials and bodies concerned. The numbers of graves recorded, by region and period, are shown in Table 12.1. In the Beaker period, well-furnished graves are found fairly equally in the three detailed study areas (the Wolds, the Peak District and Wessex), while in the Early Bronze Age it can be seen that there were many more in Wessex, and also far more in the Rest of England than in the Beaker period.

The object types included within our definition of well-furnished graves are as follows:

- All items of gold
- Items of copper and copper alloy, including daggers/knives, awls and ornaments
- All items made from jet or jet-like materials
- Items made from bone or antler, including points, belt rings, belt hooks, spatulae *etc*
- Items made from stone, including bracers, whetstones, battle-axes *etc*

Pottery was not studied in detail, as most types are covered in the literature, and neither were flint objects, as they occur in very large numbers, and they need a higher level of magnification to detect any use wear. Where pottery and flints occur in well-furnished graves, they are recorded in the detailed site database, but 'pottery only' or 'flint only' graves are not included. Initially it was intended to restrict the definition of a well-furnished grave to those which contained two or more items occurring in the list above. However, as work proceeded it became apparent that many graves which contained only one such item could also logically be included within the definition. This applied particularly to graves which contained only one item of jet or jet-like material, such as a single large V-perforated button, or stone, such as a bracer, but also to graves containing a single bone point, often in association with a pottery vessel. Previous studies of object distributions have concentrated on specific types or materials such as daggers, amber and faience. It was felt important to look closely at the distributions of other categories such as awls, items of jet and jet-like materials, bone and antler objects, and stone artefacts, as well as to undertake a fresh appraisal of dagger distributions using the revised typology developed by Stuart Needham (see Chapter 3.1).

A significant problem in the periods under consideration is the lack of modern radiocarbon dates. Also, there have been some significant changes in our understanding of the chronological definitions of the Beaker and Early Bronze Age periods in recent years. These have included the back-dating of flat-rivetted daggers of Series 2 to the Late Beaker period, and also we now have a series of dates

Table 12.1. Well-furnished graves recorded, by region and period.

Region	Beaker	Early Bronze Age	Total graves
Yorkshire Wolds	39	114	153
Peak District	34	63	97
Wessex	35	223	258
Rest of England	54	330	384
England totals	**162**	**730**	**892**

Table 12.2. The occurrence of burial rite among well-furnished graves, by region and period.

Region	Beaker inhumation	Beaker cremation	EBA inhumation	EBA cremation
Yorkshire Wolds	39	0	80	33
Peak District	33	1	26	36
Wessex	34	1	44	178
Totals	**106**	**2**	**150**	**247**

for jet buttons and necklaces in the north, dating them to a few centuries centring on 2000 cal BC (for more details see Chapter 9). A further issue is that Late Beakers may overlap with the currency of the graves belonging to Wessex Series 1. For purposes of analysis within the current project we decided on a Beaker/Early Bronze Age chronological split at around the 2000 cal BC mark, with large jet buttons placed in the Beaker period, and jet necklaces situated in the Early Bronze Age.

GRAVES AND BODIES

Although any analysis of the morphology of graves and barrows was not central to the current project, some details of the graves were recorded within the detailed site databases. However, the main emphasis was on the recording of any data concerning the age and sex of the bodies interred in order that such data could be correlated with the associated object types (see Chapter 11). As far as barrow plans are concerned it is important to note a crucial difference between the nature of burial within barrows in Wessex and within those found in the more northern regions. Most barrows in Wessex contain only one or a few centrally placed burials, while in the Peak District and the Wolds the more common pattern is to find complex multiple and often intercutting graves under a larger area of the barrow material. However, in southern England the barrows often contain complex sequences of secondary burials, many of which are well-furnished. Such contrasts have not been studied in recent years, and new detailed research in this area could be highly illuminating. The data recorded relating to the rite of burial has produced some interesting patterning; this is recorded in Table 12.2. The preponderance of inhumation burials in the Beaker period comes as no surprise, and for the Early Bronze Age we can define the level of cremation burials, which occurs at 62%. Looking at the data by region provides some further interesting information. In both the Wolds and the Peak District, there are higher levels of inhumations, while in Wessex cremations are much the preferred rite, scoring at 80%. This may mark out the Wessex region as possessing a particular character in respect of burial rite.

The criteria for age grades and quality of burial data employed within our project have been explained in Chapter 2. Quality of the age and sex data was divided into three categories, depending on how the identifications had been made, and we discounted identifications that had been inferred, for example the assumption that the body in the grave with a dagger would have been male. However, the resulting datasets are not large: there are age data for only 152 well-furnished graves, and sex data for only slightly more: from 165 well-furnished burials. The nature of the evidence for ageing and sexing, and the associated problems, have been discussed in Chapter 11.4.

A regional analysis of the reliable age data relating to well-furnished graves of the Beaker and Early Bronze Age periods is presented in Table 12.3 and Table 12.4. First, it can be noted that both the Beaker and Early Bronze Age datasets comprise mainly adults. As far as the other age categories are concerned, well-furnished Beaker graves include more mature individuals, with fewer youths and children. In the Early Bronze Age there are far more youths and more children. Regionally, starting with the Beaker period, the Peak District has relatively more youths and mature adults, while in Wessex the burials are nearly all adult or mature, with a few children, but no youths. In the Early Bronze Age the Wolds and Peak District have similar proportions of adults, but the Wolds now has more youths, and the Peak District still has no children. In Wessex there are far more adults, with equal but low proportions of youths and children. A possible distinctive signature for the Wessex region is the very high proportion of adults in the Beaker period. This pattern continues into the Early Bronze Age when adults are still predominant in Wessex in relation to the two other regions.

A regional analysis of the sex data relating to well-furnished graves is presented in Table 12.5. It is generally known that most well-furnished graves of Beaker date are of men, and the data presented here confirms that they are predominantly male. However, there are some interesting regional differences that can be discerned. The proportion of men to women is lowest in the Yorkshire Wolds, of medium value in the Peak District and highest in Wessex. In the Early Bronze Age the occurrence of male and female

Table 12.3. The occurrence of well-furnished Beaker graves with high quality age data, by region.

Age category	Age: years	Yorkshire Wolds	Peak District	Wessex	Rest of England	Total graves
Child	<12	3	0	1	1	5
Youth	12–18	1	2	0	2	5
Adult	19–40	13	5	14	28	60
Mature	>40	8	5	4	7	24
Multiple		2	1	0	2	5
Totals		**27**	**13**	**19**	**40**	**99**

Table 12.4. The occurrence of well-furnished Early Bronze Age graves with high quality age data, by region.

Age category	Age: years	Yorkshire Wolds	Peak District	Wessex	Total graves
Child	<12	9	0	4	13
Youth	12–18	18	1	4	23
Adult	19–40	46	5	27	78
Mature	>40	13	4	5	22
Multiple		5	0	2	7
Totals		**91**	**10**	**42**	**143**

Table 12.5. The occurrence of well-furnished graves with high quality sex data, by region and period. (The 'rest of England' figures for the Beaker period have not been included in the totals row, for the ease of comparison with the Early Bronze Age figures).

Region	Beaker male	Beaker female	EBA male	EBA female	Total graves
Yorkshire Wolds	13	4	19	32	68
Peak District	8	1	5	6	20
Wessex	13	1	15	13	42
Rest of England	(27)	(8)	(not recorded)		
Totals	**34**	**6**	**39**	**51**	**130**

burials is far more even than in the Beaker period. However, once again there are some clear regional variations; these are similar to those noted for the Beaker period, with the highest proportion of women occurring in the Yorkshire Wolds and the lowest in Wessex. Thus, in both periods, there seem to have been more well-furnished male graves in Wessex than in the other two regions, and this can be regarded as a further signature for this region.

OBJECT DISTRIBUTIONS

In order to investigate the possibility of regional variation amongst the various categories of object found in the Beaker and Early Bronze Age periods a series of distribution maps have been prepared, and the finds plotted are listed in Appendix 12.1 below. Inevitably these maps do not necessarily reflect the true distributions of such categories, as much as patterns of recovery which may be distorted by various factors such as the past intensity of archaeological activity or the geographical zones where barrows have survived best. Our main purpose is to see whether distributions differ for Beaker and Early Bronze Age graves, and to observe to what extent the Wessex region stands out, if at all.

The first map shows the recovery of stone objects from well-furnished Beaker graves, including items such as bracers, sponge finger stones and flint daggers (Figure 12.1). The overall distribution covers the whole of England and, if the non-grave finds of bracers were to be added, the

distribution would be much more even. No real Wessex concentration can be discerned. The recovery of grave goods made from amber, jet or jet-like materials and bone or antler from well-furnished Beaker graves is shown in Figure 12.2. The object types are buttons, belt and pulley rings, beads, tusk ornaments, toggles, bone points and bone or antler spatulae. Again, we can observe a fairly even distribution of material throughout England. There is a bias towards the eastern sector of the country, but no particular concentration in Wessex.

Turning to the metal items from well-furnished Beaker graves: objects such as gold basket ornaments, copper and copper alloy daggers, dress pins, beads and other ornaments, for the first time there is a noticeable concentration of grave goods in the Wessex area (Figure 12.3). However this is partly due to the limited distribution of the early form of tanged copper daggers, as defined by Stuart Needham. These daggers, of Needham's Association Group 1 (see Needham 2012b), are indicated by filled triangles on the map. Made from continental metal, at least some of these daggers/knives would have been introduced from near Europe by individuals crossing the Channel. Their concentration, however, lies in Wessex, the Upper Thames Valley and also Kent, so again it is not a true 'Wessex only' distribution. Also several very fine objects are not from Wessex, for example, the gold basket ornament from Northumberland. Thus, this series of maps has indicated that well-furnished Beaker graves are spread throughout England and that there are no particular concentrations,

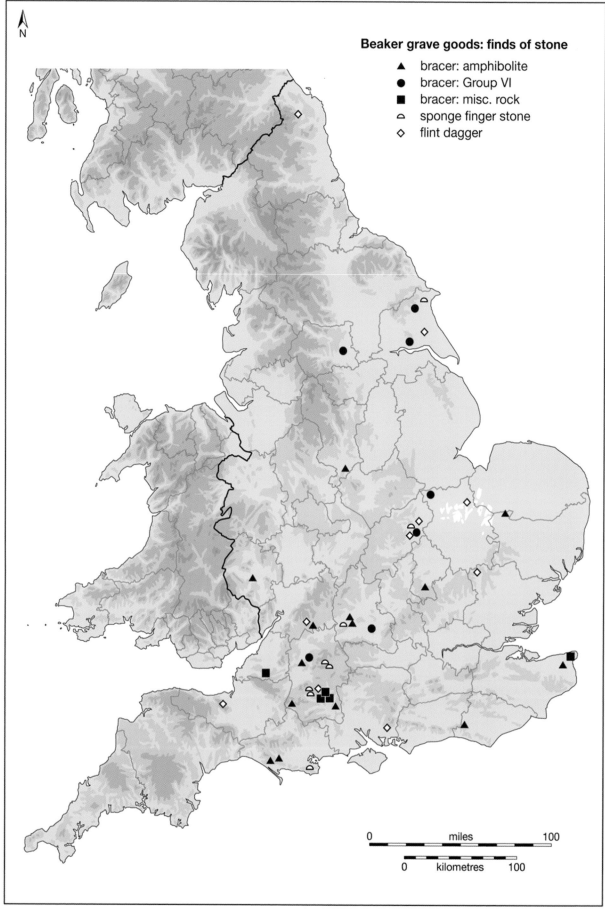

Figure 12.1. Map of recovery for finds of stone from well-furnished Beaker graves. Drawing by Henry Buglass.

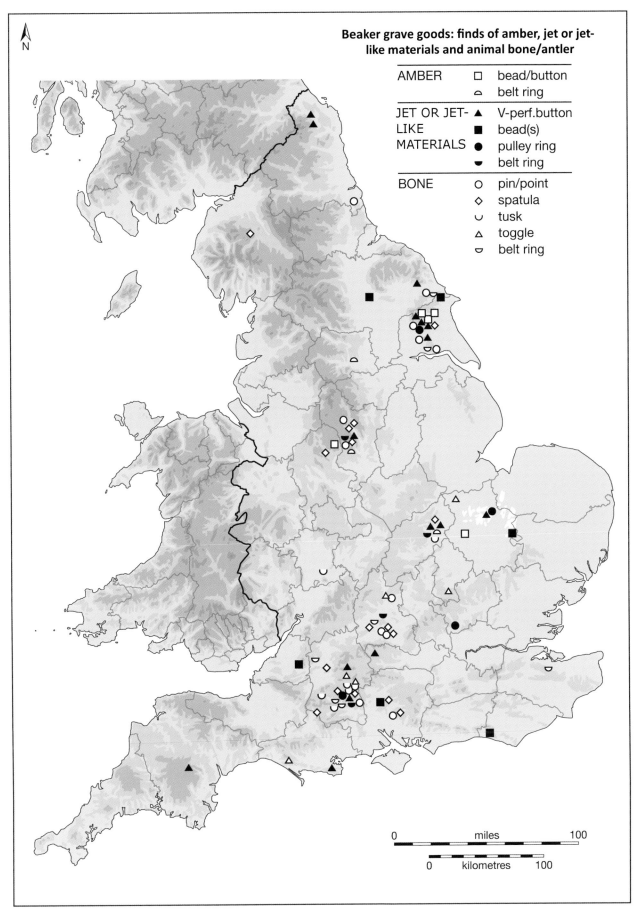

Figure 12.2. Map of recovery for finds of amber, jet and jet-like materials and animal bone/antler from well-furnished Beaker graves. Drawing by Henry Buglass.

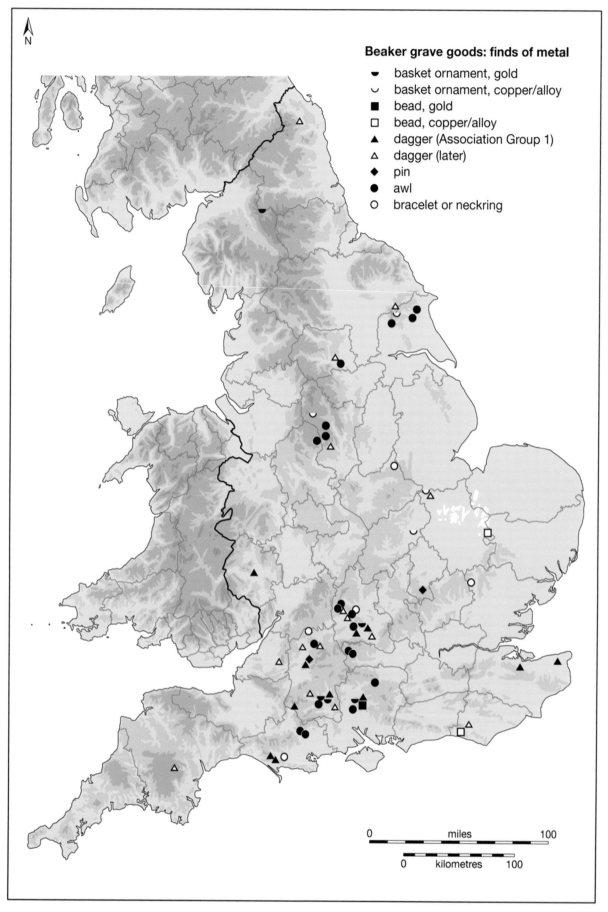

Figure 12.3. Map of recovery for finds of metal from well-furnished Beaker graves. Drawing by Henry Buglass.

apart from those reflecting zones of intense antiquarian investigation. In fact the distributions tend to mirror the overall distribution maps of all Beaker finds, such as those provided by David Clarke in his work of 1970 (Clarke 1970, 557–565).

Moving into the Early Bronze Age period, we can immediately call attention to the recent recognition of key zones of well-furnished graves that are not concentrated in the Wessex region. Perhaps most informative has been Needham's definition of a string of rich graves located along the south and south-east coasts, typified best by the inclusion of precious cups made from shale, gold or amber (Needham *et al.* 2006). These occupy a zone that he has termed the 'Channel/Southern North Sea maritory' (Needham 2009). This maritory was characterised by strong maritime connections across the Channel to Europe, and also up the eastern coast of Britain to East Anglia, and beyond to the north. All this activity was distinct, both spatially and functionally, from contemporary happenings in inland Wessex.

There were also distinct and extremely important developments in the north (Figure 12.4). Here the use of jet from Whitby on the Yorkshire coast (marked as 'W' on the map) for the manufacture of exquisite necklaces started prior to the Wessex Series graves, but the overall span of production is not yet fully documented (see Chapter 9). In England, spacer plate necklaces mainly occur in the far north, and this is just the southern edge of their major distribution which is found in Scotland. There is a small group of fine spacer plate necklaces from the Peak District, but none at all are known as far south as Wessex. A few fusiform beads which ultimately derived from such necklaces filtered down south but there is only one example known of a jet spacer plate: the new find of a decorated terminal plate from Boughton Monchelsea, Kent (Sheridan in prep., too late to be included in Figure 12.4) and another was found in the dagger grave of Kerguevarec in Brittany (Piggott 1939, figs. 1 and 3). The find spots on the map which are located in Wessex or southern England are all necklaces or bracelets made from disc beads only. These are made exclusively of non-Whitby jet materials, and probably all from shale sourced from Kimmeridge on the Dorset coast, although there is one example from Kent where the beads appear to be made from Whitby jet (Alison Sheridan pers. comm.). Disc beads were already in use during the Chalcolithic period in the south, made from shale at Chilbolton and, intriguingly, possibly from jet at Beggars Haven in Sussex.

Also from northern England, and no doubt part of this impressive jet-crafting zone, is the stunning array of large studs, probably used as ear ornaments and made, once again, from Whitby jet (see Chapter 5.6). There is also a series of smaller but taller studs which occurs from North Wales across to East Anglia, plus just one from an Early Bronze Age grave in Dorset. The idea of the flat circular studs was transferred southwards, and they occur in fired clay in the Peak District, Wales and the Midlands; there is also one example in clay within Wessex, from the very

well-furnished burial at Manton (Preshute G1a, Wiltshire). Thus the main concentration of decorative studs was in the north, with a significant outlying group of the smaller variety in East Anglia, but with only two examples known from graves in the Wessex region.

Meanwhile in East Anglia there is a distributional phenomenon of particular interest. The Little Cressingham grave (marked as 'LC' on Figure 12.4), with its amber necklace and the gold items, along with the Armorico-British B dagger is very well known, and there are also the gold-covered shale beads from Great Bircham, Norfolk and Rochford, Essex. The Little Cressingham group has close links with the south coast maritory, and with its probable further connections up the east coast to Yorkshire. It may not be a surprise to find that East Anglia provided the most southerly group of jet spacer plate necklaces and associated elements, and also decorated spacer plates made from bone (see Figure 12.4). Furthermore, there is the newly discovered Carlton Colville, Lowestoft jet lozenge ornament (Pitts 2007) which is marked as find spot 'CC' on the map. This is reminiscent of the gold lozenge from Bush Barrow, but is decorated with an intricate design executed using a highly unusual 'rocker' technique. We have discovered that spacer plates from three different locations in the East Anglian fens bear similar decoration (see Chapter 5.8 and Chapter 7.2). These are all made from Whitby jet and possibly were made by the same craftsperson. This indicates the existence of a flourishing tradition of jet working with a distinct regional technique of decoration, found only in East Anglia. This tradition may have extended rather later than the main jet necklace-producing craft centres located further north, although no absolute dating is currently available. This East Anglian craft area falls mainly within the area of Needham's Channel/Southern North Sea maritory, but it appears to have been culturally rather separate from the south coastal zone, with no precious cups present. However, it has potentially very close links with east Yorkshire, both in terms of the source of the jet material itself and the idea of fancy spacer plate necklaces.

We shall now consider the distributions of two classes of object that have received little attention within recent research: awls of copper or copper alloy and bone points. Since Andrew Fleming's work of 1971 the idea that bronze awls were concentrated in Wessex, and may have indicated the involvement of hide-working pastoralists, has been current. The histogram compiled from our site databases and lists compares the percentage occurrence of graves containing awls in each of our detailed study regions and the whole country (Figure 12.5). This diagram includes all awls belonging to both periods, Beaker and Early Bronze Age, as it was not possible to date many of the awls recorded in the HERs. However most of the awls from the three detailed study areas are of Early Bronze Age date, and this is likely to be the case also for the awls recorded for the rest of England. The overall distribution can be seen to be fairly even, but there are clearly more from the three study areas of the Yorkshire Wolds, the Peak District

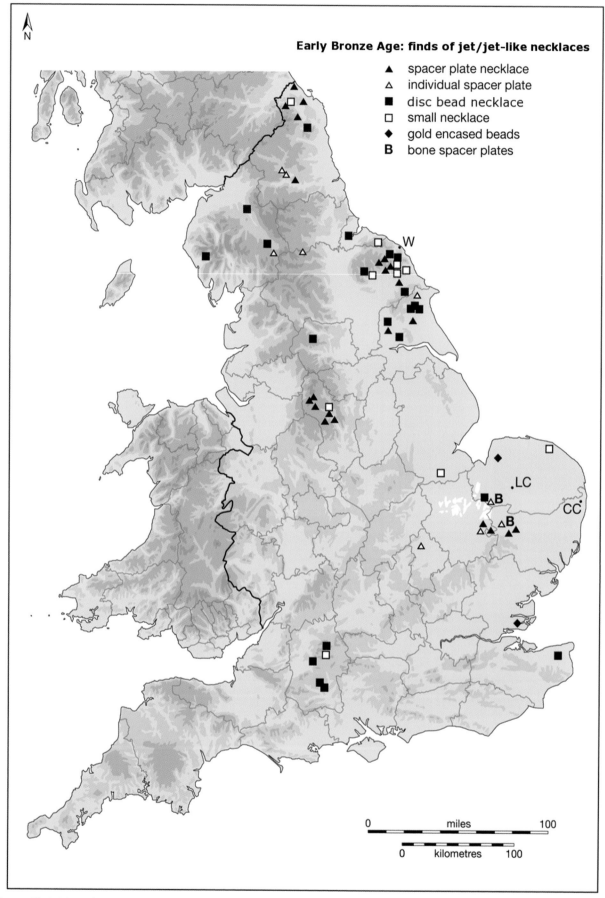

Figure 12.4. Map of recovery for necklaces of jet and jet-like materials from well-furnished Early Bronze Age graves Drawing by Henry Buglass.

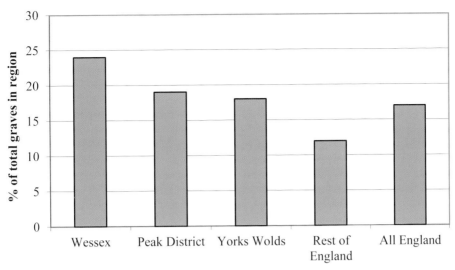

Figure 12.5. The occurrence of copper and copper alloy awls as a percentage of the total number of well-furnished graves in each region.

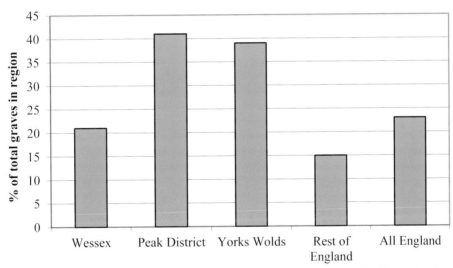

Figure 12.6. The occurrence of bone and antler points as a percentage of the total number of well-furnished graves in each region.

and Wessex. There is indeed a slight peak in Wessex, but it would be difficult to argue that awls are a defining characteristic of the Wessex region. A similar exercise was undertaken for points made from bone or antler, and in this case associations indicate that such points are almost always Early Bronze Age in date. Such points have seldom been studied in the past, and our analyses have suggested that many of them functioned as hair pins or other ornaments for the head. From the histogram (Figure 12.6) it can be seen that these items are most commonly represented in the Peak District and on the Yorkshire Wolds; occurrence in Wessex is in fact below the average figure for the whole country. In contrast with this there are some particular types of bone objects which *are* highly specific to the Wessex region only. These include: bone tweezers, all found from Wessex except for the one from the Upper Thames Valley and one from the Peak District; fancy dress pins of both bone and bronze, and a group of perforated bone plates. These display a strong geographical difference in relation to

some other types of fancy bone objects, such as the group of belt hooks, which are found country-wide.

The distributions of daggers/knives vary greatly through time. Consideration of the daggers belonging to Series 1 and 2 within the Beaker period has been included in discussion of all Beaker metal types above (see Figure 12.3). After an initial concentration in Wessex and the Upper Thames Valley, daggers/knives became widely spread throughout England. In fact there are rather fewer Series 2 flat riveted daggers from Wessex itself. Figure 12.3 only maps the daggers found in association with Beaker vessels. There are in fact many more found alone with inhumations in the non-Wessex regions. Amongst the Series 2 daggers studied in detail for the project five came from the Wolds and 15 from the Peak District. The clustering of this dagger type within the Peak District is very marked, and is clear from Gerloff's original mapping (Gerloff 1975, pl. 31).

Within the Early Bronze Age period Needham's Series 3 and 4 daggers, equating roughly to Armorico-British A

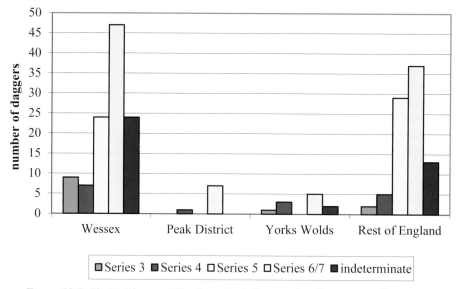

Figure 12.7. The incidence of Needham Early Bronze Age dagger types by region.

and B types, are succeeded by Series 5 which are mainly ogival daggers of the Camerton-Snowshill type. The smaller knives belong to Needham Series 6 and 7, and are less easily dated. A regional analysis was attempted by listing all daggers from graves according to type. The main sources used were Gerloff's corpus (Gerloff 1975) and more recent finds extracted from HERs. It should be noted that stray finds of daggers not found in a grave context have been excluded. From the histogram (Figure 12.7), some patterning can be discerned. Early Bronze Age daggers are fairly rare in both the Peak District and on the Yorkshire Wolds. There is a very definite concentration of Series 3 and 4 daggers in Wessex, whereas the later Series 5 (Camerton-Snowshill) daggers are more widely spread, although only in the south. The pattern of recovery for these Series 5 daggers encompasses Wessex, the southern maritory zone and the Thames valley. Thus, there appears to be an interesting chronological development through to the currency of the Wessex Series 2 graves, with a progressively wider distribution of the key dagger type. Also in Wessex there are very high number of knives (mainly of Series 7) and daggers of indeterminate type. This concentration has not shown up on previous dagger distribution maps, such as those provided by Gerloff (1975) because the indeterminate daggers have never before been fully listed or plotted. Many of the indeterminate daggers were found by Cunnington and Colt Hoare, but because they did not survive to be curated in a museum, they have never before been entered into the overall discussions. In conclusion, it can be noted that a concentration of Series 2 daggers in the Peak District and the north during the later Beaker period was succeeded by concentrations of Series 3 and 4 daggers, and of indeterminate daggers, in Wessex during the Early Bronze Age.

Another category of items which is highly concentrated in the Wessex region is that of composite necklaces. The nature of such necklaces has been described and discussed in Chapter 8. They combine beads of different shapes, sizes

and raw materials to provide visually exciting mixtures of striking and magical substances, such as jet and jet-like materials, amber, faience, gold, bone, shell and fossils. The map of recovery (Figure 12.8) includes all necklace types described in Chapter 8; these are mainly necklaces with elements of more than one raw material but also included are the simple necklaces with components of variable shape (see Appendix 12.1). The map demonstrates that composite necklaces are substantially concentrated in Wessex, with 52 deriving from the county of Wiltshire alone. However there is also a scattered distribution of composite necklaces beyond Wessex. This distribution is summarised in the histogram (Figure 12.9) which shows the fall-off in the number of necklace find-spots in relation to a hypothetical point in mid-Wiltshire. This fall-off may perhaps represent a diaspora spreading out from Wessex through some social exchange mechanism. It is interesting to note that there is no marked concentration of composite necklaces in the southern and eastern coastal maritory zones, except in the county of Dorset. They may, therefore, not have been circulating within that network of contact and exchange. However, we do know that elements of the unusual necklace from Exloo in the Netherlands most probably came from Wessex (Haveman and Sheridan 2006).

Often occurring in composite necklaces, and occasionally alone, are blue beads made from faience. Some faience bead types were widespread, but it is significant to our argument here to note that the segmented faience beads are found particularly in the Wessex region (see Sheridan and Shortland 2004, fig. 21.7.1). This, of course, may be linked to the fact that they commonly occur within the composite necklaces which, as we have seen, are also concentrated particularly in Wessex.

The major concentration of Early Bronze Age amber beads, necklaces and other items in Wessex is well documented and is illustrated in Figure 12.10, where the many find spots of individual or small groups of amber beads within Wiltshire and Dorset are represented by the

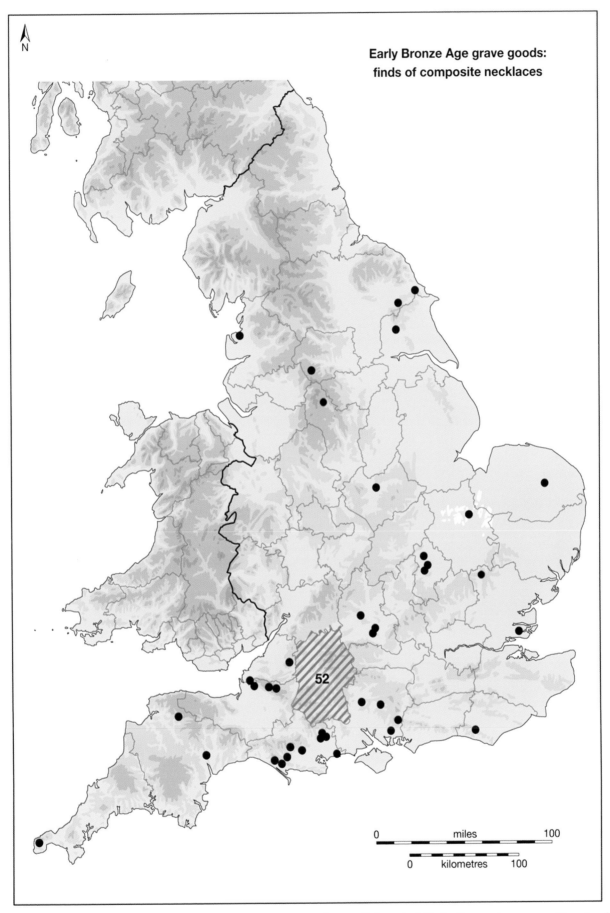

Figure 12.8. Map of recovery for finds of composite necklaces from well-furnished Early Bronze Age graves. Drawing by Henry Buglass.

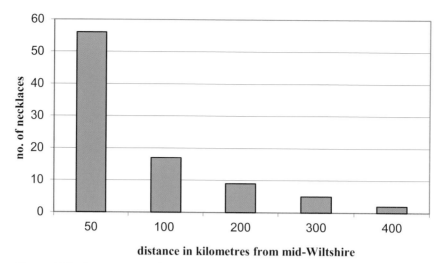

Figure 12.9. Composite necklaces: spatial occurrence in relation to mid-Wiltshire.

hatched shading. The three largest remains of amber spacer plate necklaces also occur in these two Wessex counties. However some of the larger groups occur in the coastal maritory zone, as at Little Cressingham, Norfolk, and more recently in Kent and at Mellor in Lancashire (the latter marked as 'M' on the map). Figure 12.10 also shows that many of the non-Wessex finds of amber are actually components of composite necklaces which, as we have already argued, may have come from Wessex originally. Thus the existence of a substantial concentration of amber finds in Wessex can be demonstrated.

CONCLUSIONS

The detailed study of the characteristics of well-furnished graves of Beaker and Early Bronze Age date throughout England has led to the definition of some key regional variations, some of which have been noted for the first time. Concerning the individuals buried in well-furnished graves, virtually all were inhumations in the Beaker period, while in the Early Bronze Age cremation burials became progressively more common. The main regional pattern deduced is that in the Early Bronze Age cremations were far more numerous in Wessex than in the Yorkshire Wolds or the Peak District. Age-wise almost all Beaker people buried in well-furnished graves were adults. In the Early Bronze Age there was a wider age range represented, but in Wessex adults were still dominant. Most well-furnished Beaker graves contained men. In the Early Bronze Age the occurrence of men and women became more even, but there were relatively more men in the Wessex region than in the Wolds or the Peak District.

The spatial distributions of various object categories have been illustrated in a series of maps of recovery and in histograms. In the Beaker period well-furnished graves were fairly evenly distributed throughout England, but by the Early Bronze Age a series of regional variations are apparent. Interestingly, several of the variations defined relate to areas outside the Wessex region. These include

a strong 'jet zone' in the North, the south coast maritory characterised by precious cups, the newly recognised necklace-crafting area in East Anglia, and the prevalence of bone hair pins in the Wolds and the Peak District. Meanwhile in the Thames valley well-furnished graves of the earlier Early Bronze Age are notable by their virtual absence. However in the later stages of the Wessex Series Early Bronze Age the distribution of Series 5 ogival daggers can be seen to cover Wessex, the southern maritory zone and the Thames valley. Finally metal awls display a fairly even distribution throughout England, and their definition as a type particular to Wessex cannot be upheld.

Our study has demonstrated very clearly that there is a series of specific object types that are heavily concentrated only in the Wessex region, and especially in the counties of Wiltshire and Dorset. Some of these categories are complex and exotic, while others are rather more mundane. It is this suite of artefact types that can be taken to be a defining characteristic of the 'Wessex Culture' where that term is defined as the Early Bronze Age period in the Wessex region. The object categories concerned are:

- Series 3 and 4 (Armorico-British) daggers
- Series 7 knives
- complex gold ornaments
- amber spacer plate necklaces and heirloom beads
- segmented faience beads
- bone tweezers
- fancy dress pins
- complex pendants
- perforated bone plates
- composite necklaces

Of these categories by far the most common are the components of composite necklaces; these include heirloom beads of amber and jet as well as segmented faience beads and most of the complex pendants, some of which incorporated gold elements. It is these composite necklaces that could be said to form the most significant defining feature of the Early Bronze Age in Wessex.

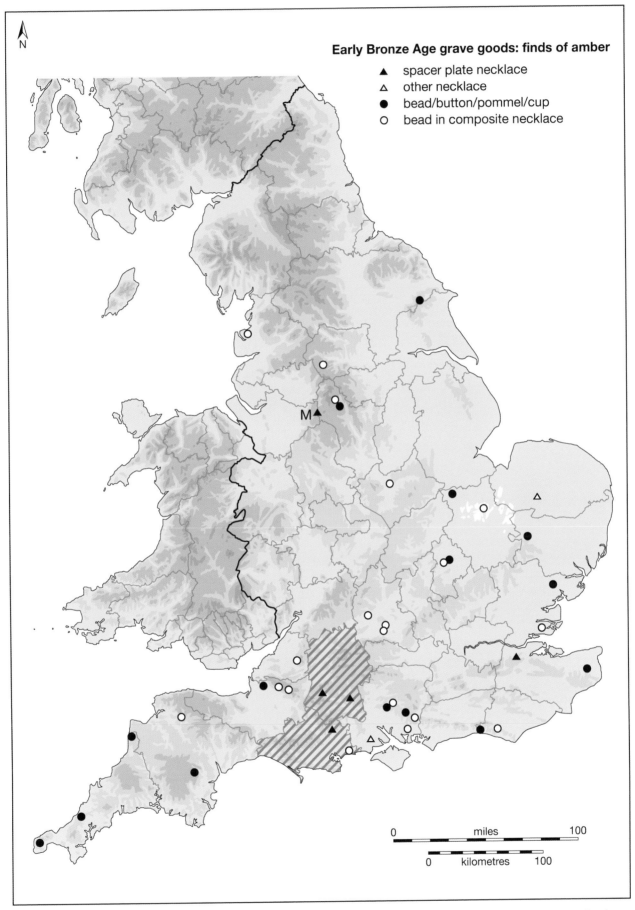

Figure 12.10. Map of recovery for finds of amber from well-furnished Early Bronze Age graves. Drawing by Henry Buglass.

Appendix 12.1

SITES MAPPED IN FIGURES 12.1–12.4, 12.8 and 12.10.

The sites are listed roughly in geographical order, from north to south. Items studied in this project are shown in italic (for the bracers see Woodward and Hunter 2011). Barrow numbering: G = Grinsell; M = Mortimer; Gr = Greenwell.

Figure 12.1. Beaker grave goods: finds of stone
Bracer: amphibolite
Aston 1 (Derbyshire); *Brandon Fields (Suffolk)*; *Sewell (Bedfordshire)*; *Wellington Quarry (Herefordshire)*; *Gravelly Guy (Oxfordshire)*; *Stanton Harcourt (Oxfordshire)*; *Shorncote (Gloucestershire)*; *Roundway G8 (Wiltshire)*; *Monkton (Kent)*; *Mere (Wiltshire)*; *Winterslow G3 (Wiltshire)*; *Pyecombe (East Sussex)*; *West Stafford (Dorset)*; *Thomas Hardye School (Dorset)*.

Bracer: Group VI
Kelleythorpe GrUN101 (East Yorkshire); *Melton Quarry (East Yorkshire)*; *Ferry Fryston (West Yorkshire)*; *Barnack (Cambridgeshire)*; *Raunds 1 (Northamptonshire)*; *Dorchester XII (Oxfordshire)*; *Hemp Knoll (Wiltshire)*.

Bracer: miscellaneous rock
Ben Bridge (Somerset); *Stonehenge (Wiltshire)*; *Amesbury Archer x 2 (Wiltshire)*; *Thanet (Kent)*.

Sponge finger stone
Rudston Gr68: no Beaker (East Yorkshire); *Raunds 1 (Northamptonshire)*; *Gravelly Guy (Oxfordshire)*; *West Overton G6b x 2 (Wiltshire)*; *Winterbourne Stoke G54 x 2 (Wiltshire)*; *Langton Matravers (Dorset)*.

Flint dagger
Wooler (Northumberland); Middleton-on-the-Wolds (East Yorkshire); Little Downham (Cambridgeshire); Raunds 1 (Northamptonshire); Raunds 6 (Northamptonshire); Great Chesterford (Essex); Shorncote (Gloucestershire); Amesbury G54 (Wiltshire); West Stogursey (Somerset); Portsdown (Hampshire).

Figure 12.2. Beaker grave goods: finds of amber, jet and jet-like materials and animal bone/antler
Amber bead/button
Kelleythorpe GrUN101 (East Yorkshire); Garton Slack M161 (East Yorshire); Acklam Wold M124 (East Yorkshire); Steep Low, Alstonefield (Staffordshire); Brampton (Cambridgeshire).

Amber belt ring
Ferrybridge (West Yorkshire); *Kniveton (Derbyshire)*; *Raunds 1 (Northamptonshire)*.

V-perforated button of jet or jet-like material
Chatton Sandyford (Northumberland); Lilburn Steads (Northumberland); Broxa Moor 4 (North Yorkshire); *Acklam Wold M124 (East Yorkshire)*; *Garton Slack Gr37 (East Yorkshire)*; *Hanging Grimston M55 (East Yorkshire)*; *Middleton-on-the-Wolds (M) (East Yorkshire)*; *Brown Edge, Hartington Middle (Derbyshire)*; *Little Downham (Cambridgeshire)*; *Raunds 1 (Northamptonshire)*; *Raunds 6 (Northamptonshire)*.

Bead of jet or jet-like material
Sutton Bank (North Yorkshire); *Folkton Gr245 (East Yorkshire)*; Waterhall Farm (Cambridgeshire); Charmy Down (Gloucestershire); Chilbolton (Hampshire); *Beggars Haven (East Sussex)*.

Jet or jet-like pulley ring
Acklam Wold M124 (East Yorkshire); *Little Downham (Cambridgeshire)*; *Tring (Hertfordshire)*; *Winterbourne Stoke G54 (Wiltshire)*.

Belt ring of jet or jet-like materials
Kenslow (Derbyshire); Raunds secondary in long barrow (Northamptonshire); Cassington (Oxfordshire); *Amesbury Archer (Wiltshire)*.

Bone/antler pin/point
Hasting Hill, Offerton (Co Durham); Elloughton (North Yorkshire); *Ganton Gr28 (East Yorkshire)*; *Acklam Wold M124 (East Yorkshire)*; Middleton-on-the-Wolds (East Yorkshire); Kenslow (Derbyshire); *Green Low (Derbyshire)*; Bicester (Oxfordshire); Barrow Hills 203 (Oxfordshire); Barrow Hills 4660 (Oxfordshire); *Amesbury Archer (Wiltshire)*; Easton Lane (Hampshire).

Bone/antler spatula
Penrith (Cumbria); *Garton Slack M163 (East Yorkshire)*; *Green Low (Derbyshire)*; *Haddon Field (Derbyshire)*; *Mouse Low, Grindon (Staffordshire)*; *Smerrill Moor (Derbyshire)*; *Raunds 1 (Northamptonshire)*; Stanton Harcourt XV1/1 (Oxfordshire); Barrow Hills 4660 (Oxfordshire); Barrow Hills 203 (Oxfordshire); *West Overton G6b (Wiltshire)*; *Amesbury Archer (Wiltshire)*; *Mere G6a (Wiltshire)*; *Amesbury G51 (Wiltshire)*; Chilbolton (Hampshire); Easton Lane (Hampshire).

Tusk
Raunds 1 (Northamptonshire); Pershore (Worcestershire); *Wilsford G1 (Wiltshire)*; *Amesbury Archer (Wiltshire)*; *Amesbury Archer Companion (Wiltshire)*; Boscombe Bowmen (Wiltshire); Sutton Veny G11a (Wiltshire).

Bone/antler toggle
Barnack (Cambridgeshire); *Sewell (Bedfordshire)*; Bicester (Oxfordshire); *Hemp Knoll (Wiltshire)*; Boscombe Bowmen (Wiltshire); Thomas Hardye School (Dorset).

Bone/antler belt ring
Melton Quarry (East Yorkshire); *Folkton Gr245 (East Yorkshire)*; Stanton Harcourt (Oxfordshire); Jug's Grave, Monkton Farleigh (Wiltshire); *Sittingbourne (Kent); Wilsford G1 x 2 (Wiltshire).*

Figure 12.3. Beaker grave goods: finds of metal

Basket ornament, gold
Alston (Northumberland); Radley 4a (Oxfordshire); Chilbolton (Hampshire); Amesbury Archer (Wiltshire); Amesbury Archer Companion (Wiltshire).

Basket ornament, copper/copper alloy
Cowlam Gr58 (East Yorkshire); *Staker Hill, Buxton (Derbyshire)*; Tallington (Leicestershire); Raunds secondary in long barrow (Northamptonshire).

Bead, gold
Chilbolton (Hampshire).

Bead, copper/copper alloy
Waterhall Farm (Cambridgeshire); *Beggars Haven (East Sussex).*

Dagger (Association Group 1)
Wellington Quarry (Herefordshire); Barrow Hills 4660 (Oxfordshire); *Sutton Courtenay (Oxfordshire)*; *Roundway G8 (Wiltshire)*; *Sittingbourne (Kent)*; Monkton, Thanet (Kent); Amesbury Archer (Wiltshire); *Mere G6a (Wiltshire)*; Chilbolton (Hampshire); Thomas Hardye School x 2 (Dorset).

Dagger (later)
West Lilburn (Northumberland); Aldro M116 (East Yorkshire); Ferrybridge (West Yorkshire); *Standlow (Derbyshire)*; *Barnack (Cambridgeshire)*; Gravelly Guy (Oxfordshire); Foxley Farm, Eynsham (Oxfordshire); Dorchester XII (Oxfordshire); Calne Without G2c (Wiltshire); East Kennet G1c (Wiltshire); Charmy Down, (Gloucestershire); Winterslow Hut (Wiltshire); *Shrewton G5k (Wiltshire)*; *Pyecombe (East Sussex)*; Fernworthy (Devon).

Pin
Sewell (Bedfordshire); Roundway G8 (Wiltshire).

Awl
Rudston Gr62 x 2 (East Yorkshire); *Aldro M116 (East Yorkshire)*; Ferry Fryston 161 (West Yorkshire); *Ilam Moor (Derbyshire)*; Minning Low (Derbyshire); Haddon Field (Derbyshire); Eynsham, Foxley Farm (Oxfordshire); Eynsham, Foxley Farm grave 18 (Oxfordshire); Tolley's Pit, Cassington (Oxfordshire); Barrow Hills 203 (Oxfordshire); Lambourn G19 (Berkshire); Lambourn 'a' (Berkshire); West Overton G6b (Wiltshire); *Amesbury G51 (Wiltshire)*;

Dummer (Hampshire); Stockbridge (Hampshire); Tarrant Launceston G8 (Dorset); *Thickthorn Down (Dorset).*

Bracelet or neckring
Knipton (Leicestershire); Berden (Essex); Yarnton (Oxfordshire); Shorncote (Gloucestershire); West Stafford (Dorset).

Figure 12.4. Early Bronze Age: finds of necklaces of jet and jet-like materials

Spacer plate necklace
Northumberland: Crookham Dene, Ford; High Cocklaw, Berwick; Stoney Vage, Wooler; Kyloe.
North Yorkshire: *NW of Pickering*; Givendale Head; West Heslerton; Lockton Pastures; Hesselskew; Egton (Allan Toft barrow).
East Yorkshire: *Calais Wold M13*; *Middleton-on-the-Wolds.*
Derbyshire: *Cow Low x 2, Green Fairfield; Windle Nook, Wormhill; Hill Head, Hasling House, Hartington Upper*; *Middleton Moor; Grind Low, Upper Haddon.*
Cambridgeshire: *Snailwell C; Soham Fen.*
Suffolk: Risby; Flempton, Risby.

Individual spacer plate
Simonburn (Northumberland); Warksburn Bridge, Wark (Northumberland); *Crosby Garrett (Cumbria)*; *Holwick in Teesdale (North Yorkshire)*; *Helperthorpe (East Yorkshire)*; *Burwell Fen (Cambridgeshire)*; Radwell (Bedfordshire).

Large necklace (disc bead necklaces)
Eglingham Gr200 (Northumberland); Santon Bridge (Cumbria); Broomrigg, Ainstable (Cumbria); Crosby Ravensworth, Crossley Cairn (Cumbria); Ingleby Barwick (Stockton-on-Tees); *Pockley (North Yorkshire);* Hesketh Moor (West Yorkshire).
East Yorkshire: *Garrowby, Painsthorpe M64; Garton Slack 75; Garton Slack VI, grave 1; Garton Slack 29, burial D; Weaverthorpe Gr44; Goodmanham Gr121.*
Wiltshire: *Manton, Preshute G1a; Wilsford G39; Winterbourne Stoke G47*; Roundway.
Monkton (Kent); Blach Burgh (Sussex).

Small necklace
Ford (Northumberland); *Egton (North Yorkshire)*; *Fylingdales (North Yorkshire)*; *Nawton, Pinderdale Wood (North Yorkshire)*; *Stranghow Moor, Moorsholm (North Yorkshire)*; *Hutton Buscel (North Yorkshire)*; *Hay Top (Derbyshire)*; Deeping St Nicholas (Lincolnshire); Southery Fen bracelet (Norfolk); Roughton (Norfolk); Childrey (Berkshire); *Tan Hill (Wiltshire).*

Gold encased beads
Great Bircham (Norfolk); Rochford (Essex).

Bone spacer plates
Feltwell Fen (Norfolk); Barton Mills (Suffolk).

Figure 12.8. Early Bronze Age grave goods: finds of composite necklaces

Note: this figure includes all the categories of necklace described in Chapter 8. The 52 sites located in Wiltshire are listed after those from other counties.

Simple necklaces with components of variable shape

Bone: *Folkton Gr71 (East Yorkshire)*.
Stone: *Bedford (Bedfordshire)*; *Kempston (Bedfordshire)*.

Composite necklaces of two or more materials

Calais Wold 114 (East Yorkshire); *Langton (East Yorkshire)*; Pilling (Lancashire); Todmorden x 2 (West Yorkshire); Abney Moor (Derbyshire); Cossington (Lincolnshire); Caistor St Edmund (Norfolk); Stonea, Wimblington (Cambridgeshire); Radwell 1 (Bedfordshire); Ashville, Abingdon (Oxfordshire); Radley 16 (Oxfordshire); Stanton Harcourt XVI, 1 (Oxfordshire); Rochford (Essex); Little Chesterford (Essex); *Marshfield (Gloucestershire)*; Chilcompton 2016 (Somerset); Ashen Hill, Chewton Mendip G11 (Somerset); Rowbarrow, Shipham G2 (Somerset); Tynings East, Cheddar (Somerset); Stockbridge Down (Hampshire); Portsdown, Southwick (Hampshire); Barnett Copse, Chalton (Hampshire); Hengistbury Head 1 (Hampshire); Easton Lane (Hampshire); *Oxsettle Bottom (East Sussex)*; Upton Pyne G4 (Devon); North Molton G17c (Devon); Boscregan (Cornwall).
Dorset: Bloxworth; Thomas Hardye School; Winterbourne St Martin G5a; Winterbourne Steepleton; Puddletown Hundred; Wimborne St Giles G6; Wimborne St Giles G8 (SE tump); Wimborne St Giles G33a.

Simple necklaces with components of variable shape: Wiltshire (n = 9)

Jet or jet-like material: *Avebury G13c*; *Durrington G14*; *Wilsford G32*.
Amber: *Aldbourne Gr276*; *Winterbourne Stoke G14*; *Norton Bavant G1*; *Wilsford G33a*.
Fossil: *Amesbury G70*; *Amesbury G71*.

Composite necklaces of two or more materials: Wiltshire (n = 43)

Described in Chapter 8, in order cited there:
Winterbourne Stoke G47; *Winterbourne Stoke G64a*; *Wilsford G16*; *Amesbury G39*; *Durrington G47*; *Winterbourne Stoke G68*; *Aldbourne Gr285 (G12)*; *Upton Lovell G2a (shaman)*; *South Newton G1*; *Warminster G10*; *Shrewton G5j*; *Upton Lovell G2e*; *Upton Lovell G1*; *Wilsford G3*; *Collingbourne Kingston G8*; *Winterbourne Stoke G67*; *Amesbury G48*; *Wilsford G46*; *Wilsford G42*;

Winterbourne Stoke G8; *Wilsford G7*; *Shrewton G5L*; *Winterslow G21*; *Preshute G1a (Manton)*; *Wilsford G8*; *Aldbourne G6*.

Composite necklaces of two or more materials: not studied or lost, listed in alphabetical order

Solstice Park (Amesbury); Amesbury G61a; Amesbury G44; Amesbury G54; Avebury G23d; Avebury G55; Collingbourne Kingston G5 (Snail Down); Collingbourne Kingston G8; Collingbourne Ducis G12; East Knoyle G1; Figheldean G12; Kingston Deverill G5; Kingston Deverill G9; Maiden Bradley G5; Wilsford G72; Winterbourne Stoke G9.

Figure 12.10. Early Bronze Age grave goods: finds of amber

Wiltshire and Dorset not mapped, except for spacer plate necklaces:
Wimborne St Giles G9 (Dorset); Upton Lovell G2e; Wilsford-cum-Lake (Wiltshire).

Spacer plate necklace

Mellor (Cheshire) (marked 'M' on Figure).

Other necklace

Little Cressingham (Norfolk); Chard (Somerset); Beaulieu (Hampshire); Whitehill Road, Southfleet (Kent).

Bead/button/pommel/cup

Acklam Wold (East Yorkshire); Abney Moor (Derbyshire); Pilsgate (Cambridgeshire); Radwell II (Bedfordshire); Pin Farm, Gazeley (Suffolk); Colchester (Essex); Cheddar G19 (Somerset); Hammeldon (Devon); Morwenstow (Cornwall); Boscregan III (Cornwall); Perranzabuloe (Cornwall); Corhampton (Hampshire); Winchester (Hampshire); Ringlemere (Kent); Hove (West Sussex).

Bead in composite necklace

Pilling (Lancashire); Todmorden (West Yorkshire); Abney Moor (Derbyshire); Cossington (Leicestershire); Stonea, Wimblington (Cambridgeshire); Radwell I (Bedfordshire); Radley 16 (Oxfordshire); Ashville, Abingdon (Oxfordshire); Stanton Harcourt XVI, 1 (Oxfordshire); Rochford (Essex); *Marshfield (Gloucestershire)*; Ashen Hill, Chewton Mendip G11 (Somerset); Chilcompton 2016 (Somerset); North Molton (Devon); Portsdown (Hampshire); Hengistbury Head 1 (Hampshire); Barnett Copse, Chalton (Hampshire); Easton Lane, Winchester (Hampshire); *Oxsettle Bottom (East Sussex)*.

13. CONCLUSIONS

The purpose of this concluding chapter is to provide an overview of the results, to present some assessment of the project's overall achievements, to comment on topics that could not be covered within the project, and to give some pointers for further related work. Observations on individual artefact types or themes are covered in the respective chapters or sub-chapters and are not pursued further here. Overall, the project involved the detailed examination of 5665 items from 780 individual graves; of these items 4778 were individual beads contained within a series of 81 necklaces. Each item has been the subject of multiple photographic views, leading to the creation of an archive of 5860 photographs containing both general and detailed images.

One of the key aims was to compare the results obtained for objects from Beaker graves with those from graves of mature Early Bronze Age date. The employment of a generalised chronological cut-off point between these two burial traditions of *c.* 2000 BC is explained in Chapter 1 and Chapter 12; the breakdown of the 780 grave groups by project period and region is shown in Table 2.3. Overall a smaller number of Beaker graves were covered within each of the four regions, and this reflects the lower occurrence of well-furnished burials within the Beaker period. Most rich burials of the mature Early Bronze Age are located in East Yorkshire and Wessex, and the project selections reflect this bias. For the 'rest of the country', many of the rich Beaker grave groups were included, but for the mature Early Bronze Age a more selective approach was adopted (see Chapter 2). This enabled the project to include as many relevant objects as possible, especially those belonging to the previously lesser studied groups of material made from stone, bone or antler and amber, as well as allowing the opportunity to pay more detailed attention to items made from gold and to the necklaces made from jet or jet-like materials, and from amber.

All the major aims of the project, which are set out in Chapter 1 and Chapter 2, have been fulfilled. All objects were recorded using standardised record forms and photographic techniques, and the information gathered was transferred to digital databases. Copies of the record forms, which include original material such as annotated sketches and full bibliographic information not covered in the digital databases, will be lodged in the archives of each relevant museum and at the Society of Antiquaries of London. Typologies for all major object categories have been devised. Sometimes these used existing published schemes, but in several cases new or revised typologies have been provided. This applies particularly to daggers (Chapter 3.1 and Appendix I), pommels (Chapter 3.2 and Appendix IV), bone points (Chapter 4.7) and to the various kinds of necklace (Chapter 7.3 and Chapter 8.6). Much attention has been paid to the identification and sourcing of the various raw materials, which often had been selected for their distinctive colours and 'magical' physical properties. This work has ranged from a reassessment of the chemical compositions of copper and copper alloy daggers to the identification of jet and the various non-jet materials that may resemble jet. One especially interesting result of the latter analyses has been the identification of the use of Whitby jet for some items from Wessex and Sussex, within both the Beaker and Early Bronze Age periods.

The results of the chemical and petrographic analysis of stone objects have been innovative. Whilst no general patterns of stone procurement, such as those determined for Beaker-age bracers (see Woodward and Hunter 2011), have been demonstrated, it has been possible to show that some objects were made from stone derived from the British south-west peninsula, whilst others were definitely made from local materials. It is interesting to note that the exploitation of Group VI tuff from Cumbria, which had been used extensively for one group of bracers, apparently did not continue into the mature Early Bronze Age period.

Innovative results have also been obtained from the detailed identification of bone and antler materials to species and body part. A summary of the species exploited is provided in Table 13.1. The figures highlight two of the surprising conclusions that resulted from studies by several project specialists. Firstly, it has been demonstrated that a series of objects, notably dagger pommels, were made from cetacean bone (whalebone), while a more varied selection of items were shown to have been manufactured

Table 13.1. The occurrence of animal raw materials by species and object type (*cattle or red deer; objects where species could not be identified are not included).

Object type	Chapter	Sheep /goat	Cattle	Pig	Large mammal*	Red deer	Deer	Cetacean/ ?cetacean	Dog/ wolf	Crane	Human	Total
Pommels	3.2				3		1	11				15
Belt hooks	3.3				5						3	8
Belt/pulley rings	3.4				5							5
Spatulae	4.5				14	25						39
Points	4.7	186	3	1	25	3	5 (roe)					223
Tweezers	4.8	9			1							10
Tubes	4.9	5								1	1	7
Plates	4.10				4							4
Toggles	4.11	3			1	1	1					6
Tools	4.12		2			2	1				1	6
Handles	4.12	1				4						5
Antlers	4.12					3	3 (roe)					6
Pendants	4.12; 5.9				1						2	3
Tusks	5.1			27								27
Teeth	5.1								25			25
Buttons	5.2	1			1			2				4
Dress pins	5.5	1			9	1	1					12
Singleton bead	5.7	1					1					2
Totals		**206**	**6**	**28**	**69**	**39**	**13**	**13**	**25**	**1**	**7**	**407**

from human bone. In both cases it can be suggested that such bone material may have been symbolically charged. In general, it can be noted that many of the bone items were made from the bones of sheep or goat. To some degree this may reflect the size and detailed morphology of the item in question, in that a particular bone may have been ideal for the manufacture, say, of a set of tweezers, or bone points. However the preponderance may reflect an underlying situation: that sheep were becoming more important within the Early Bronze Age economy. Excavated settlement sites from the period are so few that this evidence from artefacts may be of some more general importance in this respect. By contrast, it is also worth noting that the employment of bones and antlers from wild animals was found to be relatively rare.

During microscopic analysis it was important to distinguish traces of manufacture, usually in the form of cut, grinding or gouge marks, from any traces of use wear. In many cases traces of such primary shaping had been obliterated by final stages of polishing or re-polishing, but all such processes could be detected and were recorded in detail. As a result it has been possible to document the methods of production for many classes of object. In general it could be concluded that there was a significant expansion of the number of artefact types during the mature Early Bronze Age period and that this was associated with an explosion of decorative craftsmanship and the development of novel techniques of manufacture. Traces of manufacture are particularly clear on many items made from jet or jet-like materials, and detailed discussion of shaping, drilling and polishing techniques may be found within the text, especially in the descriptions of buttons (Chapter 5.2 and Chapter 5.3) and necklaces (Chapter 7.1 and Chapter 7.2).

Another main aim of the project was to determine the specific function of various categories of artefact. This was achieved by a detailed study of morphology and the location of any use wear, linked to any evidence for the placement of the object on the buried body. Many of the object categories were already known to relate to bodily adornment, and to have formed elements of special costume that may have functioned in ritual activities and ceremonies. Detailed studies of such objects within this volume, including necklaces made from many exotic and special materials, buttons, earrings, dress pins and pendants have served to provide much further detail, and have inspired ideas of how objects may have been worn and displayed on the body. It has also been possible to draw attention to some lesser known categories of body ornaments such as the studs, which were found in skull or neck positions and would have been worn in the ear or lip as studs or labrets. Belts were embellished with rings or hooks made from various materials, while use wear and body placement evidence suggests that some of the rings may have been hanging ornaments, or elements of strappage on the upper body. Buttons appear to have been used to fasten cloaks or were sewn in sets onto special jackets, and even leggings. Many sheet gold discs have now been re-interpreted as

button covers, and this emphasises the exotic significance of this form of dress ornament.

Other categories, which have previously been considered to have functioned as tools, can now be interpreted as elements of special costume, or items of potentially ritual paraphernalia. For instance, many bone points appear to have been used as hair pins or elements of headdresses, the wear on some antlers suggests that they also may have been employed in headdresses, and metal awls were most likely employed in the process of applying decoration directly to the body, in the form of tattoos or scarification. Bone tweezers could not have functioned as depilatory instruments and are more likely to have been special clips, perhaps used to secure a special hair style. Dagger pommels and antler handles show particularly strong use wear, and often had been modified for use on subsequent metal blades. Furthermore they were sometimes deposited alone in graves, and thus seem to have retained amuletic properties as individual objects. Daggers were mainly placed near the arms and hands or at the chest, and in Wessex some were placed behind the head. Use wear and morphological studies suggest that many daggers functioned as cutting knives rather than as stabbing weapons, and they may have been used during animal sacrifice rather than in human combat. Amongst the stone tools, grooved stones, previously interpreted as arrowshaft straighteners, now seem more likely to have been used to trim thicker shafts, either of bone or wood, for use on implements such as mace-heads and battle-axes. Groups of tools were often placed at the feet and may have been contained within bags or other containers made from perishable materials. Sometimes such caches of objects also contained items of personal adornment such as beads.

Patterns of association between particular object types and the age and sex of bodies found within the graves can provide evidence for differences in social function, such as rank or status, and may illuminate roles and meaning related to gender. One major trend through time can be discerned. In the Beaker period, the majority of well-furnished graves are those of men and most of the object types of that period, especially daggers, bracers, spatulae, flint daggers, bone points, buttons and awls, occur in male graves. The few well-furnished graves of women include only awls, or occasionally a bead or bracelet. In the mature Early Bronze Age period the gender pattern of daggers with men and awls with women continues, but there are now many more graves of females, and these are dominated by different styles of necklace. However, the patterns are not clear-cut, and in Wessex necklaces and awls occur in graves of both men and women. Regional differences in patterning can be discerned, and in Early Bronze Age Wessex there was a particular association between awls and composite necklaces.

The identification of heirloom items or relics depended on examining the evidence for the use of objects over time and evidence for fragmentation of an item into smaller entities that may have been retained for future exchange or curation. Object use wear was studied both by category and within individual grave groups. Excluding tools, which may have been subject to extreme wear during their primary use life, the object categories which displayed most wear were daggers, pommels and belt rings in the Beaker period and pommels, perforated stones and dress pins in the Early Bronze Age. Such items are most likely to have functioned as heirlooms. A further category which displayed significant wear in both project periods is V-perforated buttons. One of the tests used to detect the possible presence of heirloom items was to assess the variation in wear categories for objects deriving from grave groups that possessed two or more items for which a wear category was assigned during the project. It was possible to examine such variation in a total of 84 grave groups that did not contain a necklace (37 of Beaker-age and 47 Early Bronze Age). Eleven Early Bronze Age graves of this status which contained both necklaces and non-necklace items could also be considered. Necklaces most often occurred in graves which contained no further grave goods. However, the variation in wear amongst the component beads also provided good evidence for the possible presence of heirloom items. Altogether a total of 74 'necklace graves' included two or more beads with a determinate wear category and thus could be analysed in this manner. Using this large set of data it was possible to reach some important conclusions concerning the occurrence of probable heirloom items within grave groups belonging to both project periods. For the non-necklace items, 32% of the graves are likely to have contained heirlooms in the Beaker period, compared with 28% for the mature Early Bronze Age. Thus two conclusions may be drawn. Firstly the practice of employing heirlooms was already highly evident in the Beaker period, and secondly, the incidence of non-necklace heirloom deposition seems to have stayed relatively stable throughout the two periods.

Amongst the 74 necklaces with relevant recorded data, the disc bead necklaces displayed least wear, and did not appear to incorporate heirloom items. Spacer plate necklaces of jet and jet-like materials also displayed a high percentage of unworn beads, but heirloom elements were often present, and these may have derived from more than one earlier necklace. The complex amber necklaces tended to contain more worn items, although due to the nature of the material, wear categories for individual elements often could not be determined. The composite necklaces also contained many worn items, some of which, on morphological evidence, had been recycled from spacer plate necklaces of amber or jet and jet-like materials.

It was also hoped that the project might address questions relating to the definition of the 'Wessex Culture' phenomenon during the mature Early Bronze Age period. In order to investigate this topic the distributions of various artefact categories within England were studied. This analysis involved the preparation of a series of distribution maps and histograms, which may be viewed in Chapter 12. From this research it was possible to assess the concentrations of selected artefact and burial types within different parts of the country, to determine to what

extent there was any particular concentration within the Wessex region, and to investigate how overall object distributions changed between the Beaker and mature Early Bronze Age periods. In the Beaker period virtually all the well-furnished graves were inhumation burials of adult men. In the Early Bronze Age, the rite of cremation became more usual. Women were now well represented and a wider age range within both gender categories was current. Some regional variations could also be detected. In the Beaker period well-furnished graves were fairly evenly distributed throughout England, but by the Early Bronze Age a series of regional variations are also apparent. Interestingly, several of the variations defined relate to areas outside the Wessex region. These include a significant 'jet zone' in the north, the south coast maritory characterised by precious cups, the newly recognised necklace-crafting area in East Anglia, and the prevalence of bone hair pins in the Yorkshire Wolds and the Peak District. However, the distributional studies have also demonstrated that a series of object types were heavily concentrated only in the Wessex region, and especially in the counties of Wiltshire and Dorset. These object types include daggers of Series 3, 4 and 7, complex gold ornaments, amber spacer plate necklaces and heirloom beads deriving from them, segmented faience beads, bone tweezers, perforated bone plates, fancy dress pins and complex pendants. The most striking concentration of items in Wessex relates to the composite necklaces, and it is these necklaces that could be said to form the most significant defining feature of the Early Bronze Age in Wessex.

Although much has been achieved within the project, there are several areas of related research which could usefully be pursued. For logistical reasons we were not able to study the flint items or pottery vessels that were present in our selected grave groups, although the occurrence of pots of various form, flint daggers and barbed-and-tanged arrowheads was included in our databases. Detailed study of the flint items would undoubtedly produce important data and hopefully such a study could be undertaken in the future. The degree of survival (at rim level) of the ceramic vessels housed in the British Museum is indicated in diagrammatic form in the modern publication of the Greenwell Collection (Kinnes and Longworth 1985). However to assess the survival status of such vessels at the time of burial it would be necessary to study the nature of the breaks first-hand, and at the time of our research visits, the pottery at the British Museum was in closed storage. Once again, detailed study of this body of data in the future could be very illuminating. A problem that arose throughout our studies was the realisation that different materials may have become worn at different rates, and this might affect our overall analyses of relative wear categories amongst the objects in the various grave groups. What is needed is an intensive experimental programme to investigate the degree of wear traces caused by different kinds of usage within replica items made from different raw materials.

Finally it is important to draw attention to the data that will have been missing from the well-furnished graves that have been studied. This is the vast array of items and equipment made from perishable substances. It has been noted that none of the materials used for the stringing of the necklaces have survived, and a glimpse of what we may be missing has been provided by the recent finds from the grave at Whitehorse Hill, Devon (Jones *et al.* 2012; Jones forthcoming). Here a mass of plant and animal materials were preserved in association with a cremation burial within a stone cist. Preliminary examination has identified a composite object made from animal skin and textile, perhaps part of a special garment, an animal hide or pelt and a woven bag or basket, all protected between layers of matted plant material. There was also a composite necklace, two pairs of ear studs and a bracelet or armband made from strands of woven plant fibres interspersed with numerous small studs of tin. If the contents of the cist had not been waterlogged, all that would have survived would have been the beads, the small tin studs and the ear studs.

The overwhelming result of the project has been to establish that a large proportion of the items buried with individuals during the Chalcolithic and Early Bronze Age periods were objects associated with special costumes, or implements used during ritual acts and ceremonies. Most obvious are the beads and necklaces made from various materials of symbolic and supernatural significance – faience, jet and jet-like materials, amber, fossils and exotic minerals. Other categories, such as bone or metal pins and bone tweezers, were probably used to secure elaborate hairstyles, and other items were used as body ornaments (at ear, lip, forehead, wrist or ankle) or to embellish or fasten the edges of special garments. Many other items have been shown to have functioned as ritual paraphernalia, for

instance in the form of ceremonial goads, sound instruments or a mace. Only a few categories of object appear to have functioned primarily as tools – the sponge finger stones (for working animal skin), the bone or antler spatulae which were employed in the pressure flaking of flint, and the grooved stones. However many of these were used in the production of special items: the spatulae for the manufacture of fine barbed-and-tanged arrowheads and the grooved stones for the finishing of perishable shafts which were used to mount mace-heads or battle-axes. We have argued that even the metal daggers, archetypal 'weapons' of the periods concerned, often show wear patterns that indicate use as knives, perhaps used during the sacrificial despatching of animals.

Initially, from *c.* 2500 BC, the special equipment and dress ornaments occurred predominately in the rich graves of men, but well before the turn of the second millennium valuable items found in well-furnished graves were beginning to be associated with women as well. Throughout it has been shown that many items were held to be so valuable that they experienced long object biographies and were re-used and recycled as heirlooms, sometimes over several centuries. Thus particular objects were valued as exotic relics in their own right and, furthermore, oral traditions may also have linked such heirlooms to actual or mythical ancestors. We have demonstrated that these processes were in existence from the beginning of the Chalcolithic period. The presence of heirloom items in graves containing non-necklace objects was fairly constant throughout the thousand-year study period, but the proliferation of necklaces into the mature Early Bronze Age period led to a much higher incidence of heirloom objects through time.

BIBLIOGRAPHY

Abercromby, J. 1907. 'The relative chronology of some Cinerary Urn types in Great Britain and Ireland', *Proceedings of the Society of Antiquaries of Scotland* 41, 185–274.

Albarella, U. and Payne, S. 2005. 'Neolithic pigs from Durrington Walls, Wiltshire, England: a biometrical database', *Journal of Archaeological Science* 32(4), 589–99.

Albarella, U., Dobney, K., Ervynck, A. and Rowley-Conwy, P. (eds.) 2007. *Pigs and Humans. 10,000 Years of Interaction.* Oxford: Oxford University Press.

Alexander, J. and Ozanne, P. C. 1960. 'Report on the investigation of a round barrow on Arreton Down, Isle of Wight', *Proceedings of the Prehistoric Society* 26, 263–302.

Allason-Jones, L. 1996. *Roman Jet in the Yorkshire Museum.* York: The Yorkshire Museum.

Allason-Jones, L. and Jones, J. M. 1994. 'Jet and other materials in Roman artefact studies', *Archaeologia Aeliana*, 5th series, 22, 265–72.

Allason-Jones, L. and Jones, J.M. 2001. 'Identification of 'jet' artefacts by reflected light microscopy', *European Journal of Archaeology* 4(2), 233–251.

Allen, D. 1981. 'The excavation of a Beaker burial monument at Ravenstone, Buckinghamshire, in 1978', *Archaeological Journal* 138, 72–117.

Allen, M. J., Gardiner, J. and Sheridan, J. A. (eds.), 2012. *Is there a British Chalcolithic? People, Place and Polity in the Late Third Millennium.* Oxford: Oxbow/Prehistoric Society (Research Paper 4).

Annable, F. K. and Simpson, D. D. A. 1964. *Guide Catalogue of the Neolithic and Bronze Age collections in Devizes Museum.* Devizes: Wiltshire Archaeological and Archaeological Society.

Anon. 1854. *Report Presented to the Cambridge Antiquarian Society, at its Fourteenth General Meeting, May 22 1854*, 13 (bound into Volume 1 (1851–9) of *Cambridgeshire Antiquarian Society Antiquarian Communications*, 1859).

ApSimon, A. M. 1954. 'Dagger graves in the "Wessex" Bronze Age', *University of London Institute of Archaeology, 10th Annual Report*, 37–61.

Armstrong, E. C. R. 1920. *Guide to the Collection of Irish Antiquities: Catalogue of Irish Gold Ornaments in the Collection of the Royal Irish Academy.* Dublin: The Stationery Office.

Ashbee, P. 1960. *The Bronze Age Round Barrow in Britain.* London: Phoenix.

Ashbee, P. 1978. 'Amesbury Barrow 51: excavation 1960', *Wiltshire Archaeological and Natural History Magazine* 70–71, 1–60.

Ashbee, P. 1985. 'The excavation of Amesbury barrows 58, 61a, 61, 72', *Wiltshire Archaeological and Natural History Magazine* 79, 39–91.

Ashbee, P. and ApSimon, A. 1954. 'The bronze standard from Hoare's Wilsford barrow 18', in Thomas 1954, 326–30.

Ashbee, P., Bell, M. and Proudfoot, E. 1989. *Wilsford Shaft: Excavations 1960–62.* London: English Heritage Archaeological Report 11.

Baker, L., Sheridan, J. A. and Cowie, T. G. 2003. 'An Early Bronze Age 'dagger grave' from Rameldry Farm, near Kingskettle, Fife', *Proceedings of the Society of Antiquaries of Scotland* 133, 85–123.

Balkwill, C. 1978. 'The Bronze Age finds', in Parrington, M. 1978, 28.

Bamford, H. M. and Ashwin, T. 2000. 'The composite bracelet and objects of copper alloy from graves 1803 and 1906', in Ashwin, T. and Bates, S., *Excavations on the Norwich Southern Bypass, 1989–91. Part I: Excavations at Bixley, Caistor St. Edmund, Trowse, Cringleford and Little Melton,* 90. Norwich: Norfolk Museums Service, East Anglian Archaeology Report 91.

Barclay, A. 2010. 'Excavating the living dead', *British Archaeology* 115, November December 2010, 36–41.

Barclay, A. and Halpin, C. 1999. *Excavations at Barrow Hills, Radley, Oxfordshire. Vol. I: the Neolithic and Bronze Age Monument Complex.* Oxford: Oxford University Committee for Archaeology, Thames Valley Landscapes, Volume 11.

Barclay, A., Gray, M. and Lambrick, G. 1995. *Excavations at the Devil's Quoits, Stanton Harcourt, Oxfordshire 1972–3 and 1988.* Oxford: Oxford Archaeological Unit Thames Valley Landscapes: the Windrush Valley, Volume 3.

Barnatt, J. 1994. 'Excavations of an unenclosed Bronze Age cemetery, cairns, and field boundaries at Eagleston Flat, Curbar, Derbyshire 1984, 1989–90', 333–4, *Proceedings of the Prehistoric Society* 60, 287–370.

Barnatt, J. 1996. 'Barrows in the Peak District: a corpus', in Barnatt, J. and Collis, J., *Barrows in the Peak District. Recent Research,* 171–263. Sheffield: Sheffield Academic Press.

Barton, T. 1852. 'Antiquities discovered at Little Cressingham, Norfolk', *Norfolk Archaeology* 3, 1–2.

Bateman, T. 1847. 'Ornaments of Kimmeridge Coal, and on some ornaments of jewellery presumed of the Romano-British Period, found in tumuli in Derbyshire', *Journal of the British Archaeological Association* 2, 234–8.

Bateman, T. 1848. *Vestiges of the Antiquities of Derbyshire, and the Sepulchral Usages of its Inhabitants: from the most remote ages to the reformation.* London: J. R. Smith.

Bateman, T. 1861. *Ten Years' Diggings in Celtic and Saxon Grave Hills in the Counties of Derby, Stafford and York from 1848 to 1858, with Notices of Some Former Discoveries, Hitherto Unpublished and Remarks on the Crania and Pottery from the Mounds.* London: J. R. Smith and Derby: W. Bemrose and Sons.

Beck, C. W. and Shennan, S. 1991. *Amber in Prehistoric Britain.* Oxford: Oxbow Monograph 8.

Beck, H. C. 1928. 'Classification and nomenclature of beads and pendants', *Archaeologia* 77, 1–76.

Beck, H. C. and Stone, J. F. S. 1935. 'Faience beads of the British Bronze Age'. *Archaeologia* 85, 203–52.

Bennett, P., Clark, P., Hicks, A., Rady, J. and Riddler, I. 2008. *At the Great Crossroads: Prehistoric, Roman and Medieval Discoveries on the Isle of Thanet 1994–95.* Canterbury: Canterbury Archaeological Trust (Occasional Paper 4).

Beswick, P. 1994. 'Shale ring', in Barnatt, J. 1994. 'Excavations of an unenclosed Bronze Age cemetery, cairns, and field boundaries at Eagleston Flat, Curbar, Derbyshire 1984, 1989–90', 333–4, *Proceedings of the Prehistoric Society* 60, 287–370.

Borlase, W. C. 1879. 'Archaeological discoveries in the parishes of St. Just-in-Penwith and Sennen, made during the past year by the President', *Journal of the Royal Institution of Cornwall* 21, 190–212.

Borlase, W. C. 1885. 'Typical specimens of Cornish barrows', *Archaeologia* 49, 181–98.

Bradley. P. 2011. 'The basket 'earring' from the Long Barrow', in Harding, J. and Healy, F. (eds.), *A Neolithic and Bronze Age Landscape in Northamptonshire: Volume 2 Supplementary Studies,* 388–9. Swindon: English Heritage.

Bradley, R. and Edmonds, M. 1993. *Interpreting the Axe Trade.* Cambridge: Cambridge University Press.

Brailsford, J. W. 1953. *Later Prehistoric Antiquities of the British Isles.* London: British Museum.

Bray, P. J. 2009. *Exploring the Social Basis of Technology: Re-analysing regional archaeometric studies of the first copper and tin-bronze use in Britain and Ireland.* University of Oxford: Unpublished D.Phil. thesis.

Brewster, T. C. M. 1980. *The Excavation of Garton and Wetwang Slacks.* Wintringham: East Riding Archaeological Research Committee, Prehistoric Excavation Reports no. 2.

Briard, J. 1984. *Les Tumulus D'Armorique. (L'age du bronze en France, 3).* Paris: Picard.

Brindley, A. 2007. *The Dating of Food Vessels and Urns in Ireland.* Galway: National University of Ireland, Department of Archaeology, Bronze Age Studies 7.

Britton, D. 1961. 'A study of the composition of Wessex culture bronzes', *Archaeometry* 4, 39–52.

Bronk Ramsey, C. 2009. 'Bayesian analysis of radiocarbon dates', *Radiocarbon* 51, 337–60.

Brown, F., Howard-Davis, C., Brennand, M., Boyle, A., Evans, T., O'Connor, S., Spence, A., Heawood, R. and Lupton, A. 2007. *The Archaeology of the A1 (M) Darrington to Dishforth DBFO Road Scheme,* 279–89. Lancaster: Lancaster Imprints (Oxford Archaeology North) 12.

Burgess, C., Topping, P. and Lynch, F. (eds.), 2007. *Beyond Stonehenge: Essays on the Bronze Age in Honour of Colin Burgess.* Oxford: Oxbow.

Burl, A. 1979. *Prehistoric Avebury.* New Haven and London: Yale University Press.

Burleigh, R. A., Hewson, A. and Meeks, N. 1976. 'British Museum radiocarbon measurements VIII', *Radiocarbon* 18, 16–42.

Burrow, S. 2011. *Shadowland: Wales 3000–1500 BC.* Cardiff and Oxford: National Museum Wales/Oxbow.

Bussell, G. D. 1976. *A Preliminary Neutron Activation Analysis of Ornaments of Jet and Similar Materials from Early Bronze Age Sites in North Derbyshire and Yorkshire.* University of Bradford: unpublished M.A. thesis.

Bussell, G. D., Pollard, A. M. and Baird, D. C. 1982. 'The characterisation of Early Bronze Age jet and jet-like material by X-Ray fluorescence', *Wiltshire Archaeological and Natural History Magazine* 76, 27–32.

Butterworth, C. A. 1992. 'Excavations at Norton Bavant Borrow Pit, Wiltshire, 1987', *Wiltshire Archaeological and Natural History Magazine* 85, 1–26.

Cahill, M. 2005. 'Roll your own lunula', in Condit, T. and Corlett, C. (eds.) *Above and Beyond: Essays in Memory of Leo Swan,* 53–62. Bray: Wordwell.

Cahill, M. 2006. 'John Windele's golden legacy – prehistoric and later gold ornaments from Co. Cork and Co. Waterford', *Proceedings of the Royal Irish Academy* 106C, 219–337.

Callander, J. G. 1916. 'Notice of a jet necklace found in a cist in a Bronze Age cemetery, discovered on Burgie Lodge Farm, Morayshire, with notes on Scottish prehistoric jet ornaments', *Proceedings of the Society of Antiquaries of Scotland* 50 (1915–16), 201–40.

Case, H. 1977. 'An early accession to the Ashmolean Museum', in Markotic, V. (ed.) *Ancient Europe and the Mediterranean,* 19–34. Warminster.

Chapman, J. 2000. *Fragmentation in Archaeology: people, places and broken objects in the prehistory of south eastern Europe.* London: Routledge.

Chapman, J. and Gaydarska, B, 2007. *Parts and Wholes: Fragmentation in Prehistoric Context.* Oxford: Oxbow.

Christie, P. M. 1964. 'A Bronze Age round barrow on Earl's Farm Down, Amesbury', *Wiltshire Archaeological and Natural History Magazine* 59, 30–45.

Christie, P. M. 1967. 'A barrow-cemetery of the second millennium B.C. in Wiltshire, England', *Proceedings of the Prehistoric Society* 33, 336–366.

Clark, J. G. D. 1963. 'Neolithic bows from Somerset, England, and the prehistory of archery in north-west Europe', *Proceedings of the Prehistoric Society* 29, 50–98.

Clark, P. (ed.) 2009. *Bronze Age Connections: Cultural Contact in Prehistoric Europe.* Oxford: Oxbow.

Clarke, D. L. 1970. *Beaker Pottery of Great Britain and Ireland.* Cambridge: Cambridge University Press.

Clarke, D. V., Cowie, T. G. and Foxon, A. 1985. *Symbols of Power at the Time of Stonehenge.* Edinburgh: HMSO.

Close-Brooks, J. and Shepherd, I. A. G. 1997.' The finds from Cist IX', in Stewart, M. E. C. and Barclay, G. J., 'Excavations in burial and ceremonial sites of the Bronze Age in Tayside', 30. *Tayside and Fife Archaeological Journal* 3, 22–54.

Coles, B. 2006. *Beavers in Britain's Past.* Oxford: Oxbow Books.

Coles, J. and Taylor, J. J. 1971. 'The Wessex culture: a minimal view', *Antiquity* 45, 6–14.

Collins, A. E. 1980. 'A Bronze Age cremation site at Little Chesterford: interim report (Dec. 1979)', *Archaeology in Great Chesterford Bulletin* 3, 16–18.

Collins, A. E. P. and Evans, E. E. 1968. 'A cist burial at Carrickinab, Co Down', *Ulster Journal of Archaeolog,* 3, Series 31, 16–24.

Corboud, P. and Curdy, P. 2009. *Stèles préhistoriques. La nécropole néolithique du Petit-Chasseur à Sion/Prähistorische Stelen. Die neolithische Nekropole Petit-Chasseur in Sitten.* Sion/Sitten: Musées Cantonaux du Valais/Walliser Kantonsmuseen.

Corfield, M. 2012. 'The decoration of Bronze Age dagger handles with gold studs', in J.R. Trigg (ed.), *Of Things Gone but not Forgotten: Essays in Archaeology for Joan Taylor*, 75-93. British Archaeological Reports, International Series 2434. Oxford: Archaeopress.

Corney, A., Ashbee, P., Evison, V. I. and Brothwell, D. R. 1969. 'A prehistoric and Anglo-Saxon burial ground, Ports Down, Portsmouth', *Proceedings of the Hampshire Field Club and Archaeological Society* 24, 20–41.

Coutts, H. 1971. *Tayside before History: a Guide-Catalogue of the Collection of Antiquities in Dundee Museum.* Dundee: Dundee Museum and Art Gallery.

Craw, J. H. 1929. 'On a jet necklace from a cist at Poltalloch, Argyll', *Proceedings of the Society of Antiquaries of Scotland* 63 (1928–9), 1554–89.

Cunnington, M.E. 1908. 'Notes on the opening of a Bronze Age barrow at Manton near Marlborough', *Wiltshire Archaeological and Natural History Magazine* 35, 1–20.

Cunnington, W. 1806. 'Account of tumuli opened in Wiltshire', *Archaeologia* 15, 122–9.

Curtis, N. and Wilkin, N. 2012. 'The regionality of Beakers and bodies in the Chalcolithic of north-east Scotland', in Allen *et al.* (eds.), 237–56.

Curwen, E. C. 1954. *The Archaeology of Sussex.* London: Methuen.

Davis, J. B. and Thurnam, J. 1865. *Crania Britannica: Delineations and descriptions of the skulls of the aboriginal and early inhabitants of the British islands: with notices of their other remains.* London: privately published.

Davis, M. 1993. 'The identification of various jet and jet-like materials used in the Early Bronze Age in Scotland', *The Conservator* 17(1), 11–18.

Dent, J. S. 1983. 'A summary of the excavations carried out in Garton Slack and Wetwang Slack 1964–1980', *East Riding Archaeologist* 7, 1–14.

Drew, C. D. and Piggott, S. 1936. 'Two Bronze Age barrows excavated by Mr Edward Cunnington', *Proceedings of the Dorset Natural History and Archaeological Society* 58, 18–25.

Edwards, A. J. H. 1928. 'Cinerary urns from Hunterston and Seamill, West Kilbride, and a short cist at Phantassie, East Lothian', *Proceedings of the Society of Antiquaries of Scotland* 62 (1927–28), 260–3.

Edwards, B. J. N. 2007. 'An investigation into the prehistory of Pilling Moss, Lancashire', in P. Cherry (ed.), *Studies in Northern Prehistory*, 211–235. Kendal: Cumberland and Westmorland Antiquarian and Archaeological Society.

Eogan, G. 1994. *The Accomplished Art: Gold and Gold-working in Britain and Ireland during the Bronze Age.* Oxford: Oxbow Monograph 42.

Evans, C. and Appleby, G. 2008. 'Historiography and fieldwork: Wyman Abbott's Great Fengate ring-ditch (a lost manuscript found)', *Proceedings of the Prehistoric Society* 74, 171–192.

Evans, J. 1881. *The Ancient Bronze Implements, Weapons, and Ornaments of Great Britain and Ireland.* London: Longmans, Green and Co.

Evans, J. 1897. *The Ancient Stone Implements, Weapons and Ornaments of Great Britain*, 2nd edition. London: Longmans, Green and Co.

Fasham, P., Farwell, D. E. and Whinney, R. J. B. 1989. *The Archaeological Site at Easton Lane, Winchester.* Salisbury: Hampshire Field Club and Trust for Wessex Archaeology.

Fitzpatrick, A. P. 2011. *The Amesbury Archer and the Boscombe Bowmen. Bell Beaker burials at Boscombe Down, Amesbury, Wiltshire.* Salisbury: Wessex Archaeology.

Fleming, A. 1971. 'Territorial patterns in Bronze Age Wessex', *Proceedings of the Prehistoric Society* 37, 138–66.

Fowler, G. 1932. 'A skeleton of the early Bronze Age found in the Fens', *Proceedings of the Prehistoric Society of East Anglia* 6, 362–5.

Fox, A. and Stone, J. F. S. 1951. 'A necklace from a barrow in North Molton parish, North Devon', *Antiquaries Journal* 31, 25–31.

Fox, C. 1923. *The Archaeology of the Cambridge Region.* Cambridge: Cambridge University Press.

Frieman, C. 2012. 'Going to pieces at the funeral: completeness and complexity in Early Bronze Age jet "necklace" assemblages', *Journal of Social Archaeology* 12(3), 334–55.

Gardiner, J., Allen, M. J., Powell, A., Harding, P., Lawson, A. J., Loader, E., McKinley, J. I., Sheridan, J. A. and Stevens, C. 2007. 'A matter of life and death: Late Neolithic, Beaker and Early Bronze Age settlement and cemeteries at Thomas Hardye School, Dorchester', *Proceedings of the Dorset Natural History and Archaeological Society* 128, 17–52.

Garwood, P. 2011. 'Early prehistory', in Booth, P., Champion, T., Foreman, S., Garwood, P., Glass, H., Munby, J. and Reynolds, A., *On Track. The Archaeology of High Speed 1 Section 1 in Kent*, 144–9. Oxford: Oxford Wessex Archaeology.

Gerloff, S. 1975. *The Early Bronze Age Daggers in Great Britain, and a reconsideration of the Wessex Culture.* Munich: C. H. Beck'sche Verlagsbuchhandlung, Prähistorische Bronzefunde VI, 2.

Gerloff, S. 2004. 'The dagger from grave 4013/12', in Lambrick, G. and Allen, T., *Gravelly Guy, Stanton Harcourt: the Development of a Prehistoric and Romano-British Community*, 82–6. Oxford: Oxford Archaeology, Thames Valley Landscapes Monograph 21.

Gibson, A. M. 2008. 'The prehistoric pottery', in Bennett, P. *et al.*, 46–57.

Gibson, A. M. 2012. 'Report on the excavation at the Duggleby Howe causewayed enclosure, North Yorkshire', *Archaeological Journal* 168, 1–63.

Giles, M. 2008. 'Seeing red: the aesthetics of martial objects in the British and Irish Iron Age', in Garrow, D., Gosden, C. and Hill, J. D. (eds.), *Rethinking Celtic Art*, 59–77. Oxford: Oxbow Books.

Gingell, C. 1988. 'Twelve Wiltshire round barrows. Excavations in 1959 and 1961 by F. de M. and H. L. Vatcher', *Wiltshire Archaeological and Natural History Magazine* 82, 19–76.

Goddard, E. H. 1908. 'Notes on barrows at Lake, from ms note book by the Rev. E. Duke', *Wiltshire Archaeological and Natural History Magazine* 35 (1907–08), 582–6.

Graham, A. 2006. *The excavation of five Beaker burials, the Iron Age and Romano-British settlements, and the 4th century courtyard villa at Barton Field, Tarrant Hinton, Dorset 1968–1984*, 8–18. Dorchester: Dorset Natural History and Archaeological Society Monograph no. 17.

Gray, H. St. G., 1917. 'The Arthur Hull collection, Chard', *Proceedings of the Somersetshire Archaeological and Natural History Society* 63, 113–121.

Greaves, C. S. 1872. 'Remarks upon a Runic comb, jet and glass beads, arrowheads and other objects of flint lately found near Whitby', *Archaeological Journal* 29, 280–6.

Green, C. and Rollo-Smith, S. 1984. 'The excavation of eighteen round barrows near Shrewton, Wiltshire', *Proceedings of the Prehistoric Society* 50, 255–318.

Green, H. S. 1980. *The Flint Arrowheads of the British Isles.* Oxford: British Archaeological Reports British Series 75.

Greenwell, W. 1865. 'Notices of the examinations of ancient

grave-hills in the North Riding of Yorkshire', *Archaeological Journal* 22, 97–117 and 241–63.

Greenwell, W. 1868. 'Notes on the opening of Ancient British tumuli in North Northumberland', *History of the Berwickshire Naturalists' Club 5, 195–205.*

Greenwell, W. 1881. 'On barrows at Aldbourne, Wiltshire, and their contents', *Proceedings of the Society of Antiquaries of London 8, 175–9.*

Greenwell, W. 1890. 'Recent researches in barrows in Yorkshire, Wiltshire, Berkshire, etc.', *Archaeologia* 52, 1–72.

Greenwell, W. and Rolleston, G. 1877. *British Barrows.* Oxford: Clarendon Press.

Grimes, W. F. 1938. 'A barrow on Breach Farm, Llanbleddian, Glamorgan', *Proceedings of the Prehistoric Society* 4, 107–21.

Grinsell, L. V. 1957. *A History of Wiltshire. Volume 1, part 1.* London: Oxford University Press.

Grinsell, L. V. 1959. *Dorset Barrows.* Dorchester: Dorset Natural History and Archaeological Society.

Grinsell, L. V. 1968. *South Western British Prehistoric Collections.* Bristol: The City Museum.

Grinsell, L. V. 1971. *Somerset Barrows Part II: North and East.* Taunton: Somersetshire Archaeological and Natural History Society.

Grinsell, L. V. 1982. *Dorset Barrows Supplement.* Dorchester: Dorset Natural History and Archaeological Society.

Guido, M., Henderson, J., Cable, M., Bayley, J. and Biek, L. 1984. 'A Bronze Age glass bead from Wilsford, Wiltshire: Barrow G42 in the Lake group', *Proceedings of the Prehistoric Society* 50, 245–54.

Gunstone, A. J. H. 1965. 'An archaeological gazetteer of Staffordshire, part 2: the barrows', *North Staffordshire Journal of Field Studies* 5, 20–63.

Hájek, L. 1957. 'Knoflíky středevropské skupiny kultury zvoncovitých pohárů', *Památky Archeologické* 48, 389–424.

Hall, D. and Woodward, P. 1977. 'Radwell excavations, 1974–1975: the Bronze Age ring ditches', *Bedfordshire Archaeological Journal* 12, 1–16.

Harbison, P. 1969. *The Daggers and the Halberds of the Early Bronze Age in Ireland.* Munich: C. H. Beck'sche Verlagsbuchhandlung, Prähistorische Bronzefunde VI/I.

Harbison, P. 1975. *Bracers and V-perforated Buttons in the Beaker and Food Vessel Cultures of Ireland.* Bad Bramstedt: *Archaeologica Atlantica* Research Report 1.

Hardaker, R. 1974. *Early Bronze Age Dagger Pommels.* Oxford: British Archaeological Reports British Series 3.

Harding, A. 1984. *The Mycenaeans and Europe.* London: Academic Press.

Harding, A. F. 1990. 'The Wessex connection: developments and perspectives', in Bader, T. (ed.), *Orientalisch-Agäische Einflüsse in der Europäischen Bronzezeit: Ergebnisse eines Kolloquiums,* 139–54. Bonn: Römisch-Germanisches Zentralmuseum Monograph 15.

Harding, A. F. and Hughes-Brock, H. 1974. 'Amber in the Mycenean world', *Annual of the British School of Archaeology at Athens* 69, 145–72.

Harding, J. and Healy, F. 2007. *The Raunds Area Project. A Neolithic and Bronze Age Landscape in Northamptonshire.* London: English Heritage.

Harding, P., Beswick, P., McKinley, J. I., Gale, R. and Firman, R. 2005. 'Excavations at a Bronze Age barrow on Carsington Pasture by Time Team 2002', *Derbyshire Archaeological Journal* 125, 1–20.

Harrison, R. and Heyd, V. 2007. 'The transformation of Europe in the third millennium BC: the example of 'Le Petit-Chasseur

I + III' (Sion, Valais, Switzerland)', *Prähistorische Zeitschrift* 82(2), 129–214.

Hartmann, A. 1982. *Prähistorische Goldfunde aus Europa II.* Berlin: Römisch-Germanisches Zentralmuseum: Studien in den Anfängen der Metallurgie, 5.

Haveman, E. and Sheridan, J. A, 2006. 'The necklace from Exloo: new light on an old find', *Palaeohistoria* 47/48 (2005/2006), 100–39.

Hawley, W. 1910. 'Notes on barrows in south Wiltshire', *Wiltshire Archaeological and Natural History Magazine* 36, 615–28.

Hayes, R. H. 1963. 'Archaeology (2)' and 'Appendix Aiii (Neolithic-Bronze Age flint and stone axes and other implements)', in McDonnell, J. (ed.), *A History of Helmsley, Rievaulx and District,* 31–53 and 339–348. York: Stonegate Press.

Healy, F. 2012. 'Chronology, corpses, ceramics, copper and lithics', in Allen *et al.* (eds.), 144–163.

Healy, F. and Harding, J. 2004. 'Reading a burial: the legacy of Overton Hill', in Gibson, A. and Sheridan, J. A. (eds.) *From Sickles to Circles,* 176–193. Stroud: Tempus.

Hearle, J. 2011. 'Shaw Cairn revisited. The dead of Mellor Moor', *Current Archaeology* 257, 26–31.

Helms, M. W. 1988. *Ulysses' Sail.* Princeton: Princeton University Press.

Helms, M. W. 1993. *Craft and the Kingly Ideal: art, trade, and power.* Austin: University of Texas.

Henshall, A. S. 1968. 'Scottish dagger graves', in Coles, J. M. and Simpson, D. D. A. (eds.) 1968, *Studies in Ancient Europe: Essays Presented to Stuart Piggott,* 173–95. Leicester: Leicester University Press.

Heyd, V. 2007. 'Families, prestige goods, warriors and complex societies: Beaker groups and the 3rd millennium cal BC', *Proceedings of the Prehistoric Society* 73, 327–379.

Hoare, R. C. 1812. *The Ancient History of South Wiltshire.* London: William Miller.

Hoare, R. C. 1821. *The Ancient History of North Wiltshire.* London: William Miller.

Horsfield, T. 1824. *The History and Antiquities of Lewes and its Vicinity.* Lewes: J. Baxter.

Howarth, E. 1899. *Catalogue of the Bateman Collection of Antiquities in the Sheffield Public Museum.* London: Dulau and Co.

Hughes, G. 2000. *The Lockington Gold Hoard: an Early Bronze Age Barrow Cemetery at Lockington, Leicestershire,* 48–61. Oxford: Oxbow.

Hundt, H.-J. 1958. *Katalog Straubing. I. Die Funde der Glockenbecher-kultur und der Straubinger Kultur.* Kallmünz/Opf: Lassleben.

Hunter, F.J., McDonnell, J. G. and Pollard, A.M. 1993. 'The scientific identification of archaeological jet-like artefacts', *Archaeometry* 35(1), 69–89.

Hutton, J., 2008. *Excavations at Langtoft, Lincolnshire. The Freeman Land.* Cambridge: Cambridge Archaeological Unit.

Jewitt, L. 1850. *Relics of Primaeval Life in England.* Manuscript, Sheffield Galleries and Museums Trust.

Jewitt, L. 1870. *Grave-mounds and their Contents: a Manual of Archaeology.* London: Groombridge and Sons.

Jobey, G. 1980. 'Green Knowe unenclosed platform settlement and Harehope Cairn, Peeblesshire', *Proceedings of the Society of Antiquaries of Scotland* 110, 72–113.

Jockenhövel, A. 1980. *Die Rasiermesser in Westeuropa.* Munich: C. H. Beck'sche Verlagsbuchhandlung, Prähistorische Bronzefunde VIII, 3.

Johnston, D. E. 1980. 'The excavation of a bell-barrow at Sutton

Veny, Wilts.', *Wiltshire Archaeological and Natural History Magazine* 72/73, 29–50.

Jones, A. 2002. ' A biography of colour: colour, material histories and personhood in the Early Bronze Age of Britain and Ireland', in Jones, A. and MacGregor, G. (eds.), *Colouring the Past: The Significance of Colour in Archaeological Research*, 159–174. Oxford: Berg.

Jones, A.M. forthcoming. *Preserved in the peat: investigation of a Bronze Age burial on Whitehorse Hill, Dartmoor and its wider context*. Oxford: Oxbow Books.

Jones, A. M., Marchand, J., Sheridan, J. A., Straker, V. and Quinnell, H. 2012. 'Excavations at the Whitehorse Hill cist, Dartmoor', *PAST* 70, 14–16.

Kelly, E. and Cahill, M. 2010. 'Safe secrets 1 – an early Bronze Age detective story from County Roscommon', *Archaeology Ireland* (for 2010), 5–6.

Kenworthy, J. 1977. 'A reconsideration of the "Ardiffery" finds, Cruden, Aberdeenshire', *Proceedings of the Society of Antiquaries of Scotland* 108 (1976–7), 80–93.

Kinnes, I. A. 1979. *Round Barrows and Ring-ditches in the British Neolithic*. London: British Museum Occasional Paper 7.

Kinnes, I. A. 1985. *British Bronze-Age Metalwork A7–16, Beaker and Early Bronze Age Grave Groups*. London: British Museum.

Kinnes, I. A. and Longworth, I. H. 1985. *Catalogue of the Excavated Prehistoric and Romano-British Material in the Greenwell Collection*. London: British Museum Press.

Kinnes, I. A., Longworth, I. H., McIntyre, I. M., Needham, S. P. and Oddy, W. A. 1988. 'Bush Barrow gold', *Antiquity* 62, 24–39.

Kinnes, I. A., Schadla-Hall, T., Chadwick, P. and Dean, P. 1983. 'Duggleby Howe reconsidered', *Archaeological Journal* 140, 83–108.

Kirwan, R. 1872. 'Notes on the pre-historic archaeology of East Devon', *Archaeological Journal* 29, 151–65.

Kitchener, A. C. 2010. 'The elk', in O'Connor, T. and Sykes, N. (eds.), *Extinctions and Invasions: A Social History of British Fauna,* 36–42. Oxford: Oxbow books.

Ladle, L. and Woodward, A. 2009. *Excavations at Bestwall Quarry, Wareham 1992–2005*. Dorchester: Dorset Natural History and Archaeological Society Monograph 18.

Lawson, A. J. 2007. *Chalkland*. East Knoyle: Hobnob Press.

Lawson, A. J., Martin, E. A. and Priddy, D. 1981. *The Barrows of East Anglia*. Gressenhall: East Anglian Archaeology Report 12.

Leaf, L. S. 1940. 'Two Bronze Age barrows at Chippenham, Cambridgeshire', *Proceedings of the Cambridge Antiquarian Society* 36, 134–155.

Leroi-Gourhan, A. 1943. *Evolution et techniques 1: L'Homme et la Matière*. Paris: Albin Michel.

Lemonnier, P. 1976. 'La description des chaines operatoires: contribution a l'analyse des systemes techniques', *Techniques et Culture 1*: 100–151.

Lethbridge, T.C. 1949. 'Excavations of the Snailwell Group of Bronze Age Barrows', *Proceedings of the Cambridgeshire Archaeological Society* 43, 30–49.

Lethbridge, T. C., Fowler, G. and Sayce, R. U. 1932. 'A skeleton of the Early Bronze Age found in the Fens', *Proceedings of the Prehistoric Society of East Anglia* 6 (1929–32), 362–4.

Levitan, B., Audsley, A., Hawkes, C. J., Moody, A., Moody, P., Smart, P. L. and Thomas, J. 1988. 'Charterhouse Warren Farm Swallet, Mendip, Somerset. Exploration, geomorphology, taphonomy and archaeology', *Proceedings of the University of Bristol Spelaeological Society* 18 (2), 171–239.

Londesborough (Lord) 1851. 'An account of the opening of some tumuli in the East Riding of Yorkshire', *Archaeologia* 34, 251–8.

Longworth, I. H. 1984. *Collared Urns of the Bronze Age in Great Britain and Ireland*. Cambridge: Cambridge University Press.

Longworth, I. and Haith, C. 1992. 'Henry Durden and his collection', *Proceedings of the Dorset Natural History and Archaeological Society* 114, 151–160.

Low, A. 1929. 'A short cist at Culduthel, Inverness', *Proceedings of the Society of Antiquaries of Scotland* 63 (1928–29), 217–24.

Lukis, W. C. 1867. 'Notes on barrow-diggings in the parish of Collingbourne Ducis', *Wiltshire Archaeological and Natural History Magazine* 10, 85–103.

Lynch, F. M. 1993. *Excavations in the Brenig Valley: a Mesolithic and Bronze Age Landscape in North Wales*. Cardiff: Cambrian Archaeological Monographs 5.

Manby, T. G. 2009. 'The Mitchelson collection and an Early Bronze Age dagger from Lockton Warren: a question of antiquarian history and assumption', *The Ryedale Historian* 24 (2008–9), 20–30.

Mann, L. McL. 1902. 'Note on the finding of an urn, jet necklace, stone axe, and other associated objects, in Wigtownshire', *Proceedings of the Society of Antiquaries of Scotland* 36 (1901–02), 584–9.

Marsden, B. M. 1977. *Burial Mounds of Derbyshire*. Privately published.

Marsden, B. M. 2007. *The Barrow Knight. A Life of Thomas Bateman, Archaeologist and Collector (1821–61)*. Chesterfield: Bannister Publications.

Martin, A. and Allen, C. 2001. 'Two prehistoric ring ditches and an associated Bronze Age cremation cemetery at Tucklesholme Farm, Barton-under-Needwood, Staffordshire', *Transactions of the Staffordshire Archaeological and Historical Society* 39, 1–15.

Martin, E. A. 1976. 'The excavation of a tumulus at Barrow Bottom, Risby, 1975', *East Anglian Archaeology Report* 3, 43–62.

Martin, E. and Murphy, P. 1988. 'West Row Fen, Suffolk: a Bronze Age fen-edge settlement site', *Antiquity* 62, 353–358.

Mauss, M. 1947. *Manuel d'Ethnographie*. Paris: Payot.

Megaw, V. 1969. 'Problems and non-problems in palaeo-organology: a musical miscellany', in Coles, J. M. and Simpson, D. D. A. (eds.), 333–358. *Studies in Ancient Europe. Essays presented to Stuart Piggott*. Leicester: Leicester University Press.

Millett, M. and James, S. 1983. 'Excavations at Cowdery's Down, Basingstoke, Hampshire, 1978–81', *Archaeological Journal* 140, 151–279.

Moore, C. N. and Rowlands, M. 1972. *Bronze Age Metalwork in Salisbury Museum*. Salisbury: Salisbury and South Wiltshire Museum Occasional Publication.

Mortimer, J. R. 1905. *Forty Years' Researches in the British and Saxon Burial Mounds of East Yorkshire*. London: Brown.

Muller, H. 1980. 'A note on the composition of jet', *Journal of Gemmology* 17, 10–18.

Mulville, J. 2002. 'The role of cetacea in prehistoric and historic Atlantic Scotland', *International Journal of Osteoarchaeology* 12, 34–48.

Needham, S. P. 1988. 'Selective deposition in the British Early Bronze Age', *World Archaeology* 20, 229–248.

Needham, S. P. 1996. 'Chronology and periodisation in the British Bronze Age', in Randsborg, K. (ed.), *Absolute Chronology: Archaeological Europe 2500–500 BC*. Acta Archaeologica 67, 121–40.

Needham, S. P. 1999. 'Radley and the development of early metalwork in Britain', in Barclay and Halpin, 186–92.

Needham, S. P. 2000a. 'Power pulses across a cultural divide: cosmologically driven exchange between Armorica and Wessex', *Proceedings of the Prehistoric Society* 66, 151–207.

Needham, S. P. 2000b. 'The gold and copper metalwork', in Hughes, G. 2000, 23–46.

Needham, S. P. 2000c. 'The development of embossed goldwork in Bronze Age Europe', *Antiquaries Journal* 80, 27–65.

Needham, S. P. 2004. 'Migdale-Marnoch: sunburst of Scottish metallurgy', in Shepherd, I. A. G. and Barclay, G. J. (eds.) 2004, *Scotland in Ancient Europe: The Neolithic and Early Bronze Age of Scotland in their European Context*, 217–45. Edinburgh: Society of Antiquaries of Scotland.

Needham, S. P. 2005. 'Transforming Beaker culture in north-west Europe; processes of fusion and fission', *Proceedings of the Prehistoric Society* 71, 171–217.

Needham, S. P. 2007a. 'The dagger blade and hilt furnishings from Site D (Ferry Fryston), burial 2245', in Brown *et al.*, 279–89.

Needham, S. P. 2007b. 'Bronze makes a Bronze Age? Considering the systemics of Bronze Age metal use and the implications of selective deposition', in Burgess, C. *et al.* (eds.), 278–87.

Needham, S. P. 2008. 'Exchange, object biographies and the shaping of identities, 10,000–1000 B.C.', in Pollard, J. (ed.), *Prehistoric Britain*, 310–329. Oxford: Blackwell.

Needham, S. P. 2009. 'Encompassing the sea: 'maritories' and Bronze Age maritime interactions', in Clark, P. (ed.), 12–37.

Needham, S. P. 2011a. 'Gold basket-shaped ornaments from graves 1291 (Amesbury Archer) and 1236', in Fitzpatrick, 2011, 129–38.

Needham, S. P. 2011b. 'The dagger and pommel from Barrow 1', in Harding, J. and Healy, F. (eds.), *A Neolithic and Bronze Age Landscape in Northamptonshire: Volume 2: Supplementary Studies, 383–388.* Swindon: English Heritage.

Needham, S. 2012a. 'Putting capes into context: Mold at the heart of a domain', in Britnell, W. J. and Silvester, R. J. (eds.), *Reflections on the Past: Essays in Honour of Frances Lynch*, 210–36. Welshpool: Cambrian Archaeological Association.

Needham, S. 2012b. 'Case and place for the British Chalcolithic', in Allen *et al.* (eds.), 1–26.

Needham, S. P. and Bowman, S. G. E. 2005. 'Flesh-hooks, technological complexity and the Atlantic Bronze Age feasting complex', *European Journal of Archaeology* 8, 93–136.

Needham, S. and Woodward, A. 2008. 'The Clandon Barrow finery: a synopsis of success in an Early Bronze Age world'. *Proceedings of the Prehistoric Society* 74, 1–52.

Needham, S., Lawson, A. and Woodward, A. 2010. '"A noble group of barrows": Bush Barrow and the Normanton Down Early Bronze Age cemetery two centuries on', *Antiquaries Journal* 90, 1–39.

Needham, S. P., Parfitt, K. and Varndell, G. (eds.) 2006. *The Ringlemere Cup: Precious Cups and the Beginning of the Channel Bronze Age.* London: British Museum Research Publication 163.

Needham, S., Parker Pearson, M., Tyler, A., Richard, M. and Jay, M. 2010. 'A first "Wessex 1" date from Wessex', *Antiquity* 84, 363–73.

Neugebauer, C. and Neugebauer, J.-W. 1997. *Franzhausen. Das Frühbronzezeitliche Gräberfeld I. Teil 2: Materialvorlage, Tafelteil.* Vienna: Bundesdenkmalamt.

Newall, R. S. 1932. 'Barrow 85 Amesbury (Goddard's List)', *Wiltshire Archaeological and Natural History Magazine* 45, 432–58.

Norfolk Museum Service 1977. *Bronze Age Metalwork in Norwich Castle Museum.* Norwich.

O'Connor, B. J. 2010. 'From Dorchester to Dieskau: some aspects of relations between Britain and central Europe during the Early Bronze Age', in Meller, H. and Bertemes, F. (eds.), *Der Griff nach den Sternen. Internationales Symposium in Halle (Saale) Februar 2005*, 16–21. Halle: Tagungen des Landesmuseums für Vorgeschichte Halle Vol. 2.

O'Connor, S. forthcoming. 'Exotic materials used in the construction of Iron Age sword handles from South Cave, UK', in Choyke, A. and O'Connor, S. (eds.), *These Bare Bones: Raw materials and the study of worked osseous materials.* ICAZ Paris 2010 post-prints.

Ó Ríordáin, B. and Waddell, J. 1993. *The Funerary Bowls and Vases of the Irish Bronze Age.* Galway: Galway University Press.

O'Sullivan, M. 2005. Duma na nGiall. *The Mound of the Hostages, Tara.* Bray: Wordwell.

Pacitto, A. L. 1971. *Pockley, Barrow I.* Unpublished typescript for English Heritage.

Parker Pearson, M. 1999. 'The Earlier Bronze Age', in Hunter, J. and Ralston, I. B. (eds.), *The Archaeology of Britain*, 77–94. London: Routledge.

Parrington, M. 1978. *The Excavation of an Iron Age Settlement, Bronze Age Ring-ditches and Roman Features at Ashville Trading Estate, Abingdon, Oxfordshire, 1974–76.* Oxford: Oxfordshire Archaeological Unit and Council for British Archaeology.

Payne, G. 1892. *Catalogue of the Museum of Local Antiquities collected by Mr Henry Durden of Blandford, Dorsetshire.* Lewes: South Counties Press.

Piggott, C. M. 1943. 'Excavation of fifteen barrows in the New Forest, 1941–2', *Proceedings of the Prehistoric Society* 9, 1–27.

Piggott, S. 1938. 'The Early Bronze Age in Wessex', *Proceedings of the Prehistoric Society* 4, 52–106.

Piggott, S. 1939. 'Further Bronze Age "dagger graves" in Brittany', *Proceedings of the Prehistoric Society* 5, part 1, 193–5.

Piggott, S. 1958. 'Segmented bone beads and toggles in the British early and middle Bronze Age', *Proceedings of the Prehistoric Society* 24, 227–29.

Piggott, S. 1962. 'From Salisbury Plain to Siberia', *Wiltshire Archaeological and Natural History Magazine* 58, 93–7.

Piggott, S. 1973. 'The Wessex culture of the Early Bronze Age', in Crittall, E. (ed.), *A History of Wiltshire*, 1, vol 2, 352–75, Oxford: Victoria County Histories.

Piggott, S. and Stewart, M. E. C. 1958. 'Early and middle bronze age grave groups and hoards from Scotland', *Inventaria Archaeologica GB* 5th Set, GB.25–34. London.

Pitts, M. 2007. 'Unique decorated jet lozenge from Suffolk matches Stonehenge gold', *British Archaeology* 94 (May/June 2007), 6.

Pollard, A. M., Bussell, G. D. and Baird, D. C. 1981. 'The analytical investigation of Early Bronze Age jet and jet-like material from the Devizes Museum', *Archaeometry* 23, 2, 139–167.

Potter, T. W. J. 1977. 'Excavations at Stonea, Cambs.: sites of the Neolithic, Bronze Age and Roman periods', *Proceedings of the Cambridgeshire Archaeological Society* 66, 23–54.

Proudfoot, E. 1963. 'Report on the excavation of a bell barrow in the parish of Edmondsham, Dorset, England, 1959', *Proceedings of the Prehistoric Society* 29, 395–425.

Radley, J. and Plant, M. 1971. 'Tideslow: a Neolithic round barrow at Tideswell', *Derbyshire Archaeological Journal* 91, 20–30.

Rainbird Clarke, R. 1960. *East Anglia.* London: Thames and Hudson.

Rast-Eichner, A. 2012. 'Switzerland: Bronze and Iron Ages',

in Gleba, M. and Mannering, U. (eds.), *Textiles and Textile Production in Europe from Prehistory to AD 400*, 378–96.

Rayner, D. H. and Hemingway, J. E. (eds.) 1974. *The Geology and Mineral Resources of Yorkshire*. Leeds: Yorkshire Geological Society.

Richardson, J. and Vyner, B. 2011. 'An exotic Early Bronze Age funerary assemblage from Stanbury, West Yorkshire', *Proceedings of the Prehistoric Society* 77, 49–63.

Roberts, J. 1998. 'A contextual approach to the interpretation of the Early Bronze Age skeletons of the East Anglian Fens', *Antiquity* 72, 188–97.

Robinson, P. 2007. 'Some early petrological analyses of Neolithic and Bronze age lithics in Wiltshire Heritage Museum', *Wiltshire Archaeological and Natural History Magazine* 100, 187–191.

Roe, F. E. S. 1966. 'The battle-axe series in Britain', *Proceedings of the Prehistoric Society* 32, 199–245.

Roe, F. E. S. 1979. 'Typology of stone implements with shaftholes', in Clough, T. H. McK. and Cummins, W. A. (eds.), *Stone Axe Studies: Archaeological, Petrological, Experimental and Ethnographic*, 23–48. London: Council for British Archaeology Research Report 23.

Ruggles, C. 1999. *Astronomy in Prehistoric Britain and Ireland*. New Haven: Yale University Press.

Russel, A. D. 1990. 'Two Beaker burials from Chilbolton, Hampshire', *Proceedings of the Prehistoric Society* 56, 153–72.

Salzman, L.F. (ed.) 1938. *The Victoria History of the County of Cambridgeshire and the Isle of Ely*. London: Oxford University Press.

Savory, H. N. 1980. *Guide Catalogue of the Bronze Age Collections*. Cardiff: National Museum of Wales.

Scarth, H. M. 1859. 'Some account of the investigation of barrows on the line of the Roman road between Old Sarum and port at the mouth of the River Axe, supposed to be the "Ad Axium" of Ravennas', *Archaeological Journal* 16, 146–57.

Shepherd, I. A. G. 1973. *The V-bored Buttons of Great Britain*. Unpublished M.A. thesis, University of Edinburgh.

Shepherd, I. A. G. 1981. 'Bronze Age jet working in North Britain', *Scottish Archaeological Forum* 11, 43–51.

Shepherd, I. A. G. 1985. 'Jet and amber', in Clarke *et al.*, 204–16.

Shepherd, I. A. G. 2009. 'The V-bored buttons of Great Britain and Ireland', *Proceedings of the Prehistoric Society* 75, 335–369.

Sheppard, T. 1900. *Descriptive Catalogue of the Specimens in the Mortimer Museum of Archaeology and Geology at Driffield*. London: A. Brown and Sons Ltd.

Sheppard, T. 1929. *Catalogue of the Mortimer Collection*. Hull: Hull Museum.

Sheridan. J. A. 1998. 'Jet spacer plate necklace and bracelet [from East Kinwhirrie]', in Taylor, D. B., Rideout, J. S., Russell-White, C. J. and Cowie, T. G., 'Prehistoric burials from Angus: some finds old and new', *Tayside and Fife Archaeological Journal* 4, 34–7.

Sheridan, J. A. 2006. 'The National Museums' Scotland radio-carbon dating programmes: results obtained during 2005/6', *Discovery and Excavation in Scotland* 7, 204–6.

Sheridan, J. A. 2007a. 'The bone belt hook from Bargrennan pit 2', in Cummings, V. and Fowler, C., *From Cairn to Cemetery. An archaeological investigation of the chambered cairns and early Bronze Age mortuary deposits at Cairnderry and Bargrennan White Cairn, south-west Scotland*, 112–124. Oxford: British Archaeological Reports British Series 434.

Sheridan, J. A. 2007b. 'Structured space, monuments and burial', in Gardiner *et al.*, 47–8.

Sheridan, J. A. 2007c. 'Scottish Beaker dates: the good, the bad and the ugly', in Larsson, M. and Parker Pearson, M. (eds.), *From Stonehenge to the Baltic. Living with Cultural Diversity in the Third Millennium BC*, 91–123. Oxford: British Archaeological Reports International Series 1692.

Sheridan, J. A. 2007d. 'Green treasures from the magic mountain', *British Archaeology* 96, 22–7.

Sheridan, J. A. 2007e. 'Dating the Scottish Bronze Age: "There is clearly much that the material can still tell us"', in Burgess *et al.* (eds.), 162–85.

Sheridan, J. A. 2008a. 'The Bronze Age composite bead necklace', in Thomas, J., *Monument, Memory and Myth. Use and Re-use of Three Bronze Age Round Barrows at Cossington, Leicestershire*, 80–88. Leicester: Leicester Archaeology Monograph 14.

Sheridan, J.A. 2008b. 'Towards a fuller, more nuanced narrative for Chalcolithic and Early Bronze Age Britain and Ireland, 2500–1500 BC', *Bronze Age Review* 1, section 6, On-line journal, British Museum, 57–78. http://www.britishmuseum.org/pdf/BAR1_2008_6_Sheridan_c.pdf.

Sheridan, J. A. 2010a. 'The fragmentary amber spacer plate necklace from Shaw Cairn', in Noble, P., *Shaw Cairn, Mellor: An Archaeological Evaluation of an Early Bronze Age Cairn, 2010*, 83–99. Manchester: University of Manchester Archaeological Unit.

Sheridan, J. A. 2010b. 'Additional observations on the amber object', in Lewis, J., Leivers, M., Brown, L., Smith, A., Cramp, K., Mepham, L. and Phillpotts, C., *Landscape Evolution in the Middle Thames Valley. Heathrow Terminal 5 Excavations Volume 2*, CD Free Viewer, Section 10 (Glass and Amber). Oxford and Salisbury: Framework Archaeology.

Sheridan, J. A. 2012a. 'The shale stud from the Bronze Age cremation cemetery, Cefn Cwmwd', in Cuttler, R., Davidson, A. and Hughes, G., *A Corridor Through Time: the Archaeology of the A55 Anglesey Road Scheme*, 149–150. Oxford: Oxbow.

Sheridan, J. A. 2012b. 'Contextualising Kilmartin: building a narrative for developments in western Scotland and beyond, from the Early Neolithic to the Late Bronze Age', in Jones, A. M., Pollard, J., Allen, M. J. and Gardiner, J. (eds.), *Image, Memory and Monumentality; Archaeological Engagements with the Material World*, 163–83. Oxford: Oxbow/Prehistoric Society (Research Paper 5).

Sheridan, J. A. 2013. 'Chalcolithic (Copper Age) and Bronze Age Bute, *c.* 2500 – *c.* 800 BC: an assessment', in Duffy, P. (ed.), *One Island, Many Voices: Bute, Archaeology and the Discover Bute Landscape Partnership Scheme*, 53–71. Donnington: Shaun Tyas.

Sheridan, J. A. 2014. 'Gold in ancient Scotland', in Clark, N. D., *Scottish Gold: Fruit of the Nation*, 39–59. Glasgow: Hunterian Museum.

Sheridan, J. A. forthcoming a. 'The jet studs from Norton Subcourse skeleton 2'.

Sheridan, J. A. forthcoming b. 'Amesbury Solstice Park: the ornaments from inside the urn (context 1303)'. Report submitted 2005 to AC Archaeology. Already published online in http://southplanning.wiltshire.gov.uk/public-planning-application-documents/00525000/00524971_Applicants_Supporting_Information.pdf (Accessed October 2014).

Sheridan, J. A. in prep. 'The studs from Over, Barleycroft and Langtoft', in Evans, C., Knight, M. and Pollard, J., *A Book of Sites: Prehistoric and Palaeoenvironmental Investigations at Barleycroft Farm/Over, Cambridgeshire. (The Archaeology of the Lower Ouse Valley, Volume IV)*. Cambridge: Cambridge Archaeological Unit.

Sheridan, J. A. and Bradley, R. J. 2007. 'Radiocarbon dates arranged through National Museums Scotland during 2006/7', *Discovery and Excavation in Scotland* 7, 220–1.

Sheridan, J. A. and Davis, M. 1998. 'The Welsh 'jet set' in prehistory: a case of keeping up with the Joneses?', in Gibson, A. M. and Simpson, D. D. A. (eds.), *Prehistoric Ritual and Religion*, 148–62. Stroud: Sutton.

Sheridan, J. A. and Davis, M. 2001. 'The disc-bead necklace from Cist 1', in Holden, T. and Sheridan, J. A., 'Three cists and a possible Roman road at Barbush Quarry, Dunblane', 93–95. *Proceedings of the Society of Antiquaries of Scotland* 131, 87–100.

Sheridan, J. A. and Davis, M. 2002. 'Investigating jet and jet-like artefacts from prehistoric Scotland: the National Museums of Scotland project', *Antiquity* 76, 812–25.

Sheridan, J. A. and Davis, M. 2003. 'The V-perforated buttons', in Baker, L. *et al.*, 89–95.

Sheridan, J. A. and Davis, M. 2008. 'The disc bead necklace from grave 3033', in Bennett, P. *et al.*, 81–2.

Sheridan, J. A. and Shortland, A. 2003. 'Supernatural power dressing', *British Archaeology* 70, 18–23.

Sheridan, J. A. and Shortland, A. 2004. ' "...beads which have given rise to so much dogmatism, controversy and rash speculation": faience in Early Bronze Age Britain and Ireland', in Shepherd, I. A. G. and Barclay, G. J. (eds.), *Scotland in Ancient Europe*, 263–79. Edinburgh: Society of Antiquaries of Scotland.

Sheridan, J. A., Davis, M. and Hunter, F. J. 1998. 'Objects of cannel coal and similar materials', in McCullagh, R. P. J. and Tipping, R. (eds.), *The Lairg Project 1988–1996: The Evolution of an Archaeological Landscape in Northern Scotland*, 123–7. Edinburgh: Scottish Trust for Archaeological Research.

Sheridan, J. A., Kochman, W. and Aranauskas, R. 2003. 'The grave goods from the Knowes of Trotty, Orkney: reconsideration and replication', in Downes, J. and Ritchie, A. (eds.), *Sea Change: Orkney and Northern Europe in the later Iron Age AD300–80*, 177–87. Angus: Pinkfoot Press.

Sheridan, J. A., Cowie, T. G., Anderson-Whymark, H. and Grant, E. 2011. 'Radiocarbon dates arranged through National Museums' Scotland Archaeology Department during 2010/11', *Discovery and Excavation in Scotland* 12, 205.

Sheridan J. A., Jay, M., Montgomery, J., Pellegrini, M. and Cahill Wilson, J. 2013. ''Tara Boy': local hero or international man of mystery?', in O'Sullivan, M. (ed.), *Tara: From the Past to the Future*, 165–190. Dublin: Wordwell.

Sheridan, J. A., Parker Pearson, M., Jay, M., Richards, M. and Curtis, N. 2006. 'Radiocarbon dating results from the *Beaker People Project*: Scottish samples', *Discovery and Excavation in Scotland* 7, 198–201.

Sherratt, A. 1986. 'The Radley 'earrings' revised', *Oxford Journal of Archaeology* 5, 63–6.

Sherratt, A. 1987. ''Earrings' again', *Oxford Journal of Archaeology* 6, 119.

Skak-Nielsen, N. V. 2009. 'Flint and metal daggers in Scandinavia and other parts of Europe. A re-interpretation of their function in the Late Neolithic and Early Copper and Bronze Age', *Antiquity* 83, 349–358.

Smith, I. F. 1965. 'Excavation of a bell barrow, Avebury G55', *Wiltshire Archaeological and Natural History Magazine* 60, 24–46.

Smith, I. F. and Simpson, D. D. A. 1966. 'Excavation of a round barrow on Overton Hill, north Wiltshire, England', *Proceedings of the Prehistoric Society* 32, 122–155.

Smith, M. J. B. 1994. *Excavated Bronze Age Burial Mounds of North-East Yorkshire*. Durham: Architectural and Archaeological Society of Durham and Northumberland Research Report 3.

Smith, R. A. 1921. 'Irish gold crescents', *Antiquaries Journal* 1, 131–9.

Spindler, K. 1994. *The Man in the Ice*. London: Weidenfeld and Nicolson.

Stone, J. F. S. 1932. 'Excavations at Easton Down, Winterslow, 1931–2', *Wiltshire Archaeological Magazine* 46, 218–24.

Stone, J. F. S. and Hill, N. G. 1940. 'A round barrow on Stockbridge Down, Hampshire', *Antiquaries Journal* 20, 39–51.

Stuart, J. 1866. 'Notice of cairns recently examined on the Estate of Rothie, Aberdeenshire', *Proceedings of the Society of Antiquaries of Scotland* 6 (1864–66), 217–8.

Stukeley, W. 1740. *Stonehenge, a Temple Restored to the British Druids*. London: privately printed.

Stukeley, W. 1743. *Abury, a Temple of the British Druids with some others described... Volume the Second.* London: privately printed.

Sydenham, J. 1844. 'An account of the opening of some barrows in south Dorsetshire', *Archaeologia* 30, 327–8.

Taylor, H. 1950. 'The Tynings Farm barrows; third report', *Proceedings of the University of Bristol Spelaeological Society* 6 (2), 111–73.

Taylor, J. J. 1970a. 'The recent discovery of gold pins in the Ridgeway gold pommel', *Antiquaries Journal* 50, 216–21.

Taylor, J. J. 1970b. 'Lunulae reconsidered', *Proceedings of the Prehistoric Society* 36, 38–81.

Taylor, J. J. 1980. *Bronze Age Goldwork of the British Isles.* Cambridge: Cambridge University Press.

Taylor, J. J. 1985. 'Gold and silver', in Clarke, D. V. *et al.* 1985, 182–92.

Taylor, J. J. 1994. 'The first golden age of Europe was in Ireland and Britain (circa 2400–1400 B.C.)', *Ulster Journal of Archaeology* 57, 37–60.

Taylor, J. J. 1999. 'Gold reflections', in Harding, A. F. (ed.), *Experiment and Design: Archaeological Studies in Honour of John Coles*, 108–15. Oxford: Oxbow.

Taylor, J. J. 2004. 'Recognising the individual by his work: the goldsmith of Wessex and Armorica', in Perea, A., Montero, I. and García-Vuelta, Ó. (eds.), *Tecnología del Oro Antiguo: Europa y América*. Anejos de Archivo Español Arqueología 32, 339–48. Madrid: Instituto de Historia.

Taylor, J. J. 2005. 'The work of the master Wessex goldsmith: its implications', *Wiltshire Archaeological and Natural History Magazine* 98, 316–26.

Thom, A. S., Ker, J. M. D. and Burrows, T. R. 1988. 'The Bush Barrow gold lozenge: is it a solar and lunar calendar for Stonehenge?', *Antiquity* 62, 492–502.

Thomas, N. 1954. 'Notes on some Early Bronze Age grave groups', *Wiltshire Archaeological and Natural History Magazine* 55, 311–332.

Thomas, N. 1966. 'Notes on some Early Bronze Age objects in Devizes Museum', *Wiltshire Archaeological and Natural History Magazine* 61, 1–8.

Thomas, N. 2005. *Snail Down, Wiltshire. The Bronze Age Barrow Cemetery and Related Earthworks, in the parishes of Collingbourne Ducis and Collingbourne Kingston. Excavations 1953, 1955 and 1957.* Devizes: Wiltshire Archaeological and Natural History Society Monograph No. 3.

Thomas, N. and Ellwood, E. C. 2005. 'Early Bronze Age copper-alloy awls from Sites I and II; with metal analysis and classification', in Thomas, N., 219–22.

Thoms, L. 1980. *Some Short Cist Burials from Tayside*. Dundee: Dundee Museums and Art Gallery, Occasional Papers in Archaeology 2.

Thurnam, J. 1871. 'On ancient British barrows, especially those of

Wiltshire and the adjoining counties (Part II, round barrows)', *Archaeologia* 43, 285–552.

Timberlake, S. 2009. 'Copper mining and metal production at the beginning of the British Bronze Age', in Clark, P. (ed.), 94–121.

Tomalin, D. 2011. 'The character, chronology and cultural implications of the Neolithic and Bronze Age ceramics', in Harding, J. and Healy, F. (eds.), *The Raunds Area Project. A Neolithic and Bronze Age Landscape in Northamptonshire. Volume 2: Supplementary Studies*, 545–601. London: English Heritage.

Tomkeieff, S. I. 1954. *Coals and Bitumens*. London, Pergamon Press.

Varndell, G. 2000. 'Longbridge Deverill, Wiltshire: ?Early Bronze Age gold disc', *Treasure Annual Report 1998–9*, 10. London: Department of Culture, Media and Sport.

Vatcher, F. de M. and Vatcher, H. L. 1976. 'The excavation of a round barrow near Poor's Heath, Risby, Suffolk', *Proceedings of the Prehistoric Society* 42, 263–92.

Verkooijen, K. and Sheridan, J. A. forthcoming. 'Archaeological interpretations of craft-working and "The Châines that Bind.."', in Sofaer, J. and Sørensen, M. L. S. (eds.), *Creativity and Craft Production in Middle and Late Bronze Age Europe*.

Vine, P. M. 1982. *The Neolithic and Bronze Age Cultures of the Middle and Upper Trent Basin*. Oxford: British Archaeological Reports British Series 105.

Vyner, B. E. 1984. 'The excavation of a Neolithic cairn at Street House, Loftus, Cleveland', *Proceedings of the Prehistoric Society* 50, 151–95.

Vyner, B. E. forthcoming. 'The beads and ornaments from Ingleby Barwick, Stockton-on-Tees'.

Walker, K. E. and Farwell, D. E. 2000. *Twyford Down, Hampshire. Archaeological Investigations on the M3 Motorway from Bar End to Compton, 1990–93*. Winchester: Hampshire Field Club and Archaeological Society Monograph 9.

Warne, C. 1886. *The Celtic Tumuli of Dorset*. London: J. R. Smith.

Warner, R., Chapman, R. and Cahill, M. 2009. 'The gold source found at last?', *Archaeology Ireland* 23(2), 22–5.

Watkins, T. 1982. 'The excavation of an Early Bronze Age cemetery at Barns Farm, Fife', *Proceedings of the Society of Antiquaries of Scotland* 112, 48–141.

Watts, S., Pollard, A. M. and Wolff, G. A. 1997. 'Kimmeridge jet – a potential new source for British jet', *Archaeometry* 39(1), 125–43.

Wilson, P. R. 2002. *Cataractonium, Part 2: Roman Catterick and its hinterland. Excavations and Research 1958–1997*. York: Council for British Archaeology Research Report 129.

Woodward, A. 2000a. *British Barrows. A Matter of Life and Death*. Stroud: Tempus.

Woodward, A. 2000b. 'The prehistoric pottery', in Hughes, G. 2000, 48–61.

Woodward, A. 2002. 'Beads and Beakers: heirlooms and relics in the British Early Bronze Age', *Antiquity* 76, 1040–7.

Woodward, A. and Hunter, J. 2011. *An Examination of Prehistoric Stone Bracers from Britain*. Oxford: Oxbow.

Woodward, A., Hunter, J., Ixer, R., Maltby, M., Potts, P. J., Webb, P. C., Watson, J. S. and Jones, M. C. 2005. 'Ritual in some Early Bronze Age gravegoods', *Archaeological Journal* 162, 31–64.

Woodward, A., Hunter, J., Ixer, R., Roe, F., Potts, P., Webb, P., Watson, J. and Jones, M. C. 2006. 'Beaker age bracers in England: sources, function and use', *Antiquity* 80, 530–543.

Woodward, A. and Needham, S. 2012. 'Diversity and distinction: characterising the individual buried at Wilsford G58, Wiltshire', in Jones, A. M., Pollard, J., Allen, M. J. and Gardiner, J. (eds.), *Image, Memory and Monumentality. Archaeological engagements with the material world*, 116–126. Oxford: Oxbow.

Woodward, P. J. 1991. *The South Dorset Ridgeway. Survey and Excavations 1977–84*. Dorchester: Dorset Natural History and Archaeological Society Monograph 8.

INDEX TO GRAVE GROUPS AND OBJECTS STUDIED IN DETAIL

- The index relates to entries in the descriptive chapters only (Chapters 3–8).
- For definition of Yorkshire counties see Chapter 2, Table 2.5.
- Page references to illustrations, marked in bold, are placed after the text references.
- Barrow numbering is after Grinsell (G) 1957, 1959, 1971, 1982 (Dorset, Somerset and Wiltshire), Gunstone (Gu) 1965 (Staffordshire, some Derbyshire), Marsden (Ma) 1977 (Derbyshire), Mortimer (M) 1905 (Yorkshire) and Greenwell (Gr) (Kinnes and Longworth 1985; Yorkshire). Details of barrows and burials for the Peak District may be found also in Vine 1982 (catalogue) and Barnatt 1996 (index and corpus). For Wiltshire also see Annable and Simpson (1964) and Moore and Rowlands (1972). Full details of barrows, burials and references are contained within the paper record forms and project databases: for availability of these see Chapter 1, page 7. The site database contains entries for objects within the grave groups listed below that were not studied in detail e.g. pottery, flint objects, lost items.